TORTS

ASPEN PUBLISHERS

TORTS

Cases and Questions

Second Edition

Ward Farnsworth

Nancy E. Barton Scholar
Professor of Law
Boston University

Mark F. Grady

Professor of Law
UCLA Law School

Wolters Kluwer
Law & Business

AUSTIN   BOSTON   CHICAGO   NEW YORK   THE NETHERLANDS

Aspen Publishers
Attn: Permissions Department
76 Ninth Avenue, 7th Floor
New York, NY 10011-5201

To contact Customer Care, e-mail customer.care@aspenpublishers.com, call 1-800-234-1660, fax 1-800-901-9075, or mail correspondence to:

Aspen Publishers
Attn: Order Department
PO Box 990
Frederick, MD 21705

Printed in the United States of America

1 2 3 4 5 6 7 8 9 0

ISBN 978-0-7355-8294-1

Library of Congress Cataloging-in-Publication Data

Farnsworth, Ward, 1967-
     Torts : cases and questions / Ward Farnsworth, Mark F. Grady. — 2nd ed.
          p.   cm.
     Includes bibliographical references and index.
     ISBN 978-0-7355-8294-1
     1. Torts — United States. I. Grady, Mark F. II. Title.

KF1250.F37 2009
346.7303 — dc22   2009017546

About Wolters Kluwer Law & Business

Wolters Kluwer Law & Business is a leading provider of research information and workflow solutions in key specialty areas. The strengths of the individual brands of Aspen Publishers, CCH, Kluwer Law International and Loislaw are aligned within Wolters Kluwer Law & Business to provide comprehensive, in-depth solutions and expert-authored content for the legal, professional and education markets.

CCH was founded in 1913 and has served more than four generations of business professionals and their clients. The CCH products in the Wolters Kluwer Law & Business group are highly regarded electronic and print resources for legal, securities, antitrust and trade regulation, government contracting, banking, pension, payroll, employment and labor, and healthcare reimbursement and compliance professionals.

Aspen Publishers is a leading information provider for attorneys, business professionals and law students. Written by preeminent authorities, Aspen products offer analytical and practical information in a range of specialty practice areas from securities law and intellectual property to mergers and acquisitions and pension/benefits. Aspen's trusted legal education resources provide professors and students with high-quality, up-to-date and effective resources for successful instruction and study in all areas of the law.

Kluwer Law International supplies the global business community with comprehensive English-language international legal information. Legal practitioners, corporate counsel and business executives around the world rely on the Kluwer Law International journals, loose-leafs, books and electronic products for authoritative information in many areas of international legal practice.

Loislaw is a premier provider of digitized legal content to small law firm practitioners of various specializations. Loislaw provides attorneys with the ability to quickly and efficiently find the necessary legal information they need, when and where they need it, by facilitating access to primary law as well as state-specific law, records, forms and treatises.

Wolters Kluwer Law & Business, a unit of Wolters Kluwer, is headquartered in New York and Riverwoods, Illinois. Wolters Kluwer is a leading multinational publisher and information services company.

For Janet.

— W.F.

To Jeanne M. Brady
and Francis Taylor Grady.

— M.F.G.

SUMMARY OF CONTENTS

TABLE OF CONTENTS

Rains & Freedman OUT

xi

Hollenbeck out

Lombardo out
Carroll out

Blankenshp out
Bruce out
Lewis out

E. Yoma out

Eastwood out

PREFACE TO THE SECOND EDITION

This casebook is designed to help students learn about basic principles and policies of tort law, and to develop their skill in working with cases — especially their ability to distinguish cases that seem superficially similar, and to find connections between cases that are superficially different. For these purposes the best cases often are older ones that, when put side by side with others, provide grist for lively and instructive class discussions. Since the book does not aim to provide detailed information about the most recent wrinkles in tort doctrines that various states have produced, the revisions for this edition tend not to be "updates" of that kind; most of the changes instead are responses to requests and suggestions from instructors who have assigned the book — for example, that additional facts be included in case descriptions here and there, or that a favorite case be added or expanded, or that an unhelpful case be dropped. A number of instructors also asked for enlarged coverage of the Restatement (Third) of Torts; we thus have added additional excerpts to many sections of the book. And we have added notes on some recent public events of interest to the student of tort law: the 9/11 Victims' Compensation Fund (in the chapter on damages), and litigation over the painkilling drug Vioxx (in the chapter on cause in fact).

We consider the experience of those who have used a casebook to be the most valuable guide to how it might be improved. We thus are very grateful for the recommendations made to us by professors who worked with the first edition, and encourage future users to pass on additional suggestions in reply to this new one.

W.F.
M.F.G.

May 2009

PREFACE TO THE FIRST EDITION

The distinctive approach of this casebook is to present pairs and clusters of cases that contain factual similarities but arrive at different outcomes and to invite exploration of how they might be distinguished. This is a departure from the standard format of most casebooks, which typically present a lead case and then notes afterward that talk about the case just presented, ask questions about it, and make reference — usually in brief — to some related cases. There are lead cases here, as in other books; but the notes afterward consist largely of other judicial decisions presented at intermediate length: not as long as lead cases, but still fully enough to support discussion of the relationships between them. Our view is that the best way to examine an issue of tort law is not by reading a case about it, but rather by reading two cases that reach different results on related facts. We have found that this approach makes for a compelling torts course, and that it offers the following advantages in particular:

1. It makes clear to the user what to *do* with the reading: distinguish the cases and think through their implications. The apparent tension between cases is an invitation not only to work out the most that can be said to reconcile them but also to ask more broadly what underlying theory would make sense out of both results. On occasion the reader may conclude that there is no good distinction and that the cases just represent different approaches taken to the same question by two jurisdictions. But this is an argument of last resort for the lawyer, as it ought to be for the law student.

2. The book helps build skill in the lawyer's art of drawing intelligent distinctions between cases that are superficially similar and analogies between

cases that are superficially different. This is one of the aspects of legal method that a course on tort law most helpfully can teach. Despite the growing significance of statutory activity, torts remains one of the few areas of the curriculum that remains largely a matter of common law; it is an ideal place to learn how to think out arguments that the factual differences between cases ought to lead to different legal results. This approach also calls on students to infer for themselves the contours of doctrines and the policies behind them — another important practical skill to develop, and a richer way to reach an understanding of the law than by hearing the editors' views.

3. The process of sorting out decisions that are in at least superficial tension brings tort doctrines to life: conflict, including apparent conflict between cases, provides a motivation for thinking about legal problems and a basis for lively classroom discussion of them. The challenge of explaining the cases also has a puzzle-like quality that makes the process of learning the material more stimulating. The form of the question — "what is the distinction between X and Y?" — is repetitive, but the substance of it, and the thinking it calls for, is different every time it is asked.

4. The casebook's approach, properly used, yields an improved understanding of the relationship between doctrine and procedure. To grasp what it means to say that two cases conflict — to say that one was a case of liability ("L") and the other a case of no liability ("NL") — requires an appreciation of the procedural posture of each. The introduction to the book explains this in basic terms, but attaining complete comprehension of the intersection between the substance of cases and their procedural posture takes time. It is an ongoing project during the first year of law school that the book's approach is meant to support.

5. The book provides instructors with flexibility in deciding what normative ideas to explore in the course. Its presentation of cases is compatible with an emphasis on their economic logic, on matters of corrective justice, on other questions of policy, or on doctrine alone — or on some combination of these approaches.

This last point bears some elaboration. Our degree of emphasis on cases that reach different results on similar facts is unusual today, but it was more common 100 years ago in early casebooks written by Wigmore, Bohlen, Seavey and Thurston, and Ames and Smith. Those authors executed the idea quite differently, and of course they put it into the service of an intellectual agenda different from that of a twenty-first-century torts course. Indeed, the modern torts course has no consensus agenda; different instructors teach the course very differently. But we believe there was a kernel of pedagogical ingenuity in those early books that has outlived the intellectual priors they sometimes were written to advance. One of our goals has been to revive what was useful and interesting in those approaches and adapt it for use in the current environment of ideas about tort law. We have found that starting with inquiries into the distinctions between the cases serves well as a springboard for wide-ranging discussions of the policy rationales behind the doctrines and the functions and interests they serve.

With that said, our emphasis on case analysis is not exclusive. One of the book's subthemes includes periodic attention to statutes and the institutional relationships between courts and legislatures. The chapters also are seasoned with excerpts from relevant scholarly work, particularly on questions of how judges, juries, and legal actors implement and think about various legal doctrines. The seasoning is judicious; we have not attempted a thorough presentation of scholarly perspectives on most issues in the book. The literature on the law of torts is too extensive to permit this while still achieving the book's other aims. Meanwhile instructors vary widely in which secondary sources they want to discuss, and there are many excellent collections of those materials that can be assigned on a supplemental basis for those seeking greater emphasis on the theoretical work.

The text also includes many problems to consider — several dozen, interspersed within the chapters, that present the facts of real cases without their resolutions. The format of these problems resembles in an abbreviated way the examination questions students usually are asked to solve at the end of the course, not to mention the format in which tort problems come to the practicing lawyer: facts and questions, but no answers. We believe there is value in preparing and working through problems of this kind during the course, as they develop a style of analysis a bit different from the skills built by thinking about cases where the court's answer is supplied, and a bit different as well from the immediate response called for by the in-class hypothetical.

Finally, we have made a particular effort to fill the book with interesting and memorable cases. One of the rewards of studying tort law is the chance to see how various sorts of human dramas, conflicts and calamities — many of them commonplace, many others rather *outré* — have been translated into judicial accounts and given legal meaning. The cases thus include a generous sampling of the legal responses to various terrors of modern life: spilled coffee, the wreck of the *Exxon Valdez*, intrusive telemarketers, and defamation on the internet. But they also offer a good look at the law's responses to great challenges of times past: the train robbery, the marine monster, and the egg-sucking dog. Thinking about the application of similar doctrines to situations old and new alike is instructive in its own right.

The book is meant to be assigned flexibly. Starting at Chapter 3 will be the preference of many instructors; some may wish to assign Chapter 4, on duties and their limitations, later or earlier in the course than its placement indicates, or to take up the chapter on defenses based on the plaintiff's conduct earlier than its late location in the book suggests. None of this need be considered cause for alarm on the reader's part. The chapters of the book are written deliberately to be usable in various orders.

Omitted language in the cases is indicated by bracketed ellipses. Many footnotes, citations, and headings within the cases are omitted without notice.

The Table of Contents lists all the note cases within each chapter that are presented at enough length to support discussion; it does not mention secondary materials, including excerpts from the Restatements of Torts, unless they comprise leading material in a chapter.

Ward Farnsworth
Mark F. Grady

February 2004

ACKNOWLEDGMENTS

Building this book has been a labor-intensive enterprise, and I would like to thank my research assistants at the Boston University School of Law for their help with it: Patryk Silver, Hermine Hayes-Klein, Shaun Ryan, Justin Smith, Blaire Osgood, Heather Zuzenak, Lior Ohayon, Miller Brownstein, and Alon Cohen. I also wish to thank three faculty colleagues at Boston University who have taught from these materials and provided very helpful suggestions: Randy Barnett, Nancy Moore, and Kenneth Simons; Simons also was kind enough to contribute the basis for the marginal analysis exercise that appears on page 147. The manuscript also benefited very much from the recommendations of several anonymous reviewers for Aspen and Aspen's own editors, including Curt Berkowitz, Carol McGeehan, and Barbara Roth. I thank them all for their time and assistance. Finally, I thank Brian Brooks, Dan Cantor, Ronald Cass, Janet Farnsworth, Ward Farnsworth, Sr., Stephen Gilles, Russell Holmes, Adam Long, Michael Lusi, Richard Posner, Christopher Roberts, Ted Skillman, and Eugene Volokh for comments, inspiration, and other varieties of support at various points in the process.

— W.F.

My contribution to this casebook evolved over a period of years at a number of law schools: the University of Iowa, Northwestern University, UCLA, and George Mason University. My own mentor was former UCLA law professor Wesley J. Liebeler, whose incisive teaching made my part in this project possible. The students in the various torts classes I have taught helped me work out the relationships between the cases. A number of able research assistants have made substantial contributions. They are (in chronological order): Margery Huston (Iowa), Debra Ann Haberkorn (Northwestern), Jacqueline Bares (Northwestern), Erik Dyhrkopp (Northwestern), Pamela Holz (Northwestern), Jacques LeBoeuf (Northwestern), Scott Rozmus (Northwestern), Phil Mann (UCLA), and Paul Mills (UCLA).

— M.F.G.

INTRODUCTION

The purpose of this introduction is to provide the newcomer to tort law with a sense of orientation and context for the materials that follow and for a typical first course on the subject. Part 1 describes the scope of the law of torts and some major distinctions used to organize the field. Part 2 sketches the historical development of tort liability. Part 3 explains the procedural steps involved in bringing a tort suit; it also explains the use of the "liability" (L) and "no liability" (NL) designations often used in this book to describe the outcomes of the cases. Part 4 introduces some major theoretical perspectives and analytical tools used by students and scholars of tort law. All of these issues are treated only briefly; the explanations here are just meant to give the reader a nodding acquaintance with issues that will be explored in more detail during the rest of the course.

1. The Scope of the Law of Torts

The word "tort" is derived from the Latin word "tortus," meaning crooked or twisted. In French the word "tort" continues to have a general meaning of "wrong," and this remains its meaning in English legal usage as well. Tort law governs legal responsibility, or "liability," for wrongs that people inflict on each other by various means: assaults, automobile accidents, professional malpractice (for example, errors by doctors or lawyers), defamation, and so forth. Torts is the body of law that furnishes the victim of any of these forms of conduct with a remedy against the party responsible for them. The person bringing the suit (the plaintiff) claims that the defendant should be required to pay for the damage done. That is a practical and nonlegalistic description of the office of tort law, and it is incomplete in various ways; but it provides a general sense of what the subject of torts is about and suggests how this branch of law differs from others such as criminal law. Let us consider that distinction and some others in more detail.

Torts vs. crimes. Some of the conduct addressed by the law of torts also is addressed by the criminal law; indeed, in early English law the two branches were unified, with damages to the victim of a wrong awarded as part of a criminal proceeding against the wrongdoer. Today, however, there is a broad division in the law between criminal liability on the one hand and civil liability on the other. Civil actions generally refer to lawsuits brought by one party against another seeking compensation for a wrong. Criminal prosecutions are brought by a government seeking to punish the defendant. Some key distinctions between these two types of proceedings may be summarized as follows.

First, tort and criminal law often differ in the conduct they govern. Some acts are both torts and crimes; a beating, for example, may result in both a criminal prosecution and a tort suit. But other crimes are not torts. Thus a crime may be committed without injury to anyone, as when a defendant is prosecuted for driving faster than the speed limit allowed. In this case there is no occasion for a tort suit by anyone seeking damages. Likewise, many torts are not crimes. A defendant who injures someone through an act of professional malpractice typically commits no crime and will not be prosecuted, but may be required by the law of torts to pay compensation to the injured party. Even where the same conduct does give rise to both tort and criminal liability, the legal doctrines governing the two types of case tend to be quite different, with different elements of proof and different defenses available.

Second, tort and criminal law differ in the procedures they involve. A crime is regarded by the law as an offense against the public; that is why it results in a prosecution brought by the government, not by the immediate victim of the wrong. A tort suit is brought by an injured party seeking compensation for damage the defendant has caused. And because the stakes of the two proceedings for the defendant are different, the standards of proof in the two proceedings differ as well. In a criminal prosecution the defendant must be proven guilty beyond a reasonable doubt; in a tort suit the plaintiff must establish the defendant's liability by a preponderance of the evidence, a weaker standard. A tort suit and a criminal prosecution based on the same conduct may go forward at the same time, or one after the other. The two proceedings generally have no effect on each other, though findings against a defendant made in a criminal case sometimes may be regarded as settled for purposes of the tort suit as well.

Third, tort and criminal law differ in their purposes. Both are partly concerned with deterring misconduct by attaching costs to it, but deterrence is just one of the purposes classically ascribed to the criminal law — along with retribution, rehabilitation, and incapacitation of the criminal. Retribution and incapacitation rarely are thought to play any role in the law of torts; the immediate purpose of a tort suit is to secure compensation for the victim. There remains some overlap between even the apparently different purposes served by criminal and tort suits. A criminal prosecution may serve compensatory as well as punitive purposes by forcing a defendant to pay restitution to the victim of a crime, and a tort suit may serve a punitive as well as a compensatory function if the defendant is required to pay punitive damages. But the differences between the aims of tort and criminal law are large enough to result in quite different arguments about what rules and policies make sense in the two fields.

Common law vs. statutes. The law of torts comes from two principal sources: the common law and statutes. For our purposes, "common law" refers to the body of law created by judges over the course of many centuries in England and the United States. Judges deciding tort disputes in classic common law fashion reason from one case to the next, with the parties each arguing that their preferred result is the one most consistent with the decisions the court already has made. When the court decides the case it issues a written opinion explaining its decision; that opinion then becomes a precedent that can be used as authority in subsequent cases. Until well into the twentieth century most American tort law was common law — i.e., judge-made. To learn the law of torts was to know a great many cases.

Torts remains largely a common law field, but state legislatures now play a significant role in its development as well. During the past half-century it has become more common for judge-made tort doctrines to be codified, modified, or repudiated by statute, or for legislatures to make attempts to enact statutory "tort reform." Administrative agencies also supplement rules of tort liability with regulations that may cover some of the same ground. In this book we will examine a number of statutory contributions to the law of torts and consider the pros and cons of making tort law by judicial decision and by legislation. But in the main this book continues to treat torts as a common law subject, both because it largely remains so and because training in common law reasoning — the process of distinguishing cases and arguing about their precedential significance — is one of the distinctive pedagogical functions of a first-year course on tort law.

In the course of our studies we frequently will encounter the First, Second, and Third Restatements of the Law of Torts published by the American Law Institute (ALI). The ALI is an organization of lawyers, judges, and academics; the Restatements are a set of projects in which they attempt to clarify the content of the common law in various areas — torts, contracts, agency, and so forth. The creation of a Restatement begins with the appointment of a reporter (or more than one) responsible for drafting its various sections. The reporter has primary responsibility for the final result, but a Restatement is subject to comment, debate, and a vote by the membership of the ALI before it is released. The reporter generally attempts to state the best reading of the courts' position on a question — usually the position of the courts in a majority of jurisdictions, though sometimes the ALI will side with a minority view that it believes is better reasoned. Indeed, occasionally the ALI's attempt to "restate" what courts are doing will amount to a recommendation that they adopt a new framework for decision that better reflects the direction of the law. The resulting Restatements vary in the extent of their influence. In certain areas of law they have had a great impact; the Second Restatement, for example, formulated tests for products liability and invasion of privacy that have been adopted in most jurisdictions. Other sections have been less influential.

In all events, it is important to understand that the positions a Restatement takes, whether in its "black letter" statements of law or the illustrations and comments afterwards, are not law and may not reflect the position taken in some jurisdictions. Courts are under no obligation to follow the Restatements and sometimes reject them explicitly. Restatements are best viewed as useful attempts, with greater or lesser success, to summarize areas where the common law is complicated. We will consider them often in that spirit. The First Restatement of Torts, written in the 1930s, we will encounter only rarely. The Restatement (Second), written between 1964 and 1979, will make frequent appearances in the text. The new Restatement (Third) does not attempt to cover all the ground that the Second Restatement did, but we shall see that in some areas — including products liability, apportionment, and certain aspects of the negligence tort — the new work has made interesting revisions to the old and has provoked occasional controversy.

Intentional vs. unintentional torts; negligence vs. strict liability. For the sake of organization the substance of tort law can be divided along various lines. The first involves the distinction between liability for intentional and unintentional wrongs. The precise meaning of "intent" can become complicated, as we shall see, but for present purposes just think of intentional torts as those that typically involve deliberate conduct. Battery, trespass, and conversion are classic examples. Unintentional torts refer to harms caused inadvertently — "by accident," as it were. The doctrines governing liability for these two types of torts are different and are covered in different sections of the book.

The world of unintentional torts can be further divided into two types: strict liability and liability for negligence. A rule of strict liability generally requires a defendant to pay for damage caused by an activity regardless of how carefully it was conducted. A rule of negligence requires defendants to pay only for harms caused by their failure to use reasonable care — with the meaning of "reasonable" again subject to debate and qualification. Some activities are governed by the one rule and some by the other. The difference between these two types of liability is very important to an understanding of tort law as a doctrinal matter (in other words, to an understanding of how the rules work); the distinction also is central to much of the theory surrounding the law of torts.

Students of tort law have long debated whether and when liability should be imposed on a defendant without any showing of fault.

2. Historical Development

By way of additional context it will help to understand some differences between the modern divisions in the law of torts just sketched and the somewhat different distinctions that dominated the field until roughly the second half of the nineteenth century. The American legal system borrowed most of its structure from the English, and in England the roots of tort doctrine are bound up with the historical development of jurisdictional rules and requirements. Thus Henry Maine, an English legal historian of the nineteenth century, wrote that in the early common law the "substantive law has at first the look of being gradually secreted in the interstices of procedure." When the Normans invaded in 1066, England had no centralized set of courts; its legal system consisted of a variety of local courts. Over the next two hundred years the "King's courts" were established, but before bringing an action there a plaintiff had first to get permission from the Lord Chancellor of England by securing a *writ*: a document containing a standardized recital accusing the defendant of a particular type of misconduct. The plaintiff would fill in the names, dates, and place of the event. The writ directed the sheriff to produce the defendant at the next Assizes — i.e., the next session of the royal courts. The judge there was assisted in trying the case by a selection from the local citizens, known then as the "inquest" and the forerunner of what we now know as the jury.

The King's courts were in competition with the local courts that continued to be administered by English barons; as a concession to the latter, the number of writs available to gain access to the royal courts was frozen early on. More flexibility was to come later, but a lasting consequence of this initial step was that one writ became the origin of most actions we now would regard as sounding in tort: the writ of *trespass vi et armis* — "with force and arms" — alleging that the defendant had broken the King's peace, thus entitling the King's courts to jurisdiction over the dispute. The writ of trespass encompassed a range of harms much broader than suggested by its modern lay meaning of entry onto land without permission. It came to be used in cases involving collisions and accidents of all kinds, professional malpractice, and other conduct that the royal courts agreed to treat as fitting within the pigeonhole created by the trespass writ. Over time — by the fourteenth century, and then with greater clarity in the centuries that followed — the royal courts began to recognize a new form of action known as *trespass on the case* (or simply "case"). The old trespass writ came to be used in cases alleging that the defendant inflicted harm in a forcible and direct manner; case became the action used to allege that harm had been inflicted indirectly.

At first glance the distinction between trespass and case may seem to track the modern difference between intentional and unintentional torts, but that was not so. The classic illustration of the difference between trespass and case involved a log dropped by the defendant. If the log struck the plaintiff, the remedy would lie in an action for trespass because the injury was inflicted directly; if the plaintiff struck the log while driving in his carriage, the injury would be considered indirect and the remedy would lie in an action on the case. Notice that in either circumstance the defendant may have dropped the log deliberately or inadvertently.

But what of the other great modern distinction — that between strict liability and liability for negligence? The action on the case generally required a showing of some fault on the defendant's part, whether in the form of carelessness or a bad intent; the liability for negligence now familiar to us thus descends largely from old English action on the case. Legal historians differ, however, on the role that notions of fault played in early cases alleging *trespass vi et armis*. In the early leading case of Weaver v. Ward, 80 Eng. Rep. 284 (K.B. 1616), the plaintiff and defendant were fellow soldiers; the defendant shot the plaintiff while they were skirmishing with their muskets. The defendant pled that the shooting had been accidental. The court rejected this defense but said that the legal outcome might have been different if the accident had been shown to be "inevitable." Whether this amounted to strict liability or to an implied requirement that the defendant be shown to have been at fault is a matter of some debate. See, e.g., Arnold, *Accident, Mistake, and Rules of Liability in the Fourteenth Century Law of Torts*, 128 U. Pa. L. Rev. 361 (1979); Baker, An Introduction to English Legal History 337-345 (1979).

One naturally may wonder, then, how the transition was made from the old writs to the organizing ideas — negligence, strict liability, and intentional torts — sketched in the previous section of this introduction. During the nineteenth century the writ system was abolished in both England and the United States, and the distinction between trespass and case soon evaporated as well. Before this time, "torts" did not exist as an independent subject matter, so naturally the division of it into negligence, strict liability, and intentional torts did not exist, either. There simply was a collection of unrelated writs that lawyers used to bring claims for recovery in various non-contractual situations. The notion of "negligence" or "neglect" was used narrowly to refer just to situations where a defendant failed to carry out a specific duty to some plaintiff prescribed by law. As the writ system fell away, however, courts and scholars made attempts to replace it with broader efforts at conceptualization. The results of these conceptual efforts included the creation of categories and vocabulary that continue to be used now.

An important example of one of the judicial contributions was *Brown v. Kendall*, 60 Mass. 292 (1850). The defendant was trying to separate two fighting dogs by beating them with a stick; on the backswing the stick hit the plaintiff in the eye. The Chief Justice of the Supreme Judicial Court of Massachusetts, Lemuel Shaw, wrote an opinion saying that a plaintiff suing a defendant in trespass must show "either that the *intention* was unlawful, or that the defendant was *in fault*." Thus "if both plaintiff and defendant at the time of the blow were using ordinary care, or if at that time the defendant was using ordinary care, and the plaintiff was not, or if at that time, both the plaintiff and defendant were not using ordinary care, then the plaintiff could not recover." This way of talking about liability for an accidental injury is not far from the language courts would use today. *Brown v. Kendall* is regarded as a landmark in American law because it was the first to so speak of "fault" as a standard of liability with wide application.

The idea then emerged gradually that a defendant might *in general* be held liable for misfeasance: for doing some act negligently, and thus violating a duty to be careful that was not limited to a specific group of beneficiaries. This notion was pressed forward in scholarship by Oliver Wendell Holmes, Jr., later in the nineteenth century. Holmes's examination of the case law led him to argue for the existence of a general principle that underpinned various forms of liability then capable of being summarized as "torts": liability required a showing of fault, or negligence. We will look at some of Holmes's writings, and consider the meaning that the fault principle came to acquire, in chapter three of this book: The Negligence Standard.

The social significance of the negligence standard has been the subject of extensive debate. Some scholars have argued that a fault requirement is best viewed as a nineteenth century innovation that served as a subsidy to encourage developing industries — railroads, canals, and the like: firms would not be financially responsible for the injuries routinely caused by those sorts of enterprises unless they could be shown to have acted in some sense wrongfully. See, e.g., Morton Horwitz, The Transformation of American Law (1979). Others have argued that the fault requirement was in place from the outset of the nineteenth century and that it benefited many different sorts of defendants, thus undercutting the "subsidy" thesis. At various points in the book — principally in the chapters on Strict Liability and Nuisance — we shall have occasion to consider further the intersection between legal standards and industrial development.

Meanwhile some modern intentional tort actions still retain the names given to them under the old writ system: a suit for trespass to land, for example, or for replevin (a suit seeking the return of the plaintiff's goods). Traces of the old system also survive in the continued availability of certain writs in American law, such as the writ of mandamus, or of habeas corpus, or of coram nobis — none of which have much to do with tort law, however. Part of the value of understanding the English background is that it will help you to better comprehend old cases. But it also will help you to understand basic concepts and distinctions you will see in modern cases that wrestle with doctrines whose roots lie in the old forms of action.

3. *Modern Procedure: How to Understand the Posture of a Case*

This part of the introduction is meant to help you make sense out of the cases you will be reading by explaining a bit about how a legal question comes before a judge and results in a written opinion. (This is a topic that you will cover in more detail in your course on civil procedure.) It is important to understand, first, that when judges write opinions they generally are not making overall decisions about whether the defendant owes money to the plaintiff. Our legal system breaks that decision into parts. In every case you read, a plaintiff is making claims about two things: the *facts* — in other words, the events that occurred in the world ("the defendant's dog bit me"); and the *law* — in other words, the legal rules that apply to the facts ("when a dog bites someone, the dog's owner is obliged to pay compensation"). The opinions that judges write discuss propositions of the second sort: they decide legal issues, such as whether and when dog owners have to pay compensation when their dogs bite people. Judges generally do this by making certain assumptions about the facts of the case in front of them and then deciding whether the law imposes liability in those circumstances. If the factual questions in a case — such as whether the defendant's dog really did bite the plaintiff — are disputed, they typically must be decided separately by a jury (or perhaps by a judge acting as a "trier of fact"). The key distinction to grasp at this point is between (a) questions of law that result in opinions with significance for lots of cases, and (b) questions of fact that are hashed out by the parties in front of a jury, and that do not have significance for later cases (though of course they are of great importance to the parties themselves). If you want to understand the law governing dog bites, it is very important to know whether a dog owner is always liable for damage done by her dog. It is not important for you to know whether, in the case where that legal question was settled, the defendant's dog really did bite the plaintiff.

When we read opinions, we often will refer to them as resulting in "liability" (L) or "no liability" (NL). This is a useful convention because it provides a quick way to keep straight the basic outcomes of the cases we consider. The labels nevertheless require a bit of explanation. An L case is one where the court decided the issue raised in favor of the plaintiff and against the defendant — though it need not be a case where the defendant ultimately (i.e., at the end of the case) was held liable in damages. The court may simply be saying that on certain assumptions which may or may not turn out to be accurate after a trial is held, liability would be appropriate. An NL case is one where the court says that the facts it describes do not give rise to liability. A court can make statements like these at several different moments during a case. Here is a summary of them.

a. *Dismissal of a complaint.* Suppose D's dog bites P. P files a lawsuit against D seeking damages. P's lawsuit begins the way that all lawsuits begin: *P files a complaint* (a short statement of his allegations and of the legal basis of his claim against D). Now suppose D responds, as defendants sometimes do, by making a motion in court to have P's complaint *dismissed* (sometimes also known as filing a *demurrer*). A court will decide D's motion to dismiss P's complaint by assuming that all the facts alleged in the complaint are true, and then asking whether those facts would — if true — entitle the plaintiff to recover damages from the defendant. If the answer is "yes," then for our purposes this is considered a case of liability: the court is saying that if the facts of a case are thus-and-so, the defendant is required to pay damages to the plaintiff. This is true whether the decision is being made by a trial court or a court of appeals.

Note that if the facts of the case turn out later (perhaps after a trial) *not* to be as the plaintiff alleged in the complaint, then the defendant will not be held liable and will not have to pay anything to the plaintiff after all. But we still will think of the court's earlier opinion a case of "liability," because the court was saying that liability would exist under the conditions that it described (namely, the conditions alleged in the plaintiff's complaint). If, on the other hand, the court dismisses the plaintiff's complaint (or "sustains the demurrer"), then we would consider it a case of no liability — both in the sense that the defendant won the case and did not owe the plaintiff anything, and also in the sense, more important for our purposes, that the court assumed certain facts to be true and said that they would create no liability.

b. *Summary judgment.* Assuming the plaintiff's complaint is not dismissed, the next step in the life of a lawsuit is discovery: the exchange of information about the case between the parties. Witnesses have their depositions taken (in essence they are interviewed under oath, with their answers recorded by a stenographer), perhaps the plaintiff is examined by a physician who writes a report, and so forth. This process results in the creation of a record of the case: a set of documents comprising all the evidence that a jury would hear if there were a trial.

At the end of the discovery process, a defendant often will move for *summary judgment.* The defendant's claim then is that there is no point in having a trial because the plaintiff has not come up with evidence that would allow a reasonable jury to bring in a verdict in the plaintiff's favor. This time the court would decide the motion not by assuming the claims in the plaintiff's complaint are true (we are beyond that stage of the case now), but rather by assuming that all of the plaintiff's witnesses would be believed by a jury and that a jury would draw all reasonable inferences from the evidence in the plaintiff's favor. Then, as in the previous example, the court would ask whether, *given those assumptions,* the law would hold the defendant liable to the plaintiff. If the answer is yes, then we would again consider it a case of "liability," even though the defendant's actual liability would have yet to be determined by a jury. The court merely would be saying that a jury *could* find the defendant liable if it believed the plaintiff's witnesses and so forth. Conversely, if the court gave summary judgment to the defendant, then it would be a case of no liability: we would know that the facts the court assumed to be true do not make a defendant liable to a plaintiff.

When you are thinking about the facts of a case where summary judgment was granted or denied, remember that the court was giving the benefit of a doubt to the party opposing the motion (the party who wants a trial — usually the plaintiff, though occasionally the parties' roles can be reversed). You can stylize the case accordingly in your mind's eye: the court's decision is based on the assumption that a jury would draw all reasonable inferences in favor of the plaintiff; you therefore can interpret the facts of the case accordingly, just looking at the plaintiff's evidence.

[c. *Directed verdicts.*] Now suppose the defendant does not succeed in getting the plaintiff's complaint dismissed and also does not succeed in obtaining summary judgment. There is then a trial to resolve disputes about the facts of the case. After the plaintiff has presented his case, or after both sides have presented their cases, or after the jury has reached a decision, the defendant has the option of moving for *judgment as a matter of law.* This also is known in many jurisdictions as moving for a *directed verdict* if the request is made before the jury deliberates or a request for *judgment notwithstanding the verdict* ("j.n.o.v.") if the request is made after the jury has returned its decision. A judge generally decides any of these motions by just looking at the plaintiff's evidence and asking whether, if it is accepted by the jury and interpreted as favorably to the plaintiff as it reasonably can be, a rational jury could find the defendant liable. If not, it is a case of no liability. If so, it is a case of liability for our purposes. As usual, the court has made certain assumptions and has said whether those assumed facts would lead to liability.

The procedural posture just described sounds (and is) very similar to the summary judgment procedure discussed a moment ago, because in either situation the court is asking whether, if the plaintiff's witnesses are believed and all inferences are drawn in the plaintiff's favor, a rational jury could find for the plaintiff. The difference is just that summary judgment asks the question before trial (in an effort to prevent the trial from occurring if its outcome is a foregone conclusion), whereas a motion for judgment as a matter of law asks the same question after the plaintiff's evidence has been presented in court (in an effort to prevent the trial from continuing, or from ending with a judgment against the defendant that the evidence cannot support). In either case the defendant generally is arguing that the plaintiff's evidence is inadequate as a matter of law.

A variation on this last theme occurs when the defendant (or plaintiff, but assume it is the defendant for simplicity's sake) complains that the trial court gave the jury incorrect instructions. A court of appeals generally decides such claims by first deciding whether the instruction was incorrect; if so, the court then asks whether a correctly instructed jury could have brought in a verdict for the defendant if it believed all of the defendant's witnesses, etc.

[*May vs. Must.*] The explanation so far glosses over an important distinction. Occasionally a court says that if the factual assumptions it is making are found to be true, a defendant *cannot* be held liable or *must* be liable. Those are very strong precedents. In other cases — and commonly when a court denies a defendant's motion for summary judgment or judgment as a matter of law — a court offers a weaker holding: it concludes that on the facts it is assuming are true, a defendant *may* be held liable by a jury; in other words, it would be reasonable for a jury to find liability. But this does not mean the jury is required to do so. These holdings still are important because they mean that the facts the court describes entitle the plaintiff to a trial where a jury will decide whether the defendant behaved reasonably, or decide whether the plaintiff's injuries were a foreseeable result of the defendant's behavior, or answer other "jury questions." Indeed, in real tort cases that typically is the key legal determination: whether the plaintiff gets to a jury.

As a practical matter, this means that we will most often encounter two kinds of decisions in tort cases. First are the "NL" cases where the court dismissed the plaintiff's complaint or said that the defendant was entitled to summary judgment or a directed verdict. In these situations the court is saying that as a matter of law there cannot be liability on the facts the plaintiff claims to be able to prove. Second are the "L" cases where the court says there *could* be liability — cases where a jury must be permitted to find liability if it determines that the defendant acted in the way the plaintiff claims. These might more precisely be labeled "PL" cases for "potential liability," but for the sake of elegance we will stick with the "L" designation. We will only occasionally encounter cases where a court says there *must* be liability if the plaintiff's evidence is believed. Those cases will become easy to spot as you get the hang of working with the different procedural postures in which cases come before courts.

Summary. We have just surveyed the most common settings in which judges make statements about when defendants can be held liable to plaintiffs. A judge might make such a pronouncement when deciding a defendant's motion to dismiss a plaintiff's complaint; when deciding a defendant's motion for summary judgment; or when deciding a defendant's motion for a directed verdict (or judgment as a matter of law). Decisions made in these three procedural postures may be equally strong precedents. Regardless of the posture of the case, a court is making certain assumptions about the facts and then deciding whether those facts would or could lead to liability if they eventually were found to be true by a jury. Whether the story is true is another question — one very important to the parties, of course, but not important to lawyers using the case later on, claiming that it is a precedent to which future courts must stay consistent.

Decisions on the motions just described are made first by trial judges, sometimes without written opinions. A party who does not like a trial judge's decision can ask at some point — usually when the case is over in the trial court — to have the decision reviewed by a court of appeals: a panel of judges that reviews questions of law and issues opinions about them. The holdings of the resulting appellate opinions are precedents that bind all lower courts whose work the court of appeals reviews; a decision by a state supreme court, for example, is a binding precedent that must be followed by all courts in the state. The opinion may also be given some weight by courts in other states, where the decision is not binding but may be found persuasive. All else equal, courts like to be consistent with other courts elsewhere.

This book often will ask you what distinctions can be drawn between two cases you have read. If the cases were decided in different jurisdictions (as usually will be true), it is always possible that there is no good distinction between them; it may just be that the courts involved adopted different rules of law, as jurisdictions sometimes do. But attempting to draw distinctions between cases that seem to reach contradictory results is a valuable exercise regardless of whether the cases purport to be consistent with each other. When a practicing lawyer is confronted with a similar case from another jurisdiction that resulted in an unhelpful opinion, saying that the other case should be disregarded because it is from a different state is an argument of last resort. The better route is to distinguish the adverse case by showing that there are good reasons why it came out as it did that do not apply to the case "at bar." This book is intended in part to help increase your skill at creating such arguments. So when the text asks "What is the distinction between X and Y," you may consider this the equivalent of a challenge — if only as an exercise — to come up with the best argument you can that the cases can be squared with each other.

If this is your first exposure to the nuts and bolts of procedure, it no doubt will seem complicated and confusing. It all will become clearer as you work through some cases (and a separate course on civil procedure).

4. Analytical Perspectives

A course on tort law typically has several goals. One is a mastery of the doctrines that comprise the field. Another, as just discussed, is the development of a lawyerly ability to work with case law. Still another is an improved capacity to think intelligently about the problems that tort law attempts to address. This final section of the introduction to the book briefly introduces some major perspectives and analytical tools that students and scholars of tort law bring to bear on the subject.

The dominant theoretical perspectives on torts often change from one generation to the next. Most torts scholars at this writing can be broadly divided into two groups: those who believe the purpose of the law of torts is to regulate conduct and those who believe the purpose of the enterprise is to achieve some form of corrective justice. As we shall see, there are some who attempt to mix these approaches, but it will be convenient to begin by treating them as distinct.

Regulation, deterrence, and economics. In the view of the first camp of scholars, the most important aspect of a court's decision in a tort case is the impact it will have on the behavior of others in the future. The most prominent advocates of this view are economists who believe that the purpose of tort law should be to minimize the costs of accidents. Every accident or other tort creates costs for its victims; but precautions against accidents are expensive, too — as are lawsuits afterwards. The goal of the legal system, on this view, should be to keep to a minimum the *combined* costs of precautions, accidents, and litigation. Sometimes this will mean that the law should try to induce people to take more precautions than they do; sometimes it will mean that people take too many precautions already, or that it is too costly to use the legal system to try to change their behavior. The rules of tort law thus should give people incentives to take precautions that are efficient — i.e., cost-justified: precautions that prevent injuries more costly than the precautions but that allow injuries to occur if they are less costly than the precautions. The economic approach to tort law was pioneered by Guido Calabresi and Richard Posner, both of whom did seminal scholarly work in the 1960s and 1970s and later became federal appellate judges. (We will encounter their judicial work at various points in this book.) Their initial contributions have been followed by a vast economic literature analyzing the efficiency of tort doctrines.

Corrective justice. The other large branch of torts scholarship views the law of torts as a moral enterprise, the purpose of which is to produce justice between plaintiff and defendant. Some of the work in this area attempts to build formally on Aristotle's notion of corrective justice or on the work of Kant and other philosophers. Other influential efforts by legal scholars have been reasoned out less formally — from notions of personal autonomy, and the right to redress when one's personal integrity is unjustifiably invaded; from reciprocal obligations of care owed between members of the same community and the duty to compensate that arises when a party fails to live up to those obligations; or from the snug connection in tort law between a defendant's wrong and a plaintiff's right to collect damages for the resulting injuries, which might seem at odds with the economic view that tort damages are assessed just for the sake of deterring future misconduct. What these theories have in common is a deontological thrust — in other words, a perspective that evaluates rules according to their moral content, not whether they induce people to act in desirable ways. (The economic approach to tort law might be considered a moral enterprise, too, but the relevant morality is consequentialist: a variety of utilitarianism.)

Adherents to these schools of thoughts have a set of standard criticisms to exchange with each other. Economists often regard theories of corrective justice as mush — lacking in clear or persuasive guidelines for determining what conduct counts as "wrongful," unable by their terms (their self-professed hostility to instrumental thinking) to contribute to human welfare, and lacking as well in empirical content that might be verified. Moral theorists are known to dismiss the economic approach on grounds of their own: skepticism about whether people have the knowledge and rationality to be deterred by tort law in the way that economists suggest, and rejection of efficiency as a morally appealing goal for the legal system.

At the same time, some scholars have advanced "mixed theories" that draw on both traditions of argument. They may argue, for example, that appeals to efficiency actually have an underlying moral component. Meanwhile there are still others who embrace the idea that tort law should be viewed as a regulatory regime that provides incentives to people deciding what precautions to take, but who reject the economists' view that the purpose of the regulatory enterprise is just to minimize the joint cost of precautions and accidents. They may adopt other, more distributional goals, viewing tort law as a form of social insurance that protects victims of injuries from unanticipated losses and that shifts the costs of accidents onto the activities that cause them.

We will revisit some of these ideas later, and your instructor may pursue them during class discussions. In the meantime, however, these large debates over tort theory can be reduced to some questions and considerations you can ask as you start to think about the cases you read in this book. What incentives do the courts' rulings create? Are the incentives likely to have practical significance? What administrative costs does a court's holding create or avoid — in other words, what difficulties of application and what potentials for error? Is the court's decision fair — and to whom, and by what criterion? These are important questions to ask in thinking about problems of tort law and trying to assess the merits of the courts' responses to them. They also can be powerful tools for lawyers, as they serve as sources of the types of policy arguments that often are central to a court's resolution of a case.

TORTS

Chapter 1

Intentional Torts: The *Prima Facie* Case

Torts come in two general varieties: unintentional and intentional. Unintentional torts include most sorts of harms generally regarded as accidental; they are covered in later chapters. Intentional torts — the subject of this chapter — are harms inflicted more or less deliberately. For each intentional tort there is a distinct *prima facie* case consisting of certain things ("elements" of the claim) that a plaintiff must allege and then prove in order to win a lawsuit. The defendant can respond to that *prima facie* case either by denying what the plaintiff has said or by raising an affirmative defense — in other words, by alleging and then proving some additional facts that undercut the plaintiff's case, perhaps by justifying the defendant's actions. Those defenses are considered in the next chapter; this chapter is devoted to the elements of the plaintiff's *prima facie* case. We will begin by considering the tort of battery in some detail. Afterwards we will look in a bit less detail at trespass, conversion, false imprisonment, assault, and outrage (otherwise known as the intentional infliction of emotional distress).

A. BATTERY

1. Intent and Volition

Vosburg v. Putney
80 Wis. 523, 50 N.W. 403 (1891)

[The plaintiff, 14 years old at the time in question, brought an action for battery against the defendant, who was 12 years old. The complaint charged that the defendant kicked the plaintiff in the shin in a schoolroom in Waukesha, Wisconsin, after the teacher had called the class to order. The kick, though so

1

light that the plaintiff didn't feel it at first, aggravated a prior injury that the plaintiff had suffered and caused his leg to become lame. The jury rendered a special verdict as follows:

(1) Had the plaintiff during the month of January, 1889, received an injury just above the knee, which became inflamed and produced pus? A. Yes.
(2) Had such injury on the 20th day of February, 1889, nearly healed at the point of the injury? A. Yes.
(3) Was the plaintiff, before said 20th of February, lame as the result of such injury? A. No.
(4) Had the *tibia* in the plaintiff's right leg become inflamed or diseased to some extent before he received the blow or kick from the defendant? A. No.
(5) What was the exciting cause of the injury to the plaintiff's leg? A. Kick.
(6) Did the defendant, in touching the plaintiff with his foot, intend to do him any harm? A. No.
(7) At what sum do you assess the damages of the plaintiff? A. Twenty-five hundred dollars.

The trial court entered judgment for the plaintiff on the special verdict. The defendant appealed.]

LYON, J. [after stating the facts:] — The jury having found that the defendant, in touching the plaintiff with his foot, did not intend to do him any harm, counsel for defendant maintain that the plaintiff has no cause of action, and that defendant's motion for judgment on the special verdict should have been granted. In support of this proposition counsel quote from 2 Greenl. Ev. §83, the rule that "the intention to do harm is of the essence of an assault." Such is the rule, no doubt, in actions or prosecutions for mere assaults. But this is an action to recover damages for an alleged assault and battery. In such case the rule is correctly stated, in many of the authorities cited by counsel, that plaintiff must show either that the intention was unlawful, or that the defendant is in fault. If the intended act is unlawful, the intention to commit it must necessarily be unlawful. Hence, as applied to this case, if the kicking of the plaintiff by the defendant was an unlawful act, the intention of defendant to kick him was also unlawful. Had the parties been upon the play-grounds of the school, engaged in the usual boyish sports, the defendant being free from malice, wantonness, or negligence, and intending no harm to plaintiff in what he did, we should hesitate to hold the act of the defendant unlawful, or that he could be held liable in this action. Some consideration is due to the implied license of the play-grounds. But it appears that the injury was inflicted in the school, after it had been called to order by the teacher, and after the regular exercises of the school had commenced. Under these circumstances, no implied license to do the act complained of existed, and such act was a violation of the order and decorum of the school, and necessarily unlawful. Hence we are of the opinion that, under the evidence and verdict, the action may be sustained. [. . .]

Certain questions were proposed on behalf of defendant to be submitted to the jury, founded upon the theory that only such damages could be recovered as the defendant might reasonably be supposed to have contemplated as likely to result from his kicking the plaintiff. The court refused to submit such questions to the jury. The ruling was correct. The rule of damages in actions for torts was held in *Brown v. Railway Co.*, 54 Wis. 342, to be that the wrongdoer is liable for all injuries resulting directly from the wrongful act, whether they could or could not have been foreseen by him. The chief justice and the writer of this opinion dissented from the judgment in that case, chiefly because we were of the opinion that the complaint stated a cause of action *ex contractu*, and not *ex delicto*, and hence that a different rule of damages — the rule here contended for — was applicable. We did not question that the rule in actions for tort was correctly stated. That case rules this on the question of damages. [. . .]

NOTES

1. *Seven questions.* When a jury renders a *general verdict*, it simply finds the defendant liable or not liable. Sometimes, as in *Vosburg*, a judge will instead ask the jury to render a *special verdict*: a set of answers to more specific questions. A special verdict shows the basis of the jury's conclusions and thus makes it easier for a court reviewing the verdict to know what the jury thought about particular issues that may seem critical in retrospect. The defendant in *Vosburg* fastened onto one particular finding in its special verdict and claimed that it entitled him to victory. Which one?

2. *Touch football.* In Knight v. Jewett, 275 Cal. Rptr. 292 (1990), *aff'd*, 834 P.2d 696 (Cal. 1992), Knight, Jewett, and several other friends gathered at a house in Vista to watch the Super Bowl. Knight and Jewett were among those who decided to play a game of touch football during halftime using the kind of miniature football often used by children. Knight and Jewett were on different teams. The only rule they explicitly agreed upon was that to stop the player with the ball it was necessary to touch the player above the waist with two hands. Knight's understanding was that the game would not involve forceful pushing or shoving.

Soon after the game started, Jewett ran into Knight during a play; Knight told Jewett that she would leave the game if he didn't stop playing so rough. On the next play Jewett knocked Knight down and stepped on the little finger of her right hand. Jewett's account was that he had jumped up to intercept a pass and knocked Knight over as he came down; when he landed, he stepped back and onto Knight's hand. Knight's version of the events was somewhat different: as Jewett was chasing one of her teammates who had caught the ball, he came up from behind Knight and knocked her down. Knight put her arms out to break the fall and Jewett ran over her, stepping on her hand. Knight conceded in deposition testimony that Jewett did not intend to step on her hand and did not intend to hurt her.

Knight had three surgeries on the finger, but they proved unsuccessful. Ultimately the finger was amputated. She sued Jewett for battery, among other things. The trial court gave summary judgment to Jewett, and the California Supreme Court affirmed:

> A requisite element of assault and battery is intent. Here, however, there is no evidence that Jewett intended to injure Knight or commit a battery on her. Moreover, the record affirmatively shows Knight does not believe Jewett had the intent to step on her hand or injure her. Without the requisite intent, Knight cannot state a cause of action for assault and battery.

What is the superficial similarity between *Knight v. Jewett* and *Vosburg v. Putney?* What is the distinction between them?

(3.) *The piano lesson (problem).* In White v. University of Idaho, 768 P.2d 827 (Idaho 1989), Richard Neher was a professor of music at the University of Idaho. One morning he was visiting the home of one of his students, Carol White. White was seated at a counter when Neher walked up behind her and touched her back with both of his hands in a movement later described as one a pianist would make in striking and lifting the fingers from a keyboard. The resulting contact generated unexpectedly harmful injuries: White suffered thoracic outlet syndrome, requiring the removal of the first rib on the right side; she also experienced scarring of the brachial plexus nerve, which necessitated the severing of the scalenus anterior muscles in her neck. White sued Neher and the University of Idaho to recover her damages.

The University sought summary judgment on the ground that under a state statute it could not be held liable for a battery committed by one of its employees. The question thus became whether Neher's act *had* been a battery. Neher stated that he intentionally touched the plaintiff's back but said that his purpose was to demonstrate the sensation of this particular movement by a pianist, not to cause any harm. He explained that he has occasionally used this contact method in teaching his piano students. The plaintiff said that Neher's act took her by surprise, that she would not have consented to such contact, and that she found it offensive. What result on the summary judgment motion?

4. *A summing up?* From the Restatement (Second) of Torts (1965):

§18. BATTERY: OFFENSIVE CONTACT

> (1) An actor is subject to liability to another for battery if
>   (a) he acts intending to cause a harmful or offensive contact with the person of the other or a third person, or an imminent apprehension of such a contact, and

(b) an offensive contact with the person of the other directly or indirectly results.

(2) An act which is not done with the intention stated in Subsection (1, a) does not make the actor liable to the other for a mere offensive contact with the other's person although the act involves an unreasonable risk of inflicting it and, therefore, would be negligent or reckless if the risk threatened bodily harm.

Is this provision from the Second Restatement consistent with the cases seen so far?

5. *The insanity defense.* In Polmatier v. Russ, 537 A.2d 468 (Conn. 1988), the defendant, Norman Russ, opened fire on his father-in-law with a shotgun, killing him. Five hours later Russ was found in a wooded area two miles away, crying and sitting naked on a tree stump holding the shotgun and his infant daughter. Russ later described himself as a supreme being who had the power to rule the destiny of the world. He further claimed that his father-in-law was a spy for the Red Chinese who had planned to kill him. Russ was prosecuted for murder and found not guilty by reason of insanity; a psychiatrist testified that Russ suffered from a severe case of paranoid schizophrenia with auditory hallucinations. The decedent's wife then brought a civil suit against Russ for wrongful death. The same psychiatric testimony was offered. The trial court gave judgment to the plaintiff and the Connecticut Supreme Court affirmed. The court first announced its general adherence to the traditional rule against making an allowance for insanity in measuring a defendant's intent, adopting this statement of the rationale from an earlier Illinois case:

> There is, to be sure, an appearance of hardship in compelling one to respond for that which he is unable to avoid for want of the control of reason. But the question of liability in these cases is one of public policy. If an insane person is not held liable for his torts, those interested in his estate, as relatives or otherwise, might not have a sufficient motive to so take care of him as to deprive him of opportunities for inflicting injuries upon others. There is more injustice in denying to the injured party the recovery of damages for the wrong suffered by him, than there is in calling upon the relatives or friends of the lunatic to pay the expense of his confinement, if he has an estate ample enough for that purpose. The liability of lunatics for their torts tends to secure a more efficient custody and guardianship of their persons. Again, if parties can escape the consequences of their injurious acts upon the plea of lunacy, there will be a strong temptation to simulate insanity with a view of masking the malice and revenge of an evil heart.

The court then further rejected Russ's claim that his act was involuntary:

> The defendant argues that for an act to be done with the requisite intent, the act must be an external manifestation of the actor's will. The

defendant specifically relies on the Restatement (Second) of Torts §14, comment b, for the definition of what constitutes an "act," where it is stated that "a muscular movement which is purely reflexive or the convulsive movements of an epileptic are not acts in the sense in which that word is used in the Restatement. So too, movements of the body during sleep or while the will is otherwise in abeyance are not acts. An external manifestation of the will is necessary to constitute an act, and an act is necessary to make one liable [for a battery]. . . ." The defendant argues that if his "activities were the external manifestations of irrational and uncontrollable thought disorders these activities cannot be acts for purposes of establishing liability for assault and battery." We disagree.

We note that we have not been referred to any evidence indicating that the defendant's acts were reflexive, convulsive or epileptic. Furthermore, under the Restatement (Second) of Torts §2, "act" is used "to denote an external manifestation of the actor's will and does not include any of its results, even the most direct, immediate, and intended." Comment b to this section provides in pertinent part: "A muscular reaction is always an act unless it is a purely reflexive reaction in which the mind and will have no share." Although the trial court found that the defendant could not form a rational choice, it did find that he could make a schizophrenic or crazy choice. Moreover, a rational choice is not required since "[a]n insane person may have an intent to invade the interests of another, even though his reasons and motives for forming that intention may be entirely irrational." Restatement (Second) of Torts §895J, comment c. The following example is given in the Restatement to illustrate the application of comment c: "A, who is insane believes that he is Napoleon Bonaparte, and that B, his nurse, who confines him in his room, is an agent of the Duke of Wellington, who is endeavoring to prevent his arrival on the field of Waterloo in time to win the battle. Seeking to escape, he breaks off the leg of a chair, attacks B with it and fractures her skull. A is subject to liability to B for battery."

6. *The first law of nature.* In Laidlaw v. Sage, 158 N.Y. 73, 52 N.E. 679 (1899), *rev'g* 2 A.D. 374, 37 N.Y.S. 770 (1896), a mysterious stranger, later determined to be a man called Norcross, appeared one afternoon at the New York office of Russell Sage, a wealthy financier and philanthropist. The stranger was carrying a carpet bag and said that he wanted to see Sage about some railroad bonds; he claimed to have a letter of introduction from John D. Rockefeller. Sage invited Norcross in and then read the letter; it ran as follows: "The bag I hold in my hand contains ten pounds of dynamite. If I drop this bag on the floor, the dynamite will explode, and destroy this building in ruins, and kill every human being in the building. I demand $1,200,000, or I will drop the bag. Will you give it? Yes or no?" Sage returned the letter to Norcross and then started to talk, saying that he was short of time and that if Norcross's business was going to take long he should come back

later. While Sage was talking he slowly moved toward a clerk in his office who did not realize what was happening. Sage placed his hand on his clerk's shoulder and gently moved him in front of Norcross so that the clerk's body was blocking Sage from the possible blast. Norcross soon concluded that he was not going to get the money and pulled the fuse on the carpet bag; this detonated a tremendous explosion that wrecked Sage's office and much of the rest of the building. Norcross was obliterated by the blast and the clerk was injured. Russell Sage was unharmed. The clerk sued Sage for battery.

The case was tried several times due to the appellate courts' determinations of error in the trial court. The evidence in the resulting trials raised questions about whether the plaintiff might have sustained the same injuries whether or not the defendant had used him as a shield and whether the defendant had acted voluntarily. In the fourth trial the jury returned a verdict for the plaintiff and the trial court entered judgment upon it. The defendant appealed to the New York Court of Appeals, which held that the trial court misdirected the jury on whether the defendant had committed a voluntary act and that the defendant was entitled to a fifth trial of the case against him. Said the court:

> That the duties and responsibilities of a person confronted with such a danger are different and unlike those which follow his actions in performing the ordinary duties of life under other conditions is a well-established principle of law. The rule applicable [...] is stated in Moak's Underhill on Torts (page 14), as follows: "The law presumes that an act or omission done or neglected under the influence of pressing danger was done or neglected involuntarily." It is there said that this rule seems to be founded upon the maxim that self-preservation is the first law of nature, and that, where it is a question whether one of two men shall suffer, each is justified in doing the best he can for himself. [...] Indeed, the trial court recognized this doctrine in its charge, but submitted to the jury the question whether the act of the defendant was involuntary, and induced by impending danger, adding that the testimony of the defendant that everything he did, he did intentionally, was sufficient to justify it in finding that he voluntarily moved the plaintiff in the manner claimed by him. [...]
>
> [I]t is extremely difficult, upon a consideration of all the evidence in the record relating to this subject, to see how a jury was justified in finding that the defendant voluntarily interfered with the person of the plaintiff. [...]
>
> It is impossible to consider the plaintiff's injuries without a feeling of profound sympathy. His misfortune was a severe one, but sympathy, although one of the noblest sentiments of our nature, which brings its reward to both the subject and actor, has no proper place in the administration of the law. It is properly based upon moral or charitable considerations alone, and neither courts nor juries are justified in yielding to its influence in the discharge of their important and responsible duties.

Was *Laidlaw v. Sage* correctly decided? Can it be squared with *Polmatier v. Russ*? If not, which case offers a preferable view of the voluntary act requirement?

7. *Horse play*. In Keel v. Hainline, 331 P.2d 397 (Okla. 1958), approximately 40 students at a public middle school in Tulsa went to a classroom for instruction in music. The class met at 10:30 A.M., but for unknown reasons their instructor did not make an appearance until some 30 minutes later. During the instructor's absence several of the male students indulged in what they termed "horse play": they assembled at opposite ends of the classroom and threw chalkboard erasers and chalk back and forth at each other. This went on for about half an hour; it ended when an eraser thrown by one of the defendants struck the plaintiff in the face, shattering her glasses and resulting in her loss of one eye. The plaintiff had been sitting in her chair near the center of the room and studying her lessons when she was struck by the eraser; she had not been participating in the horse play. None of the defendants intended to strike or injure the plaintiff. They were throwing the erasers at each other in sport and apparently without intending to cause injury.

The plaintiff brought a suit for battery against several of the boys: the one who threw the eraser and also several of the others involved in the eraser fight. The jury brought in a verdict in her favor against all of the defendants, and the trial court entered judgment upon it. One of the defendants — the defendant at whom the fateful eraser had been thrown — appealed.

Held, for the plaintiff, that the trial court did not err in entering judgment on the jury's verdict. Said the court:

> Defendant strenuously argues that the class had not been called to order by the teacher and that the defendants were merely playing until the teacher arrived, and therefore could not be said to have been engaged in any wrongful or unlawful acts. We do not agree. We do not believe and are not willing to hold that the willful and deliberate throwing of wooden blackboard erasers at other persons in a class room containing 35 to 40 students is an innocent and lawful pastime, even though done in sport and without intent to injure. Such conduct is wrongful, and we so hold. Under such circumstances the rule applicable to this case is well stated at 4 Am. Jur. 128, Assault and Battery, sec.5, as follows: "Where, however, the basis of an action is assault and battery, the intention with which the injury was done is immaterial so far as the maintenance of the action is concerned, provided the act causing the injury was wrongful, for if the act was wrongful, the intent must necessarily have been wrongful. The fact that an act was done with a good intention, or without any unlawful intention, cannot change that which, by reason of its unlawfulness, is essentially an assault and battery into a lawful act, thereby releasing the aggressor from liability."

Keel, the defendant who appealed, also argued that he should not be held liable because everyone agreed that he did not throw the eraser that hit the plaintiff. The trial court had instructed the jury as follows:

> If you find for the plaintiff and against the defendant who actually threw the eraser, then you are instructed that if you should further find and believe from a preponderance of the evidence, that one or more of the remaining defendants, did by their acts, signs, gestures, words or demeanor, either aid, abet, encourage, procure, promote or instigate the assault and battery, then your verdict should be against all of the defendants who participated in the assault and battery, if any, either as the actual assailant or by aiding, abetting, encouraging, procuring, promoting or instigating the throwing of the eraser by the actual assailant.

The Oklahoma Supreme Court rejected Keel's argument and approved the above instruction as a correct statement of the law.

What is the relationship between *Keel v. Hainline* and *Vosburg v. Putney*? What were the intentions of the defendant who threw the eraser? Of the defendant (the appellant here) at whom the eraser was thrown?

8. *Transferred intent.* The basic doctrine that permitted the student who threw the eraser to be held liable is known as "transferred intent": if A attempts to commit a battery against B but mistakenly hits C instead, C can sue A for battery. It is no defense for A to say that he had no intent to cause contact with C. A's intentions toward B are combined with the harmful contact with C to create a battery.

9. *"Transferred" transferred intent.* The Oklahoma courts went beyond ordinary transferred intent, however, in also affirming liability for Keel, the boy at whom the eraser was thrown. This amounts to transferred intent in a different sense than was discussed a moment ago; it is a kind of liability imposed upon Keel for a secondary role in the events that produced the plaintiff's injury. What are the implications of such liability? Does it mean that if A shoots at B but mistakenly hits C, B is liable to C for battery? What if B had been goading A?

10. *Collecting the judgment. Vosburg v. Putney* and *Keel v. Hainline* both involve litigation against children, raising natural questions about how the defendants proposed to collect the judgments they won. The common law does not hold parents liable for their children's tortious acts, so judgments against children generally cannot be executed against their parents' assets. The plaintiff can collect the judgment from the child if the child has assets; and in some instances the plaintiff may also be able to renew the judgment at intervals prescribed by statute as the child grows older and accumulates property.

The common law rule respecting parents and children has been modified by statute in many jurisdictions. This North Carolina statute, §1-538.1, is typical:

> Any person or other legal entity shall be entitled to recover actual damages suffered in an amount not to exceed a total of two thousand dollars ($2,000) from the parent or parents of any minor who shall maliciously or willfully injure such person or destroy the real or personal property of such person.

To these rules compare the doctrine of respondeat superior, which generally allows employers to be sued for acts of negligence committed by their employees in the course of their employment (and also for intentional torts employees commit in furtherance of their employers' interests). Why might it be that employers routinely are held liable for torts committed by their employees while parents usually are not held liable for torts committed by their children? That question is considered in more detail in the treatment of respondeat superior later in the book.

11. *Wild pitch.* In Manning v. Grimsley, 643 F.2d 20 (1st Cir. 1981), the plaintiff was a spectator at a baseball game between the Boston Red Sox and the Baltimore Orioles at Fenway Park in Boston. He was seated in the right field bleachers, separated from the bullpen by a wire mesh fence. As Ross Grimsley, a pitcher for the Orioles, was warming up, the Red Sox fans continuously heckled him. On several occasions Grimsley gave the hecklers dirty looks. Finally Grimsley wound up as though to throw toward the bullpen plate one last time; but when he threw the ball, it flew at more than 80 miles an hour away from the plate and directly toward the hecklers in the bleachers. The ball went through the wire mesh fence and hit the plaintiff, who may or may not have been a heckler. The district court directed a verdict for the defendants on the plaintiff's battery count. The plaintiff sued Grimsley and the Orioles. The trial court gave a directed verdict to the defendants; the court of appeals reversed and remanded the case for a new trial. Said the court:

> We, unlike the district judge, are of the view that from the evidence that Grimsley was an expert pitcher, that on several occasions immediately following heckling he looked directly at the hecklers, not just into the stands, and that the ball traveled at a right angle to the direction in which he had been pitching and in the direction of the hecklers, the jury could reasonably have inferred that Grimsley intended (1) to throw the ball in the direction of the hecklers, [and] (2) to cause them imminent apprehension of being hit [. . .].
>
> The foregoing evidence and inferences would have permitted a jury to conclude that the defendant Grimsley committed a battery against the

plaintiff. This case falls within the scope of Restatement Torts 2d §13 which provides, inter alia, that an actor is subject to liability to another for battery if intending to cause a third person to have an imminent apprehension of a harmful bodily contact, the actor causes the other to suffer a harmful contact. Although we have not found any Massachusetts case which directly supports that aspect of §13 which we have just set forth, we have no doubt that it would be followed by the Massachusetts Supreme Judicial Court. [. . .] The whole rule and especially that aspect of the rule which permits recovery by a person who was not the target of the defendant embody a strong social policy including obedience to the criminal law by imposing an absolute civil liability to anyone who is physically injured as a result of an intentional harmful contact or a threat thereof directed either at him or a third person. It, therefore, was error for the district court to have directed a verdict for defendant Grimsley on the battery count. [. . .]

What is the relationship between *Grimsley* and *Keel v. Hainline* (the case of the errant eraser)? Does it follow from the appellant's liability in *Keel* that the plaintiff in *Grimsley* also could have brought suit against the hecklers?

12. *When will intent transfer?* It will aid your understanding of *Manning v. Grimsley* to note that Grimsley was found to have intended to cause the hecklers "imminent apprehension of being hit." To intentionally cause someone to have imminent apprehension of being hit is to commit an *assault,* not a battery. Since Grimsley did have a sufficient intent to commit an intentional tort, however, that intent was enough to support liability for battery.

Suppose the *Vosburg* defendant tried to kick one of his friends but missed and instead kicked the plaintiff, causing catastrophic injury to his leg. Would there be liability under the reasoning of *Manning v. Grimsley?* Would there be liability for Vosburg's friend under *Keel v. Hainline?*

2. Minimum Requirements

Having considered the intent requirement for battery, we now start our consideration of another aspect of the tort: the requirement that the defendant must commit or cause a harmful or offensive touching of the plaintiff. This element can raise several distinct types of issues that we will consider in turn. The first is how direct and invasive the contact between the parties must be before it rises to the level of "harmful or offensive."

①. *Smoke gets in your eyes.* In Leichtman v. WLW Jacor Communications, Inc., 634 N.E.2d 697 (Ohio App. 1994), the plaintiff, an antismoking advocate, alleged that he was invited to appear as a guest on a radio talk show to discuss smoking and the effects of secondary smoke. At the urging of one of the show's hosts, a second host lit a cigar and repeatedly blew smoke in the plaintiff's face. The plaintiff sued the two hosts and the radio station for battery, claiming the host blew the smoke in his face "for the purpose of causing physical discomfort, humiliation and distress." The trial court dismissed the claim. The court of appeals reversed, holding that tobacco smoke was "particulate matter" capable of making physical contact and of offending a reasonable sense of personal dignity, and thus that if the defendant intentionally directed the smoke toward the plaintiff he could be held liable for committing a battery.

2. *Liability for buses.* In Madden v. D.C. Transit System, Inc., 307 A.2d 756 (D.C. 1973), the plaintiff sought $70,000 in damages from the defendant for assault and battery. The plaintiff alleged that while standing on the traffic island near the corner of an intersection he was contacted by fumes and offensive oily substances that the defendant permitted to spew from two of its buses. The plaintiff further alleged that the defendant was aware that these regularly were discharged from its buses and that the emissions therefore were intentional. The trial court dismissed the complaint, stating that absent a showing of malice, willfulness, or specific wrongful intent, the defendant could not be held liable for the acts alleged. The plaintiff appealed, and the court of appeals affirmed.

What is the distinction between *Madden v. D.C. Transit System, Inc.* and *Leichtman v. WLW Jacor Communications, Inc.?*

3. *Just checking.* In Morgan v. Loyacomo, 1 So. 2d 510 (Miss. 1941), the plaintiff purchased an article of underwear from the defendant's store. The defendant's manager saw the purchase and suspected that the plaintiff had taken two garments but paid for only one. The manager followed the plaintiff out of the store and pursued her for a block; he then called to her in front of several other people and said he was obliged to investigate whether she had taken an article from the store without paying for it. He seized the package from under her arm, opened it, and discovered that he had been incorrect. The plaintiff sued the store for battery (as well as slander and assault). The trial court entered judgment on a verdict for the plaintiff, and the Mississippi Supreme Court affirmed: "The authorities are agreed that, to constitute an assault and battery, it is not necessary to touch the plaintiff's body or even his clothing; knocking or snatching anything from plaintiff's hand or touching anything connected with his person, when done in a rude or insolent manner, is sufficient."

What should the manager have done? The common law originally provided shopkeepers with a privilege to use reasonable force to retake their goods from thieves, but merchants using the privilege were fully liable in tort if they turned out to be mistaken in the way the defendant's manager was here. By the latter half of the twentieth century retailers commonly had moved their wares out from behind counters and onto floors where customers could inspect them, making it harder to be sure whether a theft was occurring; the privilege was broadened accordingly, sometimes by courts and sometimes by statute. See, e.g., Ariz. Rev. Stat. §13-1805(c): "A merchant, or a merchant's agent or employee, with reasonable cause, may detain on the premises in a reasonable manner and for a reasonable time any person suspected of shoplifting [ ] for questioning or summoning a law enforcement officer."

4. *Crowded world.* In Wallace v. Rosen, 765 N.E.2d 192 (Ind. App. 2002), the plaintiff, Mable Wallace, was delivering homework to her daughter at a public high school in Indianapolis. Wallace and her daughter were standing on the second floor landing of a stairwell when the school initiated a fire drill. An alarm sounded. One of the school's teachers, Rosen, led her class to the stairway where Wallace was standing. Rosen told Wallace to "move it" because a fire drill was in progress. Wallace's testimony was that Rosen put her fingers on Wallace's shoulders and turned her 90 degrees toward the open stairs. At that point Wallace slipped and fell down the stairs (she was recovering from foot surgery, and so was less stable than usual) and sustained various injuries. She sued Rosen and the school system. The trial court refused to instruct the jury that it could find the defendants liable for battery if Wallace's testimony was believed. The case proceeded on other counts, and the jury brought in a verdict for the defendants. The plaintiff appealed, claiming the trial court was mistaken in refusing to instruct the jury on battery. The court of appeals affirmed:

> Professors Prosser and Keeton [ ] made the following observations about the intentional tort of battery and the character of the defendant's action:
>
> "[I]n a crowded world, a certain amount of personal contact is inevitable and must be accepted. Absent expression to the contrary, consent is assumed to all those ordinary contacts which are customary and reasonably necessary to the common intercourse of life, such as a tap on the shoulder to attract attention, a friendly grasp of the arm, or a casual jostling to make a passage. . . .
>
> "The time and place, and the circumstances under which the act is done, will necessarily affect its unpermitted character, and so will the relations between the parties. A stranger is not to be expected to tolerate liberties which would be allowed by an intimate friend. But unless the defendant has special reason to believe that more or less will be permitted by the individual plaintiff, the test is what would be offensive to an ordinary person not unduly sensitive as to personal dignity."
>
> Prosser and Keeton on Torts §9. [. . .] The conditions on the stairway of Northwest High School during the fire drill were an example of Professors Prosser and Keeton's "crowded world." Individuals standing in the middle of a stairway during the fire drill could expect that a certain amount of personal contact would be inevitable. Rosen had a responsibility to her students to keep them moving in an orderly fashion down the stairs and out the door. Under these circumstances, Rosen's touching of

Wallace's shoulder or back with her fingertips to get her attention over the noise of the alarm cannot be said to be a rude, insolent, or angry touching.

What is the distinction between *Wallace v. Rosen* and *Morgan v. Loyacomo*? What is the distinction between *Wallace* and *White v. University of Idaho* (the L case of the piano teacher's unwelcome demonstration of technique)?

5. *Offensive contact.* From the Restatement (Second) of Torts:

§18. BATTERY: OFFENSIVE CONTACT

Comment c. Meaning of "contact with another's person." In order to make the actor liable under the rule stated in this Section, it is not necessary that he should bring any part of his own body in contact with another's person. It is enough that he intentionally cause his clothing or anything held or attached to him to come into such contact. So too, he is liable under the rule stated in this Section if he throws a substance, such as water, upon the other or if he sets a dog upon him. It is not necessary that the contact with the other's person be directly caused by some act of the actor. All that is necessary is that the actor intend to cause the other, directly or indirectly, to come in contact with a foreign substance in a manner which the other will reasonably regard as offensive. Thus, if the actor daubs with filth a towel which he expects another to use in wiping his face with the expectation that the other will smear his face with it and the other does so, the actor is liable as fully as though he had directly thrown the filth in the other's face or had otherwise smeared his face with it. [. . .]

Comment d. Knowledge of contact. In order that the actor may be liable under the statement in this Subsection, it is not necessary that the other should know of the offensive contact which is inflicted upon him at the time when it is inflicted. The actor's liability is based upon his intentional invasion of the other's dignitary interest in the inviolability of his person and the affront to the other's dignity involved therein. This affront is as keenly felt by one who only knows after the event that an indignity has been perpetrated upon him as by one who is conscious of it while it is being perpetrated.

Illustration 2. A kisses B while asleep but does not waken or harm her. A is subject to liability to B.

Comment g. Necessity of intention. The interest which one has in the inviolability of his person and, therefore, in freedom from unpermitted contacts which, while offensive to a reasonable sense of personal dignity cause no substantial or tangible bodily harm, is an interest of dignitary rather than of material value. As such, it is protected only against intentional invasion. The actor is not liable for an act which involves a risk, no matter how great and unreasonable, that it will cause only an offensive contact, although his conduct if it involved a similar risk of invading a materially valuable interest would be actionable negligence or even recklessness. So too, the actor whose conduct is negligent or reckless because of the risk involved of causing an invasion of some materially valuable interest does not become liable if it causes only an offensive contact.

Illustration 4. A throws dirty water from his window at B who is walking on a street below. A few drops fall on B's hand but do him no bodily harm. A is subject to liability to B.

§19. WHAT CONSTITUTES OFFENSIVE CONTACT

A bodily contact is offensive if it offends a reasonable sense of personal dignity.

Illustration 2. A, while walking in a densely crowded street, deliberately but not discourteously pushes against B in order to pass him. This is not an offensive touching of B.

Illustration 3. A, who is suffering from a contagious skin disease, touches B's hands, thus putting B in reasonable apprehension of contagion. This is an offensive touching of B.

6. *Cultural relativity.* A danger in offering excerpts from the Restatement is that they may be mistaken for settled rules. They are not; they are attempts to generalize from existing case law and to speculate where case law is unavailable. Regard them as suggestions, not dictates. This may be especially important in an area of law such as battery where the legal rules are contingent on conventions within the larger culture. Consider Hall, The Hidden Dimension (1966):

In the Western world, the person is synonymous with an individual inside a skin. And in northern Europe generally, the skin and even the clothes may be inviolate. You need permission to touch either if you are a stranger. This rule applies in some parts of France, where the mere touching of another person during an argument used to be legally defined as assault. For the Arab the location of the person in relation to the body is quite different. The person exists somewhere down inside the body. The ego is not completely hidden, however, because it can be reached very easily with an insult. It is protected from touch but not from words. The dissociation of the body and the ego may explain why the public amputation of a thief's hand is tolerated as standard punishment in Saudi Arabia.

Has the meaning of an "offensive" touching in the United States changed over the past 40 years?

3. *Consent and its Limits*

A second and more complex question concerning battery, to which we now will devote more time, involves whether and when a plaintiff's consent to such contact may free the defendant from liability. Sometimes a defendant will offer a plaintiff's consent as an affirmative defense, or a "privilege," to a battery claim; in other cases the consent may simply render an otherwise offensive contact inoffensive, negating an essential aspect of the plaintiff's case. We discuss consent in this section rather than in the subsequent chapter on privileges because it is closely connected to the question of whether a touching is harmful or offensive in the first place.

Mohr v. Williams
108 N.W. 818 (Minn. 1906)

wrong cite! 104 NW2d 12

BROWN, J. — Defendant is a physician and surgeon of standing and character, making disorders of the ear a specialty, and having an extensive practice in the city of St. Paul. He was consulted by plaintiff, who complained to him of trouble with her right ear, and, at her request, made an examination of that organ for the purpose of ascertaining its condition. He also at the same time examined her left ear, but, owing to foreign substances therein, was unable to make a full and complete diagnosis at that time. The examination of her right ear disclosed a large perforation in the lower portion of the drum membrane, and a large polyp in the middle ear, which indicated that some of the small bones of the middle ear (ossicles) were probably diseased. He informed plaintiff of the result of his examination, and advised an operation for the purpose of removing the polyp and diseased ossicles. After consultation with her family physician, and one or two further consultations with defendant, plaintiff decided to submit to the proposed operation. She was not informed that her left ear was in any way diseased, and understood that the necessity for an operation applied to her right ear only. She repaired to the hospital, and was placed under the influence of anaesthetics; and, after being made unconscious, defendant made a thorough examination of her left ear, and found it in a more serious condition than her right one. A small perforation was discovered high up in the drum membrane, hooded, and with granulated edges, and the bone of the inner wall of the middle ear was diseased and dead. He called this discovery to the attention of Dr. Davis — plaintiff's family physician, who attended the operation at her request — who also examined the ear, and confirmed defendant in his diagnosis. Defendant also further examined the right ear, and found its condition less serious than expected, and finally concluded that the left, instead of the right, should be operated upon; devoting to the right ear other treatment. He then performed the operation of ossiculectomy on plaintiff's left ear; removing a portion of the drum membrane, and scraping away the diseased portion of the inner wall of the ear.

This is 1st appeal...

The operation was in every way successful and skillfully performed. It is claimed by plaintiff that the operation greatly impaired her hearing, seriously injured her person, and, not having been consented to by her, was wrongful and unlawful, constituting an assault and battery; and she brought this action to recover damages therefor. The trial in the court below resulted in a verdict for plaintiff for $14,322.50. Defendant thereafter moved the court for judgment notwithstanding the verdict, on the ground that, on the evidence presented, plaintiff was not entitled to recover, or, if that relief was denied, for a new trial on the ground, among others, that the verdict was excessive; appearing to have been given under the influence of passion and prejudice. The trial court denied the motion for judgment, but granted a new trial on the ground, as stated in the order, that the damages were excessive. Defendant appealed from the order denying the motion for judgment, and plaintiff appealed from the order granting a new trial. . . .

We shall consider first the question whether, under the circumstances shown in the record, the consent of plaintiff to the operation was necessary. If, under the particular facts of this case, such consent was unnecessary, no recovery can be had, for the evidence fairly shows that the operation complained of was skillfully performed and of a generally beneficial nature. But if the consent of plaintiff was necessary, then the further questions presented become important. This particular question is new in this state. At least, no case has been called to our attention wherein it has been discussed or decided, and very few cases are cited from other courts. We have given it very deliberate consideration, and are unable to concur with counsel for defendant in their contention that the consent of plaintiff was unnecessary. The evidence tends to show that, upon the first examination of plaintiff, defendant pronounced the left ear in good condition, and that, at the time plaintiff repaired to the hospital to submit to the operation on her right ear, she was under the impression that no difficulty existed as to the left. In fact, she testified that she had not previously experienced any trouble with that organ. It cannot be doubted that ordinarily the patient must be consulted, and his consent given, before a physician may operate upon him. It was said in the case of Pratt v. Davis, 37 Chicago Leg. News, 213, referred to and commented on in Cent. Law J. 452: "Under a free government, at least, the free citizen's first and greatest right, which underlies all others — the right to the inviolability of his person; in other words, the right to himself — is the subject of universal acquiescence, and this right necessarily forbids a physician or surgeon, however skillful or eminent, who has been asked to examine, diagnose, advise, and prescribe (which are at least necessary first steps in treatment and care), to violate, without permission, the bodily integrity of his patient by a major or capital operation, placing him under an anaesthetic for that purpose, and operating upon him without his consent or knowledge." 1 Kinkead on Torts, §375, states the general rule on this subject as follows: "The patient must be the final arbiter as to whether he will take his chances with the operation, or take his chances of living without it. Such is the natural right of the individual, which the law recognizes as a legal one. Consent, therefore, of an individual, must be either expressly or impliedly given before a surgeon may have the right to operate." There is logic in the principle thus stated, for, in all other trades, professions, or occupations, contracts are entered into by the mutual agreement of the interested parties, and are required to be performed in accordance with their letter and spirit. No reason occurs to us why the same rule should not apply between physician and patient. If the physician advises his patient to submit to a particular operation, and the patient weighs the dangers and risks incident to its performance, and finally consents, he thereby, in effect, enters into a contract authorizing his physician to operate to the extent of the consent given, but no further. It is not, however, contended by defendant that under ordinary circumstances consent is unnecessary, but that, under the particular circumstances of this case, consent was implied; that it was an emergency case, such as to authorize the operation without express consent or permission. The medical profession has made signal progress in solving the problems of health and disease, and they may justly point with pride to the advancements made in supplementing nature and correcting deformities, and relieving pain and suffering. The physician impliedly contracts that he possesses, and will exercise in the treatment of patients, skill and learning, and that he will exercise reasonable care and exert his best judgment to bring about favorable results. The methods of treatment are committed almost exclusively to his judgment, but we are aware of no rule or principle of law which would extend to him free license respecting surgical operations. Reasonable latitude must, however, be allowed the physician in a particular case; and we would not lay down any rule which would unreasonably interfere with the exercise of his discretion, or prevent him from taking such measures as his judgment dictated for the welfare of the patient in a case of emergency. If a person should be injured to the extent of rendering him unconscious, and his injuries were of such a nature as to require prompt surgical attention, a physician called to attend him would be justified in applying such medical or surgical treatment as might reasonably be necessary for the preservation of his life or limb, and consent on the part of the injured person would be implied. And again, if, in the course of an operation to which the patient consented, the physician should discover conditions not anticipated before the operation was commenced, and which, if not removed, would endanger the life or health of the patient, he would, though no express consent was obtained or given, be justified in extending the operation to remove and overcome them. But such is not the case at bar. The diseased condition of plaintiff's left ear was not discovered in the course of an operation on the right, which was authorized, but upon an independent examination of that organ, made after the authorized operation was found unnecessary. Nor is the evidence such as to justify the court in holding, as a matter of law, that it was such an affection as would result immediately in the serious injury of plaintiff, or such an emergency as to justify proceeding without her consent. She had experienced no particular difficulty with that ear, and the questions as to when its diseased condition would become alarming or fatal, and whether there was an immediate necessity for an operation, were, under the evidence, questions of fact for the jury.

[Affirmed.]

NOTES

1. *Ghost surgery.* In Grabowski v. Quigley, 684 A.2d 610 (Pa. Super. 1996), the plaintiff, Grabowski, injured his back when he slipped and fell on a patch of ice. He sought treatment from defendant Quigley. As a result of their consultation Grabowski agreed that he would undergo surgery and that Quigley would perform it. Some days later Grabowski was put under anesthesia and the surgery was performed. Afterwards Grabowski encountered problems with his left foot; it dragged when he walked. Quigley recommended more surgery. Grabowski decided to seek a second opinion and requested copies of his medical records. Upon inspecting them he discovered that his first surgery largely had been performed not by Quigley, who had been in the next county during most of the operation, but by a colleague of Quigley's named Bailes. Quigley later wrote a letter about the incident to one of his superiors describing what happened when he received a telephone call informing him that Grabowski was ready for surgery:

> [Y]ou can imagine my chagrin when [approximately one hour after anesthesia had been introduced] I received a phone call that my first case was on the table already asleep. At this point we faced two options, one of reawakening [Grabowski] and informing him of the mishap or having another physician starting the case and allowing time to return and finish it. We elected to do the latter.

Grabowski's suit alleged that Quigley and Bailes were liable for battery because the surgery was not performed by the doctor to whom Grabowski gave his consent — a phenomenon known as "ghost surgery." The trial court gave summary judgment to the defendants. The court of appeals reversed:

> Over thirty years ago our Supreme Court stated that "where a patient is mentally and physically able to consult about his condition, in the absence of an emergency, the consent of the patient is 'a prerequisite to a surgical operation by his physician' and an operation without the patient's consent is a technical assault." *Smith v. Yohe*, 194 A.2d 167 (Pa. 1963). [. . .] Since Appellant has alleged facts which, if true, established that consent was not given to Bailes and/or Quigley to perform the surgery in the manner in which it occurred, he has thereby alleged sufficient facts to establish a cause of action for battery against them.

What were Grabowski's damages? Compare this item from the Restatement (Second) of Torts:

§52. CONSENT: TO WHOM GIVEN

Comment b. It should be noted that there will be many cases, as where a patient goes to a hospital and is assigned a particular doctor, but is dealing with and relying upon the hospital rather than the individual, in which the consent given to one may reasonably be interpreted to include the acts of another, or of assistants or subordinates.

2. *Objective norms.* In Brzoska v. Olson, 668 A.2d 1355 (Del. 1995), Raymond Owens, a dentist in Wilmington, tested positive in early 1989 for the Human Immunodeficiency Virus (HIV). By the summer of 1990 Owens had AIDS, and he soon exhibited open lesions, weakness, and memory loss. In February of 1991 Owens discontinued his dental practice and was hospitalized. He died a month later. A group of his patients who had not known that Owens was so afflicted brought suit against Owens's estate alleging liability for battery and other torts. None of the patients tested positive for HIV, but they sought damages for mental anguish and reimbursement of payments they made to Owens for dental treatment. The trial court gave summary judgment to the defendant. The Delaware Supreme Court affirmed. The court found, first, that Owens had not committed an offensive touching of any of the plaintiffs:

> The offensive character of a contact in a battery case is assessed by a "reasonableness" standard. In a "fear of AIDS" case in which battery is alleged, therefore, we examine the overall reasonableness of the plaintiffs' fear in contracting the disease to determine whether the contact or touching was offensive. Since HIV causes AIDS, any assessment of the fear of contracting AIDS must, *ipso facto*, relate to the exposure to HIV. Moreover, because HIV is transmitted only through fluid-to-fluid contact or exposure, the reasonableness of a plaintiff's fear of AIDS should be measured by whether or not there was a channel of infection or actual exposure of the plaintiff to the virus. [. . .]
>
> [T]he record fails to establish actual exposure to HIV. Plaintiffs argue to the contrary, noting that Dr. Owens exhibited lesions on his arms, legs, and elbow, and that he was known to have cut himself on at least one occasion while working on a patient. They have not, however, averred that the wound or lesions of Dr. Owens ever came into contact with the person of any of the plaintiffs, nor have they identified which patient was present during Dr. Owens' injury or even whether that patient was a plaintiff in this action. In fact, nothing in this record suggests any bleeding from Dr. Owens or that any wound or lesions ever came into contact with a break in the skin or mucous membrane of any of the

plaintiffs. Plaintiffs have failed to demonstrate any evidence of actual exposure to potential HIV transmission beyond mere unsupported supposition. [. . .]

Were we to authorize recovery for battery for this type of subjective, offensive touching, we would permit a common law civil tort to form the basis for recovery in an area which requires the application of medical standards and probabilities. We would thus substitute the most fragile sensibilities of the patient for the objective norms which govern the rendering of medical/dental care in the community.

The plaintiffs further alleged that Owens had misrepresented his health to many of them, denying that he had AIDS when he was asked; they alleged that they would not have consented to the dental procedures he performed if they had known that he had AIDS. The court rejected this theory of battery as well:

In our view, the tort of battery is properly limited in the medical/dental setting to those circumstances in which a health care provider performs a procedure to which the patient has not consented. In other words, "a battery consists of a touching of a substantially different nature and character than that which the patient consented." K.A.C. v. Benson, 527 N.W.2d 553 (Minn. 1995). A physician may be held liable for battery when he or she obtains the consent of the patient to perform one procedure and the physician instead performs a substantially different procedure for which consent was not obtained. A patient's consent is not vitiated, however, when the patient is touched in exactly the way he or she consented. [. . .]

Is *Brzoska v. Olson* consistent with *Grabowski v. Quigley* (the L case where the plaintiff's surgery was performed by a doctor he did not expect)? How might the cases be distinguished?

3. *Idiosyncratic objections.* In Cohen v. Smith, 648 N.E.2d 329 (Ill. App. 1995), the plaintiff was admitted to a hospital to deliver her baby. It was determined that she would need to deliver by caesarian section. She informed her doctor, who in turn informed the hospital, that her religious beliefs forbade her to be seen unclothed by a man other than her husband. The plaintiff's complaint alleged that during the ensuing procedure a male nurse employed by the hospital nevertheless saw and touched her while her clothes were off. She sued the nurse and the hospital for battery and intentional infliction of emotional distress. The trial court dismissed her complaint; the court of appeals reversed:

Although most people in modern society have come to accept the necessity of being seen unclothed and being touched by members of the opposite sex during medical treatment, the plaintiffs had not accepted these procedures and, according to their complaint, had informed defendants of their convictions. This case is similar to cases involving Jehovah's Witnesses who were unwilling to accept blood transfusions because of religious convictions. Although most people do not share the Jehovah's Witnesses' beliefs about blood transfusions, our society, and our courts, accept their right to have that belief. Similarly, the courts have consistently recognized individuals' rights to refuse medical treatment even if such a refusal would result in an increased likelihood of the individual's death. [. . .]

Accepting as true the plaintiffs' allegations that they informed defendants of their religious beliefs and that defendants persisted in treating Patricia Cohen as they would have treated a patient without those beliefs, we conclude that the trial court erred in dismissing both the battery and the intentional infliction of emotional distress counts.

What is the distinction between *Cohen v. Smith* and *Brzoska v. Olson* (the NL case of the dentist who had AIDS)?

4. *Implied consent.* In Werth v. Taylor, 475 N.W.2d 426 (Mich. App. 1991), the plaintiff, Cindy Werth, was a Jehovah's Witness. Her faith regarded it as a sin to receive a blood transfusion. Werth began to experience considerable bleeding from her uterus after giving birth to twins at the defendant hospital. Her doctor, Parsons, recommended dilation of her cervix and curettage of the uterine lining (a "D & C" procedure). Werth soon was placed under general anesthesia. The bleeding continued along with a rise in Werth's blood pressure and other alarming symptoms, causing Parsons to conclude that without a blood transfusion Werth would die. One of the other doctors present, Taylor, ordered the transfusion. Parsons informed Taylor that Werth was a Jehovah's witness; Taylor replied, "that may be, but she needs the blood."

Werth recovered fully from the procedure; she then sued Parsons, Taylor, and the hospital for battery. Her evidence was that when she had preregistered at the hospital she had filled out a form titled "Refusal to Permit Blood Transfusion." After the delivery of the twins, Parsons had talked with Werth and her husband about their view regarding transfusions. Werth recalled the conversation as follows:

[Parsons] said, "I understand that you're one of Jehovah's Witnesses and that you won't take blood," and Don and I both said, "That's correct." And she said, "You mean to tell me if your wife's dying on the table that you're not going to give her blood?" And we said — Don said, "That's — well, I don't want her to have blood, but I don't want her to die. We want the alternative treatment."

Werth's husband recalled the two of them telling Parsons that Werth did not want a transfusion under any circumstances, though he also said that he was not focused on the possibility of her death at that time because he was not under the impression that her life was at risk.

The trial court gave summary judgment to the defendants. The court of appeals affirmed:

> [T]he law implies the consent of an unconscious patient to medical procedures needed to preserve the patient's life. If a physician treats or operates on a patient without consent, he has committed an assault and battery and may be required to respond in damages. Consent may be expressed or implied. It has been held that consent is implied where an emergency procedure is required and there is no opportunity to obtain actual consent or where the patient seeks treatment or otherwise manifests a willingness to submit to a particular treatment.
>
> It is undisputed that Cindy was unconscious when the critical decision regarding the blood transfusion to avoid her death was being made. Her prior refusals had not been made when her life was hanging in the balance or when it appeared that death might be a possibility if a transfusion were not given. Clearly, her refusals were, therefore, not contemporaneous or informed. Thus, a record could not be developed regarding Cindy's refusal which would leave open an issue upon which reasonable minds could differ.

What could Werth's damages have been? What is the distinction between *Werth v. Taylor* and *Cohen v. Smith*? Between *Werth v. Taylor* and *Grabowski v. Quigley* (the L case of "ghost surgery")? Between *Werth v. Taylor* and *Mohr v. Williams*?

Was there anything Werth could have done to prevent the transfusion? Did the court mean to suggest that Werth's acts suggested actual consent to a transfusion if her life was at stake? Or was the court prepared to infer consent in these circumstances for reasons unrelated to Werth's actual wishes? The former variety of consent is known as consent implied in fact; the latter, fictitious variety is known as consent implied in law.

5. *Consent and its consequences.* From the Restatement (Second) of Torts:

§892. MEANING OF CONSENT

(1) Consent is willingness in fact for conduct to occur. It may be manifested by action or inaction and need not be communicated to the actor.

(2) If words or conduct are reasonably understood by another to be intended as consent, they constitute apparent consent and are as effective as consent in fact.

Comment c. Apparent consent. Even when the person concerned does not in fact agree to the conduct of the other, his words or acts or even his inaction may manifest a consent that will justify the other in acting in reliance upon them. This is true when the words or acts or silence and inaction, would be understood by a reasonable person as intended to indicate consent and they are in fact so understood by the other. [. . .]

Illustration 3. A, a young man, is alone with B, a girl, in the moonlight. A proposes to kiss B. Although inwardly objecting, B says nothing and neither resists nor protests by any word or gesture. A kisses B. A is not liable to B.

Illustration 4. In the course of a quarrel, A threatens to punch B in the nose. B says nothing but stands his ground. A punches B in the nose. A is not justified upon the basis of apparent consent.

§892A. EFFECT OF CONSENT

Illustration 5. In a friendly test of strength, A permits B to punch him in the chest as hard as he can. B does so. Unknown to either A or B, A has a defective heart and as a result of the blow he drops dead. A's consent is effective to bar recovery for his death.

Illustration 6. The same facts as in Illustration 5 except that, without any intent or negligence on the part of B, A is knocked over against his valuable vase, which is shattered. The same result.

Illustration 9. A consents to a fight with B. Unknown to A, B uses a set of brass knuckles. B hits A in the nose, inflicting exactly the same harm as if he had used his fist. A's consent is not effective to bar his recovery.

6. *Frontiers of liability (problem).* In <u>Neal v. Neal</u>, 873 P.2d 871 (Idaho 1994), the plaintiff, Mary Neal, discovered that her husband, Thomas, was having an affair with a woman named LaGasse. In addition to filing for divorce she sued her husband for battery. Her theory was that she would not have had sexual intercourse with her husband during the time the affair was occurring if she had known about it; thus the consent she granted to her husband was fraudulently induced and her sexual relations with him amounted to a battery. What result?

7. *Fraud and mistake.* From the Restatement (Second) of Torts:

§892B. CONSENT UNDER MISTAKE, MISREPRESENTATION, OR DURESS

Illustration 6. A consents to a friendly boxing match with B. B knows that A is unaware of the fact that A has a defective heart. B punches A in the chest and A suffers a heart attack. B is subject to liability to A for battery.

Illustration 8. A permits B to stain A's face with walnut juice, for purposes of masquerade. A is ignorant of the fact that walnut juice leaves a permanent stain and B knows that A does not know it. B is subject to liability to A for battery.

§57. FRAUD OR MISTAKE AS TO COLLATERAL MATTER

Illustration 1. A, to induce B to submit to intimate familiarities, offers her a paper which A represents to be a twenty dollar bill but which he knows to be counterfeit. B, believing the paper to be a genuine bill, submits. A is not liable to B for battery.

Illustration 2. The same facts as in Illustration 1, except that the paper is offered if B will submit to a blood transfusion. A is subject to liability to B for the harm done by the operation to which A has fraudulently induced him to submit.

Are these illustrations consistent with each other? Are they consistent with the cases we have considered?

8. *Consent to illegal acts.* In Hart v. Geysel, 294 P. 570 (Wash. 1930), two men, Cartwright and Geysel, engaged in an illegal prize fight in Seattle. Cartwright died from injuries he received in the fight, and the administrator of his estate sued Geysel for damages. Geysel defended on the ground that Cartwright had consented to the fight. The trial court dismissed the complaint, and the Washington Supreme Court affirmed:

[I]n our opinion one who engages in prize fighting, even though prohibited by positive law, and sustains an injury, should not have a right to recover any damages that he may sustain as the result of the combat, which he expressly consented to and engaged in as a matter of business or sport. To enforce the criminal statute against prize fighting, it is not necessary to reward the one that got the worst of the encounter at the expense of his more fortunate opponent.

The majority cited this discussion from the American Law Institute:

[O]ne who has sufficiently expressed his willingness to suffer a particular invasion has no right to complaint if another acts upon his consent so given. The very nature of rights of personality, which are in freedom to dispose of one's interests of personality as one pleases, fundamentally requires this to be so. There is a further principle, applicable not only in tort law but throughout the whole field of law, and perhaps more conspicuously in other subjects, to the effect that no man shall profit by his own wrongdoing. [. . .]

Clearly if a plaintiff has consented to being struck by another in the course of a brawl, his right to the control of his person and to determine by whom and how it shall be touched has not been invaded. And it is equally clear that if he has so expressed his consent to the blow that, were he not party to a breach of the peace, his assent would be an operative consent and so bar his liability, he is profiting by the illegality of his conduct if because he is party to the breach of the peace he gains a right of action which but for his criminal joinder therein he would not have had.

9. *Road rage.* In McNeil v. Mullin, 79 P. 168 (Kan. 1905), the plaintiff and the defendant, both driving horse-drawn buggies, exchanged various hostile

words. Each dismounted and removed his hat and coat. A fight ensued. The plaintiff sued the defendant to recover for injuries he suffered in the brawl. The defendant responded that the plaintiff should be barred from recovery by his consent to the fight. The trial court entered judgment on a verdict for the defendant. The Kansas Supreme Court reversed and remanded for a new trial. It held that in view of the parties' consent, neither party could claim to have acted in self-defense; but nor was the plaintiff's consent to fight a good defense against his claim against the defendant for battery:

> There is some natural repugnancy to allowing damages to be recovered by a bullying blackguard who has courted a fight and has been soundly thrashed, but the law can indulge in no sentiment regarding the matter. It can concede no legal effect to his vicious purpose. His consent to fight must be treated as utterly void, and each party must be left to suffer all consequences, civil and criminal, of his reprehensible conduct.

The court cited this passage from *Cooley on Torts* in support of its holding:

> Consent is generally a full and perfect shield, when that is complained of as a civil injury which was consented to. A man cannot complain of a nuisance, the erection of which he concurred in or countenanced. He is not injured by a negligence which is partly chargeable to his own fault. A man may not even complain of the adultery of his wife, which he connived at or assented to. If he concurs in the dishonor of his bed, the law will not give him redress, because he is not wronged. These cases are plain enough, because they are cases in which the questions arise between the parties alone. But in case of a breach of the peace it is different. The state is wronged by this, and forbids it on public grounds. If men fight, the state will punish them. If one is injured, the law will not listen to an excuse based on a breach of the law. There are three parties here; one being the state, which, for its own good, does not suffer the others to deal on a basis of contract with the public peace. The rule of law is therefore clear and unquestionable that consent to an assault is no justification.

Does the opinion in *McNeil* imply that professional boxers generally should be able to sue each other for injuries they inflict on one another? How might that case be distinguished from *McNeil*?

10. *Dueling and deterrence.* The second of the two cases just presented — *McNeil* — represents the rule followed by courts in the majority of jurisdictions: consent to an unlawful act is no defense to a claim of battery. Either participant in mutual combat can collect damages from the other. Distinguish this situation from that of self-defense, where A attacks B and B

fights back. There is no consent involved in such a case. As we will see when we consider defenses to intentional tort claims, B's battery against A may then be privileged by a plea of self-defense so long as it was not an excessive response to A's initial attack. The problem of consent considered in *Hart* and *McNeil,* by contrast, arises when two parties agree to fight — with the result sometimes referred to as a "mutual affray," akin to a duel.

Which rule — the majority or the minority (represented by *Hart,* in which neither party can collect damages) — seems more likely to discourage fights? Consider whether the legal rule is likely to have any effect on the behavior of the average person deciding whether to fight; but consider, too, whether the response of the average person is the important question from the standpoint of public policy. Note that for the law to have such consequences, it need not influence the behavior of the average person. It need only affect the behavior of some people (those "at the margin," as economists say). And some potential combatants may be more likely than others to know the legal rule or to have it transmitted to them indirectly (in which of the two cases just considered is this more likely?). In any event, it is valuable to begin thinking carefully about the possible ways that legal rules *could* influence behavior — about the "ex ante" effects of rules. In this case it may help to break the problem down by thinking it through one character at a time. Start with the winner of a fight. Which rule would he prefer: the majority's or the minority's? How might the behavior of someone who expected to be a winner be affected by the majority rule? Then ask the same questions about the loser and his behavior. Whom is it more important to deter: winners or losers? Before fights begin, of course, the participants may not know who will be the winner. What does the typical participant in a fight probably expect?

11. *Consent to crime.* From the Restatement (Second) of Torts:

§892C. CONSENT TO CRIME

(1) Except as stated in Subsection (2), consent is effective to bar recovery in a tort action although the conduct consented to is a crime.

(2) If conduct is made criminal in order to protect a certain class of persons irrespective of their consent, the consent of members of that class to the conduct is not effective to bar a tort action.

Illustration 3. A and B agree to fight a duel with pistols. A fires at B and his bullet strikes and breaks B's arm. A is not liable to B.

Illustration 7. A statute makes it rape to have sexual intercourse with a girl under the age of sixteen even with her consent. At the solicitation of A, a girl of fourteen, B has intercourse with her. A's consent does not bar her action for battery.

Illustration 10. A statute makes adultery a crime. A, a married woman, commits adultery with B. Neither is liable to the other for the contacts inseparable from their crime.

12. *Arm wrestling.* In Hollerud v. Malamis, 174 N.W.2d 626 (Mich. App. 1969), the plaintiff, Hollerud, concluded an evening of drinking with several rounds of alcoholic beverages at the defendant's establishment, the Rainbow bar. Hollerud engaged there in what he called an "Indian wrestling" match with the bartender, in the course of which he sustained injuries to his fingers that caused him lasting difficulties in his work as a bricklayer. The trial court gave summary judgment to the defendants; the court of appeals reversed:

> The trial judge concluded that Edward Hollerud willingly and knowingly participated in a friendly Indian wrestling match. Although in the ordinary case a plaintiff's consent to an assault and battery is a defense precluding a civil action, if the plaintiff, owing to his state of intoxication, was incapable of expressing a rational will and the defendant had knowledge of this state, the consent was ineffective.
>
> The separate count for assault and battery alleged that Edward Hollerud was in a drunken condition when he entered the Rainbow Bar and that the bartender knew or should have known that he was intoxicated and that Hollerud did not freely and voluntarily enter into the Indian wrestling contest. Hollerud should have been allowed to prove the effect of this alleged intoxication on his mental faculties and the trier of fact should have been allowed to determine whether he was capable of consenting to engage in an Indian wrestling contest.

Suppose the bartender had been intoxicated, too. Would this have provided him with a defense against Hollerud's claim of battery? Which of the cases considered so far would be most helpful in answering that question? If the answer is "no," why might a court be more inclined to treat intoxication as undercutting Hollerud's consent than to treat it as undercutting the bartender's intent?

13. *A demonstration of karate (problem).* In Miller v. Couvillion, 676 So. 2d 668 (La. App. 1996), the plaintiff, Ray Miller, was a sales clerk at an establishment known as Chuck's Ace Hardware. Miller was injured while attempting to assist the store's manager, Rick Savage, in performing an informal demonstration of karate in the warehouse section of the store. The men placed a cinder block pad on a forklift; Miller climbed onto the forklift and braced the pad by standing on it. Savage tried twice to break the pad with a karate chop, but was unsuccessful. An announcement then came over the public address system requesting customer assistance elsewhere in the store. As Miller began to climb down from the forklift, Savage took one last kick at the cinder block pad; the contact caused Miller to fall and injure his arm. Miller sued his employer, his insurer, and Savage, claiming that his injury was the result of an intentional tort — a battery by Savage — for which Chuck's was vicariously responsible.

Did Miller have a good claim for battery? Support your conclusion with arguments from any of the cases considered in this chapter; consider, too, how variations on these facts would lead to different legal conclusions.

B. TRESPASS

Trespass to land traditionally is known to the common law by the more formal name of trespass *quare clausum fregit* ("wherefore he broke the close"; in other words, the writ called upon the defendant to explain whether and why he entered the plaintiff's property), or "qcf" for short. It is distinct from trespass *de bonis asportatis* ("of goods carried away," referring to interference with, or damage inflicted upon, chattels, i.e., personal property). Trespass to land is distinct as well from the tort of nuisance, though the two types of claim occasionally overlap. Whereas trespass protects the right to exclusive possession of the land, nuisance law protects the right to its use and enjoyment and tends to be reserved for less tangible and direct interferences. A stranger running across your property without authorization commits a trespass but not a nuisance; a neighbor who plays unreasonably loud music may be liable for causing a nuisance but not a trespass. The law of nuisance is covered in a later chapter.

Desnick v. American Broadcasting Companies, Inc.
44 F.3d 1345 (7th Cir. 1995)

[The Desnick Eye Center and two of its surgeons sued ABC, the producer of the ABC program *Prime Time Live*, and reporter Sam Donaldson for trespass and other torts. ABC's producer had dispatched employees equipped with concealed cameras to offices of the Desnick Eye Center in Wisconsin and Indiana. Posing as patients, these persons — seven in all — requested eye examinations, and employees of the Desnick Eye Center were secretly video-taped examining them. ABC used the videotapes on an episode of *Prime Time Live* that was highly critical of Dr. Desnick and his ophthalmic clinics. Desnick sued ABC, claiming among other things that the defendants committed a trespass in insinuating the test patients into the Wisconsin and Indiana offices of the Desnick Eye Center; he claimed that he would not have consented to their presence if their true identities and motives had been known. The district court dismissed the trespass counts in the complaint, and the plaintiffs appealed.]

POSNER, *Chief Judge* [after stating the facts]: — To enter upon another's land without consent is a trespass. The force of this rule has, it is true, been diluted somewhat by concepts of privilege and of implied consent. But there is no journalists' privilege to trespass. And there can be no implied consent in any nonfictitious sense of the term when express consent is procured by a misrepresentation or a misleading omission. The Desnick Eye Center would not have agreed to the entry of the test patients into its offices had it known they wanted eye examinations only in order to gather material for a television expose of the Center and that they were going to make secret videotapes of the examinations. Yet some cases, illustrated by *Martin v. Fidelity & Casualty Co.*, 421 So. 2d 109, 111 (Ala. 1982), deem consent effective even though it was procured by fraud.

There must be something to this surprising result. Without it a restaurant critic could not conceal his identity when he ordered a meal, or a browser pretend to be interested in merchandise that he could not afford to buy. Dinner guests would be trespassers if they were false friends who never would have been invited had the host known their true character, and a consumer who in an effort to bargain down an automobile dealer falsely claimed to be able to buy the same car elsewhere at a lower price would be a trespasser in the dealer's showroom. Some of these might be classified as privileged trespasses, designed to promote competition. Others might be thought justified by some kind of implied consent — the restaurant critic for example might point by way of analogy to the use of the "fair use" defense by book reviewers charged with copyright infringement and argue that the restaurant industry as a whole would be injured if restaurants could exclude critics. But most such efforts at rationalization would be little better than evasions. The fact is that consent to an entry is often given legal effect even though the entrant has intentions that if known to the owner of the property would cause him for perfectly understandable and generally ethical or at least lawful reasons to revoke his consent.

The law's willingness to give effect to consent procured by fraud is not limited to the tort of trespass. The Restatement gives the example of a man who obtains consent to sexual intercourse by promising a woman $100, yet (unbeknownst to her, of course) he pays her with a counterfeit bill and intended to do so from the start. The man is not guilty of battery, even though unconsented-to sexual intercourse is a battery. Restatement (Second) of Torts sec. 892B, illustration 9, pp. 373-74 (1979). Yet we know that to conceal the fact that one has a venereal disease transforms "consensual" intercourse into battery. *Crowell v. Crowell*, 180 N.C. 516 (1920). Seduction, standardly effected by false promises of love, is not rape; intercourse under the pretense of rendering medical or psychiatric treatment is, at least in most states. It certainly is battery. Trespass presents close parallels. If a homeowner opens his door to a purported meter reader who is in fact nothing of the sort — just a busybody curious about the interior of the home — the homeowner's consent to his entry is not a defense to a suit for trespass. *Bouillon v. Laclede Gaslight Co.*, 148 Mo. App. 462 (1910). And likewise if a competitor gained entry to a business firm's premises posing as a customer but in fact hoping to steal the firm's trade secrets. *Rockwell Graphic Systems, Inc. v. DEV Industries, Inc.*, 925 F.2d 174, 178 (7th Cir. 1991).

How to distinguish the two classes of case — the seducer from the medical impersonator, the restaurant critic from the meter-reader impersonator? The answer can have nothing to do with fraud; there is fraud in all the cases. It has to do with the interest that the torts in question, battery and trespass, protect. The one protects the inviolability of the person, the other the inviolability of the person's property. The woman who is seduced wants to have sex with her seducer, and the restaurant owner wants to have customers. The woman who is victimized by the medical impersonator has no desire to have sex with her doctor; she wants medical treatment. And the homeowner victimized by the phony meter reader does not want strangers in his house unless they have authorized service functions. The dealer's objection to the customer who claims falsely to have a lower price from a competing dealer is not to the physical presence of the customer, but to the fraud that he is trying to perpetuate. The lines are not bright — they are not even inevitable. They are the traces of the old forms of action, which have resulted in a multitude of artificial distinctions in modern law. But that is nothing new.

There was no invasion in the present case of any of the specific interests that the tort of trespass seeks to protect. The test patients entered offices that were open to anyone expressing a desire for ophthalmic services and videotaped physicians engaged in professional, not personal, communications with strangers (the testers themselves). The activities of the offices were not disrupted, as in *People v. Segal*, 358 N.Y.S.2d 866 (Crim. Ct. 1974), another case of gaining entry by false pretenses. Nor was there any "inva[sion of] a person's private space," *Haynes v. Alfred A. Knopf, Inc.*, 8 F.3d at 1229, as in our hypothetical meter-reader case, as in the famous case of *De May v. Roberts*, 46 Mich. 160 (1881) (where a doctor, called to the plaintiff's home to deliver her baby, brought along with him a friend who was curious to see a birth but was not a medical doctor, and represented the friend to be his medical assistant), as in one of its numerous modern counterparts, *Miller v. National Broadcasting Co.*, 232 Cal. Rptr. 668, 679 (1986), and as in *Dietemann v. Time, Inc.*, 449 F.2d 245 (9th Cir. 1971), on which the plaintiffs in our case rely. *Dietemann* involved a home. True, the portion invaded was an office, where the plaintiff performed quack healing of nonexistent ailments. The parallel to this case is plain enough, but there is a difference. Dietemann was not in business, and did not advertise his services or charge for them. His quackery was private.

No embarrassingly intimate details of anybody's life were publicized in the present case. There was no eavesdropping on a private conversation; the testers recorded their own conversations with the Desnick Eye Center's physicians. There was no violation of the doctor-patient privilege. There was no theft, or intent to steal, trade secrets; no disruption of decorum, of peace and quiet; no noisy or distracting demonstrations. [. . .] "Testers" who pose as prospective home buyers in order to gather evidence of housing discrimination are not trespassers even if they are private persons not acting under color of law. The situation of the defendants' "testers" is analogous. Like testers seeking evidence of violation of anti-discrimination laws, the defendants' test patients gained entry into the plaintiffs' premises by misrepresenting their purposes (more precisely by a misleading omission to disclose those purposes). But the entry was not invasive in the sense of infringing the kind of interest of the plaintiffs that the law of trespass protects; it was not an interference with the ownership or possession of land. We need not consider what if any difference it would make if the plaintiffs had festooned the premises with signs forbidding the entry of testers or other snoops. Perhaps none, *see United States v. Centennial Builders, Inc.,* 747 F.2d 678, 683 (11th Cir. 1984), but that is an issue for another day.

[The court affirmed dismissal of the trespass counts of the complaint, and remanded for further proceedings on other issues.]

NOTES

1. *Battery and trespass.* The *Desnick* opinion illustrates the parallels between trespass and battery; notice that the court is comfortable wandering back and forth between the two torts as it discusses the significance of fraudulently induced consent. One reason for the parallels, as noted in the introduction to this book, is that during much of the history of the common law the tort of trespass covered a broad gamut of wrongs now known by other names, including both battery and trespass to land (as well as assault, false imprisonment, and other harms inflicted more or less directly). To what case in the section on battery is *Desnick* most analogous? Can *Desnick* be distinguished (need it be distinguished?) from *Neal v. Neal,* the case where the plaintiff said that her husband's extramarital affair vitiated her consent to sexual relations with him?

2. *Conditional consent.* From the Restatement (Second) of Torts (1965):

§168. CONDITIONAL OR RESTRICTED CONSENT

A conditional or restricted consent to enter land creates a privilege to do so only in so far as the condition or restriction is complied with.

Illustration 1. A, the owner of Blackacre, licenses B to drive his cow through Blackacre to B's pasture, lot X. B enters Blackacre to draw gravel from lot X, or to go to lot Y. In either case B's entry is a trespass.

Illustration 4. The A Gas Company, having mistakenly concluded that B has not paid his bill for gas, sends its servant, C, to B's house to remove the meter. C is given permission to enter to read the meter. He removes the meter. The A Company is subject to liability for a trespass.

Illustration 6. A grants to B, a contractor, a license to store his trucks in A's barn. B not only stores his trucks in A's barn, but also makes extensive repairs on such trucks while they are in the barn. While using an acetylene torch in repairing a truck, B sets fire to and burns down the barn. B is a trespasser.

Are these illustrations consistent with *Desnick v. American Broadcasting Companies?*

3. *Trespass generally.* From the Restatement (Second) of Torts:

§158. LIABILITY FOR INTENTIONAL INTRUSIONS ON LAND

One is subject to liability to another for trespass, irrespective of whether he thereby causes harm to any legally protected interest of the other, if he intentionally
(a) enters land in the possession of the other, or causes a thing or a third person to do so, or
(b) remains on the land, or
(c) fails to remove from the land a thing which he is under a duty to remove.

Illustration 1. A, against B's will, forcibly carries B upon the land of C. A is a trespasser; B is not.

Illustration 2. A tornado lifts A's properly constructed house from A's land and deposits it on B's land. This is not a trespass.

Comment i. Causing entry of a thing. The actor, without himself entering the land, may invade another's interest in its exclusive possession by throwing, propelling, or placing a thing either on or beneath the surface of the land or in the air space above it. Thus, in the absence of the possessor's consent or other privilege to do so, it is an actionable trespass to throw rubbish on another's land, even though he himself uses it as a dump heap, or to fire projectiles or to fly an advertising kite or balloon through the air above it, even though no harm is done to the land or to the possessor's enjoyment of it.

4. *Tally-ho!* In *Pegg v. Gray*, 82 S.E.2d 757 (N.C. 1954), the plaintiff owned a farm that included a herd of about 70 cattle kept in areas partitioned with barbed wire. The defendant, who lived on an adjoining farm, kept a team of hounds he used to hunt foxes. During the hunting season the defendant would loose the dogs and they often would chase foxes onto the plaintiff's property; the foxes would run in and through the plaintiffs' herds, sometimes inciting the cattle to stampede and break down the fences that enclosed them. The plaintiff sued the defendant for trespass. The trial court nonsuited the plaintiff; the North Carolina Supreme Court reversed:

[B]y natural instinct and habit an ordinary dog of most breeds is inclined to roam around and stray at times from its immediate habitat without causing injury or doing damage to persons or property. [. . .] And so, since early times the law has been and still is that the owner of a reputable dog is not answerable in damages for its entry upon the lands of another upon its own volition under circumstances amounting to an unprovoked trespass.

However, the rule is different where a dog owner or keeper for the purpose of sport intentionally sends a dog on the lands of another or releases a dog or pack of dogs with knowledge, actual or constructive, that it or they likely will go on the lands of another or others in pursuit of game. In such cases the true rule would seem to be that the owner or keeper, in the absence of permission to hunt previously obtained, is liable for trespass, and this is so although the master does not himself go upon the lands, but instead sends or so allows his dog or dogs to go thereon in pursuit of game. [. . .]

It may be conceded that since Samson, according to the folk tale of biblical lore, tied the firebrands to the tails of 300 foxes and sent them into the grain fields of the Philistines (Judges 15:4, 5) the fox has been looked upon by many persons as a noxious animal, to be exterminated. Nevertheless, to countless thousands of devotees of the chase the death of a fox, unless it be in front of hounds, is regarded as a social crime. We embrace the view [that] fox hunting as ordinarily pursued — certainly as shown by the record in this case — is pure sport to be followed in subordination to established property rights and subject to the principles governing the law of trespass.

5. *Fore!* In Malouf v. Dallas Athletic Country Club, 837 S.W.2d 674 (Tex. App. 1992), the plaintiffs lived next to the defendant's golf course in the town of Mesquite. The plaintiffs' evidence was that their automobiles were damaged on three separate occasions when balls struck by golfers on the sixth hole went astray. They brought suit against the defendant for trespass. The defendant won judgment after a bench trial. The court of appeals affirmed:

> [T]he record reflects neither legal nor factual evidence that either [the defendant] or the individual golfers intended to commit an act which violated a property right. During a game of golf, on the [defendant's] course, the individual golfers intend to hit golf balls toward hole number six. This does not violate a property right. The fact that the ball may "slice" or "hook" onto appellants' properties is an unintended consequence. [. . .] Because appellants failed to demonstrate that [the defendant country club] or the individual golfers intentionally caused the golf balls to damage appellants' personal property, we cannot say that the trial court's conclusion of law that the [club] did not trespass is erroneous.

What is the distinction between *Pegg v. Gray* (L for defendant whose dogs strayed onto plaintiff's property) and *Malouf v. Dallas Athletic Country Club*

(NL for defendant whose golfers hit stray balls onto plaintiff's property)? In view of the procedural posture of the two cases, how should their facts be stylized (in other words, what assumptions about the facts should be made) if *Malouf* is to be viewed as a case of no liability and *Pegg* described as a case of liability?

6. *Trespass vs. negligence.* It might seem odd that a golfer's errant shot could break a car's windshield without resulting in liability. But the holding just considered from *Malouf* does not necessarily imply that the plaintiffs can collect nothing; it just establishes that they were not the victims of a trespass. The plaintiffs here also would be free to press claims that the country club or the golfers were *negligent*, a different theory of liability. In fact the plaintiffs in *Malouf* did claim that the club had negligently designed its golf course — but this claim failed as well. The plaintiffs brought no claims against the individual golfers, apparently because they could not be identified. Why else might the plaintiffs be more interested in prevailing against the club?

7. *Trespass vs. battery.* What is the relationship between the standard for judging intent used in the *Pegg* and *Malouf* cases and the meaning of intent in the law of battery — e.g., in cases like *Vosburg v. Putney* or *White v. University of Idaho?* Consider these excerpts from the Second Restatement:

§164. INTRUSIONS UNDER MISTAKE

One who intentionally enters land in the possession of another is subject to liability to the possessor of the land as a trespasser, although he acts under a mistaken belief of law or fact, however reasonable, not induced by the conduct of the possessor, that he

(a) is in possession of the land or entitled to it, or

(b) has the consent of the possessor or of a third person who has the power to give consent on the possessor's behalf, or

(c) has some other privilege to enter or remain on the land.

Illustration 3. A employs a surveyor of recognized ability to make a survey of his land. The survey shows that a particular strip of land is within his boundaries. In consequence, A clears this land of timber and prepares it for cultivation. In fact, the survey is mistaken and the strip in question is part of the tract owned by his neighbor, B. A is subject to liability to B.

§166. NON-LIABILITY FOR ACCIDENTAL INTRUSIONS

Except where the actor is engaged in an abnormally dangerous activity, an unintentional and non-negligent entry on land in the possession of another, or causing a thing or third person to enter the land, does not subject the actor to liability to the possessor, even though the entry causes harm to the possessor or to a thing or third person in whose security the possessor has a legally protected interest.

Illustration 1. A is walking along the sidewalk of a public highway close to the border of B's land. Without fault on his part, A slips on a piece of ice, and falls against and breaks a plate glass window in B's store adjoining the sidewalk. A is not liable to B.

Illustration 4. A is carefully driving his well-broken horses on a highway. Frightened by a locomotive, they become unmanageable and run away, striking and damaging an iron lamp post on B's land. A is not liable to B.

Are these Restatement provisions consistent? Are they consistent with the cases just considered?

8. *A dog's breakfast.* In Van Alstyne v. Rochester Telephone Corp., 296 N.Y.S. 726 (City Ct. 1937), the plaintiff was the owner of a pair of valuable hunting dogs, Nancy and Pooch. The defendant telephone company maintained a cable that ran over the area of the plaintiff's lot where the dogs were kept. In May of 1936 the defendant's agents, present on the plaintiff's land by permit or easement, performed work on the cable. They removed the cable's insulation, which was made of lead. After performing their operations they used molten lead to seal the cable again. Nancy died of lead poisoning in June; Pooch died from the same cause another month later. The plaintiff inspected his property and found lead that appeared to have dripped when the defendant's men were sealing the cable. His theory, which the court accepted, was that the dogs died when they ate similar drops left behind by the defendant's agents.

The plaintiff sued the defendant on theories of both negligence and trespass. The court dismissed the negligence claim on the ground that the possibility of harm to the dogs — the chance that the dogs would eat the lead, and that it would prove fatal — was unforeseeable to the defendant's workers. The court nevertheless gave judgment to the plaintiff, finding that the workers trespassed when they left the lead drippings behind and that they therefore were responsible for the consequences regardless of fault:

> True, the defendant had an easement for the maintenance of its line, and presumably this expressly conferred the right of access to the plaintiff's land for purposes of repairs or extensions. But it is not to be presumed, nor is it shown, that the defendant had an express right to cast unnecessarily, or to leave in any event, articles or substances upon the premises. Lacking such an express right, the law gives him none.
>
> Such an invasion of the premises of another renders the invader liable whether it be intentional or not, or whether the loss resulting to the owner be direct or consequential. He is liable regardless of the existence or nonexistence of negligence. [...] It does not matter that the plaintiff here seeks recovery, not for direct damage to his soil or to vegetation or structures, but for consequential damages. Recovery does not depend

upon directness of the damage. The test is whether there was a direct invasion. Given that, responsibility follows. [...]

It follows that the defendant, by depositing lead on the plaintiff's premises, became an intruder, and is liable for the consequences regardless of whether the results could or should reasonably have been foreseen, or whether the acts constituted negligence. [...]

It requires no finespun reasoning to hold one responsible for a wrong done another who is without fault. But in a practical world, there must be practical limits. The law says a man in an ordinary situation should not, although in the wrong, be held for consequences which a reasonably attentive and careful man would not foresee. That rule found expression, and it endures, because it accords with the opinion of the average man.

It is a rule of action in the world at large. The immunity which it grants does not accompany the actor when he intrudes upon the property of another. There the owner is supreme. His house is his castle, and his estate his exclusive domain. There, not all the rules which govern in the world at large apply. No intrusion is so trifling as to be overlooked, and no result of the intrusion is to be without remedy because it was unusual or unexpected.

Is there a satisfactory distinction between *Van Alstyne v. Rochester Telephone Corp.* and *Malouf v. Dallas Athletic Club*? Is *Van Alstyne* consistent with the Restatement provisions (§164 and §166) that preceded it? With *Desnick v. American Broadcasting Companies*?

9. *Tort and property.* Some of the hardest and most interesting questions in the law of trespass involve the definition of the rights that accompany ownership of land. These are issues that receive fuller treatment in courses on property law, but they are important to an understanding of the trespass tort as well — an overlap that illustrates the theoretical link between the law of torts and the law of property more generally. One way to look at these topics is to think of property law, broadly understood, as involving the acquisition of rights. Tort law determines when invasions of those rights occur and how they are rectified; contract law governs how the rights are exchanged. If this model is not intuitive, it may be because while most tort cases involve personal injuries, courses on property law do not generally spend much time on the notion that one has a "property right" in one's own physical person. And meanwhile courses on tort law tend to focus more on the evaluation of the defendant's conduct than on the definition of the plaintiff's rights. But trespass cases expose the relationship between torts and property law in a more obvious way. The branch of tort law known as trespass protects property rights in a literal, conventional sense: it protects an owner's interest in exclusive possession of land. Property law determines what the content of those rights are; tort law determines when they have been violated. The two inquiries merge in the following cases, where the question of whether

anyone's rights have been invaded in a way that can support a tort suit depends on what we mean when we speak of ownership of land.

10. *Caves.* In Edwards v. Lee, 19 S.W.2d 992 (Ky. App. 1929); 24 S.W.2d 619 (Ky. App. 1930), the defendant, L. P. Edwards, discovered the entrance to a cave on his property. He named it the Great Onyx Cave, built a hotel near its mouth, widened the footpaths within it, advertised its existence, and attracted a stream of visitors who paid entrance fees and generated substantial revenue. A number of years later one of Edwards' neighbors, F. P. Lee, sued Edwards for trespass, alleging that substantial portions of the cave extended under his land. The trial court ordered a survey, determined that about one-third of the cave was owned by Lee, awarded damages to him, and enjoined Edwards from further trespassing on Lee's property. The court of appeals affirmed:

> *Cujus est solum, ejus est usque ad coelum ad infernos* (to whomsoever the soil belongs. he owns also to the sky and to the depths), is an old maxim and rule. It is that the owner of realty, unless there has been a division of the estate, is entitled to the free and unfettered control of his own land above, upon, and beneath the surface. So whatever is in a direct line between the surface of the land and the center of the earth belongs to the owner of the surface. Ordinarily that ownership cannot be interfered with or infringed by third persons. [. . .]

Logan, J., issued a memorable dissent:

> The rule should be that he who owns the surface is the owner of everything that may be taken from the earth and used for his profit or happiness. [. . .] A cave or cavern should belong absolutely to him who owns its entrance, and this ownership should extend even to its utmost reaches if he has explored and connected these reaches with the entrance.[. . .]
>
> Shall a man be allowed to stop airplanes flying above his land because he owns the surface? He cannot subject the atmosphere through which they fly to his profit or pleasure; therefore, so long as airplanes do not injure him, or interfere with the use of his property, he should be helpless to prevent their flying above his dominion. Should the waves that transmit intelligible sound through the atmosphere be allowed to pass over the lands of surface-owners? If they take nothing from him and in no way interfere with his profit or pleasure, he should be powerless to prevent their passage. [. . .]
>
> In the light of these unannounced principles which ought to be the law in this modern age, let us give thought to the petitioner Edwards, his rights and his predicament, if that is done to him which the circuit judge has directed to be done. Edwards owns this cave through right of discovery, exploration, development, advertising, exhibition, and conquest. Men fought their way through the eternal darkness, into the mysterious

and abysmal depths of the bowels of a groaning world to discover the theretofore unseen splendors of unknown natural scenic wonders. [...] They created an underground kingdom where Gulliver's people may have lived or where Ayesha may have found the revolving column of fire in which to bathe meant eternal youth. [...]

First came one to see, then another, then two together, then small groups, then small crowds, then large crowds, and then the multitudes. Edwards had seen his faith justified. [...]

Then came the horse leach's daughters crying: "Give me," "give me." Then came the "surface men" crying, "I think this cave may run under my lands." They do not know, they only "guess," but they seek to discover the secrets of Edwards so that they may harass him and take from him that which he has made his own. They have come to a court of equity and have asked that Edwards be forced to open his doors and his ways to them so that they may go in and despoil him; that they may lay his secrets bare so that others may follow their example and dig into the wonders which Edwards has made his own. What may be the result if they stop his ways? They destroy the cave, because those who visit it are they who give it value, and none will visit it when the ways are barred so that it may not be exhibited as a whole.

11. *Airspace.* In Smith v. New England Aircraft Co., 170 N.E. 385 (Mass. 1930), the plaintiffs owned a country estate near Worcester known as Lordvale; it consisted of about 270 acres. In 1927 the Worcester Airport was opened on roughly 100 acres of land adjacent to the plaintiffs' property. Within a few years the defendants regularly were flying their airplanes (biplanes and single-propeller models) over the plaintiffs' property at heights ranging from 100 to 1,000 feet. The plaintiffs brought suit for trespass. The Supreme Judicial Court began its analysis by noting that federal and state laws generally required airplanes to maintain altitudes of at least 500 feet. The Court rejected the possibility of claims against the defendants for flights above those thresholds, finding the federal statutes to be legitimate uses of the government's police power that impliedly authorized air traffic on the terms they set out. But the Court found that the occasional flights by the defendants at altitudes below 500 feet, as when they performed takeoffs and landings, presented harder problems:

The bald question in the case at bar is whether aircraft, in order to reach or leave an airport, may of right fly so low as 100 feet over brush and woodland not otherwise utilized, against the protest of the owner. Suggestions as to flight of carrier pigeons and the practice of falconry over private lands seem to us too remote and distinct from the mechanical flights of high powered aircraft to be helpful in ascertainment of rights in the case at bar. There are numerous cases holding that invasion of the airspace above the land without contact with its surface constitutes trespass. In discussing this subject it is said in Pollock on Torts (13th Ed.) p. 362: "It does not seem possible on the principles of the common law to assign any reason why an entry above the surface should not also be a trespass, unless indeed it can be said that the scope of possible trespass is limited by that of possible effective possession, which might be the most reasonable rule." Even if this suggestion of extreme limit be adopted as the test, namely, that "the scope of possible trespass is limited by that of possible effective possession," the plaintiffs seem entitled to assert that there have been trespasses upon their land. It is general knowledge that, while not extremely common in this vicinity, trees not infrequently reach heights in growth considerably in excess of 100 feet. In other parts of the country there are trees of much greater height. It is found by the master that the plaintiffs have undertaken to reforest a part of their estate by planting Norway pine and spruce. It is well known that buildings in many cities exceed 100 feet in height. Not infrequently they reach 300 feet or even more. [. . .] It would be impracticable to draw a feasible distinction as matter of right between the aircraft used by the defendants and aircraft of larger size, heavier weight and more powerful motors, and between the number and extent of use of the aircraft here involved and the much larger number and more extensive use incident to growth of air navigation.

The combination of all these factors seems to us, under settled principles of law, after making every reasonable legal concession to air navigation as commonly understood and as established under the statutes and regulations here disclosed, to constitute trespass to the land of the plaintiffs so far as concerns the take-offs and landings at low altitudes and flights thus made over the land of the plaintiffs "at altitudes as low as one hundred feet." Air navigation, important as it is, cannot rightly levy toll upon the legal rights of others for its successful prosecution. No reason has been suggested why airports of sufficient area may not be provided so that take-offs and landings of aircraft may be made without trespass upon the land of others. If, in the interest of aerial navigation, rights of flight at such low altitude over lands of others are of sufficient public importance, doubtless the power of eminent domain for acquisition of rights of way in airspaces might be authorized.

Is *Smith v. New England Aircraft Co.* consistent with *Edwards v. Lee*? If they are not consistent, is the inconsistency justifiable?

C. CONVERSION

The torts of conversion and trespass to chattels both involve interference with the personal property of another. The differences between them largely are matters of degree that can be traced back to the common law forms of action from which they descended. As noted earlier, the writ of *trespass de bonis asportatis* was available in cases where the defendant simply took the plaintiff's goods; and if a defendant was entrusted with the goods but then refused to return them, the plaintiff could seek a writ of *detinue*. These forms of action often were made unattractive, however, by the limitations, procedures, and remedies attached to them, so a new but related form of action later was made available as well: the action for *trover*, in which the plaintiff technically (and usually fictitiously) alleged that the defendant had found his goods and either damaged or failed to return them. The trover action evolved into the tort we now know as conversion, which generally entitles a plaintiff to collect damages where the defendant has interfered with the plaintiff's personal property to such an extent that the defendant is required to pay its full value — a kind of forced judicial sale of the property from the plaintiff to the defendant.

Conversion will be the primary focus of this section because it now largely supersedes the tort of trespass to chattels, but the latter action remains useful in cases where the defendant commits a minor act of interference with the plaintiff's property rights; later we shall see an example. The elements of the two torts, and the overlap between them, are sketched in these provisions from the Restatement (Second) of Torts (1965):

§217. WAYS OF COMMITTING TRESPASS TO CHATTEL

A trespass to a chattel may be committed by intentionally
(a) dispossessing another of the chattel, or
(b) using or intermeddling with a chattel in the possession of another.

§218. LIABILITY TO PERSON IN POSSESSION

One who commits a trespass to a chattel is subject to liability to the possessor of the chattel if, but only if,
(a) he dispossesses the other of the chattel, or
(b) the chattel is impaired as to its condition, quality, or value, or
(c) the possessor is deprived of the use of the chattel for a substantial time, or
(d) bodily harm is caused to the possessor, or harm is caused to some person or thing in which the possessor has a legally protected interest.

Illustration 3. A leaves his car parked in front of a store. B releases the brake on A's car and pushes it three or four feet, doing no harm to the car. B is not liable to A.

Illustration 4. A leaves his car parked near the corner. B, desiring to play a joke upon A, pushes the car around the corner where it cannot be easily seen by A. A comes out for his car, and fails to discover it for an hour. B is subject to liability for trespass to A.

§222A. WHAT CONSTITUTES CONVERSION

(1) Conversion is an intentional exercise of dominion or control over a chattel which so seriously interferes with the right of another to control it that the actor may justly be required to pay the other the full value of the chattel.

(2) In determining the seriousness of the interference and the justice of requiring the actor to pay the full value, the following factors are important:

(a) the extent and duration of the actor's exercise of dominion or control;

(b) the actor's intent to assert a right in fact inconsistent with the other's right of control;

(c) the actor's good faith;

(d) the extent and duration of the resulting interference with the other's right of control;

(e) the harm done to the chattel;

(f) the inconvenience and expense caused to the other.

Illustration 1. On leaving a restaurant, A by mistake takes B's hat from the rack, believing it to be his own. When he reaches the sidewalk A puts on the hat, discovers his mistake, and immediately re-enters the restaurant and returns the hat to the rack. This is not a conversion.

Illustration 2. The same facts as in Illustration 1, except that A keeps the hat for three months before discovering his mistake and returning it. This is a conversion.

Illustration 3. The same facts as in Illustration 1, except that as A reaches the sidewalk and puts on the hat a sudden gust of wind blows it from his head, and it goes down an open manhole and is lost. This is a conversion.

Illustration 4. Leaving a restaurant, A takes B's hat from the rack, intending to steal it. As he approaches the door he sees a policeman outside, and immediately returns the hat to the rack. This is a conversion.

§226. CONVERSION BY DESTRUCTION OR ALTERATION

One who intentionally destroys a chattel or so materially alters its physical condition as to change its identity or character is subject to liability for conversion to another who is in possession of the chattel or entitled to its immediate possession.

Illustration 4. A intentionally feeds poisonous weeds to B's horse. The horse is made ill for a few hours, but promptly recovers. This is a trespass to the horse, but not a conversion. If, however, the horse is made ill for a month, there is both a trespass and a conversion.

Illustration 5. A intentionally slashes the tire of B's automobile, ruining the tire. This is a conversion of the tire, but under ordinary circumstances in which the tire is easily replaced it is not a conversion of the automobile.

If, however, the automobile is in a desert where another tire cannot be obtained for a month, there is a conversion of the automobile.

It will be useful to note here another distinction between forms of action. In a conversion action the plaintiff seeks damages, not the return of the property. A plaintiff who instead wants the property returned brings a suit for *replevin*. In addition to allowing the plaintiff to "replevy" the property, this action also enables the recovery of damages for the loss of a chattel's use while the defendant wrongfully exercised dominion over it. Since the underlying elements of a conversion and replevin action typically are the same, we will not be considering them separately; in practice they function as different remedies for the same conduct. In the cases that follow we will see plaintiffs using both routes.

The core case of conversion is simple to understand: the defendant stole the plaintiff's goods; the plaintiff is entitled to recover damages. But conversion also covers a variety of more interesting situations where the defendant has exerted control over property that falls short of theft but is inconsistent with the plaintiff's rights of ownership, as the following cases illustrate.

(1) *The last laugh.* In Russell-Vaughn Ford, Inc. v. Rouse, 206 So. 2d 371 (Ala. 1968), the plaintiff, E. W. Rouse, paid a series of visits to the defendant's car dealership to discuss the possibility of trading in his Ford Falcon and some amount of cash for a new Ford. During his third visit one of the salesmen, Virgil Harris, asked Rouse for the keys to his Falcon. Rouse handed them over, then went to look at new cars the dealership had on display. The parties were not able to agree on terms of a trade. At this point Rouse asked for the return of the keys to his car. The salesman said he didn't know where the keys were. Rouse asked the manager and several other employees for his keys. They, too, said they were unable to help; several salesmen and mechanics sat on nearby cars and watched Rouse, laughing at him. Rouse called the Birmingham police. Upon the arrival of one of its officers, the defendant's salesman tossed the keys to Rouse, saying they had "just wanted to see him cry a while."

Rouse sued the defendant for conversion of his Falcon. The jury brought in a general verdict in Rouse's favor for $5,000. The Alabama Supreme Court affirmed:

> Initially it is argued that the facts of this case do not make out a case of conversion. [. . .] We are not persuaded that the law of Alabama supports this proposition. [. . .] A remarkable admission in this regard was elicited by the plaintiff in examining one of the witnesses for the defense. It seems that according to a salesman for Russell-Vaughn Ford, Inc., it is a rather usual practice in the automobile business to "lose keys" to cars belonging to potential customers. We see nothing in our cases which requires in a conversion case that the plaintiff prove that the defendant appropriated

the property to his own use; rather, as noted in the cases referred to above, it is enough that he show that the defendant exercised dominion over it in exclusion or defiance of the right of the plaintiff. We think that has been done here.

Further, appellants argue that there was no conversion since the plaintiff could have called his wife at home, who had another set of keys and thereby gained the ability to move his automobile. We find nothing in our cases which would require the plaintiff to exhaust all possible means of gaining possession of a chattel which is withheld from him by the defendant, after demanding its return. On the contrary, it is the refusal, without legal excuse, to deliver a chattel, which constitutes a conversion.

2. *Exceeding the scope of permission.* In Palmer v. Mayo, 68 A. 369 (Conn. 1907), the plaintiff, Frank Palmer, operated a livery business in New Haven. His evidence was that the defendant Mayo rented a horse and carriage for the stated purpose of driving to East Haven on business. While on the way there Mayo stopped at the house of a friend, one Scott. Mayo gave permission to Scott to use the carriage to drive Scott's father-in-law, Cook, to Cook's home a few blocks away. Cook and Scott drove off in the carriage and crashed it into a trolley pole, by which collision the carriage was destroyed and the horse killed. Palmer brought a suit for conversion against Mayo and Cook. Palmer's evidence was that Cook and Scott had taken the carriage to a series of saloons in West Haven and become drunk. Cook's evidence was that he was not drunk, that he was not driving the carriage (Scott was), and that when he borrowed the carriage he thought it belonged to Mayo. A jury brought in a verdict against both defendants. Cook appealed, claiming the jury had been misinstructed. The Connecticut Supreme Court affirmed:

> The defendant Cook in substance requested the court to charge the jury that he would not be liable to the plaintiff for the injury to the horse and carriage, (1) if he had no knowledge of the particular purpose for which they were hired, but supposed from Mayo's representations that they belonged to him; nor (2) if he had no control or management of the horse and carriage, but was merely riding with Scott; nor (3) if the collision with the telegraph or trolley pole and car was an "inevitable accident," caused by the horse becoming frightened and uncontrollable from the noise of a passing train, and without any negligence upon the part of this defendant. The charge was favorable to said defendant upon the first and second of these requests, excepting as the court very properly charged that Cook would be liable in any event if it was proved that he negligently drove the horse and carriage into a telegraph or trolley pole, as alleged in the complaint, and so caused the injury. As to the third request the court instructed the jury in substance that, if Mayo loaned the horse and carriage to Cook, and he knew the purpose for which they had been hired by Mayo, he would be liable even if the collision with the telegraph or trolley

pole and car was accidental and without any negligence on the part of this defendant.

The third request was rightly refused, nor should a new trial be granted upon the instruction given by the court upon the subject of that request. A bailee is liable in an action of tort for an injury to property bailed occurring during a use of it by him, or by others with his consent, which was neither expressly nor impliedly authorized by the contract of bailment, even though such injury was the result of accident, and not of negligence in the manner in which the property was used. Whether one who receives property from a bailee, without knowledge of the purpose for which it is to be used under the contract of bailment, is liable for an injury to it arising from a use not authorized by such contract, without proof of negligence, we have no occasion to decide, since the trial court charged in the defendant Cook's favor upon that question.

What should be the answer to the final question the court describes but leaves unanswered? At what point had Mayo irrevocably committed an act of conversion? At what point had Cook done so? To what case in the section on trespass is *Palmer v. Mayo* most analogous?

3. *Mistaken dominion.* In Spooner v. Manchester, 133 Mass. 270 (Mass. 1882), the defendant hired a horse and carriage from the defendant to drive from Worcester to Clinton and back. On his return trip the defendant inadvertently took a wrong turn and ended up on the road to Northborough, a town east of both Clinton and Worcester. After discovering his error he sought advice and was told that the best route to Worcester from his current position was to detour through Northborough. He proceeded accordingly; but while traveling through Northborough the horse became lame. The plaintiff sued the defendant for conversion of the horse. The case was tried without a jury. The judge found that the injury to the horse was not caused by any negligence on the defendant's part; nor was the defendant negligent in becoming lost. The trial court nevertheless gave judgment to the plaintiff. The Supreme Judicial Court of Massachusetts reversed:

> If a person wrongfully exercises acts of ownership or of dominion over property under a mistaken view of his rights, the tort, notwithstanding his mistake, may still be a conversion, because he has both claimed and exercised over it the rights of an owner; but whether an act involving the temporary use, control or detention of property implies an assertion of a right of dominion over it, may well depend upon the circumstances of the case and the intention of the person dealing with the property.
>
> In the case at bar, the use made of the horse by the defendant was not of a different kind from that contemplated by the contract between the parties, but the horse was driven by the defendant, on his return to Worcester, a longer distance than was contemplated, and on a different

road. If it be said that the defendant intended to drive the horse where in fact he did drive him, yet he did not intend to violate his contract or to exercise any control over the horse inconsistent with it. There is no evidence that the defendant was not at all times intending to return the horse to the plaintiff, according to his contract, or that whatever he did was not done for that purpose, or that he ever intended to assume any control or dominion over the horse against the rights of the owner. After he discovered that he had taken the wrong road, he did what seemed best to him in order to return to Worcester. Such acts cannot be considered a conversion.

What is the distinction between *Spooner v. Manchester* and *Palmer v. Mayo*?

4. *Acts of imposters (problem).* In Wiseman v. Schaffer, 768 P.2d 800 (Idaho 1989), the defendant, Schaffer, was the proprietor of a tow-truck business. He received a telephone request from one Larry Wiseman asking him to tow a pickup truck from the Husky Truck Stop in Port Falls to the yard of a nearby welding shop. The caller said that the $30 needed to cover the towing charge would be left on the sun visor inside the truck. Schaffer located the truck and the money and towed the truck to the welding yard as directed. The truck soon was stolen from that location. It later came out that the caller who requested the tow had been an imposter; the real Larry Wiseman had been inside the truck stop with his wife throughout the sequence of events. Neither the truck nor the imposter ever were found.

Wiseman sued Schaffer for negligence and conversion. Schaffer produced as witnesses two other tow-truck operators who said it was not unusual for them to tow unattended vehicles on the basis of authorization furnished over the phone. The jury found no negligence on the defendant's part, and the court of appeals affirmed on this point. What result on the claim for conversion?

5. *Customers of thieves.* In O'Keeffe v. Snyder, 416 A.2d 862 (N.J. 1980), the plaintiff was the famous artist Georgia O'Keeffe. She alleged that in 1946 a set of her paintings had been stolen from an art gallery run by her husband, Alfred Stieglitz. She told friends of the theft but did not report or record it. In 1975 she learned that the paintings were on display at the Crispo Gallery in New York. A man named Snyder claimed to own the paintings; he had bought them for $35,000 from one Ulrich Frank, who in turn claimed to have inherited them from his father. It was impossible to show how Frank's father had come into possession of the paintings, but evidently both Frank and Snyder were unaware that the artworks had disreputable origins. O'Keeffe brought a replevin action against Snyder to recover the paintings. The trial court gave summary judgment to Snyder. The court of appeals reversed, holding that O'Keeffe's evidence, if accepted, would entitle her to recover the paintings; the New Jersey Supreme Court agreed, subject to O'Keeffe's satisfaction of the statute of limitations. The Court held that "if the paintings were stolen, the thief acquired no title and could not transfer good

title to others regardless of their good faith and ignorance of the theft." (To satisfy the statute of limitations, the court said that O'Keeffe would have to show that she brought suit within six years of "when she first knew, or reasonably should have known through the exercise of due diligence, of the cause of action, including the identity of the possessor of the paintings.")

The rule employed in O'Keeffe's case has been stated more colorfully: "title, like a stream, cannot rise higher than its source." *Jordan v. Kancel*, 361 P.2d 894 (Kan. 1961). It also is the subject of a Latin maxim: *Nemo dat quod non habet* (known sometimes as the "nemo dat" rule), which has been variously translated as "he who hath not, cannot give," or "one cannot give what one does not have" — the application here being that a thief can transfer no better title than he himself has, i.e., none.

6. *Further acts of imposters.* In Phelps v. McQuade, 115 N.E. 441 (N.Y. 1917), the plaintiffs were jewelers. They were approached by a man falsely claiming to be one Baldwin J. Gwynne of Cleveland. The plaintiffs made inquiries to a credit bureau and determined that Baldwin Gwynne had a satisfactory rating; on this basis they delivered valuable jewelry to the man impersonating him. The imposter then sold the jewelry to a man named McQuade, who paid full value for it and had no notice of its illegitimate origins. When the plaintiffs learned what had happened, they sued McQuade to recover the jewels. The trial court gave judgment to the plaintiffs, but the New York Court of Appeals held the defendants entitled to a directed verdict. The question in the case was whether the man impersonating Baldwin Gwynne received title to the jewelry from the plaintiffs. If he did, then he was able to transfer the title to McQuade, and since McQuade was a "bona fide purchaser for value" he would not be held liable for conversion. The court found for the defendant, holding that Gwynne had indeed received title from the plaintiffs (and thus had conveyed it to McQuade). Said the court: "Where the vendor of personal property intends to sell his goods to the person with whom he deals, then title passes, even though he be deceived as to that person's identity or responsibility. Otherwise it does not. It is purely a question of the vendor's intention."

What is the distinction between *Phelps v. McQuade* and *O'Keeffe v. Snyder*? How can *Phelps* be considered consistent with the "nemo dat" rule?

7. *The innocent purchaser.* Taken together the *O'Keeffe* and *Phelps* cases illustrate an old difficulty in the law of conversion: the treatment of the later purchaser who acquires goods from a fraud or a thief. The common law has long distinguished between these last two categories. A thief acquires no title to the property he steals (his title is said to be "void"), and so can convey no title to a purchaser; nor can the purchaser pass on anything better to anybody else. Thus someone who buys goods from a thief, or who acquires the goods later in the chain of sale, is liable for conversion to the original owner. This doctrine can produce harsh results; it means that a good-faith purchaser who pays full value for goods can be required to make a second and equal

payment to their rightful owner (or to hand over the goods despite having paid for them) if they turn out to have been stolen at some earlier point in the line of ownership. *O'Keeffe* illustrates the point, as well as a constraint on the original owner's power to reclaim the goods from their eventual innocent possessor: the statute of limitations.

The result is different, however, if the victim originally lost his goods to a fraud. In that case the fraud obtains "voidable" title — voidable, that is, by the victim of the fraud once the misdeed is discovered. At that point the victim can seek damages from the fraud or can try to rescind the transaction. But until that voiding occurs the fraud does have title to the goods and is capable of passing it on to an innocent purchaser. Such a buyer is immune from a claim of conversion by the victim of the fraud. This was the reason for the finding of no liability in *Phelps*. What is the sense of the distinction the law draws between frauds and thieves?

Some of this territory now is governed by the Uniform Commercial Code, §2-403 of which provides as follows:

> (1) A purchaser of goods acquires all title which his transferor had or had power to transfer except that a purchaser of a limited interest acquires rights only to the extent of the interest purchased. A person with voidable title has power to transfer a good title to a good faith purchaser for value. When goods have been delivered under a transaction of purchase the purchaser has such power even though:
>   (a) The transferor was deceived as to the identity of the purchaser, or
>   (b) The delivery was in exchange for a check which is later dishonored, or
>   (c) It was agreed that the transaction was to be a "cash sale," or
>   (d) The delivery was procured through fraud punishable as larcenous under the criminal law.
>   (2) Any entrusting of possession of goods to a merchant who deals in goods of that kind gives him power to transfer all rights of the entruster to a buyer in ordinary course of business.
>   (3) "Entrusting" includes any delivery and any acquiescence in retention of possession regardless of any condition expressed between the parties to the delivery or acquiescence and regardless of whether the procurement of the entrusting or the possessor's disposition of the goods have been such as to be larcenous under the criminal law. [. . .]

8. *The retrieval of loot.* In Kelley Kar Company v. Maryland Casualty Co., 298 P.2d 590 (Cal. App. 1956), a man named Holland robbed the Farmers National Bank in Erick, Oklahoma. He then went to California and bought a Mercury automobile from the Kelley Kar Company. He obtained it by paying $1,000 in cash obtained from the robbery and also trading in a Buick that he had bought elsewhere — again with proceeds from the robbery. The bank's insurance company, having compensated the bank for its losses, was

subrogated to the bank's rights (i.e., it had the right to pursue any lawsuits the bank could have brought); the insurer thus sued the car dealership to collect the Buick and the stolen cash — "identifiable loot money" — that the dealer had accepted from the thief. The trial court gave judgment to the defendant. The California Supreme Court affirmed:

> One who receives stolen money in good faith and for good consideration will prevail over the unfortunate victim of the thief. [. . .] Of course no title of a stolen chattel can pass from the thief. However, the instant action does not involve a stolen chattel. The Buick automobile taken by respondent in trade was not stolen by Holland. It was purchased by him with stolen funds. Section 1744 of the Civil Code provides: "Where the seller of goods has a voidable title thereto, but his title has not been avoided at the time of the sale, the buyer acquires a good title to the goods, provided he buys them in good faith, for value, and without notice of the seller's defect of title." It is common knowledge that not every business man can delve into the problem of how or where or with what funds a chattel offered him for purchase was acquired. So long as he buys in good faith and exercises all the precautions as to title that the reasonable man would exercise and so long as he is not put on notice by an unusually low price, it must be deemed that the transaction was valid and in the normal course of business. Only bad faith on the part of such purchaser of a chattel purchased with stolen money can deprive him of ownership of the chattel.

What is the distinction between *Kelley Kar Company v. Maryland Casualty Co.* and *O'Keeffe v. Snyder*?

9. *Honor among thieves.* In Anderson v. Gouldberg, 53 N.W. 636 (Minn. 1892), the defendants took logs from the property of one Sigfrid Anderson. Anderson sued the defendants to replevy the logs. The defendants argued that Anderson tortiously had acquired the logs in the first place by trespassing on the land of a third party. The jury nevertheless brought in a verdict for Anderson, and the trial court entered judgment upon it; the Minnesota Supreme Court affirmed:

> [T]he only question is whether bare possession of property, though wrongfully obtained, is sufficient title to enable the party enjoying it to maintain replevin against a mere stranger, who takes it from him. We had supposed that this was settled in the affirmative as long ago, at least, as the early case of Armory v. Delamirie, 1 Strange, 504, so often cited on that point. When it is said that to maintain replevin the plaintiff's possession must have been lawful, it means merely that it must have been lawful as against the person who deprived him of it; and possession is good title against all the world except those having a better title. Counsel says that

possession only raises a presumption of title, which, however, may be rebutted. Rightly understood, this is correct; but counsel misapplies it. One who takes property from the possession of another can only rebut this presumption by showing a superior title in himself, or in some way connecting himself with one who has. One who has acquired the possession of property, whether by finding, bailment, or by mere tort, has a right to retain that possession as against a mere wrongdoer who is a stranger to the property. Any other rule would lead to an endless series of unlawful seizures and reprisals in every case where property had once passed out of the possession of the rightful owner.

The case of *Armory v. Delamirie,* which the court cites, is an English decision from 1722. The plaintiff found a jewel set in a socket in the course of his work as a chimney sweep. He gave the jewel to one of his superiors, who then declined to give it back; the plaintiff sued for its recovery. The court held that the finder of the stone, while having no absolute right to it, nevertheless had rights superior to all but its rightful owner. The case usually is considered in detail in courses on property law. How does *Anderson* extend *Armory?*

Suppose a sheriff seizes stolen property from a thief and the thief brings a replevin action against the sheriff, noting — correctly, let us assume — that the original owner of the property cannot be found. Such suits routinely fail. Is this consistent with *Anderson v. Gouldberg?*

10. *Frontiers of liability for conversion.* In Moore v. Regents of the University of California, 793 P.2d 479 (Cal. 1990), the plaintiff, Moore, was diagnosed with hairy-cell leukemia. As part of the treatment for the disease the defendant's doctors removed his spleen. Without Moore's knowledge the doctors then performed research on cells obtained from the spleen and determined that they had unique value; Moore's white blood cells overproduced certain proteins that help regulate the immune system. The defendants developed his cells into a "cell line" capable of reproducing indefinitely and obtained a patent on it. Some predictions within the industry suggested that the ultimate market value of the line would be approximately three billion dollars. The plaintiff brought a suit for conversion, among other claims. The trial court dismissed the complaint. The court of appeals reversed:

> Defendants' position that plaintiff cannot own his tissue, but that they can, is fraught with irony. Apparently, defendants see nothing abnormal in their exclusive control of plaintiff's excised spleen, nor in their patenting of a living organism derived therefrom. We cannot reconcile defendant's assertion of what appears to be their property interest in removed tissue and the resulting cell-line with their contention that the source of the material has no rights therein. [...]
>
> Defendants contend that plaintiff has no property right in the knowledge gained or the new things made in the course of the study of his cells.

This is an inaccurate characterization of this case. [. . .] The complaint alleges that defendants exploited plaintiff's cells, not just the knowledge gained from them. Without these small indispensable pieces of plaintiff, there could have been no three billion dollar cell-line. [. . .]

Defendants argue that even if plaintiff's spleen is personal property, its surgical removal was an abandonment by him of a diseased organ. They assert that he cannot, therefore, bring an action for conversion. [. . .] The question whether the plaintiff abandoned his spleen, or any of the other tissues taken by the defendants, is plainly a question of fact as to what his intent was at the time. [. . .] In California, absent evidence of a contrary intent or agreement, the reasonable expectation of a patient regarding tissue removed in the course of surgery would be that it may be examined by medical personnel for treatment purposes, and then promptly and permanently disposed of by interment or incineration in compliance with Health and Safety Code section 7054.4. Simply consenting to surgery under such circumstances hardly shows indifference to what may become of a removed organ or who may assert possession of it. Any use to which there was no consent, or which is not within the accepted understanding of the patient, is a conversion. It cannot be seriously asserted that a patient abandons a severed organ to the first person who takes it, nor can it be presumed that the patient is indifferent to whatever use might be made of it.

The California Supreme Court then reversed the court of appeals, ordering the dismissal of Moore's claims for conversion:

Of the relevant policy considerations, two are of overriding importance. The first is protection of a competent patient's right to make autonomous medical decisions. [. . .] This policy weighs in favor of providing a remedy to patients when physicians act with undisclosed motives that may affect their professional judgment. The second important policy consideration is that we not threaten with disabling civil liability innocent parties who are engaged in socially useful activities, such as researchers who have no reason to believe that their use of a particular cell sample is, or may be, against a donor's wishes.

[A]n examination of the relevant policy considerations suggests an appropriate balance: Liability based upon existing disclosure obligations, rather than an unprecedented extension of the conversion theory, protects patients' rights of privacy and autonomy without unnecessarily hindering research. [. . .] To be sure, the threat of liability for conversion might help to enforce patients' rights indirectly. This is because physicians might be able to avoid liability by obtaining patients' consent, in the broadest possible terms, to any conceivable subsequent research use of excised cells. Unfortunately, to extend the conversion theory would utterly sacrifice the other goal of protecting innocent parties. Since conversion is a strict liability tort, it would impose liability on all those into whose hands the cells come, whether or not the particular defendant participated in, or knew of, the inadequate disclosures that violated the patient's right to make an informed decision. In contrast to the conversion theory, the fiduciary-duty and informed-consent theories protect the patient directly, without punishing innocent parties or creating disincentives to the conduct of socially beneficial research.

The court concluded that Moore had stated a good cause of action for breach of fiduciary duty and for the performance of medical procedures without his informed consent — in both cases because the doctors failed to disclose to him their financial interest in his organs.

11. *Intangibles.* In Kremen v. Cohen, 337 F.3d 1024 (9th Cir. 2003), a man named Kremen registered the Internet domain name "sex.com" in 1994 through Network Solutions, the firm charged with assigning such designations. Soon thereafter, a con artist named Cohen, recently released from prison, sent a fraudulent letter to Network Solutions; the letter purported to be from Kremen's firm and announced that it was abandoning the domain name. Network Solutions accepted the letter at face value and gave the domain name to Cohen. Cohen used the domain name to create what the court described as a "lucrative online porn empire." Kremen sued Cohen and won $65 million in damages, but was not able to collect the judgment as Cohen fled to Mexico. Kremen then brought a suit for conversion against Network Solutions. The district court gave summary judgment to the defendant. The court of appeals, per Kozinski, J., reversed:

> Property is a broad concept that includes every intangible benefit and prerogative susceptible of possession or disposition. We apply a three-part test to determine whether a property right exists: First, there must be an interest capable of precise definition; second, it must be capable of exclusive possession or control; and third, the putative owner must have established a legitimate claim to exclusivity. Domain names satisfy each criterion. Like a share of corporate stock or a plot of land, a domain name is a well-defined interest. Someone who registers a domain name decides where on the Internet those who invoke that particular name — whether by typing it into their web browsers, by following a hyperlink, or by other means — are sent. Ownership is exclusive in that the registrant alone makes that decision. Moreover, like other forms of property, domain names are valued, bought and sold, often for millions of dollars, and they are now even subject to in rem jurisdiction, *see* 15 U.S.C. §1125(d)(2). [. . .]
>   Kremen therefore had an intangible property right in his domain name, and a jury could find that Network Solutions "wrongful[ly] dispos[ed] of" that right to his detriment by handing the domain name

over to Cohen. The district court nevertheless rejected Kremen's conversion claim. It held that domain names, although a form of property, are intangibles not subject to conversion. This rationale derives from a distinction tort law once drew between tangible and intangible property: Conversion was originally a remedy for the wrongful taking of another's lost goods, so it applied only to tangible property. Virtually every jurisdiction, however, has discarded this rigid limitation to some degree. Many courts ignore or expressly reject it. [. . .]

The district court supported its contrary holding with several policy rationales, but none is sufficient grounds to depart from the common law rule. The court was reluctant to apply the tort of conversion because of its strict liability nature. [. . .] [B]ut there is nothing unfair about holding a company responsible for giving away someone else's property even if it was not at fault. Cohen is obviously the guilty party here, and the one who should in all fairness pay for his theft. But he's skipped the country, and his money is stashed in some offshore bank account. Unless Kremen's luck with his bounty hunters improves, Cohen is out of the picture. The question becomes whether Network Solutions should be open to liability for its decision to hand over Kremen's domain name. Negligent or not, it was Network Solutions that gave away Kremen's property. Kremen never did anything. It would not be unfair to hold Network Solutions responsible and force *it* to try to recoup its losses by chasing down Cohen. This, at any rate, is the logic of the common law, and we do not lightly discard it.

The district court was worried that "the threat of litigation threatens to stifle the registration system by requiring further regulations by [Network Solutions] and potential increases in fees." Given that Network Solutions's "regulations" evidently allowed it to hand over a registrant's domain name on the basis of a facially suspect letter without even contacting him, "further regulations" don't seem like such a bad idea. And the prospect of higher fees presents no issue here that it doesn't in any other context. A bank could lower its ATM fees if it didn't have to pay security guards, but we doubt most depositors would think that was a good idea.

The district court thought there were "methods better suited to regulate the vagaries of domain names" and left it "to the legislature to fashion an appropriate statutory scheme." The legislature, of course, is always free (within constitutional bounds) to refashion the system that courts come up with. But that doesn't mean we should throw up our hands and let private relations degenerate into a free-for-all in the meantime. We apply the common law until the legislature tells us otherwise. And the common law does not stand idle while people give away the property of others.

12. *Liability for spam.* In CompuServe, Inc. v. Cyber Promotions, Inc., 962 F. Supp. 1015 (S.D. Ohio 1997), the plaintiff was an Internet service

provider. The defendant was an advertising firm that sent unsolicited e-mail advertisements, known as "spam," to hundreds of thousands of e-mail accounts, many of which were held by CompuServe's customers. CompuServe notified the defendant that it was prohibited from using CompuServe's computer equipment to process and store its advertisements; the transmissions nevertheless continued. CompuServe sued the defendant for trespass to chattels. The court granted the request for a preliminary injunction, finding that CompuServe was likely to succeed on the merits:

> Electronic signals generated and sent by computer have been held to be sufficiently physically tangible to support a trespass cause of action. It is undisputed that plaintiff has a possessory interest in its computer systems. Further, defendants' contact with plaintiff's computers is clearly intentional. Although electronic messages may travel through the Internet over various routes, the messages are affirmatively directed to their destination. [. . .]
>
> A plaintiff can sustain an action for trespass to chattels, as opposed to an action for conversion, without showing a substantial interference with its right to possession of that chattel. Harm to the personal property or diminution of its quality, condition, or value as a result of defendants' use can also be the predicate for liability. [. . .] To the extent that defendants' multitudinous electronic mailings demand the disk space and drain the processing power of plaintiff's computer equipment, those resources are not available to serve CompuServe subscribers. Therefore, the value of that equipment to CompuServe is diminished even though it is not physically damaged by defendants' conduct. [. . .]
>
> Defendants suggest that "[u]nless an alleged trespasser actually takes physical custody of the property or physically damages it, courts will not find the 'substantial interference' required to maintain a trespass to chattel claim." To support this rather broad proposition, defendants cite only two cases which make any reference to the Restatement. In *Glidden v. Szybiak*, 63 A.2d 233 (N.H. 1949), the court simply indicated that an action for trespass to chattels could not be maintained in the absence of some form of damage. The court held that where plaintiff did not contend that defendant's pulling on her pet dog's ears caused any injury, an action in tort could not be maintained. In contrast, plaintiff in the present action has alleged that it has suffered several types of injury as a result of defendants' conduct. In *Koepnick v. Sears Roebuck & Co.*, 158 Ariz. 322, 762 P.2d 609 (1988) the court held that a two-minute search of an individual's truck did not amount to a "dispossession" of the truck as defined in Restatement §221 or a deprivation of the use of the truck for a substantial time. It is clear from a reading of Restatement §218 that an interference or intermeddling that does not fit the §221 definition of "dispossession" can nonetheless result in defendants' liability for trespass.

D. FALSE IMPRISONMENT

The tort of false imprisonment protects the plaintiff's interest in freedom of movement. It generally is committed when one party confines another without authorization. The word "imprisonment" may be thought to connote formal incarceration, but today it is understood that false imprisonments can arise informally as well — in a room, a car, or anyplace else to which a party's liberty of movement might wrongfully be restricted.

Restatement (Second) of Torts

§35. FALSE IMPRISONMENT

(1) An actor is subject to liability to another for false imprisonment if

(a) he acts intending to confine the other or a third person within boundaries fixed by the actor, and

(b) his act directly or indirectly results in such a confinement of the other, and

(c) the other is conscious of the confinement or is harmed by it.

(2) An act which is not done with the intention stated in Subsection (1, a) does not make the actor liable to the other for a merely transitory or otherwise harmless confinement, although the act involves an unreasonable risk of imposing it and therefore would be negligent or reckless if the risk threatened bodily harm.

Illustration 2. Just before closing time, A, a shopkeeper, sends B into a cold storage vault to take inventory of the articles therein. Forgetting that he has done so, he locks the door of the vault on leaving the premises. If in a few moments thereafter, he remembers that B is in the vault and immediately goes back and releases B, he is not liable to B for the momentary confinement to which B has been subjected. On the other hand, if he does not remember that B is in the vault until he reaches home and, therefore, although he acts immediately, he cannot release B until B has been confined in the cold vault for so long a time as to bring on a heavy cold which develops into pneumonia, he is subject to liability to B for the illness so caused.

§36. WHAT CONSTITUTES CONFINEMENT

(1) To make the actor liable for false imprisonment, the other's confinement within the boundaries fixed by the actor must be complete.

(2) The confinement is complete although there is a reasonable means of escape, unless the other knows of it.

(3) The actor does not become liable for false imprisonment by intentionally preventing another from going in a particular direction in which he has a right or privilege to go.

Illustration 6. A by an invalid process restrains B within limits which are coterminous with the boundaries of a considerable town. A has confined B.

Illustration 7. A serves upon B an invalid writ purporting to restrain B from leaving a particular State of the United States. B submits, believing the writ to be valid. A has confined B.

Illustration 8. A wrongfully prevents B from entering the United States. A has not confined B, although B, in a sense, may be said to be confined within the rest of the habitable world.

§38. CONFINEMENT BY PHYSICAL BARRIERS

The confinement may be by actual or apparent physical barriers.

Illustration 2. A takes away the crutches of B who, being a cripple, is unable to walk without them. A has confined B.

Illustration 3. A removes a ladder which is the only available means by which B can get out of a well. A has confined B.

NOTES

1. *Deprogramming.* In Peterson v. Sorlien, 299 N.W.2d 123 (Minn. 1980), the plaintiff was a 21-year-old student at Moorhead State College in Minnesota. During her freshman year she joined a local chapter of The Way, a religious organization with a strong emphasis on fund-raising. Members were expected to obtain employment and tithe 10 percent of their earnings to the ministry, to purchase books and tapes and enroll in training programs, and to recruit others into The Way. The plaintiff did all this, and to further finance her contributions she also sold a car her parents had given to her. Her parents watched these developments with alarm. Their evidence was that as their daughter became involved in The Way her academic performance declined and she seemed increasingly distraught, irritable, and alienated from her family. The family concluded that she was in a state of psychological bondage.

At the end of her junior year, the plaintiff's father picked her up in his car and unexpectedly drove her to a house in Minneapolis where he had arranged to have her "deprogrammed." She was met there by a professional deprogrammer and a group of young people who had been involved in cults and who attempted to convince her that she had been brainwashed. At first the plaintiff responded by curling into a fetal position, crying, and covering her ears; she begged to be released, and at times she would scream hysterically and flail at her father. After a few days at the house, however, she became friendly and vivacious, having conversations with her father, going roller skating, and joining in a picnic. The plaintiff spent the next two weeks at the house in Minneapolis and traveling with one of the former cult members who had been part of the deprogramming effort. The plaintiff also spoke frequently by telephone with her fiancé, a member of the ministry who played tapes and songs to her and begged her to return to the fold.

About two weeks after she first arrived at the house, the plaintiff stepped outside, stopped a passing police car, and asked to be returned to the ministry. She sued her parents and the deprogrammers for false imprisonment and other torts. A jury brought in a verdict for the defendants and the Minnesota Supreme Court affirmed the resulting judgment:

> The period in question began on Monday, May 24, 1976, and ceased on Wednesday, June 9, 1976, a period of 16 days. The record clearly demonstrates that Susan willingly remained in the company of defendants for at least 13 of those days. [. . .] In his summation to the jury, the trial judge instructed that to deem consent a defense to the charge of false imprisonment for the entire period or for any part therein, a preponderance of the evidence must demonstrate that such plaintiff voluntarily consented. The central issue for the jury, then, was whether Susan voluntarily participated in the activities of the first three days. The jury concluded that her behavior constituted a waiver. [. . .]
>
> Although carried out under colorably religious auspices, the method of cult indoctrination, viewed in a light most favorable to the prevailing party, is predicated on a strategy of coercive persuasion that undermines the capacity for informed consent. While we acknowledge that other social institutions may utilize a degree of coercion in promoting their objectives, none do so to the same extent or intend the same consequences. Society, therefore, has a compelling interest favoring intervention. The facts in this case support the conclusion that plaintiff only regained her volitional capacity to consent after engaging in the first three days of the deprogramming process. As such, we hold that when parents, or their agents, acting under the conviction that the judgmental capacity of their adult child is impaired, seek to extricate that child from what they reasonably believe to be a religious or pseudo-religious cult, and the child at some juncture assents to the actions in question, limitations upon the child's mobility do not constitute meaningful deprivations of personal liberty sufficient to support a judgment for false imprisonment. But owing to the threat that deprogramming poses to public order, we do not endorse self-help as a preferred alternative. In fashioning a remedy, the First Amendment requires resort to the least restrictive alternative so as to not impinge upon religious belief.

Otis, J., dissented:

> [The majority furnishes] no guidelines or criteria for what constitutes "impaired judgmental capacity" other than the fact that the adult child has embraced an unorthodox doctrine with a zeal which has given the

intervenor cause for alarm, a concern which may be well-founded, ill-founded, or unfounded.

Nor do we specify whether the "cult" must be for a benign or a malevolent purpose. It is enough that the intervenor has reason to believe it is a cult i.e. "an unorthodox system of belief" and that at some juncture during the adult child's involuntary confinement, she "assents," that is to say, yields or surrenders, possibly from exhaustion or fatigue, and possibly for a period only long enough to regain her composure. [. . .]

At age 21, a daughter is no longer a child. She is an adult. Susan Peterson was not only an adult in 1976 but she was a bright, well-educated adult. For whatever reason, she was experiencing a period of restlessness and insecurity which is by no means uncommon in students of that age. But to hold that for seeking companionship and identity in a group whose proselyting tactics may well be suspect, she must endure without a remedy the degrading and humiliating treatment she received at the hands of her parents, is, in my opinion, totally at odds with the basic rights of young people to think unorthodox thoughts, join unorthodox groups, and proclaim unorthodox views. I would reverse the denial of recovery as to that cause of action.

The jury did find two of the deprogrammers liable for intentional infliction of emotional distress, and awarded the plaintiff a total of $10,000 in punitive damages against them.

2. *The iron hand.* In Eilers v. Coy, 582 F. Supp. 1093 (D. Minn. 1984), the plaintiff was a 24-year-old member of the Disciples of Jesus Christ, which the defendant's evidence depicted as "an authoritarian religious fellowship directed with an iron hand by Brother Rama Behera." Members of the plaintiff's family became concerned about changes in his personality after he joined the group. They also worried that he might have suicidal tendencies. They arranged to have the plaintiff abducted and taken for deprogramming to an institution called the Tau Center. During his first days there the plaintiff was kept handcuffed to a bed in a dormitory-style room with plywood over the windows. Once when he was allowed to use the bathroom he made a dash for one of the exits, but guards captured him and returned him to his room. After several days of resistance, however, the plaintiff pretended to consent to his confinement and became cooperative.

At the end of a week at the Tau Center, the plaintiff was taken by car to Iowa for further deprogramming. Near the outset of the journey he managed to jump out of the car and call for help. Local residents assisted him in escaping and called the police. He soon rejoined the Disciples and sued the deprogrammers for false imprisonment.

The district court gave a directed verdict to the plaintiff. The court thought that *Peterson v. Sorlien,* a controlling Minnesota precedent, was distinguishable. Do you agree?

3. *Bounty hunters*. In Bright v. Ailshie, 641 N.W.2d 587 (Mich. 2002), a man named Vincent Bright was arrested in Missouri on a drug-related charge. He identified himself to the police as his brother, Dennis Bright; he gave them Dennis's date of birth, social security number, and address. Vincent was released on bail after entering into an agreement with a bail bond company — again in his brother's name. Vincent absconded on the bond. The bail bond firm hired a bounty hunter, one Moore, to apprehend him. Moore found Dennis Bright in Detroit, took him into custody, and brought him back to Missouri. It was then determined that Dennis Bright was not the correct party and the arrest warrant was amended accordingly. Dennis Bright sued the bounty hunter and bail bond firm, among others, for false imprisonment. The trial court gave summary judgment to the defendants and the court of appeals affirmed, finding that Moore had probable cause to believe that Dennis Bright was a felon. The Michigan Supreme Court reversed. The Court held the case governed by a statute, MCL 764.16:

> A private person may make an arrest in the following situations:
>   (a) For a felony committed in the private person's presence.
>   (b) If the person to be arrested has committed a felony although not in the private person's presence.
>   (c) If the private person is summoned by a peace officer to assist the officer in making an arrest.
>   (d) If the private person is a merchant, an agent of a merchant, an employee of a merchant, or an independent contractor providing security for a merchant of a store and has reasonable cause to believe that the person to be arrested has violated section 356c or 356d of the Michigan penal code, Act No. 328 of the Public Acts of 1931, being sections 750.356c and 750.356d of the Michigan Compiled Laws, in that store, regardless of whether the violation was committed in the presence of the private person.

Said the court:

> The plain language of subsection (b) provides authority for a private person to arrest another, if the other has committed a felony. The statute does not grant arrest authority where the other has not committed a felony even if the private person has probable cause to believe the other has committed a felony. Notwithstanding the clarity of the Michigan statute, the Court of Appeals [in *People v. Bashans*, 80 Mich. App. 702 (1978)] incorrectly read a probable cause qualification into M.C.L. §764.16. This may not be done. Although such authority may have existed at common law, that authority was abrogated by our Legislature in 1927.

The court contrasted the result here with the result that might be produced by more liberal statutes such as Cal. Penal Code §837:

A private person may arrest another:

1. For a public offense committed or attempted in his presence.
2. When the person arrested has committed a felony, although not in his presence.
3. When a felony has in fact been committed, and he has reasonable cause for believing the person arrested to have committed it.

Would the plaintiff have had a good claim for false imprisonment against his brother, Vincent?

4. *The citizen's arrest.* The power of a private person to make a citizen's arrest is considered here because actions in excess of that authority can amount to false imprisonment. (If one party makes an improper citizen's arrest of another, the result sometimes may be called "false arrest" rather than false imprisonment, but in most jurisdictions nothing of substance turns on this difference in terminology.) It also is possible to view the citizen's arrest as a privilege that arises as a defense to a claim of false imprisonment. The defendant typically asserts the power to make a citizen's arrest as a defense after the plaintiff has made out a *prima facie* case; the defendant thus is assigned the burden of demonstrating that the elements of a justifiable citizen's arrest were satisfied. On this view the power to make a citizen's arrest could as well have been treated in the next chapter, which covers various privileges that can be used to justify actions that are *prima facie* intentional torts.

As *Bright v. Ailshie* illustrates, the power to make a citizen's arrest is now widely regulated by statute. In some states, however, the source of the power to make a citizen's arrest still remains the common law, the rules of which generally track the California statute excerpted above. The Restatement (Second) of Torts §119 (1965) offers these illustrations:

> *Illustration 2.* A sees B and C bending over a dead man, D. B and C each accuse the other of murdering D. A is not sure that either B or C did the killing, but he has a reasonable suspicion that either B or C killed D. A is privileged to arrest either or both.
>
> *Illustration 3.* A, while passing B's house, hears a woman's scream. He rushes into the house and discovers that the woman was screaming because B was beating her. A is privileged to arrest B.
>
> *Illustration 5.* A, a private citizen, sees B and C engaged in a mutual affray. He runs towards them. B and C both flee in different directions. A pursues B, whom he arrests after a short pursuit. A is privileged to do so. He thereupon goes in search of C. C has disappeared, and A makes inquiries as to his whereabouts and discovers that he has gone to a distant suburb of the city. He stops for a quarter of an hour to get his supper, and then takes a taxicab and follows C, whom he eventually finds some three or four hours later. A is then privileged to arrest C.

> *Illustration* 6. A is murdered by B. C, B's wife, in order to give B opportunity to escape, draws suspicion upon herself, thus leading D to believe her guilty of the murder of A. D is privileged to arrest C.

Suppose you observe a drunk driver. Do you have the power to make a citizen's arrest? For conflicting answers under different statutes, see *State v. McAteer*, 511 S.E.2d 79 (S.C. 2000), and *People v. Ciesler*, 710 N.E.2d 1270 (Ill. App. 1999). The general reason for the disagreement is that states vary in their willingness to permit citizens' arrests for misdemeanors — or they agree that such arrests are allowed if the misdemeanor is a "breach of the peace," but disagree about whether drunk driving satisfies that criterion.

5. *Shoplifters.* The common law generally recognized that same distinction between felonies and misdemeanors, and did not permit citizen's arrests for misdemeanors that were nonviolent. This created a dilemma for the shopkeeper who suspected that a customer was engaged in shoplifting. Since shoplifting usually is a misdemeanor (it depends on the value of the goods stolen) and since it is not typically considered a "breach of the peace," in most cases there was no common law privilege to detain a suspected shoplifter. The suspicious shopkeeper could invoke a limited common law privilege to use reasonable force to recover his stolen chattels, but the privilege was and is unforgiving; if it is used mistakenly, the actor is liable in damages no matter how reasonable the mistake may have been. See *Atlantic & Pacific Tea Co. v. Paul*, 261 A.2d 731 (Md. App. 1970); *Gortarez v. Smitty's Super Valu, Inc.*, 680 P.2d 807 (Ariz. 1984). In response to this problem most states have passed statutes giving shopkeepers a limited privilege to detain suspected shoplifters without liability even if their suspicions prove to be unfounded. We saw a brief example of such a statute in connection with *Morgan v. Loyacomo*, a case in the section of this chapter on battery. The statutes invariably permit the merchant to detain a suspect only in a reasonable manner and for a reasonable time. They thus generate frequent litigation by customers wrongly suspected of shoplifting who complain that they were held too long for investigation. Like many other questions of reasonableness in the law of torts, these have a tendency to go to the jury.

6. *Stek up artist.* In Baggett v. National Bank & Trust Co., 330 S.E.2d 108 (Ga. App. 1985), the plaintiff, Richard Baggett, entered the defendant's bank to deposit a check. He filled out a deposit slip from a supply provided for customer use and handed it to the teller along with his check. Unbeknownst to Baggett, on the back of the deposit slip someone had written "This is a stek up." When the teller saw this message she walked away from her window and phoned the bank manager, telling him to call the police. She then went back to the window and deposited Baggett's check. He left the bank and drove away. Meanwhile the manager had sounded the bank's silent alarm, which summoned the police; an officer soon arrived, was informed of what had happened, and issued a radio bulletin. Baggett was arrested a few minutes later. He was brought to the bank and identified by the teller as the one who

passed the note. An investigation at the scene revealed that a number of other deposit slips had similar notes written on them and that Baggett's handwriting did not match. Baggett nevertheless was taken to police headquarters and questioned further. He was released about three hours after his initial arrest. He sued the bank for false imprisonment. The trial court gave summary judgment to the bank, and the court of appeals affirmed:

> The evidence submitted by the bank in support of its motion for summary judgment establishes without dispute that the decision to arrest Baggett was made solely by the police, based on the bank employees' accurate and good faith account of what had transpired, and without any request on their part that he be detained or held in custody. We reject Baggett's contention that contrary evidence is created by two averments in his own affidavit, one to the effect that he was told by a police detective that the teller had identified him as "the guy who tried to rob her" and another to the effect that the acting manager asked him as he was being transported to the bank's conference room, "Ricky, why did you do it?'". The former statement is double hearsay and consequently without probative value, while the latter statement does not conflict with the evidence showing that the bank employees provided accurate information to police and made no effort to procure the arrest. It follows that the trial court did not err in granting summary judgment to the bank with respect to the false imprisonment claim.

Would the plaintiff have had a good claim for false imprisonment against the author of the language on the back of the deposit ticket?

7. *Standing on principle.* In Melton v. LaCalamito, 282 S.E.2d 393 (Ga. App. 1981), the plaintiff rented a U-Haul trailer in New Jersey to use in moving his belongings to Georgia. He returned the trailer to a dealership in Atlanta operated by the defendant, Melton. As he was unhitching the trailer Melton looked in the plaintiff's trunk and saw a pair of furniture pads — a type of blanket that U-Haul rented out with its trailers; the value of the pads was approximately $4 apiece. The plaintiff refused to hand them over. He said that he had obtained the blankets when his father was a U-Haul dealer in New Jersey and that they had been in his family for more than a decade; he also pointed out that his rental agreement made no mention of the pads. Melton would not yield and called the police. An officer soon arrived, as did the plaintiff's mother, who had been traveling with him. She corroborated his account of the blankets' origins. The responding officer later testified as follows:

> Q. Now, when you talked with [the plaintiff], what did you say and what did he say?
> A. [. . .] I advised the subject . . . that all we wanted to do was give the company their blankets back. Mr. Melton stated that he didn't want

to go to court or he didn't want to see the guy locked up or anything. He just wanted his company's blankets back. . . .

Q.   Now, when you said all you wanted was to get U-Haul's property back, what did he say?

A.   [Plaintiff] advised me he wasn't going to return the property. Again, he said it was property of his family. . . . Since we weren't able to get Mr. LaCalamito to return the blankets to the company, to U-Haul, we had no choice but to make an arrest.

The plaintiff was taken to jail and spent the next several hours there. It turned out that he had been telling the truth, however, and the charges against him were dismissed the next day. He sued Melton for false imprisonment. The trial court entered judgment on a jury verdict in favor of the plaintiff for $10,000 in compensatory damages and $5,000 in punitive damages. The court of appeals affirmed:

> The rule applicable in a situation such as that presented in this case is stated in W. Prosser, Law of Torts §119 (1971): "If the defendant (here Melton) merely states what he believes, leaving the decision to prosecute entirely to the uncontrolled discretion of the officer, or if the officer makes an independent investigation, or prosecutes for an offense other than the one charged by the defendant, the latter is not regarded as having instigated the proceeding; but if it is found that his persuasion was the determining factor in inducing the officer's decision, or that he gave information which he knew to be false and so unduly influenced the authorities, he may be held liable."
>
> The testimony shows that Melton indicated to the police that he did not want to go to court or to see appellee jailed. Nevertheless, during a period of discussion lasting 30 to 40 minutes, Melton continued to insist on the surrender of the furniture pads as property belonging to U-Haul. Since appellee refused to surrender the pads, the police "had no choice but to make an arrest." Under these circumstances, the jury was authorized to conclude that Melton's insistance that the pads were U-Haul property was the determining factor leading to appellee's arrest and prosecution. [. . .]

The court also found that in view of all the facts available to him, Melton did not have probable cause to support his instigation of the plaintiff's arrest.

What is the distinction between *Melton v. LaCalamito* and *Baggett v. National Bank & Trust Co.*? With these cases compare the following provision from the Restatement (Second) of Torts (1965):

§45A. INSTIGATING OR PARTICIPATING IN FALSE IMPRISONMENT

One who instigates or participates in the unlawful confinement of another is subject to liability to the other for false imprisonment.

Comment c. Instigation. If the confinement is unprivileged, the one who instigates it is subject to liability to the person confined for the false imprisonment. Instigation consists of words or acts which direct, request, invite or encourage the false imprisonment itself. In the case of an arrest, it is the equivalent, in words or conduct, of "Officer, arrest that man!" It is not enough for instigation that the actor has given information to the police about the commission of a crime, or has accused the other of committing it, so long as he leaves to the police the decision as to what shall be done about any arrest, without persuading or influencing them. Likewise it is not an instigation of a false arrest where the actor has requested the authorities to make a proper and lawful arrest, and has in no way invited or encouraged an improper one, or where he has requested an arrest at a time when it would be proper and lawful, and it is subsequently made at a time when it has become improper.

Is this Restatement provision consistent with the two cases just considered?

8. *Malicious prosecution distinguished.* When false imprisonment claims arise in the settings just considered — i.e., instigation of an arrest — they bear a family resemblance to the tort of malicious prosecution, but the two torts have different origins and different elements. False imprisonment is descended from the old tort of trespass and usually is understood to involve direct interference with the plaintiff's freedom of movement. Malicious prosecution involves more indirect steps to confine the plaintiff and thus had to be brought in the old days as an action for trespass on the case. The practical difference between the torts today generally involves the quality of the processes used to incarcerate the plaintiff. If the arrest itself is lawful — as always will be the case, for example, if a warrant for the plaintiff's arrest has been sought and obtained — then the resulting imprisonment cannot be considered "false," but the private defendant who sought the prosecution still may be held liable for malicious prosecution. False imprisonment claims arise when the arrest is made without a warrant. In that case the lawfulness of the arrest depends on whether it is supported by probable cause. If the officer relies on the defendant's importunings and they turn out to have been unsupported by probable cause, the plaintiff may be able to sue the defendant for false imprisonment. It depends on the relationship between the defendant's acts and the officer's decisions, as *Baggett* and *Melton* illustrate. Meanwhile the police officer typically will enjoy immunity from state law claims for false imprisonment or malicious prosecution, though liability remains a possibility under 42 U.S.C. §1983 if the plaintiff's federal constitutional rights were violated.

E. ASSAULT

The tort of assault typically is a companion to the tort of battery. We consider it here, a little later in the chapter, because consideration of assault also serves as a natural prologue to the modern tort of outrage, or intentional infliction of emotional distress, which will be our final topic.

Restatement (Second) of Torts

§21. ASSAULT

(1) An actor is subject to liability to another for assault if

(a) he acts intending to cause a harmful or offensive contact with the person of the other or a third person, or an imminent apprehension of such a contact, and

(b) the other is thereby put in such imminent apprehension.

(2) An action which is not done with the intention stated in Subsection (1, a) does not make the actor liable to the other for an apprehension caused thereby although the act involves an unreasonable risk of causing it and, therefore, would be negligent or reckless if the risk threatened bodily harm.

§22. ATTEMPT UNKNOWN TO OTHER

Illustration 2. A, standing behind B, points a pistol at him. C overpowers A before he can shoot. B, hearing the noise turns around and for the first time realizes the danger to which he had been subjected. A is not liable to B.

§24. WHAT CONSTITUTES APPREHENSION

Illustration 1. A, a scrawny individual who is intoxicated, attempts to strike with his fist B, who is the heavyweight champion pugilist of the world. B is not at all afraid of A, is confident that he can avoid any such blow, and in fact succeeds in doing so. A is subject to liability to B.

Comment c. Rationale. The apparent anomaly of the fact that almost from the very beginning of the common law legal protection was accorded to the interest in freedom from this one curious type of mental impression, but until recently protection was denied to the interest in freedom from other emotional disturbances which everyone recognizes as extremely distressing, such as serious fright or anxiety for the safety of oneself or a member of his family, is explainable only by the fact that the action for assault is a survival from the time when the action of trespass gave to the persons who were the victims of minor crimes a private right of action. The primary purpose of this action was to punish the wrongdoer, although the major part of the penalty imposed upon him went to the private individual aggrieved. The civil action of trespass for assault still presents a strong analogy to criminal prosecutions for an attempt to commit a crime. In reality, it was originally an action brought by the person aggrieved by the actor's attempt to commit a battery upon him.

§28. APPREHENSION OF UNINTENDED BODILY CONTACT

If the actor intends merely to put the other in apprehension of a bodily contact, he is subject to liability for an assault to the other if the other, although realizing that the actor does not intend to inflict such a contact upon him, is put in apprehension of the contact.

Illustration 1. A, an expert knife thrower, intending to frighten B, who is standing against a wall, throws a knife toward him not intending to hit him. B, though knowing A's intention, does not share A's perfect confidence in his marksmanship and is put in apprehension of being struck by the knife. A is subject to liability to B.

§32. CHARACTER OF INTENT NECESSARY

(1) To make the actor liable for an assault, the actor must have intended to inflict a harmful or offensive contact upon the other or to have put the other in apprehension of such contact.

(2) If an act is done with the intention of affecting a third person in the manner stated in Subsection (1), but puts another in apprehension of a harmful or offensive contact, the actor is subject to liability to such other as fully as though he intended so to affect him.

Illustration 1. A throws a stone at B, whom he believes to be asleep. B, who is in fact awake, sees A throwing the stone and escapes by dodging. A is subject to liability to B.

Illustration 3. A and B are trespassing in C's woods. C observes B and points a gun at him, threatening to shoot. A, at the moment, comes from behind a tree and seeing C's gun pointed in his direction is put in apprehension of being shot. C is subject to liability to A as well as to B.

1. *Sinister phone calls.* In Brower v. Ackerley, 943 P.2d 1141 (Wash. App. 1997), the plaintiff, Jordan Brower, lived in Seattle and was active in community affairs. The defendants, two brothers named Ackerley, ran a company that engaged in advertising on billboards. Brower did not like billboards, and he determined that the city had not authorized some of the billboards the Ackerleys had erected. Brower tried in various ways to persuade the city to remove the billboards. At last he succeeded in having them declared illegal. Throughout the course of this campaign Brower received anonymous telephone calls that troubled him. In the beginning the caller told Brower to "get a life." The calls took a more aggressive tone as Brower's efforts became more successful. One night the caller said, "I'm going to find out where you live and I'm going to kick your ass." He called back an hour later and said, in a voice that Brower described as "eerie and sinister," "Ooooo, Jordan, oooo, you're finished; cut you in your sleep, you sack of shit." Brower had the calls traced and determined that they came from the Ackerleys' house. Brower sued the Ackerleys on various theories, including assault; he said the calls caused him feelings of panic and terror, as well as a rising pulse, light-headedness, sweaty

palms, and sleeplessness. The trial court gave summary judgment to the Ackerleys. The court of appeals affirmed as to the assault claim:

> To constitute civil assault, the threat must be of imminent harm. As one commentator observes, it is "the immediate physical threat which is important, rather than the manner in which it is conveyed." The Restatement's comment is to similar effect: "The apprehension created must be one of imminent contact, as distinguished from any contact in the future." The Restatement gives the following illustration: "A threatens to shoot B and leaves the room with the express purpose of getting his revolver. A is not liable to B." [. . .]
>
> [The telephone calls] threatened action in the near future, but not the imminent future. The immediacy of the threats was not greater than in the Restatement's illustration where A must leave the room to get his revolver. Because the threats, however frightening, were not accompanied by circumstances indicating that the caller was in a position to reach Brower and inflict physical violence "almost at once," we affirm the dismissal of the assault claim.

The court did, however, rule that the plaintiff was entitled to a jury trial on his claim for intentional infliction of emotional distress — a topic covered in the next section of the chapter.

2. *The bat warehouse.* In Bennight v. Western Auto Supply Co., 670 S.W.2d 373 (Tex. App. 1984), Cathy Bennight worked for the defendant's retail store. The rear of the store consisted of a warehouse that was known to be infested with bats. Bennight's manager required her to work in that area despite her protests. One day she was attacked by a number of bats; none of them bit her, though one became entangled in her hair. The following day one of the bats did bite her. She had to be administered an anti-rabies treatment, and she reacted badly to it; she became blind and suffered various emotional problems as a result. State law required that Bennight's own claim against Western Auto be made through the state's workers' compensation programs. Her husband, however, brought a civil suit against Western Auto for loss of consortium. The provisions of the workers' compensation statute provided that Bennight's husband could sue only if his wife's injury was the result of an intentional tort, and not if it was accidental. A jury brought in the following special verdict:

> 1. Do you find from a preponderance of the evidence that on the occasion in question [the manager] required Cathy Bennight to work in the warehouse area against her will with the intention of causing her to be bitten by a bat or to be otherwise exposed to rabies? Answer: We do not. [. . .]
>
> 3. Do you find from a preponderance of the evidence that [Western Auto], through its manager, intentionally maintained an unsafe place to work? Answer: We do.

4. Do you find from a preponderance of the evidence that on the occasion in question [the manager] required Cathy Bennight to work in the loft against her will when he knew that such place was an unsafe place to work? Answer: We do.

The jury set Mr. Bennight's damages at $87,500. The trial court held the injury accidental and entered a judgment that the plaintiff take nothing. The court of appeals reversed and held him entitled to recover:

[T]he unlawful and intentional invasion of *one* legally protected interest of another will supply the intent necessary to hold the actor liable for the unintended consequences of his act when some *other* legally protected interest of the victim is harmed in consequence of the act. The jury's answer to special issue 1 establishes only that the manager did not intend that Cathy be bitten by a bat and exposed to rabies; it does *not* establish, as a matter of law, that he committed no intentional tort against Cathy, for as we will discuss below, the jury's answer to the remaining special issues established that he intentionally committed an assault against her and his intent in *that* regard is imputed *by operation of law* to the actual harm which did occur with catastrophic results. [. . .]

Intentionally placing Cathy in [. . .] fear [of being attacked by the bats] was an "assault," an invasion of her personality, and an independent intentional tort in and of itself. More to the point for our present purposes, the manager's intention to place Cathy in such apprehension extends by operation of law to the specific additional injury which she did receive and for which she sought recovery, *whether or not* the manager in fact intended that additional and subsequent harm.

Was the *Bennight* case rightly decided? If it was, then what is the distinction between *Bennight* and *Brower v. Ackerley*?

3. *All in good fun.* In Langford v. Shu, 128 S.E.2d 210 (N.C. 1962), Langford went to visit the house of her neighbor, one Midgie Shu. As she crossed the Shus' porch, Langford saw a wooden box there labeled "Danger, African Mongoose, Live Snake Eater." Shu explained that the box contained a mongoose that her husband had given to their children; she told Langford to have a look at the box and said that the creature would do her no harm. Langford observed the box but kept about four feet away from it, declining "to get near that thing" because she was afraid of snakes. As she was looking at the box, one of the Shu children released a spring that held it closed. A screeching sound came forth from it and a furry object sprang at Langford. In fact it was a fox tail attached to a spring. There was no mongoose. Langford was unable to appreciate the distinction, however; she turned to run and stumbled into a brick wall, tearing cartilage in her knee. She sued

Shu for assault. The trial court gave Shu judgment as a matter of law. The North Carolina Supreme Court reversed:

> Defendant in this case set the stage for her children's prank; she aided and abetted it by her answers to the plaintiff's questions about the box. Defendant had seen the box demonstrated and she knew as only the mother of boys aged nine and eleven could know, that unless she took positive steps to prevent it, they would not let such a wary and apprehensive prospect as Mrs. Langford escape without a demonstration. To reach any other conclusion would be to ignore the propensities of little boys who, since the memory of a man runneth not to the contrary, have delighted to stampede timorous ladies with snakes, bugs, lizards, mice and other rewarding small creatures which hold no terror for youngsters. It is implicit in this evidence that defendant expected to enjoy the joke on her neighbor as much as the children, and that she participated in the act with them. To say that she should not have expected one of the boys to spring "the mongoose" on plaintiff would strain credulity.

Suppose defendant threatens to shoot plaintiff with a gun. Defendant believes the gun is loaded; plaintiff knows it is not. Liability for assault?

4. *The restrained swordsman.* In Tuberville v. Savage, 86 Eng. Rep. 684 (K.B. 1669), the plaintiff sued the defendant for battery. The defendant countered that the plaintiff had provoked him by first committing an assault. The plaintiff had put his hand on his sword and said to the defendant, "If it were not assize-time, I would not take such language from you." (By referring to "assize-time," the plaintiff meant that the judges who heard civil cases were in town and thus that the courts were in session.) It was held that the plaintiff had not committed an assault and was entitled to judgment:

> [T]he declaration of the plaintiff was, that he would not assault [the defendant], the Judges being in town; and *the intention* as well as *the act* makes an assault. Therefore if one strike another upon the hand, or arm, or breast, in discourse, it is no assault, there being no *intention* to assault; but if one intending to assault, strike *at* another and miss him, this is an assault; so if he hold up his hand against another in a threatening manner and say nothing, it is an assault.

What is the distinction between *Tuberville v. Savage* and *Langford v. Shu?*

5. *Dishonorable purposes (problem).* In Newell v. Whitcher, 53 Vt. 589 (Vt. 1880), the plaintiff, Newell, was a blind woman who gave music lessons to the defendant's children in their house once a week, staying there overnight on each occasion. On the night in question Newell was awakened

by the sound of someone entering her room. It was the defendant. He sat down on her bed and leaned over her; as the court described the events, he "made repeated and persistent solicitations to her for sexual intimacy, which she repelled, and urged him to leave her room. She got up from her bed, dressed herself and sat up the residue of the night." Newell brought suit against the defendant to recover for the sickness and fright she claimed to have suffered as a result. The trial court entered judgment on a jury verdict in the plaintiff's favor. The defendant appealed. What result?

F. OUTRAGE

The tort of intentional infliction of emotional distress — often known as "IIED" or as the tort of *outrage* — is a relative newcomer to the law. The common law did not recognize freestanding liability for the infliction of emotional harm, and as late as 1934 the first Restatement of Torts explicitly repudiated the idea. The classic rationales for rejecting the tort were the difficulty of proving that the defendant's conduct caused the plaintiff's harm, the danger of fraudulent claims, and the fear of a flood of litigation. But courts have long been willing to award damages for emotional distress where it results from (or is "parasitic" upon) the commission of some other, independent tort. During the middle of the twentieth century scholars argued that courts had begun using this rule to impose liability for outrage after all; in cases where a plaintiff's distress was serious and seemed to call for relief, courts would strain to find some physical contact in the case so that it might be called a battery, or they would stretch other existing legal categories to find liability in the case and thus permit an award of damages for distress. In 1948 these arguments led the American Law Institute to recognize intentional infliction of emotional distress as its own cause of action. The elements then were further adjusted a bit in the Restatement (Second), issued in 1965, and the resulting formulation was quite influential. Most jurisdictions now subscribe to it:

§46. OUTRAGEOUS CONDUCT CAUSING SEVERE EMOTIONAL DISTRESS

(1) One who by extreme and outrageous conduct intentionally or recklessly causes severe emotional distress to another is subject to liability for such emotional distress, and if bodily harm to the other results from it, for such bodily harm.

(2) Where such conduct is directed at a third person, the actor is subject to liability if he intentionally or recklessly causes severe emotional distress

(a) to a member of such person's immediate family who is present at the time, whether or not such distress results in bodily harm, or

(b) to any other person who is present at the time, if such distress results in bodily harm.

Comment d. Extreme and outrageous conduct. The cases thus far decided have found liability only where the defendant's conduct has been extreme and outrageous. It has not been enough that the defendant has acted with an intent that is tortious or even criminal, or that he has intended to inflict emotional distress, or even that his conduct has been characterized by "malice," or a degree of aggravation that would entitle the plaintiff to punitive damages for another tort. Liability has been found only where the conduct has been so outrageous in character, and so extreme in degree, as to go beyond all possible bounds of decency, and to be regarded as atrocious, and utterly intolerable in a civilized community. Generally, the case is one in which the recitation of the facts to an average member of the community would arouse his resentment against the actor, and lead him to exclaim, "Outrageous!"

Illustration 4. A makes a telephone call but is unable to get his number. In the course of an altercation with the telephone operator, A calls her a God damned woman, a God damned liar, and says that if he were there he would break her God damned neck. B suffers severe emotional distress, broods over the incident, is unable to sleep, and is made ill. A's conduct, although insulting, is not so outrageous or extreme as to make A liable to B.

Illustration 9. A, an eccentric and mentally deficient old maid, has the delusion that a pot of gold is buried in her back yard, and is always digging for it. Knowing this, B buries a pot with other contents in her yard, and when A digs it up causes her to be escorted in triumph to the city hall, where the pot is opened under circumstances of public humiliation to A. A suffers severe emotional disturbance and resulting illness. B is subject to liability to A for both.

Illustration 10. A knows that B, a Pennsylvania Dutch farmer, is extremely superstitious, and believes in witchcraft. In order to force B to sell A his farm, A goes through the ritual of putting a "hex" on the farm, causing B to believe that it is bewitched so that crops will not grow on it. B suffers severe emotional distress and resulting illness. A is subject to liability to B for both.

Illustration 12. A is in a hospital suffering from a heart illness and under medical orders that he shall have complete rest and quiet. B enters A's sick room for the purpose of trying to settle an insurance claim. B's insistence and boisterous conduct cause severe emotional distress, and A suffers a heart attack. B is subject to liability to A if he knows of A's condition, but is not liable if he does not have such knowledge.

Daniel J. Givelber, The Right to Minimum Social Decency and the Limits of Evenhandedness: Intentional Infliction of Emotional Distress by Outrageous Conduct
82 Colum. L. Rev. 42 (1982)

The tort of intentional infliction of emotional distress by outrageous conduct differs from traditional intentional torts in an important respect: it provides no clear definition of the prohibited conduct. Battery, assault, and false imprisonment describe specific forms of behavior; while we can quibble about whether a kick in the playground should be attended with the same legal consequences as a kick in the classroom, everyone can agree that you cannot have a battery without physical contact (or an assault without at least the appearance of attempted physical contact, or a false imprisonment without restraint of the freedom of movement). The relative ease with which injury may be established is counterbalanced by the specificity of the prohibited behavior.

The term "outrageous" is neither value-free nor exacting. It does not objectively describe an act or series of acts; rather, it represents an evaluation of behavior. The concept thus fails to provide clear guidance either to those whose conduct it purports to regulate, or to those who must evaluate that conduct. The Restatement tells us that what is prohibited is conduct that is so outrageous in character, and so extreme in degree, as to go beyond all possible bounds of decency, and to be regarded as atrocious, and utterly intolerable in a civilized community.

This is a strange description of a rule of law. Those situations in which "average members of the community" are up in arms over the outrageous conduct of individuals are situations in which the evenhanded application of law is threatened. A central goal of due process is to ensure that individuals are not judged by the "passion and prejudice of the moment," but are rather evaluated by rules of universal applicability, fairly and evenhandedly applied. To suggest, as the Restatement does, that civil liability should turn on the resentments of the average member of the community appears to turn the passions of the moment into law. [. . .]

Given the open-ended nature of outrageousness, what led the proponents of the tort to recommend this test and courts to adopt it? To attempt to answer these questions we must first understand why the tort requires any limitation beyond the requirement that the defendant intended to cause the plaintiff emotional distress and succeeded.

There are a number of justifications for such a limitation. First, incivility is so pervasive in our society that it is inappropriate for the law to attempt to provide a remedy for it in every instance. The effort would tax available judicial resources as well as open the door to false claims. It would provide a judicial forum to the adjudication of private feuds. Public adjudication of common irritations and arguments would dignify most disputes far beyond their social importance (and, perhaps, retard their resolution through normal social processes). Second, there is the view that only outrageous conduct is so severe as to provide reliable confirmation that the plaintiff's suffering is genuine and reasonable. Third, there is concern for personal liberty both for its own sake and for its purported capability to enhance mental health and reduce aggression. This liberty interest includes much more than the freedom to get mad or be impolite. It also includes the freedom to exercise privacy rights even in the face of certain knowledge that it will severely distress another; extramarital affairs, divorce, and abortion are prime examples. Finally, there is the perceived social utility of mild (or not so mild) oppression. There are simply a large number of situations in which intentionally making others uncomfortable, unhappy, and upset is viewed as justified either in pursuit of one's legal rights (e.g., debt collection) or in service of a greater social good (e.g., cross-examination at trial) or for the person's "own good" (e.g., basic training). [. . .]

[T]he tort grew out of cases representing very different types of social problems. These problems — inappropriate debt collection practices and offensive practical jokes — vary in a number of respects that are relevant to whether and how the law should solve them, such as the relationship between the parties, the existence of claims of legal right, the motivations of the parties, the techniques employed, and the degree of other legal regulation of the type of activity at issue. To draw an analogy from criminal law, the events were as disparate as random street violence on the one hand and white-collar crime on the other. The traits they shared were that the defendants appeared to want the plaintiffs to suffer, and succeeded. Had the drafters of the Restatement thought in terms of the social control function of tort law, they probably would not have tried to cover these situations with a single tort. However, since the Restatement classified torts in terms of the interest of the plaintiff that was entitled to protection rather than in terms of the common features of defendant's conduct that should be discouraged, the common ground of intentionally caused severe emotional distress was thought sufficient to support the generalization that these disparate factual patterns should be covered by a single tort. [. . .]

The practical impact of the tort varies with the relationship between plaintiff and defendant. When the parties have a pre-existing economic relationship based or apparently based on contract, courts are frequently willing to uphold determinations of outrageousness. These cases reflect a common theme — they require a basic level of fair procedure and decency in dealings between people who occupy unequal bargaining positions and are bound (or apparently bound) by voluntary agreements. When the parties are not bound by contract, the cases are fewer, the results more unpredictable, and doctrine virtually nonexistent.

---

1. *Blowing off steam.* In Roberts v. Saylor, 637 P.2d 1175 (Kan. 1981), the plaintiff underwent surgery three times. The first surgeon left some sutures in the plaintiff. A second surgeon, Saylor, later performed a second operation to remove the sutures. The plaintiff then brought a malpractice suit against the first surgeon and attempted to enlist the help of Dr. Saylor. Saylor would not cooperate, however, saying (as the plaintiff later recalled it) that he "despised people" like the plaintiff "for causing doctors trouble, and we was a bunch of thieves without a gun is what he said." The plaintiff thus sued Saylor as well. That suit was settled. Three years later the plaintiff underwent a third, unrelated surgery at the same hospital, which was to be performed by a

different doctor. Shortly before the surgery began the plaintiff was lying on a gurney just outside the operating room, having received preoperative medication. The plaintiff's evidence was that Saylor saw her on the gurney as he left a nearby lounge where he was seeking advice regarding a medical problem from which he himself was suffering. Saylor entered the preoperation room and approached the plaintiff on the gurney; then, as the plaintiff recounted it, "I looked up at him and he says, 'I don't like you, I don't like you,' and he says, 'I wanted to tell you that before you went in there.' He was real hostile in the face when I looked back up at him from the cart."

The plaintiff sued Saylor for intentional infliction of emotional distress. As to the extent of her distress, her deposition ran as follows:

> Q. Well, what other damages, or what is it that you're claiming by way of damages in this case; how have you been injured or damaged by what occurred that day?
> A. Because I'm upset about it; I'm still upset. I was upset then and I'm still upset.
> Q. Well, is that all?
> A. When I seen him down there I was afraid that maybe he would come in there and try to do something to me, I didn't know. [...]
> Q. I'm trying to find out — I'm not talking about any, I'm trying to find out —
> A. Didn't do no bodily harm to me.

On cross-examination by her own attorney, plaintiff testified that as a result of defendant's conduct she was scared and didn't want to go into surgery. The trial court held Saylor entitled to summary judgment, and the Kansas Supreme Court agreed:

> It should be understood that liability does not arise from mere insults, indignities, threats, annoyances, petty expressions, or other trivialities. Members of the public are necessarily expected and required to be hardened to a certain amount of criticism, rough language and to occasional acts and words that are definitely inconsiderate and unkind. The law should not intervene where someone's feelings merely are hurt. Freedom remains to express an unflattering opinion and to blow off relatively harmless steam which comes from an uncontrollable temper. Conduct to be a sufficient basis for an action to recover for emotional distress must be outrageous to the point that it goes beyond the bounds of decency and is utterly intolerable in a civilized society. [...]

2. *Studies in bedside manner.* In Greer v. Medders, 336 S.E.2d 328 (Ga. App. 1985), the plaintiff, Greer, underwent surgery and was recovering at the hospital when his attending physician went on vacation and left Greer in the

care of a colleague, Medders. When Medders did not visit Greer for several days, Greer called Medders' office to complain. Medders soon arrived at Greer's room; the plaintiff's evidence was that Medders made the following statements in front of Greer, his wife, and a nurse who was present: "Let me tell you one damn thing, don't nobody call over to my office raising hell with my secretary . . . I don't have to be in here every damn day checking on you because I check with physical therapy . . . I don't have to be your damn doctor." Mrs. Greer interjected that Medders need not worry, as he would no longer be her husband's doctor; whereupon Medders stated: "If your smart ass wife would keep her mouth shut things wouldn't be so bad." Medders left the room, whereupon Mrs. Greer began to cry and Mr. Greer experienced episodes of uncontrollable shaking for which he required psychiatric treatment. The Greers sued Medders for intentional infliction of emotional distress. The trial court gave summary judgment to Medders. The court of appeals reversed:

> Given the fact that the alleged statements at issue in this case were made by a physician to a post-operative patient and his wife as the patient lay in a hospital bed, we cannot say as a matter of law that the statements were insufficiently abusive to support a recovery for the tort of intentional infliction of emotional distress. Accordingly, we hold that the trial court erred in awarding summary judgment in favor of Dr. Medders.

Is there a satisfactory distinction between *Greer v. Medders* and *Roberts v. Saylor*?

3. *Gorilla motif.* In Muratore v. M/S Scotia Prince, 845 F.2d 347 (1st Cir. 1988), the plaintiff, Muratore, was a passenger on a cruise ship that traveled between Maine and Nova Scotia. As she first boarded the ship two of the cruise line's employees were attempting to take pictures of the arriving passengers. Muratore said that she did not want her picture taken. When the photographers would not relent, Muratore turned and walked onto the ship backwards. The photographers nevertheless took her picture and displayed the resulting photograph of her backside near the ship's concession stand along with the other pictures they had taken; over the back of the plaintiff's head they superimposed a picture of a gorilla's face. Later during the cruise one of the photographers, this time dressed in a gorilla suit, approached Muratore again. Once more she turned her back. This time the other photographer shouted, "take the back of her — she likes things from the back." Muratore understood this remark to have lewd connotations and was embarrassed by it. The photographers tried to photograph her on other occasions as well; she spent several hours in her cabin during the cruise to avoid harassment by them. Upon her return she sued the cruise line for intentional infliction of emotional distress. The trial court found in Muratore's favor and awarded her $5,000 in compensatory damages:

The first element [of the IIED tort] focuses on the defendant-actor's state of mind: the defendant must have acted "intentionally or recklessly," or have been "certain or substantially certain" that his or her conduct would cause the plaintiff severe emotional distress. In the present case, the Court finds clear evidence that this element is satisfied. Plaintiff indicated continuously, beginning with her very first encounter with the photographers, that she did not wish to have her picture taken. [. . .] The photographers' continued harassment and taunting remarks lead the Court to conclude that the photographers' conduct was in fact intentional.

The second element goes to the nature of the conduct: the degree to which the conduct was "outrageous." [Case law] and section 46 of the Restatement (Second) of Torts suggest a rather rigorous test for "outrageousness." Comment *f* to that section, however, also makes clear that "[t]he extreme and outrageous character of the conduct may arise from the actor's knowledge that the other is particularly susceptible to emotional distress. . . ." Again, the Court concludes that Plaintiff's initial reaction to having her picture taken indicated a particular sensitivity.

The Court can perceive no valid rationale for a carrier or its agent to insist on taking photographs of a passenger over the passenger's objection, especially when the photographs are taken in the pecuniary interests of the carrier or its agent. Furthermore, the offensive conduct did not end with the initial encounter: the photographers continued to approach Plaintiff, take her picture, and make lewd comments. The Court finds the photographers' conduct, taken as a whole, to be so reprehensible as to meet the requirement of "outrageous" or "atrocious" conduct.

The third element requires a causal connection between the Defendant's actions and the Plaintiff's emotional distress. Here the Court finds that Prince of Fundy [the defendant] has little room to quibble. [. . .]

The fourth and final element focuses on the degree of Plaintiff's emotional distress. [Prior case law has] established that the emotional distress must be "severe" so that "no reasonable [person] could be expected to endure it." The Maine Supreme Judicial Court expressly added, however, that " 'shock, illness, or other bodily harm' . . . is not an absolute prerequisite for recovery of damages for intentional, as opposed to negligent, infliction of emotional distress," and that "[i]n appropriate cases, 'severe' emotional distress may be inferred from the 'extreme and outrageous' nature of the defendant's conduct alone." [. . .]

The court of appeals affirmed.

4. *The thick-skinned plaintiff.* In Pemberton v. Bethlehem Steel Corp., 502 A.2d 1101 (Md. App. 1986), the plaintiff, Pemberton, was an official for the union that represented the Bethlehem Steel Corporation's employees. He sued the corporation for intentional infliction of emotional distress and other

torts. Pemberton claimed that Bethlehem, unhappy with his conduct on behalf of the union, hired a private investigator to place him under surveillance; that the investigator obtained evidence that Pemberton was conducting an extramarital affair; and that Bethlehem anonymously sent this evidence to Pemberton's wife, ultimately precipitating their divorce. Bethlehem also obtained "mug shots" from an arrest of Pemberton that had occurred about 15 years earlier and circulated the pictures to the members of his union. The trial court gave summary judgment to the defendant. The court of appeals affirmed:

> For conduct to meet the test of "outrageousness," it must be "so extreme in degree, as to go beyond all possible bounds of decency, and to be regarded as atrocious, and utterly intolerable in a civilized community." Restatement of Torts 2d, §46. Whether the conduct complained of meets that test is, in the first instance, for the court to determine, and, in addressing that question, the court must consider not only the conduct itself but also the "personality of the individual to whom the misconduct is directed." *Harris v. Jones*, 281 Md. 560 (1977). We do not regard the sending of truthful information pertaining to the criminal conviction of an admittedly rough-and-tumble labor official to his fellow union members, the placing of such a person under the kind of surveillance indicated in this record, or the sending of truthful information about his extramarital affair to his wife to meet the test laid down in *Harris*.
>
> Nor has appellant pled or shown the degree of distress required. To satisfy the fourth requirement, a plaintiff must establish a truly devastating effect from the defendant's conduct. The emotional response must be so acute "that no reasonable person could be expected to endure it"; he must be "unable to function," "unable to attend to necessary matters." *Hamilton v. Ford Motor Credit Co., supra,* 66 Md. App. at 59-60. There is no such indication here.

Can *Pemberton v. Bethlehem Steel Corp.* be squared with *Muratore v. M/S Scotia Prince?*

5. *Villainous advices.* In Figueiredo-Torres v. Nickel, 584 A.2d 69 (Md. App. 1991), the plaintiff and his wife sought the assistance of the defendant, Herbert Nickel, a psychologist and marriage counselor. They saw Nickel together and separately. Soon Nickel and the plaintiff's wife were engaged in an affair, and Nickel was counseling the plaintiff that he and his wife ought to seek a separation. The plaintiff sued Nickel for professional negligence and for intentional infliction of emotional distress. The trial court dismissed the complaint; the court of appeals reversed:

> Nickel contends that, because Torres' wife was a consenting adult and sexual relations between consenting adults in modern society is not

extreme and outrageous conduct, the intentional infliction of emotional distress count was properly dismissed. Nickel's analysis neglects one important detail. Nickel was not "the milkman, the mailman, or the guy next door"; he was Torres' psychologist and marriage counselor.

As we recognized in [*Harris v. Jones*, 380 A.2d 611 (1977)], "the extreme and outrageous character of the defendant's conduct may arise from his abuse of a position, or relation with another person, which gives him actual or apparent authority over him, or power to affect his interests." Furthermore, "[i]n cases where the defendant is in a peculiar position to harass the plaintiff, and cause emotional distress, his conduct will be carefully scrutinized by the courts." A psychologist-patient relationship, by its nature, focuses on the psyche of the patient; and a psychologist is in a unique position to influence the patient's emotional well-being. For this reason, a psychologist-patient relationship falls squarely into the category of relationships which are carefully scrutinized by the courts. [. . .]

In addition to the allegations of sexual misconduct, Torres further alleges that, despite his knowledge that Torres "was particularly susceptible to emotional upset, anxiety and distress" and "emotionally and mentally unstable," Nickel "demoralized [Torres] by making statements, and engaging in conduct that was destructive to [Torres'] ego development and self-respect," and "caused further and greater feelings of helplessness, discouragement, shame, guilt, fear and confusion by telling him he was a 'codfish' and that his wife deserved a 'fillet'; by telling him he had bad breath and should not go near his wife, and by falsely and systematically telling [Torres] that the deterioration of [Torres'] relationship with his wife was exclusively the result of [Torres'] conduct." [. . .] Coming from a stranger, or even a friend, this conduct may not be outrageous; but we are not prepared to state as a matter of law that such behavior by a psychologist which takes advantage of the patient's known emotional problems is not extreme and outrageous conduct sufficient to support an intentional infliction of emotional distress claim.

What is the analogy between *Figueiredo-Torres v. Nickel* and *Greer v. Medders* (the L case of the doctor who scolded the patient and his wife)?

6. *Criminal conversation.* A difficulty that often arises in connection with cases like *Figueiredo-Torres v. Nickel* is that the common law regarded adulterous affairs as tortious on independent grounds: the paramour could be sued for "criminal conversation," a tort which consisted of having sexual intercourse with the spouse of another. Criminal conversation was part of a family of so-called amatory torts that also included seduction, alienation of affections, and breach of promise to marry. A majority of states have abolished all of these actions by judicial decision or by passing legislation known as "heart balm" statutes. Courts in those states often will dismiss claims for

intentional infliction of emotional distress based on adultery or other conduct that might have been the subject of an amatory tort suit at common law, reasoning that plaintiffs should not be able to avoid the legislature's intent by putting new labels on their claims. But sometimes, as in *Figueiredo-Torres v. Nickel*, IIED claims still survive on such facts. The court in the latter case relied on the following language from a similar Oregon decision:

> [C]riminal conversation consists of sexual intercourse with the spouse of another person, and the elements of alienation of affection are wrongful conduct of the defendant which is intended to cause and which actually does cause the plaintiff *the loss of the affection and consortium of the plaintiff's spouse.* The gravamen of the tort of intentional infliction of severe emotional distress, on the other hand, is that the plaintiff has suffered *a loss due to intentionally inflicted severe emotional distress.* It is the nature of *the loss* allegedly suffered by plaintiff in this case that distinguishes his claim of intentional infliction of severe emotional distress from the torts of alienation of affections and criminal conversation. He claims to have suffered severe emotional distress as a result of Johnson's alleged intentional conduct; his claimed loss is *not* the loss of his wife's society and companionship. That Johnson allegedly used his sexual relationship with plaintiff's wife as *the means* to intentionally inflict severe emotional distress on plaintiff does not transform plaintiff's claim into one for either alienation of affections or criminal conversation.

Spiess v. Johnson, 748 P.2d 1020, *aff'd*, 765 P.2d 811 (1988) (italics in original). The distinctions drawn here can be difficult to manage; perhaps unsurprisingly, courts disagree about whether liability survives these statutes in various factual situations — as when, for example, a husband discovers that he is not the father of his children. Compare G.A.W., III v. D.M.W., 596 N.W.2d 284 (Minn. App. 1999) (finding that such claims survive passage of the state's heart balm statute); and *Doe v. Doe*, 747 A.2d 617 (Md. App. 2000) (finding that they do not).

7. *Public figures.* In Hustler Magazine v. Falwell, 485 U.S. 46 (1988), *Hustler* magazine published a parody of an advertisement for Campari Liqueur. The actual Campari advertisements featured interviews with celebrities about their "first times"; this referred to the first time the celebrities had sampled Campari, but the ads also attempted to create amusement through the sexual connotations of the term. The *Hustler* parody copied the format and layout of the Campari ads; it featured the plaintiff, Jerry Falwell, stating that his "first time" was during a drunken incestuous rendezvous with his mother in an outhouse. The item contained a small disclaimer at the bottom reading, "ad parody — not to be taken seriously." Falwell sued *Hustler* for intentional infliction of emotional distress, libel, and other torts. A jury brought in a verdict for *Hustler* on the libel claim, finding

that the parody could not "reasonably be understood as describing actual facts about [Falwell] or actual events in which [he] participated," but it ruled in Falwell's favor on the emotional distress claim, awarding him $100,000 in compensatory damages and $50,000 in punitive damages. The trial court entered judgment on the verdict. The United States Supreme Court held the result unconstitutional:

> Despite their sometimes caustic nature, from the early cartoon portraying George Washington as an ass down to the present day, graphic depictions and satirical cartoons have played a prominent role in public and political debate. Nast's castigation of the Tweed Ring, Walt McDougall's characterization of Presidential candidate James G. Blaine's banquet with the millionaires at Delmonico's as "The Royal Feast of Belshazzar," and numerous other efforts have undoubtedly had an effect on the course and outcome of contemporaneous debate. Lincoln's tall, gangling posture, Teddy Roosevelt's glasses and teeth, and Franklin D. Roosevelt's jutting jaw and cigarette holder have been memorialized by political cartoons with an effect that could not have been obtained by the photographer or the portrait artist. From the viewpoint of history it is clear that our political discourse would have been considerably poorer without them.
>
> Respondent contends, however, that the caricature in question here was so "outrageous" as to distinguish it from more traditional political cartoons. There is no doubt that the caricature of respondent and his mother published in Hustler is at best a distant cousin of the political cartoons described above, and a rather poor relation at that. If it were possible by laying down a principled standard to separate the one from the other, public discourse would probably suffer little or no harm. But we doubt that there is any such standard, and we are quite sure that the pejorative description "outrageous" does not supply one. "Outrageousness" in the area of political and social discourse has an inherent subjectiveness about it which would allow a jury to impose liability on the basis of the jurors' tastes or views, or perhaps on the basis of their dislike of a particular expression. An "outrageousness" standard thus runs afoul of our longstanding refusal to allow damages to be awarded because the speech in question may have an adverse emotional impact on the audience. [. . .]
>
> We conclude that public figures and public officials may not recover for the tort of intentional infliction of emotional distress by reason of publications such as the one here at issue without showing in addition that the publication contains a false statement of fact which was made with "actual malice," *i.e.*, with knowledge that the statement was false or with reckless disregard as to whether or not it was true.

The "actual malice" standard the Court set out in the last paragraph is the same one that the Court had fashioned in prior cases, notably *New York Times v. Sullivan*, 376 U.S. 254 (1964), for claims by public figures that they have been libeled by a defendant's false statements. That doctrine is considered in the chapter of this book covering the law of defamation.

8. *Private figures*. In Van Duyn v. Smith, 527 N.E.2d 1005 (Ill. App. 1988), the plaintiff, Margaret Van Duyn, was the executive director of an abortion clinic in Peoria. The defendant was an anti-abortion activist. The plaintiff alleged, among other things, that the defendant followed her in his car on several occasions, that he confronted her at the airport and interfered with her comings and goings there, that he picketed her residence and workplace, and that he published disparaging posters featuring the plaintiff's picture. The first was a "Wanted" poster that resembled those used by the FBI to identify fugitives; it said that the plaintiff was wanted "for prenatal killing in violation of the Hippocratic Oath and Geneva Code," that she used the alias "Margaret the Malignant," and that she participated in killing for profit. At the bottom of the poster were these words: "Nothing in this poster should be interpreted as a suggestion of any activity that is presently considered unethical. Once abortion was a crime but it is not now considered a crime." The second poster bore the message "Face the American Holocaust" and featured pictures of aborted fetuses along with anti-abortion messages. The defendant distributed the posters to those living within three blocks of the plaintiff's residence. The plaintiff sued for intentional infliction of emotional distress and defamation. The trial court dismissed the complaint; the court of appeals reversed in part, reinstating the IIED claim:

> [T]he court in *Hustler Magazine* was clear in its holding that only public officials and public figures may not recover for intentional infliction of emotional distress based upon publications such as ad parodies without satisfying the *New York Times* standard of actual malice. In our view, the present case does not concern a public official, nor does it concern public figures as that status has been defined by the Supreme Court, as those who are "intimately involved in the resolution of important public questions or, by reason of their fame, shape events in areas of concern to society at large." *Associated Press v. Walker*, 388 U.S. 130 (1964). Moreover, instances of involuntary public figures are exceedingly rare.
>
> "For the most part those who attain . . . (public figure) . . . status have assumed roles of especial prominence in the affairs of society. Some occupy positions of such persuasive power and influence that they are deemed public figures for all purposes. More commonly those classed as public figures have thrust themselves to the forefront of particular public controversies in order to influence the resolution

of the issues. In either event, they invite attention and comment." *Gertz v. Robert Welch*, 418 U.S. 323, 345 (1973).

We do not consider plaintiff a public figure in this case merely because of her status as the executive director of an abortion clinic. Although she must apparently be a pro-choice advocate, we do not consider her as being in a position to influence society. [. . .] Although we do not discount defendant's right to free speech under the First Amendment, we do not read *Hustler Magazine* as requiring proof of an additional element to the tort of intentional infliction of emotional distress where the plaintiff is a private individual. Therefore, we consider it proper to take into account the posters and surrounding circumstances when determining if defendant's conduct was sufficiently outrageous to cause plaintiff to suffer severe emotional distress.

If the only alleged actions were the contents and distribution of the two posters, we would be inclined to affirm the trial court's dismissal. However, the distribution of the posters is just the last in a series of events that has spanned a two year period. We find it particularly bothersome that defendant, a seemingly well-educated person, would stoop to following, in his car, plaintiff while she was driving her car and to confronting plaintiff at the airport and preventing her ingress and egress. We believe this type of behavior, compounded with the other acts alleged, is worthy of a jury's consideration whether defendant is liable for the intentional infliction of emotional distress. [. . .]

What is the distinction between *Van Duyn v. Smith* and *Hustler Magazine v. Falwell?* Aggressive tactics of abortion protestors raise a number of interesting and difficult problems of tort law; another example is included in the chapter on invasion of privacy.

9. *Limited purpose public figures.* In Walko v. Kean College, 561 A.2d 680 (N.J. Sup. 1988), the plaintiff, Ann Walko, was an instructor at the school of education at Kean College and assistant to the dean there. The student newspaper, *The Independent*, published a parody issue titled *The Incredible*. Its contents included a mock advertisement for a telephone sex service called "Whoreline"; the ad listed the plaintiff's name along with the names of three other well-known figures on campus. The satirical advertisement evidently had something to do with a controversy on campus regarding a real telephone hotline offered by the administration. The plaintiff sued the college for intentional infliction of emotional distress. The trial court dismissed her claim:

The "Whoreline" ad that plaintiff complained of appeared surrounded by a page of obviously "fake" ads, in the middle of what was unquestionably a parody of the usual student newspaper. No reasonable person, even glancing at the offending ad, could possibly conclude that it was a factual statement of plaintiff's availability for "good telephone sex." [. . .] Given all of the surrounding circumstances, the Court is compelled to conclude that virtually everyone who read Ann Walko's name in the "Whoreline" ad would know that it was a joke . . . not a very good joke, perhaps; downright vulgar and tasteless, most readers probably would conclude; but definitely not an assertion of fact that anyone would take seriously.

The court further concluded that the plaintiff was a public figure:

Ann Walko is properly considered a "public figure" within the college community. [. . .] The concept of a limited-purpose public figure has developed in both federal and state law. The "limited" purpose has generally related to a particular issue, thus defining the person as a public figure only when the publication in controversy concerns that issue. E.g., *Gomez v. Murdoch*, 475 A.2d 622 (N.J. App. Div. 1984) (jockey is a public figure when publication relates to his professional performance). A key element, where public figure status has been so conferred on a plaintiff, is the plaintiff's own access to the media. The same concept logically applies to a particular community — whether it be a geographical, institutional, or interest-group community. [. . .]

Two key themes — the plaintiff's status in the community and the nature of the issue or controversy — and the interaction between them "reflect changing relationships between the policies of encouraging free speech and fairness to the individual." *Sisler v. Gannett Co., Inc.*, 516 A.2d 1083. That the Kean College "Hotline" which is parodied in the offending ad was the subject of a then current controversy, along with plaintiff Ann Walko's status as an instructor and administrator at Kean College, support a finding that she is a limited-purpose public figure for purposes of applying the *Hustler* decision to this case.

Is there a satisfactory distinction between *Walko v. Kean College* and *Van Duyn v. Smith*?

10. *Berating the brides (problem)*. In Murray v. Schlosser, 574 A.2d 1339 (Conn. Sup. 1990), the defendants were the hosts of a radio show broadcast in Hartford. On Thursdays the defendants conducted a feature called "Berate the Brides." They would review the photographs accompanying the wedding announcements in the *Hartford Courant* newspaper and invite their listeners to call in and vote for the "dog of the week." On the day in question the defendants named the plaintiff the dog of the week. One of the hosts concluded that the plaintiff was "too ugly even to rate"; the other host said that she wouldn't want to see her worst enemy with the plaintiff. They announced that the plaintiff had been awarded a collar and a case of Ken-L-Ration dog food. The plaintiff sued on several theories, including intentional infliction of emotional distress. What result on that count?

11. *Statutory intersections.* In addition to giving rise to possible claims of outrage, harassing behavior in the workplace also may create liability under federal civil rights statutes. Title VII of the Civil Rights Act of 1964 (42 U.S.C. §2000e et seq.) and 42 U.S.C §1981 both provide for relief to employees harassed on account of their race; Title VII also has been interpreted to permit claims for sexual harassment — whether between members of the opposite sex or the same sex — that creates an "abusive working environment." See *Harris v. Forklift Sys., Inc.,* 510 U.S. 17 (1993); *Oncale v. Sundowner Offshore Services, Inc.,* 523 U.S. 75 (1998). In certain circumstances student plaintiffs also have the right to sue school districts under a federal statute (Title IX of the Education Amendment of 1972) for sexual harassment by teachers or by other students if the school's authorities have notice of the acts and display "deliberate indifference" concerning them. The details of these statutory causes of action are beyond the scope of this book; they are considered in courses on employment law. But it is important to understand that such claims sometimes are brought alongside claims of liability for outrage, and that the substantive standards and procedural rules governing the two forms of liability can differ significantly.

Chapter 2

Intentional Torts: Privileges

Once a plaintiff has made out a *prima facie* case of battery or another intentional tort, the defendant may deny some element of the plaintiff's case — claiming, for example, that he lacked the intent necessary for a battery. But a defendant also can raise affirmative defenses: claims that while the basic elements of a battery or trespass may be made out, other circumstances also are present that excuse the defendant's behavior. In this chapter we focus primarily on two examples: the privilege created by the need to defend one's person and property, and the necessity privilege. At the end of the chapter we will briefly consider two additional privileges: public necessity and the imposition of discipline.

A. DEFENSE OF PERSON AND PROPERTY

Katko v. Briney
183 N.W.2d 657 (Iowa 1971)

[The defendants, Edward and Bertha Briney, owned an 80-acre farm in Iowa with a house on it. They did not live there; they used the house mostly for storage. After suffering a series of trespasses and break-ins at the house, the Brineys boarded up its windows and doors and posted "no trespass" signs nearby. After still another break-in Edward Briney set a trap in one of the bedrooms. He tied a 20-gauge shotgun to an iron bed with the barrel pointed at the bedroom door, then ran a wire from the doorknob to the gun's trigger so that it would fire when the door was opened. Briney first pointed the gun so an intruder would be hit in the stomach, but at his wife's suggestion it was lowered to hit the legs. He later stated that he set the gun because he "was mad and tired of being tormented," but also testified that he "did not intend to injure anyone." He nailed tin over the bedroom window. The spring gun could not be seen from the outside, and no warning of its presence was posted.

[The plaintiff broke into the house with a friend in search of antiques. He entered the bedroom and set off the gun; it removed much of his right leg. The plaintiff remained in the hospital for 40 days. He was prosecuted, pled guilty to petty larceny, was fined $50, and was paroled from a 60-day jail sentence. He then brought suit against the Brineys. At the Brineys' request the plaintiff's action was tried to a jury consisting of residents of the community where the defendants' property was located. The jury returned a verdict for the plaintiff and against the defendants for $20,000 actual and $10,000 punitive damages. The trial court entered judgment on the verdict. The Brineys appealed.]

MOORE, C. J. — [...] The main thrust of defendants' defense in the trial court and on this appeal is that "the law permits use of a spring gun in a dwelling or warehouse for the purpose of preventing the unlawful entry of a burglar or thief." They repeated this contention in their exceptions to the trial court's instructions 2, 5 and 6. They took no exception to the trial court's statement of the issues or to other instructions. [...]

Instruction 6 stated: "An owner of premises is prohibited from willfully or intentionally injuring a trespasser by means of force that either takes life or inflicts great bodily injury; and therefore a person owning a premise is prohibited from setting out 'spring guns' and like dangerous devices which will likely take life or inflict great bodily injury, for the purpose of harming trespassers. The fact that the trespasser may be acting in violation of the law does not change the rule. The only time when such conduct of setting a 'spring gun' or a like dangerous device is justified would be when the trespasser was committing a felony of violence or a felony punishable by death, or where the trespasser was endangering human life by his act." [...]

The overwhelming weight of authority, both textbook and case law, supports the trial court's statement of the applicable principles of law.

Prosser on Torts, Third Edition, pages 116-118, states:

> "... the law has always placed a higher value upon human safety than upon mere rights in property, it is the accepted rule that there is no privilege to use any force calculated to cause death or serious bodily injury to repel the threat to land or chattels, unless there is also such a threat to the defendant's personal safety as to justify a self-defense. [...] [S]pring guns and other mankilling devices are not justifiable against a mere trespasser, or even a petty thief. They are privileged only against those upon whom the landowner, if he were present in person would be free to inflict injury of the same kind."

Restatement of Torts, section 85, page 180, states: "The value of human life and limb, not only to the individual concerned but also to society, so outweighs the interest of a possessor of land in excluding from it those whom he is not willing to admit thereto that a possessor of land has, as is stated in §79, no privilege to use force intended or likely to cause death or serious harm against another whom the possessor sees about to enter his premises or meddle with his chattel, unless the intrusion threatens death or serious bodily harm to the occupiers or users of the premises. [. . .] A possessor of land cannot do indirectly and by a mechanical device that which, were he present, he could not do immediately and in person. Therefore, he cannot gain a privilege to install, for the purpose of protecting his land from intrusions harmless to the lives and limbs of the occupiers or users of it, a mechanical device whose only purpose is to inflict death or serious harm upon such as may intrude, by giving notice of his intention to inflict, by mechanical means and indirectly, harm which he could not, even after request, inflict directly were he present."

In Volume 2, Harper and James, The Law of Torts, section 27.3, pages 1440, 1441, this is found: "The possessor of land may not arrange his premises intentionally so as to cause death or serious bodily harm to a trespasser. The possessor may of course take some steps to repel a trespass. If he is present he may use force to do so, but only that amount which is reasonably necessary to effect the repulse. Moreover if the trespass threatens harm to property only — even a theft of property — the possessor would not be privileged to use deadly force, he may not arrange his premises so that such force will be inflicted by mechanical means. If he does, he will be liable even to a thief who is injured by such device." [. . .]

The legal principles stated by the trial court in [its] instructions [. . .] are well established and supported by the authorities cited and quoted *supra*. There is no merit in defendants' objections and exceptions thereto. Defendants' various motions based on the same reasons stated in exceptions to instructions were properly overruled.

Plaintiff's claim and the jury's allowance of punitive damages, under the trial court's instructions relating thereto, were not at any time or in any manner challenged by defendants in the trial court as not allowable. We therefore are not presented with the problem of whether the $10,000 award should be allowed to stand. [. . .]

Affirmed.

LARSON, J., dissenting: — [. . .] [T]he better rule is that an owner of buildings housing valuable property may employ the use of spring guns or other devices intended to repel but not seriously injure an intruder who enters his secured premises with or without a criminal intent, but I do not advocate its general use, for there may also be liability for negligent installation of such a device. What I mean to say is that under such circumstances as we have here the issue as to whether the set was with an intent to seriously injure or kill an intruder is a question of fact that should be left to the jury under proper instructions, that the mere setting of such a device with a resultant serious injury should not as a matter of law establish liability.

In the case of a mere trespass able authorities have reasoned that absolute liability may rightfully be fixed on the landowner for injuries to the trespasser because very little damage could be inflicted upon the property owner and the danger is great that a child or other innocent trespasser might be seriously injured by the device. In such matters they say no privilege to set up the device should be recognized by the courts regardless of the owner's intent. I agree.

On the other hand, where the intruder may pose a danger to the inhabitants of a dwelling, the privilege of using such a device to repel has been recognized by most authorities, and the mere setting thereof in the dwelling has not been held to create liability for an injury as a matter of law. In such cases intent and the reasonableness of the force would seem relevant to liability.

Although I am aware of the often-repeated statement that personal rights are more important than property rights, where the owner has stored his valuables representing his life's accumulations, his livelihood business, his tools and implements, and his treasured antiques as appears in the case at bar, and where the evidence is sufficient to sustain a finding that the installation was intended only as a warning to ward off thieves and criminals, I can see no compelling reason why the use of such a device alone would create liability as a matter of law. [. . .]

NOTES

1. *American Gothic.* The result in *Katko* was controversial and stirred some onlookers to mail unsolicited contributions to the Brineys to help pay the damage award Katko had obtained against them. The Brineys nevertheless were unable to satisfy the entire judgment, so Katko moved to have their house auctioned off by the sheriff. It was purchased by sympathetic neighbors who then leased it back to the Brineys. Relations between the parties later turned sour, however; the value of the property went up, and the neighbors sought to oust the Brineys from the property. For more background on *Katko v. Briney*, see Geoffrey W. R. Palmer, *The Iowa Spring Gun Case: A Study in American Gothic*, 56 Iowa L. Rev. 1219 (1971).

2. *Calibrated measures.* The common law generally confers on property owners a privilege to use only the minimum force necessary to repel trespassers and thieves; thus a landowner can ward off trespassers only with words and then by gently ushering them off the property, a battery privileged by the plea of *molliter manus imposuit* ("he gently laid hands upon"). If a peaceful but determined trespasser refuses to leave an owner's property despite the owner's protests and gentle physical encouragement, what is the owner to do? Is notice relevant? Would the outcome in *Katko v. Briney* have been different if the defendant had marked the house with clear warnings?

3. *Mistaken identity.* In Crabtree v. Dawson, 83 S.W. 557 (Ky. App. 1904), the defendant, Dawson, owned a three-story building that included various spaces used for entertaining. On the night in question a dance was conducted on the third floor and a party was thrown one floor below. A man named Noble became intoxicated and tried to enter the dance hall without paying. Dawson forcefully escorted Noble to the ground floor. After Dawson returned to the third floor he heard someone call out that "he is getting some bricks"; he then heard footsteps running rapidly up the stairs. The footsteps were those of the plaintiff, one Crabtree, a guest at the party on the second floor; Dawson mistakenly believed that it was the sound of Noble returning to attack him. Dawson picked up a musket and called, "don't come up here." The footsteps continued, and when Crabtree emerged through the doorway at the top of the stairwell Dawson hit him in the face with the butt of the musket, knocking him back down the stairs and inflicting various injuries. Crabtree sued Dawson for battery. The trial court entered judgment on a jury verdict for Dawson. The court of appeals reversed, finding that the jury had not been properly instructed — but also holding that Dawson might yet be found free from liability. Said the court:

> [I]f the defendant, at the time he struck the plaintiff, believed, and had reasonable grounds to believe, that he was Ollie Noble, and that he further believed that it was necessary, in the exercise of a reasonable judgment, to strike Noble, in order to defend himself from a threatened attack about to be made upon him by Noble, and that he used no more force than was necessary, or appeared to him to be necessary, for this purpose, then he is excused on the ground of self-defense and apparent necessity. But it was the duty of the defendant to have exercised the highest degree of care practicable under the circumstances to have ascertained whether the person whom he was about to strike was in fact the one whom he believed him to be, and from whom he apprehended danger to himself.

Although the court of appeals found in favor of Crabtree, *Crabtree v. Dawson* can be styled as a case of no liability (how?); on that reading, what is the distinction between *Crabtree v. Dawson* (NL for hitting an innocent party in the face with a musket) and *Katko v. Briney* (L for shooting a thief in the leg with a spring gun)?

4. *Escaping thieves.* In Wright v. Haffke, 196 N.W.2d 176 (Neb. 1972), the plaintiff and a confederate entered a grocery store owned and operated by the defendant, Haffke. When they reached the checkout counter, one of them knocked Haffke off balance; Haffke saw them reach into the cash register and then turn for the door. He drew a gun and shot the plaintiff in the back. The plaintiff sued Haffke, who defended on the ground that he was

privileged to use a gun to protect his property. The jury brought in a verdict for the defendant, and the Nebraska Supreme Court affirmed:

> It is plaintiff's contention that the use of a firearm in view of the circumstances herein constituted the use of unreasonable force as a matter of law. With this we do not agree. We do not believe that a person must docilely submit to robbery and the spiriting away of his property by a felon. To hold otherwise would seriously hamper the right of law-abiding individuals to peacefully enjoy their property; would encourage felons in the pursuit of their nefarious activities; and would make a farce of our criminal law. Ordinarily, a firearm may be used if reasonably necessary to prevent the commission of a felony or to arrest a felon after a felony has been committed. We do not disagree with plaintiff that the law generally places a higher value upon human life than mere rights of property. When a firearm is used, the question always is whether the force used exceeded permissible limits and is a question for the jury under proper instructions. [. . .]
>
> There is a conflict among the various jurisdictions as to whether one may resort to a firearm to prevent a theft of property. See Annotation, 100 A.L.R.2d 1012. The conflict, however, is in most instances one of degree. For minor thefts the use of a firearm would not be justified, but for more serious felonies, such as robbery, the use may be justified. In this case, the shooting occurred after the participants had committed an assault and while they were attempting to commit a robbery. Defendant owed plaintiff no duty of affirmative care, and had the right to resist the attempted robbery and to use whatever means lay within his power, necessary to that end, even to the extent of using a firearm to retain his property. It was for the jury to determine, however, whether the plaintiff was actually engaged in an attempt to commit a robbery or, if not, whether defendant had reasonable grounds to so believe.

What is the distinction between *Wright v. Haffke* and *Katko v. Briney* (the L case of the spring gun)?

5. *Watchdogs.* In Woodbridge v. Marks, 45 N.Y.S. 156 (N.Y. App. 1897), the defendant had two watchdogs that he knew to be vicious. They were chained to rods on his property that gave them about 50 feet of range apiece. The chains allowed the dogs to protect the defendant's ice house and chicken house but did not allow either dog to reach the residence or the walkways leading to it. The residence was used only in the summer and was unoccupied at the time of the incident giving rise to the case. The plaintiff's evidence was that he had entered the property in the evening in search of a man he believed was at work in the barn. The plaintiff left the defendant's walkways because he was unable to follow them in the darkness. One of the defendant's dogs met the plaintiff, threw him down, and severely injured him. He sued the

defendant to recover for his injuries. The jury brought in a verdict for the plaintiff and the court entered judgment upon it. The appellate court reversed, holding that judgment must be entered for the defendant. Said the court:

> [I]f, as a matter of law, a man whose ferocious dog bites another is liable for the injury, no matter how the dog was confined at the time, or under what circumstances the injury was done, provided only the owner knew him to be ferocious, it follows that it is practically impossible to lawfully keep a dog for the purpose of defending one's premises. If the dog must be so confined that under no circumstances can he attack or injure a trespasser, then he may as well be dead; and the rule results in this: that no dog capable of defending property can be lawfully kept by any person. In my judgment, it has not yet been decided in this state that a man may not lawfully keep and cautiously use a ferocious dog for the defense of his premises in the nighttime, or that a trespasser who comes in the way of a dog so used can recover for injuries sustained, even though his trespass is inspired by no wrongful purpose.
>
> [T]he mere keeping of a ferocious dog, knowing him to be such, for the purpose of defending one's premises, is not in itself unlawful; and, when injury follows from one so kept, the manner of his confinement and the circumstances attending the injury are all to be considered in determining the owner's liability.

The plaintiff in *Woodbridge* said his case was analogous to cases involving spring guns; the court responded elsewhere in its opinion that "the analogy is not complete." Why? What is the distinction between *Woodbridge v. Marks* and *Katko v. Briney*?

6. *Egg-sucking dog.* In Hull v. Scruggs, 2 So. 2d 543 (Miss. 1941), the plaintiff and defendant lived about a mile apart. For three weeks before the incident, the plaintiff's dog had come on to the defendant's property and sucked all the eggs which were laid by the defendant's turkeys and guinea hens. The defendant finally shot the dog and killed it. The plaintiff sued the defendant to recover for the value of the animal. The jury brought in a verdict for the plaintiff, and the defendant appealed. The Mississippi Supreme Court reversed:

> It is a fact of common knowledge that when a dog has once acquired the habit of egg-sucking there is no available way by which he may be broken of it, and that there is no calculable limit to his appetite in the indulgence of the habitual propensity. And generally he has a sufficient degree of intelligence that he will commit the offense, and return to it upon every clear opportunity, in such a stealthy way that he can seldom be caught in the act itself.
>
> When a dog of that character has for three weeks taken up his abode upon the premises of one not his owner, or else from time to time during

the course of such a period and from day to day as well as often during the night, has returned to and entered upon the premises of one not his owner, and has destroyed and continued to destroy all the eggs of the fowls kept by the owner of the premises, what shall the victimized owner of the premises do? Nobody will contend that he shall be obliged to forgo the privilege to own and keep fowls and to obtain and have the eggs which they lay; nor will it be contended that he is obliged to build extra high fences, so high as to keep out the trespassing dog, even if fences could be so built. The premises and its privileges belong to the owner thereof, not to the dog.

He must then, as the most that could be required of him, take one or the other, and when necessary all, of the three following courses: (1) He must use reasonable efforts to drive the dog away and in such appropriate manner as will probably cause him to stay away; or (2) he must endeavor to catch the dog and confine him to be dealt with in a manner which we do not enter upon because not here before us; or (3) he must make reasonable efforts to ascertain and notify the owner of the dog, so that the latter may have opportunity to take the necessary precautions by which to stop the depredations. It is undisputed in this record that the owner of the premises resorted in a reasonably diligent manner and for a sufficient length of time to each and all of the three foregoing courses of action, but his reasonable efforts in that pursuit resulted, every one of them, in failure.

What else was there reasonably left but to kill the animal? There was nothing else; and we reject the contention, which seems to be the main ground taken by appellee, that admitting all that has been said, the dog could not lawfully be killed except while in the actual commission of the offense. This is a doctrine which applies in many if not most cases, but is not available under facts such as presented by this record. After such a period of habitual depredation as shown in this case, and having taken the alternative steps aforementioned, the owner of the premises is not required to wait and watch with a gun until he can catch the predatory dog in the very act. Such a dog would be far more watchful than would the watcher himself, and the depredation would not occur again until the watcher had given up his post and had gone about some other task, but it would then recur, and how soon would be a mere matter of opportunity.

What is the distinction between *Hull v. Scruggs* and *Katko v. Briney* (the L case of the spring gun)?

7. *Dogs vs. goats.* In Kershaw v. McKown, 196 Ala. 123 (Ala. 1916), the plaintiff sued the defendant for killing his dog. The dog had been attacking the defendant's goat. The trial court instructed the jury as follows:

If you believe from the evidence that the dog here sued for was not worth greatly more than the goat, and if you further believe that the dogs were acting in a way that would lead a reasonably prudent man to conclude that it was necessary to kill these dogs in order to save the life of the goat or save it from great bodily harm, then you should render a verdict for defendant.

The jury brought in a verdict for the defendant, and the plaintiff appealed; the plaintiff made the following argument that the instruction the jury was given had been defective:

> The charges refused to plaintiff asserted the proposition that, if the goat which was being attacked was of less value than that of the dog killed, or if the value of the two was not greatly disproportionate, the verdict should be for the plaintiff for the value of the dog killed, and that, if defendant could have driven the dogs away, and thus save the goat from harm or death, then he had no right to kill the dog.

Held, for the defendant, that the jury was instructed properly:

> The most that can properly be said as a rule of law is, that there must be an apparent necessity for the defense, honestly believed to be real, and then the acts of defense must in themselves be reasonable. Acts beyond reason are excessive. The consequences of the proposed act to the aggressor should be considered in connection with the consequences of nonaction to the party defending, whether the defense be made in favor of person or property; and in case of defense of domestic animals from attacks of other animals the relative value of the animals may be a proper circumstance for the jury to consider in arriving at a conclusion whether the defense was a reasonable one under the circumstances.

How were the instructions the plaintiff wanted different from those actually used? Why should the defendant be required to pay damages if his goat was worth much less than the plaintiff's dog, but not required to pay damages if his goat was worth more, or was worth about the same amount? Suppose the dog had been of distinguished pedigree, and so "worth greatly more than the goat." What was the defendant supposed to do then?

8. *Hogs vs. chickens.* An earlier appellate court opinion in *Kershaw* explained the question of relative value in this way:

> [N]ot only out of a regard for the peace and good order of society [. . .] but from a sense of abstract right and justice, the law, as a rule, forbids the killing by one of another's hog in order to protect his own chicken because, if it permitted it, the result would be to lay down a doctrine that would allow the destruction of a $50 hog to save a 50-cent chicken, and, consequently, would be measuring the right of a chicken owner by a

standard out of all proportion to the wrong done, or suffered to be done, by the hog owner. Certainly, no man would contend that it would be right for the law to countenance the killing of a horse to save the life of a chicken that was at the time being viciously trampled upon by the horse.

12 Ala. App. 485, 488-489. Some states nevertheless reject the notion that the value of a dog should be taken into account in assessing a defendant's liability for shooting such an animal when it threatens livestock — especially when the defendant's right to kill the dog is established by statute. See, e.g., *Granier v. Chagnon*, 203 P.2d 982 (Mont. 1949) ("It matters not whether the sheep-stealing dog be a patrician or a plebeian dog. Each suffers the same fate.").

9. *Beasts of a stranger.* The problem of trespassing livestock was a familiar one to the common law. The favored response was to "distrain" (seize) the offending animal and condition its release on the owner's payment of damages. See 4 William Blackstone, Commentaries on the Laws of England 1024:

> Another injury for which distresses may be taken is where a man finds beasts of a stranger wandering in his grounds damage-feasant; that is, doing him hurt or damage by treading down his grass or the like; in which case the owner of the soil may distrain them till satisfaction be made him for the injury he has thereby sustained.

The common law license to impound trespassing animals is now widely regulated by statute; see, e.g., Del. St. Title 3 Sec. 7702:

> Any person or resident owning land in this State may take up any livestock found running at large upon the public highways or on lands owned by that person and impound the same. Such person may demand and receive a reasonable sum for the care and feeding of the animal or animals while in his care. The care and shelter provided shall be humane and shall be adequate for the size and class of livestock impounded.

10. *The single owner principle.* In Bamford v. Turnley, 122 Eng. Rep. 25, 33 (Exch. Ch. 1862), *rev'g* 122 Eng. Rep. 25 (Q.B. 1860), the defendant was a brickmaker sued by one of his neighbors for creating a nuisance. Bramwell, B., made a famous argument by analogy that "It is for the public benefit that trains should run, but not unless they pay their expenses. If one of these expenses is the burning down of a wood of such value that the railway owners would not run the train and burn down the wood if it were their own, neither is it for the public benefit that they should if the wood is not their own. If, though the wood were their own, they still would find it compensated them to run trains at the cost of burning the wood, then they obviously ought to compensate the owner of such wood, not being themselves, if they burn it

down in making their gains." Consider Bramwell's argument as a general suggestion that in deciding whether a defendant has acted wrongfully, we might ask how the situation would have been handled by a single owner who was responsible both for the source of the threat and for the property being threatened. Does this approach shed light on the cases just considered?

11. *Rules of engagement.* The law governing the privilege of self-defense contains a number of additional intricacies. The following excerpts from the Restatement (Second) of Torts illustrate them. These are best understood as attempts to summarize the law on questions where case law often is scarce; they do not represent rules that all jurisdictions can be expected to follow. They are offered here just to show the range of problems that can arise in this area of law and some proposed solutions to them.

§63. SELF-DEFENSE BY FORCE NOT THREATENING DEATH OR SERIOUS BODILY HARM

Comment l. Actor's duty to avoid force. The actor cannot reasonably believe that the use of force is necessary until he has exhausted all other reasonably safe means of preventing the other from inflicting bodily harm upon him.

Illustration 13. A in the dusk mistakes B for C. A approaches B with his cane raised as if to strike and says: "Now, C, I have my chance to punish you." B has ample time to disclose his identity before A can get within striking distance. He does not do so but awaits A's attack and knocks him down. B is subject to liability to A.

Comment m. Actor's duty to retreat. The actor, if he reasonably believes that he is threatened with the intentional imposition of bodily harm, or even of an offensive contact, may stand his ground and repel the attack by the use of reasonable force, which does not threaten serious harm or death, even though he might with absolute certainty of safety avoid the threatened bodily harm or offensive contact by retreating.

Illustration 14. A is standing on a public highway. B, who is some distance away, runs toward A, brandishing a cane and threatening to beat him. A may stand his ground, await B's attack and defend himself against it by knocking B down, although A knows that B is lame and that he can with perfect safety avoid the threatened beating by retreat. [But see Illustration 5 below.]

§65. SELF-DEFENSE BY FORCE THREATENING DEATH OR SERIOUS BODILY HARM

Illustration 1. A attempts to slap B's face. B is not privileged to shoot or stab A to prevent him from doing so, although, being much weaker than A, B cannot otherwise prevent A from slapping him.

Illustration 5. A is standing upon a public highway. B, while still some distance away, starts towards A brandishing a razor and threatening to kill him. B is lame, and A knows that he can with perfect safety avoid B's attack by running away. A is not privileged to stand his ground, await B's attack and shoot or stab B to defend himself against it.

Comment i. Standing one's ground in his dwelling place. [O]ne attacked in his dwelling place may await his assailant and use deadly force to repel him though he could prevent the assailant from attacking him by closing the door and so excluding the assailant from the premises. But the mere fact that a man is threatened with an attack while he is within his own dwelling place does not justify him in using deadly weapons if he can avoid the necessity of so doing by any alternative other than flight or standing a siege. A man can no more justify using deadly weapons when he is in his own home than he can when he is upon a public highway, if he can avoid the necessity of doing so by complying with a demand, other than a demand that he shall retreat, give up the possession of his dwelling or permit an intrusion into it, or abandon an attempt to make a lawful arrest.

Illustration 6. A is standing in the vestibule of his dwelling house. B starts toward A brandishing a razor and threatening to kill him. A is privileged to stand his ground, await B's attack and shoot or stab him, although A could with perfect safety avoid B's attack by retreating to an inner room or by closing and locking the door of the vestibule.

Illustration 7. A goes to B's dwelling place. Having gained admittance peaceably, he points a revolver at B and threatens to shoot him unless B gives him a watch which B is carrying and which is the property of B, but which A in good faith claims to be his. In determining whether B is privileged to defend himself by shooting A rather than give up the watch, the fact that the demand is made upon him in his own dwelling place instead of upon a public highway is immaterial.

§73. HARMFUL CONTACT IN DEFENSE AGAINST HARM THREATENED
     OTHERWISE THAN BY OTHER

Illustration 3. A and B are sailing in a small boat, which is about to be swamped by a squall. The boat is manifestly incapable of carrying both. A, being the stronger, pushes B into the water. A reaches shore in safety in the boat, but B drowns. A is subject to liability under a wrongful death statute for the death of B.

§76. DEFENSE OF THIRD PERSON

The actor is privileged to defend a third person from a harmful or offensive contact or other invasion of his interests of personality under the same conditions and by the same means as those under and by which he is privileged to defend himself if the actor correctly or reasonably believes that

(a) the circumstances are such as to give the third person a privilege of self-defense, and

(b) his intervention is necessary for the protection of the third person.

Illustration 4. A attacks B, knocks him down, draws a knife, and is about to stab B. C, a bystander who is a stranger to both A and B, intervenes to protect B, and strikes A on the head with a pitchfork, inflicting serious injury. C is not liable to A.

§261. PRIVILEGE OF SELF-DEFENSE OR DEFENSE OF THIRD PERSON

One is privileged to commit an act which would otherwise be a trespass to or a conversion of a chattel in the possession of another, for the purpose of defending himself or a third person against the other, under the same conditions which would afford a privilege to inflict a harmful or offensive contact upon the other for the same purpose.

Illustration 1. A, while visiting in B's house, is assaulted by B, who seizes a valuable vase to hurl at him. To protect himself, A picks up B's umbrella, and with it knocks the vase out of B's hands and breaks it and the umbrella. A is not liable to B for the value of either the umbrella or the vase.

B. PRIVATE NECESSITY

Ploof v. Putnam
81 Vt. 471, 71 A. 188 (1908)

MUNSON, J. — It is alleged as the ground of recovery that on the 13th day of November, 1904, the defendant was the owner of a certain island in Lake Champlain, and of a certain dock attached thereto, which island and dock were then in charge of the defendant's servant; that the plaintiff was then possessed of and sailing upon said lake a certain loaded sloop, on which were the plaintiff and his wife and two minor children; that there then arose a sudden and violent tempest, whereby the sloop and the property and persons therein were placed in great danger of destruction; that, to save these from destruction or injury, the plaintiff was compelled to, and did, moor the sloop to defendant's dock; that the defendant, by his servant, unmoored the sloop, whereupon it was driven upon the shore by the tempest, without the plaintiff's fault; and that the sloop and its contents were thereby destroyed, and the plaintiff and his wife and children cast into the lake and upon the shore, receiving injuries. This claim is set forth in two counts — one in trespass, charging that the defendant by his servant with force and arms willfully and designedly unmoored the sloop; the other in case, alleging that it was the duty of the defendant by his servant to permit the plaintiff to moor his sloop to the dock, and to permit it to remain so moored during the continuance of the tempest, but that the defendant by his servant, in disregard of this duty, negligently, carelessly, and wrongfully unmoored the sloop. Both counts are demurred to generally.

There are many cases in the books which hold that necessity, and an inability to control movements inaugurated in the proper exercise of a strict right, will justify entries upon land and interferences with personal property that would otherwise have been trespasses. A reference to a few of these will be sufficient to illustrate the doctrine. In *Miller v. Fandrye*, Poph. 161, trespass was brought for chasing sheep, and the defendant pleaded that the sheep were trespassing upon his land, and that he with a little dog chased them out, and that, as soon as the sheep were off his land, he called in the dog. It was argued that, although the defendant might lawfully drive the sheep from his own ground with a dog, he had no right to pursue them into the next ground; but the court considered that the defendant might drive the sheep from his land with a dog, and that the nature of a dog is such that he cannot be withdrawn in an instant, and that, as the defendant had done his best to recall the dog, trespass would not lie. [. . .] If one have a way over the land of another for his beasts to pass, and the beasts, being properly driven, feed the grass by morsels in passing or run out of the way and are promptly pursued and brought back, trespass will not lie. See Vin. Ab. Trespass, K. a, pl. 1. A traveler on a highway who finds it obstructed from a sudden and temporary cause may pass upon the adjoining land without becoming a trespasser because of the necessity. An entry upon land to save goods which are in danger of being lost or destroyed by water or fire is not a trespass. In *Proctor v. Adams*, 113 Mass. 376, 18 Am. Rep. 500, the defendant went upon the plaintiff's beach for the purpose of saving and restoring to the lawful owner a boat which had been driven ashore, and was in danger of being carried off by the sea; and it was held no trespass.

This doctrine of necessity applies with special force to the preservation of human life. One assaulted and in peril of his life may run through the close of another to escape from his assailant. 37 Hen, VII, pl. 26. One may sacrifice the personal property of another to save his life or the lives of his fellows. [. . .]

It is clear that an entry upon the land of another may be justified by necessity, and that the declaration before us discloses a necessity for mooring the sloop. But the defendant questions the sufficiency of the counts because they do not negative the existence of natural objects to which the plaintiff could have moored with equal safety. The allegations are, in substance, that the stress of a sudden and violent tempest compelled the plaintiff to moor to defendant's dock to save his sloop and the people in it. The averment of necessity is complete, for it covers not only the necessity of mooring, but the necessity of mooring to the dock; and the details of the situation which created this necessity, whatever the legal requirements regarding them, are matters of proof, and need not be alleged. It is certain that the rule suggested cannot be held applicable irrespective of circumstances, and the question must be left for adjudication upon proceedings had with reference to the evidence or the charge. [...]

Judgment affirmed and cause remanded.

NOTES

1. *Technological solutions.* Suppose that instead of appointing a servant to push away unwanted boats, Putnam had installed a locked gate that prevented strangers from using his dock, or had bought a dog to frighten away people like the Ploofs. Liability? If not, why not?

2. *Nowhere to run.* In Rossi v. DelDuca, 181 N.E.2d 591 (Mass. 1962), the plaintiff, a young girl, was walking home from school one day with a friend when they were confronted by a German Weimaraner dog. The girls tried to run away down an adjacent street. Upon discovering that it was a dead end, and with the Weimaraner in pursuit, they escaped into a field owned by the defendant. There, however, they were confronted by two Great Danes the defendant kept to guard equipment stored in the field. One of the Danes jumped on the plaintiff and bit her neck. She sued the defendant for damages under Mass. G.L. c. 140, §155, which read:

> If any dog shall do any damage to either the body or property of any person, the owner or keeper, or if the owner or keeper be a minor, the parent or guardian of such minor, shall be liable for such damage, unless such damage shall have been occasioned to the body or property of a person who, at the time such damage was sustained, was committing a trespass or other tort, or was teasing, tormenting or abusing such dog.

The defendant argued that the plaintiff was barred from recovery because she admitted that she was trespassing on the defendant's field when his dogs attacked her. The plaintiff nevertheless was held to have a good claim; in affirming the trial court's denial of the defendant's motion for a directed verdict, the court said that the pursuit of the plaintiff by the Weimaraner

> brings the case, we think, within the principle that one is privileged to enter land in the possession of another if it is, or reasonably appears to be, necessary to prevent serious harm to the actor or his property. This privilege not only relieves the intruder from liability for technical trespass [...] but it also destroys the possessor's immunity from liability in resisting the intrusion. *Ploof v. Putnam*, 81 Vt. 471, 71 A. 188 (1908)[.]

What is the distinction between *Rossi v. DelDuca* and *Woodbridge v. Marks* (the NL case in the section on the self-defense privilege where a watchdog bit a trespasser)?

Vincent v. Lake Erie Transportation Co.
109 Minn. 456, 124 N.W. 221 (1910)

O'Brien, J. — The steamship *Reynolds*, owned by the defendant, was for the purpose of discharging her cargo on November 27, 1905, moored to plaintiff's dock in Duluth. While the unloading of the boat was taking place a storm from the northeast developed, which at about 10 o'clock P.M., when the unloading was completed, had so grown in violence that the wind was then moving at 50 miles per hour and continued to increase during the night. There is some evidence that one, and perhaps two, boats were able to enter the harbor that night, but it is plain that navigation was practically suspended from the hour mentioned until the morning of the 29th, when the storm abated, and during that time no master would have been justified in attempting to navigate his vessel, if he could avoid doing so. After the discharge of the cargo the *Reynolds* signaled for a tug to tow her from the dock, but none could be obtained because of the severity of the storm. If the lines holding the ship to the dock had been cast off, she would doubtless have drifted away; but, instead, the lines were kept fast, and as soon as one parted or chafed it was replaced, sometimes with a larger one. The vessel lay upon the outside of the dock, her bow to the east, the wind and waves striking her starboard quarter with such force that she was constantly being lifted and thrown against the dock, resulting in its damage as found by the jury, to the amount of $500.

We are satisfied that the character of the storm was such that it would have been highly imprudent for the master of the *Reynolds* to have attempted to leave the dock or to have permitted his vessel to drift away from it. One witness testified upon the trial that the vessel could have been warped into a slip, and that, if the attempt to bring the ship into the slip had failed, the worst that could have happened would be that the vessel would have been blown ashore upon a soft and muddy bank. The witness was not present in Duluth at the time of the storm, and while he may have been right in his conclusions, those in charge of the dock and the vessel at the time of the storm were not required to use the highest human intelligence, nor were they required to resort to every possible experiment which could be suggested for the preservation of their property. Nothing more was demanded of them than ordinary prudence and care, and the record in this case fully sustains the contention of the appellant that, in holding the vessel fast to the dock, those in charge of her exercised good judgment and prudent seamanship.

The situation was one in which the ordinary rules regulating property rights were suspended by forces beyond human control, and if, without the direct intervention of some act by the one sought to be held liable, the property of another was injured, such injury must be attributed to the act of God, and not to the wrongful act of the person sought to be charged. If during the storm the *Reynolds* had entered the harbor, and while there had become disabled and been thrown against the plaintiffs' dock, the plaintiffs could not have recovered. Again, if while attempting to hold fast to the dock the lines had parted, without any negligence, and the vessel carried against some other boat or dock in the harbor, there would be no liability upon her owner. But here those in charge of the vessel deliberately and by their direct efforts held her in such a position that the damage to the dock resulted, and, having thus preserved the ship at the expense of the dock, it seems to us that her owners are responsible to the dock owners to the extent of the injury inflicted.

In *Depue v. Flatau*, 100 Minn. 299 (1907), this court held that where the plaintiff, while lawfully in the defendants' house, became so ill that he was incapable of traveling with safety, the defendants were responsible to him in damages for compelling him to leave the premises. If, however, the owner of the premises had furnished the traveler with proper accommodations and medical attendance, would he have been able to defeat an action brought against him for their reasonable worth?

In *Ploof v. Putnam*, 71 A. 188 (1908), the Supreme Court of Vermont held that where, under stress of weather, a vessel was without permission moored to a private dock at an island in Lake Champlain owned by the defendant, the plaintiff was not guilty of trespass, and that the defendant was responsible in damages because his representative upon the island unmoored the vessel, permitting it to drift upon the shore, with resultant injuries to it. If, in that case, the vessel had been permitted to remain, and the dock had suffered an injury, we believe the shipowner would have been held liable for the injury done.

Theologians hold that a starving man may, without moral guilt, take what is necessary to sustain life; but it could hardly be said that the obligation would not be upon such person to pay the value of the property so taken when he became able to do so. And so public necessity, in times of war or peace, may require the taking of private property for public purposes; but under our system of jurisprudence compensation must be made.

Let us imagine in this case that for the better mooring of the vessel those in charge of her had appropriated a valuable cable lying on the dock. No matter how justifiable such appropriation might have been, it would not be claimed that, because of the overwhelming necessity of the situation, the owner of the cable could not recover its value.

This is not a case where life or property was menaced by any object or thing belonging to the plaintiff, the destruction of which became necessary to prevent the threatened disaster. Nor is it a case where, because of the act of God, or unavoidable accident, the infliction of the injury was beyond the control of the defendant, but is one where the defendant prudently and advisedly availed itself of the plaintiffs' property for the purpose of preserving its own more valuable property, and the plaintiffs are entitled to compensation for the injury done.

Order affirmed.

LEWIS, J. — I dissent. It was assumed on the trial before the lower court that appellant's liability depended on whether the master of the ship might, in the exercise of reasonable care, have sought a place of safety before the storm made it impossible to leave the dock. The majority opinion assumes that the evidence is conclusive that appellant moored its boat at respondent's dock pursuant to contract, and that the vessel was lawfully in position at the time the additional cables were fastened to the dock, and the reasoning of the opinion is that, because appellant made use of the stronger cables to hold the boat in position, it became liable under the rule that it had voluntarily made use of the property of another for the purpose of saving its own.

In my judgment, if the boat was lawfully in position at the time the storm broke, and the master could not, in the exercise of due care, have left that position without subjecting his vessel to the hazards of the storm, then the damage to the dock, caused by the pounding of the boat, was the result of an inevitable accident. If the master was in the exercise of due care, he was not at fault. The reasoning of the opinion admits that if the ropes, or cables, first attached to the dock had not parted, or if, in the first instance, the master had used the stronger cables, there would be no liability. If the master could not, in the exercise of reasonable care, have anticipated the severity of the storm and sought a place of safety before it became impossible, why should he be required to anticipate the severity of the storm, and, in the first instance, use the stronger cables?

I am of the opinion that one who constructs a dock to the navigable line of waters, and enters into contractual relations with the owner of a vessel to moor at the same, takes the risk of damage to his dock by a boat caught there by a storm, which event could not have been avoided in the exercise of due care, and further, that the legal status of the parties in such a case is not changed by renewal of cables to keep the boat from being cast adrift at the mercy of the tempest.

NOTES

1. *Incomplete privilege.* Does *Vincent* contradict *Ploof v. Putnam*? If *Vincent* holds that in cases like *Ploof* the plaintiff has to pay for any damage done, what is left of the privilege in *Ploof*? If the defendant's behavior in *Vincent* was reasonable, why should he be obliged to pay anything to anyone?

2. *The single owner revisited.* Recall Baron Bramwell's suggestion in *Bamford v. Turnley* that it may be useful to consider how a conflict would be resolved if all of its elements were under the same ownership. What are the implications of this idea for cases like *Vincent*? Consider Richard A. Epstein, *A Theory of Strict Liability*, 1 J. Legal Stud. 2, 158 (1973):

> Had the Lake Erie Transportation Company owned both the dock and the ship, there could have been no lawsuit as a result of the incident. The Transportation Company, now the sole party involved, would, when faced with the storm, apply some form of cost-benefit analysis in order to decide whether to sacrifice its ship or its dock to the elements.

Regardless of the choice made, it would bear the consequences and would have no recourse against anyone else. There is no reason why the company as a defendant in a lawsuit should be able to shift the loss in question because the dock belonged to someone else. The action in tort in effect enables the injured party to require the defendant to treat the loss he has inflicted on another as though it were his own. If the Transportation Company must bear all the costs in those cases in which it damages its own property, then it should bear those costs when it damages the property of another.

Is this analysis consistent with the rules governing defense of property that were considered in the previous section of this chapter?

3. *Overnight guests.* In Texas Midland Ry. Co. v. Geraldon, 128 S.W. 611 (Tex. 1910), the plaintiff and his wife and child went to the defendant's railroad station in the late afternoon to catch a train destined for the town of Commerce. The train already had left the depot by the time they arrived. The plaintiff and his family decided to wait inside the station for the next train, which was to pass through at 5:00 the following morning. At about 10:00 that evening, however, an agent for the railroad company said it was time to close the building and ordered them out. The plaintiff's evidence was that it was raining, that his wife was vulnerable to illness, and that being forced out into the rain would put her in danger of becoming sick — and that all of these facts were made known to the agent for the railroad. When the plaintiff said he would not leave the depot, the agent summoned a marshal to oust them. Rather than be arrested, the plaintiff left the station with his family for a boarding house that was 150 to 300 yards away. By the time they arrived the rain had soaked the plaintiff's wife to her skin, and she had no change of clothes (the family's possessions had been left in boxes at the station that were nailed shut and waiting to be loaded onto the train); and as a result she did become sick and suffered various injuries. The plaintiff sued the railroad for the damages suffered by his wife. The jury found for the plaintiff and the defendant appealed. The Texas Supreme Court affirmed:

> We must assume, in deference to the verdict of the jury, that the agent of the railroad company knew that the condition of Mrs. Geraldon was such that for her to go out into the rain at night would endanger her health, and we must assume that it was raining to that extent that made it reasonably certain to the agent that injury to her health might result from putting her out of the depot into such a rain as was then falling. Under such circumstances it was not lawful for the agent of the railroad company to force Mrs. Geraldon out of the room and into the rain whereby her health might be impaired, and it appearing from the evidence that the agent of plaintiff in error having thus knowingly forced Mrs. Geraldon out of the room and into the rain, which caused her to suffer physical pain, the

railroad company was properly held responsible for the results. *Ploof v. Putnam*, 81 Vt. 471.

What is the analogy between *Texas Midland Ry. Co. v. Geraldon* and *Ploof v. Putnam*? Is the *Texas Midland* case inconsistent with *Vincent v. Lake Erie Transportation Co.*? Would you expect *Texas Midland* to be decided the same way if the facts were repeated today? If not, why not?

4. *Jumping the queue.* In London Borough of Southwark v. Williams, [1971] 2 All ER 175, a man named Williams and his family were homeless and living in London. They had no relatives to assist them, nor was the government's housing department able to help. They found empty housing owned by the borough, however, and appropriated it, becoming "squatters." When the Borough brought an action to evict them, they defended on the ground of private necessity. They were denied the use of the privilege. Said Denning, L.J.:

> There is authority for saying that in case of great and imminent danger, in order to preserve life, the law will permit an encroachment on private property. [. . .] The doctrine so enunciated must, however, be carefully circumscribed. Else necessity would open the door to many an excuse. It was for this reason that it was not admitted in *R. v. Dudley and Stephens,* where the three shipwrecked sailors, in extreme despair, killed the cabin-boy and ate him to save their own lives. They were held guilty of murder. The killing was not justified by necessity. Similarly, when a man who is starving enters a house and takes food in order to keep himself alive. Our English law does not admit the defence of necessity. It holds him guilty of larceny. Lord Hale said that "if a person, being under necessity for want of victuals or clothes, shall upon that account clandestinely, and animus furandi, steal another man's food, it is felony." The reason is because, if hunger were once allowed to be an excuse for stealing, it would open a way through which all kinds of disorder and lawlessness would pass. So here. If homelessness were once admitted as a defence to trespass, no one's house could be safe. Necessity would open a door which no man could shut. It would not only be those in extreme need who would enter. There would be others who would imagine that they were in need, or would invent a need, so as to gain entry. Each man would say his need was greater than the next man's. The plea would be an excuse for all sorts of wrongdoing. So the courts must, for the sake of law and order, take a firm stand. They must refuse to admit the plea of necessity to the hungry and the homeless; and trust that their distress will be relieved by the charitable and the good. Applying these principles, it seems to me in the circumstances of these squatters are not such as to afford any justification or excuse in law for their entry into these houses. We can sympathise with the plight in which they find themselves. We can recognise the orderly

way in which they made their entry. But we can go no further. They must make their appeal for help to others, not to us. They must appeal to the council, who will, I am sure, do all it can. They can go to the Minister, if need be. But, so far as these courts are concerned, we must, in the interest of law and order itself, uphold the title to these properties. We cannot allow any individuals, however great their despair, to take the law into their own hands and enter these premises. The court must exercise its summary jurisdiction and order the defendants to go out.

In a concurring opinion, Megaw, L.J., argued that the defendants' squatting would interfere with the Borough's system of administrative allocation:

> One factor which has to be borne in mind is that by allowing to be done what the squatting association wishes to be done there would at least be the danger that persons who are already on the council's housing list may find themselves, in relation to the obtaining of accommodation, falling behind those who are lower on the list or who have not been on the list at all; and it can well be understood that to such persons, who perhaps have been waiting their turn in the queue for a long time, it might be a matter of great heart burning, and perhaps the end of any possibility of maintaining the fairness to everyone which is inherent in an orderly queue.

What is the distinction between the *Borough of Southwark* case and *Ploof v. Putnam?* What is the distinction between *Borough of Southwark* and *Texas Midland Ry. Co. v. Geraldon?* What is different about the circumstances under which the respective defendants have appropriated the plaintiffs' property?

5. *High transaction costs?* One way to interpret cases like *Ploof* and *Vincent* is by positing that property rights must give way when human life or catastrophic property damage is threatened. The challenge for this view is to explain why *Borough of Southwark* was a case of liability for trespass. The concurring opinion in the case suggests one answer: to allow squatting by the defendants would be to unravel a program that does more than squatting to help homeless people. But what if there were no such alternative program and relatively few squatters? Would the result in the case be different?

Many economic analysts subscribe to a theory that suggests the result should not be different. They argue that the law treats rights as more flexible and less absolute in situations where it is hard to enter into voluntary transactions over them. So when it is difficult for parties to make deals with each other as a practical matter (when "transaction costs" are high), the law allows people to take each other's entitlements and pay damages; by awarding damages, the law makes the deal for the parties that they might have made for themselves if bargaining had been feasible. When transaction costs are low, the law is more likely to protect rights with "property rules" that result in stronger sanctions than the payment of damages if they are violated — e.g., fines or imprisonment.

See Calabresi and Melamed, *Property Rules, Liability Rules, and Inalienability: One View of the Cathedral*, 85 Harv. L. Rev. 1089 (1972).

Does this theory explain cases like *Ploof* and *Vincent*? In a sense bargaining was possible in those cases; the parties could have identified each other easily enough, and could have made offers that might have been accepted or rejected. So why was it held that Ploof was allowed to skip the bargaining and trespass even if Putnam did not want him there? Some economists would argue that a privilege is necessary in cases like *Ploof* because real bargaining is quite difficult in such situations. They involve not only little time to negotiate, but also bilateral monopolies: situations where each side has no alternative but to bargain with the other, which may give one of the parties inordinate leverage. Putnam, for example, would seem to be in a position to demand nearly any price from Ploof, in the same way an ordinary monopolist can demand supercompetitive prices for goods. So while voluntary transactions are possible here, the problem from an economic standpoint is that there is not a well-functioning *market* for the rights involved. If the Ploofs knew in advance that they would need use of a dock, and had been able to bargain with every dock owner on the island, presumably they would have been able to reach reasonable terms with most any of them. Perhaps it is this situation that the law tries to mimic by allowing the Ploofs to occupy Putnam's dock (subject, presumably, to the damages rule of *Vincent*).

Were transaction costs high in the *Borough of Southwark* case?

C. PUBLIC NECESSITY

1. *Mouse's case.* In Mouse's Case, 77 Eng. Rep. 1341 (K.B. 1609), the report ran as follows (note that the word "surcharge" as used below is a verb meaning "overload"):

> In an action of trespass brought by Mouse, for a casket, and a hundred and thirteen pounds, taken and carried away, the case was, the ferryman of Gravesend, took forty-seven passengers into his barge, to pass to London, and Mouse was one of them, and the barge being upon the water, a great tempest happened, and a strong wind, so that the barge and all the passengers were in danger to be drowned, if a hogshead of wine and other ponderous things were not cast out, for the safeguard of the lives of the men: it was resolved per totam Curiam, that in case of necessity, for the saving of the lives of the passengers, it was lawful to the defendant, being a passenger, to cast the casket of the plaintiff out of the barge, with the other things in it; [. . .] and the first day of this term, this issue was tried, and it was proved directly, that if the things had not been cast out of the barge, the passenger had been drowned; and that [. . .] they were ejected, some by one passenger, and some by another; and upon this the plaintiff was nonsuit[.]

It was also resolved, that although the ferryman surcharge the barge, yet for the safety of the lives of passengers in such a time and accident of necessity, it is lawful for any passenger to cast the things out of the barge: and the owners shall have their remedy upon the surcharge against the ferryman, for the fault was in him upon the surcharge; but if no surcharge was, but the danger accrued only by the act of God, as by tempest, no default being in the ferryman, everyone ought to bear his loss for the safeguard and life of a man[.]

The result, then, was that Mouse's case against the other passenger failed. (Mouse still might have been entitled to reimbursement from *all* those whose property was saved by throwing his goods overboard; this is the doctrine of general average from the law of admiralty.) What is the distinction between *Mouse's Case* and *Vincent v. Lake Erie Transportation Co.*? Is the result here consistent with what Mouse reasonably should have expected when he got onto the barge?

2. *The needs of the many outweigh the needs of the few.* In Surocco v. Geary, 3 Cal. 70 (1853), the defendant Geary, alcalde (mayor) of San Francisco, was sued for ordering the plaintiff's house destroyed in an attempt to stop the progress of a fire raging through the city in December of 1849. The plaintiffs' evidence was that they were in the process of removing their property from the building when the city blew it up, and that they otherwise would have been able to save more of their goods. The trial court gave judgment to the plaintiffs; the California Supreme Court reversed:

The right to destroy property, to prevent the spread of a conflagration, has been traced to the highest law of necessity, and the natural rights of man, independent of society or civil government. "It is referred by moralists and jurists to the same great principle which justifies the exclusive appropriation of a plank in a shipwreck, though the life of another be sacrificed; with the throwing overboard of goods in a tempest, for the safety of a vessel; with the trespassing upon the lands of another, to escape death by an enemy. . . ."

The common law adopts the principles of the natural law, and places the justification of an act otherwise tortious precisely on the same ground of necessity.

A house on fire, or those in its immediate vicinity, which serve to communicate the flames, becomes a nuisance, which it is lawful to abate, and the private rights of the individual yield to the considerations of general convenience, and the interests of society. Were it otherwise, one stubborn person might involve a whole city in ruin, by refusing to allow the destruction of a building which would cut off the flames and check the progress of the fire, and that, too, when it was perfectly evident that his building must be consumed. [. . .]

The evidence in this case clearly establishes the fact, that the blowing up of the house was necessary, as it would have been consumed had it been left standing. The plaintiffs cannot recover for the value of the goods which they might have saved: they were as much subject to the necessities of the occasion as the house in which they were situate; and if in such cases a party was held liable, it would too frequently happen, that the delay caused by the removal of the goods would render the destruction of the house useless. [. . .]

Why might it be useful to have separate doctrines of public and private necessity rather than one "necessity" doctrine that treats both situations the same way? What *problem* is the public necessity doctrine intended to address? Under the doctrine of public necessity, who bears the costs if houses are torn down to stop a fire, and who gains the benefits? How would the answers to those questions change if there were no such doctrine? Would you expect these differences to affect anyone's behavior? To answer some of these questions it may help to remember what perhaps is apparent from *Mouse's Case*: the privilege of public necessity is not just available to governments; if the defendants in the *Surocco* case had been private citizens rather than the mayor, the result would have been the same.

With Geary's approach, contrast the route taken by the Lord Mayor of London, Thomas Bludworth, during the early stages of the Great Fire of London of 1666:

> The destruction of houses to clear a way in advance of the flames was suggested to Bludworth soon after dawn, but the cautious Lord Mayor hesitated; the cost was great. "Who shall pay the charge of rebuilding the houses?" he asked those who so advised him, little appreciating the larger charge that London must needs pay. To others who again pressed him to take this necessary course he answered, that he dare not do so without the consent of the owners. Thereby he brought down upon himself universal blame.

W. G. Bell, The Great Fire of London in 1666 29-30 (1920). The fire burned for four days; more than 13,000 houses were destroyed. A later court described Bludworth's early reluctance to pull down houses as "a memorable instance of folly." *Respublica v. Sparhawk*, 1 U.S. 359 (Pa. Super. Ct. 1788).

3. *False alarm.* In Struve v. Droge, 62 How. Pr. 233 (N.Y. Sup. Ct. 1881), the plaintiff was a painter of frescoes; the defendant was his landlord. They lived in neighboring apartments. One morning the plaintiff left his apartment for the day. Soon the landlord saw smoke outside the plaintiff's window. He knocked at the plaintiff's door and received no response. Finding the plaintiff's door locked, he broke into his apartment through another entrance. He saw that there was no fire and left. It turned out that the smoke had come from a

nearby chimney. Meanwhile the landlord's efforts to break in to the plaintiff's apartment caused damage to the plaintiff's property for which he brought suit to recover. The trial court gave judgment to the defendant:

> I find, from the evidence that is before me, that the defendant broke open the plaintiff's door; that he committed the damages alleged; that there was an appearance of fire in the plaintiff's apartments, from which apartments the plaintiff was then absent; that defendant believed the premises were on fire; that his motive in breaking open the door was to subdue the fire and protect his own property as well as that of the plaintiff; that such act was lawful and justifiable; that the damage committed was accidental, and with no intent to perpetrate a wrong, but followed the opening of the door; that the breaking open of the door was justifiable in law.

The court of appeals reversed:

> The law seems to be this, that in a case of public necessity, to prevent the spreading of a fire, any individual may demolish a building, without being responsible in trespass or otherwise. If, however, such public necessity does not exist, and, in point of fact, there is no need of the destruction, the person who commits the act is responsible in damages. In Mayor of New York v. Lord (18 Wend. 132), Chancellor Walworth said, that where it became necessary to destroy the property of an individual to prevent the ravages of a fire, the persons who did the destruction were protected from personal responsibility, where they could show that the destruction of the property was necessary to produce the effect, but that they were, by the common law, bound, at their peril, to decide correctly as to such necessity, to protect themselves from liability to make good the loss.

Why this limitation on the doctrine? Is it best understood as motivated by considerations of fairness or of economics? Can the logic of *Struve v. Droge* be squared with the logic of *Crabtree v. Dawson* (the NL case from the section on self-defense where the defendant hit the plaintiff in the face with a musket because he thought the plaintiff was someone else)?

4. *Some further illustrations.* From the Restatement (Second) of Torts:

§262. PRIVILEGE CREATED BY PUBLIC NECESSITY

> One is privileged to commit an act which would otherwise be a trespass to a chattel or a conversion if the act is or is reasonably believed to be necessary for the purpose of avoiding a public disaster.
>
> *Illustration 1.* In the course of fighting a serious and widespread conflagration, A, a fireman, removes B's car lawfully parked on the highway for the purpose of gaining access to a fire plug. In so doing, A unavoidably damages the car. A is not liable for the harm thus caused.

Illustration 2. A, an agister of cattle, kills B's bull, which is in his possession, to prevent a spread of infection which is dangerous to other cattle and to human beings. If the act is reasonably necessary to prevent the spread of the disease, A is not liable to B.

Illustration 3. A, a fireman, demands that B get out of his automobile and permit the fireman to drive it to a widespread conflagration. B refuses to turn his car over to A, but offers to drive him to the fire. A is not privileged to take the car.

What result in Illustration 2 if the infection of B's bull was caused by A's earlier act of negligence?

5. *Takings.* When the public necessity defense is raised by a government, plaintiffs sometimes respond by arguing that the destruction of their property amounted to a "taking" that entitled them to compensation under *eminent domain* provisions of the federal or state constitutions. The federal version, contained in the Fifth Amendment, provides, "nor shall private property be taken for public use, without just compensation"; state constitutions typically contain similar language. The most conventional office of such provisions is to entitle property owners to compensation when the government decides to build a highway, airport, or other public facility where their homes sit. Courts disagree, however, about the applicability of such provisions to cases of the sort considered in this section. Thus in Wegner v. Milwaukee Mut. Ins. Co., 479 N.W.2d 38 (Minn. 1992), an armed suspect fled the scene of a drug bust and hid in the plaintiff's house. A SWAT team from the Minneapolis police department surrounded the residence and fired tear gas and "flash-bang" grenades through its windows; they soon captured the suspect as he tried to escape out a basement window. In the meantime the plaintiff's house sustained $70,000 in damage. The plaintiff sued the city, seeking compensation under the "just compensation" clause of Minnesota's constitution; the Minnesota Supreme Court sustained the claim:

> We are not inclined to allow the city to defend its actions on the grounds of public necessity under the facts of this case. We believe the better rule, in situations where an innocent third party's property is taken, damaged or destroyed by the police in the course of apprehending a suspect, is for the municipality to compensate the innocent party for the resulting damages. The policy considerations in this case center around the basic notions of fairness and justice. At its most basic level, the issue is whether it is fair to allocate the entire risk of loss to an innocent home-owner for the good of the public. We do not believe the imposition of such a burden on the innocent citizens of this state would square with the underlying principles of our system of justice.

For a different view, see Customer Company v. City of Sacramento, 895 P.2d 900 (Cal. 1995), where again a SWAT team damaged a plaintiff's building by firing tear gas inside to flush out a suspect. The plaintiff sought compensation under the eminent domain provision of California's constitution, which provided that "Private property may be taken or damaged for public use only when just compensation, ascertained by a jury unless waived, has first been paid to, or into court for, the owner." The California Supreme Court held the city entitled to judgment on the pleadings, finding that the attempts to smoke out the suspect to be exercises of the state's "police power" rather than its power of eminent domain.

D.   DISCIPLINE

The common law provides certain defendants with a limited privilege to impose discipline in various circumstances; this privilege permits parents and teachers (acting in place of parents, or "in loco parentis"), as well as some others, to use reasonable force to maintain order.

1. *The sea captain's privilege.* In Forbes v. Parsons, 9 F.Cas. 417 (E.D. Pa. 1839), Forbes entered into a contract to serve as cook aboard the *Suffolk*, a ship sailing from Great Britain to Philadelphia. He brought a libel (the maritime term for a lawsuit) in federal court under the admiralty jurisdiction against the ship's captain, Parsons; he claimed that Parsons committed a battery by beating him with a rope and a frying pan. The captain did not deny chastising Forbes but claimed the contact was justified by the sea captain's privilege to preserve discipline on board ship. The court agreed:

> It cannot be doubted that [Forbes's] cooking was exceedingly bad, either from want of skill or willful neglect; and the evidence is satisfactory to show that his galley and pans were kept in a very dirty condition. The bad cooking is proved by the crew, his own witnesses, as well as by the officers of the ship. [. . .] The men once went, in a body, to the captain, with the complaint that the victuals were so badly cooked that they could not eat them. The fault was not in the ship's provisions, which, it is admitted, were good. [. . .]
>
> If his deficiencies were the result of carelessness or obstinacy, [Forbes] was, doubtless, a fit object of punishment, and if he was really ignorant and incapable of the duties of the place he had assumed, he was guilty of a fraud and deception in undertaking to perform them, and comes here entitled to no particular favor. However this may be as to his cooking, it can hardly be denied that, with ordinary care and industry, he might have kept his galley and pans clean. Upon the subject of his ignorance and

incapacity, we cannot avoid to remark that it was of very serious importance to the officers and crew of a ship. To have before them a long voyage, with the disheartening prospect of having their food set before them in a condition hardly fit to be put into their mouths, was indeed a trial of patience and temper that few men would pass through and maintain their good humor. The defects of an ordinary seaman may be supplied by his comrades, but the cook stands by himself, and if he fails, no substitute, unless by an accident, can be found. To have a good dinner spoiled by the cook, is only next to having no dinner. The stomach has a wonderful control over the man and his passions, and a good-natured man, disappointed of his dinner, may become very cross. [. . .]

Having thus stated the cause and provocation given by the libellant, for the injuries he complains of, we must look to the conduct of the other party, and see whether he has exceeded the bounds of moderation, in punishing the offences of the libellant; for it must not be understood that this, or any other provocation, will justify cruel and immoderate chastisements. [. . .]

Nobody will believe that the law which governs the deportment of men on shore to each other, can be applied to their habits and conduct on board of a ship. That which would be an assault, or an assault and battery, in a drawing-room, or in the streets of our city, and punishable by indictment or a civil suit, cannot be so considered among the rough inmates of a ship at sea. The code of manners is entirely different, as is the situation and character of the men. If striking at a man, without touching him, or pointing an offensive weapon to him, or holding up the fist, were to be considered as good ground for a suit; if any rude or angry touching of the person, however lightly, is to be adjudged an assault and battery, for which damages may be recovered; no vessel could arrive without a plentiful crop of actions, equally injurious to the plaintiff and defendant. This cannot be the law of the sea practically, whatever it may be in theory. In questions of this kind, between the officers and the seamen of a ship, my desire has been to maintain a safe and proper discipline, preserving, on the one hand, a necessary and salutary obedience on the part of the seamen, and on the other, protecting him from all cruelty and undue violence, and from any severity not required for the support of the proper authority of the officer, giving a liberal consideration to the exigencies of the occasion. The officer may not, under the pretence of discipline, take advantage of some trifling fault to indulge ferocious passions, or some particular ill will against the offender. [. . .]

The court applied these principles to Forbes's claim as follows:

No serious injury appears ever to have been done to him, at any time; he went to his work, as usual, immediately after every beating, and none of the witnesses speak of the beatings as being severe, much less disabling.

The instrument used was a rope, about the size of which there is a difference between the witnesses of the libellant, and those produced on the part of the respondent. The wiping a dirty knife across his face, and the blow with a dirty frying pan, can not be considered as very aggravated or cruel assaults, nor were they followed by any serious consequences. If the articles in question were as dirty as they have been represented, we can hardly be surprised that they should suddenly have been used as the means of punishment.

2. *Legislative meddling.* Flogging on board vessels of commerce was banned by Congress in 1850 (9 Stat. 515; Rev. St. §4611).

3. *The schoolmaster's privilege.* In Lander v. Seaver, 32 Vt. 114 (1859), the plaintiff, Peter Lander, was an eleven-year-old student at a school run by the defendant, Seaver. One day after school Lander was driving his father's cow past Seaver's house; Seaver and some of Lander's schoolmates were present there. Lander called the defendant "Old Jack Seaver." At the start of school the next morning, Seaver reprimanded Lander for using insulting language and then whipped him with a rawhide. The plaintiff's evidence was that the whipping was severe. The trial court instructed the jury that if Seaver acted from proper motives and in good faith, he should not be held liable if the jury found that the punishment he administered was too severe; the court said that "if a schoolmaster was to be made liable for every error in judgment, in the opinion of a jury, when he acted with good intentions, it would be quite difficult to find a schoolmaster who would assume the authority of correction, without which a school could not well be carried on." So instructed, the jury brought in a verdict for Seaver and the trial court entered judgment upon it.

The Vermont Supreme Court reversed and remanded. The court had no difficulty with the punishment of the student for acts he committed outside the school, finding that "where the offence has a direct and immediate tendency to injure the school and bring the master's authority into contempt, as in this case, when done in the presence of other scholars and of the master, and with a design to insult him, we think he has the right to punish the scholar for such acts if he comes again to school." But the court found that the jury had been instructed improperly on the question of permissible force:

> The parent, unquestionably, is answerable only for malice or wicked motives or an evil heart in punishing his child. [...] This parental power is little liable to abuse, for it is continually restrained by natural affection, the tenderness which the parent feels for his offspring, an affection ever on the alert, and acting rather by instinct than reasoning.
>
> The schoolmaster has no such natural restraint. Hence he may not safely be trusted with all a parent's authority, for he does not act from the instinct of parental affection. He should be guided and restrained by judgment and wise discretion, and hence is responsible for their reasonable exercise. [...]

The law, as we deem it to exist, is this: — A schoolmaster has the right to inflict reasonable corporeal punishment. He must exercise reasonable judgment and discretion in determining when to punish and to what extent. In determining upon what is a reasonable punishment, various considerations must be regarded, the nature of the offence, the apparent motive and disposition of the offender, the influence of his example and conduct upon others, and the sex, age, size and strength of the pupil to be punished. Among reasonable persons much difference prevails as to the circumstances which will justify the infliction of punishment, and the extent to which it may properly be administered. On account of this difference of opinion, and the difficulty which exists in determining what is a reasonable punishment, and the advantage which the master has by being on the spot to know all the circumstances, the manner, look, tone, gestures and language of the offender (which are not always easily described), and thus to form a correct opinion as to the necessity and extent of the punishment, considerable allowance should be made to the teacher by way of protecting him in the exercise of his discretion. Especially should he have this indulgence when he appears to have acted from good motives and not from anger or malice. Hence the teacher is not to be held liable on the ground of excess of punishment, unless the punishment is *clearly* excessive and would be held so in the general judgment of reasonable men.

A less sanguine view of the teacher's prerogative was taken in Cooper v. McJunkin, 4 Ind. 290 (1853):

In one respect the tendency of the rod is so evidently evil, that it might, perhaps, be arrested on the ground of public policy. The practice has an inherent proneness to abuse. The very act of whipping engenders passion, and very generally leads to excess. Where one or two stripes only were at first intended, several usually follow, each increasing in vigor as the act of striking inflames the passions. This is a matter of daily observation and experience. Hence the spirit of the law is, and the leaning of the courts should be, to discountenance a practice which tends to excite human passions to heated and excessive action, ending in abuse and breaches of the peace. Such a system of petty tyranny cannot be watched too cautiously nor guarded too strictly. [. . .]

It can hardly be doubted but that public opinion will, in time, strike the ferule from the hands of the teacher, leaving him as the true basis of government, only the resources of his intellect and heart. Such is the only policy worthy of the state, and of her otherwise enlightened and liberal institutions. It is the policy of progress. The husband can no longer moderately chastise his wife; nor, according to the more recent authorities, the master his servant or apprentice. Even the degrading cruelties of the naval service have been arrested. Why the person of the school-boy, "with his shining morning face," should be less sacred in the eye of the law than that of the apprentice or the sailor, is not easily explained. It is regretted that such are the authorities, — still courts are bound by them. All that can be done, without the aid of legislation, is to hold every case strictly within the rule; and if the correction be in anger, or in any other respect immoderately or improperly administered, to hold the unworthy perpetrator guilty of assault and battery.

4. *Modern times.* In Rinehart v. Board of Education, 621 N.E.2d 1365 (Ohio App. 1993), the plaintiff, Rinehart, was a twelve-year-old student at an elementary school where Uhrig, one of the defendants, worked as a teacher. During the lunch hour and in front of several of his classmates, Rinehart referred to Uhrig as a "dickhead." A few minutes later his fellow students reported this to Uhrig; when Uhrig confronted Rinehart he admitted making the statement. Uhrig informed Rinehart that he was going to administer a paddling to him. He instructed Rinehart to reach down and touch his ankles and then spanked him several times with a paddle. Rinehart's evidence was that the paddling caused severe bruising, resulting in emotional distress and medical expenses. Rinehart and his father sued Uhrig and the school district. The use of corporal punishment in Ohio was governed by Ohio Rev. Code 3319.41, which read in part as follows:

Except as otherwise provided by rule of the board of education [or] the governing body of the private school, a person employed or engaged as a teacher, principal, or administrator in a school, whether public or private, may inflict or cause to be inflicted, reasonable corporal punishment upon a pupil attending such school whenever such punishment is reasonably necessary in order to preserve discipline while such pupil is subject to school authority.

The defendant Board of Education in turn had adopted the following rule:

Corporal punishment where other methods have failed may be administered by a teacher or by the Principal if not actuated by malice or anger, expressed or implied, and if there is no danger of physical injury to the student. The only acceptable corporal punishment is by the use of a properly designed paddle. Such corporal punishment shall be administered only in the presence of at least one witness who shall be a teacher, a staff member, a principal, or a parent. An exception to this corporal punishment rule may be made in cases of emergency when a student becomes an immediate threat to the safety, health or life of others and his/her removal must be made by physical force. Such removals shall be reported as soon as possible to the Principal. Also it is strongly recommended that the witness be of the same sex as the student.

The trial court gave summary judgment to the defendants. The court of appeals affirmed:

> Uhrig followed the Board's policy on corporal punishment to the letter. Paul had been "out of line" and talking earlier that same day. It is apparent from Paul's continuing course of misbehavior that other methods of discipline (including sending Paul to Saturday school as punishment for talking in class) were ineffective and had failed. None of the evidentiary material creates a genuine issue of fact as to whether Uhrig's actions were conducted with a malicious purpose or in a wanton or reckless manner.

The defendant's policy applied only if there was "no danger of physical injury to the student"; in view of the plaintiff's claimed injuries, why did the court conclude that the defendant's policy was followed "to the letter"?

5. *Instilling spirit.* In Hogenson v. Williams, 542 S.W.2d 456 (Tex. Civ. App. 1976), the plaintiff (via his parents) sued his junior high school football coach for assault, a claim equivalent to battery under Texas law. During a practice session of the seventh grade football team, the defendant became displeased with the plaintiff's performance of blocking assignments. He started yelling at the boy, then struck his helmet with force sufficient to cause him to stumble and fall to the ground, and finally grabbed his face mask. The defendant later said that he did these things to the plaintiff for the purpose of "firing him up" or "instilling spirit in him." The plaintiff soon was admitted to the hospital complaining of weakness of his left hand, left forearm and elbow region and spasms of the left neck muscles. His condition was diagnosed as a severe cervical sprain and bruising of the brachial plexus. He was discharged from the hospital after eight days and recovered several months later.

The jury, instructed that "an intent to injure is the gist of an assault," found that the defendant did not commit an assault; the jury also found that the defendant's contact with the plaintiff was done for "instruction and encouragement" without any intent to injure him. The trial court gave judgment to the defendant. The court of appeals then reversed and remanded for a new trial, finding that the definition of assault given to the jury too narrow (no intent to injure was necessary) and that the trial court had defined the disciplinary privilege too broadly:

> [W]e do not accept the proposition that a teacher may use physical violence against a child merely because the child is unable or fails to perform, either academically or athletically, at a desired level of ability, even though the teacher considers such violence to be "instruction and encouragement." [...] [A]ny force used must be that which the teacher reasonably believes necessary (1) to enforce compliance with a proper command issued for the purpose of controlling, training or educating the child, or (2) to punish the child for prohibited conduct; and in either

case, the force or physical contact must be reasonable and not dispropor-
tionate to the activity or the offense. In the event of a retrial, defensive
issues based upon privileged force should be accompanied with instructions clearly enunciating these principles.

6. *Battered wives.* A moment ago we saw the court in *Cooper v. McJunkin*
state — in 1853 — that "[t]he husband can no longer moderately chastise his
wife." A further word is in order regarding tort liability for domestic abuse;
but an understanding of the issue requires first a more general look at the
legal position occupied by married women before the twentieth century. The
common law generally did not permit married women to own property.
When a woman married, any wealth she owned immediately became her
husband's to spend during his life or dispose of at his death as he saw fit;
likewise any earnings she produced or any wealth she inherited during the
marriage. Nor, with minor exceptions, could married women make
enforceable contracts, and their participation in tort litigation was
comparably restricted: a married woman could not bring a tort suit unless
her husband joined her as a co-plaintiff, and husbands were liable for any
torts their wives committed and had to be made co-defendants in any suits
against them. These rules might seem to have complicated the prospect of a
suit for battery by a wife against an abusive husband, but in fact this
possibility was dealt with in a clear and straightforward fashion: the doctrine
of interspousal immunity forbade civil suits of any sort between husband
and wife.

Against this backdrop it is easy to understand why there is no early American
case law discussing a husband's liability for beating his wife. Wives could not
sue their husbands for anything. This did not necessarily mean that such
beatings were lawful, but it did mean that a married woman's only legal
recourse for abuse was to seek a criminal prosecution. The precise view of
such prosecutions taken by the common law courts is difficult to pin down. In
1765 the English jurist William Blackstone described the situation as follows:

> The husband also, by the old law, might give his wife moderate correc-
> tion. For as he is to answer for her misbehavior, the law thought it rea-
> sonable to intrust him with this power of restraining her, by domestic
> chastisement, in the same moderation that a man is allowed to correct his
> apprentices or children; for whom the master or parent is also liable in
> some cases to answer. But this power of correction was confined within
> reasonable bounds, and the husband was prohibited from using any vio-
> lence to his wife, aliter quam ad virum, ex causa regiminis et castigationis
> uxoris suae, licite et rationabiliter pertinet (otherwise than lawfully and
> reasonably belongs to the husband for the due government and correc-
> tion of his wife). The civil law gave the husband the same, or a larger,
> authority over his wife: allowing him, for some misdemeanors, flagellis et
> fustibus acriter verberare uxorem (to beat his wife severely with scourges

and sticks); for others, only modicam castigationem adhibere (to use moderate chastisement). But with us, in the politer reign of Charles the Second, this power of correction began to be doubted; and a wife may now have security of the peace against her husband; or, in return, a husband against his wife. Yet the lower rank of people, who were always fond of the old common law, still claim and exert their ancient privilege: and the courts of law will still permit a husband to restrain a wife of her liberty, in case of any gross misbehavior.

By the nineteenth century most American courts formally repudiated the notion that a husband had a right to beat his wife. Thus in *Fulgham v. State*, 46 Ala. 143 (1871), the Alabama Supreme Court, in affirming a husband's criminal conviction for battery of his spouse, offered this comment on the privilege Blackstone described:

> Judge Blackstone calls it merely an ancient privilege, and quotes no decided case, and possibly none such could then be found, which supports the privilege referred to by him, as a universal law. This distinguished author published his commentaries above one hundred years ago, when society was much more rude, out of the towns and cities in England, than it is at the present day in this country; and the exercise of a rude privilege there is no excuse for a like privilege here. [. . .] [T]he common law of "wife whipping" among "the lower rank of people" in Great Britain, has never been the common law of this State. It is, at best, but a low and barbarous custom, and never was a law.

It is difficult to find American cases taking a contrary view and explicitly stating that husbands had a right to chastise their wives. There are a few such examples, however; perhaps the clearest is *State v. Black*, 1 Win. 266 (N.C. 1864), where the North Carolina Supreme Court reversed a husband's conviction for battery:

> A husband is responsible for the acts of his wife, and he is required to govern his household, and for that purpose the law permits him to use towards his wife such a degree of force as is necessary to control an unruly temper and make her behave herself; and unless some permanent injury be inflicted, or there be an excess of violence, or such a degree of cruelty as shows that it is inflicted to gratify his own bad passions, the law will not invade the domestic forum or go behind the curtain. It prefers to leave the parties to themselves, as the best mode of inducing them to make the matter up and live together as man and wife should.

A few years later another defendant in the same state was prosecuted for whipping his wife. The trial court acquitted him on the ground that the lash he used for the purpose was no broader than his thumb. The North

Carolina Supreme Court affirmed, and took the opportunity to refine its position:

> [F]amily government is recognized by law as being as complete in itself as the State government is in itself, and yet subordinate to it; and that we will not interfere with or attempt to control it, in favor of either husband or wife, unless in cases where permanent or malicious injury is inflicted or threatened, or the condition of the party is intolerable. For, however great are the evils of ill temper, quarrels, and even personal conflicts inflicting only temporary pain, they are not comparable with the evils which would result from raising the curtain, and exposing to public curiosity and criticism, the nursery and the bed chamber. Every household has and must have, a government of its own, modelled to suit the temper, disposition and condition of its inmates. Mere ebullitions of passion, impulsive violence, and temporary pain, affection will soon forget and forgive; and each member will find excuse for the other in his own frailties. But when trifles are taken hold of by the public, and the parties are exposed and disgraced, and each endeavors to justify himself or herself by criminating the other, that which ought to be forgotten in a day, will be remembered for life. [...]
>
> It will be observed that the ground upon which we have put this decision, is not, that the husband has the *right* to whip his wife much or little; but that we will not interfere with family government in trifling cases. [...] Two boys under fourteen years of age fight upon the playground, and yet the courts will take no notice of it, not for the reason that boys have the *right* to fight, but because the interests of society require that they should be left to the more appropriate discipline of the school room and of home. It is not true that boys have a right to fight; nor is it true that a husband has a right to whip his wife. And if he had, it is not easily seen how *the thumb* is the standard of size for the instrument which he may use, as some of the old authorities have said; and in deference to which was his Honor's charge. A light blow, or many light blows, with a stick larger than the thumb, might produce no injury; but a switch half the size might be so used as to produce death. The standard is the *effect produced*, and not the manner of producing it, or the instrument used.

State v. Rhodes, 61 N.C. 453 (1868). This passage captures the position that many courts took well into the twentieth century: formal condemnation of domestic abuse, but a refusal to use the machinery of the criminal law to address it in any but very extreme cases. Did this amount to a privilege to engage in wife beating? Do rights have value if courts decline to enforce them?

Meanwhile the potential for *civil* liability for domestic abuse began to emerge in the second half of the nineteenth century. States passed Married Women's Property Acts that varied in their details but generally gave married women the right to own property, to sue and be sued, and to otherwise establish legal identities separate from their husbands. For many years a majority of courts nevertheless continued to retain interspousal immunity and thus reject tort suits brought by wives against their husbands to redress personal injuries. The courts reasoned that such litigation would spoil domestic harmony and would create a temptation for spouses to collude in producing fraudulent claims to extract money from insurance companies. It was not until the second half of the twentieth century that almost all jurisdictions abolished interspousal immunity for most purposes, including suits alleging battery. For a more extensive account, see Siegel, *The Rule of Love: Wife Beating as Prerogative and Privacy*, 105 Yale L.J. 2117 (1996).

Civil liability for marital rape has been particularly slow to develop. During most of the history of the common law a husband could not be prosecuted or sued for the rape of his wife. Starting in the 1970s, however, state legislatures modified their criminal provisions governing the issue. The complete exemption from prosecution for marital rape appears now to have been abolished in every jurisdiction, but many states retain it in partial form; they recognize marital rape as a crime only if the spouses are living separately or if the degree of force involved is sufficiently severe, or they recognize it but punish it less severely than other rapes. These steps on the criminal side, along with the abrogation of interspousal immunity, have been treated by courts as creating civil liability for marital rape as well. See, e.g., *In re Estate of Peters*, 765 A.2d 468 (Vt. 2000); *Henriksen v. Cameron*, 622 A.2d 1135 (Me. 1993).

Even as formal barriers to civil suits fall away, tort law appears to play a relatively minor role in redressing domestic violence. This sometimes has been attributed to the lack of assets usually held by the potential defendants in such cases as well as their lack of insurance (insurance policies typically exclude coverage for intentional acts). An additional difficulty is that until they achieve a separation or divorce, victims of torts within a marriage face a variety of obvious practical obstacles to bringing a suit; and once the divorce has been obtained, statutes of limitations and principles of res judicata may make recovery in tort difficult. For further discussion, see Wriggins, *Domestic Violence Torts*, 75 S. Cal. L. Rev. 121 (2001).

Chapter 3

The Negligence Standard

When a plaintiff sues a defendant for "negligence," the first question traditionally is whether the defendant owed the plaintiff a duty — an issue considered in a separate chapter. The second question, and the subject of this chapter, is whether the defendant breached that duty by failing to use reasonable care. Often, as in auto accident or malpractice cases where a defendant's obligation to be careful is obvious because of the risks the activity creates, the existence of a duty is taken for granted; the litigation focuses immediately on whether the defendant breached the duty by acting negligently. Thus while the question of the defendant's duty to the plaintiff may come first as a formal matter, as a practical matter the first question in many negligence cases is whether the defendant took reasonable precautions against the harm that occurred. This chapter considers a series of issues that arise in answering that question — and the related question of whether the *plaintiff* might have been negligent as well.

The word "negligence" sometimes is used to refer generally to the tort we are studying (the tort of negligence), and sometimes is used to refer more specifically to this second element of the tort (breach of the duty of care owed to the defendant) — in other words, as a sort of synonym for carelessness. So it is possible to refer to a negligent (i.e., careless) defendant who nonetheless is not held liable for the tort of negligence (consisting of duty, breach, causation, and damages). This dual usage of the word can be confusing at first; it may help to avoid speaking of defendants as behaving "negligently," and to speak instead of their failure to use due care.

A. THE REASONABLE PERSON

Restatement (Second) of Torts (1965)

§283. CONDUCT OF A REASONABLE MAN; THE STANDARD

Unless the actor is a child, the standard of conduct to which he must conform to avoid being negligent is that of a reasonable man under like circumstances.

This general formulation from the Restatement remains a common basis for a jury instruction in a negligence case. What are the attributes of the reasonable person whose behavior provides the benchmark for this judgment? Is the reasonable person of tort law simply a person with average intelligence, ability, and experience? Or is it perhaps an average person with the defendant's intelligence, ability, and experience? If there are two defendants in a case, one 15 years old and the other 50, should their conduct be measured against the same standard, or against the conduct of reasonable people aged 15 and 50, respectively, or against a generic standard?

1. *Mental Ability and Mental States*

Williams v. Hays
143 N.Y. 442, 38 N.E. 449 (1894)
157 N.Y. 541, 52 N.E. 589 (1899)

[The defendant, William Hays, was captain and part owner of the *Emily T. Sheldon*, a two-masted sailing ship bound from Maine to Annapolis with a cargo of ice. Soon after leaving port the ship encountered a storm with high winds, heavy rains, and light snow. Hays tried to sail the ship toward Cape Cod, but it became impossible for him to tell where he was. He set the ship's two sails against each other to bring the vessel to a standstill and ride out the storm. After 24 hours of this he again tried to find Cape Cod; another 12 hours later, the Thatcher Island lights (a pair of lighthouses near Gloucester) at last came into view. Though the seas remained heavy, the storm subsided, and Hays retired to his cabin. He had been on the deck of the ship and with little to eat for 48 hours. He took 15 grains of quinine (a remedy — not alcoholic — for fever and malaria, which Hays feared he might have contracted) and lay down. A few hours later, the ship's mate roused Hays to say that the crew was having trouble steering the ship. A tugboat soon passed, said that the *Sheldon*'s rudder appeared to be broken, and offered to tow the vessel to shore. Hays declined.

Another tug passed and made a similar offer; this, too, Hays refused. The testimony of the *Sheldon*'s crew was that at this point Hays was "staggering about the vessel, making irresponsive answers to questions, appeared to be in a dazed condition, and to be either drunk or insane." The crew told Hays that the *Sheldon* was being dragged toward shore by the tides, but he would take no measures in response. The ship eventually was wrecked on Peaked Hill Bar, near Provincetown. A life-saving boat soon arrived, but it took its crew several hours to coax Hays to come ashore. Hays later was able to remember nothing that had occurred that day.]

EARL, J. — [after stating the facts:] [The plaintiff, as representative of the *Sheldon*'s other owners,] brought this action against the defendant to recover damages for the loss of the vessel, alleging that it was due to his carelessness and misconduct. The defendant claims that from the time he went to his cabin, leaving the vessel in charge of his mate and crew, to the time the vessel was wrecked, and he found himself in the life saving station, he was unconscious, and knew nothing of what occurred, that in fact he was, from some cause, insane, and therefore not responsible for the loss of the vessel. The case was submitted to the jury on the theory that the defendant, if sane, was guilty of negligence causing the destruction of the vessel, but, if insane, was not responsible for her loss through any conduct on his part which, in a sane person, would have constituted such negligence as would have imposed responsibility. [The jury found for the defendant, and the plaintiff brought this appeal.]

The important question for us to determine, then, is whether the insanity of the defendant furnishes a defense to the plaintiff's claim, and I think it does not. The general rule is that an insane person is just as responsible for his torts as a sane person, and the rule applies to all torts, except, perhaps, those in which malice, and therefore intention, actual or imputed, is a necessary ingredient, like libel, slander, and malicious prosecution. In all other torts, intention is not an ingredient, and the actor is responsible, although he acted with a good and even laudable purpose, without any malice. The law looks to the person damaged by another, and seeks to make him whole, without reference to the purpose or the condition, mental or physical, of the person causing the damage. The liability of a lunatic for his torts, in the opinions of judges, has been placed upon several grounds. The rule has been invoked that, where one of two innocent persons must bear a loss, he must bear it whose act caused it. It is said that public policy requires the enforcement of the liability, that the relatives of a lunatic may be under inducement to restrain him, and that tort feasors may not simulate or pretend insanity to defend their wrongful acts, causing damage to others. The lunatic must bear the loss occasioned by his torts, as he bears his other misfortunes, and the burden of such loss may not be put upon others. [. . .] [The court quoted from *Cooley on Torts*:] "Undoubtedly, there is some appearance of hardship, even of injustice, in compelling one to respond for that which, for want of the control of reason, he was unable to avoid; that it is imposing upon a person already visited with the inexpressible

calamity of mental obscurity an obligation to observe the same care and precaution respecting the rights of others that the law demands of one in the full
possession of his faculties. But the question of liability in these cases, as well as
in others, is a question of policy; and it is to be disposed of as would be the
question whether the incompetent person should be supported at the expense
of the public, or of his neighbors, or at the expense of his own estate. If his
mental disorder makes him dependent, and at the same time prompts him to
commit injuries, there seems to be no greater reason for imposing upon the
neighbors or the public one set of these consequences, rather than the other;
no more propriety or justice in making others bear the losses resulting from his
unreasoning fury, when it is spent upon them or their property, than there
would be in calling upon them to pay the expense of his confinement in an
asylum, when his own estate is ample for the purpose." [. . .]

If the defendant had become insane solely in consequence of his efforts to
save the vessel during the storm, we would have had a different case to deal
with. He was not responsible for the storm, and while it was raging his efforts to
save the vessel were tireless and unceasing; and, if he thus became mentally
and physically incompetent to give the vessel any further care, it might be
claimed that his want of care ought not to be attributed to him as a fault. In
reference to such a case, we do not now express any opinion.

[Reversed and remanded.]

[After the case was returned to the trial court, the defendant, relying on the
last paragraph excerpted above, argued that the case should be sent again to a
jury to determine "whether or not the defendant became insane solely in
consequence of his efforts to save the vessel during the storm." The trial
judge disagreed and gave a directed verdict to the plaintiff. The defendant
appealed, and the Court of Appeals again reversed and remanded:]

HAIGHT, J. — [. . .] Upon directing a verdict in favor of the plaintiff, the trial
court said: "Assuming, as we must, for such purpose, that the condition of the
defendant was the result of exhaustion, caused by his efforts to save the ship
from the perils of the storm, and the heavy dose of quinine which he took as a
remedy, I fail to see how that presents any exception to the principle laid down
by the court of appeals, that a person of unsound mind is responsible for the
consequences of acts which in the case of a sane person would be negligent. In
other words, the standard by which he is to be judged is the same as that which
must be applied to the actions of a sane person. It certainly seems to be a cruel
doctrine; but as it is apparently based upon the principle that, as between two
innocent persons, the loss must fall upon him who caused it, rather than upon
the other, the best that can be said about it is that it is a rule which serves the
convenience of the public, to which individual rights must give way." [. . .]

We cannot give our assent to such a view of the law. To our minds it is
carrying the law of negligence to a point which is unreasonable, and, prior to
this case, unheard of, and is establishing a doctrine abhorrent to all principles

of equity and justice. In this case, as we have seen, the storm commenced on Friday, continued through Saturday and Sunday, and it was not until 5 o'clock Monday morning that the defendant was relieved from the care of his vessel. For three days and nights he had been upon duty almost continuously, and for the last 48 hours had not been below the deck. The man is not yet born in whom there is not a limit to his physical and mental endurance, and, when that limit has been passed, he must yield to laws over which man has no control. When the case was here before, it was said that the defendant was bound to exercise such reasonable care and prudence as a careful and prudent man would ordinarily give to his own vessel. What careful and prudent man could do more than to care for his vessel until overcome by physical and mental exhaustion? To do more was impossible. And yet we are told that he must, or be responsible. Among the familiar legal maxims are the following: The law intends what is agreeable to reason; it does not suffer an absurdity. Impossibility is an excuse in law, and there is no obligation to perform impossible things. Applying these maxims to the case under consideration, we think the fallacy of the reasoning below is apparent, and that it cannot and ought not to be sustained.

Reversed and remanded.

NOTES

1. *The law intends what is agreeable to reason.* What rules emerge from the two opinions of the Court of Appeals? Are they consistent? *Williams v. Hays* often is cited for the proposition that lunacy is no defense to a claim of negligence — a description of the holding that leaves out the qualifications Haight, J., added in the court's second opinion above. When are those qualifications likely to be important? Suppose a surgeon at an understaffed hospital performs surgery for 48 consecutive hours; she then capitulates to exhaustion or madness and commits an act of malpractice. What does *Williams v. Hays* suggest would be the proper instruction for the jury in such a case? What result if the defendant is an overworked associate at a large law firm, resulting in a claim of legal rather than medical malpractice?

After the second decision of the court of appeals, the plaintiff dropped his case against Hays. For details, see W. B. Hornblower, *Insanity and the Law of Negligence*, 5 Colum. L. Rev. 278 (1905).

2. *Lacking the highest order of intelligence.* In Vaughan v. Menlove, 132 Eng. Rep. 490 (C.P. 1837), the defendant built a haystack near the edge of his property. His neighbor repeatedly complained that it was a fire hazard. The defendant responded that his property was insured, and said that he would "chance it." The defendant later built a chimney through the haystack; either despite this precaution or because of it, however, the stack burst into flames. The fire spread to the defendant's barn and stables, and from there to

the plaintiff's cottages, which were entirely destroyed. The trial court told the jury that it was to decide whether the fire was caused by gross negligence on the part of the defendant; the jury further was instructed that the defendant was bound to use such reasonable caution as a prudent person would have exercised under the circumstances. The jury returned a verdict for the plaintiff. The defendant appealed, contesting the instructions given to the jury and arguing that he "ought not to be responsible for the misfortune of not possessing the highest order of intelligence."

Held, for the plaintiff, that the trial court instructed the jury correctly:

> It is contended [. . .] that the learned Judge was wrong in leaving this to the jury as a case of gross negligence, and that the question of negligence was so mixed up with reference to what would be the conduct of a man of ordinary prudence that the jury might have thought the latter the rule by which they were to decide; that such a rule would be too uncertain to act upon; and that the question ought to have been whether the Defendant had acted honestly and bona fide to the best of his own judgment. That, however, would leave so vague a line as to afford no rule at all, the degree of judgment belonging to each individual being infinitely various. [. . .] The care taken by a prudent man has always been the rule laid down; and as to the supposed difficulty of applying it, a jury has always been able to say, whether, taking that rule as their guide, there has been negligence on the occasion in question.
>
> Instead, therefore, of saying that the liability for negligence should be co-extensive with the judgment of each individual, which would be as variable as the length of the foot of each individual, we ought rather to adhere to the rule which requires in all cases a regard to caution such as a man of ordinary prudence would observe. That was in substance the criterion presented to the jury in this case[.]

What is the relationship between *Vaughan v. Menlove* and *Williams v. Hays*? Are the cases consistent? Does the same rationale underlie the two decisions?

3. *Mental disabilities*. In Lynch v. Rosenthal, 396 S.W.2d 272 (Mo. App. 1965), the plaintiff, Ronald Lynch, was a 22-year-old man with the mental capacity of a child of 10 and an I.Q. of 65. Ten years earlier the defendant's wife had taken Lynch out of the State Home for children who were "subnormal," or mentally retarded; since then Lynch had lived on the defendant's farm, helping out with chores and being treated like a member of the family. One day the defendant asked Lynch to help him with the corn picking. Lynch was instructed to walk between the corn picker and a wagon into which corn from the picker was discharged. He was to pick up any corn that fell onto the ground and put it in the wagon. While attempting to do this, Lynch stumbled into the picker. His right arm became caught in its husking

rollers, resulting in serious injuries. Lynch brought a lawsuit claiming the defendant had been negligent in failing to warn him directly that it would be dangerous to come too close to the picker. The defendant argued that Lynch had been contributorily negligent as a matter of law in coming too near the machine. Lynch's expert, a psychiatrist, testified that there are three categories of subnormal mentality: "moron, low moron, and idiot"; he said Lynch was a "low moron," and did not have the ability to appreciate the danger of moving machinery, though he could have comprehended a clear warning to stay away from it. The jury returned a verdict for Lynch, and the defendant appealed.

Held, for the plaintiff, that the evidence was sufficient to support the verdict, and that the plaintiff was not contributorily negligent as a matter of law. Said the court:

> [T]here was medical evidence to the effect that plaintiff's mental condition was such that he would understand a direct warning to stay away from [ ] machinery, which defendant did not give, but that he might not be able to understand the reason therefor. The extent of his mental deficiency was fully explored in the evidence. [. . .] Here, there is testimony to the effect that defendant directed plaintiff, a mentally subnormal person, to walk behind the picker, between it and the following wagon, which defendant himself admitted was a dangerous place to walk. The plaintiff's contributory negligence, under the evidence here, was for the jury to determine.

What was the significance in this case of Lynch's mental impairments? What is the superficial similarity between *Lynch v. Rosenthal* and *Vaughan v. Menlove* (the L case where the court said the defendant should be held to the standard of a reasonable person regardless of whether he possessed below average intelligence)? In what respects are the two cases answering different questions?

4. *Distinct defects.* From Oliver Wendell Holmes, Jr., The Common Law 86-88 (1881):

> The standards of the law are standards of general application. The law takes no account of the infinite varieties of temperament, intellect, and education which make the internal character of a given act so different in different men. It does not attempt to see men as God sees them, for more than one sufficient reason. In the first place, the impossibility of nicely measuring a man's powers and limitations is far clearer than that of ascertaining his knowledge of law, which has been thought to account for what is called the presumption that every man knows the law. But a more satisfactory explanation is, that, when men live in society, a certain average of conduct, a sacrifice of individual peculiarities going beyond a

certain point, is necessary to the general welfare. If, for instance, a man is born hasty and awkward, is always having accidents and hurting himself or his neighbors, no doubt his congenital defects will be allowed for in the courts of Heaven, but his slips are no less troublesome to his neighbors than if they sprang from guilty neglect. His neighbors accordingly require him, at his proper peril, to come up to their standard, and the courts which they establish decline to take his personal equation into account.

The rule that the law does, in general, determine liability by blameworthiness, is subject to the limitation that minute differences of character are not allowed for. The law considers, in other words, what would be blameworthy in the average man, the man of ordinary intelligence and prudence, and determines liability by that. If we fall below the level in those gifts, it is our misfortune; so much as that we must act at our peril, for the reasons just given. But he who is intelligent and prudent does not act at his peril, in theory of law. On the contrary, it is only when he fails to exercise the foresight of which he is capable, or exercises it with evil intent, that he is answerable for the consequences.

There are exceptions to the principle that every man is presumed to possess ordinary capacity to avoid harm to his neighbors, which illustrate the rule, and also the moral basis of liability in general. When a man has a distinct defect of such a nature that all can recognize it as making certain precautions impossible, he will not be held answerable for not taking them. A blind man is not required to see at his peril; and although he is, no doubt, bound to consider his infirmity in regulating his actions, yet if he properly finds himself in a certain situation, the neglect of precautions requiring eyesight would not prevent his recovering for an injury to himself, and, it may be presumed, would not make him liable for injuring another. So it is held that, in cases where he is the plaintiff, an infant of very tender years is only bound to take the precautions of which an infant is capable; the same principle may be cautiously applied where he is defendant. Insanity is a more difficult matter to deal with, and no general rule can be laid down about it. There is no doubt that in many cases a man may be insane, and yet perfectly capable of taking the precautions, and of being influenced by the motives, which the circumstances demand. But if insanity of a pronounced type exists, manifestly incapacitating the sufferer from complying with the rule which he has broken, good sense would require it to be admitted as an excuse.

Did the defendant in *Vaughan v. Menlove* have a "distinct" defect as Holmes used that expression? Did the plaintiff in *Lynch v. Rosenthal*? Holmes's understanding received the following endorsement in §289 of the Restatement (Second) of Torts (1965):

Comment n. Inferior qualities. If the actor is a child, allowance is made for his inferior qualities of mind and body, and the standard becomes that of a reasonable man with such qualities[.] If the actor is ill or otherwise physically disabled, allowance is made for such disability[.] Except in such cases, the actor is held to the standard of a reasonable man as to his attention, perception, memory, knowledge of other pertinent matters, intelligence, and judgment, even though he does not in fact have the qualities of a reasonable man. The individual who is habitually wool-gathering and inattentive, absent-minded, forgetful, ignorant or inexperienced, slow-witted, stupid, or a fool, must conform to the standards of the society in which he lives, or if he cannot conform to them must still make good the damage he does.

5. *Bridge unsafe.* In Weirs v. Jones County, 53 N.W. 321 (Iowa 1892), the defendant county determined that one of its bridges was in an unsafe condition, condemned it, and posted signs reading "Bridge unsafe" at each end. The plaintiff, unable to read English, drove his wagon over the bridge several days later. The bridge collapsed, and the plaintiff's horses and wagon fell into the stream below. He sued the county to recover for the loss of the animals and the damage to the wagon. The trial court instructed the jury as follows:

> [I]f you find from the evidence that the signboards were placed in a conspicuous place at each end of the bridge, and were of such construction as would give warning to a person of ordinary care, about to enter upon the bridge, of its unsafe condition, and if you find from the evidence that such signboards were so maintained up to and at the time plaintiff entered upon the bridge, then the fact that plaintiff was unable to read the English language, if you shall so find, would be no excuse for him[.]

So instructed, the jury brought in a verdict for the county. The plaintiff appealed, claiming the instruction was erroneous. The court of appeals affirmed:

> [T]he fact that [the plaintiff] could not read the English language should not require that the board of supervisors should put up impassable and immovable barriers, in order to protect the county from suits for damages, or to post notices or signboards of danger in all languages, so that people of every tongue might be warned of the danger. The laws of this country and the proceedings of the courts are required to be in the English language. The proceedings of the boards of supervisors, and notices ordered by them, are in the same language. The jury found that the precautions taken by the board to protect travelers were reasonably sufficient to notify persons exercising ordinary and reasonable care that the bridge was unsafe. The plaintiff cannot be allowed to claim that some standard of care shall be applied to him which is not applicable to persons in general.

What is the superficial similarity between *Weirs v. Jones County* and *Lynch v. Rosenthal*? What is the distinction between them?

6. *Reasonableness and religion.* In Friedman v. State, 54 Misc. 448 (N.Y. Cl. 1967), the plaintiff, Ruth Friedman, was a 16-year-old girl who went sightseeing with a male friend at a ski resort operated by the state of New York. Late in the afternoon they got onto the chair lift at the top of the mountain where they had been hiking and began their descent. A few minutes later the chair lift stopped moving; it had been shut down for the night by one of the resort's attendants, who did not realize that the plaintiff and her friend were still on their way down. They found themselves suspended 20 to 25 feet in the air. They called for help, but there was no response. The plaintiff lowered herself so that she was hanging from the chair, then let go and fell to the ground. She was able to walk to the base camp, where she broke in and used the phone to call for help; but in the fall she had suffered various injuries, including a broken nose, a disfiguring injury to her left nostril, trauma to her left shoulder, whiplash, and resulting "anxiety with nightmares." She brought suit against the state, which moved to dismiss the claim on the ground that the plaintiff had been contributorily negligent. The court of claims found for the plaintiff, and awarded her $35,000. Said the court:

> [I]t does not require much imagination or experience to determine that a lightly dressed 16-year-old city girl might become hysterical at the prospect of spending a night on a mountainside, suspended in the air and with no apparent reason to hope for rescue until the next morning. Secondly, we must add to the fact of expectable hysteria, the moral compulsion this young lady believed she was under, not to spend a night alone with a man.
>
> Claimants called Rabbi Herschel Stahl to testify as an expert witness on the Hebrew Law and the orthodox interpretation and observance of said Law. The Rabbi knew Miss Friedman and her family and he knew that she had been reared in an orthodox observance of her faith. Rabbi Stahl advised the Court that under the Hebrew Law, the Shulchan Arukh, there is a specific law, the Jichud, which absolutely forbids a woman to stay with a man in a place which is not available to third person. To violate this Jichud would be an overwhelming moral sin which would not only absolutely ruin this young girl's reputation but also the reputation of her parents. It was his opinion that a girl who had been trained in a 100 per cent orthodox home, as Miss Friedman was, might go even to the lengths of jumping to her death to avoid violation of the Jichud. [. . .] Rabbi Stahl's testimony established a basis for the moral compulsion that Miss Friedman believed she was under and which, in our opinion, increased the hysteria we believe a young girl might well experience regardless of faith. As stated by Justice Frankfurter in *Watts v.*

> *State of Indiana*, 338 U.S. 49, 52: "There is torture of mind as well as body; the will is as much affected by fear as by force."

The court of appeals affirmed, 297 N.Y.S.2d 850 (1969), but reduced the verdict to $20,000; it reserved judgment on the significance of any moral compulsion the plaintiff may have felt to leap from the chair lift.

What is the superficial similarity between *Friedman v. State* (as decided by the trial court in the excerpt above) and *Weirs v. Jones County*? How would you state the distinction between them? Suppose the plaintiff in *Friedman* had jumped twice as far, and that the jump therefore would have been unreasonable without the plaintiff's religious beliefs but arguably reasonable with them. What result, and on what reasoning?

7. *Contributory negligence*. In many cases plaintiffs are partly to blame for their own injuries. At common law, the doctrine of *contributory negligence* generally provided that plaintiffs whose own carelessness contributed to their injuries could collect nothing from a defendant. The doctrine was capable of producing harsh results; even if the defendant's negligence was clear and the plaintiff was only slightly at fault, the plaintiff nevertheless had to bear the entire loss. Courts ameliorated these consequences by limiting the doctrine in various ways. The most important limitation was the doctrine of *last clear chance*, which held that a plaintiff was not barred from recovery by his own negligence if the defendant had the last good opportunity to avoid the accident through the use of due care and failed to do so. The details of the doctrine varied from jurisdiction to jurisdiction, but it generally applied in cases where the plaintiff was helpless or inattentive and the defendant became aware of the danger but did not prevent it.

During the later part of the twentieth century these rules were replaced in most states by doctrines of *comparative negligence* that reduced recoveries by negligent plaintiffs in proportion to their fault but did not prevent them from recovering altogether. The shift from contributory to comparative negligence was made by judicial decisions in some states and by legislation in others, and the details of the resulting rules vary. Some states use "modified" forms of comparative negligence, allowing plaintiffs to collect only if they are not more than 50 percent responsible for their injuries; others use a "pure" rule of comparative negligence, allowing plaintiffs who are 90 percent to blame for their injuries to still bring suit to collect the remaining 10 percent. The jury may be invited to consider both how negligent each party was and the causal role that each party's negligence played in contributing to the loss. Some states also use rules of "comparative fault" that allow juries to balance the ordinary negligence of the plaintiff against the gross negligence of the defendant and to apportion liability accordingly. These rules also vary in their effect on the related but distinct defense of *assumption of the risk*. We consider the details of these doctrines and the transition between them in the chapter on Defenses later in the book.

The meaning of the negligence standard generally is the same regardless of whether the plaintiff's or defendant's conduct is being assessed; this chapter thus uses both types of cases to illustrate the meaning of the term. But can you think of situations where you would expect negligence by the plaintiff and defendant to be judged by different standards, either formally by a court or informally by a jury? What considerations bearing on the negligence standard might be present for potential plaintiffs but not for potential defendants?

8. *One degree of care*. In Fredericks v. Castora, 360 A.2d 696 (Pa. App. 1976), the plaintiff was riding in a car that was hit by two trucks. The jury found no negligence on the part of either of the trucks' drivers. The plaintiff appealed, contending that the jury should have been instructed to apply a higher standard to the defendants than it would apply to ordinary drivers; the plaintiff pointed out that both defendants were professionals who drove trucks for a living and had done so for over 20 years. The court of appeals affirmed:

> In the present case the trial court in its charge defined negligence as the want of due care under the circumstances and the failure to act as a reasonable, prudent person under the circumstances. A requirement that experienced truck drivers be subject to a higher standard of care does not impress us as being a useful concept to infuse into the law of vehicle negligence. An understanding of the ordinary standard of due care applicable to the average motorist under the multitude of changing circumstances likely to confront today's driver is already difficult to grasp and apply justly. To begin to vary the standard according to the driver's experience would render the application of any reasonably uniform standard impossible. Other jurisdictions have confronted the problem of varying degrees of care and sought to control the ceaseless variation of the concept of negligence by establishing a single standard: "Care does not increase or diminish by calling it names. We think the abstract concept of reasonable care is in itself quite difficult enough to grapple with and apply in our law without our courts gratuitously conferring honorary degrees upon it. There is only one degree of care in the law, and that is the standard of care which may reasonably be required or expected under all the circumstances of a given situation." We decline this opportunity to develop a higher standard of care for experienced truck drivers and find that the trial court did not err in its instruction on the degree of care in the present case.

9. *Supernormal strength, X-ray vision, etc.* Restatement (Second) of Torts, §298, comment d (1965), provides:

> *Necessity that the actor employ competence available*. The actor must utilize with reasonable attention and caution not only those qualities and facilities which as a reasonable man he is required to have, but also those

superior qualities and facilities which he himself has. Thus, a superior vision may enable the actor, if he pays reasonable attention, to perceive dangers which a man possessing only normal vision would not perceive, or his supernormal physical strength may enable him to avoid dangers which a man of normal strength could not avoid.

Illustration 1. A is driving a pair of well-broken horses. They become frightened and run away. A is unusually strong and could by the exercise of reasonable care in using his full muscular power bring the horses under control. He is negligent toward anyone run down by the horses if he fails to do so, although a man of ordinary muscular strength would be unable to control the horses.

From the Second Restatement, §289:

> *Illustration 12.* A is a physician. His child exhibits symptoms which A, because of his previous training and experience, should recognize as indicating that the child has scarlet fever. A fails to recognize them, and permits his child to go to school, where the child communicates the disease to B, another pupil. A is negligent in not recognizing the risk, although if he were a layman he might not be negligent.

Can these provisions be squared with the decision in *Fredericks v. Castora*? If so, what is the distinction between them? If not, which approach seems preferable?

2. *Physical Infirmities*

1. *The reasonably prudent deaf man.* In Kerr v. Connecticut Co., 140 A. 751 (Conn. 1928), the plaintiff's decedent, William Kerr, was a 58-year-old man with very poor hearing. One evening he walked home from work on Asylum Avenue in Hartford, alongside which ran the defendant's trolley line. A trolley came up behind Kerr at about 15 miles per hour. The driver saw Kerr and noticed that he was walking close enough to the tracks that he would be hit if he and the trolley both continued on their paths. The driver sounded his gong, but Kerr did not hear it and veered still closer to the tracks. The driver applied his brakes, but it was too late; the trolley knocked Kerr onto the adjacent road, and soon afterwards he died from his injuries. Kerr's administratrix sued the trolley company. The trial court found negligence on Kerr's part but no negligence on the part of the trolley driver. The plaintiff appealed and the Connecticut Supreme Court affirmed, holding that Kerr was contributorily negligent as a matter of law:

> The law required the decedent to exercise that care for his own safety which a reasonably prudent man would exercise under the same

circumstances. It is true that he had a legal right to walk where he was walking, just as any traveler has a right to walk in any part of the public highway. But as a reasonable man he was charged with knowledge that the place close to the trolley rail where he was walking was dangerous, and that a passing trolley car would necessarily strike him, and he also knew that he could not hear the bell or gong of an approaching car from the rear. It was his duty therefore to take such care as a reasonably prudent deaf man would take under those conditions.

There is nothing in the finding of facts to show that he took any precautions whatever. So far as appears, he took this position of danger and continued in it, without looking back up the "long stretch" of straight and unobstructed track from which an overtaking car would come.

2. *Blindness.* In Davis v. Feinstein, 88 A.2d 695 (Pa. 1952), the plaintiff, a blind man, was walking down 60th Street in Philadelphia, using a cane to touch the walls of abutting buildings and to tap the ground in front of him. He nevertheless fell through an open cellar door in front of the defendant's furniture store. The plaintiff sued the defendant for negligence and won a jury verdict; the trial court rejected the defendant's claim that the plaintiff should be held contributorily negligent as a matter of law. The defendant appealed, and the Pennsylvania Supreme Court affirmed:

> A blind person is not bound to discover *everything* which a person of normal vision would. He is bound to use due care under the circumstances. Due care for a blind man includes a reasonable effort to compensate for his unfortunate affliction by the use of artificial aids for discerning obstacles in his path. When an effort in this direction is made, it will ordinarily be a jury question whether or not such effort was a *reasonable* one.

What is the distinction between *Davis v. Feinstein* and *Kerr v. Connecticut Co.* (the case holding a deaf plaintiff contributorily negligent)? What is the distinction between *Davis v. Feinstein* and *Weirs v. Jones County*?

State as precisely as possible the common issue that all of the cases in this section are discussing, from *Williams v. Hays* through *Davis v. Feinstein*.

3. Age

Purtle v. Shelton
474 S.W.2d 123 (Ark. 1971)

[The defendant, Kenneth ("Bubba") Shelton, was a 17-year-old boy who accidentally shot his 16-year-old hunting companion (the plaintiff). The jury attributed an equal share of responsibility for the accident to the plaintiff and defendant. Under the state's contributory negligence rule, the plaintiff therefore recovered nothing. The plaintiff's primary claim on appeal was that the trial court erred in instructing the jury that the defendant should be found negligent only if he failed to use that degree of care which a reasonably careful minor of his age and intelligence would use in similar circumstances.]

SMITH, J. — The appellant [ ] contends that the court should have instructed the jury that Kenneth, in using a high powered rifle, was required to use the same degree of care that would be observed by an adult in like circumstances. In making that argument counsel cite our holding in *Harrelson v. Whitehead*, 365 S.W.2d 868 (Ark. 1963), where we adopted the general rule that a minor operating a motor vehicle must use the same degree of care as an adult would use. The appellant argues that motor vehicles and rifles are both dangerous and should therefore be treated alike as far as their use by a minor is concerned.

We cannot accept that argument. To begin with, the motor vehicle rule was not adopted, as our opinion in *Harrelson* reflects, solely because the driving of an automobile entails danger to others. There are other factors to be considered. A minor must be at least sixteen to operate a car by himself. He must pass an examination to demonstrate his ability to operate the vehicle on the highways. The rules governing the operation of motor vehicles are largely statutory and make no distinction, express or implied, between the degree of care to be exercised by a minor and that to be exercised by an adult. A measure of financial responsibility is required. In view of all those factors, the cases in other jurisdictions, as we pointed out in *Harrelson*, have consistently held minors to the same degree of care as adults in driving upon the highways.

In the second place, we considered the subject anew in *Jackson v. McCuiston*, 247 Ark. 862 (1969). There a farm boy almost fourteen years old was operating a tractor propelled stalk cutter — a large piece of machinery having a dangerous cutting blade. In holding that minor to an adult standard of care we quoted from three authorities. The Restatement of Torts (2d), Prosser on Torts, and Harper & James on Torts. All three authorities recognize the identical rule, that if a minor is to be held to an adult standard of care he must be engaging in an activity that is (a) dangerous to others and (b) normally engaged in only by adults. In the course of that opinion we stated that the minor "was performing a job normally expected to be done by adults."

We are unable to find any authority holding that a minor should be held to an adult standard of care merely because he engages in a dangerous activity. There is always the parallel requirement that the activity be one that is normally engaged in only by adults. So formulated, the rule is logical and sound, for when a youth is old enough to engage in adult activity there are strong policy reasons for holding him to an adult standard of care. In that situation there should be no magic in the attainment of the twenty first birthday.

We have no doubt that deer hunting is a dangerous sport. We cannot say, however, either on the basis of the record before us or on the basis of common knowledge, that deer hunting is an activity normally engaged in by adults only.

To the contrary, all the indications are the other way. A child may lawfully hunt without a hunting license at any age under sixteen. We know, from common knowledge, that youngsters only six or eight years old frequently use .22 caliber rifles and other lethal firearms to hunt rabbits, birds, and other small game. We cannot conscientiously declare, without proof and on the basis of mere judicial notice, that only adults normally go deer hunting.

In refusing to apply an adult standard of care to a minor engaged in hunting deer, we do not imply that a statute to that effect would be unwise. Indeed, we express no opinion upon that question. As judges, we cannot lay down a rule with the precision and inflexibility of a statute drafted by the legislature. If we should declare that a minor hunting deer with a high powered rifle must in all instances be held to an adult standard of care, we must be prepared to explain why the same rule should not apply to a minor hunting deer with a shotgun, to a minor hunting rabbits with a high powered rifle, to a twelve year old shooting crows with a .22, and so on down to the six year old shooting at tin cans with an air rifle. Not to mention other dangerous activities, such as the swinging of a baseball bat, the explosion of firecrackers, or the operation of an electric train. All we mean to say in this case is that we are unwilling to lay down a brand new rule of law, without precedent and without any logical or practical means of even surmising where the stopping point of the new rule might ultimately be reached. [. . .]

Affirmed.

FOGLEMAN, J. (dissenting) — [. . .] Bubba Shelton had been instructed in the skill of deer hunting by his grandfather, Melvin Tucker, a deer hunter for 30 years. Tucker testified that he had taken his grandson hunting ever since the boy was big enough to follow him in the woods with a dog, and before Bubba was big enough to carry a gun. Young Shelton, he said, had been carrying a gun ever since he was 12 or 13 years old. Tucker said that he taught the boy the safety rules of handling, shooting, loading and unloading a gun. He also taught Bubba what he called the most important thing in hunting in the woods — a certain knowledge of the identity of his target. Young Shelton, a high school senior, said that he had been deer hunting for about eight years. He had previously killed a deer. [. . .]

This court had no qualms about taking judicial notice of the hazards of automobile traffic, the frequency of accidents, often having catastrophic results, and the fact that immature individuals are no less prone to accidents, than adults, in reaching the conclusion that the time had come to require a minor to observe the same standards of care as an adult when operating an automobile. I find no logical reason for not doing the same when the use of a high powered rifle is the implement endangering the lives of all who now flock to the woods in the limited deer hunting season. Logic seems to dictate that an even higher standard be required when firearms are the death dealing instrument than is expected when the potential danger arises from the negligent use of a motor vehicle. [. . .]

BYRD, J. (dissenting) — Because a bullet fired from the gun by a minor is just as deadly as a bullet fired by an adult, I'm at a loss to understand why one with "buck fever" because of his minority is entitled to exercise any less care than any one else deer hunting. One killed by a bullet so fired would be just as dead in one instance as the other and without any more warning.

NOTES

1. *7 vs. 77.* In Roberts v. Ring, 173 N.W. 437 (Minn. 1919), the plaintiff's son, Roberts, was seven years old. As he ran across a street he was struck by an automobile driven by the defendant, who was 77 years old and had defective powers of sight and hearing. The defendant was traveling at a speed of four to five miles per hour, and said that he saw the Roberts boy when he was still about five feet in front of his car. The defendant was not able to stop, and drove his car all the way over him. The jury brought in a verdict for the defendant, and the plaintiff appealed.

Held, for the plaintiff, that the jury was not properly instructed. The court said that the trial court correctly instructed the jury to make allowances for the youth of the plaintiff's son: "Had a mature man acted as did this boy he might have been chargeable with negligence as a matter of law. But a boy of seven is not held to the same standard of care in self-protection. In considering his contributory negligence the standard is the degree of care commonly exercised by the ordinary boy of his age and maturity." But the jury incorrectly had been instructed that in deciding whether the defendant was negligent it could take into account his age and whether he suffered from any physical infirmities:

> [D]efendant's infirmities did not tend to relieve him from the charge of negligence. On the contrary they weighed against him. Such infirmities, to the extent that they were proper to be considered at all, presented only a reason why defendant should refrain from operating an automobile on a crowded street where care was required to avoid injuring other travelers. When one, by his acts or omissions causes injury to others, his negligence is to be judged by the standard of care usually exercised by the ordinarily prudent normal man.

Why hold children to a reduced standard of care but not the elderly?

2. *Motorboats vs. velocipedes.* In Dellwo v. Pearson, 107 N.W.2d 859 (Minn. 1961), the defendant, a 12-year-old boy, ran across the plaintiff's fishing line with his powerboat. This caused the plaintiff's fishing rod to break, and a piece of the reel flew into the plaintiff's eye, causing injuries for which she sought to recover. The trial court instructed the jury that "[i]n considering the matter of negligence, the duty to which defendant is held is modified because he is a child, a child not being held to the same standard of

conduct as an adult and being required to exercise only that degree of care which ordinarily is exercised by children of like age, mental capacity, and experience under the same or similar circumstances." The jury returned a general verdict for the defendant, and the plaintiffs appealed, claiming the jury had been improperly instructed. The Minnesota Supreme Court reversed:

> [I]n the circumstances of modern life, where vehicles moved by powerful motors are readily available and frequently operated by immature individuals, we should be skeptical of a rule that would allow motor vehicles to be operated to the hazard of the public with less than the normal minimum degree of care and competence.
>
> To give legal sanction to the operation of automobiles by teenagers with less than ordinary care for the safety of others is impractical today, to say the least. We may take judicial notice of the hazards of automobile traffic, the frequency of accidents, the often catastrophic results of accidents, and the fact that immature individuals are no less prone to accidents than adults. While minors are entitled to be judged by standards commensurate with age, experience, and wisdom when engaged in activities appropriate to their age, experience, and wisdom, it would be unfair to the public to permit a minor in the operation of a motor vehicle to observe any other standards of care and conduct than those expected of all others. A person observing children at play with toys, throwing balls, operating tricycles or velocipedes, or engaged in other childhood activities may anticipate conduct that does not reach an adult standard of care or prudence. However, one cannot know whether the operator of an approaching automobile, airplane, or powerboat is a minor or an adult, and usually cannot protect himself against youthful imprudence even if warned. Accordingly, we hold that in the operation of an automobile, airplane, or powerboat, a minor is to be held to the same standard of care as an adult.

What is the distinction between *Dellwo v. Pearson* and *Purtle v. Shelton?*

3. *Juvenile and adult activities.* As the opinion in *Dellwo* suggests, the law generally does not hold children to an adult standard of care when they are riding bicycles. Why? Consider that when behavior is governed by the rule of negligence, people often must coordinate their precautions; the precautions each should take often will depend on the precautions others are required to use. Drivers and pedestrians are required to use reasonable care, but each ordinarily is entitled to assume that the other will be using reasonable care as well. Drivers are not required to assume that pedestrians will walk into the street without looking. But in some situations (when?), one party may be able to see that the other probably will not be using reasonable care, and can compensate accordingly. In other situations one party's inability to measure

up to the standard of the "reasonably prudent person" may be invisible, and in that case the other party will not be able to compensate. One might argue that we should be ready to recognize people's inability to take due care in the former situations but not the latter. Indeed, this is one way to understand Holmes's argument that the law only will modify the reasonable person standard to account for "distinct defects." How helpful is this distinction in explaining the cases that have defined the reasonable person? Is being a child a "distinct defect" as Holmes used the term? In what settings is the defendant's age obvious to others?

4. *The wonder years.* In Dunn v. Teti, 421 A.2d 782 (Pa. App. 1979), the defendant swung a stick negligently, causing injuries to the plaintiff. Both parties were approximately six years old. The trial court gave summary judgment to the defendant on the ground that he was too young to be capable of negligence. The court of appeals affirmed:

> The issue with which we are confronted in this case is the minimum age below which a child is incapable of acting negligently because he lacks the attention, intelligence and judgment necessary to enable him to perceive risk and recognize its unreasonable character. The obligation to use reasonable care extends to both adults and minors, but the standard against which the acts of a child are measured to determine if they constitute negligent conduct varies from that employed for adults. When measuring the conduct of children, courts depart from the well known objective test of the care of a reasonable and prudent man, the test generally utilized to judge adult behavior, and make allowance for immaturity. A child is held to that measure of care that other minors of like age, experience, capacity and development would ordinarily exercise under similar circumstances.
>
> The application of this standard is clarified by the use of several presumptions delineating convenient points to aid in drawing the uncertain line between capacity to appreciate and guard against danger and incapacity: (1) minors under the age of seven years are conclusively presumed incapable of negligence; (2) minors between the ages of seven and fourteen years are presumed incapable of negligence, but the presumption is a rebuttable one that weakens as the fourteenth year is approached; (3) minors over the age of fourteen years are presumptively capable of negligence, with the burden placed on the minor to prove incapacity.

Cavanaugh, J., dissented:

> When determining whether a child is capable of acting negligently, the standard to be applied is that of a reasonable person of like age, intelligence and experience under the circumstances. This standard, unlike the

Majority's conclusive presumption, adequately takes into account the differing capacities of children of the same age to appreciate and cope with the dangers of a given situation.

Why is the presumption "conclusive" that a child under the age of seven cannot be capable of negligence? What is gained by such a rule that is not achieved by simply instructing the jury to compare the defendant's behavior to the (presumably low) standard set by other children of the same age? Most courts prefer to take this latter approach (see, e.g., *Standard v. Shine*, 295 S.E.2d 786 (S.C. 1982)); but most of those courts, while not adhering to the "rule of sevens" described in *Dunn v. Teti*, nevertheless still say that very young children — typically those under the age of five — are incapable of negligence. For discussion, see Dobbs, The Law of Torts §126; Restatement (Third) of Torts §10 (P.F.D. 2005).

B. RISKS AND PRECAUTIONS

United States v. Carroll Towing Co.
159 F.2d 169 (2d Cir. 1947)

[The Conners Marine Company brought this action in admiralty against the Pennsylvania Railroad for the loss of a barge, the *Anna C*. Conners owned the *Anna C* and had chartered her to the Pennsylvania in a package deal that included the services of a Conners bargee between the hours of 8 A.M. and 4 P.M. On January 2, 1944, the Pennsylvania moved the *Anna C* to the end of Pier 52 in New York Harbor. She was loaded with a cargo of flour belonging to the United States. A little later the Grace Line sent a tug it had chartered, the *Carroll*, up to Pier 52 to get another barge. The Grace Line employees — a harbormaster and his helper — had to adjust the lines of the *Anna C* in order to get to the other barge; when they were done, they improperly retied the *Anna C*'s lines. As a result, the *Anna C* later broke away from the pier and bumped into a tanker whose propeller punched a hole in the *Anna C* beneath the waterline. At the time, the Conners Company's bargee, who was supposed to be aboard the *Anna C*, was elsewhere; thus nobody discovered the leak until it was too late to pump the water from the barge. The *Anna C* sank along with her cargo. The parties affected by the accident brought various claims against one another.

[The court determined that the Grace Line's harbormaster and deckhand were negligent in retying the *Anna C* to the pier, so they were partly responsible for the ensuing damage. The court then considered whether the Conners Company also had been negligent because its bargee was not aboard the *Anna C* at the critical moment.]

LEARNED HAND, J. — [. . .] [I]f the bargee had been on board, and had done his duty to his employer, he would have gone below at once, examined the injury, and called for help from the "Carroll" and the Grace Line tug. Moreover, it is clear that these tugs could have kept the barge afloat, until they had safely beached her, and saved her cargo. This would have avoided what we shall call the "sinking damages." Thus, if it was a failure in the Conners Company's proper care of its own barge, for the bargee to be absent, the company can recover only one third of the "sinking" damages from the Carroll Company [the owner of the tugboat] and one third from the Grace Line. For this reason the question arises whether a barge owner is slack in the care of his barge if the bargee is absent.

[The court then considered whether it was negligent for the Conners Company to have an absent bargee. After reviewing cases on the subject, it continued:] It appears from the foregoing review that there is no general rule to determine when the absence of a bargee or other attendant will make the owner of the barge liable for injuries to other vessels if she breaks away from her moorings. However, in any cases where he would be so liable for injuries to others, obviously he must reduce his damages proportionately, if the injury is to his own barge. It becomes apparent why there can be no such general rule, when we consider the grounds for such a liability.

Since there are occasions when every vessel will break from her moorings, and since, if she does, she becomes a menace to those about her; the owner's duty, as in other similar situations, to provide against resulting injuries is a function of three variables: (1) The probability that she will break away; (2) the gravity of the resulting injury, if she does; (3) the burden of adequate precautions. Possibly it serves to bring this notion into relief to state it in algebraic terms: if the probability be called P; the injury, L; and the burden, B; liability depends upon whether B is less than L multiplied by P: i.e., whether $B < PL$.

Applied to the situation at bar, the likelihood that a barge will break from her fasts and the damage she will do, vary with the place and time; for example, if a storm threatens, the danger is greater; so it is, if she is in a crowded harbor where moored barges are constantly being shifted about. On the other hand, the barge must not be the bargee's prison, even though he lives aboard; he must go ashore at times. We need not say whether, even in such crowded waters as New York Harbor a bargee must be aboard at night at all[.] We leave that question open; but we hold that it is not in all cases a sufficient answer to a bargee's absence without excuse, during working hours, that he has properly made fast his barge to a pier, when he leaves her. In the case at bar the bargee left at five o'clock in the afternoon of January 3rd, and the flotilla broke away at about two o'clock in the afternoon of the following day, twenty-one hours afterwards. The bargee had been away all the time, and we hold that his fabricated story was affirmative evidence that he had no excuse for his absence. At the locus in quo — especially during the short January days and in the full tide of war activity — barges were being constantly "drilled" in and out. Certainly it was not beyond reasonable expectation that, with the inevitable haste and bustle, the work might not be done with adequate care. In such circumstances we hold — and it is all that we do hold — that it was a fair requirement that the Conners Company should have a bargee aboard (unless he had some excuse for his absence), during the working hours of daylight.

NOTES

1. *Introducing the Hand formula.* Judge Hand's style of analysis is perhaps the best-known and most widely discussed method of analyzing whether a party took reasonable care to prevent an accident. The Hand formula presents a number of difficulties in application, however, and is not without its detractors. One purpose of the cases in this section of the chapter is to explore how the formula might be applied to various cases involving claims of negligence. In each case, try to identify the three elements of the Hand formula: B, the "burden" or cost of the untaken precaution that the plaintiff claims the defendant should have used; P, the probability of the accident occurring if the precaution were not taken; and L, the loss that would result if the accident were to occur. The most usual interpretation of the Hand formula is economic: the goal is to put dollar values on B and L to the extent possible. As you read this section, consider whether there are other ways to think about the formula's elements.

To illustrate, suppose that if the defendant fails to take some precaution, such as keeping a bargee on its barge, there is a 10 percent chance that during the coming year an accident will occur; and if it does occur the total cost of the accident will be $100,000 (the typical cost of a barge). In this example, P is .10; L is $100,000; so P × L — the expected cost of the accident — is $10,000. Another way of looking at this is to say that $10,000 is the average size of the accident costs that will result if this same situation is played out repeatedly over a long period of time: we would expect one accident about every ten years if a given barge owner always fails to keep a bargee on board; the average annual cost of this to a barge owner will be $10,000 ($100,000 divided by 10 years, or multiplied by .10; if an accident occurred every 20 years, we would multiply by .05). B in this case is the cost of having a bargee. If a bargee would cost each barge owner $5,000 per year, then the Hand formula would suggest that it is negligent to fail to use one. If hiring a bargee would cost each barge owner $30,000 per year, then the Hand formula suggests that it is *not* negligent to do without one: it would be cheaper (and therefore preferable) to let the accidents occur; it would be a waste to hire a $30,000 bargee to prevent a $10,000 accident (recalling that $10,000 is the average cost of the accidents; when the accidents happen, they will cost more than that, but nine times out of ten they won't happen at all).

The illustration just considered is unrealistic because it usually is impossible to put clear numbers on each element of the Hand formula. Hand himself said that "[of the factors in the formula] care [or B] is the only one ever susceptible of quantitative estimate, and often that is not. The injuries are always a variable within limits, which do not admit of even approximate ascertainment; and, although probability might theoretically be estimated, if any statistics were available, they never are; and, besides, probability varies with the severity of the injuries. It follows that all such attempts are illusory; if serviceable at all, they are so only to the extent that they center attention upon which one of the factors may be determinative in any given situation." *Moisan v. Loftus*, 178 F.2d 148 (2d Cir. 1949). Even so, however, it may be possible to compare the *relative* relationships between B, P, and L in different cases, and so to use the formula to shed light on their outcomes.

Juries deciding negligence claims, meanwhile, are not told to apply the Hand formula. As noted in the previous section, jury instructions generally just ask whether the defendant behaved in the way that a reasonably prudent person would under the same circumstances. This test — the "reasonable man" or "reasonable person" test — rarely is supplemented with any further guidance, though occasionally a jury will be invited to compare the risks and benefits of a defendant's behavior. The Hand formula sometimes is used, however, by courts of appeal when they review jury verdicts:

> Currently, there seem to be four basic appellate stances toward the Hand formula: (1) use it routinely, sometimes even *sua sponte*, (2) use it if the appeal is couched in cost-benefit terms, (3) ignore it by disposing even of explicit cost-benefit claims under the reasonable person standard, and (4) reject it as a matter of law. A few courts (most clearly those of Louisiana and Michigan) take approach (1). No court, to my knowledge, takes approach (4). The majority of courts take either approach (2) or approach (3).

Gilles, *The Invisible Hand Formula*, 80 Va. L. Rev. 1015 (1994). Yet regardless of how much or how little the Hand formula is used explicitly by courts, it may be a useful tool for analysis. Some commentators — most famously Richard Posner — consider the Hand formula a compelling description of what judges (and perhaps juries) *do*, whether or not they say so explicitly or even realize it consciously. Appellate opinions, both modern and old, often analyze cases in terms that may resemble the Hand formula; consider this passage from the old English case of *Mackintosh v. Mackintosh*, 2 Macph. 1347 (1864):

> [I]t must be observed that in all cases the amount of care which a prudent man will take must vary infinitely according to circumstances. No prudent man in carrying a lighted candle through a powder magazine would fail to take more care than if he was going through a damp cellar. The amount of care will be proportionate to the degree of risk run, and to the magnitude of the mischief that may be occasioned.

Does this statement amount to the same point made by the Hand formula? If not, how is it different? Soon we will see additional examples of old cases that may or may not involve the type of balancing Hand describes. As you read them, consider whether more explicit thought about the Hand formula and its implications would have led to any difference in the court's result or analysis, or whether reflection on the Hand formula now makes the logic of the cases seem any clearer than the opinions themselves do.

Some commentators have argued that the Hand formula can be justified in ethical as well as economic terms:

> From an economic perspective the Hand formula makes excellent sense. The formula can be seen as designed to encourage efficient investments in safety and risk reduction; as such, it has served as a cornerstone for economic analysis. Yet despite its economic implications, the Hand formula is also conducive to an ethical explanation of the negligence liability standard. Typically the burden of risk prevention is borne in the first instance by the defendant. Take the defendant whose conduct creates a risk to others that can be measured as $100 — a risk which the defendant could prevent by incorporating a $50 precaution. If the defendant fails to adopt this precaution and hence acts negligently, the defendant's choice shows that he attaches a greater weight to his own interests than to the interests of others. By ranking his own welfare as more important than the welfare of others, the defendant's conduct can correctly be reproached as ethically improper.

Gary Schwartz, *Mixed Theories of Tort Law: Affirming Both Deterrence and Corrective Justice*, 75 Tex. L. Rev. 1801, 1819-1820 (1997). Posner offers a related suggestion. Usually his theory is thought to be that the Hand formula, or the intuition behind it, is attractive to courts because it gives people incentives to behave efficiently — i.e., to keep waste of all sorts to a minimum by either preventing accidents or allowing them to occur, whichever is cheaper. It is not necessary to his claim, however, that courts think of efficiency as an important goal; he suggests that perhaps the Hand formula reflects intuitions about blameworthiness:

> Because we do not like to see resources squandered, a judgment of negligence has inescapable overtones of moral disapproval, for it implies that there was a cheaper alternative to the accident. Conversely, there is no moral indignation in the case in which the cost of prevention would have exceeded the cost of the accident. [. . .] If indignation has its roots in inefficiency, we do not have to decide whether regulation, or compensation, or retribution, or some mixture of these best describes the dominant purpose of negligence law. In any case, the judgment of liability depends ultimately on a weighing of costs and benefits.

Posner, *A Theory of Negligence*, 1 J. Legal Stud. 29 (1972). Does this imply that *overinvestment* in safety should provoke just as much indignation as underinvestment?

These theories suggest a final question to consider as you examine the cases and problems that follow: does analysis under the Hand formula produce the same outcomes as would be generated by worrying about fairness and corrective justice?

2. *The area of ordinary prevision.* In Adams v. Bullock, 227 N.Y. 208 (1919), the defendant ran a trolley line in the city of Dunkirk. The trolleys were powered by a system of overhead wires. At one point the trolley line was crossed by a bridge that carried the tracks of the Nickle Plate and Pennsylvania railroads. As the court recounted: "Pedestrians often use the bridge as a short cut between streets, and children play on it. [. . .] [T]he plaintiff, a boy of twelve years, came across the bridge, swinging a wire about eight feet long. In swinging it, he brought it in contact with the defendant's trolley wire, which ran beneath the structure. The side of the bridge was protected by a parapet eighteen inches wide. Four feet seven and three-fourths inches below the top of the parapet, the trolley wire was strung. The plaintiff was shocked and burned when the wires came together." A jury returned a verdict for the plaintiff. The defendant appealed on the ground that the evidence was insufficient to support the verdict.

Held, for the defendant, that the trial court erred in entering judgment on the verdict. Said the court (per Cardozo, J.):

> The defendant in using an overhead trolley was in the lawful exercise of its franchise. Negligence, therefore, cannot be imputed to it because it used that system and not another. There was, of course, a duty to adopt all reasonable precautions to minimize the resulting perils. We think there is no evidence that this duty was ignored. The trolley wire was so placed that no one standing on the bridge or even bending over the parapet could reach it. Only some extraordinary casualty, not fairly within the area of ordinary prevision, could make it a thing of danger. Reasonable care in the use of a destructive agency imports a high degree of vigilance. But no vigilance, however alert, unless fortified by the gift of prophecy, could have predicted the point upon the route where such an accident would occur. It might with equal reason have been expected anywhere else. At any point upon the route, a mischievous or thoughtless boy might touch the wire with a metal pole, or fling another wire across it. If unable to reach it from the walk, he might stand upon a wagon or climb upon a tree. No special danger at this bridge warned the defendant that there was need of special measures of precaution. No like accident had occurred before. No custom had been disregarded. We think that ordinary caution did not involve forethought of this extraordinary peril. [. . .]
>
> There is, we may add, a distinction not to be ignored between electric light and trolley wires. The distinction is that the former may be insulated. Chance of harm, though remote, may betoken negligence, if needless. Facility of protection may impose a duty to protect. With trolley

wires, the case is different. Insulation is impossible. Guards here and there are of little value. To avert the possibility of this accident and others like it at one point or another on the route, the defendant must have abandoned the overhead system, and put the wires underground. Neither its power nor its duty to make the change is shown.

How might you restate the court's reasoning using the Hand formula? How might you argue that the opinion *doesn't* amount to an application of the Hand formula?

3. *A social being is not immune from social risks.* In Bolton v. Stone, [1951] A.C. 850, 1 All E.R. 1078 (H.L.), *rev'g* [1950] 1 K.B. 201, the plaintiff, Bessie Stone, lived on a residential street adjoining Lord's Cricket Ground. The grounds were enclosed on the plaintiff's side by a seven-foot fence. One day the plaintiff was standing in front of her garden gate when she was struck by a ball hit out of the Cricket Ground. There was evidence that on rare occasions over the previous 30 years balls had been hit over the fence, though none had caused injury; in any event, all agreed that the hit was excellent, covering a distance of about 78 yards, which was 20 yards beyond the fence.

The plaintiff sued the club that owned the grounds, including a negligence count among her claims. The defendants were awarded judgment after a bench trial. The Court of Appeal reversed, holding that the trial court erred in finding no negligence; the House of Lords reversed again, holding that there must be judgment for the defendants. Said Reid, L.J.:

> My Lords, it was readily foreseeable that an accident such as befell the respondent might possibly occur during one of the appellants' cricket matches. Balls had been driven into the public road from time to time, and it was obvious that if a person happened to be where a ball fell that person would receive injuries which might or might not be serious. On the other hand, it was plain that the chance of that happening was small. [. . .] It follows that the chance of a person ever being struck even in a long period of years was very small. [. . .]
>
> In the crowded conditions of modern life even the most careful person cannot avoid creating some risks and accepting others. What a man must not do, and what I think a careful man tries not to do, is to create a risk which is substantial. [. . .] In my judgment, the test to be applied here is whether the risk of damage to a person on the road was so small that a reasonable man in the position of the appellants, considering the matter from the point of view of safety, would have thought it right to refrain from taking steps to prevent the danger. In considering that matter I think that it would be right to take into account not only how remote is the chance that a person might be struck, but also how serious the consequences are likely to be if a person is struck, but I do not think that it would be right to take into account the difficulty of remedial measures.

If cricket cannot be played on a ground without creating a substantial risk, then it should not be played there at all.

Said Radcliffe, L.J.:

> My Lords, I agree that this appeal must be allowed. I agree with regret, because I have much sympathy with the decision that commended itself to the majority of the members of the Court of Appeal. I can see nothing unfair in the appellants being required to compensate the respondent for the serious injury that she has received as a result of the sport that they have organised on their cricket ground at Cheetham Hill, but the law of negligence is concerned less with what is fair than with what is culpable, and I cannot persuade myself that the appellants have been guilty of any culpable act or omission in this case. [...]
>
> It seems to me that a reasonable man, taking account of the chances against an accident happening, would not have felt himself called on either to abandon the use of the ground for cricket or to increase the height of his surrounding fences. He would have done what the appellants did. In other words, he would have done nothing. Whether, if the unlikely event of an accident did occur and his play turn to another's hurt, he would have thought it equally proper to offer no more consolation to his victim than the reflection that a social being is not immune from social risks, I do not say, for I do not think that that is a consideration which is relevant to legal liability.

In what respects do the statements from the House of Lords resemble the Hand formula? In what respects are they different?

4. *Marginal analysis.* If the Hand formula is to be used correctly as an economic matter it has to be applied at the margin. What does this mean? A typical analysis of whether a defendant was negligent involves picking an untaken precaution and asking if due care — or, here, the Hand formula — required it. But the important question is not just whether taking the precaution would have been better than doing nothing; it is whether the precaution was cost-justified considering the other precautions that also were available.

A simplified example will make the point clearer. Imagine a case like *Bolton v. Stone,* but one in which we have more precise information about the costs and effectiveness of various precautions the defendants might have taken. Suppose that the only risk at issue is the chance that a cricket ball will hit a pedestrian on the head, inflicting a $50,000 injury. Suppose further that the defendants can choose between the following precautions:

> a. They can build no fence around the cricket ground. In this case there is a 10 percent chance each year that someone will be hit by a

cricket ball and sustain a $50,000 injury — an "expected" accident cost of $5,000 per year (50,000 × 0.10).

b. They can build a fence seven feet tall. Assume that the cost of building and then maintaining the fence would be $2,000 per year, and that it would reduce the chance of the $50,000 accident each year to 2 percent — an expected annual cost of $1,000 (50,000 × 0.02).

c. They can build a fence ten feet tall. Assume that the cost of building and then maintaining this fence would be $2,500 per year, and that it would reduce the chance of an accident each year to 1.8 percent — an expected cost of $900 (50,000 × 0.018).

Given these assumptions, what does the economic interpretation of due care require the defendants to do? Spending $2,500 to build a ten-foot fence would reduce the annual expected cost of accidents from $5,000 to $900; on this view the precaution clearly seems cost-justified. But there is another option: building a seven-foot fence. The *marginal cost* (in other words, the additional, incremental cost) of moving from a seven-foot fence to a ten-foot fence is $500 per year. The *marginal benefit* of doing so is a $100 reduction each year in accident costs. So suppose the defendants build the seven-foot fence, and the plaintiff is hit by a cricket ball that goes just over it; the evidence shows that a ten-foot fence would have prevented the accident. Does the Hand formula suggest that the defendant should be held liable?

5. *Heroic measures.* In Eckert v. Long Island R. Co., 43 N.Y. 502 (1871), the plaintiff's decedent was having a conversation with another person about 50 feet from the defendant's railroad tracks in East New York when a train arrived from Queens at a speed of 12 to 20 miles per hour. The plaintiff's witnesses heard no signal from the train's whistle. The plaintiff claimed that the defendant was negligent in running its train at that speed through a thickly populated neighborhood. A child of three or four years of age was sitting on the defendant's track as the train approached and would have been run over if not removed. The plaintiff's decedent saw the child, ran to it, seized it, and threw it clear of danger. He did not have time to get clear himself, however, and was hit by the train. He died later that night. The plaintiff won a jury verdict and the trial court entered judgment upon it. The defendant appealed, claiming that the plaintiff's case should have been dismissed because he was contributorily negligent. The court of appeals affirmed:

> The evidence showed that the train was approaching in plain view of the deceased, and had he for his own purposes attempted to cross the track, or with a view to save property placed himself voluntarily in a position where he might have received an injury from a collision with the train, his conduct would have been grossly negligent, and no recovery could have been had for such injury. But the evidence further showed that

there was a small child upon the track, who, if not rescued, must have been inevitably crushed by the rapidly approaching train. This the deceased saw, and he owed a duty of important obligation to this child to rescue it from its extreme peril, if he could do so without incurring great danger to himself. Negligence implies some act of commission or omission wrongful in itself. Under the circumstances in which the deceased was placed, it was not wrongful in him to make every effort in his power to rescue the child, compatible with a reasonable regard for his own safety. It was his duty to exercise his judgment as to whether he could probably save the child without serious injury to himself. If, from the appearances, he believed that he could, it was not negligence to make an attempt so to do, although believing that possibly he might fail and receive an injury himself. He had no time for deliberation. He must act instantly, if at all, as a moment's delay would have been fatal to the child. The law has so high a regard for human life that it will not impute negligence to an effort to preserve it, unless made under such circumstances as to constitute rashness in the judgment of prudent persons. For a person engaged in his ordinary affairs, or in the mere protection of property, knowingly and voluntarily to place himself in a position where he is liable to receive a serious injury, is negligence, which will preclude a recovery for an injury so received; but when the exposure is for the purpose of saving life, it is not wrongful, and therefore not negligent unless such as to be regarded as either rash or reckless. The jury were warranted in finding the deceased free from negligence under the rule as above stated. The motion for a nonsuit was, therefore, properly denied. [. . .]

What was the untaken precaution by Eckert that formed the basis of the railroad's argument? What was its cost? How did it compare to the cost of the actions Eckert did take?

6. *The economics of* Eckert. At first the dramatic facts of the *Eckert* case might seem an unlikely occasion for application of the Hand formula. *Eckert* nevertheless has generated some discussion of the role of costs and benefits in applying the negligence standard. Consider Terry, *Negligence*. 29 Harv. L. Rev. 40, 42-44 (1915):

> The plaintiff's intestate, seeing a child on a railroad track just in front of a rapidly approaching train, went upon the track to save him. He did save him, but was himself killed by the train. The jury were allowed to find that he had not been guilty of contributory negligence. The question was of course whether he had exposed himself to an unreasonably great risk. Here the [. . .] elements of reasonableness were as follows:
>
> (a)   The magnitude of the risk was the probability that he would be killed or hurt. That was very great.

(b) The principal object was his own life, which was very valuable.

(c) The collateral object was the child's life, which was also very valuable.

(d) The utility of the risk was the probability that he could save the child. That must have been fairly great, since he in fact succeeded. Had there been no fair chance of saving the child, the conduct would have been unreasonable and negligent.

(e) The necessity of the risk was the probability that the child would not have saved himself by getting off the track in time.

Here, although the magnitude of the risk was very great and the principal object very valuable, yet the value of the collateral object and the great utility and necessity of the risk counterbalanced those considerations, and made the risk reasonable. The same risk would have been unreasonable, had the creature on the track been a kitten, because the value of the collateral object would have been small.

Compare Posner's more recent analysis:

Almost any tort problem can be solved as a contract problem, by asking what the people involved in an accident would have agreed on in advance with regard to safety measures if transaction costs had not been prohibitive. A striking example is provided by the old case of *Eckert v. Long Island Railroad*. The defendant's train was going too fast and without adequate signals in a densely populated area. A small child was sitting on the tracks oblivious to the oncoming train. Eckert ran to rescue the child and managed to throw it clear but was himself killed. The court held that Eckert had not been contributorily negligent, and therefore his estate could recover damages for the railroad's negligence. For "it was not wrongful in him to make every effort in his power to rescue the child, compatible with a reasonable regard for his own safety. It was his duty to exercise his judgment as to whether he could probably save the child without serious injury to himself." If, as implied by this passage, the probability that the child would be killed if the rescue was not attempted was greater than the probability that Eckert would get himself killed saving the child, and if the child's life was at least as valuable as Eckert's life, then the expected benefit of the rescue to the railroad in reducing an expected liability cost to the child's parents was greater than the expected cost of rescue. In that event, but for prohibitive transaction costs, the railroad would have hired Eckert to attempt the rescue, so it should be required to compensate him ex post.

Posner, Economic Analysis of Law 272 (5th ed. 1998). What is the relationship between analysis of *Eckert* under the Hand formula and the analysis Posner conducts by imagining a hypothetical contract between the parties? Is there any difference between the two approaches?

7. *Even the claims of humanity must be weighed in a balance.* In The Margharita, 140 F. 820 (5th Cir. 1905), the libelant, Martinez, was a seaman aboard a cargo ship bound from a Chilean port to Savannah. His libel alleged that he fell overboard one evening as the vessel was rounding Cape Horn. By the time he was pulled back onto the boat, a "shark or other marine monster" had bitten off his leg a few inches below the knee. There was no surgeon on the ship; the nearest place where one could be found was Port Stanley in the Falkland Islands, a detour which would have taken the ship perhaps three weeks to complete. The *Margharita* did not stop at Port Stanley or any other port, but continued without interruption on its 7,000 mile voyage to Georgia. It arrived three months later. There Martinez had a small additional portion of the leg amputated; in the later words of the court of appeals, "The result obtained was satisfactory, and according to the surgeon who performed the operation and testified for [Martinez] he now has a fairly good stump."

Martinez sued the owners of the ship for negligence in failing to seek aid for him at Port Stanley or some other port between Cape Horn and Savannah. The trial court gave judgment to Martinez, and awarded him $1,500 in damages:

> It is not difficult to conceive the unspeakable agony — indeed, torture — which the libelant must have experienced in his long voyage of more than 7,000 miles to Savannah with the ragged extremity of his cruelly wounded leg incased at times in a box of hot tar and at other times rudely bandaged by the kind, but inexperienced, hands of his shipmates. According to his own testimony his sufferings were so great that he often lost consciousness. [. . .] [It] is the duty of the courts, not only to compensate the seaman for his unnecessary and unmerited suffering when the duty of the ship is disregarded, but to emphasize the importance of humane and correct judgment under the circumstances on the part of the master.

The court of appeals reversed:

> Before surgical aid could have been obtained by putting into Port Stanley in the Falkland Islands, the nearest available point, the acute and dangerous stage resulting from the injury had passed. Before that port could have been reached the healing processes of nature were under way and had made progress. [. . .] No permanent loss or disability was occasioned by the long delay in securing surgical aid. The appellee's leg was gone, and all that a surgeon could do was to put it in condition to heal properly with the soft parts covering the ends of the bones. Therefore, the only injury resulting from the delay was the prolongation of the suffering

occasioned by the healing wound. With these conditions obtaining as to the appellee, was the master bound to deviate from his course and put into Port Stanley? The measure of a master's obligation to a seaman who is severely injured with the ship at sea is discussed by Mr. Justice Brown in [*The Iroquois*, 194 U.S. 240, 243 (1904)]:

> [...] "With reference to putting into port, all that can be demanded of the master is the exercise of reasonable judgment and the ordinary acquaintance of a seaman with the geography and resources of the country. He is not absolutely bound to put into such port if the cargo be such as would be seriously injured by the delay. Even the claims of humanity must be weighed in a balance with the loss that would probably occur to the owners of the ship and cargo. A seafaring life is a dangerous one, accidents of this kind are peculiarly liable to occur, and the general principle of law that a person entering a dangerous employment is regarded as assuming the ordinary risks of such employment is peculiarly applicable to the case of seamen."
> [...]

The accident occurred upon "one of the loneliest and most tempestuous seas in the world," and in winter. The making of an unknown harbor would have been fraught with uncertainty, and possibly with difficulties of navigation. The delay incident to a deviation from the course and stoppage would have been of somewhat indefinite duration. During this time the owners of the bark would sustain heavy loss in the wages and provisions of the crew and the demurrage of the bark.

We have examined the cases cited by appellee in support of the contention the master should have put into some intermediate harbor to secure surgical aid and relief, and it is worthy of note that in each of them, where this was held to be the duty of the master, permanent injuries and disabilities resulted from his failure to pursue this course.

How might the reasoning in this case be expressed using the Hand formula? Can the $1,500 damage award by the trial court be used as the measure of "L"? Is it of any use to try to imagine how the parties might have handled this situation by contract if they had foreseen it?

8. A *dissenting view.* In his article *Hand, Posner, and the Myth of the "Hand Formula,"* 4 Theoretical Inquiries L. 145 (2003), Professor Richard Wright takes a skeptical view of the Hand formula:

> The legal literature generally assumes that an aggregate risk utility test is employed to determine whether conduct was reasonable or negligent. However, this test is infrequently mentioned by the courts and almost never explains their decisions. Instead, they apply, explicitly or implicitly, various justice based standards that take into account the rights and relationships among the parties. [...]

Under the aggregate risk utility test, it is proper (indeed required) for you to put others at even great risk for your solely private benefit if your expected private gain outweighs the others' expected losses. However, such behavior, which treats others solely as a means to one's own ends, is condemned by common morality and the underlying principles of justice as a failure to properly respect the equal dignity and freedom of others. [...] [T]he reported cases rarely involve situations in which the sole justification offered for the defendant's creation of significant risks to another is some private (economic or non-economic) benefit to the defendant. The private benefit issue rather arises indirectly in situations involving participatory plaintiffs or socially valuable activities, in which [...] the creation of significant risks to others is deemed reasonable if and only if the risks are not too serious; they are necessary (unavoidable) in order for the participatory plaintiffs or everyone in society to obtain some desired benefit; they have been reduced to the maximum extent feasible without causing an unacceptable loss in the desired benefit; and they are significantly outweighed by the desired benefit. While the private benefits desired by those being put at risk and the equal freedom enhancing benefits to everyone in society are taken into account, the purely private benefits to the defendant (or some third party) are not taken into account.

Wright then discusses many common law cases sometimes said to illustrate the logic and use of the Hand formula, and argues that none of them actually do. Here are excerpts from his comments on three of the note cases just considered.

a. Adams v. Bullock:

Cardozo's opinion does not engage in any aggregate-risk-utility balancing, but rather employs, at most, the non balancing, prohibitive cost test for socially valuable activities. Cardozo stated that the "[c]hance of harm, *though remote*, may betoken negligence, *if needless. Facility of protection may impose a duty to protect*" (emphasis added). He did not qualify this statement by any reference to the cost of precaution. His stated reason for holding that the defendant had not been negligent is not that the burden of the precautions was greater than the risk, but rather that the risk was too remote. While noting, in dicta, that even a remote risk might be negligent if needless, Cardozo pointed out that the only way to eliminate the remote risk in this case would be to shut down the trolley or put the wires underground (which would seem to be impossible while continuing to operate the trolley, given the need for the trolley to maintain contact with the electric wires), and requiring either would be contrary to the grant of the trolley franchise: "The defendant in using an overhead trolley was in the lawful exercise of its franchise. Negligence, therefore, cannot be imputed to it because it used that system and not another." The inherent risks of the trolley system with its overhead electric wires were deemed acceptable by the community since the trolley system provided substantial transportation benefits to everyone in the community, the risks were not serious and were reduced to the maximum extent feasible while still obtaining the desired social benefits, and the social benefits greatly outweighed the risks.

b. Bolton v. Stone:

[E]ach of the Law Lords explicitly or implicitly assumed that the defendant cricket club would be liable for negligence if the risk to non-participants like Miss Stone were foreseeable and of a sufficiently high level, regardless of the expected utility to the participants or the burden of eliminating the risk. Each concluded that the risk was foreseeable, but not of a sufficiently high level to be deemed unreasonable as a matter of law, given the very low combined probability of, first, a ball's being hit into the road and, second, the ball striking someone on the little used residential side street. Although several of the Law Lords stated that the risk must be "likely" or "probable," they clearly merely meant that the risk must be significant rather than remote or minimal. The literal (greater than 50%) interpretation of "likely" or "probable" would eliminate almost all negligence cases, which could hardly have been intended. Moreover, each of the Law Lords viewed the negligence issue in *Bolton* as one that could have been decided either way by the trial court, despite the minimal risk.

c. Eckert v. Long Island Railroad Co.:

The critical passage in the majority opinion [...] states: "[...] For a person engaged in his ordinary affairs, or in the mere protection of property, knowingly and voluntarily to place himself in a position where he is liable to receive a serious injury, is negligence, which will preclude a recovery for an injury so received; but when the exposure is for the purpose of saving life, it is not wrongful, and therefore not negligent unless such as to be regarded either rash or reckless."

This "rash or reckless" test, rather than the aggregate risk utility test, is the test that the courts employ to assess the reasonableness of putting oneself at risk in order to save the life of another. In these emergency rescue situations, the courts generally hold that, no matter how much the risk to the would be rescuer may seem to exceed the expected benefit to the potential rescuee, the would be rescuer's conduct is morally praiseworthy, rather than morally blameworthy or unreasonable, unless it was "foolhardy," "wanton," "rash," or "reckless." The facts and holdings of these cases, including *Eckert*, indicate that the risk to the plaintiff rescuer is considered foolhardy, wanton, rash, or reckless only if the plaintiff put his own life at serious risk merely to save property rather than the life of another person or if there was no real or fair chance of saving the life of the person whom the plaintiff was attempting to rescue. In those circumstances, the plaintiff is failing to show proper respect for his own life by throwing it away for no good reason. However, if there is a fair chance of saving another's life, one's voluntary attempt to save the other's life, even at a great risk to oneself that exceeds the chance of saving the other, is deemed heroic and morally praiseworthy, both by ordinary persons and by the law.

How convincing are Wright's arguments? How do you think he would interpret the appellate court's decision in *The Margharita*?

9. *Untaken precautions (problem)*. In Davis v. Consolidated Rail Corp., 788 F.2d 1260 (7th Cir. 1986), the plaintiff, Davis, was an inspector for the Trailer Train Co., a lessor of cars to railroads. He made his inspections in railroad yards, among them Conrail's yard in East St. Louis. On the day of the accident at issue here, Davis, driving an unmarked van that was the same color as the Conrail vans used in the yard but that lacked the identifying "C" painted on each Conrail van, arrived at the yard and saw a train coming in from east to west. He noticed that several of the cars in the train were Trailer Train cars that he was required to inspect. The train halted and was decoupled near the front; the locomotive, followed by several cars, pulled away to the west. The remainder of the train was stretched out for three-quarters of a mile to the east; and because it lay on a curved section of the track, its rear end was not visible from the point of decoupling. An employee of Conrail named Lundy saw Davis sitting in his van, didn't know who he was, thought it queer that he was there, but did nothing.

Shortly afterward Davis began to conduct his inspection. This required him to crawl underneath the cars to look for cracks. He did not hang a metal blue flag on the train, as longstanding railroad custom and regulation required him to do. Unbeknownst to Davis, a locomotive had just coupled with the other (eastern) end of the train. It had a crew of four. Two were in the cab of the locomotive. The other two, one of whom was designated as the rear brakeman, were somewhere alongside the train; the record did not show exactly where they were, but neither was at the western end of the train, where Davis was. The crew was ordered to move the train several car lengths to the east because it was blocking a switch. The crew made the movement, but without blowing the train's horn or ringing its bell. The only warning Davis had of the impending movement was the sudden rush of air as the air brakes were activated. He tried to scramble to safety before the train started up but his legs were caught beneath the wheels of the car as he crawled out from under it. One leg was severed just below the knee; most of the foot on the other leg also was sliced off.

Davis presented three theories of the railroad's negligence to the jury; as commonly is the case, each of the three theories consisted of an untaken precaution by the railroad that might have prevented the accident. His first claim was that Conrail's employee Lundy, whose auto was equipped with a two-way radio, should have notified the crew of the train that an unknown person was sitting in a van parked near the tracks. His second theory was that before the train was moved a member of the crew should have walked its length, looking under the cars. His third theory was that it was negligent for the crew to move the train without first blowing its horn.

A jury found for Davis, assessed his damages at $3 million, but found that Davis's own negligence had been one third responsible for the accident, and therefore awarded him $2 million. The railroad appealed. In addition to denying that it was negligent in failing to take the precautions Davis described, the railroad argued that the rule regarding blue flagging relieved it from any duty of care to persons who might be injured by a sudden starting of the train, because all such persons can protect themselves by blue flagging and are careless if they fail to do so.

What result would you expect on these facts? How might the Hand formula be used to assess Davis's theories of negligence and the railroad's responses? What analysis of the case is suggested by Professor Wright's arguments?

10. *The new orthodoxy.* From the Restatement (Third) of Torts (P.F.D. 2005):

§3. NEGLIGENCE

A person acts with negligence if the person does not exercise reasonable care under all the circumstances. Primary factors to consider in ascertaining whether the person's conduct lacks reasonable care are the foreseeable likelihood that it will result in harm, the foreseeable severity of the harm that may ensue, and the burden of precautions to eliminate or reduce the risk of harm.

How does this language differ from the definition of negligence in the Second Restatement considered at the start of this chapter? Does this new formulation amount to an adoption of the Hand formula?

11. *Caught using the Hand formula.* As we conclude our examination of the Hand formula, consider a few broad questions. First, do you think the courts in the cases just considered are applying the Hand formula, consciously or otherwise? Second, is the Hand formula an appropriate way, as a normative matter, to decide whether a defendant has been negligent? What stance should the law take toward defendants who consciously use the Hand formula to decide what precautions to take? In the 1970s the Ford Motor Company was accused of deciding not to strengthen the fuel tanks in its Pinto automobiles because it was cheaper just to pay damages to people

burned or killed in fires caused by the weaker fuel tanks. One group of plaintiffs making such a claim won several million dollars from Ford in punitive damages. See *Grimshaw v. Ford Motor Co.*, 174 Cal. Rptr. 348 (Ct. App. 1981) (discussed in the chapter on damages). More recently, a jury awarded $4.9 billion in punitive damages against General Motors for placing the gas tank in its Malibu automobiles too close to the rear bumper. (The trial judge reduced the award to $1.09 billion, and GM settled with the plaintiffs for an undisclosed amount while its appeal was pending.) The plaintiffs' evidence was that GM had calculated that fires resulting from the fuel tank's placement were costing the firm only $2.40 per vehicle (in average payments to people injured in fiery collisions), and that it therefore would not make sense to spend $8.59 per vehicle to adopt a safer design. The internal memo on which this analysis was based was written in 1973. It adopted $200,000 as the value of a human life; the memo's author added that "it is really impossible to put a value on human life. This analysis tried to do so in an objective manner." After the trial ended, one of the jurors said, "We're telling GM that when they know that something . . . is going to injure people, then it's more important that they pay the money to make the car safe than to come to court and have a trial all the time." Another juror said, "We wanted to let them know that no matter how large the company may be, we as jurors, we as people all over the world, will not stand for companies having disregard for human life." See Los Angeles Times, July 10, 1999, at 1; Detroit Free Press (July 13, 1999).

Are the decisions in these cases best understood as judgments that the defendants are underestimating the size of the "L" involved when they make their Hand formula calculations? Or should the decisions be understood as condemning the defendant's decision to engage in such calculations at all? Do they tend to support the arguments from Professor Wright considered earlier? In any event, how should an automobile company decide which safety precautions to install in its vehicles and which to leave out? (Strictly speaking the plaintiffs in these cases were claiming not that the defendants were negligent, but that they sold defectively designed products; as we shall see in a later chapter, however, the standard for assessing such claims usually amounts to a comparison of the costs and benefits of the defendant's design with the costs and benefits of an alternative design proposed by the plaintiff.)

12. *Compliance errors.* So far in this section we have been considering one variety of negligence: claims that someone made a decision that violated the Hand formula — a decision not to take an injured sailor into port, or a decision to try to rescue a child sitting on a set of railroad tracks. But many negligent acts fall into a different category; they involve lapses of care in which the defendant fails to take some precaution that everyone agrees is required by reasonable prudence, as when a driver forgets to look for pedestrians. These sorts of lapses might be called "compliance errors," because they are failures to comply with an agreed-upon standard of care.

Another way of viewing this distinction is by noting that most of the cases in this section so far have involved questions about what *durable* precautions the Hand formula requires. A durable precaution generally is some safety measure that can be implemented with a single decision, such as installing a fire escape, hiring a bargee, or running wires below the ground. Compliance errors, on the other hand, typically involve momentary failures to take *repetitive* precautions, such as a driver forgetting to look both ways before entering an intersection, or a railroad's employee's failure — despite company policy — to remember to blow the horn before moving the train.

Obviously compliance errors occur frequently, and they are responsible for many accidents. But how should they be treated by the law? *Perfect* compliance with the dictates of the Hand formula might be very costly. Most people violate some rules of the road routinely when they drive; they fail to look for pedestrians, drive a bit too fast, or forget to check their tire pressure. To eradicate all of these lapses — to keep one's eyes fixed on the road at all times — would be difficult and thus "expensive" in terms of the Hand formula (high B). Perhaps what the Hand formula really requires is just the *habit* of watching the road with only occasional lapses. Yet that implies that people should be given a break when those lapses occur, since it's not worth the effort to eradicate them entirely. Should courts therefore be forgiving of the occasional lapse of due care?

The law's usual answer is "no." In a sense this amounts to a pocket of strict liability within the negligence rule, since it means that once some precaution (such as looking both ways) is considered a necessary feature of reasonable care, any failure to comply with the precaution will result in liability even if it was one of those rare lapses that even a careful person would commit. Thus if a surgeon mistakenly leaves a sponge inside a patient, there is no room for him to argue that in fact he is a very careful person and that this was a once-in-a-lifetime slipup. But suppose that the same surgeon were to purchase a machine that mechanically kept count of the number of sponges used in an operation and the number of them later removed and thrown away. The machine is more accurate than any human can be expected to be; but the machine nevertheless makes mistakes once per every million sponges that it counts. If a patient were injured by that millionth sponge, could she sue the surgeon? What argument might exist for treating this case differently from the case where the surgeon himself commits a one-in-a-million blunder?

C. CUSTOM AND THE PROBLEM OF MEDICAL MALPRACTICE

We next explore the significance of customs in defining negligence. If a defendant company takes as many precautions in its affairs as most similar companies take, can it be accused of failing to take "reasonable" care? Or suppose the defendant *failed* to take customary precautions: does this necessarily mean the defendant was negligent? When does it make sense to assume that the customary level of care in an industry is the appropriate level? The issue is especially important in the field of medical malpractice, as we shall see, but we begin by taking a broad view of the question.

The T.J. Hooper
60 F.2d 737 (2d Cir. 1932)

[Several coal barges were lost in a storm while being towed by the petitioner's two tugboats, the *Montrose* and the *Hooper*, along the New Jersey coast. The trial court found the tugboats "unseaworthy" — comparable in admiralty to a finding of negligence in an ordinary tort case — because they did not carry working radios that would have enabled them to hear about the coming bad weather and seek shelter. The tugboat company appealed.]

LEARNED HAND, *Circuit Judge* — [...] Taking the situation as a whole, it seems to us that the [masters of the tugboats] would have taken no undue chances, had they got the broadcasts [predicting foul weather].

They did not, because their private radio receiving sets, which were on board, were not in working order. These belonged to them personally, and were partly a toy, partly a part of the equipment, but neither furnished by the owner, nor supervised by it. It is not fair to say that there was a general custom among coastwise carriers so to equip their tugs. One line alone did it; as for the rest, they relied upon their crews, so far as they can be said to have relied at all. An adequate receiving set suitable for a coastwise tug can now be got at small cost and is reasonably reliable if kept up; obviously it is a source of great protection to their tows. Twice every day they can receive these predictions, based upon the widest possible information, available to every vessel within two or three hundred miles and more. Such a set is the ears of the tug to catch the spoken word, just as the master's binoculars are her eyes to see a storm signal ashore. Whatever may be said as to other vessels, tugs towing heavy coal laden barges, strung out for half a mile, have little power to manoeuvre, and do not, as this case proves, expose themselves to weather which would not turn back stauncher craft. They can have at hand protection against dangers of which they can learn in no other way.

Is it then a final answer that the business had not yet generally adopted receiving sets? There are, no doubt, cases where courts seem to make the general practice of the calling the standard of proper diligence; we have indeed given some currency to the notion ourselves. Indeed in most cases reasonable prudence is in fact common prudence; but strictly it is never its measure; a whole calling may have unduly lagged in the adoption of new and available devices. It never may set its own tests, however persuasive be its usages.

Courts must in the end say what is required; there are precautions so imperative that even their universal disregard will not excuse their omission. But here there was no custom at all as to receiving sets; some had them, some did not; the most that can be urged is that they had not yet become general. Certainly in such a case we need not pause; when some have thought a device necessary, at least we may say that they were right, and the others too slack. [...] We hold the tugs therefore because had they been properly equipped, they would have got the Arlington reports. The injury was a direct consequence of this unseaworthiness.

Decree affirmed.

NOTES

1. *The sandman.* In Ellis v. Louisville & Nashville Ry., 251 S.W.2d 577 (Ky. App. 1952), the plaintiff was responsible for maintaining mechanisms on the defendant's trains that released sand onto slippery railroad tracks to keep the wheels of the engine from spinning. Compressed air forced the sand through pipes and out onto the tracks. One of the plaintiff's tasks was to lean out over the nozzles of the pipes to confirm that the sand was falling through onto the rails. Clouds of dust would arise from the sand when he did this, and he could not avoid breathing some of it. He did other similar work with sand that also caused him to breathe dust. The plaintiff's evidence was that breathing so much dust during his 25 years of employment caused him to contract silicosis. He sued the defendant railroad, claiming it had been negligent in failing to issue him a mask that would have prevented him from inhaling the dust. The defendant put in evidence that the general practice of American railroads was not to supply masks to employees doing the plaintiff's sort of work. The trial court gave a directed verdict to the defendant railroad, and the court of appeals affirmed:

> The general rule as to common experience, usage and custom is well stated in 38 Am. Jur. "Negligence" §34, pages 679-682, from which we take these excerpts: "The common practices of the people, however, cannot be ignored in determining whether due care was exercised by an individual in a particular situation. It is not to be expected that the law will exact a degree of care in guarding any article which will make the great majority of the possessors of that article chargeable with habitual or continuous negligence. [...] Persons who are charged with a duty in relation to a particular matter or thing have a right to rely upon the sufficiency of a structure or contrivance which is in common use for the purpose and has been in fact safely used under such a variety of conditions as to demonstrate its fitness for the purpose. [...] Ordinarily, one is not considered negligent in respect of acts which conform to a common practice that has existed for years without resulting in an injury,

and that has nothing about it which shows a want of due care. [. . .] In other words, the test of negligence with respect to instrumentalities, methods, etc., is the ordinary usage and custom of mankind." [. . .]

Applying this sound rule [. . .] to the facts in this case, it is manifest defendant was not guilty of negligence in failing to furnish plaintiff safe equipment or a safe place in which to work, since the record plainly shows the practice by railroads generally throughout the nation was not to furnish masks or respirators to men doing the same character of work plaintiff had performed for defendant.

Does the holding of *Ellis v. Louisville & Nashville Ry.* necessarily represent a different rule than *The T.J. Hooper*, or are the two cases distinguishable?

2. Reason does not have to wait on usage. In MacDougall v. Pennsylvania Power and Light Co., 166 A. 589 (Pa. 1933), the plaintiff, a plumber, was hired by one Thomas Tiddy to go onto Tiddy's roof and repair a rain spout under the eaves. The defendant power company maintained a fuse box on a pole at the edge of the roof. In wet weather the outside of the box conducted electricity — and it was raining when the plaintiff went to perform the work. At one point he raised his head and bumped into the fuse box. A current entered behind his ear and exited through the base of his spine. He was knocked unconscious and fell 25 feet from the roof, sustaining various injuries. A physician testified that when he arrived at the scene of the accident to render first aid to the plaintiff, he noticed a perceptible odor of burnt flesh.

The plaintiff sued the power company, charging that it had been negligent in putting the box so near the roof of the building despite knowing that it often carried high voltage. The trial court awarded the plaintiff $10,455. The defendant appealed, arguing that "the unbending test of negligence in methods, machinery and appliances is the ordinary usage of the business," and that "no deviation by the defendant from any standard observed by those engaged in the same business was shown in this case. There is absolutely no competent testimony in this case that the equipment of the defendant or the construction of the equipment was not in accordance with the ordinary usage in the business." The Pennsylvania Supreme Court affirmed the judgment of the trial court:

Usage becomes important only when the conduct in question is not inherently dangerous. Vigilance must always be commensurate with danger. A high degree of danger always calls for a high degree of care. The care to be exercised in a particular case must always be proportionate to the seriousness of the consequences which are reasonably to be anticipated as a result of the conduct in question. Reason does not have to wait on usage; the latter must wait on reason. Ordinary common sense dictates that if in a harmless looking box there is something lurking that would kill or injure any one touching that box, the latter must be so situated, if it is possible or reasonably practicable to do so, that persons are not likely to come in contact with it. If the box must be placed where persons are likely to come in contact with it, there should be adequate warning given of its dangerous character.

Usage may sometimes be treated as a factor in the measurement of due care, and "in a few cases the courts have considered that due care is established by showing that all precautions and safeguards customarily used in the conduct of a similar business or occupation or in a similar undertaking have been adopted, although this view cannot be carried to the extent of justifying a custom which is so obviously dangerous to life and limb as to be at once recognized as such by all intelligent persons. [. . .] Customary methods or conduct do not furnish a test which is conclusive or controlling on the question of negligence, or fix a standard by which negligence is to be gauged. The standard of due care is such care as a prudent person would exercise under the circumstances of the particular case, and conformity to customary or usual conduct or methods cannot amount to more than a circumstance to be considered together with other circumstances of the case in determining whether due care has been exercised."

Is there a satisfactory distinction between *MacDougall v. Pennsylvania Power and Light Co.* and *Ellis v. Louisville & Nashville Ry.* (NL for failing to provide the plaintiff with a mask, since masks were not customary in the railroad industry)?

In most jurisdictions today, a defendant's compliance with custom or violation of it generally is considered probative evidence that the jury may consider in a negligence case, but it is not regarded as conclusive either way. Can you think of situations where it would make sense to give customary practices decisive weight in setting the standard of care?

3. *Undistorted market determinations.* In Rodi Yachts, Inc. v. National Marine, Inc., 984 F.2d 880 (7th Cir. 1993), a company called Transport Distributors, Inc. (TDI), owned a dock in Chicago. National Marine sent a barge to TDI's dock to be unloaded there. A crew supplied by National Marine lashed the barge to TDI's dock, then left the scene. Several days later, before TDI had been able to obtain a crane to unload the barge, the barge slipped free from its moorings and collided with another dock and two boats, causing more than $100,000 in damage. The owners of the damaged property brought suit against National Marine, which then impleaded TDI. The primary question in the case was the extent to which National Marine and TDI each had been negligent. TDI claimed that National Marine negligently tied its barge to the dock; National Marine claimed that TDI had been negligent in failing for several days to inspect the ropes used to tie the barge to the dock to see if they were holding up. The district court found

National Marine liable for two thirds of the plaintiffs' damages and TDI responsible for the remaining third. The defendants appealed, each claiming that the other was solely at fault. The court of appeals (per Posner, J.) reversed and remanded, holding that the district court had not made sufficient findings to support its conclusions. Said the court:

> One of the best known principles of tort law — a principle that received its canonical expression in an admiralty decision written by Learned Hand, *T.J. Hooper*, 60 F.2d 737, 740 (2d Cir. 1932) — is that compliance with custom is no defense to a tort claim. [The principle] is obviously sound when one is speaking of the duty of care to persons with whom the industry whose customary standard of care is at issue has no actual or potential contractual relation. For in that situation the costs of the injury can be made costs to the industry, and thus influence its behavior, only through the imposition of tort liability. R.H. Coase, The Problem of Social Cost, 3 J. Law & Econ. 1 (1960). It is different when the potential victims are the customers of the potential injurers. For then the latter, even if they are not subject to any tort liability, will have to ponder the possibility that if they endanger their customers they may lose them or may have to charge a lower price in order to compensate them for bearing a risk of injury. In such a case the market itself fixes a standard of care that reflects the preferences of potential victims as well as of potential injurers and then the principal function of tort law, it could be argued, is to protect customers' reasonable expectations that the firms with which they deal are complying with the standard of care customary in the industry, that is, the standard fixed by the market. This consideration is made relevant here by National Marine's argument that by departing without notice from the industry custom regarding inspections by dock operators TDI increased the risk of an accident.
>
> This case illustrates the operation of custom in both the contractual and the noncontractual setting. The owners of the dock and boats that were damaged had no actual or potential contractual relationship with the defendants. The latter in deciding what precautions to take would not be influenced, therefore, by the possible effect on transactions they might have with those owners; and as a result, the standard of care in the inland trade with regard to preventing runaway barges might be too low because it ignored some of the accident costs to which such runaways give rise. But at the present stage of this lawsuit the focus is not upon the defendants' duties toward strangers (the plaintiffs); it is upon their duties toward each other; and they had a contractual relationship with each other. It was not a direct or explicit relationship. There was no written contract, no writing at all, no money changing hands, no receipts — not even the maritime equivalent of a parking lot claim check. But a barge owner and a dock owner (or operator) are knitted together by their contracts with their customers as tightly as they would be by a contract between

themselves. Competition among barge owners and among dock owners to provide their respective legs of a unitary transportation service at the lowest possible price, coupled with tort liability to third parties, will give both types of service provider market incentives to adopt optimal safety precautions. Both face potential liability to third parties such as the plaintiffs in this case. They minimize their liability costs by allocating the responsibility for safety measures between them efficiently. They can do this explicitly or, implicitly, by abiding by the custom that the market has evolved.

Here the custom was for the barge owner (or operator) to moor the barge to the dock with a sufficient number of sound ropes, carefully fastened, and for the dock owner (or operator) to inspect the barge from time to time while it is at the dock, to make sure that the mooring lines remain securely fastened. We do not know whether National Marine violated the duty of care that custom places upon it because we do not know whether the ropes were unsound, insufficient in number (which seems highly unlikely, as we have said), or improperly fastened (also unlikely). And we do not know whether TDI violated the duty that custom imposed upon it to inspect (or in lieu therefore to notify National Marine that it was not inspecting, or to expedite the unloading), because there is no finding about what precisely the duty consists of. Since, however, these customs appear to reflect an undistorted market determination of the best way to minimize runaway barge accidents, we think the focus of the district court's inquiry should be on the parties' respective compliance with and departures from the customs and that the judge and the parties should not feel compelled to conduct a cost benefit analysis of barge transportation from the ground up.

Does the analysis in *Rodi Yachts* imply that *The T.J. Hooper* was wrongly decided on its facts? Is there a good distinction between the two cases? How might the analysis in *Rodi Yachts* apply to *MacDougall v. Pennsylvania Power and Light Co.*, or to *Ellis v. Louisville & Nashville Ry.*?

4. *Custom and contract.* The court in *Rodi Yachts* repeats the proposition that "compliance with custom is no defense to a tort claim," and says that principle "is obviously sound when one is speaking of the duty of care to persons with whom the industry whose customary standard of care is at issue has no actual or potential contractual relation." Why? Consider two scenarios. In the first, a railroad is sued when one of its trains drives through a crossing without blowing its horn and runs into the plaintiff's car. The railroad defends on the ground that it is customary in the railroad industry for trains to blow their horns only when the engineer sees an obstruction on the tracks; here, the car entered the crossing just before the train arrived. In the second scenario, a railroad is sued when one of its passengers is struck by a piece of luggage that falls out of one of the train's overhead racks.

The passenger claims that the railroad should have had enclosed baggage compartments over its seats (similar to the compartments on airplanes), rather than open racks where suitcases rest. The railroad again defends by invoking industry custom, pointing out that no railroads have such enclosed overhead compartments. Should custom be a stronger defense in one of these scenarios than in the other? Why?

5. *Medical malpractice cases.* In Brune v. Belinkoff, 354 Mass. 102 (1968), the defendant, a specialist in anesthesiology practicing in New Bedford, administered a spinal anesthetic containing eight milligrams of pontocaine to the plaintiff prior to the delivery of her child. This was the customary dose in New Bedford, but in Boston, 50 miles away, the customary dose was five milligrams or less. The defendant said that greater doses of pontocaine were needed in New Bedford because the practice of obstetricians there is to put pressure directly on the uterus during delivery. In any event, when the plaintiff attempted to get out of bed 11 hours after her delivery, she slipped and fell on the floor. She subsequently complained of numbness and weakness in her left leg and brought suit to recover for her injuries; she complained that she had been given too much pontocaine. The trial court instructed the jury to apply the traditional "locality rule" of *Small v. Howard*, 131 Mass. 131 (1880):

> [The defendant] must measure up to the standard of professional care and skill ordinarily possessed by others in his profession in the community, which is New Bedford, and its environs, of course, where he practices, having regard to the current state of advance of the profession. If, in a given case, it were determined by a jury that the ability and skill of the physician in New Bedford were fifty percent inferior to that which existed in Boston, a defendant in New Bedford would be required to measure up to the standard of skill and competence and ability that is ordinarily found by physicians in New Bedford.

So instructed, the jury returned a verdict for the defendant. The plaintiff appealed, claiming that the locality rule should be abandoned. The Supreme Judicial Court agreed, and reversed:

> We are of opinion that the "locality" rule of *Small v. Howard* which measures a physician's conduct by the standards of other doctors in similar communities is unsuited to present day conditions. The time has come when the medical profession should no longer be Balkanized by the application of varying geographic standards in malpractice cases. Accordingly, *Small v. Howard* is hereby overruled. The present case affords a good illustration of the inappropriateness of the "locality" rule to existing conditions. The defendant was a specialist practicing in New Bedford, a city of 100,000, which is slightly more than fifty miles from

Boston, one of the medical centers of the nation, if not the world. This is a far cry from the country doctor in *Small v. Howard*, who ninety years ago was called upon to perform difficult surgery. Yet the trial judge told the jury that if the skill and ability of New Bedford physicians were "fifty percent inferior" to those obtaining in Boston the defendant should be judged by New Bedford standards, "having regard to the current state of advance of the profession." This may well be carrying the rule of *Small v. Howard* to its logical conclusion, but it is, we submit, a reductio ad absurdum of the rule.

The proper standard is whether the physician, if a general practitioner, has exercised the degree of care and skill of the average qualified practitioner, taking into account the advances in the profession. In applying this standard it is permissible to consider the medical resources available to the physician as one circumstance in determining the skill and care required. Under this standard some allowance is thus made for the type of community in which the physician carries on his practice.

Notice two features of *Brune v. Belinkoff*. First, the court takes for granted that custom plays a decisive role in setting the defendant's standard of care: the question is not whether the jury thinks he acted reasonably, but whether the jury thinks he acted with the skill ordinarily found in some community of physicians, whether national or local. All courts agree on this general approach to deciding medical cases; medical malpractice is an unusual area of tort law where compliance with custom is decisive rather than just evidentiary. What is it about medical cases that might make it better to ask whether the defendant used customary care than to ask whether the defendant acted reasonably? Is the reason related to the contractual theory discussed in the *Rodi Yachts* case, or are different considerations in play?

One consequence of deferring to custom is that a plaintiff in a medical malpractice case normally must present expert testimony to show how the plaintiff's situation customarily would have been handled. This brings us to the second issue raised by *Brune*: handled in which community? No court today adheres to the strict locality rule that once required a plaintiff to show that the defendant's conduct did not measure up to the usual standard of care in the defendant's own town or city. (What are the strongest objections to such an approach?) Most courts use a national standard of care, usually with allowances similar to those noted in *Brune* if the defendant had below-average resources available. Some courts continue to use a modified locality rule, however; consider the following example.

6. *Similar localities*. In Gambill v. Stroud, 531 S.W.2d 945 (Ark. 1976), the defendant, Stroud, was a surgeon at a hospital in Jonesboro, Arkansas. He was to perform an operation on the plaintiff's wife, Yvonne Gambill, but the operation was aborted because of complications with her anesthesia; as a result of the complications, Mrs. Gambill suffered cardiac arrest and brain

damage. The plaintiff alleged that the complications were the product of Dr. Stroud's negligence. The jury was given the following instruction:

> In diagnosing the condition of and treating of a patient, a physician must possess and apply with reasonable care the degree of skill and learning ordinarily possessed and used by members of his profession in good standing engaged in the same type of service or specialty in the location in which he practices or in a similar locality. A failure to meet this standard is negligence.

So instructed, the jury brought in a verdict for the defendant. The plaintiff appealed, contending that the instruction represented a "locality rule" and so was erroneous. The Arkansas Supreme Court affirmed:

> The thrust of appellants' argument is that [the locality rule represented by the instruction] is no longer applicable to modern medicine, because doctors practicing in small communities now have the same opportunities and resources as physicians in large cities to keep abreast of advances in the medical profession, due to availability of the Journal of the American Medical Association and other journals, drug company representatives and literature, closed circuit television, special radio networks, tape recorded digests of medical literature, medical seminars and opportunities for exchange of views between doctors from small towns and those from large cities where there are complexes of medical centers and modern facilities.
>
> However desirable the attainment of this ideal may be, it remains an ideal. It was not shown in this case, and we are not convinced, that we have reached the time when the same postgraduate medical education, research and experience is equally available to all physicians, regardless of the community in which they practice. The opportunities for doctors in small towns, of which we have many, to leave a demanding practice to attend seminars and regional medical meetings cannot be the same as those for doctors practicing in clinics in larger centers. It goes without saying that the physicians in these small towns do not and cannot have the clinical and hospital facilities available in the larger cities where there are large, modern hospitals, and medical centers or the same advantage of observing others who have been trained, or have developed expertise, in the use of new skills, facilities and procedures, or consulting and exchanging views with specialists, other practitioners and drug experts, of utilizing closed circuit television, special radio networks or of studying in extensive medical libraries found in larger centers.
>
> The rule we have established is not a strict locality rule. It incorporates the similar community into the picture. The standard is not limited to that of a particular locality. Rather, it is that of persons engaged in a similar practice in similar localities, giving consideration to geographical

location, size and character of the community. The similarity of communities should depend not on population or area in a medical malpractice case, but rather upon their similarity from the standpoint of medical facilities, practices and advantages. [...]

It also seems that appellants have overlooked the impact of better medical education, modern technology, and improved means of travel and communication upon the law as it now exists. If the impact is as great as they theorize then no change in the law is necessary. These factors have already elevated the degree of skill and learning ordinarily possessed and used by members of the medical profession in every locality, if that premise is correct.

Which sorts of jurisdictions do you think would be most eager to adopt a national standard of care, and which most likely to retain a rule keyed to the type of community involved? The court in *Gambill* added that "[w]e certainly are not unaware of the difficulties experienced by small towns and rural communities in attracting qualified physicians. A complete abolition of the locality rule would certainly add to these difficulties." Tennessee provides for a similar approach by statute: a plaintiff in a medical malpractice case must establish "[t]he recognized standard of acceptable professional practice in the profession and the specialty thereof, if any, that the defendant practices in the community in which the defendant practices or in a similar community at the time the alleged injury or wrongful action occurred." T.C.A. §29-26-115. Who benefits from this rule? Who is made worse off by it?

7. *Medical care vs. facilities.* In Johnson v. Wills Memorial Hospital & Nursing Home, 343 S.E.2d 700 (Ga. App. 1986), the plaintiff's decedent, one Columbus Johnson, was a patient in the defendant's hospital. One night he began behaving strangely, running down a hospital corridor while swinging a pitcher of water and shouting "help me." He was forcibly returned to his room by two sheriff's deputies and then sedated by a nurse. A half hour later he still appeared to witnesses to be "very agitated." An orderly was stationed outside Johnson's room to ensure that he stayed there. About three hours later, the orderly reported that Johnson's room was empty; the window to the room was open and the screen had been cut. Johnson was found about eight hours later in the yard of a nearby residence. He was returned to the hospital and pronounced dead on arrival. His treating physician diagnosed the cause of death as overexposure to cold.

The plaintiff's suit alleged that the hospital, acting through its personnel, failed to adequately monitor Johnson, failed to inform the treating physician of Johnson's condition, and failed to treat him as the physician directed. The jury was instructed that the standard of care applicable to the hospital was the standard of care exercised in similar hospitals in similar communities. So instructed, the jury brought in a verdict for the defendant. The plaintiff appealed, alleging that the instruction incorrectly applied a "locality rule" to the case. The Georgia Court of Appeals affirmed:

> The "locality rule" is appropriate in a case in which the adequacy of a hospital's facilities or services is questioned. Inroads on the "local" standard of care rule have been made in cases in which a plaintiff asserts negligence in the medical care and treatment provided by a hospital's professional personnel. In the case at bar, appellant alleged in her complaint that the nursing care her late husband received was substandard and that appellee's facilities were deficient since it had failed to protect her decedent adequately. The protection of patients is not a medical function of a hospital; rather, it is a service provided by a hospital to its patients, and the ability of a small rural hospital to provide such a service is limited by its location and resources. In light of the pleadings, a charge on the locality rule was called for, and the trial court committed no error in so instructing the jury.

What is the basis for the distinction the court draws between medical care and medical facilities? Why are facilities judged by reference to custom at all? (The more usual approach would be to judge them without reference to custom or locality.)

8. *Legal malpractice.* In Cook v. Irion, 409 S.W.2d 475 (Tex. App. 1966), the plaintiff tripped and fell on a sidewalk in El Paso. There were three possible defendants she might have sued: the shopping center that owned the sidewalk, the organization of tenants occupying the shopping center, and the television station that owned the cable on which she tripped. Her lawyer, Irion, sued only the corporation that owned the shopping center. She lost. She then sued Irion for malpractice, claiming that in bringing her tort suit he should have sued the other possible defendants as well; the statute of limitations on claims against them had since expired. The plaintiff's expert was a lawyer from the town of Alpine, Texas, who testified that Irion "had failed to exercise the standard of care of the average general practitioner in the State of Texas in not suing all three of the possible defendants." The trial court gave a directed verdict to the defendant, Irion. The court of appeals affirmed, in part because the plaintiff had not offered adequate expert testimony:

> [A]n attorney practicing in a vastly different locality would not be qualified to second guess the judgment of an experienced attorney of the El Paso County Bar as to who should be joined as additional party defendants. In this case Mr. Allen practiced law in Alpine, which is 220 miles from El Paso, and it is further significant that the population of Brewster County is 6,434, as compared to 314,070 in El Paso County. As admitted by Mr. Allen, the probable make up of the jury panel is an

important consideration of whom to sue where there is an option. The importance of knowledge of the local situation is fully demonstrated by the well recognized practice among the lawyers of this State in associating local counsel in the trial of most important jury cases.

In cases of legal and other professional malpractice, as in cases of medical malpractice, the standard of care generally is set by reference to the customary behavior of professionals in the relevant community. Is the rationale for this approach in suits against lawyers as strong as it is in suits against doctors? The relevant community usually is said to be the lawyers practicing in the defendant's state. Can you think of any reason why the state, rather than the town or nation, would be the appropriate frame of reference when considering a claim of legal malpractice? Can the decision in *Cook v. Irion* be understood as a sensible exception to that usual rule?

9. *Custom and consent.* One area of medical practice where custom does not necessarily set the standard is informed consent. When a patient complains that a physician failed to disclose a risk of a procedure and that the risk then materialized, some courts will ask whether such disclosures were customary among skilled practitioners of good standing; but they also will ask — and some courts *only* will ask — whether the physician disclosed all "material" risks. The question then becomes whether the risk of the harm the patient suffered was neither so obvious nor so rare that it should not be considered "material." Evidence on that question may be supplied by experts — i.e., other physicians — but the test, strictly speaking, is not just whether the defendant made customary disclosures; even a customary level of disclosure can be found inadequate. Why does custom have less force in this context than in assessing a doctor's care in operating? The problem of informed consent in medical malpractice cases is further addressed in the chapter on cause in fact.

D. NEGLIGENCE PER SE: CRIMINAL STATUTES AND JUDGE-MADE RULES

Tort cases that we characterize as resulting in "liability" usually are cases where a court of appeals says that a jury is *permitted* to find the defendant negligent, not where a jury is required to do so. Some major exceptions to this pattern arise in cases where a defendant is held to be *negligent per se*: the court determines that the defendant has violated some sort of rule, either statutory or judge-made, and that the violation establishes the defendant's negligence as a matter of law. In other instances, however, courts may treat such violations of rules as mere evidence of negligence for the jury to consider — or as no evidence of negligence at all.

1. Violations of Criminal Statutes

Martin v. Herzog
126 N.E. 814 (N.Y. 1920)

CARDOZO, J. The action is one to recover damages for injuries resulting in death. Plaintiff and her husband, while driving toward Tarrytown in a buggy on the night of August 21, 1915, were struck by the defendant's automobile coming in the opposite direction. They were thrown to the ground, and the man was killed. At the point of the collision the highway makes a curve. The car was rounding the curve, when suddenly it came upon the buggy, emerging, the defendant tells us, from the gloom. Negligence is charged against the defendant, the driver of the car, in that he did not keep to the right of the center of the highway. Highway Law, §286, subd. 3, and section 332. Negligence is charged against the plaintiff's intestate, the driver of the wagon, in that he was traveling without lights. Highway Law, §329a, as amended by Laws 1915, c. 367. There is no evidence that the defendant was moving at an excessive speed. There is none of any defect in the equipment of his car. The beam of light from his lamps pointed to the right as the wheels of his car turned along the curve toward the left; and, looking in the direction of the plaintiff's approach, he was peering into the shadow. The case against him must stand, therefore, if at all, upon the divergence of his course from the center of the highway. The jury found him delinquent and his victim blameless. The Appellate Division reversed, and ordered a new trial.

We agree with the Appellate Division that the charge to the jury was erroneous and misleading. [. . .] In the body of the charge the trial judge said that the jury could consider the absence of light "in determining whether the plaintiff's intestate was guilty of contributory negligence in failing to have a light upon the buggy as provided by law. I do not mean to say that the absence of light necessarily makes him negligent, but it is a fact for your consideration." The defendant requested a ruling that the absence of a light on the plaintiff's vehicle was "prima facie evidence of contributory negligence." This request was refused, and the jury were again instructed that they might consider the absence of lights as some evidence of negligence, but that it was not conclusive evidence. The plaintiff then requested a charge that "the fact that the plaintiff's intestate was driving without a light is not negligence in itself," and to this the court acceded. The defendant saved his rights by appropriate exceptions.

We think the unexcused omission of the statutory signals is more than some evidence of negligence. It is negligence in itself. Lights are intended for the guidance and protection of other travelers on the highway. Highway

Law, §329a. By the very terms of the hypothesis, to omit, willfully or heedlessly, the safeguards prescribed by law for the benefit of another that he may be preserved in life or limb, is to fall short of the standard of diligence to which those who live in organized society are under a duty to conform. That, we think, is now the established rule in this state. [. . .]

In the case at hand, we have an instance of the admitted violation of a statute intended for the protection of travelers on the highway, of whom the defendant at the time was one. Yet the jurors were instructed in effect that they were at liberty in their discretion to treat the omission of lights either as innocent or as culpable. They were allowed to "consider the default as lightly or gravely" as they would (Thomas, J., in the court below). [. . .] Jurors have no dispensing power, by which they may relax the duty that one traveler on the highway owes under the statute to another. It is error to tell them that they have. The omission of these lights was a wrong, and, being wholly unexcused, was also a negligent wrong. No license should have been conceded to the triers of the facts to find it anything else.

We must be on our guard, however, against confusing the question of negligence with that of the causal connection between the negligence and the injury. A defendant who travels without lights is not to pay damages for his fault, unless the absence of lights is the cause of the disaster. A plaintiff who travels without them is not to forfeit the right to damages, unless the absence of lights is at least a contributing cause of the disaster. [. . .]

There may, indeed, be times when the lights on a highway are so many and so bright that lights on a wagon are superfluous. If that is so, it is for the offender to go forward with the evidence, and prove the illumination as a kind of substituted performance. The plaintiff asserts that she did so here. She says that the scene of the accident was illumined by moonlight, by an electric lamp, and by the lights of the approaching car. Her position is that, if the defendant did not see the buggy thus illumined, a jury might reasonably infer that he would not have seen it anyhow. We may doubt whether there is any evidence of illumination sufficient to sustain the jury in drawing such an inference; but the decision of the case does not make it necessary to resolve the doubt, and so we leave it open. It is certain that they were not required to find that lights on the wagon were superfluous. They might reasonably have found the contrary. They ought, therefore, to have been informed what effect they were free to give, in that event, to the violation of the statute. They should have been told, not only that the omission of the light was negligence, but that it was "prima facie evidence of contributory negligence"; i.e., that it was sufficient in itself unless its probative force was overcome to sustain a verdict that the decedent was at fault.

Here, on the undisputed facts, lack of vision, whether excusable or not, was the cause of the disaster. The defendant may have been negligent in swerving from the center of the road; but he did not run into the buggy purposely, nor was he driving while intoxicated, nor was he going at such a reckless speed that warning would of necessity have been futile. Nothing of the kind is shown. The collision was due to his failure to see at a time when sight should have been aroused and guided by the statutory warnings. Some explanation of the effect to be given to the absence of those warnings, if the plaintiff failed to prove that other lights on the car or the highway took their place as equivalents, should have been put before the jury. The explanation was asked for and refused.

Order affirmed.

NOTES

1. *Criminal and civil liability.* Why treat a provision of the *criminal* law as setting the standard of care for *civil* purposes? Is it because the reasonable person always complies with whatever statutes and ordinances are in place? (Can it be that a reasonable person sometimes might not comply with them?) Or is the doctrine of negligence per se better understood as a guess at what the legislature wanted when it enacted the criminal provision? Sometimes such provisions provide explicitly for civil liability if they are violated, and in that case there generally is no controversy about their application in tort suits. The difficulties arise when a statute prohibits conduct without specifying whether a violation gives an injured party a right to sue for damages.

2. *Flexible commands.* In Tedla v. Ellman, 19 N.E.2d 987 (N.Y. 1939), Anna Tedla and her brother, John Bachek, were walking along a road known as the Sunrise Highway. They were wheeling baby carriages containing junk and wood which they had collected at a nearby incinerator. It was about six o'clock on a Sunday evening in December, and it was already dark; Bachek was carrying a lantern. A car driven by the defendant, Ellman, struck them, injuring Tedla and killing Bachek. Tedla brought suit against Ellman to recover for her injuries.

Sunrise Highway was a two-lane road with no footpaths on either side. State law provided as follows:

> Pedestrians walking or remaining on the paved portion, or traveled part of a roadway shall be subject to, and comply with, the rules governing vehicles, with respect to meeting and turning out, except that such pedestrians shall keep to the left of the center line thereof, and turn to their left instead of right side thereof, so as to permit all vehicles passing them in either direction to pass on their right. Such pedestrians shall not be subject to the rules governing vehicles as to giving signals.

Tedla and Bachek were violating the statute by walking east on the eastbound or righthand roadway. At trial, however, Tedla put in evidence that the side of the road they were using was much less trafficked and thus safer than the side the law said they should use. The trial court entered judgment on a jury verdict finding that the accident was due solely to Ellman's negligence. Ellman appealed on the ground that the trial court should have held Tedla and her brother negligent as a matter of law. The court of appeals affirmed:

> The plaintiffs showed by the testimony of a State policeman that "there were very few cars going east" at the time of the accident, but that going west there was "very heavy Sunday night traffic." Until the recent adoption of the new statutory rule for pedestrians, ordinary prudence would have dictated that pedestrians should not expose themselves to the danger of walking along the roadway upon which the "very heavy Sunday night traffic" was proceeding when they could walk in comparative safety along a roadway used by very few cars. It is said that now, by force of the statutory rule, pedestrians are guilty of contributory negligence as matter of law when they use the safer roadway, unless that roadway is left of the center of the road.
>
> [The statute provides] rules of the road to be observed by pedestrians and by vehicles, so that all those who use the road may know how they and others should proceed, at least under usual circumstances. A general rule of conduct — and, specifically, a rule of the road — may accomplish its intended purpose under usual conditions, but, when the unusual occurs, strict observance may defeat the purpose of the rule and produce catastrophic results. [. . .]
>
> [W]here a statutory general rule of conduct fixes no definite standard of care which would under all circumstances tend to protect life, limb or property but merely codifies or supplements a common-law rule, which has always been subject to limitations and exceptions; or where the statutory rule of conduct regulates conflicting rights and obligations in a manner calculated to promote public convenience and safety, then the statute, in the absence of clear language to the contrary, should not be construed as intended to wipe out the limitations and exceptions which judicial decisions have attached to the common-law duty; nor should it be construed as an inflexible command that the general rule of conduct intended to prevent accidents must be followed even under conditions when observance might cause accidents. We may assume reasonably that the Legislature directed pedestrians to keep to the left of the center of the road because that would cause them to face traffic approaching in that lane and would enable them to care for their own safety better than if the traffic approached them from the rear. We cannot assume reasonably that the Legislature intended that a statute enacted for the preservation of the life and limb of pedestrians must be observed when observance would subject them to more imminent danger. [. . .]
>
> Even under that construction of the statute, a pedestrian is, of course, at fault if he fails without good reason to observe the statutory rule of conduct. The general duty is established by the statute, and deviation from it without good cause is a wrong and the wrongdoer is responsible for the

damages resulting from his wrong. Here the jury might find that the pedestrians avoided a greater, indeed an almost suicidal, risk by proceeding along the east bound roadway; that the operator of the automobile was entirely heedless of the possibility of the presence of pedestrians on the highway; and that a pedestrian could not have avoided the accident even if he had faced oncoming traffic.

What is the distinction between *Tedla v. Ellman* and *Martin v. Herzog* (where the plaintiff was found negligent per se for driving a buggy without lights in violation of statute)? Is it fair to conclude from these cases that the Hand formula trumps statutory commands when the two conflict?

3. *Never on Sunday.* In Tingle v. Chicago, B. & Q. Ry., 14 N.W. 320 (Iowa 1882), the defendant's train ran over the plaintiff's cow on a Sunday. The plaintiff sued, alleging no specific negligence on the railroad's part but pointing out that state law prohibited the operation of trains on Sundays. The trial court gave judgment to the plaintiff. The Iowa Supreme Court reversed:

> While the injury could not have been inflicted if the defendant's train had not been operated, still, as it is not claimed that the train was operated in a negligent manner, the proximate cause of the injury was not the operation of the train, but it resulted from an accident for which the defendant is not responsible.

Cf. Restatement (Second) of Torts §286, Illustration 5:

> A statute, which requires railroads to fence their tracks, is construed as intended solely to prevent injuries to animals straying onto the right of way who may be hit by trains. In violation of the statute, the A Railroad fails to fence its track. As a result, two of B's cows wander onto the track. One of them is hit by a train; the other is poisoned by weeds growing beside the track. The statute establishes a standard of conduct as to the cow hit by the train, but not as to the other cow.

4. *Sunday hat.* In White v. Levarn, 108 A. 564 (Vt. 1918), the plaintiff and defendant went squirrel hunting together on a Sunday, each armed with a shotgun. The plaintiff was wearing a hat that was the color of a gray squirrel; the defendant mistook the hat for a squirrel and shot at it, injuring the plaintiff. The plaintiff sued on the theory that hunting and discharging firearms on Sunday was forbidden by state law. The trial court gave judgment to the defendant. The Vermont Supreme Court reversed:

> Hunting and shooting wild game or other birds or animals, or discharging firearms, on Sunday (with some exceptions not material here), are unlawful by statute. The shooting which injured the plaintiff was therefore an

unlawful act voluntarily done by the defendant, and he is answerable, in an action of trespass, for the injury which happened to the plaintiff, either by carelessness or accident. . . . [C]onsent to an assault is no justification, for, since the state is wronged by it, the law forbids it on public grounds.

Is there a satisfactory distinction between *White v. Levarn* and *Tingle v. Chicago, B. & Q. Ry.*? Which decision makes more sense? How might you argue that *both* cases were wrongly decided?

5. *Uses of statutes.* From the Restatement (Second) of Torts §288B (1965):

> *Illustration 2.* A statute, construed as intended only to prevent mis-breeding of animals, provides that hogs shall be confined by fences of specified strength. In violation of the statute, A fences in his hogs with a fence of less strength. One of the hogs breaks through the fence, escapes into the highway, and is struck by B's car, as a result of which B is injured. Although the statute does not define a standard of conduct which will be adopted as a matter of law for B's action, its provisions are admissible and relevant evidence as to the necessity of a fence of the specified strength for the proper confinement of hogs.

What is the difference between the way the Restatement recommends using the statute in this example and the way it is used in *Martin v. Herzog* and *White v. Levarn*?

6. *Controlling the jury.* Much of the law of torts is focused on when questions are decided by judges and when they are left to juries. As the introduction to the book explains, a plaintiff's usual goal throughout much of a tort suit is to get in front of a jury; the defendant's usual goal is to avoid that result, obtaining a dismissal of the case as a matter of law. That is why we speak of cases as involving "liability" if the court says that the plaintiff's case was good enough to be sent to a jury (or, equivalently, that the jury would be *permitted* to find liability on the plaintiff's facts), and "no liability" if the court says that a jury would not be permitted to find liability given the plaintiff's allegations or evidence.

But notice that this description leaves out a possibility: the court could award judgment to the *plaintiff* as a matter of law. Such rulings are made relatively rarely. The reason is that in a conventional negligence case the plaintiff is assigned the burden of proving all the elements of the case, including the defendant's failure to use reasonable care. A court may be able to say that the plaintiff has failed to discharge this burden — that no rational jury could conclude from the plaintiff's evidence that the defendant was negligent. It is more difficult, however, for a court to declare that a plaintiff *has* proven the defendant's negligence as a matter of law, or (the same thing) that a rational jury would be *required* to find the defendant liable. Even if the plaintiff's evidence seems very strong, the jury usually is free to disbelieve or discount it, in which case the plaintiff must lose. Likewise, a determination that the defendant failed to act reasonably usually has to come from a jury.

Doctrines of "negligence per se" are exceptions to these general rules. Where they apply they require a finding that the defendant was negligent (or that the plaintiff was contributorily negligent). The decision is made as a matter of law by the judge. As a practical matter this can be considered precisely the point of the doctrines: a finding of negligence per se is distinctive and important not just because the defendant ends up being held negligent, but because this result is reached without resort to a jury.

These points should help you answer the question immediately above regarding the difference between §288B of the Second Restatement and the holding of *Martin v. Herzog*. What is the role of the jury in the two situations?

7. *Man's best friend.* In Selger v. Steven Brothers, Inc., 222 Cal. App. 3d 1585 (1990), dog excrement often accumulated on the sidewalk in front of the defendant's business, Steven's Nursery and Hardware. The defendant's employees usually used hoses or brooms to clean the sidewalk each morning. On the morning in question, however, the defendant's manager saw excrement on the sidewalk when he opened the store but delayed in directing an employee to clean it up. Just as the manager was issuing that instruction, he heard the plaintiff scream. She had slipped and fallen while observing a flower display outside the store. Her shoe, her clothing, and a skid mark on the sidewalk left no doubt about the cause of the accident. The plaintiff previously had undergone a hip implant, and as a result of her fall required extensive additional surgery. She sued the defendant, basing her claim of negligence on Los Angeles Municipal Code §41.46. It provided that "No person shall fail, refuse or neglect to keep the sidewalk in front of his house, place of business or premises in a clean and wholesome condition."

The trial judge instructed the jury that the defendant should be found negligent per se if it violated the ordinance. The trial court entered judgment on a jury verdict of $402,050 for the plaintiff. The defendant appealed on the ground that the trial court erred in instructing the jury on the doctrine of negligence per se. The court of appeals reversed and held the evidence against the defendant insufficient as a matter of law:

> Applying well-established authority, we hold the ordinances imposed a duty on defendant which was owed only to the city. The ordinances did not create a standard of care owed to the traveling public; therefore the trial court erred in instructing the jury that violation of the ordinances constituted negligence per se. [. . .]
>
> [B]ecause the municipality has the primary responsibility for maintaining the public sidewalks, statutes and ordinances which require the abutting landowner to maintain the sidewalk in a condition that will not endanger pedestrians have almost uniformly been interpreted not to

create a standard of care toward pedestrians but only a liability of the owner to the municipality.

Selger represents the usual result when plaintiffs slip on snow or ice and sue nearby property owners for violating similar statutes. The court in *Selger* noted, however, that "[t]he dog's owner is primarily to blame for the creation of this hazard," and that Los Angeles had a "pooper scooper" law imposing a $20 fine on dog owners who failed to clean up behind their animals. The court declined to take a position on whether the dog's owner, if found, could have been held negligent per se for violating that ordinance. What result would you expect in such a case?

8. *Ignorance as an excuse*. From the Restatement (Second) of Torts §288A (1965):

> *Comment f. Knowledge*. Where the actor neither knows nor should know of any occasion or necessity for action in compliance with the legislation or regulation, his violation of it will ordinarily be excused.
>
> *Illustration 3*. A statute provides that no vehicle shall be driven on the public highway at night without front and rear lights. While A is driving on the highway at night his rear light goes out because of the failure of an electric bulb. A has used all reasonable diligence and care in the inspection of his car, and is unaware that the light has gone out. Before he has had any reasonable opportunity to discover it, the absence of the light causes a collision with B's car, approaching from the rear, in which B is injured. A is not liable to B on the basis of the violation of the statute.

Is this provision consistent with the analysis and result in *Martin v. Herzog*?

9. *Confusing laws (problem)*. In Sparkman v. Maxwell, 519 S.W.2d 852 (Tex. 1975), the plaintiff and the defendant were involved in an automobile accident. The plaintiff was driving through an intersection with a green light when the defendant, Sparkman, traveling in the opposite direction, attempted to make a left turn in front of her. The cars collided, causing each party various injuries. Sparkman claimed that her behavior was caused by confusing traffic signals. The court recounted the facts as follows:

> Mrs. Sparkman testified that the signal facing her as she approached and entered the intersection was a red arrow pointing to the north. She did not realize at the time that it was red, but she did see an arrow pointing in the direction she wished to go. She saw "something was wrong with the light" and for that reason stopped to look at the sign. The sign indicated that she was looking at the proper signal, and she proceeded into the inter-section. Since the arrow was pointing in her direction, she decided that she should go ahead. She had no thought of its being red at the

time. She had always turned on the arrow, and in this instance the arrow was pointing in the direction she wished to go.

The light had recently been installed on a trial basis by one of the city's traffic engineers:

> As originally constructed the traffic signal consisted of three circular lens, arranged in a vertical line, a red lens at the top, a yellow lens immediately below the red, and a green lens immediately below the yellow. About two weeks before the accident, the Traffic Engineer for the City of Wichita Falls had caused a metal template to be placed inside each lens. An opening in the shape of an arrow pointing to the left was in each template, and the signal thus showed, in sequence, green, yellow and red arrows, all pointing to the left. Below the traffic signal was a sign reading "Left Turn to Fairway." When Mrs. Sparkman entered the left-turn lane on Southwest Parkway, the traffic signal showed a red arrow pointing to the left. After stopping and looking at the sign to be sure she was observing the signal that controlled the left-turn lane, she drove slowly into the intersection and collided with Mrs. Maxwell's automobile, which had entered the intersection on a green light facing traffic proceeding north on Fairway. . . .
>
> The signal was removed at the end of eight days and about an hour after the accident in this case. . . . This was the only time to [the engineer's] knowledge that either a red arrow or a yellow arrow had ever been used in Texas.

A jury found that Sparkman had not been negligent. The plaintiff sought judgment as a matter of law on the ground that Sparkman had committed negligence per se. What result?

10. *Legislative intent.* As noted earlier, the question of legislative intent usually is critical when attempting to determine whether a provision of a criminal code creates civil liability. There have been attempts in some states to settle the question with meta-provisions such as the following from California:

> (a) The failure of a person to exercise due care is presumed if:
>   (1) He violated a statute, ordinance, or regulation of a public entity;
>   (2) The violation proximately caused death or injury to person or property;
>   (3) The death or injury resulted from an occurrence of the nature which the statute, ordinance, or regulation was designed to prevent; and
>   (4) The person suffering the death or the injury to his person or property was one of the class of persons for whose protection the statute, ordinance, or regulation was adopted.

(b) This presumption may be rebutted by proof that:

(1) The person violating the statute, ordinance, or regulation did what might reasonably be expected of a person of ordinary prudence, acting under similar circumstances, who desired to comply with the law; or

(2) The person violating the statute, ordinance, or regulation was a child and exercised the degree of care ordinarily exercised by persons of his maturity, intelligence, and capacity under similar circumstances, but the presumption may not be rebutted by such proof if the violation occurred in the course of an activity normally engaged in only by adults and requiring adult qualifications.

Cal. Evid. Code §669.

11. *Legislative intent revisited.* In Vesely v. Sager, 486 P.2d 151 (Cal. 1971), the defendant was the owner of the Buckhorn Lodge, a roadhouse near the top of Mount Baldy. The plaintiff alleged that late one evening the Lodge served one of its patrons, a man named O'Connell, a series of alcoholic beverages that intoxicated him. At about 5:00 A.M., O'Connell left the lodge and proceeded to drive down the steep, narrow, and winding road that was the only way to descend the mountain. He veered into the wrong lane and ran into the plaintiff's car, causing the plaintiff various injuries. The plaintiff's suit alleged, among other things, that the defendant should be held negligent per se for violating California Bus. & Prof. Code §25602. The statute provided: "Every person who sells, furnishes, gives, or causes to be sold, furnished, or given away, any alcoholic beverage to any habitual or common drunkard or to any obviously intoxicated person is guilty of a misdemeanor." The plaintiff also cited Cal. Evid. Code §669, described above. The trial court dismissed the plaintiff's complaint. The California Supreme Court reversed:

> From the facts alleged in the complaint it appears that plaintiff is within the class of persons for whose protection section 25602 was enacted and that the injuries he suffered resulted from an occurrence that the statute was designed to prevent. Accordingly, if these two elements are proved at trial, and if it is established that Sager violated section 25602 and that the violation proximately caused plaintiff's injuries, a presumption will arise that Sager was negligent in furnishing alcoholic beverages to O'Connell. [...]
>
> [T]he Legislature has expressed its intention in this area with the adoption of Evidence Code §669, and Business and Professions Code §25602. The California Law Revision Commission's recommendation relating to Evidence Code §669 states that the presumption contained in the section "should be classified as a presumption affecting the burden of proof. In order to further the public policies expressed in the various statutes,

ordinances, and regulations to which it applies." It is clear that Business and Professions Code §25602 is a statute to which this presumption applies and that the policy expressed in the statute is to promote the safety of the people of California. To accept defendant's contentions and hold that plaintiff's complaint does not state a cause of action would be to thwart the legislative policies expressed in both statutes.

In 1978 the legislature responded to *Vesely* and cases following it with this provision:

> CAL. BUS. & PROF. CODE §25602. SALES TO DRUNKARD OR INTOXICATED PERSON; OFFENSE; CIVIL LIABILITY.
>
> (a) Every person who sells, furnishes, gives, or causes to be sold, furnished, or given away, any alcoholic beverage to any habitual or common drunkard or to any obviously intoxicated person is guilty of a misdemeanor.
> (b) No person who sells, furnishes, gives, or causes to be sold, furnished, or given away, any alcoholic beverage pursuant to subdivision (a) of this section shall be civilly liable to any injured person or the estate of such person for injuries inflicted on that person as a result of intoxication by the consumer of such alcoholic beverage.
> (c) The Legislature hereby declares that this section shall be interpreted so that the holdings in cases such as *Vesely v. Sager* [...] be abrogated in favor of prior judicial interpretation finding the consumption of alcoholic beverages rather than the serving of alcoholic beverages as the proximate cause of injuries inflicted upon another by an intoxicated person.

The California Supreme Court upheld §25602 against constitutional challenge:

> Each day the devastating effects of the drinking driver rage unabated with all of their tragic social and economic consequences. We do not speculate on the influences that might have prompted the Legislature to answer this acute and growing problem by narrowly *restricting* rather than *enlarging* civil liability. In the final analysis the Legislature must answer to an informed, and perhaps ultimately aroused, public opinion for its action. We do not substitute our judgment for its own. [...]
> The Legislature's decision to abrogate *Vesely* [...], and thereby preclude or substantially limit the liability of a provider of alcoholic beverages, may have been based upon a premise that it is unfair to require the provider (and his insurer) to share both the supervisory responsibility and the legal blame with the consumer, whose voluntary consumption of alcoholic beverages is perhaps the more direct and immediate cause

of any consequent injuries. We deem such a determination to be a rational one because for many years prior to *Vesely* the courts of this state (including ours) uniformly had followed such provider-immunity rule.

The Legislature also reasonably might have assumed that the imposition of sole and exclusive liability upon the consumer of alcoholic beverages would encourage some heightened sense of responsibility in the drinker for his acts, thereby ultimately reducing the frequency of alcohol-caused injuries. For these reasons we conclude that the general rule of immunity announced in the 1978 amendments is both founded upon a possible rational basis and reasonably related to a legitimate state purpose.

Cory v. Shierloh, 629 P.2d 8 (Cal. 1981). What do you make of this dialogue between California's Supreme Court and its legislature? Is it all a sign of well-functioning political and judicial institutions? Does it cause you to prefer one of those organs to the other as an author of solutions to social problems?

Other states vary considerably in how they interpret the civil consequences of "dram shop statutes" similar to the one considered in *Vesely*. The issue also has generated a great deal of common-law development; for further discussion, see the entry on liability of social hosts in the chapter on Duties and Limitations.

12. *Taking license*. In Brown v. Shyne, 151 N.E. 197 (N.Y. 1926), the plaintiff sought treatment from the defendant chiropractor, Shyne, for her laryngitis. She testified that on her ninth visit, Shyne "took ahold of my head, both sides of my head, and gave it a very violent turn, twist one way and then back, which gave a very bad snap," and that these manipulations later caused numbness in her arms and, finally, paralysis. The plaintiff alleged that Shyne's treatments had been negligent; she also alleged that Shyne had been negligent per se in practicing medicine without possessing the license required by the state's Public Health Law. After instructing the jury to assess whether Shyne's treatments measured up to the "standards of skill and care which prevail among those treating disease," the trial judge also gave the following instruction:

> This is a little different from the ordinary malpractice case, and I am going to allow you, if you think proper under the evidence in the case, to predicate negligence upon another theory. The public health laws of this state prescribe that no person shall practice medicine unless he is licensed so to do by the board of regents of this state and registered pursuant to statute. . . . This statute to which I have referred is a general police regulation. Its violation, and it has been violated by the defendant, is some evidence, more or less cogent, of negligence which you may consider for what it is worth, along with all the other evidence in

the case. If the defendant attempted to treat the plaintiff and to adjust the vertebrae in her spine when he did not possess the requisite knowledge and skill as prescribed by the statute to know what was proper and necessary to do under the circumstances, or how to do it, even if he did know what to do, you can find him negligent.

So instructed, the jury returned a verdict for the plaintiff, and the trial court entered judgment on it. The defendant appealed.

Held, for the defendant, that the jury instruction regarding the licensing law was error, and that the defendant could be held liable only if the jury found on retrial that his treatment of the plaintiff was in fact negligently rendered. Said the court:

> Proper formulation of general standards of preliminary education and proper examination of the particular applicant should serve to raise the standards of skill and care generally possessed by members of the profession in this state; but the license to practice medicine confers no additional skill upon the practitioner, nor does it confer immunity from physical injury upon a patient if the practitioner fails to exercise care. Here, injury may have been caused by lack of skill or care; it would not have been obviated if the defendant had possessed a license yet failed to exercise the skill and care required of one practicing medicine. True, if the defendant had not practiced medicine in this state, he could not have injured the plaintiff, but the protection which the statute was intended to provide was against risk of injury by the unskilled or careless practitioner, and, unless the plaintiff's injury was caused by carelessness or lack of skill, the defendant's failure to obtain a license was not connected with the injury.

Crane, J., dissented:

> The prohibition against practicing medicine without a license was for the very purpose of protecting the public from just what happened in this case. The violation of this statute has been the direct and proximate cause of the injury. The courts will not determine in face of this statute whether a faith healer, a patent medicine man, a chiropractor, or any other class of practitioner acted according to the standards of his own school, or according to the standards of a duly licensed physician. The law, to insure against ignorance and carelessness, has laid down a rule to be followed; namely, examinations to test qualifications and a license to practice. If a man, in violation of this statute, takes his chances in trying to cure disease, and his acts result directly in injury, he should not complain if the law, in a suit for damages, says that his violation of the statute is some evidence of his incapacity.

Suppose that an airplane crashes and it appears that the pilot was unlicensed. Or suppose that a driver with an expired driver's license strikes a pedestrian. Would these cases be distinguishable from *Brown v. Shyne*?

13. *Sheep overboard (problem).* In Gorris v. Scott, 9 L.R. Ex. 125 (1874), the defendant, a shipowner, undertook to carry the plaintiffs' sheep from a foreign port to England. The sheep were swept overboard in a storm and drowned. A statute, the Contagious Diseases (Animals) Act, had required that animals in these circumstances be kept in pens to prevent the spread of diseases among them. The defendant had failed to pen the sheep, however; assume that if he had done so, they would not have been washed overboard. A case of negligence per se?

14. *Keys in the ignition (problem).* In Ross v. Hartman, 139 F.2d 14 (D.C. Cir. 1943), the defendant's driver left a truck unlocked, with an unlocked gear shift and with the keys in the ignition, near a garage in a public alley. The driver expected an attendant to move the truck into the garage, but apparently did not notify anyone of this expectation. An unknown miscreant drove away in the truck and ran down the plaintiff. The plaintiff sued the truck driver's employer, claiming the driver had committed negligence per se by violating the following traffic ordinance:

> *Locks on Motor Vehicles.* Every motor vehicle shall be equipped with a lock suitable to lock the starting lever, throttle, or switch, or gear-shift lever, by which the vehicle is set in motion, and no person shall allow any motor vehicle operated by him to stand or remain unattended on any street or in any public place without first having locked the lever, throttle, or switch by which said motor vehicle may be set in motion.

What result would you expect in this case? What arguments for each side might be made from the cases considered above?

2. Judge-Made Rules

Oliver Wendell Holmes, Jr., The Common Law
111-129 (1881)

[A]ny legal standard must, in theory, be one which would apply to all men, not specially excepted, under the same circumstances. It is not intended that the public force should fall upon an individual accidentally, or at the whim of any body of men. The standard, that is, must be fixed. In practice, no doubt, one man may have to pay and another may escape, according to the different feelings of different juries. But this merely shows that the law does not perfectly accomplish its ends. The theory or intention of the law is not that the feeling of approbation or blame which a particular twelve may entertain should be the criterion. They are supposed to leave their idiosyncrasies on one side, and to represent the feeling of the community. The ideal average prudent man, whose equivalent the jury is taken to be in many cases, and whose culpability or innocence is the supposed test, is a constant, and his conduct under given circumstances is theoretically always the same.

Finally, any legal standard must, in theory, be capable of being known. When a man has to pay damages, he is supposed to have broken the law, and he is further supposed to have known what the law was.

If, now, the ordinary liabilities in tort arise from failure to comply with fixed and uniform standards of external conduct, which every man is presumed and required to know, it is obvious that it ought to be possible, sooner or later, to formulate these standards at least to some extent, and that to do so must at last be the business of the court. It is equally clear that the featureless generality, that the defendant was bound to use such care as a prudent man would do under the circumstances, ought to be continually giving place to the specific one, that he was bound to use this or that precaution under these or those circumstances. The standard which the defendant was bound to come up to was a standard of specific acts or omissions, with reference to the specific circumstances in which he found himself. If in the whole department of unintentional wrongs the courts arrived at no further utterance than the question of negligence, and left every case, without rudder or compass, to the jury, they would simply confess their inability to state a very large part of the law which they required the defendant to know, and would assert, by implication, that nothing could be learned by experience. But neither courts nor legislatures have ever stopped at that point. [. . .]

When a case arises in which the standard of conduct, pure and simple, is submitted to the jury, the explanation is plain. It is that the court, not entertaining any clear views of public policy applicable to the matter, derives the rule to be applied from daily experience, as it has been agreed that the great body of the law of tort has been derived. But the court further feels that it is not itself possessed of sufficient practical experience to lay down the rule intelligently. It conceives that twelve men taken from the practical part of the community can aid its judgment. Therefore it aids its conscience by taking the opinion of the jury.

But supposing a state of facts often repeated in practice, is it to be imagined that the court is to go on leaving the standard to the jury forever? Is it not manifest, on the contrary, that if the jury is, on the whole, as fair a tribunal as it is represented to be, the lesson which can be got from that source will be learned? Either the court will find that the fair teaching of experience is that the conduct complained of usually is or is not blameworthy, and therefore, unless explained, is or is not a ground of liability; or it will find the jury oscillating to and fro, and will see the necessity of making up its mind for itself. There is no reason why any other such question should not be settled, as well as that of liability for stairs with smooth strips of brass upon their edges. The exceptions would mainly be found where the standard was rapidly changing, as, for instance, in some questions of medical treatment.

If this be the proper conclusion in plain cases, further consequences ensue. Facts do not often exactly repeat themselves in practice; but cases with comparatively small variations from each other do. A judge who has long sat at nisi prius ought gradually to acquire a fund of experience which enables him to represent the common sense of the community in ordinary instances far better than an average jury. He should be able to lead and to instruct them in detail, even where he thinks it desirable, on the whole, to take their opinion. Furthermore, the sphere in which he is able to rule without taking their opinion at all should be continually growing. [. . .]

The same principle applies to negligence. If the whole evidence in the case was that a party, in full command of his senses and intellect, stood on a railway track, looking at an approaching engine until it ran him down, no judge would leave it to the jury to say whether the conduct was prudent. If the whole evidence was that he attempted to cross a level track, which was visible for half a mile each way, and on which no engine was in sight, no court would allow a jury to find negligence. Between these extremes are cases which would go to the jury. But it is obvious that the limit of safety in such cases, supposing no further elements present, could be determined almost to a foot by mathematical calculation.

The trouble with many cases of negligence is, that they are of a kind not frequently recurring, so as to enable any given judge to profit by long experience with juries to lay down rules, and that the elements are so complex that courts are glad to leave the whole matter in a lump for the jury's determination.

NOTES

1. *Stop, look, and listen.* In Baltimore & Ohio R.R. v. Goodman, 275 U.S. 66 (1927), Goodman was killed when his truck was hit by a train coming through a crossing at approximately 60 miles per hour. His administratrix sued the railroad. The Supreme Court described the facts as follows: "Goodman was driving an automobile truck in an easterly direction and was killed by a train running southwesterly across the road at a rate of not less than 60 miles an hour. The line was straight but it is said by the respondent that Goodman 'had no practical view' beyond a section house 243 feet north of the crossing until he was about 20 feet from the first rail, or, as the respondent argues, 12 feet from danger, and that then the engine was still obscured by the section house. He had been driving at the rate of 10 or 12 miles an hour but had cut down his rate to 5 or 6 miles at about 40 feet from the crossing. It is thought that there was an emergency in which, so far as appears, Goodman did all that he could." The trial court denied the defendant's motion for a directed verdict, and the jury brought in a verdict for the plaintiff. The defendant appealed.

Held, for the defendant, that the trial court should have directed a verdict in its favor. Holding that the plaintiff's failure to "stop, look and listen" was negligence as a matter of law, Holmes, J., said:

> When a man goes upon a railroad track he knows that he goes to a place where he will be killed if a train comes upon him before he is clear of the track. He knows that he must stop for the train not the train stop for him. In such circumstances it seems to us that if a driver cannot be sure otherwise whether a train is dangerously near he must stop and get out of his vehicle, although obviously he will not often be required to do more than to stop and look. It seems to us that if he relies upon not hearing the train or any signal and takes no further precaution he does so at his own risk. If at the last moment Goodman found himself in an emergency it was his own fault that he did not reduce his speed earlier or come to a stop. It is true, as said in *Flannelly v. Delaware & Hudson Co.*, that the question of due care very generally is left to the jury. But we are dealing with a standard of conduct, and when the standard is clear it should be laid down once for all by the Courts.

2. *The Wabash Cannonball.* In Pokora v. Wabash Ry., 292 U.S. 98 (1934), the plaintiff, Pokora, was struck by a train and injured when he drove his truck across a railway crossing. As Pokora left the northeast corner of the intersection where his truck had been stopped, he looked to the north for approaching trains. He did this at a point about 10 or 15 feet east of a switch that lay ahead of him. A string of box cars standing on the switch cut off Pokora's view of the tracks beyond him to the north. At the same time he listened, but heard neither bell nor whistle. Still listening, he crossed the switch; as he reached the main track he was struck by a passenger train coming from the north at a speed of 25 to 30 miles per hour.

The district court held that the plaintiff had committed contributory negligence as a matter of law and directed a verdict for the defendant. The Supreme Court reversed. In holding that the plaintiff was not guilty of contributory negligence as a matter of law, and that the issue should have been given to the jury, Cardozo, J., wrote for the Court:

> The argument is made, however, that our decision in *B. & O. R. Co. v. Goodman* is a barrier in the plaintiff's path, irrespective of the conclusion that might commend itself if the question were at large. [. . .] Here the fact is not disputed that the plaintiff did stop before he started to cross the tracks. If we assume that by reason of the box cars, there was a duty to stop again when the obstructions had been cleared, that duty did not arise unless a stop could be made safely after the point of clearance had been reached. For reasons already stated, the testimony permits the inference that the truck was in the zone of danger by the time the field of vision was enlarged. No stop would then have helped the plaintiff if he remained

seated on his truck, or so the triers of the facts might find. His case was for the jury, unless as a matter of law he was subject to a duty to get out of the vehicle before it crossed the switch, walk forward to the front, and then, afoot, survey the scene. We must say whether his failure to do this was negligence so obvious and certain that one conclusion and one only is permissible for rational and candid minds. Standards of prudent conduct are declared at times by courts, but they are taken over from the facts of life. To get out of a vehicle and reconnoiter is an uncommon precaution, as everyday experience informs us. Besides being uncommon, it is very likely to be futile, and sometimes even dangerous. If the driver leaves his vehicle when he nears a cut or curve, he will learn nothing by getting out about the perils that lurk beyond. By the time he regains his seat and sets his car in motion, the hidden train may be upon him. [...] Where was Pokora to leave his truck after getting out to reconnoiter? If he was to leave it on the switch, there was the possibility that the box cars would be shunted down upon him before he could regain his seat. The defendant did not show whether there was a locomotive at the forward end, or whether the cars were so few that a locomotive could be seen. If he was to leave his vehicle near the curb, there was even stronger reason to believe that the space to be covered in going back and forth would make his observations worthless. One must remember that while the traveler turns his eyes in one direction, a train or a loose engine may be approaching from the other.

Illustrations such as these bear witness to the need for caution in framing standards of behavior that amount to rules of law. The need is the more urgent when there is no background of experience out of which the standards have emerged. They are then, not the natural flowerings of behavior in its customary forms, but rules artificially developed, and imposed from without. Extraordinary situations may not wisely or fairly be subjected to tests or regulations that are fitting for the commonplace or normal. In default of the guide of customary conduct, what is suitable for the traveler caught in a mesh where the ordinary safeguards fail him is for the judgment of a jury. The opinion in Goodman's case has been a source of confusion in the federal courts to the extent that it imposes a standard for application by the judge, and has had only wavering support in the courts of the states. We limit it accordingly.

3) *Wake up, Louis!* In Theisen v. Milwaukee Automobile Mut. Ins. Co., 118 N.W.2d 140 (Wis. 1963), the plaintiff, Sharon Theisen, and the defendant, Louis Shepherd, were high school students who attended a cast party after their senior class play. At about 3:00 A.M. the party broke up and five girls, including the plaintiff, got into Shepherd's car to be driven home. After traveling about four miles, the car gradually veered from the right lane to the left and then onto the shoulder of the road. Shepherd had fallen asleep at the wheel. One of the girls in the front seat shouted, "Louis, lookout," but there was no reaction;

another girl hollered "Louie," but Shepherd did not move. The car proceeded 270 feet and then hit a large tree stump, causing injuries for which the plaintiff sought to recover. The Wisconsin Supreme Court held that the driver was negligent as a matter of law:

> [W]e find no justification in the common experience of mankind for one's falling asleep with his foot on the accelerator, his hands on the wheel and his auto transformed into an instrument of destruction. The process of falling asleep — normal and healthy sleep — is a matter of common experience and usually attended by premonitory warnings or is to be expected. Such warnings or reasonable expectations of sleep are especially accentuated when one is conscious of his duty to stay awake while driving and the failure to heed such warnings and permitting one-self to fall asleep while driving an automobile must be deemed negligence as a matter of law. If while driving a car one is in such a state of exhaustion that he falls asleep without any premonitory warning, he is chargeable with the knowledge of any ordinarily prudent man that such exhaustion is reasonably likely to cause sleep while driving. [. . .]
>
> We exclude from this holding those exceptional cases of loss of consciousness resulting from injury inflicted by an outside force or fainting or heart attack, epileptic seizure, or other illness which suddenly incapacitates the driver of an automobile and when the occurrence of such disability is not attended with sufficient warning or should not have been reasonably foreseen. When, however, such occurrence should have been reasonably foreseen, we have held the driver of a motor vehicle negligent as a matter of law, as in the sleep cases.
>
> The trial court excluded an offer of proof made by the defendant which would have shown Shepherd was not an habitual user of alcoholic beverages and was physically exhausted from the loss of considerable sleep for some six weeks prior to the accident practicing for the play, getting to bed later than his normal bedtime and continuing his usual farm chores. It was not error of the trial court to reject this evidence offered to prove a justification for going to sleep. On the contrary, such proof would have tended to show Shepherd should have known, as a reasonable prudent man, he was likely to have fallen asleep. Such offer of proof, of course, is immaterial under our holding that falling asleep while driving is negligence as a matter of law.

Why might *Theisen v. Milwaukee Automobile Mut. Ins. Co.* be a better candidate for a judge-made rule than *Pokora v. Wabash Ry.?*

4) *Dust storm.* In Blaak v. Davidson, 529 P.2d 1048 (Wash. 1975), the defendant was driving an 18,000-pound gasoline truck on the Pasco Kahlotus highway. Farmlands adjoining the highway had recently been plowed, leaving the soil dusty. As the defendant was proceeding towards Kahlotus, a

dust cloud engulfed his truck and completely obscured his visibility. He reduced his speed to five to ten miles per hour. As he was proceeding through the dust cloud, his truck struck the rear of the plaintiff's car, which had slowed to two to three miles per hour. No traffic citations were issued to either driver. The jury brought in a verdict for the defendant; the trial court entered judgment n.o.v. (judgment notwithstanding the verdict) for the plaintiff. The defendant appealed.

The Washington Supreme Court defined the issue in the case as follows: "When the visibility of a driver of a vehicle is completely obscured by atmospheric conditions, e.g., a dust storm, is the driver (a) negligent as a matter of law for failure to stop the vehicle, or (b) should the question of negligence ordinarily be submitted to the jury for consideration in view of the facts and surrounding circumstances?" The court adopted the latter position:

> A consideration of whether an absolute rule should be formulated must focus upon the subject matter involved and the potential variables as to facts and circumstances. In these respects, the automobile and its use in our mobile society is particularly unique. Seldom, if ever, are the facts and circumstances surrounding a collision the same. Thus, particularly with respect to automobiles, the propriety of solidifying the law into mechanistic rules for universal application is dubious, and this legal reasoning or philosophy is clearly on the wane.
>
> In this regard, human experience has proved unworkable and unjust: the attempt by Justice Holmes, in *Baltimore & Ohio R. R. v. Goodman*, to establish an absolute rule that a driver approaching a railroad must stop, look, listen and, if necessary, get out of the car before crossing the tracks. Consequently the Holmes rule in its absolute form was subsequently rejected by Justice Cardozo in *Pokora v. Wabash Ry.*, and most other jurisdictions have followed suit. Similarly, the range of vision rule, i.e., that a driver of a vehicle is negligent as a matter of law unless he can stop within the range of his vision, has undergone a process of atrophy when it became apparent that an unwavering application of the rule would be unjust.
>
> The excessive rigidity of an absolute duty to stop is underscored by the facts of the instant case. Since it is the very nature of dust clouds — as well as of fog — that their density and the corresponding lack of visibility may vary considerably within a few yards, the defendant herein could not assume that all vehicles behind him would necessarily be stopped. Moreover, the defendant's truck was loaded with gasoline; there was no place to immediately pull off the highway; and the defendant feared being rear ended on this heavily traveled road. That the defendant's fears were not solely the figment of an overactive imagination is well illustrated by the fact that a car which had stopped close to the place of the accident herein was struck by a tanker traveling in the opposite direction. In any event, it is

at least debatable whether stopping on the highway for an indeterminate period of time would be safer, with respect to other users of the highway, than slowly proceeding to a known, safe, pull out a short distance ahead.

On the basis of the foregoing analysis, we reject the rule holding a driver of a vehicle negligent as a matter of law for failure to stop when his vision is completely obscured, because such a rule would be too rigid to cope with the numerous situations presenting new or additional factors and variables. [. . .] When vision is partially or completely obscured, the jury should determine whether the defendant's failure to stop constitutes negligence under the general test of whether defendant acted as a reasonable man in view of all the facts and circumstances. Only in the most unusual and exceptional circumstances indicating clear fault and liability should the court hold defendant negligent as a matter of law.

What distinctions might you draw between *Blaak v. Davidson* and *Theisen v. Milwaukee Automobile Mut. Ins. Co.* (negligence per se when a driver falls asleep)? What analogy might be drawn between *Blaak v. Davidson* and *Tedla v. Ellman* (holding the plaintiff not negligent as a matter of law when she walked on the wrong side of the road in violation of statute)?

5. *Seat belts.* Suppose a plaintiff injured in an automobile accident concedes that he was not wearing his seat belt. Assuming there is no statutory requirement that seat belts be worn in the jurisdiction, should the court instruct the jury that this is a case of negligence per se? (What result if there *is* such a statute?) Might there be an argument for instructing the jury that as a matter of law a failure to wear a seat belt is *not* negligent? That was indeed a popular position in many jurisdictions during the era when a plaintiff's contributory negligence prevented him from recovering anything from a negligent defendant, and it remains the law in some jurisdictions today. See *Swajian v. General Motors Corp.*, 559 A.2d 1041 (R.I. 1989). What are the strongest arguments for or against treating the failure to wear a seat belt as a case of negligence as a matter of law?

6. *Not one of his more astute predictions.* In Mars Steel Corp. v. Continental Bank N.A., 880 F.2d 928 (7th Cir. 1989), a case concerning the imposition of sanctions against lawyers under the Federal Rules of Civil Procedure, Easterbrook, J., wrote: "Many judges and lawyers are concerned about the lack of uniformity in the application of Rule 11. Legitimate though this concern is, it is in the end no more serious than the same concern among physicians about uniformity in medical malpractice cases, or among manufacturers of drugs about uniformity in failure-to-warn cases. Fact-bound resolutions cannot be made uniform through appellate review, de novo or otherwise. Justice Holmes believed that courts would (at least, should) slowly reduce all of tort law to objective, readily applied rules. This is not viewed today as one of his more astute predictions."

E.   RES IPSA LOQUITUR

The negligence cases considered so far in this chapter generally have involved claims that the defendant failed to take some specific precaution that would have prevented an accident. But it is not always easy or even possible for a plaintiff to determine how an accident happened, much less to identify a specific untaken precaution that would have prevented it. At the same time, sometimes an accident seems obviously to be the result of a defendant's negligence: it probably would not have occurred unless someone had been negligent, and the defendant had control over the thing that caused the harm. Courts in such cases thus may allow a plaintiff to invoke the doctrine of *res ipsa loquitur* ("the thing speaks for itself") to establish the defendant's negligence. This section considers the elements of res ipsa loquitur and the different circumstances in which the doctrine can be used.

Byrne v. Boadle
159 Eng. Rep. 299, 2 H. & C. 722 (Exch. 1863)

[Action for negligence. The plaintiff's declaration stated that he was passing on the road in front of the defendant's premises when a barrel of flour fell on him from a window above. The defendant had a jigger-hoist and other machinery over that window for the purpose of lowering barrels. Several witnesses testified that they had seen the barrel fall on the plaintiff, but there was no other evidence of how the accident occurred. The trial court nonsuited the plaintiff on the ground that there was no evidence that the defendant was negligent for a jury to consider. At the argument that followed in the Court of Exchequer, the defendant's counsel contended, first, that no evidence connected the defendant with the occurrence, and that a complete stranger may have been supervising the lowering of flour barrels when the barrel fell on the plaintiff. Pollock, C.B., replied: "The presumption is that the defendant's servants were engaged in removing the defendant's flour. If they were not it was competent to the defendant to prove it." The defendant's attorney argued, further, that the plaintiff had failed to present any affirmative proof of the defendant's negligence, beyond the mere fact that the barrel had fallen. Counsel argued that the fact that accidents like this *could* be caused by negligence did not entitle the plaintiff to a presumption that negligence necessarily caused the barrel to fall. Said Pollock, C.B.: "There are certain cases of which it may be said res ipsa loquitur, and this seems one of them. In some cases the Courts have held that the mere fact of the accident having occurred is evidence of negligence, as, for instance, in the case of railway collisions." Said Bramwell, B.: "Looking at the matter in a reasonable way it comes to this — an injury is done to the plaintiff, who has no means of knowing whether it was the result of negligence; the defendant, who knows how it was caused, does not think fit to tell the jury." The subsequent decision of the Court of Exchequer was as follows.]

POLLOCK, C.B. — We are all of opinion that the rule must be absolute to enter the verdict for the plaintiff. The learned counsel was quite right in saying that there are many accidents from which no presumption of negligence can arise, but I think it would be wrong to lay down as a rule that in no case can presumption of negligence arise from the fact of an accident. Suppose in this case the barrel had rolled out of the warehouse and fallen on the plaintiff, how could he possibly ascertain from what cause it occurred? It is the duty of persons who keep barrels in a warehouse to take care that they do not roll out, and I think that such a case would, beyond all doubt, afford prima facie evidence of negligence. A barrel could not roll out of a warehouse without some negligence, and to say that a plaintiff who is injured by it must call witnesses from the warehouse to prove negligence seems to me preposterous. So in the building or repairing a house, or putting pots on the chimneys, if a person passing along the road is injured by something falling upon him, I think that those whose duty it was to put it in the right place are prima facie responsible, and if there is any state of facts to rebut the presumption of negligence, they must prove them. The present case upon the evidence comes to this, a man is passing in front of the premises of a dealer in flour, and there falls down upon him a barrel of flour. I think it apparent that the barrel was in the custody of the defendant who occupied the premises, and who is responsible for the acts of his servants who had the control of it; and in my opinion the fact of its falling is prima facie evidence of negligence, and the plaintiff who was injured by it is not bound to show that it could not fall without negligence, but if there are any facts inconsistent with negligence it is for the defendant to prove them.

NOTES

1. *The defendant does not think fit to tell the jury.* Note that in the comments the judges made during the argument of the case, two kinds of theories emerged to support a presumption that the defendant was negligent: the accident very likely resulted from negligence (Pollock's point); and the parties did not have the same access to evidence bearing on how the accident occurred (Bramwell's point). As you read the cases in this section, consider the presence or absence of those two rationales for the doctrine.

2. *The falling of the wedge.* In Combustion Engineering Co. v. Hunsberger, 187 A. 825 (Md. App. 1936), the plaintiff, one Hunsberger, was a workman on a project that involved rebuilding a boiler room. Hunsberger worked on the floor; the defendant's workmen were building a nearby shaft that was 30 feet tall. At one point one of the defendant's workers, a man called Durdella, was lying on a platform at the top of the shaft and

attempting to hammer a metal wedge between two plates. The wedge slipped out of place and fell down the shaft onto Hunsberger, causing injuries for which he sought to recover. The jury brought in a verdict for Hunsberger, and the trial court entered judgment upon it. The court of appeals reversed, holding the evidence of Durdella's negligence insufficient to support the verdict:

> The plaintiff's case was rested on an assumption that the mere fact of the falling of the wedge afforded evidence of negligence, and the trial court, on a prayer of the plaintiff's instructed the jury that this was true. But this court does not agree in that view. There must be evidence from which the jury might reasonably and properly conclude that there was negligence. And apart from any question of the effect on a prima facie presumption, if there should be one, of evidence of the facts produced by a defendant (*Byrne v. Boadle*, 2 H.C. 722), the court is of opinion that the mere fall of a tool being used within the building, in work of construction, cannot be presumed to result from negligence, because it cannot be supposed that such a thing is probably the result of negligence every time it occurs. On the contrary, it would seem likely that with workmen handling loose tools continually, the falling of some of them at times must be expected despite all precautions. To presume otherwise would be to presume a perfection in men's work which we know does not exist. Precautions that will ordinarily keep falling objects from an adjacent highway are required, for the work should not invade the highway. And temporary covered walks built below construction work are common sights. When objects have dropped on highways it has been presumed, prima facie, that the dropping resulted from lack of the requisite precautions to keep them off. [. . .] But as stated, it seems to the court plain that there must be some falling of small tools and other objects handled with ordinary care in the course of the work, and that therefore a particular fall cannot, of itself and without more, afford proof of negligence. [. . .]
>
> The facts given in Durdella's evidence leave it open to speculation whether despite his belief that the wedge was held fast he had driven it in more lightly than usual, or whether the plates offered unusual and unexpected resistance. That the wedge jumped out when struck would seem to indicate unexpected resistance. If there was a miscalculation on Durdella's part as to the resistance, or otherwise, that fact alone would not indicate negligence unless it could be said that every such miscalculation on the part of a workman is probably due to lack of ordinary care. And plainly, we think, it cannot.

What is the distinction between *Combustion Engineering Co. v. Hunsberger* and *Byrne v. Boadle*? Might the cases be distinguished using the Hand formula?

3. *Falling armchairs.* In Larson v. St. Francis Hotel, 188 P.2d 513 (Cal. App. 1948), the plaintiff was walking on a sidewalk in San Francisco on V-J Day, August 14, 1945, when a heavy, overstuffed armchair fell onto her head, knocking her unconscious and causing her various injuries. None of the people in the vicinity of the accident saw where the chair came from; nobody saw the chair at all until it was within a few feet of the plaintiff's head. The chair bore no identifying marks. The court nevertheless found it reasonable to infer that the chair had fallen from one of the windows of the St. Francis Hotel, the marquee of which the plaintiff had just passed; it appeared that the ejection of the chair from one of the hotel's windows was a result of "the effervescence and ebullition of San Franciscans in their exuberance of joy on V-J Day." At trial the plaintiff, after proving the foregoing facts and the extent of her injuries, rested, relying on the doctrine of res ipsa loquitur. The court granted the defendant's motion for a nonsuit; the court of appeals affirmed:

> In *Gerhart v. Southern California Gas Co.*, 56 Cal. App. 2d 425, cited by plaintiff, the court sets forth the test for the applicability of the doctrine. ". . . for a plaintiff to make out a case entitling him to the benefit of the doctrine, he must prove (1) that there was an accident; (2) that the thing or instrumentality which caused the accident was at the time of and prior thereto under the exclusive control and management of the defendant; (3) that the accident was such that in the ordinary course of events, the defendant using ordinary care, the accident would not have happened. . . . The doctrine of res ipsa loquitur applies only where the cause of the injury is shown to be under the exclusive control and management of the defendant and can have no application . . . to a case having a divided responsibility where an unexplained accident may have been attributable to one of several causes, for some of which the defendant is not responsible, and when it appears that the injury was caused by one of two causes for one of which defendant is responsible but not for the other, plaintiff must fail, if the evidence does not show that the injury was the result of the former cause, or leaves it as probable that it was caused by one or the other."
>
> Applying the rule to the facts of this case, it is obvious that the doctrine does not apply. While, as pointed out by plaintiff, the rule of exclusive control "is not limited to the actual physical control but applies to the right of control of the instrumentality which causes the injury" it is not clear how this helps plaintiff's case. A hotel does not have exclusive control, either actual or potential, of its furniture. Guests have, at least, partial control. Moreover, it cannot be said that with the hotel using ordinary care "the accident was such that in the ordinary course of events would not have happened." On the contrary, the mishap would quite as likely be due to the fault of a guest or other person as to that of defendants. The most logical inference from the circumstances shown is that the chair was thrown by some such person from a window. It thus appears

that this occurrence is not such as ordinarily does not happen without the negligence of the party charged, but, rather, one in which the accident ordinarily might happen despite the fact that the defendants used reasonable care and were totally free from negligence. To keep guests and visitors from throwing furniture out windows would require a guard to be placed in every room in the hotel, and no one would contend that there is any rule of law requiring a hotel to do that.

What is the distinction between *Larson v. St. Francis Hotel* and *Byrne v. Boadle*?

4. *Here's mud in your eye!* In Connolly v. Nicollet Hotel, 95 N.W.2d 657 (Minn. 1959), the plaintiff was walking along the sidewalk next to the defendant's hotel when she was suddenly struck in the eye with "a mud-like substance." The only place from which the falling substance could have come was the hotel. At the time the hotel was serving as headquarters for the 1953 convention of the National Junior Chamber of Commerce. The convention was lively. During its course, liquor was sold and dispensed free of charge at hospitality centers throughout the hotel. A mule was stabled in the hotel's lobby, and a small alligator was kept on the fourth floor. Bottles, ice cubes, and bags of water were thrown from the building's windows. Guns were fired in the lobby. An inspection made after the convention found that there were missing window screens, mirrors pulled off the walls in bathrooms, light fixtures and signs broken, hall lights and exit lights broken, and holes drilled through door panels; the bowl in the men's washroom was torn off the wall, and 150 face towels had to be removed from service. The day before the accident, the hotel's general manager issued a memorandum to his staff reading in part as follows:

> WE HAVE ALMOST ARRIVED AT THE END OF THE MOST HARROWING EXPERIENCE WE HAVE HAD IN THE WAY OF CONVENTIONS, AT LEAST IN MY EXPERIENCE! WHEN WE BECAME INVOLVED AND SAW WHAT THE SITUATION WAS, WE HAD NO ALTERNATIVE BUT TO PROCEED AND "TURN THE OTHER CHEEK." HOWEVER, IT INVOLVES CERTAIN EXPENSES THAT I DO NOT PROPOSE TO FOREGO WITHOUT AT LEAST AN ARGUMENT — AND MAYBE LEGAL SUIT.

The jury brought in a verdict for the plaintiff; the trial court gave judgment notwithstanding the verdict to the defendant hotel, finding that the plaintiff failed to prove negligence on the hotel's part. The court of appeals reversed:

> We have said many times that the law does not require every fact and circumstance which make up a case of negligence to be proved by direct and positive evidence or by the testimony of eye-witnesses, and the circumstantial evidence alone may authorize a finding of negligence.

Negligence may be inferred from all the facts and surrounding circumstances, and where the evidence of such facts and circumstances is such as to take the case out of the realm of conjecture and into the field of legitimate inference from established facts, a prima facie case is made.

Gallagher, J., dissented:

It is difficult to speculate as to what further precautions should reasonably have been required of defendant without making it an absolute insurer. Obviously, it could not direct its employees to enter guest rooms at random or to remain therein to prevent possible misconduct when it lacked evidence that any misconduct was occurring or was contemplated by room occupants. Not only would such procedure deprive guests of room privileges for which they had paid, but, if carried to its logical conclusion, it would require that defendant, to be exonerated from any claim of negligence, employ and station a guard in every convention guest room of the hotel during the entire convention.

In what way, if any, was the hotel negligent? What is the distinction between *Connolly v. Nicollet Hotel* and *Larson v. St. Francis Hotel* (res ipsa loquitur inapplicable when armchair falls from hotel window)?

5. *Black Angus.* In Brauner v. Peterson, 557 P.2d 359 (Wash. 1976), the plaintiff drove his car into the defendant's Black Angus cow, which had strayed onto the highway. In the plaintiff's subsequent lawsuit to recover for his damages, he produced no evidence as to how the cow escaped from the defendants' property. The trial court found for the defendants and dismissed the plaintiff's action; the Washington Supreme Court affirmed the trial judge's finding that the plaintiff's evidence was insufficient to support a verdict in his favor:

With regard to res ipsa loquitur, the presence of an animal at large on the highway is not sufficient to warrant application of the rule, i.e., the event must be of a kind not ordinarily occurring in the absence of someone's negligence. A cow can readily escape from perfectly adequate confines.

6. *Incident at the county fair.* In Guthrie v. Powell, 290 P.2d 834 (Kan. 1955), the defendants bought and sold livestock and other merchandise at the Cowley County Fair. Their main premises consisted of a two-story building, with inanimate objects for sale on the first floor and a livestock pavilion on the second floor. One day the plaintiff came onto the defendants' premises, took a seat on the first floor, and engaged in conversation with her friends. Suddenly there was a loud commotion and noise overhead, and bits of plaster and debris began to fall from the ceiling onto the plaintiff and others near her. This was immediately followed by a 600-pound steer falling

through the ceiling immediately over the plaintiff's position; the beast landed on the plaintiff, knocking her unconscious, flattening her chair, and causing her various injuries. She sued the defendants. They responded that the bare facts just recited provided no basis for holding them liable, because "reasonable conclusions other than the negligence of the defendants can be drawn to explain the occurrence." The trial court overruled the defendants' demurrer, and the Kansas Supreme Court affirmed, holding that the plaintiff was entitled to a trial and that this was an appropriate case for res ipsa loquitur.

What is the distinction between *Brauner v. Peterson* (res ipsa inapplicable when cow strays onto highway) and *Guthrie v. Powell* (res ipsa applicable when cow strays through ceiling)?

7. *Unusual occurrences.* In Wilson v. Stillwill, 309 N.W.2d 898 (Mich. 1981), the defendant, Stillwill, was an orthopedic surgeon. The plaintiff, Wilson, complained to him of trouble with his right arm. Stillwill performed an operation on the arm, and afterwards the arm became infected; as a result the arm eventually became paralyzed altogether. Wilson brought suit against Stillwill and the hospital, attempting to rely on res ipsa loquitur. The trial court gave a directed verdict to the hospital, and a jury found in favor of Stillwill. Wilson argued on appeal that his case against the hospital should have been sent to the jury under the doctrine of res ipsa loquitur; he suggested that his infection might well have been caused by the negligence of the hospital employees, such as by their not properly washing their hands, or not properly sterilizing equipment. The Michigan Supreme Court affirmed:

> The testimony showed that the defendant hospital had a post-operative infection rate well below the national average. [. . .] The plaintiffs suggest that the low incidence of infection at the defendant hospital means that infection does not ordinarily occur. From this statement they seek to apply res ipsa loquitur. Although it is true that statistically infections did not ordinarily occur at the defendant hospital, this fact does not suggest that when an infection does occur, it is the result of negligence. [. . .] The mere occurrence of a post-operative infection is not a situation which gives rise to an inference of negligence when no more has been shown than the facts that an infection has occurred and that an infection is rare.

Why not? What is the distinction between *Wilson v. Stillwill* and *Guthrie v. Powell* (the case of the cow that fell through the ceiling)?

8. *The likelihood of negligence.* What does it mean when a court says that the doctrine of res ipsa loquitur applies to a case? Consider some possible interpretations:

a. If due care had been used, the accident would have been unlikely to occur.

b. The type of accident that occurred becomes much more likely when someone is negligent than it is when due care is used.

c. When accidents of this sort occur, they usually result from negligence.

What are the differences between these formulations? Consider Guthrie, Rachlinski and Wistrich, *Inside the Judicial Mind*, 86 Cornell L. Rev. 777 (2001):

> The inverse fallacy refers to the tendency to treat the probability of a hypothesis given the evidence (for example, the probability that a defendant was negligent given that a plaintiff was injured) as the same as, or close to, the probability of the evidence given the hypothesis (for example, the probability that the plaintiff would be injured if the defendant were negligent). [...]
>
> To test whether judges would commit the inverse fallacy, we gave the judges in our study a res ipsa loquitur problem. In an item labeled "Evaluation of Probative Value of Evidence in a Torts Case," we presented all of the judges with a paragraph-long description of a case based loosely on the classic English case, *Byrne v. Boadle*:
>
> The plaintiff was passing by a warehouse owned by the defendant when he was struck by a barrel, resulting in severe injuries. At the time, the barrel was in the final stages of being hoisted from the ground and loaded into the warehouse. The defendant's employees are not sure how the barrel broke loose and fell, but they agree that either the barrel was negligently secured or the rope was faulty. Government safety inspectors conducted an investigation of the warehouse and determined that in this warehouse: (1) when barrels are negligently secured, there is a 90% chance that they will break loose; (2) when barrels are safely secured, they break loose only 1% of the time; (3) workers negligently secure barrels only 1 in 1,000 times.
>
> The materials then asked: "Given these facts, how likely is it that the barrel that hit the plaintiff fell due to the negligence of one of the workers"? The materials provided the judges with one of four probability ranges to select: 0-25%, 26-50%, 51-75%, or 76-100%.
>
> When presented with a problem like this one, most people commit the inverse fallacy and assume the likelihood that the defendant was negligent is 90%, or at least a high percentage. [...] In fact, however, the actual probability that the defendant was negligent is only 8.3%. [...] Because the defendant is negligent .1% of the time and is 90% likely to cause an injury under these circumstances, the probability that a victim would be injured by the defendant's negligence is .09% (and the probability that the defendant is negligent but causes no injury is .01%). Because the defendant is not negligent 99.9% of the time and is 1% likely to cause an injury under these circumstances, the probability that on any given occasion a victim would be injured even though the defendant

took reasonable care is 0.999% (and the probability that the defendant is not negligent and causes no injury is 98.901%). As a result, the conditional probability that the defendant is negligent given that the plaintiff is injured equals .090% divided by 1.089%, or 8.3%.

Of the 159 judges who responded to the question, 40.9% selected the right answer by choosing 0-25%; 8.8% indicated 26-50%; 10.1% indicated 51-75%; and 40.3% indicated 76-100%. Overall, the judges did well; more than 40% of them got the correct answer to a difficult question in a short period of time. Those judges who did not get the correct answer, however, exhibited a significant tendency to choose the highest range. Although we did not inquire into the reasoning process that led these judges to their answers, the number of judges who chose the highest range suggests that many committed the inverse fallacy. [. . .]

As Professor Kaye has noted, the doctrine of res ipsa loquitur (upon which the problem in our questionnaire is based) historically includes a radical misunderstanding of probability theory. According to the Restatement (Second) of Torts, a jury can infer that the defendant is negligent from the occurrence of an event that is "of a kind which ordinarily does not occur in the absence of negligence." [But e]ven if an event does not ordinarily occur when negligence is absent, the event still may be more likely to be the product of non-negligence than negligence. In the problem that we used in this study, for example, the accident was unlikely to occur when the defendant was not negligent. Nevertheless, because negligence was rare, the event was still unlikely to have been caused by negligence. Although the most recent version of the Restatement (Third) of Products Liability and drafts of the Restatement (Third) of Torts both remedy this logical error, it has lingered in the courts for over a century.

The authors refer to the Restatement (Third) of Torts; the relevant section of the proposed final draft provides as follows:

§17. RES IPSA LOQUITUR

The factfinder may infer that the defendant has been negligent when the accident causing the plaintiff's physical harm is a type of accident that ordinarily happens as a result of the negligence of a class of actors of which the defendant is the relevant member.

9. *Procedural consequences*. Where it applies, res ipsa loquitur typically permits (but does not require) a jury to find the defendant negligent on the basis of nothing more than the accident and its circumstances; the plaintiff need not put in particular evidence that the defendant should have done anything differently. Indeed, in some jurisdictions a plaintiff must choose between trying to prove "specific negligence" (particular things the defendant should have done differently) or relying on res ipsa loquitur. If a plaintiff does

rely on "res ipsa," the defendant is free to submit evidence to rebut the presumption created by the doctrine. Again, the procedural details then vary by jurisdiction. Usually the presumption created by res ipsa loquitur is treated simply as evidence for the jury to consider, so that as a practical matter the doctrine is a way for plaintiffs to avoid summary judgment despite having uncovered no untaken precaution that the defendant should have used to avoid the accident. In some jurisdictions, however, the res ipsa presumption may require judgment for the plaintiff if the defendant fails to respond with some evidence to rebut it; and occasionally courts have found the circumstantial evidence of negligence in a case so strong as to require a directed verdict for the plaintiff.

Judson v. Giant Powder Co.
107 Cal. 549, 40 P. 1020 (1895)

GAROUTTE, J. — Respondents recovered judgment for the sum of $41,164.75, as damages for acts of negligence. This appeal is prosecuted from such judgment, and from an order denying a motion for a new trial. The damages to respondents' property were occasioned by an explosion of nitroglycerine in process of manufacture into dynamite, in appellant's powder factory, situated upon the shore of the Bay of San Francisco. Appellant's factory buildings were arranged around the slope of a hill facing the bay. Nearest to respondents' property was the nitroglycerine house; next was the washing house; next were the mixing houses; then came the packing houses; and finally the two magazines used for storing dynamite. These various buildings were situated from 50 to 150 feet apart, and a tramway ran in front of them. The explosion occurred in the morning during working hours, and originated in the nitroglycerine house. There followed, within a few moments of time, in regular order, the explosion of the other buildings, the two magazines coming last; but, though last, they were not least, for their explosion caused the entire downfall and destruction of respondents' factory, residences, and stock on hand. There is no question but what the cause of this series of explosions following the first is directly traceable, by reason of fire or concussion, to the nitroglycerine explosion. Of the many employees of appellant engaged in and about the nitroglycerine factory at the time of the disaster, none were left to tell the tale. Hence any positive testimony as to the direct cause of the explosion is not to be had. The witnesses who saw and knew, like all things else around, save the earth itself, were scattered to the four winds. [...]

[The defendants-appellants argued first that the plaintiffs-respondents had assumed the risk of an explosion by selling to the defendant the land on which it built its factory. The court rejected the argument:] In making the grant, respondents had a right to assume that due care would be exercised in the conduct of the business, and certainly they have a right to demand that such care be exercised. It is argued that the explosion of all powder works is a mere matter of time; that such explosions are necessarily contemplated by every one who builds beside such works, or who brings dynamite into his dooryard. It is further contended that appellant gave to respondents actual notice of the dangerous character of its business by a previous explosion, which damaged respondents' property, and that respondents, by still continuing in business after such notice, in a degree assumed and ratified the risk, and cannot now be heard to complain. The only element of strength in this line of argument is its originality. The contention that, in the ordinary course of events, all powder factories explode, conceding such to be the fact, presents an element foreign to the case. The doctrine of fatalism is not here involved. In the ordinary course of events the time for this explosion had not arrived, and appellant had not legal right to hasten that event by its negligent acts. [. . .]

It is contended that respondents offered no evidence tending to show that the explosion of the nitroglycerine factory was occasioned by the negligence of appellant, and this contention brings us to the consideration of a most important principle of law. [. . .] Does the proof of the explosion draw with it a presumption of negligence sufficient to establish a prima facie case for a recovery? [. . .] Presumptions arise from the doctrine of probabilities. The future is measured and weighed by the past, and presumptions are created from the experience of the past. What has happened in the past, under the same conditions will probably happen in the future, and ordinary and probable results will be presumed to take place until the contrary is shown. Based upon the foregoing principles, a rule of law has been formulated, bearing upon a certain class of cases, where damages either to person or property form the foundation of the action. This rule is well declared in Shearman and Redfield on Negligence: "When a thing which causes injury is shown to be under the management of the defendant, and the accident is such as in the ordinary course of things does not happen if those who have the management use proper care, it affords reasonable evidence, in the absence of explanation by the defendant, that the accident arose from the want of care." [. . .]

In England the authorities are in entire accord. Plaintiff was passing along a highway, under a railroad bridge, when a brick used in the construction of the bridge fell and injured him. Negligence in the railroad was presumed. *Kearney v. Railway Co.*, L. R. 5 Q. B. 411. A barrel of flour rolled out of the window of a warehouse, injuring a person passing upon the street. Negligence in the warehouseman was presumed. *Byrne v. Boadle*, 2 Hurl. & C. 722. The explosion of a boiler of a steamboat is prima facie evidence of negligence. In the *Rose* case it is said: "In the present case the boiler which exploded was in the control of the employees of the defendant. As boilers do not usually explode when they are in a safe condition and are properly managed, the inference that this boiler was not in a safe condition, or was not properly managed, was justifiable." [. . .]

There is another class of cases in all essentials fully supporting our views upon this question of negligence. These cases arise in the destruction of property caused by fire escaping from locomotive engines, and, while there is some conflict in the authorities as to the true rule, it is said in Shearman and Red-field on Negligence (section 676): "The decided weight of authority and of reason is in favor of holding that, the origin of the fire being fixed upon the railroad company, it is presumptively chargeable with negligence, and must assume the burden of proving that it had used all those precautions for confining sparks and cinders (as the case may be) which have been already mentioned as necessary. This is the common law of England, and the same rule has been followed in New York, Maryland," etc., citing many other states. [...]

In the case at bar, [...] respondents placed before the court expert evidence to the effect that, if the correct process of manufacturing and handling dynamite was carefully carried out, an explosion would not occur. This evidence is stronger than in the smokestack cases, for here it declares as a certainty what there is only stated to be the probable or ordinary result; but, be that as it may, if this character of evidence was relevant and material in the smokestack cases, it is equally relevant and material here. If it was sufficient there to complete and perfect a prima facie case of negligence, it is ample here to do the same. Again, if appellant had the right, under the laws of the state, to manufacture dynamite (which is conceded), and, if by reason of the existence of such right, courts may assume that, if dynamite is properly handled in the process of manufacture, explosions will not probably occur, then respondents' case is doubly proven, for here we have, not only the presumption of the existence of certain conditions, but the evidence of witnesses as to the existence of them. [...]

Appellant was engaged in the manufacture of dynamite. In the ordinary course of things, an explosion does not occur in such manufacture if proper care is exercised. An explosion did occur, ergo, the real cause of the explosion being unexplained, it is probable that it was occasioned by a lack of proper care. The logic is unassailable, and the principle of law of presumptions of fact erected thereon is as sound as the logic upon which it is based.

For the foregoing reasons, the judgment and order are affirmed.

NOTES

1. *Double bind*. If you have studied strict liability, consider the relationship between that doctrine and res ipsa loquitur. If the plaintiffs in a case like *Judson* were to argue that the defendants should be held strictly liable for damage caused by their gunpowder factory, what response might the defendants make? Might that response then become a part of the plaintiff's argument that res ipsa loquitur should apply?

If the plaintiff obtains the benefit of the res ipsa loquitur presumption in a case like *Judson*, how — if at all — can the defendant respond? What rationale for the res ipsa doctrine is suggested by its use in cases like *Judson*? What would be the consequences of not applying res ipsa in such cases?

2. *The newspaper of record*. From The New York Times, July 10, 1892, at 1:

MIGHTY FORCE OF POWDER

TERRIFIC EXPLOSIONS IN THE VICINITY OF SAN FRANCISCO.

Five white workmen known to have been killed and a number of Chinese — seven shocks that shook buildings miles away and caused a panic.

San Francisco, July 9. — There was a terrific explosion this morning at the works of the Giant Powder Company at West Berkeley, across the bay from San Francisco. Seven distinct shocks were felt, and 300 tons of giant powder brought death and destruction to the immediate neighborhood, and caused great damage in Oakland and San Francisco. People for some moments, in both cities, were panic-stricken.

There were 180 men employed at the works when the explosion occurred, and probably it will never be known how many were killed. The majority of the workmen were Chinese.

Only five white men are known to have been killed. These include John Boe, Charles Gobertig, and Wallace Dickinson. [...]

The damage to buildings in San Francisco and Oakland will reach $100,000. In this city the scene on the principal streets was one of wild confusion. Men, pale-faced and bareheaded, rushed from business houses and anxiously looked about for some indication of where the explosion had taken place. [...]

The prisoners confined in the City Prison were in a panic. The shock came like a violent gust of wind that shook the building. Even prison officials were excited, as the rickety old building rocked to and fro from the repeated shocks. When at last the heaviest explosion came, every gas jet in the prison went out, leaving the dismal place in darkness. From without came sounds of crashing glass and cries of excited and frightened people as they ran for places of safety. Prisoners raved, cursed, and prayed in one breath. They begged piteously to be released and then swore terribly at the officials, who were deaf to their entreaties.

In Chinatown the wildest terror prevailed. Frightened Chinese did not stop to find their doors, but dashed head foremost through their windows. Several were badly cut, and one on Bartlett Alley was severely injured by jumping from a veranda on the second floor. About fifty persons sustained slight injuries in this city and in Oakland.

3. *Without a trace.* In Haasman v. Pacific Alaska Air Express, 100 F. Supp. 1 (Alaska 1951), the plaintiffs' decedents were passengers on an airplane headed to Seattle from Yakutat, Alaska. The plane vanished during the trip. No icing or storm conditions were in effect along the plane's route, and no

trace of the plane, its cargo, or its passengers ever was found. The plaintiffs sued the airline, basing their allegations of negligence on the doctrine of res ipsa loquitur. The defendants moved to dismiss the claims; the trial court denied the motion and gave judgment to the plaintiffs:

> The defendant's contention that [res ipsa loquitur] is not applicable to a case such as this is based primarily on the ground that since the plane disappeared without a trace, the defendant can have no knowledge of the cause of the loss of the plane superior to that possessed by the plaintiffs.
>
> The rule precluding the application of the doctrine where the plaintiff's knowledge is equal to that of the defendant [. . .] is applied to cases where the plaintiff has equal knowledge or where knowledge of the cause is equally accessible to the plaintiff — not to cases in which there is an equality of ignorance as in the instant case. Since inability, because of a lack of knowledge, to show specific acts of negligence is a prerequisite to the application of the doctrine itself, it follows that equality of knowledge precludes its application. But from this it does not follow that conversely equality of ignorance will likewise preclude applicability, for the function of the doctrine is to supply a fact, i.e. defendant's negligence, which must have existed in the causal chain stretching from the act or omission by the defendant to the injury suffered by the plaintiff, but which the plaintiff because of circumstances surrounding the causal chain, cannot know and cannot prove to have actually existed. I conclude, therefore, that the rule barring the application of the doctrine where there is equality of knowledge is not applicable to the case at bar.

What is the meaning of the court's distinction between equality of knowledge and equality of ignorance? What is the analogy between *Haasman v. Pacific Alaska Air Express* and *Judson v. Giant Powder Co.?*

4. *The sea itself contains many hazards.* In Walston v. Lambertsen, 349 F.2d 660 (9th Cir. 1965), the plaintiff's decedent was a member of the crew on a crab fishing boat. The boat sank, and its master and crew were drowned. The cause of the boat's disappearance was unknown. It occurred off the coast of Washington on a day when a light breeze was blowing and when the seas were calm, the weather was clear, and the visibility was about six miles. The plaintiff sued the boat's owners, claiming that the boat was unseaworthy because it was equipped with a large live crab tank that may have impaired its stability; she also based her allegations of negligence on the doctrine of res ipsa loquitur. There was a trial, and judgment was entered for the defendants. The trial judge found that "The adding of the 'live tank' to the vessel was at the instance of a competent and long experienced skipper, accomplished by a construction firm of good repute, and there is not the slightest indication that

it was improper or negligently done in any particular." The trial judge also refused to apply res ipsa loquitur to the case. The court of appeals affirmed, holding that the evidence of negligence was insufficient to support a verdict for the plaintiff:

> The appellant contends that the district court erroneously failed to apply the doctrine of res ipsa loquitur to her advantage. Our court has held that if a claimant establishes that a vessel is unseaworthy, the trial court may presume that the unseaworthiness was the proximate cause of the sinking, otherwise unexplained, of a vessel in calm seas. [. . .] A review of the opinions in these cases and all others which might seem somewhat analogous to the case at bar makes it clear that the presumption which appellant would apply has been indulged only when the claimant has been able to establish to the satisfaction of the trial court that the vessel was unseaworthy at the time it departed on its last voyage. The sea itself contains many hazards, and an inference of liability of the shipowner for the mysterious loss of his vessel should not be lightly drawn. The court below obviously and properly believed that there could be no foundation for the inference absent satisfactory proof of an unseaworthy condition which might reasonably be expected to relate directly to the sinking of the vessel.

What is the distinction between *Walston v. Lambertsen* and *Haasman v. Pacific Alaska Air Express* (L when defendant's plane disappeared without a trace)?

5. *The sleeping hitchhiker (problem).* In Archibeque v. Homrich, 543 P.2d 820 (N.M. 1975), a man named Perkins was driving from Idaho to Texas. When he reached Utah he telephoned ahead to his destination to say that he might arrive early; he said he had picked up a hitchhiker who had offered to help with the driving and would enable them to drive "straight through." Three days later Perkins' car was discovered at the bottom of a gully next to a state highway in New Mexico. Perkins and the hitchhiker were found dead inside the car; the hitchhiker was in the drivers' seat, and Perkins was on the passenger side. There were no witnesses to the crash.

Perkins' estate sued the hitchhiker's estate for negligence, relying on res ipsa loquitur. An investigation of the marks the car left behind on the road suggested that it had traveled for a while on the right hand shoulder of the highway, then veered across the road and over the left shoulder into the gully. The highway was straight, level, and dry at the point of the accident. The investigating officer suggested that the driver may have fallen asleep at the wheel, allowing the car to drift off the road to the right; the sound of the wheels hitting gravel awoke him, and he overcorrected to the left, plunging into the gully. The hitchhiker's estate countered that "in accidents such as this one an insect could have been in the car; cigarette ashes could have blown into the eyes of the driver; an animal could have run out in front of the driver; the driver could have been ill; or another vehicle could have run this vehicle off the road."

What result?

6. *Res ipsa loquitur and types of precautions.* How is it possible to say whether an accident probably was caused by negligence without knowing the details of how it occurred? Consider the amount of care and the type of care needed to safely conduct some activity — hoisting barrels, fencing in a cow, or flying an airplane. For which of these activities does reasonableness require the most care to be used? What differences exist between the kinds of precautions needed in each situation? In which case is it easiest to conclude that if there is an accident, somebody made a mistake — perhaps a "compliance error" in failing to carry out some repetitive precaution? Consider Mark F. Grady, *Res Ipsa Loquitur and Compliance Error*, 142 U. Pa. L. Rev. 887 (1994):

> The possibilities for compliance error on a Cessna are fewer than on a commercial airliner because there are not as many gauges to watch. At the birth of aviation, when a plane disappeared without a trace — Amelia Earhart's plane for instance — compliance error was much less likely to have been the cause of the disaster than in the *Haasman* crash. The reason is almost tautological: by virtue of the greater safety equipment aboard, the *Haasman* pilots had many more opportunities for compliance error than Amelia Earhart did. This theory suggests a paradox that we will see confirmed in the cases. In most instances where technology has made an activity unusually safe, that same technology has multiplied the possibilities for compliance error relative to those for unavoidable accidents. Hence, the paradox: accidents in areas with the most safety equipment are the strongest res ipsa cases. When a modern commercial airliner goes down, it is a much better res ipsa case than when a DC-3 disappears. If a nuclear reactor were to melt down, it would be an exceptionally strong res ipsa case.
>
> Crab boats are almost the opposite of commercial aircraft. The required rate of precaution is lower because the danger rate is lower. The boat travels more slowly into harm's way and fewer people are on board. Since crab boat technology is so primitive, there are many hazards that will lead to its destruction without anyone having been negligent. Indeed, the cruder safety technology leads to a higher rate of unavoidable accident than there is in the air. Also, with more rudimentary technology, the required rate of precaution is lower than on a commercial aircraft. Hence, the possibilities for compliance error are lower at sea. A strong res ipsa case is one in which the expected rate of compliance error is high relative to the normal rate of unavoidable accident. The *Haasman* air crash was that case, but the *Walston* sinking was not. [. . .]

In recent debates about the tort system, some commentators have argued that something must be seriously wrong when negligence claims are rising at the same time as objective measures of safety (fatalities per passenger mile) are improving. Far from indicating flaws in the system, this is a normal and usual relationship when technology progresses. The invention of the dialysis machine saves hundreds of lives each year, but it also adds a number of negligence claims (from compliance error) that did not exist before. The paramount purpose of the negligence system is to regulate compliance error in the use of technology. It is therefore natural that advances in technology tend to increase the number of claims.

We need to distinguish the number of claims from the claims' magnitude. The development of antiseptic techniques generally decreases the magnitude of tort claims. Consider someone accidentally injured in a hunting accident before and after Lister conducted his research on the modern antiseptic. Once good antiseptic techniques exist, negligent hunters will generally pay lower damages. Although a technology may reduce the magnitude of claims, it can still increase the number of claims. After the development of antiseptic techniques, when someone forgets to use them, there is a new negligence claim — against a doctor — which could not have existed before.

Ybarra v. Spangard
154 P.2d 687 (Cal. 1944)

GIBSON, C.J. — This is an action for damages for personal injuries alleged to have been inflicted on plaintiff by defendants during the course of a surgical operation. The trial court entered judgments of nonsuit as to all defendants and plaintiff appealed.

On October 28, 1939, plaintiff consulted defendant Dr. Tilley, who diagnosed his ailment as appendicitis, and made arrangements for an appendectomy to be performed by defendant Dr. Spangard at a hospital owned and managed by defendant Dr. Swift. Plaintiff entered the hospital, was given a hypodermic injection, slept, and later was awakened by Drs. Tilley and Spangard and wheeled into the operating room by a nurse whom he believed to be defendant Gisler, an employee of Dr. Swift. Defendant Dr. Reser, the anesthetist, also an employee of Dr. Swift, adjusted plaintiff for the operation, pulling his body to the head of the operating table and, according to plaintiff's testimony, laying him back against two hard objects at the top of his shoulders, about an inch below his neck. Dr. Reser then administered the anesthetic and plaintiff lost consciousness. When he awoke early the following morning he was in his hospital room attended by defendant Thompson, the special nurse, and another nurse who was not made a defendant.

Plaintiff testified that prior to the operation he had never had any pain in, or injury to, his right arm or shoulder, but that when he awakened he felt a sharp pain about half way between the neck and the point of the right shoulder. He complained to the nurse, and then to Dr. Tilley, who gave him diathermy treatments while he remained in the hospital. The pain did not cease but spread down to the lower part of his arm, and after his release from the hospital the condition grew worse. He was unable to rotate or lift his arm, and developed paralysis and atrophy of the muscles around the shoulder. He received further treatments from Dr. Tilley until March, 1940, and then returned to work, wearing his arm in a splint on the advice of Dr. Spangard.

Plaintiff also consulted Dr. Wilfred Sterling Clark, who had X ray pictures taken which showed an area of diminished sensation below the shoulder and atrophy and wasting away of the muscles around the shoulder. In the opinion of Dr. Clark, plaintiff's condition was due to trauma or injury by pressure or strain applied between his right shoulder and neck.

Plaintiff was also examined by Dr. Fernando Garduno, who expressed the opinion that plaintiff's injury was a paralysis of traumatic origin, not arising from pathological causes, and not systemic, and that the injury resulted in atrophy, loss of use and restriction of motion of the right arm and shoulder.

Plaintiff's theory is that the foregoing evidence presents a proper case for the application of the doctrine of res ipsa loquitur, and that the inference of negligence arising therefrom makes the granting of a nonsuit improper. Defendants take the position that, assuming that plaintiff's condition was in fact the result of an injury, there is no showing that the act of any particular defendant, nor any particular instrumentality, was the cause thereof. They attack plaintiff's action as an attempt to fix liability "en masse" on various defendants, some of whom were not responsible for the acts of others; and they further point to the failure to show which defendants had control of the instrumentalities that may have been involved. Their main defense may be briefly stated in two propositions: (1) that where there are several defendants, and there is a division of responsibility in the use of an instrumentality causing the injury, and the injury might have resulted from the separate act of either one of two or more persons, the rule of res ipsa loquitur cannot be invoked against any one of them; and (2) that where there are several instrumentalities, and no showing is made as to which caused the injury or as to the particular defendant in control of it, the doctrine cannot apply. We are satisfied, however, that these objections are not well taken in the circumstances of this case.

The doctrine of res ipsa loquitur has three conditions: "(1) the accident must be of a kind which ordinarily does not occur in the absence of someone's negligence; (2) it must be caused by an agency or instrumentality within the exclusive control of the defendant; (3) it must not have been due to any voluntary action or contribution on the part of the plaintiff." Prosser, Torts, p. 295.

There is, however, some uncertainty as to the extent to which res ipsa loquitur may be invoked in cases of injury from medical treatment. This is in part due to the tendency, in some decisions, to lay undue emphasis on the limitations of the doctrine, and to give too little attention to its basic underlying purpose. The result has been that a simple, understandable rule of circumstantial evidence, with a sound background of common sense and human experience, has occasionally been transformed into a rigid legal formula, which arbitrarily precludes its application in many cases where it is most important that it should be applied. If the doctrine is to continue to serve a useful purpose, we should not forget that "the particular force and justice of the rule, regarded as a presumption throwing upon the party charged the duty of producing evidence, consists in the circumstance that the chief evidence of the true cause, whether culpable or innocent, is practically accessible to him but inaccessible to the injured person." 9 Wigmore, Evidence, 3d Ed., §2509, p. 382.

The present case is of a type which comes within the reason and spirit of the doctrine more fully perhaps than any other. The passenger sitting awake in a railroad car at the time of a collision, the pedestrian walking along the street and struck by a falling object or the debris of an explosion, are surely not more entitled to an explanation than the unconscious patient on the operating table. Viewed from this aspect, it is difficult to see how the doctrine can, with any justification, be so restricted in its statement as to become inapplicable to a patient who submits himself to the care and custody of doctors and nurses, is rendered unconscious, and receives some injury from instrumentalities used in his treatment. Without the aid of the doctrine a patient who received permanent injuries of a serious character, obviously the result of some one's negligence, would be entirely unable to recover unless the doctors and nurses in attendance voluntarily chose to disclose the identity of the negligent person and the facts establishing liability. If this were the state of the law of negligence, the courts, to avoid gross injustice, would be forced to invoke the principles of absolute liability, irrespective of negligence, in actions by persons suffering injuries during the course of treatment under anesthesia. But we think this juncture has not yet been reached, and that the doctrine of res ipsa loquitur is properly applicable to the case before us.

The condition that the injury must not have been due to the plaintiff's voluntary action is of course fully satisfied under the evidence produced herein; and the same is true of the condition that the accident must be one which ordinarily does not occur unless some one was negligent. We have here no problem of negligence in treatment, but of distinct injury to a healthy part of the body not the subject of treatment, nor within the area covered by the operation. The decisions in this state make it clear that such circumstances raise the inference of negligence and call upon the defendant to explain the unusual result.

The argument of defendants is simply that plaintiff has not shown an injury caused by an instrumentality under a defendant's control, because he has not shown which of the several instrumentalities that he came in contact with while in the hospital caused the injury; and he has not shown that any one defendant or his servants had exclusive control over any particular instrumentality. Defendants assert that some of them were not the employees of other defendants, that some did not stand in any permanent relationship from which liability in tort would follow, and that in view of the nature of the injury, the number of defendants and the different functions performed by each, they could not all be liable for the wrong, if any.

We have no doubt that in a modern hospital a patient is quite likely to come under the care of a number of persons in different types of contractual and other relationships with each other. For example, in the present case it appears that Drs. Smith, Spangard and Tilley were physicians or surgeons commonly placed in the legal category of independent contractors; and Dr. Reser, the anesthetist, and defendant Thompson, the special nurse, were employees of Dr. Swift and not of the other doctors. But we do not believe that either the number or relationship of the defendants alone determines whether the doctrine of res ipsa loquitur applies. Every defendant in whose custody the plaintiff was placed for any period was bound to exercise ordinary care to see that no unnecessary harm came to him and each would be liable for failure in this regard. Any defendant who negligently injured him, and any defendant charged with his care who so neglected him as to allow injury to occur, would be liable. The defendant employers would be liable for the neglect of their employees; and the doctor in charge of the operation would be liable for the negligence of those who became his temporary servants for the purpose of assisting in the operation.

It may appear at the trial that, consistent with the principles outlined above, one or more defendants will be found liable and others absolved, but this should not preclude the application of the rule of res ipsa loquitur. The control at one time or another, of one or more of the various agencies or instrumentalities which might have harmed the plaintiff was in the hands of every defendant or of his employees or temporary servants. This, we think, places upon them the burden of initial explanation. Plaintiff was rendered unconscious for the purpose of undergoing surgical treatment by the defendants; it is manifestly unreasonable for them to insist that he identify any one of them as the person who did the alleged negligent act.

The other aspect of the case which defendants so strongly emphasize is that plaintiff has not identified the instrumentality any more than he has the particular guilty defendant. Here, again, there is a misconception which, if carried to the extreme for which defendants contend, would unreasonably limit the application of the res ipsa loquitur rule. It should be enough that the plaintiff can show an injury resulting from an external force applied while he lay unconscious in the hospital; this is as clear a case of identification of the instrumentality as the plaintiff may ever be able to make. [...]

[I]f we accept the contention of defendants herein, there will rarely be any compensation for patients injured while unconscious. A hospital today conducts a highly integrated system of activities, with many persons contributing their efforts. There may be, e.g., preparation for surgery by nurses and interns who are employees of the hospital; administering of an anesthetic by a doctor who may be an employee of the hospital, an employee of the operating surgeon, or an independent contractor; performance of an operation by a surgeon and assistants who may be his employees, employees of the hospital, or independent contractors; and post surgical care by the surgeon, a hospital physician, and nurses. The number of those in whose care the patient is placed is not a good reason for denying him all reasonable opportunity to recover for negligent harm. It is rather a good reason for re-examination of the statement of legal theories which supposedly compel such a shocking result.

We do not at this time undertake to state the extent to which the reasoning of this case may be applied to other situations in which the doctrine of res ipsa loquitur is invoked. We merely hold that where a plaintiff receives unusual injuries while unconscious and in the course of medical treatment, all those defendants who had any control over his body or the instrumentalities which might have caused the injuries may properly be called upon to meet the inference of negligence by giving an explanation of their conduct.

The judgment is reversed.

NOTES

1. *Something they did not appreciate.* On remand, *Ybarra v. Spangard* was retried without a jury. All of the defendants (except the hospital's owner, who was not present in the operating room) testified, and all said they had seen nothing occur which could have produced the plaintiff's injuries. The trial judge said that he thought the defendants' explanations were "honest," but that "something they did not appreciate happened in the course of the operation, in the course of handling the patient." He gave judgment to the plaintiff, and the court of appeals affirmed. Is the trial court's handling of the case on remand consistent with the *Ybarra* opinion? If the res ipsa presumption successfully induced the defendants to testify honestly, and they said that they knew nothing, then why should the presumption continue to allow the plaintiff to obtain judgments against them?

2. *Substance and procedure.* Are there uses of res ipsa loquitur that might be considered obsolete in view of the aggressive pretrial discovery now permitted to plaintiffs in tort cases? What is the difference between those two ways of forcing defendants to reveal what they know?

3. *Common knowledge.* Apart from the problem of identifying who caused the plaintiff's injury, the *Ybarra* case also raises questions about the application of res ipsa loquitur to cases of medical malpractice. How are jurors untutored in medicine to decide whether an untoward result of a complicated medical procedure "speaks for itself" and suggests that the defendant was negligent? Some states give the plaintiff in such cases the option of deciding whether to present expert witnesses; others require expert testimony in certain instances, but then struggle to distinguish between those claims of medical negligence so egregious that an inference of negligence

can be drawn by lay jurors as a matter of "common knowledge" and those where any such inference must be supported by testimony from an expert. Consider this attempt by the Nevada legislature to settle the distinction by statute:

> N.R.S. 41A.100. EXPERT TESTIMONY REQUIRED; EXCEPTIONS;
> REBUTTABLE PRESUMPTION OF NEGLIGENCE
>
> 1. Liability for personal injury or death is not imposed upon any pro-vider of medical care based on alleged negligence in the performance of that care unless evidence consisting of expert medical testimony, material from recognized medical texts or treatises or the regulations of the licensed medical facility wherein the alleged negligence occurred is pre-sented to demonstrate the alleged deviation from the accepted standard of care in the specific circumstances of the case and to prove causation of the alleged personal injury or death, except that such evidence is not required and a rebuttable presumption that the personal injury or death was caused by negligence arises where evidence is presented that the personal injury or death occurred in any one or more of the following circumstances:
>
> (a) A foreign substance other than medication or a prosthetic device was unintentionally left within the body of a patient following surgery;
>
> (b) An explosion or fire originating in a substance used in treatment occurred in the course of treatment;
>
> (c) An unintended burn caused by heat, radiation or chemicals was suffered in the course of medical care;
>
> (d) An injury was suffered during the course of treatment to a part of the body not directly involved in the treatment or proximate thereto; or
>
> (e) A surgical procedure was performed on the wrong patient or the wrong organ, limb or part of a patient's body.

4. *The author of the wrong.* In Wolf v. American Tract Society, 58 N.E. 31 (N.Y. 1900), the defendants were among 19 independent contractors working on the construction of a 23-story building in New York City. One day when work was progressing on the ninth story of the building, the plaintiff, Wolf, was on the street outside delivering pipe. A brick fell on his head. There was no evidence to suggest where the brick came from or who dropped it. Wolf sued two of the contractors at work on the building. The trial court dismissed the complaint and the Court of Appeals affirmed:

> In a case like this, where the building in process of construction is in charge of numerous contractors and their workmen, each independent of the other, and none of them subject to the control or direction of the other, some proof must be given to enable the jury to point out or identify the author of the wrong. There is no principle that I am aware of that would make all of the contractors or all the workmen engaged in erecting

this building liable *in solido*. And yet there is just as much reason for that as there is for holding two of these contractors for no other reason than that one of them had charge of the carpenter work and the other of the mason work. The plaintiff, we must assume, suffered injury from the negligence of some one; but I am not aware of any ground, in reason or law, for imputing the wrong to the two contractors who are defendants, or for selecting them from all the others as responsible to the plaintiff, unless they can conclusively show that they are not.

Cases must occasionally happen where the person really responsible for a personal injury cannot be identified or pointed out by proof, as in this case; and then it is far better and more consistent with reason and law that the injury should go without redress, than that innocent persons should be held responsible, upon some strained construction of the law developed for the occasion. The idea suggested in this case, that all or any of the 19 contractors may be held, since the plaintiff is unable by proof to identify the real author of the wrong, is born of necessity, but embodies a principle so farreaching and dangerous that it cannot receive the sanction of the courts.

Haight, J., dissented:

> Injuries of this character are not uncommon, but it is seldom that the injured party is able to show who the negligent person was; and if the principle contended for is to be sustained in its entirety, without limitation, the public has little protection from the dangers liable to occur from the construction of high buildings upon the lines of streets in our large and populous cities. A person walking along a street, who is suddenly crushed to the earth by a brick falling from a high building filled with workmen, has but slight opportunity to ascertain who the person was who caused the brick to fall, and such person seldom confesses to his misconduct. It was owing to this difficulty that the rule of presumption of negligence to which we have alluded was established. It was a rule founded upon necessity, designed for the protection of the public, and, in my judgment, should not be abrogated because the owner sees fit to contract with two or more persons to construct his building.

What is the distinction between *Wolf v. American Tract Society* and *Byrne v. Boadle* (the L case of the falling barrel)? What is the distinction between *Wolf v. American Tract Society* and *Ybarra v. Spangard*?

5. *Free fall.* In Bond v. Otis Elevator Company, 388 S.W.2d 681 (Tex. 1965), the plaintiff entered an elevator on the ninth floor of the Adolphus Tower Building in Dallas. The elevator went into "free fall"; after plummeting to the fifth or sixth floor it stopped and bounced violently on its cord. The plaintiff was thrown to the floor and injured her ankle. She sued

the owner of the building and the Otis Elevator Company. She did not attempt to prove that either defendant committed any specific act of negligence, but relied entirely on the doctrine of res ipsa loquitur. Otis installed the elevator and had a contract with the building to maintain it. In the contract, Otis provided in part that "we do not assume possession or management of any part of the equipment but such remains yours exclusively as the owner (or lessee) thereof." Neither defendant offered any explanation for the elevator's fall. The trial court found the defendants jointly and severally liable to the plaintiff. The Supreme Court of Texas held that the trial court did not err in allowing the plaintiff to rely cn res ipsa loquitur:

> It appears from the contract between Adolphus and Otis with reference to the maintenance of the elevators that the mechanism controlling the movement of the elevators is quite complicated and from the very nature of things the facts which would reveal how this "free fall" happened were peculiarly within the knowledge of respondents. If there is any explanation of this unusual occurrence of the elevator going into a "free fall", then the respondents are in a far better position to come forward with it than is the petitioner.
>
> We think that the evidence conclusively shows that the elevator was under the joint control of Adolphus Tower and Otis Elevator. A mere reading of that part of the contract quoted above shows this. Otis Elevator says that the contract places the exclusive control in Adolphus Tower. [. . .] It is true that the Adolphus Tower retained possession and management of the elevators by that contract, but with the understanding that Otis was to examine, lubricate, adjust and if in its judgment conditions warrant, it was to repair or replace all necessary equipment. In other words, what maintenance was required depended upon the judgment of Otis, not that of Adolphus Tower. It would be difficult to imagine a relationship between two parties with reference to certain equipment where joint control is more conclusively shown. The petitioner pleaded joint control and under this evidence we think the trial court was correct in its necessary holding, in support of its judgment, that both parties were in joint control of the elevator in question.
>
> We know of no case which holds that in order for the doctrine of res ipsa loquitur to apply that the instrumentality causing the injury must be under the exclusive control of a single entity. [. . .]

What is the distinction between *Bond v. Otis Elevator Company* and *Wolf v. American Tract Society* (the NL case of the falling brick)?

6. *A mystery that cannot be accounted for.* In Actiesselskabet Ingrid v. Central R. Co. of New Jersey, 216 F. 72 (2d Cir. 1914), DuPont made a contract to have dynamite shipped by railway from its plant in Kenville, New Jersey, to a port in Jersey City. DuPont also hired a crew managed by one

Healing to move the dynamite from the railroad car onto a ship Healing owned called the *Katherine W.*, which in turn was to carry it to Uruguay. One of the railroad's cars, which contained about 40,000 pounds of dynamite, exploded while the dynamite was being transferred from the train to the boat. The *Katherine W.* was demolished by the explosion, which was felt as far away as lower Manhattan; among the other ships damaged was the plaintiff's vessel, the *Ingrid*, which recently had arrived from Buenos Aires with a cargo of bones meant to be unloaded into the cars of the same railroad that was handling the dynamite. The *Ingrid* could not be salvaged and was auctioned off as scrap iron. The owners of the *Ingrid* sued DuPont, the railroad, and Healing, basing one theory of recovery on the doctrine of res ipsa loquitur. The district court dismissed the libel, and the court of appeals affirmed:

> According to the libelant's own theory as presented upon the argument, the accident might have been caused by the negligence of either the railroad company, the powder company, or Healing. It is also true that the explosion may have been caused by the act of outsiders entirely unconnected with any of the respondents. If the explosion itself is evidence of negligence, such negligence may have been that of the powder company in the manufacture of the dynamite or the packing of it in the boxes; or it may have been the negligence of the railroad company in improperly handling the car; or it may have been the negligence of Healing in carelessly transferring the boxes from the car into the lighter; or it may have been the negligence of unauthorized persons who may have interfered with some of these operations. And any one of these theories is almost as probable as another. The cause of the explosion is a mystery and cannot be accounted for.

Is there a satisfactory distinction between this case and *Bond v. Otis Elevator Co.*? Between this case and *Judson v. Giant Powder Co.*?

7. *Turkey salad (problem)*. In Samson v. Riesing, 215 N.W.2d 662 (Wis. 1974), the plaintiff attended a luncheon at the Wauwatosa Trinity Episcopal Church. The luncheon was hosted by 11 members of the Wauwatosa High School Band Mothers Association. The plaintiff ate turkey salad and dessert. She subsequently experienced salmonella poisoning and suffered permanent digestive injuries as a result. The plaintiff's evidence was that the turkey salad had been contaminated with salmonella bacteria. Nine members of the Band Mothers Association had participated in the preparation of the turkey salad. Each of the nine cooked a turkey in her own kitchen before the event; the ladies then brought the turkeys to the church kitchen where the salad was prepared. It was impossible to determine whose turkey had contaminated the batch. The plaintiff brought an action for negligence against all of the women who had cooked the turkeys and prepared the salad, attempting to rely on the doctrine of res ipsa loquitur. What result?

Chapter 4

Duties and Limitations

"Negligence" is the general term for the tort claim usually brought by victims of unintentional harm, whether their damages result from automobile collisions, from medical malpractice, or from other accidents of various varieties. A plaintiff bringing suit against a defendant for negligence traditionally must prove the existence of five elements: (1) duty; (2) breach of duty; (3) cause in fact; (4) proximate cause; and (5) damages. If you already have studied the chapter on The Negligence Standard, then the present chapter can be understood as addressing situations of a somewhat exceptional character where a plaintiff is injured by a careless defendant but is denied recovery because the defendant is said to have owed the plaintiff no duty of care. Alternatively, if this chapter provides your first exposure to the negligence tort, it can be viewed as laying groundwork by considering when and why people are obliged to behave carefully at all.

A. DUTIES ARISING FROM AFFIRMATIVE ACTS

It is natural to imagine that in a lawsuit seeking to recover damages for negligence, the defendant is being sued simply for being careless. The structure of the negligence tort is a bit more complicated than that, however; the precise claim in a negligence case is that the defendant had a duty to the plaintiff — a duty to use reasonable care — and that the defendant breached the duty. This way of thinking about negligence is important because in some situations a careless defendant may be found to have no duty at all toward a plaintiff, and so not be held liable even if his lack of care caused the plaintiff great harm. A simple example is a case where the plaintiff sues her neighbor because the neighbor saw that the plaintiff's house was on fire and did nothing about it. The neighbor might be condemned as behaving unreasonably; and because he failed to act, the plaintiff suffered great harm. But the neighbor will not be held liable because he had no duty of care to the plaintiff. His failure to make the call therefore cannot be a breach of duty, and no liability can result from it. This can be understood as the background rule of our system of tort liability for unintentional harm: people do not start out with duties to one another; a duty must be established, then a breach of the duty, before liability can arise.

So when *does* a defendant have a duty to be careful? First and most importantly, the law generally imposes duties of care on people when they engage in affirmative acts — the sorts of acts that can create risks for others. This is the most common sort of duty; indeed, it is so common that cases fitting this pattern often do not mention the existence of a duty at all: it just goes without saying that when you take an action — driving a car, for example, or performing a medical operation — you owe a duty of reasonable care to those your actions may injure. If you drive the car or perform the operation negligently, you breach that duty and become liable for whatever damage you cause. Most lawsuits to recover damages caused by accidents fall into this category. Duties arising from acts are so pervasive that some analysts consider it more useful to regard *this* as the background rule of torts: people have duties to act with reasonable care unless some exception applies — a "no duty" rule carved out for reasons of policy. Thus the Restatement (Third) of Torts (P.F.D. 2005) provides as follows

§7. DUTY.

(a) An actor ordinarily has a duty to exercise reasonable care when the actor's conduct creates a risk of physical harm.

(b) In exceptional cases, when an articulated countervailing principle or policy warrants denying or limiting liability in a particular class of cases, a court may decide that the defendant has no duty or that the ordinary duty of reasonable care requires modification.

Functionally it may not matter much whether you regard the existence of duties between people as the exception to a general "no duty" rule or as a rule to which there are "no duty" exceptions. The important point is to grasp when duties of care exist and when they don't.

An important consequence of the duties that arise from affirmative acts is the other side of the proposition: a defendant ordinarily cannot be held liable for simply doing nothing, even if that failure to act causes harm to the plaintiff. This was the point of the illustration involving the burning house: subject to various exceptions we will consider, a defendant who does nothing has no duty of care to others; doing nothing sometimes is called "nonfeasance," for which the law imposes no liability — as opposed to "misfeasance," or affirmative acts done carelessly, for which defendants may be held liable. Alas, the distinction between action and inaction sometimes turns out to be difficult to draw and defend. This chapter thus begins by examining where the law draws the line between doing nothing, and thus having no duty, and doing something, and thus having a duty to do it carefully.

Yania v. Bigan
155 A.2d 343 (Pa. 1959)

JONES, J. — A bizarre and most unusual circumstance provides the background of this appeal.

On September 25, 1957 John E. Bigan was engaged in a coal strip-mining operation in Shade Township, Somerset County. On the property being stripped were large cuts or trenches created by Bigan when he removed the earthen overburden for the purpose of removing the coal underneath. One cut contained water 8 to 10 feet in depth with side walls or embankments 16 to 18 feet in height; at this cut Bigan had installed a pump to remove the water.

At approximately 4 P.M. on that date, Joseph F. Yania, the operator of another coal strip-mining operation, and one Boyd M. Ross went upon Bigan's property for the purpose of discussing a business matter with Bigan, and, while there, were asked by Bigan to aid him in starting the pump. Ross and Bigan entered the cut and stood at the point where the pump was located. Yania stood at the top of one of the cut's side walls and then jumped from the side wall — a height of 16 to 18 feet — into the water and was drowned.

Yania's widow, in her own right and on behalf of her three children, instituted wrongful death and survival actions against Bigan contending Bigan was responsible for Yania's death. Preliminary objections, in the nature of demurrers, to the complaint were filed on behalf of Bigan. The court below sustained the preliminary objections; from the entry of that order this appeal was taken.

Since Bigan has chosen to file preliminary objections, in the nature of demurrers, every material and relevant fact well pleaded in the complaint and every inference fairly deducible therefrom are to be taken as true [. . .] Bigan stands charged with three-fold negligence: (1) by urging, enticing, taunting and inveigling Yania to jump into the water; (2) by failing to warn Yania of a dangerous condition on the land, i.e. the cut wherein lay 8 to 10 feet of water; (3) by failing to go to Yania's rescue after he had jumped into the water. [. . .]

Appellant initially contends that Yania's descent from the high embankment into the water and the resulting death were caused "entirely" by the spoken words and blandishments of Bigan delivered at a distance from Yania. The complaint does not allege that Yania slipped or that he was pushed or that Bigan made any physical impact upon Yania. On the contrary, the only inference deducible from the facts alleged in the complaint is that Bigan, by the employment of cajolery and inveiglement, caused such a mental impact on Yania that the latter was deprived of his volition and freedom of choice and placed under a compulsion to jump into the water. Had Yania been a child of tender years or a person mentally deficient then it is conceivable that taunting and enticement could constitute actionable negligence if it resulted in harm. However, to contend that such conduct directed to an adult in full possession of all his mental faculties constitutes actionable negligence is not only without precedent but completely without merit.

[I]t is urged that Bigan failed to take the necessary steps to rescue Yania from the water. The mere fact that Bigan saw Yania in a position of peril in the water imposed upon him no legal, although a moral, obligation or duty to go to his rescue unless Bigan was legally responsible, in whole or in part, for placing Yania in the perilous position. Restatement, Torts, §314. Cf. Restatement, Torts, §322. The language of this Court in *Brown v. French*, 104 Pa. 604, 607, 608, is apt: "If it appeared that the deceased, by his own carelessness, contributed in any degree to the accident which caused the loss of his life, the defendants ought not to have been held to answer for the consequences resulting from that accident. [...] He voluntarily placed himself in the way of danger, and his death was the result of his own act. [...] That his undertaking was an exceedingly reckless and dangerous one, the event proves, but there was no one to blame for it but himself. He had the right to try the experiment, obviously dangerous as it was, but then also upon him rested the consequences of that experiment, and upon no one else; he may have been, and probably was, ignorant of the risk which he was taking upon himself, or knowing it, and trusting to his own skill, he may have regarded it as easily superable. But in either case, the result of his ignorance, or of his mistake, must rest with himself — and cannot be charged to the defendants." The complaint does not aver any facts which impose upon Bigan legal responsibility for placing Yania in the dangerous position in the water and, absent such legal responsibility, the law imposes on Bigan no duty of rescue.

Recognizing that the deceased Yania is entitled to the benefit of the presumption that he was exercising due care and extending to appellant the benefit of every well pleaded fact in this complaint and the fair inferences arising therefrom, yet we can reach but one conclusion: that Yania, a reasonable and prudent adult in full possession of all his mental faculties, undertook to perform an act which he knew or should have known was attended with more or less peril and it was the performance of that act and not any conduct upon Bigan's part which caused his unfortunate death.

Order affirmed.

NOTES

1. *Failures to rescue.* The decision in *Yania v. Bigan* contains several noteworthy threads. The first involves Bigan's non-duty to rescue Yania. Did the reason involve the dangers to Bigan of undertaking such a rescue? Did it involve considerations of autonomy? Would the case have come out differently if Bigan had a life preserver on the ground next to him and could have tossed it to Yania without any risk to himself? Restatement (Second) of

Torts §314 provides: "The fact that the actor realizes or should realize that action on his part is necessary for another's aid or protection does not of itself impose upon him a duty to take such action." Illustration 4 reads as follows:

> A, a strong swimmer, sees B, against whom he entertains an unreasonable hatred, floundering in deep water and obviously unable to swim. Knowing B's identity, he turns away. A is not liable to B.

Is this illustration a fair interpretation of *Yania v. Bigan?*

Compare this statutory response from the Vermont legislature to the type of problem presented by the *Yania* case and treated in §314 of the Second Restatement:

> (a) A person who knows that another is exposed to grave physical harm shall, to the extent that the same can be rendered without danger or peril to himself or without interference with important duties owed to others, give reasonable assistance to the exposed person unless that assistance or care is being provided by others.
>
> (b) A person who provides reasonable assistance in compliance with subsection (a) of this section shall not be liable in civil damages unless his acts constitute gross negligence or unless he will receive or expects to receive remuneration. Nothing contained in this subsection shall alter existing law with respect to tort liability of a practitioner of the healing arts for acts committed in the ordinary course of his practice.
>
> (c) A person who willfully violates subsection (a) of this section shall be fined not more than $100.00.

Why do you suppose the fine for violation of the statute was set at $100? What calculations by the legislature might that figure represent?

2. *Liability for goading.* A second issue raised by *Yania v. Bigan* involves Bigan's non-liability for the role he played in goading Yania to jump into the water. Notice that this issue may be connected to his non-duty to rescue. Would it be possible to impose liability on Bigan for failing to rescue Yania without creating a general duty on the part of bystanders to rescue people in peril? How might you argue for a narrower duty on these facts? Consider Restatement (Second) of Torts (1965):

> §321. DUTY TO ACT WHEN PRIOR CONDUCT IS FOUND TO BE DANGEROUS
>
> (1) If the actor does an act, and subsequently realizes or should realize that it has created an unreasonable risk of causing physical harm to another, he is under a duty to exercise reasonable care to prevent the risk from taking effect.

(2) The rule stated in Subsection (1) applies even though at the time of the act the actor has no reason to believe that it will involve such a risk.

Illustration 3. A, carefully driving his truck, skids on an icy road, and his truck comes to rest in a position across the highway where he is unable to move it. A fails to take any steps to warn approaching vehicles of the blocked highway. B, driving his automobile with reasonable care, does not see the truck, skids on the ice and collides with it, and is injured. A is subject to liability to B.

§322. DUTY TO AID ANOTHER HARMED BY ACTOR'S CONDUCT

If the actor knows or has reason to know that by his conduct, whether tortious or innocent, he has caused such bodily harm to another as to make him helpless and in danger of further harm, the actor is under a duty to exercise reasonable care to prevent such further harm.

Comment a. The rule stated in this Section applies not only where the actor's original conduct is tortious, but also where it is entirely innocent. If his act, or an instrumentality within his control, has inflicted upon another such harm that the other is helpless and in danger, and a reasonable man would recognize the necessity of aiding or protecting him to avert further harm, the actor is under a duty to take such action even though he may not have been originally at fault. This is true even though the contributory negligence of the person injured would disable him from maintaining any action for the original harm resulting from the actor's original conduct.

Illustration 2. A, a "hit and run driver," negligently or innocently runs over B, inflicting serious wounds. Although A knows B's condition, he drives away and leaves B lying in the road. The weather is exceedingly cold, and B, unable to move, contracts pneumonia from the exposure. A is subject to liability to B for the illness, whether or not he would have been liable for the original wounds.

Can these provisions be squared with *Yania v. Bigan?*

3. *Overzealous contestants.* In Weirum v. RKO Radio General, Inc., 539 P.2d 36 (Cal. 1975), the defendant was the owner of KHJ, a Los Angeles radio station. KHJ sponsored a contest in which one of its disc jockeys, "the Real Don Steele," traveled in a conspicuous red automobile to a number of locations in the metropolitan area. Steele's location was announced on the air, and the first person to locate him and answer a simple question or possess a certain item of clothing received a cash prize. Two teenagers trying to follow Steele from one location to the next raced each other along the freeway at 80 miles per hour; they forced another car off the road, causing it to overturn and killing its driver. The driver's family sued KHJ (as well as the teenage drivers, one of whom had gone on to catch Steele and collect a prize). The jury brought in a verdict for the plaintiffs, and KHJ appealed from

an order denying its motion for judgment notwithstanding the verdict. The California Supreme Court affirmed:

> Defendant, relying upon the rule stated in section 315 of the Restatement Second of Torts, urges that it owed no duty of care to decedent. The section provides that, absent a special relationship, an actor is under no duty to control the conduct of third parties. As explained hereinafter, this rule has no application if the plaintiff's complaint, as here, is grounded upon an affirmative act of defendant which created an undue risk of harm.
>
> The rule stated in section 315 is merely a refinement of the general principle embodied in section 314 that one is not obligated to act as a "good samaritan." This doctrine is rooted in the common law distinction between action and inaction, or misfeasance and nonfeasance.
>
> Misfeasance exists when the defendant is responsible for making the plaintiff's position worse, i.e., defendant has created a risk. Conversely, nonfeasance is found when the defendant has failed to aid plaintiff through beneficial intervention. As section 315 illustrates, liability for nonfeasance is largely limited to those circumstances in which some special relationship can be established. If, on the other hand, the act complained of is one of misfeasance, the question of duty is governed by the standards of ordinary care discussed above.
>
> Here, there can be little doubt that we review an act of misfeasance to which section 315 is inapplicable. Liability is not predicated upon defendant's failure to intervene for the benefit of decedent but rather upon its creation of an unreasonable risk of harm to him.

What is the superficial similarity between *Weirum v. RKO General, Inc.* and *Yania v. Bigan*? What is the distinction between them?

4. *The obstinate engineer.* In Globe Malleable Iron & Steel Co. v. New York Cent. & H.R. R. Co., 124 N.E. 109 (N.Y. 1919), a fire broke out in the plaintiff's factory in Syracuse. The defendant's freight train, 54 cars and 2,160 feet in length, was slowly approaching from the west; the railroad tracks ran past the plaintiff's plant. The engineer saw the fire from a mile away but continued forward at a rate of two to six miles per hour. Meanwhile the Syracuse fire department was trying to reach the fire; a hose cart was on its way with its gong clanging loudly. Just as the cart reached the railroad crossing en route to the plaintiff's plant, the defendant's train came through and blocked the way. The hose cart turned east and headed for the next crossing, but again the train arrived just before the cart — as the engineer was able to observe from the train. A second hose cart tried to cross the tracks still further to the east, but once more the train made it to the intersection just before the cart. The captain of the hose cart called to someone on the engine asking why they did not stop and let the hose cart through. That person's lips were seen to move in apparent reply, but what he said was not heard.

The plaintiff's evidence was that the train would have needed only 30 or 40 feet to stop. Alternatively, the train could have stopped anyplace and in two minutes a separation could have been created to allow the hose carts to pass. Instead 15 minutes passed before the train cleared the intersections leading to the plaintiff's plant, during which time the plant suffered extensive damage. The plaintiff sued the railroad for negligence and won a jury verdict. The Appellate Division reversed, dismissing the plaintiff's complaint; the court of appeals again reversed, reinstating the verdict. Said the court:

> Steam railways with tracks on or across streets in the city of Syracuse owe some duty to the public. The street is still a street and is still devoted to street uses. Its legitimate function may not be unreasonably impaired. As to travelers upon it the railway necessarily has the right of way. But an emergency may arise which requires the temporary reversal of this rule. Knowing of such a condition the railway should yield what otherwise would be its rights. It should so manage its trains as not to increase the public hazard. A fair use of its tracks in view of its own interests and those of the public is what it is entitled to. Nothing more.

What is the distinction between the *Globe Malleable Iron & Steel Co.* case and *Yania v. Bigan*?

5. *A Clockwork Orange.* In Soldano v. O'Daniels, 141 Cal. App. 3d 443 (1983), the defendant, O'Daniels, owned Happy Jack's Saloon; he also owned the Circle Inn, a restaurant across the street. One day a patron of Happy Jack's entered the Circle Inn and informed the bartender that a man had been threatened at the saloon. He requested that the bartender either call the police or allow him to use the Circle Inn phone to do so himself. The phone was in a position where the patron could have used it without inconvenience to anyone, but the bartender refused both requests. The man being threatened at the saloon, Darrell Soldano, was soon shot and killed. Soldano's son brought suit against the owner of the two establishments. The trial court dismissed his complaint; the court of appeals reversed:

> The distinction between malfeasance and nonfeasance, between active misconduct working positive injury and failure to act to prevent mischief not brought on by the defendant, is founded on "that attitude of extreme individualism so typical of anglo-saxon legal thought." Bohlen, *The Moral Duty to Aid Others as a Basis of Tort Liability*, part I, (1908) 56 U. Pa. L. Rev. 217, 219-220. [. . .]
>
> Here there was no special relationship between the defendant and the deceased. It would be stretching the concept beyond recognition to assert there was a relationship between the defendant and the patron from Happy Jack's Saloon who wished to summon aid. But this does not end the matter. It is time to re-examine the common law rule of

nonliability for nonfeasance in the special circumstances of the instant case. [...]

[The court reviewed evidence of the public policy in favor of encouraging people to report crimes.] No rule should be adopted which would require a citizen to open up his or her house to a stranger so that the latter may use the telephone to call for emergency assistance. As Mrs. Alexander in Anthony Burgess' *A Clockwork Orange* learned to her horror, such an action may be fraught with danger. It does not follow, however, that use of a telephone in a public portion of a business should be refused for a legitimate emergency call. Imposing liability for such a refusal would not subject innocent citizens to possible attack by the "good samaritan," for it would be limited to an establishment open to the public during times when it is open to business, and to places within the establishment ordinarily accessible to the public. Nor would a stranger's mere assertion that an "emergency" situation is occurring create the duty to utilize an accessible telephone because the duty would arise if and only if it were clearly conveyed that there exists an imminent danger of physical harm. Such a holding would not involve difficulties in proof, overburden the courts or unduly hamper self-determination or enterprise.

What is the distinction between *Soldano v. O'Daniels* and *Yania v. Bigan*? What is the analogy between *Soldano v. O'Daniels* and *Globe Malleable Iron & Steel Co. v. New York Cent. & H.R. R. Co.* (the L case of the train that slowly drove past the plaintiff's plant as it burned)?

6. *The Sting.* In Stangle v. Fireman's Fund Insurance Co., 198 Cal. App. 3d 971 (1988), the plaintiff purchased a diamond ring in Honolulu in exchange for a $30,000 promissory note that was due in six months. The plaintiff testified that he bought the ring "to hold it for a short period of time and sell it for a profit." He asked one Barnabas Britt, a former girlfriend, to attempt to sell the ring in San Francisco, and told her that she would be entitled to any sale proceeds in excess of $45,000. Britt placed an advertisement offering to sell the ring for $60,000. She was contacted by a man who identified himself as Barry Richards; she met with him and agreed to sell the ring to his principal for $50,000. At Richards's direction, the sale was to take place the next day in the defendant's office building at One Market Plaza in San Francisco. Richards explained to Britt that "the person that he represented wanted the ring photographed and insured before he left the premises with it."

On the next day Britt retrieved the ring from a safe deposit box and met Richards on the fourteenth floor of the defendant's building. While Britt wrote out a bill of sale, Richards asked for the ring to have it photographed. Richards then disappeared, and neither he nor the ring ever was seen again. Britt testified that a friend of hers "was right behind" Richards when Britt went to the building's receptionist to call for assistance. Britt explained to the receptionist that the ring had been stolen, but the receptionist put her hand down on the phone and said, "I'm sorry. This is for building use only." Britt reported the theft to a security attendant and the police soon were called; but by then it was too late to apprehend the thief. The plaintiff (Britt's ex-boyfriend, who had asked her to sell the ring) sued the defendant on the theory that it had a duty, after being informed of the theft in progress, to make its telephone available to Britt. At the close of trial the defendant was granted a directed verdict. The court of appeals affirmed.

What is the distinction between *Stangle v. Fireman's Fund Insurance Co.* and *Soldano v. O'Daniels* (the L case where the bartender would not allow the phone to be used to report an assault)? What rule emerges from *Stangle* and *Soldano*? How might you explain the relationship between that rule and the principles underlying *Globe Malleable Iron & Steel Co. v. New York Cent. & H.R. R. Co.*?

7. *Theoretical perspectives.* The question of whether the law ought to impose duties on strangers to rescue one another in some circumstances has generated a great deal of scholarly commentary. Here are some examples.

a. Ames, *Law and Morals*, 22 Harv. L. Rev. 97 (1908):

It remains to consider whether the law should ever go so far as to give compensation or to inflict punishment for damage which would not have happened but for the wilful inaction of another. I exclude rare cases in which, by reason of some relation between the parties like that of father and child, nurse and invalid, master and servant and others, there is a recognized legal duty to act. In the case supposed the only relation between the parties is that both are human beings. As I am walking over a bridge a man falls into the water. He cannot swim and calls for help. I am strong and a good swimmer, or, of you please, there is a rope on the bridge, and I might easily throw him an end and pull him ashore. I neither jump in nor throw him the rope, but see him drown. Or, again, I see a child on the railroad track too young to appreciate the danger of the approaching train. I might easily save the child, but do nothing, and the child, though it lives, loses both legs. Am I guilty of a crime, and must I make compensation to the widow and children of the man drowned and to the wounded child? Macaulay, in commenting upon his Indian Criminal Code, puts the case of a surgeon refusing to go from Calcutta to Meerut to perform an operation, although it should be absolutely certain that this surgeon was the only person in India who could perform it, and that, if it were not performed, the person who required it would die. [...]

In the first three illustrations, however revolting the conduct of the man who declined to interfere, he was in no way responsible for the perilous situation, he did not increase the peril, he took away nothing from the person in jeopardy, he simply failed to confer a benefit upon a stranger. As the law stands today there would be no legal liability, either civilly or criminally, in any of these cases. The law does not compel active benevolence between man and man. It is left to one's conscience whether he shall be the good Samaritan or not.

But ought the law to remain in this condition? Of course any statutory duty to be benevolent would have to be exceptional. The practical difficulty in such legislation would be in drawing the line. But that difficulty has continually to be faced in the law. We should all be better satisfied if the man who refuses to throw a rope to a drowning man or to save a helpless child on the railroad track could be punished and be made to compensate the widow of the man drowned and the wounded child. We should not think it advisable to penalize the surgeon who refused to make the journey. These illustrations suggest a possible working rule. One who fails to interfere to save another from impending death or great bodily harm, when he might do so with little or no inconvenience to himself, and the death or great bodily harm follows as a consequence of his inaction, shall be punished criminally and shall make compensation to the party injured or to his widow and children in case of death. The case of the drowning of the man shot by the hunter differs from the others in that the hunter, although he acted innocently, did bring about the dangerous situation. Here, too, the lawyer who should try to charge the hunter would lead a forlorn hope. But it seems to me that he could make out a strong case against the hunter on common law grounds. By the early law, as we have seen, he would have been liable simply because he shot the other. In modern times, the courts have admitted as an affirmative defense the fact that he was not negligent. May not the same courts refuse to allow the defense, if the defendant did not use reasonable means to prevent a calamity after creating the threatening situation? Be that as it may, it is hard to see why such a rule should not be declared by statute, if not by the courts.

b. Epstein, A *Theory of Strict Liability*, 2 J. Legal Stud. 151, 198-203 (1973):

Once one decides that as a matter of statutory or common law duty, an individual is required under some circumstances to act at his own cost for the exclusive benefit of another, then it is very hard to set out in principled manner the limits of social interference with individual liberty. Suppose one claims, as Ames does, that his proposed rule applies only in the "obvious" cases where everyone (or almost everyone) would admit that the duty was appropriate: to the case of the man upon the bridge who refuses to throw a rope to a stranger drowning in the waters below. Even if the rule starts out with such modest ambitions, it is difficult to confine it to those limits. Take a simple case first. X as a representative of a private charity asks you for $10 in order to save the life of some starving child in a country ravaged by war. There are other donors available but the number of needy children exceeds that number. The money means "nothing" to you. Are you under a legal obligation to give the $10? Or to lend it interest-free? Does $10 amount to a substantial cost or inconvenience within the meaning of Ames' rule? It is true that the relationship between the gift to charity and the survival of an unidentified child is not so apparent as is the relationship between the man upon the bridge and the swimmer caught in the swirling seas. But lest the physical imagery govern, it is clear in both cases that someone will die as a consequence of your inaction in both cases. Is there a duty to give, or is the contribution a matter of charity?

Consider yet another example where services, not cash, are in issue. Ames insists that his rule would not require the only surgeon in India capable of saving the life of a person with a given affliction to travel across the sub-continent to perform an operation, presumably because the inconvenience and cost would be substantial. But how would he treat the case if some third person were willing to pay him for all of his efforts? If the payment is sufficient to induce the surgeon to act, then there is no need for the good Samaritan doctrine at all. But if it is not, then it is again necessary to compare the costs of the physician with the benefits to his prospective patient. It is hard to know whether Ames would require the forced exchange under these circumstances. But it is at least arguable that under his theory forced exchanges should be required, since the payment might reduce the surgeon's net inconvenience to the point where it was trivial.

Once forced exchanges, regardless of the levels of payment, are accepted, it will no longer be possible to delineate the sphere of activities in which contract (or charity) will be required in order to procure desired benefits and the sphere of activity in which those benefits can be pro-cured as of right. Where tests of "reasonableness" — stated with such confidence, and applied with such difficulty — dominate the law of tort, it becomes impossible to tell where liberty ends and obligation begins; where contract ends, and tort begins. In each case, it will be possible for some judge or jury to decide that there was something else which the defendant should have done, and he will decide that on the strength of some cost-benefit formula that is difficult indeed to apply. These remarks are conclusive, I think, against the adoption of Ames' rule by judicial innovation, and they bear heavily on the desirability of the abandonment of the good Samaritan rule by legislation as well. [...]

c. William M. Landes & Richard A. Posner, *Economics of Rescue Law*:*

Given that legal intervention and altruism are substitute methods of encouraging the internalization of the external benefits of rescues in emergency situations, the question naturally arises whether studying the pattern

---

*Adapted from Landes and Posner, *Altruism in Law and Economics*, 68 Am. Econ. Rev. Papers & Proceedings 417, 420 (1978), in Posner, Tort Law: Cases and Economic Analysis 412 (1982).

of legal intervention in rescues might provide a clue to variations over time or across societies in the level of altruism. Many foreign countries, and a single state, impose liability for failure to rescue. It may be significant that no law imposing liability for nonrescue has been found prior to 1867. This may reflect the fact that in a pre-urban society reciprocal altruism may provide an adequate substitute for legal coercion to rescue. Another suggestive feature is the predominance of fascist and communist states among the early adopters of liability for nonrescue. Liability for failure to rescue is a form of conscription for social service which would seem congenial to a state that already regards its citizens' time as public rather than private property. It may not be accidental that the first [...] state to impose liability for nonrescue is Vermont, which has the third highest tax rate (after Alaska and New York) in the United States.

d. Bender, A *Lawyer's Primer on Feminist Theory and Tort*, 38 J. Legal Educ. 34-35 (1988):

How would [the] drowning-stranger hypothetical look from a new legal perspective informed by a feminist ethic based upon notions of caring, responsibility, interconnectedness, and cooperation? [...] When our legal system trains us to understand the drowning-stranger story as a limited event between two people, both of whom have interests at least equally worth protecting, and when the social ramifications we credit most are the impositions on personal liberty of action, we take a human situation and translate it into a cold, dehumanized algebraic equation. We forget that we are talking about human death or grave physical harms and their reverberating consequences when we equate the consequences with such things as one person's momentary freedom not to act. People are decontextualized for the analysis, yet no one really lives an acontextual life. What gives us the authority to take contextual, actual problems and encode them in a language of numbers, letters, and symbols that represents no reality in any actual person's life? [...] Why should our autonomy or freedom not to rescue weigh more heavily in law than a stranger's harms and the consequent harms to people with whom she is interconnected?

B. DUTIES ARISING FROM UNDERTAKINGS

Sometimes a defendant who had no duty to a stranger may acquire a duty by undertaking to provide assistance or otherwise voluntarily assuming responsibilities. This section considers the contours of the principle: When is an "undertaking" sufficiently extensive to create a duty of care?

Hurley v. Eddingfield
59 N.E. 1058 (Ind. 1901)

[The plaintiff sued the defendant, a physician, seeking $10,000 for the wrongful death of his intestate. The trial court sustained the defendant's demurrer to the complaint, and the Indiana Supreme Court affirmed:]

BAKER, J. — The material facts alleged may be summarized thus: At and for years before decedent's death appellee was a practicing physician at Mace, in Montgomery county, duly licensed under the laws of the state. He held himself out to the public as a general practitioner of medicine. He had been decedent's family physician. Decedent became dangerously ill, and sent for appellee. The messenger informed appellee of decedent's violent sickness, tendered him his fee for his services, and stated to him that no other physician was procurable in time, and that decedent relied on him for attention. No other physician was procurable in time to be of any use, and decedent did rely on appellee for medical assistance. Without any reason whatever, appellee refused to render aid to decedent. No other patients were requiring appellee's immediate service, and he could have gone to the relief of decedent if he had been willing to do so. Death ensued, without decedent's fault, and wholly from appellee's wrongful act. The alleged wrongful act was appellee's refusal to enter into a contract of employment. Counsel do not contend that, before the enactment of the law regulating the practice of medicine, physicians were bound to render professional service to every one who applied. The act regulating the practice of medicine provides for a board of examiners, standards of qualification, examinations, licenses to those found qualified, and penalties for practicing without license. The act is a preventive, not a compulsive, measure. In obtaining the state's license (permission) to practice medicine, the state does not require, and the licensee does not engage, that he will practice at all or on other terms than he may choose to accept. Counsel's analogies, drawn from the obligations to the public on the part of innkeepers, common carriers, and the like, are beside the mark.

NOTES

1. *Villains of the common law.* What is the analogy between *Hurley v. Eddingfield* and *Yania v. Bigan* (the NL case where the defendant talked the plaintiff's decedent into jumping into a pool of water and then watched him drown)? Which is the more difficult case? What facts might you use in the *Hurley* case to argue that it is a stronger case for liability than *Yania*?

2. *Medical misfeasance.* In O'Neill v. Montefiore Hospital, 11 A.D.2d 132 (N.Y. App. 1960), the plaintiff awoke at about 5:00 A.M. and saw her husband, John O'Neill, suffering from symptoms of a heart attack. She slowly walked

him to a hospital three blocks away. When they arrived at the emergency room, the nurse on duty said that the hospital did not accept patients with their insurance plan. The nurse telephoned a doctor — Dr. Craig — who was affiliated with the O'Neills' insurance plan and passed the phone to Mr. O'Neill. The plaintiff's evidence was that after discussing his symptoms, Craig advised O'Neill to go home and return to the hospital at 8:00, when a doctor who was affiliated with O'Neill's insurance plan would be available. O'Neill's wife pressed the nurse to get immediate help for her husband, but the nurse refused and likewise advised the O'Neills to come back at 8:00. Mr. O'Neill responded that "I could be dead by 8:00." The O'Neills nevertheless headed home. When they arrived there, Mr. O'Neill collapsed to the floor and died. Mrs. O'Neill sued Craig and the hospital. The trial court dismissed the plaintiff's claims at the close of the evidence, and she appealed.

Held, for the plaintiff, that her claims should not have been dismissed and that there must be a new trial. Said the court: "The law is settled that a physician who undertakes to examine or treat a patient and then abandons him, may be held liable for malpractice."

What is the distinction between *O'Neill v. Montefiore Hospital* and *Hurley v. Eddingfield* (the NL case of the doctor who refused to aid the plaintiff's decedent)? What is the distinction between *O'Neill v. Montefiore Hospital* and *Yania v. Bigan*?

3. *Botched rescue.* In United States v. Lawter, 219 F.2d 559 (5th Cir. 1955), the plaintiff (Lawter), his wife, and two other relatives were aboard a 16-foot skiff in Biscayne Bay, Florida, when a wave drowned out their motor and further waves swamped their boat. The four passengers were cast into the water about 500 yards from shore; the depth of the bay was about four feet, but the wind was strong and the waves were rough. A U.S. Coast Guard helicopter saw the Lawters during a routine patrol flight, noted that there were no boats or vessels nearby to help them, and attempted a rescue. A cable, operated by a man named Antle, was dropped to the plaintiff's wife. Antle began to draw the cable back up to the helicopter before Mrs. Lawter could get herself into the sling attached to the end of it; she was holding on with just her hands. She was raised until her head and shoulders were above the bottom of the door of the helicopter, at which point Antle stopped the cable. Mrs. Lawter had not been raised high enough to be brought into the cabin, however, and before the cable could be raised further she lost her grip and fell into the sea, suffering fatal injuries.

Mrs. Lawter's husband sued the United States, claiming that his wife's death was caused by the Coast Guard's negligence in allowing Antle — the most inexperienced member of the crew — to operate the cable. The district court brought in a verdict for the plaintiff. The defendant appealed, arguing that the plaintiff's complaint did not state a good cause of action and that the evidence was insufficient to support the verdict. The court of appeals affirmed, stating that the Coast Guard

> not only placed the deceased in a worse position than when it took charge, but negligently brought about her death, and it is hornbook law that under such circumstances the law imposes an obligation upon everyone who attempts to do anything, even gratuitously, for another not to injure him by the negligent performance of that which he has undertaken.

What is the analogy between *United States v. Lawter* and *O'Neill v. Montefiore Hospital* (the L case where the doctor told the plaintiff's decedent to come back to the hospital in a few hours)?

4. *The* Sea Captain. In *Frank v. United States*, 250 F.2d 178 (3d Cir. 1957), the plaintiff's decedent, Daniel Frank, was a passenger aboard a 30-foot cabin cruiser, the *Sea Captain*, engaged in a fishing expedition off the New Jersey coast. The cruiser became disabled because of engine failure and anchored about 400 yards off Sandy Hook. The weather was clear but windy, and a strong tidal rip running toward the shore created breaking waves four feet or more in height. All but one of the Coast Guard boats suitable for towing the disabled cruiser were out assisting other craft in the rough seas. The only available boat, a heavy motor lifeboat, was dispatched to assist the disabled cruiser and took it in tow.

During the tow Frank attempted to walk along the deck of his own boat, holding a handrail as he proceeded. The boat heeled sharply, the handrail broke, and Frank fell into the sea. The Coast Guard crew immediately cut the tow line and tried to rescue Frank, but he drowned before they could reach him. Frank's administratrix sued the United States, claiming that Frank drowned because the Coast Guard's boat had a defective reverse gear which delayed it in reaching Frank after he fell into the sea; because the life rings in the lifeboat were so secured that they could not immediately be thrown overboard; and because the crew of the lifeboat was less than the customary Coast Guard complement. The district court found for the defendant, and the court of appeals affirmed:

> If the United States is liable at all for negligence of the Coast Guard in connection with an attempted rescue operation, the responsibility of this public agency rises no higher than that of a private salvor. [. . .] An obligation to render aid may grow out of a relationship such as master and servant or ship and crewman. But there is no such relational basis for a duty here. [. . .] We have only a diligent rescue effort which proved ineffectual for lack of adequate equipment, preparation or personnel. For such ineffectual effort a private salvor is not liable.

What is the distinction between *Frank v. United States* and *United States v. Lawter* (the L case of the bungled helicopter rescue by the Coast Guard)?

5. *The good samaritan doctrine.* In Ocotillo West Joint Venture v. Superior Court, 844 P.2d 653 (Ariz. 1993), two men named Zylka and Easley spent an afternoon golfing and drinking at the Ocotillo Golf Course. Two Ocotillo employees took away Zylka's car keys because he appeared to be intoxicated. Easley then stepped forward and offered to drive Zylka home. With that assurance, and observing Easley's apparent lack of impairment, the employees gave Zylka's keys to Easley. When the two men reached the parking lot, Easley gave the keys back to Zylka. Zylka left the golf course in his own automobile, then suffered fatal injuries in a one-car accident. Zylka's family brought a lawsuit against Ocotillo; Ocotillo attempted to bring Easley into the case, alleging that he was at least partially at fault because he volunteered to drive Zylka home and then gave the car keys back to him. The district court dismissed Ocotillo's attempt to add Easley. The court of appeals reversed, relying on the "good samaritan" doctrine laid out in §323 and §324 of the Restatement (Second) of Torts:

> §323. NEGLIGENT PERFORMANCE OF UNDERTAKING
>   TO RENDER SERVICES
>
> One who undertakes, gratuitously or for consideration, to render services to another which he should recognize as necessary for the protection of the other's person or things, is subject to liability to the other for physical harm resulting from his failure to exercise reasonable care to perform his undertaking, if
>   (a) his failure to exercise such care increases the risk of such harm, or
>   (b) the harm is suffered because of the other's reliance upon the undertaking.
>
> §324. DUTY OF ONE WHO TAKES CHARGE OF ANOTHER WHO IS HELPLESS
>
> One who, being under no duty to do so, takes charge of another who is helpless adequately to aid or protect himself is subject to liability to the other for any bodily harm caused to him by (a) the failure of the actor to exercise reasonable care to secure the safety of the other while within the actor's charge, or (b) the actor's discontinuing his aid or protection, if by so doing he leaves the other in a worse position than when the actor took charge of him.

Said the court:

> When Easley took charge of Zylka for reasons of safety he thereby assumed a duty to use reasonable care. Zylka was too drunk to drive. Under one version of the facts Ocotillo's employees had taken charge

of Zylka and effectively stopped him from driving. Easley's offer deterred the employees from their efforts to keep Zylka out of his automobile. Rather than use reasonable care to drive Zylka home or make alternative arrangements, Easley discontinued his assistance and put Zylka in a worse position than he was in when Ocotillo's employees had possession of his keys. A reasonable fact finder could conclude that Easley's actions contributed to Zylka's death, rendering Easley wholly or partially at fault.

Which of the Restatement provisions the court cited seems most applicable to Easley? What is the analogy between *Ocotillo West Joint Venture v. Superior Court* and *United States v. Lawter* (the L case of the bungled helicopter rescue by the Coast Guard)?

6. *Following the leader.* In Cuppy v. Bunch, 214 N.W.2d 786 (S.D. 1974), the defendants, Bunch and White, spent an afternoon fishing and drinking together. At the end of the day, White drove the two of them from the pond back to the town of Belle Fourche (where Bunch's car was parked); Bunch slept in White's car. When they arrived in Belle Fourche, White awakened Bunch with some difficulty. When questioned by White about his condition, Bunch said that although he did not feel well, he did not want to leave his vehicle in Belle Fourche. White advised Bunch to "follow me" or "just stay behind me." White and Bunch then left Belle Fourche, each in his own car, with White in front. Witnesses later testified that Bunch was swerving dangerously as he followed White. At one point Bunch swerved across the center line and into the path of the plaintiffs' oncoming car, causing damages for which the plaintiffs sued both Bunch and White. After a trial the court gave judgment to the plaintiffs against both defendants. The South Dakota Supreme Court reversed the judgment against White, holding that the evidence was insufficient to support a finding that White owed a duty to the plaintiffs to control Bunch. The court quoted the Restatement (Second) of Torts, §315:

> There is no duty so to control the conduct of a third person as to prevent him from causing physical harm to another unless (a) a special relation exists between the actor and the third person which imposes a duty upon the actor to control the third person's conduct, or (b) a special relation exists between the actor and the other which gives to the other a right to protection.

Said the court:

> The language in Comment b. of [Restatement] sec. 315 is appropriate: "In the absence of either one of the kinds of special relations described in this Section, the actor is not subject to liability if he fails, either intentionally or through inadvertence, to exercise his ability so to

control the actions of third persons as to protect another from even the most serious harm. This is true although the actor realizes that he has the ability to control the conduct of a third person, and could do so with only the most trivial of efforts and without any inconvenience to himself. Thus if the actor is riding in a third person's car merely as a guest, he is not subject to liability to another run over by the car even though he knows of the other's danger and knows that the driver is not aware of it, and knows that by a mere word, recalling the driver's attention to the road, he would give the driver an opportunity to stop the car before the other is run over."

The facts do not, in our opinion, indicate that White did exercise or ever was capable of exercising any control over Bunch at any time relevant to this case. Nor do the facts show that White undertook to assist Bunch which, therefore, makes sec. 324A [of the Second Restatement] inapplicable.

Is there a satisfactory distinction between *Cuppy v. Bunch* and *Ocotillo West Joint Venture v. Superior Court* (the L case where the defendant gave his drunken friend his car keys)? What is the superficial similarity between *Cuppy v. Bunch* and *Weirum v. RKO Radio General* (the L case involving the "Real Don Steele")? What is the distinction between them?

7. *Cat scratch fever (problem).* In Marsalis v. La Salle, 94 So. 2d 120 (La. App. 1957), the plaintiffs, a couple named Marsalis, were shopping in the defendant's store when Mrs. Marsalis was scratched by the defendant's Siamese cat. Mr. Marsalis asked the defendant to keep the cat under observation for 14 days until it could be determined whether the animal was rabid. The defendant agreed, but took no special precautions to keep the cat confined. Four days later the cat escaped and did not return for about a month. Two days after she had sustained the injuries, Mrs. Marsalis sought advice from a doctor; when he later learned that the cat was away without leave, he administered the Pasteur treatment to Mrs. Marsalis. She turned out to be extremely allergic to the serum and suffered ill effects. (It was later determined that the cat was not rabid.) Mr. and Mrs. Marsalis sued the defendant, who in turn argued that he owed no duty to them. What result?

8. *Promises to send help (problem).* In Bloomberg v. Interinsurance Exchange of the Automobile Club of Southern California, 207 Cal. Rptr. 853 (Cal. App. 1984), the plaintiffs' 16-year-old son was a passenger in a friend's automobile that developed engine trouble on the freeway one night. At about 1:30 A.M., the driver pulled over to a highway callbox. The California Highway Patrol put his call through to the defendant Auto Club, which said it would send a tow truck. The boys returned to the car to wait. The defendant dispatched a truck, but it was unable to find the boys' car. At about 2:25, a drunk driver crashed into the boys' car, causing fatal injuries to the plaintiffs' son. The plaintiffs sued the Auto Club. The Club moved to

have the complaint dismissed on the ground that it owed the plaintiffs' decedent no duty. What result would you expect? How would you use the cases considered in this section to support arguments for and against the existence of a duty on these facts?

C. SPECIAL RELATIONSHIPS

In cases where the defendant escapes liability for "nonfeasance," the plaintiff and defendant typically are strangers or nearly so. A different result may obtain if the parties have a "special relationship" such as innkeeper and guest or captain and crew; doing nothing against the backdrop of such a relationship may cause the defendant to be held liable if the plaintiff is injured as a result. You may recall that some of the cases already considered, such as *Weirum v. RKO Radio General* and *Soldano v. O'Daniels*, have made passing reference to this doctrine. As we shall see, it occasionally overlaps with the rules on undertakings considered in the previous part of the chapter; sometimes the creation of a special relationship resembles an undertaking, and in those instances courts may invoke either principle to support the same result.

1. *Duties to Rescue or Assist Others*

1. *Ordeal at sea.* In Petition of Trans-Pacific Fishing & Packing Co., 152 F. Supp. 44 (W.D. Wash. 1957), three crewman on a tuna fishing boat were washed overboard by a wave off the coast of Nicaragua. The court found that "[t]he seas were rough, the vessel was undergoing considerable labor, some shorting out of electrical ignition and lighting circuits resulting in small but difficult-to-control fires were being experienced in the engine room due to water leaking through a broken port and also through the deck." The captain said he did not search for the three men because it was dangerous, the vessel was hard to steer in the heavy seas, the weather was bad, and the engineer advised against it. He did send out a "May Day" call for assistance, but to no effect.

The three men swept overboard stayed briefly within sight of each other, then separated. One of them was rescued by a passing steamship after 14 hours, during which time, the court found, he experienced the "nerve-racking ordeal" of defending himself against "the savage threats of a large ocean going turtle which he finally overcame by thrusting his fingers in the turtle's eyes, — and then 'she go away', as he piteously testified." A second man was rescued by fishermen after he had spent 56 hours at sea drifting and treading water; he was hospitalized for shock and for "numerous bites of small fishes which caused much of his skin to be lost and damaged." The third man never was found. The trial court awarded damages to the two surviving men and to the mother of the third:

> It is the duty of every shipowner and ship operator to use every possible available means to rescue from the sea any and all persons and members of its crew who may be unfortunately washed overboard. In this instance the skipper and all those aboard at the time and the owner failed and neglected to do that, failed to use due care or to make any effort by turning the vessel about to attempt rescue other than to inquire of the chief engineer as to why it could not be done, failed to keep the vessel in condition so that she could be maneuvered and turned around and search for those who had been washed overboard, failed to throw out any sort of a lifeline or any kind of a floating object, failed to cast into the water any skiff or debris or life rings or other lifesaving equipment, all of which constituted negligence on the part of the owner of the vessel and the vessel's skipper[.]

What is the distinction between this case and *Yania v. Bigan* (the NL case where the defendant stood and watched as the plaintiff's decedent drowned)? Be precise about *why* the factual differences between the cases lead to different legal results. If you have read *The Margharita* (in the chapter on breach of duty), what is the distinction between that case and this one?

2. *Common carriers.* In Brosnahan v. Western Air Lines, 892 F.2d 730 (8th Cir. 1989), the plaintiff, Fred Brosnahan, took his seat in row 16 on one of the defendant's flights from Las Vegas to Rapid City. Another passenger approached and made several attempts to fit his leather garment bag in the overhead compartment above Brosnahan's seat. During one last attempt, the passenger dropped the bag on Brosnahan's head, causing him various injuries. Brosnahan sued the airline, claiming that a flight attendant should have been stationed in the coach cabin to assist passengers with carry-on items; he argued that such an attendant would have noticed the passenger struggling with his garment bag and would have intervened to prevent the accident. The jury brought in a verdict for Brosnahan, awarding him $74,600. The trial court gave judgment notwithstanding the verdict to the defendant. The court of appeals reversed and reinstated the jury's verdict:

> An airline's duty to supervise the boarding process for the protection of its passengers continues until boarding is completed, and the danger created by an airline's breach of that duty does not abate until all passengers are seated with their carry-on luggage properly stowed. Brosnahan was injured when the forces created by the airline's negligence were still in continuous operation.

3. *Duties at airports.* In Boyette v. Trans World Airlines, 954 S.W.2d 350 (Mo. App. 1997), the plaintiff's decedent, one Rutherford, booked a trip from Memphis to Sioux City on TWA. The trip involved a change of planes in St. Louis. Rutherford drank a half-dozen alcoholic beverages during the first leg of the trip. On his way through the terminal in St. Louis to reach his connecting flight, Rutherford stole an electric golf cart and began driving around the gate area. A TWA gate agent, Callier, chased Rutherford on foot until he was cornered in a nearby alcove. Callier could not pinpoint Rutherford's location and called for help. One of Rutherford's friends found him and helped him hide in a trash chute; Rutherford climbed in too far, however, and fell into a trash compactor ten feet below on the tarmac. Rutherford's friend told this to Callier, who by then had been joined by a TWA flight attendant and a police officer. They observed Rutherford in the trash compactor. He was unresponsive and appeared to be injured. Callier headed for the tarmac to get him. Soon, however, Rutherford's presence in the compactor activated the machine's electric eye, and he was compacted before Callier or his companions could locate the deactivation switch.

The administrator of Rutherford's estate brought suit against the airline, among others, claiming that his death was attributable to the defendants' negligence in chasing him into the alcove, in failing to take effective steps to protect him once he was found in the compactor, and in failing to post warnings that the chute led to the compactor. The airline defended in part on the ground that they owed no duty to Rutherford. The trial court gave summary judgment to the airline, and the court of appeals affirmed:

> Missouri has long recognized a special relationship exists between a common carrier, like [the defendant airline], and its passengers. "A common carrier has a duty to exercise the highest degree of care to safely transport its passengers and protect them while in transit." But this duty exists only so long as the special relationship of passenger and carrier exists. The carrier discharges its duty once the passenger reaches a reasonably safe place. In the instant case it is without dispute Rutherford safely reached the airport. Thus, [the defendant] fulfilled the duty it owed Rutherford as a common carrier once he reached the airport terminal. At that point [the defendant's] duty as a common carrier was discharged.

What is the distinction between *Boyette v. Trans World Airlines* and *Brosnahan v. Western Air Lines*? *Boyette* may seem an easy case because you may doubt that TWA should be held responsible for Rutherford's imprudent behavior. Focus, therefore, on the ground the court used to dispose of the case: the absence of a duty. What does this mean? What assumptions are you entitled to make about the facts of the case given its procedural posture? What would the legal result have been if Callier, on the way out the door as he headed for the tarmac, accidentally had bumped into the switch that turned on the compactor? What result if he had seen the compactor's deactivation switch but decided not to use it?

4. *Social hosts.* In Charles v. Seigfried, 651 N.E.2d 154 (Ill. 1995), the plaintiff alleged that Seigfried, an adult, hosted a party where Lynn Sue Charles, 16 years old, was served alcoholic beverages. Seigfried knowingly permitted Charles to become intoxicated (her blood alcohol level later was found to be .299) and knowingly permitted her to drive herself home. She was killed in an auto accident. Her administrator sued Seigfried. The trial court dismissed the plaintiff's complaint; the Illinois Supreme Court affirmed:

> The historic common law rule, adhered to in this State, is that there is no cause of action for injuries arising out of the sale or gift of alcoholic beverages. The rationale underlying the rule is that the drinking of the intoxicant, not the furnishing of it, is the proximate cause of the intoxication and the resulting injury. [. . .]
>
> [If a duty were imposed here] [w]e are realistic enough to know that in virtually every instance where an underage driver is involved in an alcohol-related car accident, a clever plaintiff's attorney would drag into court any and all adults who may qualify as a social host. The focus at trial would then shift from the drunk driver to the alleged social hosts. Accidents following a wedding, for example, would include the typical targets of the bride, the groom, the parents of the bride and groom, the servers, and anyone else who may have handed the underage person a drink. Ironically, these "social hosts" could be held responsible for the underage person's drinking even if that person's parents were also in attendance. Courts and jurors would then be faced with evaluating the social host's conduct. For example: Did the social host do enough to stop the underage drinker from his or her own illegal actions? Did the host check identification to determine the guests' ages? Should the host have allowed the guests to serve themselves? Should the host have allowed underage persons to be present? Could the host have done more to prevent a guest's departure? Did the host know that the guest was visibly or obviously intoxicated? We are unwilling to open up this "Pandora's Box" of unlimited liability through judicial decision. If civil liability is to be imposed in these situations, the legislature should carefully delineate the standards of conduct expected of social hosts.

What is the distinction between *Charles v. Seigfried* and *Ocotillo West Joint Venture v. Superior Court* (the L case from the section on undertakings where the drunken decedent was given his car keys by a friend)?

5. *The upheaval of prior norms.* Many states (including Illinois) have Dram Shop Acts that forbid the sale of alcohol to already intoxicated customers; most of them impose civil liability on a negligent seller when such a customer goes on to injure a third party. As for social hosts, since the mid-1980s some courts — though still a minority — have been departing from the

common law rule described in *Charles v. Seigfried*. One of the landmark decisions was *Kelly v. Gwinnell*, 476 A.2d 1219 (N.J. 1984), where the Supreme Court of New Jersey imposed liability on a social host whose drunken guest caused the death of a third party in an auto accident. Said the court:

> The dissent's emphasis on the financial impact of an insurance premium increase on the homeowner or the tenant should be measured against the monumental financial losses suffered by society as a result of drunken driving. By our decision we not only spread some of that loss so that it need not be borne completely by the victims of this widespread affliction, but, to some extent, reduce the likelihood that the loss will occur in the first place. Even if the dissent's view of the scope of our decision were correct, the adjustments in social behavior at parties, the burden put on the host to reasonably oversee the serving of liquor, the burden on the guests to make sure if one is drinking that another is driving, and the burden on all to take those reasonable steps even if, on some occasion, some guest may become belligerent: those social dislocations, their importance, must be measured against the misery, death, and destruction caused by the drunken driver. Does our society morally approve of the decision to continue to allow the charm of unrestrained social drinking when the cost is the lives of others, sometimes of the guests themselves?
>
> If we but step back and observe ourselves objectively, we will see a phenomenon not of merriment but of cruelty, causing misery to innocent people, tolerated for years despite our knowledge that without fail, out of our extraordinarily high number of deaths caused by automobiles, nearly half have regularly been attributable to drunken driving. Should we be so concerned about disturbing the customs of those who knowingly supply that which causes the offense, so worried about their costs, so worried about their inconvenience, as if they were the victims rather than the cause of the carnage? And while the dissent is certainly correct that we could learn more through an investigation, to characterize our knowledge as "scant" or insufficient is to ignore what is obvious, and that is that drunken drivers are causing substantial personal and financial destruction in this state and that a goodly number of them have been drinking in homes as well as taverns. Does a court really need to know more? Is our rule vulnerable because we do not know — nor will the Legislature — how much injury will be avoided or how many lives saved by this rule? Or because we do not know how many times the victim will require compensation from the host in order to be made whole?
>
> This Court senses that there may be a substantial change occurring in social attitudes and customs concerning drinking, whether at home or in taverns. We believe that this change may be taking place right now in New Jersey and perhaps elsewhere. It is the upheaval of prior norms by a society that has finally recognized that it must change its habits and do

whatever is required, whether it means but a small change or a significant one, in order to stop the senseless loss inflicted by drunken drivers. We did not cause that movement, but we believe this decision is in step with it.

Some courts are willing to impose liability on hosts when their guests become intoxicated, drive, and injure third parties — but not when the guests injure themselves. Why? The liability of social hosts for injuries sustained or inflicted by an intoxicated guest is framed by some courts as an inquiry into whether the host and driver had a special relationship, by others as a question of whether a duty arose as a result of the host's undertaking, and by still others as a matter of whether a duty arose from the guest's presence on the host's property (a set of issues treated in a later part of this chapter). Given the policy considerations at stake in this area, does it matter which theory of duty a court uses to arrive at its results?

6. *Institutional considerations.* What are the trade-offs involved in having the duties of social hosts settled by legislatures rather than courts? For an example of a legislative response to the issue, see Colo. Rev. St. Ann. §12-47-801(4)(a):

> No social host who furnishes any alcohol beverage is civilly liable to any injured individual or his or her estate for any injury to such individual or damage to any property suffered, including any action for wrongful death, because of the intoxication of any person due to the consumption of such alcohol beverages, except when:
>> (I) It is proven that the social host willfully and knowingly served any alcohol beverage to such person who was under the age of twenty-one years; and
>> (II) The civil action is commenced within one year after such service.
> (b) No civil action may be brought pursuant to this subsection (4) by the person to whom such alcohol beverage was served or by his or her estate, legal guardian, or dependent.
> (c) The total liability in any such action shall not exceed one hundred fifty thousand dollars.

2. *Duties to Protect Others from Third Parties*

The cases in this section generally have involved a defendant's duty to rescue or assist the plaintiff because of a special relationship between them. The last case, *Kelly v. Gwinnell*, introduced a variation on that pattern to which we now turn our full attention: cases involving a defendant's duty to protect the plaintiff from harm inflicted by a third party — a duty sometimes based on the relationship not between the plaintiff and defendant but between the defendant and the party causing the harm.

Restatement (Second) of Torts (1965)

§315. GENERAL PRINCIPLE

There is no duty so to control the conduct of a third person as to prevent him from causing physical harm to another unless

(a) a special relation exists between the actor and the third person which imposes a duty upon the actor to control the third person's conduct, or

(b) a special relation exists between the actor and the other which gives to the other a right to protection.

Tarasoff v. Regents of the University of California
551 P.2d 334 (Cal. 1976)

[This action was brought against the Regents of the University of California, psychotherapists employed by the university hospital, and campus police to recover for the murder of the plaintiffs' daughter by a psychiatric patient. The trial court dismissed the plaintiffs' complaint; the plaintiffs appealed.]

TOBRINER, J. — On October 27, 1969, Prosenjit Poddar killed Tatiana Tarasoff. Plaintiffs, Tatiana's parents, allege that two months earlier Poddar confided his intention to kill Tatiana to Dr. Lawrence Moore, a psychologist employed by the Cowell Memorial Hospital at the University of California at Berkeley. They allege that on Moore's request, the campus police briefly detained Poddar, but released him when he appeared rational. They further claim that Dr. Harvey Powelson, Moore's superior, then directed that no further action be taken to detain Poddar. No one warned plaintiffs of Tatiana's peril.

Concluding that these facts set forth causes of action against neither therapists and policemen involved, nor against the Regents of the University of California as their employer, the superior court sustained defendants' demurrers to plaintiffs' second amended complaints without leave to amend. This appeal ensued. [. . .]

Plaintiffs' first cause of action, entitled "Failure to Detain a Dangerous Patient," alleges that on August 20, 1969, Poddar was a voluntary outpatient receiving therapy at Cowell Memorial Hospital. Poddar informed Moore, his therapist, that he was going to kill an unnamed girl, readily identifiable as Tatiana, when she returned home from spending the summer in Brazil. Moore, with the concurrence of Dr. Gold, who had initially examined Poddar, and Dr. Yandell, Assistant to the director of the department of psychiatry, decided that Poddar should be committed for observation in a mental hospital. Moore orally notified Officers Atkinson and Teel of the campus police that he would request commitment. He then sent a letter to Police Chief William Beall requesting the assistance of the police department in securing Poddar's confinement.

Officers Atkinson, Brownrigg, and Halleran took Poddar into custody, but, satisfied that Poddar was rational, released him on his promise to stay away from Tatiana. Powelson, director of the department of psychiatry at Cowell Memorial Hospital, then asked the police to return Moore's letter, directed that all copies of the letter and notes that Moore had taken as therapist be destroyed, and "ordered no action to place Prosenjit Poddar in 72-hour treatment and evaluation facility."

Plaintiffs' second cause of action, entitled "Failure to Warn Of a Dangerous Patient," incorporates the allegations of the first cause of action, but adds the assertion that defendants negligently permitted Poddar to be released from police custody without "notifying the parents of Tatiana Tarasoff that their daughter was in grave danger from Posenjit Poddar." Poddar persuaded Tatiana's brother to share an apartment with him near Tatiana's residence; shortly after her return from Brazil, Poddar went to her residence and killed her. [...]

The second cause of action can be amended to allege that Tatiana's death proximately resulted from defendants' negligent failure to warn Tatiana or others likely to apprise her of her danger. Plaintiffs contend that as amended, such allegations of negligence and proximate causation, with resulting damages, establish a cause of action. Defendants, however, contend that in the circumstances of the present case they owed no duty of care to Tatiana or her parents and that, in the absence of such duty, they were free to act in careless disregard of Tatiana's life and safety.

In analyzing this issue, we bear in mind that legal duties are not discoverable facts of nature, but merely conclusory expressions that, in cases of a particular type, liability should be imposed for damage done. As stated in *Dillon v. Legg* (1968) 68 Cal. 2d 728, 734: "The assertion that liability must ... be denied because defendant bears no 'duty' to plaintiff 'begs the essential question — whether the plaintiff's interests are entitled to legal protection against the defendant's conduct. ... [Duty] is not sacrosanct in itself, but only an expression of the sum total of those considerations of policy which lead the law to say that the particular plaintiff is entitled to protection.' (Prosser, Law of Torts (3d ed. 1964) at pp. 332-333.)" [...]

Although [...] under the common law, as a general rule, one person owed no duty to control the conduct of another, nor to warn those endangered by such conduct, the courts have carved out an exception to this rule in cases in which the defendant stands in some special relationship to either the person whose conduct needs to be controlled or in a relationship to the foreseeable victim of that conduct. Applying this exception to the present case, we note that a relationship of defendant therapists to either Tatiana or Poddar will suffice to establish a duty of care; as explained in section 315 of the Restatement Second of Torts, a duty of care may arise from either "(a) a special relation ... between the actor and the third person which imposes a duty upon the actor to control the third person's conduct, or (b) a special relation ... between the actor and the other which gives to the other a right of protection."

Although plaintiffs' pleadings assert no special relation between Tatiana and defendant therapists, they establish as between Poddar and defendant therapists the special relation that arises between a patient and his doctor or psychotherapist. Such a relationship may support affirmative duties for the benefit of third persons. Thus, for example, a hospital must exercise reasonable care to control the behavior of a patient which may endanger other persons. A doctor must also warn a patient if the patient's condition or medication renders certain conduct, such as driving a car, dangerous to others. [...]

We recognize the difficulty that a therapist encounters in attempting to forecast whether a patient presents a serious danger of violence. Obviously we do not require that the therapist, in making that determination, render a perfect performance; the therapist need only exercise "that reasonable degree of skill, knowledge, and care ordinarily possessed and exercised by members of [that professional specialty] under similar circumstances." Within the broad range of reasonable practice and treatment in which professional opinion and judgment may differ, the therapist is free to exercise his or her own best judgment without liability; proof, aided by hindsight, that he or she judged wrongly is insufficient to establish negligence.

In the instant case, however, the pleadings do not raise any question as to failure of defendant therapists to predict that Poddar presented a serious danger of violence. On the contrary, the present complaints allege that defendant therapists did in fact predict that Poddar would kill, but were negligent in failing to warn. [...]

The risk that unnecessary warnings may be given is a reasonable price to pay for the lives of possible victims that may be saved. We would hesitate to hold that the therapist who is aware that his patient expects to attempt to assassinate the President of the United States would not be obligated to warn the authorities because the therapist cannot predict with accuracy that his patient will commit the crime.

Defendants further argue that free and open communication is essential to psychotherapy; that "Unless a patient ... is assured that ... information [revealed by him] can and will be held in utmost confidence, he will be reluctant to make the full disclosure upon which diagnosis and treatment ... depends." (Sen. Com. on Judiciary, comment on Evid. Code, §1014.) The giving of a warning, defendants contend, constitutes a breach of trust which entails the revelation of confidential communications. [...]

The revelation of a communication under the above circumstances is not a breach of trust or a violation of professional ethics; as stated in the Principles of Medical Ethics of the American Medical Association (1957), section 9: "A physician may not reveal the confidence entrusted to him in the course of medical attendance ... unless he is required to do so by law or unless it becomes necessary in order to protect the welfare of the individual or of the community." We conclude that the public policy favoring protection of the confidential character of patient-psychotherapist communications must yield to the extent to which disclosure is essential to avert danger to others. The protective privilege ends where the public peril begins.

Our current crowded and computerized society compels the interdependence of its members. In this risk-infested society we can hardly tolerate the further exposure to danger that would result from a concealed knowledge of the therapist that his patient was lethal. If the exercise of reasonable care to protect the threatened victim requires the therapist to warn the endangered party or those who can reasonably be expected to notify him, we see no sufficient societal interest that would protect and justify concealment. The containment of such risks lies in the public interest. For the foregoing reasons, we find that plaintiffs' complaints can be amended to state a cause of action against defendants Moore, Powelson, Gold, and Yandell and against the Regents as their employer, for breach of a duty to exercise reasonable care to protect Tatiana. [...]

Turning now to the police defendants, we conclude that they do not have any such special relationship to either Tatiana or to Poddar sufficient to impose upon such defendants a duty to warn respecting Poddar's violent intentions. Plaintiffs suggest no theory, and plead no facts that give rise to any duty to warn on the part of the police defendants absent such a special relationship. They have thus failed to demonstrate that the trial court erred in denying leave to amend as to the police defendants. [...]

Wright, C.J., and Sullivan and Richardson, JJ., concur.

NOTES

1. *Ripple effects.* A 1987 survey of 1,800 psychologists and psychiatrists in California found that 84 percent of them had heard of the *Tarasoff* decision; 49 percent were more afraid of lawsuits since *Tarasoff* was decided; and 39 percent had warned a potential victim of danger from a patient on at least one occasion since the decision, and had issued such warnings an average of 2.61 times. Forty-six percent said that they avoided counseling dangerous patients, and of those in this category 40 percent said this was due in part to fear of liability under *Tarasoff*. The authors also reported these findings:

> Therapists were then asked to determine how well they believe they can predict potential dangerousness. Few psychotherapists reported that they could assess dangerousness "very accurately" — 4.3% overall; 5.3% of psychologists, and only 1.6% of psychiatrists. Almost 30% of responding practitioners believed that they could predict potential dangerousness "somewhat accurately." Meanwhile, the overwhelming proportion of psychotherapists — 72.5% of the psychiatrists, 63.7% of the psychologists, and 66.3% of the sample who answered this question — felt that they could predict dangerousness "better than chance" or "not at all."

Rosenhan et al., *Warning Third Parties: The Ripple Effects of Tarasoff*, 24 Pac. L.J. 1165 (April 1993).

2. *New frontiers.* How might the logic of *Tarasoff* apply when a physician determines that a patient is HIV-positive? Judicial decisions on point are scarce, but some states have chosen to address the issue with statutes. Consider this example:

MARYLAND HEALTH GEN. 18-337. POSITIVE TEST RESULTS [. . .]

(b) Notice to others by health care providers. — If an individual informed of the individual's HIV positive status under §18-336 of this title refuses to notify the individual's sexual and needle-sharing partners, the individual's physician may inform the local health officer and/or the individual's sexual and needle-sharing partners of:

(1) The individual's identity; and

(2) The circumstances giving rise to the notification. [. . .]

(e) Liability of physician — Disclosure. — A physician acting in good faith to provide notification in accordance with this section may not be held liable in any cause of action related to a breach of patient confidentiality.

(f) Same — Nondisclosure. — A physician acting in good faith may not be held liable in any cause of action for choosing not to disclose information related to a positive test result for the presence of human immunodeficiency virus to an individual's sexual and needle-sharing partners.

3. *Innovative release program.* In Thompson v. County of Alameda, 614 P.2d 728 (Cal. 1980), the plaintiffs and their five-year-old son lived in the city of Piedmont, a few doors from the mother of James F., a juvenile offender confined in a county institution. The plaintiffs alleged that the county knew James had "latent, extremely dangerous and violent propensities regarding young children and that sexual assaults upon young children and violence connected therewith were a likely result of releasing [him] into the community." The county also knew that James had "indicated that he would, if released, take the life of a young child residing in the neighborhood." He had given no indication of which, if any, child he intended as his victim. The county nevertheless released James on temporary leave into his mother's custody; and "(a)t no time did [the County] advise and/or warn [the plaintiffs], the local police and/or parents of young children within the immediate vicinity of [James' mother's] house of the known facts. . . ." Within 24 hours of his release, James murdered the plaintiffs' son.

The plaintiffs' suit against the county alleged, among other things, that the county breached its duty to warn "parents of young children within the immediate vicinity" of the residence of James' mother that James was being released. The trial court dismissed the plaintiffs' complaint, and the California Supreme Court affirmed:

Unlike members of the general public, in [*Tarasoff* and a case following it] the potential victims were specifically known and designated individuals. The warnings which we therein required were directed at making those individuals aware of the danger to which they were uniquely exposed. The threatened targets were precise. In such cases, it is fair to conclude that warnings given discreetly and to a limited number of persons would have a greater effect because they would alert those particular targeted individuals of the possibility of a specific threat pointed at them. In contrast, the warnings sought by plaintiffs would of necessity have to be made to a broad segment of the population and would be only general in nature. In addition to the likelihood that such generalized warnings when frequently repeated would do little as a practical matter to stimulate increased safety measures [. . .], such extensive warnings would be difficult to give.

The court also said that imposing liability for failing to warn the neighborhood

might substantially jeopardize rehabilitative efforts both by stigmatizing released offenders and by inhibiting their release. It is also possible that, in addition, parole or probation authorities would be far less likely to authorize release given the substantial drain on their resources which such warnings might require. A stated public policy favoring innovative release programs would be thwarted.

How would you summarize the distinctions between *Thompson v. County of Alameda* and *Tarasoff v. Regents of the University of California*? What rules or guidelines emerge from the two cases?

4. *Landlord and tenant.* In Kline v. 1500 Massachusetts Avenue Corp., 439 F.2d 477 (D.C. Cir. 1970), the plaintiff, Sarah Kline, was assaulted and robbed in the common hallway of a building near Dupont Circle in Washington where she rented an apartment. Kline sued the corporation that owned the building. The incident occurred in 1966; the plaintiff had lived in the building since 1959, proceeding after the first year of her tenancy on a month-to-month basis. A doorman had been posted around the clock at the main entrance to the building when the plaintiff first arrived; there was no longer a doorman in 1966, and other entrances to the building also were either watched less closely or locked less often. In the meantime, a number of other tenants had been assaulted or robbed in the hallways of the building, and the owner had notice of this. After a bench trial the district court gave judgment as a matter of law to the defendant on the ground that it had no duty to protect its tenants from third parties. The court of appeals reversed:

As a general rule, a private person does not have a duty to protect another from a criminal attack by a third person. [. . .] Among the reasons for the [past] application of this rule to landlords are: judicial reluctance to tamper with the traditional common law concept of the landlord-tenant relationship; the notion that the act of a third person in committing an intentional tort or crime is a superseding cause of the harm to another resulting therefrom; the oftentimes difficult problem of determining fore-seeability of criminal acts; the vagueness of the standard which the land-lord must meet; the economic consequences of the imposition of the duty; and conflict with the public policy allocating the duty of protecting citizens from criminal acts to the government rather than the private sector. [. . .]

The rationale of the general rule exonerating a third party from any duty to protect another from a criminal attack has no applicability to the landlord-tenant relationship in multiple dwelling houses. The landlord is no insurer of his tenants' safety, but he certainly is no bystander. And where, as here, the landlord has notice of repeated criminal assaults and robberies, has notice that these crimes occurred in the portion of the premises exclusively within his control, has every reason to expect like crimes to happen again, and has the exclusive power to take preventive action, it does not seem unfair to place upon the landlord a duty to take those steps which are within his power to minimize the predictable risk to his tenants. [. . .]

Other relationships in which similar duties have been imposed include landowner-invitee, businessman-patron, employer-employee, school district-pupil, hospital-patient, and carrier-passenger. In all, the theory of liability is essentially the same; that since the ability of one of the parties to provide for his own protection has been limited in some way by his submission to the control of the other, a duty should be imposed upon the one possessing control (and thus the power to act) to take reasonable precautions to protect the other one from assaults by third parties which, at least, could reasonably have been anticipated. However, there is no liability normally imposed upon the one having the power to act if the violence is sudden and unexpected provided that the source of the violence is not an employee of the one in control. [. . .]

Not only as between landlord and tenant is the landlord best equipped to guard against the predictable risk of intruders, but even as between landlord and the police power of government, the landlord is in the best position to take the necessary protective measures. Municipal police cannot patrol the entryways and the hallways, the garages and the base-ments of private multiple unit apartment dwellings. They are neither equipped, manned, nor empowered to do so. In the area of the predict-able risk which materialized in this case, only the landlord could have taken measures which might have prevented the injuries suffered by appellant. [. . .]

Having said this, it would be well to state what is not said by this decision. We do not hold that the landlord is by any means an insurer of the safety of his tenants. [. . .] We do not say that every multiple unit apartment house in the District of Columbia should have those same measures of protection which 1500 Massachusetts Avenue enjoyed in

1959, nor do we say that 1500 Massachusetts Avenue should have precisely those same measures in effect at the present time. Alternative and more up-to-date methods may be equally or even more effective.

Granted, the discharge of this duty of protection by landlords will cause, in many instances, the expenditure of large sums for additional equipment and services, and granted the cost will be ultimately passed on to the tenant in the form of increased rents. This prospect, in itself, however, is no deterrent to our acknowledging and giving force to the duty, since without protection the tenant already pays in losses from theft, physical assault and increased insurance premiums.

What is the distinction between *Kline v. 1500 Massachusetts Avenue Corp.* (L for landlord when tenant is attacked by third party) and *Thompson v. County of Alameda* (NL for county when it releases murderous child into plaintiff's neighborhood)? In *Kline*, unlike in *Thompson*, the plaintiff and defendant had a contract; how might this fact be used to argue that *both* decisions were incorrect?

5. *Spotted fever.* In Bradshaw v. Daniel, 854 S.W.2d 865 (Tenn. 1993), one Elmer Johns was admitted to a hospital complaining of headaches, muscle aches, fever, and chills. The defendant, Dr. Daniel, correctly diagnosed him as suffering from the latter stages of Rocky Mountain Spotted Fever. Johns died the next day. A week later, Johns's wife was admitted to a different hospital with similar symptoms. She died of Rocky Mountain Spotted Fever a few days later. Her son sued Daniel for failing to warn her of the risk that she might have the disease. The plaintiff's evidence was that if treated promptly, the disease has a mortality rate of only 4 percent. Rocky Mountain Spotted Fever is transmitted by ticks, not by people, so Mrs. Johns could not have caught it from her husband; the plaintiff's theory, rather, was that Daniel should have warned Mrs. Johns that if her husband had contracted the disease, a member of the same cluster of ticks might have infected her as well. Daniel argued in response that he owed his patient's wife no legal duty because there was no physician-patient relationship between them, and because Rocky Mountain Spotted Fever is not a contagious disease. The trial court disagreed and denied Daniel's motion for summary judgment; on an interlocutory appeal the Tennessee Supreme Court affirmed:

> [T]his case is analogous to the *Tarasoff* line of cases adopting a duty to warn of danger and the contagious disease cases adopting a comparable duty to warn. Here, as in those cases, there was a foreseeable risk of harm to an identifiable third party, and the reasons supporting the recognition of the duty to warn are equally compelling here.

Do you agree that the reasons supporting recognition of a duty in *Tarasoff* are "equally compelling" in this case?

6. *Upon further review.* In Hawkins v. Pizarro, 713 So. 2d 1036 (Fla. App. 1998), the defendant, Dr. Pizarro, incorrectly advised a woman named Shaw that her blood test for Hepatitis-C had come back negative. Several months later Shaw met the plaintiff, Hawkins, and they soon married. In May 1995 — a year after the first test — Shaw took another test for Hepatitis-C from a different doctor. The test was positive. Shaw contacted Pizarro and asked him to re-examine her earlier test results. Upon further review, Pizarro discovered that in fact she had tested positive a year earlier. Shortly thereafter, Shaw's new husband, Hawkins, also tested positive for Hepatitis-C. Hawkins sued Pizarro; he claimed that if Shaw had been correctly informed of her first test results, she could have taken precautions to avoid infecting him. Pizarro moved for summary judgment on the ground that Hawkins was unknown to him at the time that he misread her test results, and so was not an identified third party to whom he could owe a duty of care. The trial court agreed and granted the motion, and the court of appeals affirmed.

In which of the last two cases does the doctor's behavior seem more objectionable: *Hawkins v. Pizarro* or *Bradshaw v. Daniel?* Is there a distinction between the two cases that makes sense? For a case reaching the opposite result as *Hawkins* on similar facts, see *Reisner v. Regents of the University of California*, 37 Cal. Rptr. 2d 518 (Cal. App. 1995).

7. *The problem of multiple nonrescuers.* From Saul Levmore, *Waiting for Rescue: An Essay on the Evolution and Incentive Structure of the Law of Affirmative Obligations*, 72 Va. L. Rev. 879, 934-938 (1986):

> When a victim's call for help goes unanswered, there may be more than one potential rescuer within hearing range. Indeed, it must often be the case that when B could have rescued A, B's presence at the scene only comes to the attention of the law because other potential (and often unhelpful) rescuers, C and D, were also at the scene of A's trouble. Such multiple potential rescuers pose a doctrinal problem; if no rescue is attempted, it will be unclear whether B, C, or D "caused" A's injury — and misbehavior without causation of an injury is traditionally an insufficient basis for liability. [. . .]
>
> [C]ourts have discovered a surprising number of special relationships as bases for the imposition of duties to rescue. Most significantly, these special relationships have one thing in common: when there is a special relationship there is no multiple nonrescuer problem, for such a relationship is pronounced only in circumstances in which there is one identifiable or best-situated nonrescuer. This is not to say that whenever there is but one nonrescuer, courts will insist that he and the victim had a special relationship out of which a duty to rescue arose. The presence of a single nonrescuer is at present a necessary but not a sufficient condition for liability; it is the growing number of special relationships that indicates an increasing likelihood of liability on the single nonrescuer. As indicated

earlier, the most remarkable thing about these cases in which special relationships are found is that some involve a single nonrescuer and a stranger. Liability has been found appropriate for an innkeeper who could have protected a stranger from injury by one of the innkeeper's guests, a safety engineer who could have prevented an injury to a laborer he did not employ, a psychologist who might have warned an identifiable stranger his patient was intent on harming, and, similarly, a parole board, acting as a single entity, that might have warned someone who was the target of a released convict. In these cases, there is of course no "relationship" at all. Instead, these cases contain three elements.

First, there is a single nonrescuer. Second, this nonrescuer could with little effort have prevented a serious loss. Third, this nonrescuer had no reason to think that someone else would save the day. [...]

There is another clue that suggests in a striking way that the major obstacle to holding nonrescuers liable is the historical disinclination to impose liability where multiple parties are at fault. It has long been the case that if B begins to rescue A but then abandons the rescue effort, then B will often be held liable for nonrescue even though he is said to have had no duty to rescue in the first place. Occasionally, B may have made A worse off by leaving him in a place where other rescuers were less likely to help or simply by using up time in which other rescuers might have appeared. But it is rather clear that courts do not look carefully for evidence of such causation but instead often hold B liable for what might be regarded as active, or conscious, nonrescue. Clearly, B's initial efforts single him out and "solve" any multiple party problem. B's false start allows the law to identify him — as opposed to other potential rescuers — as the nonrescuer and to see him in a light that is so similar to that which falls on a typical tortfeasor. The inclination to hold the "withdrawing rescuer," B, liable is thus a further indication that it is the problem of multiple nonrescuers that is at the heart of any difference between omissions and commissions.

How well does Levmore's theory explain the cases considered in this section?

3. *The Public Duty Doctrine*

Some of the most difficult problems in the realm of "special relationships" arise when a plaintiff complains of failures by police, fire, or other public rescue services. Such a plaintiff may encounter a number of different obstacles. One of them is *sovereign immunity*, a common law doctrine that forbids lawsuits against the government without its consent. The federal government and most states have waived this immunity for various purposes, allowing tort suits to be brought against themselves under certain circumstances. When such suits are permitted, however, establishing the existence of a duty often is difficult. It might seem obvious that police have a duty to come to the aid of people in distress; courts, however, have interpreted this as a duty that runs to the public at large, rather than to any particular individual. A plaintiff thus can only bring a lawsuit of this sort by demonstrating the existence of a special relationship with the defendant.

1. *Protection from stalkers.* In Riss v. City of New York, 240 N.E.2d 860 (N.Y. 1968), the plaintiff, Linda Riss, was dating a lawyer in the Bronx named Burton Pugach. She attempted to end their relationship when she discovered that he was married. Pugach threatened to kill or maim Riss if she left him ("If I can't have you, no one else will have you, and when I get through with you, no one else will want you"). Riss repeatedly went to the police, pleading for protection; none was provided. At a party thrown many months later to celebrate her engagement to another man, Pugach called Riss on the phone and warned her that this was her "last chance." Riss again went to the police and begged for protection. Nothing was done. The next morning, thugs hired by Pugach threw lye in Riss's face, leaving her legally blind and causing permanent scarring. (She was then given around-the-clock police protection.) Riss sued the city. The trial court gave a directed verdict to the defendant; the court of appeals affirmed:

> [T]his case involves the provision of a governmental service to protect the public generally from external hazards and particularly to control the activities of criminal wrongdoers. [. . .] The amount of protection that may be provided is limited by the resources of the community and by a considered legislative-executive decision as to how those resources may be deployed. For the courts to proclaim a new and general duty of protection in the law of tort, even to those who may be the particular seekers of protection based on specific hazards, could and would inevitably determine how the limited police resources of the community should be allocated and without predictable limits. This is quite different from the predictable allocation of resources and liabilities when public hospitals, rapid transit systems, or even highways are provided. [. . .]
>
> When one considers the greatly increased amount of crime committed throughout the cities, but especially in certain portions of them, with a repetitive and predictable pattern, it is easy to see the consequences of fixing municipal liability upon a showing of probable need for and request for protection. [. . .] To foist a presumed cure for these problems by judicial innovation of a new kind of liability in tort would be foolhardy indeed and an assumption of judicial wisdom and power not possessed by the courts.

Keating, J., dissented:

> What makes the city's position particularly difficult to understand is that, in conformity to the dictates of the law, Linda did not carry any weapon for self-defense. Thus, by a rather bitter irony she was required to rely for

protection on the City of New York which now denies all responsibility to her. [...]

Although in modern times the compensatory nature of tort law has generally been the one most emphasized, one of its most important functions has been and is its normative aspect. It sets forth standards of conduct which ought to be followed. The penalty for failing to do so is to pay pecuniary damages. At one time the government was completely immunized from this salutary control. This is much less so now, and the imposition of liability has had healthy side effects. In many areas, it has resulted in the adoption of better and more considered procedures just as workmen's compensation resulted in improved industrial safety practices. To visit liability upon the city here will no doubt have similar constructive effects. No "presumed cure" for the problem of crime is being "foisted" upon the city as the majority opinion charges. The methods of dealing with the problem of crime are left completely to the city's discretion. All that the courts can do is make sure that the costs of the city's and its employees' mistakes are placed where they properly belong.

2. *The Stockholm syndrome.* Burton Pugach was apprehended and prosecuted and served 14 years in prison. He continued to court Linda Riss during and after his prison term. A newspaper account in 1990 provided these details:

> [Linda] had never answered his letters from prison, sentimental pleadings full of Keats and Byron. "I'm not a sentimentalist," she says, "Besides, I'm blind. Who could read it?" [...] When he got out, Pugach proposed to Riss on the evening news. She and her girlfriends watched him. "He had worked out a lot. He looked like After in the Before and After ads." Her girlfriends said marry him, the woman who did her horoscope said marry him, her mother's fortune teller broke down crying and told her it was in the cards. "You don't listen to anyone," the fortune teller sobbed, pounding her chest, "You listen to me, you marry this man."

Riss married Pugach. *City Legend: What They Did for Love,* New York Newsday, April 26, 1990, at 4. In 1997 Pugach was prosecuted for threatening to kill another woman when she ended an affair they were conducting. Pugach's wife, Linda, appeared at his trial as a character witness in his favor. He was acquitted of most of the charges. *Two Tales of Soured Affairs of the Heart Intersect in a Courtroom in Queens,* New York Times, April 21, 1997, at B3; see *Pugach v. Borja,* 670 N.Y.S.2d 718 (1998).

3. *America's most wanted.* In Schuster v. City of New York, 154 N.E.2d 534 (N.Y. 1958), the plaintiff's intestate, Schuster, supplied information to the New York Police Department leading to the arrest of Willie Sutton, a criminal of national reputation. Schuster's part in Sutton's capture was

widely publicized; Schuster was described by the court as a "public spirited young man who had studied Sutton's picture on an FBI flyer that had been posted in his father's dry-goods store." After Sutton's arrest Schuster immediately received communications threatening his life. He notified the police, but they provided no protection. One evening three weeks later, Schuster was shot and killed while approaching his home.

The plaintiff's complaint alleged that the city had a duty to protect people who had thus cooperated in law enforcement; that the city failed to exercise reasonable care in supplying Schuster with police protection upon demand; and that Schuster's death was due to negligence of the city in recklessly exposing him to danger, in advising him that the threats upon his life were not seriously made, in failing to supply him with a bodyguard, and in heedlessly imparting to him a false impression of safety and lack of danger. The trial court dismissed the complaint. The court of appeals reversed, despite the fact that "[p]redictions of dire financial consequences to municipalities are waved in our faces if Schuster's estate is allowed to recover for his death":

> In our view the public (acting in this instance through the City of New York) owes a special duty to use reasonable care for the protection of persons who have collaborated with it in the arrest or prosecution of criminals, once it reasonably appears that they are in danger due to their collaboration. If it were otherwise, it might well become difficult to convince the citizen to aid and co-operate with the law enforcement officers. To uphold such a liability does not mean that municipalities are called upon to answer in damages for every loss caused by outlaws or by fire. Such a duty to Schuster bespeaks no obligation enforcible in the courts to exercise the police powers of government for the protection of every member of the general public. Nevertheless, where persons actually have aided in the apprehension or prosecution of enemies of society under the criminal law, a reciprocal duty arises on the part of society to use reasonable care for their police protection, at least where reasonably demanded or sought.
>
> In a situation like the present, government is not merely passive; it is active in calling upon persons "in possession of any information regarding the whereabouts of" Sutton, quoting from the FBI flyer, to communicate such information in aid of law enforcement. Where that has happened, as here, or where the public authorities have made active use of a private citizen in some other capacity in the arrest or prosecution of a criminal, it would be a misuse of language to say that the law enforcement authorities are merely passive. They are active in calling upon the citizen for help, and in utilizing his help when it is rendered. They have gone forward to such a stage [. . .] that inaction in furnishing police protection to such persons would commonly result, not negatively merely in withholding a benefit, but positively or actively in working an injury.

What is the distinction between *Schuster v. City of New York* and *Riss v. City of New York*? What is the analogy between *Schuster v. City of New York* and the holding of *Tarasoff v. Regents of University of California* regarding the psychotherapist's duty to warn? What is the distinction between *Schuster v. City of New York* and the part of *Tarasoff* holding that the police had no duty to warn?

4. *Take two aspirin and call me in the morning (problem)*. In Wanzer v. District of Columbia, 580 A.2d 127 (D.C. App. 1990), the plaintiff's decedent, James Lee, dialed 911 one evening. The following dialogue occurred:

Dispatcher:	What is the problem now?
Caller:	I have terrific headaches. I never had headaches in my life.
Dispatcher:	Have you taken anything for them?
Caller:	No.
Dispatcher:	How long have you had these headaches?
Caller:	About an hour.
Dispatcher:	Then you need an ambulance and you haven't tried to take an aspirin?
Caller:	No, I haven't.
Dispatcher:	Don't you think you should go take — you know, wouldn't that be logical?
Caller:	Okay, all right. [End of call.]

Nine hours later, Lee's neighbor called for an ambulance, saying that Lee was having trouble breathing and that his headaches remained terrible. An ambulance came and took Lee to a hospital. He was diagnosed as having had a stroke. He died two days later. Lee's daughter sued the District of Columbia, claiming it breached its duty to provide ambulance service to her father by negligently failing to train or supervise the dispatcher who talked to him on the night he called 911. The defendant invoked the public duty doctrine as a defense. What result?

D. DUTIES ARISING FROM THE OCCUPATION OF LAND

1. *Duties to Trespassers*

The law imposes affirmative obligations on landowners to use care toward those who come onto their property. "Doing nothing" when one is a landowner thus may result in liability if a guest is injured by a hazard on the premises as a result. As we shall see, in many jurisdictions the details of landowners' duties can vary in complex ways depending on whether the plaintiff is a trespasser, a social guest, or a business guest; in other jurisdictions those categories have been abandoned in favor of more general standards of care.

1. *The woodchuck hunt.* In Haskins v. Grybko, 17 N.E.2d 146 (Mass. 1938), the defendant raised squash. One night he went onto his lot to hunt woodchucks that had been ravaging his crop. He heard a rustling noise in the brush about 50 feet away and saw a moving object about 18 inches high. Thinking it was a woodchuck, he shot at it. A few minutes later he left the area. Rather than shooting a woodchuck, however, he had shot the plaintiff's intestate, whose body he discovered the next morning. The plaintiff brought a suit against the defendant for negligence and won in the trial court, which found "on all of the evidence that the defendant was negligent and that the degree of negligence was ordinary negligence." The Supreme Judicial Court of Massachusetts reversed:

> If the intestate was a trespasser upon the defendant's land, the latter was not liable for mere negligence. He was, however, under an obligation to refrain from intentional injury and from willful, wanton and reckless conduct. As the plaintiff failed to show that his intestate was not a trespasser upon the defendant's land when the shooting occurred, he was not entitled to recover by proving that the defendant was guilty of mere negligence, and the ruling in favor of the plaintiff was erroneous.

What result if facts similar to those in *Haskins* had arisen in public woods rather than on the defendant's private property? Suppose two trespassers are hunting on someone else's property. One of the trespassers negligently shoots the other. Liability?

2. *Trespasser at the circus.* In Herrick v. Wixom, 80 N.W. 117 (Mich. 1899), the plaintiff managed to sneak into the defendant's circus without buying a ticket. He took a seat in the audience. A clown in one of the show rings set off a large firecracker; a stray piece of the firecracker struck the eye of the plaintiff, who was about 30 feet away. The plaintiff sued the circus for negligence. The jury brought in a verdict for the circus after being instructed that "If [the plaintiff] was a mere trespasser, who forced his way in, then the defendant owed him no duty that would enable him to recover under the declaration and proofs in this case." The plaintiff appealed, claiming that the jury was not properly instructed; the Michigan Supreme Court reversed and remanded for a new trial:

> It is true that a trespasser who suffers an injury because of a dangerous condition of premises is without remedy. But, where a trespasser is discovered upon the premises by the owner or occupant, he is not beyond the pale of the law, and any negligence resulting in injury will render the person guilty of negligence liable to respond in damages. In this case the negligent act of the defendant's servant was committed after the audience was made up. The presence of plaintiff was known, and the danger to him from a negligent act was also known. The question of whether a

dangerous experiment should be attempted in his presence, or whether an experiment should be conducted with due care and regard to his safety, cannot be made to depend upon whether he had forced himself into the tent. Every instinct of humanity revolts at such a suggestion.

What is the distinction between *Herrick v. Wixom* and *Haskins v. Grybko* (the NL case of the woodchuck hunt)?

3. *Exploding outhouse.* In Cleveland Electric Illuminating Co. v. Van Benshoten, 166 N.E. 374 (Ohio 1929), the defendant was laying an underground conduit in Cleveland. During working hours its employees set up a small building over a manhole for use by its workmen as a toilet; the hole led to a sewer 20 feet below. The plaintiff was a real estate salesman who saw the building and attempted to use it without permission (the workmen were about a block away). The plaintiff's recollection of subsequent events was vague, but it appeared that while inside the structure he attempted to light a cigarette and in doing so ignited gas from the sewer, causing an explosion that deposited him on the street outside. The plaintiff sued the defendant for negligence in constructing the building and in failing to warn of its dangers. The trial court directed a verdict for the defendant, and the Ohio Supreme Court affirmed:

> The defendant did not know that the plaintiff was in its vicinity[;] con-sequently the plaintiff was neither an invitee nor a licensee, but a tres-passer, upon the defendant's property. But even so, had the defendant known that the plaintiff intended to use the building under circum-stances where ordinary care and prudence required that he should have been warned, a common-law duty or obligation might arise whereby the defendant would be required to give him warning if the defendant had reasonable cause to believe that injury might result to the plaintiff if he were not warned. [. . .]
>
> There is nothing in this record disclosing a state of facts whereby an ordinarily prudent person could reasonably have anticipated or foreseen that plaintiff would use the building for a viatic purpose, that he might ignite the gas by a lighted match, or that an injury would probably result from defendant's own act. The evidence comes wholly from the plaintiff's witnesses, and from it we are unable to perceive any duty owing by the defendant or any breach of duty committed by it.

4. *Inadvertent asphyxiation of trespassers.* In Ehret v. Village of Scarsdale, 199 N.E. 56 (N.Y. 1935), the Westchester County Small Estates Corporation laid a pipe under the surface of a street to drain water from houses it recently had built in Scarsdale. The Corporation encased part of an existing gas main inside the drain pipe. Several months later a leak opened in the gas main; the gas entered the drain pipe, worked its way into one of the Corporation's

still-vacant houses, and asphyxiated a trespasser who had entered the house and was sleeping there. The gas had been turned off the night before, but it was too late. (The gas also asphyxiated a watchman at the same house, and caused a damaging explosion at another house in the neighborhood.) The trespasser's administratrix won a judgment against the Corporation for negligence in laying its pipe. The Court of Appeals affirmed:

> If without permission or exclusion a stranger unlawfully intrudes upon the land, he voluntarily exposes himself to the risk of unsafe conditions existing thereon or of dangerous activities conducted there. In the present case the death of the plaintiff's intestate was due to a wrongful act of the owner of the land performed in a public street many months before the decedent trespassed upon the land. The rule that an owner of land is not liable to a trespasser upon his land for failure to exercise ordinary care should not be extended so far as to confer immunity upon the defendant for damages caused by his wrong under the circumstances shown here. [...]
>
> The construction of a pipe drain in a public street in a manner which created danger to person or property in nearby houses constituted a wrong. For injury resulting at any time to any person within the zone of danger, the law gives redress. A trespasser in a house belonging to the defendant may have assumed the risk that the defendant's use of its land might endanger persons thereon. He did not assume the risk that such danger would arise from a condition existing several hundred feet away in the public street, heedlessly created by the defendant or any other person.

What is the superficial similarity between *Ehret v. Village of Scarsdale* and *Cleveland Electric Illuminating Co. v. Van Benshoten* (the NL case of the exploding outhouse)? What is the distinction between them? Did the plaintiff in the *Cleveland Electric* case assume any more risks than the plaintiff in *Ehret*? What is the distinction between *Ehret v. Village of Scarsdale* and *Haskins v. Grybko* (the NL case of the woodchuck hunt)?

5. *Obligations to trespassers*. From the Restatement (Second) of Torts:

§333. GENERAL RULE

Except as stated in §§334-339, a possessor of land is not liable to trespassers for physical harm caused by his failure to exercise reasonable care (a) to put the land in a condition reasonably safe for their reception, or (b) to carry on his activities so as not to endanger them.

§334. ACTIVITIES HIGHLY DANGEROUS TO CONSTANT TRESPASSERS
        ON LIMITED AREA

A possessor of land who knows, or from facts within his knowledge should know, that trespassers constantly intrude upon a limited area thereof, is subject to liability for bodily harm there caused to them by his failure to carry on an activity involving a risk of death or serious bodily harm with reasonable care for their safety.

§337. ARTIFICIAL CONDITIONS HIGHLY DANGEROUS
      TO KNOWN TRESPASSERS

A possessor of land who maintains on the land an artificial condition which involves a risk of death or serious bodily harm to persons coming in contact with it, is subject to liability for bodily harm caused to trespassers by his failure to exercise reasonable care to warn them of the condition if (a) the possessor knows or has reason to know of their presence in dangerous proximity to the condition, and (b) the condition is of such a nature that he has reason to believe that the trespasser will not discover it or realize the risk involved.

6. *Attractive nuisance.* In Keffe v. Milwaukee & St. Paul R. Co., 21 Minn. 207 (1875), the plaintiff, who was seven years old, caught his leg in the defendant's railroad turntable. The leg later had to be amputated. The turntable revolved easily, was unfenced, and was located near the defendant's passenger depot and within 120 feet of the plaintiff's home. The trial court gave the defendant judgment on the pleadings on the ground that the plaintiff was a trespasser. The plaintiff appealed, and the Minnesota Supreme Court reversed:

> It is true that the defendant did not leave the turn-table unfastened, *for the purpose* of injuring young children; and if the defendant had no reason to believe that the unfastened turn-table was likely to attract and to injure young children, then the defendant would not be bound to use care to protect from injury the children that it had no good reason to suppose were in any danger. But the complaint states that the defendant knew that the turn-table, when left unfastened, was easily revolved; that, when left unfastened, it was very attractive, and when put in motion by them, dangerous to young children: and knew also that many children were in the habit of going upon it to play. The defendant therefore knew that by leaving this turn-table unfastened and unguarded, it was not merely inviting young children to come upon the turn-table, but was holding out an allurement, which, acting upon the natural instincts by which such children are controlled, drew them by those instincts into a hidden danger; and having thus knowingly allured them into a place of danger, without their fault, (for it cannot blame them for not resisting the temptation it has set before them,) it was bound to use care to protect them from the danger into which they were thus led, and from which they could not be expected to protect themselves.

7. *A roaring farce.* In Ryan v. Towar, 87 N.W. 644 (Mich. 1901), the Bice Manufacturing Company, which had gone out of business, still owned a small pump house with a water wheel inside in the town of Marquette. One day some

children entered the pump house through a hole in its wall (the evidence suggested that they created the hole themselves), and began to play on the wheel; one of the children was injured when she became caught between the wheel and the pit in which it turned. She sued the corporation. The trial court ordered a directed verdict for the defendants; the Michigan Supreme Court affirmed:

> The pedestrians who insist upon risking their lives by making a footpath of a railroad track, and others who habitually shorten distances by making footpaths across the corners of village lots, are none the less trespassers because the owners do not choose to resent such intrusion, and go to the expense and trouble of taking effective measures to prevent it. There is no more lawless class than children, and none more annoyingly resent an attempt to prevent their trespasses. The average citizen has learned that the surest way to be overrun by children is to give them to understand that their presence is distasteful. The consequence is that they roam at will over private premises, and as a rule this is tolerated so long as no damage is done. The remedy which the law affords for the trifling trespasses of children is inadequate. No one ever thinks of suing them, and to attempt to remove a crowd of boys from private premises by gently laying on of hands, and using no more force than necessary to put them off, would be a roaring farce, with all honors to the juveniles. For a corporation with an empty treasury, and overwhelmed with debt, to be required to [bear] the expense of preventing children from going across its lots to school, lest it be said that it invited and licensed them to do so, is to our minds an unreasonable proposition.

Notwithstanding the court's views in *Ryan v. Towar*, the opinion in *Keffe v. Milwaukee & St. Paul R. Co.* proved more influential, and later was extended to cover cases in which children were not lured onto the defendant's property by any hazard there. (The term "attractive nuisance," which still is in widespread use, thus is now a misnomer.) The prevailing doctrine is set out in the Restatement (Second) of Torts:

§339. ARTIFICIAL CONDITIONS HIGHLY DANGEROUS
            TO TRESPASSING CHILDREN

A possessor of land is subject to liability for physical harm to children trespassing thereon caused by an artificial condition upon the land if
    (a) the place where the condition exists is one upon which the possessor knows or has reason to know that children are likely to trespass, and
    (b) the condition is one of which the possessor knows or has reason to know and which he realizes or should realize will involve an unreasonable risk of death or serious bodily harm to such children, and

(c) the children because of their youth do not discover the condition or realize the risk involved in intermeddling with it or in coming within the area made dangerous by it, and

(d) the utility to the possessor of maintaining the condition and the burden of eliminating the danger are slight as compared with the risk to children involved, and

(e) the possessor fails to exercise reasonable care to eliminate the danger or otherwise to protect the children.

If you have studied the Hand formula (in the chapter on The Negligence Standard), what is the relationship between that analytical idea and the test for duty laid out above?

2. *Duties to Licensees*

1. *Inadvertent asphyxiation of licensees.* In Davies v. McDowell National Bank, 180 A.2d 21 (Pa. 1962), the plaintiffs' evidence was that Carl Davies and his wife, Mary, paid a visit one afternoon to the business office of one J. Fred Thomas. Thomas, 71 years old and in failing health, was Mrs. Davies' stepfather, and she had been helping to care for him. Mr. and Mrs. Davies found Thomas unconscious. They summoned a doctor, who succeeded in reviving Thomas; they told the doctor they would stay with Thomas until he had recovered sufficiently to be taken to their home for further care. Shortly after ten o'clock that night, a police officer visited the Thomas office and found Thomas and Mrs. Davies dead. Mr. Davies was unconscious. The cause of the deaths was carbon monoxide poisoning. Thomas's premises were heated by a gas furnace, and the damper on the heater's chimney had become rusted shut. Mrs. Davies' estate sued Thomas's estate, claiming that her death was caused by Thomas's negligence in maintaining his premises. The trial court said it would "assume that a jury could have found Thomas negligent in allowing this condition to exist" (Thomas's doctor earlier had advised him to have his furnace checked as a routine precaution to guard against harmful fumes), but the court nonetheless nonsuited the plaintiffs because there was "absolutely no testimony from which the jury could have inferred that Thomas knew of this unsafe condition." The plaintiffs appealed, and the Pennsylvania Supreme Court affirmed:

> It is asserted that under the evidence the jury could conclude that Mr. and Mrs. Davies were "business visitors" in the Thomas office on the occasion involved, and that the court below erred in concluding that they were merely social guests. If they were "business visitors" the duty of the owner would be to exercise reasonable care in maintaining the premises in a safe condition.
>
> There is no specific evidence in the record as to why they visited the Thomas office on the occasion involved. The proof does show that when the physician left they remained there in order to take Thomas to their

home when he was physically able. From the relationship existing between the parties and their past close association, the only reasonable conclusion is that they were social guests. Their mere presence upon the premises raises no presumption that they were "business visitors." That they were such may not be conjectured. Nor does the fact that a social guest performs some minor or incidental service for his host during his stay convert the status to that of "business visitor."

Social guests are gratuitous licensees. To this class, the owner of a premises is liable for bodily harm caused by a latent dangerous condition existing thereon only if he has knowledge of the condition and fails to give warning thereof, realizing that it involves an unreasonable risk to his guests and that they are not likely to discover its existence. There is not a scintilla of evidence herein to establish that the deceased, Thomas, had any previous knowledge of the existence of the latent dangerous condition upon which the cause of action is based.

What is the superficial similarity between *Davies v. McDowell National Bank* and *Ehret v. Village of Scarsdale* (the L case where the trespasser was asphyxiated by gases in the defendant's house)? What is the distinction between them?

2. *Active negligence.* In Lordi v. Spiotta, 45 A.2d 491 (N.J. 1946), the defendant invited the plaintiff and his son to come to his summer bungalow. The hot water boiler in the bungalow was heated by natural gas. One afternoon the defendant's son lit the gas heater to get water for a bath. On his way out of the house later in the day, the son asked the defendant to turn off the heater. The defendant went into the cellar and turned off the heater — or "thought he had." In fact he had not, and gas accumulated in the defendant's basement for the next several hours. That evening the defendant instructed the plaintiff to go to the basement and light the heater to provide hot water for another bath. When the plaintiff attempted to do this by striking a match, a large explosion resulted that killed the plaintiff's son. The plaintiff sued and won a jury verdict; the defendant appealed from an order denying its motion for a directed verdict. The New Jersey Supreme Court affirmed:

> Assuming that the plaintiff was a guest and as such had to take the place as he found it, so to speak — yet the so called guest rule cannot hold the proprietor of the establishment immune from answering in damages where the guest is injured by an unknown danger created by the proprietor's negligence. The dangerous condition surrounding this gas heater is analogous to creating a trap for the plaintiff. The defendant, on asking the plaintiff to go into the cellar to light the heater, certainly held out the place, for the performance of the service requested, to be free from concealed peril. We conclude that the defendant's act in regard to closing the valve controlling the gas flow, and doing it so imperfectly as to permit a gas leakage which was bound to make an accumulation of this dangerous agency, amounted to active negligence.

What is the distinction between *Lordi v. Spiotta* and *Davies v. McDowell National Bank* (the NL case where the plaintiff's decedent was asphyxiated by gas from the defendant's heater)? What if a trespasser had entered the basement of the defendant's bungalow, struck a match so that he could see, and thus ignited the gas? Could he recover from the defendant for his injuries?

3. *Obligations to licensees*. From the Restatement (Second) of Torts:

§330. LICENSEE DEFINED

A licensee is a person who is privileged to enter or remain on land only by virtue of the possessor's consent.

§341. ACTIVITIES DANGEROUS TO LICENSEES

A possessor of land is subject to liability to his licensees for physical harm caused to them by his failure to carry on his activities with reasonable care for their safety if, but only if, (a) he should expect that they will not discover or realize the danger, and (b) they do not know or have reason to know of the possessor's activities and of the risk involved.

§342. DANGEROUS CONDITIONS KNOWN TO POSSESSOR

A possessor of land is subject to liability for physical harm caused to licensees by a condition on the land if, but only if,
  (a) the possessor knows or has reason to know of the condition and should realize that it involves an unreasonable risk of harm to such licensees, and should expect that they will not discover or realize the danger, and (b) he fails to exercise reasonable care to make the condition safe, or to warn the licensees of the condition and the risk involved, and (c) the licensees do not know or have reason to know of the condition and the risk involved.
  Illustration 1. A invites his friend B to dinner. A knows that his private road has been dangerously undermined at a point where it runs along an embankment and that this is not observable to a person driving along the road. A, when giving the invitation, forgets to warn B of this. While B is driving along the road it collapses, causing serious harm to B. A is subject to liability to B.
  Illustration 2. Under facts similar to those in Illustration 2, except that A does not know that the road has been undermined but could have discovered it had he paid attention to the condition of his road, A is not liable to B.

3.   *Duties to Invitees*

1. *Invitees vs. volunteers*. In City of Boca Raton v. Mattef, 91 So. 2d 644 (Fla. 1956), Mr. Mattef, the plaintiff's decedent, was a sign painter. At a

meeting of the Boca Raton Town Council, Mattef offered to paint the town's name on the side of a water tower for $80. The Council unanimously adopted a motion awarding the job to Mattef and providing that "the Town Attorney be requested to draw the necessary contract to protect the Town's interest." The Town Attorney later advised Mattef that the contract had not been written because he did not have sufficient specifications for the job; he told Mattef to discuss them with the Town Engineer, and said that after obtaining the necessary information he would prepare the contract. Instead of doing these things, however, Mattef took his paint and equipment to the water tower and proceeded to paint the name of the town on the water tank at the top of it. When Mattef went to the tower he spoke to the superintendent of the water plant (who did not have charge of the tower) and advised him that he was going to proceed to do the painting. The superintendent made no comment on Mattef's expressed intention but did pass some of Mattef's equipment up to him. In the course of Mattef's work, a rung of a steel ladder attached to the tower broke loose. Mattef fell to the ground and was killed.

Mattef's widow brought a wrongful death suit against Boca Raton, claiming that the city breached its duty to provide Mattef with a reasonably safe place to work. The trial court instructed the jury that Mattef was an employee of the city and thus was an invitee to whom the city owed a duty of reasonable care. The jury awarded the plaintiff $25,000. The defendant appealed, claiming that the jury had been misinstructed. The Florida Supreme Court reversed and remanded for a new trial:

> Under the circumstances revealed by this record, the deceased was a volunteer. He had not yet reached the status of an invitee for the simple reason that he had not yet been invited by the appellant to enter upon the undertaking. An invitee is normally considered to be one who enters upon the premises of another for purposes connected with the business of the owner or occupant of the premises. In the matter before us, while to some extent the deceased entered the premises of the appellant in connection with the business which he had theretofore discussed with the appellant, his voluntary undertaking was certainly not pursuant to the arrangement previously made and still in its formative stages.
>
> We cannot consider the deceased to be a trespasser for the reason that he at least had implied permission to do what he did in that the head of one of the departments of the City was present and did not stop him from climbing the water tower, but on the contrary, at Mr. Mattef's request, assisted him in getting some of his brushes and equipment to the top of the tower. By a process of elimination, therefore, we come to the conclusion that when the deceased of his own volition in the fulfillment of an undertaking related to his own business of sign painting entered upon the premises of the appellant, climbed the water tower and undertook the work, he was at most a licensee. [. . .]

The licensee by permission occupies a status only slightly better than that of a trespasser insofar as the liability of the owner of the premises is concerned. Such a licensee takes the premises as he finds them and the duty of the owner of the premises is to refrain from wanton negligence or willful misconduct that would injure the licensee. If the owner has knowledge of pitfalls, booby traps, latent hazards or similar dangers, then a failure to warn such a licensee could under proper circumstances amount to wanton negligence; but there must be knowledge of the danger by the owner combined with knowledge that the licensee is about to be confronted with the danger. Beyond that, he is not obligated to make provision for the safety of the one who enters his premises under such circumstances.

Was Mattef best understood as a having been a volunteer? Suppose he had lived; do you think he would have had a good claim for any sort of recovery against the city for the value of the work he had performed? If so, why wasn't he an invitee?

2. *Stop thief!* In Jacobsma v. Goldberg's Fashion Forum, 303 N.E.2d 226 (Ill. App. 1973), the plaintiff and his wife entered the defendant's store in the Ford City shopping mall. The plaintiff soon saw a man, later identified as the store's manager, standing at the end of an aisle about 75 feet away, pointing in the direction of the plaintiff and shouting "Stop thief!" The plaintiff saw another man, who turned out to be a shoplifter, running from the manager toward him. The plaintiff pushed his wife aside and grabbed the running man. They fell to the floor. In the struggle some ladies' garments fell from under the shoplifter's coat. He then got up and ran out of the store. He was pursued unsuccessfully by the manager. Meanwhile the plaintiff had dislocated his shoulder when he fell, and he sued the defendant to recover for his injuries. He won a jury verdict. The court of appeals affirmed:

> It is conceded that the plaintiff was a business invitee upon entering the clothing store. Thus, the defendant owed him a duty to exercise ordinary care for his safety. But his injury occurred because of his attempt to restrain the shoplifter, an activity outside the normal business invitation. The defendant contends that the plaintiff was at that point a volunteer to whom the defendant owed only the duty not to willfully or wantonly cause him injury.
>
> In refusing to instruct the jury on the issue of whether the plaintiff was a volunteer, the trial court determined that he was not a volunteer as a matter of law. Whether an invitee has lost that status is generally a question of fact for the jury. But where all the facts and inferences therefrom lead to only one conclusion, the matter may be decided without recourse to a jury. The plaintiff's agent, the manager who called for help, testified that he had the authority to do so. Even if he did not have the

express authority, this would be the kind of emergency in which such authority would be implied. That the call for help was an invitation to the plaintiff is also borne out by the record. The manager called "Stop thief," and his testimony indicates that this was a general call for assistance. [. . .]

The physical positions of the three, the plaintiff, the shoplifter and the manager, who was pointing in the direction of the plaintiff, justified the plaintiff's conclusion that he was requested to assist in stopping the thief. This conclusion is further buttressed by the facts that the plaintiff was physically larger than the shoplifter and that the plaintiff was the only man other than the shoplifter and the manager in the store, which had few customers at the time. Finally, the plaintiff's purpose in attempting to restrain the shoplifter was to benefit the defendant, a purpose which has been found to be sufficient to sustain invitee status. The court did not err, therefore, in refusing the instructions on volunteer status.

The court concluded that the jury reasonably could have found that the defendant breached its duty of care to the plaintiff because it "had actual knowledge through its sales staff that the shoplifter who caused the injury had three days previously attempted to steal clothing from the defendant. With the knowledge of this man's prior crime, the defendant became charged with the responsibility to protect its invitees from other illegal acts by him."

What is the superficial similarity between *Jacobsma v. Goldberg's Fashion Forum* and *City of Boca Raton v. Mattef* (the NL case of the painter who "volunteered" to paint the water tower)? What is the distinction between them?

3. *Obligations to invitees.* From the Restatement (Second) of Torts:

§332. INVITEE DEFINED

(1) An invitee is either a public invitee or a business visitor.

(2) A public invitee is a person who is invited to enter or remain on land as a member of the public for a purpose for which the land is held open to the public.

(3) A business visitor is a person who is invited to enter or remain on land for a purpose directly or indirectly connected with business dealings with the possessor of the land.

Illustration 1. A hires a hall and gives a free public lecture on a religious topic. B, as a member of the public, attends the lecture. B is an invitee.

Illustration 2. The city of X maintains a free public library, for the use of anyone in the community. A comes to the library to read a book. A is an invitee. But if A enters to meet a friend, or merely to get out of the rain, he is not an invitee.

Comment l. If the invitee goes outside of the area of his invitation, he becomes a trespasser or a licensee, depending upon whether he goes there without the consent of the possessor, or with such consent. Thus one who goes into a shop which occupies part of a building, the rest of which is used as the possessor's residence, is a trespasser if he goes into the residential part of the premises without the shopkeeper's consent; but he is a licensee if the shopkeeper permits him to go to the bathroom, or invites him to pay a social call.

§341A. ACTIVITIES DANGEROUS TO INVITEES

A possessor of land is subject to liability to his invitees for physical harm caused to them by his failure to carry on his activities with reasonable care for their safety if, but only if, he should expect that they will not discover or realize the danger, or will fail to protect themselves against it.

§343. DANGEROUS CONDITIONS KNOWN TO OR DISCOVERABLE BY POSSESSOR

A possessor of land is subject to liability for physical harm caused to his invitees by a condition on the land if, but only if, he (a) knows or by the exercise of reasonable care would discover the condition, and should realize that it involves an unreasonable risk of harm to such invitees, and (b) should expect that they will not discover or realize the danger, or will fail to protect themselves against it, and (c) fails to exercise reasonable care to protect them against the danger.

4. *Household guests in uniform.* Suppose smoke begins to pour from the windows of a house. A firefighter enters. For reasons unrelated to the apparent fire, the railing on the basement staircase gives way, causing the firefighter to fall and suffer various injuries. The homeowner was unaware of the weak railing because he negligently had failed to inspect it. Liability for the homeowner? Is a firefighter a licensee or an invitee? What purposes do those categories serve that might bear on how firefighters are classified? Should the result be any different if the plaintiff is a meter reader arriving at the house by appointment?

5. *Challenges to the distinctions.* In Rowland v. Christian, 443 P.2d 561 (Cal. 1968), the plaintiff, Rowland, cut his hand on a cold water faucet in Christian's bathroom while he was a guest in her leased apartment. Christian had asked her landlord to fix the faucet a month earlier. The parties disputed whether the crack in the faucet was "obvious;" Christian alleged that it was, and that the plaintiff knew of it (he had used the bathroom on a prior occasion). The trial court gave summary judgment to Christian on the ground that Rowland was a licensee. The California Supreme Court reversed, rendering a landmark decision that the traditional distinctions between duties owed to trespassers, licensees, and invitees had become obsolete:

Without attempting to labor all of the rules relating to the possessor's liability, it is apparent that the classifications of trespasser, licensee, and invitee, the immunities from liability predicated upon those classifications, and the exceptions to those immunities, often do not reflect the major factors which should determine whether immunity should be conferred upon the possessor of land. Some of those factors, including the closeness of the connection between the injury and the defendant's conduct, the moral blame attached to the defendant's conduct, the policy of preventing future harm, and the prevalence and availability of insurance, bear little, if any, relationship to the classifications of trespasser, licensee and invitee and the existing rules conferring immunity. [. . .]

Although in general there may be a relationship between the remaining factors and the classifications of trespasser, licensee, and invitee, there are many cases in which no such relationship may exist. Thus, although the foreseeability of harm to an invitee would ordinarily seem greater than the foreseeability of harm to a trespasser, in a particular case the opposite may be true. The same may be said of the issue of certainty of injury. The burden to the defendant and consequences to the community of imposing a duty to exercise care with resulting liability for breach may often be greater with respect to trespassers than with respect to invitees, but it by no means follows that this is true in every case. In many situations, the burden will be the same, i.e., the conduct necessary upon the defendant's part to meet the burden of exercising due care as to invitees will also meet his burden with respect to licensees and trespassers. The last of the major factors, the cost of insurance, will, of course, vary depending upon the rules of liability adopted, but there is no persuasive evidence that applying ordinary principles of negligence law to the land occupier's liability will materially reduce the prevalence of insurance due to increased cost or even substantially increase the cost.

A man's life or limb does not become less worthy of protection by the law nor a loss less worthy of compensation under the law because he has come upon the land of another without permission or with permission but without a business purpose. Reasonable people do not ordinarily vary their conduct depending upon such matters, and to focus upon the status of the injured party as a trespasser, licensee, or invitee in order to determine the question whether the landowner has a duty of care, is contrary to our modern social mores and humanitarian values. The common law rules obscure rather than illuminate the proper considerations which should govern determination of the question of duty.

It bears repetition that the basic policy of this state set forth by the Legislature in section 1714 of the Civil Code is that everyone is responsible for an injury caused to another by his want of ordinary care or skill in the management of his property. The factors which may in particular cases warrant departure from this fundamental principle do not warrant the wholesale immunities resulting from the common law classifications, and we are satisfied that continued adherence to the common law distinctions can only lead to injustice or, if we are to avoid injustice, further fictions with the resulting complexity and confusion. We decline to follow and perpetuate such rigid classifications. The proper test to be applied to the liability of the possessor of land in accordance with section 1714 of the Civil Code is whether in the management of his property he has acted as a reasonable man in view of the probability of injury to others, and, although the plaintiff's status as a trespasser, licensee, or invitee may in the light of the facts giving rise to such status have some bearing on the question of liability, the status is not determinative.

Once the ancient concepts as to the liability of the occupier of land are stripped away, the status of the plaintiff relegated to its proper place in determining such liability, and ordinary principles of negligence applied, the result in the instant case presents no substantial difficulties. As we have seen, when we view the matters presented on the motion for summary judgment as we must, we must assume defendant Miss Christian was aware that the faucet handle was defective and dangerous, that the defect was not obvious, and that plaintiff was about to come in contact with the defective condition, and under the undisputed facts she neither remedied the condition nor warned plaintiff of it. Where the occupier of land is aware of a concealed condition involving in the absence of precautions an unreasonable risk of harm to those coming in contact with it and is aware that a person on the premises is about to come in contact with it, the trier of fact can reasonably conclude that a failure to warn or to repair the condition constitutes negligence. Whether or not a guest has a right to expect that his host will remedy dangerous conditions on his account, he should reasonably be entitled to rely upon a warning of the dangerous condition so that he, like the host, will be in a position to take special precautions when he comes in contact with it. [. . .]

6. *The healthy skeptics.* In Carter v. Kinney, 896 S.W.2d 926 (Mo. 1995), the plaintiff, Carter, was a member of a Bible study group that met at the home of the Kinneys. Carter slipped on a patch of ice on the Kinneys' driveway and broke his leg. He sued the Kinneys to recover for his injuries. The trial court gave summary judgment to the defendants, finding that Carter was not an invitee ("the record shows beyond cavil that Mr. Carter did not enter the Kinneys' land to afford the Kinneys any material benefit") and that the Kinneys therefore had no duty to protect him from unknown dangerous conditions. On appeal, Carter invited the Missouri Supreme Court to abandon the distinction between licensees and invitees; the court declined, and affirmed the summary judgment for the Kinneys:

[The Carters] argue that the current system that recognizes a lower standard of care for licensees than invitees is arbitrary and denies deserving plaintiffs compensation for their injuries. The Carters note that twenty states have abolished the distinction since 1968 and encourage Missouri to join this "trend." [The court noted that nine of those states had abolished only the distinction between licensees and invitees, while retaining separate treatment for trespassers; the other eleven, following *Rowland v. Christian*, had abandoned all of the distinctions.]

The Kinneys claim that the trend is little more than a fad. They note that twelve states have expressly rejected the abolition of the distinction since the "trend" began in 1968 and that the remaining eighteen states, including Missouri, have not directly addressed the issue and maintain the common law distinctions.

We are not persuaded that the licensee/invitee distinction no longer serves. The possessor's intentions in issuing the invitation determine not only the status of the entrant but the possessor's duty of care to that entrant. The contours of the legal relationship that results from the possessor's invitation reflect a careful and patient effort by courts over time to balance the interests of persons injured by conditions of land against the interests of possessors of land to enjoy and employ their land for the purposes they wish. Moreover, and despite the exceptions courts have developed to the general rules, the maintenance of the distinction between licensee and invitee creates fairly predictable rules within which entrants and possessors can determine appropriate conduct and juries can assess liability. To abandon the careful work of generations for an amorphous "reasonable care under the circumstances" standard seems — to put it kindly — improvident.

Though six states have abolished the distinction between licensee and invitee since Professor Keeton penned his words, he speculates that the failure of more states to join the "trend"

> may reflect a more fundamental dissatisfaction with certain developments in accident law that accelerated during the 1960's — reduction of whole systems of legal principles to a single, perhaps simplistic, standard of reasonable care, the sometimes blind subordination of other legitimate social objectives to the goals of accident prevention and compensation, and the commensurate shifting of the balance of power to the jury from the judge. At least it appears that the courts are . . . acquiring a more healthy skepticism toward invitations to jettison years of developed jurisprudence in favor of beguiling legal panacea.

W.P. Keeton, Prosser and Keeton on the Law of Torts, §62 (1984).

We remain among the healthy skeptics. The experience of the states that have abolished the distinction between licensee and invitee does not convince us that their idea is a better one. Indeed, we are convinced that they have chosen wrongly.

7. *What difference does it make?* Would *Rowland v. Christian* have come out differently if the traditional common law approach had been used in that case? More generally, how much does it matter whether courts use the

traditional approach of *Carter v. Kinney* or the newer approach of *Rowland v. Christian*? Are the legal distinctions that *Rowland* rejects simply legal fictions, as the court asserts? If (as *Rowland* suggests) a plaintiff's status as a trespasser, social guest, or business guest still should be considered a factor in determining the level of care owed by the defendant, then *Rowland v. Christian* might seem to represent only a small change in the law; it might appear just to make the application of the traditional categories a bit less rigid by turning them into factors rather than hard rules. But one way to think about "duty" doctrines is that they serve as ways of controlling juries, since a ruling that defendant has no duty or a limited duty — unlike decisions about whether the defendant used reasonable care, for example — usually is considered a determination of law to be made by a judge. Decisions about the extent of a defendant's duty under the traditional rubric thus can prevent cases from going to juries at all. How does the decision in *Rowland v. Christian* affect that distribution of labor between judge and jury?

8. *Morning train (problem).* In Rhodes v. Illinois Central Gulf Railroad, 665 N.E.2d 1260 (Ill. 1996), one of the defendant's commuter trains stopped to pick up passengers at 75th Street and Exchange Avenue in Chicago; the hour was 5:00 A.M. A passenger boarding the train told the conductor, Raymond Deany, that someone was lying in the warming house where passengers waited for the train. Deany and a colleague named Ziolkowski stepped into the doorway of the warming house and saw a man, later identified as the plaintiff's decedent, Carl Rhodes, lying face down on the floor. Deany saw a "minute amount" of blood smeared on the floor around the man's head, but no blood on the man himself. Deany and Ziolkowski returned to the train. Deany radioed his supervisor that he had seen a bleeding man lying in the warming house and that the man needed assistance (the railroad did not permit sleeping in its warming houses). The train continued on its way. Deany's supervisor passed the report to a company police dispatcher, who in turn called the Chicago police department.

Deany's train arrived back at the same station 45 minutes later. Ziolkowski saw the man still lying in the warming house. The train returned again about an hour later, at 6:40. Deany radioed his supervisor to report that the man was still there; the supervisor told Deany he had taken care of the situation. At 7:56 a conductor from another train radioed to report that a man was sleeping in the warming house. A new supervisor was on duty and relayed the information afresh to the dispatcher, who again passed it to the Chicago police. Two Chicago police officers arrived at the station at about 8:00. They thought one of the railroad's own police units was going to meet them there; finding no such unit, they left without entering the station.

At 9:00, Deany's train again stopped at the station. A passenger told Deany that a man was in the warming house who appeared to be sleeping. Deany did not report this to the supervisor because he had already reported the man twice.

Ziolkowski, whose shift had ended, went to the supervisor's office and asked if anything had been done about the man in the warming house. At this point an engineer from a commuter train also reported to the supervisor that the man and the floor were covered with blood. The supervisor called the dispatcher, who again called the Chicago police. A patrolman named Bilek arrived at the station at 10:11. Rhodes sat up with Bilek's assistance. Bilek saw bruising and cuts on Rhodes's face, but no blood; he concluded that Rhodes was intoxicated because of the smell of alcohol on his breath and clothing. Bilek asked Rhodes if he had been beaten up or had fallen. Rhodes responded slowly, nodding and speaking in a groggy voice. Two more officers arrived and took Rhodes to a hospital. When he arrived there at 11:25 he was unresponsive and was snoring with gurgling respirations. Soon he stopped breathing. Tests showed he had suffered a massive subdural hematoma (a collection of blood under the dura matter covering the brain). He died the next day. A neurosurgeon later testified for the plaintiff that if Rhodes had undergone surgery to relieve the hematoma while he still was communicating, he would more probably than not have had a good recovery.

The administrator of Rhodes's estate sued the railroad. The railroad claimed it had no duty to Rhodes. What result? How might you use any of the cases considered so far in this chapter to argue for or against liability?

9. *Your money or his life (problem).* In Boyd v. Racine Currency Exchange, 306 N.E.2d 39 (Ill. 1973), the plaintiff's decedent, Boyd, was a customer in the defendant's currency exchange. A thief entered the establishment, put a gun to the head of Boyd, and threatened to kill him if the defendant's teller, one Blanche Murphy, did not hand over the money in her drawer or open the door to the cage in which she worked. Murphy, who was standing behind bulletproof glass, did not comply, but instead dove to the floor. The robber shot Boyd in the head, killing him, and then left the premises. Boyd's administratrix sued the currency exchange, claiming it was negligent in failing to give the robber the money. The currency exchange moved to have the complaint dismissed on the ground that it had no duty to accede to the robber's demands. What result?

E. THE PRIVITY LIMITATION

Suppose A and B enter into a contract, and B performs it negligently. C is injured as a result. Clearly A has rights against B; but does C? Courts sometimes have said no, imposing limits on the duty that a defendant owes to a third party injured when the defendant breaches a contract. The limit is said to be based on the fact that C has no contract (or is not "in privity") with B. Why might such limitations on duty seem necessary?

H. R. Moch Co. v. Rensselaer Water Co.
159 N.E. 896 (N.Y. 1928)

CARDOZO, C. J. — The defendant, a water works company under the laws of this State, made a contract with the city of Rensselaer for the supply of water during a term of years. Water was to be furnished to the city for sewer flushing and street sprinkling; for service to schools and public buildings; and for service at fire hydrants, the latter service at the rate of $42.50 a year for each hydrant. Water was to be furnished to private takers within the city at their homes and factories and other industries at reasonable rates, not exceeding a stated schedule. While this contract was in force, a building caught fire. The flames, spreading to the plaintiff's warehouse near by, destroyed it and its contents. The defendant according to the complaint was promptly notified of the fire, "but omitted and neglected after such notice, to supply or furnish sufficient or adequate quantity of water, with adequate pressure to stay, suppress or extinguish the fire before it reached the warehouse of the plaintiff, although the pressure and supply which the defendant was equipped to supply and furnish, and had agreed by said contract to supply and furnish, was adequate and sufficient to prevent the spread of the fire to and the destruction of the plaintiff's warehouse and its contents." By reason of the failure of the defendant to "fulfill the provisions of the contract between it and the city of Rensselaer," the plaintiff is said to have suffered damage, for which judgment is demanded. A motion, in the nature of a demurrer, to dismiss the complaint, was denied at Special Term. The Appellate Division reversed by a divided court.

Liability in the plaintiff's argument is placed on one or other of three grounds. The complaint, we are told, is to be viewed as [including]: (1) A cause of action for breach of contract within *Lawrence v. Fox* (20 N.Y. 268); [and] (2) a cause of action for a common-law tort, within *MacPherson v. Buick Motor Company* (217 N.Y. 382). [. . .]

(1) We think the action is not maintainable as one for breach of contract.

No legal duty rests upon a city to supply its inhabitants with protection against fire. That being so, a member of the public may not maintain an action under *Lawrence v. Fox* against one contracting with the city to furnish water at the hydrants, unless an intention appears that the promisor is to be answerable to individual members of the public as well as to the city for any loss ensuing from the failure to fulfill the promise. No such intention is discernible here. On the contrary, the contract is significantly divided into two branches: one a promise to the city for the benefit of the city in its corporate capacity, in which branch is included the service at the hydrants; and the other a promise to the city for the benefit of private takers, in which branch is included the service at their homes and factories. In a broad sense it is true that every city contract, not improvident or wasteful, is for the benefit of the public. More than this, however, must be shown to give a right of action to a member of the public not formally a party. The benefit, as it is sometimes said, must be one that is not merely incidental and secondary. It must be primary and immediate in such a sense and to such a degree as to bespeak the assumption of a duty to make reparation directly to the individual members of the public if the benefit is lost. The field of obligation would be expanded beyond reasonable limits if less than this were to be demanded as a condition of liability. A promisor undertakes to supply fuel for heating a public building. He is not liable for breach of contract to a visitor who finds the building without fuel, and thus contracts a cold. The list of illustrations can be indefinitely extended. The carrier of the mails under contract with the government is not answerable to the merchant who has lost the benefit of a bargain through negligent delay. The householder is without a remedy against manufacturers of hose and engines, though prompt performance of their contracts would have stayed the ravages of fire. "The law does not spread its protection so far." (*Robins Dry Dock & Repair Co. v. Flint*, 275 U.S. 303)

So with the case at hand. By the vast preponderance of authority, a contract between a city and a water company to furnish water at the city hydrants has in view a benefit to the public that is incidental rather than immediate, an assumption of duty to the city and not to its inhabitants. [. . .] An intention to assume an obligation of indefinite extension to every member of the public is seen to be the more improbable when we recall the crushing burden that the obligation would impose. The consequences invited would bear no reasonable proportion to those attached by law to defaults not greatly different. A wrongdoer who by negligence sets fire to a building is liable in damages to the owner where the fire has its origin, but not to other owners who are injured when it spreads. If the plaintiff is to prevail, one who negligently omits to supply sufficient pressure to extinguish a fire started by another, assumes an obligation to pay the ensuing damage, though the whole city is laid low. A promisor will not be deemed to have had in mind the assumption of a risk so overwhelming for any trivial reward.

(2) We think the action is not maintainable as one for a common-law tort.

"It is ancient learning that one who assumes to act, even though gratuitously, may thereby become subject to the duty of acting carefully, if he acts at all." (*Glanzer v. Shepard*, 233 N.Y. 236, 239) The plaintiff would bring its case within the orbit of that principle. The hand once set to a task may not always be withdrawn with impunity though liability would fail if it had never been applied at all. A time-honored formula often phrases the distinction as one between misfeasance and non-feasance. Incomplete the formula is, and so at times misleading. Given a relation involving in its existence a duty of care irrespective of a contract, a tort may result as well from acts of omission as of commission in the fulfillment of the duty thus recognized by law. [. . .]

The plaintiff would have us hold that the defendant, when once it entered upon the performance of its contract with the city, was brought into such a relation with every one who might potentially be benefited through the supply of water at the hydrants as to give to negligent performance, without reasonable notice of a refusal to continue, the quality of a tort. [. . .] We are satisfied that liability would be unduly and indeed indefinitely extended by this enlargement of the zone of duty. The dealer in coal who is to supply fuel for a shop must then answer to the customers if fuel is lacking. The manufacturer of goods, who enters upon the performance of his contract, must answer, in that view, not only to the buyer, but to those who to his knowledge are looking to the buyer for their own sources of supply. Every one making a promise having the quality of a contract will be under a duty to the promisee by virtue of the promise, but under another duty, apart from contract, to an indefinite number of potential beneficiaries when performance has begun. The assumption of one relation will mean the involuntary assumption of a series of new relations, inescapably hooked together. Again we may say in the words of the Supreme Court of the United States, "The law does not spread its protection so far." [. . .]

The judgment should be affirmed with costs.

NOTES

1. *Misweighed beans.* In Glanzer v. Shepard, 135 N.E. 275 (N.Y. 1922), a seller of beans hired the defendants, who were professional weighers, to certify the weight of 905 bags of beans being sold to the plaintiffs. The plaintiffs paid the seller according to the weight of the beans certified by the defendants. Upon attempting to resell the beans, the plaintiffs found that their actual weight was less than the weight the defendants had certified. The plaintiffs sued the defendants to recover the amount they originally had overpaid to the bean seller. The trial judge gave a directed verdict to the plaintiffs. The court of appeals, per Cardozo, J., held that the trial court did not err:

> We think the law imposes a duty toward buyer as well as seller in the situation here disclosed. The plaintiffs' use of the certificates was not an indirect or collateral consequence of the action of the weighers. It was a consequence which, to the weighers' knowledge, was the end and aim of the transaction.

What is the distinction between *Glanzer v. Shepard* and *H. R. Moch Co. v. Rensselaer Water Co.* (the NL case of the company that failed to provide water to a fire hydrant near the plaintiff's burning warehouse)?

2. *Summer of Sam.* On July 13, 1977, a massive power outage terminated electrical service to more than three million Consolidated Edison customers in New York City for approximately 25 hours. The blackout led to many

lawsuits. In Food Pageant v. Consolidated Edison, 429 N.E.2d 738 (N.Y. 1981), Con Ed was found to have been grossly negligent in permitting the blackout, and was held liable to the plaintiff grocery store for damages resulting from spoiled food and lost business caused by the blackout. In Lilpan Food Corp. v. Consolidated Edison, 493 N.Y.S.2d 740 (Sup. Ct. 1985), the plaintiff supermarket sued Con Ed to recover damages for the looting of its store during the same blackout. The court dismissed the plaintiff's complaint:

> True, it may be argued that there was indeed a contractual relationship between plaintiff and Con Ed in that plaintiff was a customer for the supply of electricity to the plaintiff's market. However, the thrust of the plaintiff's case was directed, not to the failure to supply electricity to the market, but rather to the failure to supply electricity to the city, in general, including street lights and traffic lights — all of which led to the looting and vandalism of plaintiff's premises.

What is the distinction between the *Food Pageant* and *Lilpan Food Corp.* cases? What is the analogy between *Lilpan Food Corp. v. Consolidated Edison* and *H. R. Moch Co. v. Rensselaer Water Co.* (the NL case where the defendant failed to provide water to a fire hydrant near the defendant's warehouse)?

3. *Liability for blackouts.* In Conboy v. Mogeloff, 567 N.Y.S.2d 960 (App. Div. 1991), the plaintiff sought treatment from the defendant doctor for migraine headaches and episodes of unconsciousness. The defendant prescribed Fiorinal, a drug that has the side effect of causing drowsiness in some patients; the defendant advised the plaintiff that she nevertheless could drive a car. After taking Fiorinal a few days later, the plaintiff fell unconscious behind the wheel of her car and drove into a bridge abutment. The plaintiff's children were passengers in the car, and she brought suit on their behalf to recover for their injuries. The appellate division held that the plaintiff's complaint should be dismissed because the doctor owed no duty to the plaintiff's children. The court said that to establish a duty owed by a physician to a third party,

> "we have further required actual privity, or something approaching privity, such as conduct on the part of the defendant linking defendant to plaintiff which evinces defendant's understanding of plaintiff's reliance." *Eiseman v. State of New York*, 511 N.E.2d 1128 (N.Y. 1987). In this case, there are no allegations in the complaint or the bill of particulars of the children's reliance on defendant's conduct or of knowledge by defendant of any such reliance.

What is the analogy between *Conboy v. Mogeloff* and *Hawkins v. Pizarro* (the NL case from earlier in the chapter where the defendant mistakenly told his patient that she did not have Hepatitis-C, and she went on to transmit the disease to a man she later met and married)? The two cases taken together are another example of the overlap between two doctrines in the law of tort duties: here, "special relationships" and "privity." The courts use different theories to explain their decisions, but the underlying considerations sometimes may be similar.

Suppose the physician in *Conboy v. Mogeloff* had been held liable for the children's injuries. How would this affect the way that he practiced medicine or purchased insurance?

4. *Amateur hour.* In Biakanja v. Irving, 320 P.2d 16 (Cal. 1958), a man named Maroevich died. His will bequeathed all of his property to his sister. The will was prepared by the defendant, who was a notary public and not a lawyer. He neglected to have witnesses present at Maroevich's signing of the will. (According to an attorney who represented Maroevich's stepson during the subsequent probate hearing, the defendant "admonished me to the effect that I was a young lawyer, I'd better go back and study my law books some more, that anybody knew a will which bore a notarial seal was a valid will, didn't have to be witnessed by any witnesses.") As a result the will was held invalid. Maroevich's sister thus received, by intestate succession, only one-eighth of her brother's estate. She sued the defendant and recovered a judgment for the difference between the amount she would have received had the will been valid and the amount actually distributed to her. The defendant appealed, and the California Supreme Court affirmed:

> The principal question is whether defendant was under a duty to exercise due care to protect plaintiff from injury and was liable for damage caused plaintiff by his negligence even though they were not in privity of contract. [...]
> The determination whether in a specific case the defendant will be held liable to a third person not in privity is a matter of policy and involves the balancing of various factors, among which are the extent to which the transaction was intended to affect the plaintiff, the foreseeability of harm to him, the degree of certainty that the plaintiff suffered injury, the closeness of the connection between the defendant's conduct and the injury suffered, the moral blame attached to the defendant's conduct, and the policy of preventing future harm. Here, the "end and aim" of the transaction was to provide for the passing of Maroevich's estate to plaintiff. See *Glanzer v. Shepard*, 135 N.E. 275. Defendant must have been aware from the terms of the will itself that, if faulty solemnization caused the will to be invalid, plaintiff would suffer the very loss which occurred. As Maroevich died without revoking his will, plaintiff, but for defendant's negligence, would have received all of the Maroevich estate, and the fact that she received only one-eighth of the estate was directly caused by defendant's conduct.

What is the distinction between *Biakanja v. Irving* and *Conboy v. Mogeloff*? What is the analogy between *Biakanja v. Irving* and *Glanzer v. Shepard* (the L case of the misweighed beans)?

5. *Accountants*. In Ultramares Corp. v. Touche, 174 N.E. 441 (N.Y. 1931), Fred Stern & Co. hired the defendants, an accounting firm, to prepare and certify a balance sheet showing the condition of Stern's business as of December 31, 1923. The defendants' audit showed Stern to have a net worth of $1,070,715.26. Stern required extensive credit and borrowed large sums of money from banks and other lenders to finance its operations, and the defendants knew this; they also knew that Stern would use the certified balance sheet as the basis of financial dealings with banks, creditors, stockholders, and others, though the defendants did not know the specific identities of any of these parties. In reliance on the audit and balance sheet prepared by the defendants, the plaintiff made loans to Stern. In fact Stern was insolvent and could not pay back the loans; the defendants negligently had failed to discover that Stern had doctored its books. A jury returned a verdict for the plaintiff, and the defendants appealed.

Held, that the trial court should have dismissed the negligence count in the plaintiff's complaint. Said the court (per Cardozo, J.):

> If liability for negligence exists, a thoughtless slip or blunder, the failure to detect a theft or forgery beneath the cover of deceptive entries, may expose accountants to a liability in an indeterminate amount for an indeterminate time to an indeterminate class. The hazards of a business conducted on these terms are so extreme as to enkindle doubt whether a flaw may not exist in the implication of a duty that exposes to these consequences. [...]
>
> A force or instrument of harm having been launched with potentialities of danger manifest to the eye of prudence, the one who launches it is under a duty to keep it within bounds. Even so, the question is still open whether the potentialities of danger that will charge with liability are confined to harm to the person, or include injury to property. In either view, however, what is released or set in motion is a physical force. We are now asked to say that a like liability attaches to the circulation of a thought or a release of the explosive power resident in words.

The court distinguished this case from *Glanzer v. Shepard*:

> No one would be likely to urge that there was a contractual relation, or even one approaching it, at the root of any duty that was owing from the defendants now before us to the indeterminate class of persons who, presently or in the future, might deal with the Stern Company in reliance on the audit. In a word, the service rendered by the defendant in

Glanzer v. Shepard was primarily for the information of a third person, in effect, if not in name, a party to the contract, and only incidentally for that of the formal promisee. In the case at hand, the service was primarily for the benefit of the Stern Company, a convenient instrumentality for use in the development of the business, and only incidentally or collaterally for the use of those to whom Stern and his associates might exhibit it hereafter. Foresight of these possibilities may charge with liability for fraud. The conclusion does not follow that it will charge with liability for negligence.

The court summarized its conclusion as follows:

[I]f there has been neither reckless misstatement nor insincere profession of an opinion, but only honest blunder, the ensuing liability for negligence is one that is bounded by the contract, and is to be enforced between the parties by whom the contract has been made.

What is the distinction between *Ultramares Corp. v. Touche* and *Biakanja v. Irving* (the L case of the notary responsible for the invalid will)? In which of these cases is the defendant better able to predict the extent of its liability if it acts negligently? Why might such predictability be considered important?

Subsequent New York cases have refined the principle of *Ultramares* by adopting a three-part test for accountants' liability: "(1) the accountants must have been aware that the financial reports were to be used for a particular purpose or purposes; (2) in the furtherance of which a known party or parties was intended to rely; and (3) there must have been some conduct on the part of the accountants linking them to that party or parties, which evinces the accountants' understanding of that party or parties' reliance." *Credit Alliance Corp. v. Arthur Andersen & Co.*, 483 N.E.2d 110 (N.Y. 1985) (NL for negligent audit by accountant leading to bad loans); cf. *European American Bank & Trust v. Strauhs & Kaye* (L for same).

6. *Liability of artisans (problem)*. In Einhorn v. Seeley, 136 A.D.2d 122 (N.Y. App. 1988), the plaintiff, Einhorn, was raped by an unknown attacker while visiting the apartment building where her fiancé lived. Einhorn alleged that her assailant was able to enter the building because the lock on its front door was improperly installed or repaired by the defendant locksmith, who had been hired to perform the work by the building's owner. The locksmith moved to have the case dismissed on the ground that he owed no duty to the plaintiff because they were not in privity; his contract was with the owner of the building. Would you expect this argument to succeed? Assume the locksmith did perform the work negligently and that the attack on the plaintiff could not otherwise have occurred; the only question is whether the locksmith owed the plaintiff a duty of care.

F. PURE ECONOMIC LOSSES

Robins Dry Dock & Repair Co. v. Flint
275 U.S. 303 (1927)

[The plaintiffs chartered a steamboat, the *Bjornefjord*. Their agreement with the boat's owners provided that the boat would be withdrawn from service every six months for cleaning. During one of these cleanings a crack was found in the boat's propeller. The owners of the boat hired the Robins Company to install a replacement. One of Robins's employees negligently dropped the new propeller; a new one therefore had to be cast, causing a delay of two more weeks before the boat could be used by the plaintiffs. The plaintiffs paid nothing to the owners of the boat for the time the boat spent in dry dock, but they suffered losses when they were unable to use it during the two weeks needed to cast a new propeller. The plaintiffs sued Robins to collect for those losses. The district court gave judgment to the plaintiffs, and the court of appeals affirmed. This appeal followed.]

HOLMES, J. [. . .] The District Court allowed recovery on the ground that the respondents had a "property right" in the vessel, although it is not argued that there was a demise, and the owners remained in possession. This notion [was] repudiated by the Circuit Court of Appeals and rightly. The question is whether the respondents have an interest protected by the law against unintended injuries inflicted upon the vessel by third persons who know nothing of the charter. If they have, it must be worked out through their contract relations with the owners, not on the postulate that they have a right in rem against the ship.

Of course the contract of the petitioner with the owners imposed no immediate obligation upon the petitioner to third persons as we already have said, and whether the petitioner performed it promptly or with negligent delay was the business of the owners and of nobody else. But as there was a tortious damage to a chattel it is sought to connect the claim of the respondents with that in some way. The damage was material to them only as it caused the delay in making the repairs, and that delay would be a wrong to no one except for the petitioner's contract with the owners. The injury to the propeller was no wrong to the respondents but only to those to whom it belonged. But suppose that the respondent's loss flowed directly from that source. Their loss arose only through their contract with the owners — and while intentionally to bring about a breach of contract may give rise to a cause of action, no authority need be cited to show that, as a general rule, at least, a tort to the person or property of one man does not make the tort-feasor liable to another merely because the injured person was under a contract with that other unknown to the doer of the wrong. The law does not spread its protection so far. [. . .]

The decision of the Circuit Court of Appeals seems to have been influenced by the consideration that if the whole loss occasioned by keeping a vessel out of use were recovered and divided a part would go to the respondents. It seems to have been thought that perhaps the whole might have been recovered by the owners, that in that event the owners would have been trustees for the respondents to the extent of the respondents' share, and that no injustice would be done to allow the respondents to recover their share by direct suit. But justice does not permit that the petitioner be charged with the full value of the loss of use unless there is some one who has a claim to it as against the petitioner. The respondents have no claim either in contract or in tort, and they cannot get a standing by the suggestion that if some one else had recovered it he would have been bound to pay over a part by reason of his personal relations with the respondents. [. . .]

Decree reversed.

NOTES

1. *The economic loss rule.* The *Robins* case bears some resemblance to *Moch* and the other privity cases just considered (you may recall that Cardozo quoted *Robins* in the *Moch* case). *Robins* has come to stand, however, for the general notion that a plaintiff who suffers no physical injury generally cannot recover for pure economic losses caused by a defendant's negligence. The *Robins* rule thus extends to cases arising from freestanding acts of negligence not committed in the course of performing a contract. (To make the point clearer, imagine that the propeller in *Robins* had been broken by an unrelated passerby who jostled the employee who was holding it; under the holding of *Robins*, the plaintiffs would have been unable to recover against the passerby.) *Robins* was a decision made by the Supreme Court under its admiralty jurisdiction, and it thus bound other federal courts hearing maritime cases. It also has become a significant common law authority more generally, but the courts have struggled to define the limits of the principle and exceptions to it.

2. *Favorites of admiralty.* In Carbone v. Ursich, 209 F.2d 178 (9th Cir. 1953), the plaintiffs were fishermen on the *Western Pride*, a sardine fishing boat. They had no property interest in the boat or nets, but had a "lay" agreement entitling them to 61 percent of the proceeds from sale of whatever sardines they caught. During their voyage, and while the plaintiffs were pulling in a catch, the nets on their boat were fouled by the negligence of another boat, the *Del Rio*. The *Western Pride* had to be taken out of commission for four days to repair the nets. The plaintiffs sued the owners of the *Del Rio* to collect for their losses during that period. The district court gave judgment to the defendants; the court of appeals reversed, holding the plaintiffs entitled to collect their damages:

> [A] reexamination of what was said in *Robins Dry Dock* convinces us that the court was there dealing with decidedly different principles than those which should attach to the situation of these fishermen. [. . .] It is quite

evident that the court, although dealing with a well established rule of law of torts, was not thinking of the special situation of the fishermen who [...] had long been recognized as beneficiaries under a special rule which made the wrongdoer liable not only for the damage done to the fishing vessel, but liable for the losses of the fishermen as well. This long recognized rule is no doubt a manifestation of the familiar principle that seamen are the favorites of admiralty and their economic interests entitled to the fullest possible legal protection.

What is the distinction between *Carbone v. Ursich* and *Robins Dry Dock & Repair Co. v. Flint?*

3. *Villains of admiralty.* In Henderson v. Arundel Corp., 262 F. Supp. 152 (D. Md. 1966), the plaintiffs were crew members aboard the *Dredge Lyon*, a boat equipped with scooping machinery to deepen waterways. The vessel was dredging the channel of Baltimore Harbor when it collided with another boat, the *Prahsu*; the crew of the dredge was laid off for about six weeks while repairs were performed. The crew members sued the company that owned the *Prahsu*, claiming that it was responsible for the collision and thus for their lost wages. The trial court gave judgment to the defendants, relying on *Robins* and citing with approval the following passage from *Casado v. Schooner Pilgrim, Inc.*, 171 F. Supp. 78 (D. Mass. 1959):

> The only way to permit recovery here would be to say frankly, as has been done by the Ninth Circuit, that a "special rule" obtains for fishermen. *Carbone v. Ursich*, 209 F.2d 178 (9th Cir. 1953). With all respect to that learned court, I do not believe that to say "seamen are the favorites of admiralty" should be to create a corresponding class of villains on whom to impose a new type of liability. In *Carbone v. Ursich* there was only a four day interruption of fishing. But suppose a fishing vessel were sunk outright. Would all members of the crew be entitled to compensation until they obtain new employment, or if that employment were on a less profitable ship, for the difference? I believe the fundamental principles of liability should be the same, whether employees are fishermen, or factorymen.

The court of appeals affirmed without opinion. 384 F.2d 998 (4th Cir. 1967).

4. *Refined distinctions.* In Yarmouth Sea Products Ltd. v. Scully, 131 F.3d 389 (4th Cir. 1997), the defendant's racing boat, the *Coyote*, collided with the plaintiff's fishing boat, the *Lady Olive Marie*, and punctured its hull. The collision took the *Marie* out of commission and ended its fishing voyage. The captain and crew of the *Marie* sued the pilot of the *Coyote* to recover for their lost wages; they had been working under a lay agreement in which their wages consisted of a share of the catch they obtained. The trial court gave

judgment to the plaintiffs. The court of appeals affirmed; it started by denying that *Henderson*, which had been affirmed by the Fourth Circuit 30 years earlier, controlled the outcome:

> [D]redge workers are not fishermen, as are the crew members of the *Lady Olive Marie* in the case *sub judice*. Furthermore, dredge workers do not, as Yarmouth correctly argues, invest in a voyage as do fishermen on a lay, nor are they typically paid a percentage of the profits. Rather, they are compensated on the basis of a fixed wage scale. Thus, we are persuaded that *Henderson* is distinguishable from and not controlling in the instant case. Accordingly, we regard the issue of whether fishermen on lay shares can recover lost profit from a fishing voyage prematurely ended by the tortious conduct of a third party as an open issue in this circuit. [. . .]
>
> The situation of the fishermen in the instant case differs not only from that of dredge workers, but also from that of the time charterers in *Robins Dry Dock*. Unlike the purely contractual relationship between the time charterers and the vessel owners in *Robins Dry Dock*, Yarmouth and the crew of the *Lady Olive Marie* were engaged in a kind of joint venture. Both parties were entitled to a percentage of revenues from the voyage — revenues that for fishermen constituted their very livelihood, a critical fact recognized [in *Carbone* and in *Miller Industries v. Caterpillar Tractor Co.*, 733 F.2d 813, 822 (11th Cir. 1984)]. The *Miller Industries* court also noted that where the fishermen's wages are dependent on the vessel's catch and that vessel is tortiously incapacitated, their losses are as foreseeable and direct a consequence of the tortfeasor's actions as the shipowner's loss of use. Hence, they are unlike the time charterer in *Robins Dry Dock* [sic] whose contract with the shipowner is impaired "unknown to the doer of the wrong[.]"

Does *Yarmouth* succeed in harmonizing the cases? In any event, it represents the majority rule: fishermen can collect lost income when the boats on which they served are negligently disabled.

5. *Urban applications.* In 532 Madison Avenue Gourmet Foods, Inc. v. Finlandia Center, Inc., 750 N.E.2d 1097 (N.Y. 2001), the defendant owned a 39-story office building in Manhattan; the plaintiff owned a 24-hour delicatessen half a block away. The south wall of the defendant's building collapsed while renovations were being performed on it. City officials ordered Madison Avenue and the nearby side streets closed to automobile and foot traffic for two weeks and the area immediately around the defendant's building closed for a longer period. The plaintiff had to shut down the delicatessen for more than a month. The plaintiff brought suit alleging that the defendant's negligence caused the collapse and seeking to collect lost profits from the resulting five weeks during which he was forced to

close his business. The trial court dismissed the complaint. The appellate division reversed:

> A deviation from the "economic loss rule" is appropriate on the facts of this case because of defendants' alleged knowledge and reckless disregard of the risk of creating approximately 90 new windows throughout the south wall of a skyscraper, and conducting other renovation to the base of this building, which already had major pre-existing structural defects. Under such alleged scenario, defendants should have anticipated that those pre-existing problems would negatively affect the planned renovation, and could foreseeably result in injury to others. That the injuries were not catastrophic to the thousands of people who generally frequent this area was fortuitous, because the collapse took place on a Sunday, shortly after noon.
>
> Allowing the negligence cause of action here to proceed properly allocates the risk of loss and the costs of engaging in dangerous activities such as defendants are alleged to have done. Holding defendants liable for their tortious acts creates an incentive for others not to follow suit but to act reasonably with regard for the safety of others. [. . .] In this case of alleged egregious negligence, denying recovery simply because there was no incidental property damage to plaintiff's store would foreclose redress based upon a meaningless technicality. [. . .] We reject the dissent's conclusion that a neighboring plaintiff who does not suffer injury or property damage is not entitled to legal protection against the willful, grossly irresponsible behavior of defendants who cause the collapse of a wall of a skyscraper.

The New York Court of Appeals then consolidated this case with others arising from the same incident where the appellate division likewise had found liability, and ordered the complaints dismissed in all of them:

> A landowner who engages in activities that may cause injury to persons on adjoining premises surely owes those persons a duty to take reasonable precautions to avoid injuring them. We have never held, however, that a landowner owes a duty to protect an entire urban neighborhood against purely economic losses. [. . .]
>
> Policy-driven line-drawing is to an extent arbitrary because, wherever the line is drawn, invariably it cuts off liability to persons who foreseeably might be plaintiffs. [. . .] While the Appellate Division attempted to draw a careful boundary at storefront merchant-neighbors who suffered lost income, that line excludes others similarly affected by the closures — such as the law firm, public relations firm, clothing manufacturer and other displaced plaintiffs in [a related case], the thousands of professional, commercial and residential tenants situated in the towers surrounding

the named plaintiffs, and suppliers and service providers unable to reach the densely populated New York City blocks at issue in each case.

As is readily apparent, an indeterminate group in the affected areas thus may have provable financial losses directly traceable to the two construction-related collapses, with no satisfactory way geographically to distinguish among those who have suffered purely economic losses. In such circumstances, limiting the scope of defendants' duty to those who have, as a result of these events, suffered personal injury or property damage — as historically courts have done — affords a principled basis for reasonably apportioning liability.

What is the distinction between 532 *Madison Avenue Gourmet Foods, Inc. v. Finlandia Center, Inc.* and *Glanzer v. Shepard* (or for that matter *Biakanja v. Irving*) from the earlier part of this chapter covering the privity limitation?

6. *Loss of power.* In Newlin v. New England Telephone & Telegraph Co., 54 N.E.2d 929 (Mass. 1944), the plaintiff grew mushrooms in an indoor factory. The defendant company owned a telephone pole nearby. The telephone pole fell over, and in the process it took down an adjacent power line belonging to an unrelated electric company. This interrupted the flow of electrical current to the plaintiff's mushroom farm, and without it the plaintiff was unable to keep the mushrooms at a sufficiently cool temperature; the heat rose and eventually the mushrooms were ruined. The plaintiff sued the defendant to recover for his losses, claiming the telephone pole had been negligently maintained. The defendant moved to dismiss the complaint.

Held, for the plaintiff, that the complaint stated a good cause of action.

What is the distinction between *Newlin v. New England Telephone & Telegraph Co.* and 532 *Madison Avenue Gourmet Foods, Inc. v. Finlandia Center, Inc.?*

7. *Loss of goalie.* In Phoenix Professional Hockey Club, Inc. v. Hirmer, 502 P.2d 164 (Ariz. 1972), the plaintiff owned a professional hockey team. Its goalie, one Caley, was injured in an automobile accident that the plaintiff alleged was caused by the negligence of the defendant, Hirmer. Consequently the plaintiff had to hire a substitute goalie for the remainder of the season. The plaintiff sued Hirmer to recover the cost of hiring the substitute. The defendant moved to dismiss the complaint.

Held, for the defendant, that the complaint failed to state a good cause of action.

What is the distinction between *Phoenix Professional Hockey Club, Inc. v. Hirmer* and *Newlin v. New England Telephone & Telegraph Co.?*

8. *Stop the presses (problem).* In Byrd v. English, 117 Ga. 191 (1903), Byrd owned a publishing firm in Atlanta. The defendant, English, was building a house nearby. In the course of the excavations to create a basement for the

house, the defendant's agents removed earth from under an adjacent sidewalk in violation of a city ordinance. In the process they negligently severed power lines running from the Georgia Electric Light Company to Byrd's printing plant. The plant was deprived of electrical current and unable to operate for several hours until the wires were repaired. Byrd sued English to recover the profits lost while the power was out. The defendant moved to dismiss the complaint. What result?

9. *Attacking the rule.* In People Express Airlines, Inc., v. Consolidated Rail Corp., 495 A.2d 107 (N.J. 1985), a fire started at the defendant's rail yard, creating a risk that a nearby tank car full of ethylene oxide, a volatile chemical, would explode. The City of Newark ordered the evacuation of the area within a one-mile radius. The evacuated area included the north terminal at Newark International Airport, where the plaintiff's business operations were based. The feared explosion never occurred, but the plaintiff's employees were unable to work for 12 hours and many of its flights were canceled as a result. The plaintiff brought suit claiming that the fire was caused by the defendant's negligence and seeking to recover for its losses. The trial court gave summary judgment to the defendants, finding recovery barred by the economic loss doctrine. The New Jersey Supreme Court disagreed:

> Judicial discomfiture with the rule of nonrecovery for purely economic loss throughout the last several decades has led to numerous exceptions in the general rule. Although the rationalizations for these exceptions differ among courts and cases, two common threads run throughout the exceptions. The first is that the element of foreseeability emerges as a more appropriate analytical standard to determine the question of liability than a *per se* prohibitory rule. The second is that the extent to which the defendant knew or should have known the particular consequences of his negligence, including the economic loss of a particularly foreseeable plaintiff, is dispositive of the issues of duty and fault.
>
> One group of exceptions is based on the "special relationship" between the tortfeasor and the individual or business deprived of economic expectations. [The court cited a number of cases, including *Glanzer v. Shepard* and *Biakanja v. Irving.*] [. . .] A related exception in which courts have allowed recovery for purely economic losses has been extended to plaintiffs belonging to a particularly foreseeable group, such as sailors and seamen, for whom the law has traditionally shown great solicitude. *See Carbone v. Ursich,* 209 F.2d 178 (9th Cir. 1953). [. . .]
>
> These exceptions expose the hopeless artificiality of the *per se* rule against recovery for purely economic losses. When the plaintiffs are reasonably foreseeable, the injury is directly and proximately caused by defendant's negligence, and liability can be limited fairly, courts have endeavored to create exceptions to allow recovery. The scope and number of exceptions, while independently justified on various grounds, have

nonetheless created lasting doubt as to the wisdom of the *per se* rule of nonrecovery for purely economic losses. Indeed, it has been fashionable for commentators to state that the rule has been giving way for nearly fifty years, although the cases have not always kept pace with the hypothesis.

The further theme that may be extracted from these decisions rests on the specificity and strictness that are infused into the definitional standard of foreseeability. [...] The more particular is the foreseeability that economic loss will be suffered by the plaintiff as a result of defendant's negligence, the more just is it that liability be imposed and recovery allowed.

We hold therefore that a defendant owes a duty of care to take reasonable measures to avoid the risk of causing economic damages, aside from physical injury, to particular plaintiffs or plaintiffs comprising an identifiable class with respect to whom defendant knows or has reason to know are likely to suffer such damages from its conduct. A defendant failing to adhere to this duty of care may be found liable for such economic damages proximately caused by its breach of duty.

We stress that an identifiable class of plaintiffs is not simply a foreseeable class of plaintiffs. For example, members of the general public, or invitees such as sales and service persons at a particular plaintiff's business premises, or persons travelling on a highway near the scene of a negligently-caused accident, such as the one at bar, who are delayed in the conduct of their affairs and suffer varied economic losses, are certainly a foreseeable class of plaintiffs. Yet their presence within the area would be fortuitous, and the particular type of economic injury that could be suffered by such persons would be hopelessly unpredictable and not realistically foreseeable. Thus, the class itself would not be sufficiently ascertainable. An identifiable class of plaintiffs must be particularly foreseeable in terms of the type of persons or entities comprising the class, the certainty or predictability of their presence, the approximate numbers of those in the class, as well as the type of economic expectations disrupted. [...]

Among the facts that persuade us that a cause of action has been established [here] is the close proximity of the North Terminal and People Express Airlines to the Conrail freight yard; the obvious nature of the plaintiff's operations and particular foreseeability of economic losses resulting from an accident and evacuation; the defendants' actual or constructive knowledge of the volatile properties of ethylene oxide; and the existence of an emergency response plan prepared by some of the defendants (alluded to in the course of oral argument), which apparently called for the nearby area to be evacuated to avoid the risk of harm in case of an explosion. We do not mean to suggest by our recitation of these facts that actual knowledge of the eventual economic losses is necessary to the cause of action; rather, particular foreseeability will suffice.

The *People Express* case represents a break from the traditional rule; its holding remains a minority position. Can the case nevertheless be distinguished from 532 *Madison Avenue Gourmet Foods, Inc. v. Finlandia Center, Inc.?* (The New York Court of Appeals thought so, suggesting in its opinion in the latter case that its decision was not inconsistent with the New Jersey Supreme Court's decision in *People Express.*)

10. *Defending the rule.* In Barber Lines A/S v. M/V Donau Maru, 764 F.2d 50 (1st Cir. 1985), the defendants' ship, the *Donau Maru,* spilled oil into Boston Harbor. The spill prevented the plaintiff's ship, the *Tamara,* from docking at a nearby berth; the vessel was required to unload its cargo at a different pier, incurring extra docking and labor costs. The plaintiffs sued the owners of the *Donau Maru,* claiming the oil spill was caused by their negligence and seeking to recover the additional expenses to which they were put as a result. The trial court dismissed the complaint, and the court of appeals, per Breyer, J., affirmed, offering the following analysis in support of its decision to adhere to the economic loss doctrine:

> [C]ases and commentators point to pragmatic or practical administrative considerations which, when taken together, offer support for a rule limiting recovery for negligently caused pure financial harm. The number of persons suffering foreseeable financial harm in a typical accident is likely to be far greater than those who suffer traditional (recoverable) physical harm. The typical downtown auto accident, that harms a few persons physically and physically damages the property of several others, may well cause financial harm (e.g., through delay) to a vast number of potential plaintiffs. The less usual, negligently caused, oil spill foreseeably harms not only ships, docks, piers, beaches, wildlife, and the like, that are covered with oil, but also harms blockaded ships, marina merchants, suppliers of those firms, the employees of marina businesses and suppliers, the suppliers' suppliers, and so forth. To use the notion of "foreseeability" that courts use in physical injury cases to separate the financially injured allowed to sue from the financially injured not allowed to sue would draw vast numbers of injured persons within the class of potential plaintiffs in even the most simple accident cases (unless it leads courts, unwarrantedly, to narrow the scope of "foreseeability" as applied to persons suffering physical harm). That possibility — a large number of different plaintiffs each with somewhat different claims — in turn threatens to raise significantly the cost of even relatively simple tort actions. Yet the tort action is already a very expensive administrative device for compensating victims of accidents. Indeed, the legal time, the legal resources, the delay appurtenant to the tort action apparently mean that on average the victim recovers only between 28 and 44 cents of every dollar paid by actual or potential defendants, while victims who insure themselves directly recover at least between 55 and 66 cents of each premium dollar earned by insurance companies and between 85 and 90 cents of every dollar

actually paid out to investigate and satisfy claims. The added cost of the increased complexity, while unknowable with precision, seems likely significant.

At the same time many of the "financially injured" will find it easier than the "physically injured" to arrange for cheaper, alternative compensation. The typical "financial" plaintiff is likely to be a business firm that, in any event, buys insurance, and which may well be able to arrange for "first party" loss compensation for foreseeable financial harm. Other such victims will be able to sue under tort principles, for they will suffer at least some physical harm to their property. Still others may have contracts with, or be able to contract with, persons who can themselves recover from the negligent defendant. A shipowner, for example, might contract with a dock owner for "inaccessibility" compensation; and the dock owner (whose pier is physically covered with oil) might recover this compensation as part of its tort damages. Of course, such a tort suit, embodying a "contract-defined" injury, may still raise difficult foreseeability questions, cf. *Hadley v. Baxendale*, 9 Exch. 341 (1854). But the bringing of one suit, instead of several, still makes the litigation as a whole a less costly compensation device. Finally, some of the "financially injured" will have suffered harm that is, in any event, noncompensable because it is not sufficiently distinguishable from minor harms typical of ordinary living. The law does not compensate, for example, the cost of unused baseball tickets or flowers needed for apology regardless of the cause of the delay that foreseeably led to the added expense. Insofar as these considerations, taken as a whole, support recovery limitations, they reflect a fear of creating victim compensation costs that, from an administrative point of view, are unnecessarily high.

A second set of considerations focuses on the "disproportionality" between liability and fault. Those who argue "disproportionality" are not reiterating the discredited nineteenth century view that tort liability would destroy industry, investment, or capitalism. Rather, they recognize that tort liability provides a powerful set of economic incentives and disincentives to engage in economic activity or to make it safer. And, liability for pure financial harm, insofar as it proved vast, cumulative and inherently unknowable in amount, could create incentives that are perverse.

Might not unbounded liability for foreseeable financial damage, for example, make auto insurance premiums too expensive for the average driver? Is such a result desirable? After all, the high premiums would reflect not only the costs of the harm inflicted; they would also reflect administrative costs of law suits, jury verdicts in uncertain amounts, some percentage of unbounded or inflated economic claims, and lessened incentive for financial victims to avoid harm or to mitigate damage. Given the existing liability for physical injury (and for accompanying financial injury), can one say that still higher premiums are needed to make the public realize that driving is socially expensive or to provide greater incentive to drive safely (an incentive that risk spreading through insurance dilutes in any event)?

These considerations, of administrability and disproportionality, offer plausible, though highly abstract, "policy" support for the reluctance of the courts to impose tort liability for purely financial harm. While they seem unlikely to apply with equal strength to every sort of "financial harm" claim, their abstraction and generality, along with the comparative inaccessibility of the empirical information needed to confirm or to invalidate them, mean that courts cannot weigh or apply them case by case. What, for example, in cases like this one, are the added administrative costs involved in allowing all persons suffering pure financial harm to sue the shipowner instead of "channeling" suits (perhaps via contract) through traditionally injured plaintiffs? Is there a problem of "disproportionality"? How far, for example, would additional, unbounded, pure financial loss liability for negligently caused oil spills, when added to the already large potential traditional liability, affect the type of insurance carried, the incentive to mitigate losses, the incentive to transport oil safely, the likelihood that shippers will use pipelines and domestic wells instead of ships and foreign wells, and the consequences of these and other related changes? We do not know the answers to these questions, nor can judges readily answer them in particular cases.

It does not surprise us then that, under these circumstances, courts have neither enforced one clear rule nor considered the matter case by case. Rather, they have spoken of a general principle against liability for negligently caused financial harm, while creating many exceptions. [. . .] These exceptions seem designed to pick out broad categories of cases where the "administrative" and "disproportionality" problems intuitively seem insignificant or where some strong countervailing consideration militates in favor of liability. [. . .] We need not explore the exceptions in detail. Rather, we here simply point to the existence of plausible reasons underlying the judicial hesitance to award damages in a case like this one, and the need to consider exceptions by class rather than case by case. The existence of these factors, together with our comparative inability to evaluate their empirical significance, cautions us against departing from prior law.

G. THE NEGLIGENT INFLICTION OF EMOTIONAL DISTRESS

Sometimes a defendant's negligence causes the plaintiff no physical injuries but considerable fear or grief. Courts have struggled to find ways to compensate for such reactions without creating a flood of litigation from plaintiffs seeking to recover for their unhappiness. We consider the problem here because courts most often address these problems — and frame their limitations on recovery — as questions of duty.

Before considering the unsettled aspects of the law governing liability for emotional distress, recall those features of the law that *are* settled and will not be our concern here. All jurisdictions generally agree that there is liability for the *intentional* infliction of emotional distress. They also agree that if a defendant's negligence causes the plaintiff a physical injury, the defendant can be held liable not only for resulting medical expenses and lost wages but also for emotional distress of various sorts that the injury may cause. The difficult and more controversial problems involve cases where the defendant's negligence causes distress for the plaintiff without any physical harm (except, perhaps, for physical ailments caused by the distress itself). Though there are many different types of cases that can raise these questions, there are two general types of fact patterns that tend to be most common and important:

a. The first arises where the plaintiff is a direct victim of the defendant's negligence: "near miss" cases, for example, where a defendant acts negligently toward the plaintiff, narrowly avoids causing physical harm, yet puts the plaintiff in great fear; or cases where the defendant commits some negligent act that involves no physical contact, such as telling the plaintiff a terrible but mistaken piece of news.

b. The second family of cases involves the plaintiff who is not the direct victim of negligence but who is a bystander — i.e., the horrified witness of harm negligently inflicted upon another.

Cases in these two categories have provoked a range of judicial responses in the second half of the twentieth century, sometimes overlapping and sometimes distinct; most courts today allow recovery at least some of the time in both situations, but they vary in the rules they use to structure and limit the plaintiff's cause of action.

Robb v. Pennsylvania Railroad Co.
210 A.2d 709 (Del. 1965)

[The defendant railroad negligently allowed a rut to form at one of its crossings. The rear wheels of the plaintiff's car got lodged in the rut, leaving the rest of the car stuck on the tracks. After trying for several minutes to move the car, the plaintiff saw one of the defendant's trains bearing down on her. She jumped from the stalled car with seconds to spare; she had cleared the tracks by a few feet when the train hit her car, demolishing it and hurling it into the air. The plaintiff suffered no physical injuries but claimed to have suffered great fright and nervous shock that physically interfered with her ability to nurse her child and perform her work as a breeder of horses. The trial judge gave summary judgment to the defendant on the ground that the plaintiff sustained no physical impact (the "impact rule"). The plaintiff appealed.]

HERRMANN, J. The question before us for decision is this: May the plaintiff recover for the physical consequences of fright caused by the negligence of the defendant, the plaintiff being within the immediate zone of physical danger created by such negligence, although there was no contemporaneous bodily impact?

The question is still an open one in this State. Two reported Delaware cases and one unreported case border upon the field of inquiry, but none really enter it. [. . .] Two facets of the question are herewith eliminated from further consideration: First, it is accepted as settled that there can be no recovery for fright alone, not leading to bodily injury or sickness, arising from the negligence of another. The plaintiff here concedes that proposition, stating however that she does not seek to recover for fright alone but for the physical consequences thereof. Secondly, we are not here concerned with the situation wherein fright arose from the peril of another and the plaintiff was not in the path of the danger created by the negligence asserted. [. . .]

The two schools of thought in the matter at hand evolved from [cases] originating about the turn of the century. [. . .] The impact rule is based, generally speaking, upon three propositions expounded in [*Mitchell v. Rochester R. Co.*, 45 N.E. 354 (1896), and *Spade v. Lynn & Boston R. Co.*, 47 N.E. 88 (Mass. 1897)]:

1) It is stated that since fright alone does not give rise to a cause of action, the consequences of fright will not give rise to a cause of action. This is now generally recognized to be a non-sequitur, want of damage being recognized as the reason that negligence causing mere fright is not actionable. It is now generally agreed, even in jurisdictions which have adopted the impact rule, that the gist of the action is the injury flowing from the negligence, whether operating through the medium of physical impact or nervous shock.

2) It is stated that the physical consequences of fright are too remote and that the requisite causal connection is unprovable. The fallacies of this ground of the impact rule, viewed in the light of growing medical knowledge, were well stated by Chief Justice Maltbie in *Orlo v. Connecticut Co.*, 21 A.2d 402 (Conn. 1941). It was there pointed out that the early difficulty in tracing a resulting injury back through fright or nervous shock has been minimized by the advance of medical science; and that the line of cases permitting recovery for serious injuries resulting from fright, where there has been but a trivial impact in itself causing little or no injury, demonstrate that there is no insu-perable difficulty in tracing causal connection between the wrongdoing and the injury via the fright.

3) It is stated that public policy and expediency demand that there be no recovery for the physical consequences of fright in the absence of a contem-poraneous physical injury. In recent years, this has become the principal

reason for denying recovery on the basis of the impact rule. In support of this argument, it is said that fright is a subjective state of mind, difficult to evaluate, and of such nature that proof by the claimant is too easy and disproof by the party charged too difficult, thus making it unsafe as a practical matter for the law to deal with such claims. This school of thought concludes that to permit recovery in such cases would open a "Pandora's box" of fictitious and fraudulent claims involving speculative and conjectural damages with which the law and medical science cannot justly cope. [. . .]

In considering the expediency ground, the Supreme Court of Connecticut said in the *Orlo* case, supra:

> . . . There is hardly more risk to the accomplishment of justice because of disparity in possibilities of proof in such situations than in those where mental suffering is allowed as an element of damage following a physical injury or recovery is permitted for the results of nervous shock provided there be some contemporaneous slight battery or physical injury. Certainly it is a very questionable position for a court to take, that because of the possibility of encouraging fictitious claims compensation should be denied those who have actually suffered serious injury through the negligence of another.

[. . .] It is our opinion that the reasons for rejecting the impact rule far outweigh the reasons which have been advanced in its support.

The cause of action and proximate cause grounds for the rule have been discredited in the very jurisdictions which first gave them credence. [. . .] If more were needed to warrant a declination to follow the cause of action and the proximate cause arguments, reference to the fictional and mechanical ends to which the impact rule has been carried would suffice for the purpose. The most trivial bodily contact, itself causing little or no injury, has been considered sufficient to take a case out of the rule and permit recovery for serious physical injuries resulting from the accompanying fright. [. . .]

This leaves the public policy or expediency ground to support the impact rule. We think that ground untenable.

It is the duty of the courts to afford a remedy and redress for every substantial wrong. Part of our basic law is the mandate that "every man for an injury done him in his . . . person . . . shall have remedy by the due course of law . . ." Del. Const. Art. 1, §9, Del. C. Ann. Neither volume of cases, nor danger of fraudulent claims, nor difficulty of proof, will relieve the courts of their obligation in this regard. None of these problems are insuperable. Statistics fail to show that there has been a "flood" of such cases in those jurisdictions in which recovery is allowed; but if there be increased litigation, the courts must willingly cope with the task. As to the danger of illusory and fictional claims, this is not a new problem; our courts deal constantly with claims for pain and suffering based upon subjective symptoms only; and the courts and the medical profession have been found equal to the danger. Fraudulent claims may be feigned in a slight-impact case as well as in a no-impact case. Likewise, the problems of adequacy of proof, for the avoidance of speculative and conjectural damages, are common to personal injury cases generally and are surmountable, being satisfactorily solved by our courts in case after case. [. . .] We recognize that "[e]xpediency may tip the scales when arguments are nicely balanced," *Woolford Realty Co. v. Rose*, 286 U.S. 319, 330; but, in our view, such nice balance no longer exists as to the subject matter. [. . .]

We hold, therefore, that where negligence proximately caused fright, in one within the immediate area of physical danger from that negligence, which in turn produced physical consequences such as would be elements of damage if a bodily injury had been suffered, the injured party is entitled to recover under an application of the prevailing principles of law as to negligence and proximate causation. Otherwise stated, where results, which are regarded as proper elements of recovery as a consequence of physical injury, are proximately caused by fright due to negligence, recovery by one in the immediate zone of physical risk should be permitted. [. . .]

We conclude, therefore, that the Superior Court erred in the instant case in holding that the plaintiff's right to recover is barred by the impact rule. The plaintiff claims physical injuries resulting from fright proximately caused by the negligence of the defendant. She should have the opportunity to prove such injuries and to recover therefor if she succeeds. The summary judgment granted in favor of the defendant must be reversed and the cause remanded for further proceedings.

NOTES

1. *The near miss.* The *Robb* case illustrates competing judicial impulses at work in cases involving recovery for emotional distress: the desire to provide compensation where the plaintiff's suffering is clear and understandable, and the worry that doing so will open the floodgates to claims less compelling. The traditional common law rule balanced these considerations by allowing plaintiffs to recover for emotional distress only as an element of damages arising from traditional personal injuries caused by physical contact. That requirement often was stretched, as noted in the *Robb* opinion; in cases where the only real harm a plaintiff suffered was emotional, courts were prepared to strain to find a personal injury to which the claim for emotional distress could be attached as "parasitic." Thus in the celebrated case of Christy Bros. Circus v. Turnage, 144 S.E. 680 (Ga. App. 1928), a dancing horse at the plaintiff's circus evacuated its bowels into the lap of a woman sitting in the front row, causing much merriment among the spectators. She sought recovery for emotional distress; the recovery was allowed, but only because it was framed as damages for the physical injury the defendant was said to have inflicted on her. Meanwhile, in Mitchell v. Rochester Ry. Co., 45 N.E. 354 (N.Y. 1896), the defendant's car, pulled by a team of horses,

turned toward the plaintiff in the street and did not stop until the horses' heads were on either side of her. The plaintiff collapsed from fright and suffered a miscarriage. Recovery was denied because she had not been touched, the court holding that there could be no recovery for fright alone.

A few courts continue to require physical contact before awarding damages for emotional distress, but most now employ different tests. Thus we see the court in *Robb* limit recovery to a plaintiff whose emotional distress caused her physical problems and who was in the "immediate zone of physical risk" created by the defendant's negligence. A number of courts have adopted similar requirements in place of the impact rule. They can produce seemingly arbitrary results of their own, as illustrated by Richardson v. J. C. Penney, 649 P.2d 565 (Okla. App. 1982). The plaintiffs were a husband and wife whose brakes gave out while they were driving a 24-foot trailer down a winding mountain road. Although they managed to stop the vehicle without injury, the incident caused them great emotional distress. The wife was unable to recover because her distress resulted in no physical symptoms; the husband was held to have a good claim, however, because he alleged that the incident had given him an ulcer.

Other courts have gone farther than *Robb* in permitting liability, requiring neither that plaintiffs be in any zone of actual danger nor that their emotional distress cause physical injury. Instead they merely require that the emotional distress be the foreseeable result of the defendant's conduct and that the plaintiff satisfy the jury that the distress suffered was serious. The implications of such a broad position are unclear but potentially vast, causing still other courts to join in dropping the requirement that the plaintiff suffer physical injury or be within a zone of danger — but then often to permit recovery only where the negligent act breaches a pre-existing duty owed by the defendant to the plaintiff. The next cases examine the operation of some of these approaches. This corner of tort law is newer and less settled than most others in the book; as noted a moment ago, the case law from different jurisdictions is more likely here than elsewhere to be based on somewhat different tests. Here is the pending effort of the Restatement (Third) (T.D. 2007) to offer some clarity:

§46. NEGLIGENT CONDUCT DIRECTLY INFLICTING EMOTIONAL
    DISTURBANCE ON ANOTHER

An actor whose negligent conduct causes serious emotional disturbance to another is subject to liability to the other if the conduct:
    (a) places the other in immediate danger of bodily harm and the emotional disturbance results from the danger; or
    (b) occurs in the course of specified categories of activities, undertakings, or relationships in which negligent conduct is especially likely to cause serious emotional disturbance.

To gain a more particular understanding of this area of law and its difficulties, it naturally will help to consider more examples of facts that have come before the courts, how they have been handled, and whether they can be explained by reference to common principles and policies.

2. *Frightened car salesmen.* In Lawson v. Management Activities, Inc., 81 Cal. Rptr. 2d 745 (Cal. App. 1999), one of the defendant's jet aircraft crashed in Santa Ana near a Honda dealership. The employees at the dealership saw the plane go into its dive and feared that it was going to crash into them. They sued to recover for their emotional distress. The trial court dismissed the complaint. The court of appeals affirmed.

Can *Lawson v. Management Activities, Inc.* be distinguished from *Robb v. Pennsylvania Railroad Co.*?

3. *Tailspin.* In Quill v. Trans World Airlines, 361 N.W.2d 438 (Minn. 1985), the plaintiff was a passenger on a TWA flight from New York to Minneapolis. The plane was cruising at 39,000 feet when it suddenly went into an uncontrolled tailspin. It plummeted for about 40 seconds; the pilots regained control of the aircraft five seconds before it would have crashed into the ground. The plane then landed in Detroit. Neither the plaintiff nor the other passengers suffered any physical injuries. The plaintiff alleged, however, that during the plane's descent he was certain that he was about to die. His business required him to take about 60 flights each year, and on account of his experience on the defendant's plane his air travels now were accompanied by anxiety, adrenaline surges, sweaty hands, and an elevated pulse and blood pressure. The trial court allowed the case to go to a jury on the plaintiff's claim for negligent infliction of emotional distress; the jury awarded him $50,000. The court of appeals affirmed.

What is the distinction between *Quill v. Trans World Airlines* and *Lawson v. Management Activities, Inc.*? The court in the *Quill* case used a "zone of danger" rule similar to the one in *Robb*. How might you nevertheless argue that *Quill* would come out the same way under the analysis performed in *Lawson*?

4. *A confession of incompetence?* In Johnson v. Jamaica Hospital, 467 N.E.2d 502 (N.Y. 1984), the plaintiffs were parents of a girl, Kawana, who was born in the defendant's hospital in Queens. Kawana was abducted from the hospital's nursery by a stranger. She was recovered by the police four months later. The plaintiffs sued the hospital to recover for the emotional distress they suffered in the interim, alleging that the incident was the result of the hospital's negligence. The trial court held that the complaint stated a good cause of action, and the appellate division affirmed. The New York Court of Appeals reversed:

> Plaintiffs contend, and the courts below concluded, that their complaint states a cause of action because the defendant hospital owed a duty directly to them, as parents, to care properly for their child, and that it was or should have been foreseeable to defendant that any injury to Kawana, such as abduction, would cause them mental distress. There

is no basis for establishing such a direct duty. [. . .] The direct injury allegedly caused by defendant's negligence — abduction — was sustained by the infant, and plaintiffs' grief and mental torment which resulted from her disappearance are not actionable. The foreseeability that such psychic injuries would result from the injury to Kawana does not serve to establish a duty running from defendant to plaintiffs, and in the absence of such a duty, as a matter of law there can be no liability. That sound policy reasons support these decisions is evident here, for to permit recovery by the infant's parents for emotional distress would be to invite open-ended liability for indirect emotional injury suffered by families in every instance where the very young, or very elderly, or incapacitated persons experience negligent care or treatment.

There is, similarly, no basis for establishing such a duty in the contractual relationship between plaintiffs and defendant[.] [. . .] The general rule in contract cases is that absent a duty upon which liability can be based, there is no right of recovery for mental distress resulting from the breach of a contract-related duty.

Nor can a duty to refrain from causing plaintiffs emotional distress be predicated on any notion that defendant stood *in loco parentis* while caring for the infant. First, there is no basis for a finding that defendant stood *in loco parentis*. That status requires more than mere temporary care and custody; an intent to support and care for the child on a permanent basis must be shown. A finding that one stands *in loco parentis* cannot be based solely upon a relationship where, as here, one is compensated for providing services to a child. [. . .]

Meyer, J., dissented:

We have recently recognized in relation to mental distress "that the drawing of any line necessarily differentiates between close cases," *Kennedy v. McKesson Co.*, 448 N.E.2d 1332 (N.Y. 1983). But the line should not be arbitrarily or artificially drawn. Where, as here, parents have been subjected by the hospital's failure to protect their right to custody of their child to the anguish of not knowing for a period of four months where the child was, or whether she was alive or dead, there is a sufficient guarantee of genuineness and seriousness of their claim to warrant its submission to a trier of fact. To hold under such circumstances that there is no duty "is a pitiful confession of incompetence on the part of courts of justice." *Simone v. Rhode Is. Co.*, 66 A. 202 (R.I. 1907).

Would the plaintiffs have been able to recover under any of the other tests considered so far in this section?

5. *Guarantees of genuineness.* In Perry-Rogers v. Obasaju, 723 N.Y.S.2d 28 (App. Div. 2001), the plaintiffs were a couple who underwent in vitro

fertilization at the defendant's clinic. The clinic mistakenly implanted an embryo created by the plaintiffs into the uterus of another patient, a woman named Fasano. Once the child was born, Fasano at first refused to relinquish him; it took the plaintiffs four months to obtain and enforce a court order awarding them the child. The plaintiffs sued the clinic to recover for their emotional distress arising from these events. The trial court held that the complaint stated a good cause of action, and the appellate division affirmed:

> We reject defendants' argument that plaintiffs' malpractice claim must be dismissed since it seeks to recover only for emotional harm caused by the creation of human life. Plaintiffs do not seek damages for the emotional harm caused by the birth of a sick or unplanned healthy child, and would not otherwise have the court calculate the difference between existence and nonexistence. Rather, plaintiffs seek damages for the emotional harm caused by their having been deprived of the opportunity of experiencing pregnancy, prenatal bonding and the birth of their child, and by their separation from the child for more than four months after his birth. Damages for emotional harm can be recovered even in the absence of physical injury "when there is a duty owed by defendant to plaintiff, [and a] breach of that duty result[s] directly in emotional harm." *Kennedy v. McKesson Co.*, 448 N.E.2d 1332 (1983). There is no requirement that the plaintiff must be in fear of his or her own physical safety. However, "a plaintiff must produce evidence sufficient to guarantee the genuineness of the claim," *Kaufman v. Physical Measurements*, 615 N.Y.S.2d 508 (App. Div. 1994), such as "contemporaneous or consequential physical harm," which is "thought to provide an index of reliability otherwise absent in a claim for psychological trauma with only psychological consequences," *Johnson v. State of New York*, 334 N.E.2d 590 (N.Y. 1975). Here, it was foreseeable that the information that defendants had mistakenly implanted plaintiffs' embryos in a person whom they would not identify, which information was not conveyed until after such person had become pregnant, would cause plaintiffs emotional distress over the possibility that the child that they wanted so desperately, as evidenced by their undertaking the rigors of in vitro fertilization, might be born to someone else and that they might never know his or her fate. These circumstances, together with plaintiffs' medical affidavits attesting to objective manifestations of their emotional trauma, create a "guarantee of genuineness" that makes plaintiffs' claim for emotional distress viable. *Johnson v. Jamaica Hosp.*, 467 N.E.2d 502 (N.Y. 1984), is distinguishable in that it turned on the absence of a direct duty owing to the parents of a newborn who was abducted from the hospital. [. . .]

What is the distinction between *Perry-Rogers v. Obasaju* and *Johnson v. Jamaica Hospital*? Is the court's explanation satisfactory?

6. *Fear of cancer.* In Potter v. Firestone Tire and Rubber Co., 863 P.2d 795 (Cal. 1993), the plaintiffs lived next to the Crazy Horse landfill in Salinas. The defendant, Firestone, dumped toxic industrial waste in the landfill despite being told not to do so by the company managing it. The chemicals, many of which were carcinogens, seeped into the plaintiffs' wells and contaminated their water. The plaintiffs could not prove that they had suffered any physical injury as a result, but they sued Firestone to recover for their fear that their ingestion of the water eventually would cause them to develop cancer. The trial court found in favor of the four plaintiffs, concluding that their fears were reasonable; it awarded them a total of $800,000. The California Supreme Court reversed. It did agree that Firestone breached a duty to the plaintiffs and therefore might be held liable:

> [U]nless the defendant has assumed a duty to plaintiff in which the emotional condition of the plaintiff is an object, recovery is available only if the emotional distress arises out of the defendant's breach of some other legal duty and the emotional distress is proximately caused by that breach of duty. [...] Those limits on recovery for emotional distress caused by the negligent conduct of another do not aid Firestone here, however. Firestone did violate a duty imposed on it by law and regulation to dispose of toxic waste only in a class I landfill and to avoid contamination of underground water. The violation led directly to plaintiffs' ingestion of various known and suspected carcinogens, and thus to their fear of suffering the very harm which the Legislature sought by statute to avoid. [...]

The court held, however, that the plaintiffs' claims had to be measured against a more demanding standard than the trial judge had used:

> We cannot say that it would never be reasonable for a person who has ingested toxic substances to harbor a genuine and serious fear of cancer where reliable medical or scientific opinion indicates that such ingestion has significantly increased his or her risk of cancer, but not to a probable likelihood. Indeed, we would be very hard pressed to find that, as a matter of law, a plaintiff faced with a 20 percent or 30 percent chance of developing cancer cannot genuinely, seriously and reasonably fear the prospect of cancer. Nonetheless, we conclude, for the public policy reasons identified below, that emotional distress caused by the fear of a cancer that is not probable should generally not be compensable in a negligence action.
>
> As a starting point in our analysis, we recognize the indisputable fact that all of us are exposed to carcinogens every day. [...] With this consideration in mind, we believe the tremendous societal cost of otherwise allowing emotional distress compensation to a potentially unrestricted plaintiff class demonstrates the necessity of imposing some

limit on the class. Proliferation of fear of cancer claims in California in the absence of meaningful restrictions might compromise the availability and affordability of liability insurance for toxic liability risks. [. . .] In the end, the burden of payment of awards for fear of cancer in the absence of a more likely than not restriction will inevitably be borne by the public generally in substantially increased insurance premiums or, alternatively, in the enhanced danger that accrues from the greater number of residents and businesses that may choose to go without any insurance.

A second policy concern that weighs in favor of a more likely than not threshold is the unduly detrimental impact that unrestricted fear liability would have in the health care field. [. . .] Unless meaningful restrictions are placed on this potential plaintiff class, the threat of numerous large, adverse monetary awards, coupled with the added cost of insuring against such liability (assuming insurance would be available), could diminish the availability of new, beneficial prescription drugs or increase their price beyond the reach of those who need them most. [. . .]

A third policy concern to consider is that [. . .] to allow compensation to all plaintiffs with objectively reasonable cancer fears, even where the threatened cancer is not probable, raises the very significant concern that defendants and their insurers will be unable to ensure adequate compensation for those victims who actually develop cancer or other physical injuries.

7. *Fear of AIDS (problem).* In Lombardo v. New York University Medical Center, 648 N.Y.S.2d 658 (App. Div. 1996), the plaintiff was an undertaker. While preparing the corpse of a person who died of AIDS he pricked his finger on a syringe that was concealed in the folds of the shroud that cloaked the body. He sued the hospital where the patient had died, alleging that it negligently had allowed the syringe to remain in the shroud. Tests several months after the incident showed that the plaintiff had not contracted the HIV virus that causes AIDS; he nevertheless sought to recover for the emotional distress he experienced during the window of time between when he pricked his finger and when the tests came back negative. What result?

8. *The problem of bystanders.* The common law traditionally allowed no recovery by the bystander who watched an accident injure someone else. The rule requiring that the plaintiff suffer physical impact barred these claims just as it barred other claims for pure distress. But as we saw in the *Robb* case, courts gradually began to allow recovery when the distressed plaintiff was in the zone of danger caused by the defendant's negligence, even where no impact occurred. This logic has been used as well to open the door to recovery by bystanders. Thus some courts hold that a plaintiff put in reasonable fear of injury can sue to recover for the distress caused by seeing the injury befall someone else close by. A greater number of jurisdictions — indeed, a majority — have followed the lead taken by the California Supreme Court in Dillon v. Legg, 441 P.2d 912 (1968). *Dillon* involved the most common and perhaps inviting case for relief: a mother who saw her child get

hit by a car. The mother was herself in no danger, but the court nevertheless allowed her to recover for her emotional distress, offering a set of factors for courts to use in deciding whether to permit claims by a bystander: how close the bystander was to the accident; whether the bystander actually saw it occur; and how closely related the bystander was to the victim.

The states to follow *Dillon* have adjusted its holding in various ways; they are united, however, in declining to hold that plaintiffs who observe the infliction of an injury can recover only if they were in the zone of danger themselves. The California court itself later made the elements of recovery more definite and demanding in Thing v. La Chusa, 771 P.2d 814 (Cal. 1989), where recovery was limited to the plaintiff who "(1) is closely related to the injury victim; (2) is present at the scene of the injury-producing event at the time it occurs and is then aware that it is causing injury to the victim; and (3) as a result suffers serious emotional distress — a reaction beyond that which would be antici-pated in a disinterested witness and which is not an abnormal response to the circumstances." Not all courts agree. Again the Third Restatement (T.D. 1997) has made an effort at summary:

> §47. NEGLIGENT INFLICTION OF EMOTIONAL DISTURBANCE RESULTING FROM BODILY HARM TO A THIRD PERSON.
>
> An actor who negligently causes serious bodily injury to a third person is subject to liability for serious emotional disturbance thereby caused to a person who:
>   (a) perceives the event contemporaneously, and
>   (b) is a close family member of the person suffering the bodily injury.

Some courts reject this approach, and some of those that accept its outlines nevertheless differ on the details. Consider whether the following cases can be reconciled.

9. *Temporal proximity.* In Marzolf v. Stone, 960 P.2d 424 (Wash. 1998), Jeremy Marzolf was killed when his motorcycle collided with a bus. Ten minutes later his father, Barton Marzolf, happened upon the scene of the accident; emergency crews had not yet arrived. Jeremy was still alive but was badly injured, and he died soon afterwards. Barton Marzolf sued the driver of the bus and other parties for negligent infliction of emotional distress. The trial court dismissed that count of the plaintiff's complaint. The Washington Supreme Court reversed:

> A bright line rule that limits recovery for emotional distress to those who witnessed the accident is attractive in its simplicity. However, it draws an arbitrary line that serves to exclude plaintiffs without meaningful distinction. The emotional trauma caused by seeing a loved one injured at an accident scene stems not merely from witnessing the transition from health to injury, but also from witnessing the aftermath of an

accident in all its alarming detail. [. . .] Allowing recovery only to those who were present at the time of the injury-causing event creates an arbitrary distinction.

10. *Spatial proximity.* In Gain v. Carroll Mill Co., 787 P.2d 553 (Wash. 1990), James Gain, a Washington State trooper, was killed when a truck hit his squad car. His father saw live footage from the accident scene on the 11 o'clock news; he was able to read the license plate number of the police car and thus realized that his son had died in the incident. He sued the driver of the truck and other parties for negligent infliction of emotional distress. The trial court gave summary judgment to the defendants on the ground that recovery could not be had unless the plaintiff was present at the scene of the accident. The Washington Supreme Court affirmed: "We conclude that mental suffering by a relative who is not present at the scene of the injury-causing event is unforeseeable as a matter of law. We reach this conclusion after balancing the interest of the injured party to compensation against the view that a negligent act should have some end to its legal consequences."

What is the distinction between *Gain v. Carroll Mill Co.* and *Marzolf v. Stone?*

11. *The protective son.* In Barnhill v. Davis, 300 N.W.2d 104 (Iowa 1981), the plaintiff was driving his car in West Des Moines and was being followed by his mother, a woman named Maring. Her car was hit by another driver. The plaintiff's mother was slightly bruised in the accident, but six weeks later she was found to have no physical ill-effects. The plaintiff brought suit against the other driver to collect for the emotional distress he had suffered in worrying about his mother; he claimed that the distress had caused him dizziness, difficulty sleeping, and pain in his back and legs. The trial court gave summary judgment to the defendant. The Iowa Supreme Court reversed and remanded for trial: "It is reasonably foreseeable that a son, who witnesses serious injury to his mother, may suffer mental distress. [. . .] [W]e conclude Barnhill has at least minimally generated a genuine issue of material fact on whether a reasonable person would believe, and Barnhill did believe, that Maring, the direct victim, would be seriously injured or killed by the accident."

12. *Mistakes.* In Barnes v. Geiger, 446 N.E.2d 78 (Mass. App. 1983), one Frances Barnes saw a car hit a pedestrian and hurl him 60 feet into the air. The accident occurred near a place where she knew that her son was playing. She ran to the scene of the accident, fearing that he had been the victim. It turned out that the pedestrian hit by the car was an unrelated party. The next day Mrs. Barnes died of a cerebral vascular hemorrhage. Her husband sued the driver of the car, claiming that the hemorrhage had been triggered by the elevation of Mrs. Barnes' blood pressure caused by witnessing the accident. The trial court gave summary judgment to the defendant, and the court of appeals affirmed:

Whether the mistake be as to the identity of the victim, as here, or the gravity of the injury, the anxiety, perforce, is transitory, and "a fleeting instance of fear or excitement" does not present a set of circumstances against which a tortfeasor can fairly be asked to defend. Daily life is too full of momentary perturbation. Injury to a child and the protracted anguish placed upon the witnessing parent is, on the scale of human experience, tangible and predictable. Distress based on mistake as to the circumstances is ephemeral and will vary with the disposition of a person to imagine that the worst has happened. We are unwilling to expand the circle of liability [. . .] to such an additional dimension, because to do so expands unreasonably the class of persons to whom a tortfeasor may be liable.

What is the distinction between *Barnes v. Geiger* and *Barnhill v. Davis*?

13. *Dog day afternoon (problem).* In Johnson v. Douglas, 723 N.Y.S.2d 627 (Sup. Ct. 2001), the plaintiffs, a couple named Johnson, were walking their dog on a road in Lake Success when the defendant came down the street in his car at a high rate of speed. Mrs. Johnson leapt out of the car's path, narrowly escaping serious injury; the dog, Coco, was crushed by the automobile. The Johnsons sued the driver to recover for their emotional distress. What result would the cases considered in this section suggest?

H. AFTERWORD: THE DOCTRINAL ROLE OF DUTY IN TORT LITIGATION

As noted at the outset of this chapter, the traditional account of the negligence tort begins with a duty owed by the defendant to the plaintiff and then proceeds to ask whether the duty had been breached. This traditional order of operations has largely been jettisoned, however, in the current draft of the Restatement (Third) of Torts. That document describes the plaintiff's case as starting with a demonstration of fault on the defendant's part that has caused harm; it then treats "no duty" rules as exceptional arguments that defendants may be able to make to excuse themselves from liability on policy grounds. The reporter, Professor Gary Schwartz, took the view that this formulation best captured the actual current practice of the courts: duties arise so easily from affirmative acts that the existence of a duty frequently is not an issue at all in tort cases. We saw one example of this approach from the Third Restatement at the start of the chapter; here is another:

§7. DUTY

A court may determine that an actor has no duty or a duty other than the ordinary duty of reasonable care. Determinations of no duty and modifications of the duty of reasonable care are unusual and are based on special problems of principle or policy that warrant denying liability or limiting the ordinary duty of care in a particular class of cases. A defendant is not liable for any harm caused if the court determines the defendant owes no duty to the plaintiff, either in general or in relation to the particular negligence claim. If the court determines a defendant is subject to a modified duty, the defendant is subject to liability only for breach of the modified duty.

This approach has provoked objections from others who believe that it is important to ask *first* whether the defendant owed a duty to the plaintiff. See, e.g., Goldberg and Zipursky, *The Restatement (Third) and the Place of Duty in Negligence Law,* 54 Vand. L. Rev. 657 (2001):

> While we [. . .] cheerfully acknowledge a general or universal duty to take care to avoid causing physical harm to another's person or property, we maintain that it is a mistake to try to capture this notion in phrases like "duty to the world" or "duty is a non-issue," for these phrases are often interpreted to mean that the duty of due care is an obligation to behave reasonably, period — an obligation owed to no particular person or class of persons. [. . .] On this rendering, duty in its primary sense necessarily disappears from negligence. The claim that a given defendant was not under an obligation to take care to avoid injuring the plaintiff becomes unintelligible, because every defendant is defined to be under an obligation to behave reasonably, regardless of who is complaining of his conduct. In this sense, the duty-to-the-world formulation is entirely unsatisfactory in accounting for the language of duty within negligence law. [. . .]
>
> [I]t will make a difference whether courts acknowledge the element of duty in its obligation sense — as we suggest — or see "duty" as nothing more than an invitation to consider granting a policy-based exemption to liability for unreasonable conduct causing harm. A recent case from New York — *Lauer v. City of New York* — illustrates the point. The defendant was a medical examiner whose initial autopsy report on a deceased child concluded that the child had been the victim of severe trauma by an adult abusing him. The father immediately became the chief suspect in the homicide investigation, and his life predictably fell apart around him. Eighteen months later, the *New York Daily News* broke a story revealing that the medical examiner had done a second autopsy only three weeks after the first, and discovered that his initial report was mistaken, and that the death was of natural causes. Apparently fearing for his job and reputation, the medical examiner did not reveal the results of the second autopsy until the newspaper broke the story. The father sued the medical examiner for the emotional distress inflicted upon him.
>
> Chief Judge Kaye, writing for a 4-3 majority, concluded that the medical examiner could not be held liable to the father because his failure to

provide the report correcting the initial findings was not a breach of any duty owed to the father. Never did Chief Judge Kaye confront the point that, if a medical examiner is aware that a person is likely to be subject to investigation of a serious crime because of the examiner's report, then he or she will or should be aware that the person's ability to lead a normal life hinges on whether an initially erroneous report is or is not corrected. That observation naturally leads to an assertion that, under such circumstances, the examiner has an obligation to provide the suspect with the relief from the false prosecution that the examiner helped initiate and alone was situated to halt. This is a powerful and obvious argument in support of the plaintiff's claim that the examiner owed him a duty of care not to cause him emotional distress. Yet because Chief Judge Kaye appeared to treat "duty" simply as Section 6's dummy variable, she framed the question of the case in terms of whether permitting liability would open up a large vein of litigation against medical examiners. With the question thus posed, she unsurprisingly rejected plaintiff's suit. We do not mean to claim too much for this example. Certainly, we do not claim that the majority's recognition of duty in its obligation sense would have been outcome-determinative: A reasonable court could have answered this "policy" question in the affirmative, or it could have answered the obligation question in the negative. But we see no reason to doubt that the framing of the question bore on how it was resolved.

Professor Robert Rabin offered this rejoinder to the authors' analysis of *Lauer*:

> No reason to doubt? Can one really believe that the majority somehow missed the point of plaintiff's suffering because of a rote adherence to doctrine, rather than simply giving the father's emotional distress less weight than the dissent attached to it? Why wouldn't one simply conclude that, rightly or wrongly, the majority simply struck a different balance between floodgates concerns and plaintiff-protective concerns, and as a consequence, decided that the concept of duty — which embraces both sets of considerations — weighed in favor of no liability in the case? [. . .]

Do you think it matters whether duty is conceptualized as an element of recovery that must be considered first or instead as a series of exceptions to a general rule of liability for harm caused by negligent behavior?

Chapter 5

Cause in Fact

Once a plaintiff has established that the defendant acted negligently, he next must show that the negligence was the cause of his injuries. The law of torts traditionally divides this question into two parts. The first issue, and the subject of this chapter, is the requirement that the plaintiff show that the defendant's negligence was the "cause in fact" of the injuries. This typically means demonstrating that the injuries would not have occurred if the defendant had used due care; "but for" the defendant's negligence, in other words, the plaintiff would not have been hurt — though as we shall see, the question sometimes becomes a bit more complicated than that. The second issue, and the subject of the chapter that follows this one, is whether the defendant's negligence was the "proximate cause" of the plaintiff's injuries, which essentially amounts to asking whether the injuries were too remote a result of the negligence to permit recovery.

In many cases the cause in fact element is straightforward. Suppose that, as in *Davis v. Feinstein* (in the chapter on the negligence standard), the plaintiff falls through an open cellar door; he brings a suit against its owner, claiming it was negligent to have left the door open. Factual causation will not be an issue in the case: it may or may not have been negligent to fail to close the door, but it at least is clear that if the door had been closed the plaintiff would not have fallen into the cellar. In other situations, however, it may be less clear whether the defendant's untaken precautions would have made a difference. Suppose the plaintiff's decedent dies in a hotel fire. The hotel negligently had failed to install fire escapes, but the decedent was found still in his bed. Should the failure to provide fire escapes be considered a cause of his death?

A.   BUT-FOR CAUSATION

New York Central R.R. v. Grimstad
264 F. 334 (2d Cir. 1920)

[Angell Grimstad was captain of a barge that was moored in Brooklyn harbor, loaded with sugar in transit from Havana to New Brunswick. A tugboat bumped the barge. Grimstad's wife, Elfrieda, felt the resulting shock and came out from the cabin. She looked over one side of the barge and saw nothing; she crossed the deck and looked over the other side, and there saw her husband in the water about ten feet from the barge, holding up his hands. He did not know how to swim. She ran back into the cabin for a small line, but when she returned with it he had disappeared. Elfrieda Grimstad sued the owner of the barge, claiming it negligently had failed to provide lifesaving equipment on the vessel. The jury found for the plaintiff, and the trial court entered judgment on the verdict. This appeal followed.]

WARD, J. [after stating the facts:] — Obviously the proximate cause of the decedent's death was his falling into the water, and in the absence of any testimony whatever on the point, we will assume that this happened without negligence on his part or on the part of the defendant. On the second question, whether a life buoy would have saved the decedent from drowning, we think the jury were left to pure conjecture and speculation. A jury might well conclude that a light near an open hatch or a rail on the side of a vessel's deck would have prevented a person's falling into the hatch or into the water, in the dark. But there is nothing whatever to show that the decedent was not drowned because he did not know how to swim, nor anything to show that, if there had been a life buoy on board, the decedent's wife would have got it in time, that is, sooner than she got the small line, or, if she had, that she would have thrown it so that her husband could have seized it, or, if she did, that he would have seized it, or that, if he did, it would have prevented him from drowning.

The court erred in denying the defendant's motion to dismiss the complaint at the end of the case.

Judgment reversed.

NOTES

1. *Fairly and conclusively.* In Gardner v. National Bulk Carriers, Inc., 310 F.2d 284 (4th Cir. 1962), the plaintiff's decedent, Gardner, was a seaman aboard the defendant's vessel, the *S.S. Bulkcrude*, en route from New York to Corpus Christi. At around midnight one evening when the boat was traveling near the Florida Keys, Gardner was found to be missing from the ship.

He had last been seen six hours earlier. The ship did not alter its speed or course, and continued on its way to Corpus Christi, where it arrived several days later. Gardner never was seen again.

Gardner's administratrix sued the defendant under the Jones Act, a federal statute allowing seamen to recover for injuries caused by the negligence of a ship's owner or master. The trial court found the conclusion "inescapable" that Gardner had gone overboard between 6:30 P.M. and 11:40 P.M., and had died sometime thereafter, concluding that "whether he met his death by drowning, by becoming involved with the ship's propeller, or by falling victim to a shark, barracuda, or other marine life, is immaterial." The court then exonerated the ship's owners, finding that the ship's master acted reasonably: the ship had traveled over 100 miles since Gardner had last been seen; it was unknown where he had gone overboard; it was a moonless night; and as noted Gardner might already have fallen prey to marine life in the area. Citing *New York Central Ry. v. Grimstad*, the court announced its holding that "the master of the *Bulkcrude* was not negligent in failing to reverse his course for the purpose of conducting a search, and that, in any event, there was no reasonable possibility of success and, hence, there was no causal relation between the negligence, if any, and the death[.]"

The court of appeals reversed, giving judgment as a matter of law to the libelant (the maritime plaintiff):

> It can indeed be speculated, as the respondents suggest, that the seaman slipped, fainted or otherwise involuntarily went overboard, or that he entered the water bent on self-destruction. Likewise, it is conceivable that he was killed in the fall, cut to pieces by the propeller or drowned immediately; also, there may be speculation as to the precise point in time when these events occurred. But only one thing is known with certainty: often seamen who fall overboard survive for many hours in the water.
>
> The decisive question is, what was the master's duty in the present circumstances? The court found as a fact that turning back would have entailed no risk. The only thing that would have been lost in attempting rescue was time; the *Bulkcrude* might have reached its destination a half day late, at the most. [...]
>
> In the circumstances of this case, the inaction of the master established a neglect of the duty of rescue — a neglect from which a contributing cause of the seaman's death is fairly and conclusively drawn by law.

What is the distinction between *Gardner v. National Bulk Carriers* and *New York Central R.R. v. Grimstad*?

2. *Ice capades.* In Stacy v. Knickerbocker Ice Co., 54 N.W. 1091 (Wis. 1893), the defendant ice company was in the business of cutting ice that formed in Fowler Lake, in Oconomowoc, and removing it to ice houses.

The defendant hired horses from the plaintiff to help scrape snow off the surface of the ice. As one of the defendant's employees, Clifford, was hitching the horses to a scraper, two of the horses became frightened, perhaps by the sound of other scrapers. The horses reared and ran across the ice despite efforts by the defendant's employees to restrain them. After running about 100 feet the horses reached an area where the ice was thin because it recently had been harvested; a fresh snowfall made the thin ice indistinguishable from the thick, and no other signals had been erected to mark or block the area. The horses fell through the thin ice and drowned.

The plaintiff brought this action to recover the value of the horses, charging that the defendant had been negligent in three ways: by failing to erect a fence around the thin ice, as required by statute; by failing to notify its employees.of the location of the thin ice; and by failing to keep ropes and other equipment near the lake that could have been used to pull the horses out of the water before they drowned. The trial court directed a verdict for the defendant, and the Wisconsin Supreme Court affirmed:

> The testimony has been examined, and we think it demonstrates that, had all these precautions been taken, they would not have saved the horses.
>
> I. They were uncontrollable, were rearing and plunging, and getting away from the place where they became frightened as rapidly as they could. The fence of the statute (which is a single fence board nailed on 2 by 4 inch posts, 3½ feet from the surface upon which the posts stand) would have been but gossamer before those powerful horses, frantic with fright, upon whom two strong men could make no impression. [. . .]
>
> II. Exact knowledge by Clifford of the location of the thin ice is not a possible factor in the loss of the horses, for, had he been fully advised where the thin ice commenced, he was powerless to prevent the horses going upon it. He went into the water with them, and was rescued. Were he suing the plaintiff for negligence, we would have a case where the fact that he had not such knowledge might be material, but we do not regard it material here.
>
> III. We are aware of no rule of law which required the ice company to have, at the place and time of the accident, ropes and appliances suitable for use in hauling the horses out of the water. Moreover, had such ropes and appliances been there at the time, the proof is quite conclusive that they would have been of no avail. The horses fell into deep water and went under the ice, and were undoubtedly dead when the bystanders had succeeded in rescuing Clifford, who came near being drowned.

What is the superficial similarity between *Stacy v. Knickerbocker Ice Co.* and *Gardner v. National Bulk Carriers, Inc.*? What is the distinction between them?

3. *The missing sign.* In Haft v. Lone Palm Hotel, 478 P.2d 465 (Cal. 1970), the plaintiff sued the defendant motel for the wrongful death of her husband and five-year-old son, who drowned while swimming in the motel's pool. The plaintiff's family was vacationing in Palm Springs. Mr. Haft and his son were poor swimmers who could not put their faces under the water; Mrs. Haft warned them not to swim. No one witnessed the drowning of the Hafts. A guest observed them in the morning, splashing and playing on floats; about half an hour later, the same guest found their bodies submerged in the deep end.

The plaintiff established that the motel had failed to provide any of the safety measures required by statute. Specifically, the motel had failed to obey California's Health and Safety Code §24101.4, which required the motel to provide lifeguard services or to post a sign warning that no lifeguard was present. The plaintiff requested jury instructions that the defendant's failure to provide lifeguard service was a cause of the Hafts' deaths as a matter of law. "Plaintiffs argued that since defendant had failed to comply with the alternative of erecting a sign, they were under a mandatory obligation to provide lifeguard service; given this duty, plaintiffs urged that any reasonable jury would be compelled to conclude from the facts disclosed at trial that the presence of a reasonably attentive lifeguard would have averted the tragedies." The trial judge refused to instruct the jury accordingly, and the jury found for the defendant. The plaintiff appealed.

Held, for the plaintiff, that the jury was misinstructed and that there must be a new trial. Said the court:

> In failing to satisfy [the] mandatory safety requirements, which were clearly designed to protect the class of persons of which the victims were members, defendants of course were unquestionably negligent as a matter of law. [...]
>
> Defendants suggest that since their pool falls into the category of pools in which the statutory obligation would be satisfied by the posting of an adequate sign, the consequences of their failure to meet the statutory demands ought to be limited to harm caused by the non-erection of the warning notice. The language of the section makes clear, however, that the underlying requirement of this statute, for pools of either category, is the provision of "lifeguard service," and we believe that the legislative intent would be nullified if a pool owner were permitted to avoid this important requirement by pointing to the fact that he failed to comply with the statutory substitute as well. Defendants' factual argument in this case duly illustrates the manner in which the protection afforded by section 24101.4 would be undermined by an adoption of their interpretation of this requirement. Although they failed to fulfill either statutory alternative, defendants attempt to avoid liability by contending that since the decedents were the only people in the pool area, the absence of a lifeguard must have been obvious; if the absence of a lifeguard was

obvious, the argument continues, defendants' failure to post a sign notifying decedents of this absence could be of no significance. Defendants thus conclude that this negligence was not a "proximate cause" of the resulting injury. We have no doubt that this is an argument which would commonly be made by non-complying pool owners in such cases.

Although there is some superficial persuasiveness in such a position, the main strength of the argument derives not from its own merit but, instead, from the difficulty of proof facing an injured party attempting to counter this position. The sign required by section 24101.4 [...] does considerably more than indicate to potential swimmers that no lifeguard is present. It gives notice of the general hazards present in the given swimming pool and most importantly serves as a continuing warning of the potential danger to the novice swimmer; the mere absence of a lifeguard hardly provides such cautionary advice.

A pool owner, however, can facilely assert that a given individual would have gone in swimming even if there had been a "no lifeguard" sign posted; it is quite difficult, in contrast, for a plaintiff, especially in a wrongful death action, to prove that a warning sign would have had the intended cautionary effect. We do not believe that the Legislature, in giving some pool owners the option of fulfilling the lifeguard requirement by posting an adequate sign, intended, in effect, to withdraw the protection of section 24101.4 in a significant percentage of all cases. Yet, because of the uncertainty surrounding the probable effectiveness of a sign, such substantial eradication of the provision would be the practical result of an adoption of defendant's construction of section 24101.4. In view of the ease with which a pool owner can comply with this section, we cannot choose defendants' construction and remain faithful to the salutary policies underlying this provision. [...]

Upon defendants' failure to provide lifeguard services, the burden shifted to them to prove that their violation was not a proximate cause of the deaths; in the absence of such proof, defendants' causation of such death is established as a matter of law.

What is the superficial similarity between *Haft v. Lone Palm Hotel* and *Stacy v. Knickerbocker Ice Co.* (NL where the plaintiff's horses fell through ice and drowned, despite defendant's failure to mark the dangerous area or take other precautions)? What is the distinction between them? What is the analogy between *Haft v. Lone Palm Hotel* and *Gardner v. National Bulk Carriers, Inc.*?

4. *The lawyer's role*. From Mark F. Grady, *Untaken Precautions*, 18 J. Legal Stud. 139 (1989):

The most common test of cause in fact is whether the harm would have occurred *but for* the defendant's failure to have taken the untaken precaution that constituted the breach of duty. In other words, viewed ex post, would the untaken precaution have *prevented* the accident? [...] Some writers have treated actual causation as a fact of nature, but this formulation ignores the plaintiff's creative role in specifying the breach of duty and the way in which the cause-in-fact issue depends on what breach-of-duty choice the plaintiff has made. While the analysis of the breach-of-duty issue has an ex ante perspective, the test of cause in fact is whether the same untaken precaution, viewed after the accident, would have prevented it. [...]

When courts make the same untaken precaution do dual service under rules that have opposite perspectives, they create an obvious tension. From a breach-of-duty standpoint, the plaintiff may wish to allege the defendant's most trivial failing because such precautions are often highly cost-effective if only they are taken. An example would be the failure to give a signal. Nonetheless, if the plaintiff chooses a precaution that is too trivial, although he may maximize his chance of prevailing on the breach-of-duty issue, he may seriously hurt his chances of prevailing on the cause-in-fact element. When the court shifts its inquiry to cause in fact, the plaintiff is bound by the untaken precaution selected in the duty phase of the trail. Now the question is whether this duty, if performed, would have prevented this particular harm that the plaintiff has suffered. Too often an obvious breach of duty will turn out to have no causal relation to the injuries suffered. [...]

5. *Informed consent.* In Bernard v. Char, 903 P.2d 667 (Haw. 1995), the plaintiff, Bernard, complained to his dentist, the defendant Char, of an excruciating toothache. Char examined Bernard and told him that tooth number 15 — an upper left molar — was badly decayed and might be fused to the bone behind it. Bernard was advised that he could address the problem either by having the tooth extracted or with root canal surgery. Bernard could not afford root canal surgery; he was unemployed and lacked dental insurance. He therefore opted for the extraction. It became clear during the extraction procedure that the tooth was indeed fused to the bone. Char felt something "crack," and Bernard said he was "shocked" to see Char remove from his mouth "two teeth with the bone, and some meat and stuff hanging off of it." The procedure left Bernard with a dime-sized hole leading from his mouth to his sinus cavity. Char advised Bernard not to smoke cigarettes or blow his nose and told him to pack the wound with tea bags to promote clotting, but Bernard continued to bleed; he also testified that when he looked in the mirror the day after the extraction, his face was swollen to such an extent that he "looked like the elephant man." Bernard recovered after several days of bleeding episodes and a visit to the hospital.

Bernard sued Char, claiming among other things that Char negligently failed to inform him of the risks of having the tooth extracted. The jury brought in a verdict for Bernard, and after a remittitur he was awarded $35,000. Char appealed, claiming that he was entitled to a directed verdict because Bernard failed to testify that he would not have had the procedure if he had been fully informed of the risks. The Hawaii Supreme Court affirmed, holding that causation in an informed consent suit "is to be judged by an objective standard, that is, whether a reasonable person in the plaintiff-patient's position would have consented to the treatment that led to his or her injuries had the plaintiff-patient been properly informed of the risk of the injury that befell him or her." In rejecting the "subjective" approach of asking whether the plaintiff in fact would have declined the procedure, the court cited this passage from *Canterbury v. Spence*, 464 F.2d 772, 790-791 (D.C. Cir. 1972):

> [The subjective] method of dealing with the issue of causation comes in second-best. It places the physician in jeopardy of the patient's hindsight and bitterness. It places the factfinder in the position of deciding whether a speculative answer to a hypothetical question is to be credited. It calls for a subjective determination solely on testimony of a patient-witness shadowed by the occurrence of the undisclosed risk.

The court in *Bernard* added that

> [t]he practical benefits gained by application of the objective standard [include] uniformity and ease of application. [V]iewing the question from a core of reasonableness establishes an initially uniform standard among cases from which adjustments for idiosyncracies may be made. Under this rationale, the analytical exercise is grounded in objective reasonableness, but the standard may still flexibly accommodate the individual characteristics of each patient.

6. *The rights of the unreasonable.* While the objective standard used in *Bernard v. Char* and *Canterbury v. Spence* is used in a majority of jurisdictions, it has its detractors. See, e.g., Scott v. Bradford, 606 P.2d 554 (Okla. 1979), a leading case favoring a subjective inquiry:

> The *Canterbury* view certainly severely limits the protection granted an injured patient. To the extent the plaintiff, given an adequate disclosure, would have declined the proposed treatment, and a reasonable person in similar circumstances would have consented, a patient's right of self-determination is *irrevocably lost*. This basic right to know and decide is the reason for the full-disclosure rule. Accordingly, we decline to jeopardize this right by the imposition of the "reasonable man" standard.

Id. at 559 (emphasis in original).

7. *Esthetic procedures.* In Zalazar v. Vercimak, 633 N.E.2d 1223 (Ill. App. 1993), the plaintiff, Zalazar, went to Vercimak, a plastic surgeon in the town of Mendota, seeking to reduce the size of bags under her eyes. Her evidence was that Vercimak said he could make her look 20 years younger, and offered

to perform the procedure for $318, the amount of Zalazar's weekly take-home pay from the factory where she worked. After the surgery was complete, however, Zalazar suffered from bruising, numbness, and lumps on her face; she resorted to wearing sunglasses all the time. After four months most of the lumps had disappeared, but her eyes looked droopy, with the lower lid hanging away from the eyeball on each side. She ultimately received repair surgery from a hospital in Iowa City. She was satisfied with the result but continued to suffer from some droopiness, numbness, soreness, and excessive tearing in her eyes. Zalazar sued Vercimak, claiming among other things that she never had been informed of these risks of the procedure. The trial court gave a directed verdict to Vercimak on the ground that Zalazar had failed to present objective evidence that a reasonably prudent person in her position, informed of the risks, would have refused the surgery. The trial judge said that "what I have is the subjective standard. I have [plaintiff] saying that she'd not have done it. I need something more than just that." The court of appeals reversed:

> [C]ases involving esthetic cosmetic surgery differ qualitatively from procedures to address patients' medical well being. Unlike chiropractic, cobalt and X-ray treatments, and even tubal ligation, the procedure in this case involves no medically significant benefits to the patient and the alternative is simply to forego the procedure. What kind of expert can objectively weigh the benefits and risks of such a procedure in determining what a so-called "reasonable person" would have decided? We do not believe that such an expert can be found. Where no expert can objectively evaluate whether the failure to warn was the proximate cause of the patient's injury, no expert can be required.
>
> The underlying reason why courts have adopted the objective standard and required the testimony of an expert witness is not applicable in cases such as these. The objective standard and expert witness requirement within informed consent cases arose from the recognition that many medical procedures are not matters of common knowledge or within the experience of laymen. Yet, unlike most surgical procedures, the alternative to esthetic cosmetic surgery is readily apparent to the laymen on the jury.

What is the distinction between *Zalazar v. Vercimak* and *Bernard v. Char*? In *Zalazar* the doctor was arguing for an objective standard of causation; in *Bernard* the doctor was arguing for a subjective standard. Which standard is more likely to favor doctors in the long run?

8. *Framing effects and the law.* From Twerski and Cohen, *Informed Decision Making and the Law of Torts: The Myth of Justiciable Causation*, 1988 U. Ill. L. Rev. 607 (1988):

> [I]n many circumstances, descriptions of the risks of a medical procedure in terms of the chances of success or the chances of failure may have different connotations and lead to different decisions.

For example, consider the following problems presented to two groups of subjects by Professors Kahneman and Tversky. In the first problem, seventy subjects were told that, in addition to whatever they own, they have been presented with $1000. The subjects were then asked to choose between (a) a 50% chance of an additional $1000, and (b) a 100% chance of an additional $500. In the second problem, sixty-eight subjects were told that, in addition to whatever they own, they have been presented with $2000; they were then asked to choose between (a) a 50% chance of losing $1000, and (b) a 100% chance of losing $500.

A moment's reflection will reveal that the two problems are identical. In both problems, the subjects were asked to choose between (a) a gamble in which they had an even chance of ending up with either $1000 or $2000, and (b) a sure $1500. Yet the preferences expressed by the two groups of subjects were far from identical. In the first problem, 84% of the subjects selected the sure $1500 ($500 in addition to the original $1000); 16% chose the gamble. In the second problem, however, only 31% chose the sure $1500 ($2000 minus $500); 69% chose the gamble.

Professors Kahneman and Tversky theorize that the explanation for the disparity between the two groups of subjects is that "people normally perceive outcomes as gains or losses, rather than as final states of wealth or welfare." Quite obviously, then, whether the risks of a medical procedure are framed as gains or losses could have a significant impact on the patient's choice.

An example of the framing phenomenon in the medical decision-making context is provided in a study by Professors McNeil, Pauker, Sox, and Tversky. The researchers asked subjects to imagine that they had lung cancer and to choose between surgery and radiation treatment based on the information presented to them. Identical outcomes were framed differently for different subjects: they told some subjects the range of possible outcomes in terms of the probability of living at various points (e.g., 68% chance of living for more than one year), while they told others the range of possible outcomes in terms of the probability of dying (e.g., 32% chance of dying by the end of one year).

The framing of the various results in terms of survival or mortality had a significant impact. On the average, subjects preferred radiation therapy to surgery 42% of the time when the information was presented in terms of the probability of dying, but only 25% of the time when information was presented in terms of the probability of living.

1988 U. Ill. L. Rev. at 634-635 (quoting Kahneman & Tversky, *Prospect Theory: An Analysis of Decision Under Risk*, 47 Econometrica 263, 273 (1979)) (footnotes omitted). What are the implications of these studies?

The authors "suggest a radical restructuring of the informed choice doctrine. Rather than focusing on personal injury damages flowing from the hypothetical "but for," which seeks to determine what the plaintiff would have decided had the defendant provided the information, we suggest that courts should identify and value the decision rights of the plaintiff which the defendant destroyed by withholding adequate information." Id. at 608-609.

Herskovits v. Group Health Cooperative of Puget Sound
664 P.2d 474 (Wash. 1983)

[The plaintiff's decedent brought an action under Washington's wrongful death statute after the defendant failed to make an early diagnosis of his lung cancer. Mr. Herskovits had been a patient of the Group Health Cooperative for over 20 years. In December 1974, he came to the Group Health Hospital with complaints of chronic coughing and chest pain. The physician prescribed cough medicine. Herskovits's health failed to improve. Early in the summer of 1975, Herskovits consulted a physician outside Group Health, Dr. Jonathan Ostrow, and was diagnosed with cancer in the bronchus of his left lung. In July 1975, the lung was removed. Herskovits died of cancer in March 1977. His estate continued the litigation.

[The plaintiff was unable to find an expert witness who would testify that Group Health's failure to make an earlier diagnosis had "probably" or "more likely than not" caused her husband's death. Dr. Ostrow testified that there was no way of knowing how far the tumor in Herskovits's lung had developed by December 1974. He testified that, if the tumor had been diagnosed at "Stage 1" in December, Herskovits's chance of surviving for five years was 39 percent. When the tumor was diagnosed in June 1975, it was at "Stage 2." A patient's chance of surviving for five years after diagnosis with a Stage 2 tumor is 25 percent. Ostrow concluded that Group Health had probably reduced Herskovits's chance of surviving for five years from 39 percent to 25 percent.

[The defendant moved for summary judgment on the ground that the plaintiff probably would have died from lung cancer even if Group Health had diagnosed it correctly in December 1974. The trial court granted the motion and dismissed the action, holding that "under Washington law the loss of a possibility of survival is not compensable." The plaintiff appealed.]

Dore, J. — This appeal raises the issue of whether an estate can maintain an action for professional negligence as a result of failure to timely diagnose lung cancer, where the estate can show probable reduction in statistical chance for survival but cannot show and/or prove that with timely diagnosis and treatment, decedent probably would have lived to normal life expectancy. [. . .]

The main issue we will address in this opinion is whether a patient, with less than a 50% chance of survival, has a cause of action against the hospital and its employees if they are negligent in diagnosing a lung cancer which reduces his chances of survival by 14 percent. [. . .] Plaintiff contends that medical testimony of a reduction of chance of survival from 39% to 25% is sufficient evidence to allow the proximate cause issue to go to the jury. Defendant Group Health argues conversely that Washington law does not permit such testimony on the issue of medical causation and requires that medical testimony must be at least sufficiently definite to establish that the act complained of "probably" or "more likely than not" caused the subsequent disability. It is Group Health's contention that plaintiff must prove that Herskovits "probably" would have survived had the defendant not been allegedly negligent; that is, the plaintiff must prove there was at least a 51% chance of survival.

This court heretofore has not faced the issue of whether [. . .] proof that the defendant's conduct increased the risk of death by decreasing the chances of survival is sufficient to take the issue of proximate cause to the jury. Some courts in other jurisdictions have allowed the proximate cause issue to go to the jury on this type of proof. These courts emphasized the fact that defendants' conduct deprived the decedents of a "significant" chance to survive or recover, rather than requiring proof that with absolute certainty the defendants' conduct caused the physical injury. The underlying reason is that it is not for the wrongdoer, who put the possibility of recovery beyond realization, to say afterward that the result was inevitable.

Other jurisdictions have rejected this approach, generally holding that unless the plaintiff is able to show that it was more likely than not that the harm was caused by the defendant's negligence, proof of a decreased chance of survival is not enough to take the proximate cause question to the jury. These courts have concluded that the defendant should not be liable where the decedent more than likely would have died anyway.

The ultimate question raised here is whether the relationship between the increased risk of harm and Herskovits' death is sufficient to hold Group Health responsible. Is a 36% (from 39 percent to 25%) reduction in the decedent's chance for survival sufficient evidence of causation to allow the jury to consider the possibility that the physician's failure to timely diagnose the illness was the proximate cause of his death? We answer in the affirmative. To decide otherwise would be a blanket release from liability for doctors and hospitals any time there was less than a 50 percent chance of survival, regardless of how flagrant the negligence. [. . .]

Where percentage probabilities and decreased probabilities are submitted into evidence, there is simply no danger of speculation on the part of the jury. More speculation is involved in requiring the medical expert to testify as to what would have happened had the defendant not been negligent. [. . .]

We reject Group Health's argument that plaintiffs must show that Herskovits "probably" would have had a 51% chance of survival if the hospital had not been negligent. We hold that medical testimony of a reduction of chance of survival from 39% to 25% is sufficient evidence to allow the proximate cause issue to go to the jury.

Causing reduction of the opportunity to recover (loss of chance) by one's negligence, however, does not necessitate a total recovery against the negligent party for all damages caused by the victim's death. Damages should be awarded to the injured party or his family based only on damages caused directly by premature death, such as lost earnings and additional medical expenses, etc.

We reverse the trial court and reinstate the cause of action.

PEARSON, J. (concurring) — [. . .] [A]lthough the issue before us is primarily one of causation, resolution of that issue requires us to identify the nature of the injury to the decedent. Our conception of the injury will substantially affect our analysis. If the injury is determined to be the death of Mr. Herskovits, then under the established principles of proximate cause plaintiff has failed to make a prima facie case. Dr. Ostrow was unable to state that probably, or more likely than not, Mr. Herskovits' death was caused by defendant's negligence. On the contrary, it is clear from Dr. Ostrow's testimony that Mr. Herskovits would have probably died from cancer even with the exercise of reasonable care by defendant. Accordingly, if we perceive the death of Mr. Herskovits as the injury in this case, we must affirm the trial court, unless we determine that it is proper to depart substantially from the traditional requirements of establishing proximate cause in this type of case.

If, on the other hand, we view the injury to be the reduction of Mr. Herskovits' chance of survival, our analysis might well be different. Dr. Ostrow testified that the failure to diagnose cancer in December 1974 probably caused a substantial reduction in Mr. Herskovits' chance of survival. [Pearson, J., reviewed the cases and concluded that the latter way of conceptualizing the plaintiff's injury was preferable. He relied in part on King, *Causation, Valuation, and Chance in Personal Injury Torts Involving Preexisting Conditions and Future Consequences*, 90 Yale L.J. 1353 (1981).]

King's basic thesis is explained in the following passage, which is particularly pertinent to the case before us.

> Causation has for the most part been treated as an all-or-nothing proposition. Either a loss was caused by the defendant or it was not. . . . A plaintiff ordinarily should be required to prove by the applicable standard of proof that the defendant caused the loss in question. *What* caused a loss, however, should be a separate question from what the *nature and extent* of the loss are. This distinction seems to have eluded the courts, with the result that lost chances in many respects are compensated either as certainties or not at all.
>
> To illustrate, consider the case in which a doctor negligently fails to diagnose a patient's cancerous condition until it has become inoperable. Assume further that even with a timely diagnosis the patient would have had only a 30% chance of recovering from the disease and surviving over the long term. There are two ways of handling such a case.

Under the traditional approach, this loss of a not-better-than-even chance of recovering from the cancer would not be compensable because it did not appear more likely [than] not that the patient would have survived with proper care. Recoverable damages, if any, would depend on the extent to which it appeared that cancer killed the patient sooner than it would have with timely diagnosis and treatment, and on the extent to which the delay in diagnosis aggravated the patient's condition, such as by causing additional pain. A more rational approach, however, would allow recovery for the loss of the chance of cure even though the chance was not better than even. The probability of long-term survival would be reflected in the amount of damages awarded for the loss of the chance. While the plaintiff here could not prove by a preponderance of the evidence that he was denied a cure by the defendant's negligence, he could show by a preponderance that he was deprived of a 30% chance of a cure.

[. . .] Under the all or nothing approach, typified by *Cooper v. Sisters of Charity of Cincinnati, Inc.*, 272 N.E.2d 97 (Ohio 1971), a plaintiff who establishes that but for the defendant's negligence the decedent had a 51% chance of survival may maintain an action for that death. The defendant will be liable for all damages arising from the death, even though there was a 49% chance it would have occurred despite his negligence. On the other hand, a plaintiff who establishes that but for the defendant's negligence the decedent had a 49% chance of survival recovers nothing.

This all or nothing approach to recovery is criticized by King on several grounds, 90 Yale L.J. at 1376-78. First, the all or nothing approach is arbitrary. Second, it

> subverts the deterrence objectives of tort law by denying recovery for the effects of conduct that causes statistically demonstrable losses. . . . A failure to allocate the cost of these losses to their tortious sources . . . strikes at the integrity of the torts system of loss allocation.

Third, the all or nothing approach creates pressure to manipulate and distort other rules affecting causation and damages in an attempt to mitigate perceived injustices. Fourth, the all or nothing approach gives certain defendants the benefit of an uncertainty which, were it not for their tortious conduct, would not exist. Finally, King argues that the loss of a less than even chance is a loss worthy of redress.

These reasons persuade me that the best resolution of the issue before us is to recognize the loss of a less than even chance as an actionable injury. Therefore, I would hold that plaintiff has established a *prima facie* issue of proximate cause by producing testimony that defendant probably caused a substantial reduction in Mr. Herskovits' chance of survival. [. . .]

Finally, it is necessary to consider the amount of damages recoverable in the event that a loss of a chance of recovery is established. Once again,

King's discussion provides a useful illustration of the principles which should be applied.

> To illustrate, consider a patient who suffers a heart attack and dies as a result. Assume that the defendant-physician negligently misdiagnosed the patient's condition, but that the patient would have had only a 40% chance of survival even with a timely diagnosis and proper care. Regardless of whether it could be said that the defendant caused the decedent's death, he caused the loss of a chance, and that chance-interest should be completely redressed in its own right. Under the proposed rule, the plaintiff's compensation for the loss of the victim's chance of surviving the heart attack would be 40% of the compensable value of the victim's life had he survived (including what his earning capacity would otherwise have been in the years following death). The value placed on the patient's life would reflect such factors as his age, health, and earning potential, including the fact that he had suffered the heart attack and the assumption that he had survived it. The 40% computation would be applied to that base figure.

[...]

NOTES

1. *Loss of a chance.* The traditional view of "cause in fact," reflected in cases like *New York Central R.R. v. Grimstad* and *Stacy v. Knickerbocker Ice Co.*, is that a plaintiff has to show that some untaken precaution by the defendant more likely than not would have (i.e., would have been more than 50 percent likely to have) prevented the plaintiff's injuries. As noted in the introduction to this chapter, this point is straightforward enough in a case where a plaintiff definitely would not have been harmed without the defendant's negligence. Suppose the defendant negligently bumps into a barrel in a warehouse; the barrel rolls out of a window and falls onto the plaintiff's head. The defendant's negligence was a cause in fact of the plaintiff's harm: but for the defendant's act, the barrel definitely would not have fallen on the plaintiff. That is an easy case of causation in fact. An easy case of no causation in fact, as suggested earlier, would be one where a defendant negligently fails to install a fire escape but it's clear that the plaintiff's decedent would have been killed regardless of whether the fire escape was present. Perhaps he was smoking in bed and died there.

Harder cases arise when the defendant's negligence *may* have caused the plaintiff's injuries, but the plaintiff might have sustained the same injuries even without the negligence. Here are two examples drawn from cases just considered:

1. A man falls over the side of a ship and drowns. The defendant did not have any buoys on board, and this was negligence. There is no

guarantee that if there had been a buoy the man would have been saved (indeed, we will never know whether he would have lived); the buoy just would have made it *more likely* that he would have been saved. How much of an improvement in the man's odds of survival must a buoy create before we are ready to say that the failure to provide a buoy more likely than not caused his death?

2. A doctor negligently fails to diagnose a disease until it is far advanced, and the patient dies. The negligence worsened the patient's odds of surviving, but he might have died from the disease even if the doctor had diagnosed it promptly. Can we say the doctor's negligence caused the plaintiff's death? Again, the doctor's negligence did cause a greater likelihood that the plaintiff would die; but how much greater must that likelihood be before we can say for legal purposes that but for the doctor's negligence, the patient would have lived?

To clarify how the law works in these situations, consider first a case where we can imagine being able to place clear numbers on the probabilities involved. Suppose the defendant is a doctor performing a risky but important procedure. There is a 5 percent chance that the plaintiff will die even if the doctor is careful in every respect. But the doctor is negligent in some way and this raises the plaintiff's risk of death to 25 percent. The plaintiff dies. We have no way of knowing whether the death resulted from the doctor's negligence or from the original (or "background") 5 percent risk that existed anyway. (That's important; if we knew, the case would be easy.) Should the doctor be held liable?

The answer is "yes" under traditional tort principles. At first this might seem an odd case for liability because the doctor's negligence did not make it more likely than not that the plaintiff would die; the negligence only created a 25 percent chance of death, and obviously 25 percent is less than the seemingly magic 50 percent figure. But that is not the question. The question is: given that the plaintiff *did* die, how likely is it that the doctor caused the death? Very likely: the doctor's negligence caused the plaintiff's chance of death to go from 5 percent to 25 percent; chances are very good that the plaintiff's death was caused by that extra degree of risk that the doctor added, rather than by the original risk that already existed. Though the *total* risk of death was relatively small, most of the risk that did exist (four-fifths of it) was due to the doctor's negligence. The thing that was risked came to pass. There is an 80 percent chance that the doctor was to blame.

It may help you to translate the percentages into people. Saying there was a 25 percent chance that the plaintiff would die if the doctor was negligent is like saying that if this situation were repeated 100 times, 25 people would be expected to die; 20 of the deaths would be due to the doctor's negligence, and 5 of the deaths would have happened regardless of the doctor's negligence. The plaintiff's decedent, in effect, is in the imaginary group of 25 who died. There is a 4 out of 5 (80 percent) chance that the doctor's negligence caused his death. Eighty percent is greater than 50 percent, so the doctor should be held liable. This is a traditional analysis that any court would accept.

Now compare the facts of *Herskovits*. Mr. Herskovits was diagnosed with cancer late, causing his chance of survival to drop from 39 percent to 25 percent. The question was whether his doctor's negligence "caused" his death. Under the traditional analysis just described, the answer would be no. Herskovits's chance of dying went from 61 percent to 75 percent (we have reversed the likelihood-of-survival figures to create likelihood-of-death figures), and there is no reason to assume that his death was caused by that relatively small dollop of added risk that his doctor's negligence created, rather than by the large pre-existing risk. It would be different if his chance of dying had more than doubled — say, from 40 percent to 90 percent. Then we would be able to say it was more probable than not that his death was caused by the large chunk of risk that the doctor's negligence added, rather than by the somewhat smaller (40 percent) risk that already existed anyway. Here, however, Herskovits probably would have died when he did regardless of whether the defendant was negligent.

Under a traditional approach to causation, then, we ask how large a share of the risk of whatever happened was created by the defendant. In effect the plaintiff has to show that the defendant's negligence at least doubled the background likelihood of whatever injury occurred. So if a doctor's negligence causes the likelihood of death to go from 10 percent to 30 percent, then if death occurs we can say it's more likely than not that it was because of the doctor's negligence. The same goes if the doctor's negligence causes the likelihood of death to rise from 30 percent to 70 percent, or (less obviously) from 1 percent to 3 percent. The plaintiff probably won't die in the latter situation, but if he does, it's more likely than not that the death resulted from the extra risk the doctor created by being negligent. But if the doctor's negligence causes the plaintiff's risk of death to go from 30 percent to 50 percent, or even from 66 percent to 99 percent, and the plaintiff dies, we cannot say the negligence "more likely than not" was the cause of death. In the 66 percent/99 percent case, there is a one-third chance that the plaintiff died only because the doctor was negligent, and a two-thirds chance that he died for other reasons, or that he would have died no matter what the doctor did.

Importantly, this means that if a patient has less than a 50 percent chance of survival to begin with (even if the doctor uses due care), then on a traditional view of causation the doctor's negligence *never* can be considered the cause in fact of the patient's death: it always will be more likely than not that the plaintiff would have died anyway. Put differently, it is impossible for a doctor to double a plaintiff's chance of death if the plaintiff already is more than 50 percent likely to die in any event. Obviously all these figures are somewhat conjectural, but as *Herskovits* illustrates, courts often are prepared to use whatever rough numbers an expert can supply.

This analysis suggests a pair of questions. First, why did the *Herskovits* court reject these traditional rules of causation? Second, can you see how the *Herskovits* reasoning might be used in a case like *Grimstad*? Suppose Grimstad (in the opinion of the plaintiff's expert) would have had a 60 percent chance of being saved if the boat had a buoy; the absence of a buoy dropped his chances to 45 percent. Liability? It might seem so: he probably would have lived if there had been a buoy. But again that is the wrong question. The lack of a buoy merely increased his likelihood of drowning from 40 percent to 55 percent. Most of the risk that he would drown was "background risk" that existed regardless of the buoy. Should the logic of *Herskovits* allow plaintiffs with facts like these to nonetheless recover a bit for their lost chances of survival, even if the defendant's negligence only nibbled away a little at those chances?

2. *Recurring misses.* Can the problem addressed by the *Herskovits* case be considered analogous in some respects to the problem addressed in *Haft v. Lone Palm Hotel*? Consider Saul Levmore, *Probabilistic Recoveries, Restitution, and Recurring Wrongs*, 19 J. Legal Stud. 691 (1990):

> The decision [in *Haft v. Lone Palm Hotel*] is easily ridiculed. Even if a lifeguard would have reduced the Hafts' chances of death by more than 50%, the statute explicitly allowed a pool operator simply to post a notice. This notice might have reminded swimmers (and nonswimmers, like the Hafts) of the dangers of deep waters, it might have disabused Mr. Haft of any belief that a lifeguard was on duty and only momentarily out of sight, and it might have suggested to him that horseplay in the pool would be dangerous. But these possibilities surely do not add up to much; it is safe to guess that the causal connection between drownings and the absence of notice alone was quite small, say 10%, and thus well below the preponderance rule's dividing line, given that very few law-abiding pool operators employ lifeguards rather than signs.
>
> Conversely, a directed verdict for the Lone Palm Hotel plainly underdeters wrongful behavior. Most wrongdoers, such as speeding motorists, cannot ignore the possibility that they will cause harm and then lose before a jury under a preponderance-of-the-evidence rule. They may sometimes win when they should lose and lose when they should win, but the deterrence function of tort law will be satisfied at least in a rough way, even if there is some chance in who collects compensation. The full damages paid in some cases offset the complete absence of damages in other cases. In contrast, if pool operators know that the absence of both lifeguards and signs always produces a causal connection on the order of 10%, then they will never be liable under the preponderance rule and they can violate the statute with impunity. Cases like *Lone Palm* fall into the category of "recurring misses" for which the preponderance rule is not well suited. The background statistics on such matters as drowning and the efficacy of lifeguards and signs are sufficiently stable to ensure that the

preponderance rule will systematically "miss" ongoing instances of anti-social behavior that it should deter.

Unfortunately, this problem of recurring misses appears with some frequency in tort law. Many "failure-to-warn" and informed-consent cases fit this pattern because disclosure would change the behavior of some small fraction but not of most of those who are duly informed. Similarly, many cases in which a cost-justified medical or other precautionary procedure might have been taken, but was not, may be fairly described as dealing with the danger of recurring misses. . . . The identifying feature of these cases is, once again, that there is a wrongful party who is more than 0% but possibly never more than 50% likely to have caused an injury.

The two most obvious strategies for solving the underdeterrence (and undercompensation) problem presented by recurring misses are, first, to increase the use of probabilistic rules and, second, to move away from ex post, conventional tort rules to ex ante, regulatory rules. These two strategies can be mixed and matched to create a number of solutions to the problem of recurring misses. The first is simply to use regulatory or administrative sanctions to overcome the deterrence gaps in the tort system created by recurring misses. Unresponsive pool operators, like speeding motorists, could be influenced with fines or other penalties rather than with the threat of tort liability. The California statute in *Lone Palm Hotel* did, in fact, provide for a fine and for possible imprisonment for each day that a pool operator provided neither lifeguard nor notice. This first "solution," of course, calls for legislative intervention. It offers no help to a judge confronting a recurring miss, frustrated perhaps, that low levels of risk systematically elude tort sanctions.

The second solution is internal to the tort system and is to employ a probabilistic, or expected value, rule for recurring misses. A 51% "connection" would not lead to 100% liability as under the preponderance rule, but only to 51% liability; similarly, a 37% connection would lead not to no liability, but to liability for 37% of the plaintiff's losses. There might be some correction or forgiveness for very low probabilities where administrative or litigation costs are large relative to the risks that would be controlled. And this probabilistic rule could be confined to recurring misses, by judicial "certification" suspending the preponderance rule. Judges might recoil at so revolutionary an innovation, but they might nonetheless be willing to smuggle in such a probabilistic rule as part of a comparative negligence regime by insisting that there was enough of a causal connection, with plaintiff perhaps nine times more responsible than defendant. In many cases, however, it will not be possible to camouflage a probabilistic rule in this fashion.

The third solution exploits the principles of proximate cause to mimic a probabilistic rule. A judge considering *Lone Palm Hotel* might have thought it plausible that Mr. Haft would have kept his son (but not himself) out of the pool if notice had been posted, so that the jury could find that defendant "caused" the son's death but not the father's. This Solomonic allocation of injuries is unlikely to match exactly a formal probabilistic rule, but its spirit and effect can be quite similar. A fact finder can make a defendant pay only a fraction of a set of harms by finding that the defendant caused some but not all of the various separate injuries. This mechanism, however, is more usefully thought of as a precursor to comparative negligence than as a solution to the problem of recurring misses.

The fourth solution is the one that was adopted in the case: the court switched the burden of proof to the defendant to show the absence of a causal connection between its statutory violation and the deaths by drowning. I can imagine the thinking behind this decision to be as follows:

> If I decide that the plaintiff need not show causal connection and I direct a verdict for the plaintiff, then I substitute a serious problem of overdeterrence for an annoying problem of underdeterrence, for if 10% of the time the presence of a sign might have made a difference, then surely in 90% of the cases it would not. I could hope, of course, that my style of statutory construction will not be followed by all other judges in the future, and ideally if 90% of judges stick to the older rule then we will have achieved optimal deterrence through backhanded means. All this is too much to hope for.
>
> But there is another approach I might try that does not require other judges to stand up later and disagree with me. I could switch the burden of proof to the defendant so that the plaintiff escapes a directed-verdict motion. This may not do the poor plaintiff much good because the jury may be persuaded that the father knew full well what the situation was when he took the fatal swim. But if this case, and others like it, settle for about 10% of their face value, or if 10% of such juries are persuaded otherwise, then switching the burden of proof will do the job. But I am surely taking a chance, for if settlements or juries are more generous than what I have in mind, then I would have done more good with a simple no-recovery rule. But I shall take my chances, keep my own counsel, and hope for the best.

3. *Lotteries.* In Dumas v. Cooney, 1 Cal. Rptr. 2d 584 (Cal. App. 1991), the plaintiff sued his doctors for failing to diagnose his lung cancer earlier. The plaintiff went to his doctors for treatment of a separate illness in September 1984. A chest X-ray revealed something on his lung, but the defendants did not investigate further. An X-ray performed in 1986 led to a diagnosis of lung cancer. The plaintiff's expert witness testified that the plaintiff's tumor was "Stage 3A" in 1986, but was probably Stage 1 in 1984. The witness claimed that a patient in whom a Stage 1 tumor is discovered has a 67 percent chance of being free of disease five years later, while a patient in whom a Stage 2 tumor is found has a 33 percent chance of being alive and free of disease in five years. He estimated that the plaintiff's actual chance of being alive and free from disease five years was 15 to 20 percent.

The trial court instructed the jury on the doctrine of lost chance, over the defendants' objections:

> Damages for negligence in providing medical care may be based on evidence that it is a reasonable medical probability that the plaintiff would have benefited by possible cure, possible lengthening of his life, and/or improved personal comfort from more prompt diagnosis and treatment.

The jury returned a verdict for the plaintiff and the trial court entered judgment on it. The defendants appealed on the ground that the trial court had misinstructed the jury; they argued that the use of the word "possible" in the instruction permitted the jury to hold the defendants liable without finding that their negligence probably shortened the plaintiff's life. The plaintiff argued, among other things, that California should follow *Herskovits* in recognizing a right to collect for loss of a chance.

Held, for the defendants, that the trial court erred by instructing the jury on the theory of lost chance. Said the court:

> [T]he lost chance theory produces more statistical errors than a traditional analysis.
>
> Because loss of chance recovery is based on statistical probabilities, it might be appropriate to examine the statistical probabilities of achieving a "just" result with loss of chance damages. [. . .] To compare the two rules, assume a hypothetical group of 99 cancer patients, each of whom would have had a 33⅓% chance of survival. Each received negligent medical care, and all 99 died. Traditional tort law would deny recovery in all 99 cases because each patient had less than a 5[1]% chance of recovery and the probable cause of death was the pre-existing cancer not the negligence. Statistically, had all 99 received proper treatment, 33 would have lived and 66 would have died; so the traditional rule would have statistically produced 33 errors by denying recovery to all 99. The loss of chance rule would allow all 99 patients to recover, but each would recover 33⅓% of the normal value of the case. Again, with proper care 33 patients would have survived. Thus, the 33 patients who statistically would have survived with proper care would receive only one-third of the appropriate recovery, while the 66 patients who died as a result of the pre-existing condition, not the negligence, would be overcompensated by one-third. The loss of chance rule would have produced errors in all 99 cases. [. . .]
>
> Imperfect as it may be, our legal system attempts to ascertain facts to arrive at the truth. To protect the integrity of that goal, there must be some degree of certainty regarding causation before a jury may determine as fact that a medical defendant did cause the plaintiff's injury and should therefore compensate the plaintiff in damages. To dispense with this requirement is to abandon the truth-seeking function of the law. Professor King is

willing to do so in his attempt to compensate for the precise magnitude of any lost chance. Professor King's criticism of the more likely than not standard for causation, like the lost chance theory itself, is based on the erroneous premise that it is the purpose of tort law to compensate for lost chances. But tort law should not operate by the same principles that govern lotteries and insurance policies. If the acts of the defendants did not actually cause plaintiff's injury, then there is no rational justification for requiring defendants to bear the cost of plaintiff's damages.

4. *Sauce for the gander.* An additional ground of objection to recovery for lost chances was offered in Fennell v. Southern Maryland Hospital Center, Inc., 580 A.2d 206 (Md. 1990):

> If loss of chance damages are to be recognized, amendments to the wrongful death statute should also be considered. As a class, medical malpractice plaintiffs benefit from the fact that they are entitled to recover 100% of their damages from a defendant whose negligence caused only 51% of their loss because it is more probable than not that the defendant's negligence caused the loss. Reciprocally, a defendant whose negligence caused less than 50% of a plaintiff's loss pays nothing because it is probable that the negligence did not cause the loss. If a plaintiff whose decedent had a 49% chance of survival, which was lost through negligent treatment, is permitted to recover 49% of the value of the decedent's life, then a plaintiff whose decedent had a 51 percent chance of survival, which was lost through negligent treatment, perhaps ought to have recovery limited to 51% of the value of the life lost. The latter result would require a change in our current wrongful death statute.

A majority of the jurisdictions to consider the issue have permitted recovery for loss of a chance, though some have not; in Michigan the doctrine was recognized by the courts, then eliminated by statute:

> In an action alleging medical malpractice, the plaintiff has the burden of proving that he or she suffered an injury that more probably than not was proximately caused by the negligence of the defendant or defendants. In an action alleging medical malpractice, the plaintiff cannot recover for loss of an opportunity to survive or an opportunity to achieve a better result unless the opportunity was greater than 50%.

Mich. Comp. Laws Ann. §600.2912a(2). Are there reasons to prefer resolution of this issue by legislatures to resolution of it by courts?

5. *Failure to resuscitate.* In Wendland v. Sparks, 574 N.W.2d 327 (Iowa 1998), a woman named Callie was suffering from cancer, though it was in remission. She was admitted to the defendant's hospital to regain her strength. According to her expert, Callie "seemed to be doing reasonably

well and be fairly healthy in the context of a woman who obviously had a chronic illness and symptoms that were unexplained." Early one morning Callie experienced cardiac arrest. A nurse obtained a "crash" cart, which was equipped to perform electrocardiogenic shock. Another nurse contacted the defendant, Dr. Sparks. Sparks arrived at Callie's room at about the time she was drawing her last breath. He assessed the patient by feeling for a pulse, listening for heartbeats, looking for a respiratory effort, and checking her eyes. The doctor decided not to attempt CPR, and the crash cart was never used, although there was evidence in the summary judgment record that resuscitative efforts might have been successful. One nurse testified in her deposition that Dr. Sparks said, "I just can't do it to her"; the nurse characterized his decision as "an act of mercy" because Callie's prospects for quality of life if she were revived were not good.

Callie's husband sued Sparks and the hospital for negligence, relying on a lost chance theory of causation. The trial court gave summary judgment to the defendant. The Iowa Supreme Court reversed, identifying two types of probabilistic losses Callie had suffered — the lost chance that efforts at resuscitation would have been successful, and the lost chance that if she had been resuscitated she might later have been cured of her disease:

> Under the lost-chance theory, a victim who suffers from a preexisting adverse condition (in this case the patient's cancer and other diseases) and is then subjected to another source of injury (here, the failure to resuscitate) may have a claim for the second event. The rationale is that, if it were not for the second event, the victim might have survived the first. This loss of chance is to be treated and evaluated independently from the preexisting condition.

How should a jury be instructed to think about the issues of causation and damages in this case?

6. *Judge and jury.* How are juries supposed to make sense out of the statistics in cases like *Herskovits*? The answer is that all of the medical cases we have been considering in this section depend heavily on expert testimony. This is a common feature of litigation involving complex questions of causation — whether earlier medical intervention would have extended a plaintiff's life, for example, or how a plaintiff came to contract a disease, or whether a change in the design of a defendant's product would have prevented an accident. These issues do not generally lend themselves to resolution by jurors applying unvarnished common sense to the story told by the fact witnesses to a case. It therefore is standard practice for the parties to employ experts to serve as opinion witnesses, entitled (as ordinary witnesses are not) to offer their conclusions to the jury along with an explanation of the analysis that supports them. Naturally this practice produces fresh difficulties of its own, as the jurors remain charged with another task that may strain their competence: deciding which expert is right.

The trial judge mitigates these problems a bit by performing a screening function: it is up to the judge to decide whether to admit an expert's testimony at all or exclude it as too unreliable to form the basis of a verdict. For much of the twentieth century the dominant standard for admissibility was provided by *Frye v. United States*, 293 F. 1013 (D.C. Cir. 1923): expert testimony was admissible only if based on principles found by the trial judge to be generally accepted in the scientific community. In Daubert v. Merrell Dow Pharmaceuticals, Inc., 509 U.S. 579 (1993), however, the United States Supreme Court concluded that the *Frye* test had been displaced by the Federal Rules of Evidence. The Court concluded that under the Federal Rules,

> the trial judge must determine at the outset [. . .] whether the expert is proposing to testify to (1) scientific knowledge that (2) will assist the trier of fact to understand or determine a fact in issue. This entails a preliminary assessment of whether the reasoning or methodology underlying the testimony is scientifically valid and of whether that reasoning or methodology properly can be applied to the facts in issue. [. . .] Many factors will bear on the inquiry, and we do not presume to set out a definitive checklist or test.

The Court thus left open the possibility that expert testimony might be admitted despite depending on novel theories not yet generally accepted in the relevant scientific community. On the other hand, the Court also charged trial judges with making their own assessments of whether an expert is offering "scientific knowledge"; in other words, federal trial judges have to decide for themselves whether an expert's methods seem reliable. For this purpose judges can continue to consider whether the expert's methods are generally accepted, but they also may ask whether the methods have been subjected to peer review and publication, whether they have been tested in various ways, and what rate of error is associated with them; the Court emphasized that the overall standard for admissibility of such testimony is "flexible." *Daubert* itself involved testimony about whether drugs defendant sold caused birth defects, but the Supreme Court later extended these principles to cover all sorts of technical testimony, not just the medical variety. See *Kumho Tire Co. v. Carmichael*, 526 U.S. 137 (1999) (applying *Daubert* to the testimony of an expert offering to testify about a defective tire).

Since *Daubert* was an interpretation of the Federal Rules of Evidence it does not bind state courts, some of which have continued to adhere to *Frye*. In what sorts of cases would you expect it to make a difference which standard the trial judge uses? What are the costs and benefits of calling upon trial judges to make the assessments required by *Daubert*?

7. *Probable futures.* In Dillon v. Twin State Gas & Electric Co., 163 A. 111 (N.H. 1932), the defendant maintained electric wires over a public bridge that crossed a river. The plaintiff's decedent, a boy of 14, was sitting

on one of the bridge's horizontal beams. He leaned over the side, lost his balance, threw out his arm, and grabbed one of the defendant's wires to save himself from falling. The wire carried a high voltage current, and the boy was electrocuted and thrown back onto the girder. The defendant moved for a directed verdict; the motion was denied, and the defendant appealed.

Held, that the defendant's exception must be overruled. The court observed that the extent of the defendant's liability nonetheless depended on whether the jury found that the boy would have died or been maimed from the fall if the wire had not been present. Said the court:

> In leaning over from the girder and losing his balance [the decedent] was entitled to no protection from the defendant to keep from falling. Its only liability was in exposing him to the danger of charged wires. If but for the current in the wires he would have fallen down on the floor of the bridge or into the river, he would without doubt have been either killed or seriously injured. Although he died from electrocution, yet, if by reason of his preceding loss of balance he was bound to fall except for the intervention of the current, he either did not have long to live or was to be maimed. In such an outcome of his loss of balance, the defendant deprived him, not of a life of normal expectancy, but of one too short to be given pecuniary allowance, in one alternative, and not of normal, but of limited, earning capacity, in the other.
>
> If it were found that he would have thus fallen with death probably resulting, the defendant would not be liable, unless for conscious suffering found to have been sustained from the shock. In that situation his life or earning capacity had no value. To constitute actionable negligence there must be damage, and damage is limited to those elements the [wrongful death] statute prescribes.
>
> If it should be found that but for the current he would have fallen with serious injury, then the loss of life or earning capacity resulting from the electrocution would be measured by its value in such injured condition. Evidence that he would be crippled would be taken into account in the same manner as though he had already been crippled.
>
> His probable future but for the current thus bears on liability as well as damages. Whether the shock from the current threw him back on the girder or whether he would have recovered his balance, with or without the aid of the wire he took hold of, if it had not been charged, are issues of fact, as to which the evidence as it stands may lead to different conclusions.

Though at times the *Dillon* opinion sounds as if it is setting the stage for a jury determination still to come, the court appears to be affirming the denial of a directed verdict after a trial that already occurred. In any event, how might you stylize the facts and holding of *Dillon* as a case of no liability? As so stylized, what is the distinction between *Dillon* and *Herskovits*?

8. *Loss of a chance of legal victory (problem)*. In Daugert v. Pappas, 704 P.2d 600 (Wash. 1985), the plaintiff brought a legal malpractice action against his lawyer for failing to file a timely petition for review of a court of appeals decision. The defendant, Pappas, had represented the plaintiff in a contract dispute. The trial court found for Pappas's client in that action, but the court of appeals reversed, finding for the other party. The plaintiff instructed Pappas to petition the Washington Supreme Court for review of the decision the court of appeals had made. Pappas filed the petition a day late and then failed to follow the proper procedure to request an extension of time. The petition for review was therefore denied. The plaintiff then brought this action against Pappas for malpractice. At trial, both parties presented expert testimony on the likelihood that the state supreme court would have reviewed and reversed the decision in the contract case if the petition had been timely filed. Following *Herskovits*, the trial judge instructed the jury that the defendant was liable if his negligence was a "substantial factor" in causing damage to the plaintiff. The jury found that there was a 20 percent chance that the supreme court would have reviewed the decision and reversed it, and so awarded the plaintiff $71,341 — 20 percent of the damages the plaintiff incurred in losing the original contract case. Pappas appealed (via a timely petition this time) to the Washington Supreme Court.

What result? Can *Daugert v. Pappas* effectively be distinguished from *Herskovits v. Group Health Cooperative*? Are there any reasons why liability for loss of a chance might make more sense in *Herskovits* than it does here — or vice versa?

B. ALTERNATIVE LIABILITY

Summers v. Tice
199 P.2d 1 (Cal. 1948)

[The plaintiff and the two defendants went quail hunting together. Each of the defendants was armed with a 12-gauge shotgun. The three parties positioned themselves in a triangle, 75 feet apart. Defendant Tice flushed a quail into the air; the bird flew between the plaintiff and the defendants, and both defendants shot at it. The plaintiff was struck in the face by bird shot, and brought suit against the defendants for negligence. The trial court found that the defendants had been negligent in firing in the plaintiff's direction and entered judgment against both of them. The defendants appealed on the ground that the plaintiff failed to prove which of them fired the shot that hit him.]

CARTER, J. [after stating the facts:] — When we consider the relative position of the parties and the results that would flow if plaintiff was required to pin the injury on one of the defendants only, a requirement that the burden of proof on that subject be shifted to defendants becomes manifest. They are both wrong-doers both negligent toward plaintiff. They brought about a situation where the negligence of one of them injured the plaintiff, hence it should rest with them each to absolve himself if he can. The injured party has been placed by defendants in the unfair position of pointing to which defendant caused the harm. If one can escape the other may also and plaintiff is remediless. Ordinarily defendants are in a far better position to offer evidence to determine which one caused the injury. This reasoning has recently found favor in this Court. In a quite analogous situation this Court held that a patient injured while unconscious on an operating table in a hospital could hold all or any of the persons who had any connection with the operation even though he could not select the particular acts by the particular person which led to his disability. *Ybarra v. Spangard*, 25 Cal. 2d 486. There the Court was considering whether the patient could avail himself of res ipsa loquitur, rather than where the burden of proof lay, yet the effect of the decision is that plaintiff has made out a case when he has produced evidence which gives rise to an inference of negligence which was the proximate cause of the injury. It is up to defendants to explain the cause of the injury. [. . .]

It is urged that plaintiff now has changed the theory of his case in claiming a concert of action; that he did not plead or prove such concert. From what has been said it is clear that there has been no change in theory. The joint liability, as well as the lack of knowledge as to which defendant was liable, was pleaded and the proof developed the case under either theory. We have seen that for the reasons of policy discussed herein, the case is based upon the legal proposition that, under the circumstances here presented, each defendant is liable for the whole damage whether they are deemed to be acting in concert or independently.

The judgment is affirmed.

NOTES

1. *Alternative liability vs. res ipsa loquitur.* The opinion in *Summers v. Tice* cites *Ybarra v. Spangard* (considered in the chapter on breach of duty) as support for its decision. What is the relationship between the two cases? What are the differences between them?

2. *The silence of the lambs.* From the Restatement (Second) of Torts (1965):

§433A. APPORTIONMENT OF HARM TO CAUSES

Illustration 3. Five dogs owned by A and B enter C's farm and kill ten of C's sheep. There is evidence that three of the dogs are owned by A and two by B, and that all of the dogs are of the same general size and ferocity. On the basis of this evidence, A may be held liable for the death of six of the sheep, and B liable for the death of four.

§433B. BURDEN OF PROOF

Illustration 10. Over a period of three years A successively stores his furniture in warehouses operated by B, C, and D. At the end of that time A finds that his piano has been damaged by a large dent in one corner. The nature of the dent indicates that it was caused by careless handling on a single occasion. A has the burden of proving whether the dent was caused by the negligence of B, C, or D.

Illustration 11. While A's automobile is stopped at an intersection, it is struck in the rear by B's negligently driven car. Immediately afterward C's negligently driven car strikes the rear of B's car, causing a second impact upon A's car. In one collision or the other, A sustains an injury to his neck and shoulder. In A's action against B and C, each defendant has the burden of proving that his conduct did not cause the injury.

Are these illustrations consistent?

3. *E pluribus unum.* In Kingston v. Chicago & N.W. Ry. Co., 211 N.W. 913 (Wis. 1927), the plaintiff sued the defendant to obtain compensation for damage to his lumber yard. A forest fire had been burning to the northwest of the plaintiff's yard. At the same time, another fire was burning to the northeast. The two fires united about 940 feet north of the plaintiff's property, bore down upon it, and destroyed his lumber. The northeast fire had been ignited by sparks emitted from the defendant's train. The origin of the northwest fire was unknown, but the court found that it was not the product of the defendant's negligence. The fires were of equal size before they united, and either would have destroyed the plaintiff's property on its own. The jury brought in a verdict for the plaintiff, and the defendant appealed.

Held, for the plaintiff, that the judgment must be affirmed. Said the court:

> [T]he question is whether the railroad company, which is found to have been responsible for the origin of the northeast fire, escapes liability, because the origin of the northwest fire is not identified, although there is no reason to believe that it had any other than human origin. An affirmative answer to that question would certainly make a wrongdoer a favorite of the law at the expense of an innocent sufferer. The injustice of such a doctrine sufficiently impeaches the logic upon which it is founded. Where one who has suffered damage by fire proves the origin of a fire and the course of that fire up to the point of the destruction of his property, one has certainly established liability on the part of the originator of the fire. Granting that the union of that fire with another of natural origin, or with another of much greater proportions, is available as a defense the burden is on the defendant to show that, by reason of such union with a fire of such character, the fire set by him was not the proximate cause of the damage. No principle of justice requires that the plaintiff be placed under the burden of specifically identifying the origin

of both fires in order to recover the damages for which either or both fires are responsible.

What is the analogy between *Kingston v. Chicago & N.W. Ry. Co.* and *Summers v. Tice?* What is the distinction between *Kingston* and *Dillon v. Twin State Gas & Electric Co.?*

Notice the court's concession in *Kingston* that if the defendant could prove that the northwest fire had been of "natural" origin, he could not be held liable for starting the northeast fire that combined with it and destroyed the plaintiff's property. Why? What would be the distinction between such a case and *Summers v. Tice?* Most courts reject this distinction, allowing liability on facts like those in *Kingston* upon a finding by the jury that the defendant's negligence was a "substantial factor" in bringing about the harm.

4. *It did not belong to both (problem).* In Litzman v. Humboldt County, 273 P.2d 82 (Cal. App. 1954), the plaintiff, age nine, came upon an object he thought was a "flare" lying on the ground at the Humboldt County Fair. He touched a match to it and it exploded, destroying his left hand. The plaintiff's evidence was that the object in fact was an aerial bomb of the sort used in fireworks displays. Such aerial bombs had been brought onto the fair grounds by two parties: the Golden State Fireworks Manufacturing Company, which had been hired to put on a fireworks display at the fair; and one Monte Brooks, who arranged other forms of entertainment at the fair — acrobats and the like — and used aerial bombs to signify the start of the evening's show. Golden State and its aerial bombs had no connection to Brooks and his aerial bombs. The plaintiff sued both Golden State and Brooks. The trial court instructed the jury that if they were unable from the evidence to determine which of the two defendants was responsible for leaving the aerial bomb on the ground, they should exonerate both. So instructed, the jury brought in a verdict for the defendants. The plaintiff appealed, claiming that the trial court should have instructed the jury that it could find in his favor on the negligence issue under the doctrine of res ipsa loquitur set out in *Ybarra v. Spangard*, and that it could find in his favor on the causation issue under the doctrine of alternative liability set out in *Summers v. Tice.*

The defendants said in their appellate brief that "[i]n the present case [the plaintiff] admit[s] that one of the two defendants who previously had exploded fireworks probably is blameless. It could not be otherwise. Only one bomb blew off Ralph Litzman's left hand. That bomb belonged to one or the other of the defendants, Golden State or Brooks. It did not belong to both." Said the court: "We think there is no mere 'probability' about the blamelessness of one or the other of said two defendants and that the situation is as we have above stated it, that is, if one is found guilty, that finding, under the evidence in this case, exonerates the other." The court then went on to discuss whether *Ybarra* and *Summers* applied here.

What arguments might you make for and against liability on these facts?

If you have studied strict liability, then it also will be of interest to note that the plaintiff requested an instruction allowing the defendants to be held strictly liable for the plaintiff's injuries because the defendants were engaged in "ultrahazardous" activities. What arguments might you make either way on this issue?

Sindell v. Abbott Laboratories
607 P.2d 924 (Cal. 1980)

MOSK, J. — This case involves a complex problem both timely and significant: may a plaintiff, injured as the result of a drug administered to her mother during pregnancy, who knows the type of drug involved but cannot identify the manufacturer of the precise product, hold liable for her injuries a maker of a drug produced from an identical formula?

Plaintiff Judith Sindell brought an action against eleven drug companies and Does 1 through 100, on behalf of herself and other women similarly situated. The complaint alleges as follows:

Between 1941 and 1971, defendants were engaged in the business of manufacturing, promoting, and marketing diethylstilbesterol (DES), a drug which is a synthetic compound of the female hormone estrogen. The drug was administered to the plaintiff's mother and the mothers of the class she represents, for the purpose of preventing miscarriage. In 1947, the Food and Drug Administration authorized the marketing of DES as a miscarriage preventative, but only on an experimental basis, with a requirement that the drug contain a warning label to that effect.

DES may cause cancerous vaginal and cervical growths in the daughters exposed to it before birth, because their mothers took the drug during pregnancy. The form of cancer from which these daughters suffer is known as adenocarcinoma, and it manifests itself after a minimum latent period of 10 or 12 years. It is a fast-spreading and deadly disease, and radical surgery is required to prevent it from spreading. DES also causes adenosis, precancerous vaginal and cervical growths which may spread to other areas of the body. The treatment for adenosis is cauterization, surgery, or cryosurgery. Women who suffer from this condition must be monitored by biopsy or colposcopic examination twice a year, a painful and expensive procedure. Thousands of women whose mothers received DES during pregnancy are unaware of the effects of the drug.

In 1971, the Food and Drug Administration ordered defendants to cease marketing and promoting DES for the purpose of preventing miscarriages, and to warn physicians and the public that the drug should not be used by pregnant women because of the danger to their unborn children.

During the period defendants marketed DES, they knew or should have known that it was a carcinogenic substance, that there was a grave danger after varying periods of latency it would cause cancerous and precancerous growths in the daughters of the mothers who took it, and that it was ineffective to prevent miscarriage. Nevertheless, defendants continued to advertise and market the drug as a miscarriage preventative. They failed to test DES for efficacy and safety; the tests performed by others, upon which they relied, indicated that it was not safe or effective. In violation of the authorization of the Food and Drug Administration, defendants marketed DES on an unlimited basis rather than as an experimental drug, and they failed to warn of its potential danger.

Because of defendants' advertised assurances that DES was safe and effective to prevent miscarriage, plaintiff was exposed to the drug prior to her birth. She became aware of the danger from such exposure within one year of the time she filed her complaint. As a result of the DES ingested by her mother, plaintiff developed a malignant bladder tumor which was removed by surgery. She suffers from adenosis and must constantly be monitored by biopsy or colposcopy to insure early warning of further malignancy. [. . .]

Defendants demurred to the complaint. While the complaint did not expressly allege that plaintiff could not identify the manufacturer of the precise drug ingested by her mother, she stated in her points and authorities in opposition to the demurrers filed by some of the defendants that she was unable to make the identification, and the trial court sustained the demurrers of these defendants without leave to amend on the ground that plaintiff did not and stated she could not identify which defendant had manufactured the drug responsible for her injuries. Thereupon, the court dismissed the action. This appeal involves only five of ten defendants named in the complaint. [One of the eleven original defendants had been dropped from the case when it was able to show that it had not manufactured DES during the period when the plaintiff's mother took the drug.] [. . .]

This case is but one of a number filed throughout the country seeking to hold drug manufacturers liable for injuries allegedly resulting from DES prescribed to the plaintiffs' mothers since 1947. According to a note in the Fordham Law Review, estimates of the number of women who took the drug during pregnancy range from 1½ million to 3 million. Hundreds, perhaps thousands, of the daughters of these women suffer from adenocarcinoma, and the incidence of vaginal adenosis among them is 30 to 90%. Most of the cases are still pending. With two exceptions, those that have been decided resulted in judgments in favor of the drug company defendants because of the failure of the plaintiffs to identify the manufacturer of the DES prescribed to their mothers. The same result was reached in a recent California case. The present action is another attempt to overcome this obstacle to recovery. [. . .]

Plaintiff places primary reliance upon cases which hold that if a party cannot identify which of two or more defendants caused an injury, the burden of proof may shift to the defendants to show that they were not responsible for the harm. This principle is sometimes referred to as the "alternative liability" theory. [The court then summarized the facts and holding of *Summers v. Tice*.] [. . .]

Defendants assert that these principles are inapplicable here. First, they insist that a predicate to shifting the burden of proof under *Summers-Ybarra* is that the defendants must have greater access to information regarding the cause of the injuries than the plaintiff, whereas in the present case the reverse appears.

Plaintiff does not claim that defendants are in a better position than she to identify the manufacturer of the drug taken by her mother or, indeed, that they have the ability to do so at all, but argues, rather, that *Summers* does not impose such a requirement as a condition to the shifting of the burden of proof. In this respect we believe plaintiff is correct.

In *Summers*, the circumstances of the accident themselves precluded an explanation of its cause. To be sure, *Summers* states that defendants are "(o)rdinarily . . . in a far better position to offer evidence to determine which one caused the injury" than a plaintiff, but the decision does not determine that this "ordinary" situation was present. Neither the facts nor the language of the opinion indicate that the two defendants, simultaneously shooting in the same direction, were in a better position than the plaintiff to ascertain whose shot caused the injury. As the opinion acknowledges, it was impossible for the trial court to determine whether the shot which entered the plaintiff's eye came from the gun of one defendant or the other. Nevertheless, burden of proof was shifted to the defendants.

Here, as in *Summers*, the circumstances of the injury appear to render identification of the manufacturer of the drug ingested by plaintiff's mother impossible by either plaintiff or defendants, and it cannot reasonably be said that one is in a better position than the other to make the identification. Because many years elapsed between the time the drug was taken and the manifestation of plaintiff's injuries she, and many other daughters of mothers who took DES, are unable to make such identification. [. . .]

On the other hand, it cannot be said with assurance that defendants have the means to make the identification. In this connection, they point out that drug manufacturers ordinarily have no direct contact with the patients who take a drug prescribed by their doctors. Defendants sell to wholesalers, who in turn supply the product to physicians and pharmacies. Manufacturers do not maintain records of the persons who take the drugs they produce, and the selection of the medication is made by the physician rather than the manufacturer. Nor do we conclude that the absence of evidence on this subject is due to the fault of defendants. While it is alleged that they produced a defective product with delayed effects and without adequate warnings, the difficulty or impossibility of identification results primarily from the passage of time rather than from their allegedly negligent acts of failing to provide adequate warnings. Thus *Haft v. Lone Palm Hotel*, upon which plaintiff relies, is distinguishable. [. . .]

Defendants maintain that, while in *Summers* there was a 50 percent chance that one of the two defendants was responsible for the plaintiff's injuries, here since any one of 200 companies which manufactured DES might have made the product which harmed plaintiff, there is no rational basis upon which to infer that any defendant in this action caused plaintiff's injuries, nor even a reasonable possibility that they were responsible.

These arguments are persuasive if we measure the chance that any one of the defendants supplied the injury-causing drug by the number of possible tortfeasors. In such a context, the possibility that any of the five defendants supplied the DES to plaintiff's mother is so remote that it would be unfair to require each defendant to exonerate itself. There may be a substantial likelihood that none of the five defendants joined in the action made the DES which caused the injury, and that the offending producer not named would escape liability altogether. While we propose, *infra*, an adaptation of the rule in *Summers* which will substantially overcome these difficulties, defendants appear to be correct that the rule, as previously applied, cannot relieve plaintiff of the burden of proving the identity of the manufacturer which made the drug causing her injuries. [. . .]

If we were confined to the theories of *Summers* [. . .], we would be constrained to hold that the judgment must be sustained. Should we require that plaintiff identify the manufacturer which supplied the DES used by her mother or that all DES manufacturers be joined in the action, she would effectively be precluded from any recovery. As defendants candidly admit, there is little likelihood that all the manufacturers who made DES at the time in question are still in business or that they are subject to the jurisdiction of the California courts. There are, however, forceful arguments in favor of holding that plaintiff has a cause of action.

In our contemporary complex industrialized society, advances in science and technology create fungible goods which may harm consumers and which cannot be traced to any specific producer. The response of the courts can be either to adhere rigidly to prior doctrine, denying recovery to those injured by such products, or to fashion remedies to meet these changing needs. [. . .]

Where, as here, all defendants produced a drug from an identical formula and the manufacturer of the DES which caused plaintiff's injuries cannot be identified through no fault of plaintiff, a modification of the rule of *Summers* is warranted. As we have seen, an undiluted *Summers* rationale is inappropriate to shift the burden of proof of causation to defendants because if we measure the chance that any particular manufacturer supplied the injury-causing product by the number of producers of DES, there is a possibility that none of the five defendants in this case produced the offending substance and that the responsible manufacturer, not named in the action, will escape liability.

But we approach the issue of causation from a different perspective: we hold it to be reasonable in the present context to measure the likelihood that any of the defendants supplied the product which allegedly injured plaintiff by the percentage which the DES sold by each of them for the purpose of preventing miscarriage bears to the entire production of the drug sold by all for that purpose. Plaintiff asserts in her briefs that Eli Lilly and Company and

5 or 6 other companies produced 90% of the DES marketed. If at trial this is established to be the fact, then there is a corresponding likelihood that this comparative handful of producers manufactured the DES which caused plaintiff's injuries, and only a 10% likelihood that the offending producer would escape liability.

If plaintiff joins in the action the manufacturers of a substantial share of the DES which her mother might have taken, the injustice of shifting the burden of proof to defendants to demonstrate that they could not have made the substance which injured plaintiff is significantly diminished. [...]

The presence in the action of a substantial share of the appropriate market also provides a ready means to apportion damages among the defendants. Each defendant will be held liable for the proportion of the judgment represented by its share of that market unless it demonstrates that it could not have made the product which caused plaintiff's injuries. In the present case, as we have seen, one DES manufacturer was dismissed from the action upon filing a declaration that it had not manufactured DES until after plaintiff was born. Once plaintiff has met her burden of joining the required defendants, they in turn may cross-complaint against other DES manufacturers, not joined in the action, which they can allege might have supplied the injury-causing product.

Under this approach, each manufacturer's liability would approximate its responsibility for the injuries caused by its own products. Some minor discrepancy in the correlation between market share and liability is inevitable; therefore, a defendant may be held liable for a somewhat different percentage of the damage than its share of the appropriate market would justify. It is probably impossible, with the passage of time, to determine market share with mathematical exactitude. But just as a jury cannot be expected to determine the precise relationship between fault and liability in applying the doctrine of comparative fault or partial indemnity, the difficulty of apportioning damages among the defendant producers in exact relation to their market share does not seriously militate against the rule we adopt. As we said in *Summers* with regard to the liability of independent tortfeasors, where a correct division of liability cannot be made "the trier of fact may make it the best it can."

We are not unmindful of the practical problems involved in defining the market and determining market share, but these are largely matters of proof which properly cannot be determined at the pleading stage of these proceedings. Defendants urge that it would be both unfair and contrary to public policy to hold them liable for plaintiff's injuries in the absence of proof that one of them supplied the drug responsible for the damage. Most of their arguments, however, are based upon the assumption that one manufacturer would be held responsible for the products of another or for those of all other manufacturers if plaintiff ultimately prevails. But under the rule we adopt, each manufacturer's liability for an injury would be approximately equivalent to the damages caused by the DES it manufactured.

The judgments are reversed.

RICHARDSON, J. (dissenting) — [. . .] It is readily apparent that "market share" liability will fall unevenly and disproportionately upon those manufacturers who are amenable to suit in California. On the assumption that no other state will adopt so radical a departure from traditional tort principles, it may be concluded that under the majority's reasoning those defendants who are brought to trial in this state will bear effective joint responsibility for 100% of plaintiffs' injuries despite the fact that their "substantial" aggregate market share may be considerably less. This undeniable fact forces the majority to concede that, "a defendant may be held liable for a somewhat different percentage of the damage than its share of the appropriate market would justify." With due deference, I suggest that the complete unfairness of such a result in a case involving only five of two hundred manufacturers is readily manifest.

Furthermore, several other important policy considerations persuade me that the majority holding is both inequitable and improper. The injustice inherent in the majority's new theory of liability is compounded by the fact that plaintiffs who use it are treated far more favorably than are the plaintiffs in routine tort actions. In most tort cases plaintiff knows the identity of the person who has caused his injuries. In such a case, plaintiff, of course, has no option to seek recovery from an entire industry or a "substantial" segment thereof, but in the usual instance can recover, if at all, only from the particular defendant causing injury. Such a defendant may or may not be either solvent or amenable to process. Plaintiff in the ordinary tort case must take a chance that defendant can be reached and can respond financially. On what principle should those plaintiffs who wholly fail to prove any causation, an essential element of the traditional tort cause of action, be rewarded by being offered both a wider selection of potential defendants and a greater opportunity for recovery?

The majority attempts to justify its new liability on the ground that defendants herein are "better able to bear the cost of injury resulting from the manufacture of a defective product." This "deep pocket" theory of liability, fastening liability on defendants presumably because they are rich, has understandable popular appeal and might be tolerable in a case disclosing substantially stronger evidence of causation than herein appears. But as a general proposition, a defendant's wealth is an unreliable indicator of fault, and should play no part, at least consciously, in the legal analysis of the problem. In the absence of proof that a particular defendant caused or at least probably caused plaintiff's injuries, a defendant's ability to bear the cost thereof is no more pertinent to the underlying issue of liability than its "substantial" share of the relevant market. A system priding itself on "equal justice under law" does not flower when the liability as well as the damage aspect of a tort action is determined by a defendant's wealth. The inevitable consequence of such a result is to create and perpetuate two rules of law one applicable to wealthy defendants, and another standard pertaining to defendants who are poor or who have modest means. Moreover, considerable doubts have been expressed regarding the ability of the drug industry, and especially its smaller members, to bear the substantial economic costs (from both damage awards and high insurance premiums) inherent in imposing an industry-wide liability. [. . .]

I would affirm the judgments of dismissal.

NOTES

1. *Choice of weapons*. What is the difference between market share liability under *Sindell* and alternative liability under *Summers v. Tice*? If you were a defendant, which theory would you prefer to see used against you?

2. *Market share liability*. *Sindell* proved to be a highly influential decision. Many other states (not all) have followed suit in allowing market share liability in DES cases, though rarely elsewhere; the approach has been rejected in claims involving injuries caused by asbestos and lead paint. The details of the regimes that do allow market share liability vary in how they respond to various problems; consider how they should best be resolved:

a. Should the relevant market be the national or local one? Suppose that the plaintiff now lives in California, but that her mother took DES years earlier while living in New York. If a court is to use market share liability, should it assign liability to the defendant companies based on the size of the shares they held of the New York market, the California market, the national market, or by some other measure?

b. Should defendants be able to exonerate themselves in individual cases? Suppose, for example, that in one of the "market share" cases brought after *Sindell*, the plaintiff's mother remembers only that she took red pills; and suppose that one of the defendants, the Squibb firm, can show that it never made pills of that color. Should Squibb be dismissed from the case or should it still be required to contribute to a share of the plaintiff's damage award in proportion to its share of the market?

c. How large a total share of the market must all the defendants represent before they can be held liable on a market share theory? Suppose that after *Sindell* a plaintiff sues just one manufacturer — Eli Lilly, let us imagine. As usual, the plaintiff does not know whether Lilly made the DES that her mother ingested; all she can show is that Lilly had a 10 percent share of the relevant market. Should the plaintiff be able to proceed with her case and collect some of her damages from Lilly? What if the plaintiff sues four defendants who, taken together, had a 60 percent share of the market?

For discussion and one state's resolution of some of these questions, see *Hymowitz v. Eli Lilly & Co.*, 539 N.E.2d 1069 (N.Y. 1989).

3. *Legislatures vs. courts.* Courts rejecting market share liability often describe its adoption as a question for the state legislature. Thus in Mulcahy v. Eli Lilly & Co., 386 N.W.2d 67 (Iowa 1987), the court called market share liability "social engineering more appropriately within the legislative domain." And in Goldman v. Johns-Manville Sales Corp., 514 N.E.2d 691 (Ohio 1987), the court said:

> The imposition of liability upon a manufacturer for harm that it may not have caused is the very legal legerdemain, at least by our long held traditional standards, that we believe the courts should avoid unless prior warnings remain unheeded. It is an act more closely identified as a function assigned to the legislature under its power to enact laws.

What is the difference between legal innovations suitable for adoption by courts and those better left to legislatures?

4. *The seven fragrances.* In Sanderson v. International Flavors and Fragrances, Inc., 950 F. Supp. 981 (C.D. Cal. 1996), a woman brought a products liability action against manufacturers of perfumes and colognes for injuries allegedly caused by her exposure to various perfumes: Boss, Drakkar Noir, Joop! Homme, Stetson, Freesia, and Calvin Klein's Obsession ("the seven fragrances"). The plaintiff alleged that her exposure to the aldehydes in the fragrance products on over 16,000 occasions contributed to injuries including encelopathy (brain damage) and dysosmia (deranged sense of smell). Because Sanderson was unable to identify which of the seven fragrances caused her injuries, she asked the court to extend the market share theory of causation to her case. The court gave summary judgment to the defendants, finding that "plaintiff cannot shift the causation burden to defendants under *Sindell*, because plaintiff was not injured by a fungible product made by many different manufacturers and because plaintiff has in any event not joined a substantial share of the market for the products that she alleges injured her."

In deciding whether to apply market share liability, why is it important that the defendants' products be "fungible"? Why might it be important that the defendants represent a substantial share of the market? The plaintiff also attempted to rely on *Summers v. Tice*; the attempt failed. Why?

5. *Blood products (problem).* In Smith v. Cutter Biological, Inc., 823 P.2d 717 (Haw. 1991), the plaintiff was a hemophiliac. He alleged that he contracted the HIV virus, and then AIDS, from contaminated blood products supplied to him at an army hospital. The hospital dispensed blood provided by four manufacturers; the plaintiff was not able to identify which of them was the source of the contaminated batch. He sued all four, claiming that market share liability should be used to resolve the problem of causation. His argument was that during the time period when the blood products at issue were being manufactured, the defendants committed similar failures to screen donors and warn recipients. What result, and why?

6. *Managing uncertainty.* What do *Ybarra v. Spangard, Herskovits v. Group Health Cooperative, Summers v. Tice,* and *Sindell v. Abbott Laboratories* have in common? Compare what we know and what we don't know in each case, and consider how each might be understood as a response to a slightly different problem of uncertainty.

7. *Extending the principle.* Interesting problems of causation were raised by lawsuits against Merck, the manufacturer of the painkilling drug Vioxx, when evidence emerged that the drug could sometimes produce heart attacks. Merck removed the drug from the market in 2004; some industry analysts argued that it should have been removed earlier. More than 10,000 lawsuits were filed against Merck. As recounted in Issacharoff, *Private Claims, Aggregate Rights,* _____ S. Ct. Rev. (2008):

> The critical issue — basically not disputed — was that Vioxx exposure over a prolonged period resulted in some increased number of heart attacks and strokes among the exposed population. The problem is that neither cardiac event is a signature injury, one that can be traced with any certainty to Vioxx consumption as opposed to a host of other genetic or environmental causes. Put another way, the only proof of harm from Vioxx was epidemiological, which meant that even a threshold determination of liability in any individual case could only be established probabilistically by reference to the entire exposed population. Moreover, because of the extensive reliance on contested expert testimony, these cases were likely to be expensive to prosecute.
>
> Under the customary working of our tort system, these cases should have been tried on a one-at-a-time basis and one would have expected discordant results. In theory, all plaintiffs could have lost their claims because even the elevated levels of cardiac risk following Vioxx exposure could not make causation more likely than not, presumably the standard necessary to survive summary judgment. In reality, however, an otherwise healthy athlete who has an unexplained heart attack after taking Vioxx is likely to get to the jury in many if not most jurisdictions. As cases began to trickle through the litigation pipeline, a total of 18 were tried to judgment prior to the national settlement. Of these, Merck won 13 and plaintiffs won 5, though some were later reversed on appeal. In those cases that Merck lost, juries awarded large compensatory damages and sweeping punitive damages. The most salient result was that despite relying on common epidemiological evidence, some plaintiffs received nothing, while others were awarded millions.

Would market share liability have been a reasonable response to this situation? How about liability for loss of a chance, or some other departure from the traditional causation requirements? If no good solution were possible in court, can you imagine a sensible way for Merck and the plaintiffs to reach terms on a settlement?

C.   A NOTE ON APPORTIONMENT

The parts of the chapter just considered have involved lawsuits brought against multiple defendants, all of whom may sometimes have been held liable. What rules should govern the plaintiff's ability to collect damages from each of them? These commonly are labeled problems of *apportionment*. Suppose one automobile knocks the plaintiff down and another car then runs him over. He sues the two drivers for negligence. Both are found liable and the plaintiff's compensatory damages are set at $1 million. If it is possible to distinguish between the injuries caused by each of the two drivers, then the defendants' respective liabilities will be limited to the harm for which each is to blame. But if the plaintiff's injury is "indivisible" — in other words, if it is impossible to tell which defendant caused which part of the injury — the defendants are considered "joint tortfeasors"; and the common law doctrine of *joint and several liability* then provides that the plaintiff can collect the entire $1 million from either defendant. Moreover, at common law a defendant from whom the $1 million was collected would have no right to seek reimbursement from other defendants. An attempt to obtain such reimbursement is called a suit for "contribution," and the common law did not allow suits for contribution between joint tortfeasors. At least in part, however, both of these traditional rules have been modified by legislatures in every state. Courts today are more likely to hold defendants responsible only for a portion of the damages that reflects their share of responsibility for an accident, and defendants also are able to ensure that outcome through suits for contribution. Here is a sketch of the details.

1.   *The Decline of Joint and Several Liability*

Joint and several liability means that each defendant is liable for all of the plaintiff's damages. The rule takes on obvious importance in a regime where contribution between tortfeasors is not possible, because in that case one defendant may get stuck paying all the damages while any others pay nothing. But even in a regime where contribution is available, the same result can occur if one of the parties is insolvent: the plaintiff simply collects the entire award from the solvent defendant, who has no recourse as a practical matter even if his share of blame for the plaintiff's injuries was only, say, 10 percent. Such a result may seem inequitable; then again, if the plaintiff cannot collect all the damages from the solvent tortfeasor, it is the innocent plaintiff who will end up bearing 90 percent of the costs of the accident without compensation — and this may seem inequitable as well. One way to look at joint and several liability is that it allocates the risk of an insolvent defendant to other defendants rather than to the plaintiff, who is guaranteed to be able to collect full compensation if any defendant can pay it.

Joint and several liability has an all-or-nothing spirit that allies it with contributory negligence, the common law rule that denied recovery to plaintiffs
whose own negligence contributed at all to their own injuries. The decline
of joint and several liability likewise has been connected with the rise of
comparative negligence, which calls for juries to compare and apportion
responsibility for an accident between plaintiff and defendant. Comparative
negligence has come by many to be seen as inconsistent with a rule requiring
any one defendant to pay all of the plaintiff's damages regardless of his degree
of responsibility. The result was that most states, typically in the 1980s, abolished joint and several liability entirely or with respect to particular types of
cases, replacing it with *several* liability — i.e., liability limited to a defendant's
share of responsibility for the plaintiff's injuries.

The resulting legal landscape does not lend itself to generalizations. Perhaps
a dozen states have abolished joint and several liability outright in favor of
several liability; about the same number have abolished the doctrine for defendants less than 50 percent responsible for the plaintiff's damages. Some other
states provide for joint and several liability only if the plaintiff is not at all at
fault, or have retained the doctrine only with respect to certain torts, or only
with respect to "economic" damages, or only with respect to certain types of
defendants (as where injurers and their employers may both be held jointly
and severally liable). According to the Third Restatement, 16 states have
retained pure joint and several liability.

As an example of the consequences of these rules, consider *Gehres v. City of
Phoenix*, 753 P.2d 174 (Ariz. App. 1987). A man named Speck drank heavily at
a nightclub and then drove off in his car. When a Phoenix police officer
attempted to pull him over, Speck fled; a chase ensued in which Speck
drove at speeds of over 90 miles per hour. At last Speck drove into a car
occupied by the plaintiff's decedent, Violet Gehres. Speck and Gehres
both died in the collision. Gehres's husband sued Speck's estate, the nightclub,
and the City of Phoenix, claiming that each defendant had negligently contributed to the accident. A jury found Speck 95 percent responsible, the
nightclub 3 percent responsible, and the city 2 percent responsible; and it
set the plaintiff's damages at $577,600. Speck's estate was insolvent, however,
so the plaintiff collected the entire award from the nightclub and the city. The
Arizona Court of Appeals held this the correct result under common law
principles of joint and several liability.

Partly in response to this outcome, the Arizona legislature later amended its
laws to eliminate joint liability. Instead, the fault of all tortfeasors — whether or
not they are parties to the case — now is compared and each defendant is
severally liable for damages allocated "in direct proportion to that defendant's
percentage of fault." Ariz. Rev. St. §12-2506(A); *Larsen v. Nissan Motor Corp.*,
978 P.2d 119 (Ariz. App. 1999). In *Larsen* the plaintiff was injured when the
car in which she was a passenger rolled over. She sued the car's manufacturer
but not the driver, because he was her employer and so was immune from suit
under Arizona law. The jury found Nissan 8 percent responsible and the driver

92 percent responsible. The plaintiff thus was able to collect 8 percent of her damages from the defendant. Which result — *Gehres* or *Larsen* — seems preferable?

2. Contribution

The rule forbidding contribution between joint tortfeasors evidently was developed in cases where defendants acted in concert to commit intentional torts (see, e.g., *Merryweather v. Nixan*, 101 Eng. Rep. 1337 (1799)); the courts in such cases did not want to aid wrongdoers in working out a more equitable distribution of their losses between them. In most jurisdictions the rule nevertheless came to be applied to joint tortfeasors of all types until the second half of the twentieth century. All states then abandoned the rule by statute, initially favoring rules that held all defendants equally responsible for a plaintiff's injuries. Thus if a plaintiff collected an entire damage award from the first of three defendants, the first could then sue the other two for contribution and obtain reimbursement from each of them for a third of the amount paid. Again, however, the advent of comparative negligence has had its influence; now in most jurisdictions defendants can be sued for contribution in proportion to their share of responsibility for an accident, so that a defendant held to be 10 percent at fault can be required to pay 10 percent of the damages to a fellow defendant in a suit for contribution.

3. Complications

The greatest current difficulties in the law of apportionment involve cases with multiple defendants who are not on the same legal footing. For example, where one defendant has committed an intentional act while the other has committed negligence, the courts have not yet settled on a formula for apportioning damages between them; nor is there a uniform answer when one defendant is before the court while another is absent because it has immunity or cannot be found. Suppose, for example, that a worker is injured in an accident for which two parties are equally to blame: the plaintiff's employer and a visitor to the plaintiff's workplace. The employer is immune from suit under the prevailing workers' compensation statute; the plaintiff therefore sues only the visitor. Should the visitor's liability be capped at half the plaintiff's damages, or should the visitor be held liable for all the damages because there is no other defendant in the picture? While courts are divided in their handling of this problem, the trend in such circumstances is to instruct the jurors to determine the share of blame attributable to the defendant in front of them, and to take into account the responsibility of other tortfeasors even if they have not been joined as parties. Thus it becomes in the defendant's interest to argue that the absent parties are to blame for the plaintiff's injuries, while the plaintiff tends to argue the contrary.

Another family of complications arises in cases where one defendant settles with the plaintiff out of court while another defendant goes forward with litigation. Joint and several liability made this situation problematic, since the plaintiff still would seem able to collect the whole judgment from the defendant who went to court, and that defendant still would seem able to pursue contribution (once contribution was allowed) from the joint tortfeasor who settled. The traditional rule in many jurisdictions was that settlement earlier did not protect a defendant from having to pay contribution later. This rule was much criticized as discouraging settlements; an alternative since adopted by many states takes the contrary approach, providing that defendants who settle are immune from claims for contribution (the "settlement bar" rule). What effect would you expect *this* rule to have on the rate of settlement?

The rise of comparative negligence and apportionment among tortfeasors has brought with it an alternative to both of the rules just described: the settling defendant cannot be sued for contribution by a defendant who stays in the case, but the defendant who stays in is entitled to a credit to reflect the plaintiff's recovery from the settler. One approach — a "pro tanto" credit — simply reduces the damages the plaintiff is entitled to collect in court by whatever amount the settling defendant already paid. A second approach — a "pro rata" credit, also known as a "comparative share" credit — subtracts from the damages awarded to the plaintiff the fraction for which the jury determines the settling defendant was responsible. So suppose Defendant A settles with the plaintiff while Defendant B goes to trial. The jury finds Defendants A 60 percent responsible for the plaintiff's injuries, finds Defendant B 40 percent responsible, and sets the plaintiff's damages at $100,000. Under the pro rata approach, the plaintiff thus can collect $40,000 from Defendant B — not the $100,000 normally permitted in a regime of joint and several liability. Defendant A is unaffected: if he already settled for $20,000, the plaintiff made an unfortunate bargain and is stuck with it; if Defendant A settled for $200,000, then naturally he will have regrets but again they count for nothing. Defendant B still pays his $40,000.

Again, these complications all are a function of joint and several liability along with the contribution rules that states devised to go with that regime. When jurisdictions use several liability, as is increasingly common, the problems we have been considering generally go away. The court simply uses the last approach just described: the jury determines the share of responsibility of every tortfeasor, whether or not each is a party to the case; those defendants who are parties to the case pay a share of the plaintiff's damages commensurate with their responsibility for the plaintiff's injuries. Parties who settled are unaffected. There is no need for suits for contribution where several liability applies, as each party who goes to court pays no more than the share for which it is responsible in the first place.

4. Examples

The defendants in *Summers v. Tice* were held jointly and severally liable. In the DES cases applying market share liability, however, the courts have imposed liability that is several only. The California Supreme Court offered this analysis of the difference between several liability and the joint and several variety in the market share setting:

> The consequences of these methods of determining liability are markedly different. If [defendants] are jointly and severally liable, a plaintiff may recover the entire amount of the judgment from any of the defendants joined in the action. Since the plaintiff is required under *Sindell* to join the manufacturers of only a substantial share of the appropriate market for DES, it follows that if joint liability were the rule, a defendant could be held responsible for a portion of the judgment that may greatly exceed the percentage of its market share. Under several liability, in contrast, because each defendant's liability for the judgment would be confined to the percentage of its share of the market, a plaintiff would not recover the entire amount of the judgment (except in the unlikely event that all manufacturers were joined in the action) but only the percentage of the sum awarded that is equal to the market shares of the defendants joined in the action. In the one case, it would be the plaintiff who would bear the loss resulting from the fact that some producers of DES that might have been found liable under the market share theory were not joined in the action (or if a defendant became insolvent), whereas in the other such losses would fall on the defendants. Since, as we pointed out in *Sindell*, there is little likelihood that all manufacturers of DES in the appropriate market would be amenable to suit, the adoption of one or the other basis for liability could significantly affect the amount of a plaintiff's recovery and, concomitantly, a defendant's liability. [. . .]
>
> In creating the market share doctrine, this court attempted to fashion a remedy for persons injured by a drug taken by their mothers a generation ago, making identification of the manufacturer impossible in many cases. We realized that in order to provide relief to an injured DES daughter faced with this dilemma, we would have to allow recovery of damages against some defendants who may not have manufactured the drug that caused the damage. To protect such defendants against excessive liability, we considered and rejected three separate theories of liability suggested by the plaintiff, and formulated, instead, the market share concept.
>
> We explained the basis of the doctrine as follows: In order to decrease the likelihood that a manufacturer of DES would be held liable for injuries caused by products not of its making, and to achieve a reasonable approximation of its responsibility for injuries caused by the DES it produced, the plaintiff should be required to join in the action the manufacturers of a substantial share of the relevant DES market. If this were

done, the injustice of shifting the burden of proof to defendants to exonerate themselves of responsibility for the plaintiff's injuries would be diminished. Each defendant would be held liable for the proportion of the judgment represented by its market share, and its overall liability for injuries caused by DES would approximate the injuries caused by the DES it manufactured. A DES manufacturer found liable under this approach would not be held responsible for injuries caused by another producer of the drug. The opinion acknowledged that only an approximation of a manufacturer's liability could be achieved by this procedure, but underlying our holding was a recognition that such a result was preferable to denying recovery altogether to plaintiffs injured by DES.

It is apparent that the imposition of joint liability on defendants in a market share action would be inconsistent with this rationale. Any defendant could be held responsible for the entire judgment even though its market share may have been comparatively insignificant. Liability would in the first instance be measured not by the likelihood of responsibility for the plaintiff's injuries but by the financial ability of a defendant to undertake payment of the entire judgment or a large portion of it. A defendant that paid a larger percentage of the judgment than warranted by its market share would have the burden of seeking indemnity from other defendants, and it would bear the loss if producers of DES that might have been held liable in the action were not amenable to suit, or if a codefendant was bankrupt. In short, the imposition of joint liability among defendant manufacturers in a market share action would frustrate *Sindell*'s goal of achieving a balance between the interests of DES plaintiffs and manufacturers of the drug.

Brown v. Superior Court, 751 P.2d 470 (Cal. 1988).

Chapter 6

Proximate Causation

A. REMOTENESS AND FORESEEABILITY

In re Polemis
3 K.B. 560 (1921)

[Polemis was owner of the Greek steamship *Thrasyvoulos*. He and his partner chartered the ship to the defendants. In the summer of 1917, while the ship was in the defendants' care, it arrived in Casablanca with a cargo of gasoline. Some of the gasoline had leaked, creating flammable vapors in the ship's hold. The defendants' agents spread planks over the opening of a hatch on the ship, using them as a platform on which to lower the cargo after it was lifted out of the hold with a winch. One of the ropes used to operate the winch came into contact with one of the planks and caused the plank to fall into the hold; an explosion and fire immediately followed, and the ship was completely destroyed.

[A panel of arbitrators found the following facts: "(a) that the ship was lost by fire; (b) that the fire arose from a spark igniting petrol vapour in the hold; (c) that the spark was caused by the falling board coming into contact with some substance in the hold; (d) that the fall of the board was caused by the negligence of the Arabs engaged in the work of discharging; (e) that the said Arabs were employed by the charterers or their agents and were the servants of the charterers; (f) that the causing of the spark could not reasonably have been anticipated from the falling of the board, though some damage to the ship might reasonably have been anticipated." The legal question of the defendants' responsibility on these facts then came to the House of Lords, which affirmed a full award of damages to the plaintiffs.]

BANKES, L.J. According to the one view [in the case law], the consequences which may reasonably be expected to result from a particular act are material

351

only in reference to the question of whether the act is or is not a negligent act; according to the other view, those consequences are the test of whether the damages resulting from the act (assuming it to be negligent) are or are not too remote to be recoverable. [. . .] In the present case the Arbitrators have found as a fact that the falling of the plank was due to the negligence of the defendants' servants. The fire appears to me to have been directly caused by the falling of the plank. Under these circumstances I consider that it is immaterial that the causing of the spark by the falling of the plank could not have been reasonably anticipated. The appellants' junior Counsel sought to draw a distinction between the anticipation of the extent of damage resulting from a negligent act, and the anticipation of the type of damage resulting from such an act. He admitted that it could not lie in the mouth of a person whose negligent act had caused damage to say that he could not reasonably have foreseen the extent of the damage, but he contended that the negligent person was entitled to rely upon the fact that he could not have reasonably anticipated the type of damage which resulted from his negligent act. I do not think that the distinction can be admitted. Given the breach of duty which constitutes the negligence, and given the damage as a direct result of that negligence, the anticipations of the person whose negligent act has produced the damage appear to me to be irrelevant. I consider that the damages claimed are not too remote.

SCRUTTON, L.J. To determine whether an act is negligent, it is relevant to determine whether any reasonable person would foresee that the act would cause damage; if he would not, the act is not negligent. But if the act would or might probably cause damage, the fact that the damage it in fact causes is not the exact kind of damage one would expect is immaterial, so long as the damage is in fact caused sufficiently directly by the negligent act, and not by the operation of independent causes having no connection with the negligent act, except that they could not avoid its results. Once the act is negligent, the fact that its exact operation was not foreseen is immaterial. [. . .] In the present case it was negligent in discharging cargo to knock down the planks of the temporary staging, for they might easily cause some damage either to workmen or cargo in the ship. The fact that they did directly produce an unexpected result, a spark in an atmosphere of petrol vapour which caused a fire, does not relieve the person who was negligent from the damage which his negligent act directly caused.

Overseas Tankship (U.K.) Ltd. v. Morts Dock & Engineering Co., Ltd. [The Wagon Mound (No. 1)]
[1961] A.C. 388 (Privy Council)

[The defendants were owners of the S.S. *Wagon Mound*. Oil being pumped into the ship in Sydney harbor spilled into the bay; the *Wagon Mound* then headed to sea without making any effort to disperse the oil, which was carried to the plaintiffs' wharf and at first caused only minor damage there. The plaintiffs, who had been repairing another ship at the time, suspended their operations until they satisfied themselves that the oil in the water was not flammable. Two days later, however, the oil did catch fire, and the fire severely damaged the wharf and two boats docked alongside it. The trial judge found that the fire started when molten metal fell from the plaintiff's wharf onto a rag or other piece of oily cotton refuse floating in the water, which in turn acted as a wick to ignite the oil. The trial judge also made this critical finding: "The *raison d'etre* of furnace oil is, of course, that it shall burn, but I find that the defendant did not know, and could not reasonably be expected to have known, that it was capable of being set on fire when spread on water."]

Viscount Simonds. There can be no doubt that the decision of the Court of Appeal in *Polemis* plainly asserts that, if the defendant is guilty of negligence, he is responsible for all the consequences whether reasonably foreseeable or not. The generality of the proposition is perhaps qualified by the fact that each of the Lords Justices refers to the outbreak of fire as the direct result of the negligent act. There is thus introduced the conception that the negligent actor is not responsible for consequences which are not "direct", whatever that may mean.

[The Privy Council then reviewed a series of other cases that had preceded *In re Polemis* and said that "[t]he impression that may well be left on the reader of the scores of cases in which liability for negligence has been discussed is that the courts were feeling their way to a coherent body of doctrine and were at times in grave danger of being led astray by scholastic theories of causation and their ugly and barely intelligible jargon." The case law following *Polemis* likewise was reviewed, and the following conclusions reached.]

Enough has been said to show that the authority of *Polemis* has been severely shaken though lip-service has from time to time been paid to it. In their Lordships' opinion it should no longer be regarded as good law. It is not probable that many cases will for that reason have a different result, though it is hoped that the law will be thereby simplified, and that in some cases, at least, palpable injustice will be avoided. For it does not seem consonant with current ideas of justice or morality that for an act of negligence, however slight or venial, which results in some trivial foreseeable damage the actor should be liable for all consequences however unforeseeable and however grave, so long as they can be said to be "direct." It is a principle of civil liability, subject only to qualifications which have no present relevance, that a man must be considered to be responsible for the probable consequences of his act. To demand more of him is too harsh a rule, to demand less is to ignore that civilised order requires the observance of a minimum standard of behaviour.

This concept applied to the slowly developing law of negligence has led to a great variety of expressions which can, as it appears to their Lordships, be harmonised with little difficulty with the single exception of the so-called rule in *Polemis*. For, if it is asked why a man should be responsible for the natural or necessary or probable consequences of his act (or any other similar description of them) the answer is that it is not because they are natural or necessary or probable, but because, since they have this quality, it is judged by the standard of the reasonable man that he ought to have foreseen them. Thus it is that over and over again it has happened that in different judgments in the same case, and sometimes in a single judgment, liability for a consequence has been imposed on the ground that it was reasonably foreseeable or, alternatively, on the ground that it was natural or necessary or probable. The two grounds have been treated as coterminous, and so they largely are. But, where they are not, the question arises to which the wrong answer was given in *Polemis*. For, if some limitation must be imposed upon the consequences for which the negligent actor is to be held responsible — and all are agreed that some limitation there must be — why should that test (reasonable foreseeability) be rejected which, since he is judged by what the reasonable man ought to foresee, corresponds with the common conscience of mankind, and a test (the "direct" consequence) be substituted which leads to no-where but the never-ending and insoluble problems of causation. "The lawyer," said Sir Frederick Pollock, "cannot afford to adventure himself with philosophers in the logical and metaphysical controversies that beset the idea of cause." Yet this is just what he has most unfortunately done and must continue to do if the rule in *Polemis* is to prevail. [. . .]

In the same connection may be mentioned the conclusion to which the Full Court finally came in the present case. Applying the rule in *Polemis* and holding therefore that the unforeseeability of the damage by fire afforded no defence, they went on to consider the remaining question. Was it a "direct" consequence? Upon this Manning J. said: "Notwithstanding that, if regard is had separately to each individual occurrence in the chain of events that led to this fire, each occurrence was improbable and, in one sense, improbability was heaped upon improbability, I cannot escape from the conclusion that if the ordinary man in the street had been asked, as a matter of common sense, without any detailed analysis of the circumstances, to state the cause of the fire at Mort's Dock, he would unhesitatingly have assigned such cause to spillage of oil by the appellant's employees." Perhaps he would, and probably he would have added: "I never should have thought it possible." But with great respect to the Full Court this is surely irrelevant, or, if it is relevant, only serves to show that the *Polemis* rule works in a very strange way. After the event even a fool is wise. But it is not the hindsight of a fool; it is the foresight of the reasonable man which alone can determine responsibility. The *Polemis* rule by substituting "direct" for "reasonably foreseeable" consequence leads to a conclusion equally illogical and unjust.

Their Lordships conclude this part of the case with some general observations. They have been concerned primarily to displace the proposition that unforeseeability is irrelevant if damage is "direct." In doing so they have inevitably insisted that the essential factor in determining liability is whether the damage is of such a kind as the reasonable man should have foreseen. This accords with the general view thus stated by Lord Atkin in *Donoghue v. Stevenson*: "The liability for negligence, whether you style it such or treat it as in other systems as a species of 'culpa,' is no doubt based upon a general public sentiment of moral wrongdoing for which the offender must pay." It is a departure from this sovereign principle if liability is made to depend solely on the damage being the "direct" or "natural" consequence of the precedent act. Who knows or can be assumed to know all the processes of nature? But if it would be wrong that a man should be held liable for damage unpredictable by a reasonable man because it was "direct" or "natural," equally it would be wrong that he should escape liability, however "indirect" the damage, if he foresaw or could reasonably foresee the intervening events which led to its being done. Thus foreseeability becomes the effective test.

Their Lordships will humbly advise Her Majesty that this appeal should be allowed, and the respondents' action so far as it related to damage caused by the negligence of the appellants be dismissed with costs.

NOTES

1. *The sequel.* In Overseas Tankship (U.K.) Ltd. v. The Miller Steamship Co. [1967] (Wagon Mound No. 2), 1 A.C. 617, the owners of the *Wagon Mound* were sued again, this time by the owners of one of the ships destroyed in the fire. This sequel to the first Wagon Mound case illustrates the role of lawyers and litigation strategy play in framing the issues that courts decide. Recall that the trial judge in the first Wagon Mound case had found that the defendants "did not know and could not reasonably be expected to have known that [the oil] was capable of being set afire when spread on water." In the second case, however, the findings of the trial court were a bit milder; the court found that the defendants would have regarded the oil as "very difficult to ignite on water," but not impossible, and that they probably would have considered such a fire "rare" but not unheard of.

It may seem odd that the same conduct by the same defendants produced these different findings in the two trials, but Reid, J., stressed that this did not imply any failing on the part of the plaintiffs in the first case. Those plaintiffs had to worry that if the possibility of a fire had been held foreseeable, they themselves might have been found negligent in continuing the repairs at their wharf once they saw the oil there — and their contributory negligence would have been a complete bar to any recovery from the owners of the *Wagon Mound*. The plaintiffs in this second case did not have that problem, as they had no role in starting the fire and had committed no acts that could be considered negligent. They therefore had a stronger incentive to prove that the danger of fire from the spilled oil was in fact foreseeable, which they succeeded in doing to the small extent described above — and this small proof of foreseeability turned out to be enough to change the result in the case. The trial court gave judgment to the defendants, but the Privy Council reversed:

> In the present case the evidence shows that the discharge of so much oil on to the water must have taken a considerable time, and a vigilant ship's engineer would have noticed the discharge at an early stage. The findings show that he ought to have known that it is possible to ignite this kind of oil on water, and that the ship's engineer probably ought to have known that this had in fact happened before. The most that can be said to justify inaction is that he would have known that this could only happen in very exceptional circumstances; but that does not mean that a reasonable man would dismiss such risk from his mind and do nothing when it was so easy to prevent it. If it is clear that the reasonable man would have realised or foreseen and prevented the risk, then it must follow that the appellants are liable in damages.

2. *An American entry into the fray.* In Petition of Kinsman Transit Co., 338 F.2d 708 (2d Cir. 1964), a steamboat, the *Shiras*, was moored to a dock on the Buffalo River owned by the Continental Grain Company. A thaw caused large chunks of ice to come loose in one of the river's tributaries, and some of the ice drifted toward Continental's dock and piled up between the *Shiras* and the shore. The resulting pressure created by the ice caused the boat to come loose from Continental's "deadman" (the post in the ground to which the boat had been anchored). The *Shiras* floated downstream and collided with another anchored ship, the *Tewksbury*, causing it to become unmoored as well. Half an hour later the *Tewksbury* drifted into a drawbridge in downtown Buffalo, bringing down one of the bridge's towers. The *Shiras* entered the wreckage shortly thereafter, and the two ships wedged together to create a dam; together they were nearly 1,000 feet long. Soon the bridge's other tower fell down as well, and the banks of the river flooded for several miles.

The resulting claims of liability ran in several directions. One of them was that Continental negligently had maintained its deadman, which in turn had caused the *Shiras* to come loose and led to all the resulting damage. The trial court agreed that the deadman was inadequately secured and as a result held Continental liable for a share of the flood damage claimed by some 20 different plaintiffs. The court of appeals affirmed on this point. Said Friendly, J.:

> It was indeed foreseeable that the improper construction and lack of inspection of the "deadman" might cause a ship to break loose and damage persons and property on or near the river — that was what made Continental's conduct negligent. With the aid of hindsight one can also say that a prudent man, carefully pondering the problem, would have realized that the danger of this would be greatest under such water conditions as developed during the night of January 21, 1959, and that if a

vessel should break loose under those circumstances, events might transpire as they did. But such post hoc step by step analysis would render "foreseeable" almost anything that has in fact occurred; if the argument relied upon has legal validity, it ought not be circumvented by characterizing as foreseeable what almost no one would in fact have foreseen at the time.

The effect of unforeseeability of damage upon liability for negligence has recently been considered by the Judicial Committee of the Privy Council, *Overseas Tankship (U.K.) Ltd. v. Morts Dock & Engineering Co. (The Wagon Mound),* (1961) 1 All E.R. 404. The Committee there disapproved the proposition, thought to be supported by *Polemis and Furness, Withy & Co. Ltd.,* (1921) 3 K.B. 560 (C.A.), "that unforeseeability is irrelevant if damage is 'direct.'" We have no difficulty with the result of *The Wagon Mound,* in view of the finding, 1 All E.R. at 407, that the appellant had no reason to believe that the floating furnace oil would burn. On that view the decision simply applies the principle which excludes liability where the injury sprang from a hazard different from that which was improperly risked. Although some language in the judgment goes beyond this, we would find it difficult to understand why one who had failed to use the care required to protect others in the light of expectable forces should be exonerated when the very risks that rendered his conduct negligent produced other and more serious consequences to such persons than were fairly foreseeable when he fell short of what the law demanded. Foreseeability of danger is necessary to render conduct negligent; where as here the damage was caused by just those forces whose existence required the exercise of greater care than was taken — the current, the ice, and the physical mass of the Shiras, the incurring of consequences other and greater than foreseen does not make the conduct less culpable or provide a reasoned basis for insulation. The oft encountered argument that failure to limit liability to foreseeable consequences may subject the defendant to a loss wholly out of proportion to his fault seems scarcely consistent with the universally accepted rule that the defendant takes the plaintiff as he finds him and will be responsible for the full extent of the injury even though a latent susceptibility of the plaintiff renders this far more serious than could reasonably have been anticipated.

The weight of authority in this country rejects the limitation of damages to consequences foreseeable at the time of the negligent conduct when the consequences are "direct," and the damage, although other and greater than expectable, is of the same general sort that was risked. [. . .] Other American courts, purporting to apply a test of foreseeability to damages, extend that concept to such unforeseen lengths as to raise serious doubt whether the concept is meaningful; indeed, we wonder whether the British courts are not finding it necessary to limit the language of *The Wagon Mound* as we have indicated.

We see no reason why an actor engaging in conduct which entails a large risk of small damage and a small risk of other and greater damage, of the same general sort, from the same forces, and to the same class of persons, should be relieved of responsibility for the latter simply because the chance of its occurrence, if viewed alone, may not have been large enough to require the exercise of care. By hypothesis, the risk of the lesser harm was sufficient to render his disregard of it actionable; the existence of a less likely additional risk that the very forces against whose action he was required to guard would produce other and greater damage than could have been reasonably anticipated should inculpate him further rather than limit his liability. This does not mean that the careless actor will always be held for all damages for which the forces that he risked were a cause in fact. Somewhere a point will be reached when courts will agree that the link has become too tenuous — that what is claimed to be consequence is only fortuity. Thus, if the destruction of the Michigan Avenue Bridge had delayed the arrival of a doctor, with consequent loss of a patient's life, few judges would impose liability on any of the parties here, although the agreement in result might not be paralleled by similar unanimity in reasoning[. . .] We go only so far as to hold that where, as here, the damages resulted from the same physical forces whose existence required the exercise of greater care than was displayed and were of the same general sort that was expectable, unforeseeability of the exact developments and of the extent of the loss will not limit liability. Other fact situations can be dealt with when they arise.

Is the position taken in *Petition of Kinsman* more similar to the approach in the *Polemis* case or to the approach taken in *The Wagon Mound*? In what respects might it be distinct from both of them? Consider this excerpt from the Restatement (Third) of Torts (P.F.D. 2005):

§29. LIMITATIONS ON LIABILITY FOR TORTIOUS CONDUCT

An actor's liability is limited to those physical harms that result from the risks that made the actor's conduct tortious.

    . . . *Comment j. Connection with reasonable foreseeability as a limit on liability.* Many jurisdictions employ a "foreseeability" test for proximate case, and in negligence actions such a rule is essentially consistent with the standard set forth in this Section. Properly understood, both the risk standard and a foreseeability test exclude liability for harms that were sufficiently unforeseeable at the time of the actor's tortious conduct that they were not among the risks — potential harms — that made the actor negligent. Negligence limits the requirement of reasonable care to those risks that are foreseeable. Thus, when scope of liability arises in a negligence case, the risks that make an actor negligent are limited to foreseeable ones, and the factfinder must determine whether the type of harm that occurred is among those reasonably foreseeable potential harms that made the actor's conduct negligent.

How does the Restatement's approach compare to the case law seen so far?

3. *Problems of foreseeability.* Both the *Wagon Mound* and *Kinsman* cases emphasize the importance of foreseeability. But foreseeability of what? Notice that in advance of an accident there are many different features of it that may or may not have been foreseeable: whether any harm would occur at all, or whether any harm that might occur would be of the particular type or magnitude that did occur, or whether harm would occur in the *manner* (in other words, through the particular chain of events) in which it actually came to pass. Sometimes an accident may be easy to foresee in some of these senses but not others. The following cases explore the common law's treatment of them.

4. *No room for mystique.* In Doughty v. Turner, 1 Q.B. 518 (1964), the plaintiff worked in the defendants' factory. The factory contained cauldrons of molten cyanide kept at a temperature of 800 degrees centigrade, eight times the heat of boiling water; the workers hardened metal objects by dipping them into the cauldrons. Cement covers were kept on top of the cauldrons to conserve the heat within them. A worker in the factory knocked one of the covers into the cauldron it was supposed to be covering. Two workmen peered over the cauldron's edge and saw the cover slide out of view beneath the molten liquid. About two minutes later the cauldron unexpectedly erupted, throwing out a hot liquid that set fires where it landed and caused various injuries to the plaintiff, who was standing nearby. The trial court found that the defendants had not known that the immersion of the cover into the cauldron could give rise to a chemical reaction that would cause such an explosion, but the court nevertheless held that the defendants' workman was negligent in bumping the cover into the cauldron and therefore gave judgment to the plaintiff. The House of Lords reversed. Said Harman, L.J.:

> The plaintiff's argument most persuasively urged [. . .] rested, as I under-stood it, on admissions made that, if this lid had been dropped into the cauldron with sufficient force to cause the molten material to splash over the edge, that would have been an act of negligence or carelessness for which the defendants might be vicariously responsible. [. . .] So it is said here that a splash causing burns was foreseeable and that this explosion was really only a magnified splash which also caused burns[.] I cannot accept this. In my opinion, the damage here was of an entirely different kind from the foreseeable splash. Indeed, the evidence showed that any disturbance of the material resulting from the immersion of the [cover] was past an appreciable time before the explosion happened. This latter was caused by the disintegration of the hard-board under the great heat to which it was subjected and the consequent release of the moisture

enclosed within it. This had nothing to do with the agitation caused by the dropping of the board into the cyanide. I am of opinion that it would be wrong on these facts to make another inroad on the doctrine of foreseeability which seems to me to be a satisfactory solvent of this type of difficulty.

Said Diplock, L.J.:

> There is no room today for mystique in the law of negligence. It is the application of common morality and common sense to the activities of the common man. He must take reasonable care to avoid acts or omissions which he can reasonably foresee would be likely to injure his neighbour; but he need do no more than this. If the act which he does is not one which he could, if he thought about it, reasonably foresee would injure his neighbour, it matters not whether he does it intentionally or inadvertently. The judge's finding, uncontested on appeal, that in the state of knowledge as it was at the time of the accident the defendants could not reasonably have foreseen that the immersion of the asbestos cement cover in the liquid would be likely to injure anyone must lead to the conclusion that they would have been under no liability to the plaintiff if they had intentionally immersed the cover in the liquid. The fact that it was done inadvertently cannot create any liability, for the immersion of the cover was not an act which they were under any duty to take any care to avoid.

What is the analogy between *Doughty v. Turner* and *The Wagon Mound?* What is the distinction between *Doughty v. Turner* and *Petition of Kinsman?*

5. *Sensitive buildings.* In Colonial Inn Motor Lodge v. Gay, 680 N.E.2d 407 (Ill. App. 1997), the defendant was backing his car up in the parking lot of the plaintiff's hotel at a rate of approximately two miles per hour when he bumped into a heating unit protruding from the side of the building. A witness in the parking lot heard a "bang" — "it wasn't very loud, but it was loud enough that we heard it good" — and later testified that she saw that the heating unit had been dented. The defendant, however, thought his car had run into a brick wall and had done no damage, so he drove away. In fact he had severed a gas line running through the heater. The gas from the line collected in the hotel and then was ignited; the plaintiffs' expert concluded that the ignition source was a pilot light in the hotel's laundry room. The resulting explosion and fire caused extensive damage and forced the hotel to close. Its owners sued the driver to recover their damages. The trial court gave summary judgment to the defendant; the court of appeals reversed and remanded for trial. Said the court:

> The plaintiff argues that proximate cause is a jury question because there is a genuine issue of whether the damage to the building was the natural

and probable consequence of the defendant's careless driving. The plaintiff maintains that there is at least some evidence that the defendant's car struck the air-conditioning or heating unit with great force. Thus, the plaintiff asserts, the explosion was not inherently unforeseeable and proximate cause should not be decided as a matter of law. The defendant responds that the explosion was too bizarre to be a natural and probable consequence of slowly backing a car into the building. We conclude that the evidence on the issue is not so one-sided that it entitles the defendant to summary judgment.

We cannot say as a matter of law that it was not reasonably foreseeable that a collision between an automobile and the side of a building could cause the sort of injury here. Construing the evidence liberally in favor of the plaintiff, we see some basis to conclude that the impact was substantial. The sound made a person some distance off shift her attention toward the defendant. Moreover, even a slow-moving car is a large instrumentality capable of causing significant harm. The possibility that colliding with a building will disrupt a gas line or create a fire hazard is not so inherently farfetched as to merit the label "freakish" or "fantastic." Gas lines and ignition sources such as appliances are common features of buildings, including large buildings used for residential purposes. Importantly, this case does not involve the intervention of an unforeseeable third party as an intervening or additional cause. It is at least fairly arguable that, once the defendant's car hit the plaintiff's building, the sequence of events that caused the explosion was set in motion with no further action needed to bring about the injury. [. . .]

If the defendant's conduct is a substantial factor in bringing about the injury, it is not necessary that the extent of the harm or the exact manner in which it occurred could reasonably have been foreseen. A negligence defendant must take the plaintiff as he finds him, even if the plaintiff's "eggshell skull" results in his suffering an injury that ordinarily would not be reasonably foreseeable. Here, the evidence suggests that a building rather than a person may have had an "eggshell skull." That possibility alone does not foreclose liability for the injury.

What is the distinction between *Colonial Inn Motor Lodge v. Gay* and *Doughty v. Turner?*

6. *Turn off engine before fueling.* In DiPonzio v. Riordan, 679 N.E.2d 616 (N.Y. 1997), the plaintiff was a customer at the defendant's self-service gas station. As he was filling his car, another automobile drove into him and broke his leg. The other car — the one that rolled — was unoccupied; its driver had left its motor running while he filled it with gas and went to pay the attendant, and evidently it had slipped into gear while he was away. The gas station's policy was that its patrons were to turn off their engines while fueling, but the plaintiff's evidence was that the defendant failed to

enforce the policy, and that if it had done so he would not have been injured. The court of appeals held that the defendant nevertheless was entitled to summary judgment:

> When a vehicle's engine is left running in an area where gasoline is being pumped, there is a natural and foreseeable risk of fire or explosion because of the highly flammable properties of the fuel. [...] It is this class of foreseeable hazards that defines the scope of the [defendant's] purported duty.
>
> The occurrence that led to plaintiff's injury was clearly outside of this limited class of hazards. Plaintiff was injured because the parking gear of another customer's car inexplicably failed and the unattended vehicle, which had rested stationary on a level surface for more than five minutes, suddenly began to move backwards, pinning plaintiff between its rear bumper and the bumper of his own car. Because this type of accident was not among the hazards that are naturally associated with leaving a car engine running during the operation of a gas pump, the alleged misconduct of [defendant's] employees does not give rise to liability in tort.

What is the distinction between *DiPonzio v. Riordan* and *Colonial Inn Motor Lodge v. Gay*?

7. *Rat flambé (problem).* In United Novelty Co. v. Daniels, 42 So. 2d 395 (Miss. 1949), the plaintiffs' evidence was that the defendant employer instructed its employee, Daniels, to clean its coin-operated machines with gasoline. The room where the machines were located contained a lighted gas heater. While Daniels was working, a rat ran out from beneath the machine that he was cleaning and sought sanctuary beneath the heater. The heater ignited the rat's gasoline-soaked fur. The rat ran back beneath the machine that the employee was cleaning. The flames emanating from the rat apparently ignited the fumes created by Daniels' work with the gasoline. The machine exploded, killing Daniels. Daniels' family sued his employer, claiming it had been negligent in instructing Daniels to use gasoline to clean machines in a room containing a lit gas heater. The trial court entered judgment on a jury verdict for the plaintiffs. The defendant appealed on the ground that the evidence was insufficient to support the verdict. What result? Can the case be distinguished from *Doughty v. Turner*?

8. *Psychotic reaction (problem).* In Steinhauser v. Hertz Corp., 421 F.2d 1169 (2d Cir. 1970), the plaintiffs and defendants were in an automobile accident in New Jersey. The defendants' car crossed a double yellow line on the road and struck the plaintiffs' car. The occupants of the cars did not suffer any bodily injuries, but one of the passengers in the plaintiffs' car, Cynthia Steinhauser, began exhibiting unusual behavior a few minutes after the accident. She was observed to be glassy-eyed, agitated, and disturbed, and she made menacing gestures toward the defendant as he came toward the

plaintiffs' car. In the following days her condition declined. She became convinced that she was under attack, and that bullets were coming through the windows of her house; she attacked her parents; she attempted suicide. She soon was institutionalized and diagnosed as schizophrenic. At the time of trial her prognosis for recovery was poor. She and her parents sued the defendants to recover for damages associated with her condition. The plaintiffs' psychiatrist testified at trial to his conclusion that before the accident Cynthia must have had a "prepsychotic" personality and thus a predisposition to schizophrenia, and that the accident had served as the "precipitating cause" of her psychosis. What result? How might you use the prior cases in this chapter to argue for or against liability?

9. *Montezuma's revenge.* In Central of Georgia Ry. v. Price, 32 S.E. 77 (Ga. 1898), the plaintiff's evidence was that she was a passenger on the defendant's train, bound for Winchester, Georgia. Through the conductor's negligence, she was not let off at Winchester, but was carried on to Montezuma. When the train arrived there, the conductor suggested that the plaintiff spend the night at a hotel and take the morning train back to Winchester. He escorted her to a hotel and arranged to pay her expenses there. The plaintiff was taken to her room and furnished with a kerosene lamp, which she left burning after she had gone to bed. During the night the lamp exploded, setting fire to the mosquito net that covered the plaintiff's bed. She burned her hands in an attempt to extinguish the flames. She sued the railway company for her injuries and the jury returned a verdict in her favor for $400. The trial judge overruled the defendant's motion for a new trial, and the defendant appealed. The Georgia Supreme Court reversed:

> The negligence of the company consisted in passing the station where the passenger desired to alight, without giving her an opportunity to get off. Taking her version of the manner in which she was injured, the injury was occasioned by the negligence of the proprietor of the hotel or his servants in giving her a defective lamp. The negligence of the company in passing her station was therefore not the natural and proximate cause of her injury. There was the interposition of a separate, independent agency, — the negligence of the proprietor of the hotel, over whom, as we have shown, the railway company neither had nor exercised any control. The injuries to the plaintiff were not the natural and proximate consequences of carrying her beyond her station, but were unusual, and could not have been foreseen or provided against by the highest practicable care.

10. *Ambulance driver.* In Pridham v. Cash and Carry Building Center, Inc., 359 A.2d 193 (N.H. 1976), a clerk at the defendant's showroom negligently untied a rope securing some vinyl panels, causing a large pile of them to fall onto the plaintiff's decedent, Herbert Pridham. Pridham was

knocked onto his back. A doctor soon arrived and found that Pridham was unable to move his legs, so he was put onto a stretcher and carried into an ambulance. On the way to the hospital, the driver of the ambulance had a heart attack and drove into a tree. Pridham was killed in the crash. Pridham's administrator brought a wrongful death action against the defendant, claiming that Pridham's death was attributable to its clerk's negligence in handling the vinyl panels. The plaintiff won a jury verdict, and the trial court entered judgment upon it. The defendant appealed, contending that the jury had been instructed improperly. The contested instruction was as follows:

> The law provides that if the defendant is liable to the plaintiff-decedent in this case, he is also liable for any additional bodily harm resulting from normal efforts of third persons in rendering aid ... which the other's injury reasonably requires irrespective of whether such acts are done in a proper or in a negligent manner. ... If you find the defendant Cash and Carry Building Center is liable to the plaintiff, the damages awarded to the plaintiff would include all injuries suffered by the decedent Pridham at Cash and Carry; and if you also find the injuries suffered in the ambulance crash were as a result of the normal effort of third persons in rendering aid which the decedent Pridham required, then the defendant would be liable to the plaintiff for those also.

The New Hampshire Supreme Court affirmed.

Is there a satisfactory distinction between *Pridham v. Cash and Carry Building Center* and *Central of Georgia Ry. v. Price*?

11. *Injuries at the hospital.* From the Restatement (Second) of Torts (1965):

§457. ADDITIONAL HARM RESULTING FROM EFFORTS TO MITIGATE HARM CAUSED BY NEGLIGENCE

If the negligent actor is liable for another's bodily injury, he is also subject to liability for any additional bodily harm resulting from normal efforts of third persons in rendering aid which the other's injury reasonably requires, irrespective of whether such acts are done in a proper or a negligent manner.

Illustration 1. A's negligence causes B serious harm. B is taken to a hospital. The surgeon improperly diagnoses his case and performs an unnecessary operation, or, after proper diagnosis, performs a necessary operation carelessly. A's negligence is a legal cause of the additional harm which B sustains.

Comment d. Under the rule stated in this Section, the actor is answerable only for injuries which result from the risks normally recognized as inherent in the necessity of submitting to medical, surgical, or hospital treatment. He is not answerable for harm caused by misconduct which is extraordinary and therefore outside of such risks.

Illustration 4. A negligently inflicts serious harm on B. While B is in a hospital under treatment, his nurse, unable to bear the sight of his intense suffering, gives him a hypodermic injection of morphine in disobedience of the surgeon's instructions and so excessive that she knows it may be lethal. B dies as a result of the injection. A's negligence is not a legal cause of B's death.

12. *Injuries upon returning from the hospital.* From the Restatement (Second) of Torts (1965):

§460. SUBSEQUENT ACCIDENTS DUE TO IMPAIRED PHYSICAL
CONDITION CAUSED BY NEGLIGENCE

If the negligent actor is liable for an injury which impairs the physical condition of another's body, the actor is also liable for harm sustained in a subsequent accident which would not have occurred had the other's condition not been impaired, and which is a normal consequence of such impairment.

Illustration 1. Through the negligence of A, a collision occurs in which B's right leg is fractured. B is confined to a hospital for two months. At the end of that time, he is permitted by his surgeon to walk on crutches, and while he is doing so, with all reasonable care, he falls and suffers a fracture of his left arm. A's negligence is a legal cause of the second injury.

Illustration 2. The same facts as in Illustration 1, except that B attempts to descend on crutches a steep ladder into his basement. A's negligence is not a legal cause of the second injury.

13. *The speeding trolley (problem).* In Berry v. Borough of Sugar Notch, 43 A. 240 (Pa. 1899), the plaintiff was the motorman of a trolley car that traveled through the defendant's borough. One day high winds caused a large chestnut tree to fall onto the plaintiff's trolley, crushing it and causing him various injuries. The plaintiff claimed that the tree was in poor condition and that the borough therefore was negligent in allowing it to remain there. The borough countered with evidence that the plaintiff was traveling considerably in excess of the statutory speed limits for trolley cars. Did the borough thus make out a good claim of contributory negligence on the plaintiff's part?

14. *Characterization games.* From Morris on Torts (2d ed. 1980):

Once misconduct causes damage, a specific accident has happened in a particular way and has resulted in a discrete harm. When, after the event, the question is asked, "Were the particular accident and the resulting damages foreseeable?", the cases fall into one of three classes:

(1) In some cases, damages resulting from misconduct are so typical that judges and jurors cannot be convinced that they were unforeseeable. Builder negligently drops a brick on Pedestrian who is passing an urban

site of a house under construction. Even though the dent in Pedestrian's skull is microscopically unique in pattern, Builder could not sensibly maintain that the injury was unforeseeable.

(2) In some cases freakishness of the facts refuses to be downed, and any description that minimizes that oddity is viewed as misdescription. For example, in a Louisiana case (*Lynch v. Fisher*, 34 So.2d 513 (La. App. 1948)) a trucker illegally and negligently left his truck on a traveled lane of a public highway at night without setting out flares. A car crashed into the truck and caught fire. A passerby came to the rescue of the car occupants — a husband and wife. After the rescuer got them out of the car, he returned to the car to get a floor mat to pillow the injured wife's head. A pistol lay on the mat that the rescuer wanted to use. He picked it up and handed it to the husband. Unbeknownst to the rescuer, the accident had deranged the husband, and he shot the rescuer in the leg. Such a consequence of negligently failing to guard a truck with flares is so unarguably unforeseeable that no judge or juror would be likely to hold otherwise. [...]

(3) Between these extremes are cases in which consequences are neither typical nor wildly freakish. In these cases unusual details are arguably — only but only arguably — significant. If they are held significant, the consequences are unforeseeable. If they are held unimportant the consequences are foreseeable. For example, in *Hines v. Morrow* (236 S.W. 183 (Tex. Civ. App. 1922)), two men were sent out in a service truck to tow a stalled car out of a mud hole. One of them, the plaintiff, made a tow rope fast and tried to step from between the vehicles as the truck started. His artificial leg slipped into the mud hole in the road, which would not have been there had defendant-railroad not disregarded its statutory duty to maintain this part of the highway. He was unable to pull out his peg-leg and was in danger of being run over by the stalled car. He grabbed the tailgate of the service truck to use its forward force to pull him loose. A loop in the tow rope lassoed his good leg, tightened, and broke his good leg. As long as these details are considered significant facts of the case, the accident is unforeseeable. No doubt some judges would itemize the facts and hold that the railroad's neglect was not the proximate cause of the injury. As a matter of fact, courts have on occasion ruled that much less freakish injuries were unforeseeable. But in the peg-leg case, the court quoted with approval the plaintiff's lawyer's "description" of the "facts," which was couched in these words, "The case, stated in the briefest form, is simply this: Appellee was on the highway, using it in a lawful manner, and slipped into this hole, created by appellant's negligence, and was injured in undertaking to extricate himself." The court also adopted the injured man's answer to the railroad's attempt to stress unusual details: "Appellant contends [that] it could not reasonably have been foreseen that slipping into this hole would have caused the appellee to have become entangled in a rope, and the moving truck, with such dire

results. The answer is plain; the exact consequences do not have to be foreseen."

In this third class of cases, foreseeability can be determined only after the significant facts of the case have been described. If official description of the facts of the case as formulated by the court is detailed, the accident can be called unforeseeable; if it is general, the accident can be called foreseeable. Since there is no authoritative guide to the proper amount of specificity in describing the facts, the process of holding that a loss is — or is not — foreseeable is fluid and often embarrasses attempts at accurate prediction.

How convincing are Morris's claims? Try redescribing the cases considered so far in this chapter at various levels of generality to make their outcomes seem more or less foreseeable. Do the various redescriptions seem equally plausible? If not, why not?

15. *The economics of causation.* From Posner, Economic Analysis of Law:

Here now is a case where causation in a layman's sense is manifestly present but the law properly refuses to award damages. A train breaks down (as a result of the railroad's negligence), and a passenger stays in a hotel and is injured when the hotel burns down. But for the train's breaking down, the passenger would have gone on to his destination and slept in a different hotel that did not burn down that night. So there is negligence, and causation, but there is no liability. The economic reason is that the risk of a hotel fire is not a part of *PL*, the expected accident cost that the railroad could have prevented by taking *B* precautions. True, harm to this particular passenger would have been prevented but it was just as likely that the hotel in the next town would have burned down, in which event the railroad's negligence would have conferred a benefit on the passenger for which the railroad would not have been allowed to charge. To hold the railroad liable would thus be to impose (in effect) punitive damages for its negligence[...]

In some cases a defendant escapes liability for the consequences of his negligence on the ground that those consequences are unforeseeable. If this just meant that the accident had been unlikely and therefore unexpected, it would arbitrarily and drastically truncate the defendant's liability, for most accidents are low-probability events. But actually it seems to mean [...] that high costs of information prevented a party from taking any precautions against the particular accident that occurred; put differently, *B* in the Hand Formula was prohibitive once information about risk is recognized to be a cost of avoiding risk. [...]

An apparent anomaly in the tort treatment of foreseeability is the eggshell skull principle. A tort victim is permitted to recover his damages in full even though the *extent* of his injury was unforeseeable by the defendant because of the victim's unusual vulnerability. A reason for nevertheless imposing liability in such cases is that, in order for total tort damages awarded to equal tort victims' total harm, there must be liability in the eggshell skull case to balance nonliability in the "rock skull" case (i.e., where the victim has above-average resistance to damage). The alternative would be to award in every case the damages an average victim would have incurred; but this approach would distort victim's incentives (why?), as well as create severe measurement problems.

How convincing are Posner's claims? Try redescribing some of the cases considered so far in this chapter in terms of the information costs involved. Do the redescriptions seem plausible?

B. INTERVENING CAUSES

The cases and problems thus far have focused on one consideration prominent in the proximate cause inquiry: foreseeability. This section examines the related but distinct problem of intervening causes. Sometimes a defendant commits an act of negligence that produces harm when combined with a subsequent act of wrongdoing (negligence or worse) by some third party. The question then arises whether the intervening act by the third party is a "superseding cause" that cuts off the defendant's liability.

Brauer v. N.Y. Central & H.R.R. Co.
103 A. 166 (N.J. App. 1918)

[One of the defendant's trains collided with the plaintiffs wagon at a grade crossing. The plaintiffs horse was killed, his wagon was destroyed, and the wagon's contents — a keg of cider, some empty barrels, and a blanket — were stolen by unknown parties at the scene of the accident. The trial court entered judgment on a jury verdict in favor of the plaintiff, and this appeal followed.]

SWAYZE, J. — This is a case of a grade crossing collision. We are clear that the questions of negligence and contributory negligence were for the jury. If there were nothing else, the testimony of the plaintiff as to signals of the flagman would carry the case to the jury. The only question that has caused us difficulty is that of the extent of the defendant's liability. [. . .] What happened was that as a result of the collision, aside from the death of the horse and the destruction of the wagon, the contents of the wagon, consisting of empty barrels and a keg of cider, were scattered, and probably stolen by people at the scene of the accident. The driver, who was alone in charge for the plaintiff, was so stunned that one of the railroad detectives found him immediately after the collision in a fit. There were two railroad detectives on the freight train to protect the property it was carrying against thieves, but they did nothing to protect the plaintiff's property. The controversy on the question of damages is as to the right of the plaintiff to recover the value of the barrels, cider, and blanket.[. . .]

It is now argued that the defendant's negligence was not in any event the proximate cause of the loss of this property, since the act of the thieves intervened. The rule of law exempting the one guilty of the original negligence from damage due to an intervening cause is well settled. The difficulty lies in the application. Like the question of proximate cause, this is ordinarily a jury question. *Del. Lack, & West. R. R. Co. v. Salmon*, 39 N.J. Law, 299. In his opinion in the last-named case Justice Depue, speaking for this court, says that the cases in which the responsibility is laid on the original wrongdoer, though intervening agencies without his fault have interposed, are quite numerous, and he adds that they are only instances of the application of the principle of *Scott v. Shepherd*, 2 W. Bl. 892. [. . .]

We think these authorities justified the trial judge in his rulings as to the recovery of the value of the barrels, cider, and blanket. The negligence which caused the collision resulted immediately in such a condition of the driver of the wagon that he was no longer able to protect his employer's property; the natural and probable result of his enforced abandonment of it in the street of a large city was its disappearance; and the wrongdoer cannot escape making reparation for the loss caused by depriving the plaintiff of the protection which the presence of the driver in his right senses would have afforded.

"The act of a third person" said the Supreme Court of Massachusetts, "intervening and contributing a condition necessary to the injurious effect of the original negligence, will not excuse the first wrongdoer, if such act ought to have been foreseen." *Lane v. Atlantic Works*, 111 Mass. 136. [] A railroad company which found it necessary or desirable to have its freight train guarded by two detectives against thieves is surely chargeable with knowledge that portable property left without a guard was likely to be made off with. Again, strictly speaking, the act of the thieves did not intervene between defendant's negligence and the plaintiff's loss; the two causes were to all practical intent simultaneous and concurrent; it is rather a case of a joint tort than an intervening cause. [. . .] An illustration will perhaps clarify the case. Suppose a fruit vendor at his stand along the street is rendered unconscious by the negligence of the defendant, who disappears, and boys in the street appropriate the unfortunate vendor's stock in trade; could the defendant escape liability for their value? We can hardly imagine a court answering in the affirmative. Yet the case is but little more extreme than the jury might have found the present case.

The judgment is affirmed, with costs.

GARRISON, J., dissenting. The collision afforded an opportunity for theft of which a thief took advantage, but I cannot agree that the collision was therefore the proximate cause of loss of the stolen articles. Proximate cause imports unbroken continuity between cause and effect, which, both in law and in logic, is broken by the active intervention of an independent criminal actor. This established rule of law is defeated if proximate cause is confounded with mere opportunity for crime. A maladjusted switch may be the proximate cause of the death of a passenger who was killed by the derailment of the train or by the fire or collision that ensued, but it is not the proximate cause of the death of a passenger who was murdered by a bandit who boarded the train because of the opportunity afforded by its derailment. This clear distinction is not met by saying that criminal intervention should be foreseen, for this implies that crime is to be presumed, and the law is directly otherwise.

NOTES

1. *Arson.* In Watson v. Kentucky & Indiana Bridge & R.R., 126 S.W. 146 (Ky. 1910), the plaintiff's evidence was that one of the defendant's railroad cars negligently was derailed, causing its cargo of gasoline to spill out into the sheets of Louisville. The gas was ignited by a match lit by a man named Duerr. An explosion resulted that threw the plaintiff from his bed and demolished much of his house. He sued the railroad to recover for his injuries. There was a conflict in the evidence regarding how Duerr started the fire. He claimed that he had used the match to light a cigar and had started the explosion inadvertently. The railroad's witnesses, however, said that 20 minutes before the explosion they heard Duerr say to a companion, "Let us go and set the damn thing on fire." The trial court gave a directed verdict to the defendant railroad. The court of appeals reversed and remanded for a new trial, holding that the railroad's liability depended on how Duerr came to start the fire and that this was a question for the jury. Said the court:

> If the presence on Madison street in the city of Louisville of the great volume of loose gas that arose from the escaping gasoline was caused by the negligence of the appellee Bridge & Railroad Company, it seems to us that the probable consequences of its coming in contact with fire and causing an explosion was too plain a proposition to admit of doubt. Indeed, it was most probable that some one would strike a match to light a cigar or for other purposes in the midst of the gas. In our opinion, therefore, the act of one lighting and throwing a match under such circumstances cannot be said to be the efficient cause of the explosion. It did not of itself produce the explosion, nor could it have done so without the assistance and contribution resulting from the primary negligence, if there was such negligence, on the part of the appellee

Bridge & Railroad Company in furnishing the presence of the gas in the street. This conclusion, however, rests upon the theory that Duerr inadvertently or negligently lighted and threw the match in the gas. [. . .]

If, however, the act of Duerr in lighting the match and throwing it into the vapor or gas arising from the gasoline was malicious, and done for the purpose of causing the explosion, we do not think appellees would be responsible, for while the appellee Bridge & Railroad Company's negligence may have been the efficient cause of the presence of the gas in the street, and it should have understood enough of the consequences thereof to have foreseen that an explosion was likely to result from the inadvertent or negligent lighting of a match by some person who was ignorant of the presence of the gas or of the effect of lighting or throwing a match in it, it could not have foreseen or deemed it probable that one would maliciously or wantonly do such an act for the evil purpose of producing the explosion.

What is the distinction between *Watson v. Kentucky & Indiana Bridge & R.R.* and *Brauer v. New York Central & H.R.R.*?

2. *Intervening jostler.* In Village of Carterville v. Cook, 22 N.E. 14 (Ill. 1889), the defendant village maintained a sidewalk that in one area was elevated about six feet above the ground and had no railings. The plaintiff was walking along the sidewalk and using all due care when he was inadvertently jostled by another pedestrian, causing him to fall off the sidewalk and suffer various injuries. The plaintiff sued the village, claiming that its negligent failure to provide railings was a proximate cause of his damages. The jury returned a verdict in his favor. The defendant appealed.

Held, for the plaintiff, that the trial court did not err in finding the evidence sufficient to support the verdict.

3. *Heavenridge's revenge.* In Alexander v. Town of New Castle, 17 N.E. 200 (Ind. 1888), one Harvey Alexander sued the town of New Castle for negligently failing to enclose a pit that had been dug in one of its streets. A gambler named Heavenridge had been in town. Alexander engaged in a game of chance with Heavenridge in order to procure evidence for his arrest, then persuaded the town justice to appoint him special constable so that he could arrest Heavenridge personally. He did arrest Heavenridge, and the justice tried and convicted him of gaming. As Alexander was leading Heavenridge off to jail, Heavenridge seized him, threw him into the pit in the sidewalk that the defendant had left open, and made his escape. Alexander then brought this suit against the town. The trial court found for the defendant, and Alexander appealed, claiming that the evidence could not support the verdict. The Indiana Supreme Court affirmed, finding that "Heavenridge was clearly an intervening as well as an independent human agency in the infliction of the injuries of which the plaintiff complained."

What is the distinction between *Alexander v. Town of New Castle* and *Village of Carterville v. Cook?*

4. *Intentional intervening acts.* From the Restatement (Second) of Torts:

> §448. INTENTIONALLY TORTIOUS OR CRIMINAL ACTS DONE UNDER OPPORTUNITY AFFORDED BY ACTOR'S NEGLIGENCE
>
> The act of a third person in committing an intentional tort or crime is a superseding cause of harm to another resulting therefore, although the actor's negligent conduct created a situation which afforded an opportunity to the third person to commit such a tort or crime, unless the actor at the time of his negligent conduct realized or should have realized the likelihood that such a situation might be created, and that a third person might avail himself of the opportunity to commit such a tort or crime.

> §449. TORTIOUS OR CRIMINAL ACTS THE PROBABILITY OF WHICH MAKES ACTOR'S CONDUCT NEGLIGENT
>
> If the likelihood that a third person may act in a particular manner is the hazard or one of the hazards which makes the actor negligent, such an act whether innocent, negligent, intentionally tortious, or criminal does not prevent the actor from being liable for harm caused thereby.

5. *The squib case.* The opinion in *Brauer* makes reference to Scott v. Shepherd, 2 Wm. B; 892, 96 Eng. Rep. 525 (K.B. 1773). In that case the defendant, Shepherd, tossed a lighted firecracker (a "squib," as it was called) into a crowded market. It landed next to a man named Willis, who immediately flung it away to protect himself; it then landed next to one Ryal, who also hurled it away. The squib finally landed in the face of the plaintiff, Scott, where it exploded and put out one of his eyes. Scott sued Shepherd. The important question in the case was whether Scott had stated a good claim against Shepherd for trespass, the form of action used to complain of directly inflicted injuries, or whether the suit should have been brought as an action for trespass "on the case," the form of action used to bring claims for injuries inflicted indirectly. A divided court held that Shepherd had a good trespass claim. Said DeGrey, C.J.:

> I look upon all that was done subsequent to the original throwing as a continuation of the first force and first act, which will continue till the squib was spent by bursting. And I think that any innocent person removing the danger from himself to another is justifiable; the blame lights upon the first thrower. The new direction and new force flow out of the first force, and are not a new trespass. [. . .] It has been urged, that the intervention of a free agent will make a difference: but I do not consider

Willis and Ryal as free agents in the present case, but acting under a compulsive necessity for their own safety and self-preservation.

The distinction between "trespass" and "case" has evaporated, but *Scott v. Shepherd* — commonly known as the "squib case" — has retained vitality as a precedent on the question of proximate causation.

6. *She who hesitates lost.* In The Roman Prince, 275 F. 712 (S.D.N.Y. 1921), the plaintiff was in the cabin of a barge, the *C.W. Crane*. when the barge negligently was struck by the defendant's steamship (*The Roman Prince*). The plaintiff soon noticed that the barge had started to leak, but she did not think it was sinking and so declined to board another barge that was alongside hers. Half an hour later the *Crane* had sunk far enough that water was coming onto its deck. The plaintiff then tried to escape from the *Crane* onto the adjacent barge, and in doing so she stumbled and injured her knee. She brought a lawsuit claiming that the defendant was responsible for her injuries because of the negligent piloting of its ship that originally caused the collision. The trial court gave judgment to the defendant, finding that the collision was not the proximate cause of the plaintiff's injuries:

> I think the collision of the *Roman Prince* with the *Crane* cannot be regarded in a legal sense as the cause of the injuries to Mrs. Keenan. She had 15 to 25 minutes to get off the boat when she knew it was settling. She chose, because of a somewhat natural desire to stay by the vessel, to take the risk for a time of the sinking, and finally, from 20 to 30 minutes after the collision, suffered injuries because she stumbled between the two boats. If she would have avoided stumbling by leaving the *C.W. Crane* before it had settled, so that there was a long climb to the deck of the Jersey Central lighter, I think she should have left earlier; but, at any rate, I can see no reason why stumbling on her part can be reasonably attributed to the collision. If there had not been time to deliberate, and take care in leaving the *C.W. Crane* — in other words, if the facts had come within the "squib" case — we would have a different situation. *Scott v. Shepherd*, 2 W.Bl. 892. Here I think the collision was not a proximate cause of the injuries to the libelant, and the libel is accordingly dismissed, but without costs.

7. *A question of agency.* In Thompson v. White, 149 So. 2d 797 (Ala. 1963), the plaintiff was injured when the car in which she was riding was struck in the rear by a car driven by one of the defendants, Lawson White. A Gulf gasoline station recently had been opened near the point where the accident occurred. Gulf had hired clowns to perform at the side of the road. The plaintiff's evidence was that "the clowns had on clown suits and were waving something; they were facing the road and were close enough to have touched the plaintiff car; that the clowns distracted the driver of the plaintiff

car to a certain extent but not enough to interfere with her driving; that she had passed the clowns before she stopped; that the clowns 'were on a portion (of the highway) used by cars[.]" The plaintiff sued Gulf as well as White, claiming that Gulf's clowns distracted White and thus contributed to the accident. The trial court sustained Gulf's demurrer to the plaintiff's complaint; a jury brought in a verdict against White. The Alabama Supreme Court reversed the portion of the judgment in favor of Gulf and remanded for trial:

> We are of opinion that, from the evidence favorable to plaintiff, the jury could reasonably infer that the clowns were on the traveled portion of the highway, that the activities of the clowns were such as would naturally and probably distract the attention of motorists on the highway, and that the activity of the clowns did distract White and cause him to drive his car into the car in which plaintiff was riding. We are of opinion that determination of the question whether the Gulf defendants were, under the doctrine of respondeat superior, guilty of negligence was for the jury. . . . We are of opinion that the evidence reasonably supports an inference that since White's car was immediately behind the plaintiff car, the driver of which was distracted by the clowns, White was also distracted by the clowns. In that event, White was not a free agent but was acting under the influence of the clowns. DeGrey, C. J., in *Scott v. Shepherd*, 2 Blackstone 892, 900. His negligence, if any, was thus a concurring cause and not an independent, intervening cause which would insulate the Gulf defendants from liability.

As these subsequent courts have understood the "squib case," what principle does it stand for?

8. *Exercises.* Now consider the following cases, all involving "freak" accidents; in which would you expect the plaintiff's case to satisfy the proximate cause requirement?

a. Lightning strike. In Johnson v. Kosmos Portland Cement Co., 64 F.2d 193 (6th Cir. 1933), the defendant owned a barge that was moored on the Ohio River near the town of Kosmosdale. The barge recently had been used to haul oil, and as a result inflammable gases had accumulated in the barge's hold. The defendant negligently failed to remove the gases before summoning the plaintiffs' decedents to perform work on the barge using an acetylene torch. The gases were ignited, causing an explosion that killed everyone on board; but the ignition of the gases was caused not by the torch but by a bolt of lightning that struck the barge. The administrators of two of the men who died brought suits claiming that the defendant's negligent failure to rid the barge of the inflammable gases was the proximate cause of their deaths. The trial court found that the defendant's negligence was not the proximate cause of the fatal injuries suffered by the plaintiffs' decedents, and so gave judgment to the defendants. The plaintiffs appealed. What result?

b. Fire in the hole! In Henry v. Houston Lighting & Power Co., 934 S.W.2d 748 (Tex. App. 1996), the defendants' employees were drilling a hole for a utility pole when they negligently severed an underground gas line. The plaintiff, Edwin Henry, was summoned to fix the broken line. Unbeknownst to Henry, while he was doing this some other workers began to operate a mosquito fogger in a manhole on the other side of a nearby fence. Fog from the fogger drifted into the hole where Henry was working. A fellow employee, thinking the fog was smoke, shouted "Fire!" Fearing the fire would cause the leaking gas to explode, Henry sprang from the hole, rushed through the fog, and ran into a utility pole, injuring his shoulder.

Henry brought a lawsuit against the power company, claiming that his shoulder injury was attributable to its employees' negligence in originally severing the gas line. The trial court gave summary judgment to the defendants. The plaintiff appealed. What result?

c. Delayed reaction. In Clark v. E. I. DuPont de Nemours Powder Co., 146 P. 320 (Kan. 1915), defendant DuPont was hired to assist in the drilling of an oil well on the farm of a man named McDowell. After performing the work, one of DuPont's agents inadvertently left behind a pail of explosive, solidified glycerine. Joe McDowell, a son of the farm's owner and himself an oil well worker, discovered the pail and took it home to keep it out of harm's way. His mother protested against keeping so dangerous an article at the house, however, so McDowell moved the pail to a nearby graveyard and hid it there in a crevice in a stone wall. The pail remained there for over two years until it was found by the sons of the plaintiff, Clark. On the day they discovered the pail, the Clark boys did not know what it contained and left it at the graveyard. That evening, however, one of the boys described the pail to his uncle, who ventured the opinion that the substance it contained probably was some sort of animal fat. The next morning the boys returned to the graveyard. One of them picked up the pail and hit it on a rock in order to break off a piece of the substance inside to take home. This caused an explosion that injured both Clark sons. The plaintiff brought a suit claiming that his sons' injuries were attributable to the negligence of DuPont's agent in leaving the pail behind two years earlier when he was at the McDowell farm. The jury found for the plaintiff and the defendant appealed, claiming the evidence was insufficient to support the verdict.

What result would you predict on these facts? What analogies might you draw to previous cases we have considered?

d. Raging bulldozer. In Richardson v. Ham, 285 P.2d 269 (Cal. 1955), employees of the defendants' construction company were using a 26-ton bulldozer to perform work on top of a mesa. One night they negligently left the bulldozer unlocked and unattended at the work site. A pair of young men who had been drinking discovered the bulldozer, started it, drove it around the mesa for a while, and caused various sorts of damage. When they could not figure out how to stop the bulldozer, they headed it toward the eastern edge of the mesa and abandoned it. The bulldozer went over the edge of the mesa, down a hill, across a freeway, through a house, and into an automobile before at last being stopped by a retaining wall and utility pole. The plaintiffs were among the people whose property was damaged. They brought a suit claiming that their damages were attributable to the negligent failure of the defendants' employees to lock the bulldozer. The jury brought in verdicts for the defendants. The trial judge granted the plaintiffs' motions for a new trial. The defendants appealed. Construct arguments for and against liability.

e. Local cuisine. In Farmilant v. Singapore Airlines, Ltd., 561 F. Supp 1148 (N.D. Ill. 1983), the plaintiff, Farmilant, bought an airline ticket from the defendant's agent that would, with several stopovers, carry him to Madras and back: Los Angeles to Tokyo, Tokyo to Singapore, Singapore to Madras, Madras to Singapore, Singapore to Honolulu, and Honolulu to Los Angeles. He attempted to make some changes to his itinerary during the trip, however, and when he arrived in Singapore he was informed that all the flights to Madras were booked for the next three weeks. He therefore flew instead to Bombay and took a train to Madras. During a stop on the train trip Farmilant ate some local cuisine and became ill; as a result he ended up being able to spend only a few days at his final destination of Mahabalipuram. He tried to book an immediate flight back to the United States, telling the defendant's agents that he was ill and feared for his life. He was told that for the next available seat he would have to wait over a month. He booked a flight home on another carrier, and upon his return was hospitalized for 12 days. Farmilant sued the airline to recover his medical expenses, alleging that his injuries were attributable to the airline's negligence in failing to have a seat available for him on one of their flights from Singapore to Madras. Assuming that the airline was negligent, what result on the causation issue?

f. Foreseeability. In Bell v. Campbell, 434 S.W.2d 117 (Tex. 1968), the defendant, Addie Campbell, pulled onto Highway 67 near Texarkana without keeping a proper lookout or yielding the right of way. A vehicle driven by one Marshall struck Campbell's pickup truck from behind, knocking the truck off the road and causing a trailer attached to Marshall's vehicle to overturn on the highway. A crowd soon gathered. Someone began warning oncoming cars with a flashlight, and several people started removing the overturned trailer from the highway. A man named W.W. Fore, in whose car several bottles of whiskey later were found, either ignored or failed to see the warning signals. Fore struck the trailer, killing two of the people who had been trying to move it. In addition to suing Fore, the decedents' administrators also sued Campbell and Marshall, claiming that the negligence of either or both of them in causing the original accident also was the proximate cause of the decedents' deaths. What result on the latter claims?

9. *An attempt at clarification.* Professor Grady believes that problems of intervening conduct generally can be sorted into five categories, each with a handy acronym and predictable outcome:

> *Paradigm NIT ("no intervening tort"): The defendant was negligent, and no subsequent tortious act intervened between the defendant's negligence*

and the plaintiff's harm. Liability. Paradigm NIT is the most obvious situation in which the original wrongdoer's liability is preserved. The harm to the plaintiff was directly caused by the defendant because no tort by anyone else intervened between the defendant's negligence and the plaintiff's harm. This pattern results in liability so long as the other requirements of causation are satisfied: "but-for" causation, and causation in the sense that the defendant's negligence made the harm that occurred more likely to happen.

Paradigm DCE ("dependent compliance error"): The defendant negligently made the plaintiff specially vulnerable to someone else's ordinary negligence (i.e., compliance errors) or emergency response. Liability. The general idea here is that if the defendant's negligence puts the plaintiff at a higher risk of being the victim of negligence, the defendant should not be off the hook when that negligence occurs. Perhaps the very reason why the defendant is considered negligent — the risk that the defendant is creating that is bothersome — is that the defendant's conduct puts others at greater risk of being hurt by someone else's negligence. This also is the paradigm that applies when the plaintiff is hurt while trying to rescue a third party injured by the defendant's original act of negligence.

Paradigm EFR ("encouraged free radicals"): The defendant negligently created an unusually tempting opportunity for irresponsible third parties to do harm. Liability. These are cases where the defendant, a responsible person with enough assets and good judgment to be deterred by tort liability, somehow has encouraged irresponsible people ("free radicals") to wreak havoc — perhaps even to wreak havoc deliberately. This paradigm is especially appropriate when the defendant — the original wrongdoer — acted in a way that was deliberate or knowing, rather than utterly inadvertent. Ask: did the defendant really create new incentives or opportunities that made mischief by others more likely? If the defendant did encourage the free radicals, did their behavior nonetheless go beyond the defendant's encouragement?

Paradigm NCP ("no corrective precaution"): A third party willfully failed to take a corrective precaution to prevent the defendant's negligence from causing harm. No liability. The defendant avoids liability if, after the defendant commits a negligent act, some third party recognizes the risk but fails to take a precaution that would have prevented the resulting harm. The usual pattern: a defendant negligently has created a dangerous situation. A responsible person (not a free radical) appears on the scene and recognizes the danger. This intervening person for some reason, usually because of a special relationship, also has a duty of care toward the plaintiff; or the intervenor *is* the plaintiff. But the intervenor unaccountably does nothing to address the risk. Sometimes these also can be understood as cases where the intervenor's act amounts to gross negligence rather than ordinary negligence.

Paradigm IIT ("independent intervening tort"): A third party committed an intervening wrong that was independent of the defendant's negligence. No liability. These are cases where the relationship between the defendant's negligence and the third party's subsequent negligence was coincidental. *Central of Georgia Ry. v. Price* is an example. The defendant's railroad negligently took the plaintiff to the wrong stop. She stayed the night in a hotel there, and was injured in a fire. The railroad's negligence did not make it any more likely that the plaintiff would spend the night in a building that caught fire; the intervening tort (the negligence that caused the fire) thus was "independent" of the original negligence (taking the plaintiff to the wrong stop). As discussed earlier, these cases usually can be explained equally well, and more simply, by just saying there was no reasonable foreseeability: that is, the defendant's negligence did not make it any more likely that the plaintiff would become a victim of a third party's negligence.

How well do Grady's paradigms explain the cases? To the extent that the rules work, what is the sense of them? For elaboration, see Mark F. Grady, *Proximate Cause Decoded*, 50 UCLA L. Rev. 293 (2002).

C. LIMITATION OF DUTY: AN ALTERNATIVE APPROACH?

Palsgraf v. Long Island R.R. Co.
162 N.E. 99 (N.Y. 1928)

CARDOZO, C.J. Plaintiff was standing on a platform of defendant's railroad after buying a ticket to go to Rockaway Beach. A train stopped at the station, bound for another place. Two men ran forward to catch it. One of the men reached the platform of the car without mishap, though the train was already moving. The other man, carrying a package, jumped aboard the car, but seemed unsteady as if about to fall. A guard on the car, who had held the door open, reached forward to help him in, and another guard on the platform pushed him from behind. In this act, the package was dislodged, and fell upon the rails. It was a package of small size, about fifteen inches long, and was covered by a newspaper. In fact it contained fireworks, but there was nothing in its appearance to give notice of its contents. The fireworks when they fell exploded. The shock of the explosion threw down some scales at the other end of the platform many feet away. The scales struck the plaintiff, causing injuries for which she sues.

The conduct of the defendant's guard, if a wrong in its relation to the holder of the package, was not a wrong in its relation to the plaintiff, standing far away. Relatively to her it was not negligence at all. Nothing in the situation gave notice that the falling package had in it the potency of peril to persons thus removed. Negligence is not actionable unless it involves the invasion of a legally protected interest, the violation of a right. "Proof of negligence in the air, so to speak, will not do." Pollock, *Torts* (11th Ed.) p. 455. [...] The plaintiff, as she stood upon the platform of the station, might claim to be protected against intentional invasion of her bodily security. Such invasion is not charged. She might claim to be protected against unintentional invasion by conduct involving in the thought of reasonable men an unreasonable hazard that such invasion would ensue. These, from the point of view of the law, were the bounds of her immunity, with perhaps some rare exceptions, survivals for the most part of ancient forms of liability, where conduct is held to be at the peril of the actor. If no hazard was apparent to the eye of ordinary vigilance, an act innocent and harmless, at least to outward seeming, with reference to her, did not take to itself the quality of a tort because it happened to be a wrong, though apparently not one involving the risk of bodily insecurity, with reference to some one else. "In every instance, before negligence can be predicated of a given act, back of the act must be sought and found a duty to the individual complaining, the observance of which would have averted or avoided the injury." McSherry, C.J., in *West Virginia Central & P.R. Co. v. State*, 96 Md. 652, 666, 54 A. 669, 671. [...] "The ideas of negligence and duty are strictly correlative." Bowen, L. J., in *Thomas v. Quartermaine*, 18 Q. B. D. 685, 694. The plaintiff sues in her own right for a wrong personal to her, and not as the vicarious beneficiary of a breach of duty to another.

A different conclusion will involve us, and swiftly too, in a maze of contradictions. A guard stumbles over a package which has been left upon a platform. It seems to be a bundle of newspapers. It turns out to be a can of dynamite. To the eye of ordinary vigilance, the bundle is abandoned waste, which may be kicked or trod on with impunity. Is a passenger at the other end of the platform protected by the law against the unsuspected hazard concealed beneath the waste? If not, is the result to be any different, so far as the distant passenger is concerned, when the guard stumbles over a valise which a truckman or a porter has left upon the walk? The passenger far away, if the victim of a wrong at all, has a cause of action, not derivative, but original and primary. His claim to be protected against invasion of his bodily security is neither greater nor less because the act resulting in the invasion is a wrong to another far removed. In this case, the rights that are said to have been violated, are not even of the same order. The man was not injured in his person nor even put in danger. The purpose of the act, as well as its effect, was to make his person safe. If there was a wrong to him at all, which may very well be doubted it was a wrong to a property interest only, the safety of his package. Out of this wrong to property, which threatened injury to nothing else, there has passed, we are told, to the plaintiff by derivation or succession a right of action for the invasion of an interest of another order, the right to bodily security. The diversity of interests emphasizes the futility of the effort to build the plaintiff's right upon the basis of a wrong to some one else. The gain is one of emphasis, for a like result would follow if the interests were the same. Even then, the orbit of the danger as disclosed to the eye of reasonable vigilance would be the orbit of the duty. One who jostles one's neighbor in a crowd does not invade the rights of others standing at the outer fringe when the unintended contact casts a bomb upon the ground. The wrongdoer as to them is the man who carries the bomb, not the one who explodes it without suspicion of the danger. Life will have to be made over, and human nature transformed, before prevision so extravagant can be accepted as the norm of conduct, the customary standard to which behavior must conform.

The argument for the plaintiff is built upon the shifting meanings of such words as "wrong" and "wrongful," and shares their instability. What the plaintiff must show is "a wrong" to herself; i.e., a violation of her own right, and not merely a wrong to some one else, nor conduct "wrongful" because unsocial, but not "a wrong" to any one. We are told that one who drives at reckless speed through a crowded city street is guilty of a negligent act and therefore of a wrongful one, irrespective of the consequences. Negligent the act is, and wrongful in the sense that it is unsocial, but wrongful and unsocial in relation to other travelers, only because the eye of vigilance perceives the risk of damage. If the same act were to be committed on a speedway or a race course, it would lose its wrongful quality. The risk reasonably to be perceived defines the duty to be obeyed, and risk imports relation; it is risk to another or to others within the range of apprehension. This does not mean, of course, that one who launches a destructive force is always relieved of liability, if the force, though known to be destructive, pursues an unexpected path. "It was not necessary that the defendant should have had notice of the particular method in which an accident would occur, if the possibility of an accident was clear to the ordinarily prudent eye." *Munsey v. Webb*, 231 U.S. 150, 156. Some acts, such as shooting, are so imminently dangerous to any one who may come within reach of the missile however unexpectedly, as to impose a duty of prevision not far from that of an insurer. Even today, and much oftener in earlier stages of the law, one acts sometimes at one's peril. Under this head, it may be, fall certain cases of what is known as transferred intent, an act willfully dangerous to A resulting by misadventure in injury to B. These cases aside, wrong is defined in terms of the natural or probable, at least when unintentional. The range of reasonable apprehension is at times a question for the court, and at times, if varying inferences are possible, a question for the jury. Here, by concession, there was nothing in the situation to suggest to the most cautious mind that the parcel wrapped in newspaper would spread wreckage through the station. If the guard had thrown it down knowingly and willfully, he would not have threatened the plaintiff's safety, so far as appearances could warn him. His conduct would not have involved, even then, an unreasonable probability of invasion of her bodily security. Liability can be no greater where the act is inadvertent.

Negligence, like risk, is thus a term of relation. Negligence in the abstract, apart from things related, is surely not a tort, if indeed it is understandable at all.

Negligence is not a tort unless it results in the commission of a wrong, and the commission of a wrong imports the violation of a right, in this case, we are told, the right to be protected against interference with one's bodily security. But bodily security is protected, not against all forms of interference or aggression, but only against some. One who seeks redress at law does not make out a cause of action by showing without more that there has been damage to his person. If the harm was not willful, he must show that the act as to him had possibilities of danger so many and apparent as to entitle him to be protected against the doing of it though the harm was unintended. Affront to personality is still the keynote of the wrong. Confirmation of this view will be found in the history and development of the action on the case. Negligence as a basis of civil liability was unknown to mediaeval law. For damage to the person, the sole remedy was trespass, and trespass did not lie in the absence of aggression, and that direct and personal. Liability for other damage, as where a servant without orders from the master does or omits something to the damage of another, is a plant of later growth. When it emerged out of the legal soil, it was thought of as a variant of trespass, an offshoot of the parent stock. This appears in the form of action, which was known as trespass on the case. The victim does not sue derivatively, or by right of subrogation, to vindicate an interest invaded in the person of another. Thus to view his cause of action is to ignore the fundamental difference between tort and crime. He sues for breach of a duty owing to himself.

The law of causation, remote or proximate, is thus foreign to the case before us. The question of liability is always anterior to the question of the measure of the consequences that go with liability. If there is no tort to be redressed, there is no occasion to consider what damage might be recovered if there were a finding of a tort. We may assume, without deciding, that negligence, not at large or in the abstract, but in relation to the plaintiff, would entail liability for any and all consequences, however novel or extraordinary. There is room for argument that a distinction is to be drawn according to the diversity of interests invaded by the act, as where conduct negligent in that it threatens an insignificant invasion of an interest in property results in an unforeseeable invasion of an interest of another order, as, e.g., one of bodily security. Perhaps other distinctions may be necessary. We do not go into the question now. The consequences to be followed must first be rooted in a wrong.

The judgment of the Appellate Division and that of the Trial Term should be reversed, and the complaint dismissed, with costs in all courts.

ANDREWS, J. (dissenting). Assisting a passenger to board a train, the defendant's servant negligently knocked a package from his arms. It fell between the platform and the cars. Of its contents the servant knew and could know nothing. A violent explosion followed. The concussion broke some scales standing a considerable distance away. In falling, they injured the plaintiff, an intending passenger.

Upon these facts, may she recover the damages she has suffered in an action brought against the master? The result we shall reach depends upon our theory as to the nature of negligence. Is it a relative concept — the breach of some duty owing to a particular person or to particular persons? Or, where there is an act which unreasonably threatens the safety of others, is the doer liable for all its proximate consequences, even where they result in injury to one who would generally be thought to be outside the radius of danger? This is not a mere dispute as to words. We might not believe that to the average mind the dropping of the bundle would seem to involve the probability of harm to the plaintiff standing many feet away whatever might be the case as to the owner or to one so near as to be likely to be struck by its fall. If, however, we adopt the second hypothesis, we have to inquire only as to the relation between cause and effect. We deal in terms of proximate cause, not of negligence. [...]

But we are told that "there is no negligence unless there is in the particular case a legal duty to take care, and this duty must be not which is owed to the plaintiff himself and not merely to others." Salmond *Torts* (6th Ed.) 24. This I think too narrow a conception. Where there is the unreasonable act, and some right that may be affected there is negligence whether damage does or does not result. That is immaterial. Should we drive down Broadway at a reckless speed, we are negligent whether we strike an approaching car or miss it by an inch. The act itself is wrongful. If is a wrong not only to those who happen to be within the radius of danger, but to all who might have been there — a wrong to the public at large. Such is the language of the street. Such the language of the courts when speaking of contributory negligence. [...]

It may well be that there is no such thing as negligence in the abstract. "Proof of negligence in the air, so to speak, will not do." In an empty world negligence would not exist. It does involve a relationship between man and his fellows, but not merely a relationship between man and those whom he might reasonably expect his act would injure; rather, a relationship between him and those whom he does in fact injure. If his act has a tendency to harm some one, it harms him a mile away as surely as it does those on the scene. We now permit children to recover for the negligent killing of the father. It was never prevented on the theory that no duty was owing to them. A husband may be compensated for the loss of his wife's services. To say that the wrongdoer was negligent as to the husband as well as to the wife is merely an attempt to fit facts to theory. An insurance company paying a fire loss recovers its payment of the negligent incendiary. We speak of subrogation — of suing in the right of the insured. Behind the cloud of words is the fact they hide, that the act, wrongful as to the insured, has also injured the company. Even if it be true that the fault of father, wife, or insured will prevent recovery, it is because we consider the original negligence, not the proximate cause of the injury. Pollock, *Torts* (12th Ed.) 463.

In the well-known *Polemis Case*, Scrutton, L.J., said that the dropping of a plank was negligent, for it might injure "workman or cargo or ship." Because of either possibility, the owner of the vessel was to be made good for his loss. The act being wrongful, the doer was liable for its proximate results. Criticized and explained as this statement may have been, I think it states the law as it should be and as it is.

The proposition is this: Every one owes to the world at large the duty of refraining from those acts that may unreasonably threaten the safety of others. Such an act occurs. Not only is he wronged to whom harm, might reasonably be expected to result, but he also who is in fact injured, even if he be outside what would generally be thought the danger zone. There needs be duty due the one complaining, but this is not a duty to a particular individual because as to him harm might be expected. Harm to some one being the natural result of the act, not only that one alone, but all those in fact injured may complain. We have never, I think, held otherwise. [. . .]

If this be so, we do not have a plaintiff suing by "derivation or succession." Her action is original and primary. Her claim is for a breach of duty to herself — not that she is subrogated to any right of action of the owner of the parcel or of a passenger standing at the scene of the explosion.

The right to recover damages rests on additional considerations. The plaintiff's rights must be injured, and this injury must be caused by the negligence. We build a dam, but are negligent as to its foundations. Breaking, it injures property down stream. We are not liable if all this happened because of some reason other than the insecure foundation. But, when injuries do result from our unlawful act, we are liable for the consequences. It does not matter that they are unusual, unexpected, unforeseen, and unforeseeable. But there is one limitation. The damages must be so connected with the negligence that the latter may be said to be the proximate cause of the former.

These two words have never been given an inclusive definition. What is a cause in a legal sense, still more what is a proximate cause, depend in each case upon many considerations, as does the existence of negligence itself. Any philosophical doctrine of causation does not help us. A boy throws a stone into a pond. The ripples spread. The water level rises. The history of that pond is altered to all eternity. It will be altered by other causes also. Yet it will be forever the resultant of all causes combined. Each one will have an influence. How great only omniscience can say. You may speak of a chain, or, if you please, a net. An analogy is of little aid. Each cause brings about future events. Without each the future would not be the same. Each is proximate in the sense it is essential. But that is not what we mean by the word. Nor on the other hand do we mean sole cause. There is no such thing.

Should analogy be thought helpful, however, I prefer that of a stream. The spring, starting on its journey, is joined by tributary after tributary. The river, reaching the ocean, comes from a hundred sources. No man may say whence any drop of water is derived. Yet for a time distinction may be possible. Into the clear creek, brown swamp water flows from the left. Later, from the right comes water stained by its clay bed. The three may remain for a space, sharply divided. But at last inevitably no trace of separation remains. They are so commingled that all distinction is lost.

As we have said, we cannot trace the effect of an act to the end, if end there is. Again, however, we may trace it part of the way. A murder at Serajevo may be the necessary antecedent to an assassination in London twenty years hence. An overturned lantern may burn all Chicago. We may follow the fire from the shed to the last building. We rightly say the fire started by the lantern caused its destruction.

A cause, but not the proximate cause. What we do mean by the word "proximate" is that, because of convenience, of public policy, of a rough sense of justice, the law arbitrarily declines to trace a series of events beyond a certain point. This is not logic. It is practical politics. Take our rule as to fires. Sparks from my burning haystack set on fire my house and my neighbor's. I may recover from a negligent railroad. He may not. Yet the wrongful act has directly harmed the one as the other. We may regret that the line was drawn just where it was, but drawn somewhere it had to be. We said the act of the railroad was not the proximate cause of our neighbor's fire. Cause it surely was. The words we used were simply indicative of our notions of public policy. Other courts think differently. But somewhere they reach the point where they cannot say the stream comes from any one source.

Take the illustration given in an unpublished manuscript by a distinguished and helpful writer on the law of torts. A chauffeur negligently collides with another car which is filled with dynamite, although he could not know it. An explosion follows. A, walking on the sidewalk nearby, is killed. B, sitting in a window of a building opposite, is cut by flying glass. C, likewise sitting in a window a block away, is similarly injured. And a further illustration: A nursemaid, ten blocks away, startled by the noise, involuntarily drops a baby from her arms to the walk. We are told that C may not recover while A may. As to B it is a question for court or jury. We will all agree that the baby might not. Because, we are again told, the chauffeur had no reason to believe his conduct involved any risk of injuring either C or the baby. As to them he was not negligent.

But the chauffeur, being negligent in risking the collision, his belief that the scope of the harm he might do would be limited is immaterial. His act unreasonably jeopardized the safety of any one who might be affected by it. C's injury and that of the baby were directly traceable to the collision. Without that, the injury would not have happened. C had the right to sit in his office, secure from such dangers. The baby was entitled to use the sidewalk with reasonable safety.

The true theory is, it seems to me, that the injury to C, if in truth he is to be denied recovery, and the injury to the baby, is that their several injuries were not the proximate result of the negligence. And here not what the chauffeur had reason to believe would be the result of his conduct, but what the prudent would foresee, may have a bearing — may have some bearing, for the problem of proximate cause is not to be solved by any one consideration. It is all a question of expediency. There are no fixed rules to govern our judgment. There are simply matters of which we may take account. We have in a somewhat different connection spoken of "the stream of events." We have asked whether that stream was deflected — whether it was forced into new and unexpected channels. This is rather rhetoric than law. There is in truth little to guide us other than common sense.

There are some hints that may help us. The proximate cause, involved as it may be with many other causes, must be, at the least, something without which the event would not happen. The court must ask itself whether there was a natural and continuous sequence between cause and effect. Was the one a substantial factor in producing the other? Was there a direct connection between them, without too many intervening causes? Is the effect of cause on result not too attenuated? Is the cause likely, in the usual judgment of mankind, to produce the result? Or, by the exercise of prudent foresight, could the result be foreseen? Is the result too remote from the cause, and here we consider remoteness in time and space. [. . .] Clearly we must so consider, for the greater the distance either in time or space, the more surely do other causes intervene to affect the result. When a lantern is overturned, the firing of a shed is a fairly direct consequence. Many things contribute to the spread of the conflagration — the force of the wind, the direction and width of streets, the character of intervening structures, other factors. We draw an uncertain and wavering line, but draw it we must as best we can.

Once again, it is all a question of fair judgment, always keeping in mind the fact that we endeavor to make a rule in each case that will be practical and in keeping with the general understanding of mankind.

Here another question must be answered. In the case supposed, it is said, and said correctly, that the chauffeur is liable for the direct effect of the explosion, although he had no reason to suppose it would follow a collision. "The fact that the injury occurred in a different manner than that which might have been expected does not prevent the chauffeur's negligence from being in law the cause of the injury." But the natural results of a negligent act — the results which a prudent man would or should foresee — do have a bearing upon the decision as to proximate cause. We have said so repeatedly. What should be foreseen? No human foresight would suggest that a collision itself might injure one a block away. On the contrary, given an explosion, such a possibility might be reasonably expected. I think the direct connection, the foresight of which the courts speak, assumes prevision of the explosion, for the immediate results of which, at least, the chauffeur is responsible.

It may be said this is unjust. Why? In fairness he should make good every injury flowing from his negligence. Not because of tenderness toward him we say he need not answer for all that follows his wrong. We look back to the catastrophe, the fire kindled by the spark, or the explosion. We trace the consequences, not indefinitely, but to a certain point. And to aid us in fixing that point we ask what might ordinarily be expected to follow the fire or the explosion.

This last suggestion is the factor which must determine the case before us. The act upon which defendant's liability rests is knocking an apparently harmless package onto the platform. The act was negligent. For its proximate consequences the defendant is liable. If its contents were broken, to the owner; if it fell upon and crushed a passenger's foot, then to him; if it exploded and injured one in the immediate vicinity, to him also as to A in the illustration. Mrs. Palsgraf was standing some distance away. How far cannot be told from the record — apparently 25 or 30 feet, perhaps less. Except for the explosion, she would not have been injured. We are told by the appellant in his brief, "It cannot be denied that the explosion was the direct cause of the plaintiff's injuries." So it was a substantial factor in producing the result — there was here a natural and continuous sequence — direct connection. The only intervening cause was that, instead of blowing her to the ground, the concussion smashed the weighing machine which in turn fell upon her. There was no remoteness in time, little in space. And surely, given such an explosion as here, it needed no great foresight to predict that the natural result would be to injure one on the platform at no greater distance from its scene than was the plaintiff. Just how no one might be able to predict. Whether by flying fragments, by broken glass, by wreckage of machines or structures no one could say. But injury in some form was most probable.

Under these circumstances I cannot say as a matter of law that the plaintiff's injuries were not the proximate result of the negligence. That is all we have before us. The court refused to so charge. No request was made to submit the matter to the jury as a question of fact, even would that have been proper upon the record before us.

The judgment appealed from should be affirmed, with costs.

NOTES

1. *Poetic license.* The facts of the *Palsgraf* case have been extensively studied, with some investigators concluding that Cardozo subtracted and perhaps added details to his account to contribute to its rhetorical impact and support his analysis. Other details that have been unearthed about the background and aftermath of the case are interesting in their own right. At the time of the accident Helen Palsgraf was 40 years old and working as a janitor in Brooklyn. The injury for which she sued was a stammer said to be caused by the incident, and her daughter later reported that after losing the case Mrs. Palsgraf went mute. The explosion at the center of the case in fact was large; it was heard blocks away, injured more than a dozen people, and was reported on the front page of the *New York Times*. It caused a stampede, and Palsgraf's complaint said that she was knocked down either by the scale *or* the crowd, or both. The jury awarded her $6,000, which was the equivalent of about $50,000 in the year 2000. In reversing, the court of appeals awarded the railroad its costs, which amounted to about a year's pay

for Palsgraf; it is not known whether the railroad ever attempted to collect from her. See Noonan, Persons and Masks of the Law (1976); Posner, Cardozo: A Study in Reputation (1990).

2. *The so what test.* Cardozo introduces the idea that a case brought by an unforeseeable plaintiff should fail for want of a duty rather than for want of proximate cause. What possible value might there be in adding this analytical wrinkle to the inquiry into liability? What practical difference does it make whether remoteness and foreseeability are addressed as matters of "duty" or "causation"? What is the relationship between the approaches taken by Cardozo and Andrews here and the positions taken in the *Polemis* and *Wagon Mound* cases?

3. *Approaching the centennial.* Nearly a hundred years after its decision, *Palsgraf* remains one of the most famous tort cases in American law and has been subject of much scholarly discussion and debate. It is not possible to survey all that has been said about it here, but a brief sampling of some recent commentary may be of interest.

> a. From Gary Schwartz, *Cardozo as Tort Lawmaker*, 49 DePaul L. Rev. 305 (1999):

> By introducing a duty concept that is supposedly quite separate from a proximate cause concept, the Cardozo opinion prompts a long dissent by Andrews that discusses duty before it turns to proximate cause. Andrews' broad definition of duty makes it seem as though he is very strongly pro-liability. But when (and if) attention is finally focused on Andrews' treatment of proximate cause, his version of proximate cause turns out to be much less pro-liability than one might have assumed. . . . If, as Andrews states, proximate cause depends not on "logic" but rather on "expediency," "practical politics," "convenience," and "a rough sense of justice," then how in the world does a trial judge instruct the jury? Likewise, how does an appellate court determine whether a trial judge has ruled correctly? In any event, the analytic deficiencies and the anti-liability implications in Andrews' account of proximate cause are obscured by his more dramatic and unambiguous pro-liability pronouncements on the duty issue. These are pronouncements that could have been avoided altogether had Cardozo defined the issue properly as one of proximate cause rather than of duty — and had the case been fully debated in proximate cause terms. In fact, the two opinions join issue on the duty issue, a question which I regard as an irrelevancy. Worse yet, given Cardozo's emphasis on duty, there is simply no joinder on the issue of proximate cause.

> To make a bad situation worse, the Cardozo opinion is replete with grandiloquent quasi-philosophical rhetoric that captures but also confounds the reader. There is not a word in the opinion that counts as

genuine legal philosophy — that deals with the purpose or functions of the tort system. In his review of the Kaufman biography [of Cardozo], Professor Goldberg calls Cardozo "conceptual," and applies this evaluation to the *Palsgraf* opinion. I think he is right in this. But Goldberg is wrong in referring to a "pragmatic conceptualism." Rather, the Cardozo conceptualism is pretentious and essentially arid.

b. From Zipurksy, *Rights, Wrongs, and Recourse in the Law of Torts*, 51 Vand. L. Rev. 1 (1998):

Palsgraf suggests the following question: . . . Why is it not sufficient that the plaintiff has been foreseeably tortiously harmed by the defendant? . . . In short, she may not recover unless the defendant breached a tort duty to her or wronged her (relative to the set of wrongs designated under the tort law). If the defendant wronged a third party, but not the plaintiff, then that plaintiff has no right to recover. Why should this be so? The answer is that entitlement to recourse does not spring from the need precipitated by injury. It springs from the affront of being wronged by another. Because one should not have to suffer that affront passively, without response, fairness requires that one have recourse against the wrongdoer. Substantive standing cases are ones in which the plaintiff is injured, but she has not suffered the affront of being wronged by defendant. Thus, while she may have the need for compensation, she does not have a right to act against the defendant.

Cardozo's mention of the distinction between tort and crime provides another clue as to why his opinion often seems odd to modern scholars. In his insistence that Mrs. Palsgraf lacks standing to sue for a wrong to another, Cardozo appears to display a rejection of torts as an arena of public law, and this apparent rejection seems especially counterintuitive on the facts of *Palsgraf*: If the trainman acted wrongly, why not sanction him? And if Mrs. Palsgraf needed compensation, why not compensate her? When we picture tort law as a form of social insurance funded by sanctions imposed upon wrongdoers, or when we picture it as a form of regulation whose proceeds are used to compensate the injured, the case seems wrongly decided. . . . Cardozo seems to be rejecting one of the most widely accepted of Holmes's insights; he seems to be denying that tort law is really a form of public law. . . .

[O]ur scholarly tradition's treatment of *Palsgraf* is profoundly ironic. It has accepted the dissent's characterization of the issue in the case as one of proximate cause, and then it has read that issue back into the opinion of the court and understood the court to have resolved the issue in the opposite way from the dissent. In other words, scholars accept that *Palsgraf* is a proximate cause case, as Andrews said, but plaintiff loses, so Cardozo must be merely denying the existence of proximate cause in this particular instance. This is an odd way to read any case, especially a central case of our torts canon. While the traditional "proximate cause" reading of *Palsgraf* may be consistent with the outcome of the case, it is the reasoning of the case that imbues it with general importance in torts, not its outcome. The standard interpretation completely misses this reasoning. Cardozo had nothing to say about proximate cause; for him, this was crucially not a proximate cause case, and he was willing to assume arguendo that Andrews was correct about proximate cause. Thus, neither of the famous opinions in the case agrees with — or even presents — the argument most commonly attributed to it.

4. *The weakened floor.* In Edwards v. Honeywell, 50 F.3d 484 (7th Cir. 1995), a fire broke out in a house in Lawrence, a suburb of Indianapolis. The owner of the house, Baker, pushed a button on a fire alarm box that had been installed by Honeywell. This caused a signal to be sent to Honeywell's central station, where an operator in turn called the fire department. She dialed the wrong number, however, calling the Indianapolis fire department rather than the department that serviced Lawrence; she then called another wrong number before at last being transferred to the correct department. The firefighters arrived a few minutes later. One of them entered the house. The floor collapsed beneath him and he plunged to his death. His widow sued Honeywell, claiming the company was negligent in failing to keep accurate information about which fire department to call, and that as a result the fire department arrived at the scene of the blaze three minutes later than they otherwise would have — by which time the floor of the house had been critically weakened. The district court gave summary judgment to Honeywell, and the court of appeals, per Posner, C.J., affirmed. The court said that the facts lay at the intersection of the *Palsgraf* case and *H.R. Moch v. Rensselaer Water Co.* (discussed in the chapter on duty), and that the doctrines of those cases barred recovery here:

> The basic criticism of both the *Palsgraf* and [*Moch*] lines of decisions, articulated with characteristic force by Judge Friendly in *Petition of Kinsman Transit Co.*, is that since by assumption the defendant was careless (for the concept of duty would have no liability-limiting function otherwise), why should its carelessness be excused merely because either the particular harm that occurred as a consequence, or the person harmed as a consequence, was unforeseeable? If the Long Island Railroad's employees had avoided jostling the passenger carrying the bundle of fireworks, as due care required them to do, Mrs. Palsgraf would not have been injured. If the water company [in *Moch*] had kept up the pressure, as it was contractually obligated to do, the fire would not have raged out of control. And if Honeywell had used due care in identifying the fire department with jurisdiction over a fire in the Bakers' house, Edwards (we are assuming for purposes of this appeal) would not have been killed. In none of these cases would the defendant, in

order to prevent the injury of which the plaintiff was complaining, have had to exercise more care than it was required by law to exercise anyway.

[The argument on the other side] arises from the fact that a corporation or other enterprise does not have complete control over its employees, yet it is strictly liable under the principle of respondeat superior for the consequences of their negligent acts committed in the scope of their employment. It is not enough to say to the enterprise be careful and you have nothing to fear. The carelessness of its employees may result in the imposition of a crushing liability upon it. In order to know how many resources (in screening new hires and in supervising and disciplining workers after they are hired) to invest in preventing its employees from being careless, the employer must have some idea, some foresight, of the harms the employees are likely to inflict. Imposing liability for unforeseeable types of harm is unlikely, therefore, to evoke greater efforts at preventing accidents; it is likely merely to constitute the employer an insurer. The railroad in *Palsgraf* did not know that conductors who jostle boarding passengers pose a threat of injury by explosion to people standing elsewhere on the platform, and the water company in *Moch* did not know the likelihood of fires or the value of the property that might be damaged by them. [. . .]

The death of a fireman in fighting a residential fire appears to be a rare occurrence. And we have not been referred to a single case in which such a death was blamed on a malfunction, human or mechanical, in an alarm system. The problem of proving causation in such a case is [. . .] a formidable one, and the plethora of potential defendants makes it difficult (we should think) for an alarm company to estimate its likely liability even if it does foresee the kind of accident that occurred here. If "unforeseeable" is given the practical meaning of too unusual, too uncertain, too unreckonable to make it feasible or worthwhile to take precautions against, then this accident was unforeseeable. Honeywell would have difficulty figuring out how careful it must be in order to satisfy its legal obligations or how much more it ought to charge its subscribers in order to cover its contingent liability to firemen and to any others who might be injured in a fire of which the alarm company failed to give prompt notice. Similar problems of debilitating legal uncertainty would arise if the person injured were a police officer or a paramedic rather than a firefighter.

Is there any reason why the policy goals the court describes in *Edwards* would be better advanced by holding that the defendant had no duty to the plaintiff than by saying that the defendant's conduct was not the proximate cause of the plaintiff's injuries?

5. *Delirium.* In Widlowski v. Durkee Foods, 562 N.E.2d 967 (Ill. 1990), one of Durkee's employees, a man named Wells, attempted to clean an industrial tank containing nitrogen gas. Wells entered the tank without

wearing protective gear and soon was overcome by the gas; he became incoherent and delirious, and was taken to a hospital. While still delirious, he bit off part of a finger belonging to a nurse there. The nurse sued Durkee, alleging that her injuries were attributable to its negligence in failing to clean the tank and properly equip Wells before he entered it. The trial court dismissed her complaint. The court of appeals reversed:

> We believe that under the alleged facts it was reasonably foreseeable that if Wells and Durkee breached a duty of ordinary care in the manner in which the tank was being cleaned, Wells would be overcome by inhaling the nitrogen gas and a deprivation of oxygen. We also believe that it was reasonably foreseeable that Wells would thereby become delirious, agitated, reflexive and incoherent, and a danger to himself and others with whom he made direct contact. In determining whether an injury was reasonably foreseeable to warrant a duty to the injured party, it is not essential that the defendant should have foreseen the precise hazard or exact consequences and injury resulting from the defendant's action or inaction.

The Illinois Supreme Court reversed, ordering the complaint dismissed:

> [T]he burden sought to be imposed on Durkee Foods is a heavy one. Durkee Foods was not in a position to control plaintiff or any other medical personnel in the care and treatment of Wells. Furthermore, accepting plaintiff's argument at face value, liability would extend to the world at large, because it was conceivable, though highly unlikely, that Wells could have harmed anyone with whom he came into contact while in a state of delirium. However, whether a duty exists depends, in part, on the relationship between the parties.
>
> The question whether one party owes another a duty of ordinary care is "very involved, complex and indeed nebulous." The scope and boundaries of a duty are so ambiguous and indistinct that one commentator has observed: "There is a duty if the court says there is a duty." (Prosser, *Palsgraf Revisited*, 52 Mich. L. Rev. 1, 15 (1953)) The court has thus far been unwilling to "say there is a duty" unless the parties stood in such a relationship where one party is obliged to conform to a certain standard of conduct for the benefit of the other. After all, "[p]roof of negligence in the air, so to speak, will not do." (*Palsgraf v. Long Island R.R. Co.* (1928), 162 N.E. 99). For these reasons, there is no duty to guard against the "tragically bizarre" (*Cunis v. Brennan* (1974), 56 Ill. 2d 372, 377), and "liability must stop somewhere short of the freakish and the fantastic" (Prosser, *Palsgraf Revisited*, 52 Mich. L. Rev. 1, 27 (1953)). Under the circumstances of this case, public policy does not support the imposition of a duty. We hold that Durkee Foods did not owe plaintiff a duty of ordinary care.

Which approach in *Palsgraf* does the court's more closely resemble: that of Cardozo or of Andrews?

6. *Danger invites rescue.* In Wagner v. International Ry. Co., 133 N.E. 437 (N.Y. 1921), the plaintiff and his cousin Herbert were riding one night on one of the defendant's trains. Herbert was thrown from the train as it took a steep turn onto a bridge; the plaintiff's evidence was that the train's doors negligently had been left open. The train stopped once it had gotten over the bridge. The plaintiff left the train along with the conductor to search for Herbert. When they reached the bridge, the plaintiff found only his cousin's hat. The plaintiff then lost his footing, slipped, and fell off the bridge onto the ground below. (Herbert's body already was there as well.) The plaintiff brought suit against the railroad, claiming his injuries were attributable to the same original act of negligence that caused Herbert to fall off of the train. The jury brought in a verdict for the defendant railroad after being instructed that the plaintiff could win only if he had been invited by the conductor to go onto the bridge, and only if the conductor had followed him with a light. The plaintiff appealed, arguing that the jury had been improperly instructed. The court of appeals (per Cardozo, J.) reversed:

> Danger invites rescue. The cry of distress is the summons to relief. The law does not ignore these reactions of the mind in tracing conduct to its consequences. It recognizes them as normal. It places their effects within the range of the natural and probable. The wrong that imperils life is a wrong to the imperiled victim; it is a wrong also to his rescuer. The state that leaves an opening in a bridge is liable to the child that falls into the stream, but liable also to the parent who plunges to its aid. The railroad company whose train approaches without signal is a wrongdoer toward the traveler surprised between the rails, but a wrongdoer also to the bystander who drags him from the path. [. . .] The risk of rescue, if only it be not wanton, is born of the occasion. The emergency begets the man. The wrongdoer may not have foreseen the coming of a deliverer. He is accountable as if he had.
>
> The defendant says that we must stop, in following the chain of causes, when action ceases to be "instinctive." By this is meant, it seems, that rescue is at the peril of the rescuer, unless spontaneous and immediate. If there has been time to deliberate, if impulse has given way to judgment, one cause, it is said, has spent its force, and another has intervened. In this case the plaintiff walked more than 400 feet in going to Herbert's aid. He had time to reflect and weigh; impulse had been followed by choice; and choice, in the defendant's view, intercepts and breaks the sequence. We find no warrant for thus shortening the chain of jural causes. [. . .] The law does not discriminate between the rescuer oblivious of peril and the one who counts the cost. It is enough that the act, whether impulsive or deliberate, is the child of the occasion.

The defendant finds another obstacle, however, in the futility of the plaintiff's sacrifice. He should have gone, it is said, below the trestle with the others; he should have known, in view of the overhang of the cars, that the body would not be found above; his conduct was not responsive to the call of the emergency; it was a wanton exposure to a danger that was useless. We think the quality of his acts in the situation that confronted him was to be determined by the jury. [. . .] The plaintiff had to choose at once, in agitation and with imperfect knowledge. He had seen his kinsman and companion thrown out into the darkness. Rescue could not charge the company with liability if rescue was condemned by reason. "Errors of judgment," however, would not count against him if they resulted "from the excitement and confusion of the moment." The reason that was exacted of him was not the reason of the morrow. It was reason fitted and proportioned to the time and the event.

Is Cardozo's decision here consistent with his opinion in *Palsgraf?* What is the distinction between *Wagner v. International Ry. Co.* and *Edwards v. Honeywell, Inc.?*

Chapter 7

Strict Liability

One of the great thematic divides in the law of torts lies between liability for negligence and strict liability. Negligence provides the default rule governing liability for unintentional harm: defendants can be held liable only if their conduct is in some sense blameworthy. To this general rule there are many exceptions, however; areas where the law imposes liability without fault. Some of these areas are modern creations, such as the strict liability imposed on the makers of defective products or the workers' compensation statutes that govern injuries to employees. This chapter is devoted to a set of related areas in which strict liability might be considered traditional: liability for harm done by animals, liability under the English case of *Rylands v. Fletcher,* and liability for abnormally dangerous activities. We also will have a look at the doctrine of respondeat superior, which governs employers' liability for torts committed by their employees.

The "traditional" designation does not fit all of these categories in the same way. While the rules governing liability for animals are very old, *Rylands v. Fletcher* is a nineteenth-century case, and the formal notion of "abnormally dangerous activities" did not emerge until the twentieth century. But all three areas of the law share certain general features in common and can be viewed as linked in their rationales. As we shall see, the law governing liability for animals influenced the *Rylands* decision, and the *Rylands* decision has in turn influenced the emergence of liability for activities considered abnormally dangerous. Studying these areas of law together also creates a useful occasion on which to consider the merits of strict liability and negligence generally. As you read, ask whether and why fault shouldn't always be considered necessary for liability. Or ask the opposite question: why should fault *ever* be considered necessary to justify liability when the defendant is causally responsible for a plaintiff's injuries?

A. LIABILITY FOR ANIMALS

Owners of ferocious beasts are strictly liable for damage their animals cause to others; the owners are liable, in other words, regardless of what measures they took to prevent the harm from occurring. This principle has an ancient pedigree, but general statements of it hide many complications, and the rationale for the doctrine has not always been consistent — as the cases in this section illustrate.

Behrens v. Bertram Mills Circus, Ltd.
2 QB 1, 1 All ER 583, 2 WLR 404 (1957)

[The plaintiffs, Mr. and Mrs. J. H. W. Behrens, were midgets and circus performers; Mr. Behrens claimed to be the smallest man on earth. In 1953 they went on tour with their manager, a man named Whitehead, exhibiting themselves in booths for a fee. The defendants granted Whitehead a license to occupy a booth at a fun fair adjacent to their circus in London. The booth occupied by the plaintiffs was in a corridor that led into the circus; the defendants' elephants passed along the corridor on their journeys between the menagerie and the circus ring. Whitehead sat in a paybox beside the plaintiffs' booth.

[On the day of the accident at issue here, Whitehead's small Pomeranian dog, Simba, was tied to a leg of Whitehead's chair, despite the defendants' rule forbidding the presence of dogs. The elephants passed along the corridor in a single file, as usual, with the trainer walking beside the leading elephant and a groom walking beside each of the remaining elephants. As the third elephant in the procession, Bullu, passed the plaintiffs' booth, Simba ran out snapping and barking. Bullu trumpeted with fright, Simba turned back towards the booth, and Bullu went after her, followed by another elephant. As a result, the front of the booth and other parts of it were knocked down and Mrs. Behrens, who was inside the booth with her husband, was injured. The dog was killed. The trainer got the elephants back into line a few moments later. Mr. and Mrs. Behrens sued the circus, claiming it was strictly liable for damage done by its elephants.]

DEVLIN, J. — [after stating the facts:] A person who keeps an animal with knowledge (scienter retinuit) of its tendency to do harm is strictly liable for damage that it does if it escapes; he is under an absolute duty to confine or control it so that it shall not do injury to others. All animals ferae naturae, that is, all animals which are not by nature harmless, such as a rabbit, or have not been tamed by man and domesticated, such as a horse, are conclusively presumed to have such a tendency, so that the scienter need not in their case be proved. All animals in the second class, mansuetae naturae, are conclusively presumed to be harmless until they have manifested a savage or vicious propensity; proof of such a manifestation is proof of scienter and serves to transfer the animal, so to speak, out of its natural class and into the class ferae naturae. [. . .]

The particular rigidity in the scienter action which is involved in this case — there are many others which are not — is the rule which requires the harmfulness of the offending animal to be judged, not by reference to its particular training and habits, but by reference to the general habits of the species to which it belongs. The law ignores the world of difference between the wild elephant in the jungle and the trained elephant in the circus. The elephant Bullu is, in fact, no more dangerous than a cow; she reacted the same way as a cow would do to the irritation of a small dog; if perhaps her bulk made her capable of doing more damage, her higher training enabled her to be more swiftly checked. I am, however, compelled to assess the defendants' liability in this case in just the same way as I would assess it if they had loosed a wild elephant into the fun fair. This is a branch of the law which, as Lord Goddard said recently, has been settled by authority rather than reason. [. . .]

The defendants submit five answers to the scienter action. They [include] (1) that the elephants are not ferae naturae within the meaning of the rule; [and] (2) that the rule does not impose liability for every act that an animal does if it escapes control, but only for those acts which are vicious and savage, which the action of Bullu was not[.] The first submission is, in my judgment, concluded so far as this court is concerned, by the decision of the Court of Appeal in *Filburn v. People's Palace & Aquarium Co., Ltd*, which held that, as a matter of law, an elephant is an animal ferae naturae. Counsel for the defendants sought to distinguish this case on the ground that the elephants belonging to the defendants are Burmese elephants and he submits that it is open to me to hold that, while elephants generally are ferae naturae, Burmese elephants are not. In my judgment, it is not open to me to consider this submission. It is not stated in *Filburn v. People's Palace & Aquarium Co., Ltd*. what the nationality of the elephant was with which the court was there dealing, and the case must be regarded as an authority for the legal proposition that all elephants are dangerous. The reason why this is a question of law and not a question of fact is because it is a matter of which judicial notice has to be taken. The doctrine has from its formulation proceeded on the supposition that the knowledge of what kinds of animals are tame and what are savage is common knowledge. [. . .] Common knowledge about the ordinary course of nature will extend to knowledge of the propensities of animals according to their different genera, but cannot be supposed to extend to the manner of behavior of animals of the same genus in different parts of the world. Nor can one begin a process of inquiry which might lead in many directions (for example, I am told that female elephants are more docile than male, and that that is why circus elephants are usually female) and be productive of minute subdivisions which would destroy the generality of the rule.

The defendants' second contention raises a point of doubt and difficulty. It may be approached in this way. The reason for imposing a specially stringent degree of liability on the keeper of a savage animal is that such an animal has a propensity to attack mankind and, if left unrestrained, would be likely to do so. The keeper has, therefore, "an absolute duty to confine or control it so that it shall not do injury. . . ." If, however, it escapes from his control, is he liable (subject, of course, to the rules on remoteness of damage) for any injury which it causes, or only for such injury as flows naturally from its vicious and savage propensity? Counsel for the defendants submits that it is the latter part of this question which suggests the correct answer and that the rule of absolute liability applies only when an animal is acting savagely and attacking human beings. On the facts of this case, he submits that Bullu was acting, not viciously, but out of fright; she was seeking to drive off the small dog rather than to attack it; it may be that she or another elephant trampled on the dog (there is no conclusive evidence of that, and it might have been crushed by falling timber) but there is nothing to show that she trampled on it deliberately. Certainly she never attacked the wife, who was injured only indirectly. In short, if Bullu could be treated as a human being, her conduct would be described, not as vicious, but as quite excusable.

It does not, to my mind, necessarily follow that the scope of the rule is coextensive with the reason for making it. It may equally well be argued that, once the rule is made, the reason for making it is dissolved and all that then matters are the terms of the rule. That would certainly be the right approach in the case of any statutory rule of absolute liability. Is it so in the case of this rule of common law? There appears to be no authority directly on point. Counsel for the defendants derives the chief support for his contention from an argument which may be summarized as follows. If an animal mansuetae naturae manifests a vicious tendency, the scienter rule applies to it as if it were ferae naturae. [. . .] How is the principle applied? Suppose that a large dog collides with a child and knocks him down, that is an accident and not a manifestation of a vicious propensity and the scienter rule does not apply at all: if the dog bites a child, it becomes ferae naturae and the strict rule thereafter applies. It would, however, seem to be unreasonable that the strict rule should require the dog to be kept under complete restraint. Suppose that its keeper muzzles it and that while muzzled the dog playfully or accidentally knocks a child down, ought the keeper to be liable? There is a good deal of authority [. . .] to show that the keeper is not liable. [. . .]

This is an impressive argument. It does not seem to me, however, that the logic of the matter necessarily requires that an animal which is savage by disposition should be put on exactly the same footing as one which is savage by nature. Certainly, practical considerations would seem to demand that they be treated differently. It may be unreasonable to hold the owner of a biting dog responsible thereafter for everything that it does; but it may also be unreasonable to limit the liability for a tiger. If a person wakes up in the middle of the night and finds an escaping tiger on top of his bed and suffers a heart attack, it would be nothing to the point that the intentions of the tiger were quite amiable. If a tiger is let loose in a fun fair, it seems to me to be irrelevant whether a person is injured as the result of a direct attack, or because, on seeing it, he runs away and falls over. The feature of this present case which is constantly arising to blur the reasoning is the fact that this particular elephant, Bullu, was tame; but that, as I have said, is a fact which must be ignored. She is to be treated as if she were a wild elephant, and, if a wild elephant were let loose in the fun fair and were stampeding around, I do not think that there would be much difficulty in holding that a person who was injured by falling timber had a right of redress. It is not, in my judgment, practicable to introduce conceptions of mens rea and malevolence in the case of animals.

The distinction between those animals which are ferae naturae by virtue of their genus and those which become so by the exhibition of a particular habit seems to me to be this: that in the case of the former it is assumed (and the assumption is true of a really dangerous animal such as a tiger) that whenever they get out of control they are practically bound to do injury, while in the case of the latter the assumption is that they will do injury only to the extent of the propensity which they have peculiarly manifested.

It follows that, subject to any special defense, the defendants are liable for any injury done while the elephant was out of control. It does not follow (I say this because of a point that was raised in the argument) that, if an elephant slips or stumbles, its keeper is responsible for the consequences. There must be a failure of control. Here, however, there was such a failure, albeit a very temporary one. [. . .]

As liable for all injury while eleph out of control

NOTES

1. *Badly in need of simplification?* As Lord Devlin's opinion explains, the common law of liability for animals hinges on the distinction between those types of animals considered to be wild, or "ferae naturae," and those presumed to be tame, whether because they are "domitae naturae" (a species domesticated by man) or "mansuetae naturae" (a species tame by nature). The distinction between these latter two types of tameness is not generally treated as important, but much does depend on the broad distinction between species regarded as tame and wild. If the animal is of a type considered wild, its owner generally will be held strictly liable for the damage the animal causes (with exceptions we shall consider in a moment). The determination of "wildness" in this sense is made with a broad brush, as *Behrens* illustrates: all elephants are considered ferae naturae, regardless of whether the particular elephant that caused the damage has been thoroughly tamed. If the animal is of a domesticated type — e.g., a dog, cat, horse, or cow — it is presumed tame, and the owner is held strictly liable only if he is aware that the particular animal in question already had shown a propensity to cause the sort of harm it inflicted on the plaintiff.

In another part of his opinion in *Behrens*, Devlin noted the recommendation of some commentators that the rules governing liability for animals be
replaced with a single negligence standard. Said he, "I wish to express the hope
that Parliament may find time to consider this recommendation, for this
branch of the law is badly in need of simplification."

2. *Liability for bees.* In Earl v. Van Alstine, 8 Barb. 630 (N.Y. 1850), the
defendant kept 15 beehives in his yard, which was bordered by a public
highway. The plaintiff was driving his horses past the place where the bees
were kept when the bees attacked the horses; one horse died, and another was
injured. The trial court found for the plaintiff and awarded him $70.25. The
New York Court of Appeals reversed:

Peake, in his work on evidence, under the head of "Actions founded in
negligence," has the following: "If one man keep a lion, bear, or any other
wild and *ferocious* animal, and such animal escape from his confinement
and do mischief to another, the owner is liable to make satisfaction for the
mischief so done without further evidence of negligence in him; for every
person who keeps such noxious and *useless* animals must keep them at his
peril. On the contrary, if a man has a dog, a bull, or any other domestic
animal such as are usually kept and are indeed *necessary to the existence of
man*, no action is maintainable without proof of knowledge[.]" [. . .]

[I]t remains to be considered whether bees are animals of so ferocious a
disposition, that every one who keeps them, under any circumstances,
does so at his peril. If it is necessary for the plaintiff to aver and prove the
mischievous nature of the animal, nothing of the kind was done in this
case; but if courts are to take judicial notice of the nature of things so
familiar to man as bees, which I suppose they would be justified in doing,
then I would observe that however it may have been anciently, in modern
days the bee has become almost as completely domesticated as the ox or
the cow. Its habits and its instincts have been studied, and through the
knowledge thus acquired it can be controlled and managed with nearly as
much certainty as any of the domestic animals; and although it may be
proper still to class it among those ferae naturae, it must nevertheless be
regarded as coming very near the dividing line, and in regard to its propensity to mischief, I apprehend that such a thing as a *serious* injury to
persons or property from its attacks is very rare, not occurring in a ration
more frequent certainly than injuries arising from the kick of a horse, or
the bite of a dog. [. . .]

The utility of bees no one will question, and hence there is nothing to
call for the application of a very stringent rule to the case. Upon the
whole, therefore, I am clearly of the opinion that the owner of bees is
not liable *at all events* for any accidental injury they may do. The question
is still left whether the keeping of these bees so near the highway subjects
the defendant to a responsibility which would not otherwise rest upon

him. I consider this question as substantially disposed of by the evidence in the case. It appears that bees had been kept in the same situation for some eight or nine years, and no proof was offered of the slightest injury ever having been done by them. On the contrary, some of the witnesses testified that they had lived in the neighborhood and had been in the habit of passing and repassing frequently, with teams and otherwise, without ever having been molested. [. . .]

No — 8–9 yrs w/ no incident

What is the distinction between *Earl v. Van Alstine* and *Behrens v. Bertram Mills Circus?*

The net result of the *Earl* case is that Van Alstine's bees stung a horse to death, yet Van Alstine owes nothing to the horse's owner. Why? If bees of the defendant attacked other horses after the opinion in *Earl* was issued, would Van Alstine then be bound to compensate their owners? What general theory does the *Earl* case implicitly suggest should be used to explain the distinction between strict liability and negligence?

ferae naturae

3. *Liability for baboons.* In *Candler v. Smith*, 179 S.E. 395 (Ga. App. 1935), the plaintiff's car would not start, so she went into her house to call a mechanic. When she returned, she found her car occupied by a large baboon that had escaped from the defendant's zoo. The animal advanced toward the plaintiff in what she later described as a menacing manner. She turned back into her house, but tripped over the doormat and only was able to save herself from being overtaken by the animal by slamming the door in his face. The baboon returned to the automobile, seized the plaintiff's pocket-book, and destroyed its contents, including currency and other valuables. The plaintiff sued to collect damages for the nervous fright and shock caused to her by the encounter. The jury awarded her $10,000, and the defendant appealed.

Baboon escaped from zoo. Advanced on π, injured escaping it. Also caused property damage.

Held, for the plaintiff, that the defendant's motion for a new trial properly was overruled; the defendant was strictly liable for the plaintiff's injuries. (The plaintiff needlessly had alleged negligence, and the trial court incorrectly had instructed the jury that it had to find negligence to hold the defendant liable; but the jury had so found, so the errors were harmless.) Said the court:

Δ was SL

> [W]here it is alleged that a monkey or baboon (being classed as an animal ferae naturae) had escaped from its place of confinement and come upon the plaintiff's premises and there committed the injury complained of, this is sufficient to withstand a demurrer, even though it is not stated in the petition how the escape was effected. It is not necessary to allege that the owner was negligent in allowing the animal to be at large, for he is bound to keep it secure at his peril.

Keep a wild animal @ your peril — π doesn't have to allege neg l.

What is the distinction between *Candler v. Smith* and *Earl v. Van Alstine*, which declined to hold beekeepers strictly liable for injuries caused by their bees?

4. *Light work for the hangman.* In Smith v. Pelah, Hilary Term, 20 Geo. 2, 2 Strange 1265, 93 Eng. Reps. 1171, "The Chief Justice (Lord Alverstone) ruled that if a dog has once bit a man and the owner having notice thereof keeps the dog and lets him go about or lie at his door, an action will lie against him at the suit of a person who is bit though it happened by such person's treading on the dog's toes, for it was owing to his not hanging the dog on the first notice. And the safety of the King's subjects ought not afterwards to be endangered. The scienter is the gist of the action."

The point of *Smith v. Pelah* is that the defendant was strictly liable for his dog's second bite. Why? What rationale for strict liability is implied by the case?

As noted earlier, if a species of animal is held to be mansuetae naturae or domitae naturae — i.e., tame — that decision does not necessarily relieve the owner of liability for damage the animals cause. Instead the focus of the inquiry becomes the extent of the owner's knowledge that the animal had a propensity for the sort of mischief it created. If the owner had such knowledge, he is held liable for it; and the most common way for such knowledge to be shown is by demonstrating that the animal had behaved the same way in the past. Hence the apocryphal "one bite rule" of tort law — the maxim that every dog is entitled to one free bite. That is a crude approximation of the common law position; no jurisdiction quite adheres to it. An owner may be found to have had notice of a dog's viciousness even if the dog has not bitten before, and an owner may be found to have had no notice of viciousness even if the dog has bitten before.

Many states have replaced the common law approach with animal control statutes that a hold a dog owner strictly liable for any bites a dog inflicts, regardless of the dog's past record or reputation. See, e.g., *Docherty v. Sadler*, 689 N.E.2d 332 (Ill. App. 1997).

5. *The one gore rule.* In Banks v. Maxwell, 171 S.E. 70 (N.C. 1933), the plaintiff worked on the defendant's farm. The defendant instructed the plaintiff to drive a bull from its pen into a pasture. The defendant testified that "[w]hen he told me to go into the pen I at first hesitated. I had no idea what the brute was. [. . .] I picked up a club and started in, but he told me not to hit the brute with the club and I dropped it. I had not any more than dropped it until [the bull] turned on me, knocked me down and gored me." The trial court nonsuited the plaintiff, and the North Carolina Supreme Court affirmed:

> The familiar rule of liability for injuries inflicted by cattle has remained approximately constant for more than 3,000 years. This rule of liability was expressed by Moses in the following words: "If an ox gore a man or a woman that they die; then the ox shall be surely stoned and his flesh shall not be eaten, but the owner of the ox shall be quit. But if the ox were wont to push with his horn in time past, and it hath been testified to his owner,

[handwritten margin notes: Δ instructed π to drive bull from pen. Bull gored π. Nonsuit. Aff'd.]

and he hath not kept him in, but that he hath killed a man or a woman; the ox shall be stoned, and his owner also shall be put to death. If there be laid on him a sum of money, then he shall give for the ransom of his life whatsoever is laid upon him." Ex. 21:28-30.

This court declared in *Rector v. Coal Co.*, 192 N.C. 804, that a person injured by a domestic animal, in order to recover damages, must show two essential facts: (1) "The animal inflicting the injury must be dangerous, vicious, mischievous or ferocious, or one termed in the law as possessing a vicious propensity." (2) "The owner must have actual or constructive knowledge of the vicious propensity, character and habits of the animal."

In the case at bar there was no evidence offered tending to show that the bull had ever attacked a person or threatened to do so, nor that he was "wont to push with his horn in time past"; nor was there evidence that the owner had actual or constructive knowledge of any vicious propensity of the animal. It is true that a witness said that each morning when the bull was turned out of the pen "he would bellow, paw the ground, and burrow in the ground with his head." Those bred to the soil perhaps know that such acts on the part of a normal bull constituted per se no more than boastful publicity or propaganda, doubtless designed by the animal to inform his bovine friends and admirers that he was arriving upon the scene.

6. *The animate menace.* In Vaughan v. Miller Bros. "101" Ranch Wild West Show, 153 S.E. 289 (W. Va. 1930), an ape on exhibit at the defendant's circus bit off the plaintiff's finger. The plaintiff sued to recover for his injuries, alleging no negligence but asserting that the defendant was strictly liable for damage done by the animal. The West Virginia Supreme Court disagreed:

If, at common law, the ownership of wild animals was recognized and protected as lawful, how could judges consistently presume such ownership wrongful and negligent? An anomaly indeed! It is true that animals ferae naturae constantly seek to escape confinement, and, if successful, become a menace to mankind. But the tiger, unrestrained, is no more dangerous than fire, water, electricity, or gas uncontrolled. The liability of the owner of these has never been declared absolute, nor his negligence presumed from mere ownership. Why discriminate against the owner of the animate menace? [. . .]

In this country the right to exhibit wild animals is judicially recognized. "The conducting of shows for the exhibition of wild . . . animals is a lawful business." *Bostock-Ferari Amusement Co. v. Brocksmith*, 73 N. E. 281 (Ind.). Such exhibitions are licensed everywhere. Municipalities frequently maintain zoos for the benefit of the public. The idea is no longer indulged that it is prima facie negligent to keep or exhibit wild animals. [. . .] Hence the gist of modern actions against exhibitors cannot be the mere keeping of savage animals, but must be neglect to restrain them. "Latterly, however, there seems to be a disposition upon the part of the authorities to hold the more reasonable rule, that all that should be required of the keeper of such animals is that he should take that superior caution to prevent their doing mischief which their propensities in that direction justly demand of him." 1 Thompson, Comm. Neg. §841.

Vaughan represents a minority view. Is it correct? What is the court's implicit theory of when strict liability should apply? Consider this excerpt from the Restatement (Third) of Torts (P.F.D. 2005):

§24. SCOPE OF STRICT LIABILITY.

Strict liability under §§20-23 does not apply
(a) if the person suffers physical harm as a result of making contact with coming into proximity to the defendant's animal or abnormally dangerous activity for the purpose of securing some benefit from that contact or that proximity; or
(b) if the defendant maintains ownership or possession of the animal or carries on the abnormally dangerous activity in pursuance of an obligation imposed by law.

Should the victim of an animal bite at a zoo be denied recovery under part (a)?

7. *Homely brutes.* In Bostock-Ferari Amusements v. Brocksmith, 73 N.E. 281 (Ind. App. 1905), the plaintiff's evidence was that he was driving a horse-drawn buggy through the town of Vincennes when his horse spotted a large brown bear walking down the street. The bear was wearing a muzzle, and its owner and keeper was leading it, by chains attached to the animal's collar and to a ring in its nose, from the railroad station to the defendant's show where the animal was to be exhibited. The plaintiff's horse nonetheless was badly frightened by the bear, which fright resulted in various damages to the plaintiff. The jury brought in a verdict for the plaintiff for $750, and the defendant appealed.

Held, for the defendant, that the judgment must be reversed, and that there must be a new trial. Said the court:

When a person is injured by an attack by an animal ferae naturae, the negligence of the owner is presumed, because the dangerous propensity of such an animal is known, and the law recognizes that safety lies only in keeping it secure. In the case before us the injury did not result from any vicious propensity of the bear. He did nothing but walk in the charge of his owner and keeper, Peter Degeleih. He was being moved quietly upon a public thoroughfare for a lawful purpose. [. . .]

King David said, "An horse is a vain thing for safety." Modern observation has fully justified the statement. A large dog, a great bull, a baby wagon, may each frighten some horses, but their owners are not barred from using them upon the streets on that account. Nor, under the decisions, would the courts be warranted in holding that the owner of a bear, subjugated, gentle, docile, chained, would not, under the facts shown in the case at bar, be permitted to conduct the homely brute along the public streets, because of his previous condition of freedom.

What is the distinction between *Bostock-Ferari Amusements* and *Candler v. Smith* (the L case of the escaped baboon)? What is the distinction between *Bostock-Ferari Amusements v. Brocksmith* and *Behrens v. Bertram Mills Circus*?

8. *Go it, Bob.* In Baker v. Snell, 2 K.B. 825 (1908), the plaintiff was a maid employed by the defendant, an innkeeper. The defendant kept a dog he knew to be savage. The defendant's potman — an employee responsible for various chores at the inn — would let the dog out in the morning and then chain it up again before the plaintiff and the barmaids came downstairs. On the day in question, the potman brought the dog into a kitchen where the maids were at breakfast and said, "I will bet the dog will not bite any one in the room." The potman then let the dog go and said, "Go it, Bob." The dog flew at the plaintiff and bit her. The plaintiff sued the dog's owner for damages. The trial court held the defendant liable despite the potman's intervening act, saying the owner of an animal known to be savage is strictly liable for any damage it causes. The House of Lords affirmed:

> If it is true, as I think it is, that it is a wrongful act for a person to keep an animal which he knows to be dangerous, that is an authority [...] that the person so keeping it is liable for the consequences of his wrongful act, even though the immediate cause of damage is the act of a third party.

What is the analogy between *Baker v. Snell* and *Behrens v. Bertram Mills Circus*? Which is the more difficult case?

9. *Leopard scratch.* In Opelt v. Al G. Barnes Co., 183 P. 241 (Cal. App. 1919), a boy sued a circus for injuries he received from one of its leopards. The leopard was in a cage alongside an array of other caged animals; a series of posts, with guard ropes between them, separated the caged animals from the spectators by a distance that prevented either from touching the other. The plaintiff and one of his friends walked underneath one of the ropes to get a better look at the animals. The leopard reached out between the bars of his cage and scratched the plaintiff, causing the injuries that gave rise to the suit. The trial court gave judgment to the defendant, finding that the plaintiff was injured solely because he willfully placed himself within reach of the wild animal, which he knew to be ferocious. The plaintiff appealed.

Held, for the defendant, that the evidence was sufficient to support the verdict.

What is the superficial similarity between *Opelt v. Al G. Barnes Co.* and *Behrens v. Bertram Mills Circus* (the L case of the excitable elephant)? What is the distinction between them? What is the distinction between *Opelt* and *Baker v. Snell*?

10. *The hazards of the game (problem)*. In Gomes v. Byrne, 333 P.2d 754 (Cal. 1959), the court set out the facts as follows:

> Plaintiff, a salesman for the Fuller Brush Company, was canvassing in the neighborhood of defendant's home. As he walked along the sidewalk approaching the gate leading to defendant's door, the dog in the enclosed yard followed him along the inside of the fence for about fifty feet, barking continuously all the way. Plaintiff nevertheless opened the gate and walked into the yard, whereupon the dog bit him on the right lower leg, causing a puncture wound and superficial abrasions. Defendant, having heard the dog barking, went to the door and met plaintiff as he came up the steps. Plaintiff said that the dog had bitten him; defendant expressed her sorrow at the mishap; and plaintiff responded with the statement that it was one of "the hazards of the game." Plaintiff gave defendant a catalogue and left. The next day plaintiff again called at defendant's home and at that time defendant bought some merchandise from him.

The plaintiff brought suit under §3342(a) of the California Civil Code:

> The owner of any dog is liable for the damages suffered by any person who is bitten by the dog while in a public place or lawfully in a private place, including the property of the owner of the dog, regardless of the former viciousness of the dog or the owner's knowledge of such viciousness. A person is lawfully upon the private property of such owner within the meaning of this section when he is on such property in the performance of any duty imposed upon him by the laws of this state or by the laws or postal regulations of the United States, or when he is on such property upon the invitation, express or implied, of the owner.

What result?

B.   RYLANDS v. FLETCHER

Rylands v. Fletcher
Court of Exchequer, 3 H. & C. 774, 159 Eng. Rep. 737 (1865)
Exchequer Chamber, L.R. 1 Ex. 265 (1866)
House of Lords, L.R. 3 H.L. 330 (1868)

[handwritten margin note: this is wrong, he owned the mill (you'd think they'd fix in 2d ed.)]

[The defendants hired independent contractors to build a reservoir for them. One of the defendants, John Rylands, was the owner of the land on which the reservoir sat, and the other defendant, Jehu Horrocks, owned a nearby factory that used the water power that the reservoir generated. During the construction of the reservoir, the defendants' contractors discovered some old mining tunnels underneath Rylands' property but did not investigate them. It turned out that the shafts were connected to a coal mine owned by the plaintiff, Thomas Fletcher.

[When the defendants filled the reservoir, the water almost immediately broke through the bottom of it, flowed into the tunnels, and flooded the plaintiff's mine. Nobody was injured, but the plaintiff suffered damage to his property for which he sought to recover. An arbitrator found that the defendants' construction contractors had been negligent but that the defendants themselves had not been negligent. The plaintiff, however, had not sued the contractors, apparently because they had gone out of business. Based on the arbitrator's findings, the Court of Exchequer held (with Bramwell, B., dissenting) that the plaintiff was not entitled to recover against the defendants. The plaintiff appealed to the next highest court, the Court of Exchequer Chamber.]

Exchequer

BLACKBURN, J. [after stating the facts:] — The plaintiff, though free from all blame on his part, must bear the loss, unless he can establish that it was the consequence of some default for which the defendants are responsible. The question of law therefore arises, which is the obligation which the law casts on a person who, like the defendants, lawfully brings on his land something which, though harmless whilst it remains there, will naturally do mischief if it escape out of his land. It is agreed on all hands that he must take care to keep in that which he has brought on the land and keeps there, in order that it may not escape and damage his neighbours, but the question arises whether the duty which the law casts upon him, under such circumstances, is an absolute duty to keep it in at his peril, or is, as the majority of the Court of Exchequer have thought, merely a duty to take all reasonable and prudent precautions, in order to keep it in, but no more. If the first be the law, the person who has brought on his land and kept there something dangerous, and failed to keep it in, is responsible for all the natural consequences of its escape. If the second be the limit of his duty, he would not be answerable except on proof of negligence, and consequently would not be answerable for escape arising from any latent defect which ordinary prudence and skill could not detect. [. . .]

We think that the true rule of law is, that the person who for his own purposes brings on his lands and collects and keeps there anything likely to do mischief if it escapes, must keep it in at his peril, and, if he does not do so, is prima facie answerable for all the damage which is the natural consequence of its escape. He can excuse himself by shewing that the escape was owing to the plaintiff's default; or perhaps that the escape was the consequence of vis major, or the act of God; but as nothing of this sort exists here, it is unnecessary to inquire what excuse would be sufficient. The general rule, as above stated, seems on principle just. The person whose grass or corn is eaten down by the escaping cattle of his neighbour, or whose mine is flooded by the water from his neighbour's reservoir, or whose cellar is invaded by the filth of his neighbour's privy, or whose habitation is made unhealthy by the fumes and noisome vapours of his neighbour's alkali works, is damnified without any fault of his own; and it seems but reasonable and just that the neighbour, who has brought something on his own property which was not naturally there, harmless to others so long as it is confined to his own property, but which he knows to be mischievous if it gets on his neighbour's, should be obliged to make good the damage which ensues if he does not succeed in confining it to his own property. But for his act in bringing it there no mischief could have accrued, and it seems but just that he should at his peril keep it there so that no mischief may accrue, or answer for the natural and anticipated consequences. And upon authority, this we think is established to be the law whether the things so brought be beasts, or water, or filth, or stenches.

The case that has most commonly occurred, and which is most frequently to be found in the books, is as to the obligation of the owner of cattle which he brought on his land, to prevent their escape and doing mischief. The law as to them seems to be perfectly settled from early times; the owner must keep them in at his peril, or he will be answerable for the natural consequences of their escape; that is with regard to tame beasts, for the grass they eat and trample upon, though not for any injury to the person of others, for our ancestors have settled that it is not the general nature of horses to kick, or bulls to gore; but if the owner knows that the beast has a vicious propensity to attack man, he will be answerable for that too. [. . .]

But it was further said by Martin, B. [in the Court of Exchequer] that when damage is done to personal property, or even to the person, by collision either upon land or at sea, there must be negligence in the party doing the damage to render him legally responsible; and this is no doubt true, and as was pointed out by Mr. Mellish during his argument before us, this is not confined to cases of collision, for there are many cases in which proof of negligence is essential, as for instance, where an unruly horse gets on the footpath of a public street and kills a passenger: *Hammack v. White*; or where a person in a dock is struck by the falling of a bale of cotton which the defendant's servants are lowering, *Scott v. London Dock Company*; and many other similar cases may be found. But we think these cases distinguishable from the present.

Traffic on the highways, whether by land or sea, cannot be conducted without exposing those whose persons or property are near it to some inevitable risk; and that being so, those who go on the highway, or have their property adjacent to it, may well be held to do so subject to their taking upon themselves the risk of injury from that inevitable danger; and persons who by the licence of the owner pass near to warehouses where goods are being raised or lowered, certainly do so subject to the inevitable risk of accident. In neither case, therefore, can they recover without proof of want of care or skill occasioning the accident; and it is believed that all the cases in which inevitable accident has been held an excuse of what prima facie was a trespass, can be explained on the same principle, viz., that the circumstances were such as to shew that the plaintiff had taken that risk upon himself.

But there is no ground for saying that the plaintiff here took upon himself any risk arising from the uses to which the defendants should choose to apply their land. He neither knew what these might be, nor could he in any way control the defendants, or hinder their building what reservoirs they liked, and storing up in them what water they pleased, so long as the defendants succeeded in preventing the water which they there brought from interfering with the plaintiff's property. [. . .]

Judgment for the plaintiff.

[The House of Lords affirmed the decision of the Court of Exchequer Chamber:]

CAIRNS, L.J.: My Lords, the principles on which this case must be determined appear to me to be extremely simple. The Defendants, treating them as the owners or occupiers of the close on which the reservoir was constructed, might lawfully have used that close for any purpose for which it might in the ordinary course of the enjoyment of the land be used; and if, in what I may term the natural use of that land, there had been any accumulation of water, either on the surface or underground, and if, by operation of the laws of nature, that accumulation of water had passed off into the close occupied by the Plaintiff, the Plaintiff could not have complained that that result had taken place [. . .].

On the other hand if the Defendants, not stopping at the natural use of their close, had desired to use it for any purpose which I may term a non-natural use, for the purpose of introducing into the close that which in its natural condition was not in or upon it, for the purpose of introducing water either above or below ground in quantities and in a manner not the result of any operation on or under the land, and if in consequence of their doing so, the water came to escape and to pass off into the close of the Plaintiff, then it appears to me that that which the Defendants were doing they were doing at their own peril; and, if in the course of their doing it, the evil arose to which I have referred, the evil, namely, of the escape of the water and its passing away to the close of the Plaintiff and injuring the Plaintiff, then for the consequence of that, in my opinion, the Defendants would be liable [. . .].

NOTES

1. *The true rule of law.* What was the holding of the Court of Exchequer Chamber? What was the holding of the House of Lords? What are the

differences between them? How would you state the "rule" of *Rylands v. Fletcher*?

2. *Facts vs. language. Rylands v. Fletcher* is one of most influential and discussed tort cases ever decided not because cases involving leaky reservoirs have been especially common, but because the case stands for a principle that is practically important but has unclear dimensions and an uncertain rationale. Consider two ways of thinking about the significance of *Rylands*. The first involves its language: Blackburn's statement that "the person who for his own purposes brings on his lands and collects and keeps there anything likely to do mischief if it escapes, must keep it in at his peril, and, if he does not do so, is prima facie answerable for all the damage which is the natural consequence of its escape"; and the statement of Cairns, L.J., in the House of Lords that the principle applies only to non-natural uses of property. If you were to focus just on this language without reference to the facts of *Rylands*, how broadly would the holding sweep?

Another way to think about *Rylands* is to focus on its *result* — strict liability on the facts the case presented — and then to ask when other cases arise whether their facts are similar to the facts of *Rylands*. This sort of analysis, of course, requires decisions about which sorts of factual similarities matter. If the next case involves an exploding sewer pipe, is it similar to *Rylands*? Suppose the next case involves an explosion not of water but of propane gas. Does *Rylands* mean that the owner of the gas is strictly liable? Whether these cases are analogous to *Rylands* depends which features of *Rylands* seem important to the result the court reached in that case: the water, the way it was contained, the relationship between the reservoir and its surroundings, and so forth. And in the meantime there are other precedents that would compete with *Rylands* to govern the result in those new cases. Is an explosion of propane gas more like a bursting reservoir or more like a fire started by sparks from a train? Or is the propane case not usefully similar to either of those cases? The common law process often involves such decisions, made one case at a time, about which factual similarities matter and which do not.

We now proceed by examining some of the English cases interpreting *Rylands v. Fletcher*; then we will consider how American courts responded to the case.

3. *The poisonous yew.* In Crowhurst v. The Burial Board of the Parish of Amersham, Exchequer Div. Vol. IV (1878), the defendants planted a yew tree about four feet from the iron railings that enclosed their cemetery. The yew grew over and through the railings until its branches were within reach of the plaintiff's horse, which was pastured in a meadow beside the cemetery. The horse ate from branches of the yew and later was found dead in the meadow. The plaintiff had not been aware of the yew. The county court awarded the plaintiff damages, the defendant appealed, and the judgment was affirmed. Said the court, "The principle by which such a case is to be

governed is carefully expressed in the judgment of the Exchequer Chamber in *Fletcher v. Rylands.*"

In what senses (if any) is a poisonous yew tree analogous to a bursting reservoir?

4. *Impromptu reservoir.* In Rickards v. Lothian, [1913] A.C. 263 (P.C. Austrl.), the defendant was the owner of a commercial building. The plaintiff was one of his tenants. One night a trespasser entered the building, clogged the sinks in the fourth-floor lavatory, turned the water on, and left. Water accumulated and leaked into the plaintiff's rooms, damaging his stock. The Privy Council (the highest court of appeal for claims arising from British commonwealth countries), holding for the defendant, said that the case did not come within the rule of *Rylands v. Fletcher* because

> [i]t is not every use to which land is put that brings into play that principle. It must be some special use bringing with it increased danger to others, and must not merely be the ordinary use of the land or such a use as is proper for the general benefit of the community. [. . .]
>
> [T]he provision of a proper supply of water to the various parts of a house is not only reasonable, but has become, in accordance with modern sanitary views, an almost necessary feature of town life [. . .]. It would be unreasonable for the law to regard those who install and maintain such a system of supply as doing so at their own peril.

What is the distinction between *Rickards v. Lothian* and *Rylands v. Fletcher*? How would you rewrite the facts of *Rylands* to make them more like the facts of *Rickards* and thus to make *Rylands* a case of no liability on the same reasoning?

5. *Well done, Jeeves.* In Musgrove v. Pandelis, [1919] 2 K.B. 43 (C.A.), *aff'g* [1919] 1 K.B. 314, the plaintiff was the tenant of an apartment above a garage where the defendant stored his automobile. The defendant employed a chauffeur who had taken a few driving lessons but otherwise was unskilled with automobiles, which at the time were a new technology. The chauffeur was sent to clean the car and found that he had to move it first. He opened the hood, turned on the gas tap, and started the engine. An explosion and fire resulted. The chauffeur went to look for a cloth; by the time he got back, the car, the garage, and finally the plaintiff's apartment had caught fire.

Bankes, L.J., held that the motor car with gasoline in its tank was a dangerous thing to bring into the garage and thus came within the rule of *Rylands v. Fletcher*. Duke, L.J., said: "In the present case there was petrol which was easily convertible into an inflammable vapour: there was the apparatus for producing the spark: and added to those there was a person supposed to control the combustion but inexperienced and unequal to the task. Taking together the presence of the petrol and the production of the inflammable gas or those combustibles together with the inexperience of the person placed in charge of them it is impossible to say that this is not an instance of the principle laid down by Blackburn, J."

6. *Blowtorches.* In Balfour v. Barty-King, [Q.B. 1956] 2 All E.R. 555, Balfour sued the Barty-Kings for damages arising from a fire. The parties lived in separate dwellings that previously had been part of the same mansion. The Barty-Kings hired a contractor to unfreeze frozen pipes in their attic. He sought to accomplish this by using a blowtorch. The torch set fire to some felt that covered rafters near the pipes, and the fire spread to Balfour's part of the house. The court held the Barty-Kings strictly liable for the damage under *Rylands v. Fletcher*:

> It appears that although the use of a blow-lamp for the purpose of thawing out a pipe is a recognised method of thawing out a pipe in an appropriate place and appropriate circumstances, yet in other places it is not only not a recognised practice but also an extremely dangerous practice, and one which no prudent workman or contractor would have adopted. I have to have regard to all the circumstances of time and place and the practice of the trade, and, applying that test, I feel constrained to come to the conclusion that the user of the blow-lamp in these particular circumstances in this loft, so close to all this combustible material, did constitute the blow-lamp an object of the class to which the rule in *Rylands v. Fletcher* applies.

7. *Early American interpretations of Rylands v. Fletcher.* In Losee v. Buchanan, 51 N.Y. 476 (1873), a steam boiler used by the defendant Saratoga Paper Company in its Schuylerville mill exploded. Pieces of the boiler flew onto the plaintiff's premises and caused damage. The trial court rejected the plaintiff's assertion that the defendants should be held strictly liable, and the court of appeals affirmed:

> By becoming a member of civilized society, I am compelled to give up many of my natural rights, but I receive more than a compensation from the surrender by every other man of the same rights, and the security, advantage and protection which the laws give me. So, too, the general rules that I may have the exclusive and undisturbed use and possession of my real estate, and that I must so use my real estate as not to injure my neighbor, are much modified by the exigencies of the social state. We must have factories, machinery, dams, canals and railroads. They are demanded by the manifold wants of mankind, and lay at the basis of all our civilization. If I have any of these upon my lands, and they are not a nuisance and are not so managed as to become such, I am not responsible for any damage they accidentally and unavoidably do my neighbor. He receives his compensation for such damage by the general good, in which he shares, and the right which he has to place the same

things upon his lands. I may not place or keep a nuisance upon my land to the damage of my neighbor, and I have my compensation for the surrender of this right to use my own as I will by the similar restriction imposed upon my neighbor for my benefit. I hold my property subject to the risk that it may be unavoidably or accidentally injured by those who live near me; and as I move about upon the public highways and in all places where other persons may lawfully be, I take the risk of being accidentally injured in my person by them without fault on their part. Most of the rights of property, as well as of person, in the social state, are not absolute but relative, and they must be so arranged and modified, not unnecessarily infringing upon natural rights, as upon the whole to promote the general welfare.

But our attention is called to a recent English case, decided in the Exchequer Chamber [*Rylands v. Fletcher*], which seems to uphold the claim made. [. . .] It is sufficient, however, to say that the law, as laid down in [that] case, is in direct conflict with the law as settled in this country. Here, if one builds a dam upon his own premises and thus holds back and accumulates the water for his benefit, or if he brings water upon his premises into a reservoir, in case the dam or the banks of the reservoir give away and the lands of a neighbor are thus flooded, he is not liable for the damage without proof of some fault or negligence on his part. [. . .]

[T]he rule is, at least in this country, a universal one, which, so far as I can discern, has no exceptions or limitations, that no one can be made liable for injuries to the person or property of another without some fault or negligence on his part.

In this case the defendants had the right to place the steam boiler upon their premises. It was in no sense a nuisance, and the jury have found that they were not guilty of any negligence. The judgment in their favor should, therefore, have been affirmed at the General Term [. . .].

As *Losee v. Buchanan* illustrates, the initial reaction of American courts to *Rylands v. Fletcher* was hostile. Did the court in *Losee* understand *Rylands* correctly?

8. *England vs. Texas.* In Turner v. Big Lake Oil Co., 96 S.W.2d 221 (Tex. 1936), salt water overflowed from an artificial pond the defendants used in operating oil wells, causing damage to the plaintiff's pasture. The court declined to hold the defendant strictly liable:

[A] rule with reference to the adoption of the English common law is that in adopting it as the rule of decision we have done so only in so far as consistent with the conditions which obtain in this state. [. . .]

In *Rylands v. Fletcher* the court predicated the absolute liability of the defendants on the proposition that the use of land for the artificial storage of water was not a natural use, and that, therefore, the landowner was bound at his peril to keep the waters on his own land. This basis of the English rule is to be found in the meteorological conditions which obtain there. England is a pluvial country, where constant streams and abundant rains make the storage of water unnecessary for ordinary or general purposes. When the court said in *Rylands v. Fletcher* that the use of land for storage of water was an unnatural use, it meant such use was not a general or an ordinary one; not one within the contemplation of the parties to the original grant of the land involved, nor of the grantor and grantees of adjacent lands, but was a special or extraordinary use, and for that reason applied the rule of absolute liability. [. . .]

In Texas we have conditions very different from those which obtain in England. A large portion of Texas is an arid or semi-arid region. West of the 98th meridian of longitude, where the rainfall is approximately 30 inches, the rainfall decreases until finally, in the extreme western part of the state, it is only about 10 inches. This land of decreasing rainfall is the great ranch or livestock region of the state, water for which is stored in thousands of ponds, tanks, and lakes on the surface of the ground. The country is almost without streams; and without the storage of water from rainfall in basins constructed for the purpose, or to hold waters pumped from the earth, the great livestock industry of West Texas must perish. No such condition obtains in England. With us the storage of water is a natural or necessary and common use of the land, necessarily within the contemplation of the state and its grantees when grants were made, and obviously the rule announced in *Rylands v. Fletcher*, predicated upon different conditions, can have no application here.

Again, in England there are no oil wells, no necessity for using surface storage facilities for impounding and evaporating salt waters therefrom. In Texas the situation is different. Texas has many great oil fields, tens of thousands of wells in almost every part of the state. Producing oil is one of our major industries. One of the by-products of oil production is salt water, which must be disposed of without injury to property or the pollution of streams. The construction of basins or ponds to hold this salt water is a necessary part of the oil business. In Texas much of our land was granted without mineral reservation to the state, and where minerals were reserved, provision has usually been made for leasing and operating. It follows, therefore, that as to these grants and leases the right to mine in the usual and appropriate way, as, for example, by the construction and maintenance of salt water pools such as here involved, incident to the production of oil, was contemplated by the state and all its grantees and mineral lessees, that being a use of the surface incident and necessary to the right to produce oil.

9. *Bursting pipes.* In Lubin v. Iowa City, 131 N.W.2d 765 (Iowa 1964), the defendant city followed the practice of leaving its underground water pipes in place until they broke, even as each pipe approached the end of its

estimated life. The Iowa Supreme Court held the city strictly liable for the resulting damage:

> While [the rule of *Rylands v. Fletcher*] was readily followed in England, it is generally thought that it has not been widely accepted in the United States. However, Prosser in 1955 found 20 jurisdictions, including Iowa, which have accepted it in name or principle. [Prosser, *Law of Torts*, pp. 332-333.] In many other jurisdictions strict liability has been imposed on other theories for damages sustained when an escaping substance or force has invaded the real estate of another. [. . .]
>
> It is neither just nor reasonable that the city engaged in a proprietary activity can deliberately and intentionally plan to leave a watermain underground beyond inspection and maintenance until a break occurs and escape liability. A city or corporation so operating knows that eventually a break will occur, water will escape and in all probability flow onto the premises of another with resulting damage. We do not ordinarily think of watermains as being extra-hazardous but when such a practice is followed, they become "inherently dangerous and likely to damage the neighbor's property[.]" [. . .] The risks from such a method of operation should be borne by the water supplier who is in a position to spread the cost among the consumers who are in fact the true beneficiaries of this practice and of the resulting savings in inspection and maintenance costs. When the expected and inevitable occurs, they should bear the loss and not the unfortunate individual whose property is damaged without fault of his own. [. . .]
>
> The result reached here seems to be in line with modern trends. Legal scholars, with justification, accuse the courts of tending to fix tort liability, not by determining which party is at fault but by deciding which party can best stand the loss. While we cannot accept such a basis for determining liability in most tort cases, it seems to be appropriate here. Most jurisdictions which rejected *Rylands v. Fletcher* did so during that period of time when our country was still young and expanding. "Dangerous enterprises, involving a high degree of risk to others, were clearly indispensable to the industrial and commercial development of a new country and it was considered that the interests of those in the vicinity of such enterprises must give way to them, and that too great a burden must not be placed upon them. With the disappearance of the frontier, and the development of the country's resources, it was to be expected that the force of this objection would be weakened, and that it would be replaced in time by the view that the hazardous enterprise, even though it be socially valuable, must pay its way, and make good the damage inflicted. After a long period during which *Rylands v. Fletcher* was rejected by the large majority of the American courts which considered it, the pendulum has swung to acceptance of the case and its doctrine in the United States." Prosser, *Law of Torts*, p. 332.

[handwritten marginal note: miso sounds like fault...]

What is the distinction between *Lubin v. Iowa City* and *Turner v. Big Lake Oil Co.?*

10. *Escaped oil (problem).* In Walker Shoe Store v. Howard's Hobby Shop, 327 N.W.2d 725 (Iowa 1982), the plaintiff owned a shoe store; the defendant owned a hobby shop next door. The defendant heated his property with oil, which was stored in his basement in two tanks having a capacity of 550 gallons. A leak developed in one or both of the tanks, allowing oil to escape into the defendant's basement; eventually the oil was ignited by the pilot light of a hot water heater. The ensuing fire caused substantial smoke and fire damage to the plaintiff's adjacent property. The defendant produced affidavits stating that the heater had been checked regularly; the plaintiff did not respond, relying on a claim of strict liability rather than negligence. The trial court granted the plaintiff's motion for summary judgment. The defendant appealed to the Supreme Court of Iowa — the same court that decided *Lubin v. Iowa City.* What result would you expect on these facts: strict liability or liability only for negligence? Can this case be distinguished from *Lubin?*

11. *Misstated, and as misstated rejected.* In his treatise on the law of torts, William Prosser argued that when early American courts rejected *Rylands v. Fletcher,* the case "was treated as holding that the defendant is absolutely liable in all cases whenever anything under his control escapes and does damage. In other words, the law of the case was misstated, and as misstated rejected, on facts to which it had no proper application in the first place." Is this an apt criticism?

C. ABNORMALLY DANGEROUS ACTIVITIES

We now consider the most important modern branch of strict liability: its general application to "abnormally dangerous activities." Strict liability in this setting may be understood as descending from an interpretation of *Rylands v. Fletcher,* particularly if that case is given a broad reading that emphasizes the "non-natural" mismatch between the risks created by the defendant's activity and the place where the activity is carried out; indeed, some courts now speak almost interchangeably of strict liability under *Rylands* and more general strict liability for abnormally dangerous activities. But some of the criteria for applying strict liability to abnormally dangerous activities have developed independently of *Rylands,* and while state courts may disagree about the meaning of *Rylands* and whether it should be followed, every state recognizes general principles of strict liability for certain dangerous undertakings. Here the Restatements produced by the American Law Institute have been highly influential. The Institute's first Restatement of the law of torts laid out criteria for imposing strict liability on defendants engaged in "ultrahazardous" activities; the Restatement (Second) continued in the same vein, but with a shift in jargon to "abnormally dangerous" activities. As you read the Restatement's provisions and the cases that follow, consider the extent to which they overlap with the doctrines associated with *Rylands v. Fletcher*.

Restatement (Second) of Torts (1965)

§519. GENERAL PRINCIPLE

(1) One who carries on an abnormally dangerous activity is subject to liability for harm to the person, land or chattels of another resulting from the activity, although he has exercised the utmost care to prevent the harm.

(2) This strict liability is limited to the kind of harm, the possibility of which makes the activity abnormally dangerous.

§520. ABNORMALLY DANGEROUS ACTIVITIES

In determining whether an activity is abnormally dangerous, the following factors are to be considered:

(a) existence of a high degree of risk of some harm to the person, land or chattels of others;

(b) likelihood that the harm that results from it will be great;

(c) inability to eliminate the risk by the exercise of reasonable care;

(d) extent to which the activity is not a matter of common usage;

(e) inappropriateness of the activity to the place where it is carried on; and

(f) extent to which its value to the community is outweighed by its dangerous attributes.

Comments. . . .

e. Not limited to the defendant's land. In most of the cases to which the rule of strict liability is applicable the abnormally dangerous activity is conducted on land in the possession of the defendant. This, again, is not necessary to the existence of such an activity. It may be carried on in a public highway or other public place or upon the land of another.

f. "Abnormally dangerous." For an activity to be abnormally dangerous, not only must it create a danger of physical harm to others but the danger must be an abnormal one. In general, abnormal dangers arise from activities that are in themselves unusual, or from unusual risks created by more usual activities under particular circumstances. In determining whether the danger is abnormal, the factors listed in Clauses (a) to (f) of this Section are all to be considered, and are all of importance. Any one of them is not necessarily sufficient of itself in a particular case, and ordinarily several of them will be required for strict liability. On the other hand, it is not necessary that each of them be present, especially if others weigh heavily. Because of the interplay of these various factors, it is not possible to reduce abnormally dangerous activities to any definition. The essential question is whether the risk created is so unusual, either because of its magnitude or because of the circumstances surrounding it, as to justify the imposition of strict liability for the harm that results from it, even though it is carried on with all reasonable care. In other words, are its dangers and inappropriateness for the locality so great that, despite any usefulness it may have for the community, it should be required as a matter of law to pay for any harm it causes, without the need of a finding of negligence. [. . .]

i. Common usage. An activity is a matter of common usage if it is customarily carried on by the great mass of mankind or by many people in the community. It does not cease to be so because it is carried on for a purpose peculiar to the individual who engages in it. Certain activities, notwithstanding their recognizable danger, are so generally carried on as to be regarded as customary. Thus automobiles have come into such general use that their operation is a matter of common usage. This, notwithstanding the residue of unavoidable risk of serious harm that may result even from their careful operation, is sufficient to prevent their use from being regarded as an abnormally dangerous activity. On the other hand, the operation of a tank or any other motor vehicle of such size and weight as to be unusually difficult to control safely, or to be likely to damage the ground over which it is driven, is not yet a usual activity for many people, and therefore the operation of such a vehicle may be abnormally dangerous.

Although blasting is recognized as a proper means of excavation for building purposes or clearing woodland for cultivation, it is not carried on by any large percentage of the population, and therefore it is not a matter of common usage. Likewise the manufacture, storage, transportation and use of high explosives, although necessary to the construction of many public and private works, are carried on by only a comparatively small number of persons and therefore are not matters of common usage. So likewise, the very nature of oil lands and the essential interest of the public in the production of oil require that oil wells be drilled, but the dangers incident to the operation are characteristic of oil lands and not of lands in general, and relatively few persons are engaged in the activity.

The usual dangers resulting from an activity that is one of common usage are not regarded as abnormal, even though a serious risk of harm cannot be eliminated by all reasonable care. The difference is sometimes not so much one of the activity itself as of the manner in which it is carried on. Water collected in large quantity in a hillside reservoir in the midst of a city or in coal mining country is not the activity of any considerable portion of the population, and may therefore be regarded as abnormally dangerous; while water in a cistern or in household pipes or in a barnyard tank supplying cattle, although it may involve much the same danger of escape, differing only in degree if at all, still is a matter of common usage and therefore not abnormal. The same is true of gas and electricity in household pipes and wires, as contrasted with large storage tanks or high tension power lines. Fire in a fireplace or in an ordinary railway engine is a matter of common usage, while a traction engine shooting out sparks in its passage along the public highway is an abnormal danger.

Indiana Harbor Belt Ry. Co. v. American Cyanamid Co.
916 F.2d 1174 (7th Cir. 1990)

POSNER, *Circuit Judge.* American Cyanamid Company, the defendant in this diversity tort suit governed by Illinois law, is a major manufacturer of chemicals, including acrylonitrile, a chemical used in large quantities in making acrylic fibers, plastics, dyes, pharmaceutical chemicals, and other intermediate and final goods. On January 2, 1979, at its manufacturing plant in Louisiana, Cyanamid loaded 20,000 gallons of liquid acrylonitrile into a railroad tank car that it had leased from the North American Car Corporation. The next day, a train of the Missouri Pacific Railroad picked up the car at Cyanamid's siding. The car's ultimate destination was a Cyanamid plant in New Jersey served by Conrail rather than by Missouri Pacific. The Missouri Pacific train carried the car north to the Blue Island railroad yard of Indiana Harbor Belt Railroad, the plaintiff in this case, a small switching line that has a contract with Conrail to switch cars from other lines to Conrail, in this case for travel east. The Blue Island yard is in the Village of Riverdale, which is just south of Chicago and part of the Chicago metropolitan area.

The car arrived in the Blue Island yard on the morning of January 9, 1979. Several hours after it arrived, employees of the switching line noticed fluid gushing from the bottom outlet of the car. The lid on the outlet was broken. After two hours, the line's supervisor of equipment was able to stop the leak by closing a shut-off valve controlled from the top of the car. No one was sure at the time just how much of the contents of the car had leaked, but it was feared that all 20,000 gallons had, and since acrylonitrile is flammable at a temperature of 30 degrees Fahrenheit or above, highly toxic, and possibly carcinogenic, the local authorities ordered the homes near the yard evacuated. The evacuation lasted only a few hours, until the car was moved to a remote part of the yard and it was discovered that only about a quarter of the acrylonitrile had leaked. Concerned nevertheless that there had been some contamination of soil and water, the Illinois Department of Environmental Protection ordered the switching line to take decontamination measures that cost the line $981,022.75, which it sought to recover by this suit.

One count of the two-count complaint charges Cyanamid with having maintained the leased tank car negligently. The other count asserts that the transportation of acrylonitrile in bulk through the Chicago metropolitan area is an abnormally dangerous activity, for the consequences of which the shipper (Cyanamid) is strictly liable to the switching line, which bore the financial brunt of those consequences because of the decontamination measures that it was forced to take. [The district court gave summary judgment to the plaintiff on the ground that the defendant was strictly liable for the spill, and the defendant brought this appeal.]

The parties agree that the question whether placing acrylonitrile in a rail shipment that will pass through a metropolitan area subjects the shipper to strict liability is, as recommended in Restatement (Second) of Torts §520, comment 1 (1977), a question of law, so that we owe no particular deference to the conclusion of the district court. They also agree (and for this proposition, at least, there is substantial support) that the Supreme Court of Illinois would treat as authoritative the provisions of the Restatement governing abnormally dangerous activities. The key provision is section 520, which sets forth six factors to be considered in deciding whether an activity is abnormally dangerous and the actor therefore strictly liable.

The roots of section 520 are in nineteenth-century cases. The most famous one is *Rylands v. Fletcher,* but a more illuminating one in the present context is *Guille v. Swan,* 19 Johns. (N.Y.) 381 (1822). A man took off in a hot-air balloon and landed, without intending to, in a vegetable garden in New York City. A crowd that had been anxiously watching his involuntary descent trampled the vegetables in their endeavor to rescue him when he landed. The owner of the garden sued the balloonist for the resulting damage, and won. Yet the balloonist had not been careless. In the then state of ballooning it was impossible to make a pinpoint landing.

Guille is a paradigmatic case for strict liability. (a) The risk (probability) of harm was great, and (b) the harm that would ensue if the risk materialized could be, although luckily was not, great (the balloonist could have crashed into the crowd rather than into the vegetables). The confluence of these two factors established the urgency of seeking to prevent such accidents. (c) Yet such accidents could not be prevented by the exercise of due care; the technology of care in ballooning was insufficiently developed. (d) The activity was not a matter of common usage, so there was no presumption that it was a highly valuable activity despite its unavoidable riskiness. (e) The activity was inappropriate to the place in which it took place — densely populated New York City. The risk of serious harm to others (other than the balloonist himself, that is) could have been reduced by shifting the activity to the sparsely inhabited areas that surrounded the city in those days. (f) Reinforcing (d), the value to the community of the activity of recreational ballooning did not appear to be great enough to offset its unavoidable risks.

These are, of course, the six factors in section 520. They are related to each other in that each is a different facet of a common quest for a proper legal regime to govern accidents that negligence liability cannot adequately control. The interrelations might be more perspicuous if the six factors were reordered.

One might for example start with (c), inability to eliminate the risk of accident by the exercise of due care. The baseline common law regime of tort liability is negligence. When it is a workable regime, because the hazards of an activity can be avoided by being careful (which is to say, non-negligent), there is no need to switch to strict liability. Sometimes, however, a particular type of accident cannot be prevented by taking care but can be avoided, or its consequences minimized, by shifting the activity in which the accident occurs to another locale, where the risk or harm of an accident will be less ((e)), or by reducing the scale of the activity in order to minimize the number of accidents caused by it ((f)). By making the actor strictly liable — by denying him in other words an excuse based on his inability to avoid accidents by being more careful — we give him an incentive, missing in a negligence regime, to experiment with methods of preventing accidents that involve not greater exertions of care, assumed to be futile, but instead relocating, changing, or reducing (perhaps to the vanishing point) the activity giving rise to the accident. [. . .] The greater the risk of an accident ((a)) and the costs of an accident if one occurs ((b)), the more we want the actor to consider the possibility of making accident-reducing activity changes; the stronger, therefore, is the case for strict liability. Finally, if an activity is extremely common ((d)), like driving an automobile, it is unlikely either that its hazards are perceived as great or that there is no technology of care available to minimize them; so the case for strict liability is weakened.

The largest class of cases in which strict liability has been imposed under the standard codified in the Second Restatement of Torts involves the use of dynamite and other explosives for demolition in residential or urban areas. [. . .] Explosives are dangerous even when handled carefully, and we therefore want blasters to choose the location of the activity with care and also to explore the feasibility of using safer substitutes (such as a wrecking ball), as well as to be careful in the blasting itself. Blasting is not a commonplace activity like driving a car, or so superior to substitute methods of demolition that the imposition of liability is unlikely to have any effect except to raise the activity's costs.

Against this background we turn to the particulars of acrylonitrile. Acrylonitrile is one of a large number of chemicals that are hazardous in the sense of being flammable, toxic, or both; acrylonitrile is both, as are many others. A table in the record [. . .] contains a list of the 125 hazardous materials that are shipped in highest volume on the nation's railroads. Acrylonitrile is the fifty-third most hazardous on the list. Number 1 is phosphorus (white or yellow), and among the other materials that rank higher than acrylonitrile on the hazard scale are anhydrous ammonia, liquified petroleum gas, vinyl chloride, gasoline, crude petroleum, motor fuel antiknock compound, methyl and ethyl chloride, sulphuric acid, sodium metal, and chloroform. The plaintiff's lawyer acknowledged at argument that the logic of the district court's opinion dictated strict liability for all 52 materials that rank higher than acrylonitrile on the list, and quite possibly for the 72 that rank lower as well, since all are hazardous if spilled in quantity while being shipped by rail. Every shipper of any of these materials would therefore be strictly liable for the consequences of a spill or other accident that occurred while the material was being shipped through a metropolitan area. The plaintiff's lawyer further acknowledged the irrelevance, on her view of the case, of the fact that Cyanamid had leased and filled the car that spilled the acrylonitrile; all she thought important is that Cyanamid introduced the product into the stream of commerce that happened to pass through the Chicago metropolitan area. Her concession may have been incautious. One might want to distinguish between the shipper who merely places his goods on his loading dock to be picked up by the carrier and the shipper who, as in this case, participates actively in the transportation. But the concession is illustrative of the potential scope of the district court's decision.

No cases recognize so sweeping a liability. Several reject it, though none has facts much like those of the present case. [. . .] So we can get little help from precedent, and might as well apply section 520 to the acrylonitrile problem from the ground up. To begin with, we have been given no reason [. . .] for believing that a negligence regime is not perfectly adequate to remedy and deter, at reasonable cost, the accidental spillage of acrylonitrile from rail cars. Acrylonitrile could explode and destroy evidence, but of course did not here, making imposition of strict liability on [that theory] premature. More important, although acrylonitrile is flammable even at relatively low temperatures, and toxic, it is not so corrosive or otherwise destructive that it will eat through or otherwise damage or weaken a tank car's valves although they are maintained with due (which essentially means, with average) care. No one suggests, therefore, that the leak in this case was caused by the inherent properties of acrylonitrile. It was caused by carelessness — whether that of the North American Car Corporation in failing to maintain or inspect the car properly, or that of Cyanamid in failing to maintain or inspect it, or that of the Missouri Pacific when it had custody of the car, or that of the switching line itself in failing to notice the ruptured lid, or some combination of these possible failures of care. Accidents that are due to a lack of care can be prevented by taking care; and when a lack of care can [. . .] be shown in court, such accidents are adequately deterred by the threat of liability for negligence.

It is true that the district court purported to find as a fact that there is an inevitable risk of derailment or other calamity in transporting "large quantities of anything." 662 F. Supp. at 642. This is not a finding of fact, but a truism: anything can happen. The question is, how likely is this type of accident if the actor uses due care? For all that appears from the record of the case or any other sources of information that we have found, if a tank car is carefully maintained the danger of a spill of acrylonitrile is negligible. If this is right, there is no compelling reason to move to a regime of strict liability, especially one that might embrace all other hazardous materials shipped by rail as well. This also means, however, that the amici curiae who have filed briefs in support of Cyanamid cry wolf in predicting "devastating" effects on the chemical industry if the district court's decision is affirmed. If the vast majority of chemical spills by railroads are preventable by due care, the imposition of strict liability should cause only a slight, not as they argue a substantial, rise in liability insurance rates, because the incremental liability should be slight. The amici have momentarily lost sight of the fact that the feasibility of avoiding accidents simply by being careful is an argument against strict liability.

The district judge and the plaintiff's lawyer make much of the fact that the spill occurred in a densely inhabited metropolitan area. Only 4,000 gallons spilled; what if all 20,000 had done so? Isn't the risk that this might happen even if everybody were careful sufficient to warrant giving the shipper an incentive to explore alternative routes? Strict liability would supply that incentive. But this argument overlooks the fact that, like other transportation networks, the railroad network is a hub-and-spoke system. And the hubs are in metropolitan areas. Chicago is one of the nation's largest railroad hubs. In 1983, the latest year for which we have figures, Chicago's railroad yards handled the third highest volume of hazardous-material shipments in the nation. East St. Louis, which is also in Illinois, handled the second highest volume. [. . .] With most hazardous chemicals (by volume of shipments) being at least as hazardous as acrylonitrile, it is unlikely — and certainly not demonstrated by the plaintiff — that they can be rerouted around all the metropolitan areas in the country, except at prohibitive cost. Even if it were feasible to reroute them one would hardly expect shippers, as distinct from carriers, to be the firms best situated to do the rerouting. Granted, the usual view is that common carriers are not subject to strict liability for the carriage of materials that make the transportation of them abnormally dangerous, because a common carrier cannot refuse service to a shipper of a lawful commodity. Two courts, however, have rejected the common carrier exception. If it were rejected in Illinois, this would weaken still further the case for imposing strict liability on shippers whose goods pass through the densely inhabited portions of the state.

The difference between shipper and carrier points to a deep flaw in the plaintiff's case. Unlike *Guille*, [. . .] and unlike the storage cases, beginning with *Rylands* itself, here it is not the actors — that is, the transporters of acrylonitrile and other chemicals — but the manufacturers, who are sought to be held strictly liable. [. . .] A shipper can in the bill of lading designate the route of his shipment if he likes, 49 U.S.C. sec. 11710(a)(1), but is it realistic to suppose that shippers will become students of railroading in order to lay out the safest route by which to ship their goods? Anyway, rerouting is no panacea. Often it will increase the length of the journey, or compel the use of poorer track, or both. When this happens, the probability of an accident is increased, even if the consequences of an accident if one occurs are reduced; so the expected accident cost, being the product of the probability of an accident and the harm if the accident occurs, may rise. [. . .] It is easy to see how the accident in this case might have been prevented at reasonable cost by greater care on the part of those who handled the tank car of acrylonitrile. It is difficult to see how it might have been prevented at reasonable cost by a change in the activity of transporting the chemical. This is therefore not an apt case for strict liability.

The very fact that Cyanamid participated actively in the transportation of the acrylonitrile imposed upon it a duty of due care and by doing so brought into play a threat of negligence liability that, for all we know, may provide an adequate regime of accident control in the transportation of this particular chemical.

In emphasizing the flammability and toxicity of acrylonitrile rather than the hazards of transporting it, as in failing to distinguish between the active and the passive shipper, the plaintiff overlooks the fact that ultrahazardousness or abnormal dangerousness is, in the contemplation of the law at least, a property not of substances, but of activities: not of acrylonitrile, but of the transportation of acrylonitrile by rail through populated areas. [. . .] Whatever the situation under products liability law (section 402A of the Restatement), the manufacturer of a product is not considered to be engaged in an abnormally dangerous activity merely because the product becomes dangerous when it is handled or used in some way after it leaves his premises, even if the danger is foreseeable. [. . .] The plaintiff does not suggest that Cyanamid should switch to making some less hazardous chemical that would substitute for acrylonitrile in the textiles and other goods in which acrylonitrile is used. Were this a feasible method of accident avoidance, there would be an argument for making manufacturers strictly liable for accidents that occur during the shipment of their products (how strong an argument we need not decide). Apparently it is not a feasible method.

The relevant activity is transportation, not manufacturing and shipping. This essential distinction the plaintiff ignores. But even if the defendant is treated as a transporter and not merely a shipper, it has not shown that the transportation of acrylonitrile in bulk by rail through populated areas is so hazardous an activity, even when due care is exercised, that the law should seek to create — perhaps quixotically — incentives to relocate the activity to nonpopulated areas, or to reduce the scale of the activity, or to switch to transporting acrylonitrile by road rather than by rail [. . .]. It is no more realistic to propose to reroute the shipment of all hazardous materials around Chicago than it is to propose the relocation of homes adjacent to the Blue Island switching yard to more distant suburbs. It may be less realistic. Brutal though it may seem to say it, the inappropriate use to which land is being put in the Blue Island yard and neighborhood may be, not the transportation of hazardous chemicals, but residential living. The analogy is to building your home between the runways at O'Hare.

The briefs hew closely to the Restatement, whose approach to the issue of strict liability is mainly allocative rather than distributive. By this we mean that the emphasis is on picking a liability regime (negligence or strict liability) that will control the particular class of accidents in question most effectively, rather than on finding the deepest pocket and placing liability there. At argument, however, the plaintiff's lawyer invoked distributive considerations by pointing out that Cyanamid is a huge firm and the Indiana Harbor Belt Railroad a fifty-mile-long switching line that almost went broke in the winter of 1979, when the accident occurred. Well, so what? A corporation is not a living person but a set of contracts the terms of which determine who will bear the brunt of liability. Tracing the incidence of a cost is a complex undertaking which the plaintiff sensibly has made no effort to assume, since its legal relevance would be dubious [. . .].

The judgment is reversed (with no award of costs in this court) and the case remanded for further proceedings, consistent with this opinion, on the plaintiff's claim for negligence.

Reversed and remanded, with directions.

NOTES

1. *Activity levels.* One economic rationale for strict liability is that it puts pressure on parties to consider whether they ought to be engaging in some other activity altogether; a negligence standard, by contrast, considers only whether the activity the actor chose to engage in was undertaken carefully. In the context of the *Indiana Harbor Belt Railroad* case, the argument would be that applying a negligence standard amounts just to asking whether the defendant, having chosen to ship the acrylonitrile by rail near metropolitan areas, did so with reasonable care. Since strict liability would force the defendant to pay for any damage the chemical caused regardless of whether it was careful, the company will be moved to wonder whether there is some better way to ship acrylonitrile altogether. Between these poles, however, might seem to lie an intermediate possibility: a court could ask whether the defendant's decision about activity levels — here, its decision to ship the chemical by rail through Blue Island — was itself negligent, regardless of how carefully it was carried out. The economic argument for strict liability sketched above is premised on the idea that courts cannot fruitfully inquire into whether such general decisions by defendants are negligent. It has been argued, however, that Judge Posner's opinion does just that:

> On the record before the court, Posner's conclusion seems perfectly sound. But surely his ability to arrive at that conclusion undercuts the premise on which he undertook the inquiry in the first place. To conclude that spills of acrylonitrile probably could not "have been prevented at reasonable cost by a change in the activity of transporting the chemical" is, in substance, to determine that, as a rule, it is not negligent to transport acrylonitrile by rail rather than by other means or by rail through metropolitan areas rather than rerouting to avoid them. That is a rule-based determination of the very same activity-level negligence claims that Posner assumed the negligence standard could not handle.

Gilles, *Risk-Based Negligence and the Regulation of Activity Levels*, 21 J. Legal Stud. 319 (1992). Courts could, in principle, more regularly undertake the sort of analysis Gilles describes, asking not only whether defendants are reasonable in carrying on their activities but whether they are reasonable in deciding what activities to conduct. Indeed, comment b to Restatement §520 recognizes such a possibility:

> The rule stated in §519 is applicable to an activity that is carried on with all reasonable care, and that is of such utility that the risk which is involved in it cannot be regarded as so great or so unreasonable as to make it negligence merely to carry on the activity at all. If the utility of the activity does not justify the risk it creates, it may be negligence merely to carry it on, and the rule stated in this Section is not then necessary to subject the defendant to liability for harm resulting from it. [. . .]

It nevertheless is rare for courts to hold a defendant liable for negligently choosing to engage in an activity. Why?

2. *Flammable cargo.* In Siegler v. Kuhlman, 502 P.2d 1181 (Wash. 1973), the defendant's driver was scheduled to drive a truck and trailer loaded with more than 8,600 gallons of gasoline from Tumwater to Port Angeles, Washington. He performed the necessary safety checks. As he pulled onto a ramp to enter Highway 101, the trailer jerked loose from his truck, crashed through a chain-link highway fence, and came to rest upside down on a street below. Seventeen-year-old Carol House, returning home from her after-school job, drove over the puddle of gasoline created by the trailer's fall. The gasoline ignited, and the flames engulfed her car and killed her. The Washington Supreme Court held that strict liability applied:

> The basic principles supporting the *Fletcher* doctrine, we think, control the transportation of gasoline as freight along the public highways the same as it does the impounding of waters and for largely the same reasons. [. . .]
>
> In many respects, hauling gasoline as freight is no more unusual, but more dangerous, than collecting water. When gasoline is carried as cargo — as distinguished from fuel for the carrier vehicle — it takes on uniquely hazardous characteristics, as does water impounded in large quantities. Dangerous in itself, gasoline develops even greater potential for harm when carried as freight — extraordinary dangers deriving from sheer quantity, bulk and weight, which enormously multiply its hazardous properties. And the very hazards inhering from the size of the load, its bulk or quantity and its movement along the highways presents another reason for application of the *Fletcher v. Rylands* rule not present in the impounding of large quantities of water — the likely destruction of cogent evidence from which negligence or want of it may be proved or disproved. It is quite probable that the most important ingredients of proof will be lost in a gasoline explosion and fire. Gasoline is always

dangerous whether kept in large or small quantities because of its volatility, inflammability and explosiveness. But when several thousand gallons of it are allowed to spill across a public highway — that is, if, while in transit as freight, it is not kept impounded — the hazards to third persons are so great as to be almost beyond calculation. [. . .]

Transporting gasoline as freight by truck along the public highways and streets is obviously an activity involving a high degree of risk; it is a risk of great harm and injury; it creates dangers that cannot be eliminated by the exercise of reasonable care. That gasoline cannot be practicably transported except upon the public highways does not decrease the abnormally high risk arising from its transportation. Nor will the exercise of due and reasonable care assure protection to the public from the disastrous consequences of concealed or latent mechanical or metallurgical defects in the carrier's equipment, from the negligence of third parties, from latent defects in the highways and streets, and from all of the other hazards not generally disclosed or guarded against by reasonable care, prudence and foresight. Hauling gasoline in great quantities as freight, we think, is an activity that calls for the application of principles of strict liability.

What is the distinction between *Siegler v. Kuhlman* and *Indiana Harbor Belt Ry. Co. v. American Cyanamid Co.?*

3. *Fireworks.* In Klein v. Pyrodyne Corp., 810 P.2d 917 (Wash. 1991), defendant Pyrodyne was a general contractor hired to provide aerial fireworks one Fourth of July. During its fireworks display a mortar was knocked into a horizontal position and a rocket inside was discharged. The rocket flew 500 feet and exploded near a crowd of onlookers, causing them various injuries. They sued Pyrodyne. The trial court gave summary judgment to the plaintiffs on the ground that Pyrodyne was strictly liable for damage caused by its fireworks. The Washington Supreme Court affirmed:

> Any time a person ignites rockets with the intention of sending them aloft to explode in the presence of large crowds of people, a high risk of serious personal injury or property damage is created. That risk arises because of the possibility that a rocket will malfunction or be misdirected. Furthermore, no matter how much care pyrotechnicians exercise, they cannot entirely eliminate the high risk inherent in setting off powerful explosives such as fireworks near crowds.

What rationale for strict liability lies behind the court's decision? Is it a matter of fairness, efficiency, or both? Some jurisdictions have rejected strict liability for fireworks displays gone awry, finding them a matter of common usage on appropriate occasions; see Restatement (Third) of Torts (P.F.D. 2005) §20, comment j. How widespread should an activity be before it is regarded as "common" for these purposes?

4. *Firearms.* In Miller v. Civil Constructors, Inc., 651 N.E.2d 239 (Ill. App. 1995), the defendants operated a firing range located in a rural area; its main users were police offers seeking to improve their marksmanship. The plaintiff was riding on the back of a truck on a nearby road when he was struck by a bullet that ricocheted away from the range. One count of the plaintiff's resulting complaint alleged that "discharging firearms is an ultrahazardous, highly dangerous activity" and that the defendants therefore were strictly liable for the plaintiff's injuries. The trial court dismissed the plaintiff's strict liability count, and the court of appeals affirmed:

> The use of guns or firearms, even though frequently classified as danger-ous or even highly dangerous, is not the type of activity that must be deemed ultrahazardous when the [Restatement] criteria are taken into consideration. First, the risk of harm to persons or property, even though great, can be virtually eliminated by the exercise of reasonable or even "utmost" care under the circumstances. The doctrine of strict or absolute liability is ordinarily reserved for abnormally dangerous activities for which no degree of care can truly provide safety. There is a clear distinc-tion between requiring a defendant to exercise a high degree of care when involved in a potentially dangerous activity and requiring a defendant to insure absolutely the safety of others when engaging in ultrahazardous activity.
>
> Second, the use of firearms is a matter of common usage and the harm posed comes from their misuse rather than from their inherent nature alone. Third, the activity in this case was carried on at a firing range in a quarry located somewhere near the City of Freeport. We assume that the location was appropriate for such activity in the absence of further factual allegations in the complaint particularly describing the area as inappro-priate for the target practice. Finally, the target practice is of some social utility to the community; this weighs against declaring it ultrahazardous where the activity was alleged to have been performed by law enforcement officers apparently to improve their skills in the handling of weapons.

What is the distinction between *Miller v. Civil Constructors, Inc.*, and *Klein v. Pyrodyne Corp.* (applying strict liability to users of fireworks)?

5. *Blasting.* In Sullivan v. Dunham, 55 N.E. 923 (N.Y. 1900), two of the defendants were engaged to remove trees from land owned by a third. They used dynamite to remove a 60-foot elm tree on the south side of the property. The blast shattered the tree and threw a section of the stump over a nearby forest and onto a highway more than 400 feet away; there the stump struck the plaintiff's intestate and killed her. The trial court instructed the jury that the plaintiff did not have to show negligence on the defendants' part in order to recover from them. The jury returned a verdict for the plaintiff, and the court of appeals held the evidence sufficient to support the outcome.

6. *Excitable minks.* In Madsen v. East Jordan Irrigation Co., 125 P.2d 794 (Utah 1942), the plaintiff was the owner of the Madsen Mink Farm. The farm was 100 yards from the defendant's irrigation canal. The defendant used explosives in performing repairs on it. The resulting vibrations and noises caused the plaintiff's mother minks to kill 230 of their kittens; the plaintiff alleged that when minks are attending to their offspring they are highly excitable, and that when they are disturbed they tend to become terrified and kill their young. The trial court sustained the defendant's demurrer to the complaint. The plaintiff appealed, and the Utah Supreme Court affirmed:

> Had the concussion in the instant case killed the kittens directly, without the intervention of the mother minks, the majority rule of liability in concussion cases would have been applicable, but the case at bar presents the additional element of the mother minks' independent acts, thereby raising a question of proximate causation. Query: Did the mother minks' intervention break the chain of causation and therefore require an allegation of negligence?
>
> [H]e who fires explosives is not liable for every occurrence following the explosion which has a semblance of connection to it. [. . .] Whether the cases are concussion or nonconcussion, the results chargeable to the nonnegligent user of explosives are those things ordinarily resulting from an explosion.

What is the distinction between *Madsen v. East Jordan Irrigation Co.* and *Sullivan v. Dunham* (the L case of the dynamited tree)? What is the analogy between *Madsen v. East Jordan Irrigation Co.* and *Bostock-Ferari Amusements v. Brocksmith* (the NL case from the section on liability for animals where the defendant's bear frightened the plaintiff's horse)?

7. *Plummeting aircraft (problem).* In Crosby v. Cox Aircraft Co., 746 P.2d 1198 (Wash. 1987), an airplane owned by the defendant ran out of fuel and crashed into the plaintiff's garage. The trial court held that the defendant was strictly liable for the damage to the plaintiff's property. The defendant appealed. What rule would you expect to govern liability for damage on the ground caused by falling airplanes: negligence or strict liability? (Is there any reason to distinguish between plaintiffs on the ground and plaintiffs who were passengers on the plane (or their survivors)?) What arguments might you make each way based on the materials considered in this chapter?

8. *Insecticide (problem).* In Luthringer v. Moore, 190 P.2d 1 (Cal. 1948), the defendant Moore was engaged to exterminate cockroaches and other vermin in the basement of a restaurant. He made his preparations and released hydrocyanic acid gas — a deeply penetrating gas dangerous to humans — at about midnight. The plaintiff, who was employed by a pharmacy next door, arrived at work the next morning and was overcome by

the gas. She suffered various injuries as a result, and brought suit against the exterminator.

At trial, the plaintiff's expert, an exterminator named Bell, offered the following testimony:

> Q. Do you know whether hydrocyanic acid gas is a poisonous gas or a lethal gas?
> A. It definitely is.
> Q. Can you tell us what the physical characteristics of hydrocyanic acid gas are?
> A. It is a little lighter-than-air gas; a very highly penetrative gas; susceptible to moisture quite a bit, it will follow moisture; it is noninflammable; the flash point is very low so that it can be used without very much hazard of fire.
> Q. What do you mean by [the word "penetrative"]?
> A. That is one of the advantages of the gas; why they use it in fumigation. It will penetrate behind baseboards, cracks and crevices that we couldn't get at with any type of liquid insecticide. It will go through mattresses, chesterfields, furniture, some types of porous walls.
> Q. Is it difficult to keep that gas confined?
> A. Yes, because of the fact it will penetrate, you have to be careful to keep it in a definite area.
> Q. In the ordinary operation, if you go in and seal up [a room] so that you consider it is adequately sealed, you still have some leakage of gas, or not?
> A. You will have some, yes, sir, unless it is a very well built building.

The trial court instructed the jury that fumigating with hydrocyanic gas was an ultrahazardous activity for which the defendant would be strictly liable even if he had taken all reasonable precautions. So instructed, the jury returned a verdict for the plaintiff, and the defendant appealed. What result?

9. *The new Restatement and the measurement of social value.* From the Restatement (Third) of Torts (P.F.D. 2005):

> §20. STRICT LIABILITY
>
> (a) An actor who carries on an abnormally dangerous activity is subject to strict liability for physical harm resulting from the activity.
> (b) An activity is abnormally dangerous if:
> (1) the activity creates a foreseeable and highly significant risk of physical harm even when reasonable care is exercised by all actors, and
> (2) the activity is not a matter of common usage.

This provision differs most significantly from §520 of the Second Restatement in its omission of the social value of an activity as a criterion for deciding whether strict liability is appropriate. That factor in the Second Restatement occasioned some controversy, as this case excerpt illustrates:

> There are at least two reasons not to judge civil liability for unintended harm by a court's views of the utility or value of the harmful activity. One reason lies in the nature of the judgment. Utility and value often are subjective and controversial. They will be judged differently by those who profit from an activity and those who are endangered by it, and between one locality and another. The use of explosives to remove old buildings for a new highway or shopping center may be described as slum clearance or as the destruction of historic landmarks and neighborhoods. On a smaller scale, it may celebrate a traditional holiday which some may value more highly than either buildings or roads. Highly toxic materials may be necessary to the production of agricultural pesticides, or of drugs, or of chemical or bacteriological weapons, or of industrial products of all sorts; does liability for injury from their storage or movement depend on the utility of these products? Judges, like others, may differ about such values; they can hardly be described as conclusions of law.
>
> To rely on the evidence of the market place may show rather different societal values from those probably contemplated by Dean Prosser and the Restatement. While some small airplanes enhance the production of food crops, others perhaps earn a larger return flying passengers or stunt exhibitions at the county fair. Entrepreneurs may bring more money into the local economy by racing automobiles or driving them to deliberate destruction than by operating a public transit system with a comparable incidence of actual injuries. If high risk itself has market value, does this count against strict liability for a resulting calamity? The addition of this "factor" in the second Restatement was the subject of some doubt and criticism during the debate of §520 in the American Law Institute. Our cases have not required courts and counsel to enter upon such philosophical issues in deciding whether a defendant is strictly liable for harm from a hazardous activity.
>
> The second reason why the value of a hazardous activity does not preclude strict liability for its consequences is that the conclusion does not follow from the premise. In the prior cases, the court did not question the economic value of blasting, cropdusting, or storing natural gas. In an action for damages, the question is not whether the activity threatens such harm that it should not be continued. The question is who shall pay for harm that has been done. The loss has occurred. It is a cost of the activity whoever bears it. To say that when the activity has great economic value the cost should be borne by others is no more or less logical than to say that when the costs of an activity are borne by others it gains in value. This, in effect, is postulated in the argument that the industry which relies on field burning is highly valuable but could not survive the cost difference of insurance against strict liability instead of negligence.

Sometimes, moreover, the cost is borne by others engaged in the same or similar activity. That is true in this case, where plaintiffs and defendant farmed adjoining fields. The same can occur in cropdusting, in burning forest debris, or in the escape of stored water. If the accidentally impoverished neighbor is told that in the long run the losses will balance out, he may answer, like one economist, that in the long run we are all dead. Society has other ways to lighten the burdens of costly but unavoidable accidents on a valued industry than to let them fall haphazardly on the industry's neighbors.

Koos v. Roth, 652 P.2d 1255 (Or. 1982) (Linde, J.).

10. *The paradigm of reciprocity*. Professor Fletcher has argued that the decision in *Rylands v. Fletcher* can be explained by what he calls the "paradigm of reciprocity":

> I shall propose a specific standard of risk that makes sense of the Restatement's emphasis on uncommon, extra-hazardous risks, but which shows that the Restatement's theory is part of a larger rationale of liability that cuts across negligence, intentional torts, and numerous pockets of strict liability. The general principle expressed in all of these situations governed by diverse doctrinal standards is that a victim has a right to recover for injuries caused by a risk greater in degree and different in order from those created by the victim and imposed on the defendant — in short, for injuries resulting from nonreciprocal risks. Cases of liability are those in which the defendant generates a disproportionate, excessive risk of harm, relative to the victim's risk-creating activity. For example, a pilot or an airplane owner subjects those beneath the path of flight to nonreciprocal risks of harm. Conversely, cases of nonliability are those of reciprocal risks, namely those in which the victim and the defendant subject each other to roughly the same degree of risk. For example, two airplanes flying in the same vicinity subject each other to reciprocal risks of a mid-air collision. Of course, there are significant problems in determining when risks are nonreciprocal. . . .
>
> [T]he uncommon, ultra-hazardous activities pinpointed by the Restatement are readily subsumed under the rationale of nonreciprocal risk-taking. If uncommon activities are those with few participants, they are likely to be activities generating nonreciprocal risks. Similarly, dangerous activities like blasting, fumigating, and crop dusting stand out as distinct, nonreciprocal risks in the community. They represent threats of harm that exceed the level of risk to which all members of the community contribute in roughly equal shares.
>
> The rationale of nonreciprocal risk-taking accounts as well for pockets of strict liability outside the coverage of the Restatement's sections on extra-hazardous activities. For example, an individual is strictly liable for

damage done by a wild animal in his charge, but not for damage committed by his domesticated pet. Most people have pets, children, or friends whose presence creates some risk to neighbors and their property. These are risks that offset each other; they are, as a class, reciprocal risks. Yet bringing an unruly horse into the city goes beyond the accepted and shared level of risks in having pets, children, and friends in one's household. If the defendant creates a risk that exceeds those to which he is reciprocally subject, it seems fair to hold him liable for the results of his aberrant indulgence. Similarly, according to the latest version of the Restatement, airplane owners and pilots are strictly liable for ground damage, but not for mid-air collisions. Risk of ground damage is nonreciprocal; homeowners do not create risks to airplanes flying overhead. The risks of mid-air collisions, on the other hand, are generated reciprocally by all those who fly the air lanes. Accordingly, the threshold of liability for damage resulting from mid-air collisions is higher than mere involvement in the activity of flying. To be liable for collision damage to another flyer, the pilot must fly negligently or the owner must maintain the plane negligently; they must generate abnormal risks of collision to the other planes aflight.

George P. Fletcher, *Fairness and Utility in Tort Law*, 85 Harv. L. Rev. 537 (1972). Is Fletcher's theory a useful explanation of the cases considered in this chapter?

D. RESPONDEAT SUPERIOR

The doctrine of respondeat superior ("let the master answer") generally holds employers strictly liable for torts committed by their employees in the course of their work. It thus is a prominent example of *vicarious liability*: liability for one party based on the wrongs of another. It is a doctrine of great practical importance, and indeed it lurks in the background of a majority of the cases in this book. When a corporate defendant is sued because one of its employees committed a tort, the doctrine of respondeat superior usually is being invoked, often without discussion. We will, however, be giving respondeat superior and related doctrines only a brief look here; they can become quite complicated, and constitute a significant portion of a topic to which whole courses are devoted: the law of agency. We therefore will just be introducing the main points: the law's definition of a servant's "scope of employment," and how independent contractors are defined and with what consequences. The question of punitive damages against employers for torts of their employees is taken up in the chapter of this book covering damages.

One natural explanation for the doctrine of respondeat superior is that it makes it more likely that the injured plaintiff will be able to collect a judgment from a solvent defendant. But is it fair to hold employers responsible when by assumption they have done nothing wrong? Bear in mind that even without respondeat superior, it always remains possible to assert that a principal should be held liable for choosing or supervising an agent negligently. The point of respondeat superior is that where the doctrine applies, no such showing need be made. Fairness to one side, can the doctrine be defended on the ground that it tends to reduce or optimize the likely number of accidents caused by an enterprise?

Ira S. Bushey & Sons v. United States
398 F.2d 167 (2d Cir. 1968)

FRIENDLY, *Circuit Judge*. While the United States Coast Guard vessel *Tamaroa* was being overhauled in a floating drydock located in Brooklyn's Gowanus Canal, a seaman returning from shore leave late at night, in the condition for which seamen are famed, turned some wheels on the drydock wall. He thus opened valves that controlled the flooding of the tanks on one side of the drydock. Soon the ship listed, slid off the blocks and fell against the wall. Parts of the drydock sank, and the ship partially did — fortunately without loss of life or personal injury. The drydock owner sought and was granted compensation by the District Court for the Eastern District of New York in an amount to be determined; the United States appeals. [. . .]

The Government attacks imposition of liability on the ground that Lane's acts were not within the scope of his employment. It relies heavily on §228(1) of the Restatement of Agency 2d which says that "conduct of a servant is within the scope of employment if, but only if: . . . (c) it is actuated, at least in part by a purpose to serve the master." Courts have gone to considerable lengths to find such a purpose, as witness a well-known opinion in which Judge Learned Hand concluded that a drunken boatswain who routed the plaintiff out of his bunk with a blow, saying "Get up, you big son of a bitch, and turn to," and then continued to fight, might have thought he was acting in the interest of the ship. *Nelson* v. *American-West African Line*, 86 F.2d 730 (2d Cir. 1936). It would be going too far to find such a purpose here; while Lane's return to the *Tamaroa* was to serve his employer, no one has suggested how he could have thought turning the wheels to be, even if — which is by no means clear — he was unaware of the consequences.

In light of the highly artificial way in which the motive test has been applied, the district judge believed himself obliged to test the doctrine's continuing vitality by referring to the larger purposes respondeat superior is supposed to serve. He concluded that the old formulation failed this test. We do not find his analysis so compelling, however, as to constitute a sufficient basis in itself for discarding the old doctrine. It is not at all clear, as the court below suggested, that expansion of liability in the manner here suggested will lead to a more efficient allocation of resources. As the most astute exponent of this theory has emphasized, a more efficient allocation can only be expected if there is some reason to believe that imposing a particular cost on the enterprise will lead it to consider whether steps should be taken to prevent a recurrence of the accident. Calabresi, *The Decision for Accidents: An Approach to Nonfault Allocation of Costs*, 78 Harv. L. Rev. 713, 725-34 (1965). And the suggestion that imposition of liability here will lead to more intensive screening of employees rests on highly questionable premises. The unsatisfactory quality of the allocation of resource rationale is especially striking on the facts of this case. It could well be that application of the traditional rule might induce drydock owners, prodded by their insurance companies, to install locks on their valves to avoid similar incidents in the future, while placing the burden on shipowners is much less likely to lead to accident prevention. It is true, of course, that in many cases the plaintiff will not be in a position to insure, and so expansion of liability will, at the very least, serve respondeat superior's loss spreading function. But the fact that the defendant is better able to afford damages is not alone sufficient to justify legal responsibility, and this over-arching principle must be taken into account in deciding whether to expand the reach of respondeat superior.

A policy analysis thus is not sufficient to justify this proposed expansion of vicarious liability. This is not surprising since respondeat superior, even within its traditional limits, rests not so much on policy grounds consistent with the governing principles of tort law as in a deeply rooted sentiment that a business enterprise cannot justly disclaim responsibility for accidents which may fairly be said to be characteristic of its activities. It is in this light that the inadequacy of the motive test becomes apparent. Whatever may have been the case in the past, a doctrine that would create such drastically different consequences for the actions of the drunken boatswain in *Nelson* and those of the drunken seaman here reflects a wholly unrealistic attitude toward the risks characteristically attendant upon the operation of a ship. We concur in the statement of Mr. Justice Rutledge in a case involving violence injuring a fellow-worker, in this instance in the context of workmen's compensation:

> Men do not discard their personal qualities when they go to work. Into the job they carry their intelligence, skill, habits of care and rectitude. Just as inevitably they take along also their tendencies to carelessness and camaraderie, as well as emotional make-up. In bringing men together, work brings these qualities together, causes frictions between them, creates occasions for lapses into carelessness, and for fun-making and emotional flare-up. . . . These expressions of human nature are incidents inseparable from working together. They involve risks of injury and these risks are inherent in the working environment.

Hartford Accident & Indemnity Co. v. Cardillo, 112 F.2d 11, 15. [. . .]

Put another way, Lane's conduct was not so "unforeseeable" as to make it unfair to charge the Government with responsibility. We agree with a leading treatise that "what is reasonably foreseeable in this context (of respondeat superior) . . . is quite a different thing from the foreseeably unreasonable risk of harm that spells negligence. . . . The foresight that should impel the prudent man to take precautions is not the same measure as that by which he should perceive the harm likely to flow from his long-run activity in spite of all reasonable precautions on his own part. The proper test here bears far more resemblance to that which limits liability for workmen's compensation than to the test for negligence. The employer should be held to expect risks, to the public also, which arise 'out of and in the course of' his employment of labor." 2 Harper & James, *The Law of Torts* 1377-78 (1956). Here it was foreseeable that crew members crossing the drydock might do damage, negligently or even intentionally, such as pushing a Bushey employee or kicking property into the water. Moreover, the proclivity of seamen to find solace for solitude by copious resort to the bottle while ashore has been noted in opinions too numerous to warrant citation. Once all this is granted, it is immaterial that Lane's precise action was not to be foreseen. [. . .] Consequently, we can no longer accept our past decisions that have refused to move beyond the *Nelson* rule, *Brailas v. Shepard S.S. Co.*, 152 F.2d 849 (2d Cir. 1945), *Kable v. United States*, 169 F.2d 90, 92 (2d Cir. 1948), since they do not accord with modern understanding as to when it is fair for an enterprise to disclaim the actions of its employees.

One can readily think of cases that fall on the other side of the line. If Lane had set fire to the bar where he had been imbibing or had caused an accident on the street while returning to the drydock, the Government would not be liable; the activities of the "enterprise" do not reach into areas where the servant does not create risks different from those attendant on the activities of the community in general. We agree with the district judge that if the seaman "upon returning to the drydock, recognized the Bushey security guard as his wife's lover and shot him," 276 F. Supp. at 530, vicarious liability would not follow; the incident would have related to the seaman's domestic life, not to his seafaring activity, would have been the most unlikely happenstance that the confrontation with the paramour occurred on a drydock rather than at the traditional spot. Here Lane had come within the closed-off area where his ship lay, to occupy a berth to which the Government insisted he have access, and while his act is not readily explicable, at least it was not shown to be due entirely to facets of his personal life. The risk that seamen going and coming from the *Tamaroa* might cause damage to the drydock is enough to make it fair that the enterprise bear the loss. It is not a fatal objection that the rule we lay down lacks sharp contours; in the end, as Judge Andrews said in a related context, "it is all a question (of expediency,) . . . of fair judgment, always keeping in mind the fact that we endeavor to make a rule in each case that will be practical and in keeping with the general understanding of Mankind." *Palsgraf v. Long Island R.R. Co.*, 162 N.E. 99, 104 (N.Y. 1928) (dissenting opinion).

[Affirmed.]

NOTES

1. *Frolic and detour.* In Miller v. Reiman-Wuerth Co., 598 P.2d 20 (Wyo. 1979), the defendant employed a man named Grandpre on one of its construction sites. One afternoon Grandpre asked permission to leave the site to deposit his paycheck at a local bank; he was concerned that otherwise certain checks he recently had written would bounce. He was granted the permission. He drove his own car to the bank, made the deposit, and then on his way back to the worksite was involved in a collision with the plaintiffs. They sued Grandpre's employer. The trial court gave summary judgment to the defendant, and the Wyoming Supreme Court affirmed. The court summarized the plaintiffs' arguments as follows:

(1) that [Grandpre's] trip was, at least in part, for the benefit of appellee or was employment related inasmuch as it contributed to Grandpre's "happiness" and thus made him a better and more efficient employee all to appellee's benefit as evidenced by appellee's policy which made the trip possible; (2) that appellee exercised control over the trip by requiring Grandpre to return to work immediately after completing his personal activity; and (3) that the determination of these two things (and thus the determination of whether or not the trip was in the scope of employment) was a question of fact for the jury.

The court then rejected them:

To accept appellants' contention that [the defendant employer was responsible for Grandpre's conduct] would also require acceptance of the contentions that policies for employee "happiness" by allowing vacations, no Saturday work, or lunch hours, coupled with directions to return to work immediately after the end of vacation, or after one hour for lunch, or at 8:00 A.M. each working day, would place the employees in the scope of employment, without more, while on vacation, on Saturdays, during lunch hours; in fact, at all times. Under the legal definition of "scope of employment" a reasonable mind could not find activities of these types, without more, to be within the scope of employment.

What is the distinction between *Miller v. Reiman-Wuerth Co.* and *Ira S. Bushey & Sons v. United States?*

The *Miller* decision might be understood as a rough illustration of the general rule that an employer is not liable for torts committed by an employee while on a "frolic" or "detour" of his own. The doctrine finds its origin in *Joel v. Morison,* 172 Eng. Rep. 1338 (1834), where Parke, B., said:

The master is only liable where the servant is acting in the course of his employment. If he was going out of his way, against his master's implied commands, when driving on his master's business, he will make his master liable; but if he was going on a frolic of his own, without being at all on his master's business, the master will not be liable.

The classic case of frolic and detour thus is not quite *Miller*; it is the employee who departs from the route assigned by the employer to pursue recreational or other private interests. The size of the deviation from an employer's instructions needed to prevent respondeat superior from applying often is a factbound question given to the jury.

2. *An economic account.* In Konradi v. United States, 919 F.2d 1207 (7th Cir. 1990), one Farringer, a mailman, was driving to work when he collided with the car of Glenn Konradi, causing Konradi's death. Konradi's estate sued the United States under the Federal Tort Claims Act, which allows the federal government to be liable under state tort law in circumstances where private parties would be held liable. The trial court gave summary judgment to the government. The court of appeals, per Posner, J., reversed, finding summary judgment premature. The opinion began by noting the statement of the Indiana Supreme Court that "an employee on his way to work is normally not in the employment of the corporation." But the court found that "normally," which it described as a "weasel word," did much work in the Indiana cases, as there were many exceptions to the general rule; liability sometimes had been found where an employee was driving home in a company car. The court attempted to make sense of the case law by offering an economic interpretation of respondeat superior and its "scope of employment" requirement:

> Often an employer can reduce the number of accidents caused by his employees not by being more careful — he may already be using as much care in hiring, supervising, monitoring, etc. his employees as can reasonably be demanded — but by altering the nature or extent of his operations: in a word by altering not his *care* but his *activity*. This possibility is a consideration in deciding whether to impose strict liability generally. The liability of an employer for torts committed by its employees — without any fault on his part — when they are acting within the scope of their employment, the liability that the law calls "respondeat superior," is a form of strict liability. It neither requires the plaintiff to prove fault on the part of the employer nor allows the employer to exonerate himself by proving his freedom from fault. The focus shifts from changes in care to changes in activity. For example, instead of dispatching its salesmen in cars from a central location, causing them to drive a lot and thus increasing the number of traffic accidents, a firm could open branch offices closer to its customers and have the salesmen work out of those offices. The amount of driving would be less (an activity change) and with it the number of accidents. Firms will consider these tradeoffs if they are liable

for the torts of their employees committed within the scope of their employment, even if the employer was not negligent in hiring or training or monitoring or supervising or deciding not to fire the employee who committed the tort. This liability also discourages employers from hiring judgment-proof employees, which they might otherwise have an incentive to do because a judgment-proof employee, by definition, does not have to be compensated (in the form of a higher wage) for running the risk of being sued for a tort that he commits on his employer's behalf. He runs no such risk; he is not worth suing.

If it is true that one objective of the doctrine of respondeat superior is to give employers an incentive to consider changes in the nature or level of their activities, then "scope of employment" can be functionally defined by reference to the likelihood that liability would induce beneficial changes in activity. It becomes apparent for example that the employer should not be made liable for a tort committed by the employee in the employee's home, for there is no plausible alteration in the activity of the employer that would substantially reduce the likelihood of such a tort. This overstates the case a bit; one can imagine a plaintiff's arguing that if the employer had not made the employee work so hard the employee would have been more alert and therefore more careful and the accident would not have occurred. But the law has to draw some lines for ease of administration, and a rough-and-ready one is between accidents on the job and accidents off the job — including accidents while commuting — in recognition of the fact that the employer's ability to prevent accidents by employees is normally much less when the employees are not at work. Indiana recognizes, however, that the line is indeed a rough one, and it allows juries to cross it when particular circumstances make the line inapt to the purpose that it seeks to implement. [. . .]

The Postal Service, Farringer's employer, requires its rural postal carriers to furnish their own vehicle (Farringer's was a pick-up truck) in making their rounds. The alternative would be for the Service to buy or lease mail trucks for these carriers to use. A possible consequence of the choice it has made is to increase the amount of driving over what it would be if the Service furnished the vehicles. No family with one car (and precious few with two) would want to leave its car at work and thereby have to find an alternative method of commuting. The Postal Service's rule pretty much guarantees that its mailmen will drive to and from work, and by doing this it increases the amount of driving compared to a system in which, since the mailman does not need to have his own car at work, he can take a train or bus or join a car pool. One cost of more driving is more accidents, and this cost can be made a cost to the Postal Service, and thus influence its choice between furnishing its mailmen with vehicles and requiring them to furnish their own, if the scope of employment is defined for purposes of tort law as including commuting in all cases in which the employee is required to furnish a vehicle for use at work. [. . .]

All this is highly speculative. The Postal Service's rule is limited to *rural* deliverymen, and neither public transportation nor car pooling is common in rural America. [. . .] But additional evidence in this case points to employer liability. According to testimony that for purposes of this appeal (only) we must take to be true, Farringer's postmaster required the postal carriers to take the most direct route in driving to and from work, and hence not to divagate for personal business. Nor was the carrier to stop for such business, or give anyone a ride. And he was to fasten his seatbelt (this was before Indiana passed a seatbelt law). The record does not reveal the reasons for these requirements. [One] possibility, however, is that the Postal Service was trying to minimize time lost by its employees from work and its workers' compensation costs, for the government interprets the federal employees' compensation law to include the commuting accidents of postal workers. [. . .] If the Postal Service insists for time's sake that the carrier always travel to and from work by the most direct route, which may not be the safest route, the Service should be liable for the accidents that result from this directive; it has made them more likely. [. . .]

Is there a satisfactory distinction between *Konradi v. United States* and *Miller v. Reiman-Wuerth Co.* (the NL case where the employee was in an accident while returning to work from the bank)? Is the explanation of respondeat superior offered in *Konradi* persuasive? What other rationales for the doctrine are available?

3. *The unfaithful servant.* In Roth v. First Natl. State Bank of New Jersey, 404 A.2d 1182 (N.J. App. 1979), the plaintiff, Roth, ran a check-cashing business in South Kearney. Every morning he would go to the defendant's bank to deposit his most recent checks and to replenish his supply of cash. One day as Roth left the bank with a box containing $72,000, a thief put a knife to his throat while a confederate grabbed the money and ran. Police later captured the thieves but were unable to recover the money. During the investigation it came out that one of the bank's tellers, Walker, had tipped off her boyfriend, Morse, to Roth's habit of carrying away large sums of cash every morning; Morse in turn had furnished the information to the thieves. Roth sued the bank to recover for his losses. The trial court gave judgment to the bank on the ground that the teller had not been acting within the scope of her employment when she tipped off her boyfriend to Roth's habits. The court of appeals affirmed:

Our Supreme Court has referred to 1 Restatement, Agency 2d, §228 (1958), as summarizing the conventional rule to the following effect:

(1) Conduct of a servant is within the scope of employment if, but only if:
(a) it is of the kind he is employed to perform;

(b) it occurs substantially within the authorized time and space limits;

(c) it is actuated, at least in part, by a purpose to serve the master, and

(d) if force is intentionally used by the servant against another, the use of force is not unexpectable by the master.

(2) Conduct of a servant is not within the scope of employment if it is different in kind from that authorized, far beyond the authorized time or space limits, or too little actuated by a purpose to serve the master.

Ordinarily, if the employee deviates from the business of his employer and, while in the pursuit of his own ends, commits a tort, the employer is not liable. However, an act may be within the scope of employment although consciously criminal or tortious, 1 Restatement, Agency 2d, §231, as where done for the master's purposes or reasonably expectable by the latter. [...]

A fair consideration of the rationale of the scope-of-employment principle will not accommodate defendant's liability here. Not only was the employee's act outrageously criminal, and not in any sense in the service of the employer's interests, but she had no apparent connection with the effectuation of the transactions by which plaintiff made his withdrawals of cash. Walker's knowledge was seemingly a mere matter of observation on her part. Finally, the tort itself, the "tip" to Morse, was not shown to have occurred within the time-space ambit of the employment. In short, to use the language of Prosser, the "unordered and unauthorized acts" of the servant in this case are not such that it should be found, as between the plaintiff and the defendant, "expedient (as a matter of justice) to charge the master" with liability therefor. Prosser, *Law of Torts*, at 460.

What is the distinction between *Roth v. First Natl. State Bank of New Jersey* and *Ira S. Bushey & Sons v. United States*? What is the distinction between *Roth* and *Konradi v. United States* (the L case of the plaintiff hit by a mailman on his way to work)?

4. *Ill-tempered Florida bus driver (I).* In Forster v. Red Top Sedan Service, 257 So. 2d 95 (Fla. App. 1972), the two plaintiffs, a couple named Forster, were driving to the airport when the driver of a Red Top bus began trying to run them off the highway. The bus then pulled in front of the plaintiffs' car and came to an abrupt stop. The bus driver walked back to the plaintiffs' car and pulled open the door on the driver's side. He swore that no "old bastard" would delay his schedule and "hold him up from getting to the beach"; he then struck each of the Forsters in the face. The Forsters sued Red Top to recover for their injuries on a theory of respondeat superior. The trial court gave a directed verdict to Red Top. The Florida Court of Appeals reversed, finding that a reasonable jury could bring in a verdict for the plaintiffs.

5. *Ill-tempered Florida bus driver (II)*. In Reina v. Metropolitan Dade
County, 285 So. 2d 648 (Fla. App. 1973), the plaintiff was a passenger on one
of the defendant's buses. He entered into a dispute with the driver regarding
the correct fare; the dispute heightened when the driver failed to stop after
the plaintiff pulled the cord to indicate that he wanted to get off. The driver
finally stopped in the middle of the street and allowed the plaintiff to leave.
When the plaintiff reached the sidewalk he made an obscene gesture at
the driver. The driver pulled over, left the bus, chased down the plaintiff,
and beat him. The plaintiff sued the county to recover for his injuries on a
theory of respondeat superior. The trial court gave a directed verdict to the
defendant. The Florida Court of Appeals affirmed, finding *Forster v. Red Top
Sedan Service*. distinguishable. Do you agree?

6. *Apparent authority*. From the Restatement (Second) of Agency (1958):

§265. GENERAL RULE

(1) A master or other principal is subject to liability for torts which
result from reliance upon, or belief in, statements or other conduct within
an agent's apparent authority.

(2) Unless there has been reliance, the principal is not liable in tort
for conduct of a servant or other agent merely because it is within his
apparent authority or apparent scope of employment.

Illustration 1. P discharges A, his foreman, who regularly directs those
under him where to cut timber. Before the employees have been told of
A's discharge, he tells them to cut trees on B's land, which they do. P is
liable for the trespass.

Illustration 2. P discharges A, his advertising manager and spokesman,
known to be such by all local newspaper reporters. The following day,
before anyone learns of his discharge, for the purpose of harming both
P and T, A states to the reporter that T has been defrauding P, causing
P great losses. P is liable to T for the defamatory statement.

Illustration 3. P permits A to appear as his servant and A is generally
known as such. While A is driving upon his own affairs but ostensibly
upon P's affairs, he negligently runs over T, who believes A to be P's
servant. P is not thereby liable to T.

What is the distinction between the third illustration and the first two?

7. *The paper boy*. In Miami Herald Publishing Co. v. Kendall, 88 So. 2d
276 (Fla. 1956), one Molesworth was making home deliveries of the *Miami
Herald* newspaper one morning when he ran over the plaintiff with his
motorcycle. The plaintiff sued the *Herald* for damages. The *Herald* conceded
that Molesworth had been negligent but argued that it could not be held
responsible for his behavior because he was an independent contractor rather
than an employee. The trial court entered judgment on a jury verdict for the

plaintiff. The Florida Supreme Court reversed, holding as a matter of law that Molesworth was an independent contractor and that the doctrine of respondeat superior therefore did not apply:

> For nearly twenty years newsboys have delivered the *Miami Herald* under a contract identical with, or similar to, the one involved in this litigation which contains the provision, among others, that "the NEWSDEALER is a separate, independent contractor and not subject to the exercise of any control by the PUBLISHER over his *method of distributing or otherwise handling the delivery* of said newspaper within his territory other than as expressly set forth in this contract. . . ." (Italics supplied.)
>
> The contract between the appellant and Molesworth carried the provisions that the appellant would furnish Molesworth, at a stipulated price, as many copies of daily and Sunday editions as he ordered, would supply him with the names and addresses of all persons wishing the newspaper to be delivered to them in the territory assigned to Molesworth, would credit the carrier for shortages of papers, and would credit Molesworth "for subscriptions paid in advance . . ." [. . .]
>
> The appellant reminds us of a familiar criterion by which it may usually be determined whether one performing services is an independent contractor or employee, that is, roughly, if the one securing the services controls the means by which the task is accomplished, the one performing the service is an employee, if not, he is an independent contractor. The contract, says the appellant, by its very terms made the newscarrier an independent contractor, and any control exercised by appellant was directed to the result — not the manner of performance. [. . .]
>
> Our study of the contents of the contract, and particularly the part we have italicized, leads us to the belief that the instrument was intended by both parties to make Molesworth an independent contractor and we frankly say that we have this view not only because of the express conditions we have abridged but also because of the specific mention of an element we consider important, if not essential, that is, the method Molesworth was to employ in carrying the papers to the subscribers once he had received them from appellant. Not only in the contract but in the practical operation under it, the circumstances of which we will presently describe, it was left entirely to Molesworth to select the conveyance which he would use to transport the papers from the point of origin to the subscribers' front porches.
>
> We turn now to see, from the testimony favorable to the appellee's contention, the nature of the services actually performed and the supervision the appellant exercised over the manner in which its newspapers reached the subscribers through Molesworth or, as appellee puts it, the supervision of the means by which Molesworth performed his work. The newsboy began his work at 4:30 in the morning by getting the papers and folding them. He then started on his route and at 6:30 he finished.

If Molesworth overslept, the appellant's manager would go to his home and rout him out of bed. The newsboy was required to deliver the papers in an "unwrinkled condition" and to accomplish this could fold the papers "in threes or fours." Although nobody described to him the exact way to fold the papers, he was evidently told that he could not fold them in "biscuits." The agent of the appellant apparently "rode herd" on the newsboys to see that deliveries were made to the subscribers and "that everything was going all right." [. . .]

We do not find that the extra-contractual activities of the contracting parties neutralized the provisions of the agreement which to us were obviously intended to make Molesworth an independent contractor. [. . .]

What is the distinction between *Miami Herald Publishing Co. v. Kendall* and *Konradi v. United States* (the L case where the mailman ran over the plaintiff's decedent while on his way to work)?

8. *Independent contractors generally.* From the Restatement (Second) of Agency (1958):

§220. DEFINITION OF SERVANT

(1) A servant is a person employed to perform services in the affairs of another and who with respect to the physical conduct in the performance of the services is subject to the other's control or right to control.

(2) In determining whether one acting for another is a servant or an independent contractor, the following matters of fact, among others, are considered:

(a) the extent of control which, by the agreement, the master may exercise over the details of the work;

(b) whether or not the one employed is engaged in a distinct occupation or business;

(c) the kind of occupation, with reference to whether, in the locality, the work is usually done under the direction of the employer or by a specialist without supervision;

(d) the skill required in the particular occupation;

(e) whether the employer or the workman supplies the instrumentalities, tools, and the place of work for the person doing the work;

(f) the length of time for which the person is employed;

(g) the method of payment, whether by the time or by the job;

(h) whether or not the work is a part of the regular business of the employer;

(i) whether or not the parties believe they are creating the relation of master and servant; and

(j) whether the principal is or is not in business.

Comment a. Servants not performing manual labor. The word "servant" does not exclusively connote a person rendering manual labor, but one who performs continuous service for another and who, as to his physical movements, is subject to the control or to the right to control of the other as to the manner of performing the service. The word indicates the closeness of the relation between the one giving and the one receiving the service rather than the nature of the service or the importance of the one giving it. Thus, ship captains and managers of great corporations are normally superior servants, differing only in the dignity and importance of their positions from those working under them. The rules for determining the liability of the employer for the conduct of both superior servants and the humblest employees are the same; the application differs with the extent and nature of their duties.

Comment h. Factors indicating the relation of master and servant. The relation of master and servant is indicated by the following factors: an agreement for close supervision or de facto close supervision of the servant's work; work which does not require the services of one highly educated or skilled; the supplying of tools by the employer; payment by hour or month; employment over a considerable period of time with regular hours; full time employment by one employer; employment in a specific area or over a fixed route; the fact that the work is part of the regular business of the employer; the fact that the community regards those doing such work as servants; the belief by the parties that there is a master and servant relation; an agreement that the work cannot be delegated.

Illustration 5. P employs A to drive him around town in A's automobile at $4.00 per hour. The inference is that A is not P's servant. If P supplies the automobile, the inference is that A is P's servant for whose conduct within the scope of employment P is responsible.

Illustration 11. A is employed by P as resident cook for his household under an agreement in which P promises that he will in no way interfere with A's conduct in preparing the food. A is P's servant.

Is *Miami Herald Publishing Co. v. Kendall* consistent with the Restatement test offered above?

9. *Nondelegable duties.* In Yazoo & Mississippi Valley Railroad Co. v. Gordon, 186 So. 631 (Miss. 1939), a carload of cattle was being shipped by railway from Texas to Tennessee. The Yazoo Railroad hired an agent to unload the animals in Vicksburg and hold them there while they awaited a connecting train. A steer escaped from its pen, ran to a nearby highway and gored the plaintiff, who in turn sued Yazoo to recover for his injuries. The Mississippi Supreme Court held that the steer was a domestic rather than a wild animal, and that the defendant therefore should be held liable if the steer's escape was caused by negligence. The court then rejected the Yazoo

firm's argument that it should avoid liability because the animals were handled by an independent contractor:

> The appellant says that when this steer escaped, the cattle were being loaded into the car, not by its employes, but by one under contract with it so to do of such character as to make him an independent contractor. We will not determine from the evidence whether this is true, for if true, the fact would not relieve the appellant from liability. The appellant owed a duty to the public, under the circumstances hereinbefore set forth, to prevent this steer from being at large and could not delegate the performance thereof to another and thereby escape liability for its nonperformance.

What is the distinction between *Yazoo & Mississippi Valley Railroad Co. v. Gordon* and *Miami Herald Publishing Co. v. Kendall* (the NL case of the paper boy)?

10. *Peculiar risks.* As a general rule, principals are not liable for the torts of their independent contractors; this is one of the lessons of *Miami Herald Publishing Co. v. Kendall*. But as the *Yazoo* case illustrates, there is an exception to the rule for certain duties that the law does not permit to be delegated. Sometimes the principle is stated in the way the court suggested in *Yazoo*, but it can take other forms as well. Thus from the Second Restatement of Torts:

§416. WORK DANGEROUS IN ABSENCE OF SPECIAL PRECAUTIONS

One who employs an independent contractor to do work which the employer should recognize as likely to create during its progress a peculiar risk of physical harm to others unless special precautions are taken, is subject to liability for physical harm caused to them by the failure of the contractor to exercise reasonable care to take such precautions, even though the employer has provided for such precautions in the contract or otherwise.

Comment d. In order for the rule stated in this Section to apply, it is not essential that the work which the contractor is employed to do be in itself an extra-hazardous or abnormally dangerous activity, or that it involve a very high degree of risk to those in the vicinity. It is sufficient that it is likely to involve a peculiar risk of physical harm unless special precautions are taken, even though the risk is not abnormally great. A "peculiar risk" is a risk differing from the common risks to which persons in general are commonly subjected by the ordinary forms of negligence which are usual in the community. It must involve some special hazard resulting from the nature of the work done, which calls for special precautions. Thus if a contractor is employed to transport the employer's goods by truck over the public highway, the employer is not liable for the contractor's failure to inspect the brakes on his truck, or for his driving in excess of the speed limit, because the risk is in no way a peculiar one, and only an ordinary precaution is called for. But if the contractor is employed to transport giant logs weighing several tons over the highway, the employer will be subject to liability for the contractor's failure to take special precautions to anchor them on his trucks.

11. *Collateral negligence.* In Wilton v. City of Spokane, 132 P. 404 (Wash. 1913), the defendant city hired a partnership, Foster & Hindle, to build a street. The terms of the agreement made Foster & Hindle independent contractors. The contractors encountered a ledge of rock in the course of grading the street. They used dynamite to remove it; one piece of unexploded dynamite was left behind, however, and paved over. Some months later another firm was permitted to install electrical poles along the side of the new road. In the course of the drilling required for the purpose, the dynamite left behind by Foster & Hindle exploded, causing various injuries to one of the workmen. He sued the city of Spokane to recover for his injuries, arguing that it was responsible for Foster & Hindle's negligence in leaving behind the dynamite. The Washington Supreme Court held for the city:

> It is first said that the work was of such a character that it could not be let to independent contractors, and that the city could not escape liability for the negligent performance by endeavoring to so let it. The particular contention is that the work of blasting rock in an inhabited portion of a city is so inherently dangerous in itself that public policy forbids that the city be permitted to let the work to an independent contractor. But if this be the general rule, we do not think the present case falls within it. The leaving of an unexploded blast of dynamite in the rock below the surface of a street is not an incident to the work of blasting rock to make a grade for a street. Such an action is negligence and nothing else, and the city is liable for the act only in the same way, and to the same extent, that it would have been liable had the contractors left the dynamite on the surface of the street in the traveled part of the roadway on leaving the work; it is liable for injuries resulting therefrom only in the case it knew of its being so left, or by the exercise of reasonable diligence could have known of it. "But the employer is not liable where the obstruction or defect in the street causing the injury is wholly collateral to the contract work, and entirely the result of the negligence or wrongful acts of the contractor, subcontractor, or his servants. In such a case the immediate author of the injury is alone liable." Dillon's Mun. Corp. §1030. There is no evidence that the city had knowledge of the existence of this unexploded blast, and, of course, there was no sort of diligence that it could have exercised which would have made it acquainted with the fact.

What is the distinction between *Wilton v. City of Spokane* and *Yazoo & Mississippi Valley Railroad Co. v. Gordon* (the L case of the escaped steer)?

12. *Contractors mistakenly thought to be servants.* From the Restatement (Second) of Torts:

> §429. NEGLIGENCE IN DOING WORK WHICH IS ACCEPTED IN RELIANCE
>   ON THE EMPLOYER'S DOING THE WORK HIMSELF
>
> One who employs an independent contractor to perform services for another which are accepted in the reasonable belief that the services are being rendered by the employer or by his servants, is subject to liability for physical harm caused by the negligence of the contractor in supplying such services, to the same extent as though the employer were supplying them himself or by his servants.
>
> *Illustration 2.* A's wife faints. He hails a taxicab, which is so labeled as to indicate that it is operated by the B Taxicab Company, although the arrangement between the taxicab company and the driver is such as to make the driver an independent contractor. A puts his wife in the cab and accompanies her home. Through the careless driving of the taxicab driver a collision occurs in which A and his wife are hurt, as is also C, the driver of another car. The rule stated in this Section subjects the B Company to liability to A and his wife but not to C.

Are these provisions consistent with *Miami Herald Publishing Co. v. Kendall* (the NL case of the paper boy)?

13. *The figure in the carpet.* What is the logic of the different rules that apply to employees (or "servants") and independent contractors — and the exceptions to them? Is there an economic explanation of the rules regarding independent contractors that is consistent with the general rationale for respondeat superior offered in the *Konradi* case earlier in this section?

Chapter 8

Products Liability

A. HISTORICAL DEVELOPMENT

The law governing liability for defective products changed dramatically during the course of the twentieth century. We therefore begin with three landmark decisions in the development of the law in this area, followed by excerpts from the Products Liability chapter of the Restatement (Third) of Torts (1997) that discuss the general principles on which the law appears to have settled for now.

MacPherson v. Buick Motor Co.
111 N.E. 1050 (N.Y. 1916)

CARDOZO, J. The defendant is a manufacturer of automobiles. It sold an automobile to a retail dealer. The retail dealer resold to the plaintiff. While the plaintiff was in the car, it suddenly collapsed. He was thrown out and injured. One of the wheels was made of defective wood, and its spokes crumbled into fragments. The wheel was not made by the defendant; it was bought from another manufacturer. There is evidence, however, that its defects could have been discovered by reasonable inspection, and that inspection was omitted. There is no claim that the defendant knew of the defect and willfully concealed it. [...] The charge is one, not of fraud, but of negligence. The question to be determined is whether the defendant owed a duty of care and vigilance to any one but the immediate purchaser.

The foundations of this branch of the law, at least in this state, were laid in *Thomas v. Winchester*. A poison was falsely labeled. The sale was made to a druggist, who in turn sold to a customer. The customer recovered damages from the seller who affixed the label. "The defendant's negligence," it was said, "put human life in imminent danger." A poison falsely labeled is likely to injure any one who gets it. Because the danger is to be foreseen, there is a duty to avoid the injury. Cases were cited by way of illustration in which manufacturers were not subject to any duty irrespective of contract. The distinction was said to be that their conduct, though negligent, was not likely to result in injury to any one except the purchaser. We are not required to say whether the chance of injury was always as remote as the distinction assumes. Some of the illustrations might be rejected today. The principle of the distinction is for present purposes the important thing.

Thomas v. Winchester became quickly a landmark of the law. In the application of its principle there may at times have been uncertainty or even error. There has never in this state been doubt or disavowal of the principle itself. The chief cases are well known, yet to recall some of them will be helpful. [...] [E]arly cases suggest a narrow construction of the rule. Later cases, however, evince a more liberal spirit. First in importance is *Devlin v. Smith* (89 N.Y. 470). The defendant, a contractor, built a scaffold for a painter. The painter's servants were injured. The contractor was held liable. He knew that the scaffold, if improperly constructed, was a most dangerous trap. He knew that it was to be used by the workmen. He was building it for that very purpose. Building it for their use, he owed them a duty, irrespective of his contract with their master, to build it with care.

From *Devlin v. Smith* we pass over intermediate cases and turn to the latest case in this court in which *Thomas v. Winchester* was followed. That case is *Statler v. Ray Mfg. Co.* The defendant manufactured a large coffee urn. It was installed in a restaurant. When heated, the urn exploded and injured the plaintiff. We held that the manufacturer was liable. We said that the urn "was of such a character inherently that, when applied to the purposes for which it was designed, it was liable to become a source of great danger to many people if not carefully and properly constructed." It may be that *Devlin v. Smith* and *Statler v. Ray Mfg. Co.* have extended the rule of *Thomas v. Winchester*. If so, this court is committed to the extension. The defendant argues that things imminently dangerous to life are poisons, explosives, deadly weapons — things whose normal function it is to injure or destroy. But whatever the rule in *Thomas v. Winchester* may once have been, it has no longer that restricted meaning. [...]

We hold, then, that the principle of *Thomas v. Winchester* is not limited to poisons, explosives, and things of like nature, to things which in their normal operation are implements of destruction. If the nature of a thing is such that it is reasonably certain to place life and limb in peril when negligently made, it is then a thing of danger. Its nature gives warning of the consequences to be expected. If to the element of danger there is added knowledge that the thing will be used by persons other than the purchaser, and used without new tests then, irrespective of contract, the manufacturer of this thing of danger is under a duty to make it carefully. That is as far as we are required to go for the decision of this case. There must be knowledge of a danger, not merely possible, but probable. It is possible to use almost anything in a way that will make it dangerous if defective. That is not enough to charge the manufacturer with a duty independent of his contract. Whether a given thing is dangerous may be sometimes a question for the court and sometimes a question for the jury. There must also be knowledge that in the usual course of events the danger will be shared by others than the buyer. Such knowledge may often be inferred from the nature of the transaction. But it is possible that even knowledge of the danger and of the use will not always be enough. The proximity or remoteness of the relation is a factor to be considered. We are dealing now with the liability of the manufacturer of the finished product, who puts it on the market to be used without inspection by his customers. If he is negligent, where danger is to be foreseen, a liability will follow. We are not required at this time to say that it is legitimate to go back of the manufacturer of the finished product and hold the manufacturers of the component parts. To make their negligence a cause of imminent danger, an independent cause must often intervene; the manufacturer of the finished product must also fail in his duty of inspection. It may be that in those circumstances the negligence of the earlier members of the series as too remote to constitute, as to the ultimate user, an actionable wrong. We leave that question open to you. We shall have to deal with it when it arises. The difficulty which it suggests is not present in this case. There is here no break in the chain of cause and effect. In such circumstances, the presence of a known danger, attendant upon a known use, makes vigilance a duty. We have put aside the notion that the duty to safeguard life and limb, when the consequences of negligence may be foreseen, grows out of contract and nothing else. We have put the source of the obligation where it ought to be. We have put its source in the law.

From this survey of the decisions, there thus emerges a definition of the duty of a manufacturer which enables us to measure this defendant's liability. Beyond all question, the nature of an automobile gives warning of probable danger if its construction is defective. This automobile was designed to go fifty miles an hour. Unless its wheels were sound and strong, injury was almost certain. It was as much a thing of danger as a defective engine for a railroad. The defendant knew the danger. It knew also that the care would be used by persons other than the buyer. This was apparent from its size; there were seats for three persons. It was apparent also from the fact that the buyer was a dealer in cars, who bought to resell. The maker of this car supplied it for the use of purchasers from the dealer just as plainly as the contractor in *Devlin v. Smith* supplied the scaffold for use by the servants of the owner. The dealer was indeed the one person of whom it might be said with some approach to certainly that by him the car would not be used. Yet the defendant would have us say that he was the one person whom it was under a legal duty to protect. The law does not lead us to so inconsequent a conclusion. Precedents drawn from the days of travel by stage coach do not fit the conditions of travel today. The principle that the danger must be imminent does not change, but the things subject to the principle do change. They are whatever the needs of life in a developing civilization require them to be.

In England the limits of the rule are still unsettled. *Winterbottom v. Wright* (10 M. & W. 109) is often cited. The defendant undertook to provide a mail coach to carry the mail bags. The coach broke down from latent defects in its construction. The defendant, however, was not the manufacturer. The court held that he was not liable for injuries to a passenger. The case was decided on a demurrer to the declaration. [. . .] [T]he form of the declaration was subject to criticism. It did not fairly suggest the existence of a duty aside from the special contract which was the plaintiff's main reliance. [. . .]

There is nothing anomalous in a rule which imposes upon A, who has contracted with B, a duty to C and D and others according as he knows or does not know that the subject matter of the contract is intended for their use. We may find an analogy in the law which measures the liability of landlords. If A leases to B a tumble-down house he is not liable, in the absence of fraud, to B's guests who enter it and are injured. This is because B is then under the duty to repair it, the lessor has the right to suppose that he will fulfill that duty, and if he omits to do so, his guests must look to him. But if A leases a building to be used by the lessee at once as a place of public entertainment, the rule is different. There is injury to persons other than the lessee is to be foreseen, and foresight of the consequences involves the creation of a duty *Junkermann v. Tilyou R. Co.*, 213 N.Y. 404, and cases there cited). [. . .]

In this view of the defendant's liability there is nothing inconsistent with the theory of liability on which the case was tried. It is true that the court told the jury that "an automobile is not an inherently dangerous vehicle." The meaning, however, is made plain by the context. The meaning is that danger is not to be expected when the vehicle is well constructed. The court left it to the jury to say whether the defendant ought to have foreseen that the car, if negligently constructed, would become "imminently dangerous." Subtle distinctions are drawn by the defendant between things inherently dangerous and things imminently dangerous, but the case does not turn upon these verbal niceties. If danger was to be expected as reasonably certain, there was a duty of vigilance, and this whether you call the danger inherent or imminent. In varying forms that the court would not have been justified in ruling as a matter of law that the car was a dangerous thing. If there was any error, it was none of which the defendant can complain.

We think the defendant was not absolved from a duty of inspection because it bought the wheels from a reputable manufacturer. It was not merely a dealer in automobiles. It was a manufacturer of automobiles. It was responsible for the finished product. It was not at liberty to put the finished product on the market without subjecting the component parts to ordinary and simple tests. Under the charge of the trial judge nothing more was required of it. The obligation to inspect must vary with the nature of the thing to be inspected. The more probable the danger, the greater the need of caution. There is little analogy between this case and *Carlson v. Phoenix Bridge Co.*, where the defendant bought a tool for a servant's use. The making of tools was not the business on which the master was engaged. Reliance on the skill of the manufacturer was proper and almost inevitable. But that is not the defendant's situation. Both by its relation to the work and by the nature of its business, it is charged with a stricter duty.

Other rulings complained of have been considered, but no error has been found on them.

The judgment should be affirmed.

BARTLETT, C.J., dissenting. [. . .] The theory upon which the case was submitted to the jury by the learned judge who presided at the trial was that, although an automobile is not an inherently dangerous vehicle, it may become such if equipped with a weak wheel; and that if the motor car in question, when it was put upon the market was in itself inherently dangerous by reason of its being equipped with a weak wheel, the defendant was chargeable with a knowledge of the defect so far as it might be discovered by a reasonable inspection and the application of reasonable tests. This liability, it was further held, was not limited to the original vendee, but extended to a subvendee like the plaintiff, who was not a party to the original contract of sale.

I think that these rulings, which have been approved by the Appellate Division, extend the liability of the vendor of a manufactured article further than any case which has yet received the sanction of this court. It has heretofore been held in this state that the liability of the vendor of a manufactured article for negligence arising out of the existence of defects therein does not extend to strangers injured in consequence of such defects but is confined to the immediate vendee. The exceptions to this general rule which have thus far been recognized in New York are cases in which the article sold was of such a character that danger to life or limb was involved in the ordinary use thereof; in other words, where the article sold was inherently dangerous. As has already been pointed out, the learned trial judge instructed the jury that an automobile is not an inherently dangerous vehicle.

The late Chief Justice Cooley of Michigan, one of the most learned and accurate of American law writers, states the general rule thus: "The general rule is that a contractor, manufacturer, vendor, or furnisher of an article is not liable to third parties who have no contractual relations with him for negligence in the construction, manufacture, or sale of such article." (2 *Cooley on Torts* (3d ed.), 1486.)

The leading English authority in support of this rule, to which all the later cases on the same subject refer, is *Winterbottom v. Wright* (10 Meeson & Welsby, 109), which was an action by the driver of a stage coach against a contractor who had agreed with the postmaster-general to provide and keep the vehicle in repair for the purpose of conveying the royal mail over a prescribed route. The coach broke down and upset, injuring the driver, who sought to recover against the contractor on account of its defective construction. The Court of Exchequer denied him any right of recovery on the ground that there was no privity of contract between the parties, the agreement having been made with the postmaster-general alone. [...] The doctrine of that decision was recognized as the law of this state by the leading New York case of *Thomas v. Winchester* (6 N.Y. 397, 408), which, however, involved an exception to the general rule. There the defendant, who was a dealer in medicines, sold to a druggist a quantity of belladonna, which is a deadly poison, negligently labeled as extract of dandelion. The druggist in good faith used the poison in filling a prescription calling for the harmless dandelion extract and the plaintiff for whom the prescription was put up was poisoned by the belladonna. This court held that the original vendor was liable for the injuries suffered by the patient. Chief Judge Ruggles, who delivered the opinion of the court, distinguished between an act of negligence imminently dangerous to the lives of others and one that is not so, saying: "If A. builds a wagon and sells it to B., who sells it to C. and C. hires it to D., who in consequence of the gross negligence of A. in building the wagon is overturned and injured, D. cannot recover damages against A., the builder. A.'s obligation to build the wagon faithfully, arises solely out of his contract with B. The public have nothing to do with it. . . . So, for the same reason, if a horse be defectively shod by a smith, and a person hiring the horse from the owner is thrown and injured in consequence of the smith's negligence in shoeing; the smith is not liable for the injury." [...]

I do not see how we can uphold the judgment in the present case without overruling what has been so often said by this court and other courts of like authority in reference to the absence of any liability for negligence on the part of the original vendor of an ordinary carriage to any one except his immediate vendee. The absence of such liability was the very point actually decided in the English case of *Winterbottom v. Wright*, and the illustration quoted from the opinion of Chief Judge Ruggles in *Thomas v. Winchester* assumes that the law on the subject was so plain that the statement would be accepted almost as a matter of course. In the case at bar the defective wheel on an automobile moving only eight miles an hour was not any more dangerous to the occupants of the car than a similarly defective wheel would be to the occupants of a carriage drawn by a horse at the same speed; and yet unless the courts have been all wrong on this question up to the present time there would be no liability to strangers to the original sale in the case of the horse-drawn carriage.

NOTES

1. *The old rule*. The leading case *MacPherson* displaced was Winterbottom v. Wright, 10 M. & W. 109, 152 Eng. Rep. 402 (1842), mentioned in Cardozo's opinion and in the dissent. The defendant entered into a contract with the English Postmaster-General to supply a coach and keep it in good repair. The Postmaster-General then contracted with another

party, one Atkinson, to deliver mail using the coach; Atkinson in turn hired the plaintiff as a driver. The coach "gave way and broke down" while the plaintiff was driving it, allegedly due to latent defects. The plaintiff sued the supplier of the coach and lost because he was not a party to the contract by which it had been provided to the Postmaster-General. Said Lord Abinger:

> There is no privity of contract between these parties; and if the plaintiff can sue, every passenger, or even any person passing along the road, who was injured by the upsetting of the coach, might bring a similar action. Unless we confine the operation of such contracts as this to the parties who entered into them, the most absurd and outrageous consequences, to which I can see no limit, would ensue.

Baron Rolfe took a similar view:

> The breach of the defendant's duty, stated in this declaration, i[s] his omission to keep the carriage in a safe condition. [. . .] The duty [. . .] is shewn to have arisen solely from the contract; and the fallacy consists in the use of that word "duty." If a duty to the Postmaster-General be meant, that is true; but if a duty to the plaintiff be intended (and in that sense the word is evidently used), there was none.

As this last excerpt suggests, the result in *Winterbottom* seems to have been driven by certain details of the facts and choices the plaintiff made in arguing the case: he focused on the defendant's failure to keep the coach in good repair; but the only place a duty of that sort could be found was in the contract, to which the plaintiff was not a party. *Winterbottom* nevertheless came to be broadly understood as meaning that manufacturers and suppliers of products could not be held liable to anyone except those with whom they had contracts. So viewed, *Winterbottom* became a leading case in the United States as well as England, though American courts developed exceptions to its rule for inherently dangerous products — the exception that provided Cardozo with a toehold for his description of the legal landscape in *MacPherson*.

Cardozo's opinion in *MacPherson* is a landmark in American law and is considered by many to be a remarkable example of judicial craft. It reinterprets old case law to produce a new result thought to be a better fit with the conditions of its times, yet never describes itself as announcing anything new. The exception set out in *MacPherson*, creating general liability for negligence where a product may be found a "thing of danger," proceeded to swallow the rule in all jurisdictions; by the mid-1960s every state had dropped the requirement that plaintiffs must be in privity with (i.e., have a contractual relationship with) defendants before bringing suits against them to recover for injuries caused by defective products.

Escola v. Coca Cola Bottling Co.
150 P.2d 436 (Cal. 1944)

GIBSON, C.J. Plaintiff, a waitress in a restaurant, was injured when a bottle of Coca Cola broke in her hand. She alleged that defendant company, which had bottled and delivered the alleged defective bottle to her employer, was negligent in selling "bottles containing said beverage which on account of excessive pressure of gas or by reason of some defect in the bottle was dangerous . . . and likely to explode." This appeal is from a judgment upon a jury verdict in favor of plaintiff.

The bottle was admittedly charged with gas under pressure, and the charging of the bottle was within the exclusive control of defendant. As it is a matter of common knowledge that an overcharge would not ordinarily result without negligence, it follows under the doctrine of res ipsa loquitur that if the bottle was in fact excessively charged an inference of defendant's negligence would arise. If the explosion resulted from a defective bottle containing a safe pressure, the defendant would be liable if it negligently failed to discover such flaw. If the defect were visible, an inference of negligence would arise from the failure of defendant to discover it. Where defects are discoverable, it may be assumed that they will not ordinarily escape detection if a reasonable inspection is made, and if such a defect is overlooked an inference arises that a proper inspection was not made. A difficult problem is presented where the defect is unknown and consequently might have been one not discoverable by a reasonable, practicable inspection. In the *Honea* case we refused to take judicial notice of the technical practices and information available to the bottling industry for finding defects which cannot be seen. In the present case, however, we are supplied with evidence of the standard methods used for testing bottles.

A chemical engineer for the Owens-Illinois Glass Company and its Pacific Coast subsidiary, maker of Coca Cola bottles, explained how glass is manufactured and the methods used in testing and inspecting bottles. He testified that his company is the largest manufacturer of glass containers in the United States, and that it uses the standard methods for testing bottles recommended by the glass containers association. A pressure test is made by taking a sample from each mold every three hours — approximately one out of every 600 bottles — and subjecting the sample to an internal pressure of 450 pounds per square inch, which is sustained for one minute. (The normal pressure in Coca Cola bottles is less than 50 pounds per square inch.) The sample bottles are also subjected to the standard thermal shock test. The witness stated that these tests are "pretty near" infallible.

It thus appears that there is available to the industry a commonly-used method of testing bottles for defects not apparent to the eye, which is almost infallible. Since Coca Cola bottles are subjected to these tests by the manufacturer, it is not likely that they contain defects when delivered to the bottler which are not discoverable by visual inspection. Both new and used bottles are filled and distributed by defendant. The used bottles are not again subjected to the tests referred to above, and it may be inferred that defects not discoverable by visual inspection do not develop in bottles after they are manufactured. Obviously, if such defects do occur in used bottles there is a duty upon the bottler to make appropriate tests before they are refilled, and if such tests are not commercially practicable the bottles should not be re-used. This would seem to be particularly true where a charged liquid is placed in the bottle. It follows that a defect which would make the bottle unsound could be discovered by reasonable and practicable tests.

Although it is not clear in this case whether the explosion was caused by an excessive charge or a defect in the glass there is a sufficient showing that neither cause would ordinarily have been present if due care had been used. Further, defendant had exclusive control over both the charging and inspection of the bottles. Accordingly, all the requirements necessary to entitle plaintiff to rely on the doctrine of res ipsa loquitur to supply an inference of negligence are present.

The judgment is affirmed.

TRAYNOR, J., concurring. I concur in the judgment, but I believe the manufacturer's negligence should no longer be singled out as the basis of a plaintiff's right to recover in cases like the present one. In my opinion it should now be recognized that a manufacturer incurs an absolute liability when an article that he has placed on the market, knowing that it is to be used without inspection, proves to have a defect that causes injury to human beings. *MacPherson v. Buick Motor Co.*, 111 N.E. 1050 (N.Y. 1916), established the principle, recognized by this court, that irrespective of privity of contract, the manufacturer is responsible for an injury caused by such an article to any person who comes in lawful contact with it. In these cases the source of the manufacturer's liability was his negligence in the manufacturing process or in the inspection of component parts supplied by others. Even if there is no negligence, however, public policy demands that responsibility be fixed wherever it will most effectively reduce the hazards to life and health inherent in defective products that reach the market. It is evident that the manufacturer can anticipate some hazards and guard against the recurrence of others, as the public cannot. Those who suffer injury from defective products are unprepared to meet its consequences. The cost of an injury and the loss of time or health may be an overwhelming misfortune to the person injured, and a needless one, for the risk of injury can be insured by the manufacturer and distributed among the public as a cost of doing business. It is to the public interest to discourage the marketing of products having defects that are a menace to the public. If such products nevertheless find their way into the market it is to the public interest to place the responsibility for whatever injury they may cause upon the manufacturer, who, even if he is not negligent in the manufacture of the product, is responsible for its reaching the market. However intermittently such injuries may occur and however haphazardly they may strike, the risk of their occurrence is a constant risk and a general one. Against such a risk there should be general and constant protection and the manufacturer is best situated to afford such protection.

The injury from a defective product does not become a matter of indifference because the defect arises from causes other than the negligence of the manufacturer, such as negligence of a submanufacturer of a component part whose defects could not be revealed by inspection, or unknown causes that even by the device of res ipsa loquitur cannot be classified as negligence of the manufacturer. The inference of negligence may be dispelled by an affirmative showing of proper care. If the evidence against the fact inferred is "clear, positive, uncontradicted, and of such a nature that it can not rationally be disbelieved, the court must instruct the jury that the nonexistence of the fact has been established as a matter of law." *Blank v. Coffin*, 126 P.2d 868, 870. An injured person, however, is not ordinarily in a position to refute such evidence or identify the cause of the defect, for he can hardly be familiar with the manufacturing process as the manufacturer himself is. In leaving it to the jury to decide whether the inference has been dispelled, regardless of the evidence against it, the negligence rule approaches the rule of strict liability. It is needlessly circuitous to make negligence the basis of recovery and impose what is in reality liability without negligence. If public policy demands that a manufacturer of goods be responsible for their quality regardless of negligence there is no reason not to fix that responsibility openly.

In the case of foodstuffs, the public policy of the state is formulated in a criminal statute. Statutes of this kind result in a strict liability of the manufacturer in tort to the member of the public injured. [...] The statute may well be applicable to a bottle whose defects cause it to explode. In any event it is significant that the statute imposes criminal liability without fault, reflecting the public policy of protecting the public from dangerous products placed on the market, irrespective of negligence in their manufacture. While the Legislature imposes criminal liability only with regard to food products and their containers, there are many other sources of danger. It is to the public interest to prevent injury to the public from any defective goods by the imposition of civil liability generally.

The retailer, even though not equipped to test a product, is under an absolute liability to his customer, for the implied warranties of fitness for proposed use and merchantable quality include a warranty of safety of the product. This warranty is not necessarily a contractual one, for public policy requires that the buyer be insured at the seller's expense against injury. The courts recognize, however, that the retailer cannot bear the burden of this warranty, and allow him to recoup any losses by means of the warranty of safety attending the wholesaler's or manufacturer's sale to him. Such a procedure, however, is needlessly circuitous and engenders wasteful litigation. Much would be gained if the injured person could base his action directly on the manufacturer's warranty.

As handicrafts have been replaced by mass production with its great markets and transportation facilities, the close relationship between the producer and consumer of a product has been altered. Manufacturing processes, frequently valuable secrets, are ordinarily either inaccessible to or beyond the ken of the general public. The consumer no longer has means or skill enough to investigate for himself the soundness of a product, even when it is not contained in a sealed package, and his erstwhile vigilance has been lulled by the steady efforts of manufacturers to build up confidence by advertising and marketing devices such as trade-marks. Consumers no longer approach products warily but accept them on faith, relying on the reputation of the manufacturer or the trade-mark. Manufacturers have sought to justify that faith by increasingly high standards of inspection and a readiness to make good on defective products by way of replacements and refunds. The manufacturer's obligation to the consumer must keep pace with the changing relationship between them; it cannot be escaped because the marketing of a product has become so complicated as to require one or more intermediaries. Certainly there is greater reason to impose liability on the manufacturer than on the retailer who is but a conduit of a product that he is not himself able to test.

The manufacturer's liability should, of course, be defined in terms of the safety of the product in normal and proper use, and should not extend to injuries that cannot be traced to the product as it reached the market.

NOTES

1. *Multiple rationales.* The concurring opinion of Traynor, J., in the *Escola* case is the most famous judicial exposition of the arguments favoring strict liability for defective products. How many distinct rationales can you identify in his opinion? Which seem strongest today?

Greenman v. Yuba Power Products, Inc.
377 P.2d 897 (Cal. 1963)

TRAYNOR, J. Plaintiff brought this action for damages against the retailer and the manufacturer of a Shopsmith, a combination power tool that could be used as a saw, drill, and wood lathe. He saw a Shopsmith demonstrated by the retailer and studied a brochure prepared by the manufacturer. He decided he wanted a Shopsmith for his home workshop, and his wife bought and gave him one for Christmas in 1955. In 1957 he bought the necessary attachments to use the Shopsmith as a lathe for turning a large piece of wood he wished to make into a chalice. After he had worked on the piece of wood several times without difficulty, it suddenly flew out of the machine and struck him on the forehead, inflicting serious injuries. About ten and a half months later, he gave the retailer and the manufacturer written notice of claimed breaches of warranties and filed a complaint against them alleging such breaches and negligence.

After a trial before a jury, the court ruled that there was no evidence that the retailer was negligent or had breached any express warranty and that the manufacturer was not liable for the breach of any implied warranty. Accordingly, it submitted to the jury only the cause of action alleging breach of implied warranties against the retailer and the causes of action alleging negligence and breach of express warranties against the manufacturer. The jury returned a verdict for the retailer against plaintiff and for plaintiff against the manufacturer in the amount of $65,000. The trial court denied the manufacturer's motion for a new trial and entered judgment on the verdict. The manufacturer and plaintiff appeal. Plaintiff seeks a reversal of the part of the judgment in favor of the retailer, however, only in the event that the part of the judgment against the manufacturer is reversed.

Plaintiff introduced substantial evidence that his injuries were caused by defective design and construction of the Shopsmith. His expert witnesses testified that inadequate set screws were used to hold parts of the machine together so that normal vibration caused the tailstock of the lathe to move away from the piece of wood being turned permitting it to fly out of the lathe. They also testified that there were other more positive ways of fastening the parts of the machine together, the use of which would have prevented the accident. The jury could therefore reasonably have concluded that the manufacturer negligently constructed the Shopsmith. The jury could also reasonably have concluded that statements in the manufacturer's brochure were untrue, that they constituted express warranties,* and that plaintiff's injuries were caused by their breach.

The manufacturer contends, however, that plaintiff did not give it notice of breach of warranty within a reasonable time and that therefore his cause of action for breach of warranty is barred by section 1769 of the Civil Code. Since it cannot be determined whether the verdict against it was based on the negligence or warranty cause of action or both, the manufacturer concludes that the error in presenting the warranty cause of action to the jury was prejudicial.

Section 1769 of the Civil Code provides: "In the absence of express or implied agreement of the parties, acceptance of the goods by the buyer shall not discharge the seller from liability in damages or other legal remedy for breach of any promise or warranty in the contract to sell or the sale. But, if, after acceptance of the goods, the buyer fails to give notice to the seller of the breach of any promise or warranty within a reasonable time after the buyer knows, or ought to know of such breach, the seller shall not be liable therefor."

The notice requirement of section 1769, however, is not an appropriate one for the court to adopt in actions by injured consumers against manufacturers

---

*In this respect the trial court limited the jury to a consideration of two statements in the manufacturer's brochure (1) "WHEN SHOPSMITH IS IN HORIZONTAL POSITION Rugged construction of frame provides rigid support from end to end. Heavy centerless ground steel tubing insures perfect alignment of components." (2) "SHOPSMITH maintains its accuracy because every component has positive locks that hold adjustments through rough or precision work."

with whom they have not dealt. "As between the immediate parties to the sale (the notice requirement) is a sound commercial rule, designed to protect the seller against unduly delayed claims for damages. As applied to personal injuries, and notice to a remote seller, it becomes a booby-trap for the unwary. The injured consumer is seldom 'steeped in the business practice which justifies the rule,' (James, *Product Liability*, 34 Texas L. Rev. 44, 192, 197) and at least until he has had legal advice it will not occur to him to give notice to one with whom he has had no dealings." (Prosser, *Strict Liability to the Consumer*, 69 Yale L.J. 1099, 1130.) [. . .] We conclude, therefore, that even if plaintiff did not give timely notice of breach of warranty to the manufacturer, his cause of action based on the representations contained in the brochure was not barred.

Moreover, to impose strict liability on the manufacturer under the circumstances of this case, it was not necessary for plaintiff to establish an express warranty as defined in section 1732 of the Civil Code. A manufacturer is strictly liable in tort when an article he places on the market, knowing that it is to be used without inspection for defects, proves to have a defect that causes injury to a human being. Recognized first in the case of unwholesome food products, such liability has now been extended to a variety of other products that create as great or greater hazards if defective. Although in these cases strict liability has usually been based on the theory of an express or implied warranty running from the manufacturer to the plaintiff, the abandonment of the requirement of a contract between them, the recognition that the liability is not assumed by agreement but imposed by law, and the refusal to permit the manufacturer to define the scope of its own responsibility for defective products make clear that the liability is not one governed by the law of contract warranties but by the law of strict liability in tort. Accordingly, rules defining and governing warranties that were developed to meet the needs of commercial transactions cannot properly be invoked to govern the manufacturer's liability to those injured by their defective products unless those rules also serve the purposes for which such liability is imposed.

We need not recanvass the reasons for imposing strict liability on the manufacturer. They have been fully articulated in [prior cases]. The purpose of such liability is to insure that the costs of injuries resulting from defective products are borne by the manufacturers that put such products on the market rather than by the injured persons who are powerless to protect themselves. Sales warranties serve this purpose fitfully at best. In the present case, for example, plaintiff was able to plead and prove an express warranty only because he read and relied on the representations of the Shopsmith's ruggedness contained in the manufacturer's brochure. Implicit in the machine's presence on the market, however, was a representation that it would safely do the jobs for which it was built. Under these circumstances, it should not be controlling whether plaintiff selected the machine because of the statements in the brochure, or because of the machine's own appearance of excellence that belied the defect lurking beneath the surface, or because he merely assumed that it would safely do the jobs it was built to do. It should not be controlling whether the details of the sales from manufacturer to retailer and from retailer to plaintiff's wife were such that one or more of the implied warranties of the sales act arose. (Civ. Code, §1735.) "The remedies of injured consumers ought not to be made to depend upon the intricacies of the law of sales." (*Ketterer v. Armour & Co.*, 200 F. 322, 323.) To establish the manufacturer's liability it was sufficient that plaintiff proved that he was injured while using the Shopsmith in a way it was intended to be used as a result of a defect in design and manufacture of which plaintiff was not aware that made the Shopsmith unsafe for its intended use.

The judgment is affirmed.

NOTES

1. *Liability on the warranty vs. liability in tort.* The movement toward expanded products liability found outlets in both the law of torts and the law of warranty. Some jurisdictions reached results resembling strict liability through broad readings of the implied warranty thought to accompany a product when it was put into the stream of commerce; see, e.g., *Henningsen v. Bloomfield Motors, Inc.*, 161 A.2d 69 (N.J. 1960). The *Greenman* case is a milestone in the modern development of products liability law in part because it established strict liability in tort, rather than breach of warranty, as the primary theory of recovery for defective products. This pattern has been followed in most jurisdictions, though in some states counts for breach of implied warranty still sometimes are alleged along with tort theories of recovery, and from time to time may lead to recovery where the tort theory does not.

2. *The Restatements.* Two years after *Greenman* was decided, the American Law Institute's Restatement (Second) of Torts offered this formulation of the law of products liability:

§402a. SPECIAL LIABILITY OF SELLER OF PRODUCT FOR PHYSICAL HARM TO USER OR CONSUMER

(1) One who sells any product in a defective condition unreasonably dangerous to the user or consumer or to his property is subject to liability for physical harm thereby caused to the ultimate user or consumer, or to his property, if

(a) the seller is engaged in the business of selling such a product, and

(b) it is expected to and does reach the user or consumer without substantial change in the condition in which it is sold.

(2) The rule stated in Subsection (1) applies although

(a) the seller has exercised all possible care in the preparation and sale of his product, and

(b) the user or consumer has not bought the product from or entered into any contractual relation with the seller.

Section 402A proved enormously influential; it has been the most heavily cited provision of the Second Restatement and was the foundation upon which many state courts developed their law of products liability. We will examine additional provisions of the section later in this chapter.

The case law on products liability continued to grow over the next 30 years, and in 1997 the American Law Institute's Restatement (Third) of Torts offered this reformulation:

§1. LIABILITY OF COMMERCIAL SELLER OR DISTRIBUTOR FOR HARM CAUSED BY DEFECTIVE PRODUCTS

One engaged in the business of selling or otherwise distributing products who sells or distributes a defective product is subject to liability for harm to persons or property caused by the defect.

§2. CATEGORIES OF PRODUCT DEFECT

A product is defective when, at the time of sale or distribution, it contains a manufacturing defect, is defective in design, or is defective because of inadequate instructions or warnings. A product:

(a) contains a manufacturing defect when the product departs from its intended design even though all possible care was exercised in the preparation and marketing of the product;

(b) is defective in design when the foreseeable risks of harm posed by the product could have been reduced or avoided by the adoption of a reasonable alternative design by the seller or other distributor, or a predecessor in the commercial chain of distribution, and the omission of the alternative design renders the product not reasonably safe;

(c) is defective because of inadequate instructions or warnings when the foreseeable risks of harm posed by the product could have been reduced or avoided by the provision of reasonable instructions or warnings by the seller or other distributor, or a predecessor in the commercial chain of distribution, and the omission of the instructions or warnings renders the product not reasonably safe.

Comment a. History. [. . .] The liability established in this Section draws on both warranty law and tort law. Historically, the focus of products liability law was on manufacturing defects. A manufacturing defect is a physical departure from a product's intended design. See §2(a). Typically, manufacturing defects occur in only a small percentage of units in a product line. Courts early began imposing liability without fault on product sellers for harm caused by such defects, holding a seller liable for harm caused by manufacturing defects even though all possible care had been exercised by the seller in the preparation and distribution of the product. In doing so, courts relied on the concept of warranty, in connection with which fault has never been a prerequisite to liability.

The imposition of liability for manufacturing defects has a long history in the common law. As early as 1266, criminal statutes imposed liability upon victualers, vintners, brewers, butchers, cooks, and other persons who supplied contaminated food and drink. In the late 1800s, courts in many states began imposing negligence and strict warranty liability on commercial sellers of defective goods. In the early 1960s, American courts began to recognize that a commercial seller of any product having a manufacturing defect should be liable in tort for harm caused by the defect regardless of the plaintiff's ability to maintain a traditional negligence or warranty action. Liability attached even if the manufacturer's quality control in producing the defective product was reasonable. A plaintiff was not required to be in direct privity with the defendant seller to bring an action. Strict liability in tort for defectively manufactured products merges the concept of implied warranty, in which negligence is not required, with the tort concept of negligence, in which contractual privity is not required. See §2(a). [. . .]

Comment c. One engaged in the business of selling or otherwise distributing. The rule stated in this Section applies only to manufacturers and other commercial sellers and distributors who are engaged in the business of selling or otherwise distributing the type of product that harmed the plaintiff. The rule does not apply to a noncommercial seller or distributor of such products. Thus, it does not apply to one who sells foodstuffs to a neighbor, nor does it apply to the private owner of an automobile who sells it to another. It is not necessary that a commercial seller or distributor be engaged exclusively or even primarily in selling or otherwise distributing the type of product that injured the plaintiff, so long as the sale of the product is other than occasional, or casual. Thus, the rule applies to a motion picture theater's routine sales of popcorn or ice cream, either for consumption on the premises or in packages to be taken home. Similarly, a service station that does mechanical repair work on cars may also sell tires and automobile equipment as part of its regular business. Such sales are subject to the rule in this Section. However, the rule does not cover occasional sales (frequently referred to as "casual sales") outside the regular course of the seller's business. [. . .]

Comment e. Nonmanufacturing sellers or other distributors of products. The rule stated in this Section provides that all commercial sellers and distributors of products, including nonmanufacturing sellers and distributors such as wholesalers and retailers, are subject to liability for selling products that are defective. Liability attaches even when such nonmanufacturing sellers or distributors do not themselves render the products defective and regardless of whether they are in a position to prevent defects from occurring. Legislation has been enacted in many jurisdictions that, to some extent, immunizes nonmanufacturing sellers or distributors from strict liability. The legislation is premised on the belief that bringing nonmanufacturing sellers or distributors into products liability litigation generates wasteful legal costs. Although liability in most cases is ultimately passed on to the manufacturer who is responsible for creating the product defect, nonmanufacturing sellers or distributors must devote resources to protect their interests. In most situations, therefore, immunizing nonmanufacturers saves those resources without jeopardizing the plaintiff's interests. To assure plaintiffs access to a responsible and solvent product seller or distributor, the statutes generally provide that the non-manufacturing seller or distributor is immunized from strict liability only if: (1) the manufacturer is subject to the jurisdiction of the court of plaintiff's domicile; (2) the manufacturer is not, nor is likely to become, insolvent; and (3) a court determines that it is highly probable that the plaintiff will be able to enforce a judgment against the manufacturer.

B. MANUFACTURING DEFECTS

We turn now to the details of the law currently governing products liability. As explained in the Restatement excerpts above, the subject conveniently can be divided into three general areas: liability for manufacturing defects, liability for design defects, and liability for failure to warn. We begin with manufacturing defects.

Restatement (Third) of Torts: Products Liability (1997)

§2, *comment a. Rationale* [. . .] The rule for manufacturing defects stated in Subsection (a) imposes liability whether or not the manufacturer's quality control efforts satisfy standards of reasonableness. Strict liability without fault in this context is generally believed to foster several objectives. On the premise that tort law serves the instrumental function of creating safety incentives, imposing strict liability on manufacturers for harm caused by manufacturing defects encourages greater investment in product safety than does a regime of fault-based liability under which, as a practical matter, sellers may escape their appropriate share of responsibility. Some courts and commentators also have said that strict liability discourages the consumption of defective products by causing the purchase price of products to reflect, more than would a rule of negligence, the costs of defects. And by eliminating the issue of manufacturer fault from plaintiff's case, strict liability reduces the transaction costs involved in litigating that issue.

Several important fairness concerns are also believed to support manufacturers' liability for manufacturing defects even if the plaintiff is unable to show that the manufacturer's quality control fails to meet risk-utility norms. In many cases manufacturing defects are in fact caused by manufacturer negligence but plaintiffs have difficulty proving it. Strict liability therefore performs a function similar to the concept of res ipsa loquitur, allowing deserving plaintiffs to succeed notwithstanding what would otherwise be difficult or insuperable problems of proof. Products that malfunction due to manufacturing defects disappoint reasonable expectations of product performance. Because manufacturers invest in quality control at consciously chosen levels, their knowledge that a predictable number of flawed products will enter the marketplace entails an element of deliberation about the amount of injury that will result from their activity. Finally, many believe that consumers who benefit from products without suffering harm should share, through increases in the prices charged for those products, the burden of unavoidable injury costs that result from manufacturing defects.

An often-cited rationale for holding wholesalers and retailers strictly liable for harm caused by manufacturing defects is that, as between them and innocent victims who suffer harm because of defective products, the product sellers as business entities are in a better position than are individual users and consumers to insure against such losses. In most instances, wholesalers and retailers will be able to pass liability costs up the chain of product distribution to the manufacturer. When joining the manufacturer in the tort action presents the plaintiff with procedural difficulties, local retailers can pay damages to the victims and then seek indemnity from manufacturers. Finally, holding retailers and wholesalers strictly liable creates incentives for them to deal only with reputable, financially responsible manufacturers and distributors, thereby helping to protect the interests of users and consumers. [. . .]

why liability down the chain

Welge v. Planters Lifesavers Co.
17 F.3d 209 (7th Cir. 1994)

POSNER, *Chief Judge.* Richard Welge, forty-something but young in spirit, loves to sprinkle peanuts on his ice cream sundaes. On January 18, 1991, Karen Godfrey, with whom Welge boards, bought a 24 ounce vacuum sealed plastic capped jar of Planters peanuts for him at a K-Mart store in Chicago. To obtain a $2 rebate that the maker of Alka-Seltzer was offering to anyone who bought a "party" item, such as peanuts, Godfrey needed proof of her purchase of the jar of peanuts; so, using an Exacto knife (basically a razor blade with a handle), she removed the part of the label that contained the bar code. She then placed the jar on top of the refrigerator, where Welge could get at it without rooting about in her cupboards. About a week later, Welge removed the plastic seal from the jar, uncapped it, took some peanuts, replaced the cap, and returned the jar to the top of the refrigerator, all without incident. A week after that, on February 3, the accident occurred. Welge took down the jar, removed the plastic cap, spilled some peanuts into his left hand to put on his sundae, and replaced the cap with his right hand — but as he pushed the cap down

Pushing down on plastic cap of jar of Planter's Peanuts, caused it to shatter. The landlady had purch. peanuts + exactoed label off for proof of purchase.

on the open jar the jar shattered. His hand, continuing in its downward motion, was severely cut, and is now, he claims, permanently impaired.

Welge brought this products liability suit in federal district court under the diversity jurisdiction; Illinois law governs the substantive issues. Welge named three defendants (plus the corporate parent of one — why we don't know). They are K-Mart, which sold the jar of peanuts to Karen Godfrey; Planters, which manufactured the product — that is to say, filled the glass jar with peanuts and sealed and capped it; and Brockway, which manufactured the glass jar itself and sold it to Planters. After pretrial discovery was complete the defendants moved for summary judgment. The district judge granted the motion on the ground that the plaintiff had failed to exclude possible causes of the accident other than a defect introduced during the manufacturing process.

No doubt there are men strong enough to shatter a thick glass jar with one blow. But Welge's testimony stands uncontradicted that he used no more than the normal force that one exerts in snapping a plastic lid onto a jar. So the jar must have been defective. No expert testimony and no fancy doctrine are required for such a conclusion. A nondefective jar does not shatter when normal force is used to clamp its plastic lid on. The question is when the defect was introduced. It could have been at any time from the manufacture of the glass jar by Brockway (for no one suggests that the defect might have been caused by something in the raw materials out of which the jar was made) to moments before the accident. But testimony by Welge and Karen Godfrey, if believed — and at this stage in the proceedings we are required to believe it — excludes all reasonable possibility that the defect was introduced into the jar after Godfrey plucked it from a shelf in the K-Mart store. From the shelf she put it in her shopping cart. The checker at the check out counter scanned the bar code without banging the jar. She then placed the jar in a plastic bag. Godfrey carried the bag to her car and put it on the floor. She drove directly home, without incident. After the bar code portion of the label was removed, the jar sat on top of the refrigerator except for the two times Welge removed it to take peanuts out of it. Throughout this process it was not, so far as anyone knows, jostled, dropped, bumped, or otherwise subjected to stress beyond what is to be expected in the ordinary use of the product. Chicago is not Los Angeles; there were no earthquakes. Chicago is not Amityville either; no supernatural interventions are alleged. So the defect must have been introduced earlier, when the jar was in the hands of the defendants.

But, they argue, this overlooks two things. One is that Karen Godfrey took a knife to the jar. And no doubt one can weaken a glass jar with a knife. But nothing is more common or, we should have thought, more harmless than to use a knife or a razor blade to remove a label from a jar or bottle. People do this all the time with the price labels on bottles of wine. Even though mishandling or misuse, by the consumer or by anyone else (other than the defendant itself), is a defense, though a limited and (subject to a qualification noted later) partial defense, to a products liability suit in Illinois as elsewhere, and even if, as we greatly doubt, such normal mutilation as occurred in this case could be thought a species of mishandling or misuse, a defendant cannot defend against a products liability suit on the basis of a misuse that he invited. The Alka-Seltzer promotion to which Karen Godfrey was responding when she removed a portion of the label of the jar of Planters peanuts was in the K-Mart store. It was there, obviously, with K-Mart's permission. By the promotion K-Mart invited its peanut customers to remove a part of the label on each peanut jar bought, in order to be able to furnish the maker of Alka-Seltzer with proof of purchase. If one just wants to efface a label one can usually do that by scraping it off with a fingernail, but to remove the label intact requires the use of a knife or a razor blade. Invited misuse is no defense to a products liability claim. Invited misuse is not misuse.

The invitation, it is true, was issued by K-Mart, not by the other defendants; and we do not know their involvement, if any, in the promotion. As to them, the defense of misuse must fail, at this stage of the proceedings, for two other reasons. The evidence does not establish with the certitude required for summary judgment that the use of an Exacto knife to remove a label from a jar is a misuse of the jar. And in a regime of comparative negligence misuse is not a defense to liability but merely reduces the plaintiff's damages, unless the misuse is the sole cause of the accident.

Even so, the defendants point out, it is always possible that the jar was damaged while it was sitting unattended on the top of the refrigerator, in which event they are not responsible. Only if it had been securely under lock and key when not being used could the plaintiff and Karen Godfrey be certain that nothing happened to damage it after she brought it home. That is true — there are no metaphysical certainties — but it leads nowhere. Elves may have played ninepins with the jar of peanuts while Welge and Godfrey were sleeping; but elves could remove a jar of peanuts from a locked cupboard. The plaintiff in a products liability suit is not required to exclude every possibility, however fantastic or remote, that the defect which led to the accident was caused by someone other than one of the defendants. The doctrine of res ipsa loquitur teaches that an accident that is unlikely to occur unless the defendant was negligent is itself circumstantial evidence that the defendant was negligent. The doctrine is not strictly applicable to a products liability case because unlike an ordinary accident case the defendant in a products case has parted with possession and control of the harmful object before the accident occurs. But the doctrine merely instantiates the broader principle, which is as applicable to a products case as to any other tort case, that an accident can itself be evidence of liability. If it is the kind of accident that would not have occurred but for a defect in the product, and if it is reasonably plain that the defect was not introduced after the product was sold, the accident is evidence that the product was defective when sold. The second condition (as well as the first) has been established here, at least to a probability sufficient to defeat a motion for summary judgment. Normal people do not lock up their jars and cans lest something happen to damage these containers while no one is looking. The probability of such damage is too remote. It is not only too remote to make a rational person take measures to prevent it; it is too remote to defeat a products liability suit should a container prove dangerously defective.

Of course, unlikely as it may seem that the defect was introduced into the jar after Karen Godfrey bought it if the plaintiffs' testimony is believed, other evidence might make their testimony unworthy of belief — might even show, contrary to all the probabilities, that the knife or some mysterious night visitor caused the defect after all. The fragments of glass into which the jar shattered were preserved and were examined by experts for both sides. The experts agreed that the jar must have contained a defect but they could not find the fracture that had precipitated the shattering of the jar and they could not figure out when the defect that caused the fracture that caused the collapse of the jar had come into being. The defendants' experts could neither rule out, nor rule in, the possibility that the defect had been introduced at some stage of the manufacturing process. The plaintiff's expert noticed what he thought was a preexisting crack in one of the fragments, and he speculated that a similar crack might have caused the fracture that shattered the jar. This, the district judge ruled, was not enough.

But if the probability that the defect which caused the accident arose after Karen Godfrey bought the jar of Planters peanuts is very small — and on the present state of the record we are required to assume that it is — then the probability that the defect was introduced by one of the defendants is very high. In principle there is a third possibility — mishandling by a carrier hired to transport the jar from Brockway to Planters or Planters to K-Mart — but we do not even know whether a carrier was used for any of these shipments, rather than the shipper's own trucks. Apart from that possibility, which has not been mentioned in the litigation so far and which in any event, as we are about to see, would not affect K-Mart's liability, the jar was in the control of one of the defendants at all times until Karen Godfrey bought it.

Which one? It does not matter. The strict-liability element in modern products liability law comes precisely from the fact that a seller subject to that law is liable for defects in his product even if those defects were introduced, without the slightest fault of his own for failing to discover them, at some anterior stage of production. So the fact that K-Mart sold a defective jar of peanuts to Karen Godfrey would be conclusive of K-Mart's liability, and since it is a large and solvent firm there would be no need for the plaintiff to look further for a tortfeasor. This point seems to have been more or less conceded by the defendants in the district court — the thrust of their defense was that the plaintiff had failed to show that the defect had been caused by any of them — though this leaves us mystified as to why the plaintiff bothered to name additional defendants.

And even if, as we doubt, the plaintiff took on the unnecessary burden of proving that it is more likely than not that a given defendant introduced the defect into the jar, he might be able to avail himself of the rule of *Ybarra v. Spangard*, 154 P.2d 687 (Cal. 1944), and force each defendant to produce some exculpatory evidence. In fact K-Mart put in some evidence on the precautions it takes to protect containers of food from being damaged by jarring or bumping. A jury convinced by such evidence, impressed by the sturdiness of jars of peanuts (familiar to every consumer), and perhaps perplexed at how the process of filling a jar with peanuts and vacuum-sealing it could render a normal jar vulnerable to collapsing at a touch, might decide that the probability that the defect had been introduced by either K-Mart or Planters was remote. So what? Evidence of K-Mart's care in handling peanut jars would be relevant only to whether the defect was introduced after sale; if it was introduced at any time before sale — if the jar was defective when K-Mart sold it — the source of the defect would be irrelevant to K-Mart's liability. In exactly the same way, Planters' liability would be unaffected by the fact, if it is a fact, that the defect was due to Brockway rather than to itself. To repeat an earlier and fundamental point, a seller who is subject to strict products liability is responsible for the consequences of selling a defective product even if the defect was introduced without any fault on his part by his supplier or by his supplier's supplier. [. . .]

Reversed and remanded.

[handwritten margin notes, left side: "an Ybarra comparison maybe ? cd shift burden to ∆s"; "jury probably will think Brockway did it doesn't matter"; "There's /KMART on hook no matter what & so would Planters, which put peanuts in jar & moved it along)"]

[handwritten under text: "→ doesn't matter if Brockway @ fault"]

NOTES

1. *Recurring themes*. As the opinion in *Welge* suggests, the greatest difficulties in litigating a manufacturing defect case typically are problems of proof: why did the jar break? If it was defective, when was the defect introduced? Claimed manufacturing defects also can raise a number of interesting and more general legal issues, however, such as what counts as a "product" or "seller" — questions that are the focus of the cases that follow.

2. *Defective books.* In Winter v. G.P. Putnam & Sons, 938 F.2d 1033 (9th Cir. 1991), the defendant was the publisher of *The Encyclopedia of Mushrooms*. The two plaintiffs were mushroom enthusiasts who used the defendant's book as a field guide, relying on its descriptions of which wild mushrooms were safe to eat. They cooked and ate their harvest and soon became quite ill; both ultimately required liver transplants. They sued the defendant, alleging that the Encyclopedia contained incorrect information about how to identify several deadly species of mushrooms. One of the counts of their complaint alleged that the defendant should be held strictly liable for selling a defective product — viz., the book. The trial court gave summary judgment to the defendant, and the court of appeals affirmed:

> The language of products liability law reflects its focus on tangible items. In describing the scope of products liability law, the Restatement (Second) of Torts lists examples of items that are covered. All of these

are tangible items, such as tires, automobiles, and insecticides. The American Law Institute clearly was concerned with including all physical items but gave no indication that the doctrine should be expanded beyond that area.

The purposes served by products liability law also are focused on the tangible world and do not take into consideration the unique characteristics of ideas and expression. Under products liability law, strict liability is imposed on the theory that "[t]he costs of damaging events due to defectively dangerous products can best be borne by the enterprisers who make and sell these products." *Prosser & Keeton on The Law of Torts*, §98. Strict liability principles have been adopted to further the "cause of accident prevention . . . [by] the elimination of the necessity of proving negligence." Id. at 693. Additionally, because of the difficulty of establishing fault or negligence in products liability cases, strict liability is the appropriate legal theory to hold manufacturers liable for defective products. Id. Thus, the seller is subject to liability "even though he has exercised all possible care in the preparation and sale of the product." Restatement §402A comment a. It is not a question of fault but simply a determination of how society wishes to assess certain costs that arise from the creation and distribution of products in a complex technological society in which the consumer thereof is unable to protect himself against certain product defects.

Although there is always some appeal to the involuntary spreading of costs of injuries in any area, the costs in any comprehensive cost/benefit analysis would be quite different were strict liability concepts applied to words and ideas. We place a high priority on the unfettered exchange of ideas. We accept the risk that words and ideas have wings we cannot clip and which carry them we know not where. The threat of liability without fault (financial responsibility for our words and ideas in the absence of fault or a special undertaking or responsibility) could seriously inhibit those who wish to share thoughts and theories. As a New York court commented, with the specter of strict liability, "[w]ould any author wish to be exposed . . . for writing on a topic which might result in physical injury? e.g. How to cut trees; How to keep bees?" *Walter v. Bauer*, 439 N.Y.S.2d 821, 823 (Sup. Ct. 1981).

3. *Maps and legends.* In Saloomey v. Jeppesen, 707 F.2d 671 (2d Cir. 1983), the plaintiff's decedent, Willard Wahlund, was a pilot for Braniff Airlines; he also owned his own airplane, a Beechcraft Sierra. The plaintiff's evidence was that Wahlund was flying the Beechcraft from Charleston, West Virginia, to Danbury, Connecticut, using a set of navigational charts produced by the defendant, Jeppesen, that Braniff had purchased for all of its pilots. Soon after takeoff and for reasons unknown, Wahlund decided to land the plane at the airport in Martinsburg, West Virginia. The legend on Wahlund's navigational chart indicated that the Martinsburg airport was

equipped with a "full instrument landing system." The airport was not so equipped, however: it lacked a "glidescope" radio beam that would have informed Wahlund of the proper altitude to maintain for an instrument-guided landing. Wahlund proceeded toward the Martinsburg airport, communicating his intention to use its instrument landing system to air traffic controllers at Dulles International Airport near Washington. Evidently the controllers there did not detect Wahlund's misunderstanding until later. Wahlund's aircraft was traveling at a normal descent angle in line with the Martinsburg runway, apparently attempting to rely on guidance from the airport that was not being sent, when it flew into a ridge. The plane was destroyed, and Wahlund and his passengers were killed.

Wahlund's estate brought suit against Jeppesen, among others. Included among its theories of relief was a claim that Jeppesen should be held strictly liable for selling a defective product. A jury accepted this theory, as well as others that the plaintiff advanced, and brought in a verdict against Jeppesen for $1.5 million. Jeppesen moved for judgment as a matter of law on the ground that its charts were not "products" for purposes of tort law. The trial court denied the motion:

> Whether a transaction involving the sale of a map constitutes the rendition of a professional service or the sale of a tangible product poses a difficult question of semantics since there is an element of service in all "goods" whether maps or consumer durables. All require some skilled service in initial design as well as in the transformation of raw materials into finished product. [...]
>
> Given that Jeppesen mass produced and distributed its charts, its activity comes within the scope of the rationale of §402A and should not be insulated from a strict standard of liability by virtue of metaphysical and semantic quibbling.

The court of appeals affirmed:

> By publishing and selling the charts, Jeppesen undertook a special responsibility, as seller, to insure that consumers will not be injured by the use of the charts; Jeppesen is entitled — and encouraged — to treat the burden of accidental injury as a cost of production to be covered by liability insurance. [...]

What is the distinction between *Saloomey v. Jeppesen* and *Winter v. G.P. Putnam & Sons* (the NL case of the defective field guide to mushrooms)? Which element of the standard products liability case is in dispute in the two cases? What are the implications of holding Jeppesen strictly liable for defects in its maps? Suppose that in drawing its map, Jeppesen had relied on information supplied by the Martinsburg airport about its capabilities. Would Jeppesen still be liable? Or suppose that Wahlund chose to land at

Martinsburg because of the misinformation on Jeppesen's map, but flew into the ridge because his rudder failed. Would Jeppesen be liable in that case? Notice that *Jeppesen* and *Winter* might be styled as involving alleged defects in either manufacturing or design; the question of what counts as a "product" to which strict liability attaches cuts across both of those categories.

4. *This won't hurt a bit.* In Magrine v. Krasnica, 227 A.2d 539 (N.J. 1967), the plaintiff was injured when her dentist tried to use a hypodermic needle to inject a local anesthetic behind her rear tooth. The needle broke off in the plaintiff's gum. She sued the dentist to recover for her resulting injuries. The parties stipulated that the needle broke as a result of a latent defect it contained and that the dentist had committed no acts of negligence; the plaintiff's theories of liability sounded in strict products liability, breach of warranty, and breach of contract. The trial court gave judgment as a matter of law to the dentist:

> [I]n all of our recent cases strict liability was imposed (except with respect to a retail dealer) upon those who were in "a better position" in the sense that they created the danger (in making the article) or possessed a better capacity or expertise to control, inspect and discover the defect than the party injured. In these respects the dentist here was in no better position than plaintiff. He neither created the defect nor possessed any better capacity or expertise to discover or correct it than she. [. . .]
>
> Plaintiff also invokes the policy consideration of "spreading of the risks" — the concept which suggests that defendant could cover his liability by insurance, or he could be held harmless by impleading his supplier or manufacturer. The "risk distributing theory" is a relevant consideration. But again, we must appreciate the context in which it has been applied in our cases. In [prior cases] it was considered in holding liable the manfacturer or lessor, who put the goods in the stream of commerce. Such a party may fairly be assumed to have substantial assets and volume of business, and a large area of contacts over which the risk can be widely spread. It is the "large scale" enterprise which should bear the loss. The impact of liability upon such a defendant is miniscule in comparison with that of an individual dentist or physician. His means of "spreading the risk" could be by insurance or impleading his supplier or manufacturer. "Malpractice" insurance, however, does not cover implied warranty unless the policy "expressly covers contract claims."
>
> So, here, if the dentist or physician were to obtain insurance covering strict liability for equipment failure, the risk would be spread upon his patients by way of increased fees. Can anyone gainsay the fact that medical and dental costs, and insurance therefor, are already bearing hard there? Witness the constant cry over increasing medical surgical insurance premiums in New Jersey. As a matter of principle, the

spreading of losses to their patients subverts, rather than supports, the policy consideration that the loss should be imposed on those best able to withstand it, i.e., the manufacturer or other entity which puts the article into the stream of commerce. The "risk distribution" theory has some weight, but not nearly enough when laid beside other more basic considerations. [. . .]

We must consider, also, the consequences if we were to adopt the rule of strict liability here. The same liability, in principle, should then apply to any user of a tool, other equipment or any article which, through no fault of the user, breaks due to a latent defect and injures another. It would apply to any physician, artisan or mechanic and to any user of a defective article — even to a driver of a defective automobile. In our view, no policy consideration positing strict liability justifies application of the doctrine in such cases. No more should it here.

The court of appeals affirmed, concluding that "the imposition of liability on the defendant dentist cannot be justified on the basis of any of the accepted policies which underlie the doctrine of strict liability as it is presently understood." Botter, J., dissented:

As between an innocent patient and a dentist who causes injury by using a defective instrument the law should require the loss to be borne by the dentist, even if he is not negligent. [. . .] The dentist chose the instrument. The dentist is in a better position to know and prove the identity of the manufacturer or distributor. If he cannot, the patient should not be denied recovery on that account. The dentist should also know the quality of the instrument and the reliability of his source of supply. This rule may encourage greater caution in purchasing equipment and examining for defects.

Shifting the loss from A to B may not produce a net gain for society as a whole, but distribution of the loss does. Liability insurance is recognized as a means of distributing losses among the group involved in risk-producing activity. [. . .] It is pointless to say that those who purchase goods should not be compelled to pay an item of cost for insurance to protect others. The protection is for the whole group. No one knows which consumer will be injured. The cost paid by each consumer assures his own satisfaction of a judgment if he gets one. The fact is that through the cost of goods and services consumers today do pay indirectly for insurance covering losses caused by the negligent activities of their suppliers. If this is just, granting consumer protection against defective products cannot be unjust.

5. *Exact and inexact sciences.* In Newmark v. Gimbel's Inc., 258 A.2d 697 (N.J. 1969), the plaintiff was a customer at the defendant's hair-styling salon. She requested a "permanent wave." The defendant's employee applied a

solution called "Helene Curtis Candle Wave" to the plaintiff's hair. The plaintiff soon began to complain of a burning sensation. That evening her forehead began to turn red and large amounts of her hair fell out. Several days later a dermatologist diagnosed the plaintiff with dermatitis of the scalp caused by the permanent wave solution. The plaintiff brought suit alleging negligence and also claiming that the permanent wave solution was defective and that the defendant was strictly liable for breach of implied warranty. The jury found no negligence, and the trial court dismissed the strict liability claim on the ground that the defendant's salon had been providing a service rather than a product to the plaintiff. The New Jersey Supreme Court reversed and remanded for a new trial:

> Having in mind the nature of a permanent wave operation, we find that the distinction between a sale and the rendition of services is a highly artificial one. If the permanent wave lotion were sold to Mrs. Newmark by defendants for home consumption or application or to enable her to give herself the permanent wave, unquestionably an implied warranty of fitness for that purpose would have been an integral incident of the sale. Basically defendants argue that if, in addition to recommending the use of a lotion or other product and supplying it for use, they applied it, such fact (the application) would have the effect of lessening their liability to the patron by eliminating warranty and by limiting their responsibility to the issue of negligence. There is no just reason why it should. On the contrary by taking on the administration of the product in addition to recommending and supplying it, they might increase the scope of their liability, if the method of administration were improper (a result not suggested on this appeal because the jury found no negligence). [...]
>
> [W]e agree with the Appellate Division that an implied warranty of fitness of the products used in giving the permanent wave exists with no less force than it would have in the case of a simple sale. Obviously in permanent wave operations the product is taken into consideration in fixing the price of the service. The no-separate-charge argument puts excessive emphasis on form and downgrades the overall substance of the transaction. If the beauty parlor operator bought and applied the permanent wave solution to her own hair and suffered injury thereby, her action in warranty or strict liability in tort against the manufacturer-seller of the product clearly would be maintainable because the basic transaction would have arisen from a conventional type of sale. It does not accord with logic to deny a similar right to a patron against the beauty parlor operator or the manufacturer when the purchase and sale were made in anticipation of and for the purpose of use of the product on the patron who would be charged for its use. Common sense demands that such patron be deemed a consumer as to both manufacturer and beauty parlor operator.

The court distinguished this case from that of the dentist in *Magrine v. Krasnica*:

> The beautician is engaged in a commercial enterprise; the dentist and doctor in a profession. The former caters publicly not to a need but to a form of aesthetic convenience or luxury, involving the rendition of nonprofessional services and the application of products for which a charge is made. The dentist or doctor does not and cannot advertise for patients; the demand for his services stems from a felt necessity of the patient. In response to such a call the doctor, and to a somewhat lesser degree the dentist, exercises his best judgment in diagnosing the patient's ailment or disability, prescribing and sometimes furnishing medicines or other methods of treatment which he believes, and in some measure hopes, will relieve or cure the condition. His performance is not mechanical or routine because each patient requires individual study and formulation of an informed judgment as to the physical or mental disability or condition presented, and the course of treatment needed. Neither medicine nor dentistry is an exact science; there is no implied warranty of cure or relief. There is no representation of infallibility and such professional men should not be held to such a degree of perfection. Practitioners of such callings, licensed by the State to practice after years of study and preparation, must be deemed to have a special and essential role in our society, that of studying our physical and mental ills and ways to alleviate or cure them, and that of applying their knowledge, empirical judgment and skill in an effort to diagnose and then to relieve or to cure the ailment of a particular patient. Thus their paramount function — the essence of their function — ought to be regarded as the furnishing of opinions and services. Their unique status and the rendition of these *sui generis* services bear such a necessary and intimate relationship to public health and welfare that their obligation ought to be grounded and expressed in a duty to exercise reasonable competence and care toward their patients. In our judgment, the nature of the services, the utility of and the need for them, involving as they do, the health and even survival of many people, are so important to the general welfare as to outweigh in the policy scale any need for the imposition on dentists and doctors of the rules of strict liability in tort.

What do you make of the court's proposed distinction between *Newmark v. Gimbel's Inc.* and *Magrine v. Krasnica* (the NL case where the patient sued her dentist when his needle broke off in her mouth)? Can you articulate any distinctions between the cases that are more persuasive than what the court suggests?

6. *Sellers and non-sellers.* In each of the following cases, assess whether the defendant should be considered a "seller" and thus held strictly liable for defects in the products at issue.

a. In *Keen v. Dominick's Finer Foods, Inc.*, 364 N.E.2d 502 (Ill. App. 1977), the plaintiff was pushing a shopping cart in a Dominick's grocery store when the cart inexplicably tipped over; she was hurt when she tried to stop it from overturning. She sued Dominick's on a theory of strict products liability, claiming that the cart was defective.

b. In *Peterson v. Lou Bachrodt Chevrolet Co.*, 329 N.E.2d 785 (Ill. 1975), the plaintiff's decedent was killed when she was run over by an automobile that had been purchased from the defendant's used-car dealership. The plaintiff brought suit against the dealership on theories of strict products liability, alleging that the accident resulted from various defects in the car's brakes that were present when the car left the dealer's control.

c. In *Nutting v. Ford Motor Co.*, 584 N.Y.S.2d 653 (App. Div. 1992), Hewlett-Packard, the computer maker, annually bought thousands of cars for its employees to use, then auctioned them off a couple of years later. The plaintiff bought one of the HP cars at an auction, then was injured when it stalled on the highway. She sued Hewlett-Packard on theories of strict products liability. What result? What result in a similar claim against the auctioneer?

7. *Defective enchilada.* In Mexicali Rose v. Superior Court, 822 P.2d 1292 (Cal. 1992), the plaintiff was injured when he swallowed a one-inch bone contained in a chicken enchilada he was served at the defendant's restaurant. He sued on theories of negligence, breach of implied warranty, and strict liability. The basis of the latter claim was Restatement Second of Torts §402A, comment i, which calls for strict liability when food is "dangerous beyond that which would be contemplated by the ordinary consumer who purchases it, with the ordinary knowledge common to the community as to its characteristics." The trial court dismissed the claims, relying on *Mix v. Ingersoll Candy Co.*, 59 P.2d 144 (Cal. 1936), the leading California case on liability for injuries caused by food. In that case the court had held that restaurant owners were liable for damage caused by "foreign" substances in their food such as insects or glass, but generally could not be held liable for injuries caused by substances "natural" to food, such as bones. The plaintiff in *Mexicali Rose* argued that the *Mix* rule was arbitrary and urged that it be replaced by a test asking whether a reasonable consumer would have expected to find the substance — natural or otherwise — in the food. The California Supreme Court agreed that the legal test should be revised to depend on the consumer's expectations, but in applying that test the court continued to

[handwritten marginalia:] 1" bone in enchilada — consumer expectations theory — dismissed relying on Cal preced. that supplies foreign/natural — π urges adoption reas expec test as not arbitrary like f+n — Cal Sct agrees to adopt 402A reg. expec. — BVT⇒

*cited, relied on + in det. of appeals.
or f-n in det. of appeals.
+ affid. dismissal*

adhere to the distinction between foreign and natural substances. It therefore affirmed the dismissal of the plaintiff's strict liability claim:

> If the injury-producing substance is natural to the preparation of the food served, it can be said that it was reasonably expected by its very nature and the food cannot be determined unfit or defective. A plaintiff in such a case has no cause of action in strict liability or implied warranty. If, however, the presence of the natural substance is due to a restauranteur's failure to exercise due care in food preparation, the injured patron may sue under a negligence theory.

DISSENT   Mosk, J., submitted an unappetizing dissent:

> The issue presented by this case is largely semantic: what exactly do we mean when we say an object is "foreign to" or "natural to" a dish? "Natural to" surely cannot include all natural material. Salmonella is natural and feces are natural, but their presence in food surely makes the food unfit for consumption. What about a hamburger made out of chopped rat flesh? Natural food, certainly, but my colleagues would not find such a meal fit for consumption in warranty terms. So what does the term "natural to" mean? I suspect it means that any consumer should anticipate finding the object in the meal. In other words, the object should reasonably be anticipated. When we add, as the majority opinion does, that "natural" means natural to the dish as served, this conclusion becomes inescapable.

MAJ reply in fn

The majority offered this reply in a footnote:

> Unfortunately, [the dissenters] misrepresent the scope and application of our holding. The term "natural" refers to bones and other substances natural to the product served, and does not encompass substances such as mold, botulinus bacteria or other substances (like rat flesh or cow eyes) not natural to the preparation of the product served.

8. *Harm caused by food.* As noted in the Restatement excerpts earlier in this chapter, food was the first area where courts traditionally applied the sort of strict liability now associated generally with products, usually using a theory of implied warranty. (Why might foreign substances in food be a natural candidate for strict liability?) A majority of jurisdictions currently impose strict liability on providers of food for any foreign matter found in it; if a plaintiff is injured by a substance in the food that might be considered "natural," the question typically becomes whether the diner reasonably should have expected to find the substance in the food.

9. *Horribile visu (problem).* In Doyle v. Pillsbury Co., 476 So. 2d 1271 (Fla. 1985), the plaintiff's husband opened a can of Green Giant peas

distributed by the defendant; the plaintiff looked into the can and observed a large insect floating on the surface of its contents. She recoiled in alarm, fell over a chair, and suffered various injuries. She sued Pillsbury to recover for her injuries. What result?

10. *The resilient thief (problem)*. In Klages v. General Ordnance Equipment Corp., 367 A.2d 304 (Pa. Sup. 1976), the plaintiff was the night clerk at a motel in Pennsylvania. To protect himself against thieves (he had been held up once there already), he bought a "mace pen" made by the defendant. It resembled an ordinary pen but discharged mace; the literature accompanying the pen said that the mace "Rapidly vaporizes on face of assailant effecting instantaneous incapacitation . . . Instantly stops assailants in their tracks." Soon thereafter, a pair of thieves entered the motel late one night. One of them pointed a gun at the plaintiff and instructed him to open the safe. The plaintiff ducked behind the cash register and used the pen to shoot mace into the thief's face; the plaintiff testified that the shot hit the thief "right beside the nose." The thief was unmoved. He followed the plaintiff behind the counter and shot him in the head. The plaintiff survived the encounter but lost sight in one of his eyes. He sued the defendant to recover for his injuries, claiming the mace pen was defective. The basis of the plaintiff's claim was §402B of the Second Restatement:

> One engaged in the business of selling chattels who, by advertising, labels, or otherwise, makes to the public a misrepresentation of a material fact concerning the character or quality of a chattel sold by him is subject to liability for physical harm to a consumer of the chattel caused by justifiable reliance upon the misrepresentation, even though (a) it is not made fraudulently or negligently, and (b) the consumer has not bought the chattel from or entered into any contractual relation with the seller.

What result?

C. DESIGN DEFECTS

Restatement (Third) of Torts: Products Liability (1997)

§1, *comment a. History.* Questions of design defects and defects based on inadequate instructions or warnings arise when the specific product unit conforms to the intended design but the intended design itself, or its sale without adequate instructions or warnings, renders the product not reasonably safe. If these forms of defect are found to exist, then every unit in the same product line is potentially defective. Imposition of liability for design defects and for defects based on inadequate instructions or warnings was relatively infrequent until the late 1960s and early 1970s. A number of restrictive rules made recovery for such defects, especially design defects, difficult to obtain. As these rules eroded, courts sought to impose liability without fault for design defects and defects due to inadequate instructions or warnings under the general principles of §402A of the Restatement, Second, of Torts. However, it soon became evident that §402A, created to deal with liability for manufacturing defects, could not appropriately be applied to cases of design defects or defects based on inadequate instructions or warnings. A product unit that fails to meet the manufacturer's design specifications thereby fails to perform its intended function and is, almost by definition, defective. However, when the product unit meets the manufacturer's own design specifications it is necessary to go outside those specifications to determine whether the product is defective.

Sections 2(b) and 2(c) recognize that the rule developed for manufacturing defects is inappropriate for the resolution of claims of defective design and defects based on inadequate instructions or warnings. These latter categories of cases require determinations that the product could have reasonably been made safer by a better design or instruction or warning. Sections 2(b) and 2(c) rely on a reasonableness test traditionally used in determining whether an actor has been negligent. Nevertheless, many courts insist on speaking of liability based on the standards described in §§2(b) and 2(c) as being "strict."

Several factors help to explain this rhetorical preference. First, in many design defect cases, if the product causes injury while being put to a reasonably foreseeable use, the seller is held to have known of the risks that foreseeably attend such use. Second, some courts have sought to limit the defense of comparative fault in certain products liability contexts. In furtherance of this objective, they have avoided characterizing the liability test as based in negligence, thereby limiting the effect of comparative or contributory fault. Third, some courts are concerned that a negligence standard might be too forgiving of a small manufacturer who might be excused for its ignorance of risk or for failing to take adequate precautions to avoid risk. [. . .] The concept of strict liability, which focuses on the product rather than the conduct of the manufacturer, may help make the point that a defendant is held to the expert standard of knowledge available to the relevant manufacturing community at the time the product was manufactured. Finally, the liability of nonmanufacturing sellers in the distributive chain is strict. It is no defense that they acted reasonably and did not discover a defect in the product, be it manufacturing, design, or failure to warn.

Thus, "strict products liability" is a term of art that reflects the judgment that products liability is a discrete area of tort law which borrows from both negligence and warranty. It is not fully congruent with classical tort or contract law. Rather than perpetuating confusion spawned by existing doctrinal categories, §§1 and 2 define the liability for each form of defect in terms directly addressing the various kinds of defects. As long as these functional criteria are met, courts may utilize the terminology of negligence, strict liability, or the implied warranty of merchantability, or simply define liability in the terms set forth in the black letter. [. . .]

§2, *comment a. Rationale.* [. . .] In contrast to manufacturing defects, design defects and defects based on inadequate instructions or warnings are predicated on a different concept of responsibility. In the first place, such defects cannot be determined by reference to the manufacturer's own design or marketing standards because those standards are the very ones that plaintiffs attack as unreasonable. Some sort of independent assessment of advantages and disadvantages, to which some attach the label "risk-utility balancing," is necessary. Products are not generically defective merely because they are dangerous. Many product-related accident costs can be eliminated only by excessively sacrificing product features that make products useful and desirable. Thus, the various trade-offs need to be considered in determining whether accident costs are more fairly and efficiently borne by accident victims, on the one hand, or, on the other hand, by consumers generally through the mechanism of higher product prices attributable to liability costs imposed by courts on product sellers.

Subsections (b) and (c), which impose liability for products that are defectively designed or sold without adequate warnings or instructions and are thus not reasonably safe, achieve the same general objectives as does liability predicated on negligence. The emphasis is on creating incentives for manufacturers to achieve optimal levels of safety in designing and marketing products. Society does not benefit from products that are excessively safe — for example, automobiles designed with maximum speeds of 20 miles per hour — any more than it benefits from products that are too risky. Society benefits most when the right, or optimal, amount of product safety is achieved. From a fairness perspective, requiring individual users and consumers to bear appropriate responsibility for proper product use prevents careless users and consumers from being subsidized by more careful users and consumers, when the former are paid damages out of funds to which the latter are forced to contribute through higher product prices.

In general, the rationale for imposing strict liability on manufacturers for harm caused by manufacturing defects does not apply in the context of imposing liability for defective design and defects based on inadequate instruction or warning. Consumer expectations as to proper product design or warning are typically more difficult to discern than in the case of a manufacturing defect. Moreover, the element of deliberation in setting appropriate levels of design safety is not directly analogous to the setting of levels of quality control by the manufacturer. When a manufacturer sets its quality control at a certain level, it is aware that a given number of products may leave the assembly line in a defective condition and cause injury to innocent victims who can generally do nothing to avoid injury. The implications of deliberately drawing lines with respect to product design safety are different. A reasonably designed product still carries with it elements of risk that must be protected against by the user or consumer since some risks cannot be designed out of the product at reasonable cost. [. . .]

Dawson v. Chrysler Corp.
630 F.2d 950 (3d Cir. 1980)

ADAMS, *Circuit Judge*. This appeal from a jury verdict and entry of judgment in favor of the plaintiffs arises out of a New Jersey automobile accident in which a police officer was seriously injured. The legal questions in this diversity action [governed by New Jersey law] are relatively straight-forward. The public policy questions, however, which are beyond the competence of this Court to resolve and with which Congress ultimately must grapple, are complex and implicate national economic and social concerns. [. . .]

On September 7, 1974, Richard F. Dawson, while in the employ of the Pennsauken Police Department, was seriously injured as a result of an automobile accident that occurred in Pennsauken, New Jersey. As Dawson was driving on a rain-soaked highway, responding to a burglar alarm, he lost control of his patrol car, a 1974 Dodge Monaco. The car slid off the highway, over a curb, through a small sign, and into an unyielding steel pole that was fifteen inches in diameter. The car struck the pole in a backwards direction at a forty-five degree angle on the left side of the vehicle; the point of impact was the left rear wheel well. As a result of the force of the collision, the vehicle literally wrapped itself around the pole. The pole ripped through the body of the car and crushed Dawson between the seat and the "header" area of the roof, located just above the windshield. The so-called "secondary collision" of Dawson with the interior of the automobile dislocated Dawson's left hip and ruptured his fifth and sixth cervical vertebrae. As a result of the injuries, Dawson is now a quadriplegic. He has no control over his body from the neck down, and requires constant medical attention. [. . .]

The plaintiffs' claims were based on theories of strict products liability and breach of implied warranty of fitness. They alleged that the patrol car was defective because it did not have a full, continuous steel frame extending through the door panels, and a cross-member running through the floor board between the posts located between the front and rear doors of the vehicle. Had the vehicle been so designed, the Dawsons alleged, it would have "bounced" off the pole following relatively slight penetration by the pole into the passenger space.

Expert testimony was introduced by the Dawsons to prove that the existing frame of the patrol car was unable to withstand side impacts at relatively low speed, and that the inadequacy of the frame permitted the pole to enter the passenger area and to injure Dawson. The same experts testified that the improvements in the design of the frame that the plaintiffs proposed were feasible and would have prevented Dawson from being injured as he was. According to plaintiffs' expert witnesses, a continuous frame and cross-member would have deflected the patrol car away from the pole after a minimal intrusion into the passenger area and, they declared, Dawson likely would have emerged from the accident with only a slight injury.

In response, Chrysler argued that it had no duty to produce a "crashproof" vehicle, and that, in any event, the patrol car was not defective. Expert testimony for Chrysler established that the design and construction of the 1974 Dodge Monaco complied with all federal vehicle safety standards, and that deformation of the body of the vehicle is desirable in most crashes because it absorbs the impact of the crash and decreases the rate of deceleration on the occupants of the vehicle. Thus, Chrysler's experts asserted that, for most types of automobile accidents, the design offered by the Dawsons would be less safe than the existing design. They also estimated that the steel parts that would be required in the model suggested by the Dawsons would have added between 200 and 250 pounds to the weight, and approximately $300 to the price of the vehicle. It was also established that the 1974 Dodge Monaco's unibody construction was stronger than comparable Ford and Chevrolet vehicles. . . .

The jury awarded Mr. Dawson $2,064,863.19 for his expenses, disability, and pain and suffering, and granted Mrs. Dawson $60,000.00 for loss of consortium and loss of services. After the district court entered judgment, Chrysler moved for judgment notwithstanding the verdict or, alternatively for a new trial. The court denied both motions. The Dawsons then requested prejudgment interest of eight percent per annum of the damages award, accruing from the time suit was instituted to the date of the judgment. The trial judge granted the request in the amounts of $388,012.53 for Mr. Dawson and $11,274.72 for Mrs. Dawson. [. . .]

[T]he controlling issue in the case is whether the jury could be permitted to find, under the law of New Jersey, that the patrol car was defective. In *Suter v. San Angelo Foundry & Machine Co.*, 406 A.2d 140, 153 (N.J. 1979), the New Jersey Supreme Court summarized its state's law of strict liability as follows:

> If at the time the seller distributes a product, it is not reasonably fit, suitable and safe for its intended or reasonably foreseeable purposes so that users or others who may be expected to come in contact with the product are injured as a result thereof, then the seller shall be responsible for the ensuing damages.

The court, in adopting this test, specifically rejected the requirement of the Restatement (Second) of Torts §402A that the defect must cause the product to be "unreasonably dangerous to the user or consumer." In the court's view, "the Restatement language may lead a jury astray for '[i]t may suggest an idea like ultra-hazardous, or abnormally dangerous, and thus give rise to the impression that the plaintiff must prove that the product was unusually or extremely dangerous.'"

The determination whether a product is "reasonably fit, suitable and safe for its intended or reasonably foreseeable purposes" is to be informed by what the

New Jersey Supreme Court has termed a "risk/utility analysis." *Cepeda v. Cumberland Engineering Co., Inc.*, 386 A.2d 816, 825-29 (N.J. 1978). Under this approach, a product is defective if "a reasonable person would conclude that the magnitude of the scientifically perceivable danger as it is proved to be at the time of trial outweighed the benefits of the way the product was so designed and marketed." Id. at 826. The court in *Cepeda*, relying heavily on the article by Dean John Wade, referred to in *Suter*, identified seven factors that might be relevant to this balancing process:

(1) The usefulness and desirability of the product, its utility to the user, and to the public as a whole.

(2) The safety aspects of the product, the likelihood that it will cause injury, and the probable seriousness of the injury.

(3) The availability of a substitute product which would meet the same need and not be as unsafe.

(4) The manufacturer's ability to eliminate the unsafe character of the product without impairing its usefulness or making it too expensive to maintain its utility.

(5) The user's ability to avoid danger by the exercise of care in the use of the product.

(6) The user's anticipated awareness of the dangers inherent in the product and their avoidability, because of general public knowledge of the obvious condition of the product, or of the existence of suitable warnings or instructions.

(7) The feasibility, on the part of the manufacturer, of spreading the loss by setting the price of the product or carrying liability insurance.

386 A.2d at 826-27 (quoting Wade, *On the Nature of Strict Tort Liability for Products*, 44 Miss. L.J. 825, 837-38 (1973)). The court suggested that the trial judge first determine whether a balancing of these factors precludes liability as a matter of law. If it does not, then the judge is to incorporate into the instructions any factor for which there was presented specific proof and which might be deemed relevant to the jury's consideration of the matter.

Chrysler maintains that, under these standards, the district court erred in submitting the case to the jury because the Dawsons failed, as a matter of law, to prove that the patrol car was defective. Specifically, it insists that the Dawsons did not present sufficient evidence from which the jury reasonably might infer that the alternative design that they proffered would be safer than the existing design, or that it would be cost effective, practical, or marketable. In short, Chrysler urges that the substitute design would be less socially beneficial than was the actual design of the patrol car. In support of its argument, Chrysler emphasizes that the design of the 1974 Dodge Monaco complied with all of the standards authorized by Congress in the National Traffic and Motor Vehicle Safety Act of 1966.

Compliance with the safety standards promulgated pursuant to the National Traffic and Motor Vehicle Safety Act, however, does not relieve Chrysler of liability in this action. For, in authorizing the Secretary of Transportation to enact these standards, Congress explicitly provided, "Compliance with any Federal motor vehicle safety standard issued under this subchapter does not exempt any person from any liability under common law." 15 U.S.C. §1397(c) (1976). Thus, consonant with this congressional directive, we must review Chrysler's appeal on the question of the existence of a defect under the common law of New Jersey that is set forth above.

Our examination of the record persuades us that the district court did not err in denying Chrysler's motion for judgment notwithstanding the verdict. [. . .] [The Dawsons introduced into evidence] reports of tests conducted for the United States Department of Transportation, which indicated that, in side collisions with a fixed pole at twenty-one miles per hour, frame improvements similar to those proposed by the experts presented by the Dawsons reduced intrusion into the passenger area by fifty percent, from sixteen inches to eight inches. The study concluded that the improvements, "in conjunction with interior alterations, demonstrated a dramatic increase in occupant protection." There was no suggestion at trial that the alternative design recommended by the Dawsons would not comply with federal safety standards. On cross-examination, Chrysler's attorney did get the Dawsons' expert witnesses to acknowledge that the alternative design would add between 200 and 250 pounds to the vehicle and would cost an additional $300 per car. The Dawsons' experts also conceded that the heavier and more rigid an automobile, the less able it is to absorb energy upon impact with a fixed object, and therefore the major force of an accident might be transmitted to the passengers. [. . .]

On the basis of the foregoing recitation of the evidence presented respectively by the Dawsons and by Chrysler, we conclude that the record is sufficient to sustain the jury's determination, in response to the interrogatory, that the design of the 1974 Monaco was defective. The jury was not required to ascertain that all of the factors enumerated by the New Jersey Supreme Court in *Cepeda* weighed in favor of the Dawsons in order to find the patrol car defective. Rather, it need only to have reasonably concluded, after balancing these factors, that, at the time Chrysler distributed the 1974 Monaco, the car was "not reasonably fit, suitable and safe for its intended or reasonably foreseeable purposes." *Suter*, 406 A.2d at 149. [. . .]

Although we affirm the judgment of the district court, we do so with uneasiness regarding the consequences of our decision and of the decisions of other courts throughout the country in cases of this kind.

As we observed earlier, Congress, in enacting the National Traffic and Motor Vehicle Safety Act, provided that compliance with the Act does not exempt any person from liability under the common law of the state of injury. The effect of this provision is that the states are free, not only to create various standards of liability for automobile manufacturers with respect to design and structure, but also to delegate to the triers of fact in civil cases arising out of automobile accidents the power to determine whether a particular product conforms to such standards. In the present situation, for example, the New Jersey Supreme Court has instituted a strict liability standard for cases involving defective products, has defined the term "defective product" to mean any such item that is not "reasonably fit, suitable and safe for its intended or reasonably foreseeable purposes," and has left to the jury the task of determining whether the product at issue measures up to this standard.

The result of such arrangement is that while the jury found Chrysler liable for not producing a rigid enough vehicular frame, a factfinder in another case might well hold the manufacturer liable for producing a frame that is too rigid. Yet, as pointed out at trial, in certain types of accidents — head-on collisions — it is desirable to have a car designed to collapse upon impact because the deformation would absorb much of the shock of the collision, and divert the force of deceleration away from the vehicle's passengers. In effect, this permits individual juries applying varying laws in different jurisdictions to set nationwide automobile safety standards and to impose on automobile manufacturers conflicting requirements. It would be difficult for members of the industry to alter their design and production behavior in response to jury verdicts in such cases, because their response might well be at variance with what some other jury decides is a defective design. Under these circumstances, the law imposes on the industry the responsibility of insuring vast numbers of persons involved in automobile accidents.

Equally serious is the impact on other national social and economic goals of the existing case-by-case system of establishing automobile safety requirements. As we have become more dependent on foreign sources of energy, and as the price of that energy has increased, the attention of the federal government has been drawn to a search to find alternative supplies and the means of conserving energy. More recently, the domestic automobile industry has been struggling to compete with foreign manufacturers which have stressed smaller, more fuel-efficient cars. Yet, during this same period, Congress has permitted a system of regulation by ad hoc adjudications under which a jury can hold an automobile manufacturer culpable for not producing a car that is considerably heavier, and likely to have less fuel efficiency.

In sum, this appeal has brought to our attention an important conflict that implicates broad national concerns. Although it is important that society devise a proper system for compensating those injured in automobile collisions, it is not at all clear that the present arrangement of permitting individual juries, under varying standards of liability, to impose this obligation on manufacturers is fair or efficient. Inasmuch as it was the Congress that designed this system, and because Congress is the body best suited to evaluate and, if appropriate, to change that system, we decline today to do anything in this regard except to bring the problem to the attention of the legislative branch.

[Affirmed.]

pre-emption

NOTES

1. *The relevance of regulation.* One of the defenses raised and rejected in *Dawson* was that the manufacturer had complied with federal regulations in designing the car. Arguments of this kind are not uncommon in products liability cases; they require courts to decide whether a plaintiff's common law claims have been "preempted" by federal law — a question of statutory interpretation. For a more recent example, see the Supreme Court's decision in Wyeth v. Levine, 2009 WL 529172 (2009). The plaintiff received an intravenous injection of an anti-nausea drug made by Wyeth. She contracted gangrene as a result, and her arm was amputated. She claimed that Wyeth should have warned of this risk. Wyeth pointed out that the drug's labeling had been approved the Food and Drug Administration. The Court held that this was no bar to the plaintiff's claims; the majority found no conflict between the warning sought by the plaintiff and the warnings required by federal law, and no evidence of a Congressional purpose to preempt state law.

Questions of statutory interpretation to one side, what approach (or mix of approaches) makes more sense: regulation of product design by tort suits or by federal agencies?

2. *Consumer expectations.* In Green v. Smith & Nephew, 629 N.W.2d 727 (Wis. 2001), the plaintiff was a worker at a hospital who developed a mysterious rash and other symptoms of an allergy. She finally determined that she had developed an allergy to latex, and concluded that the allergy had been brought about by powdered latex gloves she wore at work, which were made by the defendant. (Her claim was not that the gloves triggered a pre-existing allergy; it was that proteins in the gloves *created* a new allergy by their interaction with her immune system.) She brought a suit alleging that the gloves were defectively designed. The trial court instructed the jury as follows:

> A product is said to be defective when it is in a condition not contemplated by the ordinary user or consumer which is unreasonably dangerous to the ordinary user or consumer, and the defect arose out of design, manufacture or inspection while the article was in the control of the manufacturer. A defective product is unreasonably dangerous to the ordinary user or consumer when it is dangerous to an extent beyond that which would be contemplated by the ordinary user or consumer possessing the knowledge of the product's characteristics which were common to the community. A product is not defective if it is safe for normal use.

The trial judge added:

> Lack of knowledge on the part of [S & N] that proteins in natural rubber latex may sensitize and cause allergic reactions to some individuals is not

a defense to the claims made by the plaintiff [Green] in this action. A manufacturer is responsible for harm caused by a defective and unreasonably dangerous product even if the manufacturer had no knowledge or could [not] have known of the risk of harm presented by the condition of the product.

The jury brought in a verdict for the plaintiff and awarded her $1 million. The Wisconsin Supreme Court affirmed, and made clear its rejection of the Restatement (Third) of Products Liability:

Comment a to §2 of the Restatement (Third) of Torts explains that 2(b) incorporates an element of foreseeability of risk of harm and a risk-benefit test. As such, 2(b) departs from the consumer-contemplation test set forth in the Restatement (Second) of Torts 402A (1965), and blurs the distinction between strict products liability claims and negligence claims. See Morden v. Continental AG, 611 N.W.2d 659 (Wis. 2000) (explaining that under Wisconsin law, foreseeability of the risk of harm is an element of negligence, not strict products liability); Meyer v. Val Lo Will Farms, Inc., 111 N.W.2d 500 (Wis. 1961) (explaining that negligence claims require a risk-benefit analysis). In this sense, for the reasons explained above, 2(b) is fundamentally at odds with current Wisconsin products liability law.

But we are more troubled by the fact that 2(b) sets the bar higher for recovery in strict products liability design defect cases than in comparable negligence cases. Section 2(b) does not merely incorporate a negligence standard into strict products liability law. Instead, it adds to this standard the additional requirement that an injured consumer seeking to recover under strict products liability must prove that there was a "reasonable alternative design" available to the product's manufacturer. Thus, rather than serving the policies underlying strict products liability law by allowing consumers to recover for injuries caused by a defective and unreasonably dangerous product without proving negligence on the part of the product's manufacturer, 2(b) increases the burden for injured consumers not only by requiring proof of the manufacturer's negligence, but also by adding an additional — and considerable — element of proof to the negligence standard. This court will not impose such a burden on injured persons.

3. *Reasonable foresight.* As the excerpts from *Green v. Smith & Nephew* show, there are two competing traditions in the law of liability for design defects: liability based on a product's failure to comport with a reasonable consumer's expectations, and liability based on a product's failure to satisfy a test that balances the risks and utility of a product's design. *Green* takes the former approach; *Dawson v. Chrysler Corp.* takes the latter. The strong trend of authority now is toward the sort of risk-utility balancing endorsed in §2(b)

of the Restatement (Third) of Products Liability. Which approach seems more attractive?

Green v. Smith & Nephew also raises another problem: the importance of reasonable foresight when holding a defendant liable. Again the trend of the decisions is contrary to Wisconsin's position. From the Restatement (Third) of Products Liability, §2, comment a:

> Most courts agree that, for the liability system to be fair and efficient, the balancing of risks and benefits in judging product design and marketing must be done in light of the knowledge of risks and risk-avoidance techniques reasonably attainable at the time of distribution. To hold a manufacturer liable for a risk that was not foreseeable when the product was marketed might foster increased manufacturer investment in safety. But such investment by definition would be a matter of guesswork. Furthermore, manufacturers may persuasively ask to be judged by a normative behavior standard to which it is reasonably possible for manufacturers to conform. For these reasons, Subsections (b) and (c) speak of products being defective only when risks are reasonably foreseeable.

4. *Design defects: "Strict" liability or negligence?* Notice that "strict liability" for design defects often may be a misleading usage. In jurisdictions that employ a risk-utility balancing test, the standard for liability tends to resemble the familiar inquiry into negligence; notice its resemblance to the Hand formula. As noted in the Restatement excerpts at the beginning of this section, however, the notion of strict liability for defective designs does retain bite in some collateral respects. The retail seller of a product found to have a design defect usually can be held liable for the damage it causes regardless of whether the retailer had a hand in the design or was careful in deciding whether to sell it. In many jurisdictions liability for defective products now is regulated by statute, and the statutory schemes vary in these and other details. Do the other standards that some jurisdictions use for assessing claimed design defects — a "consumer expectations" test, or an inquiry into whether the product was safe for its intended use — bear a greater resemblance to traditional strict liability or to liability for negligence?

The law of liability for design defects contains a number of other distinctions that courts in the past have sometimes regarded as decisive but that now are usually just considered factors for juries to consider. Whether a product's design reflected the "state of the art" when it was made is one example; this consideration may be relevant both to questions of what is technically feasible and to what is customary. Another example is whether the danger created by a product's design was "open and obvious": this once was considered by many courts a reason for denying recovery as a matter of law, but courts now generally regard it as one factor among many for a jury to evaluate in deciding whether a product's design is unreasonably dangerous.

5. *Volkswagens.* In Dreisonstok v. Volkswagenwerk A.G., 489 F.2d 1066 (4th Cir. 1974), the plaintiff was a passenger in a Volkswagen "microbus" that crashed into a telephone pole, causing her various injuries. She brought a suit against Volkswagen claiming that the bus was negligently designed and thus not crashworthy. The case was tried before a judge, who found Volkswagen liable for failing to furnish the vehicle with "sufficient energy-absorbing materials or devices or 'crush space,' if you will, so that at 40 miles an hour the integrity of the passenger compartment would not be violated." The court of appeals reversed:

> The defendant's vehicle, described as "a van type multipurpose vehicle," was of a special type and particular design. This design was uniquely developed in order to provide the owner with the maximum amount of either cargo or passenger space in a vehicle inexpensively priced and of such dimensions as to make possible easy maneuverability. To achieve this, it advanced the driver's seat forward, bringing such seat in close proximity to the front of the vehicle, thereby adding to the cargo or passenger space. This, of course, reduced considerably the space between the exact front of the vehicle and the driver's compartment. All of this was readily discernible to any one using the vehicle; in fact, it was, as we have said, the unique feature of the vehicle. The usefulness of the design is vouchsafed by the popularity of the type. It was of special utility as a van for the transportation of light cargo, as a family camper, as a station wagon and for use by passenger groups too large for the average passenger car. [. . .] There was no evidence in the record that there was any practical way of improving the "crashability" of the vehicle that would have been consistent with the peculiar purposes of its design.

What is the distinction between *Dreisonstok v. Volkswagenwerk A.G.* and *Dawson v. Chrysler Corp.*?

6. *Black Talons.* In McCarthy v. Olin Corp., 119 F.3d 148 (2d Cir. 1997), a man named Colin Ferguson boarded a Long Island Railroad train departing from New York City and opened fire on the passengers. Six people were killed; nineteen more were injured. Ferguson was armed with a semiautomatic handgun loaded with Winchester "Black Talon" bullets. The Black Talon is a hollow-point bullet designed to bend upon impact into six ninety-degree angle razor-sharp petals or "talons" that increase the wounding power of the bullet by tearing tissue and bone. Olin had pulled the Black Talon from the public market in late 1993 and restricted its sales to law enforcement personnel. Ferguson allegedly purchased the ammunition before that time. Survivors of two of the passengers who were killed in the attack sued Olin, alleging among other things that the company should be held strictly liable because the bullets were defectively designed. The district judge granted Olin's motion to dismiss the complaint for failing

to state a claim upon which relief can be granted. The court of appeals affirmed:

> To state a cause of action for a design defect, plaintiffs must allege that the bullet was unreasonably dangerous for its intended use. "[A] defectively designed product is one which, at the time it leaves the seller's hands, is in a condition not reasonably contemplated by the ultimate consumer." *Robinson v. Reed-Prentice Division of Package Mach. Co.*, 403 N.E.2d 440, 443 (N.Y. 1980). "This rule, however, is tempered by the realization that some products, for example knives, must by their very nature be dangerous in order to be functional." Id. at 443. The very purpose of the Black Talon bullet is to kill or cause severe wounding. Here, plaintiffs concede that the Black Talons performed precisely as intended by the manufacturer and Colin Ferguson. [. . .]
>
> Appellants next argue that under the risk/utility test analysis applied by New York courts, appellee should be held strictly liable because the risk of harm posed by the Black Talons outweighs the ammunition's utility. The district court properly held that the risk/utility test is inapplicable "because the risks arise from the function of the product, not any defect in the product." "There must be 'something wrong' with a product before the risk/utility analysis may be applied in determining whether the product is unreasonably dangerous or defective." *Addison v. Williams*, 546 So.2d 220, 224 (La. Ct. App. 1989).
>
> The purpose of risk/utility analysis is to determine whether the risk of injury might have been reduced or avoided if the manufacturer had used a feasible alternative design. However, the risk of injury to be balanced with the utility is a risk not intended as the primary function of the product. Here, the primary function of the Black Talon bullets was to kill or cause serious injury. There is no reason to search for an alternative safer design where the product's sole utility is to kill and maim. Accordingly, we hold that appellants have failed to state a cause of action under New York strict products liability law.

Calabresi, J., dissented, arguing that the federal court should certify the question raised by the case to the New York Court of Appeals; he contended that there were strong arguments for liability:

> [T]he fact that a product fails the risk/utility test may not be sufficient to give rise to strict liability. This is so because, as the majority notes, New York law has appeared to require that the plaintiff also show a reasonable alternative design before she will be permitted to recover in strict liability for a defectively designed product. Moreover, it has been noted (in a controversial comment in the latest tentative draft of the Third Restatement of Torts) that this requirement applies "even though the plaintiff alleges that the category of product sold by the defendant is so dangerous

that it should not have been marketed at all. [. . .]" Restatement 3rd, supra, §2 cmt. c.

In the instant case, however, a possible alternative design does exist. It consists of the elimination of the extra-destructive "talons." The proposed Restatement contains a remarkably relevant discussion:

> Several courts have suggested that the designs of some products are so manifestly unreasonable, in that they have low social utility and high degree of danger, that liability should attach even absent proof of a reasonable alternative design. In large part the problem is one of how the range of relevant alternative designs is described. For example, a toy gun that shoots hard rubber pellets with sufficient velocity to cause injury to children could be found to be defectively designed within the rule of §2(b). Toy guns that do not produce injury would constitute reasonable alternatives to the dangerous toy. Thus, toy guns that project ping pong balls, soft gelatin pellets, or water might be found to be reasonable alternative designs to a toy gun that shoots hard pellets. However, if consideration is limited to toy guns that are capable of causing injury, then no reasonable alternative will, by hypothesis, be available. In that instance, the design feature that defines which alternatives are relevant — the capacity to injure — is precisely the feature on which the user places value and of which the plaintiff complains. If a court were to adopt this characterization of the product, it could conclude that liability should attach without proof of a reasonable alternative design. The court would condemn the product design as defective and not reasonably safe because the extremely high degree of danger posed by its use or consumption so substantially outweighs its negligible utility that no rational adult, fully aware of the relevant facts, would choose to use or consume the product.

Id., §2 cmt. d.

What is the analogy between *Dreisonstok v. Volkswagenwerk A.G.* and *McCarthy v. Olin Corp.*? Both are cases of no liability; can you nevertheless articulate some possible distinctions between them?

7. *Exploding cigars.* The Third Restatement suggests a requirement that a plaintiff demonstrate the existence of a "reasonable alternative design" before liability is imposed, but it leaves open the possibility that liability may be found without an alternative design if a product's costs so outweigh its "negligible social utility" that no rational person would choose to use it. The example offered is an exploding cigar purchased from a novelty shop that sets the plaintiff's beard on fire. §2, Illus. 5. Can that case effectively be distinguished from *McCarthy v. Olin Corp.*?

8. *Causation in design defect cases.* In Price v. Blaine Kern Artista, Inc., 893 P.2d 367 (Nev. 1995), the defendant was a manufacturer of oversized masks that covered the user's head and bore caricatures of celebrities. The plaintiff, Price, was an entertainer at Harrah's Club in Reno who was injured while wearing a caricature mask of then-President George H. W. Bush. The plaintiff's evidence was that a patron at the club pushed him down from

behind, causing the weight of the mask to strain and injure his neck as he fell to the ground. His suit alleged that the mask was defectively designed because it lacked a safety harness to support his head and neck. The defendant claimed that the push from the unknown assailant was a superseding cause that insulated it from liability. The trial court gave summary judgment to the defendant; the Nevada Supreme Court reversed:

> [W]hile it is true that criminal or tortious third-party conduct typically severs the chain of proximate causation between a plaintiff and a defendant, the chain remains unbroken when the third party's intervening intentional act is reasonably foreseeable. Under the circumstances of this case, the trier of fact could reasonably find that [the defendant] should have foreseen the possibility or probability of some sort of violent reaction, such as pushing, by intoxicated or politically volatile persons, ignited by the sight of an oversized caricature of a prominent political figure. [. . .] Indeed, while the precise force that caused Price's fall is uncertain, shortly before the fall, an irate and perhaps somewhat confused patron of Harrah's took issue with the bedecked Price over Bush's policy on abortion rights. [. . .] In the final analysis, the initial cause of Price's fall appears to be of little consequence, considering the reasonable prospect that among the quantity of users of BKA's products, some of them will sooner or later fall for any number of a variety of reasons.

9. *Intervening events.* In Rodriguez v. Glock, Inc., 28 F. Supp. 2d 1064 (N.D. Ill. 1998), the plaintiff's decedent, Jose Rodriguez, was a bouncer at a nightclub in Chicago. Late one night, Rodriguez got into an altercation at the club with a man named Bedoya, an off-duty member of the Milwaukee Police Department who was carrying, in a holster, his service revolver — a handgun made by the defendant, Glock. Rodriguez grabbed Bedoya from behind and attempted to remove the revolver from its holster. The two men struggled over the weapon. When a third person tried to pull Rodriguez away, the gun discharged, fatally wounding Rodriguez. His estate brought suit against Glock, claiming the gun was defectively designed because it lacked a "safety" — an external switch to prevent the gun from being fired — and because it had an extremely short trigger-pull of half an inch. The district court gave summary judgment to Glock. It concluded that a jury might reasonably say that Rodriguez would not have been injured if the Glock had a safety, but it nevertheless found the events leading to his death unforeseeable by the defendant:

> The facts show that there was a heated struggle between Rodriguez and Bedoya for control of the weapon. Although it is not clear to what extent each intended to harm the other, the potential certainly existed. It is common knowledge that a gun is a dangerous object with the ability to inflict great bodily harm or death. Much like a knife, a chainsaw or

a car, a gun is a product which can seriously injure an individual, especially when the product is defective. Yet, the law declines to hold a manufacturer liable for every injury connected with its product. To do so would make the manufacturer an insurer of its product, a position rejected by the Illinois Supreme Court. At some point, the law relieves the manufacturer that created a condition of its liability when a third party's actions exploit the condition in a manner which the manufacturer could not reasonably foresee. That is the case here.

Common experience dictates that precautions are necessary to use a handgun properly. The recklessness involved in pointing the weapon at another human being under these circumstances, whether it is defective or not, excuses the manufacturer as the struggle was an independent superseding cause. The defect, if any, was merely a condition and could not lead to Glock's liability for Rodriguez's injury. Glock did not point the weapon at Rodriguez or struggle with him over its control, and could not have reasonably anticipated that the weapon would be used in this manner. The struggle on this occasion was so improbable and unforeseeable that it removed any potential liability from Glock for its own alleged negligence in design. Accordingly, the court concludes that the fight in the case was, as a matter of law, an intervening event which cut the causal chain.

Is there a satisfactory distinction between *Rodriguez v. Glock, Inc.* and *Price v. Blaine Kern Artista, Inc.*?

D. FAILURE TO WARN

American Tobacco Co. v. Grinnell
951 S.W.2d 420 (Tex. 1997)

CORNYN, J. [. . .] In 1952, nineteen-year-old Wiley Grinnell began smoking Lucky Strikes, cigarettes manufactured by the American Tobacco Company. Almost a year later, Grinnell changed to Pall Malls, also manufactured by American. After smoking for approximately thirty-three years, Grinnell was diagnosed with lung cancer in July 1985. Shortly thereafter, he filed this lawsuit. He died less than a year later. Grinnell's family continued this suit after his death, adding wrongful death and survival claims. The family alleges that American failed to warn of, and actively concealed, facts that it knew or should have known, including the facts that Grinnell could quickly become addicted to cigarettes and that his smoking could result in injury or death from the cancer-causing ingredients if he used the cigarettes as American intended. They also allege that, even though American knew or should have known that its cigarettes were dangerous and could not be used safely, American represented to consumers that cigarettes were not harmful, dangerous, or capable of causing injury. [The trial court gave summary judgment to the defendants on all claims. The court of appeals reversed, and this appeal followed.]

MARKETING DEFECT

A defendant's failure to warn of a product's potential dangers when warnings are required is a type of marketing defect. The existence of a duty to warn of dangers or instruct as to the proper use of a product is a question of law. Generally, a manufacturer has a duty to warn if it knows or should know of the potential harm to a user because of the nature of its product. Nevertheless, this Court has recognized that there is no duty to warn when the risks associated with a particular product are matters "within the ordinary knowledge common to the community." *Joseph E. Seagram & Sons, Inc. v. McGuire,* 814 S.W.2d 385, 388 (Tex. 1991) (holding that no legal duty exists to warn of the health risks of alcohol consumption because such risks are common knowledge). American argues that it had no duty to warn Grinnell of the risks associated with smoking its cigarettes because the dangers of smoking were common knowledge when Grinnell began smoking in 1952.

Comments i and j to Restatement section 402A incorporate common knowledge into the analysis of whether a product is "unreasonably dangerous" under that section. Comment i, which defines "unreasonably dangerous," forecloses liability against manufacturers unless a product is dangerous to an extent beyond that which would be contemplated by the ordinary consumer with knowledge common to the community:

> Many products cannot possibly be made entirely safe for all consumption, and any food or drug necessarily involves some risk of harm, if only from over-consumption. . . . That is not what is meant by "unreasonably dangerous" in this Section. *The article sold must be dangerous to an extent beyond that which would be contemplated by the ordinary consumer who purchases it, with the ordinary knowledge common to the community as to its characteristics. . . . Good tobacco is not unreasonably dangerous merely because the effects of smoking may be harmful; but tobacco containing something like marijuana may be unreasonably dangerous.*

Restatement (Second) of Torts §402A cmt. i (1965) (emphasis added). Comment j excuses a seller from the duty to warn about dangers that are generally known and recognized:

> In order to prevent the product from being unreasonably dangerous, the seller may be required to give directions or warning, on the container, as to its use. . . . But a seller is not required to warn with respect to products,

or ingredients in them, which are only dangerous, or potentially so, when consumed in excess quantity, or over a long period of time, *when the danger, or potentiality of danger, is generally known and recognized.* . . . [T]he dangers of alcoholic beverages are an example. . . .

Id. §402A cmt. j (1965) (emphasis added).

Common knowledge, in the context of comments i and j, connotes a general societal understanding of the risks inherent in a specific product or class of products. *Seagram,* 814 S.W.2d at 388. In *Seagram* we also emphasized that the standard for finding common knowledge as a matter of law is a strict one. [The court had defined "common knowledge" as encompassing "those facts that are so well known to the community as to be beyond dispute."] Thus, common knowledge is an extraordinary defense that applies only in limited circumstances. As the court in [*Brune v. Brown Forman Corp.,* 758 S.W.2d 827, 830-831 (Tex. App. 1988)] noted, common knowledge encompasses only those things "so patently obvious and so well known to the community generally, that there can be no question or dispute concerning their existence." We will find common knowledge as a matter of law only when the standard set out in *Seagram* is met. It is not met in all respects here. [. . .]

The party asserting the common-knowledge defense must establish that the dangers attributable to alcohol, tobacco, or other products were a matter of common knowledge when the consumer began using the product. Based on the summary judgment record, we hold that American established that the general ill-effects of smoking were commonly known when Grinnell started smoking in 1952. However, we also hold that American did not establish that the addictive quality of cigarettes was commonly known when Grinnell began smoking in 1952.

Regarding the general health risks associated with smoking, the Tennessee Supreme Court held as early as 1898 that these risks were "generally known." *Austin v. State,* 48 S.W. 305, 306 (Tenn. 1898), *aff'd as modified sub nom. Austin v. Tennessee,* 179 U.S. 343 (1900). On certiorari, the United States Supreme Court observed:

> [W]e should be shutting our eyes to what is constantly passing before them were we to affect an ignorance of the fact that a belief in [cigarettes'] deleterious effects, particularly upon young people, *has become very general,* and that communications are constantly finding their way into the public press denouncing their use as fraught with great danger. . . .

179 U.S. at 348 (emphasis added). Other early courts also recognized the harmful effects of smoking cigarettes. [. . .] Moreover, by 1962, when the Surgeon General's advisory committee began examining the health risks associated with smoking, there were already more than seven thousand publications of professional and general circulation examining the relationship between smoking and health. [. . .]

We conclude that the general health dangers attributable to cigarettes were commonly known as a matter of law by the community when Grinnell began smoking. We cannot conclude, however, that the specific danger of nicotine addiction was common knowledge when Grinnell began smoking. Addiction is a danger apart from the direct physical dangers of smoking because the addictive nature of cigarettes multiplies the likelihood of and contributes to the smoker's ultimate injury, in Grinnell's case, lung cancer. [. . .] This Court has also recognized the seriousness of addiction and the need for manufacturers to warn of this danger in the context of prescription drugs. We acknowledge that some authorities support the proposition that some members of the community associated addiction with smoking cigarettes earlier in this century. *Ploch v. City of St. Louis*, 345 Mo. 1069, 138 S.W.2d 1020, 1023 (1940) (cigarettes have "harmful properties" and it is common knowledge that nicotine produces "tobacco addicts"); Wiley, *The Little White Slaver*, Good Housekeeping, Jan. 1916, at 91 (people can become "slaves" to the cigarette habit and cigarette smoking can "shorten their lives"). [. . .]

[W]e cannot simply assume that common knowledge of the general health risks of tobacco use naturally includes common knowledge of tobacco's addictive quality. Indeed, as David Kessler, former head of the FDA, has pointed out:

> Before 1980, when FDA last considered its jurisdiction over tobacco products, *no* major public health organization had determined that nicotine was an addictive drug. Today, however, *all* major public health organizations in the United States and abroad with expertise in tobacco or drug addiction recognize that the nicotine delivered by cigarettes and smokeless tobacco is addictive.

Kessler et al., *The Legal and Scientific Basis for FDA's Assertion of Jurisdiction over Cigarettes and Smokeless Tobacco*, 277 JAMA 405, 406 (1997) (emphasis added). The FDA based its 1996 assertion of jurisdiction on "a wealth of epidemiologic and laboratory data establishing that tobacco users display the clinical symptoms of addiction and that nicotine has the characteristics of other addictive drugs." Id. Thus, unlike the general dangers associated with smoking, as late as 1988 and certainly in 1952, the danger of addiction from smoking cigarettes was not widely known and recognized in the community in general, or, particularly, by children or adolescents. [. . .]

Because the community's knowledge concerning the danger of nicotine addiction associated with cigarettes was not beyond dispute in 1952, the *Seagram* standard for finding common knowledge as a matter of law has not been met. [. . .] [T]he Grinnells may maintain their strict liability marketing defect claims to the extent they are based on the addictive qualities of cigarettes, if no other defenses defeat those claims.

The Grinnells assert that American breached its duty to warn users about its product's addictive nature because before January 1, 1966, the product's packages contained no warnings. A manufacturer is required to give an adequate warning if it knows or should know that potential harm may result from use of the product. In the absence of a warning, a *rebuttable* presumption arises that the "user would have read and heeded such warnings and instructions." *Magro v. Ragsdale Bros., Inc.*, 721 S.W.2d 832, 834 (Tex. 1986). A manufacturer may rebut the presumption with evidence that the plaintiff did not heed whatever warnings were given, or would not have heeded any proposed warnings.

The Grinnells assert that when Grinnell started smoking in 1952 he did not know and had heard nothing about any risk of addiction associated with smoking. The Grinnells further assert that American's failure to warn of the addictive nature of cigarettes caused Grinnell's eventual death because Grinnell testified that had he known what he later learned, he would never have started smoking. In rebuttal, American cites testimony that in the late 1950s and the 1960s, Grinnell continued smoking despite warnings from his father, coaches, and friends.

At most, the evidence relied on by American establishes that some people warned Grinnell about the general dangers of smoking. It does not conclusively establish that had Grinnell been warned that cigarettes were addictive *before* he began smoking he would have refused to follow the warnings. Grinnell testified at his deposition that if he had known of the dangers associated with smoking, including addiction, he never would have *started* smoking. At the very least, this testimony creates a fact issue regarding whether Grinnell would have heeded warnings had they been given to him before he began smoking. [. . .]

[Affirmed in part and reversed in part.]

HECHT, J., concurring in part and dissenting in part. [. . .]

For several reasons I think the Court's view is untenable.

First: In Texas, as in most places, the law is that "[g]ood tobacco is not unreasonably dangerous merely because the effects of smoking may be harmful; but tobacco containing something like marijuana may be unreasonably dangerous." Restatement (Second) of Torts §402A, cmt i, at 352 (1965); see *Joseph E. Seagram & Sons, Inc. v. McGuire*, 814 S.W.2d 385, 388 (Tex. 1991) (following comment i). Good tobacco contains nicotine. If plaintiffs are right that nicotine is addictive, then addiction is merely one of the harmful effects of the tobacco itself and cannot therefore make otherwise good tobacco unreasonably dangerous. In fact, if the agents plaintiffs claim are addictive were removed from the tobacco, it would no longer be "good tobacco." One might as well smoke a maple leaf.

Second: The distinction between addiction and habituation, important in scientific contexts, is unimportant for purposes of comment i. The two ideas mean only one thing to smokers: it's hard to quit. This is not a new discovery, suddenly revealed by the Surgeon General in a 1988 report. Almost anyone who ever smoked for any length of time and tried to stop has found it hard;

many have found it impossible. Few understood why, in terms of psychological and biochemical body processes, but the difficulty was surely no less real merely because it could not fully be explained. [. . .]

Third: The risk of addiction is subsumed in the risk of cancer and similar health problems. Addiction is a danger at all only if the dependency is unhealthy. Addiction to smoking is dangerous, not because it is expensive or offensive to others, but because it increases the risk of lung cancer. Addiction itself is never fatal, and it can be overcome. People quit smoking. But smoking, whether because of addiction, habit, or free choice, can cause cancer that is fatal. It is an odd rule that affords recovery of damages to a plaintiff who says, "I smoked even though I knew I might get lung cancer, but I never would have done it had I known I might become addicted." [. . .]

Fourth: Even if addiction is a risk of smoking separate and apart from all the other health risks that are common knowledge and were common knowledge in 1952, and even if cigarettes are unreasonably dangerous because of that risk, a product liability claim should be limited to damages caused by *that* risk, not the risk of cancer. Yet the Court allows plaintiffs in this case to recover just as if no one had ever suspected that smoking causes cancer. If cigarettes are defective only because smoking may be addictive, plaintiffs' damages should be limited to those caused by the defect. The Court places no such limits on plaintiffs' recovery.

The Court says that "no expectation of safety arises with respect to cigarettes when they are purchased." I agree, but I do not understand why that fact is not fatal to the present litigation. [. . .] I would affirm the district court's summary judgment on all plaintiffs' claims.

NOTES

1. *Skull & Crossbones*. In Graves v. Church & Dwight, 631 A.2d 1248 (N.J. App. 1993), the plaintiff, Graves, awoke late one night with heartburn. Recalling a remedy his grandmother once had offered for his malady, he went to the kitchen, poured some Arm & Hammer baking soda into a glass, filled the glass with water, and drank it. An enormous pain immediately drove him to his hands and knees. He underwent surgery later that day; his evidence was that the baking soda combined with his stomach acid to create a large volume of gas that caused a rupture in his stomach. He sued the manufacturer of the baking soda for, among other things, failure to warn of this possible consequence of ingesting its product.

Graves's expert testified that there were probably "twenty ways" to offer an effective warning on the box:

> You can use the English language. You could use a pictograph of some picture of a stomach rupturing or something along those lines following somebody ingesting this product from a glass. [. . .] [A] circle and a slash

through it would do or an X across it would do to let people know not to do that. Alternatively, you might have to spell out the hazard in words but you also need to include an instruction to avoid harm and you might show a cup or a glass with the product in it and a circle with a circle and a slash through it to indicate that one shouldn't take it this way and then back up with the written language.

Graves conceded that he had not read the label on the box of baking soda before using it and that he had taken about three times the dosage recommended there. But he characterized himself as a "compulsive" reader, especially paying attention to product labels because he had a potentially fatal allergy to nuts. It also was the case that for at least five years prior to his accident, Graves had smoked two to three packs of cigarettes a day. He was aware that cigarettes bore a warning label from the Surgeon General concerning health hazards. Graves was asked at trial whether he would have smoked cigarettes on the morning of the accident if a skull and crossbones had been on the package of cigarettes. Graves said that he hadn't thought of that.

The jury found that the baking soda was defective in failing to carry a warning of the danger of stomach rupture from its use, but it also found that this failure to warn was not a proximate cause of Graves's use of the product. Graves appealed, claiming that he was entitled to a presumption that he would have heeded a proper warning if it had been provided. The court of appeals agreed that Graves was entitled to such a presumption, but held that in this case there was sufficient evidence to rebut it:

> The evidence concerning Graves' smoking, notwithstanding warnings on cigarette packages, was admitted without objection. Such evidence, in our view, provided the jury with a basis to make an analogy between Graves smoking in the face of the health warnings on cigarettes, and his projected behavior if a warning had been on the baking soda.

2. *The heeding presumption.* As *Graves* and *Grinnell* illustrate, many jurisdictions give plaintiffs the benefit of a "heeding presumption" that they would have obeyed suitable warnings. If the defendant offers no evidence to rebut the presumption it may be considered conclusive, with the plaintiff then entitled to a directed verdict on the issue. If the defendant offers significant evidence that the plaintiff would not have obeyed a warning — either because he would not have read any warning under the circumstances or because he was prone to disobeying safety warnings in other walks of life — then it becomes a question for the jury whether an appropriate warning would in fact have prevented the plaintiff's injuries, with the burden of persuasion on the plaintiff. Here as in other areas of products liability, the details of the rule and its procedural implementation vary by jurisdiction.

3. *McWarnings.* In Brown v. McDonald's Corp., 655 N.E.2d 440 (Ohio App. 1995), the plaintiff purchased a "McLean Deluxe" sandwich — a meatless simulation of a hamburger — from a drive-through window at a McDonald's in Ohio. Soon after ingesting the sandwich she developed a rash, a tight chest, blue lips, and hives; the symptoms required a five-hour hospital stay for treatment. The plaintiff sued McDonald's, claiming that she was allergic to seafood, that the McLean contained an ingredient (carrageenan) derived from seaweed, and that the restaurant should have warned its patrons of this. Her claims were based on Ohio Rev. Code §2307.73(A)(1)(b), which imposed liability for failing to warn of a risk if

> (b) The manufacturer failed to provide the warning or instruction that a manufacturer exercising reasonable care would have provided concerning that risk, in light of the likelihood that the product would cause harm of the type for which the claimant seeks to recover compensatory damages and in light of the likely seriousness of that harm.

McDonald's conceded that it issued no warnings with the McLean Deluxe, but said that a flier was available to its customers listing the ingredients in the sandwich. The plaintiff said that she did not receive the flier and had not known it was available. McDonald's further argued that the McLean posed no risk to ordinary consumers and thus that there was no duty to warn. To this the plaintiff responded with an affidavit from a medical expert asserting that her reaction may not have been as unusual as McDonald's claimed. The trial court gave summary judgment to McDonald's. The court of appeals reversed:

> [The statute] asks whether a manufacturer exercising reasonable care would warn of that risk in light of both the *likelihood* and the seriousness of the potential harm. Within this framework, whether the plaintiff's harm was unusual or not would be a factor in calculating whether a manufacturer exercised reasonable care in its decision not to warn. The incidence of the kind of harm at issue in the case is only one factor a jury would consider in finding a duty to warn.
>
> Comment *j* to Section 402 [of the Restatement (Second) of Torts] comments specifically upon the duty to warn in relation to consumers having allergies. It states:
>
>> In order to prevent the product from being unreasonably dangerous, the seller may be required to give directions or warning, on the container, as to its use. The seller may reasonably assume that those with common allergies, as for example to eggs or strawberries, will be aware of them, and he is not required to warn against them. Where, however, the product contains an ingredient to which a substantial number of the population are allergic, and the ingredient is one whose danger is not generally known, or if known is one which the consumer would reasonably not expect to find in the product, the seller is required to give warning against it, if he has knowledge, or by the application

of reasonable, developed human skill and foresight should have knowledge, of the presence of the ingredient and the danger.

Though [McDonald's] offered evidence that it neither knew nor should have known of the risk of an adverse reaction to carrageenan, that evidence is only probative, not dispositive. Taken together with the evidence offered by the Browns, and viewing it in a light most favorable to them, it is insufficient to merit summary judgment[.]

Note that this case, like some others we have considered, can be stylized as finding "liability" in only a limited sense. What the plaintiff won here was not a damage award but rather the right to have a jury decide (a) whether McDonald's had an obligation to warn in view of her evidence of the incidence and severity of her reaction to its product, and (b) whether the steps the restaurant took to notify its patrons of the ingredients used in the product — the fliers — were adequate. As *Brown* illustrates, the issues in failure to warn cases often raise issues of reasonableness that are difficult to keep away from juries. What are the pros and cons of making it so easy for a plaintiff to create a jury question?

Is there any inconsistency between *Brown v. McDonald's Corp.* and *Graves v. Church & Dwight*? Notice not only the different evidence in the two cases but also their procedural postures: the court in *Graves* affirmed a jury verdict; the court in *Brown* sent the case to a jury, and of course might have affirmed a jury verdict in the defendant's favor if one later had been produced and appealed, just as the court in *Graves* did. Similar reasoning might be used to distinguish *Graves* from *American Tobacco Co. v. Grinnell*; but might the two cases also be distinguished on their facts?

4. *The abandonment of comment j.* Cases in this section have mentioned comment j to §402A of the Restatement (Second) of Torts (1965). In addition to the language quoted in *Brown*, comment j provided that "[w]here warning is given, the seller may reasonably assume that it will be read and heeded; and a product bearing such a warning, which is safe for use if it is followed, is not in defective condition, nor is it unreasonably dangerous." That provision proved to be controversial. In Uloth v. City Tank Corp., 384 N.E.2d 1188, 1192 (Mass. 1978), the court offered these objections:

An adequate warning may reduce the likelihood of injury to the user of a product in some cases. We decline, however, to adopt any rule that permits a manufacturer or designer to discharge its total responsibility to workers by simply warning of the dangers of a product. Whether or not adequate warnings are given is a factor to be considered on the issue of negligence, but warnings cannot absolve the manufacturer or designer of all responsibility for the safety of the product. [I]n some circumstances a warning may not reduce the likelihood of injury. For example, where the danger is obvious, a warning may be superfluous. A designer may have no duty to warn of such dangers. [. . .]

Moreover, a user may not have a real alternative to using a dangerous product, as where a worker must either work on a dangerous machine or leave his job. [. . .] Further, a warning is not effective in eliminating injuries due to instinctual reactions, momentary inadvertence, or forgetfulness on the part of a worker. One of the primary purposes of safety devices is to guard against such foreseeable situations. [. . .]

Balanced against the somewhat limited effectiveness of warnings is the designer's ability to anticipate and protect against possible injuries. If a slight change in design would prevent serious, perhaps fatal, injury, the designer may not avoid liability by simply warning of the possible injury. We think that in such a case the burden to prevent needless injury is best placed on the designer or manufacturer rather than on the individual user of a product.

The Third Restatement cited *Uloth* approvingly and concluded that "[c]omment j of the Restatement, Second, is inconsistent with the judicial abandonment of the patent danger rule and with those cases that take the position that a warning will not absolve the manufacturer from the duty to design against dangers when a reasonable, safer design could have been adopted that would have reduced or eliminated the residuum of risk that remains even after a warning is provided."

5. *Meat grinders.* In Liriano v. Hobart Corp., 170 F.3d 264 (2d Cir. 1999), the plaintiff, Liriano, was using his hand to feed meat into a meat grinder whose safety guard had been removed. His hand was drawn into the grinding mechanism and severed from his arm. The grinder had been manufactured by the defendant, Hobart, in 1961. It came equipped with a guard, bolted in place, that prevented the user's hand from coming into contact with the grinding mechanism. The machine included no warnings of the dangers of removing the guard or using the grinder without it; in 1962, however, Hobart began adding such warnings to its grinders after learning that many purchasers of its machines were taking the safety guards off. In this case it was undisputed that the Super Associated supermarket where Liriano was working had removed the guard sometime after acquiring the machine. Liriano sued both Hobart and the supermarket, claiming that they should be held liable for failing to warn that the guard was missing and that his hand could get caught in the grinder. A jury brought in a verdict for Liriano, holding him one-third responsible for his injury and assigning the remaining responsibility to the defendants, with the supermarket bearing the larger share of it. The defendants appealed, claiming the evidence was insufficient to support a verdict against them as a matter of law. The court of appeals affirmed:

Liriano was only seventeen years old at the time of his injury and had only recently immigrated to the United States. He had been on the job at Super for only one week. He had never been given instructions about how to use the meat grinder, and he had used the meat grinder only two or three times. And, as [the trial judge] noted, the mechanism that injured Liriano would not have been visible to someone who was operating the grinder. It could be argued that such a combination of facts was not so unlikely that a court should say, as a matter of law, that the defendant could not have foreseen them or, if aware of them, need not have guarded against them by issuing a warning. Nevertheless, it remains the fact that meat grinders are widely known to be dangerous. Given that the position of the New York courts on the specific question before us is anything but obvious, we might well be of two minds as to whether a failure to warn that meat grinders are dangerous would be enough to raise a jury issue.

But to state the issue that way would be to misunderstand the complex functions of warnings. [. . .] One who grinds meat, like one who drives on a steep road, can benefit not only from being told that his activity is dangerous but from being told of a safer way. As we have said, one can argue about whether the risk involved in grinding meat is sufficiently obvious that a responsible person would fail to warn of that risk, believing reasonably that it would convey no helpful information. But if it is also the case — as it is — that the risk posed by meat grinders can feasibly be reduced by attaching a safety guard, we have a different question. Given that attaching guards is feasible, does reasonable care require that meat workers be informed that they need not accept the risks of using unguarded grinders? Even if most ordinary users may — as a matter of law — know of the risk of using a guardless meat grinder, it does not follow that a sufficient number of them will — as a matter of law — also know that protective guards are available, that using them is a realistic possibility, and that they may ask that such guards be used. It is precisely these last pieces of information that a reasonable manufacturer may have a duty to convey even if the danger of using a grinder were itself deemed obvious.

Newman, J., concurred:

Those who believe that every decision in human affairs is a rational one, influenced logically by the incentives and disincentives that inhere in a given set of circumstances, will think it perverse that a manufacturer can be liable for failure to warn about the hazard of a meat-grinder originally equipped with a safety guard that has subsequently been removed even though liability might not exist had no such guard been initially installed. Surely, the devout rationalists will say, a rule of law countenancing such seemingly contradictory results will create an incentive for meat-grinder manufacturers not to install safety guards in the first place, thereby obtaining at least the chance to escape liability that, under today's decision, is deemed appropriate for jury consideration. I acknowledge that the disincentive to install a safety guard might exist, but, as with many predictions made on the assumption that a disincentive to take action will result in the action not being taken (or that an incentive to take action will result in the action being taken), I think it is extremely doubtful that meat-grinder manufacturers will elect to forgo safety guards in the hope of avoiding failure-to-warn liability for meat-grinders from which such guards have been removed. We have been well advised that the life of the law is not logic but experience, see Oliver Wendell Holmes, Jr., *The Common Law* 1 (1891), and it is often the case that the life of life itself is not logic. Though rationality guides many human actions, it does not guide them all. Despite the disincentive arguably created by the imposition of liability in this case, manufacturers might well elect to install safety guards simply because they have some concern (humanitarian, not economic) that hands should not be severed by their machines.

6. *Useful but dangerous products.* Restatement (Second) of Torts, §402(A), comment k:

> *Unavoidably unsafe products.* There are some products which, in the present state of human knowledge, are quite incapable of being made safe for their intended and ordinary use. These are especially common in the field of drugs. An outstanding example is the vaccine for the Pasteur treatment of rabies, which not uncommonly leads to very serious and damaging consequences when it is injected. Since the disease itself invariably leads to a dreadful death, both the marketing and the use of the vaccine are fully justified, notwithstanding the unavoidable high degree of risk which they involve. Such a product, properly prepared, and accompanied by proper directions and warning, is not defective, nor is it *unreasonably* dangerous. The same is true of many other drugs, vaccines, and the like, many of which for this very reason cannot legally be sold except to physicians, or under the prescription of a physician. It is also true in particular of many new or experimental drugs as to which, because of lack of time and opportunity for sufficient medical experience, there can be no assurance of safety, or perhaps even of purity of ingredients, but such experience as there is justifies the marketing and use of the drug notwithstanding a medically recognizable risk. The seller of such products, again with the qualification that they are properly prepared and marketed, and proper warning is given, where the situation calls for it, is not to be held to strict liability for unfortunate consequences attending their use, merely because he has undertaken to supply the public with an apparently useful and desirable product, attended with a known but apparently reasonable risk.

A few courts responded to comment k by holding generally that manufacturers of properly made prescription drugs could not be held liable for claimed defects in the drugs' design so long as they were accompanied by appropriate warnings. The more usual approach has been to apply comment k on a case-by-case basis. In 1997, §6 of the Restatement (Third) (Products Liability) offered a different formulation:

(c) A prescription drug or medical device is not reasonably safe due to defective design if the foreseeable risks of harm posed by the drug or medical device are sufficiently great in relation to its foreseeable thera-peutic benefits that reasonable health-care providers, knowing of such foreseeable risks and therapeutic benefits, would not prescribe the drug or medical device for any class of patients.

It is not yet clear how the courts will respond to this new Restatement provision. For an early case rejecting it, see *Freeman v. Hoffman-LaRoche*, 618 N.W.2d 827 (Neb. 2000):

[T]he [Third Restatement's] test lacks flexibility and treats drugs of unequal utility equally. For example, a drug used for cosmetic purposes but which causes serious side effects has less utility than a drug which treats a deadly disease, yet also has serious side effects. In each case, the drugs would likely be useful to a class of patients under the reasonable physician standard for some class of persons. Consequently, each would be exempted from design defect liability. But under a standard that con-siders reasonable alternative design, the cosmetic drug could be subject to liability if a safer yet equally effective design was available. As a result, the reasonable physician standard of §6(c) of the Third Restatement has been described as a standard that in effect will never allow liability. However, a standard applying a risk utility test that focuses on the pres-ence or absence of a reasonable alternative design, although also rarely allowing liability, at least allows the flexibility for liability to attach in an appropriate case.

7. *The learned intermediary.* In Brooks v. Medtronic, Inc., 750 F.2d 1227 (4th Cir. 1984), the plaintiff, Brooks, suffered a heart attack and was advised by a physician at the hospital to be fitted with a pacemaker made by Medtronic. Brooks agreed and underwent implant surgery the next day. His evidence was that later that afternoon he experienced 15 episodes of ventricular fibrillation when the pacemaker's lead came loose from his heart. Each attack required the hospital staff to apply counter electrical shock treatments to restore his heart to a normal beat. His physician soon disconnected the pacemaker, and a few days later Brooks received a different model that did not cause these problems. Brooks brought a suit against Medtronic claiming that the lead used to attach the first pacemaker was defective because the prongs at the end of it were too short to remain lodged in the heart muscle. He also claimed that Medtronic failed to warn him of

the risk that the lead might come loose. It was undisputed at trial that dislodgment of a lead is a common risk when a pacemaker is implanted; Medtronic gave all doctors, including the physician treating Brooks, written warnings of the danger, but neither Medtronic nor the physician provided any warning of it to Brooks.

The district court instructed the jury that the manufacturer had a duty to warn physicians of any dangerous characteristics of a product that were not well known to the medical community. The jury brought in a verdict for Medtronic. Brooks appealed, arguing that the jury should have been told that Medtronic also had a duty to directly warn consumers of its products of known risks associated with implant surgery. The court of appeals affirmed:

> Although ordinarily warnings must be given to the ultimate user of a product, a different approach has been developed for prescription drugs. It is settled in a substantial majority of jurisdictions that the duty a manufacturer of ethical drugs "owes to the consumer is to warn only physicians (or other medical personnel permitted by state law to prescribe drugs) of any risks or contraindications associated with that drug." *Stanback v. Parke, Davis and Co.*, 657 F.2d 642, 644 (4th Cir. 1981). If the prescribing physician has received adequate notice of possible complications, the manufacturer has no duty to warn the consumer. In that instance, the physician is called on to act as a "learned intermediary" between the manufacturer and the consumer because he is in the best position to understand the patient's needs and assess the risks and benefits of a particular course of treatment.
>
> Brooks contends, nevertheless, that the prescription drug exception does not apply on the facts of his case. Two principal reasons are advanced. First, unlike the situation in prescription drug cases, he argues that all cardiac pacemaker patients face identical risks and do not rely on doctors to act as learned intermediaries. Second, Brooks notes that Medtronic, unlike drug manufacturers, often has an opportunity to contact its users prior to surgery. In support of these arguments, Brooks places reliance on a series of cases involving injuries caused by live polio vaccines in which a few courts have expanded the scope of a drug manufacturer's duty and held that the manufacturer is required to warn the public directly of risks associated with the live vaccine. The courts in those cases have expanded the duty to warn because the vaccines — part of a special nationwide immunization program — were dispensed without the sort of individualized medical balancing at the heart of the prescription drug exception.
>
> Appellant complains that an affirmance would abrogate the patient's right to know. That prediction overstates the case. The issue raised by the appeal is not whether information should be disclosed at all; instead, the question turns on who is in a better position to disclose risks. It is the physician's duty to remain abreast of product characteristics and,

exercising an informed professional judgment, decide which facts should be told to the patient. Once adequate warnings are given to the physician, the choice of treatment and the duty to disclose properly fall on the doctor. Indeed, we have little trouble imagining — particularly with cardiac patients — situations where total disclosure by a manufacturer would not be in the patient's best interest. One in a serious medical condition of the sort experienced by Brooks as a general matter faces unwanted, unsettling and potentially harmful risks if advice, almost inevitably involved and longwinded, from non-physicians, contrary to what the doctor of his choice has decided should be done, must be supplied to him during the already stressful period shortly before his trip to the operating room. We therefore hold that the district court's duty to warn instruction was proper.

8. *Direct marketing.* In Perez v. Wyeth Laboratories, 734 A.2d 1245 (N.J. 1999), the plaintiffs were women who used Norplant, a contraceptive device consisting of capsules implanted under the skin of a woman's upper arm; the capsules distributed a low, continuous dosage of a synthetic hormone into the user's bloodstream. The plaintiffs alleged that they suffered from various side effects, including weight gain, headaches, dizziness, nausea, acne, vision problems, anemia, mood swings and depression, high blood pressure, and complications from removal of the implants that resulted in scarring. They sued Wyeth, the maker of Norplant, claiming that it failed to adequately warn them of these possible side effects. They alleged that Wyeth began a massive advertising campaign for Norplant in 1991, which it directed at women rather than at their doctors. The company advertised on television and in women's magazines such as *Glamour, Mademoiselle*, and *Cosmopolitan*. None of the advertisements warned of the side effects.

The trial court dismissed the plaintiffs' complaint on the ground that the learned intermediary doctrine shielded Wyeth from liability. The New Jersey Supreme Court reversed, holding that the doctrine does not apply in cases where the manufacturer of a drug is alleged to have marketed it directly to consumers in a misleading fashion:

> Our medical-legal jurisprudence is based on images of health care that no longer exist. At an earlier time, medical advice was received in the doctor's office from a physician who most likely made house calls if needed. [. . .] Pharmaceutical manufacturers never advertised their products to patients, but rather directed all sales efforts at physicians. In this comforting setting, the law created an exception to the traditional duty of manufacturers to warn consumers directly of risks associated with the product as long as they warned health-care providers of those risks.
>
> For good or ill, that has all changed. Medical services are in large measure provided by managed care organizations. Medicines are purchased in the pharmacy department of supermarkets and often paid for by

third-party providers. Drug manufacturers now directly advertise products to consumers on the radio, television, the Internet, billboards on public transportation, and in magazines. [. . .]

[T]he dramatic shift in pharmaceutical marketing to consumers is based in large part on significant changes in the health-care system from fee-for-service to managed care. Managed care companies negotiate directly with pharmaceutical companies and then inform prescribers which medications are covered by the respective plans. Because managed care has made it more difficult for pharmaceutical companies to communicate with prescribers, the manufacturers have developed a different strategy, marketing to consumers.

The direct marketing of drugs to consumers generates a corresponding duty requiring manufacturers to warn of defects in the product. The FDA has established a comprehensive regulatory scheme for direct-to-consumer marketing of pharmaceutical products. Given the presumptive defense that is afforded to pharmaceutical manufacturers that comply with FDA requirements, we believe that it is fair to reinforce the regulatory scheme by allowing, in the case of direct-to-consumer marketing of drugs, patients deprived of reliable medical information to establish that the misinformation was a substantial factor contributing to their use of a defective pharmaceutical product.

The court summarized what it considered to be the premises of the "learned intermediary" rule — "(1) reluctance to undermine the doctor patient-relationship; (2) absence in the era of 'doctor knows best' of need for the patient's informed consent; (3) inability of drug manufacturer to communicate with patients; and (4) complexity of the subject"; and it concluded that those rationales "are all (with the possible exception of the last) absent in the direct-to-consumer advertising of prescription drugs."

McMahon v. Bunn-O-Matic Corp.
150 F.3d 651 (7th Cir. 1998)

[The plaintiff was a passenger in a car driven by her husband. He bought a cup of coffee at a Mobil service station, and she tried to transfer the coffee into a smaller cup that would be easier for him to handle. In the process she spilled the coffee onto herself and suffered second- and third-degree burns on her legs and abdomen. She brought suit in Indiana state court against the makers of the styrofoam cup in which the coffee was served (claiming that it collapsed), and against Bunn-O-Matic, maker of the machine that she alleged kept the coffee too hot. She claimed that Bunn failed to warn consumers about the severity of burns that hot coffee can produce, and that any coffee served at more than 140 degrees is unfit for human consumption (and therefore a defective product) because of its power to cause burns more severe than consumers expect, aggravated by its potential to damage the cup and thus increase the probability of spills. The defendants removed the case to federal court on diversity grounds. The maker of the cup settled, and the district court gave summary judgment to Bunn-O-Matic. This appeal followed.]

EASTERBROOK, J. [after stating the facts] — Let us tackle the contention that Bunn should have warned the McMahons about the dangers of hot coffee. What would this warning have entailed? A statement that coffee is served hot? That it can cause burns? They already knew these things and did not need to be reminded (as both conceded in their depositions). That this coffee was unusually hot and therefore capable of causing severe burns? Warning consumers about a surprising feature that is potentially dangerous yet hard to observe could be useful, but the record lacks any evidence that 179 degrees is unusually hot for coffee. Neither side submitted evidence about the range of temperatures used by commercial coffee makers, or even about the range of temperatures for Bunn's line of products. The McMahons essentially ask us to take judicial notice that 179 degrees is abnormal, but this is not the sort of incontestable fact for which proof is unnecessary. In [previous cases courts have] reported that the industry-standard serving temperature is between 175 degrees and 185 degrees, and if this is so then the McMahons' coffee held no surprises. What is more, most consumers prepare and consume hotter beverages at home. Angelina McMahon is a tea drinker, and tea is prepared by pouring boiling water over tea leaves. Until 20 years ago most home coffee was made in percolators, where the water boiled during the brewing cycle and took some time to cool below 180 degrees. Apparently the McMahons believe that home drip brewing machines now in common use are much cooler, but the record does not support this, and a little digging on our own part turned up ANSI/AHAM CM-1-1986, which the American National Standards Institute adopted for home coffee makers. Standard 5.2.1 provides: "On completion of the brewing cycle and within a 2 minute interval, the beverage temperature in the dispensing vessel of the coffee maker while stirring should be between the limits of 170 degrees and 205 degrees. The upper finished brew temperature limit assures that the coffee does not reach the boiling point which can affect the taste and aroma. The lower temperature limit assures generally acceptable drinking temperature when pouring into a cold cup, adding cream, sugar and spoon."

What remains is the argument that Bunn should have provided a detailed warning about the severity of burns that hot liquids can cause, even if 179 degrees is a standard serving temperature. The McMahons insist that, although they knew that coffee can burn, they thought that the sort of burn involved would be a blister painful for several days (that is, a second degree burn), not a third degree burn of the sort Angelina experienced. An affidavit submitted by Kenneth R. Diller, a professor of biomedical and biomechanical engineering, observed that "full thickness third degree burn injuries would require 60 seconds of exposure [to a liquid at] 140 degrees, but only 3 seconds of exposure at 179 degrees." We may assume that ordinary consumers do not know this — that, indeed, ordinary consumers do not know what a "full thickness third degree burn" is. But how, precisely, is this information to be conveyed by a coffee maker? Bunn can't deliver a medical education with each cup of coffee. Any person severely injured by any product could make a claim, at least as plausible as the McMahons', that they did not recognize the risks ex ante as clearly as they do after the accident.

Insistence on more detail can make any warning, however elaborate, seem inadequate. Indiana courts have expressed considerable reluctance to require ever-more detail in warnings. For good reasons, laid out in *Todd v. Societe BIC, S.A.*, 9 F.3d 1216, 1218-19 (7th Cir.1993) (en banc) (Illinois law): "Extended warnings present several difficulties, first among them that, the more text must be squeezed onto the product, the smaller the type, and the less likely is the consumer to read or remember any of it. Only pithy and bold warnings can be effective. Long passages in capital letters are next to illegible, and long passages in lower case letters are treated as boilerplate. Plaintiff wants a warning in such detail that a magnifying glass would be necessary to read it. Many consumers cannot follow simple instructions (including pictures) describing how to program their video cassette recorders." Indiana has the same general understanding. See *Marshall v. Clark Equipment Corp.*, 680 N.E.2d 1102, 1105 (Ind. App. 1997). To be useful, warnings about burns could not stop with abstract information about the relation among a liquid's temperature and volume (which jointly determine not only the number of calories available to impart to the skin but also the maximum rate of delivery), contact time (which determines how many of the available calories are actually delivered), and the severity of burns. It would have to address the risk of burns in real life, starting with the number of cups of coffee sold annually, the number of these that spill (broken down by location, such as home, restaurant, and car), and the probability that any given spill will produce a severe (as opposed to a mild or average) burn. Only after understanding these things could the consumer determine whether the superior taste of hot coffee justifies the incremental risk. Tradeoffs are complex. Few consumers could understand the numbers and reach an intelligent decision on the spot at a checkout counter. Yet such a detailed warning (equivalent to the package insert that comes with drugs) might obscure the principal point that precautions should be taken to avoid spills. Indiana does not require vendors to give warnings in the detail plaintiffs contemplate. It expects consumers to educate themselves about the hazards of daily life — of matches, knives, and kitchen ranges, of bones in fish, and of hot beverages — by general reading and experience, knowledge they can acquire before they enter a mini mart to buy coffee for a journey. [...]

[The court turned to the plaintiffs' claim that the coffeemaker was defective because it kept the coffee too hot.] With warnings out of the way, the remaining theory of liability comes into focus. Indiana has codified the principles of product liability at I.C. §33-1-1.5-3. (A new statute, effective July 1, 1998, appears at I.C. §34-20-2-1 and associated sections. Our attention is confined to the version in force when Angelina McMahon was injured.) Under §33-1-1.5-3(a) any person who sells "any product in a defective condition unreasonably dangerous to any user or consumer . . . is subject to liability." If the defect in question is a design defect (as opposed to a blunder in the manufacture of a well-designed product), then "the party making the claim must establish that the manufacturer or seller failed to exercise reasonable care under the circumstances in designing the product." In other words, a design-defect claim in Indiana is a negligence claim, subject to the understanding that negligence means failure to take precautions that are less expensive than the net costs of accidents. [. . .]

Coffee at 180 degrees F is considerably more likely to cause severe burns than is coffee at 135 degrees to 140 degrees, the maximum at which [the plaintiffs' expert] believes that coffee should be served. Moreover, because it is costly to serve coffee hot (it takes electricity to keep the hotplate on), risks could be reduced for a negative outlay. How can it not be negligent to spend money for the purpose of making a product more injurious? But of course people spend money to increase their risks all the time — they pay steep prices for ski vacations; they go to baseball games where flying bats and balls abound; they buy BB guns for their children knowing that the pellets can maim. They do these things because they perceive benefits from skiing, baseball, and target practice. *Moss*, the BB gun case, holds that Indiana does not condemn products as defective just because they are designed to do things that create serious hazards. To determine whether a coffee maker is defective because it holds the beverage at 179 degrees, we must understand the benefits of hot coffee in relation to its costs. As for costs, the record is silent. We do not know whether severe burns from coffee are frequent or rare. On the other side of the ledger there are benefits for all coffee drinkers. Jack McMahon testified that he likes his coffee hot. Why did the American National Standards Institute set 170 degrees F as the minimum temperature at which coffee should be held ready to serve? [. . .]

None of this would matter if it were obvious that consumers derive no benefits from coffee served hotter than 140 degrees; then the principle of res ipsa loquitur could do the rest of the work for the McMahons. The ANSI minimum of 170 degrees F prevents us from treating as obvious the absence of benefits from temperatures above 140 degrees. What is more, even a little investigation (albeit unassisted by the parties) shows that there may be good reasons for selecting a temperature over 170 degrees, as several other courts have recognized. See Michael Sivetz & H. Elliott Foote, 2 *Coffee Processing Technology* ch. 19.2 (1963). The smell (and therefore the taste) of coffee depends heavily on the oils containing aromatic compounds that are dissolved out of the beans during the brewing process. Brewing temperature should be close to 200 degrees to dissolve them effectively, but without causing the premature breakdown of these delicate molecules. Coffee smells and tastes best when these aromatic compounds evaporate from the surface of the coffee as it is being drunk. Compounds vital to flavor have boiling points in the range of 150 degrees to 160 degrees, and the beverage therefore tastes best when it is this hot and the aromatics vaporize as it is being drunk. For coffee to be 150 degrees when imbibed, it must be hotter in the pot. Pouring a liquid increases its surface area and cools it; more heat is lost by contact with the cooler container; if the consumer adds cream and sugar (plus a metal spoon to stir them) the liquid's temperature falls again. If the consumer carries the container out for later consumption, the beverage cools still further. Our point in discussing these issues is not to endorse Sivetz & Foote; their position may be scientifically contestable. It is only to demonstrate that without evidence that a holding temperature of 180 degrees is of little worth to consumers, plaintiffs cannot show that the choice of a high temperature makes coffee defective.

It is easy to sympathize with Angelina McMahon, severely injured by a common household beverage — and, for all we can see, without fault on her part. Using the legal system to shift the costs of this injury to someone else may be attractive to the McMahons, but it would have bad consequences for coffee fanciers who like their beverage hot. First-party health and accident insurance deals with injuries of the kind Angelina suffered without the high costs of adjudication, and without potential side effects such as lukewarm coffee. We do not know whether the McMahons carried such insurance (directly or through an employer's health plan), but we are confident that Indiana law does not make Bunn and similar firms insurers through the tort system of the harms, even grievous ones, that are common to the human existence.

Affirmed.

NOTES

1. *The McDonald's coffee case.* Perhaps the most famous tort case of our times is the McDonald's coffee case — the one where, as the man on the street knows, "a lady got $3 million for spilling hot coffee on herself." The case — Liebeck v. McDonald's Corp. — has no significance as a legal precedent; it did not generate a published opinion (see 1995 WL 360309 for a brief recitation of the findings). But the case has great significance in the mythology of American law, so every lawyer should know something about its actual details. The following summary is based on newspaper accounts of the incident and the litigation that followed.

The plaintiff, Stella Liebeck, was a 79-year-old former department store clerk. On February 27, 1992, when she was riding as a passenger in her grandson's car, she bought a cup of coffee for 49 cents from a drive-through window at a McDonald's in Albuquerque, New Mexico. Her grandson parked the car.

Liebeck held the cup between her legs so that she could use the fingers of both hands to pry off the lid. The coffee spilled out. She immediately began to scream. She was wearing sweatpants, but nevertheless sustained third-degree burns over 6 percent of her body, including her thighs and genitals. She spent seven days in the hospital, then three weeks recuperating at home, then returned to the hospital for skin grafts that by all accounts were extremely painful. She lost about 20 pounds. Her medical bills were over $20,000.

Liebeck attempted to settle the case without hiring a lawyer; she had never sued anybody before. She asked McDonald's for $15,000-$20,000 to cover her medical costs (the reimbursement of which apparently would have to have been returned to Medicare) and some of the lost wages incurred by her daughter, who had stayed home to take care of her. McDonald's offered her $800. Some friends put her in touch with a lawyer who had sued McDonald's over a coffee spill once before, and with his assistance she brought a lawsuit in New Mexico state court alleging that the coffee was a defective product (both because it was too hot and because it was not accompanied by appropriate warnings) and that McDonald's had breached various implied warranties. As trial approached she offered to settle the case for $300,000. McDonald's declined. A mediator appointed by the court predicted that a jury might award her $225,000, and recommended that McDonald's settle for that amount. McDonald's declined.

The trial lasted seven days. Experts for both sides debated the reasonableness of the temperature at which McDonald's serves its coffee. The plaintiff's evidence was that McDonald's written policy was to serve its coffee at 180-190 degrees, which is about 20 degrees hotter than the coffee served by McDonald's competitors. It takes less than three seconds to produce a third-degree burn at 190 degrees; it takes 12-15 seconds at 180 degrees, and about 20 seconds at 160 degrees. Over the previous 10 years McDonald's had received more than 700 complaints from people burned by its coffee, and had settled some of the resulting claims for more than $500,000. The jurors were shown gruesome photographs of Liebeck's injuries.

The expert for McDonald's, who was paid $15,000 for his participation in the case, testified that in view of the millions of cups of coffee McDonald's sells every year, 700 complaints in a decade is "basically trivially different from zero." Some of the jurors later said that this testimony troubled them. "Each statistic is somebody badly burned," said one of the jurors. "That really made me angry." A quality assurance official from McDonald's testified that the company had not made any adjustments in response to the complaints and had no plans to do so. The lawyer for McDonald's argued that Liebeck was to blame for mishandling the coffee.

The jury found McDonald's liable. It set Liebeck's compensatory damages at $200,000, but found that she was 20 percent to blame for the accident and so reduced her award to $160,000. They also awarded $2.9 million in punitive damages against McDonald's, which represented two days of the company's profits from coffee sales. "It was our way of saying, 'Hey, open your eyes. People are getting burned,'" one of the jurors said. The judge reduced the punitive damages award to $480,000 (three times Liebeck's compensatory damages), for a total award of $640,000. While the case was on appeal, McDonald's settled it for an undisclosed amount.

What is the distinction between *Liebeck v. McDonald's Corp.* and *McMahon v. Bunn-O-Matic Corp.*? What sorts of warnings should coffee cups contain? How should sellers of coffee decide how hot to serve it?

Chapter 9

Damages

We turn now to the last element of the negligence tort, and a critical element in any tort case regardless of the theory of liability involved: damages. It is easy for beginners to regard damages as an afterthought — to suppose that the hard part in a tort case is deciding whether there is liability, and that once liability is established the calculation of the plaintiff's damages tends to be simple or mechanical. But in fact there often is room for extensive argument not only about the factual details of the plaintiff's losses but about how the losses ought to be measured as a matter of law. Indeed, in many cases the plaintiff's liability is clear from the outset, and the negotiations in the case (and the trial, if there is one) concern nothing but damages.

There are three principal types of damages that a plaintiff may seek in a tort suit: nominal damages, which are small amounts — typically a dollar — just meant to establish that the plaintiff's rights were invaded; compensatory damages, which are intended to replace what the plaintiff has lost; and punitive damages, which are intended to deter the defendant and other potential tortfeasors from committing such misconduct again. We will be spending most of our time in this chapter considering how to measure compensatory damages, which are sought in almost every tort suit. We also will consider punitive damages a bit more briefly.

A. COMPENSATORY DAMAGES

1. *Damage to Property*

United States v. Hatahley
257 F.2d 920 (10th Cir. 1958)

[The plaintiffs were members of the Navajo tribe who claimed that federal agents wrongfully seized their horses and donkeys and sold them to a horse

517

meat plant and a glue factory. The trial court found for the plaintiffs and awarded them $186,017.50. The value of each horse or donkey taken was fixed at $395; each plaintiff was awarded $3,500 for mental pain and suffering; and damages were given for one-half of the value of the diminution of the plaintiffs' herds of sheep, goats, and cattle between the time the horses and donkeys were taken in 1952 and the date of the last hearing in 1957. The United States appealed.]

PICKETT, *Circuit Judge* [after stating the facts:] — The fundamental principle of damages is to restore the injured party, as nearly as possible, to the position he would have been in had it not been for the wrong of the other party. Applying this rule, the plaintiffs were entitled to the market value, or replacement cost, of their horses and burros as of the time of taking, plus the use value of the animals during the interim between the taking and the time they, acting prudently, could have replaced the animals.

The plaintiffs did not prove the replacement cost of the animals, but relied upon a theory that the animals taken were unique because of their peculiar nature and training, and could not be replaced. The trial court accepted this theory, and relying upon some testimony that a horse or a burro could be traded among Indians for sheep, goats or cattle worth a stated price, together with the owner's testimony of the value, arrived at a market value of $395 per head. No consideration was given to replacement cost. The court rejected evidence of the availability of like animals in the immediate vicinity, and their value. This, we think, was error. It is true that animals of a particular strain and trained for a special purpose are different from animals of another strain and not so trained, but that does not mean that they cannot be replaced by animals similarly developed and trained, or which may be trained after acquisition. Ordinarily every domestic animal is developed and trained for the purpose to which the owner intends to use it. This development and training adds to its usefulness and generally increases the market value of the animal. In arriving at a fair market value of destroyed animals, the court should have considered evidence of the availability of like animals, together with all other elements which go to make up market value. In proper instances, parties and witnesses may be cross-examined on the subject.

Likewise, we think the court applied an erroneous rule, wholly unsupported by the evidence, in arriving at the amount of loss of use damage. There was testimony by the plaintiffs that because of the loss of their horses and burros they were not able to maintain and look after as much livestock as they had been able to before the unlawful taking, consequently the size of their herds was reduced. If the unlawful taking of the animals was the proximate cause of the herd reductions, the measure of damages would be the loss of profits occasioned thereby.

Applying the same formula to all plaintiffs, the court, without giving consideration to the condition, age or sex of the animals, found the value of the sheep and goats in 1952 to be $15 per head, the cattle to be $150 per head. The number of sheep, goats and cattle which each plaintiff had in 1952, as well as the number which each had at the date of the last hearing was established. This difference was multiplied by $15, in the case of sheep and goats, and by $150, in the case of cattle, and judgment was entered for one-half of the amount of the result. No consideration was given to the disposition of the livestock by the plaintiffs in reducing the herds. For example, the plaintiff Sakezzie had 600 sheep and goats and 101 head of cattle when his horses and burros were taken in 1952. At the date of the last hearing in 1957, he had 160 head of sheep and goats and 39 head of cattle. The dollar value of the difference at $15 per head for the sheep and goats, and $150 per head for the cattle, amounted to $15,900. The court found "that approximately fifty percent of this amount represents damages to the plaintiff proximately caused by deprivation of the use of plaintiff's horses, and on this basis plaintiff is entitled to recover $7,950.00 as consequential damages resulting from such deprivation." The result, insofar as it related to use damage, was arbitrary, pure speculation, and clearly erroneous. In *United States v. Huff*, 175 F.2d 678 (5th Cir. 1949), a case where the method of computing damages for loss of sheep and goats was strikingly similar to that used here, the court said:

> Moreover, there has been no sufficient showing of how much of the damage from the loss of the sheep and goats was proximately caused by the Government's failure to maintain and repair the fences under the lease, and how much of the damage resulted from the various other causes. There is no testimony whatever as to the specific dates of loss of any of the sheep and goats, or as to their age, weight, condition and fair market value at the time of the alleged losses. It therefore becomes patent that the evidence as to the loss of these animals in each case fails to rise above mere speculation and guess.

175 F.2d 680.

Plaintiffs' evidence indicated that the loss of their animals made it difficult and burdensome for them to obtain and transport needed water, wood, food, and game, and curtailed their travel for medical care and to tribal council meetings and ceremonies. Plaintiffs also testified that because of the loss of their animals they were not able to grow crops and gardens as extensively as before. These were factors upon which damages for loss of use could have been based. This does not exclude the right to damages for loss of profits which may have resulted from reduction of the number of livestock, or actual loss of the animals, if the unlawful acts of the defendant agents were the proximate cause of the loss and were proved to a reasonable degree of certainty. But the right to such damages does not extend forever, and it is limited to the time in which a prudent person would replace the destroyed horses and burros. The law requires only that the United States make full reparation for the pecuniary loss which their agents inflicted.

The District Court awarded each plaintiff the sum of $3,500 for mental pain and suffering. There is no evidence that any plaintiff was physically injured when his horses and burros were taken. There was evidence that because of the seizure of their animals and the continued activity of government agents and white ranchers to rid the public range of trespassers, the plaintiffs and their families were frightened, and after the animals were taken, they were "sick at heart, their dignity suffered, and some of them cried." There was considerable evidence that some of the plaintiffs mourned the loss of their animals for a long period of time. We think it quite clear that the sum given each plaintiff was wholly conjectural and picked out of thin air. The District Court seemed to think that because the horses and burros played such an important part in the Indians' lives, the grief and hardships were the same as to each. The equal award to each plaintiff was based upon the grounds that it was not possible to separately evaluate the mental pain and suffering as to each individual, and that it was a community loss and a community sorrow.

Apparently the court found a total amount which should be awarded to all plaintiffs for pain and suffering, and divided it equally among them. There was no more justification for such division than there would have been in using the total value of the seized animals and dividing it equally among the plaintiffs. Pain and suffering is a personal and individual matter, not a common injury, and must be so treated. While damages for mental pain and suffering, where there has been no physical injury, are allowed only in extreme cases, they may be awarded in some circumstances. Any award for mental pain and suffering in this case must result from the wrongful taking of plaintiffs' animals by agents of the United States, and nothing else. [. . .]

Reversed, and remanded for a new trial as to damages only.

NOTES

1. *General principles.* From the Restatement (Second) of Torts (1965):

§911. VALUE

(1) As used in this Chapter, value means exchange value or the value to the owner if this is greater than the exchange value.

(2) The exchange value of property or services is the amount of money for which the subject matter could be exchanged or procured if there is a market continually resorted to by traders, or if no market exists, the amount that could be obtained in the usual course of finding a purchaser or hirer of similar property or services. The rental value of property is the exchange value of the use of the property.

Comment e. Peculiar value to the owner. The phrase "value to the owner" denotes the existence of factors apart from those entering into exchange value that cause the article to be more desirable to the owner than to others. Some things may have no exchange value but may be valuable to the owner; other things may have a comparatively small exchange value but have a special and greater value to the owner. The absence or inadequacy of the exchange value may result from the fact that others could not or would not use the thing for any purpose, or would employ it only in a less useful manner. Thus a personal record or manuscript, an artificial eye or a dog trained to obey only one master, will have substantially no value to others than the owner. The same is true of articles that give enjoyment to the user but have no substantial value to others, such as family portraits. Second-hand clothing and furniture have an exchange value, but frequently the value is far less than its use value to the owner. In these cases it would be unjust to limit the damages for destroying or harming the articles to the exchange value.

Real property may also have a value to the owner greater than its exchange value. Thus a particular location may be valuable to an occupant because of a business reason, as when he has built up good will in a particular neighborhood. Even when the subject matter has its chief value in its value for use by the injured person, if the thing is replaceable, the damages for its loss are limited to replacement value, less an amount for depreciation. If the subject matter cannot be replaced, however, as in the case of a destroyed or lost family portrait, the owner will be compensated for its special value to him, as evidenced by the original cost, and the quality and condition at the time of the loss. Likewise an author who with great labor has compiled a manuscript, useful to him but with no exchange value, is entitled, in case of its destruction, to the value of the time spent in producing it or necessary to spend to reproduce it. In these cases, however, damages cannot be based on sentimental value. Compensatory damages are not given for emotional distress caused merely by the loss of the things, except that in unusual circumstances damages may be awarded for humiliation caused by deprivation, as when one is deprived of essential articles of clothing. If the article was wantonly destroyed, punitive damages can be awarded.

§912. CERTAINTY

One to whom another has tortiously caused harm is entitled to compensatory damages for the harm if, but only if, he establishes by proof the extent of the harm and the amount of money representing adequate compensation with as much certainty as the nature of the tort and the circumstances permit.

Comment f. Interference with a gift or chance for gain. [. . .] In cases in which there has been an interference with property from which a profit was expected, it may clearly appear at the trial that no profit would have been made. If so, the injured person is entitled to, but no more than, the diminution in the value of the property caused by the interference, or the total value if destroyed. Since, however, this value will normally be taken as of the time of the tort, damages will be awarded proportionate to the chance, as the situation appeared at the time of the tort, that profits would be made. When, however, there has been an interference with a right that is nontransferable and it subsequently appears that the exercise of the right would not have been profitable, the plaintiff is not entitled to substantial damages.

Illustration 16. A is one of the three remaining contestants for a prize to be awarded in a newspaper popularity contest, all three remaining contestants having received substantially the same number of votes. For the purpose of discrediting A, B, a friend of one of the other contestants, causes A to be arrested, thus destroying A's chance of winning the prize, $3000. Assuming that there was more than a mere possibility that A might have won the prize, A is entitled to damages from B based on the value of the chance that he would have received the prize, that is, in the absence of further evidence, $1000.

Illustration 17. A is a tenant for a year who has planted his crop. B, the landlord, tortiously drives him from the land in May, at which time the weather and other conditions indicate that the crop will be a very profitable one. In August an excessively dry spell burns up all the crops in the immediate neighborhood. A is nevertheless entitled to recover the value of the crop of which he was dispossessed, the value being based upon the May prices for the crop.

Illustration 18. A is one of three young women who have been selected by popular vote to take screen tests for the purpose of determining which one is to be starred in a picture. B tortiously prevents A from taking the test and another of the contestants is selected. Later, however, A is given a screen test, as a result of which it is admitted that A could not have been successful in the contest. A is not entitled to substantial damages from B.

§918. AVOIDABLE CONSEQUENCES

(1) Except as stated in Subsection (2), one injured by the tort of another is not entitled to recover damages for any harm that he could have avoided by the use of reasonable effort or expenditure after the commission of the tort.

(2) One is not prevented from recovering damages for a particular harm resulting from a tort if the tortfeasor intended the harm or was aware of it and was recklessly disregardful of it, unless the injured person with knowledge of the danger of the harm intentionally or heedlessly failed to protect his own interests.

Illustration 2. A, a trespasser upon B's pasture, negligently leaves open a gate in the fence. B sees that the gate is open but carelessly fails to close it, as a result of which B's cattle escape and are lost. B is not entitled to damages for the loss of his cattle.

Illustration 5. A destroys a fence on B's land, intending for B's cattle to escape. B sees what is happening but in the belief that A would be responsible for all harm caused by the destruction of the fence, intentionally fails to prevent his cattle from escaping as he easily could do. B is not entitled to recover damages for harm caused to his cattle by their escape.

Illustration 6. A sets fire to a haystack near B's barn, not caring whether B's barn with its contents will be destroyed. The fire spreads to the barn. B sees the fire but instead of using an available hose to put out the comparatively small blaze as a reasonable man would have done, he runs to the neighboring farm to spread the alarm. On his return it is too late to save the barn. In an action for trespass to land, B can recover damages for the loss of the barn.

Comment b. Amount by which damages are reduced. Except when the rule stated in Subsection (2) is applicable, a person who fails to avert the consequences of a tort, which he could do with slight effort, is entitled to no damages for the consequences. If harm results because of his careless failure to make substantial efforts or incur expense, the damages for the harm suffered are reduced to the value of the efforts he should have made or the amount of expense he should have incurred, in addition to the harm previously caused.

Illustration 8. A tortiously destroys B's fence. Although B knows the facts and is able to build a temporary barrier at an expense of $20, he fails to do so and his cattle worth $500 stray from the field and are lost. B is entitled to recover only $20 in addition to the value of the destroyed fence.

Comment e. When substantial expense and effort are required. A person whose body has been hurt or whose things have been damaged may not be unreasonable in refusing to expend money or effort in repairing the hurt or preventing further harm. Whether or not he is unreasonable in refusing the effort or expense depends upon the amount of harm that may result if he does not do so, the chance that the harm will result if nothing is done, the amount of money or effort required as a preventive, his ability to provide it and the likelihood that the measures will be successful. There must also be considered the personal situation of the plaintiff. A poor man cannot be expected to diminish his resources by the expenditure of an amount that might be expected from a person of greater wealth. So too, whether it is unreasonable for a slightly injured person not to seek medical advice may depend on his ability to pay for it without financial embarrassment. Likewise when a person seeks to recover damages for loss of profits or because the tortfeasor has prevented him from taking advantage of a favorable market, his financial ability to provide a substitute for that of which he has been deprived is relevant. If he has adequate resources, he must use them to minimize the loss.

§919. HARM SUFFERED AND EXPENDITURES MADE IN EFFORTS
         TO AVERT HARM

(1) One whose legally protected interests have been endangered by the tortious conduct of another is entitled to recover for expenditures reasonably made or harm suffered in a reasonable effort to avert the harm threatened.

(2) One who has already suffered injury by the tort of another is entitled to recover for expenditures reasonably made or harm suffered in a reasonable effort to avert further harm.

Illustration 2. A destroys B's fence and causes B's pigs worth approximately $50 to escape. B hunts for the pigs for a period of a week, expecting daily to find them, which he finally does. It may be found that B's efforts in searching for the pigs were reasonable, even though the value of the total time spent in searching for them exceeds their value, since it may have been reasonable to continue the search from day to day.

§920. BENEFIT TO PLAINTIFF RESULTING FROM DEFENDANT'S TORT

When the defendant's tortious conduct has caused harm to the plaintiff or to his property and in so doing has conferred a special benefit to the interest of the plaintiff that was harmed, the value of the benefit conferred is considered in mitigation of damages, to the extent that this is equitable.

Comment a. The rule stated in this Section normally requires that the damages allowable for an interference with a particular interest be diminished by the amount to which the same interest has been benefited by the defendant's tortious conduct. Thus if a surgeon performs an unprivileged operation resulting in pain and suffering, it may be shown that the operation averted future suffering. If a surgeon has destroyed an organ of the body, it may be shown in mitigation that the operation improved other bodily functions.

Comment b. Limitation to same interest. Damages resulting from an invasion of one interest are not diminished by showing that another interest has been benefited. Thus one who has harmed another's reputation by defamatory statements cannot show in mitigation of damages that the other has been financially benefited from their publication, unless damages are claimed for harm to pecuniary interests. Damages for pain and suffering are not diminished by showing that the earning capacity of the plaintiff has been increased by the defendant's act. Damages to a husband for loss of consortium are not diminished by the fact that the husband is no longer under the expense of supporting the wife.

Illustration 4. A charges B with murder. In an action for defamation in which B claims no special damages, the defendant cannot show in mitigation that the business of B, a seller of soft drinks, has been increased as the result of the charge.

Illustration 5. A charges B with being a member of a secret order. B brings an action for defamation alleging as special damage the loss of income by B as a surgeon. A can show in mitigation of damages that because of the false charge, B has been enabled to attract crowds to lectures given by him, to his great profit.

Illustration 6. A tortiously imprisons B for two weeks. In an action brought by B for false imprisonment in which damages are claimed for pain, humiliation and physical harm, A is not entitled to mitigate damages by showing that at the end of the imprisonment B obtained large sums from newspapers for writing an account of the imprisonment.

Comment c. Benefits common to the community. Although ordinarily the damages for harming land are measured by the difference in its value before and after the tort, it would be unjust to apply this measure of recovery when the tortious conduct increases values in the vicinity generally and at the same time causes special harm to the plaintiff. Therefore, the rule stated in this Section is limited to situations in which the tortious act has conferred a benefit in which the public generally does not share. Thus one whose house is continuously shaken by the operation of an adjoining factory is entitled to damages although the factory is so beneficial to the neighborhood that it enables the plaintiff to obtain more rent for his house than he did before.

Comment d. Causation. Under the rule stated in this Section to justify a diminution of damages the benefit must result from the tortious conduct. Thus one who, in boring for oil, fails to control the well, thereby causing the plaintiff's land and house to be covered with petroleum, is not entitled to have the damages reduced by showing that his success in drilling for oil in his land resulted in an increase in value of the plaintiff's land; the increase does not result from the tortious inundation but from the fact that oil is discovered. [...]

Illustration 8. A knocks B down, as a result of which B is prevented from taking a ship that later sinks with all on board. B's damages for the battery are not diminished by his escape from death resulting from A's act. B, however, cannot recover damages for failing to receive medical treatment that he would have received if he had not missed the ship and the ship had not sunk.

Illustration 9. A fraudulently persuades B to purchase Blackacre for $3000, although its value at that time is $2000. Had Blackacre been as represented, the value would have been $3500. The following week changes in the neighborhood cause Blackacre to appreciate in value to $5000. B's measure of recovery is not diminished by the subsequent rise in market value.

2. *Compensation for property.* Consider the following problems involving compensatory damages for the tortious destruction of property. It sometimes may be important to identify details not given in the problems that would affect your answers.

a. Plaintiff locks her bicycle to a lamppost near a curb. In parking his car, defendant negligently backs into the bicycle and crushes it. How should plaintiff's damages be measured? What are the options?

b. The defendant negligently crashes his car into a telephone pole; the pole is destroyed. The phone company (the owner of the pole) sues. The defendant's liability is clear. How should the plaintiff's damages be measured?

c. The plaintiff had 32 reels of film of all of her family's big events: weddings, little league games, Christmases, long-lost family members, etc. She gave them to the defendant's camera store to splice together and put onto videotape; as she handed them over, she said, "don't lose these; they are my life." The defendant lost them. How should the plaintiff's damages be measured? (Assume no contractual limitations on the store's liability.)

d. Defendant negligently burns plaintiff's house down to its foundation. Three months later a sinkhole opens and swallows up the foundation; it is clear that it would have swallowed up the entire house if the house still had been standing. What are plaintiff's damages?

e. Plaintiff is fired from her job, and remains unemployed for three months. Then, to her surprise, she obtains a new job that pays twice as well as her old one. Meanwhile she has determined that back when she was fired, she was the victim of the tort of wrongful discharge. What are her damages?

2. *Lost Earnings*

The most important elements of compensatory damages in a personal injury case (as opposed to a case involving property damage) typically are lost wages, pain and suffering, and medical expenses. We will focus on the first two of these elements because they present the most difficult and interesting problems. As we shall see, some of these elements come into play not only in lawsuits to recover for injuries suffered by the plaintiff but also in suits for *wrongful death*. A bit of background will be helpful here. At common law there was no such thing as a lawsuit for wrongful death. If someone was killed by another's negligence, neither the decedent's estate nor the decedent's family could bring a suit to collect damages; the decedent's cause of action died with him. It thus generally was cheaper to negligently kill people than to negligently injure them. This state of affairs was changed in England in 1846 by Lord Campbell's Act, and in the United States by wrongful death statutes subsequently passed in every state. The statutes differ somewhat in the sorts of suits they allow, but generally they permit the survivors of someone killed by a tortfeasor to collect for the losses — chiefly loss of economic support, but usually also "loss of society," or companionship — that they have incurred as a result of their decedent's death. Some states also allow "survival actions," in which the decedent's estate sues to collect damages in the decedent's name — i.e., any sums the decedent would have been entitled to collect from the defendant if he had lived.

Either sort of statute can raise many difficult problems of valuation, and the details of the statutory schemes, including the sorts of damages they permit survivors to collect, often vary widely from one state to the next. The general point to grasp is that if someone is sued for negligently causing a death, the basis of the lawsuit will be a statute, not the common law. In wrongful death cases it therefore becomes important to know precisely what sort of recovery the governing statute permits. Certain common problems in assessing damages nevertheless may arise in either a wrongful death suit or in an ordinary suit at common law to recover for personal injuries. For example, if a plaintiff is injured in an automobile accident, lost earnings may be an element of the resulting common law claim for damages; if a person dies in the accident, then lost earnings are likely to be an element of the statutory wrongful death suit brought by the decedent's spouse.

1. *Carpenters.* In Landers v. Ghosh, 491 N.E.2d 950 (Ill. App. 1986), Charles Landers was shot by a stranger at a gas station in Cahokia. He was taken to the emergency room at a nearby hospital. The plaintiff's evidence was that the defendant, Dr. Ghosh, was called, and said he would come soon; in fact Ghosh was about to perform an operation at another hospital, and he did not arrive to help Landers until about three hours later. Landers died during surgery. Landers's wife sued Ghosh for negligence and won a jury verdict against him. With respect to damages, the plaintiff's evidence was that Charles Landers was 22 years old when he died. He was unemployed. He had not graduated from high school, but had passed a high school equivalency exam and had been trained as a carpenter. The plaintiff's expert, one Grossman, created an estimate of Landers's lost earnings by assuming that he would have remained healthy and been fully employed as a carpenter until his late sixties; that he would have started out making between $11 and $12 per hour; and that he would have consumed 30 percent of his income himself. Grossman concluded by estimating that the total loss to Landers's family from losing his support would be $411,349. Grossman also estimated that Landers would have provided $1,000 in services around the house each year, for a value over his lifetime of about $40,000-$60,000.

The jury awarded Landers's wife a total of $400,000 — an amount meant to cover not only his wife's damages for loss of support but also her damages for loss of consortium (or "loss of society"). The verdict did not indicate how much of the amount was allocated to each of those categories. The plaintiff appealed, claiming the award was inadequate. The court of appeals affirmed:

> The plaintiff suggests that the amount of the verdict rendered here is adequate to compensate the decedent's wife only for her loss of consortium, "ignoring the other significant elements of damages discussed herein," including the absence of the decedent during the minority of

his son, estimated by the plaintiff to be of a value "well in excess of $100,000.00." From the instant record, however, it does not appear either that the jury compensated the decedent's wife solely for her loss of consortium, ignoring the other aspects of damages about which they were instructed, or that the jury awarded damages solely for the lost wages of the decedent. The jury apparently chose, as it was free to do, not to adopt the figures provided by Leroy Grossman, perhaps in part because of the seasonal nature of the occupation the decedent hoped to pursue, the effect of which the witness Grossman had not addressed in his calculations. The jury may have rejected his figures in part because of other considerations explored during cross-examination of him, in part because the decedent apparently was a smoker, or in part because the decedent appears to have been unemployed at the time of his death. Although we cannot know the reasoning of the jury in this regard, the record here does not support the conclusion that the award is palpably inadequate, that the jury ignored a proven element of damages, that the award was erroneous or the result of passion or prejudice, or that the amount of the verdict bears no reasonable relationship to the loss incurred.

2. *Oil executives*. In Pescatore v. Pan American World Airways, Inc., 887 F. Supp. 71 (E.D.N.Y. 1995), Michael Pescatore was a passenger on Pan Am flight 103 from London to New York in December 1988. A bomb exploded on the aircraft, causing the plane to come apart over Lockerbie, Scotland. The 243 passengers and 16 crew members all were killed. Survivors of many of the passengers brought wrongful death claims against Pan Am. A jury made a general finding, applicable to all of the cases, that Pan Am had committed willful misconduct in failing to determine whether every bag checked onto the airplane was matched to a passenger on the flight, and in failing to inspect any bag that was unaccompanied by a passenger. The case brought by Pescatore's wife was then submitted to a jury individually to determine her damages.

Michael Pescatore was 33 years old when he died. He had obtained an undergraduate degree in physics from Harvard, and an M.B.A. from the University of Chicago; he then went to work for British Petroleum (BP), and became the youngest vice president in the company's history. Executives from British Petroleum testified that Pescatore was "well positioned to move up in BP to the very, very high levels," was "probably the cream" of BP's young executives, and was rising through the corporate ranks "[f]aster than any contemporary." His total compensation for 1988 was estimated to have been $193,175. The plaintiff's expert estimated that her lost support over the course of Pescatore's lifetime amounted to between $25,500,000 and $73,980,000 in 1988 dollars. The defendant's expert valued the loss of support damages at approximately $2,400,000. The jury awarded Pescatore's wife $9 million in compensation for her husband's lost earnings, and an additional $5 million for loss of society. Pan Am moved for a new trial, contending the verdict was excessive; the district court denied the motion:

> Arguments that a rapidly rising executive officer, such as Michael Pescatore, would not have contributed, with reasonable foreseeability, $9 million to his wife over the ensuing thirty years border on the frivolous. Quite apart from the testimony in the case, to find the jury acted reasonably one need only consider the present compensation for top corporate officers of major corporations similar to British Petroleum. For example: (1) the aggregate compensation over the last three years for the Chief Executive Officer (CEO) of Exxon was $9,643,000; (2) the aggregate compensation over the last five years for the CEO of Amoco was $9,518,000; (3) the aggregate compensation over the last five years for the CEO of Occidental Petroleum was $22,897,000; and (4) the aggregate compensation over the last three years for the CEO of Texaco was $7,426,000. [. . .]
>
> Similarly, the arguments that an award of $5 million for loss of society, love, caring, comfort, affection and companionship, measured over a projected period of at least thirty years (circa $167,000 per year), is excessive are also without merit. The testimonials to Michael Pescatore's character, affectionate relationship with his immediate family and friends, and his deep and abiding love and affection for his wife were extensive, moving and uncontradicted. That part of plaintiff's testimony which recounted her receipt of the news of her husband's death was and is unforgettable.

The court of appeals affirmed. 97 F.3d 1 (2d Cir. 1996). Are the dramatically different recoveries in *Landers* and *Pescatore* justifiable?

3. *Housewives.* In Haddigan v. Harkins, 441 F.2d 844 (3d Cir. 1970), the plaintiff's wife was killed in a three-car automobile collision. The plaintiff sued the drivers of the other cars under Pennsylvania's wrongful death statute and won a jury verdict for $64,754.30. The court of appeals reversed because of various errors in the trial, but it affirmed the plaintiff's method of making his case for damages:

> [D]efendants urge that it was error to admit expert testimony on the economic value of services rendered by a wife and mother. Mr. Haddigan testified on direct examination that the decedent's services for her family included services each week as a cook, 17½ hours; as a dishwasher, 14 hours; as a dietician, 2 hours; as a baker, 3 hours; as a practical nurse, 1 hour; as a chambermaid, 7 hours; as a manager, 10 hours; as a seamstress, 5 hours; as a hostess, 2 hours; as a housekeeper, 16 hours; as a governess, 20 hours; as a recreation worker, 5 hours; as a handyman, 8 hours; as a laundress, 10 hours; and as a waitress, 5 hours.

(This left her 42½ hours a week, or six hours a day for all her other activities including sleeping.) Plaintiff then produced a witness, Rosner, an employment agency proprietor who specializes in placement of domestics, dishwashers, cooks, etc. Rosner was asked, without objection, to give the hourly rates of pay commanded by each of the above mentioned employment categories as of 1963 and as of 1967. Then, totaling the hours and the wages, he valued decedent's services in 1963 at $173.25 a week, and in 1967 at $236.72 a week. [. . .]

But, say the defendants, assuming there was evidence, properly admitted, to establish the value of decedent's services, the plaintiff offered little or no evidence of the cost which would have been incurred to maintain her while she performed those services. As one might expect, the attorney for plaintiff was considerably more enthusiastic in establishing the extent and value of the lost services than in establishing the cost of maintenance of decedent. There is, however, ample proof in the record from which the jury could make a fair determination.

4. *Opportunity cost.* Suppose a woman graduates from law school and takes a job at a law firm at an annual salary of $100,000. After three years she quits so that she can raise her children. Two years later she is killed by a negligent automobile driver. Some economists have suggested that in a case such as this, the appropriate damages due to the decedent's family for lost support must be at least $100,000 per year. The logic is that regardless of what the pecuniary cost would have been of replacing the decedent's services around the house, her family must have considered those services to be worth more than $100,000 — for that is what she gave up in order to stay at home (setting aside the costs of substitute child care); if her services had been worth less than $100,000 to the family, then presumably she would have kept her job. This measure of damages thus involves looking at what economists call the *opportunity cost* of the decedent's services. (Every decision to allocate resources has opportunity costs as well as costs of the more direct and familiar variety; what are the opportunity costs of your decision to attend law school?) No court takes this approach to measuring tort damages, however. What are its shortcomings?

If you find the "opportunity cost" approach attractive, consider a variation on it: suppose that Michael Pescatore had quit his job at British Petroleum a year before he died so that he could pursue his dream of becoming an oil painter, Zen master, or member of another such profession unlikely to be remunerative. Should his wife nevertheless have been entitled to collect $14 million using the "opportunity cost" theory just described? Should she at least still be able to collect the $5 million for loss of society? Is this case distinguishable from the case of the housewife?

5. *Mitigation of damages.* In Benwell v. Dean, 57 Cal. Rptr. 394 (Cal. App. 1967), the plaintiff brought a wrongful death suit to collect for the loss

of support and loss of society that she alleged had resulted from her husband's death. At trial the defendant sought to cross-examine the plaintiff about whether she had since remarried. The trial court did not allow the question. The jury awarded damages to the plaintiff, and the defendant appealed. The court of appeals affirmed:

> The majority rule is that the surviving spouse's remarriage, or the possibility thereof, does not affect the damages recoverable in an action for wrongful death of the deceased spouse. The rationale underlying the majority rule, with which California is in accord, is that the cause of action arises at the time of decedent's death and the damages are determinable as of the same time, and that the rule providing for mitigation of damages on account of the surviving spouse's remarriage is highly speculative, because it involves a comparison of the prospective earnings, services, and contributions of the deceased spouse with those of the new spouse. [. . .]
>
> Although the rule excluding evidence of remarriage may, at first blush, appear to be unreasonable and unjust, the rationale underlying the rule is best explained in *Reynolds v. Willis,* 209 A.2d 760 (Del. 1965), where it was stated that it was more reasonable to say that a defendant should not be allowed to profit by an actual or possible remarriage of the widow, just as he may not profit through monies coming to her from insurance policies purchased by her husband upon his own life, or from some other collateral source.

For an example of the minority view that a jury may consider a spouse's remarriage in calculating damages for lost support, see *Jensen v. Heritage Mutual Ins. Co.,* 127 N.W.2d 228 (Wis. 1964). Which rule makes more sense?

6. *The next Rockefeller.* In Louisville & Nashville Ry. v. Creighton, 50 S.W. 227 (Ky. 1899), the plaintiff's decedent, a child about four years old, ran across the defendant's railroad tracks in pursuit of music being played by an organ grinder on the other side. One of the defendant's trains struck the child and killed him. The incident was found to be the result of negligence on the part of the train's engineer (he, too, had been watching the organ grinder). The jury awarded the administrator of the child's estate $10,500 for lost earnings. The defendant appealed, claiming that the award was excessive. The court of appeals reversed and ordered a new trial:

> The measure of damages is the fair compensation to the estate of the child for the destruction of his capacity to earn money. The child was under four years of age. There are many diseases incidental to childhood, and it was by no means assured that this child would reach manhood. His earning capacity would be nothing, or comparatively little, until he reached puberty, or near that time. In the meantime he would have to

be supported, if he survived the dangers incidental to childhood. What his earning capacity would be after all this is largely a matter of conjecture. This court has sustained a number of verdicts for loss of life, where compensation only was allowed, from amounts ranging from $5,000 to $10,000, for adults who were vigorous and had actual money-earning capacity; but we do not think that, where compensation only is allowed, a verdict of $10,500 for the death of a little child like this ought to stand.

Guffy, J., dissented:

I do not think that this court had any right to assume that this child would not earn $10,500 over and above his expenses. If he should have had the good fortune to become the president of a railroad company, at $25,000 per year, he would in a very few years have earned more than $100,000; if it should have been his good fortune to become a judge of the Supreme Court of the United States, in a very few years he would have earned many thousand dollars; or, if it had been his good fortune to become a judge of this court, in eight years he would have earned $40,000, and, allowing $2,000 per annum for his personal expenses, he would have earned in eight years $24,000, even if he had not been reelected; and the jury had just as much right to assume that he would earn a large amount of money as this court had to assume that he would not do so. It is a well-known fact that many men earn many million dollars during life, and, if one of them should be killed by the negligence or wrongful act of any person or corporation, the recovery, under the doctrine announced in the majority opinion in this case, would amount to millions. If such a man as ex-Senator Brice, or a man like Gould, Vanderbilt, Rockefeller, or many others who might be named, had been killed, instead of the child Stock, the judgment must have been for millions of dollars, because the earning capacity could have been established beyond all question; and that, taken in connection with the probable duration of life, would have called for a judgment which would probably bankrupt almost any individual or corporation. [. . .]

If the doctrine announced in the opinion in this case is the law, then no recovery can be had, if the decedent could not have earned more than living expenses, and thus a plain and positive provision of the constitution would be abrogated or disregarded entirely. It will not do to say that nominal damages, or one cent, could be recovered in all cases, under the opinion in the case at bar; for if the power to earn money does not exceed the cost of living, as announced in the majority opinion in this case, then not even one cent can be recovered, and the result will be that persons and corporations may negligently destroy the lives of a large number of citizens with perfect impunity, and absolutely escape all pecuniary responsibility therefor[. . . .]

7. *Economic refinements.* In the cases just considered we have seen courts try to calculate the wages a party would have earned if injury or death had not intervened. Devising a fully accurate award, however, requires consideration of some additional economic matters.

a. Present value. Using a case like *Pescatore* as an example, the first point to grasp is that the plaintiff is not entitled to a lump sum representing all the support she ever would have received from the decedent if the accident had not occurred. If she were given such a lump sum at the end of the trial, she could then invest it, enjoy the interest on the investment, and thus end up with more money than she would have received if the decedent had lived. So the general practice in making damage awards for future losses is to discount them to their *present value*: the plaintiff is given an amount that, if invested safely, will grow into the correct amount once it is due. Thus if the evidence shows that the plaintiff will miss out on $100,000 in salary ten years from now, the correct damage award today is not $100,000; it is an amount that will have grown to $100,000 after sitting in the bank for ten years. The same calculations can be made for every year of the period at issue — year 11, year 30, and so forth; plaintiffs typically hire economic experts to perform such calculations and present the resulting figures to the jury. Naturally the numbers must also take into account various uncertainties — the life expectancy of the plaintiff or the plaintiff's decedent, the amount of time they would have spent in the workforce, what progress they would have made in their profession, and so forth.

One of the problems that arises in making those calculations involves inflation. The difficulty is illustrated by O'Shea v. Riverway Towing Co., 677 F.2d 1194 (7th Cir. 1982). The plaintiff was a 57-year-old cook who was injured by the defendant's negligence. Her annual wage at the time of the accident was about $7,200. The trial court awarded her $86,033 in future lost wages. The court of appeals affirmed, offering the following analysis of the figures offered by the plaintiff's economic expert:

> [T]he object of discounting lost future wages to present value is to give the plaintiff an amount of money which, invested safely, will grow to a sum equal to those wages. So if we thought that but for the accident Mrs. O'Shea would have earned $7200 in 1990, and we were computing in 1980 (when this case was tried) her damages based on those lost earnings, we would need to determine the sum of money that, invested safely for a period of 10 years, would grow to $7200. Suppose that in 1980 the rate of interest on ultra-safe (i.e., federal government) bonds or notes maturing in 10 years was 12 percent. Then we would consult a table of present values to see what sum of money invested at 12 percent for 10 years would at the end of that time have grown to $7200. The answer is $2318. But a moment's reflection will show that to give Mrs. O'Shea $2318 to compensate her for lost wages in 1990 would grossly undercompensate her. People demand 12 percent to lend money risklessly for

10 years because they expect their principal to have much less purchasing power when they get it back at the end of the time. In other words, when long-term interest rates are high, they are high in order to compensate lenders for the fact that they will be repaid in cheaper dollars. In periods when no inflation is anticipated, the risk-free interest rate is between one and three percent. Additional percentage points above that level reflect inflation anticipated over the life of the loan. But if there is inflation it will affect wages as well as prices. Therefore to give Mrs. O'Shea $2318 today because that is the present value of $7200 10 years hence, computed at a discount rate — 12 percent — that consists mainly of an allowance for anticipated inflation, is in fact to give her less than she would have been earning then if she was earning $7200 on the date of the accident, even if the only wage increases she would have received would have been those necessary to keep pace with inflation.

There are (at least) two ways to deal with inflation in computing the present value of lost future wages. One is to take it out of both the wages and the discount rate — to say to Mrs. O'Shea, "we are going to calculate your probable wage in 1990 on the assumption, unrealistic as it is, that there will be zero inflation between now and then; and, to be consistent, we are going to discount the amount thus calculated by the interest rate that would be charged under the same assumption of zero inflation." Thus, if we thought Mrs. O'Shea's real (i.e., inflation-free) wage rate would not rise in the future, we would fix her lost earnings in 1990 as $7200 and, to be consistent, we would discount that to present (1980) value using an estimate of the real interest rate. At two percent, this procedure would yield a present value of $5906. Of course, she would not invest this money at a mere two percent. She would invest it at the much higher prevailing interest rate. But that would not give her a windfall; it would just enable her to replace her lost 1990 earnings with an amount equal to what she would in fact have earned in that year if inflation continues, as most people expect it to do. (If people did not expect continued inflation, long-term interest rates would be much lower; those rates impound investors' inflationary expectations.)

An alternative approach, which yields the same result, is to use a (higher) discount rate based on the current risk-free 10-year interest rate, but apply that rate to an estimate of lost future wages that includes expected inflation. Contrary to Riverway's argument, this projection would not require gazing into a crystal ball. The expected rate of inflation can, as just suggested, be read off from the current long-term interest rate. If that rate is 12 percent, and if as suggested earlier the real or inflation-free interest rate is only one to three percent, this implies that the market is anticipating 9-11 percent inflation over the next 10 years, for a long-term interest rate is simply the sum of the real interest rate and the anticipated rate of inflation during the term.

b. *Taxes.* The Internal Revenue Code (§104(a)(2)) provides that compensatory damages, including sums awarded to a plaintiff as compensation for lost wages, are not subject to federal income tax. Many states do not tax them, either. Can you think of a rationale for these rules? Does it follow that in calculating an award for lost wages, a court should subtract out the taxes that would have had to be paid on them if they were earned in the market? Many states say so; others disagree, holding that compensatory damages should be determined without reference to taxes. What defense can be made of *this* rule? Unlike compensatory damages, punitive damages *are* taxable, see *O'Gilvie v. United States*, 519 U.S. 79 (1996); also taxed is the interest a plaintiff receives once a damage award is invested and begins generating interest.

c. *Prejudgment interest.* Bringing and winning a lawsuit can take many years; by the time damages are awarded in a wrongful death suit like *Pescatore*, the plaintiff already has been deprived of several years of support. Clearly that lost income is recoverable as part of the award. But now consider a harder question: should the plaintiff also be able to collect the interest she has missed because the damage award was paid at the end of the case rather than immediately upon her husband's death? To make the question more concrete, consider that in the actual *Pescatore* case the plaintiff's decedent died in 1988. The court entered judgment in the plaintiff's favor in 1995. As we saw, the plaintiff's basic award in the case was approximately $14 million. If she had received that award on the day of her husband's death, she would have obtained an additional seven years of interest on it; she would have gained a smaller but still significant sum if the money had been paid the day the suit was filed rather than at the end of it. Should she have been able to collect that interest from the defendant?

The traditional answer of the common law was no: prejudgment interest was permitted only as to "liquidated" amounts — in other words, only if it was clear from the outset of the suit how much money the plaintiff would be due if the defendant were found liable. This traditional rule has been modified or abandoned by judicial decision or statute in many states. See, e.g., Mass. Gen. L. ch. 231:

§6B. INTEREST ADDED TO DAMAGES IN TORT ACTIONS

In any action in which a verdict is rendered or a finding made or an order for judgment made for pecuniary damages for personal injuries to the plaintiff or for consequential damages, or for damage to property, there shall be added by the clerk of court to the amount of damages interest thereon at the rate of twelve per cent per annum from the date of commencement of the action even though such interest brings the amount of the verdict or finding beyond the maximum liability imposed by law.

Consider also Ohio St. §1343.03(C):

Interest on a judgment, decree, or order for the payment of money rendered in a civil action based on tortious conduct and not settled by agreement of the parties, shall be computed from the date the cause of action accrued to the date on which the money is paid if, upon motion of any party to the action, the court determines at a hearing held subsequent to the verdict or decision in the action that the party required to pay the money failed to make a good faith effort to settle the case and that the party to whom the money is to be paid did not fail to make a good faith effort to settle the case.

Why does this last statute link the payment of prejudgment interest to the defendant's participation in settlement talks?

In the *Pescatore* case, prejudgment interest was authorized by statute and resulted in an additional award to the plaintiff of $5 million: "There is no legitimate claim that the jury's assignment of $5,045,040.00 in interest on the award from the date of Mr. Pescatore's death to the date of the judgment is excessive. Upon examination of the jury's final figures, it is apparent that they applied the same 8.5% interest rate that was obtainable on the purchase of a five year Treasury Bond on the date of death."

8. *Insurance*. Insurance coverage provides the backdrop and motivation for most tort litigation, for the uninsured defendant rarely is worth suing. Insurance coverage can be broadly divided into two varieties. "First-party" insurance protects its holder against losses resulting from a particular event. Coverage of medical expenses or for damage suffered in automobile accidents are classic examples. "Third-party" insurance protects the insured against the threat of paying damages to another harmed by the insured's conduct. Also known as liability insurance, it is called "third-party" insurance because it causes the insurance company to pay the injured party, not the owner of the policy. The insurance policies bought by owners of homes and automobiles contain both types of coverage, as do the "comprehensive general liability" (CGL) policies the insurance industry offers on a more or less uniform basis to commercial enterprises. Liability insurance policies generally are limited to "accidents," excluding coverage for intentional torts, and often will not cover punitive damages; some states forbid any such coverage by statute. (Why?)

Insurance coverage can affect tort litigation in several ways. Naturally the existence of insurance coverage that can be used to satisfy a large damage award provides the plaintiff with an incentive to litigate. But the more complex consequence arises from the liability insurer's usual duty to defend the policyholder against all claims of personal injury or property damage. The obligation extends to claims that are groundless. The insurance company's position can be made delicate by two facts: under the typical policy it has the right to control the litigation and make decisions about whether and when to settle a case; meanwhile the company's obligation to pay is limited to whatever amount of coverage is provided in the policy. Conflicts of interest can result. Think of a tort claim for $50,000 against a defendant with a $25,000 insurance policy. The insured would very much like the company to settle the case for the policy limits or any lesser sum, thus protecting against any chance that the insured will have to pay damages. The insurance company's own interests may be different, however; it might like to turn down a settlement offer of $25,000 because it thinks its expected outcome at trial is better than that — and if it isn't, the costs of the excess judgment will be borne by someone else (the insured).

Courts have addressed such conflicts of interest in various ways. The insurer has a general obligation to act in "good faith" — and can be the subject of an action for "bad faith" if it is found to have placed its interests ahead of the interests of the insured in weighing settlement offers. As stated by the California Supreme Court in *Crisci v. Security Insurance Co.*, 426 P.2d 173 (1967), "the test is whether a prudent insurer without policy limits would have accepted the settlement offer." Other jurisdictions sometimes require some further showing of culpability on the insurance company's part before imposing liability for bad faith — a finding of "unreasonableness" or worse. How would you expect these rules to affect the dynamics of the resulting settlement negotiations between the plaintiff and the defendant's insurer?

A separate set of issues raised by the insurance company's role involves the *collateral source rule*. Suppose the plaintiff is hospitalized after being injured by the defendant's negligence. The plaintiff's first-party insurance carrier covers the resulting medical expenses. Should the plaintiff be able to recover those expenses from the defendant despite having received payment for them from a "collateral" source — i.e., the insurer? This question has generated a great deal of judicial and scholarly discussion. The common law held that the plaintiff was indeed entitled to collect damages from the defendant despite having already been made whole by the insurance company. Does this result in a windfall for the plaintiff, or is the plaintiff's contract with the insurance company best understood as a side bet in which the defendant has no legitimate interest? (If the damages due from the defendant were reduced because the plaintiff had insurance coverage, then wouldn't the plaintiff have been better off *not* buying insurance? For then the plaintiff still would have received compensation — this time from the defendant — but would have avoided paying premiums.)

Some states have changed the collateral source rule by statute, abolishing or limiting it either across the board or for certain types of claims such as those involving medical malpractice. But even where this has not been done, double recoveries by plaintiffs are not common as a practical matter. Insurance policies typically provide either that the company must be reimbursed if the insured collects damages from a defendant to cover the same costs the insurance company already has paid; or the policies provide that the insurance company is "subrogated" to the rights of the insured, meaning that the company has the power to bring a suit against the defendant to recoup the benefits it paid to its insured.

3. *Pain and Suffering; Emotional Distress; Hedonic Damages*

Damages for pain and suffering commonly are awarded to successful plaintiffs in personal injury cases. Quantifying this sort of damage is a vexing problem, however; the jurors generally are invited to fix a sum in an amount they find reasonable, with the task of helping them define "reasonableness" largely left to the lawyers. Below are excerpts from some closing arguments that have been attempted by plaintiffs' lawyers seeking compensation for their clients' pain and suffering in four personal injury cases; which (if any) do you think are proper, and which improper?

1. *The dentist hypothetical.* "You go to your dentist. Your dentist examines your mouth and he sees a bad tooth and he has to extract it. Now, physically, it is very possible for him to take that tooth out without giving you any painkiller. There is nothing that says he has to give you an anesthetic. But how many of us wouldn't pay the extra few dollars to have a painkiller to avoid that pain? I say this to you only as an example of how we do in our lives put a monetary value on pain. There is no question here that Ruby Cox has suffered with painful injuries. So when you're in there thinking about these intangibles, think what it means to suffer on a daily basis and a daily basis not only up to now but into the future. . . . You are going to hear Judge Thompson charge you about Ruby's life expectancy, which is about 31 years, and if you just multiply that out by the number of days in a year you will figure out that that comes to about 11,000 days of life expectancy, and I will say to you, members of the jury, that Ruby is entitled to fair compensation, not nominal, but fair compensation for each and every one of those days." See *Cox v. Valley Fair Corp.*, 416 A.2d 809 (N.J. 1980).

2. *The Golden Rule.* "How much are you going to give this woman? I want you, when you go back to the jury room, to figure on what she is entitled to. Dr. Brindley says she is hurt. Dr. Viers says she has lost 82% of her hearing. What is your hearing worth? Now think about it that way. Apply the Golden Rule when you come to answer this question. What's your ear worth? What's 82% loss of hearing in one of your ears worth? What would you sell your ear for? Either one of them? Now think about it that way." See *Red Top Cab Co. v. Capps*, 270 S.W.2d 273 (Tex. Civ. App. 1954).

3. *The job offer.* "In considering what is an adequate sum for this young man, suppose I was to meet one of you ladies on the street and I say to you, 'I want to offer you a job and I want to tell you a little bit about this job before you say you are going to accept it; one peculiar thing, if you take it you have to keep it for the rest of your life, you work seven days a week, no vacations, work daytime and night. The other thing is, you only get paid $3.00 a day. Here is your job — your job is to suffer Mr. Faught's disability.'" See *Faught v. Washam*, 329 S.W.2d 588 (Mo. 1959).

4. *Statutes and arguments*. In some jurisdictions, legislatures have assumed the task of regulating lawyers' ability to make arguments like these. See, e.g., this provision from New Jersey:

> (b) *Closing Statement*. After the close of the evidence and except as may be otherwise provided in the pretrial order, the parties may make closing statements in the reverse order of opening statements. In civil cases any party may suggest to the trier of fact, with respect to any element of damages, that unliquidated damages be calculated on a time-unit basis without reference to a specific sum. In the event such comments are made to a jury, the judge shall instruct the jury that they are argumentative only and do not constitute evidence.

N.J. Court Rules, 1:7-1. Does it make sense to allow lawyers to suggest that damages be calculated "on a time-unit basis" but "without reference to a specific sum"?

5. *Hang fire*. In Olin Corp. v. Smith, 990 S.W.2d 789 (Tex. App. 1999), the plaintiff, Joshua Smith, went hunting with friends near a ranch in Mason, Texas. They traveled in a Ford Bronco pickup truck; Smith rode in the passenger seat. During the drive, Smith spotted a wild pig and opened fire on it with a .22 caliber revolver out the side window of the truck. They pursued the pig past a thicket and continued to fire at it until Smith heard a "click" from his gun. Assuming it was empty, he put it on his thigh and reached for more ammunition. The gun then discharged into his left leg, which eventually had to be amputated below the knee. Smith sued Olin, the maker of the ammunition, claiming that the accident resulted from a "hang fire" — a delayed firing caused by a defect in the bullet's ignition system. A bench trial produced in a verdict for Smith; he was awarded $6,343,444, including $5,580,000 for "physical pain and mental anguish, disfigurement, and physical disability." Olin appealed, arguing among other things that the award of damages was excessive. The court of appeals affirmed:

> [A]t the time of the shooting, Joshua was 16 years of age and had a reasonable life expectancy of 55.8 years. [. . .] Extensive testimony described the months of extreme pain and mental anguish which Joshua sustained while doctors attempted to save his leg. Because Joshua's leg never properly healed, the leg was amputated below the knee and Joshua was fitted for a prosthesis.
>
> The evidence established that Joshua has undergone extensive surgical procedures and will continue to require surgery. Joshua's prosthesis will wear out from normal use every three to five years. Volumetric changes in the size of his partially severed leg require Joshua to utilize wrenches in order to keep the prosthesis properly fitted. Joshua experiences severe blistering of the skin of his leg and often complains of "phantom

pain," a sensation that feels like the toes of his amputated foot are being bent "backwards and forwards, just crunching them as hard as they can." [...] [W]e cannot say that the judgment is supported by evidence so weak as to make it manifestly unjust.

6. *Gangrene.* In Williams v. United States, 747 F. Supp. 967 (S.D.N.Y. 1990), the plaintiff, Williams, was a former inmate at the federal penitentiary in Otisville, New York. He was diabetic, and while he was imprisoned he contracted a bacterial infection in his right foot related to the diabetes. His evidence was that the prison's medical officer misdiagnosed the problem, originally believing it to be a case of athlete's foot or other fungal infection. The condition of the foot worsened until it developed a "tumor-like" appearance and discharged infectious material through a fissure on one of his toes. Later it was determined that the foot was infected with E. Coli bacteria. Williams was transferred to a hospital, but the prison failed to notify the hospital of the E. Coli diagnosis. The hospital in turn continued to mistreat Williams' ailment. At last one of the physicians noticed that Williams' foot was gangrenous, and that the gangrene was progressing up his leg. The physician recommended the immediate amputation of the leg below the knee, and Williams agreed. He then brought suit against the United States under the Federal Tort Claims Act. After a bench trial the judge found the government liable for the loss of Williams' leg. He then turned to the question of damages:

> [When the amputation occurred] Williams was 48 years of age and had a life expectancy of 24 years. Now at age 53 Williams can be expected to live for 20.5 more years, that is until the age of 73.5 years. [...]
>
> Following the amputation, Williams suffered "phantom limb pains," sharp pains "that would grab at you occasionally" and "constant throbbing and pain" related to changes in the weather, but he had no other complaints. When the shrinking process stabilized, Williams was fitted with a permanent prosthesis, and underwent physical therapy to learn to walk on it and rebuild the muscle tissue in his right thigh that had atrophied during his rehabilitation.
>
> When Williams began ambulating on the prosthesis, he experienced patellar (knee) pain in October and November 1985 due to the rubbing movement of the prosthesis against his stump and the shrinkage and expansion of his right thigh causing irritation and blisters, "which is almost like a piece of sand, pebble within the shoe." Williams must remove the prosthesis for periods of time once a month or every other month and walk with crutches to allow the sores to heal. [...]
>
> Williams tries to walk without the assistance of a cane or crutches, but must have such assistance if he walks more than four or five city blocks. [...] Williams testified that prior to the amputation, he engaged in bike

riding, swimming, roller skating and jogging, which activities he is now unable to perform. [. . .]

Williams' background has been considered for the purpose of assessing the potential for the amputation to have already affected or to prospectively affect Williams' emotional or mental state. Williams, as we have seen, has spent most of his adult life as a prison inmate; he has a history of long intravenous drug and alcohol use making him more susceptible to psychopathology than members of the general population not so afflicted; he was unable to hold a steady job during periods of time he was not incarcerated; and he has now suffered from diabetes for approximately ten years and continues to smoke, but his diabetes appears to be under control. [. . .]

In his post-trial brief, plaintiff requests an award of $1,500,000 in light of the awards for pain and suffering in prior New York cases involving below-the-knee amputations called to the court's attention by plaintiff. These cases have been carefully reviewed, and the court has taken into account the dates of the decisions and an inflationary factor. Based on all the facts and circumstances disclosed by the present record, an award to plaintiff of $500,000 (without any offset for comparative negligence) is clearly justified for his past and future pain and suffering and for the loss of his leg.

What is the best way to explain the different outcomes in *Williams v. United States* ($500,000 awarded for amputation of leg below the knee) and *Olin Corp. v. Smith* ($5 million awarded for amputation of leg below the knee)?

7. *Pre-impact fright.* In Beynon v. Montgomery Cablevision Ltd. Partnership, 718 A.2d 1161 (Md. App. 1998), the Maryland state police stopped all traffic on Interstate 495 — the "beltway" around Washington, D.C. — to permit the defendant's workers to repair a broken television cable one night at around 2:00 A.M. Traffic backed up for about a mile in both directions. The plaintiffs' decedent, Douglas Beynon, was driving a van toward the backed up traffic at full speed when he realized that a tractor-trailer was stopped in his lane less than 200 feet ahead. He slammed on his brakes, leaving 71 feet of skidmarks on the highway; he nevertheless collided with the truck at a speed of about 40 miles per hour and died on impact. His parents sued the cable company, alleging that it failed to provide adequate notice to oncoming motorists that it was performing work that would cause traffic to stop. They also brought a suit against the owner of the tractor-trailer alleging that the truck was not equipped with adequate warning lights on its rear. A jury brought in a verdict for the plaintiffs and awarded them over $1 million for economic losses and pain and suffering. They also awarded $1 million to compensate for Douglas Beynon's "preimpact fright." The trial judge reduced the latter award to $350,000, the maximum amount of noneconomic damages permitted by state statute in cases involving automobile accidents.

The defendants appealed, claiming among other things that the award for Beynon's pre-impact fright should not have been allowed. The court of appeals affirmed:

> [T]he decedent's fright is capable of objective determination by the 71½ feet of skid marks that the plaintiffs argued, and the jury apparently believed, resulted from the decedent's apprehension of impending death, and the collision itself. [. . .] Damages for "pre-impact fright" are recoverable when the decedent experiences it during the "legitimate window of mental anxiety." *Faya v. Almaraz*, 620 A.2d 327, 338 (Md. 1993), In this case, that window opened when the decedent became conscious of the fact he was in imminent danger and it closed with his death. [. . .]
>
> A rule that does not permit a decedent's estate to recover pre-impact fright damages in a survival action would be illogical in view of the fact that a victim who survives an accident similar to the one in this case would be entitled to recover damages for the emotional distress and mental anguish he or she suffered before the accident, independent of any physical injury that may have been sustained before, or after, the emotional injury. The purpose of survival statutes is to permit a decedent's estate to bring an action that the decedent could have instituted had he or she lived. Here, there is no question that, had he lived, the decedent would have been permitted to recover damages for the "pre-impact fright" he suffered before crashing into rear of the tractor-trailer.

Wilner, J., dissented:

> The Majority is comfortable allowing the jury to infer that, during the one-and-a-half to two-and-a-half seconds that Mr. Beynon was desperately trying to stop his vehicle and avoid the collision, he must have been consumed with conscious fright — anticipating his imminent death, worrying about the effect of his death on his family, chagrined at losing the opportunity to experience the pleasures of continued life, fearful of any pain that he may momentarily suffer, concerned, perhaps, about what, if any, kind of afterlife he might face. If there was any substantial evidence that any of those thoughts were, in fact, consuming Mr. Beynon during that second or two, I would agree that a recovery would be permissible. But there was no such evidence. It is rank speculation to conclude that Mr. Beynon was consciously thinking about anything other than stopping his vehicle, or, indeed, that his mind and body were engaged in anything but an instinctive reaction directed entirely at self-preservation, requiring little or no ideation at all. [. . .]
>
> In most pre-impact fright cases where an award is made, although the absolute size of the jury award is ordinarily not great, often ranging from $5,000 to $15,000, the amount per second of fright is enormous. Here,

the jury's actual award amounted to at least $400,000 per second of fright, later reduced to $140,000 per second of fright. The problem, however, is not simply one of amount. Whether the award is great or small, when grounded on nothing more than skid marks or other evasive action, it can only be a sympathy verdict based not on any substantial evidence of fright but rather on a desire either to compensate the decedent's beneficiaries for his or her death, beyond what is allowed in a wrongful death action, or to punish the wrongdoer.

Does it follow from *Benyon* that if the plaintiff's decedent *had* been able to stop his car, he still would have been entitled to $350,000?

8. *Recovery for humiliation.* From the Restatement (Second) of Torts:

§905. COMPENSATORY DAMAGES FOR NONPECUNIARY HARM

Comment d. Humiliation. One who has a cause of action for a tort may be entitled to recover as an element of damages for that form of mental distress known as humiliation, that is, a feeling of degradation or inferiority or a feeling that other people will regard him with aversion or dislike. This state of mind may result from a physical harm, an imprisonment, a defamatory statement, the disruption of the marital relation, or even the deliberate trespass to land or destruction or dispossession of chattels.

Illustration 3. A negligently causes B to lose an ear. B is entitled to damages not only for the pain and suffering, but also for the humiliation caused by his appearance.

Illustration 4. A seduces B's wife. B is entitled to damages for his humiliation.

Illustration 5. A wantonly dispossesses B of household furniture to the knowledge of B's neighbors. B is entitled to damages for humiliation.

In torts involving offense to a sense of dignity, the element of damages based on the imposition of humiliation on the injured party may have a supplementary feature in the sense of vindication that arises from a judgment for "compensatory" damages that declares publicly that he has been mistreated and that he was justified in resenting it.

Comment i. Measure of recovery. The length of time during which pain or other harm to the feelings has been or probably will be experienced and the intensity of the distress are factors to be considered in assessing the amount of damages. In determining this, all relevant circumstances are considered, including sex, age, condition in life and any other fact indicating the susceptibility of the injured person to this type of harm. [. . .]

The extent and duration of emotional distress produced by the tortious conduct depend upon the sensitiveness of the injured person. The court, however, will not permit consideration of disturbances which, conceding full weight to individuality, are wholly abnormal and unreasonable.

Thus, unless a recognizable mental disease results, there can be no recovery for a long-continued morbid propensity to fear death from rabies, if there is proof that the dog that bit the injured person was healthy, nor can there be recovery for the totally unfounded fear of a woman that an injury has prevented her from ever being able to have a child.

9. *An absurd figure?* In Douglass v. Hustler Magazine, Inc., 769 F.2d 1128 (7th Cir. 1985), the plaintiff, Robyn Douglass, was an actress who posed in the nude for a photographer. She signed a release authorizing the use of the photos in *Playboy* magazine, where some of them were published. Several years later, *Hustler* magazine also obtained and published the photographs. Douglass sued *Hustler* and the photographer for invasion of privacy. A jury awarded her $500,000 in compensatory damages, which included $300,000 for emotional distress; it also awarded her $1.5 million in punitive damages against *Hustler,* which the trial judge reduced, via remittitur, to $100,000. The judge declined the defendant's request for a new trial, ruling that "The jury's award of compensatory damages [. . .] cannot fairly be described as 'grossly excessive' or 'monstrous' or with similar pejorative adjectival terms." The court of appeals disagreed, and ordered a new trial for that and other reasons:

> The $300,000 for emotional distress is an absurd figure. Though distressed by the *Hustler* incident, Douglass suffered no severe or permanent psychiatric harm — nothing more than transitory emotional distress (some of it from obscene phone calls stimulated by the publication). The figure is ridiculous in relation to the highest judgment yet upheld on appeal in a series of cases arising from the Chicago Police Department's former practice of "strip searching" women arrested for minor crimes (mainly traffic offenses): $60,000. This was in *Mary Beth G. v. City of Chicago,* 723 F.2d 1263, 1275-76 (7th Cir.1983), where the plaintiff was strip searched in the presence of two male police officers and jeering prostitutes. We have repeatedly emphasized — and take this opportunity to emphasize again — that we will not allow plaintiffs to throw themselves on the generosity of the jury; if they want damages they must prove them.

10. *The wall of polite skepticism.* In Weller v. American Broadcasting Companies, Inc., 283 Cal. Rptr. 644 (Cal. App. 1991), the plaintiff, Michael Weller, was an antique dealer who sold a silver candelabra to the DeYoung museum in San Francisco for $65,000. The museum believed the candelabra had been made in the early nineteenth century by Paul Storr, a famous English silversmith; that it may once have belonged to the Duke of Cumberland; and that for the last century it had been in the custody of a Texas family that wished to remain anonymous. About a year later, the assistant news director at the defendant television network's affiliate, KGO,

received a tip casting doubt on the candelabra's pedigree and suggesting that the museum paid too much for it. The station went on to run a series of seven televised news reports on the candelabra, including one called "Museum Fraud?" The series suggested that the candelabra might have been stolen from the home of a well-known San Francisco sculptress who had died some years earlier, that it might have been improperly altered and restored, and that the museum may have over-paid Weller for it. Weller brought suit for defamation. The jury returned a verdict in his favor, awarding him $1 million for damage to his reputation and another $1 million for mental suffering. The defendant appealed, arguing among other things that the damages awarded for mental suffering were excessive. The court of appeals affirmed:

> In support of his claim for damages for emotional distress, Weller testified that he initially suffered from anger, worry, sleeplessness, loss of appetite and depression. He said that after several weeks these feelings "settle[d] into long-term depression." He further testified that he had very distressing conversations with the former-owner of the candelabra and her representative, who were upset that a transaction they intended to keep quiet was the subject of so much publicity. Weller also was subjected to jokes from other dealers, and was constantly embarrassed by having to explain that he was not a thief and by the "wall of polite skepticism." Weller further testified regarding the humiliation he felt in explaining these events to his family, and the sorrow he experienced because his mother died before he was vindicated by the jury verdict.
>
> In support of their contention that the damages are excessive, appellants cite numerous cases in which the courts have concluded that the damage awards were excessive. This kind of comparative analysis is simply no substitute for a review of the record in this case against the "historically honored standard of reversing as excessive only those judgments which the entire record, when viewed most favorably to the judgment, indicates were rendered as a result of passion and prejudice on the part of the jurors." *Bertero v. National General Corp.* 529 P.2d 608 (Cal. 1974). [. . .] Our review of the record, when viewed most favorably to the judgment, leads us to the conclusion that, although the damages awarded were indeed high, they are not so out of proportion with the evidence that we should infer that the judgment is the product of passion or prejudice.

What is the best way to explain the different outcomes in *Weller v. American Broadcasting Companies, Inc.* ($1 million award for emotional distress found supported by the evidence) and *Douglass v. Hustler Magazine, Inc.* ($300,000 award for emotional distress found "absurd" and excessive)?

11. *The desire for the table.* In Daugherty v. Erie Ry. Co., 169 A.2d 549 (Pa. 1961), the plaintiff was a passenger in an automobile that collided with a railroad train. He suffered disfiguring injuries to his head and face that

required him to undergo extensive surgery and wear a head cast for two months. An additional consequence of the accident was that his olfactory nerve was damaged, causing him to lose his sense of taste and smell. He brought suit against the railroad and the driver of the car. The jury brought in a verdict in his favor for $5,000. The trial court ordered a new trial on the ground that the award of damages was "so inadequate as to be patently unjust." The Pennsylvania Supreme Court affirmed:

> One of the heaviest losses sustained by the plaintiff is that of disfigurement. [. . .] [T]he trial judge said that one side of the plaintiff's face is "caved in" and the "shape of his whole head is altered." People who have known the plaintiff for years now pass him on the street without recognizing him. Persons who knew him from boyhood were unable to reconcile the plaintiff's present appearance with the way they had known him in the past. [. . .]
>
> In these days of extensive pictorial reproduction through portraits, sketches, photographs, motion pictures and television, a photogenic personality counts for more than can be estimated in dollars and cents. However, difficulty in computation should not deprive the victim of a disfiguring accident from an approximate recompense for what he loses through a crippling of his public personality. [. . .]
>
> The appellants also fail to comment on another very serious impairment sustained by the plaintiff, — his loss of the senses of taste and smell. One does not need to be a gourmand or gourmet to conclude that the consumption of food and drink represents a not inconsiderable portion of man's enjoyment of life. To be deprived of the capacity to enjoy flavorful dishes and palatable beverages is to be robbed of much of what goes into a rewarding existence because, with the "inner man" satisfied, one can work with greater zest in the accomplishment of his chosen tasks and in making his contribution to the happiness of those dependent upon him and mankind in general. The defendant has lost much of the desire for the table because he can detect no difference in food. Whether it be the rarest delicacies or the commonest kind of provender which he eats, he tastes only sawdust.

12. *Personal enjoyment.* In Hogan v. Santa Fe Trail Transportation Co., 85 P.2d 28 (Kan. 1938), the plaintiff was an accomplished violinist. Her car was hit by the defendant's truck; in the accident she broke the fifth metacarpal bone of her left hand, resulting in a permanent stiffening of her little finger. The finger was deprived of its strength and its lateral motion, leaving her unable to play the violin. She won a jury verdict for against the defendant for $5,274, of which $4,000 represented the jury's estimate of her "loss of enjoyment from being unable to play the violin." The defendant appealed, claiming this was an inappropriate basis for damages; the Kansas Supreme Court reversed, agreeing with the defendant that the award must be

reduced by $4,000. Said the court, "to hold that loss of enjoyment resulting from being unable to play the violin is too speculative and conjectural to form a sound basis for the assessment of damages." The court also cited with approval this passage from a similar Indiana case, *City of Columbus v. Strassner*, 25 N.E. 65 (Ind. 1890):

> The question of damages, like other legal propositions, should rest upon some substantial basis. The following inquiries therefore suggest themselves: What is "personal enjoyment?" How are we to ascertain to what extent it is possessed by a human being? How can its absence and the cause thereof be demonstrated? If a person for any cause has been deprived of "personal enjoyment," how are we to go about adjusting his loss upon a money basis? These questions seem to be pertinent, but unanswerable, and suggest an insuperable difficulty to the measurement of damages because of loss of "personal enjoyment."

Wedell, J., dissented:

> [T]he enjoyment in the instant case was not an imaginary enjoyment. It was a fixed and definite enjoyment which existed at the time of the injury. Nor did it constitute an incidental or merely occasional enjoyment. It was an enjoyment which grew out of and was a part of the regular and ordinary pursuits of the plaintiff's life. It was truly exactly as she stated: "It was my life work. It was just part of me." It constituted the loss of the greatest enjoyment of her life. To say that the loss of such an enjoyment and the comfort to a human being resulting from such enjoyment is compensable in no amount does not appeal to my sense of justice.

The Kansas Supreme Court effectively overruled *Hogan* in *Leiker v. Gafford*, 778 P.2d 823 (Kan. 1989). Was it right to do so? What, if anything, is wrong with *Hogan*? The damages at issue in *Daugherty* and *Hogan* are now commonly referred to as *hedonic damages*: sums meant to compensate the plaintiff not for pain and suffering but for lost pleasures of life. In what respects are the difficulties raised by hedonic damages similar to those raised by recovery for pain and suffering or for emotional distress? In what respects are the difficulties different?

13. *Thinking about hedonics.* How should lost pleasures of life be valued? When a life is lost outright, the legal system values it in conventional ways — principally by trying to compute a decedent's lost wages and awarding them to his survivors. But when injuries prevent people from experiencing the pleasures they used to enjoy, there are no obvious market measures available to use as benchmarks for valuation of the loss. Many attempts have been made to find nonobvious measures, but they generally have met with resistance in the courts. The most prominent of these attempts are known as

"willingness to pay" studies. They try to determine how much people value their lives by looking at how much they are willing to spend to reduce small risks of death.

Suppose, for example, that an airbag for an automobile costs $300, and suppose it is known that every 10,000 purchases of an airbag saves one life. In effect that means $3 million will be spent (by 10,000 consumers) to save that one life. Put differently, each purchaser evidently is willing to spend $300 to obtain the benefit of that 1/10,000 chance that it will save his own life — and this suggests that each values his life at $3 million. (If airbags were $1,000 in this example, and people stopped buying them at that price, the economic inference would be that they value their lives at less than $10 million; they would rather accept a 1/10,000 chance of death than pay $1,000 to avoid it.) Similar studies examine how much extra payment various types of workers demand to perform risky work. Assume window washers who work on top floors of tall buildings have a 1/10,000 greater chance of death than those who work near the ground; and assume that as a result window washers are prepared to accept $300 less to be assigned to low floors. Again, this would suggest that they value their lives at $3 million.

There have been many studies undertaken of these sorts, and then there have been further attempts to combine their various results to come up with an average sense of how much people seem to value their lives. Some well-known past examples generated figures in the $1 to $3 million range. That is not the end of the inquiry, for remember that the objective is to figure out how much someone valued the *pleasures* in life that they have lost. Some economists propose to do this by starting with a generic value of an "anonymous" life — say, $2 million. If we imagine a person who values her life at that amount, the valuation must (as the theory goes) come from two sources: the money she expected to earn and the pleasures she expected to enjoy. So if we subtract her expected lifetime earnings from the $2 million, then whatever is left over must reflect the value of the pleasures the plaintiff expected to derive from living. If the plaintiff is said (typically by an expert witness) to have lost 20 percent of the pleasure of living, then the plaintiff should be entitled to recover 20 percent of the sum designated as the value assigned to the enjoyment of life.

If any or all of this seems bothersome, note that government agencies often use valuations not unlike this in making regulatory decisions. The Federal Aviation Administration, the Nuclear Regulatory Commission, and other agencies have to make decisions about what precautions to require in the industries they supervise. Requiring precautions is expensive; somehow the agency has to decide whether the precautions will save enough lives to be worth the cost. Agencies sometimes use survey data of the kind just described to generate the figures they use for this purpose, and in recent times have typically ended up with numbers in the same $5 to $7 million range. If this, too, seems troubling, how else might you suggest that agencies think about whether to impose costly regulations on industries for the sake of saving a few lives over a period of many years? Are there any reasons why a procedure of this sort might make more sense for agencies than for courts? Who would you think would be more likely to want to introduce this type of "willingness to pay" evidence — plaintiffs or defendants?

In any event, almost all courts to be confronted with this sort of testimony by experts have forbidden it. Mercado v. Ahmed, 974 F.2d 863 (7th Cir. 1992), is a leading example. The plaintiff, badly injured when hit by a taxi, wanted to introduce expert testimony on the sorts of "willingness to pay" studies just described. The trial court refused to allow it, and the court of appeals affirmed:

> [W]e have serious doubts about [the expert's] assertion that the studies he relies upon actually measure how much Americans value life. For example, spending on items like air bags and smoke detectors is probably influenced as much by advertising and marketing decisions made by profit-seeking manufacturers and by government-mandated safety requirements as it is by any consideration by consumers of how much life is worth. Also, many people may be interested in a whole range of safety devices and believe they are worthwhile, but are unable to afford them. More fundamentally, spending on safety items reflects a consumer's willingness to pay to reduce *risk*, perhaps more a measure of how cautious a person is than how much he or she values life. Few of us, when confronted with the threat, "Your money or your life!" would, like Jack Benny, pause and respond, "I'm thinking, I'm thinking." Most of us would empty our wallets. Why that decision reflects less the value we place on life than whether we buy an airbag is not immediately obvious.
>
> The two other kinds of studies [the expert] relies upon are open to valid and logical criticism as well. To say that the salary paid to those who hold risky jobs tells us something significant about how much we value life ignores the fact that humans are moved by more than monetary incentives. For example, someone who believes police officers working in an extremely dangerous city are grossly undercompensated for the risks they assume might nevertheless take up the badge out of a sense of civic duty to their hometown. Finally, government calculations about how much to spend (or force others to spend) on health and safety regulations are motivated by a host of considerations other than the value of life: is it an election year? how large is the budget deficit? on which constituents will the burden of the regulations fall? what influence and pressure have lobbyists brought to bear? what is the view of interested constituents? And so on.

Some further objections are raised in McClurg, *It's a Wonderful Life: The Case for Hedonic Damages in Wrongful Death Cases*, 66 Notre Dame L. Rev. 57 (1990). But is there a better way to quantify hedonic damages?

14. *The 9/11 fund.* Congress responded to the terrorist attacks of September 11, 2001, by capping the liability that airlines and certain other defendants might face if sued by survivors of the attacks or survivors of those

who died: not more than $6 billion would be collectible ($1.5 billion for each of the four airplanes involved). But the same legislation also created a victim compensation fund to which aggrieved parties could apply for relief if they agreed not to sue the airlines, the World Trade Center, or other potential defendants. The fund was administered by a special master, Kenneth Feinberg, who had many decisions to make about how much to award to each claimant. Payments were made to nearly 5,560 claimants in all, and totaled more than $7 billion. (Ninety-four lawsuits were filed by people who opted out of the fund; all but four were settled.)

Feinberg made awards to compensate for lost earnings and also for the suffering and hedonic damages — or "non-economic losses," as they were called — suffered by those who died or were injured or were related to victims of the attacks. Here are some excerpts concerning those points from his final report:

> Faced with the unfathomable task of placing a dollar amount upon the pain, emotional suffering, loss of enjoyment of life, and mental anguish suffered by the thousands of victims of the September 11th attacks, the Special Master and the Department determined that the fairest and most rational approach was to establish a uniform figure for the pain and suffering of deceased victims and their dependents.
>
> **(1) Presumed $250,000 Non-Economic Award for Deceased Victims.** To determine an appropriate presumed non-economic loss figure for deceased victims, the Special Master and the Department [of Justice] looked to the amount of compensation available under existing federal programs for public safety officers who are killed while on duty, or members of the United States military who are killed in the line of duty while serving our nation. The presumed non-economic loss award of $250,000 for victims who died as a result of the aircraft on September 11 is roughly equivalent to the amounts received by survivors under these other federal programs. The Regulations allow claimants to attempt to demonstrate in a hearing any extraordinary circumstances that justify departure from the presumed non-economic loss award.
>
> **(2) Additional $100,000 Non-Economic Award for Spouse and Dependents of Deceased Victims/Definition of Dependent.** The Regulations also provide for an additional $100,000 for the spouse and each dependent of the deceased victim. The $100,000 figure for the spouse and each dependent includes a non-economic component of "replacement services loss." . . .

The average total award for a death claim was about $2 million, and the average payment for a claim of physical injury was about $400,000, though there was much variation among individual awards.

Does the 9/11 fund provide an appealing paradigm for use in other situations? Why not a similar fund, with similarly regular awards, for losses sustained in other disasters, man-made and natural? What would be the pros and cons of using aspects of such an approach — the public funding, and the presumptive rate of payment for non-economic damages — for accidents generally?

15. *Fixed schedules.* The notion of a fixed rate of compensation is familiar from workers' compensation statutes, which require employers to pay into a fund and then disburse compensatory awards to injured employees without litigation. Many such statutes resemble the federal Longshore and Harbor Workers' Compensation Act, 33 U.S.C. §§901-950, the compensation schedule of which provides in part:

> (c) Permanent partial disability: In case of disability partial in character but permanent in quality the compensation shall be 66 2/3 per centum of the average weekly wages, which shall be in addition to compensation for temporary total disability or temporary partial disability paid in accordance with subsection (b) or subsection (e) of this section, respectively, and shall be paid to the employee, as follows:
>
> (1) Arm lost, three hundred and twelve weeks' compensation.
> (2) Leg lost, two hundred and eighty-eight weeks' compensation.
> (3) Hand lost, two hundred and forty-four weeks' compensation.
> (4) Foot lost, two hundred and five weeks' compensation.
> (5) Eye lost, one hundred and sixty weeks' compensation.
> (6) Thumb lost, seventy-five weeks' compensation.
> (7) First finger lost, forty-six weeks' compensation.
> (8) Great toe lost, thirty-eight weeks' compensation.
> (9) Second finger lost, thirty weeks' compensation.
> (10) Third finger lost, twenty-five weeks' compensation.
> (11) Toe other than great toe lost, sixteen weeks' compensation.
> (12) Fourth finger lost, fifteen weeks' compensation. . . .
> (14) Phalanges: Compensation for loss of more than one phalange of a digit shall be the same as for loss of the entire digit. Compensation for loss of the first phalange shall be one-half of the compensation for loss of the entire digit.
> (15) Amputated arm or leg: Compensation for an arm or a leg, if amputated at or above the elbow or the knee, shall be the same as for a loss of the arm or leg; but, if amputated between the elbow and the wrist or the knee and the ankle, shall be the same as for loss of a hand or foot.
> (16) Binocular vision or per centum of vision: Compensation for loss of binocular vision or for 80 per centum or more of the vision of an eye shall be the same as for loss of the eye.
> (17) Two or more digits: Compensation for loss of two or more digits, or one or more phalanges of two or more digits, of a hand or foot may be proportioned to the loss of use of the hand or foot occasioned thereby, but shall not exceed the compensation for loss of a hand or foot.

Again, how does the fairness and the efficiency of such schedules compare to the individualized results that courts would produce?

B.   PUNITIVE DAMAGES

The purpose of an award of compensatory damages is to make the plaintiff "whole" to the extent that can be done with money. The purpose of *punitive damages* — also known as "exemplary" damages, or, in occasional times past, as "vindictive" damages — is different: it is to punish the defendant — and thus to deter the defendant, and similar parties elsewhere, from committing similar torts in the future. Punitive damages thus resemble fines in some respects; unlike a criminal fine payable to the government, however, the fine here is paid to the plaintiff. Punitive damages usually are sought in cases where the defendant has committed gross misconduct, typically with a culpable state of mind. Intentional torts thus present the most common occasion for them. The first cases in this section examine the basic justifications for punitive damages; the later cases illustrate the difficulties courts have had in deciding when they are appropriate and in what amounts.

Murphy v. Hobbs
5 P. 119 (Colo. 1884)

HELM, J. This is a civil action, brought to recover damages for malicious prosecution and false imprisonment. Plaintiff procured a verdict, and judgment was duly entered thereon. Defendant prosecutes this appeal, and assigns in support thereof numerous errors. The most important of these assignments is one which relates to the measure of damages adopted in the court below. Upon this subject the following instruction was there given:

> That the measure of damages in an action for malicious prosecution is not confined alone to actual pecuniary loss sustained by reason thereof; but if it is believed, from the evidence, that the arrest and imprisonment stated in the complaint were without probable cause, then the jury may award damages to plaintiff to indemnify him for the peril occasioned to him in regard to personal liberty, feelings, and reputation, and *as a punishment to defendant* in such further sense as they shall deem just.

By the assignment of error and argument challenging the correctness of this instruction we are called upon to consider the following question, viz.: Can damages *as a punishment* be recovered in cases like this? [. . .] Perhaps the most impressive objection to allowing damages as a punishment in cases like the one at bar, is that which relates to dual prosecutions for a single tort. Our state constitution declares that no one shall be twice put in jeopardy for the same offense. A second criminal prosecution for the same act after acquittal, or conviction and punishment therefor, is something which no English or American lawyer would defend for a moment. But here is an instance where, practically, this wrong is inflicted. The fine awarded as a punishment in the civil action does not prevent indictment and prosecution in a criminal court. On the other hand, it has been held that evidence of punishment in a criminal suit is not admissible even in mitigation of exemplary damages in a civil action. Courts attempt to explain away the apparent conflict with the constitutional inhibition above mentioned; they say that the language there used refers exclusively to criminal procedure, and cannot include civil actions. But this position amounts to a complete surrender of the evident spirit and intent of that instrument. When the convention framed and when the people adopted the constitution both understood the purpose of this clause to be the prevention of double prosecutions for the same offense. Yet, under the rule allowing exemplary damages, not only may two prosecutions, but also two convictions and punishments, be had. What difference does it make to the accused, so far as this question is concerned, that one prosecution takes the form of a civil action, in which he is called defendant? He is practically harassed with two prosecutions and subjected to two convictions; while no hypothesis, however ingenious, can cloud in his mind the palpable fact that for the same tort he suffers two punishments. [. . .]

Civil actions are instituted for the purpose of redressing private wrongs; it is the aim of civil jurisprudence to mete out as nearly exact justice as possible between contending litigants. There ought to be no disposition to take from the defendant or give to the plaintiff more than equity and justice require. Yet under this rule of damages these principles are forgotten, and judicial machinery is used for the avowed purpose of giving plaintiff that to which he has no shadow of right. He recovers full compensation for the injury to his person or property; for all direct and proximate losses occasioned by the tort; for the physical pain, if any, inflicted; for his mental agony, lacerated feelings, wounded sensibilities; and then, in addition to the foregoing, he is allowed damages which are awarded as a punishment of defendant and example to others. Who will undertake to give a valid reason why plaintiff, after being fully paid for all the injury inflicted upon his property, body, reputation, and feelings, should still be compensated, above and beyond, for a wrong committed against the public at large? The idea is inconsistent with sound legal principles, and should never have found a lodgment in the law.

The reflecting lawyer is naturally curious to account for this "heresy" or "deformity," as it has been termed. Able and searching investigations made by both jurist and writer disclose the following facts concerning it, viz.: That it was entirely unknown to the civil law; that it never obtained a foothold in Scotland; that it finds no real sanction in the writings of Blackstone, Hammond, Comyns, or Rutherforth; that it was not recognized in the earliest

English cases; that the Supreme Courts of New Hampshire, Massachusetts, Indiana, Iowa, Nebraska, Michigan, and Georgia have rejected it in whole or in part; that of late other states have falteringly retained it because "committed" so to do; [. . .] and that the rule is comparatively modern, resulting in all probability from a misconception of impassioned language and inaccurate expressions used by judges in some of the earlier English cases. [. . .]

Under the rule limiting them to compensatory damages, juries will, with proper instruction, recognize a broad distinction between a tort unaccompanied by malice, or circumstances of aggravation or disgrace, and one producing equal direct pecuniary damage, where either of these conditions exists. In the former case they consider only the actual injury to the person or property, including expenses, loss of time, bodily pain, etc., occasioned by the wrongful act. In the latter, they allow such additional sum as, in their judgment, is warranted by the circumstances of contumely, anguish, or oppression; but in both instances the damages are awarded as "compensation." The additional sum is given to the individual as a recompense for the mental suffering or wounded sensibilities, as the case may be. It often happens that this constitutes the principal element of the recovery. If, upon a crowded thoroughfare, one maliciously assaults me with blows and epithets, five dollars may fully compensate the injury inflicted to my person and clothing; but $500 may be utterly inadequate to requite the sense of insult, the personal indignity, the public disgrace and humiliation. The extra $500 exacted may operate indirectly as a punishment. It may constitute an example to others, and also deter my assailant himself from repetitions of the offense in future. In law, however, it is simply compensation for the private wrong, — a kind of indemnity which, probably, no court has ever refused to allow when warranted by the circumstances. But, under the doctrine of exemplary damages, as announced by the instruction given in this case, the jury are not required to stop with the five dollars for material injury and $500 for lacerated feelings; they may turn to the domain of criminal law, and consider the public wrong, and they may add $1,000 more as a punishment to my assailant. The arrangement is highly satisfactory to me, since I have the pleasure of pocketing the additional $1,000 to which I am not entitled; but, as we have already seen, it hardly comports with correct legal principles.

The case at bar furnishes a good illustration of the doctrine under discussion. [. . .] The jury returned a verdict for $2,780. How much of this sum was given as a punishment? Perhaps $1,000, perhaps more; yet, under our Criminal Code, $500 would have been the maximum. When defendant is on trial in the criminal court he cannot plead in bar payment of this penalty. He must, if convicted, discharge the additional fine assessed, or go to jail, if such be the sentence. Whatever may be the technical distinctions, he is, in fact, twice prosecuted, twice convicted, and twice punished for the same offense. And one of these prosecutions, convictions, and punishments is had without any regard for the leading principles obtaining in criminal procedure. [. . .]

The most difficult cases in which to exclude the rule of damages as a punishment are those where its application rests upon gross negligence, and where no criminal prosecution can be sustained. There is often a feeling that complete justice cannot be done without punitive satisfaction; but those courts which adhere to the doctrine of exemplary damages in general are by no means unanimous in applying it to this class of cases, and, when so applied, the most guarded language is used, and the most careful limitations are imposed. It is said that the negligence must be "flagrant and culpable;" so much so that malice may "well be inferred or imputed to defendant." Field, *Dam.* §84, and cases cited.

Why may not even this class of cases be safely limited to the rule of compensation? Is not this doctrine, as above explained, sufficient to meet all the reasonable demands of justice? But it is sufficient for us to say that in the case at bar the objections to double prosecutions and punishments for the same offense are decisive. [...]

[Reversed.]

Kemezy v. Peters
79 F.3d 33 (7th Cir. 1996)

POSNER, *Chief Judge.* Jeffrey Kemezy sued a Muncie, Indiana policeman named James Peters under 42 U.S.C. sec. 1983, claiming that Peters had wantonly beaten him with the officer's nightstick in an altercation in a bowling alley where Peters was moonlighting as a security guard. The jury awarded Kemezy $10,000 in compensatory damages and $20,000 in punitive damages. Peters' appeal challenges only the award of punitive damages, and that on the narrowest of grounds: that it was the plaintiff's burden to introduce evidence concerning the defendant's net worth for purposes of equipping the jury with information essential to a just measurement of punitive damages.

The standard judicial formulation of the purpose of punitive damages is that it is to punish the defendant for reprehensible conduct and to deter him and others from engaging in similar conduct. This formulation is cryptic, since deterrence is a purpose of punishment, rather than, as the formulation implies, a parallel purpose, along with punishment itself, for imposing the specific form of punishment that is punitive damages. An extensive academic literature, however, elaborates on the cryptic judicial formula, offering a number of reasons for awards of punitive damages. A review of the reasons will point us toward a sound choice between the majority and minority views [the latter being urged by Peters].

1. Compensatory damages do not always compensate fully. Because courts insist that an award of compensatory damages have an objective basis in evidence, such awards are likely to fall short in some cases, especially when the injury is of an elusive or intangible character. If you spit upon another person in anger, you inflict a real injury but one exceedingly difficult to

quantify. If the court is confident that the injurious conduct had no redeeming social value, so that "overdeterring" such conduct by an "excessive" award of damages is not a concern, a generous award of punitive damages will assure full compensation without impeding socially valuable conduct.

2. By the same token, punitive damages are necessary in such cases in order to make sure that tortious conduct is not underdeterred, as it might be if compensatory damages fell short of the actual injury inflicted by the tort.

These two points bring out the close relation between the compensatory and deterrent objectives of tort law, or, more precisely perhaps, its rectificatory and regulatory purposes. Knowing that he will have to pay compensation for harm inflicted, the potential injurer will be deterred from inflicting that harm unless the benefits to him are greater. If we do not want him to balance costs and benefits in this fashion, we can add a dollop of punitive damages to make the costs greater.

3. Punitive damages are necessary in some cases to make sure that people channel transactions through the market when the costs of voluntary transactions are low. We do not want a person to be able to take his neighbor's car and when the neighbor complains tell him to go sue for its value. We want to make such expropriations valueless to the expropriator and we can do this by adding a punitive exaction to the judgment for the market value of what is taken. This function of punitive damages is particularly important in areas such as defamation and sexual assault, where the tortfeasor may, if the only price of the tort is having to compensate his victim, commit the tort because he derives greater pleasure from the act than the victim incurs pain.

4. When a tortious act is concealable, a judgment equal to the harm done by the act will underdeter. Suppose a person who goes around assaulting other people is caught only half the time. Then in comparing the costs, in the form of anticipated damages, of the assaults with the benefits to him, he will discount the costs (but not the benefits, because they are realized in every assault) by 50 percent, and so in deciding whether to commit the next assault he will not be confronted by the full social cost of his activity.

5. An award of punitive damages expresses the community's abhorrence at the defendant's act. We understand that otherwise upright, decent, law-abiding people are sometimes careless and that their carelessness can result in unintentional injury for which compensation should be required. We react far more strongly to the deliberate or reckless wrongdoer, and an award of punitive damages commutes our indignation into a kind of civil fine, civil punishment.

Some of these functions are also performed by the criminal justice system. Many legal systems do not permit awards of punitive damages at all, believing that such awards anomalously intrude the principles of criminal justice into civil cases. Even our cousins the English allow punitive damages only in an excruciatingly narrow category of cases. But whether because the American legal and political cultures are unique, or because the criminal justice system in this country is overloaded and some of its functions have devolved upon the tort system, punitive damages are a regular feature of American tort cases, though reserved generally for intentional torts, including the deliberate use of excess force as here. This suggests additional functions of punitive damages:

6. Punitive damages relieve the pressures on the criminal justice system. They do this not so much by creating an additional sanction, which could be done by increasing the fines imposed in criminal cases, as by giving private individuals — the tort victims themselves — a monetary incentive to shoulder the costs of enforcement.

7. If we assume realistically that the criminal justice system could not or would not take up the slack if punitive damages were abolished, then they have the additional function of heading off breaches of the peace by giving individuals injured by relatively minor outrages a judicial remedy in lieu of the violent self-help to which they might resort if their complaints to the criminal justice authorities were certain to be ignored and they had no other legal remedy.

What is striking about the purposes that are served by the awarding of punitive damages is that none of them depends critically on proof that the defendant's income or wealth exceeds some specified level. The more wealth the defendant has, the smaller is the relative bite that an award of punitive damages not actually geared to that wealth will take out of his pocketbook, while if he has very little wealth the award of punitive damages may exceed his ability to pay and perhaps drive him into bankruptcy. To a very rich person, the pain of having to pay a heavy award of damages may be a mere pinprick and so not deter him (or people like him) from continuing to engage in the same type of wrongdoing. What in economics is called the principle of diminishing marginal utility teaches, what is anyway obvious, that losing $1 is likely to cause less unhappiness (disutility) to a rich person than to a poor one. [. . .] But rich people are not famous for being indifferent to money, and if they are forced to pay not merely the cost of the harm to the victims of their torts but also some multiple of that cost they are likely to think twice before engaging in such expensive behavior again. Juries, rightly or wrongly, think differently, so plaintiffs who are seeking punitive damages often present evidence of the defendant's wealth. The question is whether they must present such evidence — whether it is somehow unjust to allow a jury to award punitive damages without knowing that the defendant really is a wealthy person. The answer, obviously, is no. A plaintiff is not required to seek punitive damages in the first place, so he should not be denied an award of punitive damages merely because he does not present evidence that if believed would persuade the jury to award him even more than he is asking.

Take the question from the other side: if the defendant is not as wealthy as the jury might in the absence of any evidence suppose, should the plaintiff be required to show this? That seems an odd suggestion too. The reprehensibility of a person's conduct is not mitigated by his not being a rich person, and plaintiffs are never required to apologize for seeking damages that if awarded will precipitate the defendant into bankruptcy. A plea of poverty is a classic appeal to the mercy of the judge or jury, and why the plaintiff should be required to make the plea on behalf of his opponent eludes us. [. . .]

Affirmed.

NOTES

1. *Short-lived victory.* The Colorado Supreme Court's holding in *Murphy v. Hobbs* lasted five years; in 1889 the Colorado General Assembly abrogated the decision, providing by statute that "in all civil actions in which damages shall be assessed by a jury for a wrong done to the person, or to personal or real property, and the injury complained of shall have been attended by circumstances of fraud, malice or insult, or a wanton and reckless disregard of the injured party's rights and feelings, such jury may, in addition to the actual damages sustained by such party, award him reasonable exemplary damages." 1889 Colo. Sess. Laws 64-65 (the modern form of Colorado's statute is largely similar). Every state now permits punitive damages to be awarded in civil cases, though the rules governing the occasions for such awards vary considerably by jurisdiction.

What are the differences between the styles of argument used in *Murphy v. Hobbs* and *Kemezy v. Peters*?

2. *Meager percentages.* In Kopczick v. Hobart Corp., 721 N.E.2d 769 (Ill. App. 1999), the plaintiff was a journeyman meatcutter. He lost a finger on his left hand while operating one of the defendant's machines known as the Model 5700. The 5700 was unusual in that its blade was set at a 75-degree angle to the cutting surface, rather than perpendicular to it; Hobart believed this innovative design feature of the "slant saw" would reduce operator fatigue by providing a measure of horizontal force that would help operators more easily push meat through the saw. The plaintiff alleged that the design of the 5700 caused it to "self-feed," pulling the meat into the blade and tending to draw the operator's hands into the blade as well.

At trial the plaintiff called nine meatcutters to the stand. Each said that he had seen the 5700 model self-feed occasionally, and several had been injured by it themselves. The plaintiff offered evidence that Hobart had notice of 30 prior injuries to meatcutters due to self-feeding by the 5700; he also put into evidence a letter that had been sent from a representative of the meatcutters' union to Hobart. It read in part as follows:

> Many butchers with as many as 30 [to] 40 years of service are very fearful of this slant saw. I'm sure that if you send a Hobart representative into the [workplace] and he spoke to the people about the slant saw, that you . . . would probably call back these machines, as many car dealers call back cars that are unsafe.

A jury awarded the plaintiff $553,644 in compensatory damages and $20 million in punitive damages, finding the company guilty of "willful and wanton" misconduct. The trial court entered judgment on the verdict. The court of appeals reversed:

> [U]ncontradicted evidence established that defendant sold 5,816 Model 5700 saws from 1982 through 1992, the last calendar year before plaintiff's injury. During this same 11-year period, it is a conservative estimate that meatcutters employed the Model 5700 to make approximately 4,540,080,000 cuts of meat. [The 30 similar injuries in the past represent] roughly 0.5% of the total production of the Model 5700 and 0.0000007% of the estimated total number of cuts made with the Model 5700. Such meager percentages do not put a manufacturer of a mass-produced and inherently dangerous product on notice that its product has an unreasonably dangerous defect. This is particularly so when, as in this case, the claimed injuries arise from a risk that inheres in the product's intended use. [. . .]
>
> After a thorough review of the record, we hold that the scant evidence of defendant's pre-injury knowledge of defect, and whatever highly speculative inferences the jury might have drawn from such evidence, were insufficient to have put the question of punitive damages to the jury. Accordingly, the trial court should have granted defendant's motion for JNOV concerning the claim of willful and wanton conduct. We therefore reverse the award of punitive damages based on this claim.

3. *The Pinto case.* In Grimshaw v. Ford Motor Co., 174 Cal. Rptr. 348 (Cal. App. 1981), the plaintiff was severely injured when the Ford Pinto automobile in which he was riding was rear ended by another car, causing the Pinto to burst into flames. The collision pushed the Pinto's gas tank forward and caused it to be punctured by a flange or bolt, and as a result fuel sprayed from the punctured tank into the passenger compartment. The plaintiff alleged that the Pinto was defectively designed. In most subcompact cars the gas tank was located over the rear axle; the Pinto's styling required the tank to be placed behind the rear axle, leaving only nine or ten inches of "crush space," which the court concluded was far less than in any other American automobile. The Pinto also was designed with a less substantial bumper that any other American car produced then or later.

A jury awarded the plaintiff $2,516,000 in compensatory damages and $125 million in punitive damages. The trial court evaluated the size of the punitive damage award by reference to three criteria: "(1) Is the sum so large as to raise a presumption that the award was the result of passion and prejudice and therefore excessive as a matter of law; (2) Does the award bear a reasonable relationship to the net assets of the defendant; and (3) Does the award bear a reasonable relationship to the compensatory damages awarded." The court concluded that the award was excessive, and gave the plaintiff the choice of a reduced award of $3.5 million or a new trial. The plaintiff accepted the remittitur. Ford then appealed, arguing that the evidence was insufficient to support the finding of malice necessary under California law to support any award of punitive damages. The court of appeals affirmed:

> Ford argues that "malice" [. . .] requires *animus malus* or evil motive — an intention to injure the person harmed — and that the term is therefore conceptually incompatible with an unintentional tort such as the manufacture and marketing of a defectively designed product. This contention runs counter to our decisional law. [. . .] [N]umerous California cases [. . .] have interpreted the term "malice" [. . .] to include, not only a malicious intention to injure the specific person harmed, but conduct evincing "a conscious disregard of the probability that the actor's conduct will result in injury to others."
>
> The interpretation of the word "malice" [. . .] to encompass conduct evincing callous and conscious disregard of public safety by those who manufacture and market mass produced articles is consonant with and furthers the objectives of punitive damages. The primary purposes of punitive damages are punishment and deterrence of like conduct by the wrongdoer and others. In the traditional noncommercial intentional tort, compensatory damages alone may serve as an effective deterrent against future wrongful conduct but in commerce related torts, the manufacturer may find it more profitable to treat compensatory damages as a part of the cost of doing business rather than to remedy the defect. Governmental safety standards and the criminal law have failed to provide adequate consumer protection against the manufacture and distribution of defective products. Punitive damages thus remain as the most effective remedy for consumer protection against defectively designed mass produced articles. They provide a motive for private individuals to enforce rules of law and enable them to recoup the expenses of doing so which can be considerable and not otherwise recoverable. [. . .]
>
> Through the results of the crash tests Ford knew that the Pinto's fuel tank and rear structure would expose consumers to serious injury or death in a 20 to 30 mile-per-hour collision. There was evidence that Ford could have corrected the hazardous design defects at minimal cost but decided to defer correction of the shortcomings by engaging in a cost-benefit analysis balancing human lives and limbs against corporate profits. Ford's institutional mentality was shown to be one of callous indifference to public safety. There was substantial evidence that Ford's conduct constituted "conscious disregard" of the probability of injury to members of the consuming public. [. . .]
>
> Ford contends that the phrase "conscious disregard of its possible results" used in the two instructions [on punitive damages] would permit a plaintiff to impugn almost every design decision as made in conscious disregard of some perceivable risk because safer alternative designs are

almost always a possibility. [. . .] The jury was instructed that Ford was not required under the law to produce either the safest possible vehicle or one which was incapable of producing injury. The instructions on malice manifestly referred to conduct constituting conscious and callous disregard of a substantial likelihood of injury to others and not to innocent conduct by the manufacturer. [. . .] Plaintiffs did not argue possibility of injury; they argued that injury was a virtual certainty and that Ford's management knew it from the results of the crash tests.

What is the distinction between *Grimshaw v. Ford Motor Co.* and *Kopczick v. Hobart Corp.*?

4. *Sending the message.* In Moskovitz v. Mt. Sinai Medical Center, 635 N.E.2d 331 (Ohio 1994), the plaintiff alleged that his decedent, Margaret Moskovitz, was the victim of medical malpractice by one Harry E. Figgie III. The plaintiff's evidence was that Figgie had treated Moskovitz for difficulties with one of her legs during the period 1985-1987, and had failed to conduct or recommend a biopsy despite symptoms suggesting the presence of a tumor. Had he done so, the tumor could have been discovered and removed, leaving Moskovitz with a good chance of long-term survival. Instead, she died in 1988. The plaintiff also presented evidence that Figgie had later gone back and tampered with Moskovitz's records to make it look as though he had recommended a biopsy. The jury brought in a verdict against Figgie; in addition to compensatory damages it awarded the plaintiff $3 million in punitive damages. The Ohio Supreme Court held the award excessive and ordered a remittitur:

> Figgie's alteration of records exhibited a total disregard for the law and the rights of Mrs. Moskovitz and her family. An intentional alteration, falsification or destruction of medical records by a doctor, to avoid liability for his or her medical negligence, is sufficient to show actual malice, and punitive damages may be awarded whether or not the act of altering, falsifying or destroying records directly causes compensable harm. However, we reiterate that the purpose of punitive damages is to punish and deter. The jury's reaction in awarding $3 million in punitive damages may be understandable, given its findings of Figgie's activities, but it is wrong. Punishment does not mean confiscation. Figgie's net worth (depending on who is believed) is somewhere between $2.1 million and $3 million. We find that a portion of that net worth will send the message. [. . .] Upon a review of the record, we find that $1 million in punitive damages is the appropriate amount to be awarded.

5. *Someday he'll catch the real killer.* In Rufo v. Simpson, 103 Cal. Rptr. 2d 492 (Cal. App. 2001), the plaintiffs were the parents of Ronald Goldman and Nicole Brown Simpson, both of whom were stabbed to death in the

driveway of Nicole Simpson's home in Los Angeles. The defendant was Orenthal James Simpson, the ex-husband of Nicole Brown Simpson and a well-known sports and entertainment personality. He was prosecuted for murder and acquitted; this civil suit followed, in which a jury found him liable for the killings. To support their claims for punitive damages, the plaintiffs' experts had estimated that the defendant's net worth at the time of trial was $15,703,529, and that he had the potential to earn $2-3 million per year for the rest of his life by exploiting his name and likeness. The jury awarded the plaintiffs a total of approximately $12.5 million in compensatory damages for loss of society, and also awarded them a total of $25 million in punitive damages. The defendant appealed, claiming the award was excessive. The court of appeals affirmed:

> Simpson's contention that evidence of his future financial prospects is legally irrelevant or improper makes no sense. The ultimately proper level of punitive damages is an amount not so low that the defendant can absorb it with little or no discomfort, nor so high that it destroys, annihilates, or cripples the defendant. Whether the defendant's financial prospects are bleak or bright is relevant to the ultimate issue whether the damages will ruin him or be absorbed by him.
>
> In reviewing the [size of the] verdict the appellate court is guided by three main factors: the reprehensibility of the defendant's conduct, the actual harm suffered by the victims, and the wealth of the defendant. [. . .] In this case the first two factors, the reprehensibility of the defendant's conduct and the severity of harm to the victims, have the greatest weight legally possible. In effect the jury found that Simpson committed two deliberate, vicious murders. This is the most reprehensible conduct that society condemns and is ordinarily punished under California criminal law by a sentence of death or life imprisonment without possibility of parole. The harm suffered by the victims was the maximum possible; they were intentionally killed. This case cannot be compared to punitive damages involving a business fraud resulting only in economic harm. Considering the outrageousness of Simpson's conduct and the enormity of its consequences, the amount of $25 million, in the abstract, is not offensive and does not raise a presumption the verdict resulted from passion or prejudice. [. . .]
>
> The evidence here, viewed in the light most favorable to the judgment, shows that Simpson is a wealthy man, with prospects to gain more wealth in the future. The enormity of his misconduct shows that a large amount of punitive damages is necessary to punish him and deter him. There is no formula based on net worth for determining what amount is too much. The fundamental underlying principle is that punitive damages must not be so large they destroy the defendant. Evidence unique to this case shows this award will not destroy Simpson economically. He has pension funds worth $4.1 million that are exempt from execution to pay this award.

Despite the award of punitive damages Simpson can continue to enjoy a comfortable living.

6. *The answer to the first question was "yes."* In Kennan v. Checker Cab Co., 620 N.E.2d 1208 (Ill. App. 1993), the plaintiff, Sean Kennan, was a blind man. With the help of a passerby he hailed a taxicab operated by one of the defendant's drivers in downtown Chicago. When the cab stopped, Kennan opened the door and his guide dog, Ives, climbed onto the seat behind the driver; Kennan sat down next to the dog. After he gave the driver his destination, the driver began screaming over and over, "get out, I no take bitch." Kennan heard the rear door open and felt the driver's hand touch the back of Ives's head. He pushed the driver away. Kennan either got out of the car or was pulled out by the driver; the driver slammed him against the side of the cab and hit him in the face several times. A woman waiting at a nearby bus stop observed this and stepped between the men. She inquired of the driver: "Are you an idiot? Can't you tell the guy is blind?" The driver stopped hitting the plaintiff and said, "No, I couldn't tell he was blind, but look what the dog did to my car." The witness testified that she observed no damage to the taxicab.

Kennan suffered bruises on his face from the incident, but did not seek medical attention or lose time at work. His psychiatrist testified, however, that the altercation caused him to suffer from post-traumatic stress disorder, that he continued to view cab rides as potentially traumatic, humiliating events, and that he had to alter his commute as a result. The jury returned a verdict finding Checker liable and awarding Kennan $120,000 in compensatory damages and $193,000 in punitive damages. Checker appealed, arguing among other things that it should not be held liable for punitive damages based on its driver's conduct. The court of appeals agreed. It applied the "complicity rule" as set out in §217C of the Restatement (Second) of Agency (1958):

> Punitive damages can properly be awarded against a master or other principal because of an act by an agent if, but only if:
> (a) The principal authorized the doing and the manner of the act, or
> (b) the agent was unfit and principal was reckless in employing him, or
> (c) the agent was employed in a managerial capacity and was acting in the scope of his employment, or
> (d) the principal or a managerial agent of the principal ratified or approved the act.

The court also endorsed this discussion from a prior case:

> The complicity rule . . . seems consistent with the rationale behind the concept of punitive damages. Either as a basis for punishment or for deterrence of wrongdoers, some *deliberate corporate participation* should be shown before this sanction is applied. The complicity analysis will

allow punitive damages where the institutional conscience of the corporate master should be aroused while protecting the corporate master from liability for punitive damages when a properly supervised employee acts with requisite circumstances of aggravation.

Said the court:

> Plaintiff sought to present evidence which would establish the following: (1) Checker received a memorandum from the City of Chicago advising cab companies of their legal duty to transport blind persons; (2) prior to February 5, 1985, plaintiff was a regular user of taxis and he had made several complaints to Checker about the refusal of Checker to pick him up; and (3) other blind persons had been refused transportation by Checker taxis. When this evidence is viewed in the light most favorable to the plaintiff, it demonstrates only that Checker may have been aware of the fact that some cab drivers refused to transport blind persons. However, plaintiff's injuries were not caused by a driver refusing to transport him. Plaintiff's injuries were caused by the driver forcibly ejecting him from the cab and/or assaulting and battering him. The evidence does not establish that Checker knew of or authorized cab drivers to forcibly eject or assault and batter their customers.

7. *Provocation.* From the Restatement (Second) of Torts (1965):

§921. PROVOCATION

Compensatory damages are not diminished by the fact that the injured person provoked the tortfeasor; but the provocation is considered in determining the allowance and amount of punitive damages.

> *Illustration 1.* A insults B and runs away. B pursues A, knocks him down and breaks his glasses. A is entitled to compensatory damages for the harm done to his glasses and for any physical harm caused to him, undiminished by the fact that he insulted B. However, the jury should be instructed that while it has discretion to award punitive damages, in determining whether to do so and the amount, it should consider the fact of the insult.

What general theories used to justify punitive damages are consistent or inconsistent with the Restatement's treatment of provocation?

8. *$450 per gallon.* In In re Exxon Valdez, 1995 WL 527990 (D. Alaska 1995), the Exxon tanker *Valdez* ran aground in Prince William Sound in Alaska in 1989, causing a spill of 11 million gallons of crude oil. The plaintiffs' evidence was that the captain of the *Valdez*, Joseph Hazelwood, was an alcoholic who had been drinking on the night of the incident, and that his blood alcohol level at the time of the grounding was approximately .241. He had left the bridge of the tanker shortly before midnight on the

evening of the accident as the vessel was headed toward Bligh Reef. He instructed one of the mates to turn when he was abeam of Busby Island light. The mate made the turn too late, and the tanker ran into the reef.

Various groups of plaintiffs injured by the spill joined in a suit against Exxon. Against Hazelwood the jury awarded $5,000 in punitive damages; against Exxon the jury awarded punitive damages of $5 billion. Exxon appealed, arguing among other things that the jury was improperly instructed. There had been evidence that Exxon was reckless in permitting Hazelwood to captain the *Valdez,* and that the company's work schedules recklessly created a large risk of fatigue on the part of the vessel's crew. But the jury also was instructed that even if Exxon was not itself negligent, the company could be held liable in punitive damages if Hazelwood committed reckless acts on the night of the grounding. Exxon argued that this last instruction misstated the law. It further argued that Hazelwood had violated company policy by leaving the bridge as the tanker approached Bligh Reef; according to Exxon's Navigation and Bridge Organization Manual, "[t]he Master must be on the bridge when 'passing in the vicinity of shoals, rocks or other hazards which represent any threat to safe navigation' and when entering or leaving port." Exxon argued that in defying this instruction Hazelwood was acting outside the scope of his employment, and that in any event Exxon itself had no complicity in his misjudgments.

The district court disagreed with these arguments and entered judgment on the jury's verdict. The court used the test for liability provided by the Restatement (Second) of Agency §217C — the same test used in *Kennan v. Checker Cab Co.,* above. Why was that test thought to permit liability on these facts but not in *Kennan?* (The same test, with minor alterations, also appears at Restatement (Second) of Torts §909.)

After a series of appeals, the punitive damages in the case were reduced to $507.5 million. See *Exxon Shipping Co. v. Baker,* 128 S. Ct. 2605 (2008).

9. *Statutory measures.* Many states have enacted statutes that limit the availability of punitive damages in various ways. Pennsylvania, for example, limits the punitive damages available in medical malpractice actions to twice the amount of the plaintiff's compensatory damages, 40 Pa. St. §1301.812-A(g); Connecticut law provides the same rule for products liability cases. Conn. St. §52-240b. In Georgia, 75 percent of the punitive damage award in a product liability case is paid to the state treasury rather than to the plaintiff. Ga. St. §51-12-5.1(e)(2). And in Virginia, punitive damages in cases of all kinds are limited to $350,000. Va. St. §8.01-38.1.

Who is helped by these statutes? Who is hurt by them?

10. *Punitive damages and the due process clause.* The due process clause of the Fourteenth Amendment to the Constitution provides that no state shall "deprive any person of life, liberty, or property, without due process of law." The provision has been held to require the states to provide certain time-honored procedural safeguards (such as appellate review) before imposing punitive damages on defendants. But does the due process clause set a limit

on the sheer *size* of punitive damage awards in tort cases? The Supreme Court answered that question in the affirmative in BMW of North America v. Gore, 517 U.S. 559 (1996). The plaintiff, Gore, bought a BMW in Alabama. He later discovered that the car's paint job had been damaged during the course of its delivery to the dealership, but that the manufacturer had then repainted it so that it could be sold as "new." Gore sued BMW for fraud. A jury awarded him $4,000 in compensatory damages and $4 million in punitive damages. The Alabama Supreme Court reduced the award to $2 million. The United States Supreme Court held that the reduced award still violated BMW's rights under the due process clause. The Court said that "[t]hree guideposts, each of which indicates that BMW did not receive adequate notice of the magnitude of the sanction that Alabama might impose for adhering to the nondisclosure policy adopted in 1983, lead us to the conclusion that the $2 million award against BMW is grossly excessive: the degree of reprehensibility of the nondisclosure; the disparity between the harm or potential harm suffered by Dr. Gore and his punitive damages award; and the difference between this remedy and the civil penalties authorized or imposed in comparable cases."

Justice Scalia filed a dissenting opinion, arguing that the due process clause requires that certain procedures be followed in awarding punitive damages but imposes no limits on the size of such awards. He also contended that the majority's guideposts "mark a road to nowhere" and "provide no real guidance at all" to future courts asked to assess the constitutionality of large awards of punitive damages.

More recently, the Court struck down an award of $145 million in punitive damages in a case where the plaintiff won compensatory damages of $1 million against an insurance company for its bad-faith refusal to settle a lawsuit. *State Farm Mut. Auto. Ins. Co. v. Campbell*, 538 U.S. 408 (2003). The Court emphasized that "[a] jury must be instructed [. . .] that it may not use evidence of out-of-state conduct to punish a defendant for action that was lawful in the jurisdiction where it occurred," as appeared to have occurred in that case; the Court added that "[d]ue process does not permit courts, in the calculation of punitive damages, to adjudicate the merits of other parties' hypothetical claims against a defendant under the guise of the reprehensibility analysis, but we have no doubt the Utah Supreme Court did that here." The Court also offered the view that "few awards exceeding a single-digit ratio between punitive and compensatory damages, to a significant degree, will satisfy due process."

Cass R. Sunstein, How Law Constructs Preferences
86 Geo. L.J. 2637 (1998)

[. . .] My principal emphasis here is on the broader implications of a recent empirical study of punitive damages, undertaken by Daniel Kahneman, David Schkade, and me. Our study involved about 900 jury eligible citizens in Texas;

each was asked to evaluate punitive damage cases, by saying: (a) how outrageous the defendant's conduct was, on a bounded scale of 0 to 6; (b) how much the defendant should be punished, on the same bounded scale; and (c) how much in the way of punitive damages the defendant should be expected to pay on an unbounded scale of dollars. There were twenty eight total scenarios. The questions allowed measurement of the effects of the defendant firm's size (which was varied), the effects of harm (in all cases, compensatory damages were $200,000, but in some, the harm seemed qualitatively worse), and the effects of context (all participants read one case in isolation, others together).

Here was the basic puzzle that we sought to explore: Frequently the legal system requires judges or juries to make (normative) judgments of some kind and then to translate those judgments into dollar amounts. This is of course the task of juries who impose punitive damages. How does this translation take place? When the translation occurs, what is it that the legal system is doing? Can the task be done well?

Our basic findings were as follows:

1. People have a remarkably high degree of moral consensus on the degree of outrage and punishment that is appropriate for punitive damage cases. At least in the personal injury cases we offered, this moral consensus, on what might be called outrage and punitive intent, cuts across differences in gender, race, income, age, and education. For example, our study shows through the construction of "synthetic juries" that all white, all female, all Hispanic, all male, all poor, all wealthy, all black, all old, and all young juries are likely to come to similar conclusions about how to rank and how to rate a range of cases.

There is one exception to this generalization. Though women and men rank cases in the same way, women tend to rate cases more severely on the bounded scales, and this effect is heightened when the plaintiff is female. (It could as accurately be said that men tend to rate cases more leniently than women, and this effect is heightened when the plaintiff is female.) But this modest difference does not undermine our basic finding, which involves a striking consensus.

2. The consensus fractures when the legal system uses dollars as the vehicle to measure moral outrage. Even when there is a consensus on punitive intent, there is no consensus about the dollar amount that is necessary to produce the appropriate suffering in a defendant. Under existing law, widely shared and reasonably predictable judgments about punitive intent are turned into highly erratic judgments about appropriate dollar punishment. A basic source of arbitrariness with the existing system of punitive damages (and a problem not limited to the area of punitive damages) is the use of an unbounded dollar scale.

3. A modest degree of additional arbitrariness is created by the fact that juries have a hard time making appropriate distinctions among cases in what might be called a "no comparison condition." When one case is seen apart from other cases, people show a general tendency to place it toward the midpoint of any

bounded scale. It is therefore less likely that sensible discriminations will be made among diverse cases. This effect is, however, far less important than the effect identified in (2) in producing arbitrary awards.

4. Harm matters a great deal, even if compensatory damages are held constant. The degree of outrage evoked by the defendant's behavior was not affected by the harm that occurred, but varying the harm had a limited but statistically significant effect on punishment ratings; defendants who had done more harm to the plaintiff were judged to deserve greater punishment. Thus low harm produced an average award of $727,599 and high harm an average award of $1,171,251 — a substantially greater amount.

5. We hypothesized that the defendant firm's size would affect neither outrage nor punitive intent, but that the same degree of punitive intent would be translated into a larger amount of damages when the firm is larger than when it is smaller. As expected, we found no statistically significant effects of firm size on either outrage or punishment judgments. But large firms were punished with much larger dollar awards (an average of $1,009,994) than medium firms ($526,398). This is substantial evidence that equivalent outrage and punitive intent will produce significantly higher dollar awards against wealthy defendants.

The most basic finding that emerges from this study is that outrage and punitive intent are shared, but judgments about dollar awards are not. This is because the legal system gives people no "modulus," or standard, by which to assess different possibilities along the unbounded scale of dollars. If, for example, $2 million in punitive damages were associated with a particular, specified action, juries would have a "modulus" around which to organize their intuitions. The legal system constructs jury's preferences for punitive awards by asking them to come up with a number along the unbounded scale of dollars, subject to instructions that are usually open ended.

How might this problem be handled? Once we see that punitive awards are constructed by the legal system's particular response mode — dollars — we can specify the basis of complaints about the status quo, and generate appropriate reforms. I consider three possible approaches.

If the basic problem is simple unpredictability, the legal system might reduce that problem by asking juries not to come up with dollar amounts, but to rank the case at hand among a preselected set of exemplar cases, or to use a bounded scale of numbers rather than an unbounded scale of dollars. A conversion formula, based on previously compiled population wide data showing how punitive intent corresponds to dollar awards, might be used to generate population wide judgments about dollar amounts. Through this route, it would be possible to reduce variability and to ensure that jury judgments about appropriate dollar punishments do not reflect the likely unrepresentative views of twelve randomly selected people, but those of the population as a whole. The goal of this approach would be to come up with the community's, rather than the isolated jury's, judgment about appropriate dollar awards. This approach is highly populist, because it seeks to obtain popular convictions. The result would be a form of predictable populism.

If the basic problem is that people cannot sensibly map their moral judgments onto dollar awards, the legal system should provide a mechanism by which judges or administrators, rather than jurors, can translate the relevant moral judgments into dollar amounts. It is reasonable to question whether ordinary people can know what a given dollar amount would mean for, or do to, the defendant or those in the position of the defendant. On this view, the jury should also rank the case at hand in comparison to preselected cases, or come up with a number on a bounded scale. A conversion formula, based not on population wide data but on expert judgments about what various awards would actually mean or do, would be used to produce rational judgments about dollar amounts. This approach is a mixture of populist and technocratic elements. It is populist insofar as it relies on the community's punitive intent; it is technocratic insofar as experts come up with the relevant conversion formula. The result would be a form of technocratic populism.

If the basic problem is that people's moral judgments are not the proper basis for punitive awards, judges might, in some or all contexts, use those moral judgments as one factor to be considered among others, or the legal system might dispense with jury judgments entirely in some or all contexts. If, for example, it is believed that existing social norms are not the appropriate basis for punishment, or if deterrence rather than retribution is the appropriate goal of punitive damages, an expert body might decide on appropriate awards, or offer general guidance to trial court judges. Because this approach reduces or eliminates the jury and relies instead on specialists, it attempts a form of bureaucratic rationality.*

*Reprinted with permission of the publisher, Georgetown Law Journal © 1998.

Chapter 10

Defenses

A defendant sued for negligently inflicting harm often will attempt to fend off the claim by pointing to various features of the plaintiff's own conduct. This chapter considers such defenses. They can be divided broadly into two categories. The first, with which we begin, involves claims that the plaintiff was negligent. The second family of defenses involves claims that the plaintiff assumed the risk of the harm that occurred. These latter claims can be further divided into three types: claims that the plaintiff expressly assumed the risk by agreement; claims that the defendant had no duty to protect the plaintiff from the harm suffered because the risk of it was inherent in an activity the plaintiff chose to undertake; and claims — now more rare — that the plaintiff chose to encounter a risk negligently created by the defendant. We consider each sort of claim in turn.

A. CONTRIBUTORY AND COMPARATIVE NEGLIGENCE

The traditional common law rule was that plaintiffs whose own negligence contributed to their injuries generally could not recover anything from defendants whose negligence also contributed to them. This was the doctrine of *contributory negligence*. Most jurisdictions now have abandoned that rule in favor of *comparative negligence* doctrines that reduce the damages paid to a negligent defendant but do not prevent recovery altogether. It will help put the new rules in perspective to begin by considering the older ones.

1. *Contributory negligence: a simple example.* In Harris v. Meadows, 477 So. 2d 374 (Ala. 1985), the plaintiff, Harris, was driving down an avenue in Birmingham. The defendant, Meadows, was driving on the same street in the other direction. Meadows started to make a left turn that brought her car into the path of Harris's car. Harris testified that she blew her horn, applied

her brakes, and "moved over to the right a little bit"; the cars nevertheless collided, causing Harris various injuries for which she sought to recover. Meadows admitted that she had been negligent in making the left turn, but defended on the ground that Harris was guilty of contributory negligence. A jury found for Meadows, and Harris appealed. At trial Harris had testified as follows:

> Q. How far from her vehicle would you say you were when you really came down on your brakes in an attempt to stop?
> A. I didn't really come down on my brakes in an attempt to stop. I slowed down to see that maybe she could get on across there and not hit me. But that was not possible. She was already on me at that point.
> Q. Did you make any attempt to put on your brakes and come to a stop and let this lady turn in front of you to go into Kelly's?
> A. There wasn't time.
> Q. But you never did come down hard on your brakes, lock your brakes, skid, and attempt to stop. You were going to see if she had time to come in front of you?
> A. There was not time to make all those decisions. I just slowed down thinking she would see me coming at that point and stop her turn.
> Q. Did you ever try to mash your brakes to the floor to try to stop your vehicle to keep from hitting the Chevrolet that was turning in front of you?
> A. No, sir.

On the basis of this testimony the Alabama Supreme Court affirmed the judgment for the defendant. Said the court: "[T]here was sufficient evidence before the jury for it to conclude that Harris was guilty of contributory negligence in failing to act reasonably under the circumstances to avoid the collision. This case is perhaps illustrative of the harshness of the contributory negligence doctrine, a doctrine which [...] seems to be firmly established in our jurisprudence."

2. *All or nothing.* As the court says, *Harris v. Meadows* illustrates well the operation of contributory negligence, the traditional rule that barred plaintiffs from recovery if their own negligence contributed at all to an accident. "It has been a rule of law from time immemorial, and is not likely to be changed in all time to come, that there can be no recovery for an injury caused by the mutual default of both parties." *Pa. Ry. Co. v. Aspell*, 23 Pa. 147 (1854). About 50 years after that utterance in *Aspell* was made, however, Mississippi passed the country's first general comparative negligence statute, abolishing the "all or nothing" approach in favor of a regime in which the negligent plaintiff still could obtain a partial recovery from the defendant in many cases. Wisconsin did the same in 1931, and Arkansas in 1955; then

from the late 1960s through the 1980s almost all other states followed suit, usually by action of the legislature but in some cases by judicial decision. At this writing Alabama remains one of a few states where the doctrine of contributory negligence remains good law.

3. *The substance of the standard.* In principle, the meaning of "negligence" is the same whether the conduct being considered is the plaintiff's or the defendant's; the principles discussed in the chapter of this book covering the negligence standard apply in both directions. The traditional rule of contributory negligence was that any such negligence by the plaintiff prevented all recovery. Thus here were many cases forbidding recovery if the plaintiff's negligence, "however slight" (or "in the slightest degree"), contributed to the accident — and stating that the jury should be instructed in just those terms. See, e.g., *Crum v. Ward,* 122 S.E.2d 421 (W. Va. 1961); *Miller v. Montgomery,* 152 A.2d 757 (Pa. 1959); *Capitol Transp. Co. v. Alexander,* 242 S.W.2d 833 (Ark. 1951). The implication and result of these cases could be quite harsh, as plaintiffs who bore but a small share of blame for their injuries could collect nothing from defendants who were largely responsible. In practice, some courts appear to have judged the conduct of plaintiffs a bit more generously than the conduct of defendants to avoid such outcomes. A study of the doctrine's application in California and New Hampshire during the nineteenth century turned up a number of examples:

> In administering tort appeals, the two states' Courts developed a variety of maxim-like ideas emphasizing the lenient and forgiving quality of the contributory negligence standard. Thus, a plaintiff was not required to exercise "great care" or to behave in a "very timid or cautious" way; contributory negligence was not proven by an "indiscretion" or a mere "error of judgment," let alone by a "misjudgment" in retrospect. [. . .] If the plaintiff forgot what he knew about the particular danger, the Court could say that "people are liable to lapses of memory." Attenuating maxims like these were almost totally in lacking the Courts' opinions dealing with the possible negligence of tort defendants, who were frequently held to a standard of the "utmost care." Whatever, then, the symmetry in form of the doctrines of negligence and contributory negligence, they were administered under an emphatic, if implicit, double standard[.]

Gary Schwartz, *Tort Law and the Economy in Nineteenth-Century America: A Reinterpretation,* 90 Yale L.J. 1717, 1762 (1981).

It also is possible for a jury to create, *de facto,* a similar double standard regardless of the court's instructions. Thus, in Alibrandi v. Helmsley, 314 N.Y.S.2d 95 (Sup. Ct. 1970), the plaintiff was a truck driver who arrived at the defendant's building to pick up some packages. All the bays at the defendant's loading dock were occupied; rather than wait for one of them to open up, the plaintiff parked his truck some distance away, retrieved the boxes

himself, put them onto a cart, and then pulled the cart along while he walked
backwards down a ramp toward his truck. He tripped on a loose steel plate on
the ramp and suffered various injuries for which he sued to recover. The case
was tried to a judge rather than a jury. The judge denied recovery, holding the
plaintiff contributorily negligent as a matter of law in deciding to walk the cart
backwards down the ramp:

> I am as confident as one can be about these matters that, had the case
> been tried to a jury, the jury would have determined the sum of plaintiff's
> damages in a substantial amount, deducted a portion equivalent of the
> degree of his negligence, and returned a verdict for the difference.
> In short, as every trial lawyer knows, the jury would likely have ignored
> its instructions on contributory negligence and applied a standard of
> comparative negligence. It would be comfortable for me simply to
> guess what the jury's verdict would have been and then file a one-
> sentence decision holding defendants liable in that amount. Comfort-
> able but false. My duty is to apply the law as I understand it, and I do not
> understand that, no matter that a jury might do, a judge may pretend to
> make a decision on the basis of contributory negligence while actually
> deciding on comparative negligence.

4. *Last clear chance.* The hard results produced by contributory negligence
also were softened in a more explicit way by the doctrine of "last clear chance."
In the leading case of Davies v. Mann, 152 Eng. Rep. 588 (Exch. 1842),
Davies left his donkey to graze by the side of a highway; its legs were fettered to
prevent it from wandering. The defendant's wagon, pulled by a team of horses,
ran over the donkey and killed it. Davies was held entitled to recover despite
his negligence in letting the donkey onto the road. Said Parke, B.:

> [A]lthough the ass may have been wrongfully there, still the defendant
> was bound to go along the road at such a pace as would be likely to
> prevent mischief. Were this not so, a man might justify the driving
> over goods left on a public highway, or even over a man lying asleep
> there, or the purposely running against a carriage going on the wrong side
> of the street.

The holding of *Davies* gradually was generalized into the doctrine of last clear
chance: generally speaking, the plaintiff could recover despite committing
contributory negligence if the defendant had a sufficiently good opportunity
to avoid the accident at a point when the plaintiff did not. Typically it had to be
shown that the defendant saw the plaintiff or had some other notice of him but
failed to avoid inflicting the injury. The doctrine involves many intricacies on
which jurisdictions disagreed: whether, for example, the plaintiff must have
been helpless or merely inattentive when the defendant's chance to take precautions arose; whether it must be shown that the defendant was guilty of

something worse than negligence; whether the plaintiff must have actually perceived the plaintiff or could be held liable if he should have known the plaintiff was there; or whether it matters if the defendant created the peril faced by the plaintiff or only failed to avoid a peril created by the plaintiff himself. If the doctrine of last clear chance still retained vitality, we would be spending a section of this chapter exploring each of those issues and others like them. Given the demise of contributory negligence, however, we will content ourselves with that brief sketch of the outlines of last clear chance and the following excerpts from the Restatement (Second) of Torts:

§479. LAST CLEAR CHANCE: HELPLESS PLAINTIFF

A plaintiff who has negligently subjected himself to a risk of harm from the defendant's subsequent negligence may recover for harm caused thereby if, immediately preceding the harm,

(a) the plaintiff is unable to avoid it by the exercise of reasonable vigilance and care, and

(b) the defendant is negligent in failing to utilize with reasonable care and competence his then existing opportunity to avoid the harm, when he

(i) knows of the plaintiff's situation and realizes or has reason to realize the peril involved in it or

(ii) would discover the situation and thus have reason to realize the peril, if he were to exercise the vigilance which it is then his duty to the plaintiff to exercise.

Comment a. [...] Two explanations are commonly given for this departure from the general rule that contributory negligence bars recovery. One is that the later negligence of the defendant involves a higher degree of fault. This may be true in cases where the defendant has discovered the danger and his conduct approaches intentional or reckless disregard of it; but it fails to explain many cases in which his negligence consists merely of a failure to discover the situation at all, or in slowness, clumsiness, inadvertence, or an error of judgment in dealing with it. The other explanation is that the plaintiff's negligence is not a "proximate" or legal cause of the harm to him, because the later negligence of the defendant is a superseding cause which relieves the plaintiff of responsibility for it. This is quite out of line with modern ideas as to legal cause. Where the injury is to a third person, as for example a passenger in the actor's car, the fact that the actor has the last clear chance does not relieve the other driver of liability. The causal relation can scarcely be otherwise where the injury is to the other driver himself.

In reality the rules of the last clear chance appear to arise out of a dislike for the defense of contributory negligence, which has made the courts reject it in situations where they can regard the defendant's negligence as the final and decisive factor in producing the injury.

Illustration 1. A is driving his car negligently. In consequence he collides at an intersection with the car of B. A's car is thrown onto the other side of the road, upon which C's car is approaching. C sees the car, but instead of stopping unreasonably thinks that he can cut around it. The space is too narrow, and he collides with A's car, overturning it and breaking A's leg. C is subject to liability to A.

Illustration 3. The same facts as in Illustration 1, except that C does everything which then could be done to stop the car but is unable to do so because his brakes are negligently defective. C is not liable to A.

Illustration 4. A is negligently driving his car at night without head-lights. The absence of lights prevents A from discovering B's car, negligently stopped on the highway without lights, in time to avoid a collision with it. Although A is driving with proper care in all other respects, he collides with B's car, injuring B. A is not liable to B.

§480. LAST CLEAR CHANCE: INATTENTIVE PLAINTIFF

A plaintiff who, by the exercise of reasonable vigilance, could discover the danger created by the defendant's negligence in time to avoid the harm to him, can recover if, but only if, the defendant

    (a) knows of the plaintiff's situation, and

    (b) realizes or has reason to realize that the plaintiff is inattentive and therefore unlikely to discover his peril in time to avoid the harm, and

    (c) thereafter is negligent in failing to utilize with reasonable care and competence his then existing opportunity to avoid the harm.

Comment a. The situation dealt with in this Section differs from that dealt with in §479 in one important particular: §479 is applicable only where the plaintiff immediately before his harm could not have avoided it by the exercise of that vigilance which a reasonable man would exercise for his own protection. This Section states the rule under which a plaintiff who could have made timely discovery of his peril if he had been on the alert can recover notwithstanding his negligent inattention. In such a situation, the defendant has no reason to believe that he has the exclusive power to prevent the harm unless he not only knows or has reason to know of the plaintiff's situation but realizes or should realize that the plaintiff does not know the peril of his situation and is, therefore, in a danger from which only the defendant's careful action can protect him.

5. *Why?* From Prosser, *Comparative Negligence*, 41 Cal. L. Rev. 1 (1953):

There has been much speculation as to why the rule [of contributory negligence] found such ready acceptance in later decisions, both in England and in the United States. The explanations given by the courts themselves never have carried much conviction. Most of the decisions have talked about "proximate cause," saying that the plaintiff's negligence is an intervening, insulating cause between the defendant's negligence and the injury. But this cannot be supported unless a meaning is assigned to proximate cause which is found nowhere else. If two automobiles collide and injure a bystander, the negligence of one driver is not held to be a superseding cause which relieves the other of liability; and there is no visible reason for any different conclusion when the action is by one driver against the other. It has been said that the defense has a penal basis, and is intended to punish the plaintiff for his own misconduct; or that the court will not aid one who is himself at fault, and he must come into court with clean hands. But this is no explanation of the many cases, particularly those of the last clear chance, in which a plaintiff clearly at fault is permitted to recover. It has been said that the rule is intended to discourage accidents, by denying recovery to those who fail to use proper care for their own safety; but the assumption that the speeding motorist is, or should be, meditating on the possible failure of a lawsuit for his possible injuries lacks all reality, and it is quite as reasonable to say that the rule promotes accidents by encouraging the negligent defendant. Probably the true explanation lies merely in the highly individualistic attitude of the common law of the early nineteenth century. The period of development of contributory negligence was that of the industrial revolution, and there is reason to think that the courts found in this defense, along with the concepts of duty and proximate cause, a convenient instrument of control over the jury, by which the liabilities of rapidly growing industry were curbed and kept within bounds.

McIntyre v. Balentine
833 S.W.2d 52 (Tenn. 1992)

[Balentine's tractor collided with McIntyre's pickup truck, causing McIntyre various injuries. McIntyre sued Balentine. The evidence at trial tended to show that Balentine had been intoxicated but that McIntyre had been speeding. The jury found the two men equally at fault; the trial court thus gave judgment to the defendant, Balentine, under Tennessee's doctrine of contributory negligence. The court of appeals affirmed. This appeal followed.]

DROWOTA, J. [. . .] The common law contributory negligence doctrine has traditionally been traced to Lord Ellenborough's opinion in *Butterfield v. Forrester*, 103 Eng. Rep. 926 (1809). There, plaintiff, "riding as fast as his horse would go," was injured after running into an obstruction defendant had placed in the road. Stating as the rule that "[o]ne person being in fault will not dispense with another's using ordinary care," plaintiff was denied recovery on the basis that he did not use ordinary care to avoid the obstruction.

The contributory negligence bar was soon brought to America as part of the common law, and proceeded to spread throughout the states. This strict bar may have been a direct outgrowth of the common law system of issue pleading; issue pleading posed questions to be answered "yes" or "no," leaving common law courts, the theory goes, no choice but to award all or nothing. A number of other rationalizations have been advanced in the attempt to justify the harshness of the "all-or-nothing" bar. Among these: the plaintiff should be penalized for his misconduct; the plaintiff should be deterred from injuring himself; and the plaintiff's negligence supersedes the defendant's so as to render defendant's negligence no longer proximate. See *Prosser and Keeton on The Law of Torts*, §65 (5th ed. 1984).

In Tennessee, the rule as initially stated was that "if a party, by his own gross negligence, brings an injury upon himself, or contributes to such injury, he cannot recover;" for, in such cases, the party "must be regarded as the author of his own misfortune." *Whirley v. Whiteman*, 38 Tenn. 610, 619 (1858). In subsequent decisions, we have continued to follow the general rule that a plaintiff's contributory negligence completely bars recovery.

Equally entrenched in Tennessee jurisprudence are exceptions to the general all-or-nothing rule: contributory negligence does not absolutely bar recovery where defendant's conduct was intentional, where defendant's conduct was "grossly" negligent, where defendant had the "last clear chance" with which, through the exercise of ordinary care, to avoid plaintiff's injury, or where plaintiff's negligence may be classified as "remote." [. . .]

Between 1920 and 1969, a few states began utilizing the principles of comparative fault in all tort litigation. Then, between 1969 and 1984, comparative fault replaced contributory negligence in 37 additional states. In 1991, South Carolina became the 45th state to adopt comparative fault, leaving Alabama, Maryland, North Carolina, Virginia, and Tennessee as the only remaining common law contributory negligence jurisdictions.

Eleven states have judicially adopted comparative fault. Thirty-four states have legislatively adopted comparative fault. [. . .]

After exhaustive deliberation that was facilitated by extensive briefing and argument by the parties, amicus curiae, and Tennessee's scholastic community, we conclude that it is time to abandon the outmoded and unjust common law doctrine of contributory negligence and adopt in its place a system of comparative fault. Justice simply will not permit our continued adherence to a rule that, in the face of a judicial determination that others bear primary responsibility, nevertheless completely denies injured litigants recompense for their damages.

We recognize that this action could be taken by our General Assembly. However, legislative inaction has never prevented judicial abolition of obsolete common law doctrines, especially those, such as contributory negligence, conceived in the judicial womb. Indeed, our abstinence would sanction "a mutual state of inaction in which the court awaits action by the legislature and the legislature awaits guidance from the court," *Alvis v. Ribar*, 421 N.E.2d 886, 896 (Ill. 1981), thereby prejudicing the equitable resolution of legal conflicts. [. . .]

Two basic forms of comparative fault are utilized by 45 of our sister jurisdictions, these variants being commonly referred to as either "pure" or "modified." In the "pure" form, a plaintiff's damages are reduced in proportion to the percentage negligence attributed to him; for example, a plaintiff responsible for 90 percent of the negligence that caused his injuries nevertheless may recover 10 percent of his damages. In the "modified" form, plaintiffs recover as in pure jurisdictions, but only if the plaintiff's negligence either (1) does not exceed ("50 percent" jurisdictions) or (2) is less than ("49 percent" jurisdictions) the defendant's negligence.

Although we conclude that the all-or-nothing rule of contributory negligence must be replaced, we nevertheless decline to abandon totally our fault-based tort system. We do not agree that a party should necessarily be able to recover in tort even though he may be 80, 90, or 95 percent at fault. We therefore reject the pure form of comparative fault.

We recognize that modified comparative fault systems have been criticized as merely shifting the arbitrary contributory negligence bar to a new ground. See, e.g., *Li v. Yellow Cab Co.*, 532 P.2d 1226 (Cal. 1975). However, we feel the "49 percent rule" ameliorates the harshness of the common law rule while remaining compatible with a fault-based tort system. We therefore hold that so long as a plaintiff's negligence remains less than the defendant's negligence the plaintiff may recover; in such a case, plaintiff's damages are to be reduced in proportion to the percentage of the total negligence attributable to the plaintiff.

In all trials where the issue of comparative fault is before a jury, the trial court shall instruct the jury on the effect of the jury's finding as to the percentage of negligence as between the plaintiff or plaintiffs and the defendant or defendants. The attorneys for each party shall be allowed to argue how this instruction affects a plaintiff's ability to recover. [. . .]

[The court remanded the case for a new trial in accordance the opinion. In an appendix it included the following special verdict form for use in comparative negligence cases:]

Special Verdict Form

We, the jury, make the following answers to the questions submitted by the court:

1. Was the defendant negligent?

Answer: _____ (Yes or No)
(If your answer is "No," do not answer any further questions. Sign this form and return it to the court.)

2. Was the defendant's negligence a proximate cause of injury or damage to the plaintiff?

Answer: _____ (Yes or No)

(If your answer is "No," do not answer any further questions. Sign this form and return it to the court.)

3. Did the plaintiff's own negligence account for 50 percent or more of the total negligence that proximately caused his/her injuries or damages?

Answer: _____ (Yes or No)
(If your answer is "Yes," do not answer any further questions. Sign this form and return it to the court.)

4. What is the total amount of plaintiff's damages, determined without reference to the amount of plaintiff's negligence?

Amount in dollars: $_____

5. Using 100 percent as the total combined negligence which proximately caused the injuries or damages to the plaintiff, what are the percentages of such negligence to be allocated to the plaintiff and defendant?

Plaintiff _____%

Defendant _____%

(Total must equal 100%)

NOTES

1. *Statute vs. judicial decision.* As the opinion in *McIntyre* notes, most states have now adopted some sort of comparative negligence regime by statute rather than by judicial decision. What considerations should drive the choice between comparative and contributory negligence? Is there reason to prefer a legislative decision on the subject to a move by the courts? Here are three examples of comparative negligence statutes; notice how each differs importantly from the other two:

a. New York:

Civil Practice Law and Rules §1411. DAMAGES RECOVERABLE WHEN CON-TRIBUTORY NEGLIGENCE OR ASSUMPTION OF RISK IS ESTABLISHED

In any action to recover damages for personal injury, injury to property, or wrongful death, the culpable conduct attributable to the claimant or to the decedent, including contributory negligence or assumption of risk, shall not bar recovery, but the amount of damages otherwise recoverable shall be diminished in the proportion which the culpable conduct attributable to the claimant or decedent bears to the culpable conduct which caused the damages.

b. Colorado:

Rev. St. §13-21-111. NEGLIGENCE CASES — COMPARATIVE NEGLIGENCE AS MEASURE OF DAMAGES

(1) Contributory negligence shall not bar recovery in any action by any person or his legal representative to recover damages for negligence resulting in death or in injury to person or property, if such negligence was not as great as the negligence of the person against whom recovery is sought, but any damages allowed shall be diminished in proportion to the amount of negligence attributable to the person for whose injury, damage, or death recovery is made.

(2) In any action to which subsection (1) of this section applies, the court, in a nonjury trial, shall make findings of fact or, in a jury trial, the jury shall return a special verdict which shall state:

(a) The amount of the damages which would have been recoverable if there had been no contributory negligence; and

(b) The degree of negligence of each party, expressed as a percentage.

c. Oregon:

Rev. St. §18.470(1). CONTRIBUTORY NEGLIGENCE NOT BAR TO RECOVERY; COMPARATIVE NEGLIGENCE STANDARD; THIRD PARTY COMPLAINTS

Contributory negligence shall not bar recovery in an action by any person or the legal representative of the person to recover damages for death or injury to person or property if the fault attributable to the claimant was not greater than the combined fault of all [defendants], but any damages allowed shall be diminished in the proportion to the percentage of fault attributable to the claimant. [. . .]

Consider how each of those three states would treat a case where the jury decided that the plaintiff and the defendant were equally at fault; where the plaintiff's share of responsibility was 60 percent and the defendant's was 40 percent; and where those figures were reversed. The "not greater than" formulation (also known as the "50 percent rule") illustrated by the Oregon statute is the most common approach, being used by roughly half the states that have adopted comparative negligence in one form or another. The remaining states are about evenly divided between a "49 percent rule" such as Colorado's (and like the rule adopted in *McIntyre*) and "pure" comparative negligence after the fashion of the New York law. Would you expect the practical difference between the two types of modified comparative negligence — the 50 percent rule and the 49 percent rule — to be significant?

2. *Comparative what?* Notice an ambiguity in the statutes just considered and in the concept of comparative negligence generally: what is being

compared? One possibility is to compare how negligent each party was; another is to ask whose conduct made a greater causal contribution to the accident. To make the problem more concrete, Victor Schwartz offers a hypothetical collision between a motorcyclist and a truck in which both were negligent. Suppose it can be shown that the momentum of the truck contributed 95 percent of the force that injured the motorcyclist — but the motorcyclist was drunk and was speeding, whereas the truck driver's negligence was less flagrant. Should the motorcyclist still recover 95 percent of his damages in a regime of pure comparative fault? Schwartz, Comparative Negligence §17.01 (4th ed. 2002). The Oregon Supreme Court has answered that question in the negative, interpreting its statute to call for a comparison of negligence, not causation:

> There is no reference [in the statute] to causation, or to any question how much the fault of each contributed to the injury. [. . .] We do not mean that the allegedly faulty conduct or condition need not have affected the event for which recovery is sought; as we have said, it must have been a cause in fact. But the statute does not call for apportioning damages by quantifying the contribution of several causes that had to coincide to produce the injury.
>
> Rather, ORS 18.470 [. . .] calls upon the factfinder to assess and quantify fault. If the plaintiff's conduct is not faultless, the assessment has two purposes: to determine whether her fault is "not greater than" that of defendants, and if it is not, then to reduce the plaintiff's recovery of damages "in the proportion to the percentage of fault attributable to" the plaintiff. The question remains against what standard this "percentage of fault" [. . .] is to be measured.

Sandford v. General Motors Corp., 642 P.2d 624 (Or. 1982). There are cases elsewhere holding that the jury should compare causation, but these generally are in situations involving products liability where the defendant is held strictly liable, making an inquiry into the extent of its negligence seem out of place. See, e.g., *Murray v. Fairbanks Morse*, 610 F.2d 149 (3d Cir. 1979). In Tennessee as in many other states, the courts have avoided committing to one view or the other in ordinary negligence cases and have charged juries with comparing causation as well as negligence — and more:

> [T]he percentage of fault assigned to each party should be dependent upon all the circumstances of the case, including such factors as: (1) the relative closeness of the causal relationship between the conduct of the defendant and the injury to the plaintiff; (2) the reasonableness of the party's conduct in confronting a risk, such as whether the party knew of the risk, or should have known of it; (3) the extent to which the defendant failed to reasonably utilize an existing opportunity to avoid

the injury to the plaintiff; (4) the existence of a sudden emergency requiring a hasty decision; (5) the significance of what the party was attempting to accomplish by the conduct, such as an attempt to save another's life; and (6) the party's particular capacities, such as age, maturity, training, education, and so forth.

Eaton v. McLain, 891 S.W.2d 587 (Tenn. 1994).

3. *The question of efficiency.* The condemnation of contributory negligence usually was based on its perceived unfairness to plaintiffs. But economic analysts have focused on a different aspect of the question: which rule — contributory or comparative negligence — is more efficient? The economist's goal is to find rules to govern liability for accidents that minimize the sum of all the costs involved: the costs of the accidents themselves, but also the costs of precautions and of litigation. A possible implication of this approach is that the law should try to induce the party who can prevent an accident at least cost to take precautions against it. See G. Calabresi, The Costs of Accidents (1970). Sometimes this may be the victim of an injury rather than the party who inflicted it — the pedestrian rather than the driver. Does comparative negligence create better incentives than contributory negligence for both parties to an accident to take the right level of precautions? Does one of the rules cause more uncertainty than the other, thus creating a greater need for litigation and raising administrative costs? Is it relevant whether the rules governing comparative negligence are well known within a jurisdiction? For a rule to have an impact on incentives it need not affect the average person; it is enough if it exerts influence at the margin, causing some people to behave differently. Are there situations in which you would expect the rules governing contributory fault to significantly influence behavior?

4. *Intentional torts, etc.* One result of the rise of comparative negligence has been the modification or demise of doctrines that were developed to mitigate the effects of contributory negligence. The doctrine of last clear chance has been abolished in most jurisdictions, as noted earlier in this section; also being widely phased out is the doctrine of secondary assumption of risk, considered later in this chapter. A more complicated question involves the treatment of conduct by the defendant that is reckless, wanton, or otherwise worse than negligent. The doctrine of contributory negligence did not deprive plaintiffs of recoveries in such cases, but jurisdictions now using comparative negligence often do allow the plaintiff's negligence to be balanced against worse conduct by defendants at least some of the time. In Danculovich v. Brown, 593 P.2d 187 (Wyo. 1987), for example, the court allowed a reduction of damages on account of the plaintiff's ordinary negligence despite the defendant's gross negligence, but would not allow such a reduction if the defendant's misconduct had been "willful and wanton," reasoning that the latter sort of misbehavior involved intent and

thus was different in kind from the sort of fault meant to be compared under the state's statute. In keeping with this principle, comparative negligence, like contributory negligence, generally is held to be no defense to an intentional tort claim.

5. *Declining to balance.* A related consequence of comparative negligence is that many other rules that used to result in decisive victories for defendants have now been turned into mere factors for juries to consider. The doctrine of secondary assumption of risk is one example, as noted a moment ago. Another is the old rule that in many situations a plaintiff could not recover for injuries caused by a danger that was "open and obvious"; today the obviousness of a danger is more likely to be left for the jury to balance against the other considerations in a case, and to produce a reduced award for the plaintiff rather than a complete denial of recovery. But this preference for balancing does not always hold sway. Sometimes courts still will conclude that a plaintiff's own negligence was of a sort that should preclude any recovery, even if a negligent defendant was partly responsible for the plaintiff's injuries as well. And sometimes courts will say that a plaintiff's negligence should not cause any reduction in recovery even if it seems clearly to have contributed to the injury the plaintiff suffered. The following cases consider some examples of these decisions.

6. *Serious violations.* In Manning v. Brown, 689 N.E.2d 1382 (N.Y. 1997), the plaintiff, Manning, and her friend, Amidon, were high school classmates. Neither girl had a driver's license or learner's permit. One night they found an unattended car belonging to a friend. They discovered a set of keys in the car and drove off with it. The two of them took turns driving. At one point Manning suggested that Amidon, who then was driving, should tune the car's radio to the same station it was on when they found it, so that the car's owners would not deduce that the car had been in use. As Amidon adjusted the radio she swerved into a pole, causing Manning various injuries. Manning sued Amidon and the owners of the car, a couple named Brown, for negligence. The trial court gave summary judgment to the defendants, and the court of appeals affirmed:

> Defendant Amidon contends that plaintiff's complaint seeking damages for personal injuries should be dismissed as plaintiff was a willing participant in an illegal activity. In *Barker v. Kallash*, 479 N.Y.S.2d 201, we held, as a matter of public policy, that where a plaintiff has engaged in unlawful conduct, the courts will not entertain suit if the plaintiff's conduct constitutes a *serious* violation of the law and the injuries for which the plaintiff seeks recovery are the *direct* result of that violation. The policy derives from the rule that one may not profit from one's own wrongdoing and precludes recovery "at the very threshold of the plaintiff's application for judicial relief." *Barker v. Kallash, supra,* 479 N.Y.S.2d 201. "[R]ecovery is denied, not because plaintiff

contributed to [her] injury, but because the public policy of this State generally denies judicial relief to those injured in the course of committing a serious criminal act." Id. [. . .]

[The] difficult question is whether plaintiff's conduct constituted such a serious violation of the law that she should be precluded, as a matter of public policy, from recovery. We are persuaded that it does. [. . .] Plaintiff and Amidon, both unlicensed drivers, unjustifiably engaged in an activity which was hazardous not only to themselves but also to the public at large. An automobile is an inherently dangerous instrument in the hands of an inexperienced operator. It becomes even more dangerous when the inexperienced operator does not have permission to take the vehicle. We note that joyriding, as evidenced in the instant case, is typically characterized by more than mere unauthorized use. The unauthorized use is usually accompanied by reckless or excessively fast driving, posing a threat to innocent third parties. Such criminal conduct which puts the public at grave risk constitutes a serious violation.

Amidon was prosecuted as a juvenile and sentenced to two years in the custody of the New York State Division for Youth. Manning was not prosecuted.

7. *Pre-operative negligence.* In Fritts v. McKinne, 934 P.2d 371 (Okla. 1997), Fritts drove his pickup truck into a tree at 70 miles per hour one night while he was drunk. All of the major bones in his face were broken in the accident. The defendant, McKinne, was an otorhinolaryngologist called upon to perform a tracheostomy on Fritts so that he could breathe during surgery. Fritts suffered a ruptured artery during the procedure and bled to death. His spouse sued McKinne, alleging that he negligently had cut open the artery while performing the tracheostomy. McKinne asserted a comparative negligence defense, claiming that Fritts was responsible for his own death because he had been driving while drunk (or riding with a drunk driver; there was some dispute as to whether Fritts or a friend of his, also drunk, had been behind the wheel). The trial court permitted McKinne to present this theory to the jury, which in turn brought in a verdict in McKinne's favor. The court of appeals reversed: "Under the guise of a claim of contributory negligence, a physician simply may not avoid liability for negligent treatment by asserting that the patient's injuries were originally caused by the patient's own negligence." Why not? What is the distinction between *Fritts v. McKinne* and *Manning v. Brown*?

8. *Rescuers.* In Ouellette v. Carde, 612 A.2d 687 (R.I. 1992), the defendant, Carde, jacked up a car in his garage and set about trying to replace the muffler. The car fell off the jack, pinning Carde underneath and releasing gasoline into the garage. He worked himself free and called his neighbor, Ouellette, on the phone. During his conversation with her, Carde passed out. Ouellette rushed to his house and revived him. They decided to

leave the garage, so Ouellette pressed the button on Carde's electric garage door opener. While the door was opening, the gasoline that earlier had spilled onto the garage floor ignited, resulting in a large explosion that caused Carde and Ouellette various injuries. Ouellette sued Carde, alleging that his negligence in creating the situation was the proximate cause of her damages. Carde countered that Ouellette had herself been negligent in certain respects in her efforts to rescue him. The trial court refused to permit Carde to make these arguments or to allow the jury to consider whether Ouellette had been negligent. The Rhode Island Supreme Court affirmed:

> The law places a premium on human life, and one who voluntarily attempts to save a life of another should not be barred from complete recovery. Only if a person is rash or reckless in the rescue attempt should recovery be limited; accordingly we hold that [this] doctrine survives the adoption of the comparative-negligence statute and that principles of comparative negligence apply only if a defendant establishes that the rescuer's actions were rash or reckless. [. . .] Because defendant did not assert that plaintiff acted recklessly, the trial justice did not err in denying defendant's requested jury instruction on comparative negligence.

What principles emerge from *Ouellette v. Carde* and *Fritts v. McKinne?*

9. *Drunk driving (problem).* In Alami v. Volkswagen of America, Inc., 766 N.E.2d 574 (N.Y. 2002), a man named Alami drove his Volkswagen Jetta into a utility pole as he exited the Saw Mill Parkway in Yonkers, suffering fatal injuries. Alami's blood alcohol level at the time of his death was over the limit set for drivers by state statute. Alami's widow brought suit against Volkswagen, alleging that Alami's injuries from the crash were increased by a defect in the car's design that caused the floorboard to buckle upward during the crash. Volkswagen sought summary judgment on the ground that the plaintiff's suit was barred by *Manning v. Brown.* The trial court granted the motion and dismissed the case. The plaintiff appealed. What result?

10. *The disobedient patient (problem).* In Van Vacter v. Hierholzer, 865 S.W.2d 355 (Mo. App. 1993), Van Vacter suffered a heart attack at the age of 40. His doctors instructed him to quit smoking, to exercise, and to reduce his weight and cholesterol level. The following year his arteries were narrowing and his doctors prescribed a regimen of drug treatment. Van Vacter did not follow his doctors' directions, did not take the drugs they prescribed, and did not return for examinations as they had instructed. Several years later Van Vacter went to a hospital complaining of chest pains. A doctor there, Hierholzer, performed tests, concluded that Van Vacter's condition had stabilized, and sent him home. He died there a few hours later. His widow sued Hierholzer, claiming her negligence in sending Van Vacter home was the cause of his death. Hierholzer asked that the jury be instructed that it could reduce any recovery for the plaintiff by the extent to which Van

Vacter's death was caused by his own negligent failure to follow the instructions of his physicians during the five years before he died. The jury was so instructed and returned a verdict finding Hierholzer negligent but finding Van Vacter 93 percent responsible for his own death and awarding no damages. The plaintiff appealed, arguing that it was error to permit the jury to consider Van Vacter contributorily negligent at all. What result?

B. EXPRESS ASSUMPTION OF RISK

We turn now to a different family of defenses based on the plaintiff's conduct: claims not that the plaintiff was negligent but that the plaintiff assumed the risk of the harm that occurred and therefore should be barred from recovering from the defendant. As noted at the start of the chapter, these claims can be further divided into three types that may roughly be summarized as follows: claims that the plaintiff expressly assumed the risk by formal agreement; claims that the defendant had no duty to protect the plaintiff from the harm suffered because the risk of it was inherent in an activity the plaintiff chose to under-take; and claims — now more rare — that the plaintiff chose to encounter a risk negligently created by the defendant. We now consider each form of assumption of risk, beginning with the express variety.

1. *Any and all risk.* In Van Tuyn v. Zurich American Ins. Co., 447 So. 2d 318 (Fla. App. 1984), the plaintiff's evidence was that she was a patron at an establishment known as the Club Dallas. On the club's premises was a mechanical bull named "J.R." After observing other patrons riding the bull, the plaintiff decided to try it. She told the operator that she had never ridden before and asked that he go slowly. His response, as the plaintiff recalled it, was something to the effect of, "Don't worry about it. We'll take care of it." The plaintiff was asked to read and sign a release. She signed it without reading it. The release said:

> I fully understand that the mechanical Bucking Brama Bull known as "JR" is a dangerous amusement device.
>
> I hereby voluntarily assume any and all risk, including injury to my person and property which may be caused as a result of my riding or attempting to ride this Bucking Brama Bull.
>
> In consideration for CLUB DALLAS permitting me to ride such amuse-ment device, I hereby voluntarily release, waive, and discharge CLUB DALLAS, Marr Investments, Inc., their lessors, heirs, successors and/or assigns from any and all claims, demands, damages and causes of action of any nature whatsoever which I, my heirs, my assigns, or my successors may have against any of them for, on account of, or by reason of my riding or attempting to ride this Bucking Brama Bull. I also state that I am not

under the influence of alcohol or any other intoxicant and execute this GENERAL RELEASE, WAIVER OF CLAIM AND ASSUMPTION OF RISK AGREEMENT of my own free will and accord.

After the plaintiff had been on the bull for about 15 seconds, it began to speed up and she was thrown to the floor. She suffered various injuries, and brought a suit against the Club claiming that the operator of the bull negligently handled the mechanism that regulated the bull's speed. The trial court gave summary judgment to the defendants. The court of appeals reversed:

> An exculpatory clause, while looked on with disfavor, may operate to absolve a defendant from liability arising out of his/her own negligent acts. For such a clause to be effective, however, it must clearly state that it releases the party from liability for its own negligence.
>
> The agreement being reviewed is devoid of any language manifesting the intent to either release or indemnify Club Dallas, Marr Investments, Inc., for its own negligence. Therefore, the agreement does not, as a matter of law, bar the Appellant's recovery. [. . .]

If the release did not apply to the plaintiff's claim in this case, can you imagine a claim to which it would apply?

2. *Parachutes.* In Manning v. Brannon, 956 P.2d 156 (Okla. App. 1997), the plaintiff, Manning, took skydiving lessons from the defendant. During his training, Manning was given a detailed exculpatory contract that released the defendant from liability in the event of his injury or death. Manning watched a video tape in which an attorney explained the terms of the contract. Manning read, signed, and initialed the contract in 14 places. The release read in part as follows:

> (5) ASSUMPTION OF THE RISK. I understand and acknowledge that parachuting activities are inherently dangerous and I EXPRESSLY AND VOLUNTARILY ASSUME THE RISK OF DEATH OR OTHER PERSONAL INJURY SUSTAINED WHILE PARTICIPATING IN PARACHUTING ACTIVITIES WHETHER OR NOT CAUSED BY THE NEGLIGENCE OR OTHER FAULT of [defendant] including but not limited to equipment malfunction from whatever cause, inadequate training, and deficiencies in the landing area, or any other fault of [defendant].

On Manning's third jump, both his main and reserve chutes malfunctioned by deploying simultaneously. As instructed, he cut away his main chute. Either the reserve chute failed to fully inflate, however, or Manning was unable to properly control the jump, or he disregarded audio instructions he was receiving from a jump instructor on the ground; in any event, he spiraled into a pond, sustaining various injuries. Manning brought a lawsuit claiming that his injuries were attributable to the defendant's negligence in improperly packing his parachute or in negligently training him. The jury returned a verdict finding both parties 50 percent negligent and awarding Manning damages, and the trial court denied the defendant's motion for judgment notwithstanding the verdict. The defendant appealed.

Held, for the defendant, that the release was enforceable and that the trial court erred in denying its motion for judgment notwithstanding the verdict. Said the court:

> [T]he court must ascertain the equality of the contracting parties' bargaining power by assessing first the "importance of the subject matter to the physical or economic well-being of the party agreeing to the release" and second the "amount of free choice that party could have exercised when seeking alternate services." As to the former, Manning neither adduced evidence nor argued that parachuting was necessary or important to his physical or economic well-being. Regarding the second element, Manning again neither adduced evidence nor argued that he had no choice but to agree to be trained by and jump with Paradise as opposed to going elsewhere, parachuting without training, or choosing not to jump; in fact, the record reflects Manning was offered his money back if he did not want to jump and was offered the names of other sky-diving training facilities. Accordingly, we find no disparity in the bargaining power of the parties.

Hansen, J., dissented:

> In my view a party should not be permitted to contract to exculpate himself from responsibility for severe personal injury resulting from his acts in willful or reckless disregard for the safety of others, particularly where any negligence would create a strong potential of immediate and violent death. In such an instance, to require a participant to allow Appellants to be negligent in packing a parachute certainly violates the public policy of this state.

What is the distinction between *Manning v. Brannon* and *Van Tuyn v. Zurich American Ins. Co.* (the L case of the mechanical bull)? In thinking about the *Manning* case, is it fair to assume that the defendants did negligently pack the plaintiff's parachute? Can we assume there also would have been no liability if the defendants had forgotten altogether to include a parachute in the plaintiff's backpack, so that he plummeted to his death? How might you distinguish such a case from *Manning*?

Why does the law enforce these sorts of waivers at all? If it turns out that the defendant inexpensively could have prevented the harm the plaintiff suffered, why does anything the plaintiff signed in advance prevent the courts from saying so and assigning liability accordingly? What incentives are created by enforcing such agreements, and what incentives are created by declining to enforce them?

3. *Clerical ticket.* In Anderson v. Erie Ry. Co., 119 N.E. 557 (N.Y. 1918), a clergyman named Anderson bought a ticket to ride on the defendant's railroad at a reduced fare — a "clerical ticket." On the back of the ticket were these words: "In consideration of this ticket being sold at a reduced rate, a person accepting and using it expressly agrees to and does thereby assume all risk of accidents and damage to person and property, whether caused by negligence of the company or that of its agents or employees or otherwise." The train derailed and Anderson was killed. His administrator sued the railroad to recover and won a jury verdict. The court of appeals reversed, holding that the release barred recovery:

> The sole question presented by the appeal is whether the release from liability for negligence given by plaintiff's intestate to defendant, in consideration of the reduced rate at which the ticket was sold to him, prevents a recovery. Had the intestate, at the time of the accident, been traveling on a pass there could be but one answer to the question. A recovery could not be had. [. . .] Mr. Justice Brewer in *Northern Pacific Ry. Co. v. Adams*, 192 U. S. 440 (1904), tersely stated the reason for the rule as follows: "The railway company was not as to Adams a carrier for hire. It waived its right as a common carrier to exact compensation. It offered him the privilege of riding in its coaches without charge if he would assume the risk of negligence. He was not in the power of the company and obliged to accept its terms. They stood on an equal footing. If he had desired to hold it to its common law obligations to him as a passenger, he could have paid his fare and compelled the company to receive and carry him. He freely and voluntarily chose to accept the privilege offered, and having accepted that privilege cannot repudiate the conditions. It was not a benevolent association, but doing a railroad business for profit; and free passengers are not so many as to induce negligence on its part. So far as the element of contract controls, it was a contract which neither party was bound to enter into, and yet one which each was at liberty to make and, no public policy was violated thereby."
>
> Does an agreement to sell a ticket at a reduced rate of fare, in consideration of exemption from liability in case of negligence, change the rule? I do not think it does. No good reason can be suggested why it should. If a railroad company and a passenger be permitted to make such contract at all, then they are the sole judges of the amount of consideration which will compensate the one for being relieved from liability and the other for assuming the risk, whether it be the whole fare or anything less than that.

The usual common law rule, as *Anderson* implies, was that if a passenger signed a release promising not to sue a common carrier for injuries suffered as a result of the carrier's negligence, the release was void. What is the sense of that rule — and of the exception to it recognized by *Anderson?*

4. *The Tunkl test.* In Tunkl v. Regents of the University of California, 32 Cal. Rptr. 33 (Cal. 1963), Hugo Tunkl was admitted to the UCLA Medical Center. Upon entering he signed a document setting forth certain "Conditions of Admission." Condition number six read as follows:

> RELEASE: The hospital is a nonprofit, charitable institution. In consideration of the hospital and allied services to be rendered and the rates charged therefor, the patient or his legal representative agrees to and hereby releases The Regents of the University of California, and the hospital from any and all liability for the negligent or wrongful acts or omissions of its employees, if the hospital has used due care in selecting its employees.

Tunkl brought a lawsuit claiming that he was injured by acts of malpractice committed by employees of the medical center. A jury found that Tunkl understood or should have understood the significance of the release, and brought in a verdict for the defendants. The California Supreme Court reversed, holding the release unenforceable. The court noted case law holding that exculpatory provisions of the sort the plaintiff signed may be held unenforceable if they involve "the public interest." The court went to discuss the problem of identifying such provisions:

> If, then, the exculpatory clause which affects the public interest cannot stand, we must ascertain those factors or characteristics which constitute the public interest. The social forces that have led to such characterization are volatile and dynamic. No definition of the concept of public interest can be contained within the four corners of a formula. The concept, always the subject of great debate, has ranged over the whole course of the common law; rather than attempt to prescribe its nature, we can only designate the situations in which it has been applied. We can determine whether the instant contract does or does not manifest the characteristics which have been held to stamp a contract as one affected with a public interest.
>
> In placing particular contracts within or without the category of those affected with a public interest, the courts have revealed a rough outline of that type of transaction in which exculpatory provisions will be held invalid. Thus the attempted but invalid exemption involves a transaction which exhibits some or all of the following characteristics. It concerns a business of a type generally thought suitable for public regulation. The party seeking exculpation is engaged in performing a service of great importance to the public, which is often a matter of practical necessity for some members of the public. The party holds himself out as willing to

perform this service for any member of the public who seeks it, or at least for any member coming within certain established standards. As a result of the essential nature of the service, in the economic setting of the transaction, the party invoking exculpation possesses a decisive advantage of bargaining strength against any member of the public who seeks his services. In exercising a superior bargaining power the party confronts the public with a standardized adhesion contract of exculpation, and makes no provision whereby a purchaser may pay additional reasonable fees and obtain protection against negligence. Finally, as a result of the transaction, the person or property of the purchaser is placed under the control of the seller, subject to the risk of carelessness by the seller or his agents.

While obviously no public policy opposes private, voluntary transactions in which one party, for a consideration, agrees to shoulder a risk which the law would otherwise have placed upon the other party, the above circumstances pose a different situation. In this situation the releasing party does not really acquiesce voluntarily in the contractual shifting of the risk, nor can we be reasonably certain that he receives an adequate consideration for the transfer. Since the service is one which each member of the public, presently or potentially, may find essential to him, he faces, despite his economic inability to do so, the prospect of a compulsory assumption of the risk of another's negligence. The public policy of this state has been, in substance, to posit the risk of negligence upon the actor; in instances in which this policy has been abandoned, it has generally been to allow or require that the risk shift to another party better or equally able to bear it, not to shift the risk to the weak bargainer.

In the light of the decisions, we think that the hospital-patient contract clearly falls within the category of agreements affecting the public interest. To meet that test, the agreement need only fulfill some of the characteristics above outlined; here, the relationship fulfills all of them. [. . .] In insisting that the patient accept the provision of waiver in the contract, the hospital certainly exercises a decisive advantage in bargaining. The would-be patient is in no position to reject the proffered agreement, to bargain with the hospital, or in lieu of agreement to find another hospital. The admission room of a hospital contains no bargaining table where, as in a private business transaction, the parties can debate the terms of their contract. As a result, we cannot but conclude that the instant agreement manifested the characteristics of the so-called adhesion contract. Finally, when the patient signed the contract, he completely placed himself in the control of the hospital; he subjected himself to the risk of its carelessness.

The *Tunkl* case is well known (how can it be distinguished from *Anderson?*), and many courts in other jurisdictions have borrowed its framework (the "Tunkl test") to assess the enforceability of releases. One court summarized the resulting trend as follows:

> Generally, a written contract defines the extent of the obligations of contracting parties, and a valid exculpatory clause will preclude recovery. It was recognized long ago that parties may contractually absolve themselves from liability for the consequences of their negligent acts. [. . .] However, the law also recognized that lying behind these contracts is a residuum of public policy which is antagonistic to carte blanche exculpation from liability; and thus developed the rule that these provisions would be strictly construed with every intendment against the party seeking their protection. Responding to changes in economic and social necessities, courts then went beyond this rule of construction and found that in certain situations and relations express agreements by which one party assumes the risk of another's conduct could not, in good conscience, be accepted. Where a disparity of bargaining power has grown out of economic necessity for certain goods or services or from a monopolistic position of a seller, courts have found exculpatory agreements inimical to the public interest. Where an agreement does not represent a free choice on the part of the plaintiff, where he is forced to accept the clause by the necessities of his situation, courts have refused to enforce such agreements as contrary to public policy. This rule has been applied broadly in the employer-employee relationship; in situations where one party is charged with a duty of public service [citing cases, including *Tunkl*, involving public utilities, hospitals, and common carriers]; to agreements which attempt to exculpate one from liability for the violation of a statute or regulation designed to protect human life; and elsewhere, e.g., Uniform Commercial Code sec. 2-719(3), 12A P.S. sec. 2-719, provides that the limitation of consequential damages for injury to the person in the case of consumer goods is prima facie unconscionable.

Phillips Home Furnishings, Inc. v. Continental Bank, 331 A.2d 840, 843-844 (Pa. Super. 1974).

5. *Further attempts at summary.* From the Restatement (Second) of Torts (1965):

§496B. EXPRESS ASSUMPTION OF RISK

A plaintiff who by contract or otherwise expressly agrees to accept a risk of harm arising from the defendant's negligent or reckless conduct cannot recover for such harm, unless the agreement is invalid as contrary to public policy.

  Comment b. There is no general policy of the law which prevents the parties from agreeing that the defendant shall be under no such general or specific duty to the plaintiff. [. . . T]he parties may agree that the defendant shall not be liable even for conduct intended to invade the plaintiff's interests. Likewise they may agree that the defendant shall not be liable for conduct which would otherwise be negligent or reckless. Where such an agreement is freely and fairly made, between parties who are in an equal bargaining position, and there is no social interest with which they interfere, it will generally be upheld. Thus the plaintiff may agree, for or without consideration, that an adjoining landowner may carry on blasting operations which involve such a high degree of risk of harm to the plaintiff's house that they would otherwise be considered reckless.

Comment c. In order for an express agreement assuming the risk to be effective, it must appear that the plaintiff has given his assent to the terms of the agreement. Particularly where the agreement is drawn by the defendant, and the plaintiff's conduct with respect to it is merely that of a recipient, it must appear that the terms were in fact brought home to him and understood by him, before it can be found that he has accepted them.

Illustration 1. A, attending a theatre, checks his hat in B's check room. He is handed a ticket, on the back of which, in fine print, it is stated that B will not be liable for any loss or damage to the hat. Reasonably believing the ticket to be a mere receipt, A accepts it without reading it. B negligently loses the hat. A is not bound by the provision on the back of the ticket.

Comment d. In order for the agreement to assume the risk to be effective, it must also appear that its terms were intended by both parties to apply to the particular conduct of the defendant which has caused the harm. Again, where the agreement is drawn by the defendant and the plaintiff passively accepts it, its terms will ordinarily be construed strictly against the defendant. In particular, general clauses exempting the defendant from all liability for loss or damage will not be construed to include loss or damage resulting from his intentional, negligent, or reckless misconduct, unless the circumstances clearly indicate that such was the plaintiff's understanding and intention. On the same basis, general clauses exempting the defendant from all liability for negligence will not be construed to include intentional or reckless misconduct, or extreme and unusual kinds of negligence, unless such intention clearly appears.

Comment j. Disparity of bargaining power. An express agreement for the assumption of risk will not, in general, be enforced where there is such disparity of bargaining power between the parties that the agreement does not represent a free choice on the part of the plaintiff. The basis for such a result is the policy of the law which relieves the party who is at such a disadvantage from harsh, inequitable, and unfair contracts which he is forced to accept by the necessities of his situation. The disparity in bargaining power may arise from the defendant's monopoly of a particular field of service, from the generality of use of contract clauses insisting upon assumption of risk by all those engaged in such a field, so that the plaintiff has no alternative possibility of obtaining the service without the clause; or it may arise from the exigencies of the needs of the plaintiff himself, which leave him no reasonable alternative to the acceptance of the offered terms.

Illustration 5. In a crowded city, A drives his car around for half an hour without finding a place to park it. Having no other way to leave his car in order to transact important business, he drives it into B's garage. B gives him a ticket, of a type in general use in garages and parking places in the city, which states on its face that the car is left entirely at A's risk, and that B will not be liable for any loss or damage, even though it is due to his negligence. A reads the ticket and accepts it without comment. Through the negligence of B the car is stolen. The terms of the ticket are not effective to bar A's recovery from B for the loss of the car.

6. *Medical dilemma (problem).* In Shorter v. Drury, 695 P.2d 116 (Wash. 1985), a woman named Shorter became pregnant; the fetus died at an early stage of the pregnancy, however, and her doctor recommended a "dilation and curettage" (D and C) procedure to remove it from her uterus. Shorter was a Jehovah's Witness, and was forbidden by the tenets of the religion to accept a blood transfusion. She understood that the D and C procedure entailed a risk of bleeding, and signed a document at the hospital stating that she wanted to receive no transfusions of blood and releasing the hospital and its doctors "from any responsibility whatever for unfavorable reactions or any untoward results due to my refusal to permit the use of blood or its derivatives[.]" The procedure went badly, and Shorter began to suffer profuse bleeding. Her doctors pleaded with her to allow a transfusion, explaining that she likely would die without one. Shorter refused, and she died soon thereafter. Her husband brought a wrongful death suit against the physician and hospital, claiming that the doctor performed the D and C procedure negligently and that the release therefore had no application. What result?

7. *Khumbu flu (problem).* In Vodopest v. MacGregor, 913 P.2d 779 (Wash. 1996), the plaintiff, Vodopest, was a nurse and mountaineer. She read an article in the Boeing Alpine Club newsletter entitled, "Nepal, Himalayan Breathing Research Trek — WOULD YOU LIKE TO GO?" The article stated that in March 1990, a party of 15 trekkers would be going to the Solo Khumbu area of Nepal to "continue research on a 'Sherpa Breathing' technique for high altitude survival." The article said that "[w]e are repeating a successful research trip conducted in April of 1989" in which "seven trained breathers performed well at high altitude and were able to consistently eliminate all symptoms of altitude sickness." The trip leader was Rosemary MacGregor, a nurse and biofeedback therapist. She collaborated in organizing the trip with a professor from the University of Washington, and the University's Human Subjects Review Committee approved the venture.

Vodopest agreed to join the trek. At MacGregor's reques⁻, Vodopest signed a form entitled "Release from Liability and Indemnity Agreement," which stated that she had been informed of all dangers of the trek, including the possibility of illness, and that she released MacGregor "from all liability, claims and causes of action arising out of or in any way connected with my participation in this trek." The release also stated: "I personally assume all risks in connection with all activities, and further agree to indemnify and release Rosemary MacGregor, other group leaders, and all other participants from all liability, claims and causes of action or harm which may befall me arising from my participation in this trek."

Vodopest's evidence was that during the trek she began to exhibit symptoms of altitude sickness at 8,700 feet, and that the symptoms worsened as her altitude increased. MacGregor told Vodopest that she probably had the Khumbu flu, advised her to "breathe away" the symptoms, and said that she would be fine. Vodopest's symptoms soon became life-threatening. She developed cerebral edema, with symptoms that included shortness of breath, racing heart beat, terrible head pain, nausea, vomiting, loss of balance, and a swollen face. Another nurse on the trek administered simple neurological tests, which Vodopest failed. MacGregor suggested that Vodopest had an ear infection. The next morning Vodopest was sent down from the mountain and was ultimately diagnosed with cerebral edema from altitude sickness. As a consequence, she suffered permanent brain damage.

Vodopest sued MacGregor, claiming that her neurological damage resulted from MacGregor's negligence in promoting the use of her breathing technique rather than advising Vodopest to descend to a lower altitude as a remedy for her symptoms of altitude sickness. MacGregor moved for summary judgment based on the release Vodopest had signed. Vodopest argued that enforcing such a release in the setting of a medical research project would violate public policy. The trial court gave summary judgment to MacGregor. The plaintiff appealed. What result?

C.   PRIMARY ASSUMPTION OF THE RISK

Generally speaking, "primary" assumption of risk is a doctrine that prevents plaintiffs from recovering for injuries they suffer when they freely undertake dangerous activities. Courts often refer to it as a defense, but that may be a bit misleading; in cases where primary assumption of risk applies, the plaintiff is prevented from making out even a *prima facie* case of liability. The doctrine amounts to a way of saying that the defendant had no duty to protect the plaintiff from the harm he has suffered, or that the defendant did not breach whatever duty existed. If a plaintiff joins a tackle football game and is injured by a tackler, for example, the plaintiff cannot make out even a *prima facie* case of liability against him; the plaintiff assumed the risk of being tackled, which is equivalent to saying the tackler owed no duty at all to the plaintiff to avoid tackling him.

Murphy v. Steeplechase Amusement Co.
166 N.E. 173 (N.Y. 1929)

CARDOZO, C.J. — The defendant, Steeplechase Amusement Company, maintains an amusement park at Coney Island, N.Y. One of the supposed attractions is known as "the Flopper." It is a moving belt, running upward on an inclined plane, on which passengers sit or stand. Many of them are unable to keep their feet because of the movement of the belt, and are thrown backward or aside. The belt runs in a groove, with padded walls on either side to a height of four feet, and with padded flooring beyond the walls at the same angle as the belt. An electric motor, driven by current furnished by the Brooklyn Edison Company, supplies the needed power.

Plaintiff, a vigorous young man, visited the park with friends. One of them, a young woman, now his wife, stepped upon the moving belt. Plaintiff followed and stepped behind her. As he did so, he felt what he describes as a sudden jerk, and was thrown to the floor. His wife in front and also friends behind him were thrown at the same time. Something more was here, as every one understood, than the slowly moving escalator that is common in shops and public places. A fall was foreseen as one of the risks of the adventure. There would have been no point to the whole thing, no adventure about it, if the risk had not been there. The very name, above the gate, "the Flopper," was warning to the timid. If the name was not enough, there was warning more distinct in the experience of others. We are told by the plaintiff's wife that the members of her party stood looking at the sport before joining in it themselves. Some aboard the belt were able, as she viewed them, to sit down with decorum or even to stand and keep their footing; others jumped or fell. The tumbling bodies and the screams and laughter supplied the merriment and fun. "I took a chance," she said when asked whether she thought that a fall might be expected. Plaintiff took the chance with her, but, less lucky than his companions, suffered a fracture of a knee cap. He states in his complaint that the belt was dangerous to life and limb, in that it stopped and started violently and suddenly and was not properly equipped to prevent injuries to persons who were using it without knowledge of its dangers, and in a bill of particulars he adds that it was operated at a fast and dangerous rate of speed and was not supplied with a proper railing, guard, or other device to prevent a fall therefrom. No other negligence is charged.

We see no adequate basis for a finding that the belt was out of order. It was already in motion when the plaintiff put his foot on it. He cannot help himself to a verdict in such circumstances by the addition of the facile comment that it threw him with a jerk. One who steps upon a moving belt and finds his heels above his head is in no position to discriminate with nicety between the successive stages of the shock, between the jerk which is a cause and the jerk, accompanying the fall, as an instantaneous effect. There is evidence for the defendant that power was transmitted smoothly, and could not be transmitted otherwise. If the movement was spasmodic, it was an unexplained and, it seems, an inexplicable departure from the normal workings of the mechanism. An aberration so extraordinary, if it is to lay the basis for a verdict, should rest on something firmer than a mere descriptive epithet, a summary of the sensations of a tense and crowded moment. But the jerk, if it were established, would add little to the case. Whether the movement of the belt was uniform or irregular, the risk at greatest was a fall. This was the very hazard that was invited and foreseen.

Volenti non fit injuria. One who takes part in such a sport accepts the dangers that inhere in it so far as they are obvious and necessary, just as a fencer accepts the risk of a thrust by his antagonist or a spectator at a ball game the chance of contact with the ball. The antics of the clown are not the paces of the cloistered cleric. The rough and boisterous joke, the horseplay of the crowd, evokes its own guffaws, but they are not the pleasures of tranquillity. The plaintiff was not seeking a retreat for meditation. Visitors were tumbling about the belt to the merriment of onlookers when he made his choice to join them. He took the chance of a like fate, with whatever damage to his body might ensue from such a fall. The timorous may stay at home.

A different case would be here if the dangers inherent in the sport were obscure or unobserved, or so serious as to justify the belief that precautions of some kind must have been taken to avert them. Nothing happened to the plaintiff except what common experience tells us may happen at any time as the consequence of a sudden fall. Many a skater or a horseman can rehearse a tale of equal woe. A different case there would also be if the accidents had been so many as to show that the game in its inherent nature was too dangerous to be continued without change. The president of the amusement company says that there had never been such an accident before. A nurse employed at an emergency hospital maintained in connection with the park contradicts him to some extent. She says that on other occasions she had attended patrons of the park who had been injured at the Flopper, how many she could not say. None, however, had been badly injured or had suffered broken bones. Such testimony is not enough to show that the game was a trap for the unwary, too perilous to be endured. According to the defendant's estimate, 250,000 visitors were at the Flopper in a year. Some quota of accidents was to be looked for in so great a mass. One might as well say that a skating rink should be abandoned because skaters sometimes fall.

There is testimony by the plaintiff that he fell upon wood, and not upon a canvas padding. He is strongly contradicted by the photographs and by the witnesses for the defendant, and is without corroboration in the testimony of his companions who were witnesses in his behalf. If his observation was correct, there was a defect in the equipment, and one not obvious or known. The padding should have been kept in repair to break the force of any fall. The case did not go to the jury, however, upon any such theory of the defendant's liability, nor is the defect fairly suggested by the plaintiff's bill of particulars, which limits his complaint. The case went to the jury upon the theory that negligence was dependent upon a sharp and sudden jerk.

The judgment of the Appellate Division and that of the Trial Term should be reversed, and a new trial granted, with costs to abide the event.

NOTES

1. *The Human Kite.* In Woodall v. Wayne Steffner Productions, 20 Cal. Rptr. 572 (Cal. App. 1962), the plaintiff, Woodall, was known as "The Human Kite." The defendant hired him to perform on a street in the Los Angeles area. The performance was to be filmed and featured as a segment on a television show titled "You Asked For It." Woodall, standing on roller skates, would be lifted into the air while attached to a kite he had constructed that was tied by a 150-foot rope to the rear axle of a moving automobile. The car was to start slowly and increase its speed to about 30 miles an hour, at which time the kite would take to the air; then the driver of the car was to slow down. A failure to slow down would cause the kite to dive. Woodall told the show's producer that his main requirement in a driver for the car was that the driver had participated in stunts of this nature before. The producer told Woodall that "We have one of the best stunt drivers in Hollywood." So Woodall left his own driver at home in Cleveland, and headed for Los Angeles.

The driver supplied by the defendant was a man named Welo. Woodall's last words to Welo before the flight were, "Remember, now, don't go over 30 miles an hour," to which Welo agreed. The plaintiff's evidence was that Welo went on to drive the car over 45 miles per hour, causing the kite to turn over on Woodall and crash to the ground, injuring him. Welo later testified by deposition that "I have never represented myself to Mr. Woodall or anybody else as being a driver because I am not." Welo had indeed never held himself out to the defendant as a stunt driver, and had never been used by the defendant as a stunt driver before. Woodall sued the company that had hired him to perform the stunt and that supplied Welo as his driver. The jury brought in a verdict for Woodall, and the trial court entered judgment upon it. The defendant appealed, claiming among other things that Woodall should be barred from recovery by assumption of the risk. The court of appeals affirmed:

> It is doubtless true that plaintiff assumed any risk growing out of inexpert manipulation of the kite, a sudden windstorm, breaking loose of the tow rope which he had fastened, the kite splitting in the air, or any one of many eventualities that were not properly attributable to the [defendant's] own activities. Respondent's brief says, at page 63: "Respondent may have assumed the risk of his kite's breaking, his landing's being imperfect, a pothole in the road, a gust of wind. But that respondent

assumed the risk of the ridiculous and callous lead-foot on the accelerator, which in fact caused the accident, is denied by a mass of testimony. Every case cited by appellants simply underlines this concept. In each and every one of them, the cause of the injury was inherent in the very nature of the thing."

Concerning defendant's part in the flight, it is to be remembered that plaintiff had been assured repeatedly as to the competency and care of the driver to be furnished by defendant. That was the one feature of the venture that he could not control. He obviously surrendered his judgment as to selection of a driver to defendant and did so upon the faith of such assurances given him. *Prosser on Law of Torts*, 2nd Ed., page 311, says: "Assumption of risk must be free and voluntary. If it clearly appears from the plaintiff's words or conduct that he does not consent to relieve the defendant of the obligation to protect him, the risk will not be assumed. . . . If, however, he surrenders his better judgment upon an assurance of safety or a promise of protection, he does not assume the risk, unless the danger is so obvious and so extreme that there can be no reasonable reliance upon the assurance."

What is the distinction between *Woodall* and *Murphy v. Steeplechase Amusement Co.*? Was the plaintiff in *Woodall* arguably negligent in agreeing to perform the "human kite" stunt at all?

2. *Lobo's last stand.* In Cohen v. McIntyre, 20 Cal. Rptr. 2d 143 (1993), the defendant decided to have her dog, Lobo, neutered; Lobo had bitten three people and the defendant hoped that the surgical procedure would "mellow" him. She took the dog to the plaintiff, a veterinarian named Cohen, to be examined for this purpose. The dog snapped at Cohen when he first reached toward him. Cohen told the dog's owner that Lobo would need to be muzzled before proceeding further. The muzzle was applied and Cohen performed the examination. Once it was over, the dog was returned from the table to the floor and its owner took off the muzzle. The dog then turned on Cohen and bit him several times. Cohen sued Lobo's owner to recover for his injuries, alleging that the defendant never mentioned the dog's history as a biter and that he was not put on notice of the dog's tendencies when it "snapped insignificantly" at him on their first encounter. The trial court gave summary judgment to the defendant, and the court of appeals affirmed: "[D]efendant owed no duty of care to Cohen unless she either engaged in intentional concealment or misrepresentation, or her conduct was so reckless as to fall totally outside the range of behavior ordinarily expected of those who avail themselves of veterinary services."

What is the distinction between *Cohen v. McIntyre* and *Woodall v. Wayne Steffner Productions* (the L case of the "human kite")?

3. *Occupational hazards.* In Neighbarger v. Irwin Industries, 882 P.2d 347 (Cal. 1994), some employees of the defendant maintenance company, Irwin

Industries, were doing work at a refinery when two of them negligently tried to unplug a valve with a sharp instrument. The result was to release a stream of flammable petroleum into the work area. The plaintiffs were safety supervisors at the refinery. Their duties included participating in the refinery's fire brigade. They saw the petroleum leak, approached the valve, and tried to close it; but as they did so, the petroleum ignited and burned them. They sued Irwin to recover for their injuries. The trial court gave summary judgment to the defendants on assumption of risk grounds. The California Supreme Court reversed:

> [A] special rule has emerged limiting the duty of care the public owes to firefighters and police officers. Under the firefighter's rule, a member of the public who negligently starts a fire owes no duty of care to assure that the firefighter who is summoned to combat the fire is not injured thereby. Nor does a member of the public whose conduct precipitates the intervention of a police officer owe a duty of care to the officer with respect to the original negligence that caused the officer's intervention. [. . .] The firefighter's rule should not be viewed as a separate concept, but as an example of the proper application of the doctrine of assumption of risk, that is, an illustration of when it is appropriate to find that the defendant owes no duty of care. Accordingly, we examine the case law establishing the rule to discover the policy basis for waiving the usual duty of care and to determine whether such a policy justifies exonerating defendants from their usual duty of care in the case of private safety employees. [. . .]
>
> On the surface, the fairness element of the firefighter's rule would seem to apply equally to public firefighters and private safety employees, as both are employed to confront and control hazards that may be created by the negligence of others. However, the firefighter's rule was not intended to bar recovery for all hazards that are foreseeable in the employment context, but to eliminate the duty of care to a limited class of workers, the need for whose employment arises from certain inevitable risks that threaten the public welfare. An industrial safety supervisor faces a much broader range of risks, many of which we should be reluctant to regard as inevitably ripening into injury-causing accidents. Fire is inevitable, but industrial accidents, as a broader category, are not equally inevitable. Although we were prepared to admit that almost all fires can be traced to someone's negligence, and that it is simply too burdensome to identify that negligence for the purpose of compensating those most likely to be injured by fire, we should be hesitant to narrow the duty of care to avoid industrial accidents. [. . .]
>
> When the firefighter is publicly employed, the public, having secured the services of the firefighter by taxing itself, stands in the shoes of the person who hires a contractor to cure a dangerous condition. In effect, the public has purchased exoneration from the duty of care and should not have to pay twice, through taxation and through individual liability, for

that service. But when a safety employee is privately employed, a third party lacks the relationship that justifies exonerating him or her from the usual duty of care. The third party, unlike the public with its police and fire departments, has not provided the services of the private safety employee. Nor has the third party paid in any way to be relieved of the duty of care toward such a private employee. Having no relationship with the employee, and not having contracted for his or her services, it would not be unfair to charge the third party with the usual duty of care towards the private safety employee.

What is the distinction between *Neighbarger v. Irwin Industries* and *Cohen v. McIntyre* (the NL case of the dog bite)?

4. *Gobble gobble.* In Hendricks v. Broderick, 284 N.W.2d 209 (Iowa 1979), the plaintiff and the defendant each went turkey hunting before dawn one morning in an Iowa forest. Neither knew of the other's presence; both wore camouflage. A turkey hunter listens for the gobble of a tom turkey, then begins sending out the softer yelp of a hen turkey by using a calling device in hopes of enticing the tom to come within gunshot range. At one point Broderick heard a tom gobbling and proceeded to imitate the sounds of a female turkey. He continued the mimicking every few minutes until he detected a rustling in the brush about 60 yards away. He opened fire in that direction with his shotgun. It turned out that Hendricks had been causing the rustling, and that Broderick had shot him.

Hendricks sued Broderick for negligence. Broderick based his defense in part on the doctrines of contributory negligence and assumption of the risk. There was evidence at trial that Hendricks understood that a turkey hunter should not intrude on another hunter who is "working" a tom turkey — that is, seeking to draw the male near by imitating the sounds of a female. Broderick also testified that the following events occurred after the shooting:

Q. And when you reached [Hendricks], what did he say?
A. Well, the first thing he asked me was what size shot I used.
Q. And did he say anything further to you?
A. Well, on our way out to the car I asked him if he had heard me calling that turkey.
Q. What was his answer?
A. He said yes and he thought I was calling too loud. [...]
Q. So he criticized your style and quality of yelping, is that it?
A. Yes, sir.

The trial court instructed the jurors that they should bring in a verdict for the defendant, Broderick, if they found that the plaintiff "was negligent in that he placed himself in a position of assuming whatever risk there would be when he voluntarily went turkey hunting in Shimek Forest," and if they found that this negligence was a proximate cause of Hendricks' injuries. The jury found for the defendant. Hendricks appealed, arguing that the instruction just quoted misstated the law.

Held, for the plaintiff, that the instruction was incorrect, and that there must be a new trial. Said the court:

> Hendricks of course accepted the hazards which naturally attend turkey hunting in Shimek Forest without culpability on the part of other hunters. In an ordinary negligence case like this, however, assumption of the risk of negligence on Broderick's part is not a separate defense. [. . .] Under the particular circumstances here the contributory negligence issue was whether, if Hendricks knew or in the exercise of due care should have known that Broderick was working a turkey at the place in question, Hendricks acted as an ordinarily prudent person in entering that place. If Broderick established by a preponderance of the evidence that Hendricks did not act as an ordinarily prudent person, and also that Hendricks' conduct constituted a proximate cause of the damages, Hendricks could not recover. Lively jury arguments could be made on both sides of this question. [. . .]
>
> In the absence of evidence which does not appear here, however, a hunter does not assume whatever risk there would be by voluntarily hunting in Shimek Forest. This court stated in *Gross v. Miller*, 61 N.W. 385, 388 (1884): "Men go hunting every day, and no one reasonably anticipates that, as a result, one will negligently shoot the other." [. . .] Although Shimek is a dark and deep forest, Hendricks had a right to assume, until he knew otherwise or in the exercise of ordinary care should have known otherwise, that other hunters would exercise due care under the circumstances, including the circumstance of the nature of the forest.

What is the distinction between *Hendricks v. Broderick* and *Cohen v. McIntyre* (the NL case of the dog bite)? What is the distinction between *Hendricks v. Broderick* and *Murphy v. Steeplechase Amusements* (the NL case of the "Flopper" where assumption of risk was held to apply)?

5. *Foul ball (problem)*. In Lowe v. California League of Professional Baseball, 65 Cal. Rptr. 2d 105 (Cal. App. 1997), the plaintiff was hit in the face by a foul ball while attending a game played by the Rancho Cucamonga Quakes, a minor league baseball team. He sued the team to recover for his injuries. He alleged that the incident occurred because he was distracted by the nearby presence of "Tremor," a man wearing a dinosaur costume who served as the team's mascot; the dinosaur was standing behind the plaintiff's seat and hitting his back with its tail, causing the plaintiff to turn his attention away from the field. When he turned back to the game, the ball hit him in the face. The team claimed that Lowe assumed this risk. What result?

6. *The spectacle of savagery (problem).* In Hackbart v. Cincinnati Bengals, Inc., 601 F.2d 516 (10th Cir. 1979), the plaintiff, Hackbart, was a defensive back for the Denver Broncos football team. In the course of a game against the Cincinnati Bengals, Hackbart performed a blocking maneuver on one of the Bengals' players, Charles "Booby" Clark. The trial court found that after the play ended, Clark, "acting out of anger and frustration, but without a specific intent to injure [. . .] stepped forward and struck a blow with his right forearm to the back of the kneeling plaintiff's head and neck with sufficient force to cause both players to fall forward to the ground." The blow caused a fracture of Hackbart's neck. Hackbart sued the Bengals to recover for his injuries. After a bench trial, judgment was entered for the defendant. Said the court:

> The violence of professional football is carefully orchestrated. Both offensive and defensive players must be extremely aggressive in their actions and they must play with a reckless abandonment of self-protective instincts. The coaches make studied and deliberate efforts to build the emotional levels of their players to what some call a "controlled rage."
>
> John Ralston, the 1973 Broncos coach, testified that the pre-game psychological preparation should be designed to generate an emotion equivalent to that which would be experienced by a father whose family had been endangered by another driver who had attempted to force the family car off the edge of a mountain road. The precise pitch of motivation for the players at the beginning of the game should be the feeling of that father when, after overtaking and stopping the offending vehicle, he is about to open the door to take revenge upon the person of the other driver. [. . .]
>
> The end product of all of the organization and effort involved in the professional football industry is an exhibition of highly developed individual skills in coordinated team competition for the benefit of large numbers of paying spectators, together with radio and television audiences. It is appropriate to infer that while some of those persons are attracted by the individual skills and precision performances of the teams, the appeal to others is the spectacle of savagery. [. . .]
>
> [The plaintiff's theories] of liability are [. . .] subject to the recognized defenses of consent and assumption of the risk. Here the question is what would a professional football player in the plaintiff's circumstances reasonably expect to encounter in a professional contest? [. . .]
>
> Upon all of the evidence, my finding is that the level of violence and the frequency of emotional outbursts in NFL football games are such that Dale Hackbart must have recognized and accepted the risk that he would be injured by such an act as that committed by the defendant Clark on September 16, 1973. Accordingly, the plaintiff must be held to have assumed the risk of such an occurrence. Therefore, even if the defendant breached a duty which he owed to the plaintiff, there can be no recovery because of assumption of the risk. [. . .]

[T]o decide which restraints should be made applicable is a task for which the courts are not well suited. There is no discernible code of conduct for NFL players. The dictionary definition of a sportsman is one who abides by the rules of a contest and accepts victory or defeat graciously. Webster's Third New International Dictionary, p. 2206 (1971). That is not the prevalent attitude in professional football. There are no Athenian virtues in this form of athletics. The NFL has substituted the morality of the battlefield for that of the playing field, and the "restraints of civilization" have been left on the sidelines.

The plaintiff appealed. What result?

D. SECONDARY ASSUMPTION OF THE RISK AND THE RISE OF COMPARATIVE FAULT

"Secondary" assumption of risk cases arise when the defendant does have a duty to the plaintiff and may have breached it; as an affirmative defense, the defendant argues that the plaintiff recognized whatever danger resulted from the defendant's alleged negligence and voluntarily chose to encounter it. The traditional position of the common law was that a plaintiff who assumed the risk in this sense, like a plaintiff who was contributorily negligent, was forbidden to recover anything from the negligent defendant. But as the states gradually replaced contributory negligence with comparative negligence, which allows a plaintiff who is negligent to nevertheless collect at least some damages from the defendant, the same logic often has been applied to secondary assumption of risk. In many jurisdictions the plaintiff who assumes the risk in this sense thus will have his damages reduced accordingly, but will not be forbidden to recover altogether. Indeed, assumption of risk in the secondary sense considered here has been merged outright with comparative negligence in many jurisdictions, so that the question in every case is simply how the reasonableness of the defendant's behavior compares with the plaintiff's. ("Primary" assumption of risk, discussed in the previous section, generally remains a complete defense to a negligence claim.) We therefore treat this subject more briefly than the others in the chapter.

Marshall v. Ranne
511 S.W.2d 255 (Tex. 1974)

POPE, J. — Paul Marshall instituted this suit against John C. Ranne seeking damages for injuries he sustained when Ranne's vicious hog attacked him and severely injured his hand. The jury made findings that plaintiff Marshall was contributorily negligent and also that he voluntarily assumed the risk of the hog. The trial court rendered judgment for the defendant on the verdict. The court of civil appeals ruled that the findings of the jury concerning the plaintiff's assumption of the risk supported the judgment and affirmed. We reverse the judgments of the courts below and render judgment for the plaintiff Marshall.

The opinion of the court of civil appeals correctly states these operative facts:

> The only witness to the occurrence was plaintiff. He and defendant both lived in Dallas, but they owned neighboring farms in Van Zandt County. Plaintiff's principal occupation was raising hogs. At the time of the injury he had about two hundred on his farm. The hog in question was a boar which had escaped from defendant's farm and had been seen on plaintiff's land during several weeks before the day of the injury. According to plaintiff, defendant's boar had charged him ten to twelve times before this occurrence, had held him prisoner in his outhouse several times, and had attacked his wife on four or five occasions. On the day of the injury plaintiff had hauled in several barrels of old bread in his pickup and had put it out for his hogs at the barn. At that time he saw defendant's boar about a hundred yards behind the barn, but it came no nearer. After feeding his hogs, he went into the house and changed clothes to get ready to go back to Dallas. On emerging from the house, he looked for the boar because, as he testified, he always had to look before he made a move, but he did not see it. He started toward his pickup, and when he was about thirty feet from it, near the outhouse, he heard a noise behind him, turned around and saw the boar charging toward him. He put out his hand defensively, but the boar grabbed it and bit it severely.

Plaintiff testified that the first time the hog had jeopardized his safety was about a week or ten days before he was hurt. He did not shoot the hog because he did not consider that the neighborly thing to do, although he was an expert with a gun and had two available. He made no complaint about the hog to defendant until the day of the injury, when he wrote a note and put it on defendant's gate. The note read:

> John, your boar has gone bad. He is trying to chase me off the farm. He stalks us just like a cat stalks a mouse every time he catches us out of the house. We are going to have to get him out before he hurts someone.

This note did not come to defendant's attention until he came in late that afternoon, and the evidence does not reveal whether he saw it before plaintiff was injured. Plaintiff testified that he and defendant had previously discussed the hog's viciousness on several occasions. . . .

Marshall's argument is that he did not, as a matter of law voluntarily expose himself to the risk of the attack by the hog. The jury found that plaintiff

Marshall had knowledge of the vicious propensities of the hog and that it was likely to cause injury to persons, and also found that plaintiff, with knowledge of the nature of defendant's boar hog, voluntarily exposed himself to the risk of attack by the animal. We hold that there was no proof that plaintiff had a free and voluntary choice, because he did not have a free choice of alternatives. He had, instead, only a choice of evils, both of which were wrongfully imposed upon him by the defendant. He could remain a prisoner inside his own house or he could take the risk of reaching his car before defendant's hog attacked him. Plaintiff could have remained inside his house, but in doing so, he would have surrendered his legal right to proceed over his own property to his car so he could return to his home in Dallas. The latter alternative was forced upon him against his will and was a choice he was not legally required to accept. We approve and follow the rule expressed in Restatement (Second) of Torts s 496E (1965):

> (1) A plaintiff does not assume a risk of harm unless he voluntarily accepts the risk.
> (2) The plaintiff's acceptance of a risk is not voluntary if the defendant's tortious conduct has left him no reasonable alternative course of conduct in order to
> > (a) avert harm to himself or another, or
> > (b) exercise or protect a right or privilege of which the defendant has no right to deprive him.

The dilemma which defendant forced upon plaintiff was that of facing the danger or surrendering his rights with respect to his own real property, and that was not, as a matter of law the voluntary choice to which the law entitled him. . . .

In this case as a matter of law, the proof shows that plaintiff Marshall did not voluntarily encounter the vicious hog. We, therefore, reverse the judgments of the courts below and render judgment that plaintiff recover the sum of $4,146.00 the amount of damages found by the jury.

NOTES

1. *Flying puck syndrome.* In Kennedy v. Providence Hockey Club, 376 A.2d 329 (R.I. 1977), the plaintiff and her fiance were spectators at one of the defendant's hockey games. During a face-off, a puck flew from the ice into the stands and hit the plaintiff in the face. She brought a suit against the defendant alleging that it negligently had failed to provide her with a safe seat from which to view the game. The defendant's rink was surrounded by a plexiglass sheet that protected patrons in the first three rows of the audience. The plaintiff was seated in the fourth row. According to the plaintiff's deposition, she had attended more than 30 games in the past and had

watched others on television. During those games she had seen hockey pucks hit the plexiglass around the rink as well as fly into the crowd. Usually she sat in the seats farthest from the ice because they were least expensive, but on the day in question the only seats available were in the more expensive section closer to the ice.

The trial court gave summary judgment to the defendant, finding that the plaintiff had assumed the risk of the injury she suffered. The plaintiff appealed, arguing that assumption of risk should be treated as a form of contributory negligence; she maintained that a jury should compare her responsibility for her injury with the defendant's share and apportion liability accordingly. The Rhode Island Supreme Court affirmed the judgment in favor of the defendant:

> [C]ontributory negligence and assumption of the risk do not overlap; the key difference is, of course, the exercise of one's free will in encountering the risk. Negligence analysis, couched in reasonable man hypotheses, has no place in the assumption of the risk framework. When one acts knowingly, it is immaterial whether he acts reasonably. The postulate, then, that assumption of the risk is merely a variant of contributory fault, is not, to our minds, persuasive. [...]
>
> In the case before us Mrs. Kennedy had attended numerous hockey games and was familiar with the flying-puck syndrome. The only reasonable inference suggesting itself to us is that she knew there was a risk that the puck would take flight and come to rest somewhere in the crowd. Furthermore, the fact that the only seats available to the affianced couple were in Section F North does not make the purchase of those seats any less voluntary. Having voluntarily and knowingly encountered the risk, she can be said to have assumed it.

Does it follow from the court's discussion that the plaintiff acted unreasonably in choosing to stay in her seat?

2. *Teed off.* In Hennessey v. Pyne, 694 A.2d 691 (R.I. 1997), the plaintiff, Hennessey, lived in a condominium adjacent to a golf course. As she was returning home from church one Sunday morning, she paused to examine her flower garden. Moments later she was hit on the head by a golf ball that had been struck by the defendant, Pyne, an assistant pro at the golf course who had been attempting to play the eleventh hole. Hennessey suffered various injuries as a result, and sued Pyne to collect for them; she claimed, among other things, that Pyne negligently hit the ball and negligently failed to call out a warning before or after he hit the shot. Both parties knew golf balls often flew onto the plaintiff's property. Hennessey testified that her building was hit by balls about ten times a day during playing season, and that she had installed plexiglass over some of her windows to prevent them from being broken.

The trial court gave summary judgment to the defendant, Pyne. Hennessey appealed, and the Rhode Island Supreme Court reversed: "we believe that the question of whether Hennessey voluntarily assumed the risk of injury when she tarried to flower gaze in her own garden upon returning from church on a summer Sunday morning is a factual question to be resolved by the jury, and thus summary judgment should not have been entered against her negligence claim upon this basis."

What is the distinction between *Hennessey v. Pyne* and *Kennedy v. Rhode Island Hockey Club* (the NL case where the plaintiff was hit by a hockey puck)?

3. *Virtue is its own reward.* In Fagan v. Atnalta, 376 S.E.2d 204 (Ga. App. 1988), the plaintiff, Fagan, was a customer at a bar called The Beer Mug. The bar was staffed by a female bartender, a female waitress, and a male cook. An altercation erupted between four other customers who were shooting pool. Fagan saw the waitress and bartender trying to get the participants in the dispute to move outside through the back door of the bar. One of the men being forced to leave grabbed the bartender by her collar. Fagan grabbed the bartender from behind to prevent her from being dragged outside. This caused the belligerent parties to turn their attention to Fagan. They pulled him outside and administered a severe beating. Fagan brought a suit claiming that the owner of the bar had been negligent in failing to take appropriate security measures given an extensive history of assaults there. The trial court gave summary judgment to the defendant. The plaintiff appealed; his brief began as follows:

> In the days of chivalry and knighthood, men of courage would joust for the love of a woman. Damsels in distress would be rescued by fearless knights. It was not only a duty, but an honor to give one's life for one in imminent danger.
>
> The times have changed, like all things, and civilization bellows that chivalry is lost and gone, of another era. The final imprimatur that chivalry is lost in civilization is the courts of our society interpreting the laws to approve of cowardice and strike down the actions of a gallant knight in modern times, for almost having lost his life, in the aid of a damsel in distress.

The court of appeals nevertheless affirmed:

> Here, the appellant had a clear choice of alternative actions, stay out of the business of the management in expelling disorderly customers or voluntarily assist two female employees attempting to remove four rowdy male patrons from the premises. The appellant deliberately entered into a volatile confrontation between management and patrons. He saw the entire situation in front of him. He had the opportunity to measure the risk and testified that he was aware he would be in "big trouble" if a fight evolved from the confrontation. [. . .] [A]n adult of ordinary intelligence will be held to be aware of manifest risk or danger of

possible injury when he deliberately and voluntarily joins in an affray, as a
matter of law.

Accordingly, only one conclusion is permissible, that is, appellant saw
and recognized the risk, and deliberately interjected himself into the
affray after the bartender was grabbed by a customer being ejected.
Appellant obviously assumed the risk of injury by voluntarily confronting
four rowdy customers being ejected from a bar by management.

What is the distinction between *Fagan v. Atnalta* and *Woodall v. Wayne
Steffner Productions* (the L case of the human kite)? In stylizing the facts
and holding of *Fagan v. Atnalta*, is it reasonable to assume that the owner
of the bar was indeed negligent in failing to take precautions against assaults? Is
there a satisfactory distinction between *Fagan v. Atnalta* and *Wagner v. International Ry. Co.* (the case in the chapter on proximate cause where the court
found liability because "danger invites rescue")? Between *Fagan* and *Eckert v.
Long Island R. Co.* (the L case in the chapter on breach of duty where the
plaintiff's decedent rushed onto the defendant's railroad tracks to rescue a
child, and was killed)?

4. *A needful doctrine?* Does it make sense to have a doctrine of secondary
assumption of risk distinct from the doctrine of comparative negligence? In a
majority of jurisdictions the distinction has been abolished: the question
about the plaintiff's conduct is not whether he appreciated the risk created by
the defendant and chose to encounter it; it is just whether the plaintiff acted
reasonably. If he did act reasonably, he recovers his damages regardless of
whether he understood the risks and chose to encounter them (unless the
doctrine of *primary* assumption of risk applies, as discussed earlier). If the
plaintiff did not act reasonably, then his damages are reduced as they would
be in any case under the doctrine of comparative negligence. But as we have
seen, a few jurisdictions have held on to secondary assumption of risk as a
separate defense. Consider some circumstances where the two approaches
can differ in the results they produce:

> a. *Kennedy v. Providence Hockey Club*, considered earlier. Assume that
> the defendant was negligent in failing to have a higher plexiglass barrier
> around its rink, that the plaintiff knew this, and that the plaintiff decided
> to stay and watch the game anyway — reasonably, since the odds of her
> being hit were very remote, and no other seats were available. Should the
> plaintiff have been able to collect for her damages?
>
> b. *Eckert v. Long Island R. Co.*, considered in the chapter on the
> negligence standard. The plaintiff's decedent was killed when he ran
> onto a set of railroad tracks to rescue a child about to be hit by a train.
> The dissenter in that case argued that the plaintiff should be denied
> recovery because the rescuer had assumed the risks involved in attempt-
> ing the rescue. *Fagan v. Atnalta*, considered above, might be understood

as taking such a position. Should rescuers who volunteer for duty be able to collect for harms they knew they might be likely to suffer?

c. Suppose a passenger agrees to travel in a car despite knowing the driver to be drunk. The passenger's need for transportation is an emergency, so her decision to accept the ride is not unreasonable. The driver's intoxicated state causes him to steer the car into a telephone pole, causing the plaintiff various injuries. Should she be allowed to recover from the driver?

To what are the plaintiffs in these examples consenting? Is there any reason to hesitate before judging the reasonableness of their conduct and comparing it to the defendant's — any reason, in other words, to prefer an approach to liability other than comparative negligence? Why treat these cases differently from those where the plaintiff signs a waiver of liability and the court enforces it?

Professor Simons has suggested that secondary assumption of risk should continue to have limited application:

> In a small number of cases, assumption of risk can continue to play a valuable role in tort law. If we isolate the important common element in assumption of risk and consent doctrine, a narrow concept of *full preference* emerges. We should not simply ask whether plaintiff voluntarily and knowingly encountered the risk that defendant created, when she could have avoided that risk. Rather, we should ask whether plaintiff *fully* preferred to take the risk, i.e., whether she preferred the risky alternative that she chose *to the alternative that defendant tortiously failed to offer.*
>
> Consider a classic assumption of risk problem, the liability of the owner of a baseball park to a spectator who is hit by a ball while sitting in an unscreened seat. Suppose the owner owes and breaches a duty to provide an adequate number of screened seats in certain locations. But suppose that the spectator, aware of the risk of injury, nevertheless prefers an unscreened to a screened seat, because it provides a slightly better view. Then she fully prefers to take the risk, and should ordinarily be barred from recovery.

Kenneth W. Simons, *Assumption of Risk and Consent in the Law of Torts: A Theory of Full Preference*, 67 B.U. L. Rev. 213, 279 (1987). Does this approach produce satisfactory results in the cases we have considered?

Chapter 11

Defamation

A. INTRODUCTION

The law of defamation, comprising the torts of libel and slander, protects the plaintiff's reputation and good name against damage done by false statements. The development of this area of the law has a tortuous jurisdictional history. In the development of English law all such claims belonged first to the local courts, then to the ecclesiastical courts; for a time in the seventeenth century the "Star Chamber" — infamous secretive court for matters of national security — assumed the power to punish political libel as a crime. The power to hear libel claims finally ended up in the common law courts, which already had taken jurisdiction over claims for slander. One holdover from these early maneuverings was the continued availability, first at common law and then by statute, of criminal prosecutions for libel. Many states still recognize that possibility, though prosecutions are rare and the statutes permitting them are subject to frequent constitutional challenge. A more important holdover has been the recognition to this day of separate actions for libel and slander, with some differences in the rules that govern them. From the Restatement (Second) of Torts:

§568. LIBEL AND SLANDER DISTINGUISHED

(1) Libel consists of the publication of defamatory matter by written or printed words, by its embodiment in physical form or by any other form of communication that has the potentially harmful qualities characteristic of written or printed words.

(2) Slander consists of the publication of defamatory matter by spoken words, transitory gestures or by any form of communication other than those stated in Subsection (1).

(3) The area of dissemination, the deliberate and premeditated character of its publication and the persistence of the defamation are

factors to be considered in determining whether a publication is a libel rather than a slander.

Comment d. When publication libel, when slander. The publication of defamatory matter by written or printed words constitutes a libel. [. . .] Defamatory pictures, caricatures, statues and effigies are libels because the defamatory publication is embodied in physical form. [. . .] On the other hand, the use of a mere transitory gesture commonly understood as a substitute for spoken words such as a nod of the head, a wave of the hand or a sign of the fingers is a slander rather than a libel.

Illustration 1. A procures two men to "shadow" B. They follow him from one public place to another until the "shadowing" becomes notorious in the community. A has libeled B.

Illustration 2. A makes a gesture with his fingers in the presence of B which indicates that C has the "evil eye," a characterization that is highly disparaging in the community. A has slandered but not libeled C.

Illustration 3. A prepares a wax figure recognizable as a representation of B and places it among a number of effigies of famous murderers in "The Chamber of Horrors," where it is seen by a number of persons. A has libeled B.

The most important consequence of the distinction between libel and slander involves the recovery of damages. The common law rule, still followed in a majority of jurisdictions, is that a plaintiff who has been libeled can recover "general" damages; this means that damages are presumed without any particular proof of how the plaintiff was harmed by the libel or to what extent. The rule has considerable practical importance, for it often can be difficult to demonstrate that any clear pecuniary harm has been caused by the damage a defendant has inflicted on the plaintiff's reputation. In cases of slander, however, damages must be specifically proven (in the jargon of defamation law, "special damages" must be shown) unless the statement falls into one of four categories that make it slander *per se.* These categories traditionally include (a) utterances charging the plaintiff with criminal misconduct, usually involving moral turpitude; (b) statements that the plaintiff has a loathsome disease; (c) claims of scandalous sexual conduct on the plaintiff's part — e.g., adultery or prostitution; and (d) words bearing on the plaintiff's fitness for his occupation, whether claims of corruption, incompetence, or any other matter incompatible with the performance of the job. See §570 of the Second Restatement for more detail.

The expressions "per se" and "per quod" arise frequently in the law of defamation; they can cause confusion because they sometimes are used in different ways without explanation. The most common usage of "per se" is to refer to utterances that permit a plaintiff to collect damages without proving their specifics. Thus a spoken utterance is "slander per se" only if it fits into one of the categories described a moment ago. But in the law of libel there is a different usage of the term: written words sometimes are said to be "libel per se" if their defamatory meaning is evident on their face. If the plaintiff needs to add extrinsic facts to show that the statement was defamatory, it is a case of "libel per quod." We will see examples in the next section. Occasionally jurisdictions treat these usages as overlapping, holding that damages for libel can be recovered without specific proof only if the defamatory nature of the writing is clear on its face. But this is a minority view; the more common rule is that general damages can be collected for libel as a matter of course. In any event, a helpful suggestion was made in *Agriss v. Roadway Express, Inc.*, 334 Pa. Super. 295 (1984): "nowadays 'per se' is used so inconsistently and incoherently in the defamation context that any lawyer or judge about to use it should pause and replace it with the English words it is intended to stand for."

In most other respects, meanwhile, the distinction between libel and slander has been eroding. One usually can use libel and slander cases more or less interchangeably to illustrate general principles of the law of defamation: what qualifies as defamatory, when privileges arise that protect otherwise defamatory utterances from suit, and so forth.

The common law and the Constitution. The law of defamation looks very different today than it did before 1964. Starting with its decision that year in *New York Times v. Sullivan*, 376 U.S. 254, the United States Supreme Court has rendered a series of decisions holding that the First Amendment limits the power of the states to award damages for defamation. The common law of defamation still is critical for the lawyer to understand; the basic elements of a defamation claim today tend to be the same as ever, and in some types of cases — mostly those involving private disputes with no overtones of public interest — the common law rules continue to govern most features of a suit for libel or slander. But in other sorts of cases, and particularly in suits brought by public figures against media defendants, the law of defamation now is dominated by the constitutional obstacles that plaintiffs must overcome to win a judgment. Accordingly, the first few sections of this chapter will present the common law of defamation; the last section will then review the major Supreme Court cases on the subject and consider how they have changed the legal landscape.

B. DEFINING "DEFAMATORY"

Grant v. Reader's Digest Association
151 F.2d 733 (2d Cir. 1946)

LEARNED HAND, *Circuit Judge*. This is an appeal from a judgment dismissing a complaint in libel for insufficiency in law upon its face. The complaint alleged that the plaintiff was a Massachusetts lawyer, living in that state; that the defendant, a New York corporation, published a periodical of general circulation, read by lawyers, judges and the general public; and that one issue of the periodical contained an article entitled "I Object To My Union in Politics," in which the following passage appeared:

> And another thing. In my state the Political Action Committee has hired as its legislative agent one Sidney S. Grant, who but recently was a legislative representative for the Massachusetts Communist Party.

The innuendo then alleged that this passage charged the plaintiff with having represented the Communist Party in Massachusetts as its legislative agent, which was untrue and malicious. Two questions arise: (1) What meaning the jury might attribute to the words; (2) whether the meaning so attributed was libelous. [. . .] The innuendo added nothing to the meaning of the words, and, indeed, could not. However, although the words did not say that the plaintiff was a member of the Communist Party, they did say that he had acted on its behalf, and we think that a jury might in addition find that they implied that he was in general sympathy with its objects and methods. The last conclusion does indeed involve the assumption that the Communist Party would not retain as its "legislative representative" a person who was not in general accord with its purposes; but that inference is reasonable and was pretty plainly what the author wished readers to draw from his words. The case therefore turns upon whether it is libelous in New York to write of a lawyer that he has acted as agent of the Communist Party, and is a believer in its aims and methods.

The interest at stake in all defamation is concededly the reputation of the person assailed; and any moral obliquity of the opinions of those in whose minds the words might lessen that reputation, would normally be relevant only in mitigation of damages. A man may value his reputation even among those who do not embrace the prevailing moral standards; and it would seem that the jury should be allowed to appraise how far he should be indemnified for the disesteem of such persons. That is the usual rule. The New York decisions define libel, in accordance with the usual rubric, as consisting of utterances which arouse "hatred, contempt, scorn, obloquy or shame," and the like. However, the opinions at times seem to make it a condition that to be actionable the words must be such as would so affect "right-thinking" people[. . . .] Be that as it may, [. . .] *Katapodis v. Brooklyn Spectator, Inc.*, 287 N.Y. 17, [. . .] held that the imputation of extreme poverty might be actionable; although certainly "right-thinking" people ought not shun, or despise, or otherwise condemn one because he is poor. Indeed, the only declaration of the Court of Appeals (*Moore v. Francis*, 121 N.Y. 199) leaves it still open whether it is not libelous to say that a man is insane. [. . .] We do not believe, therefore, that we need say whether "right-thinking" people would harbor similar feelings toward a lawyer, because he had been an agent for the Communist Party, or was a sympathizer with its aims and means. It is enough if there be some, as there certainly are, who would feel so, even though they would be "wrong-thinking" people if they did. [. . .]

The lower courts in New York have passed on almost the same question in three cases. In *Garriga v. Richfield*, 20 N.Y.S.2d 544, Pecora, J., held that it was not libelous to say that a man was a Communist; in the next year in *Levy v. Gelber*, 25 N.Y.S.2d 148, Hofstadter, J., held otherwise. That perhaps left the answer open; but *Boudin v. Tishman*, 35 N.Y.S.2d 760, was an unescapable ruling, although no opinion was written. Being the last decision of the state courts, it is conclusive upon us, unless there is a difference between saying that a man is a Communist and saying that he is an agent for the Party or sympathizes with its objects and methods. Any difference is one of degree only: those who would take it ill of a lawyer that he was a member of the Party, might no doubt take it less so if he were only what is called a "fellow-traveler"; but, since the basis for the reproach ordinarily lies in some supposed threat to our institutions, those who fear that threat are not likely to believe that it is limited to party members. Indeed, it is not uncommon for them to feel less concern at avowed propaganda than at what they regard as the insidious spread of the dreaded doctrines by those who only dally and coquette with them, and have not the courage openly to proclaim themselves.

Judgment reversed; cause remanded.

NOTES

1. *Name-calling*. In Stevens v. Tillman, 855 F.2d 394 (7th Cir. 1988), Stevens was the principal of an elementary school in Chicago. Tillman was a political opponent of hers and campaigned successfully to force Stevens out of her job. Tillman called Stevens a "racist"; Stevens returned the charge, then sued Tillman for defamation. The trial court refused to send the claim to a jury, and the court of appeals affirmed:

> Stevens contends that the epithet "racist" is itself actionable because it marks her as unfit to be principal of a public school and because Tillman used the term (in conjunction with the claim that she had conducted an "investigation") to imply possession of derogatory information. [...] We do not think a court of Illinois would agree that the term itself is actionable.
>
> Illinois has competing doctrines: first, that statements impugning one's professional competence are actionable without further proof of injury; second, that "mere name-calling" is not actionable. [...] We do not think it necessary to wrestle with the subject in light of *Owen v. Carr*, the most recent word from the Supreme Court of Illinois, which held that "[l]anguage to be considered defamatory must be so obviously and naturally harmful to the person to whom it refers that a showing of special damages is unnecessary." *Owen* ruled that, as a matter of law, an accusation that an attorney filed a complaint "deliberately to intimidate" the defendants was not actionable, although the comment implied professional wrongdoing.

Accusations of "racism" no longer are "obviously and naturally harmful." The word has been watered down by overuse, becoming common coin in political discourse. [. . .] When plantation owners held blacks in chattel slavery, when 100 years later governors declared "segregation now, segregation forever," everyone knew what a "racist" was. The strength of the image invites use. To obtain emotional impact, orators employed the term without the strong justification, shading its meaning just a little. So long as any part of the old meaning lingers, there is a tendency to invoke the word for its impact rather than to convey a precise meaning. We may regret that the language is losing the meaning of a word, especially when there is no ready substitute. But we serve in a court of law rather than of language and cannot insist that speakers cling to older meanings. In daily life "racist" is hurled about so indiscriminately that it is no more than a verbal slap in the face; the target can slap back (as Stevens did). It is not actionable unless it implies the existence of undisclosed, defamatory facts, and Stevens has not relied on any such implication.

What is the distinction between *Stevens v. Tillman* and *Grant v. Reader's Digest Association*? Would *Grant* have remained a case of liability if the plaintiff had simply been referred to as a "commie" or as a "fascist"?

2. *The language of controversy.* In Dilworth v. Dudley, 75 F.3d 307 (7th Cir. 1996), Dudley, a professor of mathematics, published a book titled *Mathematical Cranks*. The book explained that the spectrum of mathematical cranks runs from those whose behavior "hardly deserves the label of crankery; 'crotchety' or 'slightly eccentric' describes it more accurately" to "people who are convinced that they have the truth, that it is revolutionary, that mathematicians are engaged in a vast conspiracy to suppress it, and that fame and wealth are rightfully theirs and that one day they will have them. Again, 'crank' is not as descriptive as another word — 'lunatic' in this case." One of the figures profiled in the book and described as a "crank" was the plaintiff, Dilworth. He sued Dudley for defamation. The trial court gave summary judgment to the defendant; the court of appeals affirmed:

The district judge granted the motion to dismiss on the ground that the word "crank" is incapable of being defamatory; it is mere "rhetorical hyperbole." This is a well-recognized category of, as it were, privileged defamation. It consists of terms that are either too vague to be falsifiable or sure to be understood as merely a label for the labeler's underlying assertions; and in the latter case the issue dissolves into whether those assertions are defamatory. If you say simply that a person is a "rat," you are not saying something definite enough to allow a jury to determine whether what you are saying is true or false. If you say he is a rat because . . . , whether you are defaming him depends on what you say in the because clause. [. . .]

Among the terms or epithets that have been held [in cases cited] to be incapable of defaming because they are mere hyperbole rather than falsifiable assertions of discreditable fact are "scab," "traitor," "amoral," "scam," "fake," "phony," "a snake-oil job," "he's dealing with half a deck," and "lazy, stupid, crap-shooting, chicken-stealing idiot." It is apparent from the list that the defamatory capability of these terms cannot be determined without consideration of context. Each of the terms has both a literal and a figurative meaning and whether it is capable of being defamatory depends on which meaning is intended, a question that can be answered only by considering the context in which the term appears. "Scab," for example, means literally one who is hired to replace a striking worker, but it is also used figuratively, to denote a worker who is not a union supporter. If as in *National Association of Letter Carriers v. Austin*, 418 U.S. 264 (1974), a person is called a "scab" in a union newsletter because he refuses to join a union, this is not defamation but merely an expression of hostility; the word is obviously being used in its figurative sense. But if a union leader were accused of having been a scab in his youth, this could well be understood to be a literal use of the word and therefore an assertion that he had engaged in conduct that demonstrated his unfitness to be a union leader. [...]

"Crank" might seem the same type of word, but we think not. A crank is a person inexplicably obsessed by an obviously unsound idea — a person with a bee in his bonnet. To call a person a crank is to say that because of some quirk of temperament he is wasting his time pursuing a line of thought that is plainly without merit or promise. [...] To call a person a crank is basically just a colorful and insulting way of expressing disagreement with his master idea, and it therefore belongs to the language of controversy rather than to the language of defamation. [...]

[W]e do [not] go so far as to hold that the word "crank" can never be defamatory. We recall that Dudley defined "crank," and had he defined it in terms that called into question Dilworth's character or sanity rather than merely his judgment or learning, we would have a different case. We hold only that where one scholar calls another a "crank" for having taken a position that the first scholar considers patently wrongheaded, the second does not have a remedy in defamation.

What is the distinction between *Dilworth v. Dudley* and *Grant v. Reader's Digest Association?*

Dilworth v. Dudley illustrates the fine lines between some of the concepts in defamation law. A plaintiff is required to show, as part of the *prima facie* case, that the defendant's statement was defamatory; the plaintiff in *Dilworth* failed on this ground. But even if the statement had been defamatory it might have been protected by a *privilege* such as "fair comment," which immunizes good faith expressions of opinion on matters of public interest. We will consider privileges later in the chapter.

3. *Scare quotes.* In Wildstein v. New York Post Corp., 243 N.Y.S.2d 386 (S. Ct. 1963), a man named Brenhouse was murdered. The *New York Post* ran a story about the incident with the headline, "SLAIN EXEC FACED LIENS OF 2 MILLIONS." The second and third paragraphs ran as follows:

> As police delved into his tangled business affairs, several women described as "associated" with Brenhouse were questioned at Hastings Police Headquarters.
>
> Among those questioned were Mrs. W. B. Wildstein who, with her husband, shared the second half of the two family house in which Brenhouse lived.

Wildstein sued the *Post* for defamation; her complaint alleged that she had no dealings with Brenhouse and that the newspaper's use of quotation marks around the word "associated" implied that she was involved in a "lewd and adulterous relationship between the plaintiff, a married woman, as aforesaid, and the deceased 'slain exec.'" The defendant moved to dismiss the complaint. The court denied the motion:

> [The article] deals with the investigation into the murder of a wealthy man involved in tangled business affairs and faced with a large lien upon his assets. To say of such a man and under such circumstances that the police questioned several women described as "associated" with him, might reasonably be held to convey the meaning of some meretricious association. The use of quotation marks around the word "associated" might be found by a jury to indicate that an inverted meaning was intended by the writer and so understood by the average reader of that newspaper in the community, and not its normal or customary meaning. There was no need to impart such emphasis or imply such connotation if the purpose was merely to indicate that the police had used the word "associated" in describing these women. The fact, if it be so, that the writer was only quoting the word used by the police would not immunize defendant from liability if it be held that it constituted a libel; one who repeats a libel must respond in damages, even if he indicates that he is quoting another.

What is the distinction between *Wildstein v. New York Post Corp.* and *Stevens v. Tillman* (the NL case where the plaintiff was called a "racist")? What is the distinction between *Wildstein* and *Dilworth v. Dudley*?

4. *The unpopular inmate.* In Saunders v. Board of Directors, WHYY-TV, 382 A.2d 257 (Del. Sup. Ct. 1978), the plaintiff, Saunders, was an inmate at the Delaware Correctional Center in Smyrna. The defendants' television station ran a news story about a search of the prison that had been conducted by the Delaware Attorney General. During the story one of the station's

reporters characterized Saunders as "an alleged F.B.I. informant." Saunders brought a suit claiming that this statement was a "slanderous and willful lie"; he said that as a result of the statement his life had been placed in danger and he had suffered physical and mental injuries. The trial court gave summary judgment to the defendants:

> It is true that a charge of informing may bring opprobrium from one's fellow inmates in the prison community. However, it is not one's reputation in a limited community in which attitudes and social values may depart substantially from those prevailing generally which an action for defamation is designed to protect. Moreover, the statement by defendants was made for general consumption by the public and was not directed specifically to the community where plaintiff contends it would be considered defamatory.

What is the distinction between *Saunders v. Board of Directors* and *Grant v. Reader's Digest Association*?

5. *Not kosher.* In Braun v. Armour & Co., 173 N.E. 845 (N.Y. 1930), the defendant ran a newspaper advertisement listing a series of dealers in meat products and stating that "These progressive dealers listed here sell Armour's Star Bacon in the new window-top carton." The plaintiff's name and address were on the list. The plaintiff sued the defendant for defamation, claiming that he exclusively sold kosher meat in accordance with the tenets of Orthodox Judaism, that bacon is a nonkosher meat product, and that the false statements in the advertisement injured the plaintiff in his reputation and business.

Held, for the plaintiff, that his complaint stated a good cause of action.

What is the distinction between *Braun v. Armour & Co.* and *Saunders v. Board of Directors, WHYY-TV*?

6. *Witchcraft (problem).* In Oles v. Pittsburg Times, 2 Pa. Super. 130 (1896), the defendant newspaper ran an article about the mysterious illness of a boy in the town of Washington. The story said that the child had been seen frothing at the mouth and barking like a dog; it continued:

> The nearest neighbors told a story of superstition almost incredible regarding the boy's parents. The Newman family, as well as many neighbors, believe the boy is possessed of devils, and that an old woman who resides on Cherry alley, this place, named Oles, is responsible for his peculiar behavior.

Oles sued the newspaper for libel, alleging that many people in her community believed in witchcraft, that the article caused them to conclude that she was responsible for the boy's illness, and that as a result she had been insulted, assaulted, and stoned in the street. What result?

7. *Nomenclature.* Sometimes it is obvious that a statement is defamatory and that it refers to the plaintiff; in other cases the contested utterance by itself may not seem defamatory or may not clearly refer to the plaintiff unless its context is known. The devices for supplying that context were known to the common law by technical names. Section 563 of the Restatement (Second) of Torts provides this sketch:

> *Comment f. "Inducement," "Colloquium," "Innuendo."* Under common law pleading, in framing a declaration for defamation, when the defamatory meaning of the communication or its applicability to the plaintiff depended upon extrinsic circumstances, the pleader averred their existence in a prefatory statement called the "inducement." In what was ordinarily called the "colloquium," he alleged that the publication was made of and concerning the plaintiff and of and concerning the extrinsic circumstances. The communication he set forth verbatim and in the "innuendo" explained the meaning of the words. The function of the innuendo was explanation; it could not change or enlarge the sense or meaning of the words. It could only explain or apply them in the light of the other averments in the declaration. The extent to which the details of these common law practices are applicable to the modern complaint under current rules of civil procedure is a matter of local practice not covered in this Restatement.

Braun v. Armour & Co. thus is a classic example of a case calling for an inducement. Stating that a dealer sells Armour's Star Bacon is not defamatory on its face; it may become defamatory, however, if it turns out that the dealer owned a kosher delicatessen. Section 565 of the Second Restatement offers this additional example:

> *Illustration 1.* A without the consent of B, an amateur golfer, publishes B's picture in an advertisement that represents B in the act of eating a chocolate bar manufactured by A's company. A number of persons understand from this advertisement that B has forfeited his amateur standing as a golfer by receiving compensation for the publication of his photograph. The communication is defamatory.

Again, the explanation in B's complaint of his amateur standing would be known as the inducement. Soon we will see additional examples of cases calling for a colloquium and innuendo — i.e., cases where the meaning or target of the defendant's words is ambiguous.

8. *Feuding clans.* In Louisville Times v. Stivers, 68 S.W.2d 411 (Ky. App. 1934), a judge named C. P. Stivers was assassinated in Louisville, evidently to prevent him from testifying in a criminal case involving members of the Baker family. A member of that family, John L. Baker, was captured in Ohio

and extradited to Kentucky to stand trial for the murder. The defendant newspaper printed an account of the story that included the following passage:

> A Kentucky feud that started in Clay county more than half a century ago may be settled in the courts of that county.
>
> Gov. George White of Ohio today approved the removal of John L. Baker, held at Cincinnati, to Manchester, Ky., to face a charge of being an accessory before the fact in the slaying of Police Judge C. P. Stivers.
>
> Baker, witnesses at an extradition hearing here last week testified, is one of the last members of the family that has fought fist fights and gun battles with the Stivers clan for fifty years.

Frank Stivers, the brother of the assassinated judge, sued the newspaper for defamation. His argument ran as follows:

> No other meaning can be given to the words used, except that the published article in the Louisville Times charges that Frank Stivers[,] Judge Stivers, and the whole Stivers generation had, for fifty years, been fighting the Bakers with firearms and fists; and further that, as a result of their attacks, there was only a single Baker left, the fugitive, John L. Baker. Is it not clear then that this amounts to a public printed charge of a number of actual crimes? [. . .]

The trial judge entered judgment on a jury verdict for the plaintiff, Stivers, and awarded him $10,000. The court of appeals reversed:

> [T]he plaintiff must be able to show he is the one against whom the article is directed, that he is the one defamed. In a comparatively small group that presents no great difficulty, as, for example, in the case of the family mentioned in the article involved in *Fenstermaker v. Tribune Publishing Co.*, 12 Utah 439, where the evidence narrowed the application to one man, his wife, and their children.
>
> As the size of the group increases, it becomes more and more difficult for the plaintiff to show he was the one at whom the article was directed, and presently it becomes impossible. As a result of that, there are men who make their living by circulating falsehoods against the Jews, the Mormons, the Catholics, the Masons, etc., taking care to mention no names, and to make only general charges against all, and thus are able to ply their nefarious trade in safety because the group is so large that no particular individual can show the article is directed at him. [. . .]
>
> According to the plaintiff, this was a defamation of the whole Stivers generation. He does not even suggest how many that may be, but it will be presumed they are numerous. [. . .] This is strictly a suit by a member of a class presumptively large for a defamation of the class. The defendant's

demurrer to the petition should have been sustained, and the same is true of its motion for a directed verdict in its favor.

9. *Of and concerning the plaintiff.* In Gross v. Cantor, 200 N.E. 592 (N.Y. 1936), the defendant, Eddie Cantor, was a comedian and one of the most famous radio personalities in the United States. He sent a telegram to *Radio Guide* magazine making statements about radio critics (known as "radio editors") working for newspapers in New York City:

> I have always had the friendliest relationship with the radio editors outside New York City. They have criticized my work but theirs [is] honest criticism with nothing personal behind it. I have a great respect for their sincerity and judgment. However, I shall continue to fight those New York radio editors who are experts at logrolling, who use their columns for delving into personalities that have nothing to do with radio and whose various rackets are a disgrace to the newspaper profession. There is but one person writing on radio in New York City who has the necessary background, dignity and honesty of purpose. Would appreciate your printing this in Radio Guide where it may be seen by radio editors throughout the country.

Radio Guide published the telegram. A radio critic sued Cantor and *Radio Guide* for defamation. By way of "inducement and colloquia" the plaintiff alleged that the leading newspapers in New York employed about 12 radio critics, that the plaintiff was known by the public as one of them, and that prior to the publication of the piece in *Radio Guide* Cantor had publicly specified the "one person" to whom he referred favorably in his telegram — and the plaintiff was not that person. The trial court dismissed the complaint. The New York Court of Appeals reversed:

> An action for defamation lies only in case the defendant has published the matter "of and concerning the plaintiff." Consequently an impersonal reproach of an indeterminate class is not actionable. "But if the words may by any reasonable application, import a charge against several individuals, under some general description or general name, the plaintiff has the right to go on to trial, and it is for the jury to decide, whether the charge has the personal application averred by the plaintiff." *Ryckman v. Delavan*, 25 Wend. 186, 202. [. . .]
>
> We cannot go beyond the face of this complaint. It does not there appear that the publication was so scattered a generality or described so large a class as such that no one could have been personally injured by it. Perhaps the plaintiff will be able to satisfy a jury of the reality of his position that the article was directed at him as an individual and did not miss the mark.

What is the distinction between *Gross v. Cantor* and *Louisville Times v. Stivers*?

10. *Defamation of groups.* From the Restatement (Second) of Torts:

§564A. DEFAMATION OF A GROUP OR CLASS

Comment a. As a general rule no action lies for the publication of defamatory words concerning a large group or class of persons. Unless the group itself is an unincorporated association, as to which see §562, it cannot maintain the action; and no individual member of the group can recover for such broad and general defamation. The words are not reasonably understood to have any personal application to any individual unless there are circumstances that give them such an application. The extreme example is the statement of David that "All men are liars," which in a sense defames all mankind and yet could not reasonably be taken to have any personal reference to each member of the human race. On the same basis, the statement that "All lawyers are shysters," or that all of a great many persons engaged in a particular trade or business or those of a particular race or creed are dishonest cannot ordinarily be taken to have personal reference to any of the class.

Comment d. Even when the group or class defamed is a large one, there may be circumstances that are known to the readers or hearers and which give the words such a personal application to the individual that he may be defamed as effectively as if he alone were named. Thus "All lawyers are shysters" may be defamatory as to an individual lawyer, when the words are uttered on an occasion when he is the only lawyer present and the context or the previous conversation indicates that the speaker is making personal reference to him.

11. *U.S.A. Confidential (problem).* In Neiman-Marcus v. Lait, 13 F.R.D. 311 (S.D.N.Y. 1952), the defendants, Jack Lait and Lee Mortimer, were reporters for the *New York Daily News* and authors of a bestselling book titled *U.S.A. Confidential.* The text included the following passages regarding employees of Neiman-Marcus, which at the time was a single but well-known department store in Dallas:

He [Stanley Marcus, president of plaintiff Neiman-Marcus Company] may not know that some Neiman models are call girls — the top babes in town. The guy who escorts one feels in the same league with the playboys who took out Ziegfeld's glorified. Price, a hundred bucks a night. The salesgirls are good, too — pretty, and often much cheaper — twenty bucks on the average. They're more fun, too, not as snooty as the models. We got this confidential, from a Dallas wolf. [. . .]

Neiman's was a women's specialty shop until the old biddies who patronized it decided their husbands should get class, too. So Neiman's put in a men's store. Well, you should see what happened. You wonder how all the faggots got to the wild and wooly. You thought those with talent ended up in New York and Hollywood and the plodders got government jobs in Washington. Then you learn the nucleus of the Dallas fairy colony is composed of many Neiman dress and millinery designers, imported from New York and Paris, who sent for their boy friends when the men's store expanded. Now most of the sales staff are fairies, too. [. . .]

Houston is faced with a serious homosexual problem. It is not as evident as Dallas', because there are no expensive imported faggots in town like those in the Neiman-Marcus set.

Three groups of plaintiffs sued Lait and Mortimer for defamation: Nine models, who constituted all of the models employed by Neiman-Marcus; 15 salesmen out of a total of 25 employed at the store; and 30 saleswomen out of a total of 382. What result as to each set of plaintiffs?

C. PUBLICATION

Publication is a necessary element of every defamation suit. The word "publication" in this setting does not necessarily refer to the printing and distribution of the statement, as the word's lay meaning would suggest. In law it is a term of art referring to any communication of the utterance to a third person. From the Restatement (Second) of Torts:

§577. WHAT CONSTITUTES PUBLICATION

(1) Publication of defamatory matter is its communication intentionally or by a negligent act to one other than the person defamed.

(2) One who intentionally and unreasonably fails to remove defamatory matter that he knows to be exhibited on land or chattels in his possession or under his control is subject to liability for its continued publication.

Illustration 2. A, a Lithuanian, engages in a violent quarrel with B on the streets in the foreign section of Chicago. In his native tongue, A accuses B of murder. No one but B understands him. A has not published a slander.

Illustration 3. The same facts as in Illustration 2, except that A is overheard by several of his countrymen. A has published a slander.

Illustration 5. A, a cartoonist, while working at his desk in an office building represents B, a member of the editorial staff, in a ludicrous attitude. A leaves the cartoon on his desk, where it can easily be seen by numerous people who pass by the desk. A stenographer subsequently sees the cartoon. A has published a libel.

Illustration 6. A writes a defamatory letter to B and sends it to him through the mails in a sealed envelope. A knows that B is frequently absent and that in his absence his secretary opens and reads his mail. B is absent from his office and his secretary reads the letter. A has published a libel.

Illustration 8. A writes a defamatory letter about B intending to send it to him through the mails. A carelessly places the letter in an envelope addressed to C, who receives and reads the letter. A has published a libel.

Illustration 9. A writes a defamatory letter about B and sends it to him through the mail in a sealed envelope. B indignantly shows the letter to his son. B, not A, has published a libel.

Illustration 11. A writes a letter to B accusing him of sexual misconduct. The defamatory matter is written in Latin, though A knows that B has no knowledge of Latin. B takes the letter to a Latin teacher to obtain a translation. A has published a libel.

Illustration 12. A writes a letter to B containing defamatory statements about C. He puts the letter in his desk and locks it up. A thief breaks open the desk and reads the letter. A has not published a libel.

NOTES

1. *Stenographers.* In Gambrill v. Schooley, 48 A. 730 (Md. App. 1901), Schooley sent a letter to Gambrill that Gambrill claimed was defamatory. Schooley defended on the ground that the letter had not been published to anyone but Gambrill; Gambrill countered that the letter had been read by Schooley's stenographer, who had typed it. The trial court held that the plaintiff stated a good claim, and the court of appeals agreed:

> [The defendant argues] that, while there was in fact a physical or mechanical reception by the stenographer of the thoughts expressed by the appellant, such reception was instantaneous only, and merely sufficient for their reduction to written characters, but that there was no comprehension and no lodgment of their meaning in the brain of the recipient, who acted as a mere phonograph, and whose function in that regard was not a mental, but purely a mechanical, process, so that there was no such perception as is requisite to constitute publication. This theory is both ingenious and subtle, but we cannot be persuaded it is sound. We cannot doubt that the dictation to Miss Willis, though taken down in stenographic characters, produced in her mind as full and complete perception of the thoughts of the appellant as a slower dictation, for the purpose of reduction to ordinary characters, would have produced in the mind of one not a stenographer. If this were not so, there could be no assurance that there would be an accurate reproduction of the matter dictated, such as common knowledge gives assurance

of from any skillful stenographer. A communication, therefore, to a stenographer, must be regarded precisely as a communication to an
ordinary amanuensis, and as establishing all that is ordinarily necessary
to constitute publication. [. . .]

[Defendant also argues] that in view of [. . .] the almost universal
employment in this country of such stenographers, and the necessity
for such employment consequent upon the demands of business, a communication to such a stenographer should be made an exception to the
general rule, and be held not to be an actionable publication. But we
cannot adopt this view. [. . .] Neither the prevalence of any business
customs or methods, nor the pressure of business which compels resort
to stenographic assistance, can make that legal which is illegal, nor make
that innocent which would otherwise be actionable. Nor can the fact that
the stenographer is under contractual or moral obligation to regard all his
employer's communications as confidential alter the reason of the matter.

The court quoted approvingly from the English case of *Pullman v. Walter
Hill & Co.* (English) 1 Q.B. 529 (1891), where Lopes, L.J., stated:

It is said that business cannot be carried on if merchants may not employ
their clerks to write letters for them in the ordinary course of business.
I think the answer to this is very simple. I have never yet heard that it is in
the usual course of a merchant's business to write letters containing
defamatory statements. If a merchant has occasion to write such a letter,
he must write it himself and make a copy of it himself, or he must take the
consequences.

The court in *Gambrill* continued:

[T]here was no question of privilege in *Pullman v. Walter Hill & Co.*, and
there is none here, as the appellant owed no duty in the matter to any one.
The typewriter had no conceivable interest in hearing or seeing the letters,
and there could be, therefore, no privilege between her and the appellant.

2. *Stenographers (II).* In Chalkley v. Atlantic Coast Line Railroad Co., 143
S.E. 631 (Va. 1928), Chalkley was a telegraph operator. His supervisor sent
him a notice of dismissal; the notice accused Chalkley of drinking while
on duty. Chalkley sued for libel. The defendant replied that the notice of
dismissal had not been published to anyone but Chalkley. Chalkley countered
that the notice had been read by the stenographer who typed it. The trial court
dismissed the complaint, and the Virginia Supreme Court affirmed, holding
that there was no publication:

Perhaps the case most often cited and relied on for this view — the sound
view as we think — is *Owen v. J. S. Ogilvie Pub. Co.*, 53 N.Y. Supp. 1033

(1898). The court there laid down the rule that the dictation by the manager of a corporation to a stenographer of the firm, of a libelous letter concerning firm business, does not constitute a publication of the letter. There the fact that the manager and the stenographer were servants of a common master, engaged in their respective employments, was emphasized; and the case was regarded as distinct from one where the person giving the dictation and the stenographer bore the relation of master and servant, rather than co-employees of a common master, for it was said: "[. . .] Under such circumstances we do not think that the stenographer is to be regarded as a third person, in the sense that either the dictation or the subsequent reading can be regarded as a publication by the corporation. It was a part of the manager's duty to write letters for the corporation, and it was the duty of the stenographer to take such letter in shorthand, copy it out, and read it for the purpose of correction. [. . .] The writing and the copying were but parts of one act, *i.e.*, the production of the letter. Under such conditions we think the dictation, copying and mailing are to be treated as only one act of the corporation; and, as the two servants were required to participate in it, there was no publication of the letter, in the sense in which that term is understood, by delivering to and reading by a third person." [. . .]

The case of *Gambrill v. Schooley*, 95 Md. 48 (1901), is generally cited as the leading case enforcing the contrary view. We think, however, that [the case is distinguishable because] in *Gambrill v. Schooley* there was no privilege; that the matter communicated was libelous *per se*; and that the stenographer had no duty whatever to perform in connection with the communication. Here, however, the communication was privileged and the typist had a duty to discharge in the ordinary course of business in connection with the transcription of the communication.

Can you articulate the sense of the distinction between *Chalkley v. Atlantic Coast Line Railroad Co.* and *Gambrill v. Schooley*?

3. *The dignity of labor.* The most common judicial response to the fact patterns just considered is to find that statements are published when made to secretaries and stenographers, and to treat the privileged nature of the statements as a separate question. Some courts adhere to the line drawn in *Chalkley* to distinguish that case from *Gambrill*, finding liability in the one situation but not the other; others find liability in all such situations. An example of the latter approach is Rickbeil v. Grafton Deaconess Hospital, 23 N.W.2d 247 (N.D. 1946): "To hold that a stenographer is not an individual but a mere cog in the machine because of modern development necessitated by the changes in business methods is a derogation of human personality, and not in harmony with the modern conception of the dignity of labor."

4. *Graffiti.* In Scott v. Hull, 259 N.E.2d 160 (Ohio App. 1970), the defendants owned a building. The plaintiff alleged that in October 1968 an

unknown party painted graffiti defaming the plaintiff on one of the building's exterior walls. The words were painted in ten-inch letters and were visible to large numbers of passersby. In November the plaintiff sent a certified letter to the defendants informing them of the graffiti and demanding its removal within 48 hours. When the graffiti remained on the wall in late February, the plaintiff sued the defendants for defamation. The trial court dismissed the complaint, and the court of appeals affirmed:

> [L]iability to respond in damages for the publication of a libel must be predicated on a positive act, on something done by the person sought to be charged, malfeasance in the case of an intentional defamatory publication and misfeasance in the case of a negligent defamatory publication. Nonfeasance, on the other hand, is not a predicate for liability.
>
> The only claim against the defendants here, at best, is nonfeasance, not that they published the graffiti by some positive act on their part, but that they published the graffiti merely by failing to remove same after its existence was called to their attention and demand made upon them to do so. The viewing by the public was not at their invitation or a result of any positive act on their part.

5. *The writing on the wall.* In Hellar v. Bianco, 244 P.2d 757 (Cal. App. 1952), the plaintiff received a telephone call from a stranger asking to visit her and apparently suggesting that they might share intimacies. The plaintiff declined. The caller explained to the plaintiff that he had obtained her name and number from a writing on the wall of the men's room at a nearby tavern. The plaintiff's husband called the tavern and instructed the bartender to remove the writing from the restroom wall. The bartender replied that he was working alone, that he was busy, and that he would remove the writing when he got around to it. The plaintiff's husband summoned a constable and they arrived at the tavern later that night. They found the message still on the wall. The inscription indicated, in the court's paraphrase, that the plaintiff "was an unchaste woman who indulged in illicit amatory ventures"; it then offered her phone number and told callers to "ask for Isabelle." The plaintiff sued the owner of the tavern for defamation. The trial court gave a directed verdict to the defendant. The court of appeals reversed:

> Persons who invite the public to their premises owe a duty to others not to knowingly permit their walls to be occupied with defamatory matter. [. . .] The theory is that by knowingly permitting such matter to remain after reasonable opportunity to remove the same the owner of the wall or his lessee is guilty of republication of the libel. [. . .] Republication occurs when the proprietor has knowledge of the defamatory matter and allows it to remain after a reasonable opportunity to remove it. While there is in the record no evidence of actual knowledge on the part of the defendants the knowledge of an agent, while acting in the

scope of his authority, is imputed to the principal. From the testimony given the jury could have found that the bartender, to whom appellant's husband imparted knowledge of the existence of the slanderous matter and of its location, was in general control of the establishment, with the duty of supervising the premises, including the rest rooms. While he was not told of the exact terminology of the writing, undoubtedly because neither appellant nor her husband had been given that terminology by the stranger who called appellant on the phone, yet the bartender was told enough about the defamatory nature of it to put him upon inquiry and to charge him with the duty of removing the writing from respondents' wall. [. . .] It was also a question for the jury whether, after knowledge of its existence, respondents negligently allowed the defamatory matter to remain for so long a time as to be chargeable with its republication, occurring when the husband and the group with him visited the rest room and saw the writing.

What is the distinction between *Hellar v. Bianco* and *Scott v. Hull*?

6. *Ripple effects.* In Overcast v. Billings Mutual Insurance Co., 11 S.W.3d 62 (Mo. 2000), the plaintiff, Overcast, filed for insurance benefits when his house burned down. The defendant insurance company performed an investigation, found evidence that flammable liquids had been poured onto the carpets in the house, and concluded that it was a case of arson. The defendant's agent, Cobb, sent a registered letter to Overcast explaining that coverage was being denied because "the loss resulted from an intentional act committed by you or at your direction." Overcast soon attempted to buy insurance from another company for some farm buildings he owned. The company's agent asked Overcast if he had ever had an insurance claim denied in the past. In reply Overcast showed the agent the letter he had received from Cobb. The agent said that she would not be able to issue Overcast a policy. After seeking coverage from other firms with the same result, Overcast sued the defendant for defamation. Cobb testified that he used registered mail precisely to avoid publishing the arson claim to anyone other than Overcast, but he also testified that he knew the letter's contents would affect Overcast's ability to obtain insurance elsewhere. The trial court entered judgment on a jury verdict in favor of Overcast, and the Missouri Supreme Court affirmed:

> Communication of defamatory matter only to the plaintiff who then discloses it to third parties ordinarily does not subject defendant to liability. However, an exception, which applies here, is recognized by this Court where "the utterer of the defamatory matter intends, or has reason to suppose, that in the ordinary course of events the matter will come to the knowledge of some third person." *Herberholt v. DePaul Community Health Center*, 625 S.W.2d 617 (Mo. 1981). There was testimony that Cobb was concerned that he would be sued for defamation. His sending

the letter registered mail, return receipt requested, deliver to addressee only, was his unsuccessful attempt to avoid a publication to third parties. There was testimony by agents from other insurance companies that insurance applications ask if the applicant had ever had a claim denied and the reasons for the denial. The evidence was sufficient to show that in the ordinary course of business, Cobb was aware that the allegation that Overcast was an arsonist would need to be published and would be published to third parties.

7. *Self-defamation (problem).* In Sullivan v. Baptist Memorial Hospital, 995 S.W.2d 569 (Tenn. 1999), the plaintiff, Sullivan, was a nurse at the defendant's hospital, Baptist Memorial in Memphis. She also worked part-time at St. Francis hospital nearby. Baptist fired Sullivan when the hospital received evidence that she was stealing equipment and taking it to St. Francis, where the facilities evidently were not quite as strong. When Sullivan applied for work at other hospitals she was asked why she had left Baptist; in reply she explained the hospital's stated reason for her dismissal. Upon hearing this, the other hospitals declined to hire her. She sued Baptist for defamation. What result? Can this situation be distinguished from *Overcast v. Billings Mutual Insurance Co.?*

8. *Notes on publication.* From the Restatement (Second) of Torts:

§581. TRANSMISSION OF DEFAMATION PUBLISHED BY THIRD PERSON

(1) Except as stated in subsection (2), one who only delivers or transmits defamatory matter published by a third person is subject to liability if, but only if, he knows or has reason to know of its defamatory character.

(2) One who broadcasts defamatory matter by means of radio or television is subject to the same liability as an original publisher.

Comment b. Meaning of "delivers or transmits." The word "delivers," as used in Subsection (1), refers to the transfer of possession of a physical embodiment of the defamatory matter. It includes selling, renting, giving or otherwise transferring or circulating a book, paper, magazine, document or phonograph record containing defamation published by a third person. It includes similar dealing with a defamatory picture or statue. The word "transmits" includes in addition the conveyance of defamatory words by methods other than physical delivery, as in the case of a telegraph company putting through a call.

On the other hand, neither term properly applies to one who merely makes available to another equipment or facilities that he may use himself for general communication purposes. This is true of the supplier of a typewriter, a dictating machine or a loudspeaker. It is also true of a telephone company, whether the telephone is in a pay station or a private home, or even, it has been held, using equipment installed on the telephone for the purpose of conveying recorded messages.

Illustration 1. A, while riding in the subway, gives to B his copy of the evening newspaper. B accepts the paper and reads a news item defamatory of C. A does not know of the article. A is not liable to C for publishing a libel.

Illustration 3. A sends to B a copy of a tabloid newspaper containing a statement defaming C. A marks the defamatory statement to bring it to the attention of B. A is subject to liability to C for publishing a libel.

Comment e. Bookstores and libraries. Bookshops and circulating or lending libraries come within the rule stated in this Section. The vendor or lender is not liable, if there are no facts or circumstances known to him which would suggest to him, as a reasonable man, that a particular book contains matter which upon inspection, he would recognize as defamatory. Thus, when the books of a reputable author or the publications of a reputable publishing house are offered for sale, rent or free circulation, he is not required to examine them to discover whether they contain anything of a defamatory character. If, however, a particular author or a particular publisher has frequently published notoriously sensational or scandalous books, a shop or library that offers to the public such literature may take the risk of becoming liable to any one who may be defamed by them.

Comment f. Transmission of messages. One who, whether gratuitously or for hire, carries or transmits a written message for another is not liable for the defamatory character of the message unless he knows or has reason to know that the message is libelous. Thus a telegraph company that transmits a communication innocent on its face is not liable to one who by reason of extrinsic facts is libeled by it. This is true of messages sent by a secret code or in a foreign language; for while the operator knows that any such message may be defamatory, he usually has no reason to believe that a particular message is libelous, and it would be an unreasonable burden to require him to make the investigation necessary to satisfy himself of the innocence of the message. [. . .]

9. *Dissemination.* In Emmens v. Pottle, 16 Q.B. Div. 354 (1885), the plaintiff alleged that a magazine sold at the defendants' newsstand in London defamed him. He sued the defendants for libel. A jury brought in a verdict for the defendants after finding that they were unaware of the defamatory content of the magazine. The plaintiff appealed, stating his case as follows:

Why should a newsvendor be able to disseminate a libel without being in any way responsible for it? This would be a very dangerous doctrine. The publisher of the paper may be a man of straw or a bogus company.

A grocer is liable if he sells an adulterated article, even if he has taken every care to obtain a pure article.

Said Lord Esher:

Taking the view of the jury to be right, that the defendants did not know that the paper was likely to contain a libel, and, still more, that they ought not to have known this [...] having used reasonable care — the case is reduced to this, that the defendants were innocent disseminators of a thing which they were not bound to know was likely to contain a libel. That being so, I think the defendants are not liable for the libel. If they were liable, the result would be that every common carrier who carries a newspaper which contains a libel would be liable for it, even if the paper were one of which every man in England would say that it was not likely to contain a libel. To my mind the mere statement of such a result shews that the proposition from which it flows is unreasonable and unjust. The question does not depend on any statute, but on the common law, and, in my opinion, any proposition the result of which would be to shew that the Common Law of England is wholly unreasonable and unjust, cannot be part of the Common Law of England.

Bowen, L.J., agreed:

A newspaper is not like a fire; a man may carry it about without being bound to suppose that it is likely to do an injury. It seems to me that the defendants are no more liable than any other innocent carrier of an article which he has no reason to suppose likely to be dangerous. But I by no means intend to say that the vendor of a newspaper will not be responsible for a libel contained in it, if he knows, or ought to know, that the paper is one which is likely to contain a libel.

10. *Radio days.* In Coffey v. Midland Broadcasting Co., 8 F. Supp. 889 (W.D. Mo. 1934), a radio show was produced by the Remington Company at the studios of the Columbia Broadcasting Company in New York. The show was sent by telephone to radio stations around the country; those stations then broadcast the show locally. One place the show aired was Kansas City, where the Midland Broadcasting Company owned a radio station and paid to receive content from Columbia. During the show the plaintiff was mentioned and referred to as an ex-convict who had spent time in the penitentiary. He sued Midland, among others, for defamation. The district court held that the complaint stated a good claim against Midland:

I see no essential distinction between a situation in which the owner of a broadcasting station in Kansas City sells the privilege of speaking over the station for thirty minutes to X who, speaking in the local studio of the station, suddenly and unexpectedly utters a defamatory sentence concerning A and a situation in which the same station sells the same privilege to X, who, speaking in New York, projects his defamation by telephonic means into the identical broadcasting apparatus in the Kansas City station. [. . .] The situations essentially are identical. The greater simplicity of the first of the situations stated makes its consideration more convenient.

In my thought, then, I put the primary offender in the local studio of KMBC at Kansas City. I assume his good reputation; [. . .] I assume a sudden utterance by him of defamatory words not included in the manuscript, an utterance so quickly made as to render impossible its prevention; I assume, in short, a complete absence of the slightest negligence on the part of the owner of the station. With those assumptions is the owner of KMBC liable to one of whom the primary offender has falsely spoken as an ex-convict who has served time in a penitentiary?

The conclusion seems inescapable that the owner of the station is liable. It is he who broadcasted the defamation. He took the utterance of the speaker which came to him in the form of pulsations in the air. Those waves of air he changed into electrical impulses. Them he threw out upon the ether knowing they would be caught up by thousands and changed again into sound waves and into a human voice. He intended to do these things. But for what he has done the victim of the defamation never would have been hurt.

I conceive there is a close analogy between such a situation and the publication in a newspaper of a libel under circumstances exonerating the publisher of all negligence. The latter prints the libel on paper and broadcasts it to the reading world. The owner of the radio station "prints" the libel on a different medium just as widely or even more widely "read." In the case of the newspaper publisher absence of negligence is no defense. Yet he is not helpless. He knows that without any fault of him or of any of his employees some one some time surreptitiously may insert in his paper some line of libel. He takes that risk. He can insure himself against resulting loss through the subscription and advertising rates he charges or otherwise. The owner of a broadcasting station knows that some time some one may misuse his station to libel another. He takes that risk. He too can insure himself against resulting loss.

Learned counsel for nonresident defendants contends with earnestness and with subtle and finely reasoned argument that a more precise analogy is that between the situation here and that of a telephone company which, without negligence, carries over its wire words of defamation to some listener. [. . .] But the analogy does not persist. The telephone company, assuming the absence of negligence, but carries a message (in a sealed envelope, as it were) from the sender to a single person.

The operator of the broadcasting station publishes the message to the world. If this distinction is a practical one rather than theoretical, it is nevertheless a most significant distinction and quite enough to support an entirely different measure of responsibility.

The case here certainly is not like that in which one only provides another with an instrumentality which that other, all unsuspected by him who furnished it, uses to inflict injury. Here the instrumentality is operated by the owner for another who has hired him to operate it.

What is the superficial similarity between *Coffey v. Midland Broadcasting Co.* and *Emmens v. Pottle*? What is the distinction between them? Can *Coffey* be squared with Restatement §581?

Zeran v. America Online, Inc.
129 F.3d 327 (4th Cir. 1997)

[The plaintiff, Zeran, was the victim of a hoax. Shortly after the bombing of the Alfred P. Murrah federal building in Oklahoma City in 1995, a posting appeared on an Internet bulletin board announcing the sale of "Naughty Oklahoma T-Shirts" containing tasteless slogans. One of them read "Visit Oklahoma — It's a Blast"; another said "Rack'em, Stack'em and Pack'em — Oklahoma 1995"; another crudely referenced the children killed in the bombing. The posting said that the shirts could be ordered by telephone, and the phone number listed was Zeran's. Zeran had nothing to do with the posting, however; it was created by someone who opened a trial account on America Online using a false name and whose real identity remains unknown. Zeran began to receive harassing phone calls and immediately asked America Online to remove the postings, but they remained on the Internet for a week. Zeran sued America Online for defamation. The district court gave summary judgment to the defendant on the ground that Zeran's claims were barred by the Communications Decency Act of 1996, 47 U.S.C. §230. This appeal followed.]

WILKINSON, *Chief Judge* — [After stating the facts:] The relevant portion of §230 states: "No provider or user of an interactive computer service shall be treated as the publisher or speaker of any information provided by another information content provider." 47 U.S.C. §230(c)(1). By its plain language, §230 creates a federal immunity to any cause of action that would make service providers liable for information originating with a third-party user of the service. Specifically, §230 precludes courts from entertaining claims that would place a computer service provider in a publisher's role. Thus, lawsuits seeking to hold a service provider liable for its exercise of a publisher's traditional editorial functions — such as deciding whether to publish, withdraw, postpone or alter content — are barred.

The purpose of this statutory immunity is not difficult to discern. Congress recognized the threat that tort-based lawsuits pose to freedom of speech in the new and burgeoning Internet medium. The imposition of tort liability on service providers for the communications of others represented, for Congress, simply another form of intrusive government regulation of speech. Section 230 was enacted, in part, to maintain the robust nature of Internet communication and, accordingly, to keep government interference in the medium to a minimum. [. . .]

Zeran argues, however, that the §230 immunity eliminates only publisher liability, leaving distributor liability intact. Publishers can be held liable for defamatory statements contained in their works even absent proof that they had specific knowledge of the statement's inclusion. W. Page Keeton et al., *Prosser and Keeton on the Law of Torts* §113, at 810 (5th ed. 1984). According to Zeran, interactive computer service providers like AOL are normally considered instead to be distributors, like traditional news vendors or book sellers. Distributors cannot be held liable for defamatory statements contained in the materials they distribute unless it is proven at a minimum that they have actual knowledge of the defamatory statements upon which liability is predicated. [. . .] Zeran contends that he provided AOL with sufficient notice of the defamatory statements appearing on the company's bulletin board. This notice is significant, says Zeran, because AOL could be held liable as a distributor only if it acquired knowledge of the defamatory statements' existence.

Because of the difference between these two forms of liability, Zeran contends that the term "distributor" carries a legally distinct meaning from the term "publisher." Accordingly, he asserts that Congress' use of only the term "publisher" in §230 indicates a purpose to immunize service providers only from publisher liability. He argues that distributors are left unprotected by §230 and, therefore, his suit should be permitted to proceed against AOL. We disagree. Assuming *arguendo* that Zeran has satisfied the requirements for imposition of distributor liability, this theory of liability is merely a subset, or a species, of publisher liability, and is therefore also foreclosed by §230.

The terms "publisher" and "distributor" derive their legal significance from the context of defamation law. Although Zeran attempts to artfully plead his claims as ones of negligence, they are indistinguishable from a garden variety defamation action. Because the publication of a statement is a necessary element in a defamation action, only one who publishes can be subject to this form of tort liability. Restatement (Second) of Torts §558(b) (1977); Keeton et al., supra, §113, at 802. Publication does not only describe the choice by an author to include certain information. In addition, both the negligent communication of a defamatory statement and the failure to remove such a statement when first communicated by another party — each alleged by Zeran here under a negligence label — constitute publication. In fact, every repetition of a defamatory statement is considered a publication. Keeton et al., supra, §113, at 799.

In this case, AOL is legally considered to be a publisher. "[E]very one who takes part in the publication . . . is charged with publication." Id. Even distributors are considered to be publishers for purposes of defamation law:

> Those who are in the business of making their facilities available to disseminate the writings composed, the speeches made, and the information gathered by others may also be regarded as participating to such an extent in making the books, newspapers, magazines, and information available to others as to be regarded as publishers. They are intentionally making the contents available to others, sometimes without knowing all of the contents — including the defamatory content — and sometimes without any opportunity to ascertain, in advance, that any defamatory matter was to be included in the matter published.

Id. at 803. AOL falls squarely within this traditional definition of a publisher and, therefore, is clearly protected by §230's immunity. [..]

Zeran simply attaches too much importance to the presence of the distinct notice element in distributor liability. The simple fact of notice surely cannot transform one from an original publisher to a distributor in the eyes of the law. To the contrary, once a computer service provider receives notice of a potentially defamatory posting, it is thrust into the role of a traditional publisher. The computer service provider must decide whether to publish, edit, or withdraw the posting. In this respect, Zeran seeks to impose liability on AOL for assuming the role for which §230 specifically proscribes liability — the publisher role. [. . .]

Zeran next contends that interpreting §230 to impose liability on service providers with knowledge of defamatory content on their services is consistent with the [statute's] purposes. Zeran fails, however, to understand the practical implications of notice liability in the interactive computer service context. Liability upon notice would defeat the dual purposes advanced by §230 of the CDA. Like the strict liability imposed [in *Stratton Oakmont, Inc. v. Prodigy Servs. Co.*, 1995 WL 323710 (N.Y. Sup. Ct. 1995)], liability upon notice reinforces service providers' incentives to restrict speech and abstain from self-regulation.

If computer service providers were subject to distributor liability, they would face potential liability each time they receive notice of a potentially defamatory statement — from any party, concerning any message. Each notification would require a careful yet rapid investigation of the circumstances surrounding the posted information, a legal judgment concerning the information's defamatory character, and an on-the-spot editorial decision whether to risk liability by allowing the continued publication of that information. Although this might be feasible for the traditional print publisher, the sheer number of postings on interactive computer services would create an impossible burden in the Internet context. Because service providers would be subject to liability only for the publication of information, and not for its removal, they would have a natural incentive simply to remove messages upon notification, whether the contents were defamatory or not. Thus, like strict liability, liability upon notice has a chilling effect on the freedom of Internet speech.

Similarly, notice-based liability would deter service providers from regulating the dissemination of offensive material over their own services. Any efforts by a service provider to investigate and screen material posted on its service would only lead to notice of potentially defamatory material more frequently and thereby create a stronger basis for liability. Instead of subjecting themselves to further possible lawsuits, service providers would likely eschew any attempts at self-regulation.

More generally, notice-based liability for interactive computer service providers would provide third parties with a no-cost means to create the basis for future lawsuits. Whenever one was displeased with the speech of another party conducted over an interactive computer service, the offended party could simply "notify" the relevant service provider, claiming the information to be legally defamatory. In light of the vast amount of speech communicated through interactive computer services, these notices could produce an impossible burden for service providers, who would be faced with ceaseless choices of suppressing controversial speech or sustaining prohibitive liability. Because the probable effects of distributor liability on the vigor of Internet speech and on service provider self-regulation are directly contrary to §230's statutory purposes, we will not assume that Congress intended to leave liability upon notice intact.

Zeran finally contends that the interpretive canon favoring retention of common law principles unless Congress speaks directly to the issue counsels a restrictive reading of the §230 immunity here. This interpretive canon does not persuade us to reach a different result. Here, Congress has indeed spoken directly to the issue by employing the legally significant term "publisher," which has traditionally encompassed distributors and original publishers alike. [. . .]

D. DEFENSES

1. *Conditional Privileges*

Watt v. Longsdon
1 K.B. 130 (1930)

[Browne and Watt worked in Casablanca for the Scottish Petroleum Company. Browne sent a letter to another employee, Longsdon, who worked in London and had been appointed as liquidator for the firm. The letter described troubling discoveries that Browne had made about his colleague, Watt:

> Now to come to the amazing tangle. For some few days [. . .] we had noticed that the housemaid's attitude had completely changed and she was being very familiar with [Watt]. I put this down to cheek on the part of a person of that class. [. . .] On Saturday afternoon the servant herself called and said she wanted to speak to me privately. My wife and I received her, of course, very coldly and told her that her attitude in demanding money from Mr. Watt was disgusting and we could do nothing for her. Judge of our surprise when she replied that she had been Mr. Watt's mistress for over two months and after all his promises to her she thought herself quite justified in demanding sufficient money to keep her until she could find another job. Of course I asked for details as it seemed too amazing to be true, especially as she is an old woman, stone deaf, almost blind, with dyed hair!!! She was however able to give me a mass of details which left not the slightest doubt and the cook was also able to corroborate the fact that the servant was in the habit of spending part of the night with Mr. Watt.

[The letter went on to say that Watt had been conducting "orgies" in his flat and plotting ways to "compromise" Browne's wife, and that Watt was a "perfect beast and a perjurer." It concluded: "All our sympathy goes out to Mrs. Watt who can never hope to be happy again unless she separates herself from a man who has shown himself to be a blackguard, a thief, a liar and to whom friendship was a totally unknown thing, and who lived and lives exclusively to satisfy his own passions and lust."

[Longsdon, the recipient of Browne's letter, was a friend of Mrs. Watt; she once had cared for him when he had been sick. Longsdon wrote back to Browne that he was not surprised by these disclosures and that he felt obliged to share them with Mrs. Watt: "To me it is wrong, wicked and I will say cruel, that she, the one most concerned, should be in the dark to these disgusting and degrading happenings. To think the man will return to her and take up his life with her as an innocent and wholesome being is to me too appalling. Surely to God she should be told and give her [sic] the chance to decide what she wishes to do. To me, to hide such facts from a friend, no matter how great or how small a one, is iniquitous." Longsdon asked Browne to obtain a sworn statement supporting the claims in the letter, "for an interferer between husband and wife nearly always comes off the worst"; but Longsdon forwarded the letter to Mrs. Watt before this was done. She soon filed for divorce. Longsdon also sent the letter on to the chairman of the company's board of directors, one Singer.

[Watt brought this suit for defamation against Longsdon, complaining of his publication of the letter to Mrs. Watt and to the chairman of the board and also complaining of Longsdon's letter replying to Browne. In the trial court

Horridge, J., gave judgment to Longsdon on the ground that the statements in the letters were privileged. The court of appeal reversed.]

SCRUTTON, L.J. This case raises, amongst other matters, the extremely difficult question, equally important in its legal and social aspect, as to the circumstances, if any, in which a person will be justified in giving to one partner to a marriage information which that person honestly believes to be correct, but which is in fact untrue, about the matrimonial delinquencies of the other party to the marriage. The question becomes more difficult if the answer in law turns on the existence or non-existence of a social or moral duty, a question which the judge is to determine, without any evidence, by the light of his own knowledge of the world, and his own views on social morality, a subject matter on which views vary in different ages, in different countries, and even as between man and man. [. . .]

By the law of England there are occasions on which a person may make defamatory statements about another which are untrue without incurring any legal liability for his statements. These occasions are called privileged occasions. A reason frequently given for this privilege is that the allegation that the speaker has "unlawfully and maliciously published," is displaced by proof that the speaker had either a duty or an interest to publish, and that this duty or interest confers the privilege. But communications made on these occasions may lose their privilege: (1.) they may exceed the privilege of the occasion by going beyond the limits of the duty or interest, or (2.) they may be published with express malice, so that the occasion is not being legitimately used, but abused. [. . .] The classical definition of "privileged occasions" is that of Parke B. in *Toogood v. Spyring*, a case where the tenant of a farm complained to the agent of the landlord, who had sent a workman to do repairs, that the workman had broken into the tenant's cellar, got drunk on the tenant's cider, and spoilt the work he was sent to do. The workman sued the tenant. Parke B. gave the explanation of privileged occasions in these words: "In general, an action lies for the malicious publication of statements which are false in fact, and injurious to the character of another (within the well-known limits as to verbal slander), and the law considers such publication as malicious, unless it is fairly made by a person in the discharge of some public or private duty, whether legal or moral, or in the conduct of his own affairs, in matters where his interest is concerned. In such cases, the occasion prevents the inference of malice, which the law draws from unauthorized communications, and affords a qualified defence depending upon the absence of actual malice. If fairly warranted by any reasonable occasion or exigency, and honestly made, such communications are protected for the common convenience and welfare of society; and the law has not restricted the right to make them within any narrow limits." It will be seen that the learned judge requires: (1.) a public or private duty to communicate, whether legal or moral; (2.) that the communication should be "fairly warranted by any reasonable occasion or exigency"; (3.) or a statement in the conduct of his own affairs where his interest is concerned. [. . .] The question whether the occasion was privileged is for the judge, and so far as "duty" is concerned, the question is: Was there a duty, legal, moral, or social, to communicate? As to legal duty, the judge should have no difficulty; the judge should know the law; but as to moral or social duties of imperfect obligation, the task is far more troublesome. The judge has no evidence as to the view the community takes of moral or social duties. All the help the Court of Appeal can give him is contained in the judgment of Lindley L.J. in *Stuart v. Bell*: "The question of moral or social duty being for the judge, each judge must decide it as best he can for himself. I take moral or social duty to mean a duty recognized by English people of ordinary intelligence and moral principle, but at the same time not a duty enforceable by legal proceedings, whether civil or criminal. My own conviction is that all or, at all events, the great mass of right-minded men in the position of the defendant would have considered it their duty, under the circumstances, to inform Stanley of the suspicion which had fallen on the plaintiff." Is the judge merely to give his own view of moral and social duty, though he thinks a considerable portion of the community hold a different opinion? Or is he to endeavour to ascertain what view "the great mass of right-minded men" would take? It is not surprising that with such a standard both judges and text-writers treat the matter as one of great difficulty in which no definite line can be drawn.

[After further discussion of the precedents, Lord Scrutton concluded that a privilege would arise on the following conditions:] [E]ither (1.) a duty to communicate information believed to be true to a person who has a material interest in receiving the information, or (2.) an interest in the speaker to be protected by communicating information, if true, relevant to that interest, to a person honestly believed to have a duty to protect that interest, or (3.) a common interest in and reciprocal duty in respect of the subject matter of the communication between speaker and recipient. [. . .]

In my opinion Horridge J. went too far in holding that there could be a privileged occasion on the ground of interest in the recipient without any duty to communicate on the part of the person making the communication. But that does not settle the question, for it is necessary to consider, in the present case, whether there was, as to each communication, a duty to communicate, and an interest in the recipient. First as to the communication between Longsdon and Singer, I think the case must proceed on the admission that at all material times Watt, Longsdon, and Browne were in the employment of the same company, and the evidence afforded by the answer to the interrogatory put in by the plaintiff that Longsdon believed the statements in Browne's letter. In my view on these facts there was a duty, both from a moral and a material point of view, on Longsdon to communicate the letter to Singer, the chairman of his company, who, apart from questions of present employment, might be asked by Watt for a testimonial to a future employer. Equally, I think Longsdon receiving the letter from Browne, might discuss the matter with him, and ask for further information, on the ground of a common interest in the affairs of the company, and to obtain further information for the chairman. [...] As to the communications to Singer and Browne, in my opinion the appeal should fail, but as both my brethren take the view that there was evidence of malice which should be left to the jury, there must, of course, be a new trial as to the claim based on these two publications.

The communication to Mrs. Watt stands on a different footing. I have no intention of writing an exhaustive treatise on the circumstances when a stranger or a friend should communicate to husband or wife information he receives as to the conduct of the other party to the marriage. I am clear that it is impossible to say he is always under a moral or social duty to do so; it is equally impossible to say he is never under such a duty. It must depend on the circumstances of each case, the nature of the information, and the relation of speaker and recipient. It cannot, on the one hand, be the duty even of a friend to communicate all the gossip the friend hears at men's clubs or women's bridge parties to one of the spouses affected. On the other hand, most men would hold that it was the moral duty of a doctor who attended his sister in law, and believed her to be suffering from a miscarriage, for which an absent husband could not be responsible, to communicate that fact to his wife and the husband. [T]he decision must turn on the circumstances of each case, the judge being much influenced by the consideration that as a general rule it is not desirable for any one, even a mother in law, to interfere in the affairs of man and wife. Using the best judgment I can in this difficult matter, I have come to the conclusion that there was not a moral or social duty in Longsdon to make this communication to Mrs. Watt such as to make the occasion privileged, and that there must be a new trial so far as it relates to the claim for publication of a libel to Mrs. Watt. The communications to Singer and Browne being made on a privileged occasion, there must be a new trial of the issue as to malice defeating the privilege. There must also be a new trial of the complaint as to publication to Mrs. Watt, the occasion being held not to be privileged. [...]

GREER, L.J. — [...] In my judgment no right minded man in the position of the defendant, a friend of the plaintiff and of his wife, would have thought it right to communicate the horrible accusations contained in Mr. Browne's letter to the plaintiff's wife. The information came to Mr. Browne from a very doubtful source, and in my judgment no reasonably right-minded person could think it his duty, without obtaining some corroboration of the story, and without first communicating with the plaintiff, to pass on these outrageous charges of marital infidelity of a gross kind, and drunkenness and dishonesty, to the plaintiff's wife. As regards the publication to the plaintiff's wife, the occasion was not privileged, and it is unnecessary to consider whether there was evidence of express malice. As regards the publication to the chairman of the company, who owned nearly all the shares, and to Mr. Browne, I think on the facts as pleaded there was between the defendant and the recipients of the letters a common interest which would make the occasion privileged, but I also think there is intrinsic evidence in the letter to Browne, and evidence in the hasty and unjustifiable communication to the plaintiff's wife, which would be sufficient to entitle the plaintiff to ask for a verdict on these publications on the ground of express malice. [. . .]

NOTES

1. *Frank explanation.* In Flowers v. Smith, 80 S.W.2d 392 (Tex. App. 1934), the plaintiff, Flowers, was a purchaser of electricity from West Texas Utilities. One of the company's agents, E. E. Smith, came to Flowers's house, removed the electrical meter from the porch, and moved it to the top of a 30-foot pole. Flowers's wife called Smith to ask why he had done this. Smith replied, "I will be frank with you. It is because your husband has been wiring around the meter." Mr. Flowers sued Smith for defamation, saying that Smith had accused him of stealing electrical current. Smith defended on the ground that even if his statements were false they were made in good faith and were conditionally privileged as a matter of common interest. The trial court dismissed the complaint, concluding that the words were indeed privileged and that the privilege was conclusive since Flowers had not alleged any malice on Smith's part. The court of appeals affirmed, citing *Watt v. Longsdon* for its general statement of the law but concluding that here the privilege was present.

What is the distinction between *Flowers v. Smith* and *Watt v. Longsdon?*

2. *Conditional privileges.* The privilege at issue in *Watt* and found in *Flowers* is known now as the "common interest" privilege. It is an example of a *conditional* privilege available in defamation cases. The privilege is conditional because it applies only so long as it is not abused. The most common form of abuse is bad faith: the privilege applies only if the defendant believed he was speaking the truth. Courts vary in how they define additional prerequisites for the assertion of a conditional privilege. The most common statement of limitation, and one endorsed in the Second Restatement, is that the privilege is forfeited by "actual malice" — i.e., knowledge that a statement is false or recklessness as to its truth or falsity. Many courts also consider a conditional privilege forfeited if the circumstances to justify it are present but the speaker is motivated by dishonorable considerations:

> Where a person speaks upon a privileged occasion, but the speaker is motivated more by a desire to harm the person defamed than by a purpose to protect the personal or social interest giving rise to the privilege, then it can be said that there was express malice and the privilege is destroyed. Strong, angry, or intemperate words do not alone show express malice; rather, there must be a showing that the speaker used his privileged

position "to gratify his malevolence." *Myers v. Hodges*, 53 Fla. 197 (1907). If the occasion of the communication is privileged because of a proper interest to be protected, and the defamer is motivated by a desire to protect that interest, he does not forfeit the privilege merely because he also in fact feels hostility or ill will toward the plaintiff. The incidental gratification of personal feelings of indignation is not sufficient to defeat the privilege where the primary motivation is within the scope of the privilege.

Randolph v. Beer, 695 So. 2d 401 (Fla. App. 1997). Notice the difference between actual and express malice. Express malice is malice in the lay sense, but "actual" malice is not; the latter depends on the plaintiff's knowledge of the statement's falsity and may exist where the plaintiff has no malicious intentions at all. Actual malice is the more important category in modern defamation law because important constitutional doctrines depend on it. We will examine them in the next section of the chapter.

The opinion in *Watt v. Longsdon* can be viewed as setting out general criteria for deciding when a conditional privilege exists. In situations that arise with some regularity, however, courts have no need to repair to those criteria; rather, the criteria have been reduced to discrete doctrines establishing privileges for various occasions on a categorical basis: employment references provided for students or former employees, for example, usually are subject to a conditional privilege, as are many other statements about employees made within a workplace; credit reports likewise are privileged.

Those specific rules to one side, the general "common interest" privilege covers a variety of circumstances where the publisher and recipient of the words share a legitimate interest in their subject matter. Business partners, co-tenants, members of a religious order, and participants at a seminar all are examples of parties whose statements to one another regarding their common interests normally are cloaked in a conditional privilege.

There also are some other conditional privileges, related to the common interest privilege just sketched, that have a certain miscellaneous quality in their coverage. A conditional privilege can arise if the speaker has a strong interest that can only be protected by making the utterance. A privilege to publish a statement also arises when it appears necessary to protect the interests of another — whether the recipient of the words or a third party — but only if the publisher has a duty to provide that protection either as a formal matter or according to general standards of conduct in the community. The Second Restatement offers these illustrations:

§594. PROTECTION OF THE PUBLISHER'S INTEREST

Illustration 1. A sees B, a stranger, about to drive off in a car that appears in every particular to be A's car. A calls to a policeman to prevent B from stealing his car. The privilege applies although the car actually belongs to B.

§595. PROTECTION OF INTEREST OF RECIPIENT OR A THIRD PERSON

Illustration 1. A sees a man whom he erroneously believes to be B, a chauffeur of C, taking his family for a drive, in a car that A supposes to belong to C. A belongs to the same golf club as C and writes to C informing him that B, his chauffeur, has been using his car to take his wife and children for drives. The publication of this defamatory matter is not privileged, although it would be if C had said to A, "I hear my chauffeur is using my car without my permission to take his family out. Do you know anything about it?"

In view of the various categories just surveyed, were the privileges at issue in *Watt v. Longsdon* and *Flowers v. Smith* quite the same?

3. *Rumors.* From the Restatement (Second) of Torts:

§602. PUBLICATION OF DEFAMATORY RUMOR

One who upon an occasion giving rise to a conditional privilege publishes a defamatory rumor or suspicion concerning another does not abuse the privilege, even if he knows or believes the rumor or suspicion to be false, if
    (a) he states the defamatory matter as rumor or suspicion and not as fact, and
    (b) the relation of the parties, the importance of the interests affected and the harm likely to be done make the publication reasonable.
Illustration 2. A informs his daughter B that there is a rumor that C, B's fiance, is an embezzler. The fact that A believes the rumor to be false does not constitute an abuse of the privilege.

4. *Limitations.* From the Restatement (Second) of Torts:

§604. EXCESSIVE PUBLICATION

One who, upon an occasion giving rise to a conditional privilege for the publication of defamatory matter to a particular person or persons, knowingly publishes the matter to a person to whom its publication is not otherwise privileged, abuses the privilege unless he reasonably believes that the publication is a proper means of communicating the defamatory matter to the person to whom its publication is privileged.
Illustration 1. A, a director of a bank, on his way to a meeting of the directors, while walking in the lobby where a number of depositors are present, in a loud voice says to a fellow director that he suspects the cashier of dishonesty. A has abused the privilege.
Illustration 2. A, from a hotel window, shouts to a policeman in the street to come at once to prevent a murder in an adjoining room of the hotel. A has not abused the privilege.

5. *The fair report privilege.* From the Restatement (Second) of Torts:

§611. REPORT OF OFFICIAL PROCEEDING OR PUBLIC MEETING

The publication of defamatory matter concerning another in a report of an official action or proceeding or of a meeting open to the public that deals with a matter of public concern is privileged if the report is accurate and complete or a fair abridgement of the occurrence reported.

Comment a. Character of privilege. The privilege of the publication of reports of defamatory statements covered in this Section is not an absolute privilege. It is, however, somewhat broader in its scope than the conditional privileges covered [elsewhere]. The basis of this privilege is the interest of the public in having information made available to it as to what occurs in official proceedings and public meetings. The privilege is therefore one of general publication and is not limited to publication to any person or group of persons. For the same reason the privilege exists even though the publisher himself does not believe the defamatory words he reports to be true and even when he knows them to be false. Abuse of the privilege takes place, therefore, when the publisher does not give a fair and accurate report of the proceeding. [. . .]

Illustration 2. A attends a murder trial as a spectator. In the course of the trial a witness makes false statements of fact that defame B. That evening at dinner A orally gives his friend C a complete and accurate report of the trial, including this testimony. A's report is privileged.

A person cannot confer this privilege upon himself by making the original defamatory publication himself and then reporting to other people what he had stated. This is true whether the original publication was privileged or not. Nor may he confer the privilege upon a third person, even a member of the communications media, by making the original statement under a collusive arrangement with that person for the purpose of conferring the privilege upon him.

6. *Self-defense.* In Israel v. Portland News Pub. Co., 53 P.2d 529 (Or. 1936), one W. Frank Akin, an accountant, was conducting an investigation into the fiscal management of the Port of Portland. When he was murdered under mysterious circumstances, the defendant's newspaper, the *Morning Oregonian*, published a story that ran in part as follows:

Traces of "another woman" in the W. Frank Akin murder mystery were revealed yesterday in a startling story unfolded to state police by Mark M. Israel, jeweler and loan broker, of 2034 Northeast Twenty-first avenue. [. . .] Israel, who said Akin had checked his books and made out his income tax reports for about four years, told Linville that the murdered man had told him on a number of occasions that a woman, with whom he had an affair, had repeatedly threatened his life.

"I talked with Akin lots of times," Israel said, "and he told me about his woman and added that the only reason he kept seeing her was that he was afraid she would kill him. He said she had threatened to do so a number of times and on several occasions went so far as to point a gun at him. [. . .]

"He confided in me often when he used the balcony of my store, the Century Loan & Jewelry Company, at Third and Washington streets, for an office. After this affair had lasted some time, Akin told me that he had confessed his infidelity to his wife and offered to give her a divorce. Mrs. Akin, I was told forgave her husband, but told him that he could leave with the other woman any time he desired." [. . .]

In a later edition of the newspaper that same day, a follow-up story appeared titled "Akin's Widow Flays Gossip." It ran in part as follows:

The scandalous tale related to police by Mark Israel, pawnshop dealer, about a "jealous woman" in the life of W. Frank Akin, slain port investigator, was branded absolutely false Thursday by the widow of the murdered man.

"It is silly, in the first place," she said, "to suppose Frank might have confided in Israel on any private matter. He had no regard for Israel's integrity and frequently said so after being engaged to audit the books of that firm.

"He told me he knew Israel was stealing from his own father-in-law and he said he had no use for that kind of a man. Israel hated him after that, and he hated Israel. Can you imagine the police believing that those two would have confided in each other? That Frank would have confided secrets of his private life to him?"

Israel sued the newspaper for defamation. The trial judge instructed the jury that statements made by Akin's wife were conditionally privileged. So instructed, the jury brought in a verdict for the defendant. The judge ordered a new trial and the defendant appealed. The Oregon Supreme Court held that the statements were indeed privileged:

The law seems to be well-settled that when one is attacked by defamatory matter published in the press, one may resort to the same methods to reply to or rebut the charges made.

"Every man has a right to defend his character against false aspersion. It is one of the duties which he owes to himself and to his family. Therefore, communications made in fair self-defence are privileged. If a person is attacked in a newspaper, he may write to the paper to rebut the charges, and may at the same time retort upon his assailant, where such retort is a necessary part of his defence or fairly arises out of the charges he has made. A man who commences a newspaper war cannot subsequently come to the court as plaintiff to complain that he has had the worst of the fray. But in rebutting an accusation the party should not state what he knows at the time to be untrue, or intrude unnecessarily into the private life or character of his assailant. The privilege extends only to such retorts as are fairly an answer to the attacks." *Newell on Libel and Slander* (4th Ed.) §429, p. 456. [. . .]

The text seems to be well supported by the authorities and by common sense and reason. The law does not look with disapproval on an act which a high-class, good citizen would perform. Mrs. Akin was, and still is, a teacher in the public schools of Portland, Ore. One of the essential elemental qualifications for that position is a good moral character. She was charged with conniving at and consenting to the alleged adulterous conduct of her late husband. She owed a duty to herself as well as to the community to refute that charge so far as she could, in the same manner in which it was made. If her refutation was pertinent and grew out of or was reasonably connected with the defamatory matter published by respondent, and was published in good faith and without malice, she would not be liable. It is no light matter to a school teacher to be accused of a low moral character.

7. *Puffing the product.* In Sternberg Mfg. Co. v. Miller, DuBrul & Peters Mfg. Co., 170 F. 298 (8th Cir. 1909), the parties were competing manufacturers of cigar molds. As recounted by the court, the Miller firm published a pair of notices to cigar makers around the country:

> [In the notices, Miller was] representing itself to be the sole owner of all patents for making cigar molds known as the "vertical top," alleging that it had brought a line of suits against all manufacturers of that particular mold and warning all persons against infringement. The two articles so alleged to have been published by plaintiff contained much laudation and puffing of the value of its patents and of its manufactured product, strong assertion of exclusive right to manufacture the vertical top mold, and a precautionary warning of danger to all who should attempt to infringe its rights.

In reply, the Sternberg firm published a circular of its own to the same cigar manufacturers:

> A recent threatening circular sent out to the cigar makers of the country by the Miller, Du Brul & Peters Manufacturing Company is a remarkable document. A valid patent secures an inventor a monopoly for seventeen years. For that time a valid patent is better than a trust because it is lawful. The gentlemen composing said company claim in their circular that beginning thirty years ago they have taken out 149 patents, but they don't state how many of the 149 are now alive. A patent issued

30 years ago has been dead for 13 years. We made the same style of molds ten years ago that we are making today. Why do they resort to lawsuits at this late day? The answer is easy. Simply because their patents are no longer a protection. [. . .] After a "live and let live" career of thirty years, [Miller] now proposes to kill off competition by using the courts as a club. It wants to use injunctions and in this way gain the power of a trust. The cigar makers know the class of people who resort to injunctions. The trust will push the price away up and force you to pay it. No injunction will be issued against us. We have made the best cigar mold on the market for years, have infringed no patent, and won't be bluffed out of business. [. . .]

The Miller firm sued the Sternberg firm for defamation. Sternberg argued that its statements were privileged. The trial court declined to so instruct the jury, which then gave a verdict to the plaintiff. The court of appeals affirmed:

The charge that defendant could not libel the plaintiff in retaliation for its offenses was clearly right. One can no more take the law into his own hand, and counteract the effect of one libel with another, than he can take satisfaction for a past physical assault by administering one to the assailant.

Is there a satisfactory distinction between *Sternberg Mfg. Co. v. Miller, DuBrul & Peters Mfg. Co.*, and *Israel v. Portland News Pub. Co.*?

2. Absolute Privileges

As we have seen, conditional privileges are lost if abused. But the law of defamation also affords a few *absolute* privileges that provide complete immunity from suit for their holders regardless of whether their statements are made in good faith or with proper motives. These privileges are regulated, however, by limits on the occasions when they will apply.

1. *Crossfire.* In Roush v. Hey, 475 S.E.2d 299 (W. Va. 1996), the plaintiff, Judith Roush, divorced her husband in 1988 and won custody of their two children. While the younger child was still in her custody, Roush moved in with a man to whom she was not married. Her ex-husband petitioned to regain custody of the child. The case was assigned to Judge John Hey. Judge Hey entered an order offering Mrs. Roush these alternatives: (1) marry the person with whom she had been living, (2) move out of the house where she had been cohabiting with the person not her husband, or (3) lose custody of her daughter. While this decision was pending on appeal, Judge Hey appeared on the CNN program *Crossfire*, a show that featured debate over politically contentious issues. Also featured as a guest on the show was Gloria

Allred, a well-known attorney specializing in cases involving women's rights. The host was Patrick Buchanan. Judge Hey offered the following views:

> [Allred] is talking about love and affection as if this were a stable family unit; this is not perhaps the first boyfriend, now, I won't get into the merits of this particular case, but I will give you hypotheticals. She's painted it as if it were a loving family unit; normally the boyfriend with whom they're . . . to use your word Mr. Buchanan, not mine, "shacked up" with today, in front of the children — teenage, impressionable children, is not necessarily going to be the boyfriend with whom she is living next week or even tomorrow. [. . .]
>
> My primary concern, now I want to make this clear, is for the welfare of that child and I don't think it is in the welfare, the best interest of a child 13 years old to see her mother sleeping with a man that is not her father, and next week there may be a different man in the house, and the third week there may be a third one.
>
> I'm not into sexy kink, Ms. Allred. I don't care what two consenting adults do in the privacy of their own quarters, but it genuinely concerns me when they do it in the presence of children — that concerns me.

Mrs. Roush sued Judge Hey for defamation. Hey sought summary judgment on the ground that his statements were absolutely privileged by the doctrine of judicial immunity. The trial court granted the motion; the West Virginia Supreme Court reversed, holding the remarks unprivileged:

> Because determining what is a judicial act is encumbered with doubt and confusion, we need to search for characteristics or markers which might be common to all judicial acts. [. . .] The first factor is whether the act was a function normally performed by a judge. This turns on the nature of the act itself and not on the identity of the actor. The second factor is whether the parties dealt with the judge in his judicial capacity; this factor looks to the expectation of the parties. [. . .]
>
> If we were to cloak Judge Hey's remarks with the cover of judicial immunity, then we would be saying that any act performed by a judge, no matter under what circumstances, should be exempt from personal liability. We are prepared to protect the sanctity of the judicial immunity doctrine, but we are not prepared to make it so sweeping so as to mock the doctrine. We hold, then, that an appearance by a judge on a nationally televised program, dedicated to contentious discussion of politically and socially sensitive issues, in order to vindicate a position expressed in a decision relating to the custody of a child, is not a function normally performed by a judge.
>
> Next, we analyze the second factor of whether the parties dealt with Judge Hey in his judicial capacity. This factor requires an examination of the expectations of the parties. [. . .] A judicial act requires the kind of

discretion or judgment aligned with the adjudication of a controversy (that is expected), and not the justification of that decision expressed during a public debate with someone taking a view in opposition to that decision (that is not expected). The only appropriate forum to argue the qualitative merits of Judge Hey's decision is the West Virginia Supreme Court of Appeals (that is expected), and not a nationally televised program such as "Crossfire" (that is not expected). The only people who should be involved in arguing the merits of Judge Hey's decision are the lawyers for the respective parties (that is expected), and not the trial judge and another stranger to the case arguing the opposite view (that is not expected).

The court also noted that Judge Hey's remarks may have violated the Code of Judicial Conduct, which provided that "a judge shall not make any public or nonpublic comment about any pending or impending proceeding which might reasonably be expected to affect its outcome or impair its fairness[.]"

2. *Contemplated litigation.* In Sriberg v. Raymond, 345 N.E.2d 882 (Mass. 1976), the plaintiff, Sriberg, was president of Roll Form Products, Inc. The defendant, Raymond, was a lawyer for the Southwest Truck Body Company. Roll Form entered into a contract with Southwest to purchase a subsidiary business of Southwest's called Mac-Fab Products; the Shawmut Credit Corporation of Boston was to handle various financial details of the transfer. A couple of weeks before the sale was scheduled to close, Roll Form announced that it would not go through with the deal. In response, Raymond sent a letter to Sriberg — with a copy delivered to Shawmut — that read in part as follows:

> Your persistence, against this backdrop, of a meritorious basis for repudiation is a sham. Your conduct in this respect is reckless, willful and malicious. Your decision to pursue that course is a tragic mistake. It severely injures Mac-Fab as well as Southwest and, in view of the full manifestation of management control your people have exerted over Mac-Fab in the industry, a vast monetary amount will be required to duplicate the posture in which Mac-Fab and Southwest would have been had you closed your purchase as agreed in writing. It is quite obvious that you now are attempting to appropriate Mac-Fab's business without payment.
>
> If these demands are not met, suit will be instituted against Roll Form and Shawmut for actual and exemplary damages, including without limitation damages for Roll Form's misappropriation of Mac-Fab's business information communicated in connection with this purchase and in confidence, as well as for Roll Form's taking and asportation of Mac-Fab's customer orders and Roll Form's severe injury to the business reputation of Mac-Fab and its management. Injunctive relief likewise will be sought in the foregoing respects.
>
> Mr. Sriberg, this choice is yours!

The transaction was not completed. Sriberg sued Raymond for libel. Raymond claimed that the letter was absolutely privileged; the Supreme Judicial Court of Massachusetts agreed:

> The Restatement of Torts, §586 (1938), provides that "[a]n attorney at law is absolutely privileged to publish false and defamatory matter of another in communications preliminary to a proposed judicial proceeding, or in the institution of, or during the course and as a part of a judicial proceeding in which he participates as counsel, if it has some relation thereto." [. . .]
>
> The public policy of permitting attorneys complete freedom of expression and candor in communications in their efforts to secure justice for their clients commends itself to us. The basic elements of such a policy were recognized early in this Commonwealth by Chief Justice Shaw in the following terms: "[I]t is, on the whole, for the public interest, and best calculated to subserve the purposes of justice, to allow counsel full freedom of speech, in conducting the causes, and advocating and sustaining the rights, of their constituents; and this freedom of discussion ought not to be impaired by numerous and refined distinctions." It appears desirable to install the privilege where such statements are made by an attorney engaged in his function as an attorney whether in the institution or conduct of litigation or in conferences and other communications preliminary to litigation. Where a communication to a prospective defendant relates to a proceeding which is contemplated in good faith and which is under serious consideration, it is our view that the privilege should attach. This is subject to the provisions that such proceeding is not to be employed as a shield of immunity for defamation where there is not serious consideration of suit.

What is the distinction between *Sriberg v. Raymond* and *Roush v. Hey*?

3. *Judicial proceedings.* The particular privileges involved in *Roush* and *Sriberg* are generally referred to as involving "judicial proceedings"; also covered under this heading are statements by jurors, witnesses, and parties to litigation. The *Roush* case illustrates one limit on the privilege. Another is that the remarks must be relevant to the case:

> The ends of justice can be effectually accomplished by placing a limit upon the party or counsel who avails himself of his situation to gratify private malice by uttering slanderous expressions and making libelous statements, which have no relation to, or connection with, the cause in hand or the subject-matter of inquiry. The person whose good name suffers has, or ought to have, the right to vindicate his reputation by an appeal to the courts, instead of taking the law into his own hands. The law would be a vain thing indeed to shut the gates of justice in his face, and at the same time fetter his hands by the command: "Thou shalt not kill."

Myers v. Hodges, 44 So. 357 (Fla. 1907). But the test for relevance is a forgiving one:

> It is enough if the offending statement may possibly bear on the issues in litigation now or at some future time. Presumably there is some residual test of rationality, but it would seem that the barest rationality, divorced from any palpable or pragmatic degree of probability, suffices.

Seltzer v. Fields, 244 N.Y.S.2d 792 (App. Div. 1963). The Second Restatement provides these additional details on judicial and related privileges:

§585. JUDICIAL OFFICERS

Comment c. [...] The exercise of the judicial function is also not confined to tribunals created by legislative provisions. Thus, in a grievance proceeding arising under a collective bargaining agreement, the arbiter is exercising a judicial function, and the indications are that the protection of this Section extends to him as well.

§590. LEGISLATORS

A member of the Congress of the United States or of a State or local legislative body is absolutely privileged to publish defamatory matter concerning another in the performance of his legislative functions.

Comment a. Unlike the privileges of judicial officers and others participating in judicial proceedings, those legislative officers designated in this Section are absolutely privileged in publishing defamatory matter while they are performing a legislative function although the defamatory matter has no relation to a legitimate object of legislative concern. [...] The privilege does not protect a legislator who in private or public discussion outside of his legislative function explains his reasons for voting on past, pending or proposed legislation or who otherwise discusses the legislation, or who engages in other activities incidentally related to legislative affairs but not a part of the legislative process itself.

§591. EXECUTIVE AND ADMINISTRATIVE OFFICERS

An absolute privilege to publish defamatory matter concerning another in communications made in the performance of his official duties exists for

> (a) any executive or administrative officer of the United States; or
>
> (b) a governor or other superior executive officer of a state.

Comment c. All of the state courts that have considered the question have agreed that the absolute privilege stated in Clause (b) protects the superior officers of the state governments, including at least the governor, the attorney-general or the heads of state departments whose rank is the equivalent of cabinet rank in the Federal Government. A good number of the States have gone further, and have extended the absolute privilege to state officers of various ranks below that of cabinet level. The greater number of the state courts have not made the extension to the point of the federal rule and some have expressly confined the absolute privilege to superior officers of the States. This leaves the inferior state officers in these States with only a conditional privilege[.]

Comment d. The privilege stated in this Section is absolute. Hence no action for defamation can be maintained against any one of the designated executive officers irrespective of his purpose in making the publication. There are certain testimonial privileges applicable not only to chief executive officers and departmental heads but also to inferior officers of the State and Nation which, on grounds of public policy, make inadmissible as evidence in a court certain reports and other communications between servants of the State. These rules sometimes afford indirect protection to subordinate officers by preventing the presentation of proof necessary to establish liability. The statement of the rules governing the admissibility of these privileged communications is not within the scope of this Restatement.

Illustration 2. A, a janitor of a governmental office building in Washington, issues a "press release" to newspapers, radio and television, describing his work and its difficulties, in the course of which he makes several statements defamatory of B, who works in the building. A has no privilege to make the publication.

Illustration 3. A, the Attorney-General of State X, issues a press release explaining the delay of his office in prosecuting certain offenses against the State, in the course of which he accuses B of suppressing evidence that might lead to a conviction. A is absolutely privileged, and is not liable to B.

Illustration 4. The same facts as in Illustration 3, except that A is not Attorney-General, but is a local district attorney. A has only a conditional privilege [. . .] even if it is found that the press release is within the scope of his official duties.

§592. HUSBAND AND WIFE

A husband or a wife is absolutely privileged to publish to the other spouse defamatory matter concerning a third person.

4. *Judge vs. lawyer (problem).* In Yoder v. Workman, 224 F. Supp. 2d 1077 (S.D.W.Va. 2002), the defendant, Workman, was a Justice on the West Virginia Supreme Court. Truman Chafin, the majority leader in the state Senate, was embroiled in a custody dispute with his ex-wife that found its way to Workman's court. Chafin argued that Workman should recuse herself from the case because Workman and Chafin's ex-wife were acquainted; Chafin also filed a lawsuit against Workman arguing that his civil rights were violated by her refusal to step aside. A few days later

Workman did recuse herself, and she posted the following press release on the court's website:

> *Mr. Chafin and his stable of lawyers* have engaged in a vitriolic campaign of judge-shopping. This campaign of spurious and unethical legal actions and false allegations against me has been designed to stalk, harass and defame me as a member of the Judiciary because the legal rulings in which I participated with the other Justices of the Supreme Court did not suit them.

John Yoder, the lawyer who had filed the complaint in Chafin's civil rights suit against Workman, now brought a suit of his own against Workman for defamation. What result?

5. *Truth.* From the Restatement (Second) of Torts:

§581A. TRUE STATEMENTS

One who publishes a defamatory statement of fact is not subject to liability for defamation if the statement is true.

Comment a. To create liability for defamation there must be publication of matter that is both defamatory and false. There can be no recovery in defamation for a statement of fact that is true, although the statement is made for no good purpose and is inspired by ill will toward the person about whom it is published and is made solely for the purpose of harming him. [. . .]

Comment b. At common law the majority position has been that although the plaintiff must allege falsity in his complaint, the falsity of a defamatory communication is presumed. It has been consistently held that truth is an affirmative defense which must be raised by the defendant and on which he has the burden of proof. The practical effect of this rule has been eroded, however, by the recent Supreme Court holdings that the First Amendment to the Constitution requires a finding of fault on the part of the defendant regarding the truth or falsity of the communication. Pending further elucidation by the Supreme Court, the Institute does not purport to set forth with precision the extent to which the burden of proof as to truth or falsity is now shifted to the plaintiff.

For further developments on this last question, see *Philadelphia Newspapers v. Hepps*, 475 U.S. 767 (1986), later in this chapter.

6. *Nunc pro tunc.* In Beggarly v. Craft, 31 Ga. 309 (1860), the defendant, Beggarly, lived with his family in Atlanta. The plaintiff, Craft, rented an apartment nearby. Beggarly attempted to persuade the owner of Craft's building to oust her; in the course of those efforts he spoke these words: "She is a girl of bad character; she is a whore; I believe her to be a whore; she keeps

the same kind of company that such women keep." Craft sued Beggarly for slander. Beggarly defended by asserting that his statements were true, and to prove them he offered evidence that two months after the words were spoken Craft did perform acts of prostitution. The trial court refused to admit this evidence, and the Georgia Supreme Court affirmed:

> [T]he Court was right in rejecting the plea and proof of actual prostitution, two months after the words were spoken. Whether offered in order to draw the inference, that, if the plaintiff was actually unchaste in August, she was probably not free from the taint of pollution in June, or to diminish the damages on account of the degradation to which the witness swore she subsequently yielded, we hold, it would be dangerous in the extreme to allow such proof. The charge made was well calculated to stimulate assaults upon the virtue of a young woman, however innocent she might be in her deportment, and then it would become the interest of the defendant to conspire to bring about the result which he imputed. No authority is produced in support of this attempt, and policy forbids the allowance of such testimony.

7. *The libel-proof plaintiff.* In Guccione v. Hustler Magazine, Inc., 800 F.2d 298 (2d Cir. 1986), the plaintiff, Bob Guccione, was publisher of *Penthouse* magazine. He was the subject of an article in the November 1983 issue of *Hustler* magazine written by Larry Flynt, its publisher. The article was accompanied by a photograph of Guccione, fully clothed, posing next to some nude models. The article said, "Considering he is married and also has a live-in girlfriend, Kathy Keeton . . . we wonder if he would let either of them pose nude with a man[.]" Guccione sued *Hustler* for libel. He claimed that the article implied that he was committing adultery in 1983 and living then with his wife and girlfriend simultaneously. In fact Guccione had married Muriel Guccione in 1956, separated from her in 1964, and divorced her in 1979; he had been cohabiting with Keeton since 1966. The district court, calling the case a "grudge match," entered judgment on a $2,600,000 jury verdict in favor of Guccione. The court of appeals reversed:

> [T]he undisputed facts establish the defense of substantial truth as a matter of law. New York law recognizes that an alleged libel is not actionable if the published statement could have produced no worse an effect on the mind of a reader than the truth pertinent to the allegation. [. . .] This is not to suggest that every person guilty of even a single episode of marital infidelity has no recourse if, years after the fact, he is accused in print of currently committing adultery. However, the undisputed facts of this case — the extremely long duration of Guccione's adulterous conduct, which he made no attempt to conceal from the general public, and the relatively short period of time since his divorce — make it fair

to say that calling Guccione an "adulterer" in 1983 was substantially true. Of course, "former long-time adulterer" would have been more precise.

The undisputed facts also establish that Guccione's libel complaint fails because Guccione was "libel-proof with respect to the accusation of adultery printed in the *Hustler* article. We have recognized that a plaintiff's reputation with respect to a specific subject may be so badly tarnished that he cannot be further injured by allegedly false statements on that subject. See *Cardillo v. Doubleday & Co., Inc.*, 518 F.2d 638 (2d Cir. 1975). It has also been recognized that a plaintiff may have had his reputation so badly damaged by true statements in a particular publication that minor false accusations within the same publication cannot result in further meaningful injury. See *Simmons Ford, Inc. v. Consumers Union*, 516 F. Supp. 742 (S.D.N.Y.1981). The libel-proof plaintiff doctrine is to be applied with caution, since few plaintiffs will have so bad a reputation that they are not entitled to obtain redress for defamatory statements, even if their damages cannot be quantified and they receive only nominal damages. But in those instances where an allegedly libelous statement cannot realistically cause impairment of reputation because the person's reputation is already so low or because the true portions of a statement have such damaging effects, even nominal damages are not to be awarded. Instead, the claim should be dismissed so that the costs of defending against the claim of libel, which can themselves impair vigorous freedom of expression, will be avoided. [. . .]

What is the distinction between *Guccione v. Hustler Magazine, Inc.* and *Beggarly v. Craft?*

8. *Bad answer.* In Buckner v. Spaulding, 26 N.E. 792 (Ind. 1891), the substance of the court's opinion was brief:

> The complaint alleges that the defendant, here the appellant, slandered the plaintiff by falsely charging her with adultery with one Williams. The answer is, in substance, that the plaintiff did have sexual intercourse with one Bloder. The answer is so clearly bad that discussion is unnecessary. It is no answer to a slanderous charge that the plaintiff was guilty of a specific act of adultery with one man to allege that she was guilty of a specific act of adultery with another man.

To similar effect is Prosser and Keeton on the Law of Torts §116:

> Specific charges cannot be justified by showing the plaintiff's general bad character; and if the accusation is one of particular misconduct, such as stealing a watch from A, it is not enough to show a different offense, even though it be a more serious one, such as stealing a clock from A, or six watches from B.

What is the distinction between *Buckner v. Spaulding* and *Guccione v. Hustler Magazine, Inc.?*

E. CONSTITUTIONAL DEVELOPMENTS

1. *Public Plaintiffs*

New York Times Co. v. Sullivan
376 U.S. 254 (1964)

[The plaintiff, Sullivan, was one of three elected commissioners of Montgomery, Alabama, and was in charge of its police department. He claimed that the *New York Times* libeled him by printing a full-page advertisement titled "Heed Their Rising Voices"; the ad protested an "unprecedented wave of terror" against civil rights demonstrators in the South. Sullivan complained about these two paragraphs in particular:

> In Montgomery, Alabama, after students sang "My Country, 'Tis of Thee" on the State Capitol steps, their leaders were expelled from school, and truckloads of police armed with shotguns and tear-gas ringed the Alabama State College Campus. When the entire student body protested to state authorities by refusing to re-register, their dining hall was padlocked in an attempt to starve them into submission.
>
> Again and again the Southern violators have answered Dr. King's peaceful protests with intimidation and violence. They have bombed his home almost killing his wife and child. They have assaulted his person. They have arrested him seven times — for 'speeding,' 'loitering' and similar 'offenses.' And now they have charged him with 'perjury' — a felony under which they could imprison him for ten years. . . .

[Sullivan claimed that he was indirectly defamed by the references to the police in these paragraphs. The defendants admitted that some of the claims in the advertisement were false: the police did not "ring" the campus, for example, but only gathered nearby; King had been arrested four times rather than seven; and the dining hall had not been padlocked. Witnesses testified that they understood the ad to refer to Sullivan, and Sullivan in turn proved that he had not been commissioner when some of the events occurred. The jury awarded Sullivan $500,000 in general damages. The Alabama Supreme Court affirmed. The United States Supreme Court reversed.]

BRENNAN, J. We are required in this case to determine for the first time the extent to which the constitutional protections for speech and press limit a

State's power to award damages in a libel action brought by a public official against critics of his official conduct.

[The opinion began by establishing two preliminary points: that a judgment in a defamation suit amounts to "state action" constrained by the First and Fourteenth Amendments; and that the statements were not exempt from constitutional concern by virtue of being part of a paid advertisement. The opinion then continued:]

Respondent relies heavily, as did the Alabama courts, on statements of this Court to the effect that the Constitution does not protect libelous publications. Those statements do not foreclose our inquiry here. None of the cases sustained the use of libel laws to impose sanctions upon expression critical of the official conduct of public officials. [. . .] Like insurrection, contempt, advocacy of unlawful acts, breach of the peace, obscenity, solicitation of legal business, and the various other formulae for the repression of expression that have been challenged in this Court, libel can claim no talismanic immunity from constitutional limitations. It must be measured by standards that satisfy the First Amendment.

The general proposition that freedom of expression upon public questions is secured by the First Amendment has long been settled by our decisions. [. . .] Thus we consider this case against the background of a profound national commitment to the principle that debate on public issues should be uninhibited, robust, and wide-open, and that it may well include vehement, caustic, and sometimes unpleasantly sharp attacks on government and public officials. The present advertisement, as an expression of grievance and protest on one of the major public issues of our time, would seem clearly to qualify for the constitutional protection. The question is whether it forfeits that protection by the falsity of some of its factual statements and by its alleged defamation of respondent.

Authoritative interpretations of the First Amendment guarantees have consistently refused to recognize an exception for any test of truth — whether administered by judges, juries, or administrative officials — and especially one that puts the burden of proving truth on the speaker. The constitutional protection does not turn upon "the truth, popularity, or social utility of the ideas and beliefs which are offered." *N.A.A.C.P. v. Button*, 371 U.S. at 445. As Madison said, "Some degree of abuse is inseparable from the proper use of every thing; and in no instance is this more true than in that of the press." 4 *Elliot's Debates on the Federal Constitution* (1876), p. 571. [. . .] That erroneous statement is inevitable in free debate, and that it must be protected if the freedoms of expression are to have the "breathing space" that they "need . . . to survive," *N.A.A.C.P. v. Button*, 371 U.S. at 433, was also recognized by the Court of Appeals for the District of Columbia Circuit in *Sweeney v. Patterson*, 128 F.2d 457, 458 (1942), *cert. denied*, 317 U.S. 678. Judge Edgerton spoke for a unanimous court which affirmed the dismissal of a Congressman's libel suit based upon a newspaper article charging him with anti-Semitism in opposing a judicial appointment. He said:

> Cases which impose liability for erroneous reports of the political conduct of officials reflect the obsolete doctrine that the governed must not criticize their governors. . . . The interest of the public here outweighs the interest of appellant or any other individual. The protection of the public requires not merely discussion, but information. Political conduct and views which some respectable people approve, and others condemn, are constantly imputed to Congressmen. Errors of fact, particularly in regard to a man's mental states and processes, are inevitable. . . . Whatever is added to the field of libel is taken from the field of free debate.

Injury to official reputation error affords no more warrant for repressing speech that would otherwise be free than does factual error. Where judicial officers are involved, this Court has held that concern for the dignity and reputation of the courts does not justify the punishment as criminal contempt of criticism of the judge or his decision. This is true even though the utterance contains "half-truths" and "misinformation." Such repression can be justified, if at all, only by a clear and present danger of the obstruction of justice. If judges are to be treated as "men of fortitude, able to thrive in a hardy climate," surely the same must be true of other government officials, such as elected city commissioners. Criticism of their official conduct does not lose its constitutional protection merely because it is effective criticism and hence diminishes their official reputations.

If neither factual error nor defamatory content suffices to remove the constitutional shield from criticism of official conduct, the combination of the two elements is no less inadequate. This is the lesson to be drawn from the great controversy over the Sedition Act of 1798, 1 Stat. 596, which first crystallized a national awareness of the central meaning of the First Amendment. That statute made it a crime, punishable by a $5,000 fine and five years in prison, "if any person shall write, print, utter or publish . . . any false, scandalous and malicious writing or writings against the government of the United States, or either house of the Congress . . . , or the President . . . , with intent to defame . . . or to bring them, or either of them, into contempt or disrepute; or to excite against them, or either or any of them, the hatred of the good people of the United States." The Act allowed the defendant the defense of truth, and provided that the jury were to be judges both of the law and the facts. Despite these qualifications, the Act was vigorously condemned as unconstitutional in an attack joined in by Jefferson and Madison. [. . .]

Although the Sedition Act was never tested in this Court, the attack upon its validity has carried the day in the court of history. Fines levied in its prosecution were repaid by Act of Congress on the ground that it was unconstitutional. [. . .] The invalidity of the Act has also been assumed by Justices of this Court. These views reflect a broad consensus that the Act, because of the restraint it imposed upon criticism of government and public officials, was inconsistent with the First Amendment.

There is no force in respondent's argument that the constitutional limitations implicit in the history of the Sedition Act apply only to Congress and not to the States. It is true that the First Amendment was originally addressed only to action by the Federal Government, and that Jefferson, for one, while denying the power of Congress "to controul the freedom of the press," recognized such a power in the States. But this distinction was eliminated with the adoption of the Fourteenth Amendment and the application to the States of the First Amendment's restrictions.

What a State may not constitutionally bring about by means of a criminal statute is likewise beyond the reach of its civil law of libel. The fear of damage awards under a rule such as that invoked by the Alabama courts here may be markedly more inhibiting than the fear of prosecution under a criminal statute. Alabama, for example, has a criminal libel law which subjects to prosecution "any person who speaks, writes, or prints of and concerning another any accusation falsely and maliciously importing the commission by such person of a felony, or any other indictable offense involving moral turpitude," and which allows as punishment upon conviction a fine not exceeding $500 and a prison sentence of six months. Alabama Code, Tit. 14, §350. Presumably a person charged with violation of this statute enjoys ordinary criminal-law safeguards such as the requirements of an indictment and of proof beyond a reasonable doubt. These safeguards are not available to the defendant in a civil action. The judgment awarded in this case — without the need for any proof of actual pecuniary loss — was one thousand times greater than the maximum fine provided by the Alabama criminal statute, and one hundred times greater than that provided by the Sedition Act. And since there is no double-jeopardy limitation applicable to civil lawsuits, this is not the only judgment that may be awarded against petitioners for the same publication. Whether or not a newspaper can survive a succession of such judgments, the pall of fear and timidity imposed upon those who would give voice to public criticism is an atmosphere in which the First Amendment freedoms cannot survive. Plainly the Alabama law of civil libel is "a form of regulation that creates hazards to protected freedoms markedly greater than those that attend reliance upon the criminal law." *Bantam Books, Inc. v. Sullivan*, 372 U.S. 58 (1963).

The state rule of law is not saved by its allowance of the defense of truth. [. . .] A rule compelling the critic of official conduct to guarantee the truth of all his factual assertions — and to do so on pain of libel judgments virtually unlimited in amount — leads to a comparable "self-censorship." Allowance of the defense of truth, with the burden of proving it on the defendant, does not mean that only false speech will be deterred. Even courts accepting this defense as an adequate safeguard have recognized the difficulties of adducing legal proofs that the alleged libel was true in all its factual particulars. Under such a rule, would-be critics of official conduct may be deterred from voicing their criticism, even though it is believed to be true and even though it is in fact true, because of doubt whether it can be proved in court or fear of the expense of having to do so. They tend to make only statements which "steer far wider of the unlawful zone." The rule thus dampens the vigor and limits the variety of public debate. It is inconsistent with the First and Fourteenth Amendments.

The constitutional guarantees require, we think, a federal rule that prohibits a public official from recovering damages for a defamatory falsehood relating to his official conduct unless he proves that the statement was made with "actual malice" — that is, with knowledge that it was false or with reckless disregard of whether it was false or not. An oft-cited statement of a like rule, which has been adopted by a number of state courts, is found in the Kansas case of *Coleman v. MacLennan*, 78 Kan. 711, 98 P. 281 (1908) [. . .].

Such a privilege for criticism of official conduct is appropriately analogous to the protection accorded a public official when *he* is sued for libel by a private citizen. In *Barr v. Matteo*, 360 U.S. 564 (1959), this Court held the utterance of a federal official to be absolutely privileged if made "within the outer perimeter" of his duties. The States accord the same immunity to statements of their highest officers, although some differentiate their lesser officials and qualify the privilege they enjoy. But all hold that all officials are protected unless actual malice can be proved. The reason for the official privilege is said to be that the threat of damage suits would otherwise "inhibit the fearless, vigorous, and effective administration of policies of government" and "dampen the ardor of all but the most resolute, or the most irresponsible, in the unflinching discharge of their duties." *Barr v. Matteo*, supra. Analogous considerations support the privilege for the citizen-critic of government. It is as much his duty to criticize as it is the official's duty to administer. As Madison said, "the censorial power is in the people over the Government, and not in the Government over the people." It would give public servants an unjustified preference over the public they serve, if critics of official conduct did not have a fair equivalent of the immunity granted to the officials themselves.

We conclude that such a privilege is required by the First and Fourteenth Amendments.

We hold today that the Constitution delimits a State's power to award damages for libel in actions brought by public officials against critics of their official conduct. Since this is such an action, the rule requiring proof of actual malice is applicable. While Alabama law apparently requires proof of actual malice for an award of punitive damages, where general damages are concerned malice is "presumed." Such a presumption is inconsistent with the federal rule. [. . .] Since the trial judge did not instruct the jury to differentiate between general and punitive damages, it may be that the verdict was wholly an award of one or the other. But it is impossible to know, in view of the general verdict returned. Because of this uncertainty, the judgment must be reversed and the case remanded.

Since respondent may seek a new trial, we deem that considerations of effective judicial administration require us to review the evidence in the present record to determine whether it could constitutionally support a judgment for respondent. [. . .] Applying these standards, we consider that the proof presented to show actual malice lacks the convincing clarity which the constitutional standard demands, and hence that it would not constitutionally sustain the judgment for respondent under the proper rule of law. The case of the individual petitioners requires little discussion. Even assuming that they could constitutionally be found to have authorized the use of their names on the advertisement, there was no evidence whatever that they were aware of any erroneous statements or were in any way reckless in that regard. The judgment against them is thus without constitutional support.

As to the *Times*, we similarly conclude that the facts do not support a finding of actual malice. The statement by the *Times*' Secretary that, apart from the padlocking allegation, he thought the advertisement was "substantially correct," affords no constitutional warrant for the Alabama Supreme Court's conclusion that it was a "cavalier ignoring of the falsity of the advertisement (from which), the jury could not have but been impressed with the bad faith of the *Times*, and its maliciousness inferable therefrom." The statement does not indicate malice at the time of the publication; even if the advertisement was not "substantially correct" — although respondent's own proofs tend to show that it was — that opinion was at least a reasonable one, and there was no evidence to impeach the witness' good faith in holding it. The *Times*' failure to retract upon respondent's demand, although it later retracted upon the demand of Governor Patterson, is likewise not adequate evidence of malice for constitutional purposes. Whether or not a failure to retract may ever constitute such evidence, there are two reasons why it does not here. First, the letter written by the *Times* reflected a reasonable doubt on its part as to whether the advertisement could reasonably be taken to refer to respondent at all. Second, it was not a final refusal, since it asked for an explanation on this point — a request that respondent chose to ignore. Nor does the retraction upon the demand of the Governor supply the necessary proof. It may be doubted that a failure to retract which is not itself evidence of malice can retroactively become such by virtue of a retraction subsequently made to another party. But in any event that did not happen here, since the explanation given by the *Times*' Secretary for the distinction drawn between respondent and the Governor was a reasonable one, the good faith of which was not impeached.

Finally, there is evidence that the *Times* published the advertisement without checking its accuracy against the news stories in the *Times*' own files. The mere presence of the stories in the files does not, of course, establish that the *Times* "knew" the advertisement was false, since the state of mind required for actual malice would have to be brought home to the persons in the *Times*' organization having responsibility for the publication of the advertisement. With respect to the failure of those persons to make the check, the record shows that they relied upon their knowledge of the good reputation of many of those whose names were listed as sponsors of the advertisement, and upon the letter from A. Philip Randolph, known to them as a responsible individual, certifying that the use of the names was authorized. There was testimony that the persons handling the advertisement saw nothing in it that would render it unacceptable under the *Times'* policy of rejecting advertisements containing "attacks of a personal character"; their failure to reject it on this ground was not unreasonable. We think the evidence against the *Times* supports at most a finding of negligence in failing to discover the misstatements, and is constitutionally insufficient to show the recklessness that is required for a finding of actual malice.

We also think the evidence was constitutionally defective in another respect: it was incapable of supporting the jury's finding that the allegedly libelous statements were made "of and concerning" respondent. Respondent relies on the words of the advertisement and the testimony of six witnesses to establish a connection between it and himself. [. . .] There was no reference to respondent in the advertisement, either by name or official position. A number of the allegedly libelous statements — the charges that the dining hall was padlocked and that Dr. King's home was bombed, his person assaulted, and a perjury prosecution instituted against him — did not even concern the police; despite the ingenuity of the arguments which would attach this significance to the word "They," it is plain that these statements could not reasonably be read as accusing respondent of personal involvement in the acts in question. The statements upon which respondent principally relies as referring to him are the two allegations that did concern the police or police functions: that "truckloads of police . . . ringed the Alabama State College Campus" after the demonstration on the State Capitol steps, and that Dr. King had been "arrested . . . seven times." These statements were false only in that the police had been "deployed near" the campus but had not actually "ringed" it and had not gone there in connection with the State Capitol demonstration, and in that Dr. King had been arrested only four times. The ruling that these discrepancies between what was true and what was asserted were sufficient to injure respondent's reputation may itself raise constitutional problems, but we need not consider them here. Although the statements may be taken as referring to the police, they did not on their face make even an oblique reference to respondent as an individual. Support for the asserted reference must, therefore, be sought in the testimony of respondent's witnesses. But none of them suggested any basis for the belief that respondent himself was attacked in the advertisement beyond the bare fact that he was in overall charge of the Police Department and thus bore official responsibility for police conduct; to the extent that some of the witnesses thought respondent to have been charged with ordering or approving the conduct or otherwise being personally involved in it, they based this notion not on any statements in the advertisement, and not on any evidence that he had in fact been so involved, but solely on the unsupported assumption that, because of his official position, he must have been. [. . .]

The judgment of the Supreme Court of Alabama is reversed and the case is remanded to that court for further proceedings not inconsistent with this opinion.

BLACK, J., with whom DOUGLAS, J., joins (concurring). I concur in reversing this half-million-dollar judgment against the New York Times Company and the four individual defendants. In reversing the Court holds that "the Constitution delimits a State's power to award damages for libel in actions brought by public officials against critics of their official conduct." I base my vote to reverse on the belief that the First and Fourteenth Amendments not merely "delimit" a State's power to award damages to "public officials against critics of their official conduct" but completely prohibit a State from exercising such a power. The Court goes on to hold that a State can subject such critics to damages if "actual malice" can be proved against them. "Malice," even as defined by the Court, is an elusive, abstract concept, hard to prove and hard to disprove. The requirement that malice be proved provides at best an evanescent protection for the right critically to discuss public affairs and certainly does not measure up to the sturdy safeguard embodied in the First Amendment. Unlike the Court, therefore, I vote to reverse exclusively on the ground that the Times and the individual defendants had an absolute, unconditional constitutional right to publish in the Times advertisement their criticisms of the Montgomery agencies and officials. [. . .]
[Concurring opinion of Goldberg, J., omitted.]

NOTES

1. *Convincing clarity.* The Court in *New York Times v. Sullivan* concluded that the plaintiff's proof of the defendant's actual malice lacked "the convincing clarity which the constitutional standard demands." This statement and others that followed in later cases have been understood to require that in cases where the *New York Times* standard applies, actual malice must be established by "clear and convincing evidence," and not merely by the preponderance of the evidence standard that governs most issues in a tort case.

2. *Public figures.* In Curtis Publishing Co. v. Butts, 388 U.S. 130 (1967), the Supreme Court broadened the holding of *New York Times v. Sullivan* to cover "public figures" in addition to public officials. In Gertz v. Robert Welch, Inc., 418 U.S. 323 (1974), the Court elaborated further, holding that the "public figure" designation

> may rest on either of two alternative bases: In some instances an individual may achieve such pervasive fame or notoriety that he becomes a public figure for all purposes and in all contexts. More commonly, an

individual voluntarily injects himself or is drawn into a particular public controversy and thereby becomes a public figure for a limited range of issues. In either case such persons assume special prominence in the resolution of public questions.

The second sort of plaintiff described in this passage has come to be known as a "limited purpose public figure." We will consider the *Gertz* case in more detail in a moment.

3. *Monkey business.* In Hutchinson v. Proxmire, 443 U.S. 111 (1979), Hutchinson was director of research at the Kalamazoo State Mental Hospital in Michigan. He received a series of grants from federal agencies to study objective ways of measuring aggression in animals — clenching of the teeth and the like. The defendant, Proxmire, was a United States Senator from Wisconsin. He was the creator of the "Golden Fleece" award, a prize he distributed each month for egregious cases of wasteful government spending. In April 1975 Proxmire gave the Golden Fleece award to the agencies that funded Hutchinson's work; he also issued a press subjecting the work to ridicule, referring to "the transparent worthlessness of Hutchinson's study of jaw-grinding and biting by angry or hard-drinking monkeys." Hutchinson responded that Proxmire had misrepresented his work, and several newspapers reported this. Hutchinson also sued Proxmire for defamation. Proxmire claimed Hutchinson was a public figure who therefore had to prove "actual malice" to prevail. The Supreme Court disagreed:

> It is not contended that Hutchinson attained such prominence that he is a public figure for all purposes. Instead, respondents have argued that the District Court and the Court of Appeals were correct in holding that Hutchinson is a public figure for the limited purpose of comment on his receipt of federal funds for research projects. That conclusion was based upon two factors: first, Hutchinson's successful application for federal funds and the reports in local newspapers of the federal grants; second, Hutchinson's access to the media, as demonstrated by the fact that some newspapers and wire services reported his response to the announcement of the Golden Fleece Award. Neither of those factors demonstrates that Hutchinson was a public figure prior to the controversy engendered by the Golden Fleece Award; his access, such as it was, came after the alleged libel. [. . .] Clearly, those charged with defamation cannot, by their own conduct, create their own defense by making the claimant a public figure.
>
> Hutchinson did not thrust himself or his views into public controversy to influence others. Respondents have not identified such a particular controversy; at most, they point to concern about general public expenditures. But that concern is shared by most and relates to most public expenditures; it is not sufficient to make Hutchinson a public figure. If it

were, everyone who received or benefited from the myriad public grants
for research could be classified as a public figure — a conclusion that our
previous opinions have rejected.

Moreover, Hutchinson at no time assumed any role of public prominence in the broad question of concern about expenditures. Neither his
applications for federal grants nor his publications in professional journals can be said to have invited that degree of public attention and
comment on his receipt of federal grants essential to meet the public
figure level. [. . .]

Finally, we cannot agree that Hutchinson had such access to the media
that he should be classified as a public figure. Hutchinson's access was
limited to responding to the announcement of the Golden Fleece Award.
He did not have the regular and continuing access to the media that is
one of the accouterments of having become a public figure.

4. *Open season.* In Wolston v. Reader's Digest Association, 443 U.S. 157
(1979), Ilya Wolston was summoned to appear before a grand jury
investigating claims of espionage in 1958. He did not respond to the
subpoena, was prosecuted for contempt of court, and pled guilty; he was
given a suspended sentence and put on probation. These events were
reported in about a dozen newspaper stories in Washington and New York. In
1974 Reader's Digest published a book titled *KGB: The Secret Work of Soviet
Agents.* The book included the name of the plaintiff, Wolston, on a list of
"Soviet agents who were convicted of espionage or falsifying information or
perjury and/or contempt charges following espionage indictments, or who
fled to the Soviet bloc to avoid prosecution[.]" Wolston, who had never been
prosecuted for espionage, sued for defamation. The trial court gave summary
judgment to Reader's Digest because it found that Wolston could not prove
actual malice — a showing required of him because the court concluded that
he was a public figure: "[Wolston] became involved in a controversy of a
decidedly public nature in a way that invited attention and comment, and
thereby created in the public an interest in knowing about his connection
with espionage[.]" The Supreme Court reversed:

> We do not agree with respondents and the lower courts that petitioner can
> be classed as [a] limited-purpose public figure. First, the undisputed facts
> do not justify the conclusion of the District Court and Court of Appeals
> that petitioner "voluntarily thrust" or "injected" himself into the forefront
> of the public controversy surrounding the investigation of Soviet espio-
> nage in the United States. It would be more accurate to say that petitioner
> was dragged unwillingly into the controversy. The Government pursued
> him in its investigation. Petitioner did fail to respond to a grand jury
> subpoena, and this failure, as well as his subsequent citation for con-
> tempt, did attract media attention. But the mere fact that petitioner vol-
> untarily chose not to appear before the grand jury, knowing that his action

might be attended by publicity, is not decisive on the question of public-figure status. [. . . P]etitioner never discussed this matter with the press and limited his involvement to that necessary to defend himself against the contempt charge. It is clear that petitioner played only a minor role in whatever public controversy there may have been concerning the investigation of Soviet espionage. We decline to hold that his mere citation for contempt rendered him a public figure for purposes of comment on the investigation of Soviet espionage.

Petitioner's failure to appear before the grand jury and citation for contempt no doubt were "newsworthy," but the simple fact that these events attracted media attention also is not conclusive of the public-figure issue. [. . .] To accept such reasoning would in effect re-establish the doctrine advanced by the plurality opinion in *Rosenbloom v. Metromedia, Inc.*, 403 U.S. 29 (1971), which concluded that the *New York Times* standard should extend to defamatory falsehoods relating to private persons if the statements involved matters of public or general concern. We repudiated this proposition in *Gertz* and in *Firestone*, however, and we reject it again today. A libel defendant must show more than mere newsworthiness to justify application of the demanding burden of *New York Times*. [. . .] [Petitioner] did not in any way seek to arouse public sentiment in his favor and against the investigation.

This reasoning leads us to reject the further contention of respondents that any person who engages in criminal conduct automatically becomes a public figure for purposes of comment on a limited range of issues relating to his conviction. We declined to accept a similar argument in *Time, Inc. v. Firestone*, supra, 424 U.S. 448 (1976) where we said, [. . .] "[W]hile participants in some litigation may be legitimate 'public figures,' either generally or for the limited purpose of that litigation, the majority will more likely resemble respondent, drawn into a public forum largely against their will in order to attempt to obtain the only redress available to them or to defend themselves against actions brought by the State or by others." [. . .] We think that these observations remain sound, and that they control the disposition of this case. To hold otherwise would create an "open season" for all who sought to defame persons convicted of a crime.

5. *Involuntary public figures.* In Dameron v. Washington Magazine, Inc., 779 F.2d 736 (D.C. Cir. 1985), the defendant's magazine ran an article about an airplane crash that occurred in 1982. At one point the article noted that failures of air traffic control rarely cause accidents:

> Since [1956] — despite hair-raising talk among controllers about computer malfunctions, fatigue-induced errors, and reports of "near misses" in mid-air — it is believed that no major crash has been caused solely by controller errors. They have been assigned partial blame in a few accidents, including the 1974 crash of a TWA 727 into Mt. Weather in

Virginia upon approach to Dulles (92 fatalities), the 1977 Southern Airways crash in Georgia, and the 1978 collision of a Pacific Southwest Airlines jet with a light plane over San Diego (142 fatalities).

The plaintiff, Dameron, was the only air traffic controller on duty at Dulles Airport on the day of the crash at Mt. Weather. His complaint alleged that he never had been found blameworthy for the accident and had been exonerated in a tort suit brought by the kin of the deceased. The trial court gave summary judgment to the defendant; the court of appeals affirmed, finding that Dameron was a public figure:

> [T]he Supreme Court has recognized that it is possible, although difficult and rare, to become a limited-purpose public figure *involuntarily*. In *Gertz* the Supreme Court noted that it is "possible to become a public figure through no purposeful action of [one's] own" although it added that "the instances of *truly* involuntary public figures must be exceedingly rare." Id. at 345 (emphasis added). We think that within the very narrow framework represented by the facts of this case, such has been Dameron's fate. By sheer bad luck, Dameron happened to be the controller on duty at the time of the Mt. Weather crash. As in *Gertz*, Dameron "assume[d a] special prominence in the resolution of [a] public question[ ]." *Gertz* at 351. He became embroiled, through no desire of his own, in the ensuing controversy over the causes of the accident. He thereby became well known to the public in this one very limited connection. The numerous press reports on the Mt. Weather crash introduced by the defendants in their motion for summary judgment amply demonstrate this. Dameron's name and likeness were often used in these reports. It was in that same very limited connection that *The Washingtonian*'s brief and oblique reference to him surfaced years later.

What is the distinction between *Dameron v. Washington Magazine, Inc.* and *Wolston v. Reader's Digest Association*? What is the distinction between *Dameron* and *Hutchinson v. Proxmire*?

6. *Scandalous priorities (problem).* In Clyburn v. News World Communications, 903 F.2d 29 (D.C. Cir. 1990), a woman named Medina collapsed from a drug overdose at an apartment in the District of Columbia. She died four days later. Her boyfriend, Clyburn, was interviewed by prosecutors and by a reporter from the *Washington Post*. Clyburn said that he had been with Medina when she collapsed and that he had called 911. He later admitted that he had not been alone and that someone else had made the call to the paramedics. The defendant's newspaper, the *Washington Times*, also ran a series of articles about Medina's death. Some of the articles mentioned Clyburn, noting that he was present when Medina collapsed, that he was a friend of the mayor, Marion Barry, and that he was the head of a consulting

firm that had contacts with the D.C. government. Another of the articles —
the one that precipitated this suit — stated that Medina's collapse had
occurred during a party where a number of high-ranking officials in the D.C.
government were present. Citing anonymous sources, the article reported
that Medina's boyfriend, Clyburn, had delayed calling an ambulance to give
the partygoers time to flee the scene. Clyburn sued the publisher of the *Times*
for libel. The *Times* sought summary judgment on the ground that Clyburn
had no evidence of actual malice and that he could not win without it
because he was a public figure. What result on this last issue, given the facts
provided here?

7. *Absence of malice.* In St. Amant v. Thompson, 390 U.S. 727 (1968),
St. Amant was a candidate for public office in Louisiana. He made a speech
in which he tried to show connections between his opponent and Edward
Partin, the president of a local union alleged by St. Amant to be corrupt.
St. Amant quoted in his speech from an affidavit given to him by a member
of Partin's union, one Albin. The quoted part of the affidavit included
charges of bribery; it said that "money had passed hands" from Partin to a
sheriff in Baton Rouge, Herman Thompson. Thompson sued St. Amant for
defamation. The jury brought in a verdict for Thompson and the Louisiana
Supreme Court affirmed, finding sufficient evidence that St. Amant had
acted recklessly. The Supreme Court of the United States reversed the grant
of summary judgment, finding inadequate evidence of actual malice:

> St. Amant had no personal knowledge of Thompson's activities; he relied
> solely on Albin's affidavit although the record was silent as to Albin's
> reputation for veracity; he failed to verify the information with those in
> the union office who might have known the facts; he gave no consider-
> ation to whether or not the statements defamed Thompson and went
> ahead heedless of the consequences; and he mistakenly believed he
> had no responsibility for the broadcast because he was merely quoting
> Albin's words.
>
> These considerations fall short of proving St. Amant's reckless
> disregard for the accuracy of his statements about Thompson. "Reckless
> disregard," it is true, cannot be fully encompassed in one infallible def-
> inition. Inevitably its outer limits will be marked out through case-by-case
> adjudication, as is true with so many legal standards for judging concrete
> cases, whether the standard is provided by the Constitution, statutes, or
> case law. Our cases, however, have furnished meaningful guidance for
> the further definition of a reckless publication. [...] These cases are
> clear that reckless conduct is not measured by whether a reasonably
> prudent man would have published, or would have investigated before
> publishing. There must be sufficient evidence to permit the conclusion
> that the defendant in fact entertained serious doubts as to the truth of his

publication. Publishing with such doubts shows reckless disregard for truth or falsity and demonstrates actual malice.

It may be said that such a test puts a premium on ignorance, encourages the irresponsible publisher not to inquire, and permits the issue to be determined by the defendant's testimony that he published the statement in good faith and unaware of its probable falsity. Concededly the reckless disregard standard may permit recovery in fewer situations than would a rule that publishers must satisfy the standard of the reasonable man or the prudent publisher. But *New York Times* and succeeding cases have emphasized that the stake of the people in public business and the conduct of public officials is so great that neither the defense of truth nor the standard of ordinary care would protect against self-censorship and thus adequately implement First Amendment policies. [. . .]

The defendant in a defamation action brought by a public official cannot, however, automatically insure a favorable verdict by testifying that he published with a belief that the statements were true. The finder of fact must determine whether the publication was indeed made in good faith. Professions of good faith will be unlikely to prove persuasive, for example, where a story is fabricated by the defendant, is the product of his imagination, or is based wholly on an unverified anonymous telephone call. Nor will they be likely to prevail when the publisher's allegations are so inherently improbable that only a reckless man would have put them in circulation. Likewise, recklessness may be found where there are obvious reasons to doubt the veracity of the informant or the accuracy of his reports.

By no proper test of reckless disregard was St. Amant's broadcast a reckless publication about a public officer. Nothing referred to by the Louisiana courts indicates an awareness by St. Amant of the probable falsity of Albin's statement about Thompson. Failure to investigate does not in itself establish bad faith.

8. *Almost what he said.* In Masson v. New Yorker Magazine, Inc., 501 U.S. 496 (1991), the plaintiff, Masson, was a psychoanalyst made the subject of a profile in the *New Yorker* magazine. Masson alleged that the article quoted him uttering statements that were damaging to himself but that he had not made, including a description of himself as an "intellectual gigolo." The quotation evidently was based on Masson's description of himself as someone whose company famous analysts enjoyed but with whom they would not want to be seen in public. Masson sued Janet Malcolm (the author of the article), the *New Yorker*, and Knopf, the publisher of a book based on Malcolm's article that included the damaging quotations. The trial court gave summary judgment to the defendants, and the court of appeals affirmed; the Supreme Court reversed the grant of summary judgment, but held that knowingly

misquoting the plaintiff did not necessarily make the defendants guilty of actual malice:

> We reject the idea that any alteration beyond correction of grammar or syntax by itself proves falsity in the sense relevant to determining actual malice under the First Amendment. An interviewer who writes from notes often will engage in the task of attempting a reconstruction of the speaker's statement. That author would, we may assume, act with knowledge that at times she has attributed to her subject words other than those actually used. Under petitioner's proposed standard, an author in this situation would lack First Amendment protection if she reported as quotations the substance of a subject's derogatory statements about himself. [. . .]
>
> If an author alters a speaker's words but effects no material change in meaning, including any meaning conveyed by the manner or fact of expression, the speaker suffers no injury to reputation that is compensable as a defamation. [. . .] We conclude that a deliberate alteration of the words uttered by a plaintiff does not equate with knowledge of falsity for purposes of *New York Times Co. v. Sullivan*[,] unless the alteration results in a material change in the meaning conveyed by the statement. The use of quotations to attribute words not in fact spoken bears in a most important way on that inquiry, but it is not dispositive in every case. [. . .]
>
> We agree with the dissenting opinion in the Court of Appeals that "[f]airly read, intellectual gigolo suggests someone who forsakes intellectual integrity in exchange for pecuniary or other gain." A reasonable jury could find a material difference between the meaning of this passage and petitioner's tape-recorded statement that he was considered "much too junior within the hierarchy of analysis, for these important training analysts to be caught dead with [him]."

On remand the Ninth Circuit dismissed the claims against Knopf, holding that when it published the article as a book it was entitled to rely on the fact-checking it expected had been performed by the *New Yorker*. Later juries found that the *New Yorker* and Malcolm had acted without actual malice.

9. *Kato did it (problem)*. In Kaelin v. Globe Communications Corp., 162 F.3d 1036 (9th Cir. 1998), the plaintiff was Kato Kaelin, a friend of O. J. Simpson's who gained temporary fame as a witness when Simpson was tried for the murder of his ex-wife and her friend. A week after Simpson was acquitted, the *National Examiner* ran the following front-page headline:

COPS THINK KATO DID IT!
. . . he fears they want him for perjury, say pals . . .

The story explaining the headline appeared on page 17 of the magazine; it said that Kaelin's friends were worried that Kaelin would be prosecuted for perjury. Kaelin sued the publisher for libel, claiming that the headline implied that the police thought Kaelin had committed the murders for which Simpson was acquitted. The news editor of the *Examiner* offered the following deposition testimony:

> *Q.* Okay. Did you have any concerns when you saw this headline [before publication] about the way this headline was framed?
>
> *A.* I wasn't mad about it.
>
> *Q.* What do you mean by that?
>
> *A.* Journalistically I didn't think it was the best headline in the world.
>
> *Q.* Were you concerned that it implied that Kato had committed the murders or played some role in them?
>
> *A.* No, I just didn't think it was very accurate to the story. It could have been better. [. . .]
>
> *Q.* [. . . Did] the National Examiner have in its possession [. . .] any information that a police officer anywhere thought that Kato Kaelin was involved in Nicole Brown Simpson's and Ronald Goldman's murders?
>
> *A.* No. [. . .]
>
> *Q.* . . . What did you think, on September 22nd, 1995 about what the words "Cops Think He Did It" meant? What is the "it" to which this statement — ?
>
> *A.* Perjury.
>
> *Q.* Perjury?
>
> *A.* Mm-hmm.
>
> *Q.* Did you have any concern that a reader might connect the "Cops Think He Did It" with the other information in the article that refers to allegations that Mr. Kaelin was involved in the murders themselves?
>
> *A.* I was a bit concerned about it, yes, but in fact I thought the second part of the headline coped with that . . .

The defendant sought summary judgment. What result?

10. *This just in (problem).* Meisler v. Gannett Co., 12 F.3d 1026 (11th Cir. 1994), the plaintiff, Meisler, lived in Alabama but was part owner of the Dairyland Greyhound Park, a dog racing track in Kenosha, Wisconsin. The Wisconsin Racing Board ordered a disciplinary hearing against Meisler and his three Alabama partners to investigate allegations that they had committed fraud. At the hearing the director of the Racing Board announced a settlement: two of the other partners had been found culpable and would pay fines and divest themselves of their ownership interests in the dog track; Meisler and the other

remaining partner would acquire those interests. The Associated Press soon issued a wire service report marked "URGENT" and reading in part as follows:

> BOARD OKs DAIRYLAND AFTER ACCEPTING SETTLEMENT
> MADISON, Wis. (AP) — The State Racing Board Thursday granted an operating license for 1991 to the troubled Dairyland Greyhound Park Inc. after accepting a settlement that removes the race track's Alabama investors.

The story ended with the notation "MORE." Half an hour later, another item came across the AP wire also marked URGENT and clarifying that only two of the Alabama partners — and not Meisler — had been removed from their ownership roles. A reporter for the USA *Today* newspaper saw the first AP story but did not look for or read the second one. He adapted the first into an item on the paper's "News From Every State" feature for Wisconsin. It read:

> KENOSHA — Dairyland Greyhound Park can reopen Jan. 2, state racing board said. Board removed 4 controversial Alabama investors from track ownership, ordered 4 to pay state $1 million as part of settlement for state racing board violations this year. . . .

USA *Today* ran a correction of its story a week later. Meisler sued the newspaper for defamation. The newspaper sought summary judgment. In his opposition papers, Meisler included evidence that both the first and second wire reports had arrived in the office of the USA *Today* reporter before he filed his story. Meisler also submitted an affidavit from an expert witness who testified, as the court recounted it, "that it was common knowledge in the industry that 'URGENT' signifies that the news event had just occurred and that AP had rushed the wire. 'MORE,' he said, indicates that additional wires on the same story would be forthcoming. He expressed the opinion that no responsible publisher would have published a news item based upon the initial AP wire without consulting subsequent wires." What result?

11. *The rumor (problem)*. In Martin v. Wilson Publishing Co., 497 A.2d 322 (R.I. 1985), the plaintiff, George Martin, was a Rhode Island businessman who owned a construction firm and a real estate holding company. In 1969 he became interested in real estate in the village of Shannock, a former mill town. He bought a series of properties there: first a mansion, then 22 structures — mill houses — near the town center, which he renovated and turned into rental units. He made a series of additional purchases totaling about 125 acres of property. He made frequent visits to Shannock and appeared several times in front of local regulatory boards to obtain permits to go forward with his plans for the properties. Over the

years he also was the subject of occasional newspaper stories and appeared in a film about Shannock made by the state's Department of Community Affairs.

In 1977 the defendant's newspaper, the *Chariho Times*, published an article titled "The New Face of Shannock Village." The article discussed Martin's purchases and his plans to turn the old mill in town into an apartment complex and small shopping center. The article said that town residents were anxious about Martin's plans. One of its passages read as follows:

> Some residents stretch available facts when they imagine Mr. Martin is connected with the 1974 rash of fires in the village (the abandoned depot, the back of the Shannock Spa, and even that old barn he loved). Local fire officials feel that certain local kids did it for kicks. The same imaginations note that the fire at the old Shannock mill before he bought it made it cheaper (but less valuable), or that the fire there since he bought it might have been profitable (though derelict buildings, such as it was, are customarily uninsurable).

Martin sued for defamation, saying he had nothing to do with the fires. What result?

2. Private Plaintiffs

Gertz v. Robert Welch, Inc.
418 U.S. 323 (1974)

[A Chicago police officer named Nuccio shot and killed a young man named Ronald Nelson. Nuccio was convicted of second-degree murder. Nelson's family then hired a lawyer, Elmer Gertz, to bring a civil suit for damages against Nuccio. A magazine called *American Opinion*, an organ of the John Birch Society published by the respondent, Robert Welch, ran an article called "Frame-Up: Richard Nuccio and the War on Police." The article falsely claimed that Gertz was a Communist, that he had a long police record, and that he was the architect of a plot to frame Nuccio and discredit the police department. The magazine's editor said that he had made no effort to verify the article's claims but that he had no reason to doubt their truth.

[Gertz sued the publisher for libel. A jury awarded him $50,000. The trial judge nevertheless gave judgment to the defendant on the ground that while Gertz was not a public figure, the defamatory statements concerned a matter of public interest; that Gertz therefore had to show actual malice to win; and that he had failed to do so.]

POWELL, J. The principal issue in this case is whether a newspaper or broadcaster that publishes defamatory falsehoods about an individual who is neither a public official nor a public figure may claim a constitutional privilege against liability for the injury inflicted by those statements. [. . .]

We begin with the common ground. Under the First Amendment there is no such thing as a false idea. However pernicious an opinion may seem, we depend for its correction not on the conscience of judges and juries but on the competition of other ideas. But there is no constitutional value in false statements of fact. Neither the intentional lie nor the careless error materially advances society's interest in "uninhibited, robust, and wide-open" debate on public issues. *New York Times Co. v. Sullivan*, 376 U.S., at 270. [. . .] The need to avoid self-censorship by the news media is, however, not the only societal value at issue. If it were, this Court would have embraced long ago the view that publishers and broadcasters enjoy an unconditional and indefeasible immunity from liability for defamation. Such a rule would, indeed, obviate the fear that the prospect of civil liability for injurious falsehood might dissuade a timorous press from the effective exercise of First Amendment freedoms. Yet absolute protection for the communications media requires a total sacrifice of the competing value served by the law of defamation.

The legitimate state interest underlying the law of libel is the compensation of individuals for the harm inflicted on them by defamatory falsehood. We would not lightly require the State to abandon this purpose[. . . .] Some tension necessarily exists between the need for a vigorous and uninhibited press and the legitimate interest in redressing wrongful injury. [. . .] In our continuing effort to define the proper accommodation between these competing concerns, we have been especially anxious to assure to the freedoms of speech and press that "breathing space" essential to their fruitful exercise. To that end this Court has extended a measure of strategic protection to defamatory falsehood.

The *New York Times* standard defines the level of constitutional protection appropriate to the context of defamation of a public person. Those who, by reason of the notoriety of their achievements or the vigor and success with which they seek the public's attention, are properly classed as public figures and those who hold governmental office may recover for injury to reputation only on clear and convincing proof that the defamatory falsehood was made with knowledge of its falsity or with reckless disregard for the truth. This standard administers an extremely powerful antidote to the inducement to media self-censorship of the common-law rule of strict liability for libel and slander. And it exacts a correspondingly high price from the victims of defamatory falsehood. Plainly many deserving plaintiffs, including some intentionally subjected to injury, will be unable to surmount the barrier of the *New York Times* test. Despite this substantial abridgment of the state law right to compensation for wrongful hurt to one's reputation, the Court has concluded that the protection of the *New York Times* privilege should be available to publishers and broadcasters of defamatory falsehood concerning public officials and public figures. We think that these decisions are correct, but we do not find their holdings justified solely by reference to the interest of the press and broadcast media in immunity from liability. Rather, we believe that the *New York Times* rule states an accommodation between this concern and the limited state interest present in the context of libel actions brought by public persons. For the reasons stated below, we conclude that the state interest in compensating injury to the reputation of private individuals requires that a different rule should obtain with respect to them.

Theoretically, of course, the balance between the needs of the press and the individual's claim to compensation for wrongful injury might be struck on a case-by-case basis. As Mr. Justice Harlan hypothesized, "it might seem, purely as an abstract matter, that the most utilitarian approach would be to scrutinize carefully every jury verdict in every libel case, in order to ascertain whether the final judgment leaves fully protected whatever First Amendment values transcend the legitimate state interest in protecting the particular plaintiff who prevailed." *Rosenbloom v. Metromedia,* Inc., 403 U.S., at 63, 91 S. Ct., at 1829 (footnote omitted). But this approach would lead to unpredictable results and uncertain expectations, and it could render our duty to supervise the lower courts unmanageable. Because an ad hoc resolution of the competing interests at stake in each particular case is not feasible, we must lay down broad rules of general application. Such rules necessarily treat alike various cases involving differences as well as similarities. Thus it is often true that not all of the considerations which justify adoption of a given rule will obtain in each particular case decided under its authority.

With that caveat we have no difficulty in distinguishing among defamation plaintiffs. The first remedy of any victim of defamation is self-help — using available opportunities to contradict the lie or correct the error and thereby to minimize its adverse impact on reputation. Public officials and public figures usually enjoy significantly greater access to the channels of effective communication and hence have a more realistic opportunity to counteract false statements than private individuals normally enjoy. Private individuals are therefore more vulnerable to injury, and the state interest in protecting them is correspondingly greater.

More important than the likelihood that private individuals will lack effective opportunities for rebuttal, there is a compelling normative consideration underlying the distinction between public and private defamation plaintiffs. An individual who decides to seek governmental office must accept certain necessary consequences of that involvement in public affairs. He runs the risk of closer public scrutiny than might otherwise be the case. And society's interest in the officers of government is not strictly limited to the formal discharge of official duties. [. . .]

Those classed as public figures stand in a similar position. Hypothetically, it may be possible for someone to become a public figure through no purposeful action of his own, but the instances of truly involuntary public figures must be exceedingly rare. For the most part those who attain this status have assumed roles of especial prominence in the affairs of society. Some occupy positions of such persuasive power and influence that they are deemed public figures for all purposes. More commonly, those classed as public figures have thrust themselves to the forefront of particular public controversies in order to influence the resolution of the issues involved. In either event, they invite attention and comment.

Even if the foregoing generalities do not obtain in every instance, the communications media are entitled to act on the assumption that public officials and public figures have voluntarily exposed themselves to increased risk of injury from defamatory falsehood concerning them. No such assumption is justified with respect to a private individual. He has not accepted public office or assumed an "influential role in ordering society." *Curtis Publishing Co. v. Butts*, 388 U.S. at 164 (Warren, C.J., concurring). He has relinquished no part of his interest in the protection of his own good name, and consequently he has a more compelling call on the courts for redress of injury inflicted by defamatory falsehood. Thus, private individuals are not only more vulnerable to injury than public officials and public figures; they are also more deserving of recovery. [. . .]

We hold that, so long as they do not impose liability without fault, the States may define for themselves the appropriate standard of liability for a publisher or broadcaster of defamatory falsehood injurious to a private individual. This approach provides a more equitable boundary between the competing concerns involved here. It recognizes the strength of the legitimate state interest in compensating private individuals for wrongful injury to reputation, yet shields the press and broadcast media from the rigors of strict liability for defamation. At least this conclusion obtains where, as here, the substance of the defamatory statement "makes substantial danger to reputation apparent." This phrase places in perspective the conclusion we announce today. Our inquiry would involve considerations somewhat different from those discussed above if a State purported to condition civil liability on a factual misstatement whose content did not warn a reasonably prudent editor or broadcaster of its defamatory potential. Such a case is not now before us, and we intimate no view as to its proper resolution.

[The Court then said that "the strong and legitimate state interest in compensating private individuals for injury to reputation [. . .] extends no further than compensation for actual injury.] For the reasons stated below, we hold that the States may not permit recovery of presumed or punitive damages, at least when liability is not based on a showing of knowledge of falsity or reckless disregard for the truth.

The common law of defamation is an oddity of tort law, for it allows recovery of purportedly compensatory damages without evidence of actual loss. Under the traditional rules pertaining to actions for libel, the existence of injury is presumed from the fact of publication. Juries may award substantial sums as compensation for supposed damage to reputation without any proof that such harm actually occurred. The largely uncontrolled discretion of juries to award damages where there is no loss unnecessarily compounds the potential of any system of liability for defamatory falsehood to inhibit the vigorous exercise of First Amendment freedoms. Additionally, the doctrine of presumed damages invites juries to punish unpopular opinion rather than to compensate individuals for injury sustained by the publication of a false fact. More to the point, the States have no substantial interest in securing for plaintiffs such as this petitioner gratuitous awards of money damages far in excess of any actual injury.

We would not, of course, invalidate state law simply because we doubt its wisdom, but here we are attempting to reconcile state law with a competing interest grounded in the constitutional command of the First Amendment. It is therefore appropriate to require that state remedies for defamatory falsehood reach no farther than is necessary to protect the legitimate interest involved. It is necessary to restrict defamation plaintiffs who do not prove knowledge of falsity or reckless disregard for the truth to compensation for actual injury. We need not define "actual injury," as trial courts have wide experience in framing appropriate jury instructions in tort actions. Suffice it to say that actual injury is not limited to out-of-pocket loss. Indeed, the more customary types of actual harm inflicted by defamatory falsehood include impairment of reputation and standing in the community, personal humiliation, and mental anguish and suffering. Of course, juries must be limited by appropriate instructions, and all awards must be supported by competent evidence concerning the injury, although there need be no evidence which assigns an actual dollar value to the injury.

We also find no justification for allowing awards of punitive damages against publishers and broadcasters held liable under state-defined standards of liability for defamation. In most jurisdictions jury discretion over the amounts awarded is limited only by the gentle rule that they not be excessive. Consequently, juries assess punitive damages in wholly unpredictable amounts bearing no necessary relation to the actual harm caused. And they remain free to use their discretion selectively to punish expressions of unpopular views. Like the doctrine of presumed damages, jury discretion to award punitive damages unnecessarily exacerbates the danger of media self-censorship, but, unlike the former rule, punitive damages are wholly irrelevant to the state interest that justifies a negligence standard for private defamation actions. They are not compensation for injury. Instead, they are private fines levied by civil juries to punish reprehensible conduct and to deter its future occurrence. In short, the private defamation plaintiff who establishes liability under a less demanding standard than that stated by *New York Times* may recover only such damages as are sufficient to compensate him for actual injury.

[The Court rejected the argument that Gertz was a public figure.] We therefore conclude that the *New York Times* standard is inapplicable to this case and that the trial court erred in entering judgment for respondent. Because the jury was allowed to impose liability without fault and was permitted to presume damages without proof of injury, a new trial is necessary. We reverse and remand for further proceedings in accord with this opinion.

[The concurring opinion of Justice Blackmun, and dissenting opinions of Chief Justice Burger and Justices Douglas and Brennan, are omitted; Chief Justice Burger would have reinstated the jury's verdict, while Douglas and Brennan thought the majority's decision insufficiently protective of speech.]

WHITE, J. (dissenting). For some 200 years — from the very founding of the Nation — the law of defamation and right of the ordinary citizen to recover for false publication injurious to his reputation have been almost exclusively the business of state courts and legislatures. Under typical state defamation law, the defamed private citizen had to prove only a false publication that would subject him to hatred, contempt, or ridicule. Given such publication, general damage to reputation was presumed, while punitive damages required proof of additional facts. The law governing the defamation of private citizens remained untouched by the First Amendment because until relatively recently, the consistent view of the Court was that libelous words constitute a class of speech wholly unprotected by the First Amendment, subject only to limited exceptions carved out since 1964.

But now, using that Amendment as the chosen instrument, the Court, in a few printed pages, has federalized major aspects of libel law by declaring unconstitutional in important respects the prevailing defamation law in all or most of the 50 States. That result is accomplished by requiring the plaintiff in each and every defamation action to prove not only the defendant's culpability beyond his act of publishing defamatory material but also actual damage to reputation resulting from the publication. Moreover, punitive damages may not be recovered by showing malice in the traditional sense of ill will; knowing falsehood or reckless disregard of the truth will not be required.

I assume these sweeping changes will be popular with the press, but this is not the road to salvation for a court of law. As I see it, there are wholly insufficient grounds for scuttling the libel laws of the States in such wholesale fashion, to say nothing of deprecating the reputation interest of ordinary citizens and rendering them powerless to protect themselves. I do not suggest that the decision is illegitimate or beyond the bounds of judicial review, but it is an ill-considered exercise of the power entrusted to this Court, particularly when the Court has not had the benefit of briefs and argument addressed to most of the major issues which the Court now decides. I respectfully dissent. [. . .]

The impact of today's decision on the traditional law of libel is immediately obvious and indisputable. No longer will the plaintiff be able to rest his case with proof of a libel defamatory on its face or proof of a slander historically actionable per se. In addition, he must prove some further degree of culpable conduct on the part of the publisher, such as intentional or reckless falsehood or negligence. And if he succeeds in this respect, he faces still another obstacle: recovery for loss of reputation will be conditioned upon "competent" proof of actual injury to his standing in the community. This will be true regardless of the nature of the defamation and even though it is one of those particularly reprehensible statements that have traditionally made slanderous words actionable without proof of fault by the publisher or of the damaging impact of his publication. [. . .]

So too, the requirement of proving special injury to reputation before general damages may be awarded will clearly eliminate the prevailing rule, worked out over a very long period of time, that, in the case of defamations not actionable per se, the recovery of general damages for injury to reputation may also be had if some form of material or pecuniary loss is proved. Finally, an inflexible federal standard is imposed for the award of punitive damages. No longer will it be enough to prove ill will and an attempt to injure.

These are radical changes in the law and severe invasions of the prerogatives of the States. They should at least be shown to be required by the First Amendment or necessitated by our present circumstances. Neither has been demonstrated. [. . .]

The Court evinces a deep-seated antipathy to "liability without fault." But this catch-phrase has no talismanic significance and is almost meaningless in this context where the Court appears to be addressing those libels and slanders that are defamatory on their face and where the publisher is no doubt aware from the nature of the material that it would be inherently damaging to reputation. He publishes notwithstanding, knowing that he will inflict injury. With this knowledge, he must intend to inflict that injury, his excuse being that he is privileged to do so — that he has published the truth. But as it turns out, what he has circulated to the public is a very damaging falsehood. Is he nevertheless "faultless"? Perhaps it can be said that the mistake about his defense was made in good faith, but the fact remains that it is he who launched the publication knowing that it could ruin a reputation.

In these circumstances, the law has heretofore put the risk of falsehood on the publisher where the victim is a private citizen and no grounds of special privilege are invoked. The Court would now shift this risk to the victim, even though he has done nothing to invite the calumny, is wholly innocent of fault, and is helpless to avoid his injury. I doubt that jurisprudential resistance to liability without fault is sufficient ground for employing the First Amendment to revolutionize the law of libel, and in my view, that body of legal rules poses no realistic threat to the press and its service to the public. The press today is vigorous and robust. To me, it is quite incredible to suggest that threats of libel suits from private citizens are causing the press to refrain from publishing the truth. I know of no hard facts to support that proposition, and the Court furnishes none.

The communications industry has increasingly become concentrated in a few powerful hands operating very lucrative businesses reaching across the Nation and into almost every home. Neither the industry as a whole nor its individual components are easily intimidated, and we are fortunate that they are not. Requiring them to pay for the occasional damage they do to private reputation will play no substantial part in their future performance or their existence. [...]

Not content with escalating the threshold requirements of establishing liability, the Court abolishes the ordinary damages rule, undisturbed by *New York Times* and later cases, that, as to libels or slanders defamatory on their face, injury to reputation is presumed and general damages may be awarded along with whatever special damages may be sought. Apparently because the Court feels that in some unspecified and unknown number of cases, plaintiffs recover where they have suffered no injury or recover more than they deserve, it dismisses this rule as an "oddity of tort law." The Court thereby refuses in any case to accept the fact of wide dissemination of a per se libel as prima facie proof of injury sufficient to survive a motion to dismiss at the close of plaintiff's case. [...]

NOTES

1. *Matters of private concern.* In Dun & Bradstreet, Inc. v. Greenmoss Builders, Inc., 472 U.S. 749 (1985), the defendant, Dun & Bradstreet, issued a credit report wrongly stating that the plaintiff had filed for bankruptcy. A jury awarded the plaintiff presumed and punitive damages without any showing of actual malice. The Supreme Court affirmed. Writing for a plurality of three, Justice Powell said that the rules in *Gertz* only applied to cases involving speech on matters of public concern, and that the credit report did not qualify:

> In *Gertz*, we found that the state interest in awarding presumed and punitive damages was not "substantial" in view of their effect on speech at the core of First Amendment concern. This interest, however, *is* "substantial" relative to the incidental effect these remedies may have on speech of significantly less constitutional interest. The rationale of the common-law rules has been the experience and judgment of history that "proof of actual damage will be impossible in a great many cases where, from the character of the defamatory words and the circumstances of publication, it is all but certain that serious harm has resulted in fact." W. Prosser, *Law of Torts* §112. As a result, courts for centuries have allowed juries to presume that some damage occurred from many defamatory utterances and publications. Restatement of Torts §568, Comment *b*, p. 162 (1938) (noting that Hale announced that damages were to be presumed for libel as early as 1670). This rule furthers the state interest in providing remedies for defamation by ensuring that those remedies are effective. In light of the reduced constitutional value of speech involving no matters of public concern, we hold that the state interest adequately supports awards of presumed and punitive damages — even absent a showing of "actual malice."

Burger, C.J., and White, J., concurred, resulting in five votes for the proposition that plaintiffs can recover presumed and punitive damages without showing actual malice so long as the speech at issue was not of public concern. The dissenters would have extended *Gertz* to cover all such cases.

2. *Falsity.* In Philadelphia Newspapers v. Hepps, 475 U.S. 767 (1986), the defendant's newspaper published a story saying that Maurice Hepps had links to organized crime. Hepps sued for libel. The trial court told the jury that Hepps bore the burden of proving that the statements were false. The Pennsylvania Supreme Court disagreed, holding that the burden was on the defendant to prove that its statements were true if it wished to have the benefit of such a defense. The United States Supreme Court reversed:

> There will always be instances when the factfinding process will be unable to resolve conclusively whether the speech is true or false; it is in those cases that the burden of proof is dispositive. Under a rule forcing the plaintiff to bear the burden of showing falsity, there will be some cases in which plaintiffs cannot meet their burden despite the fact that the speech is in fact false. The plaintiff's suit will fail despite the fact that, in some abstract sense, the suit is meritorious. Similarly, under an alternative rule placing the burden of showing truth on defendants, there would be some cases in which defendants could not bear their burden despite the fact that the speech is in fact true. Those suits would succeed despite the fact that, in some abstract sense, those suits are unmeritorious. Under either rule, then, the outcome of the suit will sometimes be at variance with the outcome that we would desire if all speech were either demonstrably true or demonstrably false.
>
> This dilemma stems from the fact that the allocation of the burden of proof will determine liability for some speech that is true and some that is false, but *all* of such speech is *unknowably* true or false. Because the burden of proof is the deciding factor only when the evidence is ambiguous, we cannot know how much of the speech affected by the allocation of the burden of proof is true and how much is false. In a case presenting a configuration of speech and plaintiff like the one we face here, and where the scales are in such an uncertain balance, we believe that the Constitution requires us to tip them in favor of protecting true speech. To ensure that true speech on matters of public concern is not deterred, we hold that the common-law presumption that defamatory speech is false cannot stand when a plaintiff seeks damages against a media defendant for speech of public concern. [. . .]
>
> We recognize that requiring the plaintiff to show falsity will insulate from liability some speech that is false, but unprovably so. Nonetheless, the Court's previous decisions on the restrictions that the First Amendment places upon the common law of defamation firmly support our

conclusion here with respect to the allocation of the burden of proof. In attempting to resolve related issues in the defamation context, the Court has affirmed that "[t]he First Amendment requires that we protect some falsehood in order to protect speech that matters." *Gertz*, 418 U.S., at 341. Here the speech concerns the legitimacy of the political process, and therefore clearly "matters." [. . .]

We note that our decision adds only marginally to the burdens that the plaintiff must already bear as a result of our earlier decisions in the law of defamation. The plaintiff must show fault. A jury is obviously more likely to accept a plaintiff's contention that the defendant was at fault in publishing the statements at issue if convinced that the relevant statements were false. As a practical matter, then, evidence offered by plaintiffs on the publisher's fault in adequately investigating the truth of the published statements will generally encompass evidence of the falsity of the matters asserted.

3. *Matters of opinion.* In Milkovich v. Lorain Journal Co., 497 U.S. 1 (1990), the plaintiff, Milkovich, was the coach of a high-school wrestling team that got into a fight with a team visiting from another school. The fight resulted in hearings and litigation in which Milkovich and others testified. The defendant newspaper ran an editorial reading in part: "Anyone who attended the meet [. . .] knows in his heart that Milkovich and Scott lied at the hearing after each having given his solemn oath to tell the truth." Milkovich sued for libel, claiming that the newspaper had accused him of perjury. The Ohio courts determined that the article contained "constitutionally protected opinion" and thus gave summary judgment to the defendant. The Supreme Court reversed, declining to find expressions of opinion constitutionally privileged; it took the position that no such privilege was needed in view of its holding in *Hepps*:

> If a speaker says, "In my opinion John Jones is a liar," he implies a knowledge of facts which lead to the conclusion that Jones told an untruth. Even if the speaker states the facts upon which he bases his opinion, if those facts are either incorrect or incomplete, or if his assessment of them is erroneous, the statement may still imply a false assertion of fact. Simply couching such statements in terms of opinion does not dispel these implications; and the statement, "In my opinion Jones is a liar," can cause as much damage to reputation as the statement, "Jones is a liar." As Judge Friendly aptly stated: "[It] would be destructive of the law of libel if a writer could escape liability for accusations of [defamatory conduct] simply by using, explicitly or implicitly, the words 'I think.'" *Cianci v. New Times Publishing Co.*, 639 F.2d 54, 64 (CA2 1980). It is worthy of note that at common law, even the privilege of fair comment did not extend to "a false statement of fact, whether it was expressly stated

or implied from an expression of opinion." Restatement (Second) of Torts, §566, Comment *a* (1977). [. . .]

[W]e think *Hepps* stands for the proposition that a statement on matters of public concern must be provable as false before there can be liability under state defamation law, at least in situations, like the present, where a media defendant is involved. Thus, unlike the statement, "In my opinion Mayor Jones is a liar," the statement, "In my opinion Mayor Jones shows his abysmal ignorance by accepting the teachings of Marx and Lenin," would not be actionable. *Hepps* ensures that a statement of opinion relating to matters of public concern which does not contain a provably false factual connotation will receive full constitutional protection.

The Court concluded that a jury might be able to conclude that the defendant implied Milkovich had committed perjury, and that this was sufficiently capable of being proven true or false to permit recovery under the First Amendment.

4. *Fair comment.* The common law position was that statements of opinion as well as statements of fact could be defamatory if they subjected the plaintiff to opprobrium. But the consequences of this view were greatly softened by the privilege of "fair comment," which protected the good faith expression of defamatory opinions on matters of public interest so long as they were based on true or privileged facts. Thus in Carr v. Hood, 170 Eng. Rep. 983 (1808), Carr sued for libel when several of his books were attacked by a reviewer. Ellenborough, L.J., dismissed the action:

> Where is the liberty of the press if an action can be maintained on such principles? Perhaps the plaintiff's *Tour through Scotland* is now unsaleable; but is he to be indemnified by receiving a compensation in damages from the person who may have opened the eyes of the public to the bad taste and inanity of his compositions? [. . .] We really must not cramp observations upon authors and their works. They should be liable to criticism, to exposure, and even to ridicule, if their compositions be ridiculous[.]

In *Milkovich* the Supreme Court saw no need to find such a privilege in the Constitution because *Hepps* already had held that no liability can attach to statements of public interest unless they are proven false — and an opinion cannot be proven false, though the factual basis for it might be. In principle the common law privilege thus continues to survive distinct from *Hepps* and *Milkovich*; in practice, however, most cases where fair comment would serve as a defense also are cases where the plaintiff now is required by the Supreme Court's cases to show that the defendant's statements contained a "provably false factual connotation." This latter requirement tends to overshadow the common law doctrine by immunizing pure opinion from liability regardless of whether all the elements of the fair comment privilege are satisfied. The following cases illustrate some of the difficulties that can arise at the borderline between fact and opinion.

5. *The ambulance chaser.* In Flamm v. American Association of University Women, 201 F.3d 144 (2d Cir. 2000), the defendants published a directory of lawyers willing to help women involved in higher education bring discrimination suits against their employers. The entry regarding the plaintiff, Leonard Flamm, contained the only negative notation in the book; it read as follows:

> Mr. Flamm handles sex discrimination cases in the area of pay equity, harassment, and promotion. Note: At least one plaintiff has described Flamm as an "ambulance chaser" with interest only in "slam dunk cases."

Flamm sued the publishers of the directory for libel. The district court dismissed the complaint on the ground that the language challenged by Flamm "could not reasonably be construed as a statement of objective fact":

> Here [. . .] the phrase "ambulance chaser" is not being used in its literal sense. Moreover, it is coupled with the comment "with interest only in 'slam dunk cases.'" As used here, the words together simply do not have a precise and readily understood meaning. Indeed, an "ambulance chaser" is not someone who is interested only in "slam dunk cases," but rather, he is someone who is much less selective and who must "chase" after cases. Hence, even though the statement that a lawyer is an ambulance chaser standing alone arguably could be understood to accuse the lawyer of verifiable acts of criminal and unethical behavior, "the loose nature of the language, [and] the 'general tenor' of the remarks made" here, are such that a reasonable reader would not conclude that defendants were making factual assertions about Flamm. [. . .]
>
> [U]ltimately I conclude that the questions of whether a particular case is a "slam dunk" and whether a particular lawyer is "interested only in slam dunk cases" are difficult propositions to prove or disprove. I cannot envision conducting a trial, for example, where the parties try to prove or disprove whether each of a long series of cases was a "slam dunk."

The court of appeals reversed:

> The description "an 'ambulance chaser' with interest only in 'slam dunk cases'" can reasonably be interpreted to mean an attorney who improperly solicits clients and then takes only easy cases. This reading, which separates to a degree the "ambulance chaser" characterization from the "slam dunk cases" language, is especially plausible because, in the challenged statement as printed, each of those phrases was separately

enclosed in quotation marks. It would not be unreasonable to read the "ambulance chaser" excerpt literally, because it could have been unrelated to the "slam dunk cases" reference in whatever passage the AAUW was quoting. [. . .]

The AAUW also argues that "ambulance chaser" cannot be read in the literal sense of a lawyer who "has engaged in improper activities to solicit and obtain clients" because dictionary definitions of "ambulance chaser" typically refer to solicitation of negligence or accident victims. See, e.g., *Black's Law Dictionary* 80 (7th ed. 1999); *Webster's Ninth Collegiate Dictionary* 77 (9th ed. 1984). This peculiar argument, challenging the alleged meaning of "ambulance chaser" as overly literal because not literal enough, is without merit. Although "rhetorical hyperbole" and "lusty and imaginative expression" may not be actionable, there is at the same time no requirement that the defamatory meaning of a challenged statement correspond to its literal dictionary definition. It is sufficient, for the purpose of defeating this motion to dismiss, that the challenged statement reasonably implies the alleged defamatory meaning.

6. *Dueling phantoms.* In Phantom Touring, Inc. v. Affiliated Publications, Inc., 953 F.2d 724 (1st Cir. 1992), the plaintiff produced a comedic version of the musical *The Phantom of the Opera*; it was not connected with the very successful Broadway musical of the same name produced by Andrew Lloyd Webber. The *Boston Globe* ran a series of articles questioning whether the plaintiff's advertisements made clear to the public that its musical was not the famous one. The *Globe's* theater critic, one Kelly, said that Ken Hill, the author of the less-famous *Phantom*, had been "thriving off the confusion created by the two productions." The article quoted a drama critic for the *Washington Post* who said that Hill's version "bears as much resemblance to its celebrated counterpart as Jell-O does to Baked Alaska," and who further described the show as "a rip-off, a fraud, a scandal, a snake-oil job." Another article suggested that the confusion was intentional:

> When it was suggested to Josiah Spaulding, who heads the [Wang theater], that, surely, he must be aware the incoming "Phantom" — a musical comedy by Ken Hill — is deliberately confusing people; that, in fact, it wouldn't be on tour at all if the Webber "Phantom" had not become the megahit it has, he said to me, "We're not in the business of denying any genre to come here and rent the hall."

The trial court dismissed the plaintiff's defamation complaint. The court of appeals affirmed:

> Arguably, the connotation of deliberate deception is sufficiently factual to be proved true or false, and therefore is vulnerable under *Milkovich*. To

rebut the implied assertion, appellant might be able to present objective evidence demonstrating longstanding plans to take its "Phantom" on a nationwide tour of the United States, or evidence showing that the "Original London production" language in its advertising was developed before Webber's "Phantom" rose to prominence, and thus was not designed to deceive consumers.

Whether or not the allegation of intentional deception meets the "provable as true or false" criterion, however, we think the context of each article rendered the language not reasonably interpreted as stating "actual facts" about appellant's honesty. The sum effect of the format, tone and entire content of the articles is to make it unmistakably clear that Kelly was expressing a point of view only. As such, the challenged language is immune from liability.

The nonfactual nature of [the] articles is indicated at first glance by the format. Both appeared as a regularly run theater column, a type of article generally known to contain more opinionated writing than the typical news report. The structure and tone of the language reinforced this subjective design. [. . .] Kelly's snide, exasperated language indicated that his comments represented his personal appraisal of the factual information contained in the article.

Of greatest importance, however, is the breadth of Kelly's articles, which not only discussed all the facts underlying his views but also gave information from which readers might draw contrary conclusions. In effect, the articles offered a self-contained give-and-take, a kind of verbal debate between Kelly and those persons responsible for booking and marketing appellant's "Phantom." Because all sides of the issue, as well as the rationale for Kelly's view, were exposed, the assertion of deceit reasonably could be understood only as Kelly's personal conclusion about the information presented, not as a statement of fact.

What is the distinction between *Phantom Touring, Inc. v. Affiliated Publications, Inc.* and *Flamm v. American Assoc. of University Women*?

7. *Fact and opinion.* In Stevens v. Tillman, 855 F.2d 394 (7th Cir. 1988), also considered at the start of this chapter, Stevens was the principal of an elementary school in Chicago; Tillman was a political opponent of hers and campaigned successfully to force Stevens out of her job. Stevens sued Tillman for defamation. Easterbrook, J., offered these views on the distinction between fact and opinion:

Gertz requires a court to separate "fact" from "opinion," a task we have carried out when necessary without producing a useful definition of "opinion." The parties press different views on us, but we resist the temptation to come up with a new and "better" definition, in part because fact cannot be separated from opinion by ever-more-elaborate definitions. Every statement of opinion contains or implies some proposition of fact, just as every statement of fact has or implies an evaluative component. [. . .] One may say "George Stigler did not deserve the Nobel Prize" because one believes that Frank Knight should have received it; but Knight died before Stigler received the prize, and on learning that there are no posthumous Nobel Prizes this person too might favor Stigler. The statement "no one will ever build a heavier-than-air flying machine" is opinion in 1900 and false in 1905. The statement "Paul Morphy was a better composer than Wolfgang Amadeus Mozart" appears to be an egregiously erroneous statement of either opinion or fact — until you realize that the speaker must have meant "composer of chess puzzles". [. . .]

Courts trying to find one formula to separate "fact" from "opinion" therefore are engaged in a snipe hunt, paralleling the debates between positivist and deontological thinkers in philosophy. Perhaps the Constitution requires the search for this endangered species, but more likely the difference between "fact" and "opinion" in constitutional law responds to the pressure the threat of civil liability would place on kinds of speech that are harmless or useful, not on the ability to draw a line that has vexed philosophers for centuries. It is the cost of searching for "truth" — including the cost of error in condemning speech that is either harmless or in retrospect turns out to be useful, a cost both inevitable and high in our imprecise legal system — that justifies the constitutional rule. Like other attempts to compare things that can be neither quantified nor reduced to a common metric (how much does the value of free speech "weigh" compared with the value of reputational injury?), this will never yield a rule.

8. *Peking duck (problem).* In Mr. Chow of New York v. Ste. Jour Azur S.A., 759 F.2d 219 (2d Cir. 1985), the defendants were publishers of the *Gault/ Millau Guide to New York*, a book of restaurant reviews. Its review of the plaintiff's Chinese restaurant ran in part as follows:

> While his London restaurant enjoys an honorable reputation (although it is clearly overrated) the branch which the clever Mr. Chow has just opened in New York is simply astounding from a culinary point of view. [. . . T]he dishes on the menu (very short) have only the slightest relationship to the essential spirit of Chinese cuisine. With their heavy and greasy dough, the dumplings, on our visit, resembled bad Italian ravioli, the steamed meatballs had a disturbingly gamy taste, the sweet and sour pork contained more dough (badly cooked) than meat, and the green peppers which accompanied it remained still frozen on the plate. The chicken with chili was rubbery and the rice, soaking, for some reason, in oil, totally insipid. [. . .] At a near-by table, the Peking lacquered duck (although ordered in advance) was made up of only one dish (instead of the three traditional ones), composed of pancakes the size of a

saucer and the thickness of a finger. [...] We do not know where Mr. Chow recruits his cooks, but he would do well to send them for instruction somewhere in Chinatown. There, at least, they still know the traditions. It is, however, true, that when one sees with what epicurian airs his customers exclaim at canned lychees, one can predict for him a long and prosperous life uptown. About $25, without the drinks.

The plaintiff brought suit for defamation. How should analysis proceed?

9. *Taking stock.* At this point it may help to summarize the changes wrought in the common law by the Supreme Court cases considered in this chapter. Public figures have to prove that defendants acted with actual malice — not with spite, but with knowledge of falsity or recklessness as to truth or falsity — to win defamation cases (with the meaning of "public figure" subject to the complications considered earlier). When private plaintiffs bring suits over statements of public concern, the Court has held that they must prove the statements were false and prove at least negligence on the defendant's part; they also must show actual malice if they want presumed or punitive damages. In defamation suits brought by private plaintiffs regarding statements of no public concern, the common law continues to apply without qualification. Cases resembling *Watt v. Longsdon* or *Overcast v. Billings Mutual Insurance Co.*, considered earlier in this chapter, thus have not been affected by the Supreme Court's rulings — or so it seems; it is not yet entirely clear whether the Court's holdings in *Hepps* and *Milkovich* may have some application to entirely private disputes.

These rules can be turned into some practical generalizations about modern defamation cases. *Gertz* said that in cases involving private plaintiffs and matters of public concern the states are free to impose liability on whatever terms they like, so long as there is some requirement of fault. In practice most states have responded by requiring such plaintiffs to prove negligence. But defamation suits based on claims of negligence do not turn out to be terribly common. Plaintiffs in the many defamation suits brought against media defendants — i.e., publishers and broadcasters — usually are at least limited-purpose public figures who have to show actual malice, not just negligence, to win. If a plaintiff cannot make such a showing, there can be no liability at all for the defendant; if a plaintiff can make such a showing, the defendant can be held liable for presumed and punitive damages. Meanwhile the cases brought by entirely private plaintiffs often involve matters not of public concern to which the constitutional rigmarole has no application.

Notice, then, that much of the common law of defamation remains relevant all the time: the plaintiff always must show that the statement was defamatory, was reasonably interpreted as regarding him, and was "published"; meanwhile, the defendant can interpose common law privileges of both the conditional and absolute variety. The significance of the Supreme Court's decisions is that they have erected barriers to recovery in some types of cases that are higher than were known to the common law and that therefore tend to dominate the resulting litigation. Would you expect the Supreme Court's interventions in defamation law to have increased or decreased the number of lawsuits against media defendants? What effect would you expect the decisions to have had on the expense of those suits for either side?

Chapter 12

Invasion of Privacy

A. HISTORICAL BACKGROUND

In 1890 a young couple, Mr. and Mrs. Samuel Warren, were among the social elite of Boston, and found their affairs distastefully reported in the city's *Saturday Evening Gazette* and other newspapers. There was then no such tort as invasion of privacy, so the Warrens had no legal recourse. Samuel Warren was, however, a lawyer and the partner of Louis Brandeis, who would go on to be appointed to the Supreme Court 26 years later; Warren and Brandeis were moved to write an article, *The Right to Privacy*, that appeared in the Harvard Law Review and proved to have a large influence on the development of the law. Said the authors:

> That the individual shall have full protection in person and in property is a principle as old as the common law; but it has been found necessary from time to time to define anew the exact nature and extent of such protection. Political, social, and economic changes entail the recognition of new rights, and the common law, in its eternal youth, grows to meet the new demands of society. [. . .] Recent inventions and business methods call attention to the next step which must be taken for the protection of the person, and for securing to the individual what Judge Cooley calls the right "to be let alone." Instantaneous photographs and newspaper enterprises have invaded the sacred precincts of private and domestic life; and numerous mechanical devices threaten to make good the prediction that "what is whispered in the closet shall be proclaimed from the house-tops." [. . .]
>
> Of the desirability — indeed of the necessity — of some such protection, there can, it is believed, be no doubt. The press is overstepping in every direction the obvious bounds of propriety and of decency. Gossip is no longer the resource of the idle and of the vicious, but has become a trade, which is pursued with industry as well as effrontery. To satisfy a prurient

taste the details of sexual relations are spread broadcast in the columns of the daily papers. To occupy the indolent, column upon column is filled with idle gossip, which can only be procured by intrusion upon the domestic circle. The intensity and complexity of life, attendant upon advancing civilization, have rendered necessary some retreat from the world, and man, under the refining influence of culture, has become more sensitive to publicity, so that solitude and privacy have become more essential to the individual; but modern enterprise and invention have, through invasions upon his privacy, subjected him to mental pain and distress, far greater than could be inflicted by mere bodily injury. Nor is the harm wrought by such invasions confined to the suffering of those who may be the subjects of journalistic or other enterprise. In this, as in other branches of commerce, the supply creates the demand. Each crop of unseemly gossip, thus harvested, becomes the seed of more, and, in direct proportion to its circulation, results in the lowering of social standards and of morality. Even gossip apparently harmless, when widely and persistently circulated, is potent for evil. It both belittles and perverts. It belittles by inverting the relative importance of things, thus dwarfing the thoughts and aspirations of a people. When personal gossip attains the dignity of print, and crowds the space available for matters of real interest to the community, what wonder that the ignorant and thoughtless mistake its relative importance. Easy of comprehension, appealing to that weak side of human nature which is never wholly cast down by the misfortunes and frailties of our neighbors, no one can be surprised that it usurps the place of interest in brains capable of other things. Triviality destroys at once robustness of thought and delicacy of feeling. No enthusiasm can flourish, no generous impulse can survive under its blighting influence.

Warren and Brandeis went on to explore the basis of the right to privacy, analogizing it to an author's copyright in unpublished materials. They also proposed some restrictions and refinements to the tort they proposed: that it would be limited in the same manner as defamation suits, and would not apply to an exposure "of public or general interest"; that truth would not be a defense; that malice would not be required to make out a *prima facie* case; and a few other points.

The article now is considered one of the most influential ever written, but its ideas did not enter the law immediately. The first case to consider its arguments, *Roberson v. Rochester Folding Box Co.*, 64 N.E. 442 (N.Y. 1902), rejected them. A flour manufacturer had reproduced a portrait of the plaintiff on its advertisements without her consent. The plaintiff claimed that she was "greatly humiliated by the scoffs and jeers" of people who recognized her face from the advertisement, causing her sickness and nervous shock. The court dismissed her claims of an infringed right to privacy:

The so-called "right of privacy" is, as the phrase suggests, founded upon the claim that a man has the right to pass through this world, if he wills, without having his picture published, his business enterprises discussed, his successful experiments written up for the benefit of others, or his eccentricities commented upon either in handbills, circulars, catalogues, periodicals, or newspapers; and, necessarily, that the things which may not be written and published of him must not be spoken of him by his neighbors, whether the comment be favorable or otherwise. [. . .]

If such a principle be incorporated into the body of the law through the instrumentality of a court of equity, the attempts to logically apply the principle will necessarily result not only in a vast amount of litigation, but in litigation bordering upon the absurd, for the right of privacy, once established as a legal doctrine, cannot be confined to the restraint of the publication of a likeness, but must necessarily embrace as well the publication of a word picture, a comment upon one's looks, conduct, domestic relations or habits. And, were the right of privacy once legally asserted, it would necessarily be held to include the same things if spoken instead of printed, for one, as well as the other, invades the right to be absolutely let alone. An insult would certainly be in violation of such a right, and with many persons would more seriously wound the feelings than would the publication of their picture. And so we might add to the list of things that are spoken and done day by day which seriously offend the sensibilities of good people to which the principle which the plaintiff seeks to have imbedded in the doctrine of the law would seem to apply. I have gone only far enough to barely suggest the vast field of litigation which would necessarily be opened up should this court hold that privacy exists as a legal right enforceable in equity by injunction, and by damages where they seem necessary to give complete relief.

The legislative body could very well interfere and arbitrarily provide that no one should be permitted for his own selfish purpose to use the picture or the name of another for advertising purposes without his consent. In such event no embarrassment would result to the general body of the law, for the rule would be applicable only to cases provided for by the statute. The courts, however, being without authority to legislate, are required to decide cases upon principle, and so are necessarily embarrassed by precedents created by an extreme, and therefore unjustifiable, application of an old principle.

The New York legislature responded by creating a statutory right to privacy; its terms were limited to cases where a person's picture was used for business purposes without consent. Most other states eventually came to recognize some form of privacy tort as a matter of common law. The courts varied in what they understood the tort to cover, however, and the resulting disarray led William Prosser to write an article sorting privacy claims into four types: disclosure of embarrassing facts about the plaintiff; intrusion on the plaintiff's seclusion; appropriation of the plaintiff's name or likeness;

and publicity placing the plaintiff in a false light. These categories became the basis for an influential section of the Restatement (Second) of Torts, §652, which Prosser drafted; they form the basis around which the rest of this chapter is organized.

B.   DISCLOSURE OF EMBARRASSING PRIVATE FACTS

Restatement (Second) of Torts

§652D.   PUBLICITY GIVEN TO PRIVATE LIFE

One who gives publicity to a matter concerning the private life of another is subject to liability to the other for invasion of his privacy, if the matter publicized is of a kind that

    (a) would be highly offensive to a reasonable person, and

    (b) is not of legitimate concern to the public.

Comment a. Publicity. The form of invasion of the right of privacy covered in this Section depends upon publicity given to the private life of the individual. "Publicity," as it is used in this Section, differs from "publication," as that term is used in §577 in connection with liability for defamation. "Publication," in that sense, is a word of art, which includes any communication by the defendant to a third person. "Publicity," on the other hand, means that the matter is made public, by communicating it to the public at large, or to so many persons that the matter must be regarded as substantially certain to become one of public knowledge. The difference is not one of the means of communication, which may be oral, written or by any other means. It is one of a communication that reaches, or is sure to reach, the public.

Thus it is not an invasion of the right of privacy, within the rule stated in this Section, to communicate a fact concerning the plaintiff's private life to a single person or even to a small group of persons. On the other hand, any publication in a newspaper or a magazine, even of small circulation, or in a handbill distributed to a large number of persons, or any broadcast over the radio, or statement made in an address to a large audience, is sufficient to give publicity within the meaning of the term as it is used in this Section. The distinction, in other words, is one between private and public communication.

Illustration 2. A, a creditor, posts in the window of his shop, where it is read by those passing by on the street, a statement that B owes a debt to him and has not paid it. This is an invasion of B's privacy.

Illustration 3. A, a motion picture exhibitor, wishing to advertise a picture to be exhibited, writes letters to a thousand men in which he makes unprivileged and objectionable statements concerning the private life of B, an actress. This is an invasion of B's privacy.

Briscoe v. Reader's Digest Association
483 P.2d 34 (Cal. 1971)

[Marvin Briscoe hijacked a truck in Kentucky in 1956. Soon afterwards he abandoned crime and led an honest life among friends and family members unaware of his past activities. In 1967 Reader's Digest published an article titled. "The Big Business of Hijacking." The article discussed the looting of trucks and at one point referred to Briscoe: "Typical of many beginners, Marvin Briscoe and (another man) stole a 'valuable-looking' truck in Danville, Ky., and then fought a gun battle with the local police, only to learn that they had hijacked four bowling-pin spotters." There was nothing in the article to indicate that the hijacking occurred in 1956. Briscoe sued Reader's Digest for invasion of privacy, claiming that while the article may have been newsworthy his name was not; he alleged that as a result of its publication his daughter and friends learned of his past for the first time, and that they had scorned and abandoned him as a result. The trial court dismissed the complaint, and this appeal followed.]

PETERS, J. [after stating the facts:] — Acceptance of the right to privacy has grown with the increasing capability of the mass media and electronic devices with their capacity to destroy an individual's anonymity, intrude upon his most intimate activities, and expose his most personal characteristics to public gaze. [ ] In a society in which multiple, often conflicting role performances are demanded of each individual, the original etymological meaning of the word "person" — mask — has taken on new meaning. Men fear exposure not only to those closest to them; much of the outrage underlying the asserted right to privacy is a reaction to exposure to persons known only through business or other secondary relationships. The claim is not so much one of total secrecy as it is of the right to *define* one's circle of intimacy — to choose who shall see beneath the quotidian mask. Loss of control over which "face" one puts on may result in literal loss of self-identity, and is humiliating beneath the gaze of those whose curiosity treats a human being as an object.

A common law right to privacy, based on Warren and Brandeis' article, is now recognized in at least 36 states. California has recognized the right to privacy for 40 years.

The right to keep information private was bound to clash with the right to disseminate information to the public. We early noted the potential conflict between freedom of the press and the right of privacy, as did Warren and Brandeis themselves, who suggested that the right should not apply to matters of "public or general interest." The instant case, pitting a rehabilitated felon's right to anonymity against a magazine's right to identify him, compels us to consider the character of these competing interests. [...]

There can be no doubt that reports of current criminal activities are the legitimate province of a free press. The circumstances under which crimes occur, the techniques used by those outside the law, the tragedy that may befall the victims — these are vital bits of information for people coping with the exigencies of modern life. Reports of these events may also promote the values served by the constitutional guarantee of a public trial. Although a case is not to be "tried in the papers," reports regarding a crime or criminal proceedings may encourage unknown witnesses to come forward with useful testimony and friends or relatives to come to the aid of the victim.

It is also generally in the social interest to identify adults currently charged with the commission of a crime. While such an identification may not presume guilt, it may legitimately put others on notice that the named individual is suspected of having committed a crime. Naming the suspect may also persuade eye witnesses and character witnesses to testify. For these reasons, while the suspect or offender obviously does not consent to public exposure, his right to privacy must give way to the overriding social interest. [ ] In general, therefore, truthful reports of *recent* crimes and the names of suspects or offenders will be deemed protected by the First Amendment. [ ] The instant case, however, compels us to consider whether reports of the facts of *past* crimes and the identification of *past* offenders serve these same public-interest functions.

We have no doubt that reports of the facts of past crimes are newsworthy. Media publication of the circumstances under which crimes were committed in the past may prove educational in the same way that reports of current crimes do. The public has a strong interest in enforcing the law, and this interest is served by accumulating and disseminating data cataloguing the reasons men commit crimes, the methods they use, and the ways in which they are apprehended. Thus in an article on truck hijackings, Reader's Digest certainly had the right to report the *facts* of plaintiff's criminal act.

However, identification of the *actor* in reports of long past crimes usually serves little independent public purpose. Once legal proceedings have terminated, and a suspect or offender has been released, identification of the individual will not usually aid the administration of justice. Identification will no longer serve to bring forth witnesses or obtain succor for victims. Unless the individual has reattracted the public eye to himself in some independent fashion, the only public "interest" that would usually be served is that of curiosity.

There may be times, of course, when an event involving private citizens may be so unique as to capture the imagination of all. In such cases — e.g., the behavior of the passengers on the sinking Titanic, the heroism of Nathan Hale, the horror of the Saint Valentine's Day Massacre — purely private individuals may by an accident of history lose their privacy regarding that incident for all time. There need be no "reattraction" of the public eye because the public interest never wavered. An individual whose name is fixed in the public's memory, such as that of the political assassin, never becomes an anonymous member of the community again. But in each case it is for the trier of fact to determine whether the individual's infamy is such that he has never left the public arena; we cannot do so as a matter of law.

The Restatement of Torts some time ago balanced the considerations relevant here, concluding that criminals "are the objects of legitimate public interest during a period of time after their conduct . . . has brought them to the public attention; until they have reverted to the lawful and unexciting life led by the great bulk of the community, they are subject to the privileges which publishers have to satisfy the curiosity of the public as to their leaders, heroes, villains and victims." (§867, comment c.) Where a man has reverted to that "lawful and unexciting life" led by others, the Restatement implies that he no longer need "satisfy the curiosity of the public." [. . .]

One of the premises of the rehabilitative process is that the rehabilitated offender can rejoin that great bulk of the community from which he has been ostracized for his anti-social acts. In return for becoming a "new man," he is allowed to melt into the shadows of obscurity. [ ] We are realistic enough to recognize that men are curious about the inner sanctums of their neighbors — that the public will create its heroes and villains. We must also be realistic enough to realize that full disclosure of one's inner thoughts, intimate personal characteristics, and past life is neither the rule nor the norm in these United States. We have developed a variegated panoply of professional listeners to whom we confidentially "reveal all"; otherwise we keep our own counsel. The masks we wear may be stripped away upon the occurrence of some event of public interest. But just as the risk of exposure is a concomitant of urban life, so too is the expectation of anonymity regained. It would be a crass legal fiction to assert that a matter once public never becomes private again. Human forgetfulness over time puts today's "hot" news in tomorrow's dusty archives. In a nation of 200 million people there is ample opportunity for all but the most infamous to begin a new life.

Plaintiff is a man whose last offense took place 11 years before, who has paid his debt to society, who has friends and an 11-year-old daughter who were unaware of his early life — a man who assumed a position in "respectable" society. Ideally, his neighbors should recognize his present worth and forget his past life of shame. But men are not so divine as to forgive the past trespasses of others, and plaintiff therefore endeavored to reveal as little as possible of his past life. Yet, as if in some bizarre canyon of echoes, petitioner's past life pursues him through the pages of Reader's Digest, now published in 13 languages and distributed in 100 nations, with a circulation in California alone of almost 2,000,000 copies. [. . .]

In *Time, Inc. v. Hill*, the United States Supreme Court considered some of these same balancing problems with regard to a different form of invasion of privacy, that of placing the individual in a false light in the public eye. The New York statute construed in *Time* did not create a right of action for the truthful report of newsworthy people or events. The Supreme Court stated, however, that "[t]his limitation to newsworthy persons and events does not of course foreclose an interpretation . . . to allow damages where 'Revelations may be so intimate and so unwarranted in view of the victim's position as to outrage the community's notions of decency.'" 385 U.S. at 383, fn. 7.

Thus a truthful publication is constitutionally protected if (1) it is newsworthy and (2) it does not reveal facts so offensive as to shock the community's notions of decency.

We have previously set forth criteria for determining whether an incident is newsworthy. We consider "(1) the social value of the facts published, (2) the depth of the article's intrusion into ostensibly private affairs, and (3) the extent to which the party voluntarily acceded to a position of public notoriety." *Kapellas v. Kofman*, 459 P.2d 912.

On the assumed set of facts before us we are convinced that a jury could reasonably find that plaintiff's identity as a former hijacker was not newsworthy. First, as discussed above, a jury could find that publication of plaintiff's identity in connection with incidents of his past life was in this case of minimal social value. There was no independent reason whatsoever for focusing public attention on Mr. Briscoe as an individual at this time. A jury could certainly find that Mr. Briscoe had once again become an anonymous member of the community. Once legal proceedings have concluded, and particularly once the individual has reverted to the lawful and unexciting life led by the rest of the community, the public's interest in knowing is less compelling.

Second, a jury might find that revealing one's criminal past for all to see is grossly offensive to most people in America. Certainly a criminal background is kept even more hidden from others than a humiliating disease or the existence of business debts The consequences of revelation in this case — ostracism, isolation, and the alienation of one's family — make all too clear just how deeply offensive to most persons a prior crime is and thus how hidden the former offender must keep the knowledge of his prior indiscretion.

We do not hold today that plaintiff must prevail in his action. It is for the trier of fact to determine (1) whether plaintiff had become a rehabilitated member of society, (2) whether identifying him as a former criminal would be highly offensive and injurious to the reasonable man, (3) whether defendant published this information with a reckless disregard for its offensiveness, and (4) whether any independent justification for printing plaintiff's identity existed. We hold today only that, as pleaded, plaintiff has stated a valid, cause of action, sustaining the demurrer to plaintiff's complaint was improper, and that the ensuing judgment must therefore be reversed. . . .

NOTES

1. *Where are they now?* In Sidis v. F-R Publishing Co., 113 F.2d 806 (2d Cir. 1940), the plaintiff, William J. Sidis, was well known to newspaper readers as a child prodigy in 1910. When he was 11 years old he lectured to distinguished mathematicians on the subject of Four-Dimensional Bodies; he graduated from Harvard at the age of 16. He then sought, however, to live a modest and unobtrusive life, and succeeded in this until the defendant's magazine, the *New Yorker*, printed a profile of him in 1937. The article

appeared in a section titled "Where Are They Now?" and was subtitled "April Fool!" The court furnished the following description of it:

> The author describes [Sidis's] early accomplishments in mathematics and the wide-spread attention he received, then recounts his general breakdown and the revulsion which Sidis thereafter felt for his former life of fame and study. The unfortunate prodigy is traced over the years that followed, through his attempts to conceal his identity, through his chosen career as an insignificant clerk who would not need to employ unusual mathematical talents, and through the bizarre ways in which his genius flowered, as in his enthusiasm for collecting streetcar transfers and in his proficiency with an adding machine. The article closes with an account of an interview with Sidis at his present lodgings, "a hall bedroom of Boston's shabby south end." The untidiness of his room, his curious laugh, his manner of speech, and other personal habits are commented upon at length, as is his present interest in the lore of the Okamakam-messett Indians. The subtitle is explained by the closing sentence, quoting Sidis as saying "with a grin" that it was strange, "but, you know, I was born on April Fool's Day."

Sidis sued for invasion of privacy. The trial court dismissed his complaint, and the court of appeals affirmed:

> [T]he article is merciless in its dissection of intimate details of its subject's personal life, and this in company with elaborate accounts of Sidis' passion for privacy and the pitiable lengths to which he has gone in order to avoid public scrutiny. The work possesses great reader interest, for it is both amusing and instructive; but it may be fairly described as a ruthless exposure of a once public character, who has since sought and has now been deprived of the seclusion of private life. [...]
>
> [W]e are not yet disposed to afford to all of the intimate details of private life an absolute immunity from the prying of the press. Everyone will agree that at some point the public interest in obtaining information becomes dominant over the individual's desire for privacy. Warren and Brandeis were willing to lift the veil somewhat in the case of public officers. We would go further, though we are not yet prepared to say how far. At least we would permit limited scrutiny of the "private" life of any person who has achieved, or has had thrust upon him, the questionable and indefinable status of a "public figure."
>
> William James Sidis was once a public figure. As a child prodigy, he excited both admiration and curiosity. Of him great deeds were expected. In 1910, he was a person about whom the newspapers might display a legitimate intellectual interest, in the sense meant by Warren and Brandeis, as distinguished from a trivial and unseemly curiosity. But the precise motives of the press we regard as unimportant. And even if

Sidis had loathed public attention at that time, we think his uncommon achievements and personality would have made the attention permissible. Since then Sidis has cloaked himself in obscurity, but his subsequent history, containing as it did the answer to the question of whether or not he had fulfilled his early promise, was still a matter of public concern. The article in The New Yorker sketched the life of an unusual personality, and it possessed considerable popular news interest.

We express no comment on whether or not the news worthiness of the matter printed will always constitute a complete defense. Revelations may be so intimate and so unwarranted in view of the victim's position as to outrage the community's notions of decency. But when focused upon public characters, truthful comments upon dress, speech, habits, and the ordinary aspects of personality will usually not transgress this line. Regrettably or not, the misfortunes and frailties of neighbors and "public figures" are subjects of considerable interest and discussion to the rest of the population. And when such are the mores of the community, it would be unwise for a court to bar their expression in the newspapers, books, and magazines of the day.

Can *Sidis v. F-R Publishing Co.* be reconciled with *Briscoe v. Reader's Digest Association*? Is there anything Sidis could have done to restore his right not to be the subject of such an article?

2. *Descriptive vs. normative analysis.* From Note, *The Right of Privacy: Normative-Descriptive Confusion in the Defense of Newsworthiness*, 30 U. Chi. L. Rev. 722 (1963):

> The *Sidis* case exposes a crucial dilemma pervading the privacy field: Is the term "newsworthy" a descriptive predicate, intended to refer to the fact that there is widespread public interest? Or is it a value predicate, intended to indicate that the publication in question is a meritorious contribution and that the public's interest is praiseworthy? [...] The publisher has almost certainly published any given report because he judged it to be of interest to his audience, and believed that it would encourage them to purchase his publications in anticipation of more of the same. [...] But if "newsworthy" has normative meaning, the courts are evaluating the public's interest. If adequate standards for this judgment cannot be found, then the limitations on free expression created by the tort of invasion of privacy may be in danger of attack on constitutional grounds.

What was the answer to these questions in *Sidis*? What should be the answer to them generally? Should newsworthiness be a question for a judge or a jury?

3. *Abortion protesters.* In Doe v. Mills, 536 N.W.2d 824 (Mich. App. 1995), the defendants were anti-abortion protesters. One of the protesters

climbed into a dumpster outside an abortion clinic one night and found a piece of paper indicating that the plaintiffs were scheduled to have abortions on the next day. The defendants created large signs displaying the names of the plaintiffs and urging them not to "kill their babies"; they stood with the signs at the entrance to the clinic's parking lot. The plaintiffs sued the protesters for invasion of privacy. The trial court gave summary judgment to the defendants on the ground that the facts disclosed about the plaintiffs were not offensive and were of public interest:

> The words on the placards that were carried by the defendants conveyed the message that plaintiffs were contemplating and or scheduling an abortion. This is the disclosed information. Would plaintiffs seriously suggest or argue that one who contemplates or schedules an abortion has committed an act that is highly offensive to a reasonable person?
>
> It is this court's opinion that abortion, no matter how one views this subject, is unquestionably a matter of great public concern. [...] Because abortions are so controversial in our society, events surrounding abortions do attract considerable public attention, witness the heavy picketing of abortion clinics and the extensive amount of publicity the subject of abortion receives.

The court of appeals reversed:

> Plaintiffs [allege] that the publicity given by defendants was highly offensive and was deliberately calculated to embarrass and humiliate them, which it allegedly did. We cannot say that a reasonable person would not be justified in feeling seriously aggrieved by such publicity. Rather, we find that plaintiffs' allegations are sufficient to constitute a question for the jury regarding whether embarrassing private facts were involved in a public disclosure.
>
> [E]ven though the abortion issue may be regarded as a matter of public interest, the plaintiffs' identities in this case were not matters of legitimate public concern, nor a matter of public record, but, instead, were purely private matters. We conclude, therefore, that plaintiffs' allegations are sufficient to meet the minimum prima facie showing necessary to establish that the information disclosed must concern a private matter.

Presumably the defendants believed that the plaintiffs' identities were matters of public interest. Is there a politically neutral basis for the appellate court's conclusion to the contrary?

4. *Ten minutes of fame.* In Neff v. Time, Inc., 406 F. Supp. 858 (W.D. Pa. 1976), a photographer for Sports Illustrated was taking pictures of a professional football game between the Cleveland Browns and the Pittsburgh Steelers. The plaintiff was a spectator seated near the field. At one point

plaintiff and the fans around him were jumping up and down, waving banners and drinking beer; when they saw the photographer and learned that he was from Sports Illustrated, they began "screaming and howling and imploring the photographer" to take pictures of them. The photographer took over 7,200 pictures at the game; 30 of them were photos of this group of spectators. He edited the pictures and submitted 100 of them to the magazine for consideration. A committee at Sports Illustrated reviewed them and selected for publication a picture of the plaintiff with the zipper of his pants open. They used it to illustrate an article titled "A Strange Kind of Love."

Plaintiff sued the magazine for invasion of privacy. He claimed that the photograph implied that he was a "crazy, drunken slob," and, when combined with the title of the article, that he was "a sexual deviate." The district court gave summary judgment to the defendant:

> Although Neff's fly was not open to the point of being revealing, the selection was deliberate and surely in utmost bad taste; subjectively, as to Neff, the published picture could have been embarrassing, humiliating and offensive to his sensibilities. Without doubt the magazine deliberately exhibited Neff in an embarrassing manner. [. . .] It seems to us that art directors and editors should hesitate to deliberately publish a picture which most likely would be offensive and cause embarrassment to the subject when many other pictures of the same variety are available. Notwithstanding, the courts are not concerned with establishing canons of good taste for the press or the public.
>
> The article about Pittsburgh Steeler fans was of legitimate public interest; the football game in Cleveland was of legitimate public interest; Neff's picture was taken in a public place with his knowledge and with his encouragement; he was catapulted into the news by his own actions; nothing was falsified; a photograph taken at a public event which everyone present could see, with the knowledge and implied consent of the subject, is not a matter concerning a private fact. A factually accurate public disclosure is not tortious when connected with a newsworthy event even though offensive to ordinary sensibilities.

5. *The Seven Year Itch.* In Daily Times Democrat v. Graham, 162 So. 2d 474 (Ala. 1964), the plaintiff attended the Cullman County Fair in Alabama with her sons. The boys wanted her to take them through the "Fun House," and she obliged. On the way out of the attraction, and unknown to the plaintiff, was a device that blew jets of air up from the ground. The effect in plaintiff's case was to blow her dress up and leave her visible in her underwear from the waist down. A photographer for the defendant took a picture of the plaintiff at that moment, and the defendant printed it on the front page of its newspaper four days later. The plaintiff sued for invasion of privacy and won a jury verdict. On appeal the newspaper offered this

quotation from a Pennsylvania case rejecting a claim by a plaintiff photographed in public:

> On the public street, or in any other public place, the plaintiff has no right to be alone, and it is no invasion of his privacy to do no more than follow him about. Neither is it such an invasion to take his photograph in such a place, since this amounts to nothing more than making a record, not differing essentially from a full written description of a public sight which anyone present would be free to see.

The Alabama Supreme Court affirmed; it accepted the quoted statement, but responded that "When a legal principle is pushed to an absurdity, the principle is not abandoned, but the absurdity avoided":

> One who is a part of a public scene may be lawfully photographed as an incidental part of that scene in his ordinary status. Where the status he expects to occupy is changed without his volition to a status embarrassing to an ordinary person of reasonable sensitivity, then he should not be deemed to have forfeited his right to be protected from an indecent and vulgar intrusion of his right of privacy merely because misfortune overtakes him in a public place.

What is the distinction between *Daily Times Democrat v. Graham* and *Neff v. Time, Inc.*? Restatement §652D, Illustration 4, provides as follows:

> While A is walking on the street, B takes a motion picture of a scene and activities on the street, which he exhibits to the public in a newsreel. The picture shows A walking past the camera with a rip in the seat of his trousers. This is not an invasion of A's privacy.

Can this illustration be reconciled with *Daily Times Democrat v. Graham*?

6. *Constitutional constraints.* In Cox Broadcasting Corp. v. Cohn, 420 U.S. 469 (1975), the plaintiff was a man whose daughter was raped and murdered. A reporter on one of the defendant's news broadcasts revealed the victim's name; it had not been made public by the police, but the reporter discovered it by reading an indictment that was available in the courtroom where her attackers were put on trial. The plaintiff sought damages for invasion of privacy. The Georgia Supreme Court held that he had stated a good cause of action, but the United States Supreme Court reversed, holding that the suit was foreclosed by the First Amendment:

> We are reluctant to embark on a course that would make public records generally available to the media but forbid their publication if offensive to the sensibilities of the supposed reasonable man. Such a rule would make it

very difficult for the media to inform citizens about the public business and yet stay within the law. The rule would invite timidity and self-censorship and very likely lead to the suppression of many items that would otherwise be published and that should be made available to the public.

In a later case, *Florida Star v. B.J.F.*, 491 U.S. 524 (1989), the Court extended the rule in *Cox* to cover the public disclosure of a rape victim's name obtained from a nonpublic source. The holding was limited; the particular statute creating the plaintiff's cause of action was found defective in various respects:

> We do not hold that truthful publication is automatically constitutionally protected, or that there is no zone of personal privacy within which the State may protect the individual from intrusion by the press, or even that a State may never punish publication of the name of a victim of a sexual offense. We hold only that where a newspaper publishes truthful information which it has lawfully obtained, punishment may lawfully be imposed, if at all, only when narrowly tailored to a state interest of the highest order, and that no such interest is satisfactorily served by imposing liability under [the Florida statute] to appellant under the facts of this case.

Does *Briscoe v. Reader's Digest Association* survive these holdings?

Haynes v. Alfred A. Knopf, Inc.
8 F.3d 1222 (7th Cir. 1993)

POSNER, *Chief Judge.* — Luther Haynes and his wife, Dorothy Haynes nee Johnson, appeal from the dismissal on the defendants' motion for summary judgment of their suit against Nicholas Lemann, the author of a highly praised, best-selling book of social and political history called *The Promised Land: The Great Black Migration and How It Changed America* (1991), and Alfred A. Knopf, Inc., the book's publisher. The plaintiffs claim that the book libels Luther Haynes and invades both plaintiffs' right of privacy. [. . .]

[The subject of the defendants' book was the migration of millions of black men and women from the rural South to cities in the northern part of the United States between 1940 and 1970. The book told its story through case studies, and one of the principal studies involved Ruby Lee Daniels and Luther Haynes, the plaintiff. The book describes how Daniels and Haynes met in Chicago in the 1940s; the court's opinion recounts this part of the book's narrative as follows.]

When [Haynes] met Ruby Daniels he had a well-paying job in an awning factory. They lived together, and had children. But then "Luther began to drink too much. When he drank he got mean, and he and Ruby would get into ferocious quarrels. He was still working, but he wasn't always bringing his paycheck home." Ruby got work as a maid. They moved to a poorer part of the city. The relationship went downhill. "It got to the point where [Luther] would go out on Friday evenings after picking up his paycheck, and Ruby would hope he wouldn't come home, because she knew he would be drunk. On the Friday evenings when he did come home — over the years Ruby developed a devastating imitation of Luther, and could re-create the scene quite vividly — he would walk into the apartment, put on a record and turn up the volume, and saunter into their bedroom, a bottle in one hand and a cigarette in the other, in the mood for love. On one such night, Ruby's last child, Kevin, was conceived. Kevin always had something wrong with him — he was very moody, he was scrawny, and he had a severe speech impediment. Ruby was never able to find out exactly what the problem was, but she blamed it on Luther; all that alcohol must have gotten into his sperm, she said."

Ruby was on public aid, but was cut off when social workers discovered she had a man in the house. She got a night job. Luther was supposed to stay with the children while she was at work, especially since they lived in a dangerous neighborhood; but often when she came home, at 3:00 a.m. or so, she would "find the older children awake, and when she would ask them if Luther had been there, the answer would be, 'No, ma'am.'" Ruby's last aid check, arriving providentially after she had been cut off, enabled the couple to buy a modest house on contract — it "was, by a wide margin, the best place she had ever lived." But "after only a few months, Luther ruined everything by going out and buying a brand-new 1961 Pontiac. It meant more to him than the house did, and when they couldn't make the house payment, he insisted on keeping the car" even though she hadn't enough money to buy shoes for the children. The family was kicked out of the house. They now moved frequently. They were reaching rock bottom. At this nadir, hope appeared in the ironic form of the Robert Taylor Homes, then a brand-new public housing project, now a notorious focus of drug addiction and gang violence. Ruby had had an application for public housing on file for many years, but the housing authority screened out unwed mothers. Told by a social worker that she could have an apartment in the Taylor Homes if she produced a marriage license, she and Luther (who was now divorced from his first wife) were married forthwith and promptly accepted as tenants. "The Haynes family chose to rejoice in their good fortune in becoming residents of the Robert Taylor Homes. As Ruby's son Larry, who was twelve years old at the time, says, 'I thought that was the beautifullest place in the world.'"

Even in the halcyon days of 1962, the Robert Taylor Homes were no paradise. There was considerable crime, and there were gangs, and Ruby's son Kermit joined one. Kermit was not Luther's son and did not recognize his authority. The two quarreled a lot. Meanwhile Luther had lost his job in the awning factory "that he had had for a decade, and then bounced around a little.

He lost jobs because of transportation problems, because of layoffs, because of a bout of serious illness, because of his drinking, because he had a minor criminal record (having been in jail for disorderly conduct following a fight with Ruby), and because creditors were after him." He resumed "his old habit of not returning from work on Fridays after he got his paycheck." One weekend he didn't come home at all. In a search of his things Ruby discovered evidence that Luther was having an affair with Dorothy Johnson, a former neighbor. "Luther was not being particularly careful; he saw in Dorothy, who was younger than Ruby, who had three children compared to Ruby's eight, who had a job while Ruby was on public aid, the promise of an escape from the ghetto, and he was entranced." The children discovered the affair. Kermit tried to strangle Luther. In 1965 Luther moved out permanently, and eventually he and Ruby divorced. [. . .]

After divorcing Ruby, Luther Haynes married Dorothy Johnson. He is still married to her, "owns a home on the far South Side of Chicago, and has worked for years as a parking-lot attendant; only recently have he and Ruby found that they can speak civilly to each other on the phone." [. . .]

In *Melvin v. Reid*, 297 P. 91 (Cal. 1931), the plaintiff was a former prostitute, who had been prosecuted but acquitted of murder. She later had married and (she alleged) for seven years had lived a blameless respectable life in a community in which her lurid past was unknown — when all was revealed in a movie about the murder case which used her maiden name. The court held that these allegations stated a claim for invasion of privacy. The Hayneses' claim is similar although less dramatic. They have been a respectable married couple for two decades. Luther's alcohol problem is behind him. He has steady employment as a doorman. His wife is a nurse, and in 1990 he told Lemann that the couple's combined income was $60,000 a year. He is not in trouble with the domestic relations court. He is a deacon of his church. He has come a long way from sharecropping in Mississippi and public housing in Chicago and he and his wife want to bury their past just as Mrs. Melvin wanted to do and in *Melvin v. Reid* was held entitled to do. Cf. *Briscoe v. Reader's Digest Ass'n*, 483 P.2d 34 (1971). In Luther Haynes's own words, from his deposition, "I know I haven't been no angel, but since almost 30 years ago I have turned my life completely around. I stopped the drinking and all this bad habits and stuff like that, which I deny, some of [it] I didn't deny, because I have changed my life. It take me almost 30 years to change it and I am deeply in my church. I look good in the eyes of my church members and my community. Now, what is going to happen now when this public reads this garbage which I didn't tell Mr. Lemann to write? Then all this is going to go down the drain. And I worked like a son of a gun to build myself up in a good reputation and he has torn it down." [. . .]

Evolution along the divergent lines marked out by *Melvin* and *Sidis* continued — until *Cox Broadcasting Corp. v. Cohn*, 420 U.S. 469 (1975), which may have consigned the entire *Melvin* line to the outer darkness.

[. . .] [D]espite the limited scope of the holdings of *Cox* and *Florida Star*, the implications of those decisions for the branch of the right of privacy that limits the publication of private facts are profound, even for a case such as this in which, unlike *Melvin v. Reid*, the primary source of the allegedly humiliating personal facts is not a public record. [. . .] The Court must believe that the First Amendment greatly circumscribes the right even of a private figure to obtain damages for the publication of newsworthy facts about him, even when they are facts of a kind that people want very much to conceal. [. . .] People who do not desire the limelight and do not deliberately choose a way of life or course of conduct calculated to thrust them into it nevertheless have no legal right to extinguish it if the experiences that have befallen them are newsworthy, even if they would prefer that those experiences be kept private. The possibility of an involuntary loss of privacy is recognized in the modern formulations of this branch of the privacy tort, which require not only that the private facts publicized be such as would make a reasonable person deeply offended by such publicity but also that they be facts in which the public has no legitimate interest.

The two criteria, offensiveness and newsworthiness, are related. An individual, and more pertinently perhaps the community, is most offended by the publication of intimate personal facts when the community has no interest in them beyond the voyeuristic thrill of penetrating the wall of privacy that surrounds a stranger. The reader of a book about the black migration to the North would have no legitimate interest in the details of Luther Haynes's sex life; but no such details are disclosed. Such a reader does have a legitimate interest in the aspects of Luther's conduct that the book reveals. For one of Lemann's major themes is the transposition virtually intact of a sharecropper morality characterized by a family structure "matriarchal and elastic" and by an "extremely unstable" marriage bond to the slums of the northern cities, and the interaction, largely random and sometimes perverse, of that morality with governmental programs to alleviate poverty. Public aid policies discouraged Ruby and Luther from living together; public housing policies precipitated a marriage doomed to fail. No detail in the book claimed to invade the Hayneses' privacy is not germane to the story that the author wanted to tell, a story not only of legitimate but of transcendent public interest. [. . .]

Well, argue the Hayneses, at least Lemann could have changed their names. But the use of pseudonyms would not have gotten Lemann and Knopf off the legal hook. The details of the Hayneses' lives recounted in the book would identify them unmistakably to anyone who has known the Hayneses well for a long time (members of their families, for example), or who knew them before they got married; and no more is required for liability either in defamation law or in privacy law. Lemann would have had to change some, perhaps many, of the details. But then he would no longer have been writing history. He would have been writing fiction. [. . .]

Affirmed.

NOTES

1. *The economics of privacy.* Does *Cox Broadcasting v. Cohn* dictate the result in *Haynes*? Can the result in *Haynes* be reconciled with *Briscoe v. Reader's Digest*? Elsewhere the author of the *Haynes* opinion has written at length about the legal regulation of privacy and expressed skepticism about the branch of the law on which Haynes was relying:

> We would think it wrong (and inefficient) if the law permitted a seller in hawking his wares to make false or incomplete representations of their quality. But people "sell" themselves as well as their goods by professing high standards of behavior to induce others to engage in advantageous social or business dealings with them, while concealing facts that these acquaintances need in order to evaluate their character. There are practical reasons for not imposing a general legal duty of full and frank disclosure of one's material personal shortcomings. But shouldn't a person be allowed to protect himself from disadvantageous transactions by ferreting out concealed facts about individuals which are material to the implicit or explicit representations that those individuals make concerning their moral qualities? It is no answer that people have "the right to be let alone," for few people want to be let alone. Rather, they want to manipulate the world around them by selective disclosure of facts about themselves. [. . .] It is not clear why society should assign the property right in such information to the individual to whom it pertains [.]

Posner, The Economics of Justice (1981). What would be the application of this reasoning to the *Haynes* case? To the other cases in this chapter?

C. INTRUSION UPON SECLUSION

Restatement (Second) of Torts

§652B. INTRUSION UPON SECLUSION

One who intentionally intrudes, physically or otherwise, upon the solitude or seclusion of another or his private affairs or concerns, is subject to liability to the other for invasion of his privacy, if the intrusion would be highly offensive to a reasonable person.

Nader v. General Motors Corp.
255 N.E.2d 765 (N.Y. 1970)

FULD, C.J. — The plaintiff, an author and lecturer on automotive safety, has, for some years, been an articulate and severe critic of General Motors' products from the standpoint of safety and design. According to the complaint — which, for present purposes, we must assume to be true — the appellant, having learned of the imminent publication of the plaintiff's book "Unsafe at any Speed," decided to conduct a campaign of intimidation against him in order to "suppress plaintiff's criticism of and prevent his disclosure of information" about its products. To that end, the appellant authorized and directed the other defendants to engage in a series of activities which, the plaintiff claims in his first two causes of action, violated his right to privacy.

Specifically, the plaintiff alleges that the appellant's agents (1) conducted a series of interviews with acquaintances of the plaintiff, "questioning them about, and casting aspersions upon (his) political, social . . . racial and religious views . . . ; his integrity; his sexual proclivities and inclinations; and his personal habits"; (2) kept him under surveillance in public places for an unreasonable length of time; (3) caused him to be accosted by girls for the purpose of entrapping him into illicit relationships; (4) made threatening, harassing and obnoxious telephone calls to him; (5) tapped his telephone and eavesdropped, by means of mechanical and electronic equipment, on his private conversations with others; and (6) conducted a "continuing" and harassing investigation of him. These charges are amplified in the plaintiff's bill of particulars, and those particulars are, of course, to be taken into account in considering the sufficiency of the challenged causes of action.

The threshold choice of law question requires no extended discussion. In point of fact, the parties have agreed — at least for purposes of this motion — that the sufficiency of these allegations is to be determined under the law of the District of Columbia. [. . .] Turning, then, to the law of the District of Columbia, it appears that its courts have not only recognized a common-law action for invasion of privacy but have broadened the scope of that tort beyond its traditional limits. Thus, in the most recent of its cases on the subject, *Pearson v. Dodd*, 410 F.2d 701, the Federal Court of Appeals for the District of Columbia declared:

> We approve the extension of the tort of invasion of privacy to instances of *intrusion*, whether by physical trespass or not, into spheres from which an ordinary man in a plaintiff's position could reasonably expect that the particular defendant should be excluded.

It is this form of invasion of privacy — initially termed "intrusion" by Dean Prosser in 1960 (*Privacy*, 48 Cal. L. Rev. 383, 389 et seq.; *Torts*, §112) — on which the two challenged causes of action are predicated.

Quite obviously, some intrusions into one's private sphere are inevitable concomitants of life in an industrial and densely populated society, which the law does not seek to proscribe even if it were possible to do so. "The law does not provide a remedy for every annoyance that occurs in everyday life." *Kelley v. Post Pub. Co.*, 327 Mass. 275, 278. However, the District of Columbia courts have held that the law should and does protect against certain types of intrusive conduct, and we must, therefore, determine whether the plaintiff's allegations are actionable as violations of the right to privacy under the law of that jurisdiction. To do so, we must, in effect, predict what the judges of that jurisdiction's highest court would hold if this case were presented to them. In other words, what would the Court of Appeals for the District of Columbia say is the character of the "privacy" sought to be protected? More specifically, would that court accord an individual a right, as the plaintiff before us insists, to be protected against any interference whatsoever with his personal seclusion and solitude? Or would it adopt a more restrictive view of the right, as the appellant urges, merely protecting the individual from intrusion into "something secret," from snooping and paying into his private affairs?

The classic article by Warren and Brandeis — to which the court in the *Pearson* case referred as the source of the District's common-law action for invasion of privacy — was premised, to a large extent, on principles originally developed in the field of copyright law. The authors thus based their thesis on a right granted by the common law to "each individual . . . of determining, ordinarily, to what extent his thoughts, sentiments and emotions shall be communicated to others." Their principal concern appeared to be not with a broad "right to be let alone" but, rather, with the right to protect oneself from having one's private affairs known to others and to keep secret or intimate facts about oneself from the prying eyes or ears of others.

In recognizing the existence of a common-law cause of action for invasion of privacy in the District of Columbia, the Court of Appeals has expressly adopted this latter formulation of the nature of the right. Quoting from the Restatement, Torts (§867), the court in the *Jaffe* case, 366 F.2d at 653, has declared that "[l]iability attaches to a person 'who unreasonably and seriously interferes with another's interest in *not having his affairs known to others.*'" (Emphasis supplied.) And, in *Pearson*, where the court extended the tort of invasion of privacy to instances of "intrusion," it again indicated, contrary to the plaintiff's submission, that the interest protected was one's right to keep knowledge about oneself from exposure to others, the right to prevent "the obtaining of the information by improperly intrusive means." In other jurisdictions, too, the cases which have recognized a remedy for invasion of privacy founded upon intrusive conduct have generally involved the gathering of private facts or information through improper means.

It should be emphasized that the mere gathering of information about a particular individual does not give rise to a cause of action under this theory. Privacy is invaded only if the information sought is of a confidential nature and the defendant's conduct was unreasonably intrusive. Just as a common-law copyright is lost when material is published, so, too, there can be no invasion of privacy where the information sought is open to public view or has been voluntarily revealed to others. In order to sustain a cause of action for invasion of privacy, therefore, the plaintiff must show that the appellant's conduct was truly "intrusive" and that it was designed to elicit information which would not be available through normal inquiry or observation.

The majority of the Appellate Division in the present case stated that *all of "[t]he activities complained of"* in the first two counts constituted actionable invasions of privacy under the law of the District of Columbia. We do not agree with that sweeping determination. At most, only two of the activities charged to the appellant are, in our view, actionable as invasions of privacy under the law of the District of Columbia. However, since the first two counts include allegations which are sufficient to state a cause of action, we could — as the concurring opinion notes — merely affirm the order before us without further elaboration. To do so, though, would be a disservice both to the judge who will be called upon to try this case and to the litigants themselves. In other words, we deem it desirable, nay essential, that we go further and, for the guidance of the trial court and counsel, indicate the extent to which the plaintiff is entitled to rely on the various allegations in support of his privacy claim.

Turning, then, to the particular acts charged in the complaint, we cannot find any basis for a claim of invasion of privacy, under District of Columbia law, in the allegations that the appellant, through its agents or employees, interviewed many persons who knew the plaintiff, asking questions about him and casting aspersions on his character. Although those inquiries may have uncovered information of a personal nature, it is difficult to see how they may be said to have invaded the plaintiff's privacy. Information about the plaintiff which was already known to others could hardly be regarded as private to the plaintiff. Presumably, the plaintiff had previously revealed the information to such other persons, and he would necessarily assume the risk that a friend or acquaintance in whom he had confided might breach the confidence. If, as alleged, the questions tended to disparage the plaintiff's character, his remedy would seem to be by way of an action for defamation, not for breach of his right to privacy.

Nor can we find any actionable invasion of privacy in the allegations that the appellant caused the plaintiff to be accosted by girls with illicit proposals, or that it was responsible for the making of a large number of threatening and harassing telephone calls to the plaintiff's home at odd hours. Neither of these activities, howsoever offensive and disturbing, involved intrusion for the purpose of gathering information of a private and confidential nature.

As already indicated, it is manifestly neither practical nor desirable for the law to provide a remedy against any and all activity which an individual might find annoying. On the other hand, where severe mental pain or anguish is inflicted through a deliberate and malicious campaign of harassment or intimidation, a remedy is available in the form of an action for the intentional infliction of emotional distress — the theory underlying the plaintiff's third cause of action. But the elements of such an action are decidedly different from those governing the tort of invasion of privacy, and just as we have carefully guarded against the use of the prima facie tort doctrine to circumvent the limitations relating to other established tort remedies, we should be wary of any attempt to rely on the tort of invasion of privacy as a means of avoiding the more stringent pleading and proof requirements for an action for infliction of emotional distress.

Apart, however, from the foregoing allegations which we find inadequate to spell out a cause of action for invasion of privacy under District of Columbia law, the complaint contains allegations concerning other activities by the appellant or its agents which do satisfy the requirements for such a cause of action. The one which most clearly meets those requirements is the charge that the appellant and its codefendants engaged in unauthorized wiretapping and eavesdropping by mechanical and electronic means. The Court of Appeals in the *Pearson* case expressly recognized that such conduct constitutes a tortious intrusion, and other jurisdictions have reached a similar conclusion. In point of fact, the appellant does not dispute this, acknowledging that, to the extent the two challenged counts charge it with wiretapping and eavesdropping, an actionable invasion of privacy has been stated.

There are additional allegations that the appellant hired people to shadow the plaintiff and keep him under surveillance. In particular, he claims that, on one occasion, one of its agents followed him into a bank, getting sufficiently close to him to see the denomination of the bills he was withdrawing from his account. From what we have already said, it is manifest that the mere observation of the plaintiff in a public place does not amount to an invasion of his privacy. But, under certain circumstances, surveillance may be so "overzealous" as to render it actionable. Whether or not the surveillance in the present case falls into this latter category will depend on the nature of the proof. A person does not automatically make public everything he does merely by being in a public place, and the mere fact that Nader was in a bank did not give anyone the right to try to discover the amount of money he was withdrawing. On the other hand, if the plaintiff acted in such a way as to reveal that fact to any casual observer, then, it may not be said that the appellant intruded into his private sphere. In any event, though, it is enough for present purposes to say that the surveillance allegation is not insufficient as a matter of law.

Since, then, the first two causes of action do contain allegations which are adequate to state a cause of action for invasion of privacy under District of Columbia law, the courts below properly denied the appellant's motion to dismiss those causes of action. It is settled that, so long as a pleading sets forth allegations which suffice to spell out a claim for relief, it is not subject to dismissal by reason of the inclusion therein of additional nonactionable allegations. [. . .]

The order appealed from should be affirmed, with costs, and the question certified answered in the affirmative.

[Concurring opinion of Breitel, J., omitted.]

NOTES

1. *Goons*. In Figured v. Paralegal Technical Services, 555 A.2d 663 (N.J. App. 1989), the plaintiff, Barbara Figured, was in an automobile accident in which she claimed to have suffered physical and emotional injuries.

The liability carrier for the other driver in the accident hired the defendant firm to investigate the plaintiff's claims. Figured's evidence was that she received a phone call one morning from a neighbor who said there were two suspicious-looking cars driving back and forth in front of Figured's house. When Figured soon left her house to go to a doctor's appointment she saw two cars parked nearby, with two men standing nearby watching her. Both cars pursued her as she drove off. When she pulled into a parking lot of a store about five miles away, the two cars followed; one of the drivers got out and walked slowly around the front of Figured's car, coming within arm's length of her and "staring" and "peering" at her face. On another day Figured left a family birthday party elsewhere in the state and saw one of the same cars following her. It pursued her closely for over 40 miles. When she pulled into a rest area, the other car pulled over as well and parked facing her.

Figured sued the agency for invasion of privacy. The trial court gave summary judgment to the defendants. The court of appeals affirmed:

> The allegations do not reveal an intrusion which would be "highly offensive" to a reasonable person: The thrust of this aspect of the tort is, in other words, that a person's private, personal affairs should not be pried into. . . . The converse of this principle is, however, of course, that there is no wrong where defendant did not actually delve into plaintiff's concerns, or where plaintiff's activities are already public or known. [. . .]
>
> [B]y making a claim for personal injuries appellant must expect reasonable inquiry and investigation to be made of her claim and to this extent her interest in privacy is circumscribed. [. . .] [T]he defendants' activities all took place in the open, either on public thoroughfares or in areas where members of the public had the right to be. [. . .] [*Bisbee v. Conover Agency*, 452 A.2d 689 (N.J. App. 1982)] supports the proposition that whatever the public may see from a public place cannot be private.

2. *Spies.* In Johnson v. K-Mart Corp., 723 N.E.2d 1192 (Ill. App. 2000), K-Mart became concerned about theft and drug use at one of its distribution plants. It hired a security company, Confidential Investigative Consultants (CIC), to perform undercover investigations of its employees. CIC sent two of its investigators into K-Mart's plant, one of them posing as a janitor, and the other — actually the wife of the first — posing as a worker in the repacking department. The investigators would have conversations with other employees at work and at social gatherings, and every few days would write reports of what they had learned about them; the reports were sent on to the employer. The reports included information about employees' families (e.g., the criminal conduct of employees' children, incidents of domestic violence, and impending divorces); employees' romantic interests and sex lives; employees' future employment plans (which were looking for new jobs and which were planning to quit without giving notice); complaints about the

defendant; and various other personal matters (e.g., one employee's prostate problems, and characterization of other employees as alcoholics).

Eventually a disgruntled former employee who knew of the undercover operation exposed it to a current K-Mart worker, and as a result K-Mart discontinued the program. Fifty-five employees sued K-Mart for invasion of privacy. The trial court gave summary judgment to K-Mart; the court of appeals reversed:

> [T]he circuit court entered summary judgment in favor of defendant, finding that there was no unauthorized intrusion because plaintiffs had voluntarily disclosed the complained-of information to the investigators and that defendant's actions did not amount to an offensive or objectionable intrusion. We find that the circuit court erred in entering summary judgment in favor of defendant. We believe that a genuine issue of fact exists regarding whether there was an unauthorized intrusion. It is true, as defendant argues, that plaintiffs willingly provided these personal details to the investigators. However, we believe that the means used by defendant to induce plaintiffs to reveal this information were deceptive. Specifically, we believe that the act of placing private detectives, posing as employees, in the workplace to solicit highly personal information about defendant's employees was deceptive. A disclosure obtained through deception cannot be said to be a truly voluntary disclosure. Plaintiffs had a reasonable expectation that their conversations with "coworkers" would remain private, at least to the extent that intimate life details would not be published to their employer. [. . .]
>
> Defendant admitted that it had no business purpose for gathering information about employees' personal lives. Yet, defendant never instructed the investigators to change their practices or to stop including the highly personal information in their reports. We find that a material issue of fact exists regarding whether a reasonable person would have found defendant's actions to be an offensive or objectionable intrusion.

What is the distinction between *Johnson v. K-Mart Corp.* and *Figured v. Paralegal Technical Services*? What is the distinction between *Johnson v. K-Mart Corp.* and those parts of *Nader v. General Motors Corp.* finding no liability?

3. *Quackery.* In Dietemann v. Time, Inc., 449 F.2d 245 (9th Cir. 1971), the plaintiff was a journeyman plumber who also claimed to be a scientist; he purported to practice the art of healing with clay, minerals, and herbs in his home. He accepted contributions from his patients but did not charge for his services and did not advertise. Two employees of *Life* Magazine came to him pretending to seek help. One of them, Metcalf, said that she had a lump in her breast; plaintiff examined her using a wand and some other gadget, and announced his conclusion that she had eaten rancid butter eleven years, nine

months, and seven days earlier. This dialogue was transmitted from a wireless microphone in the employee's purse to a parked car outside, where it was recorded by another employee of the magazine accompanied by a local prosecutor. Meanwhile the other employee admitted to the plaintiff's house took pictures of the plaintiff using a hidden camera. A month later the plaintiff was arrested for practicing medicine without a license, and soon afterwards *Life* published an article called "Crackdown on Quackery" that featured the plaintiff; it included a photograph of him from the undercover visit. Plaintiff sued for invasion of privacy, and after a bench trial was awarded $1,000. The court of appeals affirmed:

> Plaintiff's den was a sphere from which he could reasonably expect to exclude eavesdropping newsmen. He invited two of defendant's employees to the den. One who invites another to his home or office takes a risk that the visitor may not be what he seems, and that the visitor may repeat all he hears and observes when he leaves. But he does not and should not be required to take the risk that what is heard and seen will be transmitted by photograph or recording, or in our modern world, in full living color and hi-fi to the public at large or to any segment of it that the visitor may select. A different rule could have a most pernicious effect upon the dignity of man and it would surely lead to guarded conversations and conduct where candor is most valued, e.g., in the case of doctors and lawyers.
>
> The defendant claims that the First Amendment immunizes it from liability for invading plaintiff's den with a hidden camera and its concealed electronic instruments because its employees were gathering news and its instrumentalities "are indispensable tools of investigative reporting." We agree that newsgathering is an integral part of news dissemination. We strongly disagree, however, that the hidden mechanical contrivances are "indispensable tools" of newsgathering. Investigative reporting is an ancient art; its successful practice long antecedes the invention of miniature cameras and electronic devices. The First Amendment has never been construed to accord newsmen immunity from torts or crimes committed during the course of newsgathering. The First Amendment is not a license to trespass, to steal, or to intrude by electronic means into the precincts of another's home or office. It does not become such a license simply because the person subjected to the intrusion is reasonably suspected of committing a crime.

What is the analogy between *Dietemann v. Time, Inc.* and those portions of *Nader v. General Motors Corp.* that find potential liability? What is the distinction between *Dietemann* and those portions of the *Nader* case that find no liability?

4. *The prying eye.* In Desnick v. American Broadcasting Co., 44 F.3d 1345 (7th Cir. 1995), a case reprinted at length in the chapter on intentional torts,

the plaintiff, Desnick, was the owner of a chain of ophthalmic clinics; the defendants were producers of *PrimeTime Live*, a documentary television series that ran an expose on Desnick's methods. The defendants sent employees into Desnick's clinics with hidden cameras. They posed as patients and recorded instances of Desnick's employees advising them to undergo cataract surgery that they did not need. Desnick sued ABC for trespass, claiming that the investigators had gained access to his premises by lying about their intentions. He also sued for invasion of privacy. The court of appeals dismissed both claims, believing that *Dietemann v. Time, Inc.* was distinguishable. Do you agree? What is the distinction between the *Desnick* case and *Johnson v. K-Mart Corp.*?

5. *Abusive telemarketers.* In Irvine v. Akron Beacon Journal, 147 Ohio App. 3d 428 (Ohio App. 2002), the plaintiffs received several "hang up" calls on their telephone, and were unable to trace them using the phone's caller ID system. They therefore filed a criminal harassment complaint and obtained a trap on their phone line that enabled them to determine that the calls were coming from the defendant's subscription offices. The plaintiff's evidence, as it later developed, was that the defendant used automatic dialing machines to maximize the number of residences that its telemarketers were able to reach. Sometimes the autodialer would call multiple numbers at once, then connect the telemarketer to whichever phone was answered first while disconnecting the other. The autodialer also was programmed after hours to call recently disconnected phone numbers in the region to determine whether they had yet been reassigned to new residents; the defendant had found that new residents made promising targets for its telemarketing, so if the number had been reassigned it would then be called during business hours by a live person. The result of these methods, possibly in combination with malfunctions in the defendant's computer system, was that the plaintiffs received many hang-up calls, including three in the middle of the night. They sued the defendant for invasion of privacy. A jury found for the plaintiffs, awarding $250 in compensatory damages to each member of the family, plus $100,000 in punitive damages. The court of appeals affirmed:

> Beacon Journal contends that reasonable minds could only conclude, and that the jury lost its way in reaching a conclusion to the contrary, that Beacon Journal did not call the Irvines "with such persistence and frequency as to amount to a course of hounding" or to become a "substantial burden to [their] existence." This court does not agree. [. . .] Although Beacon Journal again focuses solely on the three late-night phone calls, there was evidence before the jury that the Irvines received many other phone calls from Beacon Journal. [Plaintiffs] testified that they received hundreds of phone calls from Beacon Journal. During some calls, the caller identified himself or herself as being from the Beacon Journal. Many of the calls were "hang-up" calls, however. [. . .]

Middle-of-the-night hang-up calls would be disturbing to anyone, but Beacon Journal apparently did not even factor that consideration into its decision-making process. Beacon's staff set the machine to run all night, everyone went home, and when they came back the next day the data were waiting for them. [...] The jury could reasonably conclude that Beacon Journal had acted in conscious disregard to the rights of others and that its conduct had a great probability of causing substantial harm.

What is the distinction between *Irvine v. Akron Beacon Journal* and *Figured v. Paralegal Technical Services?*

6. *Final indignity.* In Estate of Berthiaume v. Pratt, 365 A.2d 792 (Me. 1976), Henry Berthiaume was referred to the defendant, Pratt, for surgical treatment of cancer of the larynx. Pratt performed a laryngectomy on Berthiaume, and then a radical neck dissection. During this period Pratt took a number of photographs of Berthiaume for his own use; they were not to be shown to students or used as illustrations in articles. The plaintiff's evidence was that a few weeks after the treatment concluded, Berthiaume was close to death in his hospital bed with his wife nearby. Pratt arrived with a nurse and placed a blue towel under Berthiaume's head. He explained that the towel was meant to create a color contrast for photographs they were about to take. Berthiaume protested the taking of the pictures by raising a clenched fist and attempting to move his head out of the camera's range; in the corridor Berthiaume's wife told Pratt that she "didn't think that Henry wanted his picture taken." Pratt nevertheless took several pictures, which he later explained were meant to complete his record of the case. Berthiaume died later that day. His wife brought suit as representative of his estate, seeking damages from Pratt for invasion of privacy. The trial court gave a directed verdict to the defendant. The Supreme Judicial Court of Maine reversed, adopting this language from an earlier Pennsylvania case with similar facts:

[A]n individual has the right to decide whether that which is his shall be given to the public and not only to restrict and limit but also to withhold absolutely his talents, property, or other subjects of the right of privacy from all dissemination. The facial characteristics or peculiar cast of one's features, whether normal or distorted, belong to the individual and may not be reproduced without his permission. Even the photographer who is authorized to take a portrait is not justified in making or retaining additional copies for himself.

A man may object to any invasion, as well as to an unlimited invasion. Widespread distribution of a photograph is not essential nor can it be said that publication in its common usage or in its legal meaning is necessary. It may be conceded that the doctrine of privacy in general is still suffering the pains of its birth and any doctrine in its inception borrows from established precedent. An analogy to the laws of libel, however, is not justified under the circumstances of this case. The author of a libel is the creator and there can be no offense until the contents are communicated to another. One cannot invade the rights of another merely by expressing his thoughts on paper. Two persons are necessary. One's right of privacy, however, may be invaded by a single human agency. Plaintiff's picture was taken without her authority or consent. Her right to decide whether her facial characteristics should be recorded for another's benefit or by reason of another's capriciousness has been violated. The scope of the authorization defines the extent of the acts necessary to constitute a violation. If plaintiff had consented to have her photograph taken only for defendant's private files certainly he would have no right to exhibit it to others without her permission. Can it be said that his rights are equally extensive when even that limited consent has not been given?

What is the distinction between *Estate of Berthiaume v. Pratt* and *Figured v. Paralegal Technical Services?*

7. *Hair thief.* In Froelich v. Werbin, 548 P.2d 482 (Kan. 1976), a man named Hamilton sued his ex-wife, Burneta Adair, for defamation. She had stated that Hamilton was a homosexual and that he had a male lover, one William Froelich. One of Adair's defenses in the defamation case was that the statements were true. The plaintiff's evidence was that Adair asked a friend, Werbin, to obtain a sample of Froelich's hair from a hospital in Wichita to which he had been admitted; Adair's plan was to match Froelich's hair to hair she had found in Hamilton's underclothes. Adair's friend paid an orderly at the hospital to retrieve specimens of Adair's hair from a hairbrush and from a band-aid that had been used to secure an intravenous needle to his arm and that had ripped out a bit of hair upon its removal. When Froelich learned that this had been done he sued Adair and Werbin for invasion of privacy. The trial court gave a directed verdict to the defendant, and the Kansas Supreme Court affirmed:

> Froelich failed as a matter of law to establish an invasion of his right of privacy. There is no evidence in the record to show physical intrusion into a privately secluded place which Froelich had secured for himself. The plaintiff introduced no evidence that the hair was taken from plaintiff Froelich's hospital room. There was no evidence that hair was taken from the person of the plaintiff. In fact, both court and counsel throughout the trial assumed that the hair was taken from a piece of adhesive tape which had been thrown into a trash container in a utility room. Plaintiff offered no evidence to establish that the plaintiff's state of mind was disturbed at the time the hair was obtained by the orderly. The evidence was undisputed that the plaintiff did not know that the hair had been obtained by Marlett until three or four months later.

What is the distinction between *Froelich v. Werbin* and *Estate of Berthiaume v. Pratt*? What is the superficial similarity between *Froelich* and *Johnson v. K-Mart Corp.*? What is the distinction between them?

8. *Peeping tom.* In Harkey v. Abate, 346 N.W.2d 74 (Mich. App. 1984), the plaintiffs were a mother and daughter who were patrons at the defendant's roller skating rink and who used the public restrooms on their visit. They later learned that the defendant had installed see-through panels in the ceiling of the restroom that permitted surreptitious observation of the bathroom stalls. They sued the owner of the roller rink for invasion of privacy. He denied having looked at the plaintiffs through the one-way glass, and the plaintiffs conceded that they could not prove that he did. The trial court gave summary judgment to the defendant. The court of appeals reversed:

> The installation of viewing devices as alleged by plaintiff is a felony in this state. M.S.A. §28.807(4). Though this statute does not specifically impose civil liability for such conduct, nor does plaintiff's complaint assert liability based on its violation, it does constitute, at a minimum, a legislative expression of public policy opposed to such conduct.
>
> The type of invasion of privacy asserted by plaintiff does not depend upon any publicity given to the person whose interest is invaded, but consists solely of an intentional interference with his or her interest in solitude or seclusion of a kind that would be highly offensive to a reasonable person. Clearly, plaintiff and her daughter in this case had a right to privacy in the public restroom in question. In our opinion, the installation of the hidden viewing devices alone constitutes an interference with that privacy which a reasonable person would find highly offensive. And though the absence of proof that the devices were utilized is relevant to the question of damages, it is not fatal to plaintiff's case.

What is the distinction between *Harkey v. Abate* and *Froelich v. Werbin* (the NL case of the theft of the plaintiff's hair)?

9. *Keeping the restrooms safe.* In Elmore v. Atlantic Zayre, Inc., 341 S.E.2d 905 (Ga. App. 1986), a customer at a Zayre department store complained to the management that homosexual activities were occurring in one of its public restrooms. The store's loss prevention manager visited the restroom and found the indications there suspicious, so he and another member of the security staff went to a storage room above the restroom where a crack in the floor enabled them to see down into the restroom stalls. They observed the plaintiff engaged in sexual acts with another man; they called the police, and based on their observations the plaintiff was arrested for sodomy. He sued Zayre, claiming it had invaded his privacy by "spying on him in a private

place." The trial judge gave summary judgment to the defendant. The court of appeals affirmed:

> An individual clearly has an interest in privacy within a toilet stall. However, the law recognizes that the right of privacy is not absolute [and that it] must be kept within its proper limits, and in its exercise must be made to accord with the rights of those who have other liberties, as well as the rights of any person who may be properly interested in the matters which are claimed to be of purely private concern.
>
> In the instant case, the toilet stall which appellant was occupying was in a restroom provided by appellee Zayre's for use by its customers. Thus, appellee Zayre's had an overriding responsibility to its patrons to keep that restroom free of crime, safe, and available for its intended purpose.

Can *Elmore v. Atlantic Zayre* be reconciled with *Harkey v. Abate*? With *Johnson v. K-Mart Corp.*?

10. *Reality TV (problem).* In Shulman v. Group W Productions, 955 P.2d 469 (Cal. 1998), the plaintiffs, Ruth and Wayne Shulman, were injured when their car skidded off a highway in California, tumbled down an embankment, and came to rest upside down in a drainage ditch. A rescue helicopter soon arrived. In addition to a medic, a nurse, and a pilot, the helicopter contained a cameraman employed by the defendant. The nurse was wearing a microphone as well. Audio and video recordings were made of the ensuing rescue and were broadcast as a nine-minute segment on a television show called "On Scene: Emergency Response." The broadcast included footage of the plaintiffs being extricated from the vehicle using the mechanical device known as the "jaws of life"; footage of the plaintiffs being moved to the helicopter on a stretcher; dialogue between the nurse and Ruth Shulman in which she seemed disoriented, repeated questions several times, and was reassured by the nurse; and footage of the plaintiffs in the helicopter during the trip to the hospital, when Ruth Shulman had an oxygen mask over her face. The plaintiffs were not identified by name, though the nurse could be heard using the name "Ruth." The segment closed with the narrator saying: "Thanks to the efforts of the crew of Mercy Air, the firefighters, medics and police who responded, patients' lives were saved." Then a written epilogue appeared on the screen: "[The nurse's] patient spent months in the hospital. She suffered severe back injuries. The others were all released much sooner."

The Shulmans brought a suit for invasion of privacy against the company that produced the segment. They testified that they had not known that the incident was recorded and learned of it only when they saw it themselves on television. They claimed that the defendants had violated their rights by publishing private facts about them and by intruding on their right to seclusion. What result?

D. APPROPRIATION OF NAME OR LIKENESS

As we saw at the beginning of the chapter, New York's courts rejected early invasion of privacy claims, prompting the state legislature to address the issue with a statute. The New York law was written in response to the problem of plaintiffs who found their likenesses used without their consent, and so naturally was focused on that aspect of the privacy tort — sometimes known as the "right of publicity." Thus §51 of New York's Civil Rights law provides in relevant part:

> [A]ny person whose name, portrait or picture is used within this state for advertising purposes or for the purposes of trade without the written consent first obtained as above provided may maintain an equitable action in the supreme court of this state against the person, firm, or corporation so using his name, portrait or picture, to prevent and restrain the use thereof; and may also sue and recover damages for any injuries sustained by reason of such use[.]

The statute was an important and influential early step in the development of the right of publicity. Most jurisdictions have since followed suit, establishing a similar right by statute or, more often, by judicial decision. New York remains an important jurisdiction for publicity claims because of the many celebrities who live there, but when such cases arise they continue to be treated as matters of statutory interpretation, not common law. Indeed, in New York the statute governs invasion of privacy claims of all sorts; there is no cause of action in the state for public disclosure of embarrassing private facts or for intrusion upon seclusion. To avoid the idiosyncracies of the New York statute and the results it sometimes produces, we will focus in this section on the common law right of publicity.

Restatement (Second) of Torts

§652C. APPROPRIATION OF NAME OR LIKENESS

One who appropriates to his own use or benefit the name or likeness of another is subject to liability to the other for invasion of his privacy.

Comment d. Incidental use of name or likeness. The value of the plaintiff's name is not appropriated by mere mention of it, or by reference to it in connection with legitimate mention of his public activities; nor is the value of his likeness appropriated when it is published for purposes other than taking advantage of his reputation, prestige, or other value associated with him, for purposes of publicity. No one has the right to object merely because his name or his appearance is brought before the public, since neither is in any way a private matter and both are open to public observation. It is only when the publicity is given for the purpose of appropriating to the defendant's benefit the commercial or other values associated with the name or the likeness that the right of privacy is invaded. The fact that the defendant is engaged in the business of publication, for example of a newspaper, out of which he makes or seeks to make a profit, is not enough to make the incidental publication a commercial use of the name or likeness. Thus a newspaper, although it is not a philanthropic institution, does not become liable under the rule stated in this Section to every person whose name or likeness it publishes.

White v. Samsung Electronics America, Inc.
971 F.2d 1395 (9th Cir. 1992)

GOODWIN, *Senior Circuit Judge*. [. . .] Plaintiff Vanna White is the hostess of "Wheel of Fortune," one of the most popular game shows in television history. An estimated forty million people watch the program daily. Capitalizing on the fame which her participation in the show has bestowed on her, White markets her identity to various advertisers.

The dispute in this case arose out of a series of advertisements prepared for Samsung by Deutsch. The series ran in at least half a dozen publications with widespread, and in some cases national, circulation. Each of the advertisements in the series followed the same theme. Each depicted a current item from popular culture and a Samsung electronic product. Each was set in the twenty-first century and conveyed the message that the Samsung product would still be in use by that time. By hypothesizing outrageous future outcomes for the cultural items, the ads created humorous effects. For example, one lampooned current popular notions of an unhealthy diet by depicting a raw steak with the caption: "Revealed to be health food. 2010 A.D." Another depicted irreverent "news"-show host Morton Downey Jr. in front of an American flag with the caption: "Presidential candidate. 2008 A.D."

The advertisement which prompted the current dispute was for Samsung video-cassette recorders (VCRs). The ad depicted a robot, dressed in a wig, gown, and jewelry which Deutsch consciously selected to resemble White's hair and dress. The robot was posed next to a game board which is instantly recognizable as the Wheel of Fortune game show set, in a stance for which White is famous. The caption of the ad read: "Longest-running game show. 2012 A.D." Defendants referred to the ad as the "Vanna White" ad. Unlike the other celebrities used in the campaign, White neither consented to the ads nor was she paid.

[White brought suit against Samsung and Deutsch, alleging that they had violated her common law right of publicity and other rights. The district court gave summary judgment to Samsung; White took this appeal.]

White [argues] that the district court erred in granting summary judgment to defendants on White's common law right of publicity claim.

In *Eastwood v. Superior Court*, 198 Cal.Rptr. 342 (1983), the California court of appeal stated that the common law right of publicity cause of action "may be pleaded by alleging (1) the defendant's use of the plaintiff's identity; (2) the appropriation of plaintiff's name or likeness to defendant's advantage, commercially or otherwise; (3) lack of consent; and (4) resulting injury." The district court dismissed White's claim for failure to satisfy *Eastwood*'s second prong, reasoning that defendants had not appropriated White's "name or likeness" with their robot ad. We agree that the robot ad did not make use of White's name or likeness. However, the common law right of publicity is not so confined. [. . .]

The "name or likeness" formulation referred to in *Eastwood* originated not as an element of the right of publicity cause of action, but as a description of the types of cases in which the cause of action had been recognized. The source of this formulation is Prosser, *Privacy*, 48 Cal. L. Rev. 383, 401-07 (1960), one of the earliest and most enduring articulations of the common law right of publicity cause of action. In looking at the case law to that point, Prosser recognized that right of publicity cases involved one of two basic factual scenarios: name appropriation, and picture or other likeness appropriation.

Even though Prosser focused on appropriations of name or likeness in discussing the right of publicity, he noted that "[i]t is not impossible that there might be appropriation of the plaintiff's identity, as by impersonation, without the use of either his name or his likeness, and that this would be an invasion of his right of privacy." Id. at 401, n. 155. At the time Prosser wrote, he noted however, that "[n]o such case appears to have arisen."

Since Prosser's early formulation, the case law has borne out his insight that the right of publicity is not limited to the appropriation of name or likeness. In *Motschenbacher v. R. J. Reynolds Tobacco Co.*, 498 F.2d 821 (9th Cir. 1974), the defendant had used a photograph of the plaintiff's race car in a television commercial. Although the plaintiff appeared driving the car in the photograph, his features were not visible. Even though the defendant had not appropriated the plaintiff's name or likeness, this court held that plaintiff's California right of publicity claim should reach the jury.

In [*Midler v. Ford Motor Co.*, 849 F.2d 460 (9th Cir. 1988),] this court held that, even though the defendants had not used Midler's name or likeness, Midler had stated a claim for violation of her California common law right of publicity because "the defendants . . . for their own profit in selling their product did appropriate part of her identity" by using a Midler sound-alike. Id. at 463-64.

These cases teach not only that the common law right of publicity reaches means of appropriation other than name or likeness, but that the specific means of appropriation are relevant only for determining whether the defendant has in fact appropriated the plaintiff's identity. The right of publicity does not require that appropriations of identity be accomplished through particular means to be actionable. [. . .] It is not important *how* the defendant has appropriated the plaintiff's identity, but *whether* the defendant has done so. *Motschenbacher* [and] *Midler* teach the impossibility of treating the right of publicity as guarding only against a laundry list of specific means of appropriating identity. A rule which says that the right of publicity can be infringed only through the use of nine different methods of appropriating identity merely challenges the clever advertising strategist to come up with the tenth.

Indeed, if we treated the means of appropriation as dispositive in our analysis of the right of publicity, we would not only weaken the right but effectively eviscerate it. The right would fail to protect those plaintiffs most in need of its protection. Advertisers use celebrities to promote their products. The more popular the celebrity, the greater the number of people who recognize her, and the greater the visibility for the product. The identities of the most popular celebrities are not only the most attractive for advertisers, but also the easiest to evoke without resorting to obvious means such as name, likeness, or voice. [. . .]

Viewed separately, the individual aspects of the advertisement in the present case say little. Viewed together, they leave little doubt about the celebrity the ad is meant to depict. The female-shaped robot is wearing a long gown, blond wig, and large jewelry. Vanna White dresses exactly like this at times, but so do many other women. The robot is in the process of turning a block letter on a game-board. Vanna White dresses like this while turning letters on a game-board but perhaps similarly attired Scrabble-playing women do this as well. The robot is standing on what looks to be the Wheel of Fortune game show set. Vanna White dresses like this, turns letters, and does this on the Wheel of Fortune game show. She is the only one. Indeed, defendants themselves referred to their ad as the "Vanna White" ad. We are not surprised.

Television and other media create marketable celebrity identity value. Considerable energy and ingenuity are expended by those who have achieved celebrity value to exploit it for profit. The law protects the celebrity's sole right to exploit this value whether the celebrity has achieved her fame out of rare ability, dumb luck, or a combination thereof. We decline Samsung and Deutch's invitation to permit the evisceration of the common law right of publicity through means as facile as those in this case. Because White has alleged facts showing that Samsung and Deutsch had appropriated her identity, the district court erred by rejecting, on summary judgment, White's common law right of publicity claim.

The Parody Defense

In defense, defendants cite a number of cases for the proposition that their robot ad constituted protected speech. The only cases they cite which are even remotely relevant to this case are *Hustler Magazine v. Falwell*, 485 U.S. 46, 108 S.Ct. 876, 99 L. Ed. 2d 41 (1988) and *L. L. Bean, Inc. v. Drake Publishers, Inc.*, 811 F.2d 26 (1st Cir. 1987). Those cases involved parodies of advertisements run for the purpose of poking fun at Jerry Falwell and L. L. Bean, respectively. This case involves a true advertisement run for the purpose of selling Samsung VCRs. The ad's spoof of Vanna White and Wheel of Fortune is subservient and only tangentially related to the ad's primary message: "buy Samsung VCRs." Defendants' parody arguments are better addressed to non-commercial parodies. The difference between a "parody" and a "knock-off" is the difference between fun and profit. [. . .]

In remanding this case, we hold only that White has pleaded claims which can go to the jury for its decision.

KOZINSKI, *Circuit Judge* (dissenting from the order rejecting the suggestion for rehearing en banc). Saddam Hussein wants to keep advertisers from using his picture in unflattering contexts. Clint Eastwood doesn't want tabloids to write about him. Rudolf Valentino's heirs want to control his film biography. The Girl Scouts don't want their image soiled by association with certain activities. George Lucas wants to keep Strategic Defense Initiative fans from calling it "Star Wars." Pepsico doesn't want singers to use the word "Pepsi" in their songs. Guy Lombardo wants an exclusive property right to ads that show big bands playing on New Year's Eve. Uri Geller thinks he should be paid for ads showing psychics bending metal through telekinesis. Paul Prudhomme, that household name, thinks the same about ads featuring corpulent bearded chefs. And scads of copyright holders see purple when their creations are made fun of.

Something very dangerous is going on here. Private property, including intellectual property, is essential to our way of life. It provides an incentive for investment and innovation; it stimulates the flourishing of our culture; it protects the moral entitlements of people to the fruits of their labors. But reducing too much to private property can be bad medicine. Private land, for instance, is far more useful if separated from other private land by public streets, roads and highways. Public parks, utility rights-of-way and sewers reduce the amount of land in private hands, but vastly enhance the value of the property that remains.

So too it is with intellectual property. Overprotecting intellectual property is as harmful as underprotecting it. Creativity is impossible without a rich public domain. Nothing today, likely nothing since we tamed fire, is genuinely new: Culture, like science and technology, grows by accretion, each new creator building on the works of those who came before. Overprotection stifles the very creative forces it's supposed to nurture.

The panel's opinion is a classic case of overprotection. Concerned about what it sees as a wrong done to Vanna White, the panel majority erects a property right of remarkable and dangerous breadth: Under the majority's opinion, it's now a tort for advertisers to *remind* the public of a celebrity. Not to use a celebrity's name, voice, signature or likeness; not to imply the celebrity endorses a product; but simply to evoke the celebrity's image in the public's mind. This Orwellian notion withdraws far more from the public domain than prudence and common sense allow. It conflicts with the Copyright Act and the Copyright Clause. It raises serious First Amendment problems. It's bad law, and it deserves a long, hard second look. [...]

Consider how sweeping this new right is. What is it about the ad that makes people think of White? It's not the robot's wig, clothes or jewelry; there must be ten million blond women (many of them quasi-famous) who wear dresses and jewelry like White's. It's that the robot is posed near the "Wheel of Fortune" game board. Remove the game board from the ad, and no one would think of Vanna White. But once you include the game board, anybody standing beside it — a brunette woman, a man wearing women's clothes, a monkey in a wig and gown — would evoke White's image, precisely the way the robot did. It's the "Wheel of Fortune" set, not the robot's face or dress or jewelry that evokes White's image. The panel is giving White an exclusive right not in what she looks like or who she is, but in what she does for a living.

This is entirely the wrong place to strike the balance. Intellectual property rights aren't free: They're imposed at the expense of future creators and of the public at large. Where would we be if Charles Lindbergh had an exclusive right in the concept of a heroic solo aviator? If Arthur Conan Doyle had gotten a copyright in the idea of the detective story, or Albert Einstein had patented the theory of relativity? If every author and celebrity had been given the right to keep people from mocking them or their work? Surely this would have made the world poorer, not richer, culturally as well as economically.

This is why intellectual property law is full of careful balances between what's set aside for the owner and what's left in the public domain for the rest of us: The relatively short life of patents; the longer, but finite, life of copyrights; copyright's idea-expression dichotomy; the fair use doctrine; the prohibition on copyrighting facts; the compulsory license of television broadcasts and musical compositions; federal preemption of overbroad state intellectual property laws; the nominative use doctrine in trademark law; the right to make soundalike recordings. All of these diminish an intellectual property owner's rights. All let the public use something created by someone else. But all are necessary to maintain a free environment in which creative genius can flourish.

The intellectual property right created by the panel here has none of these essential limitations: No fair use exception; no right to parody; no idea-expression dichotomy. It impoverishes the public domain, to the detriment of future creators and the public at large. Instead of well-defined, limited characteristics such as name, likeness or voice, advertisers will now have to cope with vague claims of "appropriation of identity," claims often made by people with a wholly exaggerated sense of their own fame and significance. Future Vanna Whites might not get the chance to create their personae, because their employers may fear some celebrity will claim the persona is too similar to her own. The public will be robbed of parodies of celebrities, and our culture will be deprived of the valuable safety valve that parody and mockery create.

Moreover, consider the moral dimension, about which the panel majority seems to have gotten so exercised. Saying Samsung "appropriated" something of White's begs the question: *Should* White have the exclusive right to something as broad and amorphous as her "identity"? Samsung's ad didn't simply copy White's schtick — like all parody, it created something new. True, Samsung did it to make money, but White does whatever she does to make money, too; the majority talks of "the difference between fun and profit," but in the entertainment industry fun *is* profit. Why is Vanna White's right to exclusive for-profit use of her persona — a persona that might not even be her own creation, but that of a writer, director or producer — superior to Samsung's right to profit by creating its own inventions? Why should she have such absolute rights to control the conduct of others, unlimited by the idea-expression dichotomy or by the fair use doctrine?

To paraphrase only slightly *Feist Publications, Inc. v. Rural Telephone Service Co.*, 499 U.S. 340 (1991), it may seem unfair that much of the fruit of a creator's labor may be used by others without compensation. But this is not some unforeseen byproduct of our intellectual property system; it is the system's very essence. Intellectual property law assures authors the right to their original expression, but encourages others to build freely on the ideas that underlie it. This result is neither unfair nor unfortunate: It is the means by which intellectual property law advances the progress of science and art. We give authors certain exclusive rights, but in exchange we get a richer public domain. The majority ignores this wise teaching, and all of us are the poorer for it. [. . .]

NOTES

1. *Advertisements for news.* In Anderson v. Fisher Broadcasting Co., 712 P.2d 803 (Or. 1986), the plaintiff was in an automobile accident. A cameraman from the defendant's television station arrived on the scene and shot film of it; in the videotape the plaintiff's face was bloodied and he was in evident pain while receiving treatment. The defendant's station did not use the footage on its newscast. It instead used the footage on an advertisement for a report it planned to run about a new system for dispatching emergency help. The plaintiff sued, claiming the defendant violated his right to privacy by "appropriating to defendant's own use and advantage" the pictures its photographer had taken of him. The trial court held the defendant entitled to summary judgment; the Oregon Supreme Court agreed:

> When actors, athletes or other performers object, not to a loss of anonymity, but to unauthorized exploitation of their valuable public identities, the remedy should reflect the wrongful appropriation of a "right to publicity" that has economic value to the plaintiff as well as to the

defendant, rather than damages for psychic distress at a loss of "privacy." When a person who neither has nor wants a marketable public identity demands damages for unauthorized publicity, such a person may claim injury to a noneconomic rather than an economic interest in his or her privacy; but it is not always obvious, as it is not in this case, why the loss of privacy is different when it occurs in a "commercial" rather than a "noncommercial" form of publication. If the plaintiff can show no psychic injury at all, for instance an infant whose picture has been used in an advertisement for baby food rather than in a magazine or television report on child care, the answer must be that the advertiser, but not the reporter, has unjustly enriched himself by appropriating something for which he is expected to pay, an answer that begs the question.

Our system relies for freedom of information, ideas, and entertainment, high or low, primarily on privately owned media of communication, operating at private cost and seeking private profit. Books, newspapers, films, and broadcasts are produced and distributed at private cost and for private profit, that is to say, "commercially," and the use of materials from the lives of living persons in such publications can enrich authors, photographers, and publishers just as their use in advertisements, for instance the writers and publishers of the New Yorker magazine in *Sidis v. F-R Pub. Corporation.* [. . .] Publication of an accident victim's photograph is not appropriation for commercial use simply because the medium itself is operated for profit.

There is another reason why an unauthorized use of a person's name or image to sell goods or services can be a tortious appropriation when the same use in the content of material published to be sold is not. The use may make it appear that the person has consented to endorse the advertised product, with or without being paid to do so. When that impression is in fact false, the appropriation of the person's identity places the person in a false light [. . . .] Such an inference is most likely to be drawn about professional performers, who are widely known to be paid for endorsing products in print and television advertisements and even for using their sponsors' sports clothes and equipment in their work. [. . .] This theory is not available, however, to a person whose image, with no established public familiarity, appears in a commercial context only incidentally, perhaps as one of several persons in a public scene, or otherwise under circumstances that plainly are not presented so as to convey any endorsement by that person.

What is the distinction between *Anderson v. Fisher Broadcasting Co.* and *White v. Samsung Electronics?*

2. *The human cannonball.* In Zacchini v. Scripps-Howard Broadcasting Co., 433 U.S. 562 (1977), the plaintiff, Hugo Zacchini, was the performer of a carnival act in which he was shot from a cannon into a net 200 feet away. In

this case he was performing at the Geauga County Fair in Ohio. A reporter from one of the defendant's television stations attended the fair with a video camera. Zacchini asked the reporter not to film his performance, but the reporter did so; the station's daily newscast then aired the tape, which included all 15 seconds of Zacchini's act. The newscaster described the act as a "thriller" and said that "you really need to see it in person" to appreciate it. Zacchini sued for invasion of privacy. The Ohio Supreme Court found that Zacchini's *prima facie* case was strong enough to get him to a jury, but that the broadcast of his act was privileged by the First Amendment as a matter of public interest. The United States Supreme Court reversed:

> Wherever the line in particular situations is to be drawn between media reports that are protected and those that are not, we are quite sure that the First and Fourteenth Amendments do not immunize the media when they broadcast a performer's entire act without his consent. The Constitution no more prevents a State from requiring respondent to compensate petitioner for broadcasting his act on television than it would privilege respondent to film and broadcast a copyrighted dramatic work without liability to the copyright owner.
>
> The broadcast of a film of petitioner's entire act poses a substantial threat to the economic value of that performance. As the Ohio court recognized, this act is the product of petitioner's own talents and energy, the end result of much time, effort, and expense. Much of its economic value lies in the "right of exclusive control over the publicity given to his performance"; if the public can see the act free on television, it will be less willing to pay to see it at the fair. The effect of a public broadcast of the performance is similar to preventing petitioner from charging an admission fee. "The rationale for (protecting the right of publicity) is the straightforward one of preventing unjust enrichment by the theft of good will. No social purpose is served by having the defendant get free some aspect of the plaintiff that would have market value and for which he would normally pay." Kalven, *Privacy in Tort Law: Were Warren and Brandeis Wrong?*, 31 Law & Contemp. Prob. 326, 331 (1966). Moreover, the broadcast of petitioner's entire performance, unlike the unauthorized use of another's name for purposes of trade or the incidental use of a name or picture by the press, goes to the heart of petitioner's ability to earn a living as an entertainer. Thus, in this case, Ohio has recognized what may be the strongest case for a "right of publicity" involving, not the appropriation of an entertainer's reputation to enhance the attractiveness of a commercial product, but the appropriation of the very activity by which the entertainer acquired his reputation in the first place.
>
> Of course, Ohio's decision to protect petitioner's right of publicity here rests on more than a desire to compensate the performer for the time and effort invested in his act; the protection provides an economic incentive

for him to make the investment required to produce a performance of interest to the public. [...]

What is the distinction between *Zacchini v. Scripps-Howard Broadcasting Co.* and *Anderson v. Fisher Broadcasting Co.?*

3. *Falsehoods.* In Eastwood v. National Enquirer, 198 Cal. Rptr. 342 (Cal. App. 1984), Clint Eastwood, the famous actor, was featured in a cover story by the *National Enquirer.* On the cover were the words "Clint Eastwood in Love Triangle with Tanya Tucker" beneath a picture of Eastwood and Tucker together. The story inside said that Eastwood was "involved in a romantic tug-of-war" between Tucker, a country music singer, and Sandra Locke, an actress. It reported various details, such as Eastwood's "fun-filled romantic evenings" with Tucker, Locke's camping at Eastwood's doorstep and begging him to keep her, and more along the same lines. Eastwood sued the *Enquirer* for invasion of privacy, claiming that the story was false and that the *Enquirer* published it with "actual malice" (i.e., that the magazine either knew the story was false or was reckless as to its truth or falsity). Among other things he claimed damages for the unauthorized commercial appropriation of his name and likeness. The trial court dismissed those claims; the court of appeals reversed:

> *Enquirer* argues that the failure of Eastwood to allege the appearance of an "endorsement" of the *Enquirer* is fatal to stating a cause of action for commercial appropriation. [...] [T]he appearance of an "endorsement" is not the *sine qua non* of a claim for commercial appropriation. [...] Here, the *Enquirer* used Eastwood's personality and fame on the cover of the subject publication and in related telecast advertisements. To the extent their use attracted the readers' attention, the *Enquirer* gained a commercial advantage. [...]
>
> We have no doubt that the subject of the *Enquirer* article (the purported romantic involvements of Eastwood with other celebrities) is a matter of public concern, which would generally preclude the imposition of liability. However, Eastwood argues that the article, and thereby the related advertisements, are not entitled to either constitutional protection or exemption from liability as a news account because the article is a calculated falsehood.
>
> The spacious interest in an unfettered press is not without limitation. This privilege is subject to the qualification that it shall not be so exercised as to abuse the rights of individuals. [...] [W]herever the line in a particular situation is to be drawn between news accounts that are protected and those that are not, we are quite sure that the First Amendment does not immunize *Enquirer* when the entire article is allegedly false.

What is the distinction between *Eastwood v. National Enquirer* and *Anderson v. Fisher Broadcasting Co.?*

4. *Artistic expression.* In Rogers v. Grimaldi, 695 F. Supp. 112 (S.D.N.Y. 1988), *aff'd*, 875 F.2d 994 (2d Cir. 1989), Federico Fellini directed a movie called "Ginger and Fred." The film was a work of fiction depicting a reunion of two retired Italian dancers who once had made a living in cabarets imitating Ginger Rogers and Fred Astaire, and thus had earned the nicknames Ginger and Fred. In the movie the two fictitious dancers are called upon to reprise a dance routine on television that they have not performed for 30 years. Ginger Rogers sued for invasion of privacy on a misappropriation theory. The district court gave summary judgment to the defendants:

> [T]he relevance of "Ginger" in both the Film's title and screenplay is apparent at two levels. First, the title accurately refers to the fictionalized nicknames of the Film's two central characters. Second, the screenplay establishes the reference to Rogers and Astaire as the basis for the Film's characters' livelihood and thereby recognizes the Rogers and Astaire phenomenon as a known element of modern culture.
>
> In addition, the record here establishes that the Film's satirical vision of television entertainment in the 1980's rests in part on the contrast provided by the old hoofers' imitation of Hollywood entertainment in a bygone era. The director's affidavit evinces Fellini's intent to evoke an American cultural symbol the existence of which Rogers concedes in her complaint. There is nothing in the record to suggest that Fellini intended to use Rogers' name to deceive the public into flocking to his movie under the mistaken belief that the Film was about the true Rogers and Astaire. [. . .]
>
> [Rogers' claims] fail as a matter of law because the Film is a work of protected artistic expression. It is not an "ordinary subject of commerce," a simple "commodity" or a piece of "merchandise." Under the cited authorities, the Film does not meet the requirements for "trade or advertising" or an "advertisement in disguise" for a "collateral commercial product." Thus, the Film enjoys the full protection of the First Amendment.

The court of appeals affirmed. What is the distinction between *Rogers v. Grimaldi* and *White v. Samsung Electronics?*

5. *Enrichment vs. exploitation.* In Estate of Presley v. Russen, 513 F. Supp. 1339 (D.N.J. 1981), the defendant was the producer of "The Big El Show," a concert featuring an Elvis Presley impersonator performing Presley's music. The impersonator wore his hair in Presley's style, wore the same sorts of clothes that Presley did, and imitated Presley's body movements and style of

singing; the district court found that when photographs of the real Presley and the imitator were put side by side, it was difficult to tell which was which. Presley's estate sued on various theories, including misappropriation. The district court entered a preliminary injunction against the defendant's performances, finding the plaintiff likely to succeed on the merits after trial:

> [T]he purpose of the portrayal in question must be examined to determine if it predominantly serves a social function valued by the protection of free speech. If the portrayal mainly serves the purpose of contributing information, which is not false or defamatory, to the public debate of political or social issues or of providing the free expression of creative talent which contributes to society's cultural enrichment, then the portrayal generally will be immune from liability. If, however, the portrayal functions primarily as a means of commercial exploitation, then such immunity will not be granted. [. . .]
>
> In the present case, the defendant's expressive activity, THE BIG EL SHOW production, does not fall clearly on either side. Based on the current state of the record, the production can be described as a live theatrical presentation or concert designed to imitate a performance of the late Elvis Presley. The show stars an individual who closely resembles Presley and who imitates the appearance, dress, and characteristic performing style of Elvis Presley. The defendant has made no showing, nor attempted to show, that the production is intended to or acts as a parody, burlesque, satire, or criticism of Elvis Presley. As a matter of fact, the show is billed as "A TRIBUTE TO ELVIS PRESLEY." In essence, we confront the question of whether the use of the likeness of a famous deceased entertainer in a performance mainly designed to imitate that famous entertainer's own past stage performances is to be considered primarily as a commercial appropriation by the imitator or show's producer of the famous entertainer's likeness or as a valuable contribution of information or culture. After careful consideration of the activity, we have decided that although THE BIG EL SHOW contains an informational and entertainment element, the show serves primarily to commercially exploit the likeness of Elvis Presley without contributing anything of substantial value to society.

What is the distinction between *Estate of Presley v. Russen* and *Rogers v. Grimaldi*?

6. *Parodies.* In Cardtoons, L.C. v. Major League Baseball Players Association, 95 F.3d 959 (10th Cir. 1996), Cardtoons was a producer of trading cards. The cards featured caricatures of major league baseball players on the front and satirical commentary about their careers on the back. One of the cards, for example, lampooned the famous player Rickey Henderson; it depicted a player resembling him but named "Egotisticky Henderson."

The character on the card was patting himself on the back, and was accompanied by text in which Henderson presented an award to himself and, wiping tears from his eyes, congratulated himself for all that he had accomplished.

The MLBPA, acting as assignee of the publicity rights of all major league ballplayers, threatened to sue Cardtoons, which in turn sought a declaratory judgment establishing its right to produce the cards. The district court gave judgment to the defendant; the Tenth Circuit affirmed, finding that Cardtoons had invaded the baseball players' rights of publicity but that the invasion was privileged by the First Amendment:

> Cardtoons' interest in publishing its parody trading cards implicates some of the core concerns of the First Amendment. "Parodies and caricatures," noted Aldous Huxley, "are the most penetrating of criticisms." A parodist can, with deft and wit, readily expose the foolish and absurd in society. Parody is also a valuable form of self-expression that allows artists to shed light on earlier works and, at the same time, create new ones. Thus, parody, both as social criticism and a means of self-expression, is a vital commodity in the marketplace of ideas. [. . .]
>
> Because celebrities are an important part of our public vocabulary, a parody of a celebrity does not merely lampoon the celebrity, but exposes the weakness of the idea or value that the celebrity symbolizes in society. Cardtoons' trading cards, for example, comment on the state of major league baseball by turning images of our sports heroes into modern-day personifications of avarice. In order to effectively criticize society, parodists need access to images that mean something to people, and thus celebrity parodies are a valuable communicative resource. Restricting the use of celebrity identities restricts the communication of ideas. [. . .]
>
> The incentive effect of publicity rights [. . .] has been overstated. Most sports and entertainment celebrities with commercially valuable identities engage in activities that themselves generate a significant amount of income; the commercial value of their identities is merely a by-product of their performance values. [. . .] The argument that publicity rights provide valuable incentives is even less compelling in the context of celebrity parodies. Since celebrities will seldom give permission for their identities to be parodied, granting them control over the parodic use of their identities would not directly provide them with any additional income. It would, instead, only allow them to shield themselves from ridicule and criticism. The only economic incentive gained by having control over the use of one's identity in parody is control over the potential effect the parody would have on the market for nonparodic use of one's identity. MLBPA claims, for example, that publication of the parody cards will decrease demand for traditional baseball cards because Cardtoons and other makers of parody trading cards would compete with manufacturers of licensed cards in the same limited trading card market. Parody,

however, rarely acts as a market substitute for the original, and there is no evidence in this record that convinces us otherwise. Even if there is some substitutive effect, and card collectors with limited resources decide to buy parody cards instead of traditional, licensed cards, the small amount of additional income generated by suppressing parody cards will have little, if any, effect on the incentive to become a major league baseball player.

The incentives argument would be even more tenuous, indeed perverse, if good-humored celebrities were to license use of their identities for parody. The right of publicity would then provide an incentive to engage in the socially undesirable behavior that might give rise to a reason to parody. Although part of any parody's market appeal depends upon the prominence of the celebrity, the critical element of the parody's value hinges on the accuracy of the caricature or criticism. Society does not have a significant interest in allowing a celebrity to protect the type of reputation that gives rise to parody.

What is the distinction between *Cardtoons, L.C. v. Major League Baseball Players Association* and *White v. Samsung Electronics*? What is the distinction between the *Cardtoons* case and *Estate of Presley v. Russen*?

7. *Puns.* In Carson v. Here's Johnny Portable Toilets, Inc., 698 F.2d 831 (6th Cir. 1983), the plaintiff, Johnny Carson, was a famous comedian and host of *The Tonight Show*; his broadcasts always began with his sidekick, Ed McMahon, announcing, "Here's Johnny." The defendant was a maker of portable restrooms. The defendant's founder admitted that he chose the name "Here's Johnny" for his firm because it was Carson's slogan on his television program. He said he coupled those words with a second pun, "the World's Foremost Commodian," to make "a good play on a phrase." Carson sued the defendant on a misappropriation theory, alleging that it had invaded his right of publicity. After a bench trial the district court gave judgment to the defendant, finding that Carson's right to publicity extended only to his name and likeness. The Sixth Circuit reversed:

> It is not fatal to appellant's claim that appellee did not use his "name." Indeed, there would have been no violation of his right of publicity even if appellee had used his name, such as "J. William Carson Portable Toilet" or the "John William Carson Portable Toilet" or the "J. W. Carson Portable Toilet." The reason is that, though literally using appellant's "name," the appellee would not have appropriated Carson's identity as a celebrity. Here there was an appropriation of Carson's identity without using his "name."
>
> [A]ppellant Carson's achievement has made him a celebrity which means that his identity has a pecuniary value which the right of publicity should vindicate. Vindication of the right will tend to encourage

achievement in Carson's chosen field. Vindication of the right will also tend to prevent unjust enrichment by persons such as appellee who seek commercially to exploit the identity of celebrities without their consent.

What is the distinction between *Carson v. Here's Johnny Portable Toilets, Inc.* and *Rogers v. Grimaldi*? What is the distinction between *Carson v. Here's Johnny Portable Toilets* and *Cardtoons, L.C. v. Major League Baseball Players Association*?

8. *Commemorative posters (problem)*. In Montana v. San Jose Mercury News, 40 Cal. Rptr. 2d 639 (Cal. App. 1995), the plaintiff was Joe Montana, quarterback for the San Francisco 49ers football team. In 1990, after the 49ers won their fourth Super Bowl, the defendant newspaper published a "souvenir section" commemorating the occasion. The front page of the section featured an artist's rendering of Montana. Within two weeks the newspaper had reproduced the picture of Montana in poster form and was selling the posters to the public for five dollars apiece. Montana sued for invasion of privacy on a misappropriation theory. What result?

E.   FALSE LIGHT

Restatement (Second) of Torts

§652E.   PUBLICITY PLACING PERSON IN FALSE LIGHT

One who gives publicity to a matter concerning another that places the other before the public in a false light is subject to liability to the other for invasion of his privacy, if
    (a) the false light in which the other was placed would be highly offensive to a reasonable person, and
    (b) the actor had knowledge of or acted in reckless disregard as to the falsity of the publicized matter and the false light in which the other would be placed.

Caveat: The Institute takes no position on whether there are any circumstances under which recovery can be obtained under this Section if the actor did not know of or act with reckless disregard as to the falsity of the matter publicized and the false light in which the other would be placed but was negligent in regard to these matters.

Comment a. Nature of Section. The form of invasion of privacy covered by the rule stated in this Section does not depend upon making public any facts concerning the private life of the individual. On the contrary, it is essential to the rule stated in this Section that the matter published concerning the plaintiff is not true. The rule stated here is, however, limited to the situation in which the plaintiff is given publicity. [. . .]

Comment b. Relation to defamation. The interest protected by this Section is the interest of the individual in not being made to appear before the public in an objectionable false light or false position, or in other words, otherwise than as he is. In many cases to which the rule stated here applies, the publicity given to the plaintiff is defamatory, so that he would have an action for libel or slander under the rules stated in Chapter 24. In such a case the action for invasion of privacy will afford an alternative or additional remedy, and the plaintiff can proceed upon either theory, or both, although he can have but one recovery for a single instance of publicity.

It is not, however, necessary to the action for invasion of privacy that the plaintiff be defamed. It is enough that he is given unreasonable and highly objectionable publicity that attributes to him characteristics, conduct or beliefs that are false, and so is placed before the public in a false position. When this is the case and the matter attributed to the plaintiff is not defamatory, the rule here stated affords a different remedy, not available in an action for defamation.

Illustration 3. A is a renowned poet. B publishes in his magazine a spurious inferior poem, signed with A's name. Regardless of whether the poem is so bad as to subject B to liability for libel, B is subject to liability to A for invasion of privacy.

Comment c. Highly offensive to a reasonable person. The rule stated in this Section applies only when the publicity given to the plaintiff has placed him in a false light before the public, of a kind that would be highly offensive to a reasonable person.

Illustration 7. A and other police officers of a city maintain in the police department a "Rogues Gallery" of photographs, fingerprints and records of those convicted of crime. B is accused of robbery, arrested, fingerprinted and jailed. He is released when the accusation proves to be a matter of mistaken identity and another man is convicted of the crime. Although B never has been convicted of any crime, A insists, over B's objection, in including B's photograph and fingerprints in the Rogues Gallery. A has invaded the privacy of B.

Illustration 9. A is the pilot of an airplane flying across the Pacific. The plane develops motor trouble, and A succeeds in landing it after harrowing hours in the air. B Company broadcasts over television a dramatization of the flight, which enacts it in most respects in an accurate manner. Included in the broadcast, however, are scenes, known to B to be false, in which an actor representing A is shown as praying, reassuring passengers, and otherwise conducting himself in a fictitious manner that does not defame him or in any way reflect upon him. Whether this is an invasion of A's privacy depends upon whether it is found by the jury that the scenes would be highly objectionable to a reasonable man in A's position.

NOTES

1. *Desperate hours.* In Time, Inc. v. Hill, 385 U.S. 374 (1967), the family of the plaintiff, James Hill, was taken hostage in their home outside Philadelphia by three escaped convicts in 1952. After 19 hours they were released unharmed; they said afterwards that the convicts had treated them with courtesy and without violence. Though the plaintiffs soon moved to Connecticut and sought to avoid publicity, their story attracted considerable interest. It inspired a novel titled *The Desperate Hours,* and a play based on the novel. *Life* magazine reported on the play in one of its issues; its report ran in part as follows:

> Three years ago Americans all over the country read about the desperate ordeal of the James Hill family, who were held prisoners in their home outside Philadelphia by three escaped convicts. Later they read about it in Joseph Hayes's novel, *The Desperate Hours,* inspired by the family's experience. Now they can see the story re-enacted in Hayes's Broadway play based on the book, and next year will see it in his movie, which has been filmed but is being held up until the play has a chance to pay off.
>
> The play, directed by Robert Montgomery and expertly acted, is a heart-stopping account of how a family rose to heroism in a crisis. LIFE photographed the play during its Philadelphia tryout, transported some of the actors to the actual house where the Hills were besieged. On the next page scenes from the play are re-enacted on the site of the crime.

The pictures on the subsequent pages included an enactment of Hill's son being "roughed up" by one of the convicts, entitled "brutish convict"; a picture of his daughter biting the hand of a convict to make him drop a gun, entitled "daring daughter"; and a picture of the father throwing his gun through the door after a "brave try" to save his family is foiled.

Hill sued the publisher of *Life* magazine for invasion of privacy on a false light theory. The complaint alleged that the *Life* article was intended, to, and did, give the impression that the play *The Desperate Hours* mirrored the Hill family's experience, which, to the knowledge of the defendant, "was false and untrue." The defendant argued that the article was "a subject of legitimate news interest" and that it was "published in good faith without any malice whatsoever." A jury brought in a verdict for the plaintiff, and the trial court entered judgment upon it. The United States Supreme Court set the verdict aside and remanded for a new trial:

> We hold that the constitutional protections for speech and press preclude the application of the New York statute to redress false reports of matters of public interest in the absence of proof that the defendant published the report with knowledge of its falsity or in reckless disregard of the truth.

The guarantees for speech and press are not the preserve of political expression or comment upon public affairs, essential as those are to healthy government. One need only pick up any newspaper or magazine to comprehend the vast range of published matter which exposes persons to public view, both private citizens and public officials. Exposure of the self to others in varying degrees is a concomitant of life in a civilized community.

The risk of this exposure is an essential incident of life in a society which places a primary value on freedom of speech and of press. [. . .] As James Madison said, "Some degree of abuse is inseparable from the proper use of every thing, and in no instance is this more true than in that of the press." We create a grave risk of serious impairment of the indispensable service of a free press in a free society if we saddle the press with the impossible burden of verifying to a certainty the facts associated in news articles with a person's name, picture or portrait, particularly as related to nondefamatory matter. Even negligence would be a most elusive standard, especially when the content of the speech itself affords no warning of prospective harm to another through falsity. A negligence test would place on the press the intolerable burden of guessing how a jury might assess the reasonableness of steps taken by it to verify the accuracy of every reference to a name, picture or portrait.

In this context, sanctions against either innocent or negligent misstatement would present a grave hazard of discouraging the press from exercising the constitutional guarantees. Those guarantees are not for the benefit of the press so much as for the benefit of all of us. A broadly defined freedom of the press assures the maintenance of our political system and an open society. Fear of large verdicts in damage suits for innocent or merely negligent misstatement, even fear of the expense involved in their defense, must inevitably cause publishers to "steer . . . wider of the unlawful zone," *New York Times Co. v. Sullivan*, 376 U.S. at 279, and thus create the danger that the legitimate utterance will be penalized.

But the constitutional guarantees can tolerate sanctions against calculated falsehood without significant impairment of their essential function. We held in *New York Times* that calculated falsehood enjoyed no immunity in the case of alleged defamation of a public official concerning his official conduct. Similarly, calculated falsehood should enjoy no immunity in the situation here presented us. [. . .]

Turning to the facts of the present case, the proofs reasonably would support either a jury finding of innocent or merely negligent misstatement by *Life*, or a finding that *Life* portrayed the play as a reenactment of the Hill family's experience reckless of the truth or with actual knowledge that the portrayal was false. [. . .] We do not think, however, that the instructions confined the jury to a verdict of liability based on a finding that the statements in the article were made with knowledge of their falsity or in reckless disregard of the truth.

2. *Absence of malice.* For an example of the implications of *Time, Inc. v. Hill*, consider Zeran v. Diamond Broadcasting, Inc., 203 F.3d 714 (10th Cir. 2000), where the plaintiff was the victim of a hoax (a case related to this one is presented in the chapter on defamation). Shortly after the bombing of the Alfred P. Murrah federal building in Oklahoma City, a posting appeared on an Internet bulletin board announcing the sale of "Naughty Oklahoma T-Shirts" containing tasteless slogans. One of them read "Visit Oklahoma — It's a Blast"; another said "Rack'em, Stack'em and Pack'em — Oklahoma 1995"; another crudely referenced the children killed in the bombing. The posting said that the shirts could be ordered by telephone. The phone number listed belonged to the plaintiff in Seattle. The plaintiff had nothing to do with the posting, however; it was created by someone who opened a trial account on America Online using a false name and whose real identity was never discovered. The plaintiff began to receive harassing phone calls and immediately asked America Online to remove the postings, but they remained on the Internet for a week.

The defendant owned KRXO, a radio station in Oklahoma City. The station broadcast a morning talk show called the "Shannon and Spinozi show." One of the hosts, Shannon, received an email that contained the posting about the T-shirts. He did not attempt to call the number it listed because (he said) it was before business hours. Shannon read the posting on the air, including the plaintiff's telephone number. He urged his listeners to call "Ken ZZ03" (the name given on the posting; the plaintiff's name, Kenneth Zeran, was not used in the posting or on the air) and tell him what they thought of him for offering such products. On that day the plaintiff received approximately 80 angry phone calls laced with obscenities. He had to be put on anti-anxiety medication as a result, and later described it as the worst day of his life. He sued the defendant for invasion of privacy on a false light theory. The district court gave summary judgment to the defendant, and the court of appeals affirmed:

> The district court granted summary judgment to Defendant on this claim on the ground that Plaintiff had failed to offer proof that Defendant's employees either knew the postings were fictitious or acted recklessly, as that term is defined by the controlling authorities. The district court was influenced by the fact that Plaintiff's own expert found that they did not satisfy the level of culpability necessary to impose liability, opining only that "Mark Shannon and Ron Benton were extremely negligent and violated standards of professional conduct when hosting the Shannon and Spinozi Show on May 1, 1995." We affirm on the same basis.
>
> In order to establish reckless disregard, Plaintiff must demonstrate actual knowledge of probable falsity. "The only extent that an investigation enters into the consideration of the premises is if the investigation is made and through it, actual knowledge is imparted." *Jurkowski v. Crawley*, 637 P.2d 56, 60 (Okla.1981). [. . .] Plaintiff's expert's affidavit,

regardless of its content, is not relevant for the same reason. Plaintiff's expert could not possibly have had personal knowledge concerning the relevant question, namely, whether Shannon and Spinozi had an actual, subjective awareness that what they were repeating on the air was probably false.

3. *Larry Flynt's niche.* In Douglass v. Hustler Magazine, 769 F.2d 1128 (7th Cir. 1985) (also considered in the chapter on damages), the plaintiff, Robyn Douglass, was an actress and model. In 1974 she posed in the nude for a photographer named Augustin Gregory. The pictures were intended for a feature in *Playboy* magazine. In subsequent years Douglass appeared in *Playboy* eight times, and also found work in commercials and movies; she had a starring role in the movie *Breaking Away.* Meanwhile Gregory became the photography editor at *Hustler* magazine. In 1981 *Hustler* published photographs from the Gregory's 1974 sessions with Douglass. When Douglass complained to *Hustler* that it had no authority to publish pictures of her, the magazine produced releases Gregory had supplied to them that she appeared to have signed. Douglass sued *Hustler* for invasion of privacy, claiming that the magazine had cast her in a false light and also appropriated her commercial right to her likeness. Her evidence was that the releases Gregory supplied to *Hustler* were forgeries and that publication of her pictures in *Hustler* had caused her emotional distress as well as ending her career in Chicago because advertisers thought she had voluntarily appeared in what they considered an extremely vulgar magazine. An economist testified that the present value of Douglass's lost earnings from the publication was $716,565 at the time of trial. The trial court entered judgment on a verdict for Douglass, and the court of appeals affirmed the finding of liability:

> Douglass argues that the *Hustler* feature casts her in a false light [because it] insinuates that she is the kind of person willing to be shown naked in *Hustler*. Nothing in the feature itself suggests that the nude photographs of her are appearing without her permission and against her will, and readers might well assume that she had cooperated in the preparation of the feature in order to stimulate interest in her films. Moreover, she had been described in a previous issue of *Hustler* as a forthcoming "Hustler celebrity-exclusive," and in another issue *Hustler*'s chairman, Larry Flynt, had announced in an editorial column that he does not publish photographs of women without their consent. It is (or so a jury could find) as if *Hustler* had said, "Robyn Douglass is proud to pose nude for *Hustler* magazine." To complete this part of her argument Douglass asserts that voluntary association with *Hustler* as a nude model is degrading. [. . .]
>   The question whether she was [. . .] being depicted in a degrading association with *Hustler* invites attention to the difference between libel and false light. It would have been difficult for Douglass to state this claim as one for libel. For what exactly is the imputation of saying (or here,

implying) of a person that she agreed to have pictures of herself appear in a vulgar and offensive magazine? That she is immoral? This would be too strong a characterization in today's moral climate. That she lacks good taste? This would not be defamatory. The point is, rather, that to be shown nude in such a setting before millions of people — the readers of the magazine — is degrading in much the same way that to be shown beaten up by criminals is degrading (although not libelous, despite the analogy to being reported to have been raped), though of course if Douglass consented to appear nude in this setting she is responsible for her own debasement and can get no judicial redress.

Hustler argues that publication of "Robyn Douglass Nude" could not be degrading to one who had posed nude for *Playboy*. This fact distinguishes the case from the two cases that give the most support to Douglass's false-light claim: *Wood v. Hustler Magazine, Inc.*, 736 F.2d 1084 (5th Cir. 1984), where the plaintiff was not a model or actress and her nude photo (taken by her husband) had not been published previously and had not been intended to be published; and *Braun v. Flynt*, 726 F.2d 245 (5th Cir. 1984), where the photo of the plaintiff that was published on the same page with offensive matter in another "provocative" magazine published by Flynt (*Chic*) was not a nude photo; the plaintiff was wearing a bathing suit. (It should be apparent by now that this little niche of the law of privacy is dominated by Larry Flynt's publications.)

To evaluate *Hustler*'s contention required the jury to compare the two magazines. [The court reviewed in detail the contents of sample copies of *Playboy* and *Hustler*.] Although many people find *Playboy*, with its emphasis on sex and nudity, offensive, the differences between it and *Hustler* are palpable. *Playboy*, like *Hustler*, contains nude pictorials, but the erotic theme is generally muted, though there are occasional photographs that an earlier generation would have considered definitely obscene. And unlike *Hustler*, *Playboy* does not carry sexual advertisements, does not ridicule racial or religious groups, and avoids repulsive photographs — though most of the jokes and cartoons have sex as their theme, and not all are in good taste. We cannot say that it would be irrational for a jury to find that in the highly permissive moral and cultural climate prevailing in late twentieth-century America, posing nude for *Playboy* is consistent with respectability for a model and actress but that posing nude in *Hustler* is not (not yet, anyway), so that to portray Robyn Douglass as voluntarily posing nude for *Hustler* could be thought to place her in a false light even though she had voluntarily posed nude for *Playboy*.

What is the superficial similarity between *Douglass v. Hustler Magazine* and *Zeran v. Diamond Broadcasting, Inc.*? What is the distinction between them?

4. *Involuntary campaign appearances.* In Cox v. Hatch, 761 P.2d 556 (Utah 1988), the plaintiffs were postal workers in Utah. In 1982 Orrin Hatch,

a United States Senator from Utah, visited the plaintiffs' post office and they posed for pictures with him. One of the resulting photographs was printed in an eight-page political flier Hatch later distributed, the "Senator Orrin Hatch Labor Letter." The photograph was not captioned. The plaintiffs were shown smiling at Senator Hatch, who was looking at their work. The accompanying article presented claims that the Republican Party was committed to creating a better life for union members. The plaintiffs brought a suit alleging that the photograph reasonably could be construed as an implicit endorsement of Hatch on their part. They denied having endorsed him; indeed, because they were postal employees they were forbidden by federal law to publicly approve or endorse any political candidate or actively participate in a political campaign. They claimed that after the publication of the photograph, they were investigated by their employer and the union as to the extent of their involvement in Hatch's campaign.

The trial court dismissed the plaintiffs' claims, and the Utah Supreme Court affirmed. The court first held that the pictures and their use was not defamatory:

> The tort of defamation protects only reputation. A publication is not defamatory simply because it is nettlesome or embarrassing to a plaintiff, or even because it makes a false statement about the plaintiff. Thus, an embarrassing, even though false, statement that does not damage one's reputation is not actionable as libel or slander. If no defamatory meaning can reasonably be inferred by reasonable persons from the communication, the action must be dismissed for failure to state a claim.
>
> Here, the photograph shows the plaintiffs with Senator Hatch in a work setting, and it appears in a political advertisement dealing with labor issues. At most, the photograph can be construed to imply that the plaintiffs are members of the Republican Party or that they supported Hatch's reelection. However, attribution of membership in a political party in the United States that is a mainstream party and not at odds with the fundamental social order is not defamatory, nor is attribution of support for a candidate from one of those parties.

The court then went on to affirm the dismissal the invasion of privacy claims as well:

> [The complaint fails to] state a claim for placing the plaintiffs in a "false light" under §652E. Under that section, the false light "must be highly offensive to a reasonable person." Restatement, supra, §652D. For essentially the same reasons that the photograph was not susceptible to a defamatory meaning, it was not "highly offensive to a reasonable person."

The Court also said that the claims properly were dismissed on First Amendment grounds: "we hold that pictures of public officials and candidates for public office taken in public or semi-public places with persons who either pose with them or who inadvertently appear in such pictures may not be made the basis for an invasion of privacy or abuse of personal identity action."

Note that Restatement §652E, Illustration 4, provides as follows:

> A is a Democrat. B induces him to sign a petition nominating C for office. A discovers that C is a Republican and demands that B remove his name from the petition. B refuses to do so and continues public circulation of the petition, bearing A's name. B is subject to liability to A for invasion of privacy.

Can the Restatement illustration be squared with *Cox v. Hatch*?

5. *The fertile centenarian.* In Peoples Bank & Trust Co. v. Globe International Publishing, Inc., 978 F.2d 1065 (8th Cir. 1992), the plaintiff was a 97-year-old woman living in the Ozarks of northern Arkansas. She delivered newspapers and operated a newsstand in the region for more than 50 years; she was well known there, and had occasionally been the subject of newspaper stories. The defendant was the publisher of a tabloid called the *Sun*, which ran a picture of the plaintiff on its cover with the headline "Pregnancy forces granny to quit work at age 101." The accompanying story featured another picture of the plaintiff along with a fictitious account of a woman in Australia named Audrey Wiles who was said to have quit her paper route at the age of 101 because an extramarital affair with a millionaire client on her route had left her pregnant. Readers were told that Wiles became pregnant by one "Will," a "reclusive millionaire" she met on her newspaper route: "I used to put Will's paper in the door when it rained, and one thing just kind of led to another."

This issue of the *Sun* was a sell-out in the part of Arkansas where the plaintiff lived. She brought suit for defamation, false light invasion of privacy, and outrage. The defendant claimed that the story and the paper in which it appeared reasonably must be understood as fictitious; the issue in question also contained articles about encounters between Winston Churchill and UFOs, etc. The jury found for the defendant on the defamation claim but for the plaintiff on the other claims. It awarded her $650,000 in compensatory damages and $850,000 in punitive damages. The trial court denied the defendant's motion for judgment as a matter of law, and the Eighth Circuit affirmed:

> Globe does not dispute that the published story was false; indeed, its principal defense is that the story was "pure fiction." Nor does Globe dispute that the story would be highly offensive to a reasonable person, or that it was in fact highly offensive to Mitchell. The central issue on appeal is the existence of actual malice: whether Globe intended, or recklessly failed to anticipate, that readers would construe the story as conveying actual facts or events concerning Mitchell. Globe contends

that, as a matter of law, no reader reasonably could construe the story as conveying actual facts about Mitchell, and that no evidence supports a finding that Globe intended that result. [. . .]

Globe argues only that the assertion of pregnancy could not reasonably be believed, and therefore must render the whole story an obvious, non-actionable "fiction." Every other aspect of the charged story, however — such as the implication of sexual impropriety and that Mitchell was quitting her life-long profession — is subject to reasonable belief. Even the report of the pregnancy — a physical condition, not an opinion, metaphor, fantasy, or surrealism — could be proved either true or false. In the context of this case, therefore, we cannot say as a matter of law that readers could not reasonably have believed that the charged story portrayed actual facts or events concerning Mitchell. We decline to reverse the verdict of the jury that arrived at the same conclusion. [. . .]

The format and style of the *Sun* suggest it is a factual newspaper. Globe advertises the *Sun* as publishing "the weird, the strange, and the outlandish *news* from around the globe," and nowhere in the publication does it suggest its stories are false or exaggerated. The *Sun* also mingles factual, fictional, and hybrid stories without overtly identifying one from the other. At trial, even its own writers could not tell which stories were true and which were completely fabricated.

The court remanded, however, for a reduction of the plaintiff's compensatory damages.

What is the distinction between *Peoples Bank & Trust Co. v. Globe International Publishing* and *Cox v. Hatch*?

6. *The personal character of the right.* In Mineer v. Williams, 82 F. Supp. 2d 702 (E.D. Ky. 2000), a woman named Erica Fraysure disappeared; various facts surrounding her disappearance caused authorities to suspect foul play. Fraysure's mother appeared on the Montel Williams show, a nationally syndicated television program, along with a psychic named Sylvia Browne. She asked Browne to use her psychic powers to determine Erica Fraysure's whereabouts and fate. Browne said there was someone who had information about Fraysure's disappearance, and that his name was "Chris." On the following day, an acquaintance of Fraysure's named Chris Mineer shot and killed his girlfriend and himself. (It was not alleged that he heard the television broadcast.) A few months later Sylvia Browne appeared again on Williams' show, and Williams implied that she correctly had implicated Mineer in Erica Fraysure's disappearance. Said Williams:

[Mineer] murdered his girlfriend and was implicated in the case that Sylvia talked about. So if you want to wonder whether or not this woman is talking fact or fiction, she gave up the name to this family during the break, and the next thing you know, the guy who probably committed the murder to begin with, realized the law is on my tail, he killed himself and his other girlfriend.

Chris Mineer's mother sued Williams for invasion of privacy on a false light theory; she alleged that Mineer never had been implicated by the police in Fraysure's disappearance. The court dismissed the claim because Mineer had died, relying on §6521 of the Restatement (Second) of Torts:

§6521. PERSONAL CHARACTER OF RIGHT OF PRIVACY

Except for the appropriation of one's name or likeness, an action for invasion of privacy can be maintained only by a living individual whose privacy is invaded.

Comment b. In the absence of statute, the action for the invasion of privacy cannot be maintained after the death of the individual whose privacy is invaded. In a few states particular statutes permit the survival of an action for invasion of privacy that has occurred before death. In a smaller number of states there is statutory authorization for an action on the part of surviving relatives for invasion of the privacy of one who is already deceased, with the invasion occurring after his death. Since appropriation of name or likeness is similar to impairment of a property right and involves an aspect of unjust enrichment of the defendants or his estate, survival rights may be held to exist following the death of either party.

What is the logic of this provision?

7. *Reservations.* Although a majority of jurisdictions recognize "false light" invasion of privacy claims, not all do. Some have rejected the cause of action on the ground that it overlaps heavily with defamation claims but without the many doctrines of defamation law that limit its reach and thus protect the freedom of speech. Thus in Cain v. Hearst Corp., 878 S.W.2d 577 (Tex. 1994), the Texas Supreme Court rejected false light as a theory of liability:

Actions for defamation in Texas are subject to numerous procedural and substantive hurdles. For example, accounts of governmental proceedings, public meetings dealing with a public purpose, or any "reasonable and fair comment on or criticism of an official act" are privileged under Texas Civil Practice & Remedies Code Section 73.002. Broadcasters are generally not liable in defamation for broadcasts made by third parties. Tex. Civ. Prac. & Rem. Code §73.004 (1986). Qualified privileges against defamation exist at common law when a communication is made in good faith and the author, the recipient or a third person, or one of their family members, has an interest that is sufficiently affected by the communication. A communication may also be conditionally privileged if it affects an important public interest. Damages awarded for defamatory statements may be mitigated by factors such as public apology, correction, or retraction. See also Restatement (Second) of Torts §652E cmt. e (1977) (listing other possible limitations on the defamation action, including bond posting requirements and proof of special damages).

These technical restrictions serve to safeguard the freedom of speech. Every defamation action that the law permits necessarily inhibits free speech. As the Supreme Court stated with respect to political speech in *New York Times v. Sullivan*, 376 U.S. 254, 272 (1964), "[w]hatever is added to the field of libel is taken from the field of free debate." While less compelling, these same considerations are also at play in private, non-political expression. Thus, the defamation action has been narrowly tailored to limit free speech as little as possible.

Courts in many jurisdictions have preserved their protection of speech by holding false light actions to the same strictures as defamation actions. As comment e to section 652E of the Restatement reasons:

> [w]hen the false publicity is also defamatory . . . it is arguable that limitations of long standing that have been found desirable for the action for defamation should not be successfully evaded by a proceeding upon a different theory of later origin, in the development of which the attention of the courts has not been directed to the limitations.

Permitting plaintiffs to bring actions for false light without the limits established for defamation actions may inhibit free speech beyond the permissible range. On the other hand, no useful purpose would be served by the separate tort if these restrictions are imposed. As the court observed in *Renwick v. News & Observer Publishing Co.*, 312 S.E.2d 405 (1984):

> Given the First Amendment limitations placed upon defamation actions by [*New York Times v.*] *Sullivan* and upon false light invasion of privacy actions by [*Time, Inc. v.*] *Hill*, we think that such additional remedies as we might be required to make available to plaintiffs should we recognize false light invasion of privacy claims are not sufficient to justify the recognition in this jurisdiction of such inherently constitutionally suspect claims for relief.

Hightower, J., dissented, concluding that the rule of *Time, Inc. v. Hill* was adequate to keep the false light tort within constitutional bounds.

Chapter 13

Nuisance

A *nuisance* arises in classic form when a landowner interferes with a neighbor's ability to use and enjoy his property. Though only a small corner of the law of torts, nuisances are of disproportionately great theoretical interest because they raise basic questions about liability in pointed form. Whereas much tort law involves a party being put at risk by the conduct of a stranger, nuisances typically involve two parties who know each other and live side by side, with one inflicting certain costs on the other. In this sense a nuisance might seem like just another intentional tort, but in nuisance cases the injury usually is a byproduct of some activity that may produce considerable public and private benefits, making analysis a challenge.

Note that a "public nuisance" is quite distinct from the private nuisances we will be considering here. A public nuisance involves a land use that is an offense against the state because it violates a law, typically a criminal statute. It can be abated on a suit by a prosecutor or public agency, but no private right to sue arises unless a party suffers "special" damages — damages distinct from those suffered by the public at large. Our concern here, by contrast, is with those nuisances one private party inflicts on another, and that can be redressed by — and in most cases only by — a lawsuit by the one against the other.

A. DEFINITIONS AND STANDARDS

Bamford v. Turnley
3 B.&S. 66, 122 Eng. Rep. 27 (Ex. Ch. 1862)

[The plaintiff claimed that the defendant, his neighbor, was committing a nuisance by using his land for making bricks.]

POLLOCK, C.B. The question in this case is, whether the direction of the Lord Chief Justice, professing to be founded on the decision of the Court of Common Pleas in *Hole v. Barlow* (4 C.B.N.S. 334) [an earlier nuisance case involving brickmaking, in which defendant prevailed], was right, and in my judgment substantially it was right, viz., taking it to have been as stated in the case, viz., "that if the jury thought that the spot was convenient and proper, and the burning of the bricks was, under the circumstances, a reasonable use by the defendant of his own land, the defendant would be entitled to a verdict." I do not think that the nuisance for which an action will lie is capable of any legal definition which will be applicable to all cases and useful in deciding them. The question so entirely depends on the surrounding circumstances, — the place where, the time when, the alleged nuisance, what, the mode of committing it, how, and the duration of it, whether temporary or permanent, occasional or continual, — as to make it impossible to lay down any rule of law applicable to every case, and which will also be useful in assisting a jury to come to a satisfactory conclusion: — it must at all times be a question of fact with reference to all the circumstances of the case.

Most certainly in my judgment it cannot be laid down as a legal proposition or doctrine, that anything which, under any circumstances, lessens the comfort or endangers the health or safety of a neighbour, must necessarily be an actionable nuisance. That may be a nuisance in Grosvenor Square which would be none in Smithfield Market, that may be a nuisance at midday which would not be so at midnight, that may be a nuisance which is permanent and continual which would be no nuisance if temporary or occasional only. A clock striking the hour, or a bell ringing for some domestic purpose, may be a nuisance, if unreasonably loud and discordant, of which the jury alone must judge; but although not unreasonably loud, if the owner, from some whim or caprice, made the clock strike the hour every ten minutes, or the bell ring continually, I think a jury would be justified in considering it to be a very great nuisance. In general, a kitchen chimney, suitable to the establishment to which it belonged, could not be deemed a nuisance, but if built in an inconvenient place or manner, on purpose to annoy the neighbours, it might, I think, very properly be treated as one. The compromises that belong to social life, and upon which the peace and comfort of it mainly depend, furnish an indefinite number of examples where some apparent natural right is invaded, or some enjoyment abridged, to provide for the more general convenience or necessities of the whole community; and I think the more the details of the question are examined the more clearly it will appear that all that the law can do is to lay down some general and vague proposition which will be no guide to the jury in each particular case that may come before them. [...]

I think the word "reasonable" cannot be an improper word, and too vague to be used on this occasion, seeing that the question whether a contract has been reasonably performed with reference to time, place and subject matter, is one that is put to a jury almost as often as a jury is assembled. If the act complained of be done in a convenient manner, so as to give no unnecessary annoyance, and be a reasonable exercise of some apparent right, or a reasonable use of the land, house or property of the party under all the circumstances, in which I include the degree of inconvenience it will produce, then I think no action can be sustained, if the jury find that it was reasonable, — as the jury must be taken to have found that it was reasonable that the defendant should be allowed to do what he did, and reasonable that the plaintiff should submit to the inconvenience occasioned by what was done. [. . .]

[T]he judgment of the court below [for defendant] ought to be affirmed.

MARTIN, B. read the judgment of BRAMWELL, B. I am of opinion that this judgment should be reversed. The defendant has done that which, if done wantonly or maliciously, would be actionable as being a nuisance to the plaintiff's habitation by causing a sensible diminution of the comfortable enjoyment of it. This, therefore, calls on the defendant to justify or excuse what he has done. And his justification if this: He says that the nuisance is not to the health of the inhabitants of the plaintiff's house, that it is of a temporary character, and is necessary for the beneficial use of his, the defendant's land, and that the public good requires he should be entitled to do what he claims to do.

The question seems to me to be, Is this a justification in law, — and, in order not to make a verbal mistake, I will say, — a justification for what is done, or a matter which makes what is done no nuisance? It is to be borne in mind, however, that, in fact, the act of the defendant is a nuisance such that it would be actionable if done wantonly or maliciously. The plaintiff, then, has a prima facie case. The defendant has infringed the maxim Sic utere tuo ut alienum non laedas. Then, what principle or rule of law can he rely on to defend himself? It is clear to my mind that there is some exception to the general application of the maxim mentioned. The instances put during the argument, of burning weeds, emptying cesspools, making noises during repairs, and other instances which would be nuisances if done wantonly or maliciously, nevertheless may be lawfully done. It cannot be said that such acts are not nuisances, because, by the hypothesis, they are; and it cannot be doubted that, if a person maliciously and without cause made close to a dwelling-house the same offensive smells as may be made in emptying a cesspool, an action would lie. Nor can these cases be got rid of as extreme cases, because such cases properly test a principle. Nor can it be said that the jury settle such questions by finding there is no nuisance, though there is. For that is to suppose they violate their duty, and that, if they discharged their duty, such matters would be actionable, which I think they could not and ought not to be. There must be, then, some principle on which such cases must be excepted. It seems to me that that principle may be deduced from the character of these cases, and is this, viz., that those acts necessary for the common and ordinary use and occupation of land and houses may be done, if conveniently done, without subjecting those who do them to an action. This principle would comprehend all the cases I have mentioned, but would not comprehend the present, where what has been done was not the using of land in a common and ordinary way, but in an exceptional manner — not unnatural nor unusual, but not the common and ordinary use of land. There is an obvious necessity for such a principle as I have mentioned. It is as much for the advantage of one owner as of another; for the very nuisance the one complains of, as the result of the ordinary use of his neighbour's land, he himself will create in the ordinary use of his own, and the reciprocal nuisances are of a comparatively trifling character. The convenience of such a rule may be indicated by calling it a rule of give and take, live and let live.

Then can this principle be extended to, or is there any other principle which will comprehend, the present case? I know of none: it is for the defendant to shew it. None of the above reasoning is applicable to such a cause of nuisance as the present. It had occurred to me, that any not unnatural use of the land, if of a temporary character, might be justified; but I cannot see why its being of a temporary nature should warrant it. What is temporary, — one, five, or twenty years? If twenty, it would be difficult to say that a brick kiln in the direction of the prevalent wind for twenty years would not be as objectionable as a permanent one in the opposite direction. If temporary in order to build a house on the land, why not temporary in order to exhaust the brick earth? I cannot think then that the nuisance being temporary makes a difference.

But it is said that, temporary or permanent, it is lawful because it is for the public benefit. Now, in the first place, that law to my mind is a bad one which, for the public benefit, inflicts loss on an individual without compensation. But further, with great respect, I think this consideration misapplied in this and in many other cases. The public consists of all the individuals of it, and a thing is only for the public benefit when it is productive of good to those individuals on the balance of loss and gain to all. So that if all the loss and all the gain were borne and received by one individual, he on the whole would be a gainer. But whenever this is the case, — whenever a thing is for the public benefit, properly understood, — the loss to the individuals of the public who lose will bear compensation out of the gains of those who gain. It is for the public benefit there should be railways, but it would not be unless the gain of having the railway was sufficient to compensate the loss occasioned by the use of the land required for its site; and accordingly no one thinks it would be right to take an individual's land without compensation to make a railway. It is for the public benefit that trains should run, but not unless they pay their expenses. If one of those expenses is the burning down of a wood of such value that the railway owners would not run the train and burn down the wood if it were their own, neither is it for the public benefit they should if the wood is not their own. If, though the wood were their own, they still would find it compensated them to run trains at the cost of burning the wood, then they obviously ought to compensate the owner of such wood, not being themselves, if they burn it down making their gains. So in like way in this case a money value indeed cannot easily be put on the plaintiff's loss, but it is equal to some number of pounds or pence, £10, £50 or what not: unless the defendant's profits are enough to compensate this, I deny that it is for the public benefit he should do what he has done; if they are, he ought to compensate.

The only objection I can see to this reasoning is, that by injunction or by abatement of the nuisance a man who would not accept a pecuniary compensation might put a stop to works of great value, and much more than enough to compensate him. This objection, however, is comparatively of small practical importance; it may be that the law ought to be amended, and some means be provided to legalise such cases, as I believe is the case in some foreign countries on giving compensation; but I am clearly of opinion that, though the present law may be defective, it would be much worse, and be unjust and inexpedient, if it permitted such power of inflicting loss and damage to individuals, without compensation, as is claimed by the argument for the defendant.

In the result, then, I think it should be overruled, — which practically is the question here; and that our judgment should be for the plaintiff.

Judgment reversed, and entered for the plaintiff for 40s.

NOTES

1. *The obligation to compensate.* In Jost v. Dairyland Power Cooperative, 172 N.W.2d 647 (1970), the plaintiffs were farmers who lived near the defendant's coal-burning power plant. They alleged that sulfurous gases emitted by the defendant's operation damaged their crops: it whitened their alfalfa leaves, killed their pine trees, made it difficult to raise flowers, and damaged their apple trees, sumac, and grapes. The trial judge found these injuries substantial and awarded the plaintiffs damages for the resulting reduction in the market value of their properties. On appeal the defendant complained that it had not been allowed to put in evidence that it used due care in building and operating its plant, and that the plant's economic utility outweighed the costs it imposed on the plaintiffs. The Wisconsin Supreme Court rejected both claims and affirmed the judgment:

> There was no attempt to hinge plaintiffs' case on the theory that the defendant was not exercising due care. Under the plaintiffs' theory, which we deem to be a correct one, it is irrelevant that defendant was conforming to industry standards of due care if its conduct created a nuisance. [. . .] [F]reedom from negligence is no defense if the consequences of the continued conduct nevertheless cause substantial injury to a claimant. In any event it is apparent that a continued invasion of a plaintiff's interests by non-negligent conduct, when the actor knows of the nature of the injury inflicted, is an intentional tort, and the fact the hurt is administered non-negligently is not a defense to liability. [. . .]
>
> [T]he court properly excluded all evidence that tended to show the utility of the Dairyland Cooperative's enterprise. Whether its economic

or social importance dwarfed the claim of a small farmer is of no consequence in this lawsuit. It will not be said that, because a great and socially useful enterprise will be liable in damages, an injury small by comparison should go unredressed. We know of no acceptable rule of jurisprudence that permits those who are engaged in important and desirable enterprises to injure with impunity those who are engaged in enterprises of lesser economic significance. Even the government or other entities, including public utilities, endowed with the power of eminent domain — the power to take private property in order to devote it to a purpose beneficial to the public good — are obliged to pay a fair market value for what is taken or damaged. To contend that a public utility, in the pursuit of its praiseworthy and legitimate enterprise, can, in effect, deprive others of the full use of their property without compensation, poses a theory unknown to the law of Wisconsin, and in our opinion would constitute the taking of property without due process of law.

2. *The utility of the conduct.* In Carpenter v. Double R Cattle Company, 701 P.2d 222 (Idaho 1985), the plaintiffs resided near the defendants' cattle feedlot. Their evidence was that the feedlot was occupied by several thousand cows, and that it generated noxious odors, swarms of insects, and water pollution that damaged their properties. The trial judge instructed the jury to determine whether the defendants' invasion of the plaintiffs' rights was unreasonable, and said that the "gravity of any harm" and "utility of defendants' conduct" both should be weighed in making that determination. The court also instructed the jury to take into account "the interests of the community as a whole," the "general public good," and the "social value" of the defendants' conduct. The trial judge empaneled an advisory jury, and it brought in a verdict for the defendants; the trial court entered judgment upon the verdict. The plaintiffs appealed, claiming among other things that the jury improperly was told to balance the harm caused by the defendants against the utility of their conduct. The Idaho Supreme Court affirmed:

> [I]n a nuisance action seeking damages the interests of the community, which would include the utility of the conduct, should be considered in the determination of the existence of a nuisance. [. . .] The State of Idaho is sparsely populated and its economy depends largely upon the benefits of agriculture, lumber, mining and industrial development. To eliminate the utility of conduct and other factors listed by the trial court from the criteria to be considered in determining whether a nuisance exists, as the appellant has argued throughout this appeal, would place an unreasonable burden upon these industries. We see no policy reasons which should compel this Court to accept appellant's argument and depart from our present law. Accordingly, the judgment of the district court is affirmed and the Court of Appeals decision is set aside.

Bistline, J., dissented:

> The majority today continues to adhere to ideas on the law of nuisance that should have gone out with the use of buffalo chips as fuel. [. . .] The majority's rule today suggests that part of the cost of industry, agriculture or development must be borne by those unfortunate few who have the fortuitous luck to live in the immediate vicinity of a nuisance producing facility. Frankly, I think this naive economic view is ridiculous in both its simplicity and its outdated view of modern economic society. The "cost" of a product includes not only the amount it takes to produce such a product but also includes the external costs: the damage done to the environment through pollution of air or water is an example of an external cost. In the instant case, the nuisance suffered by the homeowners should be considered an external cost of operating a feedlot and producing beef for public consumption. I do not believe that a few should be required to pay this extra cost of doing business by going uncompensated for a nuisance of this sort. If a feedlot wants to continue, I say fine, providing compensation is paid for the serious invasion (the odors, flies, dust, etc.) of the homeowner's interest. My only qualification is that the financial burden of compensating for this harm should not be such as to force the feedlot (or any other industry) out of business. The true cost can then be shifted to the consumer who rightfully should pay for the *entire* cost of producing the product he desires to obtain.
>
> The majority today blithely suggests that because the State of Idaho is sparsely populated and because our economy is largely dependent on agriculture, lumber, mining and industrial development, we should forego compensating those who suffer a serious invasion. If humans are such a rare item in this state, maybe there is all the more reason to protect them from the discharge of industry.

3. *Strict liability vs. negligence.* The *Jost* and *Carpenter* cases illustrate competing traditions in the law of nuisance. The tradition epitomized by *Jost* imposes strict liability once substantial damage is found; when this standard is used, the assessment of whether the defendant's conduct is socially valuable comes into play at the remedial stage when deciding whether to award damages or an injunction — an issue we will consider later. The *Carpenter* case differs in permitting the value of the defendant's conduct to excuse the costs it imposes on the plaintiff. This latter approach can be termed a negligence standard, but the term may be misleading. First, the issue is not whether the defendant was careful or careless in a conventional sense; it is whether the utility of the defendant's conduct outweighs the burdens it creates for others. Second, notions of negligence typically are associated with the infliction of unintentional harm, while a nuisance is a variety of intentional tort. So perhaps the better word for the criterion used in

Carpenter is reasonableness. Which of these cases is consistent with the approach of Pollock, C.B., in *Bamford v. Turnley*, and which with the approach of Baron Bramwell?

Consider some difficulties that arise with each of these approaches. If a plaintiff wins under a strict liability approach, it might be said that the *defendant's* property usage therefore is being impaired, since the property no longer can be used for its former purpose. Why should the rights of the plaintiff extend so far? Isn't it a general lesson of negligence law that a defendant who inflicts harm on a plaintiff nevertheless escapes liability if preventing the accident would have cost more than allowing the accident to occur? And doesn't the application of that logic to nuisance cases suggest that the utility of the defendant's conduct should be relevant, and that it should sometimes excuse the conduct even where the damage to the plaintiff's property is significant? If you favor strict liability in nuisance cases, do you believe there is something wrong with negligence as a standard for tort liability more generally, or with the formulation of it just offered? Finally, how can strict liability be squared with the social need for factories, airports, and other uses of land that inevitably impose costs on nearby property owners?

If your instincts favor liability only for unreasonableness or negligence, what do you make of the dissent in the *Carpenter* case? Should not the price of a product reflect all the costs created by its manufacture? And doesn't mere liability for negligence — i.e., letting the value of the defendant's conduct excuse the damage it causes to others — give the defendant a private right to condemn the property of others for his own use, and without compensation? Notice that to make this last complaint hold up, one needs a baseline definition of "property" — in other words, an understanding of what rights come with ownership. Otherwise it is circular to say that the factory creates costs for its neighbors, or that the owners of the factory are condemning the property of the surrounding neighbors; for without a clear idea of what comes with a property right, it is possible to reply to both of those claims by arguing that the factory's owners are just exercising *their* rights. If a definition of those rights by reference to costs and benefits is rejected, what alternative is more attractive, and why?

4. *Epstein's theory.* Professor Epstein has suggested one way to relieve the tensions that strict liability creates. His view is that owners have certain rights in their property, including the right not to have their interests physically invaded by others — a right protected by a regime of strict liability. But he argues that the stringent requirement to compensate for such invasions can be relaxed as the following conditions become more prominent in a case:

1. High administrative costs for claim resolution;
2. High transaction costs for voluntary reassignment of rights;
3. Low value to the interested parties of the ownership rights whose rearrangement is mandated by the public rule;
4. Presence of implicit in-kind compensation from all to all that precludes any systematic redistribution of wealth among the interested parties.

Richard A. Epstein, *Nuisance Law: Corrective Justice and Its Utilitarian Constraints*, 8 J. Legal Stud. 49 (1979). The best examples of nuisances that Epstein's theory would excuse are those discussed in Bramwell's opinion in *Bamford v. Turnley*: "burning weeds, emptying cesspools, making noises during repairs," for which Bramwell would assign no liability because the right to do such things "is as much for the advantage of one owner as of another; for the very nuisance the one complains of, as the result of the ordinary use of his neighbour's land, he himself will create in the ordinary use of his own, and the reciprocal nuisances are of a comparatively trifling character." Says Epstein:

> [Bramwell's] rule of live and let live clearly satisfies the four requisites set out above for the abolition of the private cause of action without any form of explicit substitute compensation. The large number of interested private parties and the protean forms of nuisance-like behavior both make it extremely unlikely that private agreements could soften the rigors of a pure corrective justice theory of nuisance law. Likewise, the administrative costs needed to resolve those low-level claims within the legal system would be very high, particularly in light of the small amounts in controversy. Finally, there is a high degree of implicit in-kind compensation between parties. The nuisances here are of such common and frequent occurrence that it is safe to assume that virtually all persons will be in separate individual instances both wrongdoers and victims. The high frequency and low intensity of claims suggest that they will, in sharp contrast to the accident case, most likely balance out. Any special effort to award individual compensation would, no matter how approached, only eat up the wealth of all the interested parties, leaving them all worse off than before. In general, private causes of action should be abrogated, leaving only informal social pressures in their place.

An example of a decision departing from Epstein's approach is the English case of *Andreae v. Selfridge & Co.*, 1 Ch. 1 (1938). The defendants were owners of Selfridge's, a London department store. They bought property next to the plaintiff's hotel, the Wigmore, and set out to build a new store on the lot. To accomplish this they demolished the existing houses on the site and excavated 60 feet into the ground using cranes and pneumatic drills that generated enormous amounts of dust and grit. As a result the Wigmore lost business and eventually was sold to the defendants. The trial court awarded damages to the plaintiff for all costs imposed on it by the defendants' actions: "All these acts may be very convenient, but I think that if you build in that kind of way and demolish in that kind of way [and] have caused pecuniary loss to your neighbour it is but fair that you should compensate your neighbour for what you have done rather than that he should suffer." The court of appeals reversed and remanded, however, holding that the defendants should be liable only for the costs they imposed when they failed to use reasonable efforts to keep the damage they caused to a minimum:

> People coming to this hotel, who were accustomed to a quiet outlook at the back, coming back and finding demolition and building going on, may very well have taken the view that the particular merit of this hotel no longer existed. That would be a misfortune for the plaintiff; but assuming that there was nothing wrong in the defendant company's works, assuming the defendant company was carrying on the demolition and building, productive of noise though it might be, with all reasonable skill, and taking all reasonable precautions not to cause annoyance to its neighbours, then the plaintiff might lose all her clients in the hotel because they had lost the amenities of an open and quiet place behind, but she would have no cause of complaint.

Epstein's view of the appellate decision is unfavorable: "[The defendants' construction] far exceeded in magnitude the low-level harms to which the live and let live rule properly applies. Allowing the defendant a partial justification in *Andreae* worked a major and impermissible redistribution of wealth between strangers, for there is no remote likelihood, let alone real prospect, that the plaintiff would at some future time inflict an uncompensated harm of equal severity upon the defendant."

5. *Coase's theory.* Ronald Coase advanced a quite different vision of nuisance law in his celebrated paper *The Problem of Social Cost*, 3 J. Law & Econ. 1 (1960). Coase takes an economist's view of the subject: when there is a conflict between two parties' uses of some resource, the goal is to ensure that the more valuable use prevails. Indeed, Coase views this as the inevitable outcome in many instances because parties can continue to bargain with each other after their case has been adjudicated. Thus if bargaining between the parties is easy (i.e., if "transaction costs" are low), a court's decision is irrelevant from the standpoint of efficiency because the parties can bargain their way to the efficient result if the court's decision differs from it. For example, if the plaintiff values the right to be free from the defendant's noise or odors more than the defendant values the right to create them, the plaintiff either will win the right to shut down the defendant's operations or will lose in court but then pay the defendant to shut down. The court's decision will affect who pays whom but will not ultimately affect which party's use will yield to the other's. This is known as the Coase theorem: in a world of zero transaction costs, all rights would end up in the hands of whoever values them the most regardless of what the legal system says about who owns them. (There is no formal "theorem" stated in Coase's famous article; this is just an attempt to state the implications of his analysis.)

If ensuring that resources are put to their most valuable uses is taken to be the legal system's goal, conventional notions of "causation" — of which party is causing trouble to which — can come to seem vacuous. Coase illustrates the point by reference to the old English case of *Bryant v. Lefever*, 4 C.P.D. 172 (1879). The defendants built a house next to the plaintiff's property with a wall that blocked the flow of smoke out of the plaintiff's chimney and caused it to back up into the plaintiff's house. The court held that the defendants lawfully had used their property and so were not liable for the damage: "It is the plaintiff who causes the nuisance by lighting a coal fire in a place the chimney of which is placed so near the defendants' wall, that the smoke does not escape, but comes into the house." Coase analyzed the case as follows:

> The smoke nuisance was caused both by the man who built the wall *and* by the man who lit the fires. Given the fires, there would have been no smoke nuisance without the wall; given the wall, there would have been no smoke nuisance without the fires. Eliminate the wall *or* the fires and the smoke nuisance would disappear. On the marginal principle it is clear that *both* were responsible and *both* should be forced to include the loss of amenity due to the smoke as a cost in deciding whether to continue the activity which gives rise to the smoke. And given the possibility of market transactions, this is what would in fact happen. Although the wall-builder was not liable legally for the nuisance, as the man with the smoking chimneys would presumably be willing to pay a sum equal to the monetary worth to him of eliminating the smoke, this sum would therefore become for the wall-builder a cost of continuing to have the high wall[.]

On this view, the decisions of courts in nuisance cases often may seem irrelevant from the standpoint of efficiency. But Coase takes the point further and suggests that where bargaining between parties after judgment is not feasible, courts should use remedies to create the same outcome the parties would reach if they could bargain. In other words, the party who can put the rights to the more valuable use should prevail. Indeed, if the court can determine which party values the rights more it should assign them accordingly in all cases, thus saving the parties the cost of negotiating afterwards. These determinations would require difficult judgments about the value of neighbors' competing activities, but Coase suggests that precisely such judgments may lurk behind the legalisms that courts invoke when deciding nuisance cases. "The courts do not always refer very clearly to the economic problem posed by the cases brought before them but it seems probable that in the interpretation of words and phrases like 'reasonable' or 'common or ordinary use' there is some recognition, perhaps largely unconscious and certainly not very explicit, of the economic aspects of the questions at issue." As an example Coase cites with approval *Andreae v. Selfridge & Co.* — the same case Epstein condemns as an illegitimate transfer of wealth from one stranger to another.

6. *The search for Coasean bargains.* What are the implications for Coase's theory if it turns out that parties are uninterested in bargaining after judgment? An empirical study of some recent nuisance lawsuits suggested that such negotiations may be rare:

> A study of twenty old-fashioned nuisance cases litigated to judgment revealed no bargaining after judgment in any of them. Nor did any of the lawyers contacted believe that bargaining after judgment would have occurred if judgment had been given to the loser. They attributed the lack of bargaining after judgment to acrimony between the parties, and to attitudes toward their rights that would have made the parties reluctant to bargain over them. The size of the sample considered here is small, so it would not be wise to draw from these results aggressive generalizations about how nuisance cases ought to be decided. We do not know just how often these sorts of problems — of enmity, and of resistance on various grounds to treating certain rights as commodities — are sufficient to foreclose the possibility of bargaining after judgment. But in view of the consistency of the results recounted here, it does seem reasonable to conclude that these problems often can be substantial impediments to bargaining after judgment in nuisance cases. [. . .]
>
> These results raise a number of questions worthy of further exploration. Why might parties have the attitudes toward cash exchanges that the lawyers in these cases describe? To what extent do similar attitudes toward cash exchanges exist in other non-market contexts? What stance should the law take toward the parties' feelings in cases like these? [. . .] [I]f it turns out that parties do not bargain over their rights when transaction costs are low (or if we know they wouldn't because we see them refusing to bargain for reasons that have nothing to do with transaction costs in the sense of feasibility problems), then the broad project of using law to create bargains for parties when transaction costs are high becomes more complicated to defend.

Farnsworth, *Do Parties to Nuisance Cases Bargain After Judgment? A Glimpse Inside the Cathedral,* 66 U. Chi. L. Rev. 373 (1999).

7. *The Restatements.* The approaches used in *Carpenter* and *Jost,* and roughly advocated by Coase and Epstein, also roughly track the recommendations of the First and Second Restatements respectively. Section 822 of the First Restatement (1939) provided for nuisance liability where the defendant's invasion of the plaintiff's rights was "substantial and unreasonable." It then offered this provision on the meaning of "unreasonable":

§826. "GRAVITY" OF HARM AND "UTILITY" OF CONDUCT

> An intentional invasion of another's interest in the use and enjoyment of land is unreasonable under the rules stated in §822, unless the utility of the actor's conduct outweighs the gravity of the harm.

At first this provision might appear to call for a straight balancing of the profitability of the defendant's conduct and the costs it imposes on its neighbors, but the comments to the section suggest a broader perspective. "The utility of the conduct depends to a great extent upon whether its primary purpose has social value and upon how much social value it has. It has social value if the general public good is in some way advanced or protected by the encouragement or achievement of such purposes." §828, comment d. The "suitability of the conduct to the character of the locality" and "impracticability of preventing or avoiding the invasion" also are to be accounted for in measuring utility. But the point remains that the value of the defendant's conduct has the potential to excuse it from liability altogether. The Second Restatement (1977) took a somewhat different view. Section 822 again provides for nuisance liability only if the defendant's land use is "unreasonable"; but then §826 runs as follows:

§826. UNREASONABLENESS OF INTENTIONAL INVASION

An intentional invasion of another's interest in the use and enjoyment of land is unreasonable if
    (a) the gravity of the harm outweighs the utility of the actor's conduct, or
    (b) the harm caused by the conduct is serious and the financial burden of compensating for this and similar harm to others would not make the continuation of the conduct not feasible.

Comment d to §822 states that "an invasion may be regarded as unreasonable even though the utility of the conduct is great and the amount of harm is relatively small," and comment g adds that "Liability for damages is imposed in those cases in which the harm or risk to one is greater than he ought to be required to bear under the circumstances, at least without compensation." These provisions leave open the possibility that the benefits of a defendant's activities may excuse the costs they impose on a neighbor, but it creates a presumptive obligation to provide compensation in such cases. The authors' uncertainty is evident, however. Why the exemption for cases where compensation would make continuation of the defendant's conduct infeasible?

8. *Reminders of mortality.* In Rockenbach v. Apostle, 47 N.W.2d 636 (Mich. 1951), the defendants sought to open a funeral home in the city of Muskegon Heights. The street they chose was largely residential, though one of the homes was used by its owner as a watch repair shop and another for physiotherapy baths, and there was a grocer on the next block. The plaintiffs were nearby residents who complained that the funeral home would create excess traffic, spread disease into the neighborhood, reduce their property values, and have a depressing influence upon them. Said one resident: "Every time you see a body you think of yourself, pretty soon you got to die too and they carry you in and out too. The presence of hearses and funeral cars would have the same effect on me." The defendants countered with testimony from

three funeral directors who said that undertaking establishments had no depressing influence upon them, or upon others so far as they knew.

The trial court entered an injunction against the opening of the funeral home, and the Michigan Supreme Court affirmed. The court found that "[t]he evidence in this case would not support a finding that the establishment proposed by the defendants will in its operation become a nuisance by reason of noises, odors, fumes, flies, or dissemination of disease. [. . .] [T]here is no probative value in any testimony to show that a parking problem or traffic congestion will necessarily arise." In nevertheless affirming the injunction, the court quoted with approval these passages from earlier Michigan cases:

> We think it requires no deep research in psychology to reach the conclusion that a constant reminder of death has a depressing influence upon the normal person. Cheerful surroundings are conducive to recovery for one suffering from disease, and cheerful surroundings are conducive to the maintenance of vigorous health in the normal person. Mental depression, horror, and dread lower the vitality, rendering one more susceptible to disease, and reduce the power of resistance. [. . .] [T]he not infrequent taking in and out of dead bodies; the occasional funeral, with its mourners and funeral airs, held in the part of the house designed for a chapel; the unknown dead in the morgue, and the visits of relatives seeking to identify them; the thought of autopsies, of embalming; the dread, or horror, or thought, that the dead are or may be lying in the house next door, a morgue; the dread of communicable disease, not well founded, as we have seen, but nevertheless present in the mind of the normal layman — all of these are conducive to depression of the normal person; each of these is a constant reminder of mortality. These constant reminders, this depression of mind, deprive the home of that comfort and repose to which its owner is entitled.
>
> It is not necessary to show danger from disease or unpleasantness of odors arising from the maintenance of such a business in order to enjoin it. Emotions, caused by the constant contemplation of death, as well as the realization that the bodies of deceased persons are often, if not continuously, on such premises as those here in question, are more acute in their painfulness, in many cases, than suffering perceived through the senses; and mental pain and suffering are elements of damage, in the eyes of the law.

The court noted that the city's zoning ordinances required the defendants to obtain consent for the placement of the funeral home by a five-sevenths vote of the city council, and that the defendants had succeeded in doing this. While recognizing some division of authority on the deference owed by courts to zoning decisions, the court concluded that the injunction should stand:

> The weight of authority is to the effect that an ordinance which allows the establishment or maintenance of a funeral home or undertaking

establishment in a district zoned either for residential or commercial purposes is permissive only, and not controlling as to whether such undertaking establishment would constitute a nuisance which might be enjoined by an equity court. However, proof of the existence of such a zoning ordinance is admissible as evidence of the character of the district, and bearing on the question of nuisance. A nuisance will not be upheld solely on the ground that it has been permitted by municipal ordinance.

Is the court in this case applying strict liability, a negligence standard, or neither? Would it be more accurate to say that the defendants' funeral home was found to be an interference with the plaintiffs' use and enjoyment of their properties, or vice versa? How does one decide which party's use of property is creating the interference and which is on the receiving end of it? Consider as well the relationship between the court's decision and the zoning ordinance the defendants had satisfied. Are there institutional reasons to prefer that matters such as these be resolved by ordinance rather than by judicial decision? Should zoning decisions be understood to bind courts hearing common law nuisance complaints?

9. *Unfounded fears.* In Adkins v. Thomas Solvent Co., 467 N.W.2d 715 (Mich. 1992), the plaintiffs lived near the defendant's manufacturing plant in Battle Creek. They alleged that their wells had been contaminated by toxic chemicals and industrial wastes improperly stored on the defendant's property. After discovery it became clear to all the parties that while chemicals may have leaked from the defendant's storage containers, they never had reached, or would reach, many of the plaintiffs' properties; a subterranean geological barrier separated their groundwater from the defendant's factory. Those plaintiffs who were beyond the zone of danger nevertheless continued to press their nuisance claims, arguing that their property values had been reduced by public concern over contaminants in the general area. The trial court gave summary judgment to the defendants, and the Michigan Supreme Court affirmed:

> The crux of the plaintiffs' complaint is that publicity concerning the contamination of ground water in the area (although concededly not their ground water) caused diminution in the value of the plaintiffs' property. This theory cannot form the basis for recovery because negative publicity resulting in unfounded fear about dangers in the vicinity of the property does not constitute a significant interference with the use and enjoyment of land. [...] [D]iminished property value based on unfounded fear is not a substantial interference in and of itself.
>
> We do not agree with the dissent's suggestion that wholly unfounded fears of third parties regarding the conduct of a lawful business satisfy the requirement for a legally cognizable injury as long as property values decline. Indeed, we would think it not only "odd" but anachronistic

that a claim of nuisance in fact could be based on unfounded fears regarding persons with AIDS moving into a neighborhood, the establishment of otherwise lawful group homes for the disabled, or unrelated persons living together, merely because the fears experienced by third parties would cause a decline in property values.

Levin, J., dissented:

[The plaintiffs should] be allowed to recover damages in nuisance on proofs introduced at a trial tending to show that the defendants actually contaminated soil and ground water in the neighborhood of plaintiffs' homes with toxic chemicals and industrial wastes, that the market perception of the value of plaintiffs' homes was actually adversely affected by the contamination of the neighborhood, and thus that plaintiffs' loss was causally related to defendants' conduct.

Even if potential buyers were to be made aware that the soil and water supply for plaintiffs' homes is not contaminated, and thus were unfettered by "unfounded fear," they nonetheless would pay no more for plaintiffs' homes than the claimed reduced market value. Thus, to the extent that the value of plaintiffs' homes has declined because of well-founded concern about the contamination of soil and ground water in the neighborhood, educating potential buyers that plaintiffs' homes are not in fact contaminated would not necessarily rectify damage suffered by plaintiffs because of the contamination.

Although it would undoubtedly be considered "anachronistic" to enjoin the placement of a woman with leprosy in a residential district in 1992, the public understanding, or misunderstanding, of leprosy in 1898 justified such action. The court reaching that conclusion [*Baltimore v. Fairfield Improvement Co.*, 39 A. 1081 (Md. 1898)] expatiated on "the popular belief of [leprosy's] perils founded on the Biblical narrative, on the stringent provisions of the Mosaic law that show how dreadful were its ravages and how great the terror which it excited, and an almost universal sentiment, the result of a common concurrence of thought for centuries [that] cannot in this day be shaken or dispelled by mere scientific asseveration or conjecture." If equally overpowering fears now grip the public with regard to toxic waste, radioactive contamination, or similar modern perils, this Court may not properly dismiss such fears out of hand.

The dissent also cited this language from *Everett v. Paschall*, 111 P. 879 (Wash. 1910), where the court held that a sanitarium for patients with tuberculosis was a nuisance despite findings that it posed no danger of contagion to nearby residents:

If dread of the disease and fear induced by the proximity of the sanitarium, in fact, disturb the comfortable enjoyment of the property of the appellants, we question our right to say that the fear is unfounded or unreasonable, when it is shared by the whole public to such an extent that property values are diminished. The question is, not whether the fear is founded in science, but whether it exists; not whether it is imaginary, but whether it is real, in that it affects the movements and conduct of men. Such fears are actual, and must be recognized by the courts as other emotions of the human mind. [...] Regard should be had for the notions of comfort and convenience entertained by persons generally of ordinary tastes and susceptibilities. The nuisance and discomfort must affect the ordinary comfort of human existence as understood by the American people in their present state of enlightenment. The theories and dogmas of scientific men, though provable by scientific reference, cannot be held to be controlling unless shared by the people generally.

What is the superficial similarity between *Adkins v. Thomas Solvent Co.* and *Rockenbach v. Apostle*? What is the distinction between them? How might the dissenter in *Adkins* have distinguished the hypothetical case described by the majority in which people with AIDS are considered a nuisance?

B. COMING TO THE NUISANCE

How should analysis proceed if the defendant's activity was well established before the plaintiff arrived nearby and started complaining about it? Blackstone described the common law's position as follows:

If my neighbor makes a tan-yard so as to annoy and render less salubrious the air of my house or gardens, the law will furnish me with a remedy; but if he is first in possession of the air, and I fix my habitation near him, the nuisance is of my own seeking, and may continue.

2 Wm. Blackstone, Commentaries on the Laws of England 402 (17th ed. 1830). The situation Blackstone describes remains familiar, and sometimes is known today as the problem of "coming to the nuisance." The response of the courts to such cases, however, has proven more complex than his statement suggests.

1. *Pioneers.* In Oehler v. Levy, 139 Ill. App. 294 (1908), the plaintiffs were owners of apartment buildings on Lincoln Street in Chicago. The defendant owned stables next door where he kept approximately 20 horses and a number of wagons that he used to deliver newspapers. The plaintiffs complained that the stables were a nuisance: the manure that accumulated

there created noxious odors, the horses were noisy when harnessed in the middle of the night, and the defendant's servants produced a great deal of foul language audible to the building's tenants. The defendant argued that the claim nevertheless should fail because the stables had been in place before the apartments were built; the plaintiffs had "come to the nuisance." Said the court:

> The question involved is an interesting and delicate one. Should pioneers in any direction on the outskirts of a growing city or in its purely manufacturing and business quarters, be entitled to hold in its place, against the changing conditions of the neighborhood, a business legitimate in itself, but injurious and hurtful to residences and their occupants? This question seems to be answered for Illinois, so far as a judicial dictum can answer it, by the language of Judge Magruder, speaking for the Supreme Court in *Laflin & Rand Powder Co. v. Tearney,* in the following words: "Carrying on an offensive trade for any number of years in a place remote from buildings and public roads does not entitle the owner to continue it in the same place after houses have been built and roads have been laid out in the neighborhood, to the occupants of which and the travelers upon which it is a nuisance. As the city extends, such nuisances should be removed to the vacant ground beyond the immediate neighborhood of the residence of the citizens. This public policy as well as the health and comfort of the population of the city demand." This seems also to be the doctrine laid down in other jurisdictions, which [is] the probable justification for the assertions of text writers that "the doctrine of coming to a nuisance is now exploded," and that the most recent authorities hold that the fact that complainant came to such a nuisance is immaterial and will not prevent the issuance of an injunction.
>
> It may easily be conceived that the rights of the parties carrying on a legitimate business, which would be nevertheless a nuisance in a residence district, and of persons who wished to establish a residence in some particular locality, might under some circumstances be very different from the ones in the mind of writers who conceive of the residence use of property as always the higher use. Legally we take it, for the purposes of a discussion like this, the higher use must always be considered that which is economically the more profitable. The principle which would allow an injunction in favor of one who came with a residence to a nuisance of such a character in a locality where that highest and most profitable use of the land was for residences, would not justify such an injunction in favor of a person who undertook to build a residence and demand such an injunction in a locality where the highest and most profitable economic use for the land in that vicinity was for trades and callings which could not be made inoffensive or even harmless to resident householders. We are laying down, therefore, no universal rule that an

injunction will always issue in favor of a householder either prior or subsequent in such holding to a neighbor in an offensive business.

To a certain extent the change in values of certain pieces of land works automatically the change in the characteristics of the neighborhood, but cases, such as the one at bar seems to present to us, occur where the changes in a populous city make it clear, as the court in the *Tearney* case indicates, that public policy and individual health and comfort demand that the courts should so enforce the old maxim "*Sic utere tuo ut alienum non laedas*" as to require the removal of a business *per se* entirely legitimate from a neighborhood where it had been in entire good faith and legally established[.]

The court held that the stables were a nuisance and entered an injunction requiring the defendant to reduce the noise and odors created by them.

2. *In the highest degree unreasonable.* The notion that plaintiffs should be denied recovery if they "came to the nuisance" was rejected in stronger language in United States v. Luce, 141 F. 385 (1905). The court said that such a doctrine

would be so unreasonable and oppressive as to work its own condemnation. If, by way of illustration, one should purchase a lot of land one hundred feet square in an uninhabited section and erect and operate upon it a bone boiling establishment, or other factory, causing noxious, noisome or physically discomforting and annoying odors or stenches to spread over the surrounding country within a radius of half a mile from such mill or factory, he would furnish the means of destroying the ordinary enjoyment of human existence throughout an area more than 2188 times as large as the lot owned by him and devoted to the offensive business. It would be in the highest degree unreasonable and absolutely repugnant to the sense of justice that he should in the supposed case have a right to subordinate to his own selfish ends the beneficial enjoyment of land of others having an area in comparison with which that of the lot acquired by him is so insignificant. The establishment of the offensive business in such case could not prevent the then owners of the residue of the land within the sphere of the noisome odors from building and occupying dwelling houses thereon, nor deprive them of the right to have and enjoy reasonably pure and inoffensive air in and about their homes. Such right they would possess by virtue of their ownership and occupancy of the land; and that right undoubtedly would pass to their grantees or others taking title mediately or immediately from them. Indeed, were such right not capable of passing to others, the value of the land in the hands of those subsequently parting with the title would be seriously impaired or, perchance, wholly destroyed, by the erection and operation of the offensive business, and those succeeding to the title would be without remedy or redress of any kind for the continuance of the nuisance. But such clearly is not the law.

3. *The burdens of prosperity.* In Powell v. Superior Portland Cement, Inc., 129 P.2d 536 (Wash. 1942), the plaintiff lived in the same town as the defendant firm, which manufactured cement from the large deposits of limestone in the region. In the late nineteenth century the town had been called Baker and had consisted of some logging camps and few homes. Soon after the defendant began its operations in 1908, however, the town was renamed Concrete. By the time the plaintiff brought suit, Concrete had a school that housed 300 students, and about half of the town's residents depended on the defendant's firm for their livelihood. The plaintiff claimed that the defendant's plant was a nuisance because it regularly doused his property with dust. The trial court found that the dust could be eliminated through the use of new machinery, but that its installation would be very expensive; it would require the defendant's plant to be reconstructed entirely and would limit its use. As for the plaintiff's injuries, the court found that

> an appreciable and substantial quantity of dust reaches the plaintiff's property from the defendant's plant and that this quantity is sufficient to produce an unpleasant and uncomfortable situation on the premises during a considerable part of the time. This dust [. . .] permeates the house and out-buildings whether the windows and doors are closed or not; it tends to adhere to the surfaces which it reaches if even slightly moistened, because of its propensity for setting or scaling. This commonly occurs upon the sides of the buildings or personal property out of doors, and upon foliage, especially if there is any dew, and tends to change their appearance. It causes these articles to assume a grayish color, rather unnatural and unattractive. It interferes with household affairs, such as the washing and drying of clothes, and increases the frequency with which the house and its contents must be cleaned and dusted. [. . .] The deposit of dust makes painting difficult and decreases the life of the paint. It damages the roof and shortens the life of the roof. [. . .] The court finds that a normal, ordinary individual, such as the plaintiff, is subject to substantial inconvenience and discomfort by the repeated and recurring discharges of dust upon the plaintiff's premises by the defendant.

On this basis the trial court found in favor of the plaintiff and awarded him $500. The Washington Supreme Court reversed:

> Respondent, who has resided in Concrete thirty-five years, did not acquire until 1934 the property which is involved in this action. He purchased the property with knowledge of conditions. [. . .] Respondent knew that living in the surroundings herein described necessarily entailed some discomfort. That burden he assumed when he acquired his

property in a community the character of which had been established for many years. [. . .]

That a certain amount of smoke, fumes, gases, and noises will necessarily be produced and emitted by manufacturing plants is inevitable, but that persons who dwell near manufacturing plants, like persons who dwell near railroads or on busy city streets, must put up with a certain amount of resulting annoyance and discomfort is self-evident. The prosperity of an industrial community depends on its industrial activities, and it would be inconsistent with sound public policy to prohibit these activities at the behest of a comparatively few who are annoyed thereby. Every form of industrial activity has its disagreeable factors. Industries, like individuals, have "the defects of their qualities." In mining and manufacturing communities people must expect that their homes will be more difficult to keep clean than if they lived in an agricultural community. A certain amount of noise also is inseparable from industrial activity. The burdens of prosperity must be taken with its benefits.

There is no doubt that respondent's property will sell for as much for any use with the plant, alleged to constitute the nuisance, in operation as it would if the operation should cease (in fact, what value the property has is because of the populating of the town by operation of the plant); therefore, no recovery can be had for the claimed reduction of its value for use as a home.

What is the distinction between *Powell v. Superior Portland Cement* and *Oehler v. Levy*? Does it follow from *Powell* that a factory cannot be a nuisance if its presence adds more value to neighboring properties than it subtracts by emitting fumes, dust, and the like?

4. *Company towns.* Areas dependent on factories have long presented challenges for the common law of nuisance. The most famous example is the classic English case of St. Helen's Smelting Co. v. Tipping, 11 H.L. Cas. 642, 11 Eng. Rep. 1483 (1865). The plaintiff had bought an estate of more than 1,000 acres that was about a mile and a half from the defendant's copper smelting works. He claimed that the gases from the defendant's works ruined his hedges and trees, made his cattle unhealthy, and in other ways reduced the value of the property. The House of Lords recounted the trial court's instructions to jury as follows:

> The learned Judge told the jury that an actionable injury was one producing sensible discomfort; that every man, unless enjoying right obtained by prescription or agreement, was bound to use his own property in such a manner as not to injure the property of his neighbors; that there was no prescriptive right in this case; that the law did not regard trifling inconveniences; that everything must be looked at from a reasonable point of view; and therefore, in an action for nuisance to property, arising from noxious vapours, the injury to be actionable must be such as visibly

to diminish the value of the property and the comfort and enjoyment of it. That when the jurors came to consider the facts, all the circumstances, including those of time and locality, ought to be taken into consideration; and that with respect to the latter it was clear that in counties where great works had been erected and carried on, persons must not stand on their extreme rights and bring actions in respect of every matter of annoyance, for if so, the business of the whole country would be seriously interfered with.

A jury brought in a verdict for the plaintiff, finding that his enjoyment of his property had been "sensibly diminished"; the jury found that the smelting works were "conducted in a proper manner, in as good a manner as possible," but when asked whether they thought the business was carried on in a proper place, they answered, "We do not." The House of Lords affirmed. Said the Lord Chancellor:

> My Lords, in matters of this description it appears to me that it is a very desirable thing to mark the difference between an action brought for a nuisance upon the ground that the alleged nuisance produces material injury to the property, and an action brought for a nuisance on the ground that the thing alleged to be a nuisance is productive of sensible personal discomfort. With regard to the latter, namely, the personal inconvenience and interference with one's enjoyment, one's quiet, one's personal free- dom, anything that discomposes or injuriously affects the senses or the nerves, whether that may or may not be denominated a nuisance, must undoubtedly depend greatly on the circumstances of the place where the thing complained of actually occurs. If a man lives in a town, it is necessary that he should subject himself to the consequences of those operations of trade which may be carried on in his immediate locality, which are actually necessary for trade and commerce, and also for the enjoyment of property, and for the benefit of the inhabitants of the town and of the public at large. [. . .] But when an occupation is carried on by one person in the neighbourhood of another, and the result of that trade, or occupation, or business, is a material injury to property, then there unquestionably arises a very different consideration. I think, my Lords, that in a case of that description, the submission which is required from persons living in society to that amount of discomfort which may be necessary for the legitimate and free exercise of the trade of their neigh- bours, would not apply to circumstances the immediate result of which is sensible injury to the value of the property.

Said Lord Cranworth:

> I perfectly well remember, when I had the honour of being one of the Barons of the Court of Exchequer, trying a case in the county of Durham,

where there was an action for injury arising from smoke, in the town of Shields. It was proved incontestably that smoke did come and in some degree interfere with a certain person; but I said, "You must look at it not with a view to the question whether, abstractedly, that quantity of was a nuisance, but whether it was a nuisance to a person living in the town of Shields"; because, if it only added in an infinitesimal degree to the quantity of smoke, I held that the state of the town rendered it altogether impossible to call that an actionable nuisance. There is nothing of that sort, however, in the present case.

Said Lord Wensleydale:

My Lords, I entirely agree in opinion with both my noble and learned friends in this case. In these few sentences I think everything is included: The defendants say, "If you do not mind you will stop the progress of works of this description." I agree that it is so, because, no doubt, in the county of Lancaster above all other counties, where great works have been created and carried on, and are the means of developing the national wealth, you must not stand on extreme rights and allow a person to say, "I will bring an action against you for this and that, and so on." Business could not go on if that were so. Everything must be looked at from a reasonable point of view; therefore the law does not regard trifling and small inconveniences, but only regards sensible inconveniences, injuries which sensibly diminish the comfort, enjoyment, or value of the property which is affected.

5. *The Committee on Noxious Vapours.* Brenner, *Nuisance Law and the Industrial Revolution*, 3 J. Legal Stud. 403 (1974), provides interesting evidence of the actual conditions in the town of St. Helen's in the year before Tipping brought his lawsuit. The Lords Select Committee on Noxious Vapours had made a study of St. Helens in 1863. There were large numbers of smelting works, alkali works, and collieries in the neighborhood of the town; the collieries produced over two million tons of coal each year. The effects of the vapors produced by all the factories, as recounted in the report, were dramatic:

Farms recently well-wooded, and with hedges in good condition, have now neither tree nor hedge left alive; whole fields of corn are destroyed in a single night, especially when the vapours fall upon them while in bloom; orchards and gardens, of which there were great numbers in the neighbourhood of St. Helens, have not a fruit tree left alive; pastures are so deteriorated that graziers refuse to place stock upon them; and some of the witnesses have attributed to the poisonous nature of the grass the fact that their sheep and cattle have lost their young in considerable numbers.

From Brenner's article:

> As for the health of the people, the evidence is abundant and conclusive that life expectancy in counties such as Lancashire and Glamorganshire was substantially lower than elsewhere; that coughing, nausea, and prostration from gases were regular features of day-to-day life in factory towns; and that the incidence of serious respiratory diseases in these towns was greater than in the nation at large. [...] The Vicar of Widnes, who himself had felt ill in church from chemical vapors and who complained of throat afflication from them, said that the gases "cause people to be constantly sick. I have seen three people vomiting in the streets, in the middle of the day, and the workmen said that it was attributable to the chlorine gas coming upon them." [...]
>
> From this evidence alone, I conclude that the law of nuisance as it was known at the beginning of the nineteenth century was not being applied in industrial towns. The man who breathed chlorine gas on the job was not entitled to bring an action in nuisance against his employer. But when he got home at night and found the air was bad there, too, he should have had such a right, as occupier, yet no such actions seem to have been reported.

Given the ghastly conditions that Brenner describes, why do you suppose the case reports from the nineteenth century are not full of reports of nuisance cases being brought to complain about them?

6. *Statutes.* In most American jurisdictions nowadays the fact that a plaintiff "came to the nuisance" is just one consideration among many for a court to weigh in deciding whether the defendant's conduct is reasonable; it does not have decisive significance. But once again the territory previously controlled by the common law has in some places been taken over by legislatures. Thus Indiana provides by statute that:

> (c) An agricultural or industrial operation or any of its appurtenances is not and does not become a nuisance, private or public, by any changed conditions in the vicinity of the locality after the agricultural or industrial operation, as the case may be, has been in operation continuously on the locality for more than one (1) year if:
>   (1) there is no significant change in the hours of operation;
>   (2) there is no significant change in the type of operation; and
>   (3) the operation would not have been a nuisance at the time the agricultural or industrial operation began on that locality.
> (d) This section does not apply whenever a nuisance results from the negligent operation of an agricultural or industrial operation or its appurtenances.

Ind. Code §34-19-1-4. The statute's effects are illustrated by *Erbrich Products v. Wills*, 509 N.E.2d 850 (Ind. App. 1987). Chlorine gas escaped from the defendant's bleach factory in 1984 and caused injuries to its neighbors. They brought suit on several theories, including nuisance, but the nuisance claims were dismissed under the statute just excerpted: the factory had not been a nuisance when it opened in 1932, because the neighborhood then surrounding it was industrial even if that no longer was the case. Who benefits from a statute of this sort, and who pays for it?

C. SENSITIVITY AND SPITE

The classic nuisance case involves a defendant innocently engaged in an activity that has the unfortunate side effect of bothering the neighbors. But not all defendants are innocent in this way, and not all plaintiffs have the same tolerance for noise or other annoyances. When parties differ along these dimensions, the law is presented with special challenges: should it take into account the particular sensitivities of peculiar plaintiffs? Should it look askance at defendants who deliberately choose to incommode their neighbors? The cases that follow consider those questions.

1. *The extrasensitive plaintiff.* In Rogers v. Elliott, 15 N.E. 768 (Mass. 1888), the evidence of the plaintiff, Rogers, was that he suffered sunstroke and was taken for recovery to a house across the street from a Catholic church. The church possessed a large, loud bell, and when it rang it threw the plaintiff into convulsions. The plaintiff's doctor went to the pastor, one Elliott, explained the circumstances to him, and asked if he would refrain from ringing the bell. Elliott refused. When he later was cross-examined Elliott explained as follows: "If a man was sick and that would kill him, I should probably not stop the bell. People are dying every day. I would not stop ringing the bell for my sister or my brother. I should permit the bell to be rung if it killed the man by doing it; but I should not will it, although I could stop it." Elliott added that "I did have some trouble with Mr. Rogers at one time. He had me arrested, and the case was tried in the police court. I was tried for assault and battery. The trouble was about church matters, and I was discharged." The trial court gave a directed verdict to the defendant, and the Supreme Judicial Court affirmed:

> The right to make a noise for a proper purpose must be measured in reference to the degree of annoyance which others may reasonably be required to submit to. In connection with the importance of the business from which it proceeds, that must be determined by the effect of noise

upon people generally, and not upon those, on the one hand, who are peculiarly susceptible to it, or those on the other, who, by long experience, have learned to endure it without inconvenience; not upon those whose strong nerves and robust health enable them to endure the greatest disturbances without suffering, nor upon those whose mental or physical condition makes them painfully sensitive to everything about them. [. . .]

If one's right to use his property was to depend upon the effect of the use upon a person of peculiar temperament or disposition, or upon one suffering from an uncommon disease, the standard for measuring it would be so uncertain and fluctuating as to paralyze industrial enterprises. The owner of a factory containing noisy machinery, with dwelling-houses all about it, might find his business lawful as to all but one of the tenants of the houses, and as to that one, who dwelt no nearer than the others, it might be a nuisance. The character of his business might change from legal to illegal, or illegal to legal, with every change of tenants of an adjacent estate, or with an arrival or departure of a guest or boarder at a house near by; or even with the wakefulness or the tranquil repose of an invalid neighbor on a particular night. Legal rights to the use of property cannot be left to such uncertainty. [. . .]

In the case at bar it is not contended that the ringing of the bell for church services in the manner shown by the evidence materially affected the health or comfort of ordinary people in the vicinity, but the plaintiff's claim rests upon the injury done him on account of his peculiar condition. However his request should have been treated by the defendant upon considerations of humanity, we think he could not put himself in a place of exposure to noise, and demand as of legal right that the bell should not be used. The plaintiff, in his brief, concedes that there was no evidence of express malice on the part of the defendant, but contends that malice was implied in his acts. In the absence of evidence that he acted wantonly, or with express malice, this implication could not come from his exercise of his legal rights. How far, and under what circumstances, malice may be material in cases of this kind, it is unnecessary to consider.

2. *Poor planning.* In Amphitheaters, Inc. v. Portland Meadows, 198 P.2d 847 (Or. 1948), the plaintiff and defendant owned adjoining properties. During 1945-1946, the plaintiff built a drive-in outdoor movie theater on his lot, while the defendant built a horse racing track. The theater was completed and opened for business in August of 1946; the racetrack began operations two weeks later. The racetrack was equipped for use at night, and so included 350 lights mounted in clusters atop poles 80 feet high. The cluster of lights nearest to the plaintiff's movie screen was about 800 feet away, which was close enough to seriously impair the quality of the images the plaintiff projected there; on one occasion the plaintiff felt obliged to refund the admission fees of its patrons. The defendant installed hoods over the lights to

reduce their tendency to spill over onto the plaintiff's property, but they were not effective. The plaintiff brought suit claiming that the lights were a nuisance. The trial court gave a directed verdict to the defendant, and the Oregon Supreme Court affirmed:

> This court has repeatedly quoted the ancient maxim, Sic utere tuo ut alienum non laedas. In this connection we quote the words of Lord Esher in *Yarmouth v. France*, 19 Q.B.D. 647, 653, as follows: "I need hardly repeat that I detest the attempt to fetter the law by maxims. They are almost invariably misleading; they are for the most part so large and general in their language that they always include something which really is not intended to be included in them." And to this we add the crisp comment of Justice Holmes: "Decisions . . . often are presented as hollow deductions from empty general propositions like sic utere tuo ut alienum non laedas, which teaches nothing but a benevolent yearning." 8 Harv. L. Rev. 3. [. . .]
>
> Again it is held that whether a particular annoyance or inconvenience is sufficient to constitute a nuisance depends upon its effect upon an ordinarily reasonable man, that is, a normal person of ordinary habits and sensibilities. [This doctrine] appears to have had its origin in Aldred's Case, (1601) 9 Coke 57b, 77 Eng. Reprint 816. The rule announced in that case, "Lex non favet delicatorum votis," ["The law favours not the vows of the squeamish" — ED.] [. . .] has been applied in many cases involving smoke, dust, noxious odors, vibration and the like, in which the injury was not to the land itself but to the personal comfort of dwellers on the land. [. . .]
>
> The same doctrine is followed by Joyce, *Law of Nuisances*, §26: ". . . But the doing of something not in itself noxious does not become a nuisance merely because it does harm to some particular trade of a delicate nature in the adjoining property where it does not affect any ordinary trade carried on there nor interfere with the ordinary enjoyment of life. A man who carries on an exceptionally delicate trade cannot complain because it is injured by his neighbor doing something lawful on his property, if it is something which would not injure an ordinary trade or anything but an exceptionally delicate trade."

3. *Computers vs. televisions (problem).* In Page County Appliance Center v. Honeywell, Inc., 347 N.W.2d 171 (Iowa 1984), the plaintiff owned a store that sold televisions in the town of Shenandoah. The defendants included Central Travel Service, a travel agency two doors down from the plaintiff's business, and Honeywell, which installed new computers in the travel agency's offices in 1980. Radiation leaked from the computers and affected the televisions on display in the plaintiff's showrooms down the street, distorting the pictures they displayed. Plaintiff brought suit on a nuisance theory. Assuming Iowa recognizes the previous two cases as good law, what result?

4. *The last straw.* There are few generalizations about nuisance law that hold up across all jurisdictions; the defense that the plaintiff is hypersensitive is yet another example of a rule observed in most states but not all of them. Thus, in Poole v. Lowell Dunn Co., 573 So. 2d 51 (Fla. App. 1991), the plaintiffs were a couple who bought a house about two miles away from the defendant's quarry. The defendant soon began blasting in the quarry, and plaintiffs' evidence was that the blasting caused their pool and house to crack, distressed their child, and created difficulties in their marriage that eventually led to a divorce. They brought suit on theories of strict liability and nuisance; the nuisance count was necessary to the plaintiffs' case because it permitted them to seek damages for emotional distress. The defendants requested and the jury received the following instruction:

> If you find, by the greater weight of the evidence, it establishes that the gravity of the harm to the Plaintiff outweighs the utility of the Defendants' conduct, the test to be applied in determining whether a particular nuisance or inconvenience is such degree to constitute a nuisance, it is the effect of the condition on an ordinary, reasonable person with a reasonable disposition and ordinary health and sensibility. The law does not provide for those who are hypersensitive, and if the greater weight or the claim [*sic*] does not support the Plaintiffs, then the verdict is for the Defendants.

The jury found for the defendants. The plaintiffs appealed, claiming among other things that the jury should not have been given the instruction on hypersensitivity. The court of appeals agreed and ordered a new trial. The court found the quoted instruction

> incorrect because, under Florida law, the tortfeasor takes the plaintiff as he finds him. A plaintiff's "hypersensitivity" does not affect the causal relationship between the defendant's conduct and the plaintiff's damages. The defendant's initial wrongful conduct is the proximate cause of the plaintiff's damages despite the fact that the wrong may not have caused that same *degree of damage* to an ordinary person.

What are the implications of this decision? Suppose the plaintiffs' relations were in precarious shape already, and that the aggravation caused by the blasting was simply the last straw that caused their marriage to collapse. Would they be allowed to collect damages? Most jurisdictions agree that a tortfeasor takes his victim as he finds him — the "eggshell skull rule." Yet most of them consider it a good defense to a nuisance claim that the plaintiff is hypersensitive. Can these two positions be reconciled?

5. *Sauce for the goose.* In Christie v. Davey, 1 Ch. 316 (1893), the parties lived in adjoining residences in Brixton, a district of London. The plaintiffs

were Mr. and Mrs. J. F. Holder Christie. Mrs. Christie was a music teacher; in her house she instructed pupils in piano, violin, and singing. The defendant, Mr. H. Fitzer Davey, was an engraver of wood who also worked in his home. Davey sent the Christies a letter that ran in part as follows:

> During this week we have been much disturbed by what I at first thought were the howlings of your dog, and, knowing from experience that this sort of thing could not be helped, I put up with the annoyance. But, the noise recurring at a comparatively early hour this morning, I find I have been quite mistaken, and that it is the frantic effort of some one trying to sing with piano accompaniment, and during the day we are treated by way of variety to dreadful scrapings on a violin, with accompaniments. If the accompaniments are intended to drown the vocal shrieks or teased catgut vibrations, I can assure you it is a failure, for they do not. I am at last compelled to complain, for I cannot carry on my profession with this constant thump, thump, scrape, scrape, and shriek, shriek, constantly in my ears. It may be a pleasure or source of profit to you, but to me and mine it is a confounded nuisance and pecuniary loss, and, if allowed to continue, it must most seriously affect our health and comfort. We cannot use the back part of our house without feeling great inconvenience through this constant playing, sometimes up to midnight and even beyond. Allow me to remind you of one fact, which must most surely have escaped you — that these houses are only semi-detached, so that you yourself may see how annoying it must be to your unfortunate next-door neighbour. If it is not discontinued I shall be compelled to take very serious notice of it.

The plaintiffs said that in consequence of the tone of the letter they did not respond to it.

Within a day of the letter's arrival the plaintiffs found that whenever music was played in their house the defendant and his servants would commence the creation of various noises: performing "mock concerts" with concertinas, horns, flutes, pianos, and other musical instruments, blowing whistles, knocking on trays or boards, hammering, shrieking and shouting, and imitating what was being played in the plaintiffs' house. The plaintiffs' solicitor wrote to Davey that "your disgraceful proceedings are the cause of very much discomfort and annoyance to our clients, and seriously interfere with their professional pursuits and engagements[.]" The defendant's reply ran this way:

> [Y]ou say that I interfere with your clients' professional pursuits. Just so; this is simply reversing my complaint, and what is sauce for the goose is sauce for the gander. [. . .] It is my intention during these winter months to endeavour to perfect myself on the following instruments — viz., flute, concertina, cornopean, horn, and piano, which my child is learning to

accompany me. I used to play them at one time, both in a church band and an amateur troupe; but I have been out of practice lately, but hope soon to regain my former proficiency.

The plaintiffs brought an action in Chancery court to enjoin the defendant from creating further disturbances. The defendant counterclaimed, seeking an injunction against the noise emanating from the plaintiffs' house. The defendants' lawyer argued that "The Plaintiffs in fact seek to restrain the Defendant from making a noise, in order that they may be the better able to make a noise themselves. They admit that music is almost continually going on in their house. Plaintiffs who thus act themselves are not entitled to prevent their neighbour from playing on any instrument he likes." North, J., found in favor of the Christies:

> I think I am bound to interfere for the protection of the Plaintiffs. In my opinion the noises which were made in the Defendant's house were not of a legitimate kind. [. . .] I am satisfied that they were made deliberately and maliciously for the purpose of annoying the Plaintiffs. If what has taken place had occurred between two sets of persons both perfectly innocent, I should have taken an entirely different view of the case. But I am persuaded that what was done by the Defendant was done only for the purpose of annoyance, and in my opinion it was not a legitimate use of the Defendant's house to use it for the purpose of vexing and annoying his neighbours.
>
> I now come to the Defendant's counter-claim. [. . .] In my opinion, the giving of lessons for seventeen hours a week in the house of musicians, who gain their living by the exercise of their profession, does not give the Defendant any legal ground of complaint. Nor do I think that the additional circumstance that [. . .] the Plaintiffs occasionally have musical performances in the evening, will create a legal nuisance. [. . .] If there were the slightest ground for believing that what has been done by the Plaintiffs' household had been done maliciously, for an improper purpose, I might have regarded the case with a very different view. But, in my opinion, there is no foundation for such a suggestion, and I can see no ground for granting an injunction against the Plaintiffs. So far I have left out of consideration the playing of the violoncello by the Plaintiffs' son. He has for some years learnt the violoncello and has had lessons away from home. It seems to be his habit to go down into the kitchen and there practise the violoncello from ten o'clock to eleven at night. I am willing to believe that he may often have played as late as a quarter-past eleven. [. . .] I will say this for his guidance in future, that it would be only reasonable that he should cease playing at eleven o'clock, or as soon as possible afterwards. I do not mean that he is not to finish a piece which he is actually playing and to stop precisely at eleven; but I think he should not begin any fresh piece after eleven.

Is there a satisfactory distinction between *Christie v. Davey* and *Rogers v. Elliott* (the NL case of the church bell that sent the plaintiff into convulsions)?

6. *Sinister designs.* In Mayor of Bradford v. Pickles, App. Cas. 587, All Eng. Rep. 984 (1895), the plaintiffs were owners of a waterworks corporation. The corporation possessed land that contained springs serving as its source of water. One of these properties was called Trooper Farm. The defendant, Pickles, lived next to Trooper Farm and uphill from it. The water that later reached the plaintiffs' springs first had to pass through Pickles's property. Pickles began digging shafts on his land that diminished and discolored the groundwater flowing to the farm. He announced his intention to continue digging his tunnels, claiming that he planned to mine the stone buried there. The plaintiffs brought suit alleging, among other things, that Pickles had no real intention of mining, and that he was blocking the flow of groundwater to their land for improper motives, viz., to force them to buy him out. The case worked its way to the House of Lords, which found in favor of Pickles. Said MacNaghten, L.J.:

> [The plaintiffs] say that Mr. Pickles' action in the matter is malicious, and that because his motive is a bad one, he is not at liberty to do a thing which every landowner in the country may do with impunity if his motives are good. Mr. Pickles, it seems, was so alarmed at this view of the case that he tried to persuade the Court that all he wanted was to unwater some beds of stone which he thought he could work at a profit. In this innocent enterprise the Court found a sinister design. And it may be taken that his real object was to shew that he was master of the situation, and to force the corporation to buy him out at a price satisfactory to himself. Well, he has something to sell, or, at any rate, he has something which he can prevent other people enjoying unless he is paid for it. Why should he, he may think, without fee or reward, keep his land as a store-room for a commodity which the corporation dispense, probably not gratuitously, to the inhabitants of Bradford? He prefers his own interests to the public good. He may be churlish, selfish, and grasping. His conduct may seem shocking to a moral philosopher. But where is the malice? Mr. Pickles has no spite against the people of Bradford. He bears no ill-will to the corporation. They are welcome to the water, and to his land too, if they will pay the price for it. So much perhaps might be said in defence or in palliation of Mr. Pickles' conduct. But the real answer to the claim of the corporation is that in such a case motives are immaterial. It is the act, not the motive for the act, that must be regarded. If the act, apart from motive, gives rise merely to damage without legal injury, the motive, however reprehensible it may be, will not supply that element.

What is the distinction between *Mayor of Bradford v. Pickles* and *Christie v. Davey*?

7. *Spite fences.* In Barger v. Barringer, 66 S.E. 439 (N.C. 1909), the plaintiff, Barger, was the chief of police in the town of West Hickory. He registered a complaint that the stables kept by his neighbor, Barringer, were filthy, and as a result of the complaint Barringer was forced to remove the stables from his property. The plaintiff's evidence was that Barringer sought revenge by building an eight-foot fence along their property line that greatly darkened Barger's house. The trial court found for the defendant, Barringer; the Supreme Court of North Carolina reversed:

> Light and air are as much a necessity as water, and all are the common heritage of mankind. While, for legitimate purposes, a person's rights in them may sometimes be curtailed without consulting his comfort or convenience, the common welfare of all forbids that this should be needlessly permitted in order to gratify one of the basest and most degrading passions that sometimes takes possession of the human heart. [. . .]
>
> There are many annoyances arising from legitimate improvements and businesses which those living near must endure, but no one should be compelled by law to submit to a nuisance created and continued for no useful end, but solely to inflict upon him humiliation, as well as physical pain. The ancient maxim of the common law, "Sic utere tuo ut alienum non laedas," is not founded in any human statute, but in that sentiment expressed by Him who taught good will toward men, and said, "Love thy neighbor as thyself." Freely translated, it enjoins that every person in the use of his own property should avoid injury to his neighbor as much as possible. No one ought to have the legal right to make a malicious use of his property for no benefit to himself, but merely to injure his fellow man. To hold otherwise makes the law an engine of oppression with which to destroy the peace and comfort of a neighbor, as well as to damage his property for no useful purpose, but solely to gratify a wicked and debasing passion. The doctrine of private nuisances is founded upon this humane and venerable maxim of the law. If it can be successfully invoked to prevent the keeping of stables and hogpens so near one's neighbor as to cause discomfort, why cannot he, whom it is sought to needlessly and maliciously deprive of air and sunlight, also seek the aegis of its protection? The right thus to injure one's neighbor with impunity cannot long continue to exist anywhere in an enlightened country where God is acknowledged and the Golden Rule is taught.

Hoke, J., dissented:

> We are all, I trust, striving, at times somewhat blindly, to attain to the perfect righteousness of the great Teacher as well as Savior of men, but in the present stage of our development, and with our limited human ken, it has been found best to confine litigation in our civil courts to the enforcement of rights, and the redress of wrongs growing out of an invasion of

those rights, done or threatened, and not allow causes of action to be based upon motive alone. For here we enter upon the domain of taste and temperament, involving questions entirely too complex, varied, and at times fanciful for satisfactory inquiry and determination by municipal courts. [. . .] If plaintiff can succeed in this, the next grievance will very likely be found in the shape of the roof or the color of the paint, and the defendant, who had supposed that he was the owner of a piece of property, no doubt descended to him from his fathers, will find that in the evolution of things modern he is only an occupant, holding subject to the capricious whims of some supersensitive and overly aesthetic but influential neighbor.

Is there a satisfactory distinction between *Barger v. Barringer* and *Mayor of Bradford v. Pickles?*

8. *Spite buildings.* In Fontainebleau Hotel Corp. v. Forty-Five Twenty-Five, Inc., 114 So. 2d 357 (Fla. App. 1959), plaintiff and defendant were the owners of neighboring luxury hotels, the Fontainebleau and the Eden Roc, on the east coast of Florida. The owner of the Fontainebleau announced an intention to build a 14-story addition to the building. The addition was to be 160 feet tall and sit 20 feet from the Eden Roc's property. One consequence of the addition would be to block afternoon sunlight from reaching the Eden Roc during much of the year, throwing a shadow over its swimming pool and beach. The Eden Roc brought a lawsuit to enjoin construction of the addition, claiming that the Fontainebleau's decision to build the addition so near to the Eden Roc was motivated by spite, and claiming as well that the Eden Roc possessed an easement of light that the addition would obstruct. The trial court entered the injunction. The court of appeals reversed:

> No American decision has been cited, and independent research has revealed none, in which it has been held that — in the absence of some contractual or statutory obligation — a landowner has a legal right to the free flow of light and air across the adjoining land of his neighbor. Even at common law, the landowner had no legal right, in the absence of an easement or uninterrupted use and enjoyment for a period of 20 years, to unobstructed light and air from the adjoining land. And the English doctrine of "ancient lights" has been unanimously repudiated in this country.
>
> There being, then, no legal right to the free flow of light and air from the adjoining land, it is universally held that where a structure serves a useful and beneficial purpose, it does not give rise to a cause of action, either for damages or for an injunction under the maxim *sic utere tuo ut alienum non laedas*, even though it causes injury to another by cutting off the light and air and interfering with the view that would otherwise be

available over adjoining land in its natural state, regardless of the fact that the structure may have been erected partly for spite.

We see no reason for departing from this universal rule. If, as contended on behalf of plaintiff, public policy demands that a landowner in the Miami Beach area refrain from constructing buildings on his premises that will cast a shadow on the adjoining premises, an amendment of its comprehensive planning and zoning ordinance, applicable to the public as a whole, is the means by which such purpose should be achieved. (No opinion is expressed here as to the validity of such an ordinance, if one should be enacted pursuant to the requirements of law.) But to change the universal rule — and the custom followed in this state since its inception — that adjoining landowners have an equal right under the law to build to the line of their respective tracts and to such a height as is desired by them (in the absence, of course, of building restrictions or regulations) amounts, in our opinion, to judicial legislation.

What is the distinction between *Fontainebleau Hotel Corp. v. Forty-Five Twenty-Five, Inc.* and *Barger v. Barringer*? (Not all jurisdictions recognize liability for spite fences, but Florida is one that generally does — notwithstanding the *Fontainebleau* decision.)

9. *The fox farm (problem).* In Hollywood Silver Fox Farm, Ltd. v. Emmett, 2 K.B. 468 (1936), the plaintiff, one Captain Chandler, bred silver foxes in the county of Kent southeast of London. Near the edge of his land he posted a sign inscribed "Hollywood Silver Fox Farm." The defendant, Emmett, lived next door, and the sign was visible from his land. He was planning to sell his property and believed the visibility of Chandler's sign would reduce its value, so he asked Chandler to remove it. Chandler refused. Soon thereafter Emmett instructed his son to discharge a 12-bore gun loaded with black powder at the boundary of his land nearest to Chandlers' pens. The resulting noise greatly disturbed Chandlers' vixens, who were very nervous as it was breeding season. This exercise was repeated on four consecutive evenings; on the last of them, Emmett accompanied his son and was met at the border of the property by Chandler. In reply to Chandler's protest, Emmett asked if he intended to remove the notice-board, saying at the same time that he was acquainted with the law and that he knew he had a right to shoot as he pleased on his own land. Chandler did not remove the sign but sued Emmett to recover for his damages; his evidence was that the noise caused by the defendant's gun caused one of the vixens to devour her four cubs and caused others not to mate at all. What result? (Chandler cited *Christie v. Davey* as authority for a judgment in his favor; Emmett relied on *Mayor of Bradford v. Pickles.*) Do extrasensitivity cases such as *Rogers v. Elliott* have any bearing here?

10. *Paint it black.* There is a division of authority among American courts on liability for spite fences; a majority now hold them tortious, but a substantial number do not. Thus in Koblegard v. Hale, 53 S.E. 793 (W. Va. 1906), the defendant, Hale, lived next door to a lot where a church was under construction. Trustees of the church brought a suit alleging that Hale had built a ten-foot fence along his property line and announced his intention to paint the fence black on the side facing the church; the fence was as high as the ten large windows on the eastern side of the church, and prevented light from reaching them. The plaintiffs said that Hale did this to "get even" because the church obstructed sunlight that formerly shone on his property, and that the creation of the fence was motivated entirely by spite. The trial court found the fence to be a nuisance. The Supreme Court of West Virginia reversed and ordered the complaint dismissed, saying that "[w]e do not think that the motive or intent of appellants in building the fence is material in determining what right appellees have in the light and air the obstruction of which they seek to enjoin." The court also quoted approvingly the view of an Ohio court that "[a] man may be compelled to keep his gas, smoke, odors, and noises at home; but he cannot be compelled to send his light and air abroad." A similar view was taken in Metzger v. Hochrein, 83 N.W. 308 (Wis. 1900), another case rejecting liability for erection of a spite fence:

> If one is so constituted as not to be susceptible to those feelings which a reasonably well-balanced man is supposed to possess, and is so consti- tuted as to obtain more pleasure out of needlessly annoying others than by securing and retaining their respect as a manly member of society, his sovereign right in his own property, to use it as he may so far as that use does not physically extend outside his boundaries to the detriment of others, may be so exercised as to violate the moral obligations which every member of society owes to his neighbors, without any penalty being visited upon him for his misconduct, of which he can be made conscious.

Which view of spite fences is most persuasive: the view permitting them or the view that finds them a nuisance?

11. *More statutes.* In some jurisdictions the question of spite fences has been settled by statute. This Massachusetts provision is typical:

> A fence or other structure in the nature of a fence which unnecessarily exceeds six feet in height and is maliciously erected or maintained for the purpose of annoying the owners or occupants of adjoining property shall be deemed a private nuisance. Any such owner or occupant injured in the comfort or enjoyment of his estate thereby may have an action of tort for damages under chapter two hundred and forty-three.

Mass. Gen. Laws Ann. 49 §21. The Supreme Judicial Court of Massachusetts found the statute constitutional in an opinion by Justice Holmes that suggested there may be limits on how far such measures lawfully can go:

> [T]o a large extent the power to use one's property malevolently in any way which would be lawful for other ends is an incident of property which cannot be taken away even by legislation. It may be assumed that under our constitution the legislature would not have power to prohibit putting up or maintaining stores or houses with malicious intent, and thus to make a large part of the property of the commonwealth dependent upon what a jury might find to have been the past or to be the present motives of the owner. But it does not follow that the rule is the same for a boundary fence, unnecessarily built more than six feet high. It may be said that the difference is only one of degree. Most differences are, when nicely analyzed. At any rate, difference of degree is one of the distinctions by which the right of the legislature to exercise the police power is determined. Some small limitations of previously existing rights incident to property may be imposed for the sake of preventing a manifest evil; large ones could not be, except by the exercise of the right of eminent domain.

Rideout v. Knox, 19 N.E. 390 (Mass. 1889).

D. REMEDIES

Most of the cases in this book involve suits seeking damages — i.e., money — from the defendant. This is only natural in cases involving liability for accidents; the harm has been completed in such situations, leaving the plaintiff with nothing to do but seek compensation for it. Nuisance cases are different because they frequently involve ongoing acts by defendants that impose costs on plaintiffs, thus making feasible another type of remedy: an injunction ordering the defendant to desist. The choice between awarding such "equitable" relief (so called because injunctions used to be available only from courts of equity) and awarding damages presents a number of complications that we now consider.

1. *Balancing the equities.* In Madison v. Ducktown Sulphur, Copper & Iron Co., 83 S.W. 658 (Tenn. 1904), the defendants owned copper mines in Ducktown. The plaintiffs owned farms in the nearby mountains. The defendants processed the ore from their mines by putting it into piles and setting them on fire. The smoke generated by the piles tended to destroy the plaintiffs' crops and damage their health, causing them headaches and coughing. The court also found that there was no other way to process the ore than by

burning the piles, and that the defendants had spent approximately $200,000 on unsuccessful efforts to reduce the resulting noxious vapors. Meanwhile the plaintiffs owned about 600 acres, and altogether these properties were worth about $900. In 1903 the total tax revenues for Polk County, where Ducktown was situated, were $2,585,931; half of this ($1,279,533) was collected from the defendants. Before the defendants' companies began operations there were 200 people living in the district of the mines. At the time of the court's decision there were 12,000 people, most of them dependent on the mines either as employees or as suppliers of materials that the defendants required. It was found that one of the defendants paid out roughly $500,000 each year in wages.

The court of chancery appeals granted the plaintiffs' request for an injunction. The Tennessee Supreme Court reversed:

> The question now to be considered is, what is the proper exercise of discretion, under the facts appearing in the present case? Shall the complainants be granted, in the way of damages, the full measure of relief to which their injuries entitle them, or shall we go further, and grant their request to blot out two great mining and manufacturing enterprises, destroy half of the taxable values of a county, and drive more than 10,000 people from their homes? We think there can be no doubt as to what the true answer to this question should be.
>
> In order to protect by injunction several small tracts of land, aggregating in value less than $1,000, we are asked to destroy other property worth nearly $2,000,000, and wreck two great mining and manufacturing enterprises, that are engaged in work of very great importance, not only to their owners, but to the state, and to the whole country as well, to depopulate a large town, and deprive thousands of working people of their homes and livelihood, and scatter them broadcast. The result would be practically a confiscation of the property of the defendants for the benefit of the complainants — an appropriation without compensation. The defendants cannot reduce their ores in a manner different from that they are now employing, and there is no more remote place to which they can remove. The decree asked for would deprive them of all of their rights. We appreciate the argument based on the fact that the homes of the complainants who live on the small tracts of land referred to are not so comfortable and useful to their owners as they were before they were affected by the smoke complained of, and we are deeply sensible of the truth of the proposition that no man is entitled to any more rights than another on the ground that he has or owns more property than that other. But in a case of conflicting rights, where neither party can enjoy his own without in some measure restricting the liberty of the other in the use of property, the law must make the best arrangement it can between the contending parties, with a view to preserving to each one the largest measure of liberty possible under the circumstances. We see no escape from the conclusion in

the present case that the only proper decree is to allow the complainants a reference for the ascertainment of damages, and that the injunction must be denied to them, except in the qualified manner below indicated.

2. *The humblest suitor.* In Whalen v. Union Bag & Paper Co., 101 N.E. 805 (N.Y. 1913), the defendants operated a pulp mill on Kayaderosseras creek in Saratoga county. The mill had cost more than $1 million to build and employed between four and five hundred people. The plaintiff owned a 225-acre farm downstream from the mill. The defendant's works discharged sulphur, lime, and other material into the stream, leaving it unsuitable for use by the plaintiff. The Appellate Division found that the plaintiff's damages were $100 per year, and awarded him that sum; it denied the request for an injunction, stating that "[t]he creek runs through mere pasture and meadow land of the plaintiff; and, while the water of the creek is made foul and offensive from the aggregate pollution, the injury to the plaintiff is insignificant compared to the injury which would result to the defendant in compelling it to discontinue the operation of its pulp mill." Betts, J., dissented: "It has always been the boast of equity that any substantial injustice might be corrected by it to even the humblest suitor, and that the financial size of such a suitor's antagonist was not important." The New York Court of Appeals reversed and ordered the injunction granted:

> Although the damage to the plaintiff may be slight as compared with the defendant's expense of abating the condition, that is not a good reason for refusing an injunction. Neither courts of equity nor law can be guided by such a rule, for if followed to its logical conclusion it would deprive the poor litigant of his little property by giving it to those already rich. It is always to be remembered in such cases that "denying the injunction puts the hardship on the party in whose favor the legal right exists, instead of on the wrongdoer." *Pomeroy's Eq. Juris*, vol. 5, §530. In speaking of the injustice which sometimes results from the balancing of injuries between parties, the learned author from whom we have just quoted sums up the discussion by saying, "The weight of authority is against allowing a balancing of injury as a means of determining the propriety of issuing an injunction." To the same effect is the decision in *Weston Paper Co. v. Pope*, 155 Ind. 394: "The fact that the appellant has expended a large sum of money in the construction of its plant, and that it conducts its business in a careful manner and without malice, can make no difference in its rights to the stream. Before locating the plant the owners were bound to know that every riparian proprietor is entitled to have the waters of the stream that washes his land come to it without obstruction, diversion, or corruption, subject only to the reasonable use of the water, by those similarly entitled, for such domestic purposes as are inseparable from and necessary for the free use of their land; they were bound also to know the character of their proposed business, and to take notice of

the size, course, and capacity of the stream, and to determine for themselves at their own peril whether they should be able to conduct their
business upon a stream of the size and character of Brandywine creek
without injury to their neighbors; and the magnitude of their investment
and their freedom from malice furnish no reason why they should escape
the consequences of their own folly." This language very aptly expresses
the rule which we think should be applied to the case at bar.

Which of these two cases — *Madison* or *Whalen* — is more persuasive? (Is it
possible to view them as consistent?)

3. *The significance of bargaining after judgment.* Do you imagine that
the court's decision in *Whalen* was the last word in the case? It is natural
to distinguish between injunctions and damages by supposing that an
injunction forces a defendant to stop what he is doing, while damages allow
him to keep doing it but to pay for the damage he causes. Economists view
the remedies differently, however: an injunction does not necessarily stop the
defendant; rather, it gives the plaintiff the *right* to stop him, and thus forces
the defendant to negotiate with the plaintiff and pay him some amount if he
wants to continue his conduct. Thus the difference between damages and an
injunction is that when damages are awarded the court determines the value
of the parties' rights, whereas an injunction forces a negotiation in which the
parties determine those values on their own. Notice that a finding of no
liability can be understood to force the same sort of negotiation: the losing
plaintiff still can offer to pay the defendant to desist from his conduct. Indeed,
even an award of damages can serve as the starting point for additional
negotiations if the damage award does not accurately capture the values that
parties place on their rights.

These points are applications of the Coase theorem, which we discussed at
the start of the chapter. They might suggest that courts should favor injunctions
as remedies when transactions between the parties are feasible: an injunction
will force the parties to determine the value they place upon the rights through
negotiation, and this valuation will be more accurate than one performed by a
court. On this view damages can be understood as a second-best remedy for use
in cases where bargaining after judgment will be difficult, perhaps because the
parties are too numerous; the damage award becomes a court's rough attempt
to arrange the bargain for the parties that they would arrange themselves if
bargaining were feasible. From this point the economic analysis turns to
whether and when parties can be expected to bargain after judgment — in
other words, how one can know whether transaction costs are high. The sim-
plest case of high transaction costs arises in disputes with large numbers of
parties, actual or potential. If a hundred plaintiffs complain about the defendant's conduct, it will be costly for the defendant to negotiate with each of
them. The situation is made worse by the prospect of strategic behavior: the last
plaintiff of the hundred might hold out for an especially large payment,

knowing that without his consent the defendant will have to shut down.
Indeed, every complainant might like to hold out and become the last to
agree. Similar problems can arise even if there are only two parties, for then
they are locked into a "bilateral monopoly": the plaintiff can demand more
than he really requires to be fully compensated for his losses because the
defendant has nobody else to whom he can turn in search of a better offer,
and vice versa.

These sorts of considerations generally are not discussed by courts in deciding whether to award injunctions or damages, at least explicitly, but speculation about them has formed the basis of a small academic industry. Of course
there remain the skepticisms mentioned earlier in the chapter about whether
parties to nuisance cases really do bargain after judgment. Would such bargaining have been likely in *Madison* and *Whalen*? If not, why not? Consider
three reasons why bargaining might not occur or succeed: too much enmity
may exist between the parties; the parties who prevail may be profoundly
attached to their rights and not want to sell them for any price their adversaries
are willing to pay; or one side may engage in strategic behavior, and their
bluffing may cause the other party to walk away from the bargaining table.
If we knew these problems were likely to arise, would they justify an award of
damages rather than an injunction?

If bargaining after judgment would have been likely in these cases, what do
you suppose the negotiations would have sounded like? Why would leaving the
parties to their negotiations not make more sense than awarding damages? In
the *Madison* case, for example, the court's decision could be understood to
effectively force the plaintiffs to sell their homes to the defendants at a price
determined by the court; would a private negotiation between the parties have
been more or less likely to result in a transfer of the plaintiffs' rights to the
defendant at an appropriate price? (What *would* be an appropriate price?)

Keep in mind that most cases settle before a judgment is entered. Should
this affect the choice of remedy in cases litigated to judgment? Suppose it is
clear from a jurisdiction's case law that the plaintiff will be entitled to an
injunction rather than damages if he presses forward to trial. How would
you expect this to affect settlement negotiations with the defendant?

4. *Permanent damages.* In Boomer v. Atlantic Cement Co., 257 N.E.2d
870 (N.Y. 1970), the defendant owned a cement plant near Albany. It was
one of the largest cement factories in the world, representing an investment
of over $45 million and employing more than 300 people. The plant used the
most effective available technology for reducing its pollution. The plaintiffs
were seven residents who lived near the plant; the trial court found that the
dust emitted by the defendant's blasting and manufacturing had caused the
value of the plaintiffs' properties to drop by about 50 percent apiece, for a
total loss in value of $185,000. The court denied the plaintiffs' request for an
injunction in view of "[t]he defendant's immense investment in the Hudson
River Valley, its contribution to the Capital District's economy and its

immediate help to the education of children in the Town of Coeymans through the payment of substantial sums in school and property taxes." The court of appeals agreed, overturning the *Whalen* decision and ordering that the plaintiffs be awarded permanent damages:

> The parties could settle this private litigation at any time if defendant paid enough money and the imminent threat of closing the plant would build up the pressure on defendant. If there were no improved techniques found, there would inevitably be applications to the court at Special Term for extensions of time to perform on showing of good faith efforts to find such techniques.
>
> Moreover, techniques to eliminate dust and other annoying byproducts of cement making are unlikely to be developed by any research the defendant can undertake within any short period, but will depend on the total resources of the cement industry nationwide and throughout the world. The problem is universal wherever cement is made.
>
> For obvious reasons the rate of the research is beyond control of defendant. If at the end of 18 months the whole industry has not found a technical solution a court would be hard put to close down this one cement plant if due regard be given to equitable principles.
>
> On the other hand, to grant the injunction unless defendant pays plaintiffs such permanent damages as may be fixed by the court seems to do justice between the contending parties. All of the attributions of economic loss to the properties on which plaintiffs' complaints are based will have been redressed.

Jasen, J., dissented:

> I see grave dangers in overruling our long-established rule of granting an injunction where a nuisance results in substantial continuing damage. In permitting the injunction to become inoperative upon the payment of permanent damages, the majority is, in effect, licensing a continuing wrong. It is the same as saying to the cement company, you may continue to do harm to your neighbors so long as you pay a fee for it. Furthermore, once such permanent damages are assessed and paid, the incentive to alleviate the wrong would be eliminated, thereby continuing air pollution of an area without abatement.

The case was remanded to the trial court for a determination of damages. Most of the plaintiffs settled. The one who did not, Kinley, owned a 283-acre dairy farm. The defendant's expert testified that the value of the property without the nearby nuisance would be $210,000, but that it now was worth $105,000. The plaintiff's expert said the property would have been worth $420,500 without the nuisance, but that with the nuisance it was worth $25,000. The plaintiff also put in evidence of another nearby parcel of real estate that had been purchased for $3,438 and sold for $32,500 a year later when an adjoining landowner needed to purchase it to expand his business. The plaintiff argued that the value of a servitude on his property should be assessed using a similar multiplier, and that the "special market value" of the property, given the defendant's need for it, thus was $840,000. The trial court rejected this theory and awarded the plaintiff $175,000. What, if anything, was wrong with the plaintiff's argument that he should be entitled to $840,000?

5. *Compensated injunctions.* In Spur Industries v. Del E. Webb Development Co., 494 P.2d 700 (Ariz. 1972), the defendant, Spur Industries, operated a cattle feedlot about 15 miles west of Phoenix. Spur began using its property as a feedlot in 1956. In 1959 the plaintiff, Del Webb, began planning the creation of a community for senior citizens to be known as Sun City; it purchased 20,000 acres of land not far from the defendant's lot. Meanwhile Spur was expanding the lot in the direction of Sun City and in 1959 bought another 80 acres of property. Each party continued to expand. By 1967 Spur was feeding up to 30,000 head of cattle and generating a million pounds of manure each day; Sun City had continued to grow, and now was within 500 feet of Spur's feedlot. Del Webb brought a suit contending that the feedlot was a nuisance, diminishing the comfort of Sun City's residents and making it harder to sell properties on the edge of the development nearest the defendant's land. The Arizona Supreme Court ordered that Del Webb's request for an injunction should be granted, but that Del Webb should be required to pay Spur's costs in relocating:

> There was no indication in the instant case at the time Spur and its predecessors located in western Maricopa County that a new city would spring up, full-blown, alongside the feeding operation and that the developer of that city would ask the court to order Spur to move because of the new city. Spur is required to move not because of any wrongdoing on the part of Spur, but because of a proper and legitimate regard of the courts for the rights and interests of the public.
>
> Del Webb, on the other hand, is entitled to the relief prayed for (a permanent injunction), not because Webb is blameless, but because of the damage to the people who have been encouraged to purchase homes in Sun City. It does not equitably or legally follow, however, that Webb, being entitled to the injunction, is then free of any liability to Spur if Webb has in fact been the cause of the damage Spur has sustained. It does not seem harsh to require a developer, who has taken advantage of the lesser land values in a rural area as well as the availability of large tracts of land on which to build and develop a new town or city in the area, to indemnify those who are forced to leave as a result.
>
> Having brought people to the nuisance to the foreseeable detriment of Spur, Webb must indemnify Spur for a reasonable amount of the cost of moving or shutting down. It should be noted that this relief to Spur is

limited to a case wherein a developer has, with foreseeability, brought into a previously agricultural or industrial area the population which makes necessary the granting of an injunction against a lawful business and for which the business has no adequate relief.

The *Spur Industries* case attracted great attention because of its unprecedented choice of remedy. In the same year that the case was decided, Calabresi and Melamed had published a widely noticed article identifying four ways a claimed right might be protected by the law: (1) with a property right for its holder (i.e., the right to obtain an injunction against its infringement); (2) with a "liability rule" (damages due to the plaintiff); (3) with a property right for the defendant (i.e., no liability at all); or (4) with damages due to the *defendant* upon compliance with the plaintiff's demands. Calabresi and Melamed, *Property Rules, Liability Rules, and Inalienability: One View of the Cathedral*, 85 Harv. L. Rev. 1089 (1972). This last possibility — "Rule 4," or the "compensated injunction" — was exotic; *Spur Industries* was, and is, the only known nuisance case to adopt it. Compare Dobris, *Boomer Twenty Years Later: An Introduction, With Some Footnotes About "Theory,"* 54 Alb. L. Rev. 171, 180 (1990) (describing the compensated injunction as "a novelty item from some academic rubber goods catalog"); and Melamed, Remarks: A *Public Law Perspective*, 106 Yale L.J. 2209 (1997) (arguing that "Rule 4" remedies are widely used in public law contexts). What incentives does the Rule 4 remedy create? Would it have made sense as a remedy in any other cases considered in this chapter?

TABLE OF CASES

Hackbart v. Cincinnati Bengals, Inc., 604
Haddigan v. Harkins, 529
Haft v. Lone Palm Hotel, 311
Harkey v. Abate, 721
Harris v. Meadows, 571
Hart v. Geysel, 25
Haskins v. Grybko, 256
Hawkins v. Pizarro, 250
Haynes v. Alfred A. Knopf, Inc., 706
Hellar v. Bianco, 630
Henderson v. Arundel Corp., 282
Hendricks v. Broderick, 602
Hennessey v. Pyne, 608
Henry v. Houston Lighting & Power Co., 375
Herrick v. Wixom, 256
Herskovits v. Group Health Cooperative of Puget
  Sound, 317
Hogan v. Santa Fe Trail Transportation Co., 546
Hogenson v. Williams, 116
Hollerud v. Malamis, 28
Hollywood Silver Fox Farm, Ltd. v. Emmett, 782
Hull v. Scruggs, 91
Hurley v. Eddingfield, 230
Hustler Magazine v. Falwell, 79
Hutchinson v. Proxmire, 667

In re Exxon Valdez, 564
In re Polemis, 351
Indiana Harbor Belt Ry. Co. v. American Cyanamid
  Co., 419
Ira S. Bushey & Sons v. United States, 434
Irvine v. Akron Beacon Journal, 718
Israel v. Portland News Pub. Co., 647

Jacobsma v. Goldberg's Fashion Forum, 265
Johnson v. Douglas, 303
Johnson v. Jamaica Hospital, 296
Johnson v. K-Mart Corp., 715
Johnson v. Kosmos Portland Cement Co., 374
Johnson v. Wills Memorial Hospital & Nursing
  Home, 168
Jost v. Dairyland Power Cooperative, 753
Judson v. Giant Powder Co., 201

Kaelin v. Globe Communications Corp., 673
Katko v. Briney, 85
Keel v. Hainline, 8
Keen v. Dominick's Finer Foods, Inc., 477
Keffe v. Milwaukee & St. Paul R. Co., 259
Kelley Kar Company v. Maryland Casualty Co., 48
Kelly v. Gwinnell, 240
Kemezy v. Peters, 555
Kennan v. Checker Cab Co., 563
Kennedy v. Providence Hockey Club, 607
Kerr v. Connecticut Co., 133
Kershaw v. McKown, 92
Kingston v. Chicago & N.W. Ry. Co., 334
Klages v. General Ordnance Equipment Co., 479
Klein v. Pyrodyne Corp., 427

Kline v. 1500 Massachusetts Avenue Corp., 247
Knight v. Jewett, 3
Koblegard v. Hale, 783
Konradi v. United States, 438
Kopczick v. Hobart Corp., 558
Kremen v. Cohen, 52

Laidlaw v. Sage, 6
Lander v. Seaver, 113
Landers v. Ghosh, 527
Langford v. Shu, 68
Larson v. St. Francis Hotel, 195
Lawson v. Management Activities, Inc., 296
Leichtman v. WLW Jacor Communications, Inc.,
  11
Liebeck v. McDonald's Corp., 513
Lilpan Food Corp. v. Consolidated Edison, 276
Liriano v. Hobart Corp., 503
Litzman v. Humboldt County, 335
Lombardo v. New York University Medical Center,
  300
London Borough of Southwark v. Williams, 104
Lordi v. Spiotta, 262
Losee v. Buchanan, 412
Louisville & Nashville Ry. v. Creighton, 531
Louisville Times v. Stivers, 622
Lowe v. California League of Professional Baseball,
  603
Lubin v. Iowa City, 414
Luthringer v. Moore, 429
Lynch v. Rosenthal, 126

MacDougall v. Pennsylvania Power and Light Co.,
  161
MacPherson v. Buick Motor Co., 449
Madden v. D.C. Transit System, Inc., 12
Madison v. Ducktown Sulphur, Copper & Iron Co.,
  784
Madsen v. East Jordan Irrigation Co., 429
Magrine v. Krasnica, 473
Malouf v. Dallas Athletic Country Club, 34
Manning v. Brannon, 588
Manning v. Brown, 584
Manning v. Grimsley, 10
Mars Steel Corp. v. Continental Bank N.A., 191
Marsalis v. La Salle, 235
Marshall v. Ranne, 605
Martin v. Herzog, 171
Martin v. Wilson Publishing Co., 675
Marzolf v. Stone, 301
Masson v. New Yorker Magazine, Inc., 672
Mayor of Bradford v. Pickles, 779
McCarthy v. Olin Corp., 490
McIntyre v. Balentine, 577
McMahon v. Bunn-O-Matic Corp., 509
McNeil v. Mullin, 25
Meisler v. Gannett Co., 674
Melton v. LaCalamito, 62
Mercado v. Ahmed, 549
Metzger v. Hochrein, 783
Mexicali Rose v. Superior Court, 477

INDEX